THIS EDITION WRITTEN AND RESEARCHED BY

Sarina Singh,

Trent Holden, Abigail Hole, Kate James, Amy Karafin,

Anirban Mahapatra, Kevin Raub

welcome to
South India

Soul Stirring

Two words: stunningly unforgettable. This is the India for those seeking the happy-go-lucky beach life of Goa; the ancient Hindu temples of Tamil Nadu and Karnataka; the upbeat urban jungles of Mumbai (Bombay) and Bengaluru (Bangalore); the breezy palm-fringed backwaters of tropical Kerala; the trekking and wildlife-watching opportunities of forested sanctuaries; and the remarkably unfettered tribal culture of Andhra Pradesh. With its ability to inspire, frustrate, thrill and confound all at once, this part of the world certainly presents an extraordinary spectrum of travel experiences. Some of these can be challenging, particularly for the first-time visitor: the poverty is confronting, Indian bureaucracy can be exasperating and the crush of humanity sometimes turns the simplest task into an epic battle. Even veteran travellers find their sanity frayed at some point, yet this is all part of the India ride. Love it or loathe it – and most visitors' see-saw between the two – South India will jostle your entire being, and no matter where you go or what you do, the memories you gather will blaze brightly long after your trip comes to a close.

Luscious Landscapes

South India comprises thousands of kilometres of coastline that frame fertile plains and curvaceous hills, all kept glis-

Like a giant wedge plunging into the Indian Ocean, peninsular South India is the steamy heartland of the subcontinent, and a lush contrast to the snow-capped mountains and sun-crisped plains of the north.

(below) Souvenirs of Hindu gods for sale, Sri Meenakshi Temple (p364), Tamil Nadu
(left) Turmeric workers, Mattancherry, Kerala

teningly lush by the double-barrelled monsoon. The region's tropical splendour is one of its greatest tourist drawcards with thick coconut groves, luminescent rice paddies, fragrant spice gardens and verdant tea plantations proffering plenty of green respite. And then there are the waterways. Azure seas gently lap crescents of sun-warmed sand and boats cruise along the slender rivers and glassy lagoons of Kerala's renowned backwaters. Aficionados of the great outdoors can look forward to paddling in the shimmering waters of one of many beautiful beaches, scouting for big jungle cats on heart-racing wildlife safaris, or simply inhaling fresh country air on meditative forest walks.

Deliciously Festive

With a tremendous variety of diverse dishes, South India is deliciously rewarding. From traditional southern favourites such as *idlis* (fermented rice cakes) and papery dosas (savoury crepes) to a melange of regional and global offerings, there's certainly no dearth of culinary adventures. Food also plays a prominent part in many of the region's festivals, with wildly colourful sweets usually taking centre stage. Given its rich collection of religious denominations, South India's festival scene is a wonderfully mixed platter – from larger-than-life celebrations with elephants and body-twisting acrobats, to pint-sized harvest fairs honouring a locally worshipped deity.

❯ South India & Kerala

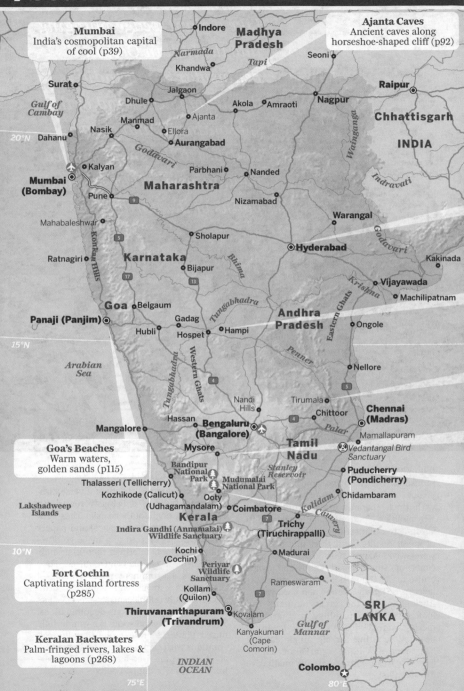

Mumbai
India's cosmopolitan capital
of cool (p39)

Ajanta Caves
Ancient caves along
horseshoe-shaped cliff (p92)

Indore

**Madhya
Pradesh**

Seoni

Narmada

Tapi

Khandwa

Raipur

Surat

Jalgaon

Dhule

Akola   Amraoti   **Nagpur**

Chhattisgarh

*Gulf of
Cambay*

Manmad

Ajanta

INDIA

Nasik

Elløra

20°N   Dahanu

Aurangabad

Godavari

Wainganga

Kalyan

Parbhani   Nanded

Indravati

**Mumbai
(Bombay)**

Pune

Maharashtra

Nizamabad

Warangal

Mahabaleshwar

Sholapur

Godavari

Ratnagiri

Karnataka

Bijapur

Bhima

◉**Hyderabad**

Kakinada

**Andhra
Pradesh**

Krishna

Vijayawada

Tungabhadra

◉ Machilipatnam

Goa Belgaum

Gadag

Hampi

Ongole

Panaji (Panjim) ◉

Hubli

Hospet

Eastern Ghats

Penner

15°N

*Arabian
Sea*

Tungabhadra

Western Ghats

Nellore

Penner

Nandi
Hills

Tirumala

**Chennai
(Madras)**

Hassan

**Bengaluru
(Bangalore)**

Chittoor

Mamallapuram

Goa's Beaches
Warm waters,
golden sands (p115)

Mysore

**Tamil
Nadu**

Vedantangal Bird
Sanctuary

Bandipur
National
Park

*Stanley
Reservoir*

**Puducherry
(Pondicherry)**

Thalasseri (Tellicherry)

Mudumalai
National Park

Kozhikode (Calicut)

Ooty
(Udhagamandalam)

Chidambaram

**Lakshadweep
Islands**

Coimbatore

Kolidam

Kerala

Indira Gandhi (Annamalai)
Wildlife Sanctuary

**Trichy
(Tiruchirappalli)**

Cauvery

Kochi
(Cochin)

Madurai

Fort Cochin
Captivating island fortress
(p285)

Periyar
Wildlife
Sanctuary

10°N

Kollam
(Quilon)

Rameswaram

**SRI
LANKA**

**Thiruvananthapuram
(Trivandrum)**

Kovalam

*Gulf of
Mannar*

Keralan Backwaters
Palm-fringed rivers, lakes &
lagoons (p268)

Kanyakumari
(Cape
Comorin)

*INDIAN
OCEAN*

Colombo

75°E

80°E

Mangalore

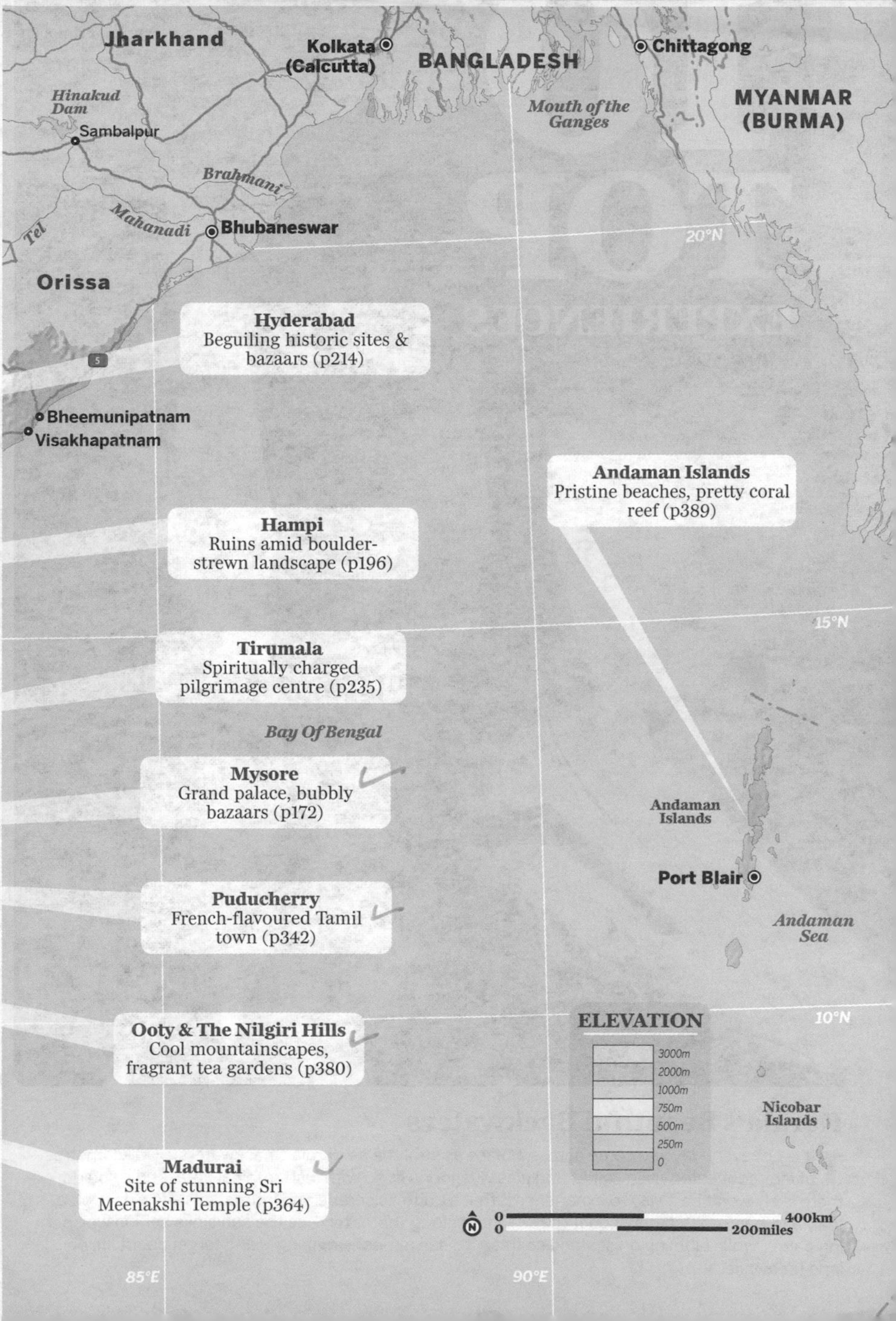

Jharkhand

Kolkata ◉
(Calcutta)

BANGLADESH

◉ **Chittagong**

Hinakud Dam
Sambalpur

Mouth of the Ganges

MYANMAR (BURMA)

Brahmani

Mahanadi ◉ **Bhubaneswar**

Tel

20°N

Orissa

Hyderabad
Beguiling historic sites & bazaars (p214)

◦ **Bheemunipatnam**
◦ **Visakhapatnam**

Andaman Islands
Pristine beaches, pretty coral reef (p389)

Hampi
Ruins amid boulder-strewn landscape (p196)

15°N

Tirumala
Spiritually charged pilgrimage centre (p235)

Bay Of Bengal

Mysore
Grand palace, bubbly bazaars (p172)

Andaman Islands

Puducherry
French-flavoured Tamil town (p342)

Port Blair ◉

Andaman Sea

ELEVATION

10°N

Ooty & The Nilgiri Hills
Cool mountainscapes, fragrant tea gardens (p380)

| 3000m |
| 2000m |
| 1000m |
| 750m |
| 500m |
| 250m |
| 0 |

Nicobar Islands

Madurai
Site of stunning Sri Meenakshi Temple (p364)

Ⓝ 0 / 0 400km / 200miles

85°E

90°E

© XALIMAGEBROKER

10 TOP EXPERIENCES

Kerala's Beautiful Backwaters ✓

1 It is not every day you come across a place as sublime as Kerala's backwaters: 900 kilometres of interconnected rivers, lakes and glassy lagoons lined with lush tropical flora. And if you do, there likely won't be a way to experience it that's quite as serene and intimate as a few days on a teak-and-palm-thatch houseboat (p268). Float along the water – as the sun sinks behind whispering palms, while nibbling on seafood so fresh it's still almost wriggling – and forget about life on land for awhile.

2 Silken sand, gently crashing waves, thick coconut groves, hot pink sunsets…yes, if there's one place that effortlessly fulfils every glossy tourist brochure cliché, it's Goa (p115). Apart from a few exceptions Goa's beaches are a riot of activity, with a constant cavalcade of roaming sarong vendors, stacks of ramshackle beachside eateries and countless oiled bodies slowly baking on row after row of sun lounges. Goa is also known for its inland spice plantations and lovely heritage buildings, most notably the handsome cathedrals built during Portuguese reign. Market, Anjuna

© PIXAL IMAGEBROKER

Ajanta's Ancient Caves

3 They may have been ascetics, but the 2nd-century-BC monks who created the Ajanta caves (p92) certainly had an eye for the dramatic. The 30 rock-cut forest grottoes punctuate the side of a horseshoe-shaped cliff and originally had individual staircases leading down to the river. The architecture and towering stupas made these caves inspiring places to meditate and live, but the real bling came centuries later, in the form of exquisite carvings and paintings depicting the Buddha's former lives. Makes living in a cave look pretty darn good.

KEREN SU/LONELY PLANET IMAGES ©

© FRANCK GUIZIOU/HEMIS/CORBIS

Enigmatic Hampi

4 Today's surreal boulder-scape of Hampi (p196) was once the glorious Vijayanagar, capital of a powerful Hindu empire. Still glorious in ruins, its temples and royal structures combine with the terrain in mystical ways: giant rocks balance on skinny pedestals near an ancient elephant garage, temples tuck into crevices between boulders, and round coracle boats float by rice paddies and bathing buffaloes near a gargantuan bathtub for a queen. Watching the sunset cast a rosy glow over the extraordinary landscape, you might just forget what planet you're on.
Virupaksha Temple, Hampi

Ooty & the Nilgiri Hills

5 The plunging valleys, pancake-flat plains and palm-ringed beaches are all well and good, but it can get mighty hot down there! India's princes and British colonials long used the country's mountain towns such as Ooty (p380) as cool refuges from the relentless summer heat, and today the hill stations still have plenty of forests, crisp mountain air and sprawling tea plantations. Curl up under a blanket with a steaming cup of local tea, peer over the misty hills at the mountain birds swooping by and experience India's chilled-out side.

ANDERS BLOMQVIST/LONELY PLANET IMAGES ®

Mumbai's Architectural Gems

6 Mumbai (p39) has always had a knack of weaving disparate strands together to make a richly unique cultural tapestry. The architectural result is a fabulously diverse mix of buildings: the art deco and modern towers are undeniably flash, but it's the eclectic Victorian-era structures – the neo-Gothic, Indo-Saracenic and Venetian Gothic hodgepodge – which have made Mumbai the flamboyant beauty that she is. All those slender spires, curvaceous arches and puffy onion domes make for a truly riveting amble through the city's former incarnations. University of Mumbai Library

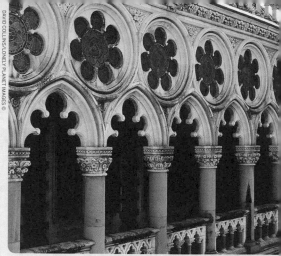

DAVID COLLINS/LONELY PLANET IMAGES ©

Puducherry Savoir Faire ✓

© OCEAN/CORBIS

7 A little pocket of France in Tamil Nadu? *Pourquoi pas?* In this former French colony (p342), mustard-coloured houses line cobblestone rues, austere cathedrals are adorned with architectural frou-frou, and the croissants are the real deal. But Puducherry is also a classic Tamil town – with all the history and hubbub that go along with that – and a classic retreat town, too, with the Sri Aurobindo Ashram at its heart. Turns out that yoga, *pain au chocolat*, Hindu deities and colonial-era architecture make for a *très* atmospheric mix.

Madurai's Sri Meenakshi Temple ✓

8 Built in the 17th-century, Madurai's brilliant Sri Meenakshi Temple (p364) is dedicated to Sundareswarer (a form of Shiva) and his consort, Meenakshi (an incarnation of the Goddess Parvati). 'Meenakshi' translates to 'fish-eyed' which, in classic Tamil literature, is a flattering reference to perfect eyes. The complex is a feast of deftly crafted pillars, friezes and figurines which are flanked by ornate gopurams (pyramidal gateway towers). A star attraction is the 1000-Pillared Hall, its chunky columns artfully embellished with delicately sculptured celestial beings.

© DAVID H WELLS/AGE FOTOSTOCK/PHOTOLIBRARY

RICHARD I'ANSON/LONELY PLANET IMAGES ©

Historic Hyderabad

9 If you're a history buff, you'll get your fill in Hyderabad (p214). The city has oodles of historic attractions, including the landmark Charminar – a graceful edifice with fluted minarets and elegant arches. Bazaars are another highlight, with fabrics, pearls, scented oils among the many treasures to be found. And then there's the food. Acclaimed for its traditional Mughal-style cuisine, notably spicy kebabs and biryani (steamed rice with meat and/ or vegetables), Hyderabadi fare gets a hearty round of applause for its deliciously inventive preparations. Charminar, Hyderabad

CRAIG PERSHOUSE/LONELY PLANET IMAGES ©

Majestic Mysore

10 Welcome to Mysore (p172) – a city whose etymology is linked to the spot where a brave goddess conquered a ferocious demon. Apart from its formidable history, this is the place to take a leisurely wander through frenetic old bazaars filled with the intoxicating aroma of sandalwood, fresh flowers and incense. Mysore is also known for its convivial festivals. Dussehra – which celebrates the triumph of good over evil – is one of the most spectacular occasions with merry street parades and the dazzling lighting-up of the city's enormous palace. Maharaja's Palace, Mysore

need to know

Currency
» Indian Rupees (₹)

Language
» Hindi, English & regional dialects

When to Go

Mumbai
GO Nov-Feb

Hyderabad
GO Nov-Mar

Bengaluru
GO Nov-Mar

Chennai
GO Nov-Feb

Thiruvananthapuram
GO Nov-Mar

Desert, dry climate
Mild to hot summers, cold winters
Tropical climate, rain year round
Tropical climate, wet dry seasons
Warm to hot summers, mild winters

High Season
(Dec-Mar)

» Pleasant weather, mostly. Peak tourists. Peak prices. Pre-book flights & accommodation.

» It starts heating up in February.

Shoulder Season
(Jul-Nov)

» Hot, humid conditions on the plains; cooler in the mountainous areas.

» The south coast experiences heavy rain any time from October to early December.

Low Season
(Apr-Jun)

» April is hot; May & June hotter. Competitive hotel prices.

» From June the monsoon starts. Fatiguing humidity.

» Beat the heat (but not the crowds or bargain hotel rates) by fleeing to the cool hills.

Your Daily Budget

Prices (especially accommodation) vary widely across the country – consult regional chapters for on-the-ground costs.

Budget

» Stay at cheap guesthouses with shared bathrooms, or hostels.

» Eat at roadside stalls or basic restaurants.

» Travel locally by bus, occasionally autorickshaw.

Midrange

» Good accommodation (with private bathrooms) & restaurants.

» Travel locally by autorickshaw and taxi.

Top End

» Accommodation & dining out – the sky is the limit!

» Hire a car with driver – but don't miss the adventure of an autorickshaw ride.

Money

» Most urban centres have ATMS. It's wise to carry cash or travellers cheques as back-up. MasterCard & Visa are the most widely accepted credit cards.

Visas

» Most people travel on the standard six-month tourist visa. Tourist visas are valid from the date of issue, not the date you arrive in India.

Mobile Phones

» Getting connected can be complicated in some states due to security issues. To avoid expensive roaming costs get hooked up to the local mobile-phone network.

Driving/Transport

» South India has expansive rail, bus and air connections. Within towns, taxis and/or rickshaws are commonly available. Hiring a car with driver doesn't cost a fortune.

Websites

» **Lonely Planet** (www.lonelyplanet.com/india) Destination information, the Thorn Tree Forum and more.

» **Incredible India** (www.incredibleindia.org) Official India tourism site.

» **World Newspapers** (www.world-newspapers.com/india.html) Links to India's English-language publications.

» **Art India** (www.artindia.net) Performing arts information, especially dance & music.

» **Festivals of India** (www.festivalsofindia.in) All about Indian festivals.

Exchange Rates

Australia	A$1	₹48
Canada	C$1	₹46
Euro zone	€1	₹63
Japan	¥100	₹56
New Zealand	NZ$1	₹35
UK	UK£1	₹73
US	US$1	₹45

For current exchange rates see www.xe.com

Important Numbers

From outside India, dial your international access code, India's country code then the number (minus '0', which is used when dialling domestically).

Country code	✆91
International access code	✆00
Ambulance	✆102
Fire	✆101
Police	✆100

Arriving in South India

» Mumbai, Chennai South India's two major international gateway cities have prepaid-taxi booths at their airport terminals. These enable you to book a taxi for a fixed price (including luggage), thus avoiding commission scams or other shenanigans. Many hotels will arrange airport pick-ups with advance notice – these are often complimentary with top-end hotels but for a fee at others; advance arrangements are wise if you're a solo traveller and your flight lands late at night.

Don't Leave Home Without...

» Getting a visa (p490) and travel insurance (p484)

» Seeking advice about vaccinations (p502)

» Nonrevealing clothes (women and men)

» Well-concealed money belt

» Sunscreen and sunglasses

» Small flashlight for poorly lit streets and/or power cuts

» Earplugs – noise can be a nuisance

» Slip-on shoes – handy for visiting sacred sites

» Tampons – sanitary pads are widely available but tampons are usually restricted to big (or touristy) towns

» Mosquito repellent

if you like...

Forts & Palaces

Historically South India has a uniquely colourful tapestry of wrangling dynasties, interwoven with the influx of seafaring traders and conquerors. Today some of their legacies can be seen in the region's remarkable collection of palaces and forts.

Mysore The Maharaja's Palace is one of India's largest and most spectacular royal buildings. Within the walls of this grand Indo-Saracenic complex are rare artworks, stained glass, mosaic floors and beautifully carved wooden fittings (p172).

Maharashtra The land of Shivaji is almost as much of a fort junkie as Rajasthan (which has a particularly prolific royal heritage) with defensive masterpieces like Daulatabad, camouflaged on a hilltop, and Janjira, an island fortress (p77).

Hyderabad The rugged Golconda Fort, whose gem vault once stored the Hope and Koh-i-Noor diamonds, complements the ethereal palaces of the City of Pearls (p214).

Bidar Fort So weathered and peaceful you'll just have to trust that once upon a time it was the seat of a powerful sultanate (p209).

Beaches

South India has the country's most breathtaking stretches of coastline, with standout beaches found in tropical Goa and Kerala. Seaside resort towns usually spring to life around sunset, when locals gather to take leisurely strolls and enjoy beachside snacks sold by roving vendors.

Kerala Kovalam and Varkala, with their gorgeous crescent-shape sugar-white beaches, rustling palm trees, lighthouse (Kovalam) and dramatic cliffs (Varkala), are an absolute vision (p247).

Goa Everything they say about the beaches is true (p115) – even when overrun with tourists, they're still somehow lovely. Vagator and Palolem are two of the prettiest, as is Gokarna, just nearby in Karnataka (p155).

Mumbai Hit Chowpatty beach, as the afternoon melts into dusk, to snack on unusual and creative local delicacies, people-watch, and see just how hot-pink the sunset can get (p39).

Bazaars

Megamalls may be popping up like monsoon frogs in South India's larger cities, but the traditional outdoor bazaars – with their tangle of lanes lined with shops selling everything from freshly ground spices and floral bouquets to kitchen utensils and colourful saris – can't be beat.

Goa Tourist-oriented flea markets have become huge attractions at several spots on the north coast, while the local bazaars of Panjim and, especially, Margao make for atmospheric wandering (p115).

Mumbai Among modern malls, this megalopolis has wonderful old markets conveniently dedicated to themes: Mangaldas (fabric), Zaveri (jewellery), Crawford (meat and produce) and Chor (random antique pieces) (p68).

Mysore Iconic Devaraja Market is about 125 years old and filled with about 125 million flowers, fruits and vegetables (p172).

» Powdered pigments, Devaraja Market (p172)

Grand Temples & Ancient Ruins

No one does grand temples (or little temples, for that matter) like the subcontinent. From the psychedelic Technicolor Hindu towers of Tamil Nadu to the faded splendour of Ajanta and Ellora's Buddhist cave temples, the range is as vast as it is spectacular.

Tamil Nadu Tamil Nadu is prime temple territory, with towering, fantastical structures – such as the striking Sri Meenakshi Temple of Madurai (p364) – that soar skyward in riotous rainbows of masterfully sculpted deities.

Ajanta & Ellora These magnificent old rock-cut cave temples, clinging to a horseshoe-shaped gorge, are revered not only for their spiritual significance but also for their architectural prowess (p84).

Hampi The rosy-hued temples and crumbling palaces of what was once the mighty capital of Vijayanagar are strewn among otherworldly-looking boulders and hills (p196).

Local Festivals

Apart from embracing a range of countrywide festivals, South India has its own vibrant collection of locally celebrated events. These range from sacred temple processions to flamboyant beachside affairs.

Kerala Keralan festivals are nothing short of fabulous, especially when it comes to elephant processions and boat races. The Nehru Trophy Snake Boat Race sees elegant 125-ft-long canoes in a lively rowing showdown. (p248).

Chennai Festival of Music & Dance For six weeks, the city fills up on Carnatic (and some non-Carnatic) music, dance and drama (p312).

Tamil Nadu Pongal, in mid-January, celebrates the close of the harvest season. Pots of *pongal* (a mixture of rice, sugar, dhal and milk) are prepared and fed to decorated cows (p312).

Goa The four-day Carnival (p116) in Goa kicks off Lent with colourful parades, concerts and plenty of merrymaking.

Mumbai Mumbai hosts interesting art performances and exhibitions during its two-week Kala Ghoda Festival (p40).

City Sophistication

It's true that most Indians live in villages, but city people here had attained high planes of sophistication when classiness was just a glimmer in the West's eye. India's cities have riveting arts scenes, terrific multicuisine restaurants and oodles of style.

Mumbai Mumbai has it all – fashion, film, art, dining and a buzzing nightlife scene – on an elaborate stage of fanciful architecture and scenic water views (p39).

Hyderabad The ancient architecture of several extraordinarily wealthy dynasties sits just across town from a refined restaurant, nightlife and arts scene (p214).

Bengaluru This cosmopolitan metropolis is the hub of India's IT industry. The city's lungs are its leafy gardens which are sandwiched between knots of high-rise office blocks and peeling apartments (p157).

Puducherry A pleasant coastal town known for its faded French flavour, Puducherry is India at its eclectic best. The French Quarter has charming alleys and mustard-coloured villas (p342).

If you like... natural health
Kerala has many centres specialising in ayurvedic healing (p247).

If you like... luxury train trips
The 'Deccan Odyssey' is seven nights of the best of Maharashtra and Goa (p25).

If you like... diving
The Andaman Islands have some world-class diving opportunities, with coral gardens and marine life (p389).

Hill Stations

South India is blessed with sunshine and hills to escape from it when summer rolls in. The foundation for today's hill-station resort culture is largely thanks to locals – especially royalty and colonials – who traditionally fled to escape the heat of the plains.

Tamil Nadu The Tamil hill stations of the Western Ghats are full of thick pine forests, little tea houses, sprawling cardamom plantations and architectural Raj-era flourishes (p372).

Matheran A popular weekend retreat for Mumbaikars, Matheran is not only delightfully scenic and easygoing (largely thanks to its ban on cars) but also has a quaint narrow-gauge toy train plying the 21kms to the main road (p77).

Meditation & Yoga

The art of wellbeing has long been ardently pursued in the south. Today there is a variety of treatments on offer that strive to heal mind, body and spirit, with meditation and yoga courses especially abundant.

Maharasthra The Vipassana International Academy, in Igatpuri, has intensive meditation courses in the Theravada Buddhist tradition (p77). Meanwhile, the famous Osho International Meditation Resort (p105) runs on the teachings of its charismatic founder, the late Bhagwan Shree Rajneesh.

Tamil Nadu Puducherry's Sri Aurobindo Ashram (p342) was founded by the renowned Sri Aurobindo. Its courses seek to synthesise yoga and modern science.

Coimbatore The Isha Yoga Center (p378) has a variety of residential courses and retreats.

Puttaparthi Prasanthi Nilayam (p238) is the ashram of the controversial but very popular guru Sri Sathya Sai Baba.

Traveller Enclaves

Sometimes you don't want to race around in a bid to absorb as much as you can before your trip ends. Sometimes you want to chill with fellow backpackers: swap travel tales, read, take afternoon naps, play cards, drink beer....

Hampi The stunning beauty of Hampi's landscape and architecture makes everyone want to stay for a while, which has led to a well-developed traveller community (p196).

Arambol Goa is one big traveller enclave, but Arambol may be its epicentre. Lots of shops and services combine with a splendid beach and cheap sleeps; no wonder we all end up there sooner or later (p144).

month by month

1 **Carnival**, January or February

2 **Pongal**, January

3 **Ganesh Chaturthi**, August or September

4 **Navratri** and **Dussehra,** September or October

5 **Diwali**, October or November

Most festivals follow the Indian lunar (or Islamic) calendar, which means dates can vary from year to year – consult tourist offices for exact dates.

January

Post-monsoon cool lingers throughout the country, although it never gets truly cool in the most southerly states. Pleasant weather and several festivals make it a popular time to travel (book ahead!).

Free India
Republic Day commemorates the founding of the Republic of India on 26 January 1950; the biggest celebrations are in Delhi, which holds a huge military parade along Rajpath and the Beating of the Retreat three days later.

Kite Festival
Sankranti, the Hindu festival marking the sun's passage into Capricorn, is celebrated in many ways across India – from banana-giving to dips in the Ganges to cockfights. But it's the mass kite-flying in Maharasthra (among other states) that steals the show.

Southern Harvest
The Tamil festival of Pongal, equivalent to Sankranti, marks the end of the harvest season. Families prepare pots of *pongal* (a mixture of rice, sugar, dhal and milk), symbolic of prosperity and abundance, then feed them to decorated cows.

Celebrating Saraswati
On Vasant Panchami, Hindus dress in yellow and place books, musical instruments and other educational objects in front of idols of Saraswati, the goddess of learning, to receive her blessing. This festival may fall in February.

February

The weather is comfortable in most nonmountainous areas, with summer heat percolating, especially in the southernmost states. It's still peak travel season; sunbathing and swimming remain hot on the agenda.

The Prophet Mohammed's Birthday
The Islamic festival of Eid-Milad-un-Nabi celebrates the birth of the Prophet Mohammed with prayers and processions. It falls in the third month of the Islamic Calendar: around 4 February (2012), 24 January (2013) and 13 January (2014).

Tibetan New Year
Losar is celebrated by Tantric Buddhists all over India for 15 days, with the most important festivities during the first three. Losar is usually in February or March, though dates can vary between regions.

Shivaratri
This day of Hindu fasting recalls the *tandava* (cosmic victory dance) of Lord Shiva. Temple processions are followed by the chanting of mantras and anointing of linga (phallic images of Shiva). Shivaratri can also fall in March.

Carnival in Goa
The four-day party kicking off Lent is particularly big in Goa. Sabado Gordo, Fat Saturday, starts it off with parades of elaborate

floats and costumed dancers, and the revelry continues with street parties, concerts and general merrymaking.

March

The last month of the main travel season, March is full-on hot in most of the country. Wildlife are easier to spot as they come out to search for water, and Holi, celebrated mainly by Hindus, lends a festive air.

★ Holi
More widely celebrated in the North, but still embraced by many southerners, Holi celebrates the onset of spring. Held in February or March, merrymakers hurl coloured water and *gulal* (powder) on one another. The night before Holi, bonfires symbolise the demise of the demoness Holika.

★ Rama's Birthday
During Ramanavami, which lasts anywhere from one to nine days, Hindus celebrate the birth of Rama with processions; music, fasting and feasting; readings and enactments of scenes from the Ramayana; and, at some temples, ceremonial weddings of Rama and Sita idols.

April

The hot has well and truly arrived in south India, and with the rise in temperature also comes a rise in competitive travel deals and a drop in tourist traffic.

★ Easter
The Christian holiday marking the Crucifixion and Resurrection of Jesus Christ is celebrated simply in Christian communities with prayer and good food. It's nowhere near as boisterous as Carnival, earlier in the year, but good vibes abound. Easter may also be in March.

★ Mahavir's Birthday
Mahavir Jayanti commemorates the birth of Jainism's 24th and most important *tirthankar* (teacher and enlightened being). Temples are decorated and visited, Mahavir statues are given ritual baths, processions are held and offerings are given to the poor. The festival can also fall in March.

May

In most of the country it's hot. Really hot. Festivals slow down as the humidity builds up in anticipation of the rain. Hill stations are hopping, though.

★ Buddha's Birthday
Commemorating Buddha's birth, nirvana (enlightenment) and *parinirvana* (total liberation from the cycle of existence, or passing away), Buddha Jayanti is quiet but moving: devotees dress simply, eat vegetarian, listen to dharma talks, and visit monasteries or temples.

June

June's not a popular travel month in India, unless you're trekking up north.

The rainy season, or pre-monsoon extreme heat, has started just about everywhere else.
See regional chapters for state-specific festivals.

July

Now it's raining almost everywhere, with a number of remote roads being washed out. Consider doing a rainy-season meditation retreat, an ancient Indian tradition.

★ Snake Festival
The Hindu festival Naag Panchami is dedicated to Ananta, the serpent upon whose coils Vishnu rested between universes. Women return to their family homes and fast, while serpents are venerated as totems against flooding and other evils. Falls in July or August.

★ Brothers and Sisters
On Raksha Bandhan (Narial Purnima), girls fix amulets known as *rakhis* to the wrists of brothers and close male friends to protect them in the coming year. Brothers reciprocate with gifts and promises to take care of their sisters.

★ Ramadan (Ramazan)
Thirty days of dawn-to-dusk fasting mark the ninth month of the Islamic calendar. Muslims traditionally turn their attention to God, with a focus on prayer and purification. Ramadan begins around 20 July (2012), 9 July (2013) and 28 June (2014).

August

It's still high monsoon season: wet wet wet. Some folks swear by visiting tropical areas, like Kerala or Goa, at this time of year: the jungles are lush, bright green and glistening in the rain.

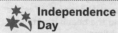 Independence Day

This public holiday on 15 August marks the anniversary of India's independence from Britain in 1947. Celebrations are a countrywide expression of patriotism, with flag-hoisting ceremonies – the biggest one is in Delhi – parades and patriotic cultural programs.

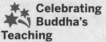 Celebrating Buddha's Teaching

Drupka Teshi commemorates Siddhartha Gautama's first teaching, in which he explained the Four Noble Truths to his disciples in Sarnath. The festival may also fall in July.

Krishna's Birthday

Janmastami celebrations can last a week in Krishna's birthplace, Mathura (Uttar Pradesh); elsewhere the festivities range from fasting to *puja* (prayers) and offering sweets to drawing elaborate *rangoli* (rice-paste/powder) designs outside the home. Janmastami is sometimes in July.

Parsi New Year

Parsis celebrate Pateti, the Zoroastrian new year, especially in Mumbai. Houses are cleaned and decorated with flowers and rangoli, the family dresses up and eats special fish dishes and sweets, and offerings are made at the Fire Temple.

Eid al-Fitr

Muslims celebrate the end of Ramadan with three days of festivities, starting 30 days after the start of the fast. Prayers, shopping, gift-giving and, for women and girls, *mehndi* (henna designs) may all be part of the celebrations.

September

The rain begins to ease up somewhat, but with temperatures still relatively high throughout southern Indian the moisture-filled air can create a fatiguing steam-bath-like environment.

Ganesh's Birthday

Hindus celebrate Ganesh Chaturthi, the birth of the elephant-headed god, with verve, particularly in Mumbai. Clay idols of Ganesh are paraded through the streets before being ceremonially immersed in rivers, tanks (reservoirs) or the sea. Ganesh Chaturthi may also fall in August.

Durga Puja

The conquest of good over evil, exemplified by the goddess Durga's victory over the demon Mahishasura. Celebrations occur around Dussehra and in some places images of the goddess are displayed then ritually immersed in rivers and water tanks.

October

Although the southeast coast (and southern Kerala) can still be rainy, this is when India starts to get its travel mojo on. October, aka shoulder season, brings festivals, reasonably comfy temperatures, and post-rain lushness.

Gandhi's Birthday

The national holiday of Gandhi Jayanti is a solemn celebration of Mohandas Gandhi's birth, on 2 October, marked with prayer meetings. Schools and businesses close for the day.

Navratri

This Hindu 'Festival of Nine Nights' leading up to Dussehra celebrates the goddess Durga in all her incarnations. Special dances are performed, and the goddesses Lakshmi and Saraswati are also celebrated. Festivities are particularly vibrant in Maharashtra. Navratri sometimes falls in September.

Dussehra

Colourful Dussehra celebrates the victory of the Hindu god Rama over the demon-king Ravana and the triumph of good over evil. Dussehra is especially prominent in Mysore (p172), which hosts one of India's grandest parades.

Festival of Lights

In the lunar month of Kartika, in October or November, Hindus celebrate Diwali (Deepavali) for five days, giving gifts, lighting fireworks, and burning butter and oil lamps (or hanging lanterns) to lead Lord Rama home from exile. One of India's prettiest festivals.

★ Eid al-Adha

Muslims commemorate Ibrahim's readiness to sacrifice his son to God by slaughtering a goat or sheep and sharing it with family, the community and the poor. It'll be held around 26 October in 2012, 15 October in 2013 and 4 October in 2014.

November

The climate is reasonably pleasant in most places, but rain sweeps parts of Tamil Nadu and Kerala. It's a good time to be

anywhere low-altitude, notwithstanding, as the temperatures are just right.

★ Guru Nanak's Birthday

Nanak Jayanti, birthday of Guru Nanak, founder of Sikhism, is celebrated with prayer readings, *kirtan* (Sikh devotional singing) and processions for three days. The festival may also be held on 14 April, thought to be Nanak's actual 1469 birth date.

★ Muharram

During this month of grieving and remembrance, Shi'ia Muslims commemorate the martyrdom of the Prophet Mohammed's grandson Imam, an event known as Ashura, with beautiful processions.

It begins around 15 November (2012), 4 November (2013) and 25 October (2014).

December

December is peak tourist season for a reason: the weather is lovely, the humidity is lower than usual, the mood is festive and the beach is simply sublime.

★ Christmas Day

Christians celebrate the birth of Jesus Christ on December 25th. The festivities are especially big in Goa and Kerala, which see musical events, elaborate decorations and special Masses, while Mumbai's Catholic neighbourhoods become festivals of lights.

itineraries

Whether you've got six days or 60, these itineraries provide a starting point for the trip of a lifetime. Want more inspiration? Head online to lonelyplanet.com/thorntree to chat with other travellers.

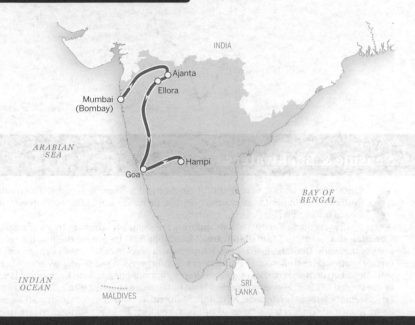

2 weeks
Goa, Caves & Cities

Begin in cosmopolitan **Mumbai**, the beating heart of Bollywood and site of some of the nation's best shopping, eating and drinking opportunities. Take a sunset stroll along Marine Drive, a curvaceous ocean-side promenade dubbed the 'Queen's Necklace' because of its sparkling night lights. Catch a ferry to **Elephanta Island** – just 9km from Mumbai's historic Gateway of India – to marvel at its stunning rock-cut temples and impressive triple-faced sculpture of Lord Shiva. Next, head northeast to explore the ancient cave art at **Ajanta** and **Ellora**. Located within 100km of each other, the Buddhist caves of Ajanta are clustered along a horseshoe-shaped gorge, while those of Ellora – which contain a mix of Hindu, Jain and Buddhist shrines – are situated on a 2km-long escarpment. After soaking up cave culture, slide southwest to tropical **Goa** for some soul-reviving sand-castle therapy. Wander through a lush Goan spice plantation, visit Portuguese-era cathedrals, shop at colourful flea markets and feast on fresh seafood before travelling east to **Hampi** in neighbouring Karnataka. Ramble around Hampi's enigmatic boulder-strewn landscape and imagine what life here was like when it was a centre of the mighty Vijayanagar Empire.

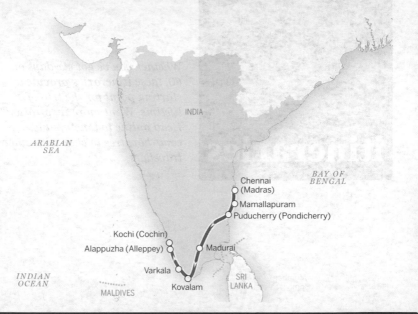

3 weeks
Seaside & Backwaters

South India is blessed with beautiful beaches and tropical waterways. The south-western shoreline is the star attraction, but there are a number of southeastern coastal towns that also deserve exploration.

After spending a couple of days enjoying the sights and culinary treats of steamy **Chennai**, slide south to **Mamallapuram** (Mahabalipuram) to admire the fine bas-relief work of the World Heritage–listed Shore Temple, which peers over the Bay of Bengal. Travel further south to French-flavoured **Puducherry** (Pondicherry), a pretty coastal town where you can fuel up on robust curries or delicate crepes after rambling around the cobbled lanes of the French Quarter. Sunset is a perfect time to take an unhurried stroll along Puducherry's scenic beachside promenade. Next stop, **Madurai**, to marvel at the striking Sri Meenakshi Temple, abode of a triple-breasted fish-eyed goddess. This sprawling sacred complex is a veritable feast of masterfully carved pillars, friezes and brightly coloured figurines. It's now time to dip your toes in the warm waters of **Kovalam**, one of Kerala's premier beach resorts or, if you prefer more of a backpacker vibe, **Varkala** – further north – with its dramatic sea-cliffs and long sandy beaches. Both are super spots to soak up the sun, indulge in rejuvenating Ayurvedic treatments and tuck into wonderfully fresh seafood. When you're all beached out, make a beeline to **Alappuzha** (Alleppey), gateway to Kerala's famed back-waters. Take a languid houseboat cruise along the palm-fringed network of shimmering rivers, glassy lagoons and slender canals that pass tiny fishing villages, expansive emerald green rice paddies and thick coconut groves. While gliding along the silken waterways, keep your eyes peeled for boats carting bulging bags of coir (coconut fibre), copra (dried coconut kernels) and cashews – major exports of this region. If you're in Alappuzha on the second Saturday of August, don't miss the spectacular Nehru Trophy Snake Boat Race. Next, head north to **Kochi** (Cochin) – a knot of islands and peninsulas connected by bridges and ferries – where you can stay at a gorgeous colonial-era mansion in evocative Fort Cochin; see traditional Chinese fishing nets fluttering in the breeze like giant perforated moths; catch a Kathakali performance; and peruse the eclectic mix of historic sites that include magnificent Portuguese-era cathedrals.

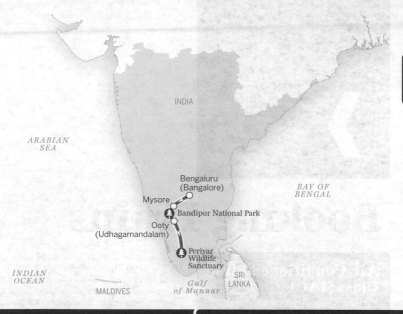

INDIA

ARABIAN
SEA

Bengaluru
(Bangalore)

BAY OF
BENGAL

Mysore

Bandipur National Park

Ooty
(Udhagamandalam)

Periyar
Wildlife
Sanctuary

INDIAN
OCEAN

SRI
LANKA

MALDIVES

Gulf
of Mannar

2 weeks
Cities & Sacred Sites

Delve into **Chennai's** rich history with a wander around the Government Museum before going to the ancient Shiva Kapaleeshwarar Temple with its *gopuram* (gateway tower). Take a look at San Thome Cathedral, a soaring Roman Catholic church, before checking out the military memorabilia at the Fort St George museum. Travel south to **Mamallapuram** (Mahabalipuram) to explore the superb rock-cut shrines that hark back to the Pallava dynasty. Next, head to **Puducherry** (Pondicherry) to feast your eyes on the faded buildings of the French Quarter; the 18th-century Church of Our Lady of the Immaculate Conception; and the Sri Manakula Vinayagar Temple. Time to move on to **Tiruvannamalai** to see the Arunachaleswar Temple, one of the country's largest sacred complexes. For more spiritual sustenance head to Chidambaram, site of the Nataraja Temple (one of South India's holiest Shiva sites) followed by a trip to **Madurai** to savour the Sri Meenakshi Temple, another architectural superstar. Wrap up your tour in **Hyderabad**, home to historic monuments that include the Golconda Fort and the Charminar.

2 weeks
Cities & Sanctuaries

Spend a few days indulging in the culinary and shopping delights of **Bengaluru** (Bangalore). For a taste of the city's royal past visit the 18th-century Tipu Sultan Palace and whimsical Bengaluru Palace, then go to the breezy Lalbagh Botanical Gardens – home to over 1000 different plant species that include centuries-old trees. The next stop is **Mysore**. Shop for sandalwood and silk in the city's vibrant bazaars and gawp at the Maharaja's Palace, an uber-grand complex topped with rhubarb-red and chalky-white domes. Slide south to the sprawling **Bandipur National Park**, in southern Karnataka, to scout for wild elephants, chitals (spotted deer), sloth bears, Indian bison and elusive tigers. Slip further south to the cool hill town of **Ooty** (Udhagamandalam), one of South India's most loved summer holiday retreats. Enjoy stunningly panoramic views from the Doddabetta Lookout, row a boat on the rippling lake and scoff salty snacks in the bubbly bazaar. Descend to peaceful **Periyar Wildlife Sanctuary** in Kumily (Kerala) and join a wildlife-spotting trek – apart from teeming birdlife that includes kingfishers and owls, the jungle is home to lion-tailed macaques, elephants and even otters.

Booking Trains

Air-Conditioned First Class (1AC)

The most expensive class of train travel; two-or four-berth compartments with locking doors and meals included.

Air-Conditioned 2-Tier (2AC)

Two-tier berths arranged in groups of four and two in an open-plan carriage. The bunks convert to seats by day and there are curtains for some semblance of privacy.

Air-Conditioned 3-Tier (3AC)

Three-tier berths arranged in groups of six in an open-plan carriage; no curtains.

AC Executive Chair

Comfortable, reclining chairs and plenty of space; usually found on Shatabdi express trains.

Sleeper Class

Open plan carriages with three-tier bunks and no AC; but the open windows afford great views.

Unreserved 2nd Class

Wooden or plastic seats and *a lot* of people – but cheap!

Travelling on an Indian train is a reason to travel all by itself. India's rail network is one of the world's most extensive and the prices are very reasonable. Bookings open 90 days before departure and seats fill up quickly – an estimated 17 to 20 million people travel by train in India *every day*. So if you have a route mapped out and dates locked in, you can book your train tickets before you even arrive in the country. Here's the lowdown on how to do it.

Booking Tickets

Booking online is the easiest way to buy train tickets. The railway reservation system is open from 1.30am to 11.30pm every day (IST) so keep this in mind when trying to book online, particularly if you are abroad. The following websites all issue e-tickets, which are valid for train travel. You may have to show your passport as ID along with the printout of your booking reference when you are on the train.

The following websites all accept international credit cards.

Indian Railway Catering and Tourism Corporation Limited (www.irctc.co.in) Set up by the Ministry of Railways; you can book regular trains as well as tourist trains such as the Deccan Odyssey.

Cleartrip (www.cleartrip.com) An excellent, easy to use and reliable website that charges a small fee (₹20) on top of the regular ticket price.

Make My Trip (www.makemytrip.com) Similar to Cleartrip with very good reports from travellers.

South India offers an enticing choice of tailored train journeys for tourists seeking to ride the rails with flair. Fares usually include accommodation on board, tours, admission fees and all or most meals, and there are normally child concessions – inquire when booking.

In Maharashtra, the *Deccan Odyssey* (www.deccan-odyssey-india.com) offers seven nights of luxury covering the main tourist spots of Maharashtra and Goa. The train leaves from Mumbai (Bombay), heading south through the resorts and fort towns of the Konkan Coast to Goa, then looping inland to Pune, Aurangabad (for Ellora), Jalgaon (for Ajanta) and Nasik. From October to March, fares per person per night start at US$650/500/425 for single/double/triple occupancy (US$500/390/315 in September and April). You can do the trip for a minimum of three days (two nights).

The *Golden Chariot* (www.thegoldenchariot.co.in) takes visitors through Karnataka in style. Two tour packages are available: Bengaluru (Bangalore)–Bengaluru (Monday to Monday) and Bengaluru–Goa (Monday to Sunday). It runs throughout the year. Rates per person for the seven-night tour are US$4795/3465/2800 for single/double/triple occupancy.

Yatra (www.yatra.com) This travel booking website has an Indian version (www.yatra.in) and a UK site (www.yatra.com/UK/index.html).

Reservations

You must make a reservation for all chair-car, sleeper, and 1AC, 2AC and 3AC carriages. No reservations are required for general (2nd-class) compartments. Bookings are strongly recommended for all overnight journeys and if you plan on travelling during Indian holidays or festivals. For more information on trains, tickets and fares see p500.

Trains & Classes

Trains and seats come in a variety of classes and not all classes are available on every train.

» Express and mail trains usually have general (2nd class) compartments with unreserved seating and more comfortable compartments that you can reserve.

» Shatabdi express trains are same-day services with seating only, in AC Chair and Executive Chair cars.

» Rajdhani express trains are long-distance overnight services between Delhi and state capitals with a choice of 1AC, 2AC, 3AC and 2nd class.

» New to the rails are eight women-only trains, which service New Delhi, Mumbai, Chennai and Kolkata.

» Some cities also have suburban train networks, but these are very crowded during peak hours.

» In the higher sleeper categories bedding is provided but it doesn't hurt to bring your own.

» In all classes, a padlock and a length of chain are useful for securing your luggage to the baggage racks.

Train Passes

The IndRail Pass permits unlimited rail travel for the period of its validity, but it offers limited savings and you must still make reservations. Passes are available for from one to 90 days of travel. The easiest way to book these is through the IndRail pass agency in your home country. They can also book any necessary train reservations for you. Overseas travel agencies and station ticket offices in major Indian cities also sell the pass – click on the Information/International Tourist link on www.indianrail.gov.in for further details, including prices. There's no refund for either lost or partially used tickets.

Volunteering

Choosing an Organisation

Consider how your skill-set may benefit an organisation and community, and choose a cause that you're passionate about.

Time Required

Think realistically about how much time you can devote to a project. Some charities offer week-long placements but you're more likely to be of help if you commit for at least a month.

Money

Often giving up your time is not enough; many charities will expect volunteers to cover their own costs including accommodation, food and transport.

Working 9 to 5

Make sure you know what you're signing up for; many volunteer programs expect you to work full-time, five days a week.

Transparency

Ensure that the organisation you choose is reputable and transparent about how they spend their money. Where possible, get feedback from former volunteers.

Many charities and international aid agencies work in India and there are numerous opportunities for volunteers. It may be possible to find a placement after you arrive in India, but charities and nongovernment organisations (NGOs) normally prefer volunteers who have applied in advance and been approved for the kind of work involved.

There are some excellent local charities and NGOs, some of which have opportunities for volunteers; for listings check www.indianngos.com. The **Concern India Foundation** (☏011-26224482/3; www.concern indiafoundation.org; Room A52, 1st fl, Amar Colony, Lajpat Nagar 4) may be able to link volunteers with current projects around the country; contact them well in advance for information. In Delhi, the magazine *First City* lists various local NGOs that welcome volunteers and financial aid.

Aid Programs in South India

The following are listings of programs in South India that may have opportunities for volunteers; it's best to contact them before turning up on their doorstep. Donations may also be welcomed.

Caregiving

There are opportunities for volunteer work in this field, particularly those with a medical, health or teaching background.

AGENCIES OVERSEAS

There are scores of international volunteering agencies, and it can be bewildering trying to assess which ones have ethical policies. Agencies that offer short projects in lots of different countries whenever you want to go are almost always tailoring projects to the volunteer rather than finding the right volunteer for the work that needs to be done. Look for projects that will derive benefits from your existing skills. To find sending agencies in your area, read Lonely Planet's *Volunteer,* the *Gap Year Book* and the *Career Break Book,* or try one of the following agencies:

» **Ethical Volunteering** (www.ethicalvolunteering.org) has some excellent guidelines for choosing an ethical sending agency.

» **Voluntary Service Overseas** (VSO; www.vso.org.uk) is a British organisation that places volunteers in various professional roles, though the time commitment can be up to several years.

» **Indicorps** (www.indicorps.org) matches volunteers to projects across India in all sorts of fields, particularly social development. There are special fellowships for people of Indian descent living outside India.

» **Kerala Link** (www.kerala-link.org) is a UK-registered charity that places volunteers at one of their partner institutions located in rural Kerala, including a special-needs children's school.

Maharashtra

» **Sadhana Village** (☎020-25380792; www.sadhana-village.org; Priyankit, 1 Lokmanya Colony, Pune) is a residence for intellectually disabled adults; minimum commitment of two months for volunteers.

Community

Many community volunteer projects work to provide health care and education to villages.

Andhra Pradesh

» The **Confederation of Voluntary Associations** (☎040-24572984; www.covanetwork.org; 20-4-10, Charminar, Hyderabad) is an umbrella organisation for around 800 NGOs in Andhra Pradesh. Volunteers are matched by their skills; long-term volunteers preferred.

Karnataka

» In Bengaluru, **Equations** (☎080-25457607; www.equitabletourism.org; 415, 2nd C Cross, 4th Main Rd, OMBR Layout, Banaswadi Post) promotes 'holistic tourism' and protects local communities from exploitation through lobbying, local training programs and research publications.

» Across the river from Hampi, the **Kishkinda Trust** (☎08533-267777; www.thekishkindatrust.org; Royal Street, Anegundi) devotes itself to social empowerment and sustainable community development through a number of avenues, such as rural tourism.

Mumbai

» The **Concern India Foundation** (☎022-22852270; www.concernindia.org; 3rd fl, Ador House, 6 K Dubash Marg) supports development-oriented organisations to establish sustainable projects run by local people. Six months minimum; many of the field jobs require Hindi.

Tamil Nadu

» In Chennai, the **Rejuvenate India Movement** (RIM; ☎044-22235133; www.rejuvenateindiamovement.org) can arrange short- and long-term placements for skilled volunteers on development projects run by partner NGOs in Tamil Nadu.

Environment & Conservation

The following are just some of the charities focused on environmental education and sustainable development:

Andaman Islands

» **ANET** (Andaman & Nicobar Environmental Team; ☎03192 280081; www.anetindia.org; North Wandoor) is an environmental NGO that accepts volunteers to assist with activities from field projects to general maintenances.

HANDY WEBSITES

» **World Volunteer Web** (www.worldvolunteerweb.org) Information and resources for volunteering around the world.

» **Working Abroad** (www.workingabroad.com) Volunteer and professional work opportunities in over 150 countries.

» **Worldwide Volunteering** (www.worldwidevolunteering.org.uk) Enormous database offering information on worldwide volunteering opportunities.

Karnataka

» **Ashoka Trust for Research in Ecology & the Environment** (ATREE; ☑080-23635555; www.atree.org; Royal Enclave, Sriramapura, Jakkur Post, Bengaluru) takes volunteers who have experience or a keen interest in conservation and environmental issues.

Maharashtra

» **Nimbkar Agricultural Research Institute** (☑02166-222396; www.nariphaltan.org; Phaltan-Lonand Rd, Tambmal, Phaltan) focuses on sustainable development, animal husbandry and renewable energy. Volunteer internships lasting two to six months are available for agriculture, engineering and science graduates to assist with the research.

Tamil Nadu

» In Kotagiri, the **Keystone Foundation** (www.keystone-foundation.org) strives to improve environmental conditions in the Nilgiris while working with and creating better living standards for indigenous communities.

Working with Animals

From stray dogs to injured goats, opportunities for animal lovers are plentiful.

Andhra Pradesh

» **Blue Cross of Hyderabad** (☑040-23544355; www.bluecrosshyd.in; Rd No 35, Jubilee Hills, Hyderabad) runs a large shelter with over 1000 animals. It works to rescue and adopt sick animals, and vaccinate and sterilise stray dogs. Volunteers can help care for shelter animals (dogs, cats and livestock), or in the office.

» **Karuna Society for Animals & Nature** (☑08555-287214; www.karunasociety.org; 2/138C Karuna Nilayam, Prasanthi Nilayam Post, Anantapur) rescues and treats sick, abandoned and mistreated animals. Volunteers can help with caretaking operations; a one-month, full-time minimum commitment is needed, as are anti-rabies vaccinations

Goa

» **International Animal Rescue** (IAR; ☑2268328/272; www.internationalanimalrescue.org; Animal Tracks, Madungo Vaddo, Assagao) runs its Animal Tracks rescue facility in Assagao, and visitors and volunteers (both short- and long-term) are always welcome to assist vets and tend to sick strays.

» The animal welfare group **GAWT** (see p151) also has volunteer opportunities.

Mumbai

» The **Welfare of Stray Dogs** (☑022-64222838; www.wsdindia.org; Yeshwant Chambers, B Bharocha Rd, Kala Ghoda) works to improve the lives of street dogs. Volunteers can walk dogs, mind kennels, treat animals (training and rabies shot required), manage stores, educate kids in school programs or fundraise.

Working with Children

The following are just a selection of the many excellent charities working with children in India.

Goa

» **Children Walking Tall** (☑09822-124802; www.childrenwalkingtall.com, the 'Mango House', near Vrundavan Hospital, Karaswada, Mapusa) has opportunities for volunteer child care workers, teachers and medics at its projects for homeless children and orphans near Mapusa (minimum three months). Every volunteer needs a criminal-background check.

» **El Shaddai** (☑6513286/7; www.childrescue.net; El Shaddai House, Socol Vaddo, Assagao) aids impoverished and homeless children. A one-month commitment is required and volunteers undergo a rigorous vetting process, which can take up to six months, so apply well in advance.

Mumbai

» **Child Rights & You** (CRY; off Map p44); ☑022-23096845; www.cry.org; 189A Anand Estate, Sane Guruji Marg, Mahalaxmi) fundraises for more than 300 projects India-wide. Volunteers can assist with campaigns (online and on the ground), research, surveys and media. A six-week commitment is required.

» **Saathi** (☎022-23009117; www.saathi.org; Agripada Municipal School, Farooque Umarbhouy Lane, Agripada) works with adolescent youths living on the street. Volunteers should be willing to commit to at least three months and work full-time (six days per week). Those interested in working directly with adolescents should speak some Hindi. You can take a tour of the neighbourhood where Saathi works for a ₹1000 donation.

» The **Vatsalya Foundation** (off Map p44; ☎022-24962115; www.thevatsalyafoundation. org; Anand Niketan, King George V Memorial, Dr E Moses Rd, Mahalaxmi) works with Mumbai's street children, focusing on rehabilitation into mainstream society. There are long- and short-term opportunities in teaching and sports activities.

Tamil Nadu

» The NGO **Rural Institute for Development Education** (RIDE; off Map p337; ☎044-27268223; www.rideindia.org) works with villages around Kanchipuram to remove children from forced labour and into transition schools. Volunteers can contribute in teaching, administrative and support roles.

Working with Women

See www.indianngos.com for more charities working to empower and educate women.

Mumbai

» Volunteers can support English and art classes, design workshops or do research or data analysis at **Apne Aap Women Worldwide** (☎022-23004201; www.apneaap.org; Chandramani Budh Vihar Municipal School, ground fl, 13th Lane, Kamathipura), an anti-trafficking organisation that works in legal protection and provides learning and livelihood training to women's and teenage girls' groups.

Travel with Children

Top Regions for Kids

Goa

Gorgeous white sand beaches make Goa the perfect family choice for lazing the days away with swimming, sand castles, boat trips, and an excursion to a spice plantation near Ponda to bathe with an elephant.

Kerala

Backwater houseboat adventures, elephant spotting at wildlife reserves, tea-picking in firefly studded plantations, and some serious beach time await beside the ocean.

Fascinating, frustrating, thrilling and fulfilling; India is every bit as much a great adventure for children as it is for parents. Though the sensory overload may be, at times, overwhelming for younger kids and even short journeys by bus or train can prove rigorous for the entire family, the colours, scents, sights and sounds of India more than compensate by setting young imaginations ablaze. Gaze at twinkling Diwali candles with your under-tens, dig your heels into white sand beaches while your toddlers build a sand-temple or two; tuck into family-sized thalis at a bus station lunch joint or trek through forests with your teenagers: perfect moments like these make the occasional aches and pains of Indian travel worthwhile. By taking your children along for the ride you'll not only be creating fantastic childhood memories but also likely to foster a fascination and fondness for this incredible, riotous country that will last a lifetime.

India for Kids

A Warm Welcome

In many respects, travel with children in India can be a delight, and warm welcomes are frequent. Smaller charges in particular will be constantly coddled and offered treats and smiles and warm welcomes. Hotels will almost always come up with an extra bed or two, and restaurants with a familiar meal.

Before You Go

Remember to visit your doctor to discuss vaccinations, health advisories and other health-related issues involving your children well in advance of travel. For more tips on travel in India, and first-hand accounts of travels in the country, pick up Lonely Planet's *Travel with Children*.

What to pack

If you're travelling with a baby or toddler, there are several items worth packing in quantity: disposable or washable nappies, nappy rash cream (Calendula cream works well against heat rash, too), extra bottles, a good stock of wet wipes, infant formula and jarred or rehydratable food. You can get all these items in many parts of India, too, but often prices are at a premium and brands may not be those you recognise. Another good idea is a fold-up baby bed; a pushchair, though, is optional, since there are few places with pavements even enough to use it successfully. For older children, make sure you bring good sturdy footwear, a hat or two, a few less-precious toys – that won't be mourned if lost or damaged – and a swimming jacket, life jacket or water wings for the sea or pool. Finally, child-friendly insect repellent and sun lotion are a must.

Railway porters will produce boiled sweets from their pockets; clucking old ladies will pinch rosy toddler cheeks; domestic tourists will thrill at taking a photograph or two beside your bonny, bouncing baby.

But while all this is fabulous for outgoing children it may prove tiring, or even disconcerting, for those of a more retiring disposition. The key, as a parent on the road in India, is to stay alert to children's needs and to remain firm in fulfilling them. If, for instance, your four-year-old starlet is happy to be photographed for the umpteenth time, there's probably no harm in allowing it; if, on the other hand, they're feeling camera-shy, you may find it easiest to practise a little paparazzi evasion. Remember, though, that the attention your children will inevitably receive is almost always good-natured; kids are the centre of life in many Indian households, and your own will be treated – usually for better rather than worse – just the same.

Eating

There is plenty on Indian menus countrywide to satisfy even the most sensitive childhood palates, but if you're travelling in the most family-friendly regions of India, such as Goa, Kerala or the big cities, feeding your brood is even easier. Here you will find street snacks to keep busy children topped up, and familiar Western dishes in abundance. While on the road, easy portable snacks such as bananas, samosas, *puri* (puffy dough pockets) and packaged biscuits (Parle G brand are a perennial hit) will keep diminutive hunger pangs at bay. Adventurous eaters and vegetarian children, meanwhile, will delight in experimenting with the vast range of tastes and textures available at the Indian table: *paneer* (unfermented cheese) dishes, simple dhals (mild lentil curries), creamy kormas, buttered naans (tandoori breads), pilaus (rice dishes) and Tibetan *momos* (steamed or fried dumplings) are all firm favourites while few children, no matter how culinarily unadventurous, can resist the finger-food fun of a vast South Indian dosa (savoury crepe) served up for breakfast.

Sleeping

India offers such an array of accommodation – from beach huts to heritage boutiques to five-star fantasies – that you're bound to be able to find something that will appeal to the whole family. Even the swishest of hotels are almost always child-friendly, as are many budget hotels, whose staff will usually rustle up an extra mattress or two; most places won't mind cramming several children into a regular-sized double room along with their parents. Travelling with a baby, it can make sense to pack the lightest possible travel cot you can find (companies such as KidCo make excellent pop-up tent-style beds) since hotel cots may prove precarious. If your budget stretches to it, a good way to maintain familial energy levels is to mix in

CHILDREN'S HIGHLIGHTS

» Hampi Make like the Flintstones on the boulder-strewn shores of the Tungabhadra River, crossable by coracle; explore magical ancient ruins, and stop for a tasty dosa at the riverside Mango Tree.

» Elephants in Karnataka Visit the pachyderm retirees at the Dubare Forest Reserve near Madikeri; get busy bathing and feeding them, and then hop on for a ride.

» Goa's dolphins Splash out on a dolphin-spotting boat trip from almost any Goan beach to see the sleek grey mammals cavorting among the waves.

» Hill Station Monkeys Head up to a hill station for close encounters with the manifold monkeys that will readily sneak into your bedroom and steal your precious packet of Hobnobs if you give them half a chance. Be aware that monkeys can carry rabies.

Funnest Forms of Transport

» Auto-rickshaw Hurtle the back alleys to create a scene worthy of Indiana Jones.

» Hand-pulled rickshaw, Matheran A narrow-gauge toy train takes visitors most of the way up to this cute, monkey-infested hill station, after which your children can choose to continue to the village on horseback or in a clunky, bumpy hand-pulled rickshaw.

» Backwater boat, Allapuzha Take a cruise or rent a houseboat to trawl Kerala's beautiful, mangrove-infested backwaters. If you happen to hit town on the second Saturday in August, take the kids along to see the spectacular Nehru Trophy Snake Boat race.

Best Beachfront Kick-backs

» Palolem, Goa Hole up in a beachfront palm-thatched hut and watch your kids cavort at beautiful Palolem beach, which sports the shallowest, safest waters in Goa.

» Patnem, Goa Just up the leafy lane from Palolem, quieter Patnem draws scores of long-stayers with children to its nice sand beach and cool, calm, child-friendly beach restaurants.

» Havelock Island Splash about in the shallows at languid Havelock Island, part of the Andaman Island chain, where, for older, adventurous children, there's spectacular diving on offer.

---

a few top-end stays throughout your travels. The very best five stars come equipped with children's pools, games rooms and even children's clubs, while an occasional night with a warm bubble bath, room-service macaroni cheese and the Disney channel will revive even the most disgruntled young traveller's spirits.

On the Road

Travel in India, be it by taxi, local bus, train or air, can be arduous for the whole family. Plan fun, easy days to follow longer bus or train rides, pack plenty of diversions (iPads or laptops with a stock of movies downloaded make invaluable travel companions, as do the good old-fashioned story books and cheap toys and games available widely across India), but most of all don't be put off: it might take you a while to get there (and there are few words more daunting than 'delay' to

already frazzled parents), but chances are it will be well worth it when you do.

Health

The availability of a decent standard of healthcare, particularly in the most traveller-frequented parts of India, makes keeping children healthy while on the road easier than you might think. It's almost always easy to track down a doctor at short notice, most hotels will be able to recommend a reliable one, and prescriptions are quickly and cheaply filled over the counter at numerous pharmacies. In general, the most common concerns for on-the-road parents include heat rash, skin complaints such as impetigo, insect bites or stings and tummy troubles, all of which can be treated swiftly and effectively, particularly with the help of a well-equipped first aid kit. For more information on Health see p502.

regions at a glance

South India is a wonderfully diverse patchwork of states. The vernacular vary, the customs are distinctive and the topography spectacularly manifold. South India's mind-shaking mix of state-of-the-art and timeless tradition mean that no matter where you choose to travel you'll be rewarded with an invigorating assault on the senses.

For travellers, South India's remarkable diversity is most often apparent in its extraordinary wealth of architecture, wildlife, landscapes, festivals, handicrafts and cuisine. And then there's spirituality – the beating heart of the entire nation – which faithfully pulsates all the way from the jagged peaks of the Himalayas to the lush jungles of the southern plains.

Mumbai

Architecture ✓✓✓
Gastronomy ✓✓✓
Nightlife ✓✓✓

Colonial Relics
The British left striking colonial-era architecture in Mumbai, highlighted by Unesco-listed Chhatrapati Shivaji Terminus, the High Court and the University of Mumbai.

Culture & Cuisine
Mumbai's collision of cultures means it's a haven for foodies. A kaleidoscope of flavour from all over India vies for tastebud attention with imported cuisines the world over. Yum.

Bollywood & Booze
As India's financial powerhouse and the world's most prolific film industry, Mumbai parties hard...even on Wednesdays! The subcontinent's wildest bars, hottest clubs and exclusive Bollywood bashes showcase a tipsier side of India.

p39

Maharashtra

Caves ✓✓✓
Beaches ✓✓
Wine ✓✓

Caves
The World Heritage Sites of Ajanta and Ellora house the most exquisite collection of cave paintings and rock sculptures dating back to India's golden ages.

Beaches
Strung out along Maharashtra's Konkan Coast are some of the most secluded but beautiful beaches, custom-made for romantics, adventurers, loners and philosophers alike.

Wine
Nasik, the *grand cru* of India's up-and-coming wine industry, proudly flaunts a few world-class drops in the many excellent cellars around town.

p77

Goa

Beaches ✓✓✓
Food ✓✓
Architecture ✓✓✓

Beaches
They're so beautiful that they're practically a cliché, but even the most hardcore travellers can't resist Goa's stunning beachscapes. Lots of them are backed by shady palm-tree groves.

Food
Goa has fresh, fresh seafood and a long tradition of preparing it in brilliant ways, often with the ubiquitous coconut. Sometimes it's the random shack on the beach that does it best.

Architecture
Portuguese colonialism's most attractive legacy may be its pretty buildings. Mansions in Quepem and Chandor, houses in Panjim, Old Goa's grand religious structures, and little homes and churches across the state are pure eye candy.

p115

Karnataka

Temples ✓✓✓
National Parks ✓✓
Cuisine ✓✓

Temples
From the Hoysala beauties at Belur, Halebid and Somnathpur to the electric Virupaksha Temple in Hampi or the quaint shrines in Gokarna and Udupi, Karnataka is strewn with fantastic temples that overwhelm you with their ambience and ritual finery.

National Parks
The Nilgiri Biosphere Reserve boasts some of the most pristine forests in India, and there's abundant wildlife to be sighted in national parks such as Bandipur, Kabini and Nagarhole.

Cuisine
Start off with the delectable Udupi vegetarian thali, then move on to some fiery Mangalorean seafood, and finally wash it all down with fresh draught in beertown Bengaluru.

p155

Andhra Pradesh

Religious Sights ✓✓✓
Food ✓✓
Beaches ✓

Religious sites
Hindus flock to Sri Venkateswara Temple at Tirumala. There are ancient ruins of once-flourishing Buddhist centres across the state, while Hyderabad has grand Islamic architecture. Further south, devotees jet in to Puttaparthi to see Sai Baba.

Food
Biryani is a local obsession. The taste will leave you salivating long after your departure. Meanwhile 'hyderabadi haleem' has been patented so that it can't be served unless it meets strict quality standards.

Beaches
Vishakhapatnam has a gorgeous stretch of coastline. Tourism is geared towards the domestic market, bringing a unique and festive atmosphere.

p211

Kerala

Backwaters ✓✓✓
Food ✓✓✓
Wildlife ✓✓

Backwaters
Kerala's backwaters are vast lakes and long canals that spread like tendril inland. One of India's most relaxing and beautiful experiences is to stay overnight on a houseboat or take a canoe trip.

Food
Delicious, delicate cuisine flavoured with coconut and myriad spices – Kerala's table is born of a melting pot of influences and remarkable geography.

Wildlife
Kerala has a concentration of national parks inland where, amid lush mountainous landscapes you can spot wild elephants, tigers, lions, and myriad bird and other wildlife.

p247

Tamil Nadu

Temples ✓✓✓
Hill Stations ✓✓
Heritage Hotels ✓

Temples
The amazing architecture, rituals and colourful festivals of Tamil Nadu's Hindu temples draw pilgrims from around the county; major temples have soaring *gopurams* (gateway towers) and intricately carved, pillared *mandapams* (pavilions).

Hill Stations
The hill stations of the Westerns Ghats offer cool weather, the chance to hike to gorgeous mountain vistas, bustling festival seasons, and cosy colonial-era guesthouses with open fires.

Heritage Hotels
Restored spots to lay your head include the picturesque houses of Puducherry's French Quarter, the palace hotels of the hill stations and the Chettiar mansions of the south.

p309

Andaman Islands

Diving & Snorkelling ✓✓✓
Beaches ✓✓✓
Tribal Groups ✓✓

Diving
Exploring the underwater jungles of coral and tropical fish is what lures most visitors to the islands; perfect for beginners or dive masters alike.

Beaches
Whether you're searching for that picture-postcard beach, or miles of deserted coastline – here you'll find some of the nicest beaches in India.

Ethnic groups
An anthropologist's dream, the Andamans are home to fascinating tribal groups; some still literally living in the Stone Age. Most reside on outlying islands, which tourists are prohibited from visiting, but elsewhere you'll encounter an interesting mix of South and Southeast Asian settlers.

p389

Look out for these icons:

 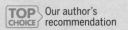 Our author's recommendation

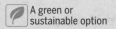 A green or sustainable option

 No payment required

On the Road

Going Green
Woman selling herbs and green leafy vegetables at a market in Hyderabad

GREG ELMS/LONELY PLANET IMAGES ©

Mumbai (Bombay)

Best Places to Eat

» Khyber (p61)
» Peshawri (p65)
» Five Spice (p62)
» Trishna (p63)
» Culture Curry (p65)

Best Places to Stay

» Taj Mahal Palace, Mumbai (p56)
» Iskcon (p60)
» YWCA (p57)
» Hotel Moti (p57)
» Residency Hotel (p58)

Why Go?

Mumbai is a beautiful mess, full of dreamers and hard-labourers, actors and gangsters, stray dogs and exotic birds, artists and servants, fisherfolk and *crorepatis* (millionaires), and lots more. Its crumbling architecture in various states of Technicolor dilapidation is a reminder that Mumbai once dreamt even bigger, leaving a brick-and-mortar museum around its maze of chaotic streets as evidence that its place in the world has always been a poetic disaster.

Today Mumbai is home to the most prolific film industry, one of Asia's biggest slums and the largest tropical forest in an urban zone. It's India's financial powerhouse, fashion epicentre and a pulse point of religious tension. Between the fantastical architecture and the modern skyscrapers, the fine dining and frenetic streets, the urban grit and suburban glamour, the madness and the mayhem, there's a cinematic cityscape set to a playful and addictive raga – a complex soundtrack that dances to the beat of its own *desi* drum.

When to Go
Mumbai (Bombay)

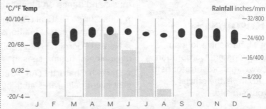

Apr–May Some like it hot...some like it *hot*.

Aug–Sep Mumbai goes Ganesh crazy during its biggest and most exciting festival, Ganesh Chaturthi.

Oct–Feb Put away the scuba gear as the monsoons retreat for Mumbai's 'cool' season.

Fast Facts

» Population: 16.4 million

» Area: 444 sq km

» Area code: ☏022

» Languages: Marathi, Hindi, Gujarati, English

» Sleeping prices: **$** below ₹1000, **$$** ₹1000 to ₹4000, **$$$** above ₹4000

Top Tips

Many international flights arrive after midnight. Save yourself some moon-lit hassle by carrying detailed landmark directions for your hotel – many airport taxi drivers don't speak English and can dwindle precious sleep time hunting it down.

Eicher City Map Mumbai (₹250) is an excellent street atlas, worth picking up if you'll be spending some time here.

Resources

» Maharashtra Tourism Development Corporation (www.maharashtratourism .gov.in) is the official tourism site.

A Mouthful of Mumbai

Mumbai is a city shaped by flavours from all over India and the world. Throw yourself into the culinary kaleidoscope by sampling Parsi *dhansak* (meat with curried lentils and rice), Gujarati or Keralan thalis ('all-you-can-eat' meals), Mughlai kebabs, Goan vindaloo and Mangalorean seafood. And don't forget, if you see Bombay duck on a menu, it's actually *bombil* fish dried in the sun and deep-fried.

Streetwise, don't miss Mumbai's famous beach *bhelpuri,* readily available at Girgaum Chowpatty, a flavour summersault of crisp-fried thin rounds of dough mixed with puffed rice, lentils, lemon juice, onions, herbs, chilli and tamarind chutney piled high on takeaway plates. Other street stalls offering rice plates, samosas, *pav bhaji* (spiced vegetables and bread) and *vada pav* (deep-fried spiced lentil-ball sandwich) do a brisk trade around the city.

DON'T MISS

For many, a visit to cosmopolitan Mumbai is all about dining, nightlife and shopping, but the city offers far more than nocturnal amusement and retail therapy. Nowhere is that more evident than in the spectacular maze of Gothic, Victorian, Indo-Saracenic and art deco architecture, remnants of the British colonial era and countless years of European influence. **Chhatrapati Shivaji Terminus (Victoria Terminus)**, **High Court**, **University of Mumbai**, **Taj Mahal Palace hotel** and the **Gateway of India** are just the most prominent – little architectural jewels dot the urban quagmire throughout the metropolis and stumbling upon them is one of Mumbai's great joys.

Top Mumbai Festivals

» Mumbai Festival (Jan, citywide, p54) A showcase of Mumbai music, dance and culture

» Elephanta Festival (Feb, Elephanta Island, p54) Classical music and dance on Elephanta Island

» Kala Ghoda Festival (Feb, citywide, p54) Two weeks of art performances and exhibitions

» Nariyal Poornima (Aug, Colaba, p54) Commemorates the beginning of fishing season

» Ganesh Chaturthi (Aug/Sep, citywide, p54) Mumbai's biggest event celebrates all things Ganesh

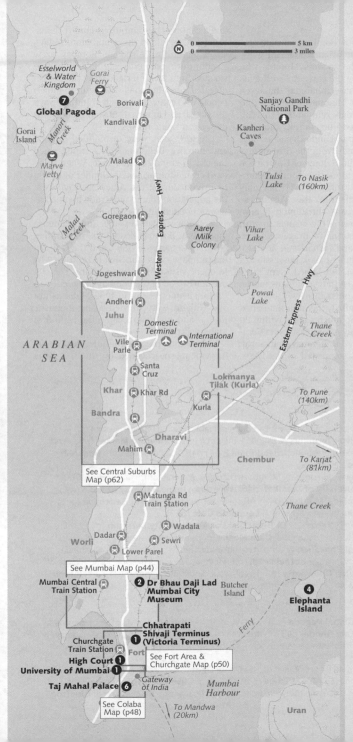

Mumbai Highlights

❶ Marvel at the magnificence of Mumbai's colonial-era architecture: **Chhatrapati Shivaji Terminus** (p46), **University of Mumbai** (p46) and **High Court** (p47)

❷ Ogle the Renaissance-revival interiors of the **Dr Bhau Daji Lad Mumbai City Museum** (p47)

❸ Dine like a Maharaja at one of India's best **restaurants** (p61)

❹ Behold the commanding triple-headed Shiva at **Elephanta Island** (p76)

❺ Get lost amid the clutter in Mumbai's ancient **bazaars** (p68)

❻ Sleep in one of the world's iconic hotels, the **Taj Mahal Palace, Mumbai** (p56)

❼ Pay serene respects to an astonishing feat of spiritually fuelled engineering at the **Global Pagoda** (p51)

History

In 1996 the city of Bombay officially became Mumbai. The original Marathi name is derived from the goddess Mumba, who was worshipped by the early Koli residents whose fisherfolk have inhabited the seven islands that form Mumbai since the 2nd century BC. Amazingly, remnants of this culture remain huddled along the city shoreline today. A succession of Hindu dynasties held sway over the islands from the 6th century AD until the Muslim Sultans of Gujarat annexed the area in the 14th century, eventually ceding it to Portugal in 1534. The only memorable contribution the Portuguese made to the area was christening it Bom Bahai, before throwing the islands in with the dowry of Catherine of Braganza when she married England's Charles II in 1661. The British government took possession of the islands in 1665, but leased them three years later to the East India Company for the paltry annual rent of UK£10.

Then called Bombay, the area flourished as a trading port. So much so that within 20 years the presidency of the East India Company was transferred to Bombay from Surat. Bombay's fort was completed in the 1720s,

and a century later ambitious land reclamation projects joined the islands into today's single landmass. Although Bombay grew steadily during the 18th century, it remained isolated from its hinterland until the British defeated the Marathas (the central Indian people who controlled much of India at various times) and annexed substantial portions of western India in 1818.

The fort walls were dismantled in 1864 and massive building works transformed the city in grand colonial style. When Bombay became the principal supplier of cotton to Britain during the American Civil War, the population soared and trade boomed as money flooded into the city.

A major player in the Independence movement, Bombay hosted the first Indian National Congress in 1885, and the Quit India campaign was launched here in 1942 by frequent visitor Mahatma Gandhi. The city became capital of the Bombay presidency after Independence, but in 1960 Maharashtra and Gujarat were divided along linguistic lines – and Bombay became the capital of Maharashtra.

The rise of the pro-Maratha regionalist movement, spearheaded by the Shiv Sena

MUMBAI IN...

Two Days

Start at the grandaddy of Mumbai's colonial-era giants, the old Victoria Terminus, **Chhatrapati Shivaji Terminus** (CST; p46) and stroll up to **Crawford Market** (p68) and the maze of bazaars here. Lunch at **Rajdhani** (p64), with a juice shake from **Badshah Snacks & Drinks** (p64).

Spend the afternoon admiring Mumbai's marvellous architecture at the **High Court** (p47) and the **University of Mumbai** (p46). Walk down to the **Gateway of India** (p43) and **Taj Mahal Palace, Mumbai** (p43). After sunset, eat streetside at **Bademiya** (p61). Swap tall tales with fellow travellers at **Leopold's Café** (p66).

The next day, visit the ornate **Dr Bhau Daji Lad Mumbai City Museum** (p47), then head to Kemp's Corner for lunch at **Café Moshe** (p63) and some shopping. Make your way down to **Mani Bhavan** (p47), the museum dedicated to Gandhi, and finish the day wandering the tiny lanes of **Kotachiwadi** (p59) followed by a beach sunset and a plate of *bhelpuri* at **Girguam Chowpatty** (p47). A blowout dinner at **Khyber** (p61) won't let you forget Mumbai soon.

Four Days

Head out to the **Global Pagoda** (p51) and return in the afternoon to visit the museums and galleries of **Kala Ghoda** (p43). In the evening, head to Bandra for a candle-lit dinner at **Sheesha** (p65), followed by some seriously hip bar action with a view at **Aer** (p66) in Worli.

Another day could be spent visiting the **Dhobi Ghat** (p49) and the nearby **Mahalaxmi Temple** (p50) and **Haji Ali's Mosque** (p49). Lunch at **Olive Bar & Kitchen** (p67) at Mahalaxmi Racecourse and then rest up for a night of avant-garde clubbing at **Bluefrog** (p67) in Worli.

(Hindu Party; literally 'Shivaji's Army'), shattered the city's multicultural mould by actively discriminating against Muslims and non-Maharashtrians. The Shiv Sena won power in the city's municipal elections in 1985. Communalist tensions increased and the city's cosmopolitan self-image took a battering when nearly 800 people died in riots following the destruction of the Babri Masjid in Ayodhya in December 1992.

The riots were followed by a dozen bombings on 12 March 1993, which killed more than 300 people and damaged the Bombay Stock Exchange and Air India Building. The July 2006 train bombings, which killed more than 200 people, and November 2008's coordinated attacks on 10 of the city's landmarks, which lasted three days and killed 173 people, are reminders that tensions are never far from the surface.

India's '26/11' – as the Mumbai attacks have come to be known – was a wake-up call for the city. Security is now intense at many of the city's prominent landmarks, well-known hotels and important financial and government buildings. Entire streets have been sealed off in some cases, providing impromptu cricket pitches for the city's numerous street youth. But Mumbai soldiers on, content to up the ante of inconvenience to maintain the Mumbaikar spirit, a defiant Marathi manner that steadies the city as India's commercial hub and a global financial powerhouse.

◉ Sights

Mumbai, the capital of Maharashtra, is an island connected by bridges to the mainland. The city's (off-limits) naval docks dominate the island's eastern seaboard. The city's commercial and cultural centre is at the southern, claw-shaped end of the island known as South Mumbai. The southernmost peninsula is Colaba, traditionally the travellers' nerve centre, with most of the major attractions, and directly north of Colaba is the busy commercial area known as Fort, where the old British fort once stood. It's bordered on the west by a series of interconnected, fenced grassy areas known as maidans (pronounced may-*dahns*).

Though just as essential a part of the city as South Mumbai, the area north of here is collectively known as 'the suburbs'. The airport and many of Mumbai's best restaurants, shopping and nightspots are here, particularly in the upmarket suburbs of Bandra and Juhu.

The opening of the cable-stayed Bandra-Worli Sea Link in 2009 cut travel time between the two areas from one hour to seven minutes, making these upmarket suburbs easily accessible to travellers.

COLABA

For mapped locations of all the following sights, see Map p48.

Sprawling down the city's southernmost peninsula, Colaba is a bustling district packed with street stalls, markets, bars and budget to midrange lodgings. **Colaba Causeway** (Shahid Bhagat Singh Marg) dissects the promontory and Colaba's jumble of side streets and gently crumbling mansions.

Sassoon Dock (off Map p48) is a scene of intense and pungent activity at dawn (around 5am) when colourfully clad **Koli fisherfolk** sort the catch unloaded from fishing boats at the quay. The fish drying in the sun are *bombil,* the fish used in the dish Bombay duck. Photography at the dock is forbidden.

TOP CHOICE **Taj Mahal Palace, Mumbai** LANDMARK
This iconic hotel (p56) is a fairy-tale blend of Islamic and Renaissance styles jostling for prime position among Mumbai's famous landmarks. Facing the harbour, it was built in 1903 by the Parsi industrialist JN Tata, supposedly after he was refused entry to one of the European hotels on account of being 'a native'.

Gateway of India MONUMENT
This bold basalt arch of colonial triumph faces out to Mumbai Harbour from the tip of Apollo Bunder. Derived from the Islamic styles of 16th-century Gujarat, it was built to commemorate the 1911 royal visit of King George V. It was completed in 1924. Ironically, the gateway's British architects used it just 24 years later to parade off their last British regiment as India marched towards Independence.

These days, the gateway is a favourite gathering spot for locals and a top spot for people-watching. Giant-balloon sellers, photographers, beggars and touts rub shoulders with Indian and foreign tourists, creating all the hubbub of a bazaar. Boats depart from the gateway's wharfs for Elephanta Island and Mandwa.

KALA GHODA

'Black Horse', the area between Colaba and Fort, contains most of Mumbai's main galleries and museums alongside a wealth of

Mumbai

1 km
0.5 miles

Arabian Sea

Haji Ali's Mosque

Dr Bhau Daji Lad Mumbai City Museum

Mahalaxmi Dhobi Ghat

Reay Rd

Reay Rd Train Station

Sandhurst Train Station

BYCULLA

Byculla Train Station

Victoria Gardens (Veermata Jijabai Bhonsle Udyan)

Patanwala Marg

Victoria Rd

S Balwant singh Rd

Jail Rd

J Jijibhoy Rd

Sir JJ Rd

Clare Rd

Dhabu St

Mutton St

Maulana Azad Rd

Morland Rd

J Boman Behram Marg

Foras Rd

Grant Rd

Sardar V Patel Rd

To Child Rights & You (500m)

Mahalaxmi Train Station

Bapurao Jagtap Marg

Maulana Azad Rd

To Vatsalya Foundation (600m);
Four Seasons (700m);
Bluefrog (1km); Zenzi Mills (1km);
Cathay Pacific (1.6km);
Iyengar Yogashraya (1.7km)

Mahalaxmi Racecourse

Willingdon Sports Club Golf Course

Mumbai Central Train Station

Falkland Rd

Tardeo Rd

Grant Rd Train Station

Dr D Bhadkamkar Rd (Lamington Rd)

OPERA HOUSE

To Nehru Centre (200m)

Lala Lajpat Rai Rd

Vatsalabai Desai Chowk

Kemp's Corner

G Deshmukh Rd (Peddar Rd)

A Kranti Marg

August Kranti Maidan

Laburnum Rd

Sitaram Patkar Rd

Tata Garden

Hanging Gardens

Priyardashini Park

colonial-era buildings. The best way to see these buildings is on a guided (p53) or self-guided (p55) walking tour.

TOP CHOICE **Chhatrapati Shivaji Maharaj Vastu Sangrahalaya (Prince of Wales Museum)** MUSEUM
(Map p50; www.themuseummumbai.com; K Dubash Marg; Indian/foreigner ₹25/300, camera/video ₹200/1000; ⊙10.45am-6pm Tue-Sun) Mumbai's biggest and best museum, this domed behemoth is an intriguing hodgepodge of Islamic, Hindu and British architecture displaying a mix of dusty exhibits from all over India. Opened in 1923 to commemorate King George V's first visit to India (back in 1905, while he was still Prince of Wales), its flamboyant Indo-Saracenic style was designed by George Wittet – who also did the Gateway of India.

The museum has undergone a ₹12 million upkeep renovation, which introduced a fascinating new miniature-painting gallery and a new gallery dedicated to Vishnu. Elsewhere, the vast collection includes impressive Hindu and Buddhist sculpture, terracotta figurines from the Indus Valley, porcelain and some particularly vicious weaponry.

FREE **Jehangir Art Gallery** ART GALLERY
(Map p50; 161B MG Rd; ⊙11am-7pm) Hosts interesting shows by local artists. Most works are for sale. Rows of hopeful artists often display their work on the pavement outside.

National Gallery of Modern Art ART GALLERY
(Map p48; MG Rd; Indian/foreigner ₹10/150; ⊙11am-6pm Tue-Sun) On Mahatma Ghandi (MG) Rd. Has a bright, spacious and modern exhibition space showcasing changing exhibitions by Indian and international artists.

Keneseth Eliyahoo Synagogue SYNAGOGUE
(Map p50; www.jacobsassoon.org; Dr VB Gandhi Marg; admission free, camera ₹100; ⊙9am-6pm) Built in 1884, this impossibly sky-blue synagogue still functions and is tenderly maintained by the city's dwindling Jewish community (and protected to Baghdad Green Zone levels by Mumbai's finest).

FORT
Lined up in a row and vying for your attention with aristocratic pomp, many of Mumbai's majestic Victorian buildings pose on the edge of **Oval Maidan**. This land, and the **Cross** and **Azad Maidans** immediately to the north, was on the oceanfront in those days, and this series of grandiose structures faced west directly out to the Arabian Sea.

Mumbai

For mapped locations of the following sights see Map p50.

TOP CHOICE **Chhatrapati Shivaji Terminus (Victoria Terminus)** HISTORICAL BUILDING

Imposing, exuberant and overflowing with people, this is the city's most extravagant Gothic building, the beating heart of its railway network, and an aphorism for colonial India. As historian Christopher London put it, 'the Victoria Terminus is to the British Raj what the Taj Mahal is to the Mughal empire'. It's a meringue of Victorian, Hindu and Islamic styles whipped into an imposing Daliesque structure of buttresses, domes, turrets, spires and stained-glass windows.

Designed by Frederick Stevens, it was completed in 1887, 34 years after the first train in India left this site. Today it's the busiest train station in Asia. Officially renamed Chhatrapati Shivaji Terminus (CST) in 1998, it's still better known locally as VT. It was added to the Unesco World Heritage list in 2004.

University of Mumbai (Bombay University) HISTORICAL BUILDING

Looking like a 15th-century French-Gothic masterpiece plopped incongruously among Mumbai's palm trees, this university on Bhaurao Patil Marg was designed by Gilbert Scott of London's St Pancras Station fame. There is an exquisite **University Library** and **Convocation Hall**, as well as an 80m-high **Rajabai Clock Tower**, decorated with detailed carvings, but since the 2008 terror attacks on Mumbai the public is no longer allowed inside the grounds. The architecture is best admired by strolling along Bhaurao Patil Marg as trees obscure much of the splendour when viewed from the Oval Maidan.

High Court
HISTORICAL BUILDING

(Eldon Rd) A hive of daily activity, packed with judges, barristers and other cogs in the Indian justice system, the High Court is an elegant 1848 neo-Gothic building. The design was inspired by a German castle and was obviously intended to dispel any doubts about the authority of the justice dispensed inside, though local stone carvers presumably saw things differently: they carved a one-eyed monkey fiddling with the scales of justice on one pillar. You are permitted (and it is highly recommended) to walk around inside the building and check out the pandemonium and pageantry of public cases that are in progress – just walk right in! You'll have to surrender your camera to the guards, then make your way through the maze-like building to the original building's courtyard opposite Court 6.

St Thomas' Cathedral
CHURCH

(Veer Nariman Rd; ⊙6.30am-6pm) Recently restored to its former glory, this charming cathedral is the oldest English building standing in Mumbai (construction began in 1672, though it remained unfinished until 1718). The cathedral is an interracial marriage of Byzantine and colonial-era architecture, and its airy, whitewashed interior is full of exhibitionist colonial memorials.

GIRGUAM CHOWPATTY AREA
For mapped locations of the following sights see Map p44.

Marine Drive & Girguam Chowpatty BEACH
Built on land reclaimed from Back Bay in 1920, Marine Drive (Netaji Subhashchandra Bose Rd) arcs along the shore of the Arabian Sea from Nariman Point past Girguam Chowpatty (where it's known as Chowpatty Seaface) and continues to the foot of Malabar Hill. Lined with flaking art deco apartments, it's one of Mumbai's most popular

ⓘ EXILE ON MAIN STREET

Street numbers on buildings are basically nonexistent in Mumbai and street signs sometimes come in English, sometimes in Hindi, sometimes both, a lot of the time not at all. But signs outside legitimate businesses often include the street address, so look for those to orient yourself when street signs fail you.

promenades and sunset-watching spots. Its twinkling night-time lights earned it the nickname 'the Queen's Necklace'.

Girguam Chowpatty (often referred to as 'Chowpatty Beach' in English, though this means 'Beach Beach' and often confuses locals) remains a favourite evening spot for courting couples, families, political rallies and anyone out to enjoy what passes for fresh air. Eating an evening time *bhelpuri* at the throng of stalls found here is an essential part of the Mumbai experience. Forget about taking a dip: the water is toxic.

FREE **Mani Bhavan** MUSEUM
(☎23805864; www.gandhi-manibhavan.org; 19 Laburnum Rd; ⊙9.30am-6pm) As poignant as it is tiny, this museum is in the building where Mahatma Gandhi stayed during visits to Bombay from 1917 to 1934. The museum showcases the room where the leader formulated his philosophy of satyagraha (nonviolent protest) and launched the 1932 Civil Disobedience campaign that led to the end of British rule. Exhibitions include a photographic record of his life, along with dioramas and original documents, such as letters he wrote to Adolf Hitler and Franklin D Roosevelt. Nearby, August Kranti Maidan is where the campaign to persuade the British to 'Quit India' was launched in 1942.

MALABAR HILL
Mumbai's most exclusive neighbourhood of sky-scratchers and private palaces, **Malabar Hill** (Map p44) is at the northern promontory of Back Bay and signifies the top rung for the city's social and economic climbers.

Surprisingly, one of Mumbai's most sacred and tranquil oases lies concealed among apartment blocks at its southern tip. **Banganga Tank** (off Map p44) is a precinct of serene temples, bathing pilgrims, meandering, traffic-free streets and picturesque old *dharamsalas* (pilgrims' rest houses). The wooden pole in the centre of the tank is the centre of the earth: according to legend, Lord Ram created the tank by piercing the earth with his arrow.

For some of the best views of Girguam Chowpatty and the graceful arc of Marine Drive, visit the small **Kamala Nehru Park** (Map p44).

BYCULLA
TOP CHOICE **Dr Bhau Daji Lad Mumbai City Museum** MUSEUM
(Map p44; Dr Babasaheb Ambedkar Rd; Indian/ foreigner ₹10/100; ⊙10am-5.30pm Thu-Tue)

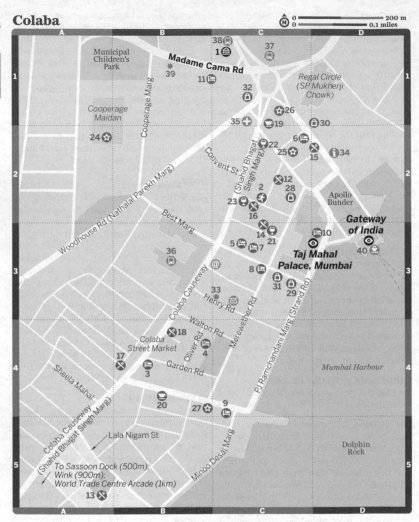

Jijamata Udyan – aka Veermata Jijabai Bhonsle Udyan and formerly named Victoria Gardens – is a lush and sprawling mid-19th-century garden and zoo. It's home to this gorgeous museum, originally built in Renaissance revival style in 1872 as the Victoria & Albert Museum. It reopened in 2007 after an impressive and sensitive four-year renovation. In addition to extensive structural work, the building's Minton tile floors, gilt ceiling moulding, and ornate columns, chandeliers and staircases were restored to their former, historically accurate glory. Even the sweet mint-green paint choice was based on historical research. Also restored were the museum's 3500-plus objects centering on Mumbai's history – clay models of village life, photography and maps, archaeological finds, costumes, a library of books and manuscripts, industrial and agricultural exhibits, and silver, copper, Bidriware, laquerware, weaponry and exquisite pottery, all set against the museum's very distracting, very stunning decor. Skip the zoo.

MAHALAXMI TO WORLI

For mapped locations of the following sights see Map p44.

TOP CHOICE **Haji Ali's Mosque**　　　MOSQUE

Floating like a sacred mirage off the coast, this mosque, one of Mumbai's most striking symbols, is an exquisite Indo-Islamic shrine. Built in the 19th century on the site of a 15th-century structure, it contains the tomb of the Muslim saint Haji – legend has it that Haji Ali died while on a pilgrimage to Mecca and his casket miraculously floated back to this spot. A long causeway reaches into the Arabian Sea, providing access to the mosque. Thousands of pilgrims, especially on Thursdays and Fridays, cross it to make their visit, many donating to the beggars who line the way; but at high tide, water covers the causeway and the mosque becomes an island. Once inside, pilgrims fervently kiss the dressings of the tomb.

Erosion has taken its toll on the concrete structure, and at press time, renovations had been ongoing since 2008. The structural upgrade includes beautiful white Rajasthani marble – the same used for the Taj Mahal. The dargah will remain open, but access may be limited.

FREE **Mahalaxmi Dhobi Ghat**　　　LANDMARK

If you've had washing done in Mumbai, chances are your clothes have already visited this 140-year-old **dhobi ghat** (place where clothes are washed). The whole hamlet is Mumbai's oldest and biggest human-powered washing machine: every day hundreds of people beat the dirt out of thousands of kilograms of soiled Mumbai clothes and linen in 1026

MUMBAI (BOMBAY)

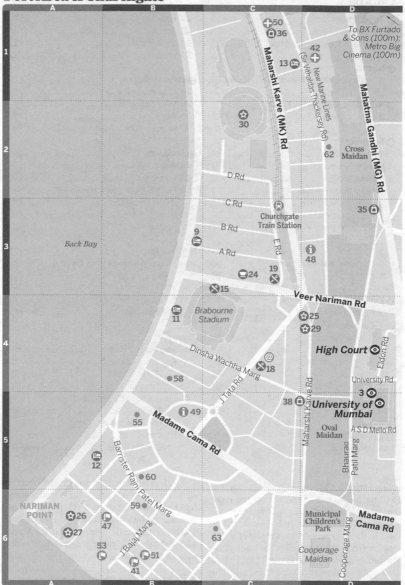

open-air troughs. The best view, and photo opportunity, is from the bridge across the railway tracks near Mahalaxmi train station.

Mahalaxmi Temple HINDU TEMPLE
It's only fitting that in money-mad Mumbai one of the busiest and most colourful temples is dedicated to Mahalaxmi, the goddess of wealth. Perched on a headland, it is the focus for Mumbai's Navratri (Festival of Nine Nights) celebrations in September/October.

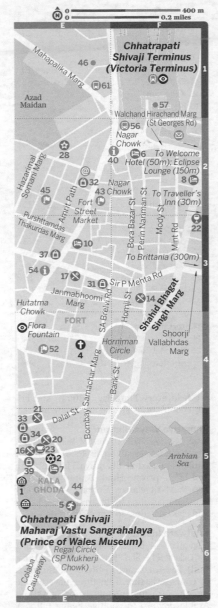

11am-5pm). The architecture is striking: the tower looks like a giant cylindrical pineapple, the planetarium a UFO.

GORAI ISLAND

TOP CHOICE **Global Pagoda** LANDMARK
(www.globalpagoda.org; Near Esselworld, Gorai Creek; 9am-6pm) Rising up like a mirage from polluted Gorai Creek and the lush but noisy grounds of the Esselworld and Water Kingdom amusement parks, the breathtaking structure is a 96m-high stupa modelled after Burma's Shwedagon Pagoda. The dome, which is designed to hold 8000 meditators and houses relics of Buddha, was built entirely without supports using an ancient technique of interlocking stones. It just snatched the record away from Bijapur's Golgumbaz for being the world's largest unsupported dome. The pagoda also has a museum dedicated to the life of the Buddha and his teaching – it's affiliated with teacher SN Goenka, and an on-site meditation centre offers 10-day meditation courses. To get here, take the train from Churchgate to Borivali, then an autorickshaw (₹28) to the ferry landing, where the Esselworld ferries (return ₹35) come and go every 30 minutes. The last ferry back is 5.25pm.

🏃 Activities

Birdwatching WILDLIFE-WATCHING
Mumbai has surprisingly good birdwatching opportunities. Sanjay Gandhi National Park is popular for woodland birds, while the marshlands of industrial Sewri (pronounced *shev*-ree) swarm with birds in winter. Contact the **Bombay Natural History Society** (BNHS; Map p50; 22821811; www.bnhs.org; Hornbill House, Dr Salim Ali Chowk, Shaheed Bhagat Singh Rd, Kala Ghoda) or Sunjoy Monga at **Yuhina Eco-Media** (9323995955) for information on upcoming trips.

Outbound Adventure OUTDOOR ADVENTURE
(9820195115, www.outboundadventure.com) Runs one-day rafting trips on the Ulhas River near Karjat, 88km southeast of Mumbai, from July to early September (₹1600 per person). After a good rain, rapids can get up to Grade III+, though usually the rafting is much calmer, with lots of twists and zigzags. OA also organises camping and canoeing trips.

📖 Courses

Kaivalyadhama Ishwardas Yogic Health Centre YOGA
(Map p44; 22818417; www.kdhammumbai.com; 43 Marine Dr, Girgaum Chowpatty; 6.30-10am

Nehru Centre CULTURAL COMPLEX
(off Map p44; 24964676; www.nehru-centre. org; Dr Annie Besant Rd, Worli) This cultural complex includes a planetarium, theatre, gallery and an interesting history exhibition **Discovery of India** (admission free;

& 3.30-7pm Mon-Sat) Several yoga classes are held daily at the Kaivalyadhama Ishwardas Yogic Health Centre. Fees include a ₹600 (students/seniors ₹500/400) monthly membership fee and a ₹500 admission fee.

Yoga Institute YOGA
(Map p62; ☑26122185; www.theyogainstitute.org; Shri Yogendra Marg, Prabhat Colony, Santa Cruz East; per 1st/2nd month ₹400/300) The Yoga Institute, near Santa Cruz station, has daily classes as well as weekend and weeklong programs.

Iyengar Yogashraya YOGA
(off Map p44; ☑24948416; www.bksiyengar.com; Elmac House, 126 Senapati Bapat Marg, Lower Parel; per class ₹130) Has classes in Iyengar yoga, including some for the developmentally disabled. There is a ₹113 admission fee.

BollyDancing Mumbai DANCING
(Map p44; ☑9821130788; www.BollyDancing.co.in; Napean Sea Rd, opp Walsingham School, Malabar Hill) The family-run institute runs choreographed Bollywood dance classes as well as BollySalsa, a salsa-fusion with a fitness edge. Hour-long beginner classes (₹450 per hour)

are held every Thursday (1.30pm) and Friday (noon); or by special arrangement.

Bharatiya Vidya Bhavan LANGUAGE
(Map p44; ☑23871860; cnr KM Munshi Marg & Ramabai Rd, Girgaum; per hr ₹500) Professor Shukla is based at Bharatiya Vidya Bhavan and offers private Hindi, Marathi, Gujarati and Sanskrit classes. Contact this worldly octogenarian directly to arrange a syllabus and class schedule to suit your needs.

Khatwara Institute HANDICRAFTS, COOKING
(Shri Khatwari Darbar; Map p62; ☑26042670, cnr Linking Rd & Shri Khatwari Darber Marg, Khar West) The Khatwara Institute offers dozens of courses, lasting from three days to one month, for women only (sorry guys!) in Arabic *mehndi* (decorative henna tattoos), 'basic' *mehndi,* block printing, embroidery, sewing and cooking, among other things. Call Vanita for details.

☞ **Tours**

Fiona Fernandez's *Ten Heritage Walks of Mumbai* (₹395) contains excellent walking tours in the city, with fascinating historical background.

The Government of India tourist office (p71) can arrange **multilingual guides** (per half-/full day ₹600/750). Guides using a foreign language other than English will charge at least ₹225 extra.

🖋 **Reality Tours & Travel**   DHARAVI TOUR
(Map p48; ☏9820822253; www.realitytoursandtravel.com; 1/26 Akbar House, Nawroji F Rd, Colaba; short/long tours ₹500/1000) Runs socially responsible tours of Dharavi (p56). Photography is strictly forbidden and funds from the tour plus 80% of post-tax profits go to the agency's own NGO, **Reality Gives** (www.realitygives.org), which runs a kindergarten and community centre in Dharavi. Enter the office through SSS Corner store on Nawroji F Rd.

Bombay Heritage Walks   WALKING
(☏23690992; www.bombayheritagewalks.com) Run by two enthusiastic architects, has the best city tours. Private two-hour guided tours are ₹1500 for up to three people, ₹500 for each additional person.

MTDC   CITY TOUR
(Maharashtra Tourism Development Corporation; Map p48; ☏22841877; Apollo Bunder; 1hr tour ₹120; ⊙8.30am-4pm Tue-Sun & 5.30-8pm Sat & Sun) Runs open-deck bus tours of illuminated heritage buildings on weekends at 7pm and 8.15pm. They depart from and can be booked at the booth near Apollo Bunder.

Cruises   CRUISE
(☏22026364; ⊙9am-7pm) A cruise on Mumbai Harbour is a good way to escape the city and a chance to see the Gateway of India as it was intended. Ferry rides (₹60, 30 minutes) depart from the Gateway of India.

Traansway International   CITY TOUR
(☏9920488712; traanswaytours@gmail.com; per 1-/2-/3-person tour ₹2500/3500/4500) Runs five-hour day or night tours of South Mumbai's sights. Prices include pick-up and drop-off.

H2O Water Sports Complex   CRUISE
(Map p44; ☏23677546; www.drishtigroup.com; Marine Dr, Mafatlal Beach; ⊙10am-10pm Oct-May)

BOLLYWOOD DREAMS

Mumbai is the glittering epicentre of India's gargantuan Hindi-language film industry. From silent beginnings with a cast of all-male actors (some in drag) in the 1913 epic *Raja Harishchandra* and the first talkie, *Lama Ara* (1931), it now churns out more than 1000 films a year – more than Hollywood. Not surprising considering it has a captive audience of one-sixth of the world's population, as well as a sizable Non-Resident Indian (NRI) following.

Every part of India has its regional film industry, but Bollywood continues to entrance the nation with its escapist formula in which all-singing, all-dancing lovers fight and conquer the forces keeping them apart. These days, Hollywood-inspired thrillers and action extravaganzas vie for moviegoers' attention alongside the more family-oriented saccharine formulas.

Bollywood stars can attain near godlike status in India and star-spotting is a favourite pastime in Mumbai's posher establishments.

Extra, Extra!

Studios sometimes want Westerners as extras to add a whiff of international flair (or provocative dress, which locals often won't wear) to a film. It's become so common, in fact, that 100,000 junior actors nearly went on strike in 2008 to protest, among other things, losing jobs to foreigners, who work for less.

If you're still game, just hang around Colaba where studio scouts, recruiting for the following day's shooting, will find you. A day's work pays ₹500. You'll get lunch, and other snacks if you start early or finish late. Transport is usually by 2nd-class train unless there are enough tourists to justify private transport. The day can be long and hot with loads of standing around the set; not everyone has a positive experience. Complaints range from lack of food and water to dangerous situations and intimidation when extras don't 'comply' with the director's orders. Others describe the behind-the-scenes peek as a fascinating experience. Before agreeing to anything, always ask for the scout's identification and go with your gut.

Arranges 45-minute day (₹170 per person, minimum four people) and night (₹280, 7pm to 11pm) cruises.

Taj Yacht　　　　　　　　　　　　CRUISE
(up to 10 people per 2hr ₹48,000) For the luxury version, hire this yacht; contact the Taj Mahal Palace, Mumbai (p56) for details.

✦ Festivals & Events

Mumbai Festival　　　　　MUSIC, DANCE
Based at several stages around the city, it showcases the food, dance and culture of Mumbai in January.

Banganga Festival　　　　　　　MUSIC
(www.maharashtratourism.gov.in) A two-day classical-music festival held in January at the Banganga Tank.

Kala Ghoda Festival　　　ARTS, CULTURE
(www.kalaghodaassociation.com) Getting bigger and more sophisticated each year, this two-week-long offering in February has a packed program of arts performances and exhibitions.

eElephanta Festival　　　　　　MUSIC
(www.maharashtratourism.gov.in) Classical music and dance on Elephanta Island in February.

Nariyal Poornima　　　　　　　HINDU
(www.rakhifestival.com) Festivals in the tourist hub of Colaba kick off with this celebration in August at the start of the fishing season after the monsoon.

Ganesh Chaturthi　　　　　　　HINDU
Mumbai's biggest annual festival – a 10- to 11-day event in August or September in celebration of the elephant-headed deity Ganesh – sweeps up the entire city. On the first, third, fifth, seventh and 10th days of the festival families and communities take their Ganesh statues to the seashore and auspiciously drown them: the 10th day, which sees millions descending on Girgaum Chowpatty to submerge the largest statues, is pure mayhem.

Colaba Festival　　　　　　　　ARTS
A small October arts festival in Colaba that sometimes overlaps with Diwali festivities.

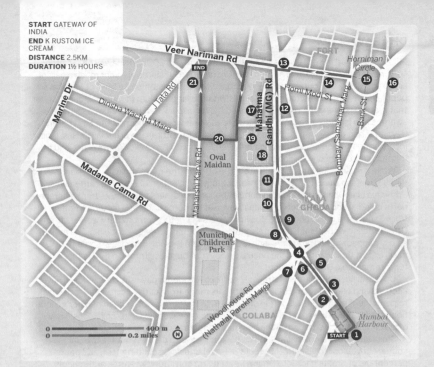

Walking Tour
Mumbai

Its distinctive mix of colonial-era and art deco architecture is Mumbai's defining feature.

Starting from the ❶ **Gateway of India** walk up Chhatrapati Shivaji Marg past the members-only colonial relic ❷ **Royal Bombay Yacht Club** on one side and the art deco residential-commercial complex ❸ **Dhunraj Mahal** on the other, towards ❹ **Regal Circle**. The best view of the surrounding buildings – including the old ❺ **Sailors Home**, which dates from 1876 and is now the Maharashtra Police Headquarters, the art deco ❻ **Regal** cinema and the old ❼ **Majestic Hotel**, now the Sahakari Bhandar cooperative store – is from the circle's centre.

Continue up MG Rd, past the beautifully restored facade of the ❽ **National Gallery of Modern Art**. Opposite is the ❾ **Chhatrapati Shivaji Maharaj Vastu Sangrahalaya**. Back across the road is the 'Romanesque Transitional' ❿ **Elphinstone College** and the ⓫ **David Sassoon Library & Reading Room**, where members escape the afternoon heat lazing on planters' chairs on the upper balcony.

Continue north to admire the vertical art deco stylings of the ⓬ **New India Assurance Company Building**. On a traffic island ahead lies the pretty ⓭ **Flora Fountain**, erected in 1869 in honour of Sir Bartle Frere, the Bombay governor responsible for dismantling the fort.

Turn east down Veer Nariman Rd, walking towards ⓮ **St Thomas' Cathedral**. Ahead lies the stately ⓯ **Horniman Circle**, an arcaded ring of buildings laid out in the 1860s around a circular and beautifully kept botanical garden. The circle is overlooked from the east by the neoclassical ⓰ **Town Hall**.

Backtrack to Flora Fountain, continuing west and turning south on to Bhaurao Patil Marg to see the august ⓱ **High Court** in full glory and the ornately decorated ⓲ **University of Mumbai**. The university's 80m-high ⓳ **Rajabai Clock Tower** is best observed from within the ⓴ **Oval Maidan**. Turn around to compare the colonial edifices with the row of art deco beauties lining Maharshi Karve (MK) Rd, culminating in the wedding cake tower of the ㉑ **Eros Cinema**.

DHARAVI SLUM

Mumbaikars had mixed feelings about the stereotypes in 2008's runaway hit, *Slumdog Millionaire* (released in Hindi as *Slumdog Crorepati*). But slums are very much a part of – some would say the foundation of – Mumbai city life. An astonishing 55% of Mumbai's population lives in shantytowns and slums, and the largest slum in Mumbai (and Asia, for that matter) is Dharavi. Originally inhabited by fisherfolk when the area was still creeks, swamps and islands, it became attractive to migrant workers, from South Mumbai and beyond, when the swamp began to fill in as a result of natural and artificial causes. It now incorporates 1.75 sq km sandwiched between Mumbai's two major railway lines and is home to more than one million people.

While it may look a bit shambolic from the outside, the maze of dusty alleys and sewer-lined streets of this city within a city are actually a collection of abutting settlements. Some parts of Dharavi have mixed populations, but in others inhabitants from different parts of India, and with different trades, have set up homes and tiny factories. Potters from Saurashtra live in one area, Muslim tanners in another; embroidery workers from Uttar Pradesh work alongside metalsmiths; while other workers recycle plastics as women dry pappadams in the searing sun. Some of these thriving industries, some 10,000 in all, export their wares, and the annual turnover of business from Dharavi is thought to top a remarkable US$665 million.

Up close, life in the slums is strikingly normal. Residents pay rent, most houses have kitchens and electricity, and building materials range from flimsy corrugated-iron shacks to permanent multistorey concrete structures. Many families have been here for generations, and some of the younger Dharavi residents even work in white-collar jobs. They often choose to stay, though, in the neighbourhood they grew up in.

Slum tourism is a polarising subject, so you'll have to decide your feelings for yourself. If you opt to visit, Reality Tours & Travel does a fascinating tour, and pours a percentage of profits back into Dharavi, setting up community centres and schools. Some tourists opt to visit on their own, which is OK as well – just don't take photos. Take the train from Churchgate station to Mahim (₹12), exit on the west side and cross the bridge into Dharavi.

Prithvi Theatre Festival THEATRE
(www.prithvitheatre.org) A showcase of what's going on in contemporary Indian theatre, held in November; also includes performances by international troupes and artists.

🛏 Sleeping

You'll need to recalibrate your budget here: Mumbai has the most expensive accommodation in India. Book ahead at Christmas and in Diwali season.

Colaba is compact, has the liveliest foreigner scene and many of the budget and midrange options. Fort is more spread out and convenient to sights and the main train stations (CST and Churchgate). Most of the top-end places are dotted around the suburbs; hotels in Juhu are convenient for the trendy Bandra district.

To stay with a local family, contact the Government of India tourist office for a list of homes participating in Mumbai's **paying-guest scheme** (r with full board; ₹1500-2500; 🌢).

A 4% (more common at budget end) or 10% tax should be added to all prices listed here unless otherwise stated.

COLABA

For mapped locations of the following venues see Map p48.

🏆 **Taj Mahal Palace,
Mumbai** HERITAGE HOTEL $$$
(Map p48; ☏66653366; www.tajhotels.com; Apollo Bunder, Colaba; s/d tower from ₹21,500/23,000, palace from ₹25,250/26,750; 🌢✻@🌢🌢) The hotel formerly known as the Taj Mahal Palace & Tower debuted its new name and new spaces on Indian Independence Day 2010, the result of a meticulous restoration following the November 2008 terrorist attacks that nearly brought this 1903 Mumbai landmark to its knees. But with its sweeping arches, staircases and domes, it has risen again, defiantly opulent. Some 285 rooms have been lavishly restored in gorgeous fuchsia, saffron and celadon colour schemes, and

security is Fort Knox level – guests can only access their own floor via elevator keys. All of the hotel bars – including the legendary **Harbour Bar**, Mumbai's first licensed bar – and restaurants have been redesigned, rounding out a triumphant return for one of Mumbai's most enduring symbols.

YWCA
GUESTHOUSE **$$**

(22025053; www.ywcaic.info; 18 Madame Cama Rd; s/d/t/q incl breakfast, dinner & taxes ₹2024/3000/4200/6000; ✴@☎) The YWCA presents a frustrating dilemma: It's immaculate and surprisingly good, considering it's a cool ₹1000 cheaper than most in its class. Rates include tax, breakfast, dinner, 'bed tea', free wi-fi *…and a newspaper,* so it's the best value (and location, for that matter) within miles. But there's a trade-off here with a series of unorthodox rules, including the very stubborn policy of not allowing early check-in – even if your room is ready – unless you pay extra.

Hotel Moti
GUESTHOUSE **$$**

(22025714; hotelmotiinternational@yahoo.co.in; 10 Best Marg; s/d/tr with AC incl tax from ₹1800/2000/3200; ✴@) This traveller's haven occupies the ground floor of a gracefully crumbling, beautiful colonial-era building. Simple rooms have whispers of charm and some nice surprises, like ornate stucco ceilings and Western showers. Some are huge and all have fridges filled with soft drinks and bottled water, which is charged at cost – one of the many signs of the pragmatic and friendly management.

Sea Shore Hotel
GUESTHOUSE **$**

(22874237; 4th fl, Kamal Mansion, Arthur Bunder Rd; s/d without bathroom ₹500/700) In a building housing several budget guesthouses, the Sea Shore will go above and beyond your expectations for the price, mainly due to a spiffy new makeover that has turned ratty plywood walls and shoebox-sized rooms into simple but near hotel-quality accommodation, with communal bathrooms and sinks that approach those of design hotels. On the floor below, the same owners offer **India Guest House** (22833769; s/d without bathroom ₹350/450) with the same new bathrooms but no further renovations at research time.

Hotel Suba Palace
HOTEL **$$$**

(22020636; www.hotelsubapalace.com; Battery St; s/d with AC incl breakfast ₹4400/5170; ✴@☎) Teetering precariously on the edge of boutique hotel, the Suba Palace oozes soothing neutral tones, from the tiny taupe shower tiles in the contemporary bathrooms to the creamy crown moulding and beige quilted headboards in the tastefully remodelled rooms. Comfy, quiet and central.

Salvation Army Red Shield Guest House
GUESTHOUSE **$**

(22841824; red_shield@vsnl.net; 30 Mereweather Rd; dm incl breakfast ₹225, d/tr/q with full board ₹725/991/1368, d with AC & full board ₹1199; ✴@) Salvy's is a Mumbai institution popular with travellers counting every rupee. The large, ascetic dorms are clean, though ratty mattresses encourage bed bugs. All rooms have their own bathroom; some are not attached but you get a private key. Dorm beds cannot be reserved in advance so come just after the 9am kickout to ensure a spot.

Ascot Hotel
HOTEL **$$$**

(66385566; www.ascothotel.com; 38 Garden Rd; d with AC incl breakfast from ₹6000; ✴@☎) Marble-meets-modern at this classy hotel with hardwood hallways leading to boutiquey rooms with big headboards, bathtubs, desks, new LCD TVs, and lots of natural light and tree views.

MUMBAI FOR CHILDREN

Rina Mehta's www.mustformums.com has the Mumbai Mums' Guide, with info on crèches, health care and even kids' salsa classes in the city. *Time Out Mumbai* (₹50) often lists fun things to do with kids.

Little tykes with energy to burn will love the Gorai Island amusement parks, **Esselworld** (www.esselworld.in; adult/child ₹510/380; ⊙11am-7pm) and **Water Kingdom** (www.waterkingdom.in; adult/child ₹510/380; ⊙11am-7pm). Both are well maintained and have lots of rides, slides and shade. Combined tickets are ₹710/580 (adult/child). Low-season weekday ticket prices are lower. It's a ₹35 ferry ride from Borivali jetty.

BNHS (p51) and Yuhina Eco-Media (p51) often conduct nature trips for kids while **Yoga Sutra** (Map p44; 32107067; www.yogasutra.co.in; Chinoy Mansions, Bhulabhai Desai Rd, Cumballa Hill; drop-in classes ₹300) has kids' yoga classes, taught in English.

The decriminalisation of homosexuality – a law on the Indian books for 148 years – by Delhi's High Court in July 2009 means India is out of the closet, but cosmopolitan Mumbai has been slow on the uptake.

The pioneering GLBTQ magazine *Bombay Dost* (www.bombaydost.co.in) organises **Sunday High**, a twice-monthly screening of queer-interest films, usually in the suburbs, and is an excellent resource on happenings around town. You can pick up a copy at Oxford Bookstore (p70) in Churchgate as well as the Humsafar Trust (p483) offices around town. **Queer Ink** (www.queer-ink.com) is an online Indian bookstore specialising in gay and lesbian books and magazines of every ilk.

The **Kashish-Mumbai International Queer Film Festival** (www.mumbaiqueerfest.com) made its debut in 2010 and is expected to become an annual event. *XXWHY*, a documentary short by Mumbai-based filmmaker Dr Bharaty Manjula about Kerala's first out female-to-male transgender, was the big winner in the inaugural event.

Around town, no dedicated gay and lesbian bars/clubs have yet opened but gay-friendly 'safe house' venues often host private gay parties on specific nights – see the following. Check out Gay Bombay (www.gaybombay.org) for listings.

Azaardbaazaar
BOUTIQUE

(Map p62); 16th/33rd Rd, Bandra; ⊘closed Monday) Billed as India's first GLBTQ pride store, tucked in a garage off 33rd Rd.

Just Around the Corner
CAFE

(Map p62); cnr 24th & 30th Rd, Bandra West; mains ₹95-375; ⊘lunch) This great cafe is a popular meeting point for the GLBTQ crowd, but it's popular with everyone for its tolerance across the board.

Voodoo Pub
NIGHTCLUB

(Map p48; ☑22841959; Kamal Mansion, Arthur Bunder Rd, Colaba; cover ₹300) This dark and sweaty bar has unofficially hosted Mumbai's only regular gay night on Saturdays since 1994 – long before it was trendy (or legal) to do so. There is little going on other nights of the week, but staff are screened for open-mindedness and it's considered gay friendly all week long.

Eclipse Lounge
NIGHTCLUB

(off Map p50; 11/13 Walchand Hirachand Marg, Ballard Estate) Formerly known as Let's Scream, the dark and iffy Eclipse was quick to point out it isn't gay, but does often host private gay parties.

Bentley's Hotel
HOTEL **$$**

(☑22841474; www.bentleyshotel.com; 17 Oliver Rd; s/d incl breakfast & tax from ₹1690/2090; ⊛) Colonial charm aplenty, with old-school floor tiles and wooden furniture; its location spread out over several buildings on Oliver St and Henry Rd can all seem a bit *The Shining*–like isolated.

Regent Hotel
HOTEL **$$$**

(☑22871853/4; www.regenthotelcolaba.com; 8 Best Marg; r/tr with AC incl breakfast & tax ₹4290/4620; ⊛@) An upper-scale Arabian-flavoured hotel with marble surfaces and soft pastels aplenty. The retro-chic breakfast area fills the 1st floor hallway, so avoid rooms 101–110 if you plan to sleep in.

FORT, CHURCHGATE & MARINE DRIVE

For mapped locations of the following venues see Map p50, unless otherwise stated.

TOP CHOICE Residency Hotel
HOTEL **$$**

(Map p50; ☑22625525; www.residencyhotel.com; 26 Rustom Sidhwa Marg, Fort; s/d from ₹2500/2700; ⊛@⊛) This polarising hotel can be hit or miss. On one hand, the small rooms in the original building – where a waft of sweet lemongrass graces the lobby – are older but come with fridges, flat-screen TVs and flip-flops (thongs), while the newly annexed building next door houses a far more modern design-style hotel with rain showers, leather-walled elevators and free wi-fi. But during our visit, a Londoner was overheard complaining, 'One of our rooms smells like cigarettes, the other like urine', so it's a gamble.

Welcome Hotel
HOTEL $$

(off Map p50; 🖉 6631488; welcome _hotel@vsnl. com; 257 Shahid Bhagat Singh Rd; s/d incl breakfast from ₹2783/3278, without bathroom from ₹1397/1595; 🌡 📶) Its reputation as immaculate was crushed when a cockroach scurried across our authoring desk but, all things considered, this is a cleaner-than-most midrange choice. New top-floor executive rooms evoke a different hotel altogether – a boutique makeover has turned them into something more LA than Bombay. Rates include evening tea in the rooms. For value under ₹2000, it's tough to beat.

Sea Green Hotels
HOTEL $$

(Map p50; s/d ₹2500/3150; 🌡 📶) Seagreen Hotel (🖉 66336525; www.seagreenhotel.com; 145 Marine Dr); Sea Green South Hotel (🖉 22821613; www.sea greensouth.com; 145A Marine Dr) These identical art deco hotels have spacious but spartan AC rooms, originally built in the 1940s to house British soldiers. Snag a sea-view room – they're the same price – and you've secured top value in this price range (even with the 10% service charge).

West End Hotel
HOTEL $$$

(Map p50; 🖉 22039121; www.westendhotelmum bai.com; 45 New Marine Lines; s/d with AC from ₹3900/4500; 🌡 📶) This accidentally retro hotel boasts a nonchalant funky vibe built around old-fashioned rooms that are spacious, with bathtubs, shagalicious rugs and modish daybeds.

Trident
HOTEL $$$

(Oberoi Hotel; Map p50; 🖉 66324343; www.trid enthotels.com; Marine Dr, Nariman Point; s/d from ₹18,750/20,000; 🌡 @ 📶 ☰) The Trident is, along with the Oberoi, part of the Oberoi

Hotel complex. But the Trident wins out both on price and on the spiffy, streamlined design of its restaurants, bars and pool area. The rates above are rack, but you can get the rooms for half depending on occupancy.

InterContinental
HOTEL $$$

(🖉 39879999; www.intercontinental.com; 135 Marine Dr, Churchgate; r incl breakfast from ₹19,500; 🌡 @ 📶 ☰) Very sleek for an InterContinental. All earth tones and Buddha chic, the spacious deluxe rooms are sizeable in their own right, while the halfmoon corner suites mirror the curved elegance of Marine Drive's Queen's Necklace. The stunning **Dome** bar and restaurant stylishly graces the rooftop and overlooks the sea, while **Koh** turns Thai food on its head at the lobby level.

Traveller's Inn
GUESTHOUSE $

(Map p50; 🖉 22644685; 26 Adi Marzban Rd, Ballard Estate; dm ₹500, r ₹900, with AC ₹1150; 🌡 @ 📶) On a quiet, tree-lined street, the tiny Traveller's Inn underwent a spiffy renovation in 2010 and now boasts bigger rooms (and thinner hallways); and new air-con units, lockers and windows, making a good budget choice that much better.

Hotel Lawrence
GUESTHOUSE $

(🖉 22843618; 3rd fl, ITTS House, 33 Sai Baba Marg; s/d/tr without bathroom incl breakfast & tax ₹600/700/900) A bottom-barrel guesthouse tucked away in a little side lane offering clean crashpads that are popular with shoestring meditators – and a management that tends to enforce moral judgements on guests.

Hotel City Palace
HOTEL $$

(🖉 22666666; www.hotelcitypalace.net; 121 City Tce, Walchand Hirachand Marg; s/d without bathroom from ₹803/1350, r with bathroom from ₹2200; 🌡) Organised and clean, across from CST. If you just got off an overnight

DON'T MISS

KOTACHIWADI

This storied *wadi* (hamlet) is a bastion clinging onto Mumbai life as it was before highrises. A Christian enclave of elegant two-storey wooden mansions, it's 500m northeast of Girgaum Chowpatty (Map p44), lying amid Mumbai's predominantly Hindu and Muslim neighbourhoods. These winding laneways allow a wonderful glimpse into a quiet life free of rickshaws and taxis. It's not large by any means, but you can lose considerable moments wandering these fascinating alleyways – no doubt in shock that the hustle and bustle of the real Mumbai is but steps away.

To find it, aim for **St Teresa's Church** (Map p44) on the corner of Jagannath Shankarsheth Marg (JS Marg) and RR Roy Marg (Charni Rd), then head directly opposite the church on JS Marg and duck down the second and third lanes on your left.

MUMBAI (BOMBAY)

train, the rooms are no bigger than a sleeper compartment, so you won't suffer any disorientation at wake up.

THE SUBURBS

There are several midrange hotels on Nehru Rd Extension in Vile Parle East near the domestic airport, but rooms are overpriced and only useful for early or late flights. Juhu is convenient for Juhu Beach and for the restaurants, shops and clubs in Bandra.

TOP CHOICE **Iskcon** GUESTHOUSE **$$**
(Map p62; ☏26206860; guesthouse.mumbai@ pamho.net; Hare Krishna Land, Juhu; s/d incl tax ₹2095/2495, with AC incl tax ₹2395/2995; ❋@) If you are looking for an experience rather than a shelter, this efficiently managed guesthouse, part of Juhu's lively Hare Krishna complex, is one of Mumbai's most interesting choices. The lobby looks out into the temple, while rooms in the two flamingo-pink towers have pretty lacquered *sankheda* (lacquered country wood) furniture from Gujarat and those in the original tower have semicircular balconies. The whole things feel like you are in the thick of India, which is more than can be said for most of the resort or business-oriented hotels out this way. Don't miss the evening *aarti* (candle-lighting ritual).

Four Seasons Hotel HOTEL **$$$**
(off Map p44; ☏24818000; www.fourseasons.com; 114 Dr E Moses Rd, Worli; r from ₹15,200; ❋@☎☲) This modern Four Seasons is everything you expect it to be: exemplary service, psychic staff, everything classic yet slick as oil. Now with the addition of its fashionable rooftop lounge **Aer** (p66), it's hip as hopscotch, too.

Hotel Kemps Corner HOTEL **$$**
(Map p44; ☏23634646; 131 August Kranti Marg; s/d from ₹2700/3800; ❋☎) A general spiffing -up of the place means the prices at this friendly midrange are no longer the deal they once were, but it remains a great spot in the heart of the Kemp's Corner fashion bonanza (which is a lot less frenzied than Colaba or Fort) and walking distance to Haji Ali Mosque and Girgaum Chowpatty. Service comes with more smiles than most, though it takes a serious dive on Sundays.

Juhu Residency BOUTIQUE HOTEL **$$$**
(Map p62; ☏67834949; www.juhuresidency.com; 148B Juhu Tara Rd, Juhu; s/d with AC incl breakfast from ₹5000; ❋@☎) A makeover two years ago turned this into a quasi-boutique hotel, with sleek marble floors, king-size beds (in the premium rooms), dark woods and artistic bedspreads imported from Singapore. There are three restaurants for 18 rooms, and one, the **Melting Pot**, garners accolades for its Indian cuisine. A great choice if you're looking for something hip and intimate that won't cost you a fortune.

Hotel Suba International BOUTIQUE HOTEL **$$$**
(Map p62; ☏67076707; www.hotelsubainterna tional.com; Sahar Rd, Vile Parle East; s/d with AC incl breakfast from ₹6000/7000; ❋☎) Brand-spanking new at time of research, this hi-tech boutique business hotel is just 1km from the international terminal, 3km from the domestic. It's laid out in slick blacks and glossy marble, with clean lines and lots of masculine hardwoods and design-forward touches. All the electronics in the rooms are controlled wirelessly by iPod Touch! If it's full, its sister property in Andheri East, **Hotel Suba Galaxy** (Map p62; ☏26821188; www. hotelsubagalaxy.com; NS Phadke Rd, Andheri East; s/d with AC incl breakfast from ₹3200/6000; ❋☎), isn't as shiny but is an acceptable alternative.

Sun-n-Sand HOTEL **$$$**
(Map p62; ☏66938888; www.sunnsandhotel. com; 39 Juhu Beach, Juhu; r with AC from ₹7500; ❋@☎☲) The Sun-n-Sand has been offering up beachfront hospitality for decades. The newly renovated 4th floor offers shiny new hardwood floors and some bathtubs, but the best rooms remain the sea-facing ones (from ₹8500): lots of silk and the pleasant burnt-orange motif complement the pool, palm-tree and ocean views from the huge window. It's off Juhu Rd, near the old Holiday Inn.

ITC Maratha HOTEL **$$$**
(Map p62; ☏28303030; www.itcwelcomgroup. in; Sahar Rd, Andheri East; s/d incl breakfast & tax from ₹22,000/23,500; ❋@☎☲) The five-star with the most luxurious Indian character, from the Jaipur-style lattice windows around the atrium to the silk pillows on the beds to Peshawri, one of the best restaurants in town.

Hotel Columbus HOTEL **$$**
(Map p62; ☏42144343; www.hotelcolumbus.in; 344 Nanda Patkar Rd, Vile Parle East; r with AC from ₹3000; ❋@☎) The best midrange in the domestic airport area, with gussied-up super deluxe rooms (₹4000) with stylised wood-grain accents, flat-screen TVs and an aspiration for high design.

Citizen Hotel HOTEL **$$$**
(Map p62; ☏66932525; www.citizenhotelmum bai.com; Juhu Tara Rd, Juhu; s/d with AC incl

breakfast from ₹7000/7500; ❄@🖥️) The Citizen's location is what you're paying for here, but rooms are also well maintained, with marble floors and marble-top furniture, flat-screen TVs, wi-fi access, fridges – and, of course, excellent beach views.

✗ Eating

In this gastro-epicentre a cornucopia of flavours from all over India collides with international trends and tastebuds. Colaba is home to most of the cheap tourist haunts, while Fort and Churchgate skew more upscale, a trend that continues as you head north to Mahalaxmi and the Central Suburbs, where you'll find Mumbai's most exciting, cutting-edge and expensive restaurants.

For self-caterers, the **Colaba market** (Map p48; Lala Nigam St) has fresh fruit and vegetables. **Saharkari Bhandar Supermarket** (Map p48; ☑22022248; cnr Colaba Causeway & Wodehouse Rd; ⊙10am-8.30pm) and, even better, **Suryodaya** (Map p50; ☑22040979; Veer Nariman Rd; ⊙7.30am-8.30pm) are well-stocked supermarkets.

COLABA

For mapped locations of the following venues see Map p48.

Indigo   FUSION, EUROPEAN **$$$**
(☑66368980; 4 Mandlik Marg; mains ₹525-945; ⊙lunch & dinner) Over a decade in and still a star, Colaba's finest eating option is a gourmet haven serving inventive European cuisine, a long wine list, sleek ambience and a gorgeous roof deck lit with fairy lights. Favourites include excellent kiwi margaritas, tea-grilled quail (₹625), anise-rubbed white salmon (₹725) and inventive takes on traditional cuisine like juniper-berry-cured tandoori chicken (₹625). Its cool quotient has chilled a bit with the focus on the suburbs, but it remains a high-gastronomy favourite.

Bademiya   INDIAN **$**
(Tulloch Rd; meals ₹50-100) If you can walk by this street-stall-on-steroids without coming away with a chicken tikka roll in hand, you are a better person than us. This whole street buzzes nightly with punters from all walks of Mumbai life lining up for spicy, fresh grilled treats. If Mumbai street food scares the bejesus out of you, this is the spot to get over it.

Indigo Delicatessen   CAFE **$$**
(Pheroze Bldg, Chhatrapati Shivaji Marg; mains ₹245-495; ⊙9am-midnight) Indigo's casual and less expensive sister is just as big a draw as the original, with cool tunes, warm decor and massive wooden tables. It has breakfast all day (₹155 to ₹295), casual meals, French press coffee, wines (₹300 to ₹690 per glass) and is also a bakery and deli.

Theobroma   CAFE **$**
(Colaba Causeway; confections ₹40-85) Theobroma calls its creations 'food of the gods' – and it ain't lying. Dozens of perfectly executed cakes, tarts and chocolates, as well as sandwiches and breads, go well with the coffee here. The genius pistachio-and-green-cardamom truffle (₹30) or decadent chocolate overload brownie (₹65) should send you straight into a glorious sugar coma. A bigger location has opened in Bandra West (Map p62).

Wich Latte   CAFE **$$**
(Map p48; Western Breeze Bldg, Colaba; sandwiches ₹120-175) Churning out excellent coffee but trumping both Coffee Day and Barista when it comes to food, Wich Latte bills itself as India's first sandwich cafe. For breakfast, the bagelwiches are an excellent homesick remedy and throughout the day there are salads, sandwiches and pizza. There's also a convenient location in Kala Ghoda (Map p50), but it opens from lunch onwards.

New Laxmi Vilas   SOUTH INDIAN **$**
(19A Ram Mansion, Nawroji F Rd; mains ₹23-85) A budget eatery that serves great South India specialities.

KALA GHODA & FORT

TOP CHOICE **Khyber**   NORTH INDIAN **$$$**
(Map p50; ⊙40396666; 145 MG Rd, Fort; mains ₹225-450; ⊙lunch & dinner) Like Bukhara in Delhi, Khyber is an iconic restaurant the thought of which will spark Pavlovian drooling for years to come. The burnt-orange, Afghan-inspired interiors are a multitiered and cavernous maze of moody Mughal royalty art embedded in exposed brick, tasteful antique oil lanterns and urns, and railway-trestle ceilings. As mouth-watering Punjabi/North Indian kebabs, biryanis and curries saunter their way to a who's who of Mumbai's elite, your tastebuds will do a happy dance – before the disheartening realisation: too much food, too little space. Highlights of the meat-centric menu include the Reshmi Kebab Masala, a transcendent dish of cream and yoghurt-marinated chicken drowning in the restaurant's intricate red masala; and its pièce de résistance, *raan* (a whole leg of slow-cooked lamb).

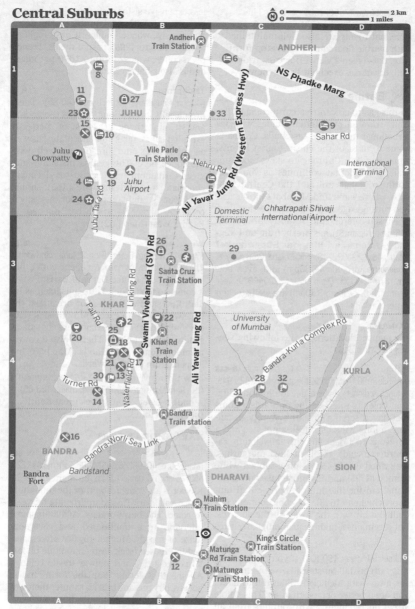

0 — 2 km
0 — 1 miles

MUMBAI (BOMBAY)

ANDHERI

NS Phadke Marg

Andheri Train Station

JUHU

Juhu Chowpatty

Vile Parle Train Station

Juhu Airport

Nehru Rd

Ali Yavar Jung Rd (Western Express Hwy)

Sahar Rd

International Terminal

Domestic Terminal

Chhatrapati Shivaji International Airport

Santa Cruz Train Station

Linking Rd

KHAR

Swami Vivekanada (SV) Rd

Pali Rd

Juhu Tara Rd

Khar Rd Train Station

Ali Yavar Jung Rd

University of Mumbai

Bandra-Kurla Complex Rd

KURLA

Waterfield Rd

Turner Rd

BANDRA

Bandra-Worli Sea Link

Bandstand

Bandra Fort

Bandra Train station

DHARAVI

SION

Mahim Train Station

King's Circle Train Station

Matunga Rd Train Station

Matunga Train Station

Five Spice   INDO-CHINESE **$$**
(Map p50; 296A Perin Nariman St, Sangli Bank Bldg, Fort; mains ₹220-275; ☺lunch & dinner) A 30-minute wait is commonplace at this overheated, near-divey Indo-Chinese Godsend that's so good, it'll make you downright angry you can't eat Chinese like this at home. The menu is packed with chicken, lamb, prawn and veg dishes, all tantalising, so choosing is an issue. We went for the chicken in burnt chilli sauce (₹235) and dumped it on a bed of burnt chilli rice (₹185) –

quite possibly the best thing since the fortune cookie. Of course, there's one in Bandra (Map p62).

Trishna SEAFOOD $$$
(Map p50; ☎22614991; Sai Baba Marg, Kala Ghoda; mains ₹170-575; ⊙lunch & dinner) An outstanding and intimate seafood restaurant focused on Mangalorean preparations. The crab with butter, black pepper and garlic and Hyderabadi fish tikka are house specialities that warrant the hype, while service is underbearing, friendly and helpful. One of the best seafooders in town. Reservations unnecessary before 8pm.

Brittania PARSI $$
(off Map p50; Wakefield House, 11 Sprott Rd, Ballard Eatte; mains ₹100-250; ⊙lunch Mon-Sat) The kind of place traveller's tales are made of – this Mumbai icon, and its endearing owner, has been going since 1923. The signature dish is the berry *pulao* (₹250) – spiced and boneless mutton or chicken buried in basmati rice and tart barberries, imported to

the tune of 1000kg per year from Iran. The owner, Boman Kohinoor – born the year his father opened the place – will take your order and chat your ear off. Dead simple, dead delicious.

Café Moshe CAFE $$
(Map p50; Fabindia, 1st fl, Jeroo Bldg, MG Rd, Kala Ghoda; light meals ₹120-270; ⊙lunch & dinner) After shopping downstairs, refuel with Moshe's excellent salads, sandwiches, baked goods, coffees and smoothies. There's also a Moshe's in Kemp's Corner (Map p44); and Colaba (Map p48), where you'll find an extended menu, including the famed marinated garlic, mushroom, leek and capsicum open-faced sandwich with melted mozzarella on brown bread.

Mahesh Lunch Home SEAFOOD $$$
(Map p50; ☎22023965; 8B Cowasji Patel St, Fort; mains ₹150-600; ⊙lunch & dinner) A great place to try Mangalorean seafood in Mumbai. It's renowned for its ladyfish, pomfret, lobster and crabs; the *rawas tikka* (marinated

DABBA-WALLAHS

A small miracle of logistics, Mumbai's 5000 *dabba*-wallahs (*dabba* means food container; also called tiffin-wallahs) work tirelessly to deliver hot lunches to office workers throughout the city.

Lunch boxes are picked up each day from restaurants and homes and carried on heads, bicycles and trains to a centralised sorting station. A sophisticated system of numbers and colours (many wallahs are illiterate) identifies the destination of each lunch. More than 200,000 meals are delivered – always on time, come (monsoon) rain or (searing) shine.

This system has been used for centuries and, on average, there's only about one mistake per six million deliveries. No wonder *dabba*-wallahs take immense pride in their work.

white salmon) and tandoori pomfret are outstanding. There's also a branch on Juhu Tara Rd (Map p62).

Badshah Snacks & Drinks   INDIAN $
(Map p44; snacks ₹30-110) Opposite Crawford market, Badshah's been serving snacks, fruit juices and its famous *falooda* (rose-flavoured drink made with milk, cream, nuts and vermicelli – like swallowing a bed of roses!) to hungry bargain-hunters for more than 100 years.

Rajdhani   INDIAN $$
(Map p44; 361 Sheikh Memon St, Kalbadevi; thali ₹249; ☺lunch & dinner Mon-Sat, lunch Sun) Opposite Mangaldaas Market, Rajdhani is famous for its Gujarati and Rajasthani thalis. On Sundays, dinner isn't served and thali prices jump ₹50.

CHURCHGATE
For mapped locations of the following venues, see Map p50.

TOP CHOICE Koh   THAI $$$
(InterContinental Marine Dr; ☑39879999; mains ₹495-925; ☺lunch & dinner) India's first signature Thai restaurant is Mumbai's hottest dining destination. Celebrity chef Ian Kittichai works his native cuisine into an international frenzy of flavour that starts with the 'liquid gastronomy', which might be a jasmine and honey martini or a Bloody Mary made with lemongrass-infused vodka and *sriracha* chilli; from there the envelope is further pushed into revelational dishes like the 12-hour lamb shank Massaman curry – pair it with hot-stone garlic rice – that throws preconceived notions about Thai food to the Mumbai curb.

Samrat   SOUTH INDIAN $$
(☑42135401; Prem Ct, J Tata Rd; lunch/dinner thalis ₹220/260; ☺lunch & dinner) If this is your first thali, strap yourself in – the cavalcade of taste and texture will leave you wondering what the hell just happened – *then* they bring the rice. With a dizzying number of concoctable bites, it's as adventurous and diverse as India itself. Samrat is the anchor behind a pure-veg empire in the same location, which includes **210°C**, an outdoor cafe and bakery, and **Relish**, a funky spot that's home to Asian-Mexican-Lebanese fusion.

K Rustom   SWEETS $
(87 Stadium House, Veer Nariman Rd; dessert ₹40; ☺lunch & dinner) Nothing but a few metal freezers, but the ice-cream sandwich (₹40) has been pleasing Mumbaikar palettes since 1953. Delish.

GIRGAUM CHOWPATTY
For mapped locations of the following venues see Map p44.

TOP CHOICE New Kulfi Centre   SWEETS $
(cnr Chowpatty Seaface & Sardar V Patel Rd; kulfi per 100gm ₹20-40; ☺9am-1.30am) Serves the best *kulfi* (firm-textured ice cream served in killer flavours like pistachio, rose and saffron) you'll have anywhere, which means it will rock your pants off. When you order, the *kulfi* is placed on a betel-nut leaf and then weighed on an ancient scale – which makes it even better.

Cream Centre   CAFE $$
(Chowpatty Seaface; mains ₹100-249; ☺lunch & dinner) This sleek and contemporary Indian diner is hugely popular for its pure-veg hodgepodge of Indian, Mexican and Lebanese as well as its extensive menu of sizzling sundaes (₹195 to ₹220), which take 'hot fudge' to the boiling point!

MAHALAXMI TO WORLI
For mapped locations of the following venues see Map p44.

Tote on the Turf
FUSION $$$
(Map p44; ☑61577777; Near Gate No 5 & 6, Mahalaxmi Racecourse, Mahalaxmi; mains ₹485-985; ⊙lunch & dinner) Funky, all-white tree-branch interiors and ridiculously beautiful crowds aside, this hip new restaurant from the folks who own Indigo dishes out Euro-fusion, split into veg (like green garlic risotto with palm hearts, cherry tomatoes and chilli feta) and non-veg (grilled chicken with stuffed Bhavnagri chilli and mustard sauce). Don't dismiss the thin, wood-fired pizzas, which caused a bit of order envy on our visit.

Cafe Noorani
NORTH INDIAN $$
(Tardeo Rd, Haji Ali Circle; mains ₹120-180; ⊙lunch & dinner) This almost-retro diner is a requisite stop before or after visiting Haji Ali Mosque. On the menu is the gamut of Moghlai and Punjabi staples, all done well and cheap. The chicken tikka biryani is so good, you'll forgive a bite or two of gristle.

THE SUBURBS
North Mumbai is home to the city's trendiest dining, centered on Bandra West and Juhu. For mapped locations of the following venues see Map p62.

TOP CHOICE Peshawri
NORTH INDIAN $$$
(☑28303030; ITC Maratha, Sahar Rd; mains ₹700-1675; ⊙lunch & dinner) Make this Indian northwest frontier restaurant, just outside the international airport, your first or last stop in Mumbai. It's pricy as hell, but you won't regret forking out the ₹2700 (feeds two easily) for the exquisite Sikandari *raan* (leg of spring lamb braised in malt vinegar, cinnamon, black cumin) – it will forever skew your standards of lamb. The buttery dhal Bukhara (a thick black dhal cooked for a day; ₹700) is also memorable.

Culture Curry
SOUTH INDIAN $$
(Kataria Rd, Matunga West; mains ₹209-459; ⊙lunch & dinner) As the Culture Curry folks rightly point out, there's a lot more to southern food than *idli* and dosas. Exquisite dishes from all over the south, ranging from Andhra and Coorg to Kerala, are the specialty here. Vegies are particularly well served: the Kooru Curry (kidney and green beans in coconut gravy; ₹179) is extraordinary. The same owners run **Goa Portuguesa** (attached), specialising in fiery Goan dishes, where the 'Chicken Chilly Fry' is also a knockout (₹299). From Matunga station, it's about 750m west on Katinga Rd on the left.

Sheesha
NORTH INDIAN $$
(☑66770555; 7th fl, Shoppers Stop, Linking Rd, Bandra West; mains ₹145-295; ⊙lunch & dinner) With maybe the most beautiful ambience in town, Sheesha's alfresco rooftop lair has glass lanterns hanging from wooden beams, comfy couches and coloured-glass lamps high above the city and shopping madness below. You almost forget about the food, though you shouldn't; the countless kebabs and curries are outstanding. Otherwise, it's all hookah action (no alcohol). Order double apple: 'It's way better than apple', as one Desi beauty put it. Reserve on weekends.

Lemongrass
SOUTHEAST ASIAN $$
(Carlton Ct, cnr of Turner & Pali Rds, Bandra West; mains ₹215-400; ⊙lunch & dinner) In a good spot for watching Bandra streetlife, Lemongrass serves up tasty Southeast Asian fare from Myanmar (Burma) to Indonesia. The veg or meat *khowsuey* (Burmese noodles with a coconut broth; ₹400) is superb; and the service is above and beyond for its price: staff fronted our rickshaw fare when we didn't have small change; and the owner told us, 'If you don't like the food, send it back'. No, he didn't know who we were.

Salt Water Cafe
FUSION $$$
(87 Chapel Rd, Bandra; mains ₹180-500) This foodie find offers one of Mumbai's most ambitious menus. It made a name for itself for marrying dramatically opposing flavours (green peppercorn chicken with grape jus, cardamom and carrot mash) but most of the menu is just mouth-watering global fusion. The aesthetically cold design is as much of a contrast to India as some of the recipes, and service grinds to a crawl at lunchtime, b' it's a lovely spot to twist up your tasteb' after a curry overdose.

Prithvi Cafe
CAFE $
(Map p62; Juhu Church Rd, Juhu; light meals ₹70-140) You'd never know it was there, but this bohemian cafe attached to the Prithvi Theatre is a cultural hub of intellectuals, artists and theatre types who tuck themselves away in the lush, bamboo-heavy spot for all-day breakfast, cheap kebab value meals, sandwiches and savoury croissants. The non-veg combo is distinctly average, but the vibe more than makes up for it. Try the Irish coffee instead!

🍷 Drinking
Mumbai's lax attitude to alcohol means that there are loads of places to drink – from

hole-in-the-wall beer bars and chichi lounges to brash, multilevel superclubs – but the 25% liquor tax means bills can bring sticker shock.

If it's the caffeine buzz you're after, Barista and Café Coffee Day cafes are ubiquitous in Mumbai.

Kala Ghoda Café
CAFE

(Map p50; 10 Ropewalk Ln, Fort) An artsy, modern and miniscule cafe that's a favourite among journalists and other creative types, who come for the organic Arabica and Robusta coffee sourced from sustainable plantations, organic teas, small bite sandwiches and salads, and charming breakfasts – and then fight for one of the few tables. Even the *jaggery* (natural sugar) is organic. It's across the street from Trishna, but uses the English street name.

Mocha Bar
CAFE

(⊙10am-1.30am); Churchgate (Map p50; 82 Veer Nariman Rd); Juhu (Map p62; 67 Juhu Tara Rd) This atmospheric Arabian-styled cafe is often filled to the brim with bohemians and students deep in esoteric conversation, Bollywood gossip, or just a hookah pipe. Cosy, low-cushioned seating (including some old cinema seats), exotic coffees, shakes and teas, and global comfort cuisine promote an intellectually chilaxed vibe.

First Floor
CAFE

(Map p44; Sitaram Bldg, Dr Dadabhai Naoroji Rd; ⊙7pm-4am) This local's secret is the come-down cafe of choice; there's no alcohol, but the party ends up here, anyway – especially on Wednesdays and Saturdays – when the cool kids pack the house from 1.30am to 4am to sop up the drunkenness over a Continental mix of burgers, Mexican, Italian and sheeshas. It's above Zaffran, a worthy Muglai restaurant in its own right.

Haji Ali Juice Centre
JUICE BAR

(Lala Lajpatrai Rd, Haji Ali Circle; ⊙5am-1.30am Mon-Sat) An excellent juice megastand, strategically placed at the entrance to Haji Ali Mosque. A great cool off after the hot sun, overwater pilgrimage.

Samovar Café
CAFE

(Map p50; Jehangir Art Gallery, 161B MG Rd, Kala Ghoda; meals ₹60-90; ⊙closed Sun) This intimate place inside the art gallery overlooks the gardens of the Prince of Wales Museum.

Cha Bar
TEAHOUSE

(Map p50; Oxford Bookstore, Apeejay House, 3 Dinsha Wachha Marg, Churchgate; teas ₹30-80; ⊙10am-9.30pm) Thirteen pages of exotic teas, including organic and ayurvedic; and tasty snacks amid lots of books.

SOUTH MUMBAI

For mapped locations of the following venues see Map p48, unless otherwise indicated.

Cafe Mondegar
BAR

(☑22020591; Metro House, 5A Shahid Bhagat Singh Rd, Colaba) Like Leopold's, 'Mondys' draws a healthy foreign crowd, too, but with a better mix of friendly Indians, who all cosy up together in the much smaller space, bonding over the excellent jukebox, one of Mumbai's few. Good music, good people.

Busaba
BAR, LOUNGE

(☑22043779; 4 Mandlik Marg) Red walls and contemporary Buddha art give this loungey restaurant-bar a nouveau Tao. It's next to Indigo so gets the same trendy crowd but serves cheaper, more potent cocktails (₹330 to ₹480). There's a low-key DJ Wednesdays to Sundays from 8.30pm. The upstairs restaurant serves pan-Asian (mains ₹350 to ₹575); its back room feels like a posh treehouse. Reserve ahead if you want a table.

Leopold's Café
BAR

(cnr Colaba Causeway & Nawroji F Rd) Love it or hate it, most tourists end up at this Mumbai travellers' institution at one time or another. Around since 1871, Leopold's has wobbly ceiling fans, open-plan seating and a rambunctious atmosphere conducive to swapping tales with random strangers. Although there's a huge menu, the lazy evening beers – especially the 3L yards – are the real draw.

Café Universal
BAR

(Map p50; 299 Shahid Bhagat Singh Rd; ⊙9am-11pm Mon-Sat, 4-11pm Sun) A little bit of France near CST. The Universal has an art nouveau look to it, with butterscotch-colour walls, a wood-beam ceiling and marble chandeliers, and is a cosy place for happy hour and Kingfisher drafts (₹100).

Dome
BAR

(Map p50; Hotel InterContinental, 135 Marine Dr, Churchgate) This white-on-white rooftop lounge has awesome views of Mumbai's curving seafront while cocktails beckon the hip young things of Mumbai nightly.

THE SUBURBS

TOP CHOICE Aer
BAR/LOUNGE

(off Map p44; Four Seasons Hotel, 33rd fl, 114 Dr E Moses Rd, Worli) With astounding city views on one side and equally impressive sea views on the other, we'll be damned if this isn't India's most impressive tipple. Aer is a slick, open-air rooftop lounge with its share of plush couches as well as weird, uncomfortable plastic 'lounge chairs' that cater more to form than function. You'll need to remortgage your home for something shaken and stirred (₹600), but the ₹250 Kingfishers are a steal at these views. A DJ spins low-key house and techno nightly from 9pm, but who cares? It's all about the eye candy, both near and far.

Shiro
LOUNGE

(☑66156969; Bombay Dyeing Mills Compound, Worli) Shiro has its share of detractors, who squabble: Overpriced! Too pretentious! Snippy service! Sub-par food! (Maybe...but we adored our crispy spicy avocado sushi roll). Regardless, its status as a shock-and-awe venue for a cocktail cannot be denied. Water pours from the hands of towering Japanese faux-stone goddesses into lotus ponds, which reflect shimmering light on the walls. It's totally over the top, but the drinks are excellent and the DJs spin some mean house (Saturdays) and retro (Fridays).

Olive Bar & Kitchen
BAR

(Map p62; ☑26058228; Pali Hill Tourist Hotel, 14 Union Park, Khar West; ⊙7.30pm-1.30am) Hip, gorgeous and snooty, this longtime Mediterranean-style restaurant and bar has light and delicious food (mains ₹525 to ₹950), soothing DJ sounds and pure Ibiza-meets-Mykonos decor (even the host is Greek). Thursday and weekends are packed. There's a second branch at Mahalaxmi Racecourse.

WTF!
BAR

(Map p62; 8 Vora Bldg, 3rd Khar Rd, Khar) Hilariously named and an equally good time, rambunctious WTF! (pronounced as letters) is a small venue divided in two rooms, one a lipstick-red den of pop culture kitsch and Formica, the other dumbed down with the cricket likely to be on the big screen. The DJ spins right in your face beside the front door – a loud and brash wall of international pop trash. Staff wouldn't call us a taxi at the end of the night, though – WTF?

Toto's Garage
BAR

(Map p62; ☑26005494; 30 Lourdes Heaven, Pali Naka, Bandra West; ⊙6pm-1am) Forget the beautiful people. Toto's is a down-to-earth local dive done up in a mechanic's theme where you can go in your dirty clothes, drink pitchers of beer and listen to music that gave us

guilty pleasure with the back-to-back-to-back Savage Garden–Linkin Park–AC/DC set. Get there early or you won't get a seat.

Elbo Room
PUB

(Map p62; St Teresa's Rd, Khar West) A genuine bar that approaches resto-lounge but thankfully falls short. Instead, it's a pub reminiscent of home and a good bet for wines by the glass (₹275 to ₹700) screening both English Premier League and Bundesliga football matches. The Italian-Indian menu is best enjoyed on the terrace while the serious drinkers – no shortage of expats among them – stay inside.

☆ Entertainment

The daily English-language tabloid *Mid-Day* incorporates a guide to Mumbai entertainment. Newspapers and *Time Out Mumbai* (p71) list events and film screenings, while www.nh7.in has live music listings. The cutting-edge **Bombay Elektrik Projekt** (www.bombayelektrik.com) organises everything from live DJs to poetry slams to short film screenings.

It would be a crime not to see a movie in India's film capital. Unfortunately, Hindi films aren't shown with English subtitles. The cinemas we've listed all show English-language movies, along with some Bollywood numbers.

Big clubs nights are (oddly) Wednesday, as well as the traditional Friday and Saturday; there's usually a cover charge. Dress codes apply so don't rock up in shorts and sandals. The trend in Mumbai of late is towards resto-lounges as opposed to full on nightclubs – serious tax implications on discos versus lounges and restaurants means folks got a little clever.

TOP CHOICE Bluefrog
LIVE MUSIC

(off Map p44; ☑6158; www.bluefrog.co.in; D/2 Mathuradas Mills Compound, NM Joshi Marg, Lower Parel; admission after 9pm Sun & Tue-Thu ₹300, Fri & Sat ₹500; ⊙7pm-1am Tue-Sun) The most exciting thing to happen to Mumbai's music scene in a long time, Bluefrog is a concert space, production studio, restaurant and one of Mumbai's most happening spaces. It hosts exceptional local and international acts, and has space-age, orange-glowing 'pod' seating in the intimate main room.

Valhalla
RESTO-LOUNGE

(Map p50; ☑67353535; 1st fl, East Wing, Eros Theatre Bldg, Churchgate) This discreet resto-lounge

MUMBAI (BOMBAY)

caters to Mumbai's bold and beautiful, who turn up here amid aubergine walls and baroque aesthetics on Friday and Saturday club nights when everywhere else closes (it's unofficially open until 4am or so). Getting in isn't easy – you need to call ahead and get on the list – but if you manage it, you'll rub elbows with a very high-profile crowd.

Not Just Jazz By the Bay   LIVE MUSIC
(Map p50; ☑22851876; 143 Marine Dr; admission weekdays/weekends ₹100/300; ☺noon-3.30am) This is the best, and frankly the only, jazz club in South Mumbai. True to its name, there are also live pop, blues and rock performers most nights from 10pm, but Sunday, Monday and Tuesday are reserved for karaoke. By day, there's a well done all-you-can-eat buffet (₹325).

Trilogy   NIGHTCLUB
(Map p62; Hotel Sea Princess, Juhu Tara Rd, Juhu; cover per couple after 11pm ₹1000; ☺closed Tue) Mumbai's newest club at time of writing is all attitude – rumour has it that staff size up potentials for looks and charge a varying admission accordingly. That bodes well for those who make it past face patrol. The trilevel space is gorgeous, highlighted by a black granite dance floor lit up by 1372 LED cube lights that go off like an epileptic Lite-Brite in an Indian power surge. The imported sound system favours house and hip-hop while the bartenders look imported from Ed Hardy's employee pool.

Polly Esther's   NIGHTCLUB
(Map p48; Gordon House Hotel, Battery St, Colaba; cover per couple Wed, Fri & Sat ₹800-1500) The city's fashionistas feel nauseous at its mere mention, but this mirror-plated, cheesy nightclub wallowing in retro gaudiness remains a fun choice to mingle with middle-class Mumbai. The *Saturday Night Fever* illuminated dance floor stays packed with gossiping 20-somethings and ogling tourists. Wednesday is free for the gals and all but ₹200 is recoupable in drinks most nights.

Wankhede Stadium   SPORT
(Mumbai Cricket Association; Map p50; ☑22795500; www.mumbaicricket.com; D Rd, Churchgate) Test matches and One Day Internationals are played a few times a year in season (October to April). Contact the Cricket Association for ticket information; for a test match you'll probably have to pay for the full five days.

Cooperage Football Ground   SPORT
(Map p48; ☑22024020; MK Rd, Colaba; tickets ₹20-25) Home to FC Air India, Mumbai FC and ONGC FC. Hosts national-league and local football (soccer) matches between October and February. Tickets are available at the gate.

National Centre for the Performing Arts   THEATRE
(NCPA; Map p50; ☑66223737, box office 22824567; www.ncpamumbai.com; cnr Marine Dr & Sri V Saha Rd, Nariman Point; tickets ₹200-500; ☺box office 9am-7pm) Spanning 800 sq metres, this cultural centre is the hub of Mumbai's music, theatre and dance scene. In any given week, it might host Marathi theatre, poetry readings and art exhibitions, Bihari dance troupes, ensembles from Europe or Indian classical music. The Experimental Theatre occasionally has English-language plays. Many performances are free. The box office is at the end of NCPA Marg.

Prithvi Theatre   THEATRE
(Map p62; ☑26149546; www.prithvitheatre.org; Juhu Church Rd, Juhu) At Juhu Beach, this is a good place to see both Hindi and English-language theatre. It hosts an excellent annual international theatre festival and there's a charming cafe, too.

Regal   CINEMA
(Map p48; ☑22021017; Opposite Regal Circle, Shahid Bhagat Singh Rd, Colaba; tickets ₹100-200) Check out the art deco architecture.

Eros   CINEMA
(Map p50; ☑22822335; MK Rd, Churchgate; tickets ₹80-120)

Metro Big   CINEMA
(off Map p50; ☑39894040; MG Rd, New Marine Lines, Fort; tickets ₹100-600) This grand dame of Bombay talkies was just renovated into a multiplex.

Sterling   CINEMA
(Map p50; ☑66220016; Marzaban Rd, Fort; tickets ₹120-180)

🔒 Shopping

Mumbai is India's great marketplace, with some of the best shopping in the country.

You can buy just about anything in the dense bazaars north of CST (Map p44). The main areas are Crawford Market (fruit and veg), Mangaldas Market (silk and cloth), Zaveri Bazaar (jewellery), Bhuleshwar Market (fruit and veg) and Chor Bazaar (antiques and furniture). Dhabu St is lined with fine leather goods and Mutton St specialises in antiques, reproductions and fine junk.

LOCAL KNOWLEDGE

PRAMOD SIPPY: DJ PRAMZ

A Mumbai turntable veteran, DJ Pramz has spun the black circles in the city for over half his lifetime. Here are his top picks.

Cosiest Club

Bonobo (Map p62); Kenilworth, Phase 2, Off Linking Rd, Bandra West) is a home away from home. They don't impose a dress code neither do they charge an entry. It's a walk-in and offers some really good cocktails at very good prices. It doesn't take long for one to establish their comfort level. As a DJ, I love performing there because of the 'no main-stream music' policy and of course because the owners are very much on the same page as me. They are young entrepreneurs who understand the global trends and are ready to experiment and do things differently.

Most Stunning Club

Wink (off Map p48; Vivanta by Taj – President Hotel, 90 Cuffe Pde, Cuffe Parade) is a beautifully designed bar with a demarcated area for quick meals. The drinks and service are easily the best in town. Their Winktinis are world-renowned and the music is nothing short of spectacular. I love to perform here because they are open-minded and, in spite of being situated in a five-star [hotel], they don't entertain requests that fall outside the ambit of the DJ. It's frequented by a large expatriate crowd who are usually [hotel] guests. Although the space is bright and unlike a club, the pulsating music on weekends makes the vibe quite groovy.

Most Celebrated Club

Zenzi Mills (off Map p44; Mathuradas Mills Compound, Senapati Bapat Marg, Lower Parel; ⊙closed Sun) is a paradise of sorts for all alternative music aficionados. It's basically an offshoot of the legendary Zenzi (Bandra), which essentially laid the foundation for alternative entertainment in the city. Zenzi widened its horizon by launching Mills, which had everything that the original Zenzi lacked – a state-of-the-art sound system, a beautiful set-up for visuals, a split level space. It works for artists of all alternative genres as the club is open to experimentation. A lot of deep-rooted sentiments are attached to it and it has become immortal for many in their hearts, but word is out that it's undergoing an image makeover and will be seen in an all-new form and feel. What it's going to be like is yet a mystery, though.

Crawford Market (Mahatma Phule Market) is the last outpost of British Bombay before the tumult of the central bazaars begins. Bas-reliefs by Rudyard Kipling's father, Lockwood Kipling, adorn the Norman Gothic exterior.

Snap up a bargain backpacking wardrobe at Fashion Street, the strip of stalls lining MG Rd between Cross and Azad maidans (Map p50), or in Bandra's Linking Rd, near Waterfield Rd (Map p62) – hone your bargaining skills. Kemp's Corner has many good shops for designer threads.

Various state-government emporiums sell handicrafts in the World Trade Centre Arcade (off Map p48) near Cuffe Parade. Small antique and curio shops line Merewether Rd behind the Taj Mahal Palace (Map p48). They aren't cheap, but the quality is a step up from government emporiums. If you prefer Raj-era

bric-a-brac, head to Chor Bazaar (Map p44): the main area of activity is Mutton St, where you'll find a row of shops specialising in antiques (and many ingenious reproductions, so beware) and miscellaneous junk.

Fabindia CLOTHING
(Map p50; Jeroo Bldg, 137 MG Rd, Kala Ghoda) Founded as a means to get traditional fabric artisans' wares to market, Fabindia has all the vibrant colours of the country in its trendy cotton and silk fashions, materials and homewares in a modern-meets-traditional Indian shop. If you are too cool for Indian-wear, try here. The Santa Cruz outpost (Map p62) is also good.

Bombay Electric CLOTHES
(Map p48; www.bombayeletric.in; 1 Reay House, Best Marg, Colaba) High fashion is the calling

THE GREAT WALL OF MUMBAI

An artistic initiative similar to Berlin's East Side Gallery, though without the 28 years of oppression and isolation, the **Wall Project** (Map p62; www.thewallproject.com) was started by a group of ex-art/design students who decided to paint their neighbours' walls with local themes and artsy graffiti. This soon spread into a public project that has splashed colourful murals on everything from houses to hospitals all over the suburb of Bandra. The idea quickly began spreading like kaleidoscopic Kudzu – a spray-painted virus that has turned crumbling structures and neglected walls into a living museum of contemporary urban culture. At time of writing, hundreds of artists (and nonartists) have painted some 600 murals, the longest stretch of which starts at Mahim station (West) on Tulsi Pipe Rd (Senapati Bapat Marg) and runs along the Western Railway to Matunga Rd station – nicknamed as the Great Wall of Mumbai.

Anyone can visit and paint the wall, as long as the art is not sexually explicit, political, religious or commercial. Grab some acrylic distemper paint – recommended due to harsh weather conditions – and get your art on!

at this trendy unisex boutique next to the Taj Mahal Palace hotel. It sources fabrics (for its own hip brand, Gheebutter) and weaved scarfs and jackets from NGOs in Madhya Pradesh and Gujarat, as well as select antiques and handicrafts. It's a sharp spot to pick up *kurtas* (long shirts), dress shirts and stylish T-shirts.

Phillips   ANTIQUES, CURIOS
(Map p48; www.phillipsantiques.com; Wodehouse Rd, Colaba) The 150-year-old Phillips has nizam-era royal silver, wooden ceremonial masks, Victorian glass and various other gorgeous things that you never knew you wanted. It also has high-quality reproductions of old photos, maps and paintings, and a warehouse shop of big antiques.

Shrujan   HANDICRAFTS
Breach Candy (Map p44; Sagar Villa, Warden Rd, opposite Navroze Apts; ⊙closed Sun); Juhu (Map p62; Hatkesh Society, 6th North South Rd, JVPD Scheme; ⊙closed Sun) Selling the intricate embroidery work of women in 114 villages in Kutch, Gujarat, the nonprofit Shrujan aims to help women earn a livelihood while preserving the spectacular embroidery traditions of the area. The sophisticated clothing, wall hangings and purses make great gifts.

Biba   CLOTHING
(Map p44; 1 Hughes Rd, Kemp's Corner; ⊙10.30am-9pm Mon-Sat) You'll be impossibly fashionable in LA or London in these sundresses! Also in Khar West (p62).

Bombay Store   HANDICRAFTS
(Map p50; Western India House, Sir PM Rd, Fort; ⊙10.30am-8pm Mon-Sat, to 6.30pm Sun) A classy selection of rugs, clothing, teas,

stationery, aromatherapy, brass sculptures and, perhaps most interestingly, biodegradable Ganesh idols for use in the Ganesh Chaturthi festival.

Good Earth   HANDICRAFTS
(Map p48; 2 Reay House, Colaba) This Delhi transplant hawks gorgeous, eco-leaning housewares, candles, cosmetics and glassware. Funky coasters, hand-decorated china, stylish coffee mugs – all higher end and artsy.

Oxford Bookstore   BOOKSTORE
(Map p50; www.oxfordbookstore.com; Apeejay House, 3 Dinsha Wachha Marg, Churchgate; ⊙8am-10pm) Mumbai's best, with a tea bar.

Crossword   BOOKSTORE
(Map p44; Mohammedbhai Mansion, NS Patkar Marg, Kemp's Corner) Enormous.

Khadi & Village Industries Emporium
CLOTHING
(Khadi Bhavan; Map p50; 286 Dr Dadabhai Naoroji Rd, Fort; ⊙10.30am-6.30pm Mon-Sat) Khadi Bhavan is dusty, 1940s timewarp with ready-made traditional Indian clothing, material, shoes and handicrafts that are so old they're new again.

Cotton Cottage   CLOTHING
(Map p50; Agra Bldg, 121 MG Rd, Kala Ghoda; ⊙10am-9pm) Stock up on simple cotton *kurtas* and various pants – *salwars, churidars, patiala* – for the road.

Mini Market/Bollywood Bazaar
ANTIQUES, CURIOS
(Map p44; ☑23472427; 33/31 Mutton St; ⊙11am-8pm Sat-Thu) Sells original vintage Bollywood posters and other movie ephemera

as well as odd and interesting trinkets.
Call if you get lost.

Kala Niketan
CLOTHING
(Map p50; 95 MK Rd; ☺9.30am-7.30pm Mon-Sat)
Sari madness on Queens Rd.

Mélange
CLOTHING
(Map p44; 33 Altamount Rd, Kemp's Corner;
☺closed Sun) High-fashion ladies garments
from over 100 Indian designers in a chic
exposed-brick space.

Chimanlals
HANDICRAFTS
(Map p50; 210 Dr Dadabhai Naoroji Rd,
Fort; ☺9.30am-6pm Mon-Fri, to 5.30pm Sat)
Beautiful writing materials made from
traditional Indian paper. Enter from
Wallace St.

Rhythm House
MUSIC STORE
(Map p50; ☺22842835; 40 K Dubash Marg, Fort;
☺10am-8.30pm Mon-Sat, 11am-8.30pm Sun)
Nonpirated CDs; tickets to concerts, plays
and festivals.

BX Furtado & Sons
MUSIC STORE
(off Map p50; www.furtadosonline.com; Jer Mahal,
Dhobitalao; ☺10am-8pm Mon-Sat) The best
place in Mumbai for musical instruments
– sitars, tablas, accordions and local and
imported guitars. The branch around the
corner on Kalbadevi Rd is pianos and
sheet music only.

Central Cottage
Industries Emporium
HANDICRAFTS, SOUVENIRS
(Map p48; ☺22027537; Chhatrapati Shivaji Marg,
Colaba; ☺closed Sun) Limited souvenir shop-
ping at government-restricted prices.

Standard Supply Co
PHOTOGRAPHY
(Map p50; ☺22612468; Image House, Walchand
Hirachand Marg, Fort; ☺10am-7pm Mon-Sat)
Everything you could possibly need for
digital and film photography.

ⓘ Information

Internet Access
Portasia (Kitab Mahal, Dr Dadabhai Naoroji
Rd, Fort; per hr ₹25; ☺9am-9pm Mon-Sat)
Entrance is down a little alley; look for the
'cybercafe' sign hanging from a tree.

Sify iWay (per 2hr ₹100) Churchgate (Prem Ct,
J Tata Rd; ☺8.30am-9.30pm); Colaba (Donald
House, 1st fl, Colaba Causeway; ☺8.30am-
9.30pm) The Colaba branch entrance is on JA
Allana Marg.

Media
To find out what's going on in Mumbai, check out
the free *burrp! Know Your City* (www.mumbai.
burrp.com), available in most hotels; the
Hindustan Times' Café insert or **Time Out
Mumbai** (www.timeoutmumbai.net; ₹50).

Medical Services
Bombay Hospital (Map p50; ☑22067676,
ambulance 22067309; www.bombayhospital.
com; 12 New Marine Lines)

Breach Candy Hospital (Map p44;
☑23672888; www.breachcandyhospital.org;
60 Bhulabhai Desai Rd, Breach Candy) Best in
Mumbai, if not India.

Royal Chemists (Map p50; ☑22004041-3; 89A
Maharshi Karve Rd, Churchgate; ☺8.30am-
8.30pm Mon-Sat)

Sahakari Bhandar Chemist (Map p48;
☑22022399; Colaba Causeway, Colaba;
☺10am-8.30pm)

Money
ATMs are everywhere and foreign-exchange
offices changing cash and travellers cheques are
also plentiful.

Akbar Travels Colaba (Map p48; ☑22823434;
30 Alipur Trust Bldg; ☺10am-7pm); Fort (Map
p50; ☑22633434; Terminus View, 167/169 Dr
Dadabhai Naoroji Rd; ☺10am-7pm Mon-Fri, to
6pm Sun)

Thomas Cook (☺9.30am-6pm Mon-Sat)
Colaba (Map p48; ☑22882517-20; Colaba
Causeway); Fort (Map p50; ☑61603333; 324
Dr Dadabhai Naoroji Rd)

Post
The **main post office** (Map p50; ☺10am-6pm
Mon-Sat) is an imposing building behind Chha-
trapati Shivaji Terminus (CST; Victoria Termi-
nus). **Poste restante** (☺9am-8pm Mon-Sat) is
at Counter 1. Letters should be addressed c/o
Poste Restante, Mumbai GPO, Mumbai 400 001.
Bring your passport to collect mail. The **EMS
Speedpost parcel counter** (☺11.30am-7.30pm
Mon-Fri) is across from the stamp counters. Op-
posite the post office, under the tree, are parcel-
wallahs who will stitch up your parcel for ₹40.

Colaba post office (Map p48; Henry Rd)
Convenient branch.

Blue Dart/DHL Churchgate (Map p50; www.
bluedart.com; Khetan Bhavan, J Tata Rd;
☺10am-8pm Mon-Sat); Nariman Point (Map
p44; www.dhl.co.in; Embassy Centre; ☺9am-
8.30pm Mon-Sat) Private express-mail company.

Telephone
Justdial (☑69999999; www.justdial.com) and
☑197 provide directory enquiries.

Tourist Information
Government of India tourist office (Map p50;
☑22074333; www.incredibleindia.com; 123
Maharshi Karve Rd; ☺8.30am-7pm Mon-Fri, to
2pm Sat) Provides information for the entire
country.

Government of India tourist office airport booths domestic (📞26156920; ⏰7am-midnight); international (📞26813253; ⏰24hr)

Maharashtra Tourism Development Corporation booth (MTDC; Map p48; 📞22841877; Apollo Bunder; ⏰8.30am-4pm Tue-Sun, 5.30-8pm weekends) For city bus tours.

MTDC reservation office (Map p50; 📞22841877; www.maharashtratourism.gov.in; Madame Cama Rd, opposite LIC Bldg, Nariman Point; ⏰9.45am-5.30pm Mon-Sat) Information on Maharashtra and bookings for MTDC hotels and the *Deccan Odyssey* train package. This is also the only MTDC office that accepts credits cards.

Travel Agencies

Akbar Travels (Map p50; 📞22633434; www.akbartravelsonline.com; Terminus View, 167/169 Dr Dadabhai Naoroji Rd, Fort; ⏰10am-7pm Mon-Fri, to 6pm Sun)

Magnum International Travel & Tours (Map p48; 📞61559700; 10 Henry Rd, Colaba; ⏰10am-5.30pm Mon-Fri, to 4pm Sat)

Thomas Cook (Map p50; 📞22048556-8; 324 Dr Dadabhai Naoroji Rd, Fort; ⏰9.30am-6pm Mon-Sat)

Visa Extensions

Foreigners' Regional Registration Office (FRRO; Map p50; 📞22620446; Annexe Bldg No 2, CID, Badaruddin Tyabji Rd, near Special Branch) Does not officially issue extensions on tourist visas; even in emergencies it will direct you to Delhi (p491). However, some travellers have managed to procure an emergency extension here after much waiting and persuasion.

❶ Getting There & Away

Air

AIRPORTS Mumbai is the main international gateway to South India and has the busiest network of domestic flights. **Chhatrapati Shivaji International Airport** (📞domestic 26264000, international 26813000; www.csia.in), about 30km from the city centre, has been undergoing a $2 billion modernisation since 2006. At time of writing, the airport comprises three domestic (1A, 1B and 1C) and one international terminal (2A). However, the domestic side is accessed via Vile Parle and is known locally as Santa Cruz airport, while the international, with its entrance 4km away in Andheri, goes locally by Sahar. Both terminals have ATMs, foreign-exchange counters and tourist-information booths. A free shuttle bus runs between the two every 30 minutes for ticket holders only. By 2014 the shiny new terminal T2 is expected to be open, serving both domestic and international flights, with the existing Santa Cruz terminal being converted to cargo only.

INTERNATIONAL AIRLINES Travel agencies are often better for booking international flights, while airline offices are increasingly directing customers to their call centres. The following airline ticket offices are clinging to life in Mumbai:

Air India (Map p50; 📞27580777, airport 26156633; www.airindia.com; Air India Bldg, cnr Marine Dr & Madame Cama Rd, Nariman Point; ⏰9.15am-6.30pm Mon-Fri, to 5.15pm Sat & Sun)

Cathay Pacific (off Map p44; 📞66572222, airport 66859002/3; www.cathaypacific.com; 2 Brady Gladys Plaza, Senapati Bapat Marg, Lower Parel; ⏰9.30am-6.30pm Mon-Sat)

Emirates Airlines (Map p50; 📞40974097; www.emirates.com; 3 Mittal Chambers, 228 Nariman Point; ⏰9am-5.30pm Mon-Sat)

El Al Airlines (Map p50; 📞66207400, airport 66859425/6; www.elal.co.il; 6th fl, NKM International House, BM Chinai Marg, Nariman Point; ⏰9.30am-5.30pm Mon-Fri, to 1pm Sat)

Qantas (Map p50; 📞61111818; www.qantas.com.au; 4th fl, Sunteck Centre, 37-40 Subhash Rd, Vile Parle; ⏰9am-1.15pm & 2.30-5.30pm Mon-Fri)

Swiss (Map p50; 📞67137240; www.swiss.com; 2nd fl, Vashani Chambers, 9 New Marine Lines; ⏰9am-5.30pm Mon-Sat)

Thai Airways (Map p50; 📞61395599; www.thaiair.com; 2A Mittal Towers A Wing, Nariman Point; ⏰9.30am-5.30pm Mon-Fri, to 4pm Sat)

Major nonstop domestic flights from Mumbai include the following:

DESTINATION	SAMPLE LOWEST ONE-WAY FARE (₹)	DURATION (HR)
Bengaluru	2533	1½
Chennai	3482	1¾
Delhi	3483	2
Goa	2532	1
Hyderabad	2282	1¼
Jaipur	2533	1¾
Kochi	3483	1¾
Kolkata	3882	2¾

DOMESTIC AIRLINES The following all have ticketing counters at the domestic airport; most open 24 hours.

GoAir (📞call centre 1800 222111, airport 26264789; www.goair.in)

Indian Airlines (Map p50; 📞22023031, call centre 1800 1801407; www.indian-airlines.nic.in;

Air India Bldg, cnr Marine Dr & Madame Cama Rd, Nariman Point)

IndiGo (☎call centre 1800 1803838; www.goindigo.in)

Jet Airways (Map p48; ☎call centre 39893333, airport 26266575; www.jetairways.com; Amarchand Mansion, Madame Cama Rd; ☻9.30am-6pm Mon-Fri, to 1pm Sat)

JetLite (☎call centre 1800 225522; www.jetlite.com)

Kingfisher/Kingfisher Red (Map p50;☎call centre 1800 2331310, airport 26262605; www.flykingfisher.com; Nirmal Bldg, Marine Dr, Nariman Point; ☻9am-7pm Mon-Sat, 10am-2pm Sun)

SpiceJet (☎call centre 1800 1803333, airport 26156155; www.spicejet.com)

Bus

Numerous private operators and state governments run long-distance buses to and from Mumbai.

Private buses are usually more comfortable and simpler to book but can cost significantly more than government buses; they depart from Dr Anadrao Nair Rd near Mumbai Central train station (Map p44). Fares to popular destinations (like Goa) are up to 75% higher during holiday periods. To check on departure times and current prices, try **National CTC** (Map p44; ☎23015652; Dr Anadrao Nair Rd; ☻7am-10pm).

More convenient for Goa and southern destinations are the private buses run by **Chandni Travels** (Map p50; ☎22713901) that depart three times a day in front of Azad Maidan, just south of the Metro cinema. Ticket agents are located near the bus departure point.

Long-distance government-run buses depart from **Mumbai Central bus terminal** (Map p44; ☎23074272/1524) by Mumbai Central train station. Buses service major towns in Maharashtra and neighbouring states. They're cheaper and more frequent than private services, but the quality and crowd levels vary.

Popular long-distance bus fares include the following:

DESTINATION	PRIVATE NON-AC/AC SLEEPER ₹	GOVERN-MENT NON-AC ₹	DURA-TION (HR)
Ahmedabad	250/600	N/A	13
Aurangabad	250/600	368	10
Mahabaleshwar	450/500*	270	7
Paniji	300/700	N/A	14-18
Pune	200**	170-250	4
Udaipur	350/1400	N/A	16

* AC Sitting; **AC Sitting

Train

Three train systems operate out of Mumbai, but the most important services for travellers are Central Railways and Western Railways. Tickets for either system can be bought from any station, in South Mumbai or the suburbs, that has computerised ticketing.

Central Railways (☎134), handling services to the east, south, plus a few trains to the north, operates from CST. The **reservation centre** (Map p50; ☎139; ☻8am-8pm Mon-Sat, to 2pm Sun) is around the side of CST where the taxis gather. **Foreign tourist-quota tickets** (Counter 52) can be bought up to 90 days before travel, but must be paid in foreign currency or with rupees backed by an encashment certificate or ATM receipt. Indrail passes (p25) can also be bought at Counter 52. You can buy nonquota tickets with a Visa or MasterCard at the much faster credit-card counters (10 and 11) for a ₹30 fee. Refunds for Indians and foreigners alike are handled at Counter 8.

Some Central Railways trains depart from Dadar (D), a few stations north of CST, or Churchgate/Lokmanya Tilak (T), 16km north of CST.

Western Railways (☎131, 132) has services to the north (including Rajasthan and Delhi) from Mumbai Central train station (MC; ☎23061763, 23073535), usually called Bombay Central (BCT). The **reservation centre** (Map p50; ☻8am-8pm Mon-Sat, to 2pm Sun), opposite Churchgate train station, has a **foreign tourist-quota counter** (Counter 14). The same rules apply as at CST station. The creditcard counter is No 6.

❶ Getting Around

To/From the Airports

INTERNATIONAL The prepaid-taxi booth that is located at the international airport has set fares for every neighbourhood in the city; Colaba, Fort and Marine Dr are AC/non-AC ₹495/395, Bandra West ₹310/260 and Juhu ₹235/190. There's a ₹10 service charge and a charge of ₹10 per bag. The journey to Colaba takes about 45 minutes at night and 1½ to two hours during the day. Tips are not required.

Autorickshaws queue up at a little distance from arrivals, but don't try to take one to South Mumbai: they can only go as far as Mahim Creek. You can catch an autorickshaw (around ₹40) to Andheri train station and catch a suburban train (₹7, 45 minutes) to Churchgate or CST. Only attempt this if you arrive during the day outside of rush 'hour' (6am to 11am) and are not weighed down with luggage.

Minibuses outside arrivals offer free shuttle services to the domestic airport and Juhu hotels.

DESTINATION	TRAIN NO & NAME	SAMPLE FARE (₹)	DURATION (HR)	DEPARTURE
Agra	12137 *Punjab Mail*	410/1098/1501/2533	22	7.40pm CST
Ahmedabad	12901 *Gujarat Mail*	232/594/802/1350	9	9.50pm MC
Aurangabad	17057 *Devagiri Express*	176/463/632/1061	7	9.05pm CST
	17617 *Tapovan Express*	102/363*	7	6.10am CST
Bengaluru	16529 *Udyan Express*	363/991/1364/2298	25	8.05am CST
Bhopal	12137 *Punjab Mail*	325/857/1167/1958	14	7.40pm CST
Chennai	11041 *Chennai Express*	383/1046/1440**	27	2.00pm CST
Delhi	12951 *Rajdhani Express*	1495/1975/3305†	16	4.40pm MC
	12137 *Punjab Mail*	442/1187/1623/2743	25½	7.10pm CST
Margao	10103 *Mandavi Express*	288/782/1073/1799	11½	6.55am CST
	12051 *Shatabdi Express*	283/787/1073/1799	9	5.10am CST
Hyderabad	12701 *Hussainsagar Express*	312/823/1119/1876	14½	9.50pm CST
Indore	12961 *Avantika Express*	320/847/1151/1931	14½	7.05pm MC
Jaipur	12955 *Jaipur Express*	383/1021/1394/2348	18	6.50pm MC
Kochi	16345 *Netravati Express*	430/1178/1624***	26½	11.40am T
Kolkata	12859 *Gitanjali Express*	508/1883*	30½	6.00am CST
	12809 *Howrah Mail*	508/1374/1883/3190	33	8.35pm CST
Pune	12125 *Pragati Express*	76/267*	3½	5.10pm CST
Varanasi	11093 *Mahanagari Express*	422/1157/1593***	2½	12.10am CST
Trivandrum	16345 *Netravati Express*	1277/1762#	30	11.40am T

Station abbreviations: CST (Chhatrapati Shivaji Terminus); MC (Mumbai Central); T (Lokmanya Tilak); D (Dadar)

Note: fares are for sleeper/3AC/2AC/1AC except for: * AC/Non-AC, ** sleeper/3AC/2AC, *** Non-AC/3AC/2AC, # 3AC/2AC, † 3AC/2AC/1AC

A taxi from South Mumbai to the international airport should be between ₹350 and ₹400 by negotiating a fixed fare beforehand; official baggage charges are ₹10 per bag. Add 25% to the meter charge between midnight and 5am. We love the old-school black-and-yellows, but there are also AC, metered call taxis run by **Meru** (☑44224422; www.merucabs.com), charging ₹20 for the first kilometre and ₹14 per kilometre thereafter (25% more at night). Routes are tracked by GPS, so no rip-offs!

DOMESTIC Taxis and autorickshaws queue up outside both domestic terminals. The prepaid counter is outside arrivals. A non-AC/AC taxi to Colaba or Fort costs ₹350/400, day or night, plus ₹10 per bag. For Juhu, ₹150/200.

A cheaper alternative is to catch an autorickshaw between the airport and Vile Parle train station (₹20 to ₹30), and a train between Vile Parle and Churchgate (₹7, 45 minutes). Don't attempt this during rush hour (6am to 11am).

Boat

Both **PNP** (☑22885220) and **Maldar Catamarans** (☑22829695) run regular ferries to Mandwa (oneway ₹110), useful for access to Murud-Janjira and other parts of the Konkan Coast, avoiding the long bus trip out of Mumbai. Their ticket offices are at Apollo Bunder (near the Gateway of India; Map p48).

Bus

Mumbai's single- and double-decker buses are good for travelling short distances. Fares around South Mumbai cost ₹3 for a section; pay the conductor once you're aboard. The service is run by **BEST** (Map p48; www.bestundertaking. com), which has a depot in Colaba (the website has a useful search facility for bus routes across the city). Just jumping on a double-decker (such as bus 103) is an inexpensive way to see South Mumbai. Day passes are available for ₹25.

In the table following are some useful routes; all of these buses depart from the bus stand at the southern end of Colaba Causeway and pass Flora Fountain.

DESTINATION	BUS NO
Breach Candy	132, 133
CST & Crawford Market	1, 3, 21, 103, 124
Churchgate	70, 106, 123, 132
Girgaum Chowpatty	103, 106, 107, 123
Haji Ali	83, 124, 132, 133
Hanging Gardens	103, 106
Mani Bhavan	123
Mohammed Ali Rd	1, 3, 21
Mumbai Central train station	124, 125

Car

Cars are generally hired for an eight-hour day and an 80km maximum, with additional charges if you go over. For an AC car, the best going rate is about ₹1000.

Agents at the Apollo Bunder ticket booths near the Gateway of India can arrange a non-AC Maruti with driver for a half-day of sightseeing for ₹1000 (going as far as Mahalaxmi and Malabar Hill). Regular taxi drivers often accept a similar price.

Metro

Mumbai's US$8.17 billion metro project has broken ground. The Colaba–Bandra–Airport line will most benefit tourists, but is several years away from completion.

Motorcycle

Allibhai Premji Tyrewalla (Map p44; www. premjis.com; 205/207 Dr D Bhadkamkar Rd; ⏱10am-7pm Mon-Sat), around for almost 100

TAXI TROUBLE

We won't name names, but Mumbaikar taxis and rickshaws *might* occasionally like to take advantage of foreign faces. If you find yourself in either with an old-fashion meter (outside on the left-hand dash), you are vulnerable. Print out handy conversion charts from the **Mumbai Traffic Police** (www.trafficpo licemumbai.org/Tariffcard_Auto_taxi_form. htm) – end of discussion (until the next price hike).

years, sells new and used motorcycles with a guaranteed buy-back option. For two- to three-week 'rental' periods you'll still have to pay the full cost of the bike upfront. The company prefers to deal with longer-term schemes of two months or more, which work out cheaper anyway. A used 150cc or 225cc Hero Honda Karizma costs ₹25,000 to ₹80,000, with a buy-back price of around 60% after three months (higher-cc Enfields are sometimes available). A smaller bike (100cc to 180cc) starts at ₹25,000. The company can also arrange shipment of bikes overseas (around ₹24,000 to the UK).

Taxi & Autorickshaw

Every second car on Mumbai's streets seems to be a black-and-yellow Premier taxi (India's version of a 1950s Fiat). They're the most convenient way to get around the city, and in South Mumbai drivers *almost* always use the meter without prompting. Autorickshaws are confined to the suburbs north of Mahim Creek.

Drivers don't always know the names of Mumbai's streets (especially new names) – the best way to find something is by using nearby landmarks. A 2010 fare increase means taxi meters start at ₹16 during the day (₹20 after midnight) for the first 1.6km and ₹10 per kilometre after this (₹12 after midnight). If you get a taxi with the old-fashion meters, the fare will be roughly 16 times the amount shown. The minimum autorickshaw fare is ₹11.

Train

Mumbai has an efficient but overcrowded suburban train network.

There are three main lines, making it easy to navigate. The most useful service operates from Churchgate heading north to stations such as Charni Rd (for Girgaum Chowpatty), Mumbai Central, Mahalaxmi (for the Dhobi Ghat; p49), Vile Parle (for the domestic airport), Andheri (for the international airport) and Borivali (for Sanjay Gandhi National Park). Other suburban lines operate from CST to Byculla (for Veermata Jijabai Bhonsle Udyan, formerly Victoria Gardens), Dadar and as far as Neral (for Matheran). Trains run from 4am till 1am. From Churchgate, 2nd-/1st-class fares are ₹4/41 to Mumbai Central, ₹7/78 to Vile Parle or Andheri, and ₹9/104 to Borivali.

'Tourist tickets' permit unlimited travel in 2nd/1st class for one (₹50/170), three (₹90/330) or five (₹105/390) days.

Avoid rush hours when trains are jam-packed, even in 1st class; watch your valuables, and gals, stick to the ladies-only carriages.

WORTH A TRIP

SANJAY GANDHI NATIONAL PARK

It's hard to believe that within 90 minutes of the teeming metropolis you can be surrounded by this 104-sq-km **protected tropical forest** (☑28866449; adult/child ₹30/15, 2-/4-wheeler vehicle ₹15/50; ☉7.30am-6pm). Here, bright flora, birds, butterflies and elusive wild leopards replace pollution and crowds, all surrounded by forested hills on the city's northern edge. Urban development and shantytowns try to muscle in on the fringes of this wild region, but its status as a national park has allowed it to stay green and calm.

In addition to well-worn trekking trails to Shilonda waterfall and Vihar and Tulsi lakes, there is a lion and tiger safari and Kanheri caves to occupy day-trippers escaping the Mumbai mayhem. Inside the main northern entrance is an information centre with a small exhibition on the park's wildlife. The best time to see birds is October to April and butterflies August to November.

GREATER MUMBAI

Elephanta Island

In the middle of Mumbai Harbour, 9km northeast of the Gateway of India, the rock-cut temples on **Elephanta Island** (http://asi.nic.in/; Indian/foreigner ₹10/250; ⊘caves 9am-5.30pm Tue-Sun) are a Unesco World Heritage Site and worth crossing the waters for. Home to a labyrinth of cave-temples carved into the basalt rock of the island, the artwork represents some of the most impressive temple carving in all of India. The main Shiva-dedicated temple is an intriguing latticework of courtyards, halls, pillars and shrines, with the magnum opus a 6m-tall statue of Sadhashiva – depicting a three-faced Shiva as the destroyer, creator and preserver of the universe. The enormous central bust of Shiva, its eyes closed in eternal contemplation, may be the most serene sight you witness in India.

The temples are thought to have been created between AD 450 and 750, when the island was known as Gharapuri (Place of Caves). The Portuguese renamed it Elephanta because of a large stone elephant near the shore, which collapsed in 1814 and was moved by the British to Mumbai's Jijamata Udyan.

The English-language guide service (free with deluxe boat tickets) is worthwhile; tours depart every hour on the half-hour from the ticket booth. Beware of touts that meet you at the jetty and try to convince you to employ their services – the included English guide will met you at the entrance to the temples. Ask for government-issued ID if in doubt.

If you explore independently, pick up Pramod Chandra's *A Guide to the Elephanta Caves* from the stalls lining the stairway. There's also a small **museum** on-site, which has some informative pictorial panels on the origin of the caves.

⊙ Getting There & Away

Launches (economy/deluxe ₹105/130) head to Elephanta Island from the Gateway of India every half-hour from 9am to 3.30pm Tuesday to Sunday. Buy tickets at the booths lining Apollo Bunder. The voyage takes just over an hour.

The ferries dock at the end of a concrete pier, from where you can walk (around three minutes) or take the **miniature train** (₹10) to the **stairway** (admission ₹5) leading up to the caves. It's lined with handicraft stalls and patrolled by pesky monkeys. Wear good shoes.

Maharashtra

Best Places to Eat

» Malaka Spice (p108)
» Biso (p102)
» Khyber (p82)
» The Grapevine (p112)
» Prem's (p108)

Best Places to Stay

» Verandah in the Forest (p101)
» Hotel Sunderban (p107)
» Lemon Tree (p85)
» Beyond (see boxed text, p82)
» Osho Meditation Resort Guesthouse (p107)

Why Go?

India's third-largest (and second-most populous) state, Maharashtra is smattered with lazy beaches, lofty mountains, virgin forests and historic hot spots, all complemented by the incredible sights, sounds, smells and tastes of India.

Starting up north around Nasik, the state yields a curious blend of spirituality, meditation and chardonnay. Next comes cosmopolitan Pune, a city as famous for its sex guru as its food-and-beverage circuit. Slip westward and you are rewarded with a rash of golden sands, crumbling forts and emerald forests along the lonely shores of the Arabian Sea. For an off-beat experience, head east to spy tigers prowling in dense tropical jungle, or saunter south for overwhelming temples, zany palaces and brawny action in wrestling pits. Sounds like your kind of melting pot? Dive right in.

When to Go
Nasik

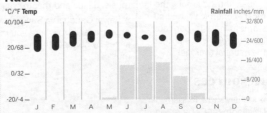

Jan It's party time in Nasik's wineries, marked by grape harvesting and crushing galas.

Sep The frenzied and energetic Ganesh Chaturthi celebrations reach fever pitch.

Dec Winter's a lovely time for the secluded beaches of Murud, Ganpatipule and Tarkarli.

FORTS GALORE

In terms of medieval forts and citadels, Maharashtra comes second perhaps only to Rajasthan. The best of the lot is Daulatabad Fort (p88), a bastion that once played a cameo as India's capital. Equally intriguing is Janjira (p98), a 12th century island fortress that was once an outpost for the seafaring African traders. Best of all are the many forts closely associated with the life of Chhatrapati Shivaji, including the Raigad Fort (p112), and Shivneri Fort (p111), where the Maratha leader was born.

Fast Facts

» Population: 112.4 million

» Area: 307,690 sq km

» Capital: Mumbai

» Main languages: Marathi, Hindi, English

» Sleeping prices: **$** below ₹1000, **$$** ₹1000 to ₹4000, **$$$** above ₹4000

Money Matters

Maharashtra is among the most economically well-off states in India. Its per-capita income is 60% higher than the national average.

Resources

» Maharashtra Tourism Development Corporation (MTDC; www.maharashtra tourism.gov.in)

» Maharashtra State Road Transport Corporation (MSRTC; www.msrtc.gov.in)

Top Yoga & Meditation Centres

The **Vipassana International Academy** in Igatpuri (p83) has long been a destination for those wishing to put mind over matter through an austere form of Buddhist meditation. The boundaries of yoga, on the other hand, are constantly pushed at the **Ramamani Iyengar Memorial Yoga Institute** in Pune (p107) and the **Kaivalyadhama Yoga Hospital** in Lonavla (p102). For a more lavish and indulgent form of spiritual engagement, there's the super-luxurious **Osho International Meditation Resort** in Pune (p105), where one can meditate in style, while flexing a few muscles in the unique game of 'zennis' (Zen tennis).

DON'T MISS

The ancient caves of **Ellora** and **Ajanta** are among India's top architectural and artistic wonders. Rock art and cave paintings reach sublime levels of beauty and perfection at these World Heritage Sites.

Top Festivals

» Naag Panchami (Aug, Pune, p103, Kolhapur, p113) A traditional snake-worshipping festival.

» Ganesh Chaturthi (Sep, Pune, p103) Celebrated with fervour all across Maharashtra; Pune goes particularly hysteric in honour of the elephant-headed deity.

» Dussehra (Sep & Oct, Nagpur, p96, Aurangabad, p84) A Hindu festival, but it also marks the Buddhist celebration of the anniversary of the famous humanist and Dalit leader BR Ambedkar's conversion to Buddhism.

» Ellora Ajanta Aurangabad Festival (Nov, Aurangabad, p84) A cultural festival bringing together the best classical and folk performers from across the region, while promoting a number of artistic traditions and handicrafts on the side.

» Kalidas Festival (Nov, Nagpur, p96) Commemorates the literary genius of legendary poet Kalidas through spirited music, dance and theatre sessions.

» Sawai Gandharva Sangeet Mahotsav (Dec, Pune, p103) An extravaganza where you can see unforgettable performances by some of the heftiest names in Indian classical music.

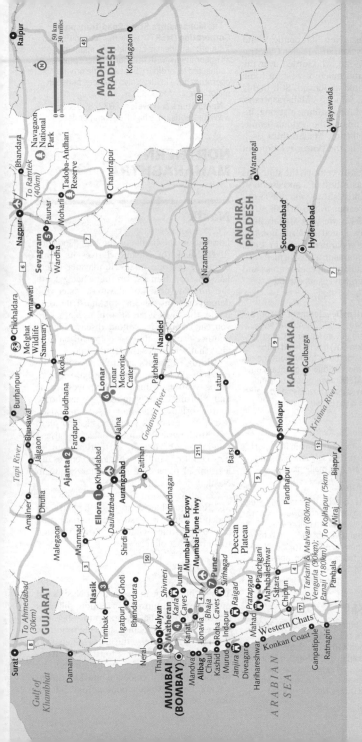

Maharashtra Highlights

1 Drop your jaw at the awe-inspiring beauty of the monumental **Kailasa Temple**, the jewel in Ellora Caves' crown (p89)

2 Be mesmerised by antique Buddhist art in the ancient cave galleries of **Ajanta** (p92)

3 Sip on a glass of zinfandel or sauvignon, and lose yourself

in a holy confluence of faith and ritual in **Nasik** (p80)

4 Gallop on a horse to Echo Point, or simply outrun the toy train chugging up the hill in **Mattheran** (p100)

5 Rediscover the Gandhian way of life at the **Sevagram Ashram** in Sevagram (p97)

6 Brush up on your astronomy skills while ambling

around the primordial **Lonar Meteorite Crater** (p96)

7 Learn more about India's diverse cultures and traditions at the fantastic museums of **Pune** (p103)

History

Maharashtra was given its political and ethnic identity by Maratha leader Chhatrapati Shivaji (1627–80), who lorded over the Deccan plateau and much of western India from his stronghold at Raigad. Still highly respected today among Maharashtrans, Shivaji is credited for instilling a strong, independent spirit among the region's people, as well as establishing Maharashtra as a dominant player in the power relations of medieval India.

From the early 18th century, the state was under the administration of a succession of ministers called the Peshwas who ruled until 1819, ceding thereafter to the British. After Independence (1947), western Maharashtra and Gujarat were joined to form Bombay state, only to be separated again in 1960, when modern Maharashtra was formed with the exclusion of Gujarati-speaking areas and with Mumbai (Bombay) as its capital.

ⓘ Information

Maharashtra Tourism Development Corporation (MTDC; Map p44; ☏02222845678; www.maharashtratourism.gov.in; Madame Cama Rd; ⊙10am-5.30pm Mon-Sat) has its head office in Mumbai. Most major towns throughout the state have offices, too, but they're generally only useful for booking MTDC accommodation and tours. While Sunday is not a business day, many government offices also remain closed on alternate Saturdays.

ⓘ Getting There & Away

Mumbai (p72) is Maharashtra's main transport hub, although Pune (p110), Jalgaon (p96) and Aurangabad (p88) are also major players.

ⓘ Getting Around

Because the state is so large, internal flights (eg Pune to Nagpur) can help speed up your explorations. Airfares vary widely on a daily basis. AC Indica taxis are readily available, too, and charge around ₹7 per kilometre. For long trips, factor in a minimum daily distance of 250km, and a daily driver's allowance of ₹100.

HOTEL TAXES

In Maharashtra, hotel rooms below ₹1200 are charged a 4% tax, while those priced higher are slapped a 10% tax. Some hotels may also charge an extra 10% expenditure tax. At popular tourist getaways, tariffs can shoot up manifold over weekends, and holidays such as Diwali, Holi, Christmas and New Year.

The **Maharashtra State Road Transport Corporation** (MSRTC; www.msrtc.gov.in) has a superb semideluxe bus network spanning all major towns, with the more remote places connected by ordinary buses. Some private operators have luxury Volvo services between major cities.

Neeta Tours & Travels (☏02228902666; www.neetabus.in) is highly recommended.

NORTHERN MAHARASHTRA

Nasik

☏0253 / POP 1.2 MILLION / ELEV 565M

Located on the banks of the holy Godavari River, Nasik (or Nashik) derives its name from the episode in the Ramayana where Lakshmana, Rama's brother, hacked off the *nasika* (nose) of Ravana's sister, the demon enchantress Surpanakha. True to its name, the town is an absorbing place, and you can't walk far without discovering yet another exotic temple or colourful bathing ghat that references the Hindu epic.

Adding to Nasik's spiritual flavour is the fact that the town serves as a base for pilgrims visiting Trimbak (33km west; p84) and Shirdi (79km southeast), once home to the original Sai Baba (see the boxed text, p84). Every 12 years, Nasik also plays host to the grand Kumbh Mela, the largest religious gathering on earth that shuttles between four Indian religious centres on a triennial basis. The next congregation in Nasik is due in 2015.

Mahatma Gandhi Rd, better known as MG Rd, a few blocks north of the Old Central bus stand, is Nasik's commercial hub. The temple-lined Godavari flows through town just east of here.

◉ Sights

Ramkund   GHAT

This bathing ghat in the heart of Nasik's old quarter sees hundreds of Hindu pilgrims arriving daily to bathe, pray and – because the waters provide moksha (liberation of the soul) – to immerse the ashes of departed friends and family. For a tourist, it's an intense cultural experience, heightened by the presence of a colourful **market** downstream. It's OK to take photographs, but try not to be intrusive.

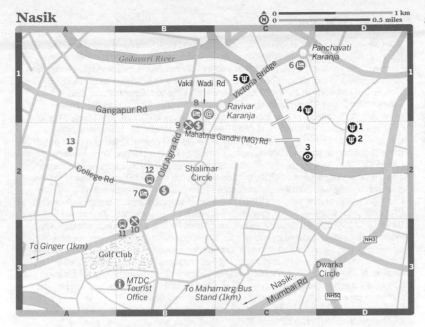

Temples
HINDU TEMPLES

A short walk uphill east of Ramkund is the **Kala Rama Temple**, the city's holiest shrine. Dating to 1794 and containing unusual black-stone representations of Rama, Sita and Lakshmana, the temple stands on the site where Lakshmana sliced off Surpanakha's nose. Nearby is the **Gumpha Panchavati**, where Sita supposedly hid while being assailed by the evil Ravana.

The ramshackle **Sundar Narayan Temple**, at the western end of Victoria Bridge, contains three black Vishnu deities, while the modern **Muktidham Temple**, about 7km southeast of the city near the train station, has 18 muralled chapters of the Bhagavad Gita lining its interior walls.

All the temples are open from 6am to 9pm.

🛏 Sleeping & Eating

Panchavati
HOTEL $$

(www.panchavatihotels.com; 430 Chandak Wadi, Vakil Wadi Rd) To save yourself the hassle of scouting for a comfy bed in town, head straight for this excellent complex, comprising four hotels (and a few popular restaurants) that cover every pocket from budget to top-end, and deliver each rupee's worth. Kicking off at the cheaper end is **Panchavati Guest House** (☏2578771; s/d from ₹500/600; ✲), which has

slightly cramped but clean rooms and prompt service. A more inviting option is **Panchavati Yatri** (☏2578782; s/d from ₹1100/1350; ✲), which features excellent rooms with hot showers, spot-on service, cooperative staff and an in-house health club. **Hotel Panchavati**

From wimpy raisins to full-bodied wines, the grapes of Nasik have come a long way. The town had been growing grapes meant for regular consumption since time immemorial. However, it was only in the early '90s that a couple of entrepreneurs realised that Nasik, with its fertile soils and cool climate, boasted conditions similar to Bordeaux. In 1997 industry pioneer **Sula Vineyards** (☎09970090010; www.sulawines.com; Govardhan, Gangapur–Savargaon Rd; ⏰11am-10pm) fearlessly invested in a crop of sauvignon blanc and chenin blanc, and the first batch of domestic wines hit the shelves in 2000. It hasn't looked back.

These days, the wine list in most of Nasik's wineries stretch to include zinfandel, shiraz, merlot and cabernet as well as a few reserves and champagnes, and most of these drops can be sampled first-hand by visiting one of the estates. **York Winery** (☎02532230700; www.yorkwinery.com, Gangavarhe, Gangapur–Savargaon Rd; ⏰3pm-10pm) offers wine-tasting sessions (₹100) in a top-floor room that has scenic views of the lake and surrounding hills. Sula Vineyards, located 15km west of Nasik, rounds off a vineyard tour with a wine-tasting session (₹150) that features six of its best. It's also possible to stay at some wineries. For an extremely indulging experience, head 3km inland to **Beyond** (☎09970090010; www.sulawines.com; d from ₹6000; ✦✦), an enchanting luxury resort set by a lake bordered by rolling hills, where you can roam the landscape on bicycles, go kayaking on the still waters or laze the hours away at the spa. Or you could try Chateau Indage, another of Nasik's wine biggies, that operates **Tiger Hill Vineyards Resort & Spa** (☎02532336274; www.indagegroup.com; Vilholi, Mumbai–Agra NH3; d from ₹3500; ✦), a stylish getaway-cum-wine bar 10km south of town, where you can pair its signature chardonnay with a relaxing grapeseed-oil massage.

During harvest season (January to March), some wineries also organise grape-crushing festivals, marked by unbridled revelry. Events are usually advertised on the wineries' websites.

(☎2575771; s/d from ₹1299/1499; ✦), fronting the complex, is pricier with classy rooms; it caters largely to business travellers. Last of all is the sumptuous **Panchavati Millionaire** (☎2312318; s/d ₹1600/1950; ✦), a moody affair where lavish rooms are complemented by cosy sit-in areas that are perfect for a steaming morning cuppa.

Hotel Samrat HOTEL $$
(☎2577211; www.hotelsamratnasik.com; Old Agra Rd; s/d from ₹900/1175; ✦) You'll find little to complain about at the Samrat. Inviting rooms have large windows, are tastefully decorated in brown and beige, with pine-themed furniture thrown in for good measure. Located right next to the bus stand, its spick-and-span vegetarian restaurant is open 24 hours, making it popular as a refuelling stop.

Hotel Abhishek HOTEL $
(☎2514201; www.hotelabhishek.com; Panchavati Karanja; s/d ₹345/450, with AC ₹600/675; ✦) Located off the Panchavati Karanja roundabout, this pleasant budget option packs hot showers, TV and appetising vegetarian food into its well-kept, value-for-money rooms. A few minutes' walk uphill from the Godavari River, it sits amid all the ritualistic action,

and is a vantage point from which to be totally overwhelmed by sacred India at its noisiest but best.

Ginger HOTEL $$
(☎6616333; www.gingerhotels.com; Plot P20, Satpur MIDC, Trimbak Rd; s/d ₹1799/2299; ✦✦) In another town, Ginger could easily have been our top choice. In Nasik, however, it loses out to its rivals mainly due to its location, which is a couple of kilometres west of the central district. Primarily a business hotel, it features do-it-yourself service, but there are luxe features and conveniences aplenty, and the rooms are as fresh as the autumn breeze.

TOP CHOICE **Khyber** AFGHANI $$
(Panchavati Hotel Complex; mains ₹180-230) Taste one succulent morsel of any of Khyber's signature dishes and you might start wondering if you are actually in Kandahar. The Khyber is, without doubt, one of Nasik's top-notch fine-dining establishments, and it works up a great ambience (soft lighting, sparkling glassware, teak furniture) to go with its wide range of delectable offerings. The *murgh shaan-e-khyber*, juicy pieces of

chicken marinated with herbs and cooked in a creamy gravy, is not to be missed.

Annapoorna Lunch Home FAST FOOD $
(MG Rd; mains ₹50) This fast-moving joint has all the usual quick eats rolling endlessly off its culinary assembly line. No surprises on offer, but it would be hard to find fault with the pan-fresh food that's cheaper than peanuts. Peak lunch hours are a bad time to walk in, as you might have trouble finding a seat.

Talk of the Town MULTICUISINE $$
(Old Agra Rd; mains ₹150-180) Next to the New Central bus stand, this place attracts more tipplers than eaters, although that's no indication of the quality of its food. An upscale place comprising dining rooms at split levels, it offers a good selection of coastal, North Indian and Chinese dishes, best washed down with a refreshing pint of lager.

❶ Information

Cyber Café (Vakil Wadi Rd; per hr ₹20; ☺10am-10pm) Near Panchavati Hotel Complex.
MTDC tourist office (☑2570059; T/I, Golf Club, Old Agra Rd; ☺10.30am-5.30pm Mon-Sat) About 1km south of the Old Central bus stand.
State Bank of India (Old Agra Rd; ☺11am-5pm Mon-Fri, 11am-1pm Sat) Opposite the Old Central bus stand. Changes cash and travellers cheques and has an ATM.
HDFC Bank (MG Rd) Has a 24-hour ATM.

❶ Getting There & Around

Bus

Nasik's **Old Central bus stand** (CBS) is useful for those going to Trimbak (₹27, 45 minutes). A block south, the **New Central bus stand** has services to Aurangabad (semideluxe ₹199, 4½ hours) and Pune (semideluxe/deluxe ₹213/360, 4½ hours). South of town, the **Mahamarg bus stand** has services to Mumbai (semideluxe ₹211, four hours) and Shirdi (₹90, 2½ hours).

Private bus agents based near the CBS run buses to Pune, Mumbai, Aurangabad and Ahmedabad. Fares are marginally lower than those charged on state buses. Note that buses depart from Old Agra Rd, and that most Mumbai-bound buses terminate at Dadar in Mumbai.

Train

The Nasik Rd train station is 8km southeast of the town centre, but a useful **railway reservation office** (1st fl, Commissioner's Office, Canada Corner; ☺8am-8pm Mon-Sat) is 500m west of the CBS. The *Panchavati Express* is the fastest

train to Mumbai (2nd class/chair ₹75/263, 3½ hours, 7am), and the *Tapovan Express* is the only convenient direct train to Aurangabad (2nd class/chair ₹66/233, 3½ hours, 9.50am). An autorickshaw to the station costs about ₹70.

Around Nasik

BHANDARDARA

The picturesque village of Bhandardara is nestled deep in the folds of the Sahyadris, about 70km from Nasik. A little-visited place surrounded by craggy mountains, it remains one of Maharashtra's best-kept travel secrets and, with an absence of checkbox travellers, makes a fantastic getaway from the bustle of urban India. However, you don't need to be a rocket scientist to figure out that the scene might be very different in the near future – visit while you can.

Most of Bhandardara's habitation is thrown around the spectacular **Arthur Lake**, a horseshoe-shaped reservoir fed by the waters of the Pravara River. The lake is barraged on one side by the imposing **Wilson Dam**, a colonial-era structure dating back to 1910. If you like walking, consider a hike to the summit of **Mt Kalsubai**, which at 1646m was once used as an observation point by the Marathas. Alternately, you could hike to the ruins of the **Ratangad Fort**, another of Shivaji's erstwhile strongholds, which has wonderful views of the surrounding ranges.

The charming **Anandvan Resort** (☑9920311221; www.anandvanresorts.com; d from ₹5500; ✽), an ecoresort with a choice of comfy cottages and villas overlooking Arthur Lake, allows you to camp in style. The **MTDC Holiday Resort** (☑0242457032; d from ₹1200; ✽), located further down the hill, is also a good place to spend the night.

Bhandardara can be accessed by taking a local bus from Nasik's Mahamarg bus stand to Ghoti (₹30, one hour), from where an autorickshaw ride costs ₹60. A taxi from Nasik can also drop you at your resort for about ₹1200.

IGATPURI

Heard of *vipassana,* haven't you? Well head to Igatpuri to see where (and how) it all happens. Located about 44km south of Nasik, this village is home to the headquarters of the world's largest *vipassana* meditation institution, the **Vipassana International Academy** (☑02553244076; www.dhamma.org), which institutionalises this strict form of meditation first taught by Gautama Buddha in the 6th century BC and reintroduced to India by teacher SN Goenka in the '60s. Ten-day residential courses (advance bookings compulsory) are held throughout the year, though authorities warn that it requires rigorous discipline, and dropping out midway isn't encouraged. Basic accommodation, food and meditation instruction are provided free of charge, but donations upon completion of the course are accepted.

TRIMBAK

The moody **Trimbakeshwar Temple** stands in the centre of Trimbak, 33km west of Nasik. It's one of India's most sacred temples, containing a *jyoti linga,* one of the 12 most important shrines to Shiva. Only Hindus are allowed in, but non-Hindus can peek into the courtyard. Nearby, the waters of the Godavari River flow into the **Gangadwar bathing tank**, where all are welcome to wash away their earthly sins. You also have the option of a four-hour return hike up the **Brahmagiri Hill**, where you can see the Godavari dribble forth from a spring.

Regular buses run from the CBS in Nasik to Trimbak (₹26, 45 minutes).

Aurangabad

📞0240 / POP 892,400 / ELEV 515M

Aurangabad lay low through most of the tumultuous history of medieval India and only hit the spotlight when the last Mughal emperor, Aurangzeb, made the city his capital from 1653 to 1707. With the emperor's death came the city's rapid decline, but the brief period of glory saw the building of some fascinating monuments, including a Taj Mahal replica (Bibi-qa-Maqbara), that continue to draw a steady trickle of visitors today. These monuments, alongside other historic relics such as a group of ancient Buddhist caves, make Aurangabad a good choice for a fairly decent weekend excursion. But the real reason for traipsing all the way here is because the town is an excellent base for exploring the World Heritage Sites of Ellora and Ajanta.

Silk fabrics were once Aurangabad's chief revenue generator, and the town is still known across the world for its hand-woven Himroo and Paithani saris (see Shopping, p87).

The train station, cheap hotels and restaurants are clumped together in the south of the town along Station Rd East and Station Rd West. The MSRTC bus stand is 1.5km to the north of the train station. Northeast of the bus stand is the buzzing old town with its narrow streets and Muslim quarters. Interestingly, Aurangabad also has a sizeable Buddhist community who follow in the footsteps of eminent humanist and social leader BR Ambedkar, and celebrate his conversion to Buddhism during Dussehra.

⊙ Sights

Bibi-qa-Maqbara   MONUMENT
(Indian/foreigner ₹5/100; ⊙dawn-10pm) Built by Aurangzeb's son Azam Khan in 1679 as a mausoleum for his mother Rabia-ud-Daurani, Bibi-qa-Maqbara is widely known as the 'poor man's Taj'. With its four minarets flanking a central onion-domed mausoleum, the white structure bears striking resemblance to the original Taj Mahal in Agra. It is much less grand, however, and apart from having a few marble adornments, most of the structure is finished in lime mortar. Apparently the prince had conceived the entire mausoleum in white marble like the Taj, but was

---

SAI BABA OF SHIRDI

His iconic status as a national guru is legendary. And his divinity, to some, is unquestionable. But Sai Baba, for all his popularity, remains one of India's most enigmatic figures. No one knows where he came from, what his real name was, or when he was born. Having stepped out of an obscure childhood, he first appeared in the town of Shirdi near Nasik around the age of 16 (in the mid-1800s). There, he advocated religious tolerance, which he practised by sleeping alternately in a mosque and a Hindu temple as well as praying in them both. The masses took to him right away, and by the time Sai Baba died in 1918, the many miracles attributed to him had seen him gather a large following. Today, his temple complex in Shirdi draws an average of 40,000 pilgrims a day. Interestingly, in Andhra Pradesh, another widely respected holy man Sathya Sai Baba (1926–2011) claimed to be the reincarnation of the original Sai Baba (see p238).

thwarted by his frugal father who opposed his extravagant idea of draining state coffers for the purpose. However, despite the use of cheaper material and the obvious weathering, it's a sight far more impressive than the average gravestone. The central onion dome was being restored during research, and should be back in its untarnished glory by the time you visit.

Aurangabad Caves
CAVE
(Indian/foreigner ₹5/100; ⊘dawn-dusk) Architecturally speaking, the Aurangabad Caves aren't a patch on Ellora or Ajanta, but they do throw some light on early Buddhist architecture and, above all, make for a quiet and peaceful outing. Carved out of the hillside in the 6th or 7th century AD, the 10 caves, comprising two groups 1km apart (retain your ticket for entry into both sets), are all Buddhist. Cave 7, with its sculptures of scantily clad lovers in suggestive positions, is particularly arty. The caves are about 2km north of Bibi-qa-Maqbara. A return autorickshaw from the mausoleum shouldn't cost more than ₹150.

Panchakki
GARDEN
(Indian/foreigner ₹5/20; ⊘6.15am-9.15pm) The garden complex of Panchakki, literally meaning 'water wheel', takes its name from the hydro-mill which, in its day, was considered a marvel of engineering. Driven by water carried through earthen pipes from the river 6km away, it was once used to grind grain for pilgrims. You can still see the humble machine at work today.

Baba Shah Muzaffar, a Sufi saint and spiritual guide to Aurangzeb, is buried here. His **memorial garden** is flanked by a series of fish-filled tanks, near a large shade-giving banyan tree.

Shivaji Museum
MUSEUM
(Dr Ambedkar Rd; admission ₹5; ⊘10.30am-6pm Fri-Wed) This simple museum is dedicated to the life of the Maratha hero Shivaji. Its collection includes a 500-year-old chain-mail suit and a copy of the Quran handwritten by Aurangzeb.

☞ Tours

Classic Tours (p88) and the **Indian Tourism Development Corporation** (ITDC; ☑2331143) both run daily bus tours to the Ajanta and Ellora Caves. The trip to Ajanta Caves costs ₹400 and the tour to Ellora Caves, ₹270; prices include a guide but don't

cover admission fees. The Ellora tour also includes all the other major Aurangabad sites along with Daulatabad Fort and Aurangzeb's tomb in Khuldabad, which is a lot to swallow in a day. All tours start and end at the MTDC Holiday Resort. During quiet periods, operators often pool resources and pack their clients into a single bus.

For private tours, try **Ashoka Tours & Travels** (p88), which owns a decent fleet of taxis and can personalise your trip around Aurangabad and to Ajanta and Ellora.

🛌 Sleeping

TOP CHOICE **Lemon Tree**
HOTEL $$$
(☑6603030; www.lemontreehotels.com; R7/2 Chikalthana, Airport Rd; s/d incl breakfast from ₹3499/4499; ❄ 🅟 ☷) Fresh as lemonade, this swish, all-new boutique hotel (spread lazily around what we thought was the best swimming pool in the Deccan) makes you want to stay back in Aurangabad even after you're done sightseeing. The rooms are done up in vivid tropical shades offset against snow-white walls, and are super snug to boot. Adding a dash of class is the prim Citrus Café, and the Slounge bar, where you can down a drink while hustling a fellow traveller in to a game of pool. It's one place you're sure to have a nice stay.

MTDC Holiday Resort
HOTEL $$
(☑2331513; Station Rd East; d from ₹1100, with AC from ₹1300; ❄) Set around a lovely lawn and shaded by robust canopies, this curiously disorganised hotel is one of the better state-owned operations in Maharashtra. The large residential blocks have recently received a facelift, and the rooms, though lacking in character, are spacious and tidy. Service is prompt, there's also a well-stocked bar, a decent restaurant and a couple of travel agencies and souvenir shops on-site. Come between March and July and you will pay 20% less.

Hotel Panchavati
HOTEL $
(☑2328755; www.hotelpanchavati.com; Station Rd West; s/d ₹525/625, with AC ₹775/900; ❄) This place is fast establishing itself as one of the more reputed hotels in Aurangabad (quite a turnaround from the days when it took some serious stick from travellers). Generally packed to the gills with guests, it offers a range of compact but thoughtfully appointed rooms, with comfortable beds and patterned rugs on the floor that match the

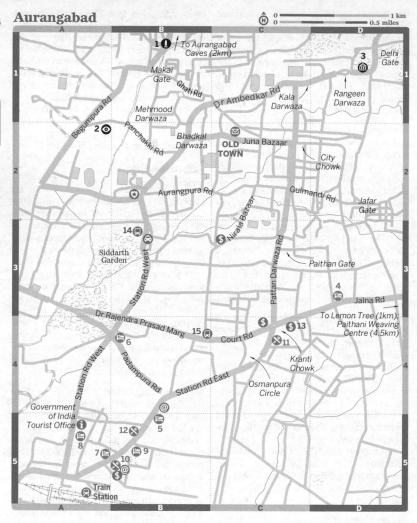

upholstery and pastel walls. The managers are efficient and friendly and the hotel sits easily at the top of the value-for-money class.

VITS   HOTEL $$$
(☎2350701; www.vitshotelaurangabad.com; Station Rd East; s/d incl breakfast ₹5500/6500; ❋❄❆) Located close to the train station, snazzy-lobbied VITS goes by the motto 'Guest. Rest. Best'. What that basically means is you have a delightfully luxurious room to flop about in, packed with all the usual luxe features you'd find in top-range

hotels. A branch of the Four Fountains chain of spas located within the hotel considerably ups the indulgence quotient.

Hotel Nandanvan   HOTEL $
(☎2338916; Station Rd East; s/d ₹450/550, with AC ₹650/750; ❋) Unusually large but clean rooms are on offer at this well-run hotel, set in a prime location close to Kailash Restaurant. The real dealmakers, of course, are the loos, which are cleaner than those of most other budget options in town. The noise coming off the main road might get to you at times, though.

Aurangabad

Hotel Amarpreet   HOTEL $$
(☏6621133; www.amarpreethotel.com; Jalna Rd; s/d from ₹2800/3600; ❄@) We have to hand it to Amarpreet for trying hard. The rooms might trigger the occasional hunch that you'd have got more bang for your buck elsewhere, but the all-smiles management makes up for it with polite service, excellent housekeeping and a great selection of food and booze. Ask for a room in the western wing, with superb views of Bibi-qa-Maqbara.

Tourist's Home   HOTEL $
(☏2337212; Station Rd West; d ₹400, with AC ₹1000; ❄) This one's as basic as it gets. Although recently given a makeover, most rooms here are barebones, but well-ventilated. There are quite a few rules and regulations to be adhered to, going by the noticeboard at the entrance, but the management is friendly. And it's close to the train station, which is a positive.

✖ Eating

China Town   CHINESE $$
(Hotel Amarpreet, Jalna Rd; mains ₹180-200) For a place like Aurangabad, this in-house restau-

rant at Hotel Amarpreet tosses up Chinese dishes of a surprisingly fine quality. A good range of noodles is on offer, which goes extremely well with the numerous chicken and lamb preparations all presented appetisingly in the restaurant's well-dressed interiors.

Swad Veg Restaurant   INDIAN $
(Kanchan Chamber, Station Rd East; mains ₹70-80) This place has come a long way since its formative years, and now offers a fantastic range of Indian snacks and staples – plus a few pizzas, ice creams and shakes – in its prim and clean basement premises. Try the Gujarati thali (₹110), an endless train of dishes that diners gobble up under the benevolent gaze of patron saint swami Yogiraj Hanstirth, whose portrait illuminates a far wall of the restaurant.

Tandoor   NORTH INDIAN $$
(Shyam Chambers, Station Rd East; mains ₹160-180) Offering fine tandoori dishes and flavoursome North Indian veg and non-veg options in a weirdly Pharaonic atmosphere, Tandoor is one of Aurangabad's top standalone restaurants. A few Chinese dishes are also on offer, but patrons clearly prefer the dishes coming out of, well, the tandoor.

Kailash   INDIAN $
(Station Rd East; mains ₹70-80) Adjacent to Hotel Nandanvan, this busy pure-veg restaurant is a smart glass-and-chrome place where you can sit back after a long day out and wolf down a variety of local delicacies brought to your table by smartly dressed waiters.

Prashanth   INDIAN $
(Siddharth Arcade, Station Rd East; mains ₹70-90) Located near the railway station bang opposite the MTDC Holiday Resort, Prashanth has consistently won accolades from travellers for its delightful vegetarian-only dishes, epic fruit juices and enjoyable patio setting. Eat your heart out.

🛍 Shopping

Hand-woven Himroo material is a traditional Aurangabad speciality (though people have differing opinions regarding its aesthetic appeal). Made from cotton, silk and silver threads, it was developed as a cheaper alternative to Kam Khab, the more ornate brocade of silk and gold thread woven for royalty in the 14th century. Most of today's Himroo shawls and saris are mass-produced using power looms, but some showrooms in the city still run traditional workshops, thus preserving this dying art.

Himroo saris start at ₹1000 (cotton and silk blend). Paithani saris, which are of a superior quality, range from ₹5000 to ₹300,000 – before you baulk at the price, bear in mind that some of them take more than a year to make. If you're buying, ensure you're spending your money on authentic Himroo, and not 'Aurangabad silk'.

One of the best places to come and watch weavers at work is the **Paithani Weaving Centre** (Jalna Rd; ⊙11.30am-8pm), behind the Indian Airlines office.

ℹ Information

Internet Access

Internet Browsing Hub (Station Rd East; per hr ₹15; ⊙8am-10pm)

Sai Internet Café (Station Rd East; per hr ₹15; ⊙8am-10pm)

Money

ICICI, State Bank of India (SBI), State Bank of Hyderabad (SBH) and HDFC Bank have several ATMs along Station Rd East, Court Rd, Nirala Bazaar and Jalna Rd.

State Bank of India (Kranti Chowk; ⊙11am-5pm Mon-Fri, 11am-1pm Sat) Handles foreign exchange.

Post

Post office (Juna Bazaar; ⊙10am-6pm Mon-Sat)

Tourist Information

Government of India tourist office (☑2331217; Krishna Vilas, Station Rd West; ⊙8.30am-6pm Mon-Sat) A friendly and helpful tourist office with a decent range of brochures.

MTDC office (☑2331513; MTDC Holiday Resort, Station Rd East; ⊙10am-5.30pm Mon-Sat)

Travel Agencies

Ashoka Tours & Travels (☑9890340816; Hotel Panchavati, Station Rd West) Personalised city and regional tours, car hire and hotel pick-ups. Run by former Lonely Planet recommended autorickshaw driver Ashok T Kadam.

Classic Tours (☑2337788; www.classictours .info; MTDC Holiday Resort, Station Rd East) Trusty place to book transport and tours.

ℹ Getting There & Away

Air

The **airport** is 10km east of town. En route are the offices of **Indian Airlines** (☑2485241; Jalna Rd) and **Jet Airways** (☑2441392; Jalna Rd).

There are daily flights to Delhi, with a stopover in Mumbai. Fares start from around ₹1500.

Bus

Buses leave regularly from the **MSRTC bus stand** (Station Rd West) to Pune (semideluxe/deluxe ₹228/390, five hours) and Nasik (semideluxe ₹199, five hours). **Private bus agents** are located around the corner where Dr Rajendra Prasad Marg becomes Court Rd; a few sit closer to the bus stand. Deluxe overnight bus destinations include Mumbai (with/without AC ₹280/220, sleeper ₹610, eight hours), Ahmedabad (₹410, 15 hours) and Nagpur (₹390, 12 hours).

Ordinary buses head to Ellora from the MSRTC bus stand every half hour (₹28, 45 minutes) and hourly to Jalgaon (₹122, four hours) via Fardapur (₹80, two hours). The T-junction near Fardapur is the drop-off point for Ajanta (see p95 for more details).

Train

Aurangabad's **train station** (Station Rd East) is not on a main line, but two heavily-booked trains, the Tapovan Express (2nd class/chair ₹102/338, 7½ hours, 2.35pm) and the Janshatabdi Express (2nd class/chair ₹127/420, 6½ hours, 6am) run direct to/from Mumbai. For Hyderabad (Secunderabad), take the Devagiri Express (sleeper/2AC ₹224/822, 10 hours, 4.05am). To reach northern or eastern India, take a bus to Jalgaon and board a train there.

ℹ Getting Around

Autorickshaws are as common here as mosquitoes in a summer swamp. The **taxi stand** is next to the MSRTC bus stand; share jeeps also depart from here for destinations around Aurangabad, including Ellora and Daulatabad. Expect to pay ₹600 for a full-day tour in a rickshaw, or ₹900 in a taxi.

Around Aurangabad

DAULATABAD

This one's straight out of a Tolkien fantasy. A most beguiling structure, the 12th-century hilltop fortress of Daulatabad is located about 15km from Aurangabad, en route to Ellora. Now in ruins, the citadel was originally conceived as an impregnable fort by the Yadava kings. Its most infamous highpoint came in 1328, when it was christened Daulatabad (City of Fortune) by eccentric Delhi sultan Mohammed Tughlaq and made the capital – he even marched the entire population of Delhi 1100km south to populate it. Ironically, Daulatabad – despite being better positioned strategically than Delhi –

soon proved untenable as a capital due to an acute water crisis, and Tughlaq forced the weary inhabitants all the way back to Delhi, which had by then been reduced to a ghost town.

Daulatabad's central bastion sits atop a 200m-high craggy outcrop known as Devagiri (Hill of the Gods), surrounded by a 5km **fort** (Indian/foreigner ₹5/100; ☺6am-6pm). The climb to the summit takes about an hour, and leads past an ingenious series of defences, including multiple doorways designed with odd angles and spike-studded doors to prevent elephant charges. A tower of victory, known as the **Chand Minar** (Tower of the Moon), built in 1435, soars 60m above the ground to the right – it's closed to visitors. Higher up, you can walk into the **Chini Mahal**, where Abul Hasan Tana Shah, king of Golconda, was held captive for 12 years before his death in 1699. Nearby, there's a 6m **cannon**, cast from five different metals and engraved with Aurangzeb's name.

Part of the ascent goes through a pitch-black, bat-infested, water-seeping, spiralling tunnel. Guides (₹450) are available near the ticket counter to show you around, and their flame-bearing assistants will lead you through the dark passageway for a small tip. But on the way down you'll be left to your own devices, so carry a torch. The crumbling staircases and sheer drops can make things difficult for the elderly, children and those suffering from vertigo or claustrophobia.

KHULDABAD

Time permitting, take a pit-stop in the scruffy-walled settlement of Khuldabad (Heavenly Abode), a quaint and cheerful little Muslim pilgrimage village just 3km from Ellora. Buried deep in the pages of history, Khuldabad is where a number of historic figures lie interred, including emperor Aurangzeb, the last of the Mughal greats. Despite matching the legendary King Solomon in terms of state riches, Aurangzeb was an ascetic in his personal life, and insisted that he be buried in a simple tomb constructed only with the money he had made from sewing Muslim skullcaps. An unfussy affair of modest marble in a courtyard of the **Alamgir Dargah** (☺7am-8pm) is exactly what he got.

Generally a calm place, Khuldabad is swamped with pilgrims every April when a robe said to have been worn by the Prophet Mohammed, and kept within the dargah (shrine), is shown to the public. Across the road from the Alamgir Dargah, another shrine contains strands of the Prophet's beard and lumps of silver from a tree of solid silver, which is said to have miraculously grown at this site after a saint's death.

Ellora

♫ 02437

Give a man a hammer and chisel, and he'll create art for posterity. Come to the World Heritage Site-listed **Ellora cave temples** (Indian/foreigner ₹10/250; ☺dawn-dusk Wed-Mon), located 30km from Aurangabad, and you'll know exactly what we mean. The epitome of ancient Indian rock-cut architecture, these caves were chipped out laboriously over five centuries by generations of Buddhist, Hindu and Jain monks. Monasteries, chapels, temples – the caves served every purpose, and they were stylishly embellished with a profusion of remarkably detailed sculptures. Unlike the caves at Ajanta (p92), which are carved into a sheer rock face, the Ellora caves line a 2km-long escarpment, the gentle slope of which allowed architects to build elaborate courtyards in front of the shrines, and render them with sculptures of a surreal quality.

Ellora has 34 caves in all: 12 Buddhist (AD 600–800), 17 Hindu (AD 600–900) and five Jain (AD 800–1000). The grandest, however, is the awesome Kailasa Temple (Cave 16), the world's largest monolithic sculpture, hewn top to bottom against a rocky slope by 7000 labourers over a 150-year period. Dedicated to Lord Shiva, it is clearly among the best that ancient Indian architecture has to offer.

Historically, the site represents the renaissance of Hinduism under the Chalukya and Rashtrakuta dynasties, the subsequent decline of Indian Buddhism and a brief resurgence of Jainism under official patronage. The increasing influence of Tantric elements in India's three great religions can also be seen in the way the sculptures are executed, and their coexistence at one site indicates a lengthy period of religious tolerance.

Official guides can be hired at the ticket office in front of the Kailasa Temple for ₹700. Most guides have an extensive knowledge of cave architecture, so try not to skimp. If your tight itinerary forces you to choose between Ellora or Ajanta, Ellora wins hands down.

Ellora Caves

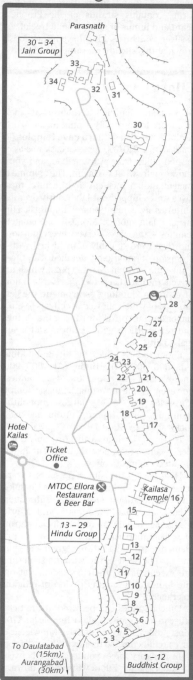

Parasnath

30 – 34
Jain Group

33

34

32   31

30

29

28

27
26

25

24 23

22   21

20

19

18

17

Hotel
Kailas

Ticket
Office

MTDC Ellora
Restaurant
& Beer Bar

Kailasa
Temple 16

15

13 – 29
Hindu Group

14

13

12

11

10

9

8

7

6

5
4
3
1 2

To Daulatabad
(15km);
Aurangabad
(30km)

1 – 12
Buddhist Group

Sights

Kailasa Temple
HINDU TEMPLE

Halfway between a cave and a religious shrine, this **rock-cut temple**, built by King Krishna I of the Rashtrakuta dynasty in AD 760, was built to represent Mt Kailasa (Kailash), Shiva's Himalayan abode. To say that the assignment was daring would be an understatement. Three huge trenches were bored into the sheer cliff face with hammers and chisels, following which the shape was 'released', a process that entailed removing 200,000 tonnes of rock, while taking care to leave behind those sections that would later be used for sculpting. Covering twice the area of the Parthenon in Athens and being half as high again, Kailasa is an engineering marvel that was executed straight from the head with zero margin for error. Modern draughtsmen might have a lesson or two to learn here.

Size aside, the temple is remarkable for its prodigious sculptural decoration. The temple houses several intricately carved panels, depicting scenes from the Ramayana, the Mahabharata and the adventures of Krishna. Also worth admiring are the immense **monolithic pillars** that stand in the courtyard, flanking the entrance on both sides, and the southeastern gallery that has 10 giant and fabulous panels depicting the different avatars of Lord Vishnu. Kailasa is a temple, still very much in use; you'll have to remove your shoes to enter the main shrine.

After you're done with the main enclosure, bypass the hordes of snack-munching day trippers to explore the temple's many dank, bat urine-soaked corners with their numerous forgotten carvings. Afterwards, hike up a foot trail to the south of the complex that takes you to the top perimeter of the 'cave', from where you can get a bird's-eye view of the entire temple complex.

Buddhist Caves
CAVES

The southernmost 12 caves are Buddhist *viharas* (monasteries), except Cave 10, which is a *chaitya* (assembly hall). While the earliest caves are simple, Caves 11 and 12 are more ambitious, and on par with the more impressive Hindu temples.

Cave 1, the simplest *vihara,* may have been a granary. **Cave 2** is notable for its ornate pillars and the imposing seated Buddha, which faces the setting sun. **Cave 3** and **Cave 4** are unfinished and not well-preserved.

Cave 5 is the largest *vihara* in this group, at 18m wide and 36m long; the rows of stone benches hint that it may once have been an assembly hall.

Cave 6 is an ornate *vihara* with wonderful images of Tara, consort of the Bodhisattva Avalokitesvara, and of the Buddhist goddess of learning, Mahamayuri, looking remarkably similar to Saraswati, her Hindu equivalent. Cave 7 is an unadorned hall, but from here you can pass through a doorway to Cave 8, the first cave in which the sanctum is detached from the rear wall. Cave 9 is notable for its wonderfully carved fascia.

Cave 10 is the only *chaitya* in the Buddhist group and one of the finest in India. Its ceiling features ribs carved into the stonework; the grooves were once fitted with wooden panels. The balcony and upper gallery offer a closer view of the ceiling and a frieze depicting amorous couples. A decorative window gently illuminates an enormous figure of the teaching Buddha.

Cave 11, the Do Thal (Two Storey) Cave, is entered through its third basement level, not discovered until 1876. Like Cave 12, it probably owes its size to competition with the more impressive Hindu caves of the same period.

Cave 12, the huge Tin Thal (Three Storey) Cave, is entered through a courtyard. The locked shrine on the top floor contains a large Buddha figure flanked by his seven previous incarnations. The walls are carved with relief pictures, like those in the Hindu caves.

Hindu Caves   CAVES

Where calm and contemplation infuse the Buddhist caves, drama and excitement characterise the Hindu group (Caves 13 to 29). In terms of scale, creative vision and skill of execution, these caves are in a league of their own.

All these temples were cut from the top down, so it was never necessary to use scaffolding – the builders began with the roof and moved down to the floor.

Cave 13 is a simple cave, most likely a granary. Cave 14, the Ravana-ki-Khai, is a Buddhist *vihara* converted to a temple dedicated to Shiva sometime in the 7th century.

Cave 15, the Das Avatara (Ten Incarnations of Vishnu) Cave, is one of the finest at Ellora. The two-storey temple contains a mesmerising Shiva Nataraja, and Shiva emerging from a lingam (phallic image) while Vishnu and Brahma pay homage.

Caves 17 to 20 and 22 to 28 are simple monasteries.

Cave 21, known as the Ramesvara Cave, features interesting interpretations of familiar Shaivite scenes depicted in the earlier temples. The figure of goddess Ganga, standing on her makara (mythical sea creature), is particularly notable.

The large Cave 29, the Dumar Lena, is thought to be a transitional model between the simpler hollowed-out caves and the fully developed temples exemplified by the Kailasa. It has views over a nearby waterfall you can walk down to.

Jain Caves   CAVES

The five Jain caves may lack the artistic vigour and ambitious size of the best Hindu temples, but they are exceptionally detailed. The caves are 1km north of the last Hindu temple (Cave 29) at the end of the bitumen road.

Cave 30, the Chhota Kailasa (Little Kailasa), is a poor imitation of the great Kailasa Temple and stands by itself some distance from the other Jain temples.

In contrast, Cave 32, the Indra Sabha (Assembly Hall of Indra), is the finest of the Jain temples. Its ground-floor plan is similar to that of the Kailasa, but the upstairs area is as ornate and richly decorated as the downstairs is plain. There are images of the Jain *tirthankars* (great teachers) Parasnath and Gomateshvara, the latter surrounded by wildlife. Inside the shrine is a seated figure of Mahavira, the last *tirthankar* and founder of the Jain religion.

Cave 31 is really an extension of Cave 32. Cave 33, the Jagannath Sabha, is similar in plan to 32 and has some well-preserved sculptures. The final temple, the small Cave 34, also has interesting sculptures. On the hilltop over the Jain temples, a 5m-high image of Parasnath looks down on Ellora.

🛏 Sleeping & Eating

Hotel Kailas   HOTEL $$
(☑244446; www.hotelkailas.com; d ₹1500, cottages from ₹2000; ✹) The sole decent hotel near the site, this place should be considered only if you can't have enough of Ellora in a single day. The comfy cottages here come with warm showers; those with cave views are ₹500 pricier. There's a good restaurant (mains ₹100) and a lush lawn tailor-made for an evening drink.

The spotless MTDC Ellora Restaurant & Beer Bar (mains ₹60-90; ⊙9am-5pm), located within the complex, is a good place to settle in for lunch, or pack takeaways in case you want to picnic beside the caves.

ℹ Getting There & Away

Buses regularly ply the road between Aurangabad and Ellora (₹28); the last bus departs from Ellora at 8pm. Share jeeps leave when they're full with drop-off outside the bus stand in Aurangabad (₹40). A full-day autorickshaw tour to Ellora, with stops en route, costs ₹600; taxis charge around ₹900.

Ajanta

📞 02438

Fiercely guarding its horde of priceless artistic treasures from another era, the **Buddhist caves of Ajanta** (Indian/foreigner ₹10/250; video ₹25; ⊙9am-5.30pm Tue-Sun), 105km northeast of Aurangabad, could well be called the Louvre of ancient India. Much older than Ellora, its venerable twin in the World Heritage Sites listings, these secluded caves date from around the 2nd century BC to the 6th century AD and were among the earliest monastic institutions to be constructed in the country. Ironically, it was Ellora's rise that brought about Ajanta's downfall, and historians believe the site was abandoned once the focus had shifted to the newly-built caves of Ellora. Upon being deserted, the caves were soon reclaimed by wilderness and remained forgotten until 1819, when a British hunting party led by officer John Smith stumbled upon them purely by chance.

The primary reason to visit Ajanta is to admire its renowned 'frescoes', actually temperas, which adorn many of the caves' interiors. With few other examples from ancient times matching their artistic excellence and fine execution, these paintings are of unfathomable heritage value. It's believed that the natural pigments for these paintings were mixed with animal glue and vegetable gum to bind them to the dry surface. Many caves have small, crater-like holes in their floors, which acted as palettes during paint jobs.

Despite their age, the paintings in most caves remain finely preserved today, and many attribute it to their relative isolation from humanity for centuries. However, it would be a tad optimistic to say that decay hasn't set in. Signposts placed at the entrance of the complex list a series of 'Dos and Don'ts' intended to reduce human impact on this vulnerable site. Please comply.

Authorised guides are available to show you around for ₹600.

◉ Sights & Activities

The Caves   CAVES

The 30 caves of Ajanta line the steep face of a horseshoe-shaped rock gorge bordering the Waghore River flowing below. They are sequentially numbered from one end to the other, barring Caves 29 and 30. The numbering has nothing to do with their chronological order; the oldest caves are actually in the middle and are flanked by newer caves on both sides.

Caves 3, 5, 8, 22 and 28 to 30 remain either closed or inaccessible. Other caves might be closed from time to time due to restoration work – Cave 10, the grandest of them all, was being scaffolded on the outside during research. During rush periods, viewers are allotted 15 minutes within the caves, many of which have to be entered barefoot (socks allowed).

Five of the caves are *chaityas* while the other 25 are *viharas*. Caves 8, 9, 10, 12, 13 and part of 15 are early Buddhist caves, while the others date from around the 5th century AD (Mahayana period). In the simpler, more austere early Buddhist school, the Buddha was never represented directly – his presence was always alluded to by a symbol such as the footprint or wheel of law.

Cave 1, a Mahayana *vihara*, was one of the last to be excavated and is the most beautifully decorated. This is where you'll find a rendition of the **Bodhisattva Padmapani**, the most famous and iconic of the Ajanta artworks. A verandah in front leads to a large congregation hall, housing sculptures and narrative murals known for their splendid perspective and elaborate detailing of dress, daily life and facial expressions. The colours in the paintings were created from local minerals, with the exception of the vibrant blue made from Central Asian lapis lazuli. Look up to the ceiling to see the carving of four deer sharing a common head.

Cave 2 is also a late Mahayana *vihara* with deliriously ornamented columns and capitals, and some fine paintings. The ceiling is decorated with geometric and floral patterns. The murals depict scenes from the Jataka tales, including Buddha's mother's

Ajanta Caves

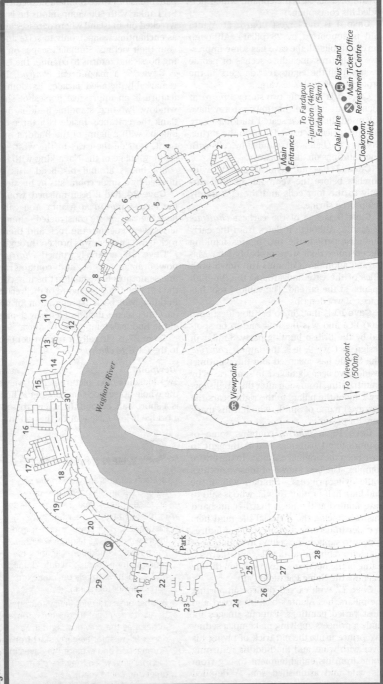

100 m

0

To Fardapur
T-junction (4km);
Fardapur (5km)

Bus Stand

Main Ticket Office

Refreshment Centre

Chair Hire

Cloakroom;
Toilets

Main Entrance

1

2

3

4

5

6

7

8

9

10

11

12

13

14

15

16

17

18

19

20

21

22

23

24

25

26

27

28

29

30

Waghore River

Viewpoint

To Viewpoint
(500m)

Park

dream of a six-tusked elephant, which heralded his conception.

Cave 4 is the largest *vihara* at Ajanta and is supported by 28 pillars. Although never completed, the cave has some impressive sculptures, including scenes of people fleeing from the 'eight great dangers' to the protection of Avalokitesvara.

Cave 6 is the only two-storey *vihara* at Ajanta, but parts of the lower storey have collapsed. Inside is a seated Buddha figure and an intricately carved door to the shrine. Upstairs the hall is surrounded by cells with fine paintings on the doorways.

Cave 7 has an atypical design, with porches before the verandah leading directly to the four cells and the elaborately sculptured shrine.

Cave 9 is one of the earliest *chaityas* at Ajanta. Although it dates from the early Buddhist period, the two figures flanking the entrance door were probably later Mahayana additions. Columns run down both sides of the cave and around the 3m-high dagoba at the far end. The vaulted roof has traces of wooden ribs.

Cave 10 is thought to be the oldest cave (200 BC) and was the first one to be spotted by the British hunting party. Similar in design to Cave 9, it is the largest *chaitya*. The facade has collapsed and the paintings inside have been damaged, in some cases by graffiti dating from soon after their rediscovery. One of the pillars to the right bears the engraved name of Smith, who left his mark here for posterity.

Cave 16, a *vihara*, contains some of Ajanta's finest paintings and is thought to have been the original entrance to the entire complex. The best known of these paintings is the 'dying princess' – Sundari, wife of the Buddha's half-brother Nanda, who is said to have fainted at the news that her husband was renouncing the material life (and her) in order to become a monk. Carved figures appear to support the ceiling in imitation of wooden architectural details, and there's a statue of the Buddha seated on a lion throne teaching the Noble Eightfold Path.

Cave 17, with carved dwarfs supporting the pillars, has Ajanta's best-preserved and most varied paintings. Famous images include a princess applying make-up, a seductive prince using the old trick of plying his lover with wine, and the Buddha returning home from his enlightenment to beg from his wife and astonished son. A detailed panel tells of Prince Simhala's expedition to Sri Lanka: with 500 companions he is shipwrecked on an island where ogresses appear as enchanting women, only to seize and devour their victims. Simhala escapes on a flying horse and returns to conquer the island.

Cave 19, a magnificent *chaitya*, has a remarkably detailed facade; its dominant feature is an impressive horseshoe-shaped window. Two fine, standing Buddha figures flank the entrance. Inside is a three-tiered dagoba with a figure of the Buddha on the front. Outside the cave, to the west, sits a striking image of the Naga king with seven cobra hoods around his head. His wife, hooded by a single cobra, sits by his side.

Cave 24, had it been finished, would be the largest *vihara* at Ajanta. You can see how the caves were constructed – long galleries were cut into the rock and then the rock between them was broken through.

Cave 26, a largely ruined *chaitya*, is now dramatically lit, and contains some fine sculptures that shouldn't be missed. On the left wall is a huge figure of the 'reclining Buddha', lying back in preparation for nirvana. Other scenes include a lengthy depiction of the Buddha's temptation by Maya.

Cave 27 is virtually a *vihara* connected to the Cave 26 *chaitya*.

Viewpoints VIEWPOINT

Two lookouts offer picture-perfect views of the whole horseshoe-shaped gorge. The first is a short walk beyond the river, crossed via a bridge below Cave 8. A further 40-minute

WHEN IN AJANTA...

» Flash photography is strictly prohibited within the caves, due to its adverse effect on natural dyes used in the paintings. Authorities have installed rows of tiny pigment-friendly lights which cast a faint glow within the caves, but additional lighting is required for glimpsing minute details, and you'll have to rely on long exposures for photographs.

» Most buses ferrying noisy tourists to Ajanta don't get there until noon, so either stay the previous night in Fardapur or push for an early start from Aurangabad and explore the caves in the morning, when they are pleasantly quiet and uncrowded.

uphill walk (not to be attempted during the monsoons) leads to the lookout from where the British party first spotted the caves.

🛏 Sleeping & Eating

Accommodation options close to the caves are limited and you're better off using Aurangabad or Jalgaon as a base.

MTDC Holiday Resort HOTEL $
(☎244230; Aurangabad-Jalgaon Rd, Fardapur; d with/without AC ₹900/700; ❄) This government hotel has been given a much-needed overhaul, and it now sits pretty amid lawns just by the main road in Fardapur. Rooms are decent, and the open-air beer bar clinches the deal. It's by far the best lodging option around here.

MTDC Ajanta Tourist Complex HOTEL $$
(☎09422204325; Fardapur T-junction; cottages ₹1200; ❄) Located just behind the shopping 'plaza' and the bus stand is this mint-fresh resort, featuring five charming and well-appointed cottages nestled amid grassy lawns overlooking the hills. However, you'll have to forage for your own food from the stalls nearby.

As far as stuffing your face goes, there is a string of cheap, unappetising restaurants in the plaza (at Fardapur T-Junction). You could pack a picnic and enjoy it in the shady park below Caves 22 to 27. There's also a buzzing refreshment centre by the main ticket office (at Ajanta caves), which serves an overpriced vegetarian thali (₹80) and warm beer.

ℹ Information

A cloakroom adjoining the toilets near the main ticket office is a safe place to leave gear (₹5 per item for four hours), in case you are visiting Ajanta en route from Aurangabad to Jalgaon or vice versa. The caves are a short, steep climb from the ticket office; the elderly can opt for a chair carried by four bearers (₹400).

On a rather perplexing note, the authorities were constructing a brand new complex near the T-junction during research, where they reportedly intended to replicate the major caves within modern, climate-controlled domes!

ℹ Getting There & Away

Buses from Aurangabad (p88) or Jalgaon (p96) will drop you off at the T-junction (where the highway meets the road to the caves), 4km from the site. From here, after paying an 'amenities' fee (₹7), race to the departure point for the

green-coloured 'pollution-free' buses (with/ without AC ₹12/7), which zoom up to the caves. Buses return on a regular basis (half-hourly, last bus at 6.15pm) to the T-junction.

All MSRTC buses passing through Fardapur stop at the T-junction. After the caves close you can board buses to either Aurangabad or Jalgaon outside the MTDC Holiday Resort in Fardapur, 1km down the main road towards Jalgaon. Taxis are available in Fardapur; ₹900 should get you to Jalgaon.

Jalgaon

☎0257 / POP 368,000 / ELEV 208M

Apart from being a handy base for exploring Ajanta 60km away, Jalgaon is really nothing more than a convenient transit town. A grubby settlement, it stands on the passing rail trade, connecting northern Maharashtra to all major cities across India. Indeed, it's a place to consider if you're moving out of the state towards northern India, or vice versa.

🛏 Sleeping & Eating

Most of the hotels in Jalgaon have 24-hour check out. Power cuts are common, so carry a torch for emergencies.

Hotel Plaza HOTEL $
(☎2227354; hotelplaza_jal@yahoo.com; Station Rd; d with/without AC ₹900/500; ❄@) It's amazing how Hotel Plaza continues to impress travellers day after relentless day. There's nothing fancy on offer here, but for the money you pay it's a bumper deal. Rooms are squeaky clean, the sheets fresh, and the effusive owner a mine of useful information.

Hotel Royal Palace HOTEL $$
(☎2233555; Jai Nagar, Mahabal Rd; d from ₹975; ❄🛰) It's worth suffering the 15-minute rickshaw ride from the train station to this smart hotel. Luxuriant by Jalgaon's standards, it has a range of spotlessly clean and prim rooms, and a decent multicuisine restaurant serving eminently edible north Indian, coastal, Chinese and Continental fare.

Hotel Arya INDIAN $
(Navi Peth; mains ₹50-80) Vegetarian-only grub on offer; try one of the lip-smacking Punjabi delights. You may have to queue for a table during meals.

ℹ Information

You can find a couple of banks, ATMs and internet cafes on Nehru Rd, which runs along the top of Station Rd.

❶ Getting There & Away

Several express trains connecting Mumbai (sleeper/2AC ₹211/721, eight hours), Delhi (sleeper/2AC ₹375/1362, 18 hours) and Kolkata (sleeper/2AC ₹442/1623, 26 hours) stop at Jalgaon **train station**. The *Sewagram Express* goes to Nagpur (sleeper/2AC ₹207/709, eight hours, 10pm).

Buses to Fardapur (₹40, 1½ hours) depart half-hourly from the **bus stand** starting at 6am, continuing to Aurangabad (₹122, four hours).

Jalgaon's train station and bus stand are about 2km apart (₹20 by autorickshaw). Luxury bus offices on Railway Station Rd offer services to Aurangabad (₹140, 3½ hours), Mumbai (₹275, nine hours), Pune (₹275, nine hours) and Nagpur (ordinary/sleeper ₹330/360, 10 hours).

Lonar Meteorite Crater

If you like off-beat adventures, travel to Lonar to explore a prehistoric natural wonder. About 50,000 years ago, a meteorite slammed into the earth here, leaving behind a massive crater, 2km across and 170m deep. In scientific jargon, it's the only hypervelocity natural impact crater in basaltic rock in the world. In lay terms, it's as tranquil and relaxing a spot as you could hope to find, with a shallow green lake at its base and wilderness all around. The lake water is supposedly alkaline and excellent for the skin. Scientists think that the meteorite is still embedded about 600m below the southeastern rim of the crater.

The crater's edge is home to several **Hindu temples** as well as wildlife, including langurs, peacocks, deer and an array of birds.

MTDC Tourist Complex (☏07260221602; d with/without AC ₹1100/900; ❄) has a prime location just across the road from the crater, and offers eight rooms of relatively good value, considering the location.

❶ Getting There & Away

There are a couple of buses a day between Lonar and Aurangabad (₹125, 3½ hours). It's also possible to visit Lonar on a day trip from Aurangabad or Jalgaon if you hire a car and driver, and don't mind dishing out about ₹2200.

Nagpur

☏0712 / POP 2.1 MILLION / ELEV 305M

In the heart of India's orange country, Nagpur is located way off the main tourist routes. Apart from being at its festive best during Dussehra, the city – as such – is hopelessly devoid of sites. Nonetheless, it makes a good base for venturing out to the far eastern corner of Maharashtra. First up, it's close to the temples of Ramtek (p97) and the ashrams of Sevagram (p97). Besides, Nagpur is also a convenient stop for those heading to the isolated **Tadoba-Andhari Tiger Reserve**, 150km south of Nagpur, which has some of India's most dense forest teeming with wildlife, including the famed Bengal tigers.

If you have some time to kill in the evening, take a stroll in the city's Civil Lines area, dotted with some fantastic buildings and mansions dating back to the Raj era, now used as government offices.

🛏 Sleeping & Eating

Nagpur's hotels cater primarily to business-people, not tourists. Needless to say, they're frightfully overpriced. Stay in the Central Ave area if you're on a budget, or have a train to catch in the wee hours. Otherwise, consider moving to Ramdaspeth, closer to the city centre.

Hotel Centre Point HOTEL $$
(☏2420910; fax 2446260; www.centrepointgroup.org; 24 Central Bazar Rd, Ramdaspeth; s/d from ₹3750/4250; ❄ 🛜 ☲) A trusted address that's been setting the standards of luxury in Nagpur for sometime now. Rooms are plush, with fluffy beds, high-speed internet access and cheerful paintings adorning the walls. It's located in the heart of the business and entertainment district.

Hotel Blue Diamond HOTEL $
(☏2727461; www.hotelbluediamondnagpur.com; 113 Central Ave; s/d ₹400/500, with AC ₹1250/1350; ❄) The mirrored ceiling in reception is straight out of a bad '70s nightclub and the rooms are pretty much the type you'd expect above a seedy '70s nightclub. There's a dungeon-like bar on the mezzanine floor. AC rooms have LCD TVs and crumpled linoleum flooring.

The Pride Hotel HOTEL $$$
(☏2291102; fax 2290440; www.pridehotel.com; opp. airport, Wardha Rd; s/d from ₹5500/6250; ❄ 🛜 ☲) Located close to the airport and away from the din of the city, this sleek business hotel is a good stopover option for touch-and-go travellers. Royal Lancers, its lobby bar, and Puran Da Dhaba, a souped-up version of a traditional Punjabi eatery, are good places to settle in for the evening.

Krishnum SOUTH INDIAN $
(Central Ave; mains ₹40-50) This popular place dishes out South Indian snacks and fruit juices of agreeable quality. It also has branches in other parts of town.

Picadilly Checkers FAST FOOD $
(VCA Complex, Civil Lines; mains ₹60-80) A favourite eating joint for Nagpur's college brigade. A good range of all-vegetarian quick bites are on offer.

The dozens of *dhabas* (snack bars), food stalls and fruit stands opposite the train station rouse in the evening. Summer is the best time to sample the famed oranges.

ℹ Information

Computrek (18 Central Ave; per hr ₹20; ⊙10am-10pm) Internet access on the main drag.
MTDC (☑2533325; near MLA Hostel, Civil Lines; ⊙10am-5.45pm Mon-Sat) Manned by helpful staff.
State Bank of India (Kingsway; ⊙11am-2pm Mon-Fri) A two-minute walk west of the train station. Deals in foreign exchange.
State Bank of India, ICICI Bank, Axis Bank and HDFC Bank have ATMs along Central Ave and in Ramdaspeth.

ℹ Getting There & Away

Air
Most domestic airlines, including **Indian Airlines** (☑2533962) and **Jet Airways** (☑5617888), operate daily flights to Delhi (from ₹3500, 1½ hours), Mumbai (from ₹2500, 1½ hours) and Kolkata (from ₹2500, 1½ hours), as well as linking Hyderabad, Ahmedabad, Bengaluru, Chennai and Pune. Taxis/autorickshaws from the airport to the city centre cost ₹350/200.

Bus
The main **MSRTC bus stand** is 2km south of the train station and hotel area. Ordinary buses head regularly for Wardha (₹57, three hours) and Ramtek (₹35, 1½ hours). There are two buses to Jalgaon (₹326, 10 hours), and three to Hyderabad (₹317, 12 hours).

Train
From Nagpur's **train station**, the *Vidarbha Express* departs for Mumbai (sleeper/2AC ₹140/1159, 14 hours, 5.15pm), and heading north to Kolkata is the *Gitanjali Express* (sleeper/2AC ₹379/1378, 17½ hours, 7.05pm). Several expresses bound for Delhi and Mumbai stop at Jalgaon (for Ajanta caves; sleeper/2AC ₹207/709, seven hours).

Around Nagpur

RAMTEK
About 40km northeast of Nagpur, Ramtek is believed to be the place where Lord Rama, of the epic Ramayana, spent some time during his exile with his wife Sita and brother Lakshmana. The place is marked by a cluster of **temples** (⊙6am-9pm) about 600 years old, which sit atop the Hill of Rama and have their own population of resident monkeys. Autorickshaws will cart you the 5km from the bus stand to the temple complex for ₹50. You can return to town via the 700 steps at the back of the complex. On the road to the temples you'll pass the delightful **Ambala Tank**, lined with small shrines. You can take a boat ride (₹20 per head) around the lake if you want.

Not far away from the main temple cluster, **Rajkamal Resort** (☑07114202761; d with/without AC ₹1200/900; ☀) has large, featureless rooms with TVs, and a basic restaurant-bar.

Buses run half-hourly between Ramtek and the MSRTC bus stand in Nagpur (₹35, 1½ hours). The last bus to Nagpur is at 7pm.

SEVAGRAM
☑07152
Located about 85km from Nagpur, Sevagram (Village of Service) was chosen by Mahatma Gandhi as his base during the Indian Independence Movement. Throughout the freedom struggle, the village played host to several nationalist leaders, who would regularly come to visit the Mahatma at his **Sevagram Ashram** (☑284753; ⊙6am-5.30pm).

The overseers of this peaceful ashram, built on 40 hectares of tree-lined farmland, have carefully restored and conserved the original huts that Gandhi lived and worked in, which now house some of his personal effects, including items of stationery, wooden sandals and his walking stick. Overall, it's a wonderful daylong excursion, although slightly out of the way.

Very basic lodging is available in the **Yatri Nivas** (☑284753; d ₹100), across the road from the entry gate (advance booking recommended), and simple vegetarian meals can be served in the ashram's dining hall with prior notice.

Just 3km from Sevagram, Paunar village is home to the **Brahmavidya Mandir Ashram** (☑288388; ⊙4am-noon & 2-8pm). Founded by Vinoba Bhave, a nationalist and disciple of Gandhi, the ashram is run almost entirely by women. Modelled on *swaraj* (self-sufficiency), it's operated on a social system of consensus with no central management.

Sevagram can be reached by taking a Wardha-bound bus from Nagpur (₹50, three hours).

TADOBA-ANDHARI RESERVE
Now under India's Project Tiger directorate, this little-explored national park – with

THE LEGEND OF 'BABA' AMTE

The legend of Murlidhar Devidas 'Baba' Amte (1914–2008) is oft-repeated in humanitarian circles around the world. Hailing from an upper-class Brahmin family in Wardha, Amte was snugly ensconced in material riches and on his way to becoming a successful lawyer, when he witnessed a leper die unattended in the streets one night. It was an incident that changed him forever.

Soon after, Amte renounced worldly comforts, embracing an austere life through which he actively worked for the benefit of leprosy patients and those belonging to marginalised communities. In the primitive forested backyards of eastern Maharashtra, he set up his ashram called Anandwan (Forest of Joy). A true Gandhian, Amte believed in self-sufficiency, and his lifelong efforts saw several awards being conferred upon him, including the Ramon Magsaysay Award in 1985.

Amte's work has been continued by his sons Vikas and Prakash and their wives – the latter couple also won the Magsaysay Award in 2008. The family now runs three ashrams in these remote parts to care for the needy, both humans and animals. Volunteering opportunities are available; contact the ashram on mss@niya.org or lbp@bsnl.in.

a healthy population of Bengal tigers – lies 150km south of Nagpur. Less visited than most other forests in India, this is a place where you can get up close with wildlife (which also includes gaurs, chitals, nilgais and sloth bears) without having to jostle past truckloads of shutter-happy tourists. The trade-off is that you'll have to make do with basic amenities and low comfort levels. The park remains open through most of the year.

The **MTDC Resort** (d with/without AC ₹1500/1200) in nearby Moharli has a string of decent rooms and dining facilities. The resort can also arrange jungle safaris in jeeps and minibuses. Bookings can be made at the MTDC's Nagpur office (see p97). If you're travelling in groups of six or more, MTDC has an all-inclusive overnight package out of Nagpur (₹3750 per person), which is recommended since it takes care of logistical hassles. Call in advance.

Several state buses ply between Nagpur and Chandrapur through the day (₹110, 3½ hours).

SOUTHERN MAHARASHTRA

Konkan Coast

Despite being flanked on both ends by two of India's top urban centres, it's laudable how the Konkan Coast manages to latch on to its virginal bounties. A little-explored shoreline running southward from Mumbai all the way to Goa, it is a picturesque strip of land peppered with flawless beaches, tropical green paddy fields, rolling hills and decaying forts. Travelling through this peaceful and quaint region can be sheer bliss. However, remember that accommodation is scant, the cuisine unsophisticated though tasty, and the locals unaccustomed to tour groups, especially foreigners. Since transport is both limited and unreliable, a good option is to rent a taxi in Mumbai and drift slowly down the coast to Goa. What you'll get in return is an experience that money can't buy.

MURUD
02144 / POP 12,500

Even if you don't plan on going the whole stretch, the sleepy fishing hamlet of Murud – 165km from Mumbai – should definitely be on your itinerary. Once you step on to its lazy beaches and feel the white surf rush past your feet, you'll be happy you came.

Sight-wise, Murud is home to the magnificent island fortress of **Janjira** (admission free; ⊙7am-5.30pm), standing about 500m offshore. The citadel was built in 1140 by the Siddis, descendants of sailor-traders from the Horn of Africa, who settled here and allegedly made their living through piracy. No outsider ever made it past the fort's 12m-high walls which, when seen during high tide, seem to rise straight from the sea. Unconquered through history, the fort finally fell to the spoils of nature. Today, its ramparts are slowly turning to rubble as wilderness reclaims its innards.

The only way to reach Janjira is by boat (₹20 return, 15 minutes) from Rajpuri Port.

Boats depart from 7am to 5.30pm daily, but require a minimum of 20 passengers. You can also have a boat to yourself (₹400), and most oarsmen will double as guides for a negotiable fee (around ₹350). To get to Rajpuri from Murud, take an autorickshaw (₹50) or hire a bicycle (₹50 per hour) from the Golden Swan Beach Resort.

Back in Murud you can waste away the days on the beach, joining in with karate practice or playing cricket with local youngsters. Alternately, you could peer through the gates of the off-limits **Ahmedganj Palace**, estate of the Siddi Nawab of Murud, or scramble around the decaying mosque and tombs on the south side of town.

Sleeping & Eating

Golden Swan Beach Resort HOTEL $$
(274078; www.goldenswan.com; Darbar Rd; d incl full board with/without AC from ₹3500/2000;) With only a thicket of palms separating it from the beach, this upscale hotel offers accommodation in cosy rooms and cottages looking out to the sea. The non-AC rooms are in a charming old bungalow located five minutes away from the main property.

Sea Shell Resort HOTEL $$
(09833667985; www.seashellmurud.com; Darbar Rd; d with/without AC ₹2500/2000;) A very smart place with breezy sea-facing rooms, this place scores quite well with Mumbai's weekend travellers. A teeny swimming pool at the entrance is a welcome addition, and dolphin safaris can be arranged upon prior request.

Hotel Shoreline HOTEL $$
(02232258882; www.ajinkyaholidays.com; Darbar Rd; d from ₹3000;) It's slightly boxy and brassy in contrast to its surroundings, but it's centrally located and should be alright for a night or two. Only the more expensive rooms face the sea.

New Sea Rock Restaurant FAST FOOD $
(Rajpuri; 9am-9pm) Perched on a cliff overlooking the beach at Rajpuri, this quick-eats joint has an awesome view of Janjira, which looms ahead. A perfect place to steal a million-dollar sunset for the price of a chai (₹10). The proprietors also arrange kayak rides and other water sports during the high season.

Vinayaka Restaurant INDIAN $
(Darbar Rd; mains ₹100) A great place to tuck into a delicious and fiery Malvani thali, served with pink kokam syrup to smother the spices.

ⓘ Getting There & Away

AC catamarans (₹100, two hours) from the Gateway of India in Mumbai cruise to Mandva pier between 6am and 7pm. The ticket includes a free shuttle bus to Alibag (30 minutes), otherwise an autorickshaw will be about ₹150. Rickety local buses from Alibag head down the coast to Murud (₹35, two hours). Alternatively, buses from Mumbai Central bus stand take almost six hours to Murud (ordinary/semideluxe ₹117/158).

Avoid the train. The nearest railhead is at Roha, two hours away and badly connected.

GANPATIPULE
02357

Primarily a temple town, Ganpatipule has been luring a steady stream of sea-lovers over the years with its clean waters and pristine sands stretching to the horizon. Located about 375km from Mumbai, it's a village that snoozes through much of the year, except during holidays such as Diwali or Ganesh Chaturthi. These are times when hordes of boisterous 'tourists' turn up to visit the seaside **Ganesha Temple** (6am-9pm) housing a monolithic Ganesha (painted a bright orange), supposedly discovered 1600 years ago.

About 40km southward, Ratnagiri is the largest town on the southern Maharashtra coast and the main train station for Ganpatipule (it's on the Konkan Railway). You'll also find several ATMs strung along Ratnagiri's main street. But once you've refilled your wallet and gone shopping for conveniences, the only sight worth checking out – apart from a dirty beach – are the remnants of the **Thibaw Palace** (Thibaw Palace Rd; admission free; 10am-5.30pm Tue-Sun), where the last Burmese king, Thibaw, was interned under the British from 1886 until his death in 1916.

Sleeping & Eating

MTDC Resort HOTEL $$
(235248; d with/without AC from ₹1500/1300;) Spread over a prime complex just off Ganpatipule's beach, this is the best place to camp. It's a smart, well-kept place with an assortment of rooms and cottages, and packs in a **Bank of Maharashtra** that changes travellers cheques, along with a beer bar. Try the Konkani huts, themed on rural Malvani homes, for a unique experience.

Hotel Vihar Deluxe HOTEL $$
(02352222944; Main Rd, Ratnagiri; d with/without AC ₹1800/1000;) This gigantic operation is one of a few functional but featureless hotels that line the main strip in Ratnagiri. Rooms are adequate (the loos quite good), and the

WORTH A TRIP

GET MAROONED

Apart from its main sands, the Konkan Coast also features a string of less-explored but heavenly beaches that could arm-wrestle the Maldives any given day. About 17km north of Murud, well connected by share autorickshaws (₹50), lies **Kashid**, a fantastic beach where you can cosy up with your favourite paperback while sipping on tender coconuts. South of Murud is **Diveagar**, swarming with colonies of sand bubbler crabs, scenic **Harihareshwar**, famous for its seaside temple, and serene **Vengurla**, 10km from Tarkarli, a place you probably wouldn't mind being shipwrecked. Most of these places are connected by back roads where public transport is scant, so they are best visited in a hired cab. You might have to ask for directions often, or stay in village homes for the odd night. Be generous with how much you give.

food – especially the seafood – is commendable. A hearty South Indian breakfast is complimentary.

Tarang Restaurant   INDIAN $
(MTDC Resort; mains ₹80-100) Barring beachside stalls, this is one of the few places where you can grab a decent meal in Ganpatipule.

❶ Getting There & Away

Ordinary buses shuttle between Ganpatipule and Ratnagiri (₹40, 1½ hours). One semideluxe MSRTC bus heads out at 8.45am to Mumbai (₹369, 10 hours), and departs from Mumbai at 8pm. From Ratnagiri's **train station**, the *Janshatabdi Express* goes to Mumbai (2nd class/chair ₹142/460, 5½ hours, 5.50pm). The return train heading for Goa (2nd class/chair ₹122/390, 3½ hours) is at 10.45am. From Ratnagiri's **old bus stand**, semideluxe buses leave for Goa (₹221, seven hours) and Kolhapur (₹135, four hours).

TARKARLI & MALVAN
📞 02365

A government tourism promo parades this place as comparable to Tahiti, and for once, you can rest assured that these guys are not exaggerating! Within striking distance of Goa, about 200km from Ratnagiri, pristine Tarkarli has white sands and sparkling blue waters that rekindle memories of the Andamans or Ko Phi Phi in Thailand. What's lacking is a well-oiled tourist industry and urban comforts, but do you care?

The monstrous **Sindhudurg Fort**, built by Shivaji and dating from 1664, lies on an offshore island and can be reached by frequent ferries (₹30) from Malvan. MTDC can arrange snorkelling trips to the clear waters around the fortress.

Of the few hotels and resorts available, the good old **MTDC Holiday Resort** (📞252390; d from ₹1800; ❉) is still your best

bet. Enquire at the resort about backwater tours on its fabulous **houseboats** (standard/luxury incl full board ₹6500/7500).

The closest train station is Kudal, 38km away. Frequent buses (₹25, one hour) cover the route from Malvan **bus stand** (📞252034). An autorickshaw from Kudal to Malvan or Tarkarli is about ₹400. Malvan has buses daily to Panaji (₹70, three hours) and a couple of services to Ratnagiri (₹130, five hours).

Matheran
📞 02148 / POP 5100 / ELEV 803M

Literally meaning 'Jungle Above', Matheran is a tiny patch of peace and quiet capping a craggy Sahyadri summit within spitting distance from Mumbai's heat and grime. Endowed with shady forests criss-crossed with foot trails and breathtaking lookouts, it is easily the most elegant of Maharashtra's hill stations.

The credit for discovering this little gem goes to Hugh Malet, erstwhile collector of Thane district, who chanced upon it during one of his excursions in 1850. Soon it became a hill station patronised by the British and populated by Parsi families.

Getting to Matheran is really half the fun. While speedier options are available by road, nothing beats arriving in town on the narrow-gauge toy train (mini train) that chugs laboriously along a 21km scenic route to the heart of the settlement. Motor vehicles are banned within Matheran, making it an ideal place to give your ears and lungs a rest and your feet some exercise.

◉ Sights & Activities

You can walk along shady forest paths to most of Matheran's viewpoints in a matter of hours, and it's a place well-suited to stress-free ambling. To catch the sunrise, head to **Panorama Point**, while **Porcupine Point** (also known as Sunset Point) is the most popular (read: packed) as the sun drops. **Louisa Point** and **Little Chouk Point** also have stunning views of the Sahyadris and if you're visiting **Echo Point**, give it a yell. Stop at **Charlotte Lake** on the way back from Echo Point, but don't go for a swim – this is the town's main water supply and stepping in is prohibited. You can reach the valley below **One Tree Hill** down the path known as **Shivaji's Ladder**, supposedly trod upon by the Maratha leader himself.

Horses can be hired along MG Rd for rides to the lookout points; they cost about ₹250 per hour (negotiable).

🛏 Sleeping & Eating

Hotels in Matheran are low in quality and unreasonably high in tariff, so if you're not feeling generous, make your visit a day trip from Mumbai. Check-out times vary wildly (as early as 7am), as do high and low season rates. Matheran shuts shop during the monsoons.

TOP
CHOICE **Verandah**
In The Forest   HERITAGE HOTEL **$$**
(☑230296; www.neemranahotels.com; Barr House; d incl breakfast from ₹3000) This wonderfully preserved 19th-century bungalow thrives on undiluted nostalgia. Step past the threshold of one of its quaintly luxurious rooms or suites and find yourself reminiscing about bygone times in the company of ornate candelabras, antique teak furniture, Victorian canvases, grandfather clocks and a rush of other memorabilia. The eponymous verandah is probably the most beautiful location from where to admire Matheran's woods, and there's a good selection of food and beverages to keep you company through idle hours.

Lord's Central Hotel   HERITAGE HOTEL **$$**
(☑230228; www.matheranhotels.com; MG Rd; d incl full board from ₹3600; ❋@❋) Owned by a gracious Parsi family over six generations, this charming colonial-style affair is one of Matheran's most reputed establishments, and guarantees a pleasant stay within its old-world portals. The rooms are comfy, the swimming pool deck offers fabulous views of the valley and distant peaks, and a jumbo chess board out on the lawns is a nice place to down a beer before an awesome Parsi lunch.

Hope Hall Hotel   HOTEL **$$**
(☑230253; MG Rd; d from ₹2000) 'Since 1875', says a plaque at reception, and frankly, the age shows! However, it's a cheerful place and going by the scores of 'thank you' notes left by guests, it must be an okay place to stay.

Hookahs & Tikkas   INDIAN **$$**
(MG Rd; mains ₹50-110) Operating from a balcony overlooking the main road, this place serves a range of kebabs and savoury Indian fare, as well as hookahs with flavoured tobacco.

Rasna   INDIAN **$**
(MG Rd; mains ₹80-100) This restaurant opposite Naoroji Lord Garden serves tasty vegetarian food. Try the popular Punjabi (North Indian) thali (₹90).

❶ Information

Entry to Matheran costs ₹25 (₹15 for children), which you pay on arrival at the train station or the Dasturi car park.

On the main road into town, **Vishwas Photo Studio** (MG Rd; ☉9.30am-10pm) sells useful miniguides (₹25) and photographic accessories, and doubles as a tourist office. The **Union Bank of India** (MG Rd; ☉10am-2pm Mon-Fri, to noon Sat) has an ATM.

❶ Getting There & Away

Taxi

Share taxis run from Neral to Matheran's Dasturi car park (₹60, 30 minutes). Horses (₹180) and hand-pulled rickshaws (₹200) wait here to whisk you in a cloud of red dust to Matheran's main bazaar. You can also walk this stretch in a little over an hour.

Train

The toy train (2nd class/1st class ₹35/210) chugs between Matheran and Neral Junction five times daily. The service is suspended during monsoons. From Mumbai, express trains to Neral Junction include the 7.10am *Deccan Express* or the 8.40am *Koyna Express* (2nd class/chair ₹46/165, 1½ hours). Other expresses from Mumbai stop at Karjat, down the line from Neral, from where you can backtrack on a local train. From Pune, you can reach Karjat by the *Sinhagad Express* (2nd class/chair ₹47/165, two hours, 6.05am).

❶ Getting Around

Apart from hand-pulled rickshaws and horses, walking is the only other transport option in Matheran.

Lonavla

📞02114 / POP 55,600 / ELEV 625M

Cheekily masquerading as a hill station, Lonavla is an overdeveloped (and overpriced) mercantile town about 106km southeast of Mumbai. It's far from attractive, with its main drag consisting almost exclusively of garishly lit shops flogging *chikki,* the rockhard, brittle sweet made in the area.

The only reason you'd want to come here is to visit the nearby Karla and Bhaja Caves which, after those at Ellora and Ajanta, are the best in Maharashtra.

Hotels, restaurants and the main road to the caves lie north of the train station (exit from platform 1). Most of the Lonavla township and its markets are located south of the station.

The petrol pump opposite Hotel Rama Krishna now has three ATMs dispensing cash. Internet access is available at **Balaji Cyber Café** (1st fl, Khandelwal Bldg, New Bazaar; per hr ₹15; ⏱12.30-10.30pm), immediately south of the train station.

🏃 Activities

Founded in 1924, the **Kaivalyadhama Yoga Hospital** (📞273039; www.kdham.com; Indian/foreigner incl full board ₹9000/US$320), set about 2km from Lonavla en route to the Karla and Bhaja Caves, combines yoga courses with naturopathic therapies. Room rates cover accommodation, yoga sessions, programs and lectures over seven days. Two-, three- and four-week packages are also offered.

Mumbai-based **Nirvana Adventures** (📞022-26053724; www.flynirvana.com) offers various paragliding courses (Indian/foreigner including full board from ₹6500/€250) or 10-minute tandem flights (₹2000) at Kamshet, 25km from Lonavla.

🛏 Sleeping & Eating

Lonavla's hotels suffer from inflated prices and low standards. All hotels listed here have a 10am check-out.

Hotel Adarsh   HOTEL **$$**
(📞272353; near Bus Stand; d from ₹2500; 🌡🖥) This is clearly the best-value place in town. Centrally located, it has smart rooms and good service, and seems to be preferred by local yuppies. The terrace pool gives you another good reason to stay.

Hotel Lonavla   HOTEL **$$**
(📞272914; Mumbai-Pune Rd; d from ₹1195) Fanonly rooms here, but it's cheap by Lonavla's standards. Bulk bookings can often leave you without a room, so enquire in advance. They insist that you clear your bills every third day (who stays that long anyway?).

Lonavla & Around

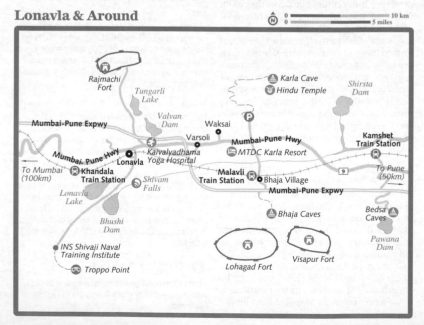

TOP CHOICE **Biso** ITALIAN $$
(Citrus Hotel, DT Shahani Rd, mains ₹180-220) This could be a delightfully redeeming feature of your Lonavla trip. A top-class alfresco restaurant thrown around the lawns of a sleek business hotel about 15 minutes east of the bus stand, Biso serves an excellent selection of pastas, wood oven-fired pizzas and desserts for its upmarket clientele. The penne in basil sauce and the farmhouse pizza are dishes you won't quickly forget.

Hotel Rama Krishna INDIAN $$
(Mumbai-Pune Rd; mains ₹120-150) This place is famed for its meaty fare, especially the kebabs, and can brim over with travelling parties during meals.

ℹ Getting There & Away

Lonavla is serviced by MSRTC buses departing the **bus stand** to Dadar in Mumbai (ordinary/semideluxe ₹65/94, two hours) and Pune (ordinary/semideluxe ₹55/80, two hours). Luxury AC buses (about ₹130) also travel to both cities.

All express trains from Mumbai to Pune (2nd class/chair ₹57/195, three hours) stop at Lonavla **train station**. From Pune, you can also reach Lonavla by taking an hourly shuttle train (₹15, two hours).

Karla & Bhaja Caves

While they pale in comparison to Ajanta or Ellora, these rock-cut caves (dating from around the 2nd century BC) are among the better examples of Buddhist cave architecture in India. They are also low on commercial tourism, which make them ideal places for a quiet excursion. Karla has the most impressive single cave, but Bhaja is a quieter site to explore.

Karla Cave CAVES
(Indian/foreigner ₹5/100; ⊘9am-5pm) Karla Cave, the largest early Buddhist *chaitya* in India, is reached by a 20-minute climb from a mini-bazaar at the base of a hill. Completed in 80 BC, the *chaitya* is around 40m long and 15m high, and sports similar architectural motifs as *chaityas* in Ajanta and Ellora. Excluding Ellora's Kailasa Temple, this is probably the most impressive cave temple in the state.

Karla Cave is also the only site in Maharashtra where the original woodwork, more than two centuries old, has managed to survive. A semicircular 'sun window' filters light in towards a dagoba or stupa (the cave's representation of the Buddha), protected by a carved wooden umbrella, the only remaining example of its kind. The cave's roof also retains ancient teak buttresses. The 37 pillars forming the aisles are topped by kneeling elephants. The carved elephant heads on the sides of the vestibule once had ivory tusks.

There's a Hindu **temple** in front of the cave, thronged by pilgrims whose presence adds colour to the scene.

Bhaja Caves CAVES
(Indian/foreigner ₹5/100; ⊘8am-6pm) Across the expressway, it's a 3km jaunt from the main road to the Bhaja Caves, where the setting is lusher, greener and quieter than at Karla Cave. Thought to date from around 200 BC, 10 of the 18 caves here are *viharas,* while Cave 12 is an open *chaitya,* earlier than that at Karla, containing a simple dagoba. Beyond this is a strange huddle of 14 stupas, five inside and nine outside a smaller cave.

Once you're done exploring the Bhaja Caves, you can embark on a trek to the ruined twin-forts of **Lohagad** and **Visapur**. You could also check out the picturesque **Pawana Dam**, down a road about 20km east from the Karla–Bhaja access point.

🛏 Sleeping & Eating

MTDC Karla Resort HOTEL $$
(✆02114-282230; d with/without AC from ₹1300/900; ✸) Set off the highway, close to Karla–Bhaja access point. Rooms and cottages are well-kept, and there's a good restaurant.

ℹ Getting There & Away

Karla and Bhaja can be visited over a single day from Lonavla. Take a local bus (₹10, 30 minutes) to the access point, from where it's about a 6km return walk on each side to the two sites. An autorickshaw charges about ₹450 from Lonavla for the tour, including waiting time.

Pune

🎵020 / POP 3.7 MILLION / ELEV 535M
With its healthy mix of small-town wonders and big-city blues, Pune (also pronounced Poona) is a city that epitomises 'New India'. Once little more than a pensioners' town and an army outpost, it is today an unpretentious, cosmopolitan place inhabited by a cheerful and happy population. A thriving centre of academia and business, Pune is also known globally for its numero-uno export, the late guru Bhagwan Shree Rajneesh and his ashram, the Osho International Meditation Resort (p105).

Pune

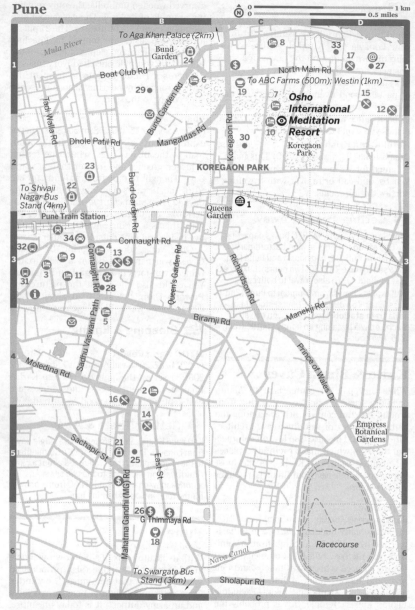

Pune was initially given pride of place by Shivaji and the ruling Peshwas, who made it their capital. The British took the city in 1817 and, thanks to its cool and dry climate, soon made it the Bombay Presidency's monsoon capital. Globalisation knocked on Pune's doors in the 1990s, following which it went in for an image overhaul. However, the colonial charm was retained by preserving its old buildings and residential areas, bringing about a pleasant coexistence of the old and new which (despite the pollution and hectic traffic) makes Pune a wonderful place to explore. In September **Ganesh Chaturthi** brings on a tide of festivities across the city, and provides a fantastic window for exploring the city's cultural side.

The city sits at the confluence of the Mutha and Mula Rivers. Mahatma Gandhi (MG) Rd, about 1km south of Pune train station, is the main commercial street. Koregaon Park, northeast of the train station, is the undisputed chill-out zone, home to some of the best hotels, restaurants, coffee shops and of course, the Osho Ashram.

◉ Sights & Activities

TOP
CHOICE **Osho International Meditation Resort** MEDITATION

(☎66019999; www.osho.com; 17 Koregaon Park) You'll either like it or hate it. A splurge of an institution, this ashram, located in a leafy, upscale northern suburb, has been drawing thousands of *sanyasins* (seekers), many of them Westerners, ever since the death of Osho (see the boxed text, p106) in 1990. With its placid swimming pool, sauna, 'zennis' and basketball courts, massage and beauty parlour, bookshop and a luxury boutique guest house (p107), it is, to some, the ultimate place to indulge in stress-busting meditation. Alternately, there are detractors who point fingers at the ashram's blatant commercialisation and accuse it of marketing a warped version of the mystic East to gullible Westerners.

The main centre for meditation and the nightly white-robed spiritual dance is the Osho Auditorium (no coughing or sneezing, please). The Osho Samadhi, where the guru's ashes are kept, is also open for meditation. The commune's 'Multiversity' runs a plethora of courses in meditation and other esoteric techniques. If you wish to take part, or even just meditate, you'll have to pay ₹1150/1550 (Indian/foreigner), which covers registration, a mandatory on-the-spot HIV test (sterile needles used), introductory sessions and your first day's meditation pass. You'll also need two robes (one maroon and one white, from ₹200 per robe). For subsequent days, a daily meditation pass costs ₹300/700 (Indian/foreigner), and you can come and go as you please. If you want further involvement, you can also sign up for a 'work as meditation' program.

The curious can watch a video presentation at the visitor centre and take a 10-minute silent tour of the facilities (₹10; adults only, cameras and phones prohibited) at 9.15am and 2pm daily. Tickets have to be booked at least a day in advance (9.30am to 1pm and 2pm to 4pm). It's also worth checking out the 5-hectare garden, **Osho Teerth** (admission free; ☺6-9am & 3-6pm), behind the commune, and accessible all day for those with a meditation pass.

TOP CHOICE **Raja Dinkar Kelkar Museum** MUSEUM
(www.rajakelkarmuseum.com; 1377-1378 Natu Baug, Bajirao Rd; Indian/foreigner ₹20/200; ☺9.30am-5.30pm) This fascinating museum is one of Pune's true delights. Housing only a fraction of the 20,000-odd objects of Indian daily life painstakingly collected by Dinkar Kelkar (who died in 1990), it's worth an entire day out. The quirky pan-Indian collection includes hundreds of hookah pipes, writing instruments, lamps, textiles, toys, entire doors and windows, kitchen utensils, furniture, puppets, jewellery, betel-nut cutters and an amazing gallery of musical instruments. During research, the museum was scouting for a new address with more display space, where it could do justice to the vast unseen portion of the collection currently rotting away in strongrooms.

Tribal Cultural Museum MUSEUM
(28 Queen's Garden; admission ₹10; ☺10.30am-5.30pm Mon-Sat) About 1.5km east of the train station, near the army cantonment, this small museum showcases an excellent collection of tribal artefacts (jewellery, utensils, musical instruments, even black magic accessories) sourced from remote tribal belts. It's a great place to familiarise yourself with tribal traditions and cultures of the region. Don't forget to check out the section featuring ornate papier-mâché festival masks, to the rear of the building.

Aga Khan Palace PALACE
(Ahmednagar Rd; Indian/foreigner ₹5/100; ☺9am-5.45pm) Set amid a wooded 6.5-hectare plot across the Mula River in Yerwada, the grand Aga Khan Palace (housing the **Gandhi National Memorial**) is easily Pune's biggest crowd-puller. Built in 1892 by Sultan Aga Khan III, this lofty building was where the Mahatma and other prominent nationalist leaders were interned by the British for about two years following Gandhi's Quit India resolution in 1942. Both Kasturba **Gandhi**, the Mahatma's wife, and Mahadeobhai Desai, his secretary for 35 years, died here in confinement. You'll find their shrines (containing their ashes) in a quiet garden to the rear.

OSHO: GURU OF SEX

Ever tried mixing spirituality with primal instincts, and garnishing the potent concoction with oodles of panache? Well, Bhagwan Shree Rajneesh (1931–90) certainly did. Osho, as he preferred to be called, was one of India's most flamboyant 'export gurus' to market the mystic East to the world, and undoubtedly the most controversial. Initially based in Pune, he followed no particular religion or philosophy, and outraged many across the world with his advocacy of sex as a path to enlightenment. A darling of the international media, he quickly earned himself the epithet 'sex guru'. In 1981, Rajneesh took his curious blend of Californian pop psychology and Indian mysticism to the USA, where he set up an agricultural commune in Oregon. There, his ashram's notoriety, as well as its fleet of (material and thus valueless!) Rolls Royces grew, until raging local paranoia about its activities moved the authorities to charge Osho with immigration fraud. He was fined US$400,000 and deported. An epic journey then began, during which Osho and his followers, in their search for a new base, were either deported from or denied entry into 21 countries. By 1987, he was back at his Pune ashram, where thousands of foreigners soon flocked for his nightly discourses and meditation sessions.

They still come in droves. To house them all, the capacious Osho Auditorium was unveiled in 2002, which saw the centre's name being changed from 'Osho Commune International' to 'Osho International Meditation Resort'. Such is the demand for the resort's facilities that prices are continually on the rise, with luxury being redefined every day. Interestingly, despite Osho's comments on how nobody should be poor, no money generated by the resort goes into helping the disadvantaged. That, resort authorities maintain, is up to someone else.

Within the main palace, you can peek into the room where Gandhi used to stay. Photos and paintings exhibit moments in his extraordinary career, but it's poorly presented.

Shaniwar Wada
FORT

(Shivaji Rd; Indian/foreigner ₹5/100; ⊘8am-6pm) The remains of this fortressed palace of the Peshwa rulers are located in the old part of the city. Built in 1732, Shaniwar Wada was destroyed in a fire in 1828, but the massive walls and plinths remain, as do the sturdy palace doors with their daunting spikes. In the evenings, there is an hour-long **sound-and-light show** (admission ₹25; ⊘8.15pm Thu-Tue).

Katraj Snake Park & Zoo
ZOO

(Pune–Satara Hwy; adult/child ₹3/2; ⊘10.30am-6pm Thu-Tue) There's a mediocre selection of Indian wildlife on show at the Katraj Snake Park & Zoo. But a trip to this faraway park on Pune's southern outskirts makes sense if you want to know more about snakes, of which there are plenty.

Pataleshvara Cave Temple
TEMPLE

(Jangali Maharaj Rd; ⊘6am-9.30pm) Set across the river is the curious rock-cut Pataleshvara Cave Temple, a small and unfinished (though living) 8th-century temple, similar in style to the grander caves at Elephanta Island off the Mumbai coast. Adjacent is the **Jangali Maharaj Temple** (⊘6am-9.30pm), dedicated to a Hindu ascetic who died here in 1818.

Ramamani Iyengar Memorial Yoga Institute
YOGA

(☑25656134; www.bksiyengar.com; 1107 B/1 Hare Krishna Mandir Rd, Model Colony) To attend classes at this famous institute, 7km northwest of the train station, you need to have been practising yoga for at least eight years.

🛏 Sleeping

Pune's main accommodation hubs are around the train station and Koregaon Park. Most midrange hotels have check-out at noon, and accept credit cards. Some families rent out rooms starting at about ₹400 (without bathroom) to around ₹700 (with bathroom). Rickshaw drivers will know where to look.

TOP CHOICE Hotel Sunderban
HOTEL $$

(☑26124949; www.tghotels.com; 19 Koregaon Park; s/d incl breakfast from ₹2500/3000; ❀🛜) Set around a manicured lawn right next to the Osho Resort, this renovated art deco bungalow effortlessly combines classy antiquity with boutique appeal. The huge non-AC rooms in the main building sport a variety of dated furniture, and have a generally quaint air. The pricier rooms are across the lawns, in a sleek, glass-fronted building. An additional draw is the fantastic in-house fine-dining restaurant, Dario's (see p108).

TOP CHOICE Osho Meditation Resort Guesthouse
HOTEL $$$

(☑66019900; www.osho.com; Koregaon Park; s/d ₹3900/4400; ❀) This uber-chic designer place will only allow you in if you come to meditate at the Osho International Meditation Resort (p105). The rooms and common spaces in this stylish property are an elegant exercise in modern aesthetics, as minimalist as they are chic. Add to that other ultra luxe features, such as purified fresh air supply in all rooms! Be sure to book well in advance; it's perpetually rushed.

Hotel Surya Villa
HOTEL $$

(☑26124501; www.hotelsuryavilla.com; 294/2 Koregaon Park; s/d from ₹1200/1500, with AC ₹1600/2000; ❀@) A cheerful place with bright, airy and spacious rooms and squeaky-clean loos, this is clearly the best of Pune's midrange options. It stands just off the Koregaon Park backpacker hub, so you're always clued in to the coolest developments in town. There's free internet for guests at the book kiosk below.

Homeland
HOTEL $$

(☑26123203; www.hotelhomeland.net; 18 Wilson Garden; s/d ₹900/1100, with AC from ₹1300/1500; ❀) A surprisingly restful place tucked away from the din of the train station, Homeland is excellent value for money. The labyrinthine corridors lead to rooms with freshly painted walls and clean sheets, and the restaurant downstairs shows movies in the evenings.

Hotel Srimaan
HOTEL $$

(☑26136565; srimaan@vsnl.com; 361/5 Bund Garden Rd; s/d ₹2200/2900; ❀@) The fact that Srimaan has dropped its tariffs actually makes this centrally-located place quite a steal. Jackson Pollock-inspired paintings lend their colour to the small but luxurious rooms. The pricier rooms have lovely windows with soothing green views outside. A good Italian joint called La Pizzeria is available on-site.

Samrat Hotel
HOTEL $$

(☑26137964; thesamrathotel@vsnl.net; 17 Wilson Garden; s/d incl breakfast from ₹1800/2200; ❀🛜) A sparkling modern hotel with excellent rooms opening around a central, top-lit foyer, this place sure knows how to make you feel at home. The staff is courteous and eager to please, and the well-appointed rooms meet every expectation you could have from hotels in this price bracket.

Westin
HOTEL $$$

(☎67210000; www.starwoodhotels.com; 36/3B Koregaon Park Annexe; d incl breakfast from ₹6000; ❋✸❄) Sprawled out like a giant luxury yacht on Koregaon Park's eastern fringes is this mint-fresh business hotel, combining the best of luxury and leisure with impeccable service. The rooms offer lovely views of the river course below.

Hotel Ritz
HOTEL $$

(☎26122995; fax 26136644; 6 Sadhu Vaswani Path; s/d incl breakfast from ₹2550/2750; ❋) Plush, friendly, atmospheric: three words that sum it all up for the Ritz, a Raj-era building that holds its own in town. The pricey rooms are in the main building, while the cheaper ones are located in an annexe next to the garden restaurant, which serves good Gujarati and Maharashtrian food.

National Hotel
HOTEL $

(☎26125054; 14 Sasoon Rd; s/d/q ₹750/850/1100, cottages s/d/q ₹650/750/950) What the National can't provide in terms of comfort, it compensates for with antique charm. Housed in a crumbling colonial-era mansion opposite the train station, the low-end rooms in this hotel can border on suffocating, and may not match your idea of 'clean'. The cottages across the garden are more liveable, and come with tiled sit-outs.

Grand Hotel
HOTEL $

(☎26360728; grandhotelpune@gmail.com; MG Rd; d from ₹770, s without bathroom ₹290) Well, it's anything but grand at this budget address. The cheapest beds here (and in all of Pune) are a series of hole-in-the-wall cabins next to the bar. The doubles are converted family homes, not the most luxurious of their kind either. But then, look at how much you're paying, and take comfort in the fact that the patio is a great place to nurse an evening beer.

Hotel Ashirwad
HOTEL $$

(☎26128687; hotelashir@gmail.com; 16 Connaught Rd; s/d from ₹3500/4000; ❋❄) A large, smooth-moving joint, this place stands out for its well-kept (though unremarkable) rooms and the popular Akshaya vegetarian restaurant downstairs, which serves a good range of Punjabi and Mughlai fare.

Eating

Pune is a great place for those with an adventurous palate. Predictably, there are a host of well-priced, high-quality eateries, many around Koregaon Park. Unless otherwise mentioned, the following are open noon to 3pm and 7pm to 11pm daily; last orders at 10.45pm.

TOP CHOICE Malaka Spice
ASIAN FUSION $$

(Lane 5, North Main Rd, Koregaon Park; mains ₹220-250) A definitive stop on Pune's food circuit, this upscale alfresco restaurant serves mouth-watering Southeast Asian fare that is given a creative tweak or two by its star chefs. Dishes such as the squid and broccoli tauche, or the burnt garlic and shrimp rice, are simply to die for. There's a souvenir shop too, if you'd like to buy something to remember your hearty meal here.

TOP CHOICE Prem's
MULTICUISINE $$

(North Main Rd, Koregaon Park; mains ₹180-220; ⊙8am-11pm) In a quiet, tree-canopied courtyard tucked away behind a commercial block, Prem's is perfect for those lazy, beer-aided lunch sessions that great holidays are centred around. Its relaxed ambience attracts droves of loyalists throughout the day, who slouch around the tables and put away countless pints before wolfing down their 'usual' orders. The noisy sizzlers are a hit with everyone, so don't leave without trying one.

Dario's
ITALIAN $$

(Hotel Sunderban; mains ₹250-280) This bistro serves only the best of Italian cuisine, made from a selection of local organic produce and handpicked rations flown straight in from Italy. There's a yummy selection of homemade penne, gnocchi and spaghetti on offer, while dishes such as the *torta bombardino* (onion quiche with fresh salad) explode on your palate with a hundred flavours.

Flag's
MULTICUISINE $$

(G2 Metropole, Bund Garden Rd; mains ₹230-250) This super-popular place serves timeless favourites from all corners of the world with Lebanese chicken, Mongolian cauliflower, New Orleans seafood platter and *yakisoba* (fried Japanese noodles) all rubbing shoulders under one roof. There's also a super-hot lunch buffet that goes for a super-cool ₹249.

Vaishali
FAST FOOD $

(FC Rd; mains ₹40-70; ⊙10am-10pm) Old-timers can't stop raving about this institution, known for its range of delicious snacks and meals. The scrumptious *sev potato dal puri* (₹45), a favourite of locals, has fed generations of college-goers in Pune, and still garners respect across the board.

Arthur's Theme
CONTINENTAL $$

(Lane 6, North Main Rd, Koregaon Park; mains ₹200-230) Start off with Don Quixote (deep fried cheese croquettes) or Cleopatra (grilled chicken cubes), before moving on to King Morgan (tiger prawns in herbs and olive oil) or Lancelot (chicken in cranberry sauce). A wacky (and tasty) way to brush up on your history lessons.

Juice World
CAFE $

(2436/B East St; snacks ₹50-60; ⊙8am-11.30pm) As well as producing delicious fresh fruit juices and shakes, this casual cafe with outdoor seating serves inexpensive but wholesome snacks such as pizza and *pav bhaji* (spiced vegetables and bread).

The Place: Touche the Sizzler
MULTICUISINE $$

(7 Moledina Rd; mains ₹180-200) The perfect old-school eating option. A variety of smoking sizzlers, and other assorted Indian fare, is on offer at this family-style eatery in the heart of Pune's business district. The ambience is quaint (read: slightly mothballed), but the overall experience more than makes up for it.

Swiss Cheese Garden
CONTINENTAL $$

(ABC Farms; mains ₹250-300) About a kilometre east of Koregaon Park, this restaurant leads a pack of smart eateries (many advocating organic food) situated within a leafy campus called ABC Farms. The pastas and the cheese fondues are good.

🍷 Drinking & Entertainment

Pune puts a great deal of effort into its nocturnal activities, yet some pubs tend to shut up shop as quickly as they open, so ask around for the latest hot spots. Most are open from 7pm to around 1.30am.

1000 Oaks
NIGHTCLUB

(2417 East St) This one is an old favourite among Pune's tipplers, featuring a cosy pub-style bar, a compact dance floor and a charming, foliaged and moodily lit sit-out area for those who prefer it quieter. There's live music on Sundays, to go with your favourite poison.

Mocha
CAFE

(North Main Rd, Koregaon Park) This funky café with quirky decor and friendly staff features a brilliant selection of coffees from around the world, from the famed Jamaican Blue Mountain to Indian Peaberry. There are flavoured hookahs on offer too. Carry some form of ID to show at the gate.

Arc Asia
BAR

(ABC Farms) An extremely classy affair, rounding off the ABC Farms experience. A great stock of malts, scotches and beers, with groovy music on the PA.

Inox
CINEMA

(Bund Garden Rd) A state-of-the-art multiplex where you can take in the latest blockbuster from Hollywood or Mumbai.

Shopping

Pune has some good shopping options.

Bombay Store
SOUVENIRS

(322 MG Rd; ⊙10.30am-8.30pm Mon-Sat) The best spot for general souvenirs.

Pune Central
CLOTHING

(Bund Garden Rd, Koregaon Park) This glass-fronted mall is full of Western high-street labels and premium Indian tags.

Crossword
BOOKSTORE

(1st fl, Sohrab Hall, RBM Rd, ⊙10.30am-9pm) An excellent collection of fiction, nonfiction and magazines.

Either Or
CLOTHING

(24/25 Sohrab Hall, 21 Sasoon Rd; ⊙10.30am-8pm Fri-Wed) Modern designer Indian garments and accessories available at this popular boutique.

Fabindia
CLOTHING

(Sakar 10, Sasson Rd, ⊙10am-8pm) For Indian saris, silks and cottons, as well as diverse accessories and handmade products.

ℹ Information

Internet Access
You'll find several internet cafes along Pune's main thoroughfares.

Arihant Communications (North Main Rd, Koregaon Park; per hr ₹30; ⊙9am-11pm) Opposite Lane 5. Lightning-fast broadband connection.

Maps
Destination Finder (₹65) provides a great map of the city, along with some key travel information.

Money

Citibank has a 24-hour ATM on North Main Rd. HSBC dispenses cash at its main branch on Bund Garden Rd. You'll find ICICI Bank and State Bank of India ATMs at the railway station, an Axis Bank ATM on MG Rd and an HDFC Bank ATM on East St.

Thomas Cook (☑66007903; 2418 G Thimmaya Rd; ⊙9.30am-6pm Mon-Sat) Cashes travellers cheques and exchanges foreign currency.

Post

Main post office (Sadhu Vaswani Path; ⊙10am-6pm Mon-Sat)

DHL (Bund Garden Rd; ⊙10am-8pm Mon-Sat)

Tourist information

MTDC tourist office (☑26126867; I Block, Central Bldg, Dr Annie Besant Rd; ⊙10am-5.30pm Mon-Sat) Buried in a government complex south of the train station. There's also an **MTDC desk** at the train station (⊙9am-7pm Mon-Sat, to 3pm Sunday).

Travel Agencies

Rokshan Travels (☑26136304; rokshantravels @hotmail.com; 1st fl, Kumar Plaza, MG Rd; ⊙10am-6pm) These guys shine when it comes to getting you on the right bus, train or flight without a glitch. They also book taxis.

Yatra.com (☑65006748; www.yatra.com; North Main Rd; ⊙10am-7pm Mon-Sat) The city office of the reputed internet ticketing site of the same name.

ℹ Getting There & Away

Air

Airline contact information in Pune:

GoAir (airline code G8; ☑9223222111; www.goair.in)

Indian Airlines (airline code IC; ☑26052147; www.indian-airlines.nic.in; 39 Dr B Ambedkar Rd)

IndiGo (airline code 6E; ☑9910383838; www.goindigo.in)

Jet Airways (airline code 9W; ☑02239893333; www.jetairways.com; 243 Century Arcade, Narangi Baug Rd)

Kingfisher Airlines (airline code IT; ☑1800 2333131; www.flyingkingfisher.com; Gera Garden, Koregaon Rd)

SpiceJet (airline code SG; ☑1800 1803333; www.spicejet.com)

Airlines listed above fly daily from Pune to Delhi (from ₹3100, two hours), Bengaluru (from ₹2200, 1½ hours), Nagpur (from ₹2100, 1½ hours), Goa (from ₹3500, 1½ hours), Chennai (from ₹2300, 1½ hours) and hopping flights to Kolkata (from ₹3500, four hours).

Bus

Pune has three bus stands: **Pune train station stand** for Mumbai, Goa, Belgaum, Kolhapur, Mahabaleshwar and Lonavla; **Shivaji Nagar bus stand** for Aurangabad, Ahmedabad and Nasik; and **Swargate bus stand** for Sinhagad, Bengaluru and Mangalore. Deluxe buses shuttle from the train-station bus stand to Dadar (Mumbai) every hour (₹260, four hours).

Several private buses head to Panaji (Panjim) in Goa (ordinary/sleeper ₹330/450, 12 hours), Nasik (semideluxe/deluxe ₹180/280, five hours) and Aurangabad (₹170, six hours). Try **Brright Travels** (☑26114222; Connaught Rd).

Taxi

Share taxis (up to four passengers) link Pune with Mumbai airport around the clock. They leave from the **taxi stand** in front of Pune train station (per seat ₹500, 2½ hours). Several tour operators hire out long-distance taxis over days or even weeks for intrastate travelling. Try **Simran Travels** (☑26153222; North Main Rd, Koregaon Park).

Train

The computerised **booking hall** is to the left of Pune's main station building. The 7.15am *Deccan Queen*, 6.05am *Sinhagad Express* and 6.35pm *Indrayani Express* are fast commuter trains to

MAJOR TRAINS FROM PUNE

DESTINATION	TRAIN NO & NAME	FARE (₹)	DURATION (HR)	DEPARTURE
Bengaluru	16529 *Udyan Exp*	330/1232	21	11.45am
Chennai	12163 *Chennai Exp*	371/1348	19½	12.10am
Delhi	11077 *Jhelum Exp*	430/1624	27	5.20pm
Hyderabad	17031 *Hyderabad Exp*	246/910	13½	4.35pm
Mumbai CST	12124 *Deccan Queen*	67/237	3½	7.15am

Express fares are sleeper/2AC; *Deccan Queen* fares are 2nd class/chair. To calculate 1st class and other fares see p501.

Mumbai (2nd class/chair ₹67/237, 3½ hours). For other long-distance trains, see the boxed text, opposite.

ⓘ Getting Around

The airport is 8km northeast of the city, and boasts a swanky new building. An autorickshaw there costs about ₹100; a taxi is ₹250.

Autorickshaws can be found everywhere.

A ride from the train station to Koregaon Park costs about ₹35 (₹60 at night).

Turtle-paced city buses leave the PMT depot (opposite Pune train station) for Swargate (bus 4) and Shivaji Nagar (bus 5) and Koregaon Park (bus 159).

Some garages in Koregaon Park hire out motorcycles for ₹300 a day, petrol extra. The boys hanging out at Hotel Surya Villa will know where to look.

Around Pune

SINHAGAD

The ruined **Sinhagad** (admission free; ☉dawn-dusk) or Lion Fort, about 24km southwest of Pune, was wrested by Maratha leader Shivaji from the Bijapur kings in 1670. In the epic battle (where he lost his son Sambhaji), Shivaji used monitor lizards yoked with ropes to scale the fort's craggy walls. Today, it's a sad picture of its past, but worth visiting for the sweeping views.

From Sinhagad village, share jeeps (₹40) can cart you 10km to the base of the summit. Bus 50 runs frequently to Sinhagad village from Swargate (₹20, 45 minutes).

SHIVNERI

Situated 90km northwest of Pune above the village of Junnar, **Shivneri Fort** (admission free; ☉dawn-dusk) holds the distinction of being the birthplace of Shivaji. Within the ramparts of this ruined fort are the old royal stables, a mosque dating back to the Mughal era and several rock-cut reservoirs. The most important structure is Shivkunj, the pavilion in which Shivaji was born.

About 4km from Shivneri, on the other side of Junnar, is an interesting group of Hinayana Buddhist caves called **Lenyadri** (Indian/foreigner ₹5/100; ☉dawn-dusk). Of the 30-odd caves, Cave 7 is the most impressive, and interestingly houses an image of the Hindu lord Ganesh.

A bus (₹70, two hours, 7.15am) goes to Junnar from Pune's Shivaji Nagar terminus. A return bus leaves Junnar at 11.30am. A day cab from Pune will cost around ₹1600.

Mahabaleshwar

 02168 / POP 12,700 / ELEV 1372M

Up in the Western Ghats, Mahabaleshwar – founded in 1828 by British governor Sir John 'Boy' Malcolm – was, at one time, the summer capital of the Bombay presidency. However, what was once a pretty town oozing old-world charm is today a jungle of mindless urban construction. Swarms of raucous holiday-makers who throw the place into a complete tizzy only make things worse. Mahabaleshwar's only face-saver is the delightful views it offers, but they're not half as good in practice, given that you'll have to combat the riotous tourists while appreciating them.

The hill station virtually shuts down during the monsoons (June to September), when an unbelievable 6m of rain falls.

The action can be found in the main bazaar (Main Rd, also called Dr Sabane Rd) – a 200m strip of holiday tack. The bus stand is at the western end. You have to cough up a ₹20 'tourist tax' on arrival.

◉ Sights & Activities

Viewpoints   VIEWPOINT
The hills are alive with music, though it's usually blasted out of car stereos as people race to tick off all the viewpoints. To beat them, start very early in the morning, and you can savour fine views from **Wilson's Point** (Sunrise Point), within easy walking distance of town, as well as **Elphinstone**, **Babington**, **Kate's** and **Lodwick Points**.

The sunset views at **Bombay Point** are stunning; but you won't be the only one thinking so! Much quieter, thanks to being 9km from town, is **Arthur's Seat**, on the edge of a 600m cliff. Attractive waterfalls around Mahabaleshwar include **Chinaman's**, **Dhobi's** and **Lingmala Falls**. A nice walk out of town is the two-hour stroll to Bombay Point, and then following **Tiger Trail** back in (maps are available from the MTDC tourist office).

☞ Tours

Leaving the bus stand thrice from 2.15pm, the MSRTC conducts a Mahabaleshwar sightseeing round (₹80, 4½ hours) taking in nine viewpoints plus Old Mahabaleshwar. Alternatively, taxi drivers will give a three-hour tour for about ₹500. Tours are also available to lookout points south of town (₹400, 2½ hours), Panchgani (₹450, three hours) and Pratapgad Fort (₹500, three hours).

🍴 Sleeping & Eating

Hotel prices soar during weekends and peak holidays (November to June). At other times you might get hefty discounts. Most hotels are around the main bazaar, while dozens of resort-style lodges are scattered around the village. Check out is usually at 8am or 9am.

Hotel Panorama HOTEL $$
(☏260404; www.panoramaresorts.net; Main Rd; d with/without AC from ₹3500/3000; ❄☀) Business meets leisure at Mahabaleshwar's most reputed midtown luxury address. Very professionally managed, it boasts clean, comfy and tastefully appointed rooms, and there's some great grub at the restaurant. There's a dunk-sized pool, and a water channel where you might want to ride swan-headed paddle boats.

MTDC Resort HOTEL $
(☏260318; Bombay Point Rd; d from ₹700) This large-scale operation is situated about 2km southwest from town, and comes with quieter and greener surroundings. Rooms smack of government aesthetics, but it's cheap, so all's forgiven. Taxis can drop you here from the city centre for about ₹80.

Hotel Vyankatesh HOTEL $$
(☏260575; hotelvkt@yahoo.com; Main Rd; d ₹1500) A typically overpriced hotel cashing in on Mahabaleshwar's never-ending tourism boom. Located behind a souvenir store, this place has slightly dreary rooms, but so have lots of hotels around town.

TOP CHOICE Grapevine MULTICUISINE $$
(Masjid Rd; mains ₹140-160) Skip this place, and you've missed half the fun in town. Tucked pleasantly away behind the main drag, this tiny eatery serves a delectable range of Indian, Continental and Thai dishes, along with some excellent Parsi fare including the signature *dhansak*. A charming wrought-iron table set-up tastefully lends the interiors a Mediterranean air, and the restaurant also boasts a smart wine list to complement your food.

Hotel Rajmahal INDIAN $
(Main Rd; mains ₹50-70) A good place to dig into some lip-smacking veg delights.

Aman Restaurant INDIAN $
(Main Rd; mains ₹80-100) Little more than a roadside stall, Aman can pull out some amazing kebabs and other meaty bites.

ℹ Information

State Bank of India (Main Rd; ⊙11am-5pm Mon-Fri, 11am-1pm Sat) Handles foreign currency.

Bank of Baroda Has an ATM on Masjid Rd.

RB Travels (☏260251; Main Rd) Local tours, ticketing, taxi hire and bus services.

Joshi's Newspaper Agency (Main Rd; per hr ₹50; ⊙10am-7pm) Slow internet access.

MTDC tourist office (☏260318; Bombay Point Rd) At the MTDC Resort south of town.

ℹ Getting There & Away

From the **bus stand** state buses leave regularly for Pune (semideluxe ₹123, 3½ hours) via Panchgani (₹15, 30 minutes). There's one ordinary bus to Goa (₹274, eight hours, 8.30am) via Kolhapur (₹139, five hours), while seven buses ramble off to Mumbai Central Station (ordinary/semideluxe ₹174/234, seven hours).

Private agents in the bazaar book luxury buses to destinations within Maharashtra, and Goa (seat/sleeper ₹600/800, 12 hours, with a changeover at Surur). Remember to ask where they intend to drop you. Buses to Mumbai (₹450, 6½ hours) generally don't go beyond Borivali, while those bound for Pune (₹230) will bid you adieu at Swargate.

ℹ Getting Around

Taxis and Maruti vans near the bus stand will take you to the main viewpoints or to Panchgani; you can haggle.

Cycling is also an option, but be careful of speeding traffic especially on the outskirts. Bikes can be hired from **Vasant Cycle Mart** (Main Rd; ⊙8am-8pm) for ₹50 per day.

ℹ SOLO BLUES

If you're a single traveller, do not schedule a night in Mahabaleshwar. Local laws bar hotels from renting out rooms to loners, especially men. Make sure you have an early departure plan in place, even if you visit for the day.

Around Mahabaleshwar

PRATAPGAD FORT

The windy **Pratapgad Fort** (maintenance fee ₹5; ⊙7am-7pm), built by Shivaji in 1656, straddles a high mountain ridge 24km west of Mahabaleshwar. In 1659, Shivaji agreed to meet Bijapuri General Afzal Khan here, in an attempt to end a stalemate. Despite

BERRIES, ANYONE?

Fruity Mahabaleshwar is India's berry-growing hub, producing some of the country's finest strawberries, raspberries and gooseberries. Harvested from November to June, the best crops come around February and can be bought fresh at Mahabaleshwar's bazaar. You can also pick up fruit drinks, sweets, squashes, fudges or jams from reputed farms such as **Mapro Gardens** (☑02168240112; ⊙10am-1pm & 2pm-6.30pm), halfway between Mahabaleshwar and Panchgani.

a no-arms agreement, Shivaji, upon greeting Khan, disembowelled his enemy with a set of iron *baghnakh* (tiger's claws). Khan's tomb (out of bounds) marks the site of this painful encounter at the base of the fort.

Pratapgad is reached by a 500-step climb that affords brilliant views. Guides are available for ₹150. The state bus (₹80 return, one hour, 9.30am) does a daily shuttle from Mahabaleshwar, with a waiting time of around one hour. A return taxi ride is about ₹500.

RAIGAD FORT

Some 80km from Mahabaleshwar, all alone on a high and remote hilltop, stands the enthralling **Raigad Fort** (Indian/foreigner ₹5/100; ⊙8am-5.30pm). Having served as Shivaji's capital from 1648 until his death in 1680, the fort was later sacked by the British, and some colonial structures added. But monuments such as the royal court, plinths of royal chambers, the main marketplace and Shivaji's tomb still remain, and it's worth a daylong excursion.

You can hike a crazy 1475 steps to the top. But for a more 'levitating' experience, take the vertigo-inducing **ropeway** (⊙8.30am-5.30pm), which zooms up the cliff and offers an eagle-eye view of the deep gorges below. A return ticket costs ₹160. Guides (₹200) are available within the fort complex. **Sarja Restaurant** (mains ₹30), adjoining the ropeway's base terminal, is a good place for lunch or snacks.

Public transport to Raigad is infrequent, so it's best to hire a cab at Mahabaleshwar (₹1300). Squeeze both Pratapgad and Raigad into your day's itinerary, and you've got a deal.

Kolhapur

☑0231 / POP 505,500 / ELEV 550M

A rarely-visited town, Kolhapur is the perfect place to get up close and personal with the flamboyant side of India. Only a few

hours from Goa, this historic town boasts an intensely fascinating temple complex and a friendly population. In August, Kolhapur is at its vibrant best, when **Naag Panchami**, a snake-worshipping festival, is held in tandem with one at Pune. Gastronomes take note: the town is also the birthplace of the famed, spicy Kolhapuri cuisine, especially chicken and mutton dishes.

The old town around the Mahalaxmi Temple is 3km southwest of the bus and train stations, while the 'new' palace is a similar distance to the north. Rankala Lake, a popular spot for evening strolls, is 5km southwest of the stations.

⊙ Sights

TOP CHOICE **Shree Chhatrapati Shahu Museum**   MUSEUM

(Indian/foreigner ₹13/30; ⊙9.30am-5.30pm) 'Bizarre' takes on a whole new meaning at this 'new' palace, an Indo-Saracenic behemoth designed by British architect 'Mad' Charles Mant for the Kolhapur kings in 1884. The ground floor houses a madcap museum, featuring countless trophies from the eponymous king's trigger-happy jungle safaris, which were put to some ingenious uses, including walking sticks made from leopard vertebrae, and ashtrays fashioned out of tiger skulls and rhino feet. Then, there's an armoury, which houses enough weapons to stage a mini coup. The horror-house effect is brought full circle by the taxidermy section. However, don't forget to visit the durbar hall, a rather ornate affair, where the kings once held court sessions. Photography is strictly prohibited.

Old Town   AREA

Kolhapur's atmospheric old town is built around the lively and colourful **Mahalaxmi Temple** (⊙5am-10.30pm) dedicated to Amba Bai, or the Mother Goddess. The temple's origins date back to AD 10, and it's one of the most important Amba Bai temples in India. Non-Hindus are welcome. Nearby, past a foyer in the Old Palace, is **Bhavani Mandap** (◷6am-8pm), dedicated to the goddess Bhavani.

Kolhapur is famed for the calibre of its wrestlers and at the **Motibag Thalim**, a courtyard beside the entrance to Bhavani Mandap, young athletes train in a muddy pit. You are free to walk in and watch, as long as you don't mind the sight of sweaty, semi-naked men and the stench of urine emanating from the loos. Professional matches are held between June and December in the **Kasbagh Maidan**, a red-earth arena a short walk south of Motibag Thalim.

Shopaholics, meanwhile, can browse for the renowned Kolhapuri leather sandals, prized the world over for their intricate needlework. Most designs are priced from ₹300 to ₹500. The break-in blisters on your feet come free.

🛏 Sleeping & Eating

Hotel Tourist   HOTEL $
(◹2650421; www.hoteltourist.co.in; Station Rd; s/d incl breakfast from ₹700/900; ❋) Recently given a facelift, this is one of the nicest places on the main street, and is acclaimed for its excellent service. Cosy though minimalist rooms offer great value (especially the AC ones), and there's an excellent restaurant serving great veg food.

Hotel Pavillion   HOTEL $$
(◹2652751; www.hotelpavillion.co.in; 392 Assembly Rd; s/d ₹950/1150, with AC from ₹1300/1450; ❋@) Located at the far end of a leafy park-cum-office area, this place guarantees a peaceful stay in large, clean rooms with windows that open out to delightful views of seasonal blossoms. It's very close to the MTDC office.

Hotel Pearl   HOTEL $$
(◹6684451; hotelpearl@yahoo.com; New Shahupuri; s/d incl breakfast from ₹1900/2100; ❋@) Modelled on big-city business hotels, this place has good rooms, a spa, a travel desk and a decent multicuisine restaurant.

Surabhi   INDIAN $
(Hotel Sahyadri Bldg; mains ₹70-80) A great place to savour Kolhapur's legendary snacks such as the spicy *misal* (similar to *bhelpuri*), thalis and lassi. Saawan Dining Hall, located alongside, serves non-veg food.

🛈 Information

Axis Bank has a 24-hour ATM near Mahalaxmi Temple.

SBI has a 24-hour ATM on Indumati Rd, parallel to Station Rd.

Internet Zone (Kedar Complex, Station Rd; per hr ₹20; ◷8am-11pm) Internet access.

MTDC tourist office (◹2652935; Assembly Rd; ◷10am-5.30pm Mon-Sat) Opposite the Collector's Office.

State Bank of India (Udyamnagar; ◷10am-2pm Mon-Sat) A short autorickshaw ride southwest of the train station near Hutatma Park. Handles foreign exchange.

🛈 Getting There & Around

Autorickshaws are abundant in Kolhapur and most drivers are honest with their billing. Most carry conversion charts to calculate fares from outdated meters.

From the **bus stand**, services head regularly to Pune (semideluxe/deluxe ₹228/390, five hours) and Ratnagiri (ordinary/semideluxe ₹100/135, four hours). Most private bus agents are on the western side of the square at Mahalaxmi Chambers, across from the bus stand. Overnight services with AC head to Mumbai (seat/sleeper ₹380/650, nine hours) and non-AC overnighters go to Panaji (₹210, 5½ hours).

The **train station** is 10 minutes' walk west of the bus stand. Three daily expresses, including the 10.50pm *Sahyadri Express,* zoom to Mumbai (sleeper/2AC ₹227/832, 13 hours) via Pune (₹161/574, eight hours). The *Rani Chennama Express* makes the long voyage to Bengaluru (sleeper/2AC ₹294/1097, 17½ hours, 2.20pm).

Services at Kolhapur airport were suspended in mid-2010 due to safety concerns.

Goa

Best Places to Eat

» Upper House (p125)

» Le Poisson Rouge (p136)

» Thalassa (p142)

» Seasonal beach shacks (all over)

» Plantain Leaf (p136)

Best Places to Stay

» Nilaya Hermitage (p136)

» Mayfair Hotel (p124)

» Marbella Guest House (p132)

» Backwoods Camp (p130)

» Dunes (p144)

Why Go?

It's green, it's glistening and it's gorgeous: just three of the reasons why Goa has allured travellers for decades. Two million visitors come each year for the silken sand, crystalline shores, cocohut culture and *susegad* – a Portuguese-derived term that translates loosely to 'laid-backness'.

But there's more to discover here than the pleasure of warm sand between your toes. Goa is as beautiful and culturally rich as it is tiny and hassle-free, so you can go bird-watching in a butterfly-filled forest, marvel at centuries-old cathedrals, venture out to white-water waterfalls or meander the capital's charming alleyways, all in between lazy beach days (or weeks). Pour in a dash of Portuguese-influenced food and architecture, infuse with a colourful blend of religious traditions, pepper with parties, and you've got a heady mix that makes Goa easy to enjoy and extremely hard to leave.

When to Go
Goa (Panaji)

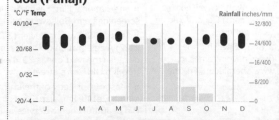

Early Nov The rains are over and the waterfalls are full – but the beaches aren't.

Early Dec Festivals galore and great weather, just before the high-peak prices and crowds.

Mar Carnival. Enough said.

MAIN POINTS OF ENTRY

Tiny Dabolim Airport handles all flights, Margao Railway Station is the state's largest and best connected, and Mapusa and Panaji bus terminals are your best bet for long-distance rides.

Fast Facts

» Population: 1.5 million

» Area: 3701 sq km

» Capital: Panaji (Panjim)

» Telephone code: ☎0832

» Main languages: Konkani, Marathi, English and Hindi

» Sleeping prices: **$** below ₹1000, **$$** ₹1000 to ₹2500, **$$$** above ₹2500

Top Tip

Don't swim wasted! And stay away during Christmas and New Year's, when the parties are raging but so are the prices and the hordes.

Resources

» Goa Tourism (www.goa-tourism.com) Good background and tour info.

» Goa World (www.goa-world.com) General info on Goan culture.

» Goa's English dailies (www.navhindtimes.in, www.oheraldo.in) For the news.

Food

Goans tend to be hearty meat and fish eaters, and fresh seafood is a staple, as is the quintessential Goan lunch 'fish-curry-rice': fried mackerel steeped in coconut, tamarind and chilli sauce. The good, genuine cooking can be hard to find in the tourist areas, but hunt around and you'll be rewarded with your best souvenir: memories of a stellar vindaloo (fiery dish in a marinade of vinegar and garlic) or *xacuti* (a spicy chicken or meat dish cooked in red coconut sauce).

DON'T MISS

There's little chance of missing the **beach** – it's spectacular and it's everywhere – but don't give in to the temptation to laze on it nonstop. **Yoga** is ubiquitous in Goa – in both long-course and short-class form – and even for dabblers, it's the perfect yin to beach-lounging's yang. Palolem has lots of **trekking** and even canyoning opportunities, and **birds**, **forests** and **waterfalls** are just waiting to be enjoyed inland. Goa has a fascinating **history** that also shouldn't be missed: set aside some time to explore evocative Panaji (Panjim), Old Goa, Quepem and Chandor.

Top State Festivals

» Feast of the Three Kings (6 Jan, Chandor, p147) Boys re-enact the story of the three kings bearing gifts for Christ.

» Shigmotsav (Shigmo) of Holi (Feb/Mar, statewide) Goa's version of the Hindu festival Holi sees coloured powders thrown about and parades in most towns.

» Sabado Gordo (Feb/Mar, Panaji, p120) A procession of floats and street parties on the Saturday before Lent.

» Carnival (Mar, statewide) A four-day festival kicking off Lent; the party's particularly jubilant in Panaji.

» Fama de Menino Jesus (2nd Mon in Oct, Colva, p150) Colva's Menino Jesus statue is paraded through town.

» International Film Festival of India (Nov, Panaji, p120) Film screenings and Bollywood glitterati everywhere.

» Feast of St Francis Xavier (3 Dec, Panaji, p120, Old Goa, p127) A celebration of Goa's patron saint; once every decade (the next one is 2014), the saint's body is carried through Old Goa's streets.

» Feast of Our Lady of the Immaculate Conception (8 Dec, Margao, p145, Panaji, p120) Fairs and concerts are held, as is a beautiful church service at Panaji's Church of Our Lady of the Immaculate Conception.

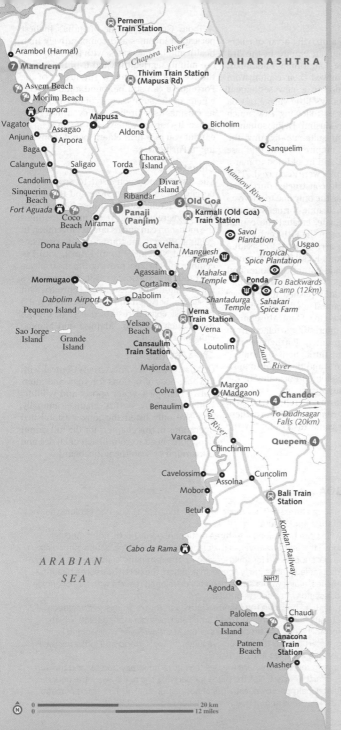

Goa Highlights

1 Wander the Portuguese quarters of **Panaji** (Panjim; p120) and linger over lunch at one of its ravishing restaurants

2 Indulge in barefoot luxury on quiet white-sand **beaches** in the state's sleepy southern stretches

3 Open up your chakras while doing **yoga** to the rhythm of ocean waves and swaying palms

4 Dream of times gone by in the mansions of **Quepem** (p149) and **Chandor** (p147)

5 Shiver in the shadows of grand cathedrals and observe the countryside from a hilltop chapel in **Old Goa** (p127)

6 Feel the wind in your hair while you **ride your bicycle or scooter** through palm-tree jungles and rice-paddy fields

7 Worship the sun away from the northern crowds on the beautiful beach at **Mandrem** (p143)

History

Goa went through a dizzying array of rulers from Ashoka's Mauryan empire in the 3rd century BC to the long-ruling Kadambas, who in AD 1054 moved their capital from present-day Chandor to a new settlement called Govepuri, today's little village of Goa Velha. The centuries following saw much conflict, with the Muslim Delhi sultanate and then Bahmani sultanate fighting the Hindu Vijayanagar empire for control; these were violent times, and in addition to many, deaths, Hindu temples were also razed. (Tiny Tambdi Surla temple, constructed during the Kadamba reign, was the only one to survive.) The Adil Shahs of Bijapur, formerly part of the Bahmani sultanate, created the capital we now call Old Goa in the 15th century.

The Portuguese arrived in 1510, seeking control of the region's lucrative spice routes by way of Goa's wide natural harbours and plentiful waterways. They defeated the Bijapur kings and steadily pushed their power from their grand capital at Old Goa out into the provinces. (The Goa State Museum in Panaji has lots of interesting artefacts from this period.) Soon after, Portuguese rule and religion spread throughout the state – sometimes by force – and the Goan Inquisition brought repression and brutality in the name of Christianity. It was not until 1961, when the Indian army marched into Goa, that almost five centuries of Portuguese occupation finally came to an end on the subcontinent.

Today Goa enjoys one of India's highest per-capita incomes and comparatively high health and literacy rates, with tourism, iron-ore mining, agriculture and fishing forming the basis of its economy. The legacy of the Portuguese can still be found almost everywhere, in the state's scores of old mansions, its cuisine, its churches and even in its language; it's rare nowadays, but if you keep an ear out you may hear elderly people conversing in Portuguese.

Climate

The annual monsoon used to scour Goa's beaches clean between June and the end of September reliably, but things have gone a little haywire in recent years, and sometimes the monsoon can end as late as November. In general, though, the tourist season stretches from mid-November to mid-April, with December to February proving the most pleasant (and busiest) time to visit. Temperatures and humidity increase after February. Out of season, between April and October, you'll find most coastal resorts deserted, though towns such as Panaji, Mapusa and Margao chug on as usual.

🏃 Activities

Goa has, of late, become Activity Central, with a whole host of options for yoga and alternative therapies, water sports and wildlife-watching. Many outfits change annually, so we've only listed the longer-established operations in this chapter; for the full gamut of options, head to your beach of choice and ask around or scan the noticeboards.

WHERE TO GOA...

Goa is tiny. With enough time (and discipline to get off the beach), you can explore the state's beaches, nature *and* culture.

Very generally, Goa can be split up into three distinct regions: north, south and central. The north, above the Mandovi River, is the place for those seeking action, shopping and activities in equal supply, and for folks looking for the remnants – and they are only remnants – of Goa's fabled trance party scene. In addition, the north has some beautiful almost-empty beaches, along with a string of highly developed resorts with lots of choice in restaurants, hotels and water-sports outfits.

In central Goa, nestling between the Mandovi and Zuari Rivers, things get decidedly more cultural. Here sits Panaji (Panjim), Goa's small and loveable state capital, which slings itself comfortably along the broad banks of the Mandovi River, while inland lie spice plantations, waterfalls and the glorious vestiges of Goa's grand and glittering past in the form of mansions, temples and cathedrals.

Things slow down in the south, where the beaches grow generally quieter and the sun lounges are spaced further apart. Not the place for partying the night away, the beaches here cater to a quieter, calmer crowd, with lots of homespun charm. This is the place to sit back, unwind, and perhaps spot a hatching turtle or two.

YOGA & ALTERNATIVE THERAPIES

Every imaginable form of yoga, meditation, reiki, ayurvedic massage and other spiritually orientated health regime is practised, taught and relished in Goa. Palolem and Patnem, in the south of the state, and Arambol (Harmal), Mandrem, Anjuna and Calangute in the north all have courses in ayurveda, yoga, reiki and the like. Mandrem and Arambol have reputable yoga centres, and Calangute has an excellent ayurveda clinic.

WILDLIFE-WATCHING

Goa is a nature lover's paradise, perfect for wildlife-watching, with an abundance of brilliant birdlife and a fine (but well concealed) collection of fauna, including sambars, barking deer and the odd leopard. Head to Cotigao Wildlife Sanctuary to scout out birds and beasts alike, or to Backwoods Camp. Day Tripper in Calangute offers various nature-related tours, while John's Boat Tours in Candolim runs birdwatching boat trips, along with crocodile- and dolphin-spotting rides. At almost any beach, though, you'll find someone with a boat eager to show you those adorable grey mammals of the sea.

WATER SPORTS

Based in Baga, Barracuda Diving, offers scuba-diving courses and trips. Parasailing and jet-skiing are readily available on the beaches at Baga, Benaulim and Colva, and you can try paragliding at Anjuna and Arambol.

Dangers & Annoyances

One of the greatest – and most deceptive – dangers in Goa is to be found right in front of your beautiful bit of beach: the Arabian Sea, with its strong currents and dangerous undertows, claims dozens of lives per year, many of them foreigners who knew how to swim. Though some of Goa's beaches are now overseen by lifeguards during daylight hours, it's extremely important to heed local warnings on the safety of swimming, and don't, whatever you do, venture into the water after drinking or taking drugs.

Other dangers and annoyances are of the rather more universal kind. Keep your valuables under lock and key, especially if you're renting an easy-to-penetrate cocohut, and don't walk along empty stretches of beach alone at night.

DRUGS

Acid, ecstasy, cocaine, charas (hashish), marijuana and all other forms of recreational drugs are illegal in India (though still very much available in Goa), and purchasing or carrying drugs is fraught with danger. Goa's Fort Aguada jail is filled with prisoners, including some foreigners, serving lengthy sentences for drug offences, and being caught in possession of even a small quantity of illegal substances can mean a 10-year stay in a cockroach-infested cell.

ℹ Information

The **Goa Tourism Development Corporation** (GTDC; www.goa-tourism.com) provides maps and information, operates (not-great) hotels throughout the state and runs a host of one-day and multiday tours. Its main office is in Panaji, but you can book its tours and get a simple map of Goa at any of its hotel branches. Panaji's Indiatourism office also has information on Goa.

ACCOMMODATION Accommodation prices in Goa are generally higher than in most other states of India and vary wildly depending on the season. High-season prices, often more than twice the mid-season rates, run from early December to early February, while prices climb higher still during the crowded Christmas and New Year period (around 22 December to 3 January). Mid-season runs from the end of October through November (when most beach shacks are just being built) and from February to April, and low season runs through the rainy season (April to October). All accommodation rates listed in this chapter are for the high season. Note, however, that prices can fluctuate incredibly from year to year, and some hotels may bump up their high-season tariffs more than others. Always call ahead for rates. In addition, the Goan government levies a hotel tax of either 5% (for rooms costing less than ₹750), 7% (₹750 to ₹1500), 10% (₹1500 to ₹3000) or 12% (over ₹3000).

Most accommodation options have a standard noon checkout, except in Panaji, where most hotels cruelly demand you depart at 9am.

ℹ Getting There & Away

AIR Goa's sole and diminutive airport, Dabolim, is in the centre of the state, 29km south of Panaji, 30km north of Margao and an easy taxi or bus ride from any of the state's beaches. Few international flights go here directly; those that do are package-holiday charters, mostly from Russia and Britain. Independent travellers from the UK could check **Thomson** (www.thomsonfly.com), and from Germany, **Condor** (www.condor.com);

ℹ DIAL 108 IN EMERGENCIES

In any emergency in Goa, dial 108. This will connect you to the police, fire brigade or medical services.

both offer flight-only fares. Generally, the quickest way to reach Goa from overseas is to take a flight into Mumbai (Bombay), and then a one-hour hop by domestic airline down to Goa. There are lots of domestic flights each day, starting from around ₹3500 (cheaper if you book well in advance).

Dabolim Airport has a money-exchange office, a GTDC counter, charter-airline offices, an ATM and two prepaid taxi booths.

BUS Plenty of long-distance interstate buses – both 'government' and 'private' – operate to and from Panaji, Margao, Mapusa and Chaudi, near Palolem. Fares for private operators are higher than for government buses, and they fluctuate throughout the year; in peak season, they can be triple the price of the state operators. (Some would say that they're also three times more comfortable, but this isn't always the case.) A tip for overnight journeys: sleeper buses, counter-intuitively, can be less comfortable than seaters. The seats keep you from getting tossed around with every bump and turn.

TRAIN The **Konkan Railway** (www.konkan railway.com), the main train line running through Goa, runs between Mumbai and Mangalore. Its biggest station in Goa is Margao's Madgaon station, from which there are several useful daily services to Mumbai. Other smaller, useful stations on the line include Pernem for Arambol, Thivim for Mapusa and the northern beaches, Karmali (Old Goa) for Panaji, and Canacona for Palolem.

Other train lines out of Margao head to Chennai; Pune; Ahmedabad (Amdavad) and Vadodara (Baroda) in Gujarat; Ernakulam (for Kochi) and Thiruvananthapuram (Trivandrum) in Kerala; Hubli in Karnataka and even Delhi.

Book tickets online (see p500); at Madgaon station; at the train reservation office at Panaji's Kadamba bus stand; or at any travel agent vending train tickets (though you'll probably pay a small commission). Only the stations at Margao and Vasco da Gama (near Dabolim Airport) have foreign-tourist-quota booking counters. Make sure you book as far in advance as possible for sleepers, since they fill up very quickly.

See p148 for detailed train information.

ⓘ Getting Around

TO/FROM THE AIRPORT Dabolim's two pre-paid taxi counters – one in the arrivals hall and the other just outside – make arriving easy; buy your ticket here and you'll be ushered to a cab.
BUS Goa has an extensive network of buses, shuttling to and from almost every town and village. They run frequently and have no numbers, and fares rarely exceed ₹30. Buses are in fairly good condition and tend to be pretty efficient operations.
CAR & MOTORCYCLE It's easy in Goa to organise a private car with a driver for long-distance day trips. Prices vary, but you should bank on

paying from ₹1000 (if you're lucky) to ₹1500 for a full day out on the road (usually defined as eight hours and 80km). It's also possible, if you have the nerves and the skills, to procure a self-drive car. A small Maruti will cost from ₹600 to ₹900 per day and a jeep around ₹1000, excluding petrol; there are few organised rental outlets, so ask around for someone with a car willing to rent it to you. Note the slightly mystifying signposts posted on Goa's major National Highway 17 (NH17), which advise of different speed limits (on the largely single-carriageway road) for different types of vehicles.

You'll rarely go far on a Goan road without seeing a tourist whizzing by on a scooter or motorbike, and renting (if not driving) one is a breeze. You'll likely pay from ₹200 to ₹300 per day for a scooter, ₹400 for a smaller Yamaha motorbike, and ₹500 for a Royal Enfield Bullet. These prices can drop considerably if you're renting for more than a day or if it's an off-peak period.

Bear in mind that Goan roads are treacherous, filled with human, bovine, canine, feline, mechanical and avian obstacles, as well as a good sprinkling of potholes and hairpin bends. Take it slowly, try not to drive at night (when black cows can prove dangerous), don't attempt a north–south day trip on a 50CC scooter, and the most cautious of riders might even consider donning a helmet, which is technically the law.

TAXI Taxis are widely available for town-hopping, and, as with a chauffeured car, a full day's sightseeing, depending on the distance, will be around ₹1500. Motorcycles, known as 'pilots', are also a licensed form of taxi in Goa. They're cheap, easy to find, and can be identified by a yellow front mudguard – and even the heftiest of backpacks seem to be no obstacle.

CENTRAL GOA

Panaji (Panjim)

POP 98,915

Panaji (more commonly known as Panjim) has yellow houses with purple doors, cats lying in front of bicycles parked beneath oyster-shell windows, and paddle-wheel boats moseying along the river that laps the city's northern boundary. Oh, and a giant church on a hill that looks like a fancy white wedding cake. It's a friendly, manageable and walkable city – maybe India's cutest capital – and its Portuguese-era colonial charms make it a perfect place to while away a day or two. Stroll the peaceful streets, take a kitschy river cruise, eat vindaloos and end the evening in a cosy local bar.

WHEN IN ROME...

Venture beyond the tourist areas and you're sure to find a Goan who will sadly shake their heads and say that Goa has changed for the worse. The spread of serious drug use among locals, overdevelopment and environmental damage, and Goa's growing reputation within India as a place for bad behaviour are the dark underbelly to its tropical paradise. You can help repair Goa's image by following a few simple steps:

» Away from the beaches, adopt the same, more modest dress that you would in other parts of the country. This generally means shoulders and knees covered, and keeping your shirts on. Nude or topless sunbathing was recently banned in Goa and can result in fines.

» Keep your naughtiest behaviour confined to appropriate venues. Partying into the night with illegal substances at a family guesthouse might disturb the owners, though they may not say anything.

» Women should be cautious when partying; rape, sadly, is on the rise in Goa, and though we don't believe (as many do) that bikinis are to blame, it makes sense to be in control of your surroundings.

Panaji's also a natural base for exploring Goa's historic hinterland, and if the timing's right, the place to be for its many festivals, which include the street party that is **Sabado Gordo** on the Saturday before Lent, a madcap **Carnival**, and, in December, the **Feast of St Francis Xavier** and the **Feast of Our Lady of the Immaculate Conception**. If you happen to be here in November, Panaji is also host to the excellent **International Film Festival of India** (www.iffi.gov.in, www.iffigoa.org), India's largest and most glittering film festival. Panajimites know how to throw a festival – but they also know how to nap: the city mostly shuts down between 1pm and 3pm.

◉ Sights & Activities

Panaji is a city of long, leisurely strolls, through the sleepy Portuguese-era Sao Tomé, Fontainhas and Altinho districts, for a spot of shopping on 18th June Rd, and down along the languid Mandovi River.

Church of Our Lady of the Immaculate Conception
CHURCH

Panaji's spiritual and geographical centre is its gleamingly picturesque main church, consecrated in 1541. When Panaji was little more than a sleepy fishing village, this place was the first port of call for sailors from Lisbon, who would clamber up here to thank their lucky stars for a safe crossing before continuing to Old Goa, the state's capital until the 19th century, further east up the river.

If your visit coincides with 8 December, be sure to call in for the Feast of Our Lady of the Immaculate Conception, which sees a special church service and a lively fair spilling away from the church to mark the date.

FREE Goa State Museum
MUSEUM

(☑2438006; www.goamuseum.nic.in; EDC Complex, Patto; ◷9.30am-5.30pm Mon-Sat) This large museum, in a strangely uncentral area southwest of the Kadamba bus stand, has a sleepy feel and an intriguing hodgepodge of exhibits. In addition to the usual Hindu and Jain sculptures and bronzes, the museum has a good collection of wooden Christian sculptures, a room devoted to the history of print in Goa (replete with hulking, old-school presses), an exhibition on Goa's freedom fighters, and a few nice examples of Portuguese-era furniture, including an elaborately carved table used during the notoriously brutal Portuguese Inquisition in Goa.

Houses of Goa Museum
MUSEUM

(☑2411276; Torda; adult/child ₹100/25; ◷10.30am-7.30pm Tue-Sun) This little museum was created by a well-known local architect, Gerard da Cunha, to illuminate the history of Goan architecture. Interesting displays on building practices and European and local design will change the way you see those old Goan homes, apparent statewide in various states of glory and decrepitude. Next door is the **Mario Gallery** (☑2410711; admission free; ◷10am-5.30pm Mon-Fri, to 1pm Sat), with works by one of India's favourite cartoonists, Mario Miranda. The museum and gallery are north of Panaji in the Torda neighbourhood. To get here, take a Mapusa-bound bus and get off at Okukora Circle, also known as Kokeru; a rickshaw from here and back, including waiting time, costs ₹100. From Panaji, a taxi or rickshaw will cost you about ₹300 one-way.

Panaji (Panjim)

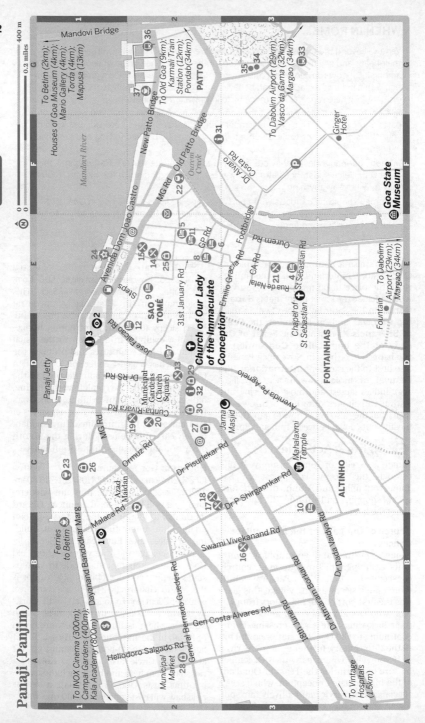

GOA CENTRAL GOA

To INOX Cinema (300m);
Campal Gardens (400m);
Kala Academy (800m)

Ferries
to Betim

To Betim (2km);
Houses of Goa Museum (4km);
Mario Gallery (4km);
Torda (4km);
Mapusa (13km)

Mandovi Bridge

Mandovi River

Panaji Jetty

Dayanand Bandodkar Marg

MG Rd

Heliodoro Salgado Rd

Municipal
Market

Azad
Maidan

Malaca Rd

Ormuz Rd

General Bernado Guedes Rd

Gen Costa Alvares Rd

Swami Vivekanand Rd

Dr P Shirgaonkar Rd

Dr Pisurlekar Rd

Cunha-Rivara Rd

Dr RS Rd

Municipal
Gardens
(Church
Square)

Jose Falcão Rd

Avenida Dom João Castro

Steps

SAO
TOMÉ

31st January Rd

Church of Our Lady
of the Immaculate
Conception

Emilio Gracia Rd

Rua de Natal

Jama
Masjid

Mahalaxmi
Temple

ALTINHO

FONTAINHAS

Chapel of
St Sebastian

St Sebastian Rd

CA Rd

Ourem Rd

Avenida Pe Agnelo

18th June Rd

Dr Atmaram Borkar Rd

Dr Dada Vaidya Rd

To Vintage
Hospitals
(1.5km)

New Patto Bridge

Old Patto Bridge

Ourem Creek

MG Rd

GP Rd

Footbridge

PATTO

To Old Goa (9km);
Karmali Train
Station (12km);
Pondad(34km)

Dr Alvaro
Costa Rd

Ginger
Hotel

P

Fountain

To Dabolim
Airport (29km);
Margao (34km)

To Dabolim Airport (29km);
Vasco da Gama (32km);
Margao (34km)

Goa State
Museum

1
2
3
5
11
6
8
4
21
14
15
24
25
9
12
7
13
29
30
32
20
27
19
26
23
17
18
16
10
22
31
36
37
35
34
33
28

400 m
0.2 miles

N

Secretariat Building HISTORIC BUILDING
(Avenida Dom Joao Castro) This colonial-era
building is on the site of Bijapur Sultan Yusef
Adil Shah's summer palace. The current structure dates from the 16th century and became
the Portuguese viceroy's official residence in
1759. Nowadays it houses less exciting government offices but is worth a gaze as the oldest,
and one of the prettiest, buildings in town,
though it may still be under renovation when
you visit. Immediately to the west, the com-
pelling **statue** of a man bearing down upon
a supine female form depicts Abbé Faria, a
Goan priest, 'father of hypnotism' and friend
of Napoleon, in melodramatic throes.

Menezes Braganza Institute HISTORIC BUILDING
(Malaca Rd) This beautiful early 20th-century
affair is worth dropping into to see the pretty blue-and-white *azulejos* (glazed ceramic-
tile compositions) in the entrance hall. The

Panaji Central Library (◷9.30am-1.15pm &
2-6.30pm Mon-Sat) is a pleasantly retro place
to read the paper and some magazines.

Campal AREA
The Campal neighbourhood, to the west of
Panaji proper, is home to some green spaces
that are perfect for whiling away an afternoon. Goa's premier cultural centre, **Kala
Academy** has a lovely campus, with a snack
bar; an art gallery; a lighthouse, pier and
benches along the water; and a library with
great books on Indian arts. East of this is
Campal Gardens (Bhagwan Mahaveer Bal
Vihar), a peaceful, expansive park with play-
grounds and river views.

⚲ Courses

Holiday on the Menu COOKING
(www.holidayonthemenu.com; courses from
US$149) This London-based outfit offers a

variety of Goan-cooking holidays, ranging from a Saturday 'Curry Morning' to a one-week program that includes trips to a spice plantation and a local market, based in the picturesque village of Betim, just across the river north of town.

☞ Tours

The Goa Tourism Development Corporation (GTDC) operates a range of boat trips along the Mandovi River, including daily hour-long **cruises** (₹150; ☺6pm & 7.15pm) and two-hour **dinner cruises** (₹450; ☺8.45pm) aboard the *Santa Monica*. All include a live band and dancers – sometimes lively, sometimes lacklustre – performing Goan folk songs and dances. Cruises depart from the Santa Monica jetty beside the New Patto Bridge, where the **GTDC boat counter** (☎2437496) also sells tickets.

Three private companies also offer one-hour **night cruises** (adult/child ₹150/free; ☺6pm, 7pm & 8.30pm) departing from Santa Monica jetty. The GTDC cruises are a little more staid, while others – maybe because of the bars and DJs – can get rowdy with groups of local male tourists.

GTDC also runs a two-hour **Goa By Night bus tour** (₹200; ☺6.30pm Tue & Sun), which leaves from the same jetty and includes a river cruise and packs in as much as possible.

You can take your own free tour aboard the local ferries that depart frequently (whenever full) at the dock next to Quarterdeck; locals have reported seeing dolphins on evening rides. Avoid rush hour, when the boats are crammed.

🛌 Sleeping

As in the rest of Goa, prices vary wildly in Panaji depending on supply and demand. Lots of rock-bottom-priced options pepper 31st January Rd, but most consist of a cell-like room, with a 9am checkout, for ₹500 or less. Inspect a few before you decide. Some are full of bachelors where it would be odd – and potentially problematic – for gals to stay, so if unsure, ask at reception if the hotel is a 'family' place.

TOP CHOICE **Mayfair Hotel**　　　HOTEL **$$**
(☎2223317; Dr Dada Vaidya Rd; s/d from ₹900/1200; ✳) Bright rooms at this friendly family-run hotel have mango-yellow accents, woodblock-print curtains and either balconies on the street side or windows overlooking the backyard garden (think palms, flowers and cats

chasing butterflies). Beautiful ground-floor oyster-shell windows and good old-fashioned service make it atmospheric, too, and loving details like balcony lanterns at Diwali time make it feel homey. Be sure to get recommendations from the chatty mother and daughters at reception, and check out the fun Mario Miranda mosaic in the lobby. Discounts are given for stays of more than two nights.

Casa Nova　　　GUESTHOUSE **$$$**
(☎9423889181, 7709886212; www.goaholidayaccommodation.com; Gomes Pereira Rd; ste ₹3100) Here's your chance to actually stay in one of Panaji's gorgeous old Portuguese-style homes – if you can get a booking. Casa Nova consists of just one stylish, exceptionally comfy suite, accessed via a little alley and complete with arched windows, wood-beam ceilings and mod cons like a kitchenette. Sister property **Casa Morada** (☎9822196007, 9881966789; agomes@tbi.in; Gomes Pereira Rd; s/d incl breakfast ₹5000/10,000) is as fancy as Nova is modern. Its two bedrooms and sitting room are full of antique furniture and objets d'art (ergo the no children, no pets policy), with real art on the walls and floors of elegant pale-green marble.

Crown　　　HOTEL **$$$**
(☎2400060; www.thecrowngoa.com; Jose Falcao Rd; d/ste incl breakfast from ₹5000/10,000; ✳@🛜✈) Perched high above Panaji, with lovely views from its cool and peaceful pool area, this is a great option for a little bit of luxury in the midst of the city. The Crown was recently renovated, and the result is airy, tastefully done rooms in mustards and whites (some with balconies) with supermodern bathrooms. The staff is competent without being stuffy. The price includes breakfast and, for stays of more than two nights, pick-up/drop-off at the airport or train station.

Afonso Guest House　　　HOTEL **$$**
(☎2222359, 9764300165; St Sebastian Rd; r ₹1500) Run by the friendly Jeanette, this place in a pretty, old Portuguese-era town house offers spacious, well-kept rooms with wood-plank ceilings and a pinch of character. The little rooftop terrace, meanwhile, makes for sunny breakfasting (dishes from ₹20 to ₹30). It's a simple, serene stay in the heart of the most atmospheric part of town with just two small faults: checkout is 9am and it doesn't take bookings.

Pousada Guest House　　　HOTEL **$**
(☎2422618; sabrinateles@yahoo.com; Luis de Menezes Rd; d/tr/f ₹420/735/900, with AC

₹630/840/1000; ✹) The four rooms in this little place in the centre of town are nothing special – the two doubles are downstairs, dark and a little small even – but they're clean; civilised; owner Sabrina is friendly and no-nonsense; and of course, the price is right.

Republica Hotel
HOTEL **$**

(☏2224630; Jose Falcao Rd; s/d from ₹400/700, d with AC ₹1000; ✹) The Republica is a story of unexplored potential, an architectural beauty that's been left to the elements – though its dilapidation is, in part, its charm. We thought the welcome could be warmer, and the rooms, though a bit worn, are pricey, but the elderly, ramshackle wooden building has balconies railed with ornate wrought-iron banisters, some rooms have three walls of stained glass, and the air hangs heavy with *saudade* and faded grandeur.

Casa Paradiso
HOTEL **$$**

(☏2230092; www.casaparadisogoa.com; Jose Falcao Rd; r ₹2000-2500; ✹) Just steps away from Panaji's Church of Our Lady of the Immaculate Conception, the newish Casa is a central, if a tad overpriced, option with friendly staff and bright rooms.

Bharat Lodge
GUESTHOUSE **$$**

(☏2224862, 9890193688; Sao Tomé St; d without/with AC ₹1000/1600; ✹) A good, clean option in a pretty, recently renovated old building. Rooms have TVs, but could be cheaper.

Comfort Guest House
GUESTHOUSE **$**

(☏6642250; 31st January Rd; r ₹500) Wasn't yet open at research time, but we heard good things about it.

✕ Eating

You'll never go hungry in Panaji, where food is enjoyed fully and frequently. A stroll down 18th June or 31st January Rds will turn up a number of great, cheap canteen-style options, as will a quick circuit of the Municipal Gardens.

TOP CHOICE Upper House
GOAN **$$**

(Cunha-Rivara Rd; mains ₹95-295; ⊙11am-10pm) Fans of Goan seafood *and* vegetarians alike can rejoice in the food at this new spot specialising in home-style regional dishes. Local favourites such as crab *xec xec* (crab cooked in a roasted-coconut gravy), pork vindaloo, and fish-curry-rice are done the old-fashioned way (the latter even comes with salt-water mango pickle, rarely found outside

Goan mothers' kitchens), and even the veg adaptations (eg mixed veg and mushroom *xacuti*) are show-stoppers. Upper House also serves the best *pav* (Portuguese-style bread) you've ever tasted, while the *alebale* dessert (pancake stuffed with jaggery and coconut) might make you wet your pants it's so good. The restaurant's on the 1st floor of the building next to Hindu Pharmacy.

Sher-E-Punjab
NORTH INDIAN **$$**

(18th June Rd; mains ₹70-140; ⊙10.30am-11.30pm) A cut above the usual lunch joint, Sher-E-Punjab caters to well-dressed locals with its generous, carefully spiced Punjabi dishes: even a humble *mattar paneer* (unfermented cheese and pea curry) is memorable here. There's a pleasant garden terrace out back, too, open seasonally. The food at the fancier branch of **Sher-E-Punjab** (Hotel Aroma, Cunha-Rivara Rd; mains ₹120-270; ⊙11am-3pm & 7-10.30pm) is equally tasty.

George Bar & Restaurant
GOAN **$$**

(Church Sq; mains ₹75-160; ⊙9.30am-10.30pm) Slightly cramped wooden tables and a healthy mix of drunks and families make for a good local, down-to-earth vibe. Seafood's the name of the game here, and it's done especially well in *pilau* (rice cooked in stock; often spelled *pulao* in Goa) and other Goan classics. George is also one of those rare birds in Goa that does good veg; try the biryani or the delish veg *pilau*.

Hotel Vihar
VEGAN **$**

(MG Rd; mains ₹50-80, thalis ₹45-70; ⊙7.30am-10pm) A vast menu of 'pure veg' food, great big thalis and a plethora of fresh juices make this clean, simple canteen a popular place for locals and visitors alike. Sip a hot chai, invent your own juice combination, and dig into one of the fresh thalis or tiffins.

Viva Panjim
GOAN **$**

(31st January Rd; mains ₹65-120; ⊙11am-3.30pm & 7-10.30pm Mon-Sat, 7-10.30pm Sun) Though it's crazy touristy these days, this little side-street eatery, with a couple of tables out on the street itself, still delivers tasty Goan classics – there's a whole page of the menu devoted to pork dishes – as well as the standard Indian fare. Veggies, though, will leave disappointed.

Hospedaria Venite
GOAN **$$**

(31st January Rd; mains ₹180-260; ⊙9am-10.30pm) The atmospheric Venite is a long-time tourist favourite: its tiny, rickety balcony tables make the perfect lunchtime spot. But perhaps success has gone to Venite's head: the food was never great, and now it's exorbitantly priced, too. Maybe visit for a cold beer or snack in the evening instead and chill out on the balcony before moving on.

Legacy of Bombay INDIAN $$
(Hotel Fidalgo, 18th June Rd; mains ₹90-150) Slightly fancy, slightly pricey, really good pure-veg.

Satkar Vegetarian Restaurant INDIAN $
(18th June Rd; thalis ₹55-70, mains ₹50-80) Casual, cheap, pretty good pure-veg.

 Drinking

Panaji's got pick-me-up pit stops aplenty, especially in Sao Tomé and Fontainhas. Mostly simple little bars with a few plastic tables and chairs, they're a great way to get chatting with locals.

Down the Road BAR
(MG Rd; ⊙11am-2am) This restaurant's balcony overlooking the creek and Old Patto Bridge makes for a good and comfy cocktail spot. The ground-floor bar is also Panaji's only real late-nighter, with occasional live music.

Quarterdeck BAR
(Dayanand Bandodkar Marg; ⊙11am-10.45pm) The prices here are on the high side, but the spot right on the water makes up for that.

 Entertainment

Kala Academy CULTURAL PROGRAMS
(✆2420451; www.kalaacademy.org; Dayanand Bandodkar Marg) On the west side of the city at Campal is Goa's premier cultural centre, which features an excellent program of dance, theatre, music and art exhibitions throughout the year. Many plays are in Konkani, but there are occasional English-language productions; call to find out what's on when you're in town.

INOX CINEMA
(✆2420999; www.inoxmovies.com; Old GMC Heritage Precinct; tickets ₹180-200) This comfortable multiplex cinema shows Hollywood and Bollywood blockbusters alike; films change on Fridays.

Casino boats ply the Mandovi waters each night, offering lose-your-savings fun to all who step aboard. **Casino Royale** (✆6519471/2; www.casinoroyalegoa.com; entry

₹3500; ⊙6pm-8am) is the largest; various age and dress restrictions apply.

 Shopping

Panaji's **municipal market** is a great place for people-watching and buying necessities.

Khadi Gramodyog Bhavan HANDICRAFTS
(Dr Atmaram Borkar Rd; ⊙9am-noon & 3-7pm Mon-Sat) Goa's only outpost of the government's Khadi & Village Industries Commission has an excellent range of hand-woven cottons (the towels and men's kurtas are particularly good), along with oils, soaps, spices and other handmade products that come straight from – and directly benefit – regional villages.

Barefoot HANDICRAFTS
(31st January Rd; ⊙10am-8pm Mon-Sat) Barefoot is part of Panaji's new wave of very high end shops specialising in design of one kind or another. Barefoot, though pricey, has some nice gifts, ranging from traditional Christian paintings on wood to jewellery to beaded coasters.

Panaji has several good bookstores, all with a range of books on Goa and the region.

Book Fair BOOKSTORE
(Hotel Mandovi, Dayanand Bandodkar Marg; ⊙9am-9pm) A small, well-stocked bookstore in the Hotel Mandovi lobby; you'll find *Fish Curry & Rice,* the Goa Foundation's environmental sourcebook, here (see p131).

Singbal's Book House BOOKSTORE
(Church Sq; ⊙9.30am-1pm & 3.30-7.30pm Mon-Sat) Lots of books and newspapers and heaps of character at this slightly grumpy establishment that, incidentally, had a cameo role in the *Bourne Supremacy.*

Vision World Book Depot BOOKSTORE
(Church Sq; ⊙9.30am-8pm) A good selection of self-help and spiritual titles, among other things.

 Information

ATMs are everywhere, especially on 18th June Rd and around the Thomas Cook office.

Cozy Nook Travels (18th June Rd; per hr ₹35; ⊙9am-9pm) Superfriendly internet joint, with a quiet ISD booth.

Goa Tourism Development Corporation (GTDC; ✆2424001/2/3; www.goa-tourism.com; Dr Alvaro Costa Rd; ⊙9.30am-1.15pm & 2-5.45pm Mon-Sat) Pick up maps of Goa and Panaji here and book one of GTDC's host of tours.

Indiatourism (Government of India tourist office; ☏2223412; www.incredibleindia.com; 1st fl, Communidade Bldg, Church Sq; ◷9.30am-6pm Mon-Fri, to 2pm Sat) Helpful staff can provide a list of qualified guides for tours and trips in Goa. A half-/full-day tour for up to five people costs ₹600/750.

Main post office (MG Rd; ◷9.30am-5.30pm Mon-Sat)

Oliveira Fernandes & Sons Business Centre (MG Rd; per hr ₹30; ◷9am-midnight) Best internet cafe with the best name.

Thomas Cook (☏2221312; Dayanand Bandodkar Marg; ◷9.30am-6pm Mon-Sat) Changes travellers cheques commission-free and handles currency exchange, wire transfers, cash advances on credit cards, and air bookings.

Vintage Hospitals (☏6644401-05, ambulance 2232533; www.vintage3.com; Cacula Enclave, St Inez) A couple of kilometres southwest of Panaji, Vintage is a reputable hospital with all the fixings.

❶ Getting There & Away

AIR A taxi from Panaji to Dabolim Airport takes about an hour, and costs ₹500.

BUS All government buses depart from the **Kadamba bus stand** (☏local enquiries 2438034), with local services heading out every few minutes. To get to South Goan beaches, take a bus to Margao and change there; Ponda buses also stop at Old Goa.

Calangute ₹14, 45 minutes
Candolim ₹12, 30 minutes
Mapusa ₹10, 20 minutes
Margao express; ₹26, 45 minutes
Old Goa ₹8, 15 minutes

State-run long-distance services also depart from the **Kadamba bus stand** (☏interstate enquiries 2438035; ◷reservations 8am-8pm). Private operators have booths outside Kadamba, but the buses depart from the interstate bus stand next to New Patto Bridge. One reliable company is **Paulo Travels** (☏2438531; www.paulotravels.com; Kardozo Bldg). Some high-season government and private long-distance fares:

Bengaluru ₹550-800, 15 hours, five daily
Bengaluru private; ₹800-1300, 14-15 hours
Hampi private; ₹700-800, 10-11 hours
Hubli ₹150, six hours, hourly
Mumbai private ₹600-1500, 12-14 hours
Pune ₹450, 11 hours, nine daily
Pune private; ₹700-1200, 10-11 hours

Kadamba station has an ATM, an internet cafe – and a Ganesh temple.

TRAIN Panaji's closest train station is Karmali (Old Goa), 12km to the east, where many long-distance services stop. Panaji's **Konkan Railway reservation office** (☏2712940; ◷8am-8pm Mon-Sat) is on the 1st floor of the Kadamba bus stand. See p147 for details on trains out of Margao, many of which stop at Karmali.

❶ Getting Around

It's easy enough to get around Panaji on foot, and it's unlikely you'll even need a pilot or autorickshaw, which is good because they charge a lot: a rick from Kadamba to your hotel will cost ₹50. Frequent buses run between Kadamba and the municipal market (₹5).

To Old Goa, a taxi costs around ₹300, an autorickshaw ₹150. Lots of taxis hang around the Municipal Gardens, while you'll find autorickshaws and pilots in front of the post office, on 18th June Rd, and just south of the church.

Old Goa

From the 16th to the 18th centuries, when Old Goa's population exceeded that of Lisbon or London, this capital of Goa was considered the 'Rome of the East'. You can still sense that grandeur as you wander the grounds, with its towering churches and cathedral and majestic convents. Its rise under the Portuguese, from 1510, was meteoric, but cholera and malaria outbreaks forced the abandonment of the city in the 1600s. In 1843 the capital was officially shifted to Panaji.

Some of the churches, the cathedral and a convent or two are still in use, but many of the other historical buildings have become museums. It's a fascinating day trip, but it can get crowded: consider visiting on a weekday morning, when you can take in Mass at Sé Cathedral or the Basilica of Bom Jesus (remember to cover your shoulders and legs in the churches and cathedral), and definitely stop by if you're around in the 10 days leading up to the **Feast of St Francis Xavier** on 3 December.

◉ Sights

Sé Cathedral CHURCH
The largest church in Old Goa, the Sé de Santa Catarina, is also the largest in Asia, at over 76m long and 55m wide. Construction began in 1562, under orders from Portugal's King Dom Sebastião, and the finishing touches were made 90 years later. Fairly plain all-round, the cathedral has three especially notable features: the first, up in the belfry, is the **Golden Bell**, the largest bell in Asia; the second is in the screened chapel inside

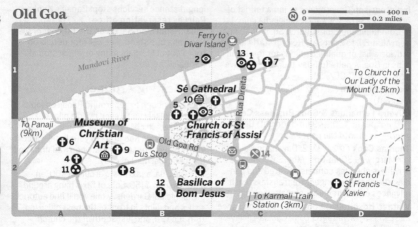

to the right, known as the **Chapel of the Cross of Miracles**, wherein sits a cross said to have miraculously, and vastly, expanded in size after its creation by local shepherds in 1619. The third is the massive gilded reredos (ornamental screen behind the altar), which depicts the life of St Catherine, to whom the cathedral is dedicated and who came to a sticky end in Alexandria, Egypt, where she was beheaded.

Next to the cathedral, in the old archbishop's house, **Kristu Kala Mandir Art Gallery** (admission ₹10; ◷9.30am-5.30pm Tue-Sun) has a hodgepodge of contemporary Christian art and religious objects, including old church confessionals and altar pieces. The decorative wall frescoes may be the gallery's prettiest holdings.

Church of St Francis of Assisi   CHURCH
The gorgeous interior of this 1661 church, built over a 16th-century chapel, is filled with gilded and carved woodwork, murals depicting the life of St Francis, frescoes of decorative flowers and various angels, 16th-century Portuguese tombstones, and another stunning reredos.

Just behind the church, the former convent houses the **Archaeological Museum** (admission ₹10; ◷8am-5pm), whose small but worthwhile collection includes a portrait gallery of Portuguese viceroys, a couple of bronze statues, fragments of Hindu temple sculpture, and some interesting 'hero stones', carved to commemorate Hindu warriors who perished in combat.

TOP CHOICE Museum of Christian Art   MUSEUM
(http://christianartmuseum.goa-india.org; adult/child ₹30/free; ◷9.30am-5pm) This excellent museum, in a positively stunning space in the restored 1627 **Convent of St Monica**, has a fine collection of 16th- and 17th-century Christian art from Old Goa and around the state. There are some exquisite pieces here – wooden sculptures glittering with gilt and polychrome, processional lamps, tabernacle doors, polychrome paintings and other religious objects from Old Goa's prime – that are almost, but not quite, outdone by the atmospheric interior. The four-storey-high ceilings, exposed wood beams and terracotta-work, and all-around beauty of the place are worth a visit in their own right.

Basilica of Bom Jesus   CHURCH
Famous throughout the Roman Catholic world for its rather grizzled and grizzly long-term resident, the basilica's vast, gilded interior forms the last resting place of Goa's patron saint, St Francis Xavier (except for his diamond-encrusted fingernail, which sits in Chandor). In 1541, the saint embarked on a mission to put right the sinful, heady lifestyles of Goa's Portuguese colonials. Construction of the imposing red-stone basilica was completed in 1605; St Francis himself is housed in a **mausoleum** to the right, in a glass-sided coffin amid a shower of gilt stars.

Church of Our Lady of the Mount   CHURCH
For a wonderful view of the city hike up to this hilltop church, also known as **Capela de Monte**, 2km east of Sé Cathedral; it's especially worth the trip for a spectacular sunset. (Locals will warn you not to go solo; the site is a bit remote.) The church is rarely open but was recently restored and, with its exceptional acoustics, now hosts concerts

during the Feast of St Francis Xavier in December, the Monte Music Festival in February, and at other times during the year.

Monastery of St Augustine   HISTORIC SITE
The melancholy, evocative ruins of this once vast and impressive Augustinian monastery are all that remain of a huge structure founded in 1572 and abandoned in 1835. The building's facade came tumbling down in 1942; all that remains, amid piles of rubble, is the towering skeletal belfry, though the bell itself was rescued and now hangs in Panaji's Church of Our Lady of the Immaculate Conception.

There are plenty of other monuments in Old Goa to explore, including the **Church of St Cajetan**, **Viceroy's Arch**, **Adil Shah Palace Gateway**, **Chapel of St Anthony**, **Chapel of St Catherine**, **Albuquerque's Steps**, the **Convent & Church of St John**, **Sisters' Convent** and the **Church of Our Lady of the Rosary**.

✖ Eating

Little tourist restaurants with chai and snacks are peppered around; the basic **Sanjay Cafe** (Old Goa Rd; thalis ₹35, tiffins ₹25-30) has the best food in town.

❶ Getting There & Away

Frequent buses from Old Goa head to Panaji's Kadamba bus stand (₹8, 25 minutes) from Old Goa Rd, just beside the Tourist Inn and at the main roundabout to the east.

Ponda & Around

The workaday inland town of Ponda, 29km southeast of Panaji, has two big drawcards in the vicinity – Hindu temples and spice plantations – and is worth a day away from the beach. Temple aficionados, however, might be a little disappointed; most were built or rebuilt after the originals were destroyed by the Portuguese, so they're not as ancient as those elsewhere in India.

The 18th-century hilltop **Mangueshi Temple** at Priol, 5km northwest of Ponda, is dedicated to Manguesh, a god known only in Goa, while 1km away at Mardol is the **Mahalsa Temple**, also dedicated to a specifically Goan deity. The 1738 **Shantadurga Temple**, meanwhile, just west of Ponda, is dedicated to Shantadurga, the goddess of peace, and is one of the most famous shrines in Goa.

The **Tropical Spice Plantation** (☏2340329; www.tropicalspiceplantation.com; admission incl lunch ₹400; ☺9am-4pm), 5km northeast of Ponda, is touristy, but you'll get an entertaining 45-minute tour of the 120-acre plantation's 'demo garden' followed by a buffet lunch. Elephant rides and bathings are available for ₹600, but seeing the elephants uncomfortably tied on short leashes all day may make this part less appealing. **Sahakari Spice Farm** (☏2312394; www.sahakarifarms .com; admission incl lunch ₹400; ☺9am-4pm), 2km from Ponda, is practically the same thing.

Nearby, the 200-year-old family **Savoi Plantation** (☏2340272, 9423888899; www .savoiplantation.com; ☺9am-4.30pm), whose motto is 'Organic Since Origin', is much mellower, less touristed and elephant-free. You'll find a warm welcome from knowledgeable guides keen to walk you through the 100-acre plantation at your own pace. Local crafts are for sale, and you're welcomed with fresh *kokum* juice, cardamom bananas and other organic treats. Savoi also recently built a couple of **cottages** (d incl meals ₹5000).

There are regular buses to Ponda from Panaji (₹18, 45 minutes) and Margao, after which you'll need to arrange a taxi to visit the temples or spice farms. Taxis from Panaji charge ₹1000 for a day trip to the area (up to eight hours and 80km).

Dudhsagar Falls

On the eastern border with Karnataka, Dudhsagar Falls (603m) are Goa's most impressive waterfalls, and the second highest in India, best seen as soon as possible after the rains. To get here, take the 8.13am train to Colem from Margao (check return times in advance; there are only three trains daily in each direction), and from there, catch a jeep for the bumpy 40-minute trip to the falls (₹300 return per person, or ₹1800 for the six-passenger jeep). It's then a short but rocky clamber to the edge of the falls themselves. A simpler, but more expensive, option is to take a full-day **GTDC tour** (₹700; ⊘9am-6pm Wed & Sun) from Panaji, Mapusa or Calangute (book at the office in Panaji), or arrange an excursion with the Day Tripper travel agency in Calangute or Speedy Travels in Anjuna.

NORTH GOA

Mapusa

POP 40,100

The pleasantly bustling market town of Mapusa (pronounced 'Mapsa') is the largest town in northern Goa, and is most often visited for its busy **Friday Market** (⊘8am-

6.30pm), which attracts scores of buyers and sellers from neighbouring towns and villages, and a healthy intake of tourists from the northern beaches. It's a good place to pick up the usual embroidered bedsheets and the like at prices lower than in the beach resorts. You'll probably pass through Mapusa eventually anyway, as it's a major transport hub for northern Goa buses.

Mapusa is also home to the exceptionally awesome **Other India Bookstore** (⊋2263306; www.otherindiabookstore.com; Mapusa Clinic Rd; ⊘9am-5pm Mon-Fri, to 1pm Sat), specialising in 'dissenting wisdom' – a small but spectacular selection of books on nature, farming, politics, education and natural health. To find it, go up the steps on the right as you walk down Mapusa Clinic Rd, and follow signs; it's at the end of a dingy corridor.

There's little reason to stay the night in Mapusa when the beaches of the north coast are all so close, but if you do, go for **Hotel Vilena** (⊋2263115; Feira Baixa Rd; d without/with AC ₹525/725, without bathroom ₹420; ✷). There are plenty of nice, old-fashioned cafes within the market area. The thalis are excellent at busy **Ashok Snacks & Beverages** (thalis & mains ₹35-70; ⊘6am-10.30pm Mon-Sat, to 4pm Sun), overlooking the market. It's a simple place full of local families and folks on their lunch break. **Hotel Vrundavan** (thalis ₹38-55, tiffins ₹12-50; ⊘7am-10pm Wed-Mon), an all-veg place bordering the municipal gardens, is another great joint with good chai and snacks.

ℹ Information

There are plenty of ATMs scattered about town.
Mapusa Clinic (⊋2263343; ⊘consultations 10.30am-1.30pm Mon-Sat, 3.30-7pm Mon, Wed & Fri) A well-run medical clinic, with 24-hour

---

WORTH A TRIP

BACKWOODS CAMP

In a forest in the Mahaveer Sanctuary full of butterflies and birds, **Backwoods Camp** (⊋9822139859; www.backwoodsgoa.com) could not be in a more magical, serene spot. The resort is about 1km from Tambdi Surla temple, and for birdwatching enthusiasts it offers one of Goa's richest sources of feathered friends, with everything from Ceylon frogmouths and Asian fairy bluebirds to puff-throated babblers and Indian pittas putting in a regular appearance. Accommodation is in comfortable tents on raised platforms, bungalows and farmhouse rooms (all with attached bathroom), and the camp makes valiant attempts to protect this fragile bit of the Goan ecosystem through measures including waste recycling, replanting indigenous tree species and employing local villagers. One-, two- and three-day birdwatching excursions, including guide, transport from Ponda, accommodation at the camp and all meals, cost from ₹4000, ₹6000 and ₹8000 per person, respectively.

GREEN GOA?

Goa's environment has suffered from an onslaught of tourism over the last 40 years, but also from the effects of logging, mining and local customs (rare turtle eggs have traditionally been considered a dining delicacy). Construction proceeds regardless of what the local infrastructure or ecosystem can sustain, while plastic bottles pile up in vast mountains. There are, however, a few easy ways to minimise your impact on Goa's environment:

» Take your own bag when shopping and refill water bottles with filtered water wherever possible. The 5L Bisleri water bottles come with a deposit and are returnable to be reused; invest in these when you can. Better yet, bring a water filter with you.

» Rent a bicycle instead of a scooter, and ask around if you don't find any: bicycle rentals are declining as a result of our scooter infatuation, but they'll bounce back if the demand is there.

» Dispose of cigarette butts, which are nonbiodegradeable, in bins; birds and sealife may mistake them for food and choke.

Turtles are currently protected by the **Forest Department** (www.goaforest.com), which operates huts on beaches, such as Agonda, where turtles arrive to lay eggs. Drop into these or check out the website to find out more about the department's work. Also doing good work is the **Goa Foundation** (☑2256479, 2263305; www.goafoundation.org; St Britto's Apts, G-8 Feira Alta, Mapusa), the state's main environmental pressure group. It has spearheaded a number of conservation projects since its inauguration in 1986, and its website is a great place to learn more about Goan environmental issues. The group's excellent *Fish Curry & Rice* (₹400), a sourcebook on Goa's environment and lifestyle, is sold at Mapusa's Other India Bookstore. The Foundation occasionally runs volunteer projects; call or swing by for details.

emergency services. Be sure to go to the 'new' Mapusa Clinic, behind the 'old' one.

Pink Panther Travel Agency (☑2250352, 2263180; panther_goa@sancharnet.in; ☉10am-6pm Mon-Fri, to 1.30pm Sat) Train and air tickets (both international and domestic), currency exchange and property consultancy services.

Softway (☑2262075; per hr ₹20; Chandranath Apts; ☉9am-10pm Mon-Sat, 10am-9.30pm Sun) Fast internet and ice cream in a shopping complex just past the post office (opposite the police station).

❶ Getting There & Away

If you're coming to Goa by bus from Mumbai, Mapusa's **Kadamba bus stand** (☑2232161) is the jumping-off point for the northern beaches. Local services run every few minutes; just look for the correct destination on the sign in the bus windscreen – and try to get an express. For buses to the southern beaches, take a bus to Panaji, then Margao, and change there.

Local services:

Anjuna ₹10, 20 minutes
Arambol ₹20, 1½ hours
Calangute/Candolim ₹10/12, 20/35 minutes
Panjim ₹10, 20 minutes
Thivim ₹10, 20 minutes

Interstate services run out of the same lot, but private operators have their offices next to the bus stand. There's generally little difference in price, comfort or duration between private services.

Long-distance services:

Bengaluru government; ₹500, 12 hours, one daily at 5pm
Bengaluru private; non-AC ₹1500, AC ₹1600-2000
Mumbai private; non-AC ₹1500, AC ₹1600-2000
Pune government; non-AC ₹380-500, AC ₹600, three daily, in evening
Pune private; non-AC ₹1200, AC ₹1200-1500

There's a prepaid taxi stand outside the bus terminal; it has a handy sign of prices. Cabs to Anjuna or Calangute cost ₹200, Arambol ₹400, and Margao ₹800; autorickshaws typically charge ₹50 less than taxis.

Thivim, about 12km northeast of town, is the nearest train station on the Konkan Railway. Local buses meet trains; an autorickshaw into Mapusa from Thivim costs around ₹150.

Candolim, Sinquerim & Fort Aguada

POP 8600

Candolim's vast beach, which curves round as far as smaller Sinquerim beach in the south, is largely the preserve of older, slow-roasting package tourists from the UK, Russia and Scandinavia, and is fringed with beach shacks, all offering sun beds and shade in exchange for your custom. Its best-known feature, though, may be the hulking *River Princess* tanker which ran aground here in the late 1990s. This massive industrial creature, marooned just a few dozen metres offshore, with tourists sunbathing in her sullen shadow, is a surreal, and oddly pretty, sight.

Candolim's beach is pleasant, the town is mellow, and there are some great hotels here, but it's somewhat fading and lacks the personality of many other beach towns. The post office, supermarkets, travel agents, internet cafes, pharmacies and plenty of banks with ATMs are all on the main Fort Aguada Rd, which runs parallel to the beach.

◉ Sights & Activities

Fort Aguada   FORT, AREA
(⊙8.30am-5.30pm) Guarding the mouth of the Mandovi River and hugely popular with Indian tour groups, Fort Aguada was constructed by the Portuguese in 1612 and is the most impressive of Goa's remaining forts. It's worth braving the crowds and hawkers at the moated ruins on the hilltop for the views; unfortunately, there was no entry at research time to the fort's four-storey **Portuguese lighthouse**, built in 1894 and the oldest of its type in Asia. But just down the road is the peninsula's active **lighthouse** (Indian/foreigner/child ₹10/25/3; ⊙3-5.30pm), which you can climb for extraordinary views. It's a pleasant 2km ride along a hilly, sealed road to the fort, or you can walk via a steep, uphill path past Marbella Guest House. Beneath the fort is the **Fort Aguada Jail**, whose cells were originally fort storehouses, and **Johnny's Mansion**, owned by a famously wealthy Goan and often used as a set for Indian films. Neither is open to the public.

Calizz   MUSEUM
(☑3250000; www.calizz.com; Fort Aguada Rd; adult/child ₹300/free; ⊙10am-7pm) A highlight of Candolim, this impressive compound is filled with traditional Goan houses and

some 75,000 artefacts. The museum won a National Tourism Award for its innovativeness, but it's the pretty houses that will blow you away. Resident historians conduct 45-minute tours that bring the state's cultural history to life.

Boat Cruises   BOATING
Some of the most popular boat trips around town are run by **John's Boat Tours** (☑6520190, 9822182814; www.johnboattrips.com), including dolphin-watching cruises (₹900), boat trips to Anjuna Market (₹600), a Grand Island snorkelling excursion (₹1200), and even overnight houseboat cruises (₹5000 per person, full board). For something more low-key (read: cheaper), head to the **excursion boat jetty** along the Nerul River; independent local boat conductors here operate trips to Anjuna (₹300) and dolphin cruises (₹200; dolphins guaranteed) that pass by Coco Beach, Fort Aguada Jail, the fort, and – of course – 'Johnny's Millionaire House'.

🛏 Sleeping

Candolim has a surprising range of great accommodation. Most of the best-value (and cheapest) budget choices are in the lush area in northern Candolim between the road and the beach; wander through the tiny trails and you're sure to find something. The little road up to the Marbella Guest House also has private houses offering double rooms for around ₹500 per night.

TOP CHOICE Marbella Guest House   HOTEL $$$
(☑2479551; www.marbellagoa.com; d/ste from ₹3000/4100; ✴) You might be put off by the name, but this place has not a touch of Spain's Costa del Sol about it. A stunning Portuguese-era villa filled with antiques and backed by a lush, peaceful courtyard garden, the Marbella is a romantic and sophisticated old-world remnant. Its kitchen serves up some imaginative dishes, and its penthouse suite is a dream of polished tiles and four-posters. Sadly for kids with a keen sense of style, no guests under 12 are permitted.

Beach Nest   GUESTHOUSE $
(☑2489866; d ₹800-1000) Even the sand in the yard is swept tidily clean each day at this spotless and exceedingly friendly little place that's just a quick jungle-footpath walk to the beach. Upstairs rooms have balcony, kitchenettes and fridges, the owners are smiley and helpful, and the atmosphere's serene and homey.

D'Mello's Sea View Home
HOTEL $$

(☑2489650; dmellos_seaview_home@hotmail.com; d ₹1200-1800) Lovely breezy rooms are the principle attraction at D'Mello's, right at the edge of the beach. Rooms in the sea-facing building are divine, with only three walls: the fourth is your balcony, with huge, stunning views of the ocean. Even interior rooms are stylish, with perky colours and chic cotton bedspreads. All rooms are fastidiously clean and have mosquito nets, and the place is professionally (if a bit impersonally) run.

Villa Ludovici Tourist Home
GUESTHOUSE $

(☑2479684; Fort Aguada Rd; d incl breakfast ₹1000) Well-worn, creaky rooms in a grand old Portuguese-style villa.

Candolim Villa Horizon View
HOTEL $$

(☑2489105; www.candolimvilla.com; d with AC ₹1500-2250; ✹@🛜🏊) Simple AC rooms are set around a small swimming pool at this friendly, professional place.

Vivanta by Taj
HOTEL $$$

(☑6645858; www.vivantabytaj.com; Sinquerim, r with AC from ₹10,000; ✹@🛜🏊) Upmarket Taj hotel.

🍴 Eating & Drinking

Candolim's plentiful beach shacks are popular places to eat; **Pete's Shack** (mains ₹90-230), on the northern end of the strip, may be the most elegant.

TOP CHOICE **Café Chocolatti**
CAFE, BAKERY $$

(Fort Aguada Rd; baked goods ₹40-100, mains ₹120-180; ⊘9am-7pm Mon-Sat) When you're tired of thalis or simply seeking sanctuary, treat yourself at this lovely tearoom, set in a green garden light years from the bustle of the beach. The cafe serves sandwiches and salads, but the chocolate's the star. Order a slice of double-chocolate cake and sink back into cocoa heaven.

Stone House
MULTICUISINE, BAR $$

(Fort Aguada Rd; mains ₹90-300; ⊘10am-3pm & 6pm-midnight) Surf 'n' turf's the thing at this venerable old Candolim venue, inhabiting a stone house and a leafy front courtyard. 'Swedish Lobster' cooked in beer tops the list, followed by other bold plates like flattened beef steak with mushroom and onion in spicy Goan sauce (₹250). There's quality live music most nights of the week.

Republic of Noodles
ASIAN FUSION $$$

(Fort Aguada Rd; mains ₹375-450; ⊘11am-3.30pm & 7-11pm) For a sophisticated dining experience, the RoN delivers with its dark bamboo interior, Buddha heads and floating candles. Delicious, huge noodle plates, wok stir-fries and clay-pot dishes are the order of the day – consider the coconut and turmeric curry of red snapper – and there are some exciting dishes for the veggies too.

Bob's Inn
MULTICUISINE, BAR $$

(Fort Aguada Rd; mains ₹90-200; ⊘10.30am-4pm & 6.30pm-midnight) Great fish dishes, relaxed ambience and old dudes – foreigners and locals alike – chillaxing at the community table. The African wall hangings, thatch everywhere, and terracotta sculptures are a nice backdrop to the *rava* (semolina wheat) fried mussels or the prawns 'chilly fry' with potatoes.

ℹ Getting There & Away

Buses run frequently to Panaji (₹12, 30 minutes) and Mapusa (₹12, 35 minutes) and stop at the turn-off near John's Boat Tours. Calangute buses (₹5, 15 minutes) start at the Fort Aguada bus stop and can be flagged down on Fort Aguada Rd.

Calangute & Baga

POP 15,800

Once a refuge of wealthy Goans, and later a 1960s hot spot for naked, revelling hippies, Calangute today is popular with extended Indian families, groups of Indian bachelors and partying foreigners. If you want to experience authentic Indian (or Russian) tourism full-on, come to Calangute. The northern beach area can get crowded – including the water, which fills up with people, boats and jet skis – but the southern beach is more relaxed. Baga, to the north, meanwhile, is the place for drinking and dancing, and Northern Baga, across the Baga River, is surprisingly tranquil, with budget accommodation bargains clinging to the coast.

🏃 Activities

Water Sports

You'll find numerous jet-ski and parasailing operators on Calangute and Baga beaches; H20 Adventure is the most established. Parasailing costs around ₹600 per ride, jet-skiing costs ₹1000 per 15 minutes, and water-skiing can be had for about ₹1200 per 10 minutes.

Barracuda Diving
DIVING

(☑2279409-14, 9822182402; www.barracudadiving.com; Sun Village Resort, Baga; courses from ₹4000) This long-standing diving school

Calangute

Calangute

Activities, Courses & Tours

Sleeping

Eating

Drinking

Entertainment

Shopping

Information

offers a range of dives and courses, including a free 'Try Scuba' family session every Monday. It's also exceptional for its 'Project A.W.A.R.E', which undertakes marine-conservation initiatives and annual underwater and beach clean-ups.

Yoga & Ayurveda

**Ayurvedic Natural
Health Centre** AYURVEDA, YOGA
(☑2409275; www.healthandayurveda.com; Chogm Rd, Saligao; massages from ₹1200; ⊙7.30am-7.30pm) This highly respected centre, 5km inland, offers a range of massages and other ayurvedic treatments lasting from one hour to three weeks. Herbal medicines and consultations with an ayurvedic doctor are also available. For the more serious, professional courses are given here in ayurveda, yoga and other regimes; enquire well in advance. For the more spontaneous, drop-in yoga classes (₹300) are held daily. Some, but not all, buses from Baga/Calangute to Mapusa stop in Saligao, just near the centre; check before boarding.

Boat Trips

Local fishers congregate around northern Baga beach, offering dolphin-spotting trips (₹400 per person), visits to Anjuna Market (₹200 per person) and whole-day excursions to Arambol and Mandrem (₹1000 per person). Call friendly **Eugenio** (☑9226268531).

☞ Tours

Day Tripper (☑2276726; www.daytrippergoa.com; Gaura Vaddo, Calangute; ⊙9am-5.30pm Mon-Sat Nov-Apr), one of Goa's best tour agencies, runs a variety of trips around Goa, including two weekly to Dudhsagar Falls (₹1175) and another sailing through the mangroves of the Cumbarjua River (₹1300), as well as longer trips.

GTDC tours can be booked online (www.goa-tourism.com) or at **Calangute Residency** (☑2276024), by the beach.

🛏 Sleeping

Calangute and Baga's sleeping options are manifold. Generally, the quietest hotels lie in south Calangute, and across the bridge north of Baga.

CALANGUTE

Casa de Goa HOTEL $$$
(☑2277777/9999; www.casadegoa.com; Tivai Vaddo; r/ste/cottages ₹5000/6000/7000; ❄@🤶🏊) The beautiful Casa de Goa is popular with Indian families and books up months in

advance – for good reason. Portuguese-style yellow-ochre buildings surround a pretty pool courtyard, decor is bright and fresh, and the big, clean rooms have safes, flatscreen TVs and new fridges, with other high-end and thoughtful touches. Cottages are across the street from the main hotel and may not get wi-fi.

Ospy's Shelter
GUESTHOUSE $
(✆2279505; oscar_fernandes@sify.com; d ₹600-700) Tucked away in a quiet, lush little area full of palms and sandy paths between the beach and St Anthony's Chapel, are a bunch of family-run guesthouses. Ospy's, just a two-minute walk to the beach, is our favourite. Spotless upstairs rooms have fridges and balconies and look brand new even though they're not, and the whole place has a cosy family feel. Check out the gorgeous old floor tiles on the ground floor.

Johnny's Hotel
HOTEL $
(✆2277458; s ₹400, d ₹600-900) Twelve basic rooms in this backpacker-popular place make for a sociable stay, with regular classes available in yoga, reiki and the tantalisingly titled 'metamorphic technique'. A range of apartments and houses are available for longer-stayers. Johnny's is also home to a popular cafe: stop in for baked beans on toast for breakfast (₹100) or spice up lunchtime with a Goan 'veg vindaloo' (₹70).

Garden Court Resort
GUESTHOUSE $
(✆2276054; luarba@dataone.in; r ₹500-600, with AC ₹700-800, 1-/2-/3-bedroom apts ₹1000/1500/2500; ❄) Fronted by a Portuguese-style home, rooms here are set among pretty gardens and have balconies and cathedral-ish windows. Apartments rented for short stays when available.

BAGA

Cavala Seaside Resort
HOTEL $$
(✆2276090; www.cavala.com; s/d/ste incl breakfast from ₹850/1300/2200; ❄🛜🏊) Classy, ivy-clad Cavala has been charming Baga-bound travellers for more than 30 years, and continues to deliver clean, simple, nicely furnished rooms among a large complex with two swimming pools (₹150 for nonguests). There's a good vibe about the place and friendly staff, and the bar-restaurant cooks up a storm most evenings, with frequent live music.

Divine Guest House
GUESTHOUSE $$
(✆2279546, 9370273464; www.indivinehome.com; s/d from ₹700/1000; ❄@🛜) The Divine welcomes you with a 'Praise the Lord' gatepost

Baga

Baga

To Arpora (2km); Anjuna (5.5km)

Baga Bus Stand

BAGA

Church

ARABIAN SEA

Tito's Rd
To Calangute (1.5km)

Calangute–Baga Rd

WORTH A TRIP

NILAYA HERMITAGE

Spend a night at what may be Goa's most sophisticated luxury hotel, 5km from the beach atop a verdant hill at Arpora, and you'll be signing the guest book with the likes of Sean Connery, Manish Arora and Kate Moss. At **Nilaya Hermitage** (☏2276793/94; www.nilaya.com; Arpora; d incl breakfast, dinner & spa €350; ✳@🖥🏊), red-stone laterite structures undulate around a swimming pool, and the 10 luxury rooms and four stunning tents could not be more elegantly styled. Everything is done in the colour of lapis lazuli or warm whites, set off by old brass, chunky wood and perfect touches. The food is as dreamy as the surroundings, and the spa's sublime.

and keeps perky reminders throughout the place, so only stay here if you don't mind cheerful proselytising. Rooms are sweet and homey, with bright colours, lots of kitsch and the odd individual touch, all at a quiet riverside location.

Nani's Bar & Rani's Restaurant
GUESTHOUSE $$
(☏2276313; www.naniranigoa.com; r without/with AC ₹1300/1500; ✳@) Nani's is as charming as it is well situated, with clean, simply furnished rooms (think fresh paint, a working phone) set around a garden and a gorgeous colonial bungalow that overlook the water.

Melissa Guest House
GUESTHOUSE $
(☏2279583; d ₹500) Neat little rooms, all with attached bathrooms and hot-water showers, comprise this quiet, good-value little place, pleasantly located in a lush spot near the water. Upstairs, **Johnny's** (☏2914000; d ₹600) is almost as good.

✖ Eating

Calangute and Baga have everything from fresh fish cooked up on the beach to the finest Scottish smoked salmon. The main beach strip is thick with vendors selling grilled corn, *pav bhaji* (spiced vegetables and bread) and luminescent candyfloss, as well as the usual beach-shack cuisine. Dining gets more sophisticated to the north and south. The market area, meanwhile, is filled with chai-and-thali joints, and vendors at Baga's bus-stand area sell chai, omelettes and other nonveg snacks for super cheap.

CALANGUTE

TOP
CHOICE **Plantain Leaf**
INDIAN $
(thalis ₹70-90, mains ₹75-150) On the 1st floor, at a slight remove from the business of the intersection below, is the pure-veg Plantain Leaf. The many Indian families that fill the booths here know a good thing when they

see it: the tea is good, the place is cosy, busy and bright, and the veg thali might be the best you'll get in Goa.

Infantaria
BAKERY, ITALIAN $$
(Calangute-Baga Rd; pastries ₹50-100, mains ₹110-275; ◷7.30am-midnight) Next to the São João Batista church is this delish bakery-turned-awesome-Italian-restaurant, loaded with homemade croissants, little flaky pastries, real coffee, Goan and Italian specialities, and lots of booze. The noticeboard here is a hotbed for all things current and counter-current.

A Reverie
CONTINENTAL $$$
(Holiday St; mains ₹315-575; ◷7pm-2am) A gorgeous lounge-bar, all armchairs, cool jazz and sparkling crystals, this is the place to spoil yourself with the likes of Serrano ham, grilled asparagus, French wines and Italian cheeses. Try the delectable cream prawn velouté with fennel soup (₹250) or splurge on the smoked French mallard duck breast in madeira jus with sour cherries (₹995).

Casandré
GOAN, MULTICUISINE $$
(mains ₹60-140; ◷8.30am-3pm & 6pm-midnight) Housed in an old Portuguese-style bungalow, this dim and tranquil retreat seems mightily out of place amid the tourist tat of Calangute's main beach drag. With a long and old-fashioned menu encompassing everything from 'sizzlers' to Goan specialities, and a cocktail list featuring the good old gimlet, this is a loveable time warp.

BAGA

Le Poisson Rouge
FRENCH $$$
(mains ₹310-390; ◷7pm-midnight) Baga manages to do fine dining with aplomb, and this French-slanted experience is one of the picks of the place. Simple local ingredients are combined into winning dishes such as beetroot carpaccio (₹185) and red-snapper

masala (₹390), and served up beneath the stars.

J&A's
ITALIAN $$$

(mains ₹305-445) A pretty cafe set around a gorgeous Portuguese-style villa, this little slice of Italy is a treat even before the sumptuous, if rather pricey, food arrives. The jazz-infused garden and twinkling evening lights make for a romantic setting, too. Add to this triple-filtered water, electric car and composted leftovers, and you've got an experience that's as earth-friendly as it is indulgent.

Lila Café
CAFE $$

(mains ₹110-270; ⊙8.30am-6pm Wed-Mon) German-run place with home-baked breads, perfect, frothy cappuccinos and power-house mains like goulash with spaetzle.

Britto's
MULTICUISINE, BAR $$

(mains ₹95-260; ⊙8.30am-midnight) A Baga institution. Tip: stick to the Goan seafood dishes.

Drinking & Entertainment

Baga's club scene bubbles on long after the parties further north have been locked down. If you're up for a night of decadent drinking or dancing on the tables, you're in the right place. For something lower-key, go for the bars on Calangute's main seaside road.

Jerry's Place
BAR

Also known as JJJ, Jerry's Place is a cute little Calangute bar-resto that's just dingy enough to keep things interesting. Snacks and basic Indian meals (from ₹50) are available, and surprisingly decent rooms (₹800) are just upstairs.

Café Mambo
NIGHTCLUB

(⌨9822765002; www.titos.in; couple ₹500; ⊙10.30pm-3am) Mambo's is Baga's club of the moment: it's slightly sophisticated (relative to Baga), with nightly DJs pumping out mostly commercial house and hip hop, and the occasional (Western) retro nights. Tito's, just next door, used to be Baga's 'it' club. It's still worth a visit, especially for Bollywood nights. Cover, rules and hours are the same as Mambo's, and for both clubs, women enter free, but unaccompanied gents don't enter at all.

Kerkar Art Complex
CULTURAL PROGRAMS

(⌨2276017, 9923958016; www.subodhkerkar.com; Holiday St; ⊙10am-7pm) Showcasing the work of local artist Dr Subodh Kerkar, this Calang-

ute complex is most notable for the open-air music and dance recitals – on Tuesday and Thursday nights and some weekends – hosted by its multicuisine restaurant, Waves (mains ₹300-500; ⊙11am-3pm & 7pm-2am).

Sun Set
BAR, MULTICUISINE

(⊙7.30am-10.30pm) Just a little spot to watch the sunset and the boats with a drink; at low tide, you can walk through the water back to Baga beach.

Shopping

Both Mackie's Saturday Nite Bazaar (www.mackiesnitebazaar.com), in Baga, and the larger Ingo's Saturday Nite Bazaar (www.ingosbazaar.com), in Arpora, about 2km northeast of Baga, start around 6pm and are fun alternatives to Anjuna's Wednesday market. They were running at the time of research but have been cancelled from time to time in recent years for reasons unclear. Ask around to see if they're on.

Karma Collection
SOUVENIRS

(www.karmacollectiongoa.com; ⊙9.30am-10.30pm) This fixed-price shop in Baga has the usual patchwork wall hangings, but also antiques from across South Asia.

Literati Bookshop & Cafe
BOOKSTORE

(⌨2277740; www.literati-goa.com; ⊙10am-6.30pm Mon-Sat) A refreshingly different bookstore, in the owners' Calangute home. Ask about readings and other events.

Tara Travels
BOOKSTORE

(⊙9am-midnight Mon-Sat) A good selection of new and secondhand books in Baga; it's also a book exchange and travel agency.

Information

Currency exchange offices, ATMs, pharmacies and tons of internet cafes cluster around Calangute's main market and bus stand area, with several more (of everything) along the Baga and Candolim roads.

MGM International Travels (www.mgmtravels.com; Umta Vaddo, Calangute; ⊙9.30am-6.30pm Mon-Sat) A long-established and trusted travel agency with competitive prices on domestic and international air tickets.

Thomas Cook (⌨2282455; Calangute-Anjuna Rd, Calangute; ⊙9am-6pm Mon-Sat) Currency exchange and the like.

Getting There & Around

Frequent buses to Panaji (₹14, 45 minutes) and Mapusa (₹10) depart from the Baga and Calangute bus stands, and a local bus (₹5) runs between the Baga and Calangute stands every few minutes; catch it anywhere along the way. A prepaid taxi from Dabolim Airport to Calangute costs ₹645.

Anjuna

Dear old Anjuna, that stalwart on India's hippy scene, still drags out the sarongs and sandalwood each Wednesday for its famous – and once infamous – flea market. Though it continues to pull in droves of backpackers and long-term hippies, midrange tourists are also increasingly making their way here. The town itself might be a bit ragged around the edges these days, but that's all part of its cosy charm, and Anjuna remains a favourite of long-stayers and first-timers alike.

🏃 Activities

Anjuna's charismatic, rocky **beach** runs for almost 2km from the northern village area to the flea market. The northern end shrinks to almost nothing when the tide washes in, but when the tide goes out, it becomes a lovely, and surprisingly quiet, stretch of sand. For more action, **paragliding** (tandem rides ₹1500) sometimes takes place on market days off the headland at the southern end of the beach.

If you're looking to embellish yourself while in town, try **Andy's Tattoo Studio** (www.andys-tattoo-studio-anjuna-goa.com; ⊘noon-7pm Mon-Sat), behind the San Francisco Restaurant and brimming with attitude. Drop in to make an appointment and get a quote for your permanent souvenir.

Yoga

There's lots of yoga, reiki and ayurvedic massage offered around Anjuna; look for notices at Café Diogo and the German Bakery. Drop-in classes are organised by **Avalon Sunset** (www.yogainternationalorganisation.com; classes ₹300-400) and at **Brahmani Yoga** (☑9370568639; www.brahmaniyoga.com; classes

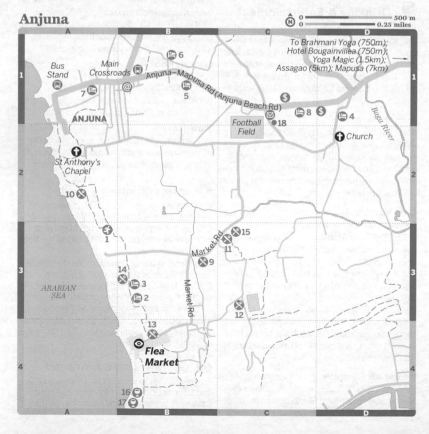

Anjuna

₹500), next to Hotel Bougainvillea. Also consider staying at Yoga Magic or the Ashtanga Purple Valley Yoga Retreat, both lovely resorts with longer-term yoga programs.

🛏 Sleeping

Most accommodation and other useful services are sprinkled along the beach, or down shady inland lanes. Dozens of rooms of the largely concrete cell variety run along Anjuna's northern clifftop stretch; most come in at ₹400 to ₹600 per night. There are also plenty of small, family-run guesthouses tucked back from the main beach strip, offering nicer double rooms for a similar price; take your pick from the dozens of 'Rooms to Let' signs.

Hotel Bougainvillea HERITAGE HOTEL **$$**
(Granpa's Inn; ☎2273270/71; www.granpasinn.com; d/ste incl breakfast & tax from ₹2200/2950; ❄🛜⊠) This old-fashioned hotel in a 200-year-old yellow mansion is ridiculously pretty. Elegant rooms have that rare combination of charm and luxury, and the pool

area is gorgeous, with lots of trees around. The grounds are so lush and shady, in fact, that the place seems a good few degrees cooler than the rest of Anjuna.

Vilanova GUESTHOUSE **$**
(☎6450389, 9225904244; mendonca90@rediffmail.com; d without/with AC ₹700/900; ❄) Big, clean rooms have fridge, TV, 24-hour hot water and window screens and are set in three Portuguese-style bungalows in a cute little compound. There are good vibes and a comfortable family atmosphere, with friendly staff and a good-value restaurant. We almost hate to tell anyone about it!

🍃 Yoga Magic GUESTHOUSE **$$$**
(☎6523796; www.yogamagic.net; s/d huts ₹4500/6000, ste ₹6000/8000; 🛜) Solar lighting, vegetable farming and compost toilets are just some of the worthy initiatives practised in this ultraluxurious yoga resort, where hand-printed textiles, reclaimed-wood furniture and organic, gourmet vegetarian food are the order of the day. 'Huts' are of the stunning, dramatic Rajasthani variety. Rates include breakfast; daily yoga classes cost an extra ₹400 per session.

Faiz'd GUESTHOUSE **$**
(☎9619855350; tents ₹800) The spacious, high-end tents here are lined with embroidered fabric, have tile floors and attached bathrooms, and are set in pretty grounds – like a little tent village – with winding, lamp-lit paths. The location, a stone's throw from the beach, isn't bad, either.

Palacete Rodrigues HERITAGE HOTEL **$$**
(☎2273358, 9422056467; www.palacetegoa.com; s/d from ₹850/1000, d/ste with AC ₹1550/1750; ❄) This old-fashioned mansion, filled with antiques, odd corners and bags of fun, tacky charm, is as cool and quirky as they come. Choose your theme: rooms come in Chinese, Vietnamese, Portuguese and, of course, Goan flavours.

Paradise GUESTHOUSE **$**
(☎9922541714; janet_965@hotmail.com; Anjuna-Mapusa Rd; d ₹600-800, with AC ₹1500; ❄) The friendly, homey Paradise is fronted by an old Portuguese house, and its clean rooms are set in rustic grounds full of crowing roosters and sleeping cats. Proprietor Janet and her enterprising family also run a general store, restaurant, internet cafe (₹40 per hour), travel agency, money exchange, Western Union services and beauty parlour (₹250 for

GOA'S FLEA MARKET EXPERIENCE: GOAN, GOAN, GONE?

Wednesday's weekly flea market at Anjuna is as much part of the Goan experience as a day on a deserted beach. More than two decades ago, it was the sole preserve of hippies smoking jumbo joints and convening to compare experiences on the heady Indian circuit. Nowadays, things are far more staid and mainstream, and package tourists seem to beat out independent travellers in both numbers and purchasing power. A couple of hours here and you'll never want to see a mirrored bedspread, brass figurine or floaty Indian cotton dress again in your life. That said, it's still a good time, and you can find some interesting one-off souvenirs and clothing in among the tourist tat. Remember to bargain hard and take along equal quantities of patience and stamina, applicable to dealing with local and expat vendors alike.

head massages). You name it and Janet can probably arrange it for you.

Florinda's Guest House GUESTHOUSE **$**
(☎9890216520, 9762331032; r ₹400-900) One of the better cheapies near the beach, Florinda's has clean rooms, with 24-hour hot water and window screens, set around a garden with the world's tiniest pool.

Peace Land GUESTHOUSE **$**
(☎2273700; s/d ₹450/600; ☎) Rooms here are small but arranged around a tranquil courtyard garden. There's also a pool table here, a chill-out area and a small shop selling basic provisions. Customer service could use some help though.

Purple Valley Yoga Retreat GUESTHOUSE **$$$**
(☎2268364; www.yogagoa.com; 142 Bairo Alto, Assagao; ☒) This popular yoga resort in nearby Assagao offers one- and two-week residential courses in Ashtanga yoga; weekly rates, which include accommodation, classes and meals, begin at £480 per person.

Sea Wave Inn HOTEL **$**
(Sea Queen; ☎2274455; seaqueenanjuna@gmail.com; Anjuna-Mapusa Rd; r without/with AC ₹800/1000; ☒) Good rooms and friendly staff, and the outdoor restaurant, which shows movies and sports on a big screen, is a fun night-time hang-out.

✕ Eating & Drinking

Inside the flea market on market days (Wednesdays), look for the teensy **Maria's Tea Stall** (snacks from ₹10), selling tasty chai and snacks made by colourful elderly local Maria herself. **Curlie's** (mains ₹80-250; ☺9am-3am) and **Shiva Valley** (mains ₹80-240; ☺8am-midnight), both big, loud bar-restaurants, are good for an evening sunset drink, an alternative crowd and the odd im-

promptu party. Head to either to find out what's on.

Shore Bar MULTICUISINE **$$**
(mains ₹120-400) Anjuna has lots of cliffside cafes with the standard traveller-orientated menus, happy hours and stunning coastal views, but the food is overwhelmingly mediocre. Shore Bar is the exception: the grilled baguettes, seafood, and especially coffees are supergood (at a price), the walls are adorned with cool art, and loungy day beds and sofas are full of happy, mellow dreadlocked customers. Shore also has a no-commission art gallery and rooms out back. There were rumours at research time about relocating; we hope it's still there by the time you arrive.

German Bakery MULTICUISINE **$$**
(pastries ₹30-50, mains ₹70-170; ☎) Leafy and filled with prayer flags, jolly lights and atmospheric curtained nooks, this is a perfect place for a relaxed dinner. Innovative tofu dishes are a speciality: this may be your only chance to try tofu tikka (₹150). There's live music and sometimes Middle Eastern dancers on Wednesday night and round-the-clock wi-fi (₹100 per hour).

Café Diogo CAFE **$**
(Market Rd; snacks ₹30-100; ☺8am-5pm) Probably the best fruit salads in the world are sliced and diced at Café Diogo, a small locally run cafe on the way to the market. Also worth a munch are the generous toasted avocado, cheese and mushroom sandwiches.

Whole Bean Tofu Shop & Vegetaria CAFE **$$**
(Market Rd; mains ₹60-150; ☺8am-5pm) One of the only places in Goa where vegans can eat well, this tofu-filled health-food cafe focuses on all things created from that most versatile of beans. Breakfasts include eggs (for the nonvegans) and a surprisingly good tofu scramble with onions and toast (₹130).

6Pack Bar & Restaurant MULTICUISINE, BAR **$$**
(Market Rd; mains ₹60-200; 9am-midnight)
Everyone loves 6Pack for its excellent 'traditional' – that's code for beef – cheeseburgers (₹170), pool table, and festive vibe when sports are shown on the big screen upstairs.

Avalon Sunset MULTICUISINE **$**
(mains ₹50-140;) Nice views but so-so food; we only mention it for the wi-fi (₹40 per hour).

❶ Information

Anjuna has three ATMs, clustered together about 100m east of **Bank of Baroda** (9.30am-2.30pm), which gives cash advances on Visa and MasterCard.

Om Sai Internet (Anjuna-Mapusa Rd; per hr ₹40; 10.30am-11pm Mon-Sat)

Speedy Travels (2273266; 9am-6.30pm Mon-Sat, 10am-1pm Sun) Reliable agency for air and train ticket booking, a range of tours (including one to Dudhsagar Falls), and credit-card advances or currency exchange.

❶ Getting There & Away

Buses to Mapusa (₹10) depart every half-hour or so from the main bus stand near the beach; some from Mapusa continue on to Vagator and Chapora. Two daily buses to Calangute depart from the main crossroads. Cabs and pilots gather at both stops, and you can hire scooters and motorcycles easily from the crossroads.

Vagator & Chapora

Dramatic red-stone cliffs, dense green forests and a crumbling 17th-century **Portuguese fort** provide Vagator and its diminutive neighbour Chapora with one of the prettiest

settings on the north Goan coast. Once known for their wild trance parties and heady, hippy lifestyles, things have slowed down considerably these days, though Chapora – reminiscent of Star Wars' Mos Eisley Cantina – remains a fave for smokers, with the smell of charas hanging heavy in the air. It also has slightly more personality than Vagator, but fewer eating and sleeping options.

If you're keen to see the remnants of the trance scene, hang around long enough in Vagator and you'll likely be handed a flyer for a party (many with international DJs), which can range from divine to dire. You may also catch wind of something going down in a hidden location. If you're lucky, it won't have been closed down by the time you get there.

🛏 Sleeping

VAGATOR
You'll see lots of signs for 'rooms to let' in private homes and guesthouses along Ozran Beach Rd and on side roads too. Most charge around ₹500 per double.

TOP CHOICE **Shalom** GUESTHOUSE **$**
(2273166; d ₹800-1000) Arranged around a placid garden not far from the path down to Little Vagator Beach, this place, run by a

Vagator & Chapora

WHERE'S THE PARTY?

Though Goa was long legendary among Western visitors for its all-night, open-air Goan trance parties, a central government 'noise pollution' ban on loud music in open spaces between 10pm and 6am has largely curbed its often notorious, drug-laden party scene: Goa simply does not party the way it used to. With a tourist industry to nurture, however, authorities tend to turn a blind eye to parties during the peak Christmas–New Year period. Late nights are also allowed in interior spaces, which is why clubs carry on without problems. If you're looking for the remainder of the real party scene, though, you'll need to cross your fingers, keep your ear close to the ground, and wait out for word in Vagator or Anjuna.

friendly family (whose home is on site), has a variety of extremely well-kept rooms, and a two-bedroom apartment for long-stayers.

Janies GUESTHOUSE $
(☎2273635, 9850057794; janiesricardo@yahoo.com; d ₹800, 1-/2-bed bungalow ₹1200/1500) A great choice for long-stayers, run by a very friendly woman and with a simple but homey vibe. The two double rooms each come equipped with fridge and TV, and the three large bungalows have either one or two bedrooms and full-on kitchen.

Bean Me Up Soya Station HOTEL $
(☎2273479; www.myspace.com/beanmeupindia; d ₹680, without bathroom ₹475; ☎) The rooms around a leafy, parachute-silky courtyard might look a bit cell-like from the outside, but step in and you'll be pleased to find that the billowing silks and mellow, earthy shades follow you there. Scooters are available for rent, and there's a great vegetarian restaurant.

Paradise on the Earth BEACH HUTS $
(☎2273591; www.moondance.co.nr; huts without bathroom ₹500-1000) Simple bamboo huts (not too common in these parts) clinging to the cliff above Little Vagator Beach are great value for the beachside location, though the name might be a little overkill.

Garden Villa GUESTHOUSE $
(☎6529454, 9822104780; Vagator Beach Rd; r ₹250-500) Big, clean, cheap and friendly, on pretty grounds near Vagator Beach. Room No 14 has an old four-poster.

CHAPORA

Head down the road to the harbour and you'll find lots of rooms – and whole homes – for rent; check out a few before you commit.

Casa de Olga GUESTHOUSE $
(☎2274355, 9822157145; r ₹1500, without bathroom ₹500) This exceedingly welcoming family place has rooms arranged around a pretty

garden in a variety of sizes. The cheaper ones are basic (but comfy and clean), while the pricier ones have hot showers, kitchenette with fridge, and balcony. It's in a pretty spot near the harbour, too.

✖ Eating

VAGATOR

A few eating options cluster around the entrance to Little Vagator Beach, along with the usual slew of much-of-a-muchness beach shacks down on the sands.

TOP CHOICE **Thalassa** GREEK $$
(☎9850033537; mains ₹180-400; ⏰4pm-midnight) Authentic and ridiculously good Greek food is served here alfresco on a breezy terrace to the sound of the sea just below. Go for the specials; when we visited, beef stifado (₹270) and lamb meatballs in red sauce (₹320) were on the list. But veggie dishes also excel. The *spanakorizo* (spinach and rice cooked with Greek olive oil and herbs and topped with feta; ₹230) is hearty and deceptively simple: the fresh ingredients and expert preparation are what made us swoon. Reservations essential. Thalassa also has **huts** (₹1000), which are almost as classy as the restaurant.

TOP CHOICE **Yangkhor Moonlight** TIBETAN, MULTICUISINE $$
(mains ₹70-200) Superfresh food is glorified in the Tibetan and even the Italian dishes here. The veg *momo* (Tibetan dumpling) soup (₹80)? You'll die. The pasta? F-ing delish. The chairs and tablecloths are plastic and the walls are lime green, but – maybe because of the friendly service and the soft Chinese pop music – it's cosy to boot.

Mango Tree Bar & Café MULTICUISINE $$
(mains ₹90-210; ⏰9am-4pm) With loud reggae, crappy service, dark-wood furniture and mango-colour walls, a sometimes rambunc-

tious bar scene, terracotta lanterns, and a good vibe, Mango Tree is an ever-popular place for all that and for its really good food. Films or sports are screened most nights.

Bean Me Up

Soya Station   MULTICUISINE, VEGAN **$$**

(Ozran Beach Rd; mains ₹120-250; 8am-4pm & 7-11pm) Oh, veggies and vegans, you've had a hard time in Goa. Come here and relax in the garden, full of tall trees and black pepper vines, and eat tofu Thai curry (₹230) or seitan fried onion (₹130) to your heart's delight, followed by lusciously egg-less desserts. The all-veg restaurant also has breakfasts, juices and even a bar, and an on-site shop sells tofunaise and soysage.

CHAPORA

Chapora's eating situation is not as evolved as Vagator's. Little restaurants pepper the centre (such as it is), but they're reliable only for caloric intake. **Sunrise Restaurant** (mains ₹70-150) is nothing special but good enough, with friendly service, while the very popular **Scarlet Cold Drinks** (juices & snacks ₹20-80) and **Jai Ganesh Fruit Juice Centre** (juices ₹20-70) are both in close proximity to the thickest gusts of charas smoke. Scarlet has an exceptionally good noticeboard, while Jai Ganesh has cold coffee and avocado lassis.

Drinking & Entertainment

Aside from secretive parties, there's not as much going on in Vagator and Chapora these days; gone are the all-nighters and the beach trance is now turned off promptly at 10pm. But Chapora's extremely mellow hole-in-the-wall bars are a certain kind of entertainment; Vagator's **Nine Bar** (6pm-4am) and **Hill Top**, on the Anjuna road, are still thumping on; and the Russians, having taken the party crown away from the Israelis, seem to create nightlife in various spots around town.

🔒 Shopping

Rainbow Bookshop   BOOKSTORE

(10am-2pm & 3-7pm) In Vagator, this lovely little shop, run by a charming elderly gentleman, stocks a good range of secondhand and new books.

ℹ Information

Vagator's sole ATM is at **Corporation Bank** on the road to Anjuna. Plenty of internet places are scattered around town, but **Mira Cybercafe**

2000 (Ozran Beach Rd; 9am-2pm & 3-11pm; per hr ₹40) is best.

ℹ Getting There & Away

Frequent buses run from Chapora, through Vagator, to Mapusa (₹10) throughout the day, many via Anjuna. The buses start in Chapora village, but there are a couple of other stops in Chapora and Vagator. We couldn't find any bicycles to rent here, sadly (ask around; it's a supply-and-demand thing), but prices for scooters/motorbikes tend to be around ₹200/300 per day in high season.

Morjim & Asvem

Morjim and Asvem, a pretty strip of mostly empty sand, is one of the very few beaches where sunbathing doesn't attract hordes of hawkers, dogs and onlookers. The water, though, does suffer from a bit of river run-off pollution and cannot ever be described as crystal clear. Nonetheless, rare olive ridley turtles nest at the beach's southern end from September to February, so this is a protected area, which, in theory at least, means no development and no rubbish. Morjim and Asvem have a handful of low-key beach shacks and several places to stay and eat, including the beachfront **Goan Café** (✆2244394; www.goancafe.com; huts ₹1150-1350, without bathroom ₹800, apt from ₹1250; ❄), whose three brother-owners might well be the friendliest and most helpful hotel owners in Goa; **Meems' Beach Resort** (✆3290703; www.meemsbeachresort.com; d/q huts from ₹1500/3500; 🛜), which has a range of huts and rooms also right on the beach, along with free wi-fi and an atmospheric restaurant; and **La Plage** (mains ₹215-315), known for its high-caliber French food.

Mandrem

Peaceful, quiet, hidden Mandrem has in recent years become a refuge for those seeking a break from the traveller scenes of Arambol and Anjuna – and those who avoided the scene to begin with. The beach is beautiful, and there's little to do but laze on it. Coco-huts can be had for around ₹500. It's not easy to get here by public transport; hire a scooter or cab in Arambol.

There's lots of yoga around, mostly taught by foreigners each season. **Himalaya Yoga Valley** (✆9922719982; www.yogagoaindia.com) specialises in hatha and ashtanga teacher-training courses, but also has walk-in classes (₹300) twice daily.

Sleeping & Eating

GOA NORTH GOA

Dunes
TOP CHOICE · BEACH HUTS $

(☎2247219; www.dunesgoa.com; d/q huts ₹950/1500; @) Pretty huts here are peppered around a palm-forest allée leading to the beach, and at night, globe lamps light up the place like a palm-tree dreamland. Dunes also has friendly, helpful staff, a good restaurant on the beach, and clean, cosy, muslin-lined huts with mosquito nets and balconies with comfy chairs or couches. It's a peaceful, feel-good kind of place, with yoga classes, yoga teachers -to-be hanging around drinking healthful juices, and a marked absence of trance.

Cuba Retreat
HOTEL $$

(☎2645775; www.cubagoa.com; d without/with AC ₹1250/1550; ✳) The sheets here are tucked in *tight* (we heart fastidiousness!) and rooms are clean and tidy as anything, but Cuba really scores for its retro white-and-kelly-green exterior, kind staff and good bar-restaurant in the courtyard, which is also home to a hanging swing.

Oasis on the Beach
BEACH HUTS $$

(☎9822163886; r/huts ₹1500/2000) A great, slightly higher-end beach-hut option, Oasis has some huts with balconies overlooking the sea, and an excellent ayurvedic-massage centre (massages from ₹1000). Oasis's beachfront restaurant gets rave reviews, too, especially for its seafood and tandoori dishes.

Villa River Cat
GUESTHOUSE $$$

(☎2247928; www.villarivercat.com; d ₹2000-3800; ✳) This unusual circular guesthouse is filled with art, antiques and a lot of spunk, but it should be even spunkier (and friendlier) for the price.

Arambol (Harmal)

Arambol first emerged in the 1960s as a mellow paradise for long-haired long-stayers, and ever since, travellers attracted to the hippy atmosphere have been drifting up to this blissed-out corner of Goa, setting up camp and, in some cases, never leaving. As a result, in the high season the beach and the road leading down to it (the town is basically one road) can get pretty crowded – with huts, people and nonstop stalls selling the usual tourist stuff. If you're looking for a committed traveller vibe, this is the place to come; if you're seeking laid-back languidness, you might be better off heading down the coast to Mandrem or Morjim.

🏃 Activities

Himalayan Iyengar Yoga Centre
YOGA

(www.hiyogacentre.com) A popular spot for Iyengar yoga, with five-day courses (beginning on Fridays; ₹3000), intensive workshops, children's classes, and teacher training all available. The centre is a five-minute walk from the beach, off the main road; look for the big banner. HI also has **huts** (s/d without bathroom ₹250/300) for students.

Arambol Hammocks
PARAGLIDING

(☎9822389005; www.arambol.com; per 20min ₹1800; ⊙9am-6pm) Paragliding and kite surfing are getting big in Arambol, and several operators give lessons and rent equipment on the very south of Arambol beach. At the north end, Arambol Hammocks is a more established paragliding option, and it also sells…hammocks.

🏨 Sleeping

Accommodation in Arambol is almost all of the budget variety, and it pays to trawl the cliffside to the north and south of Arambol's main beach stretch for the best hut options. It's almost impossible to book in advance: simply turn up early in the day to check out who's checking out. The area around the Narayan temple (take a left turn off the main road as you enter town), also has several guesthouses of similar quality.

Chilli's
HOTEL $

(☎9921882424; s/d ₹300/400) This clean and simple place, owned by superfriendly and helpful Derick Fernandes, is one of Arambol's best nonbeachside bargains. Chilli's offers 10 nice, no-frills rooms on the beach road, near the beach entrance, all with attached bathroom, fan and hot-water shower; there's an honour system for buying bottled water, self-service, from the fridge on the landing.

Shree Sai Cottages
BEACH HUTS $$

(☎3262823, 9420767358; shreesai_cottages@ yahoo.com; huts without bathroom ₹1000) A short walk north from the main Arambol beach, Shree Sai has a calm, easygoing vibe and really cute hut-cottages with little balconies and lovely views out over the water. Maybe the best of the beach-hut bunch.

Om Ganesh
BEACH HUTS $

(☎9404436447; r & huts ₹800) Popular huts right on the edge of the water, as well as rooms, managed by the friendly Sudir. The seaside Om Ganesh Restaurant is also a great place for lunch or dinner. Note that everyone in the area will tell you that their place is Om Ganesh; it's a family enterprise. Call ahead to avoid confusion.

Lamuella GUESTHOUSE $
(☏9822486314; s/d ₹600/900) Cute, charming rooms with curtains made from saris, built-in cathedral-arch shelving, pretty mosaic tiles around mirrors and little balconies. Far from the beach though.

✖ Eating & Drinking

Sparkly and parachute-silk-draped places to eat are everywhere in Arambol. Many change annually, but **21 Coconuts** (for seafood) and **Relax Inn** (for Italian) are mainstays. For simpler fare, head up to Arambol village, by the bus stop, where small local joints will whip you up a thali (₹40) and a chai (₹4).

Shimon MIDDLE EASTERN $
(light meals ₹60-120; ◷9am-11pm) If you can navigate the surly service and total lack of ambience, then fill up on an exceptional falafel (₹90) at Israeli-owned Shimon before hitting the beach. For something more unusual, go for *sabikh* (₹100), aubergine slices stuffed into pita bread with boiled egg, potato, salad and spicy relishes. Follow either up with Turkish coffee (₹35).

Fellini ITALIAN $$
(mains ₹140-280; ◷11am-11pm) Pizza's the big deal here – the menu has no fewer than 41 different kinds – and the pastas, calzones and paninis, especially with seafood, are also tasty. The tiramisu (₹60) will keep you up at night, thinking back on it fondly.

Double Dutch MULTICUISINE $$
(mains ₹110-290) An ever-popular option for its steaks, salads, Thai and Indonesian dishes, and famous apple pies, all in a pretty garden setting. The noticeboard here is also worth a peruse, maybe while munching on a plateful of cookies or a huge sandwich.

German Bakery BAKERY, MULTICUISINE $
(Welcome Inn; pastries ₹20-60, mains ₹40-75) This rather dim and dingy corner cafe is surprisingly popular, with so-so pastries (eg lemon cheese pie, ₹50), big breakfasts (₹100 to ₹140) and Arambol's best masala chai.

Outback Bar MULTICUISINE $$
(mains ₹70-150) Seafood's a speciality at this place tucked away from the Arambol action.

❶ Information

Internet outfits, travel agents and money changers are as common as monsoon frogs on the road leading down to Arambol's beach, while several agencies toward the top of the road also offer parcel services by post, FedEx and DHL. The closest ATM is in Siolim, about 12km south.

JBL Enterprises (per hr ₹40; ◷8.30am-10.30pm) Internet cafe, travel agency, money and ISD: one-stop shopping.

❶ Getting There & Around

Buses to Mapusa (₹20, 1½ hours) depart from Arambol village every half-hour. It's only about 1.5km from the main beach area, but you're lucky if you get a cab, or even an autorickshaw, for ₹50. A prepaid taxi to Arambol from Dabolim Airport costs ₹975; from Mapusa it's ₹400.

Lots of places in Arambol rent scooters and motorbikes, for ₹200 and ₹300, respectively, per day; we like Derick's, at Chilli's, the best.

SOUTH GOA

Margao (Madgaon)

POP 94,400

The capital of Salcete province, Margao (also known as Madgaon) is the main population centre of south Goa and is a friendly, bustling market town of a manageable size for getting things done, or for getting in and out of the state. If you're basing yourself in south Goa, it's great for shopping, organising travel arrangements or simply enjoying the busy energy of big-city India without big-city hassles. It's also your best base for visiting Chandor, Quepem or Dudhsagar Falls.

◉ Sights

Margao has plenty of shopping opportunities, and the covered **MMC New Market** (◷8.30am-9pm Mon-Sat) is one of the most colourful in all of Goa. It's also worth a walk around the lovely, small **Largo de Igreja** district, home to lots of atmospherically crumbling and gorgeously restored old Portuguese homes, and the quaint and richly decorated 17th-century **Church of the Holy Spirit**, particularly impressive when a Sunday morning service is taking place. The church also hosts services at 4pm on weekdays but is open erratically at other times.

The administrative heart of the city, the Municipal Building, is home to the dusty and awesome **Municipal Library** (◷8am-8pm

Margao (Madgaon)

bright-yellow building tucked away behind the Bank of India, Om Shiv does a fine line in 'executive' rooms, which all have AC, balcony and an ordered air. But it's mostly worth recommending for the suites, which have exceptional views, or as a Tanish backup.

✗ Eating

SwaD INDIAN $
(New Market; veg thalis ₹40-75, mains ₹60-85) Margao's best veg food, hands down, is at the family-friendly, lunch-break favourite SwaD, across from Lotus Inn. The thalis are reliably delish, as are the snacks, South Indian tiffins, mains and all the other stuff on the 12-page menu of pure-veg scrumptiousness.

Longhuino's GOAN, MULTICUISINE $$
(Luis Miranda Rd; mains ₹60-150) Since 1950, quaint old Longhuino's bar and restaurant, with its old wooden chairs and slow service, has been serving up tasty Goan, Indian and Chinese dishes popular with locals and tourists alike. Go for the pork vindaloo (₹90) or the fried mussels with salad (₹120).

Café Tato INDIAN $
(Valaulikar Rd; thalis ₹50, mains ₹50-80; ☺Mon-Sat) A favourite local lunch spot: tasty

Mon-Fri, 9am-noon & 4-7pm Sat & Sun), which has some great books on Goa and a retro reading room where you can read the paper along with lots of gents in button-downs.

☐ Sleeping

Hotel Tanish HOTEL $
(☏2735656; Reliance Trade Centre, Valaulikar Rd; s/d ₹600/850, s/d/ste with AC ₹750/1050/1600; ✤) The best place to stay in town – incongruously located on the top floor of a mall – has really kind staff and tidy, well-equipped rooms with great views of the surrounding countryside. Suites come with a bathtub, big TV and views all the way to Colva. Just make sure to ask for an outside-facing room; some overlook the mall interior. The hotel is near Grace Church.

Om Shiv Hotel HOTEL $$
(☏2710294; www.omshivhotel.com; Cine Lata Rd; s/d/ste with AC from ₹1100/1400/2500; ✤) In a

vegetarian fare in a bustling backstreet canteen.

Shopping

Golden Heart Emporium BOOKSTORE
(Confidant House, Abade Faria Rd; ☺10am-1.30pm & 4-7pm Mon-Sat) One of Goa's best bookstores, crammed with fiction, nonfiction and illustrated books on the state's food, architecture and history.

❶ Information

Banks offering currency exchange and 24-hour ATMs are all around town, especially near the municipal gardens and along Luis Miranda Rd.
Apollo Victor Hospital (☑2728888; Station Rd, Malbhat) Reliable medical services.
Cyberlink (Abade Faria Rd; per hr ₹20; ☺8.30am-7.30pm Mon-Sat) Not the best, but it'll do.
DHL (Gurusai Plaza, Isidoro Baptista Rd; ☺10am-7pm Mon-Sat)
Main post office (☺9am-1.30pm & 2.30-5pm Mon-Sat) North of the Municipal Gardens.
Margao Residency (☑2715096; www.goa -tourism.com) Book GTDC trips here.
Reliance Cybercafe (1st fl, Reliance Trade Centre, Valaulikar Rd; per hr ₹30; ☺9.30am-7pm) Fastest and friendliest.
Thomas Cook (Mabai Hotel Bldg; ☺9.30am-6pm Mon-Sat)

❶ Getting There & Around

BUS Government and private long-distance buses both depart from **Kadamba bus stand**, about 2km north of the municipal gardens. Private buses ply interstate routes several times a day and can be booked at offices all over town; try **Paulo Travel Masters** (☑2702922; 1st fl, Bella Vista Apt, Luis Miranda Rd; ☺8am-7.30pm). Sample long-distance high-season fares:
Bengaluru ₹400, 14 hours, one daily in evening
Bengaluru private; without/with AC ₹1000/1500, 13 hours
Gokarna ₹95, one daily
Hampi private; ₹1000-1200, nine hours
Hospet ₹240, 10 hours, one daily in evening
Mumbai private; without/with AC ₹800/1400, 14 hours
Palolem ₹27, one hour, every 30 minutes
Panaji express; ₹26, 45 minutes, every few minutes
Pune ₹400, 12 hours, one daily in evening
Pune private; without/with AC ₹800/1100, 11 hours
Vasco da Gama 'shuttle'; ₹35, 45 minutes, hourly (stops near Dabolim Airport on request)

Local buses to Benaulim (₹7), Betul (₹15), Colva (₹10) and Palolem (₹27) also swing by the bus stop on the east side of the Municipal Gardens every 15 minutes or so.
TAXI Taxis are plentiful around the municipal gardens, train station and Kadamba bus stand, and they'll go anywhere in Goa, including Palolem (₹700), Panaji (₹700), Calangute (₹900), Anjuna (₹1100) and Arambol (₹1600). Except for the train station, where there's a prepaid booth, you'll have to negotiate the fare with the driver.
Autorickshaws and pilots are the most popular way to get around town; most trips cost ₹50 and ₹30, respectively.
TRAIN Margao's well-organised train station, about 2km south of town, serves the Konkan Railway and other routes. Its **reservation hall** (☑information 2712790, PNR enquiry 2700730; ☺8am-2pm & 2.15-8pm Mon-Sat, 8am-2pm Sun) is on the 1st floor. Services to Mumbai, Mangalore, Ernakulam and Thiruvananthapuram are the most frequent. See p127 for more train information.

Chandor

The lush village of Chandor, 15km east of Margao, makes a perfect day away from the beaches, and it's here, more than anywhere else in the state, that the once opulent lifestyles of Goa's former landowners, who found favour with the Portuguese aristocracy, are still visible in its strings of quietly decaying colonial-era mansions. If you're around in January, Chandor hosts the colourful **Feast of the Three Kings** on the 6th, during which local boys re-enact the arrival of the three kings from the Christmas story.

Braganza House, built in the 17th century, is possibly the best example of what Goa's scores of once grand and glorious mansions have today become. Built on land granted by the King of Portugal, the house was divided from the outset into two wings, to house two sides of the same big family. The **West Wing** (☑2784201; ☺9am-5pm) belongs to one set of the family's descendants, the Menezes-Bragança, and is filled with gorgeous chandeliers, Italian marble floors, 250-year-old, locally made rosewood furniture, and antique treasures from Macau, Portugal, China and Europe. The elderly Mrs Aida Menezes-Bragança nowadays lives here alone, but will show you around with the help of her assistant. Between them, they struggle valiantly with the upkeep of a beautiful but needy house, whose grand history oozes from every inch of wall, floor and furniture. Next door, the

MAJOR TRAINS FROM MARGAO (MADGAON)

DESTINATION	TRAIN NO & NAME	FARE (₹)	DURATION (HR)	DEPARTURES
Ahmedabad (via Vadodara)	6338 Okha Express	371/1013/1394	20	10.45am Thu, Sat
Chennai (Madras)	7312 Vasco-da-Gama-Chennai Express	343/936/1286	21	3.15pm Thu
Delhi	2431 Rajdhani Express	2035/2615	27	10.15am Tue, Thu, Fri
Hubli	7312 Vasco-da-Gama-Chennai Express	124/316/427	6	3.15pm Thu
Ernakulam	2618 Lakshadweep Express	325/857/1167	14½	7.25pm
	6345 Netravati Express	345/827/1137	15½	10.40pm
Mangalore	2618 Lakshadweep Express	214/544/732	5	7.30pm
Mumbai (Bombay)	0112 Konkan Kanya Express	288/782/1073	12	6pm
	0104 Mandovi Express	288/782/1073	12	9.30am
	2052 Jan Shatabdi Express	197/680	9	2.30pm
Pune	2779 Goa Express	264/688/930	13	3.45pm
Thiruvananthapuram	2432 Rajdhani Express	1355/1770	17	12.40pm Mon, Wed, Thu
	6345 Thiruvananthapuram-Netravati Express	347/947/1302	18	10.40pm

Rajdhani fares are 3AC/2AC; Shatabdi fares are 2S/CC; Express fares are sleeper/3AC/2AC.

East Wing (☏2784227, 2857630; ☉10am-6pm) is owned by the Braganza-Pereiras, descendants of the other half of the family. It's nowhere near as grand: paint peels from windows, ceilings sag and antiques are mixed in with cheap knick-knacks and seaside souvenirs. But it's beautiful in its own, lived-in way (check out the kerosene fridge) and has a small but striking family chapel, which contains a carefully hidden fingernail of St Francis Xavier (see p128). Both homes are open daily, and there's almost always someone around to let you in. The owners rely on donations for the hefty costs of maintenance: if you choose to donate, ₹100 per visitor per house is reasonable, though anything extra is welcomed.

Down the road, the original building of the **Fernandes House** (☏2784245; ranferns@yahoo.co.in; admission ₹200; ☉9am-6pm), about 1km east of the church, dates back more than 500 years, while the Portuguese section was tacked on by the Fernandes family in 1821. The secret basement hideaway, full of gun holes and with an escape tunnel to the river, was used by the family to flee attackers.

The best way to get here is by cab from Margao: taxis charge ₹350 round trip, including waiting time.

Colva & Benaulim

POP 10,200

Colva and Benaulim, with their broad, open beaches, are not the first place backpackers head – most tourists here are of the domestic or ageing European varieties – but are, as a result, slightly less sceney than Palolem or the beach towns up north. Of the two, Benaulim has the greater charm, though out of high season it sometimes has the sad feel of a deserted seaside town. Perhaps the biggest reason to stay at either is to explore this part of the southern coast (which stretches north as far as Velsao and south as far as the mouth of the Sal River at Mobor), which in many parts is empty and gorgeous. The inland road that runs this length is perfect for gentle cycling and scootering, with lots of picturesque Portuguese-era mansions and whitewashed churches along the way.

Sights & Activities

TOP CHOICE Goa Chitra   MUSEUM
(☑6570877; www.goachitra.com; St John the Baptist Rd, Mondo Vaddo, Benaulim; admission ₹200; ⏰9am-6pm Tue-Sun) Artist and restorer Victor Hugo Gomes first noticed the slow extinction of traditional objects – everything from farming tools to kitchen utensils to altarpieces – as a child in Benaulim. But it wasn't until he was older that he realised the traditional, and especially agricultural, local knowledge was disappearing with them. He created this ethnographic museum from the more than 4000 cast-off objects that he collected from across the state over 20 years (he often had to find elderly people to explain their uses). In addition to the organic traditional farm out back, you'll see tons of tools and household objects, Christian artefacts and some fascinating farming implements, including a massive grinder for making coconut oil, which, ingeniously, attaches to a bull who does all the hard work. Goa Chitra is 3km east of Maria Hall.

The beach entrances of Colva and Benaulim throng with dudes keen to sell you **parasailing** (per ride ₹600), **jet-skiing** (per 15min ₹700), and one-hour **dolphin-watching trips** (per person ₹300).

Sleeping

COLVA
Sam's Cottages   HOTEL $
(☑2788753; r ₹500) Up away from the fray, north of Colva's main drag, you'll find Sam's, a cheerful place with superfriendly owners, spacious, spick-and-span rooms – that were getting a major upgrade when we visited – and pretty and peaceful grounds.

Skylark Resort   HOTEL $$
(☑2788052; www.skylarkresortgoa.com; r without /with AC from ₹2300/3000; ❄☀) Clean and fresh rooms here have pretty, locally made teak furniture and block-print bedspreads, which gives them much more ambience than the hotel's generic exterior. The pool outside is also pleasant, and you can always just lounge here if you can't deal with the three-minute walk to the beach.

Casa Mesquita   GUESTHOUSE $
(☑2788173; r ₹300) With just three rooms that go beyond simple and a phone number that may or may not work, this old mansion on the main coast road is the place to go if you like atmosphere. Goodness knows when rooms were last cleaned, but the elderly inhabitants are friendly, the paint's suitably peeling, and the ghosts of better days linger lovingly in the shadows.

Soul Vacation   HOTEL $$$
(☑2788144/47; www.soulvacation.in; r incl breakfast ₹6300-7000; ❄☎☀) Tasteful rooms are arranged around gardens and a gorgeous pool area at the sleek Soul Vacation, 400m from Colva Beach. New luxury rooms are capacious and sophisticated in cool blues and whites – totally worth the extra money. It's a relaxing (if slightly pretentious) place to unwind.

La Ben   HOTEL $$
(☑2788040; www.laben.net; Colva Beach Rd; r without/with AC ₹1100/1400; ❄) Neat, clean and not entirely devoid of atmosphere,

---

THE FOUNDING FATHER OF QUEPEM

When Father José Paulo de Almeida looked out his oyster-shell doors and windows, he saw the Church of the Holy Cross beyond the palm trees out front, the river that functioned as his road into and out of the forest out back, and below, lush gardens elaborately designed with cruciform patterns. The Portuguese priest and nobleman arrived in Goa in 1779 and set up the town of Quepem not long after. Today the **Palácio do Deão** (☑2664029, 9823175639; www.palaciododeao.com; ⏰10am-5pm Sat-Thu) may look a lot like it did when he lived there, with original woodwork, furniture, religious effects and even the garden design all lovingly restored in the past few years by Goan couple Ruben and Celia Vasco da Gama, who researched the mansion's original features in the dean's hometown in Portugal. The Vasco da Gamas also host lunches and teatime on the back verandah; call for reservations and prices. All donations to the Palácio are used to continue restoration work and eventually create a cultural centre here.

Stop by the Church of the Holy Cross, the small and sweet church across the way, while you're here. A taxi from Margao, 14km away, will cost ₹550 round trip, including waiting time, but the bus (₹10, every few minutes) stops just a few minutes' walk down the road.

COLVA'S MENINO JESUS

Colva's 18th-century **Our Lady of Mercy Church** has been host to several miracles, it's said. Inside, closely guarded under lock and key, lives a little statue known as the 'Menino' (Baby) Jesus, which is thought to miraculously heal the sick and which only sees the light of day during the **Fama de Menino Jesus festival**, on the second Monday in October. Then, the little image is paraded about town, dipped in the river, and installed in the church's high altar for pilgrims to pray to. At other times of year, you can still visit the church in the early evening, and if you have any afflictions, you might choose to stop on your way in to buy a plastic ex-voto shaped like the body part in question (similar to those used in Mexican or Eastern Orthodox churches) for offering to the Baby Jesus.

this place is particularly known for its rooftop restaurant.

BENAULIM

There are lots of homes around town advertising simple rooms to let. This, combined with a couple of decent budget options, make Benaulim a better bet for backpackers than Colva.

Palm Grove Cottages HOTEL $$
(☏2770059/411; www.palmgrovegoa.com; d without/with AC incl tax from ₹1600/2000; ❄) Old-fashioned, secluded charm is to be had amid the dense foliage at Palm Grove Cottages, hidden among a thicket of trees on a road winding slowly south out of Benaulim. Guest rooms are atmospheric (some have balconies), and the ever-popular Palm Garden Restaurant graces the garden. New rooms (₹2700) – more grand than cosy – were being constructed at the time of research.

D'Souza Guest House GUESTHOUSE $
(☏2770583; d ₹600) This traditional blue house is run by a superfriendly local Goan family and comes with bundles of homey atmosphere, a lovely garden and just three spacious, clean rooms – making it best to book ahead. There's an imposter **D'Souza Guest House** (☏2771307; Vasvaddo Beach Rd; d ₹500) that's not as homey but also a good option; rooms are compact but airy and clean.

Blue Corner BEACH HUTS $$
(☏9850455770; www.blue-cnr-goa.com; huts ₹1600) The friendly (but overpriced) Blue Corner has simple beach huts (which sometimes lose electricity or running water) on a cosy spot right on the beach. The restaurant (mains ₹80 to ₹150) gets good reviews from guests.

Rosario's Inn GUESTHOUSE $
(☏2770636; r without/with AC ₹350/600; ❄) Across a football field flitting with young players and dragonflies, Rosario's is a large

establishment with very clean, simple rooms. Sheets are bright and tucked in tight, kids are playing in the garden, and good vibes abound.

Taj Exotica HOTEL $$$
(☏6683333; www.tajhotels.com; r from ₹20,500; ❄@☷) Set in 56 acres of stunning tropical gardens, the Exotica is luxurious but not the freshest Taj we've ever seen.

✗ Eating & Drinking

COLVA

Colva's beach has plenty of shacks offering the standard fare. At the roundabout near the church, you'll find chai shops and thali places, fruit, vegetable and fish stalls, and, at night, *bhelpuri* vendors.

Sagar Kinara INDIAN $
(Colva Beach Rd; thalis ₹65-85, mains ₹70-120) A pure-veg restaurant with tastes to please even committed carnivores, this great place is super-efficient and serves up cheap and delicious North and South Indian cuisine. You might have to wait for a table among throngs of Indian families who love it as much as we do.

Leda Lounge & Restaurant CONTINENTAL, BAR $$
(mains ₹125-200; ◔7.30am-midnight) Somewhat pricey Western favourites – pizzas, salads, sandwiches – meet fancy drinks – Mojitos, Long Island iced teas – at this comfy, cosmopolitan cafe-lounge. It's a hip environment (relative to Colva), replete with contemporary -print sofas lit by artful woven-basket chandeliers. There's often live music too.

BENAULIM

Malibu Restaurant INDIAN, ITALIAN $$
(mains ₹80-180) With a secluded garden setting full of flowers, cool breezes and butterflies, the relatively inland Malibu is one of

Benaulim's tastier and more sophisticated dining experiences, with great renditions of Italian favourites and live jazz and blues on Tuesday evenings.

Pedro's Bar & Restaurant
GOAN, MULTICUISINE $$
(Vasvaddo Beach Rd; mains ₹70-220; ☺9am-midnight) In a large, shady garden set back from the beachfront and popular with local and international tourists alike, Pedro's offers standard Indian, Chinese and Italian dishes, as well as a good line in Goan choices and some super 'sizzlers'.

Johncy Restaurant
GOAN, MULTICUISINE $$
(Vasvaddo Beach Rd; mains ₹75-195; ☺9.30am-1am) Like Pedro's beside it, Johncy dispenses standard beach-shack favourites from its location just off the sands. Staff are obliging, and food, if not exciting, is fresh and filling.

ℹ Information

Colva has plenty of banks and ATM machines strung along the east–west Colva Beach Rd, and a post office on the lane that runs past the eastern end of the church. Benaulim has a single '24-hour' Bank of Baroda ATM, which is sometimes locked, and most of its useful services (pharmacies, supermarkets, travel agents) are clustered around Benaulim village, which runs along the east–west Vasvaddo Beach Rd. Internet joints:

Click Nooks (Vasvaddo Beach Rd; per hr ₹30; ☺9am-10pm)

Sify Cyber Café (Colva Beach Rd; per hr ₹30; ☺9am-11pm)

ℹ Getting There & Around

COLVA Buses run from Colva to Margao every few minutes (₹10, 20 minutes) until around 7pm.

BENAULIM Buses from Benaulim to Margao are also frequent (₹7, 15 minutes); they stop at the intersection by Maria Hall. Some from Margao continue south to Varca and Cavelossim. Rickshaws and pilots charge ₹150 to ₹200 for Margao, and ₹50 to ₹60 for the five-minute ride to the beach. Benaulim gets green points for ubiquitous bicycle rentals for ₹50 per day; scooters will cost you ₹200.

Benaulim to Palolem

Immediately south of Benaulim are the beach resorts of **Varca** and **Cavelossim**, with wide, pristine sands and a line of roomy five-star hotels set amid landscaped grounds fronting the beach. The most luxe is the (somewhat snooty) **Leela Goa** (☑6621234; www.theleela.com; r from ₹25,000; ✱@☞☎) at Mobor, 3km south of Cavelossim. Just beyond it, at the end of the peninsula, you'll find one of the most picturesque spots in Goa, with simple beach shacks serving good food. The **Cafe Beach Hut** (mains ₹70-200) is at another pretty beach-shack spot; the turnoff is halfway between Cavelossim town and Mobor, opposite Old Anchor Dalmia Resort.

If you're here with your own transport, you can cross the Sal River at Cavelossim on the rusting tin-tub **ferry**, which will run until the nearby bridge is completed in late 2012-ish. Ferries run approximately every 30 minutes between 6.15am and 8.30pm; they're free for pedestrians and ₹7 for cars, or you can charter the whole damn thing anytime for ₹55. To reach it, turn at the 'Village Panchayat Cavelossim' sign close to Cavelossim's whitewashed church, then continue 2km to the river. On the other side is the very charming fishing village of **Betul**.

From Betul on south to Agonda, the road winds over gorgeous, undulating hills thick with palm groves. It's worth stopping off at the bleak old Portuguese fort of **Cabo da Rama** (look for the green, red and white signposts leading the way), which has a small church within the fort walls, stupendous views and several old buildings rapidly becoming one with the trees. (You can also reach the fort by bus from Chaudi, near Palolem; it stops 5km from the fort.)

Back on the main road there's a turnoff to **Agonda**, a small village with a wide,

---

PUPPY LOVE

Pick up some gifts, donate clothes and other stuff you don't want, and borrow books from the lending library at Colva's **Goa Animal Welfare Trust Shop** (☺9.30am-1pm & 4-7pm Mon-Sat), next to Skylark Resort. You can also learn more about the work of **GAWT** (☑2653677; www.gawt.org; Old Police Station, Curchorem; ☺9am-4pm), which operates a shelter in Curchorem (near Margao) and a smaller **shelter** (☑9665636264) behind the Chaudi bus stand near Palolem, both serving sick, stray and injured animals. Volunteers are welcome at the shelters, even for a few hours, to walk or play with the dogs.

empty beach on which rare olive ridley turtles sometimes lay their eggs. The water here can be unsafe for swimming at times, which has kept Agonda from getting too popular, but it's also not the idyllic secret of south Goa that it once was. Nevertheless, the pace is still slow and mellow. There's plenty of accommodation to choose from, including 10 million beach huts. For a step up, **Chattai** (✆9822481360; www.chattai.co.in; huts ₹1600), at the north end of the beach, has lovely huts with attached bathrooms and front porches.

There's lots of yoga and ayurveda in Agonda – look out for notices – and plenty of beach restaurants serving up the usual grub. *Pav bhaji* and chai can be had at the cluster of tiny eateries beside the church. The excellent organic restaurant **Blue Planet**, formerly of Palolem, was moving to Agonda at research time.

Palolem & Around

Palolem's stunning crescent beach was, as recently as 15 years ago, another of Goa's undiscovered gems, with few tourists and even fewer facilities to offer them. Nowadays, it's no longer quiet or hidden, and remains one of Goa's most beautiful spots, with a friendly, laid-back pace and lots of budget accommodation along the sands. Nightlife's still sleepy here – there are no real clubs, and the place goes to bed when the music stops at 10pm. But if you're looking for a nice place to lay up, rest a while, swim in calm seas and choose from an infinite range of yoga, massages and therapies on offer, this is your place.

If even Palolem's version of action is too much for you, head south, along the small rocky cove named **Colomb Bay**, which hosts several basic places to stay, to **Patnem Beach**, where a fine selection of beach huts, and a less pretty – but infinitely quieter – stretch of sand awaits.

Note that Palolem, even more so than other beach towns, operates seasonally; many places aren't up and running until November.

🏃 Activities

Yoga
Palolem and Patnem are the places to be if you're keen to yoga, belly dance, reiki, t'ai chi or tarot the days away. There are courses and classes on offer all over town, with locations and teachers changing seasonally. Bhakti Kutir (p153) offers daily drop-in yoga classes, as well as longer residential courses, but it's just a single yogic drop in the area's ever-changing alternative-therapy ocean. You'll find info on local yoga, and even cooking, classes at Butterfly Book Shop (p834).

Beach Activities
Kayaks are available for rent on both Patnem and Palolem beaches; an hour's paddling will cost ₹200 to ₹300, including dry bag. Fishermen and other boat operators hanging around the beach offer rides to beautiful **Butterfly Beach**, north of Palolem, for ₹800 to ₹1000 for two people, including one hour's waiting time.

Trekking
Cotigao Wildlife Sanctuary NATURE RESERVE (✆2965601; admission/camera ₹5/25; ⏱7am-5.30pm) About 9km south of Palolem is this beautiful, remote-feeling sanctuary.

Palolem

Palolem

0 ———— 200 m
0 ———— 0.1 miles

To Dreamcatcher (300m);
Ordo Sounsar (400m)

To Chaudi (2km);
Canacona Train Station (3km);
Agonda (8km); Cotigao Wildlife
Sanctuary (9km)

ARABIAN SEA

Mosque ⊙

To Patnem (700m)

Don't expect to bump into its more exotic residents (including gaurs, sambars, leopards and spotted deer), but blazingly plumed birds, frogs, snakes and monkeys are plentiful. Trails are marked; set off early morning for the best sighting prospects from one of the sanctuary's two forest watchtowers, 6km and 9km from the entrance. A rickshaw/taxi from Palolem to the sanctuary will charge ₹500/600 including a couple of hours' waiting time, and two buses (at 1pm and 6.15pm) also go here from Chaudi, making the park's two cottages (₹400 and ₹750) a convenient option.

Goa Jungle Adventure   OUTDOOR ADVENTURE
(☑9850485641, 9922173517; www.goajungle.com; trekking/canyoning trips from ₹1200/1500) Run by a couple of very professional, very gregarious French guys, this adventure outfit gets rave reviews from travellers for its trekking and canyoning trips. (Canyoning, as owner Emmanuel puts it, is 'part jumping, part abseiling and part sliding' down a cliff.) Trips run from a half-day to several days, and rafting trips are also occasionally offered. Shoes can be rented for ₹150 per day.

🛏 Sleeping

PALOLEM
Most of Palolem's accommodation is of the simple beach-hut variety. Since the huts are dismantled and rebuilt with each passing season, standards can vary greatly from one year to the next. Walk along the beach and check out a few before making your decision; a simple hut without attached bathroom will cost around ₹600.

Palolem Guest House   HOTEL $$
(☑2644879; www.palolemguesthouse.com; r ₹750-2300; ✺) Towels here have 'Palolem Guest House' embroidered on them: that's the kind of old-school hotel this is (though reception could use some friendliness training). Comfortable rooms are arranged around a leafy garden just a quick walk from the beach, and the food in the courtyard restaurant is excellent.

Bhakti Kutir   HOTEL $$$
(☑2643472; www.bhaktikutir.com; cottages ₹2500-4000; @) Ensconced in a thick wooded grove between Palolem and Patnem Beaches, Bhakti's well-equipped rustic cottages are a little on the pricey side, but still make for a unique jungle retreat. There are daily drop-in yoga classes (₹200) and ayurvedic

massages, and the outdoor restaurant (mains ₹120 to ₹240), beneath billowing parachute silks, turns out yummy, imaginative, healthful stuff.

Ordo Sounsar   BEACH HUTS $$
(☑9822488769; www.ordosounsar.com; huts ₹2000-2500, without bathroom ₹1500) Beach huts they might be, but set as far north up Palolem beach as it's possible to go, across a rickety bridge spanning a wide creek, this hidden haven makes a cool, quiet alternative to some of the elbow-to-elbow options further on down the sands. Friendly owner Serafin prides himself on the restaurant's Goan dishes.

Ciaran's   BEACH HUTS $$$
(☑2643477; www.ciarans.com; huts incl breakfast ₹4000; ✺🛜) You can barely call the gorgeous lodgings here 'huts'. With actual windows, stone floors, full-length mirrors, wood detailing and nicer bathrooms than you'll find in most hotels, they're more like small chalets, all arranged around peaceful gardens right at the beach. It's the perfect balance of rustic and sophisticated. Plus, the wi-fi's free.

Dreamcatcher   BEACH HUTS $$
(☑2644873; www.dreamcatcher.in; huts from ₹2000, without bathroom ₹1000) Stylish huts are peppered around a lush garden on the beach, and yoga's offered every day. There's a four-day minimum stay (but you'd probably stay that long anyway).

My Soulmate   HOTEL $
(Shirley's Residency; ☑9823785250; mysoulmate@gmail.com; r ₹700-800, with AC ₹1000; ✺) A good spot close to the beach (behind Rainbow Travels), and the best hotel name ever.

PATNEM
Long-stayers will revel in Patnem's choice of village homes and apartments available for rent. A very basic house can cost ₹10,000 per month, while a fully equipped apartment can run up to ₹40,000.

Papaya's   BEACH HUTS $$
(☑9923079447; www.papayasgoa.com; huts ₹2000-3500; 🛜) Lovely huts head back into the palm grove from Papaya's popular restaurant. Each is lovingly tended to, with lots of wood and floating muslin, as well as a porch, and the staff are incredibly keen to please.

Micky Huts & Rooms BEACH HUTS $
(☑9850484884; huts/r ₹400/600) If you don't blanche at basic, this is the best bargain on the whole of Patnem beach, run by the friendliest and most obliging local family you could imagine. There's no signpost: just head for the huge patch of bamboo beside the small stream towards the northern end of the beach, and enquire at the restaurant.

Sea View Resort HOTEL $$
(☑2643110, 9850477147; www.seaviewpatnem.com; r ₹1000-2500, with AC ₹2800-3500; ❋@) The friendly management here, clean rooms – many with balconies, some with kitchens – and neighbourhoody garden setting just a quick walk from Patnem beach makes Sea View a reliable, comfy option.

✗ Eating

Both Palolem and Patnem's beaches are lined with beach shacks, offering all-day dining and fresh, fresh seafood as the catch comes in and the sun goes down. Many of these change seasonally, but as of press time, **Ma-Rita's** was winning the readers' choice award.

TOP CHOICE Café Inn CAFE $$
(light meals ₹70-240) This huge, fun semi-outdoor place has loud music, servers in saris and a cafeteria vibe (in a good way). The snacks, shakes, burgers and salads are great, but it's the evening barbecue (from 6pm to 10pm) that will really blow you away: pick your base, toppings, sauces and bread to create a grilled mix-and-match masterpiece.

German Bakery BAKERY, MULTICUISINE $$
(pastries ₹25-80, mains ₹95-170) Tasty baked treats and excellent coffee are the star at the Nepali-run German Bakery, but the Western breakfasts and Italian and Indian dinners are also super good. It also occasionally has yak cheese from Nepal – how cool is that? Oh, and the whole thing is set in a peaceful garden festooned with flags.

Casa Fiesta MEXICAN, MULTICUISINE $$
(mains ₹70-200) Fiesta, like all the restaurants around here, has a little bit of everything on the menu. Its speciality, though, is Mexican, and it makes a valiant attempt at it (and does surprisingly well). The mellow hut ambience is also working, as are the evening barbecues.

Home CONTINENTAL $$
(☑2643916; www.homeispatnem.com; mains from ₹100) A hip, relaxed veg restaurant, Home also rents out nicely decorated, light rooms (₹1000 to ₹2500); call to book or ask at the restaurant.

Shiv Sai MULTICUISINE $
(thalis ₹40-50, mains ₹40-100) A local lunch joint knocking out tasty thalis, including Goan fish and veggie versions, and a good line in Western breakfasts like banana pancakes (₹40).

🔒 Shopping

Butterfly Book Shop BOOKSTORE
(☑9341738801; ⊘9am-9.30pm Mon-Sat) A great bookshop with some neat gifts and a range of books on yoga, meditation and spirituality.

ℹ Information

Palolem's main road is lined with travel agencies, internet places, and money changers – but no ATMs. For those, head to nearby Chaudi, which also has a supermarket, several pharmacies and all the other amenities you might need. An autorickshaw from Palolem to Chaudi costs ₹50, or you can walk the flat 2km in a leisurely 45 minutes.

Sun-n-Moon Travels (per hr ₹40; ⊘8am-midnight) Quick internet.

ℹ Getting There & Around

BUS Services to Margao (₹27, one hour, every 30 minutes) and Chaudi (₹5, every 15 minutes), the nearest town, depart from the bus stand down by the beach and stop at the Patnem turn-off. Chaudi has good bus connections, but for Panaji, better to go to Margao and catch an express from there. Buses from Chaudi:

Agonda ₹9, half-hourly

Cabo da Rama ₹18, 9am (return buses depart Cabo da Rama at 3pm)

Gokarna ₹70, 2pm

Karwar ₹30, half-hourly

Mangalore ₹200, two daily

Margao ₹24, every 10 minutes

Mysore ₹310, one daily

Panaji ₹50, 6.20pm and 7.15pm

TAXI & AUTORICKSHAW An autorickshaw from Palolem to Patnem costs ₹50, as does a rick from Palolem to Chaudi. A prepaid taxi from Dabolim Airport to Palolem costs ₹1000, but going the other way, you might get it for ₹800.

TRAIN Many trains that run north or south out of Margao (see p147) stop at the **Canacona Train Station** (☑2643644, 2712790).

Karnataka & Bengaluru

Includes »

Best Places to Eat

» Karavalli (p166)

» Koshy's Bar & Restaurant (p167)

» Mango Tree (p200)

» Malgudi Café (p177)

» Namaste Café (p196)

Best Places to Stay

» Kabini River Lodge (p185)

» Taj West End (p163)

» Parklane Hotel (p176)

» Green Hills Estate (p188)

» SwaSwara (p195)

Why Go?

Rounding off the southern extent of the Deccan Plateau, sprawling Karnataka is an inexhaustible goldmine of natural, cultural and artistic variety. Complemented by an ultra-professional tourism industry and an inherently friendly population, it's a travellers' haven that makes for fun, stress-free and thoroughly enjoyable gallivanting all the way.

At the nerve centre of this mind-boggling state is silicon-capital Bengaluru (Bangalore), overfed with the good life. Scattered around the epicurean city are rolling hills rife with spice and coffee plantations, a historic town adorned in brocaded regal splendour, a paradisaical nature reserve and a group of awesome rock-cut temples dating back to medieval times. Only a stone's throw away is the Karnataka coastline, with shimmering beaches and colourful temple towns. Bringing your pleasure trip full circle are the World Heritage–listed monuments of Hampi and Pattadakal, and the forgotten battlements and ruins of Bijapur and Bidar. You're unlikely to return home disappointed.

When to Go
Bengaluru

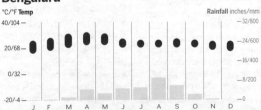

Jan The best season to watch tigers and elephants in Karnataka's pristine national parks.

Oct Mysore's Dasara (Dussehra) carnival brings night-long celebrations and a jumbo parade.

Dec The coolest time to explore the northern districts' forts, palaces, caves and temples.

ON THE ROCKS

Magnificent bluffs and rounded boulders stand tall all over Karnataka. Anegundi (p201) and Hampi (p196) have graded boulders for some easy climbing. Challenging rock faces can be found in Badami (p204), Ramnagar, 40km south of Bengaluru, Savandurga, 50km west of the capital, and Turahalli, on Bengaluru's southern outskirts.

Fast Facts

» Population: 61.1 million
» Area: 191,791 sq km
» Capital: Bengaluru (Bangalore)
» Main languages: Kannada, Hindi, English
» Sleeping prices: **$** below ₹1000, **$$** ₹1000 to ₹4000, **$$$** above ₹4000

Jungle Jaunt

Jungle Lodges & Resorts Ltd (Map p164; ☑080-25597944; www.jungle lodges.com; Shrungar Shopping Complex, MG Rd, Bengaluru; ⊙10am-5.30pm Mon-Sat), is a top-class government-run organisation promoting low-impact and sustainable eco-tourism in the state's many wildlife parks and reserves. Book your getaways in their Bengaluru office or online.

Resources

» Karnataka Tourism (KSTDC) (www.karnataka tourism.org)
» Bengaluru city guide (www.discoverbangalore. com)

Savoury South

The diverse and delectable cuisine of Karnataka is perhaps reason enough for you to visit this state. The highest-flying of all local delicacies is the spicy *pandhi* (pork) masala, a flavourful Kodava signature dish. Mangalore, out on the coast, tosses up a train of fiery dishes – mostly seafood. The crunchy prawn *rawa* (semolina) fry and the sinful chicken ghee roast are two of Mangalore's many dishes to have gathered a pan-Indian following. Vegetarians, meanwhile, can head to Udupi to sample its legendary veg thalis. Oh, and did we mention the classic steak-and-beer joints of Bengaluru?

DON'T MISS

The **temples** of Hampi, Pattadakal, Belur and Halebid, and Somnathpur are some of India's best archaeological sites, embellished with sculptures of stellar quality.

Top State Festivals

» Udupi Paryaya (Jan, Udupi, p193) Held in even-numbered years, with a procession and ritual marking the handover of swamis at the town's Krishna Temple.

» Classical Dance Festival (Jan/Feb, Pattadakal, p206) Some of India's best classical dance performances.

» Vijaya Utsav (Jan, Hampi, p196) A three-day extravaganza of culture, heritage and the arts at the foot of Hampi's Matanga Hill.

» Tibetan New Year (Feb, Bylakuppe, p189) Lamas in Tibetan refugee settlements take shifts leading nonstop prayers that span the weeklong celebrations.

» Vairamudi Festival (Mar/Apr, Melkote, p181) Lord Vishnu is adorned with jewels at Cheluvanarayana Temple, including a diamond-studded crown belonging to Mysore's former maharajas.

» Ganesh Chaturthi (Sep, Gokarna, p194) Families march their Ganesh idols to the sea at sunset.

» Dussehra (Oct, Mysore, see the boxed text, p173) Also spelt 'Dasara' in Mysore. The Maharaja's Palace is lit up in the evenings and a vibrant procession hits town to the delight of thousands.

» Lakshadeepotsava (Nov, Dharmasthala, p192) Thousands and thousands of lamps light up this Jain pilgrimage town, offering spectacular photo ops.

» Huthri (Nov/Dec, Madikeri, p186) The Kodava community celebrates the start of the harvesting season with ceremony, music, traditional dances and much feasting for a week.

History

A rambling playfield of religions, cultures and kingdoms, Karnataka has been ruled by a string of charismatic rulers through history. India's first great emperor, Chandragupta Maurya, made the state his retreat when he embraced Jainism at Sravanabelagola in the 3rd century BC. From the 6th to the 14th century, the land was under a series of dynasties such as the Chalukyas, Cholas, Gangas and Hoysalas, who left a lasting mark in the form of stunning caves and temples across the state.

In 1327, Mohammed Tughlaq's army sacked Halebid. In 1347, Hasan Gangu, a Persian general in Tughlaq's army led a rebellion to establish the Bahmani kingdom, which was later subdivided into five Deccan sultanates. Meanwhile, the Hindu kingdom of Vijayanagar, with its capital in Hampi, rose to prominence. Having peaked in the early 1550s, it fell in 1565 to a combined effort of the sultanates.

In subsequent years, the Hindu Wodeyars of Mysore grew in stature and extended their rule over a large part of southern India. They remained largely unchallenged until 1761, when Hyder Ali (one of their generals) deposed them. Backed by the French, Hyder Ali and his son Tipu Sultan set up capital in Srirangapatnam and consolidated their rule. However, in 1799, the British defeated Tipu Sultan and reinstated the Wodeyars. Historically, this flagged off British territorial expansion in southern India.

Mysore remained under the Wodeyars until Independence – post-1947, the reigning maharaja became the first governor. The state boundaries were redrawn along linguistic lines in 1956 and the extended Kannada-speaking state of Mysore was born. It was renamed Karnataka in 1972, with Bangalore (now Bengaluru) as the capital.

ℹ Information

The website of **Karnataka Tourism** (KSTDC; www.karnatakatourism.org) has lots of relevant information.

Several government offices in Karnataka remain closed on alternate Saturdays.

ACCOMMODATION In Karnataka, luxury tax is 4% on rooms costing ₹151 to ₹400, 8% on those between ₹401 and ₹1000, and 12% on anything over ₹1000. Some midrange and top-end hotels may add a further service charge.

ℹ Getting There & Away

The main gateway to Karnataka is Bengaluru, serviced by most domestic airlines and some international carriers.

Coastal Mangalore is a transit point for those going north to Goa, or south to Kerala. Hubli, in central Karnataka, is a major railway junction for routes going into Maharashtra and northern India.

ℹ Getting Around

The **Karnataka State Road Transport Corporation** (KSRTC) has a superb bus network across the state. Taxis with drivers are easily available in major towns. For long trips, most taxis charge around ₹7 per kilometre for a minimum of 250km, plus a daily allowance of ₹150 for the driver.

SOUTHERN KARNATAKA

Bengaluru (Bangalore)

🖉 080 / POP 5.7 MILLION / ELEV 920M

Despite its grim consequences in real life, getting 'Bangalored' has always had sunnier implications for travellers. The hub of India's booming IT industry, cosmopolitan Bengaluru is the numero uno city in the Indian deep south, blessed with a benevolent climate, a handful of interesting sights and a progressive dining, drinking and shopping scene. Located within close range of Kerala and Tamil Nadu, it's also a great base for those venturing out across southern India.

In recent times, Bengaluru has seen a mad surge of development, coupled with traffic congestion and rising pollution levels. However, it's a city that has also taken care to preserve its greens and its colonial heritage. So while urbanisation continually pushes its boundaries outward, the central district (dating back to the Raj years) remains more or less unchanged. Of interest to travellers are Gandhi Nagar (the old quarters); Mahatma Gandhi (MG) Rd, the heart of British-era Bangalore; and the Central Business District (CBD), north of MG Rd, across the greens.

Locally known as Majestic, Gandhi Nagar is a crowded area where Bengaluru's central bus stand and the City train station are located. A few historical relics lie to its south, including Lalbagh Botanical Gardens and Tipu Sultan's palace.

About 4km east are the high streets bounded by Mahatma Gandhi (MG), Brigade, St Mark's and Residency (FM Cariappa) Rds. This is Bengaluru's cosmopolitan hub, with parks, tree-lined streets, churches, grand houses and military establishments. In between are sandwiched the golf club, the racecourse and the cricket stadium.

Karnataka Highlights

1 Be bowled over by the awesome royal palace and the technicolour Devaraja Market in **Mysore** (p172)

2 Savour aromatic coffee while recharging your soul in the cool highlands of the **Kodagu Region** (p186)

3 Drink yourself under the table, or stab into top-notch global cuisine in **Bengaluru** (p157)

4 Stride across the deserted ramparts of the 15th century fort in **Bidar** (p209)

5 Marvel at the gravity-defying boulders, and wander among the melancholic ruins of **Hampi** (p196)

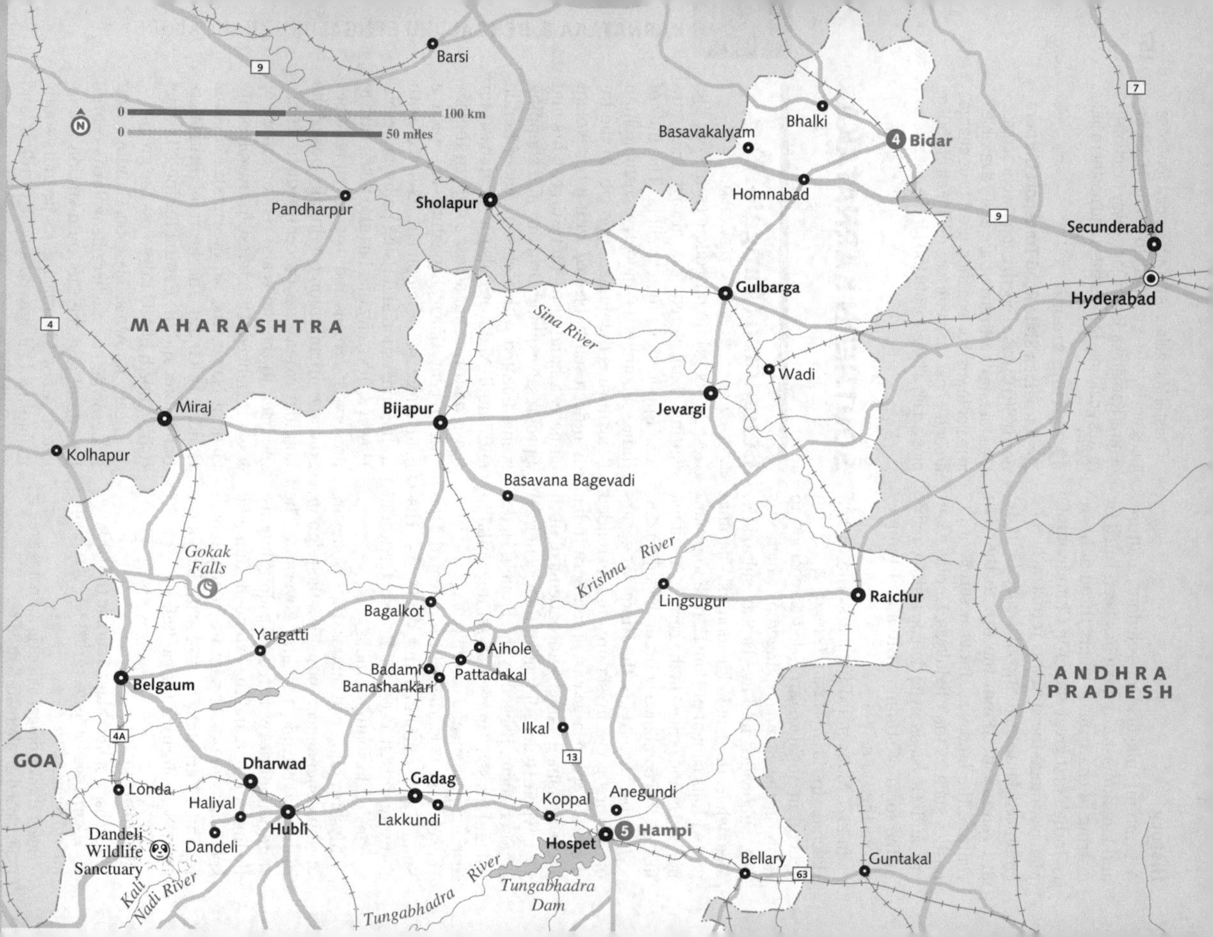

ANDHRA PRADESH

MAHARASHTRA

GOA

Hyderabad
Secunderabad
Bidar
Bhalki
Basavakalyam
Homnabad
Gulbarga
Wadi
Jevargi
Raichur
Lingsugur
Guntakal
Bellary
Anegundi
Hampi
Hospet
Koppal
Ilkal
Tungabhadra Dam
Basavana Bagevadi
Basavana Bagevadi
Krishna River
Sina River
Barsi
Sholapur
Bijapur
Pandharpur
Miraj
Kolhapur
Belgaum
Yargatti
Dharwad
Hubli
Haliyal
Dandeli
Dandeli Wildlife Sanctuary
Lönda
Gokak Falls
Aihole
Pattadakal
Badami
Banashankari
Bagalkot
Gadag
Lakkundi
Tungabhadra River
Kali River
Nadi River

0   50 miles
0   100 km

N

6 Soak up the electric ambience of the atmospheric Krishna Temple in **Udupi** (p193)

7 Spy on lazy tuskers and listen to exotic birds in the forests bordering the serene **Kabini Lake** (p185)

Finding your way around Bengaluru can be difficult at times. In certain areas, roads are named after their widths (eg 80ft Rd). The city also follows a system of mains and crosses: 3rd cross, 5th main, Residency Rd, for example, refers to the third lane on the fifth street branching off Residency Rd.

History

Literally meaning 'Town of Boiled Beans', Bengaluru supposedly derived its name from an ancient incident involving an old village woman who served cooked pulses to a lost and hungry Hoysala king. Kempegowda, a feudal lord, was the first person to earmark Bengaluru's extents by building a mud fort in 1537. The town remained obscure until 1759, when it was gifted to Hyder Ali by the Mysore maharaja.

The British arrived in 1809 and made it their regional administrative base in 1831, renaming it Bangalore. During the Raj era, the city played host to many a British officer, including Winston Churchill, who enjoyed life here during his greener years and famously left a debt (still on the books) of ₹13 at the Bangalore Club.

Now home to countless software, electronics and business outsourcing firms, Bengaluru's knack for technology developed early. In 1905 it was the first Indian city to have electric street lighting. Since the 1940s, it has been home to Hindustan Aeronautics Ltd (HAL), India's largest aerospace company. And if you can't do without email, you owe it all to a Bangalorean – Sabeer Bhatia, the inventor of Hotmail, grew up here.

The city's name was changed back to Bengaluru in November 2006, though few care to use it in practice.

◉ Sights

Cubbon Park
GARDEN

(Map p160) In the heart of Bengaluru's business district is Cubbon Park, a sprawling 120-hectare garden named after former British commissioner Sir Mark Cubbon. Under its leafy boughs, groups of Bengaluru's residents converge to steal a moment from the rat race that rages outside. Idlers, thinkers, lovers, dreamers and health freaks, you'll find them all here, immersed in their own indulgences.

On the fringes of Cubbon Park are the red-painted Gothic-style **State Central Library** and two municipal museums. For the gadget-oriented traveller, there's the **Visvesvaraya Industrial and Technical Museum** (Map p160; Kasturba Rd; admission ₹15; ⊙10am-6pm Mon-Sat), which showcases a wide range of electrical and engineering displays, from a replica of the Wright brothers' 1903 flyer to

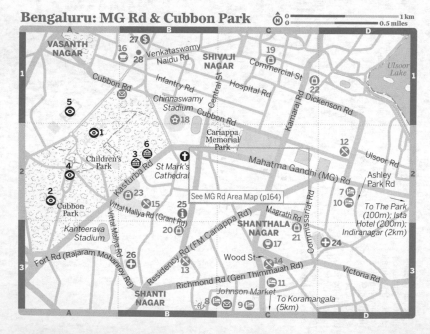

Bengaluru: MG Rd & Cubbon Park

KARNATAKA & BENGALURU SOUTHERN KARNATAKA

21st-century virtual-reality games. The **Government Museum** (Kasturba Rd; admission ₹4; ◷10am-5pm Tue-Sun) to the south houses a collection of stone carvings and relics. The attached **Venkatappa Art Gallery** (admission free; ◷10am-5pm Tue-Sun) preserves several works and personal memorabilia of K Venkatappa (1887–1962), court painter to the Wodeyars.

At the northwestern end of Cubbon Park are the colossal neo-Dravidian-style **Vidhana Soudha**, built in 1954, and the neoclassical **Attara Kacheri**, that houses the High Court. Both are closed to the public.

Bengaluru Palace PALACE
(off Map p162; Palace Rd; Indian/foreigner ₹100/200, camera/video ₹500/1000; ◷10am-6pm) The private residence of the Wodeyars, erstwhile maharajas of the state, Bengaluru Palace preserves a slice of bygone royal splendour for you to see. Aged retainers show you around the building, designed to resemble Windsor Castle, and you can marvel at the lavish interiors and galleries featuring hunting trophies, family photos and a collection of nude portraits. Ask before you get clicking. The palace grounds, interestingly, are now Bengaluru's hottest concert arena, having hosted rock 'n' roll biggies such as Iron Maiden, the Rolling Stones, Aerosmith and Deep Purple.

Lalbagh Botanical Gardens GARDEN
(off Map p162; admission ₹10; ◷5.30am-7.30pm) Spread over 96 acres of landscaped terrain, the expansive Lalbagh gardens were laid out in 1760 by Hyder Ali. You can take a guided tour in a ten-seater ecofriendly buggy (per head ₹100), and learn about the centuries-old trees and collections of plants from around the world. A beautiful glasshouse, modelled on the original Crystal Palace in London, is the venue for flower shows in the weeks preceding Republic Day (26 January) and Independence Day (15 August). Walk in early on Sundays and you can hear the police band perform at the Police Bandstand.

Karnataka Chitrakala Parishath ART GALLERY
(Map p162; www.karnatakachitrakalaparishath.com; Kumarakrupa Rd; admission ₹10; ◷10.30am-5.30pm Mon-Sat) This visual arts gallery is Bengaluru's premier art institution. A wide range of Indian and international contemporary art is on show in its galleries (open

Bengaluru: MG Rd & Cubbon Park

10.30am to 7pm), while permanent displays showcase lavish gold-leaf works of Mysore-style paintings and folk and tribal art from across Asia. A section is devoted to the works of Russian master Nicholas Roerich, known for his vivid paintings of the Himalayas, and his son Svetoslav.

Tipu Sultan's Palace   PALACE
(Map p162; Albert Victor Rd; Indian/foreigner ₹5/100, video ₹25; ⊗8.30am-5.30pm) Close to the vibrant Krishnarajendra (City) Market stands the elegant palace of Tipu Sultan, notable for its teak pillars and ornamental frescoes. Though not as beautiful (or well-maintained) as Tipu's summer palace in Sri-rangapatnam, it's an interesting monument, and worth an outing when combined with other nearby sights such as the **Krishnara-jendra (City) Market** (Map p162), the massive **Jama Masjid** (Map p162; Silver Jubilee (SJ) Park Rd; admission free), the remains of Kem-pegowda's **fort** (Map p162) and the ornate **Venkataraman Temple** (Map p162; Krishnara-jendra Rd; ⊗8.30am-6pm).

Bull Temple & Dodda Ganesha Temple   HINDU TEMPLES
(Bull Temple Rd, Basavangudi; ⊗7am-8.30pm) Built by Kempegowda in the 16th-century Dravidian style, the Bull Temple contains a huge granite monolith of Nandi and is one of Bengaluru's most atmospheric temples. Nearby is the **Dodda Ganesha Temple** (Bull Temple Rd, Basavangudi; ⊗7am-8.30pm), with an equally enormous Ganesh idol. The temples are about a kilometre south of Tipu Sultan's Palace, down Krishnarajendra Rd.

Iskcon Temple   HINDU TEMPLE
(Hare Krishna Hill, Chord Rd; ⊗7am-1pm & 4-8.30pm) Built by the International Society of Krishna Consciousness (Iskcon), also referred to as the Hare Krishnas, this shiny temple, 8km northwest of the town centre, is lavishly decorated in a mix of ultra-contemporary and traditional styles. The Sri Radha Krishna Mandir has a stunning shrine to Krishna and Radha. The temple is a 20-minute autorickshaw ride from MG Rd, near Yeshvantpur train station.

HAL Aerospace Museum & Heritage Centre   MUSEUM
(Airport-Varthur Rd; admission ₹20, camera/video ₹25/45; ⊗9am-5pm Tue-Sun) For a peek into India's aeronautical history, visit this wonderful museum past the old airport, where you can see some of the indigenous aircraft

Bengaluru: Chickpet & Gandhi Nagar

models designed by HAL. Interesting exhibits include the infamous MIG-21, homegrown models such as the Marut and Kiran, and a vintage Canberra bomber. You can also engage in mock dogfights at the simulator machines (₹10) on the top floor.

🏃 Activities

Ayurveda & Yoga

The staff at **Chiraayu Ayurvedic Health & Rejuvenation Centre** (☑25500855; 6th block, 17th D Main, Koramangala; ⊗8.30am-6pm) take their practice seriously, so don't make vague demands like 'I'd like a massage!' Make an appointment, discuss your problems, and the resultant therapy – prescribed by in-house experts – could range from a day-long session to long-term programs. Allergy, diabetes, asthma and other critical diseases can be treated.

Based in the eastern suburb of White-field, **Ayurvedagram** (☑27945430; www.ayurvedagram.com; Hemmandanhalli) is a reputed ayurvedic treatment centre that customises packages for individual disorders. For a more lavish experience, try **Soukya** (☑28017000; www.soukya.com; Soukya Rd, Samethanahalli, Whitefield; ⊗6am-8.30pm), an internationally renowned place set on a picture-perfect 30-acre organic farm that offers some of the best programs in ayurvedic therapy and yoga (per hour therapy Indian/foreigner ₹2750/US$55). Long-term packages are also available.

Stylish **Urban Yoga Centre** (☑32005720; www.urbanyoga.in; 100ft Rd, Indiranagar; ⊙6.30am-9pm) has a smart yoga studio offering a range of classes, and sells yoga clothes, accessories and books.

Outdoor Adventure

Getoff ur ass (☑26722750; www.getoffurass.com; 858 1D Main Rd, Giri Nagar 2nd Phase) has perfect recipes for outward-bound adventures, including rafting, kayaking, trekking and mountaineering in Karnataka and elsewhere. It also sells and rents outdoor gear.

☞ Tours

Bangalore Walks   WALKING
(☑9845523660, 9845068416; www.bangalorewalks.com) A must-do. Choose between a traditional walk, medieval walk, garden walk or Victorian walk to get under Bengaluru's skin. Held on Saturdays and Sundays (7am to 10am), the walks (adult/child ₹500/300) are all about knowing and loving Bengaluru in a way that many locals have forgotten. There's a scrummy breakfast en route. Book in advance; each walk takes a maximum of 15 people.

Bus Tours   SIGHTSEEING
The state tourism department runs a couple of city bus tours, all of which begin at Badami House. The basic city tour runs twice daily at 7.30am and 2pm (ordinary/deluxe ₹170/190), while a 16-hour tour to Srirangapatnam, Mysore and Brindavan Gardens

departs daily at 6.30am (ordinary/deluxe ₹530/680). There are longer tours to other destinations; enquire at the Karnataka Tourism offices.

⊨ Sleeping

Hotel tariffs are skyrocketing in Bengaluru even as you read this. Decent rooms are perpetually in short supply, and a good night's sleep will set you back by at least ₹1000. Serviced apartments are frequently a better deal than many midrange and top-end hotels. Most hotels have 24-hour checkout. Book early.

Stacks of hotels line Subedar Chatram (SC) Rd, east of the bus stands and train station. It's a loud and seedy area, but convenient if you're in transit. For longer stays, consider moving into town, preferably closer to MG Rd. All hotels listed here have hot water, at least in the mornings.

TOP CHOICE **Taj West End**   HERITAGE HOTEL **$$$**
(Map p162; ☑66605660; www.tajhotels.com; Racecourse Rd; s/d incl breakfast from ₹11,600/12,800; ❄️🛜❄️) The West End saga flashbacks to 1887, when it was incepted by a British family as a 10-room hostel for passing army officers. Since then, nostalgia has been a permanent resident at this lovely property which – spread over 20 acres of tropical gardens – has evolved as a definitive icon of Indian luxury hospitality. Its pearly mansions and villas seamlessly mix heritage with modern comforts, with verandahs overlooking the verdant greens that come alive with the chirping of exotic birds every day. Get antiquated in style.

KARNATAKA & BENGALURU SOUTHERN KARNATAKA

TOP CHOICE Casa Piccola Cottage

HERITAGE HOTEL $$

(Map p160; ☎22270754; www.casapiccola.com; 2 Clapham Rd; r incl breakfast from ₹3600; ❀🐾)
Located on a quiet back lane in Richmond Town, this beautifully renovated 1915 cottage is a tranquil sanctuary from the city madness. With an uncanny ability to make you feel immediately at home, it offers a personalised brand of hospitality that has garnered it a solid reputation. Its studio rooms are high on old-world charm, and the gazebo in the garden is a nice place to tuck into your free breakfast.

Ashley Inn

GUESTHOUSE $$

(Map p160; ☎41233415; www.ashleyinn.in; 11 Ashley Park Rd; s/d incl breakfast from ₹1800/2200; ❀🐾)
Once in a while, we all come across a hotel that gets it right without trying too hard. Ashley Inn is one such place. Seconds from the MG Rd mayhem, with eight pleasant rooms in soothing colours, this sweet guesthouse evokes that homely feeling you sometimes desperately yearn for while on the move.

Tom's

HOTEL $$

(Map p160; ☎25575875; 1/5 Hosur Rd; s/d incl breakfast from ₹1199/1399; ❀🐾) Long favoured for its unbelievably low tariffs, cheerful Tom's allows you to stay in the heart of town for a song. Yes, there's been some cost-cutting since we last visited, but rooms are spacious, the linen spotless, and the staff professional. Ask for a north-facing room; they come with balconies.

Villa Pottipati

HERITAGE HOTEL $$

(☎23360777; www.neemranahotels.com; 142 8th Cross, 4th Main, Malleswaram; s/d incl breakfast from ₹4000/4500; ❀@☀) Located a little off-centre, this heritage building was once the garden home of an expat Andhra family. Needless to say, it's flooded with memories in the form of numerous artefacts scattered within its rooms. Dollops of quaintness are added by features such as antique four-poster beds and arched doorways, while the overall ambience gains from a garden full of ageless trees, seasonal blossoms and a dunk-sized pool.

Hotel Ajantha

HOTEL $

(Map p160; ☎25584321; www.hotelajantha.in; 22A MG Rd; s/d from ₹475/750, d with AC from ₹999; ❀) Old Indian tourism posters and stacks of potted foliage welcome you into this oldie located off MG Rd, with a range of par-for-the-course rooms in a semi-quiet compound. Being dirt cheap, it's insanely popular with budget travellers, so book well ahead.

Tricolour Hotel

HOTEL $$

(Map p162; ☎41279090; www.ibchotels-resorts.com; 15 Tank Bund Rd; s/d ₹1300/1600; ❀@) This pseudo-boutique hotel should be your first option if you want to sleep in relative comfort while being close to the bus and train stations. It's both classy and contemporary, with primly laid-out rooms and cheerful, sky-lit foyers. Col Sanders sells his legendary fried chicken at the glitzy mall next door.

JP Cordial

HOTEL $$

(p162; ☎40214021; www.jpcordial.com; 68 SC Rd; d incl breakfast Indian/foreigner from ₹3600/US$95; ❀@) A rather pleasant business hotel straddling the maddening commotion on SC Rd, this designer place meets requisite luxury standards, and the amiable staff is always ready to meet your requirements. It's one of the better mid-rangers in this part of town.

Casa Piccola Service Apartments HOTEL **$$**
(Map p160; ☎22270754; www.casapiccola.com; Wellington Park Apartments, Wellington St; r from ₹2400; ❄) One of Bengaluru's many sleek serviced apartments, this place offers a set of well-appointed two- and three-bedroom flats located within a residential complex on a shared basis. Tastefully done up in pastel shades, they're stocked with all amenities. It's owned by the Oberoi family, who run the Casa Piccola Cottage across the lane.

Ista Hotel HOTEL **$$$**
(off Map p160; ☎25558888; www.istahotels.com; 1/1 Swami Vivekananda Rd, Ulsoor; d from ₹8099; ❄@❄) With its name meaning 'sacred space', Ista delivers accommodation happiness in a cool, minimalist style. The smallish but elegant rooms with king-sized windows offer sweeping vistas across Ulsoor lake. The bar and restaurant, opening on to the rooftop pool, are swell, and the spa will pamper you with diverse treatments kicking off at around ₹1300.

Hotel Empire International HOTEL **$$**
(Map p164; ☎25593743; www.hotelempire.in; 36 Church St; s/d incl breakfast from ₹1550/1850; ❄@) Consistency is the Empire's middle name. The bright and airy rooms are as clean and well-serviced, the front desk as professional and courteous, and the overall vibe as cheerful as on our previous visits. Combined with its location in the heart of all the action and nightlife, it's a sure deal.

Monarch HOTEL **$$**
(Map p164; ☎25591915; www.monarchhotels.in; 54 Brigade Rd; s/d incl breakfast from ₹25000/3500; ❄❀) Between you and us, a night at the Monarch should be costing twice as much. Don't tell them, though. Just lie back in one of their super-comfy rooms and make the most of their innumerable facilities (free wi-fi, 24-hour currency exchange counter, courier service and a dozen others). Then follow it up with a rocking evening on the town.

Brindavan Hotel HOTEL **$**
(Map p164; ☎25584000; 108 MG Rd; s/d from ₹750/900; ❄) Being located conveniently off central Bengaluru's main drag, this budget dive is perennially booked out, and you need to call well in advance if you want to check into one of its plain and characterless (though tidy and airy) rooms. There's an in-house astro-palmist, if you're interested.

Hotel Adora HOTEL **$**
(Map p162; ☎22200024; 47 SC Rd; s/d from ₹425/650) A largish and popular budget option near the stations, with unfussy rooms with clean sheets. Downstairs is a good veg restaurant, Indraprastha. Walk-in reservations only.

The Park HOTEL **$$$**
(off Map p160; ☎25594666; 14/7 MG Rd; s/d incl breakfast from ₹15,000/16,000) A swanky designer hotel with oodles of glitz and glam. Home to the reputed Italian restaurant, **i-t.ALIA**.

✕ Eating

Bengaluru's adventurous dining scene keeps pace with the whims and rising standards of its hungry, moneyed masses. Unless stated otherwise, all restaurants are open from noon to 3pm, and 7pm to 11pm. It's best to book a table in some (telephone numbers listed).

If and when the state government passes a much-discussed anti cow-slaughter bill, beef may go off the menus in many mid-range restaurants.

MG ROAD AREA

TOP CHOICE Karavalli   SEAFOOD $$$

(Map p164; 66604545; The Gateway Hotel; 66 Residency Rd; mains ₹450-500) The Arabian Sea is some 500km away, but you'll have to come only as far as this superb spot to savour South India's finest coastal cuisines. It's designed like a seaside villa, and the decor is a stylish mash of thatched roofs and vintage woodwork. The juicy Lobster Balchao is an eternal favourite, as are the fiery Mangalorean fishy delights. And there's the divine Bebinca with vanilla ice-cream for dessert.

Oye! Amritsar   NORTH INDIAN $$

(Map p164; 4th fl, Asha Enclave, Church St; mains ₹150-180) Pining for some good old Punjabi fare in South India? This is where you'll find it all. A *dhaba*-style eatery with funky souped-up decor, this restaurant serves some lip-smacking dishes from the northern state, best washed down with a glass of yoghurt-based lassi.

The Only Place   STEAKHOUSE $$

(Map p164; 13 Museum Rd; mains ₹200-220) Juicy steaks, brawny burgers and the classic shepherd's pie – no one serves them better than this time-tested restaurant which has many an expat loyalist in town. It's a place that doesn't encourage much conversation, simply because you've got your mouth full most of the time.

Queen's Restaurant   INDIAN $

(Map p164; Church St; mains ₹80-100) This reputed joint serves some quick and tasty Indian morsels such as a range of vegetable and dhal preparations, to go with fluffy and hot chapati. The interiors are rustic, with painted motifs adorning earthy walls.

Ebony   MULTICUISINE $$

(Map p164; 41783344; 13th fl, Barton Centre, 84 MG Rd; mains ₹150-180) Serves the best Parsi food in town, along with some delectable Thai, French and Indian dishes. The interiors are classy, and the rooftop location heavenly.

Palm Grove   SOUTH INDIAN $

(Ballal Residency, 74/3 3rd Cross, Residency Rd; mains ₹80-100; 7am-10.30pm) One of the best places in Bengaluru's central district where you can tuck into authentic South Indian veg fare, such as dosas, vadas and multicourse thalis.

OTHER AREAS

TOP CHOICE Mavalli Tiffin Rooms   SOUTH INDIAN $

(MTR; Map p162; Lalbagh Rd; mains ₹40-60; 6.30-11am, 12.30-2.45pm, 3.30-7.30pm & 8-9.30pm) A legendary name in South Indian comfort food, this super-popular eatery, commonly called MTR, has had Bengaluru eating out of its hands since 1924. Head up to the dining room upstairs, queue for a table, and then admire the dated images of southern beauties etched on smoky glass as waiters bring you savoury local fare, capped by frothing filter coffee served in silverware. It's a definitive Bengaluru experience; don't leave town without trying it.

Caperberry   CONTINENTAL $$

(Map p160; 25594567; 121 Dickenson Rd; mains ₹240-270) A smart blend of European monochromes and glittering South Indian goldwork create a sophisticated ambience at this fancy restaurant specialising in Spanish food. Paella, or pear and asparagus salad? Take your pick from the extensive menu, and match it with a sangria on the side.

Windsor Pub   MULTICUISINE $$

(7 Kodava Samaja Bldg, 1st Main Vasanthnagar; mains ₹220-280) The awesome fillet steak belted out by this relaxed eatery near Bangalore Palace qualifies as the ultimate death-row meal for many a Bengaluru foodie. And that's not forgetting the flavoursome Mangalorean fish fries, or the tangy *pandhi* (pork) masala from Kodagu's hills. Beer flows freely from the taps as you gleefully stuff your face.

Harima   JAPANESE $$

(off Map p160; 41325757; 4th fl, Devatha Plaza, Residency Rd; mains ₹250-280) Tempura, sashimi, sushi and that refreshing sip of sake. Flavourful Japanese staples form the core of this restaurant's repertoire, noted for its minimalist interiors. It's one of Bengaluru's most underrated places, but you'll certainly spread the word once you've been there.

Olive Beach   MEDITERRANEAN $$$

(Map p160; 41128400; 16 Wood St, Ashoknagar; mains ₹350-400) Lodged within an elegant villa in upscale Ashoknagar is this fantastic fine-dining restaurant, with food that evokes wistful memories of sunny Tuscany (or whatever your fave Mediterranean getaway might be). Spinach and goat cheese pizza, anyone? Or crumbled sausage and cauliflower risotto, maybe? The roasted pumpkin and sage ravioli sure has a few admirers, too.

Sunny's   ITALIAN $$
(Map p160; ✉41329366; 34 Vittal Mallya Rd; mains ₹280-300) Cheese and olive oil conspire to work up some mouth-watering Mediterranean flavours at this popular restaurant specialising in Italian food. Its wide range of pastas, pizzas, salads and desserts are a hit with Bengaluru's expat community.

Barbeque Nation   MUGHLAI $$
(100Ft Rd, Indiranagar; meals ₹450) Good news for kebab lovers. This stylish place has an endless supply of the grilled meaty delights for you to gorge on. Meals feature unlimited portions of a set menu which changes on a daily basis. And the meat is skewered live at your table to suit your tastes! Eat till you're beat.

Gramin   INDIAN $$
(✉41104104; 20, 7th Block Raheja Arcade, Koramangala; mains ₹140-160) A wide choice of flavourful and breezy North Indian fare is on offer at this extremely popular all-veg place. Try the excellent range of lentils, best had with oven-fresh rotis, or the veg kebabs.

🍷 Drinking

BARS & LOUNGES
Despite Bengaluru's rock-steady reputation as a place to get sloshed in style, local laws require pubs and discos to shut shop at 11.30pm (opening time is usually 7.30pm). However, given the wide choice of chic watering holes around, you can indulge in a spirited session of pub-hopping in this original beer town of India. The trendiest nightclubs will typically charge you a cover of around ₹1000 per couple, but it's often redeemable against drinks or food.

TOP CHOICE **Koshy's Bar & Restaurant**   BAR
(Map p164; 39 St Mark's Rd; ◷9am-11.30pm) They say half of Bengaluru's court cases are argued around Koshy's teetering tables, and many hard-hitting newspaper articles written over its steaming coffees. Having quenched the collective thirst of the city's intelligentsia for decades, this buzzy and joyful pub is where you can put away pints of beer and classic British meals (mains ₹170 to ₹200) in-between fervent discussions.

Plan B   PUB
(Map p160; 20 Castle St, Ashoknagar) 'Finish your beer. There are sober kids in India', says a poster adorning this chilled-out pub's robust interiors. And to aid you in this eminently enjoyable task, there's a whole line of awesome bites from peanut masala to porky platters, and some ageless music (remember 'My Sharona'?). The place brims over with motorsports buffs on F1 racedays.

Shiro   BAR
(Map p160; UB City) A sophisticated lounge to get sloshed in style, Shiro has elegant interiors complemented by arty Buddha busts and Apsara figurines. Its commendable selection of cocktails and drinks draw rave reviews from patrons, who often fight off their Saturday night hangovers by converging again for Sunday brunch.

B Flat   BAR
(100ft Rd, Indiranagar) A pub and jazz bar that often features live performances by some of India's best bands, this place is on the radar of every jazz and blues junkie in town. There's a ₹200 entry fee, offset against moody guitar solos.

13th Floor   BAR
(Map p164; 13th fl, Barton Centre, 84 MG Rd) Come early to grab a spot on the terrace sit-out, with all of Bengaluru glittering at your feet. The atmosphere is that of a relaxed cocktail party, and you can tap your feet to a good selection of retro music.

Beach   BAR
(100ft Rd, Indiranagar) Couldn't make it to Goa? Then come to this slick beach-bum's lounge, and feel the sand between your toes (literally), as you dance away to some groovy music. Women drink free on Wednesdays, and there's the occasional quiz night for you to flaunt your GK.

CAFES & TEAHOUSES
Bengaluru is liberally sprinkled with good chain cafes. Those such as **Café Coffee Day** (Map p164; Brigade Rd; ◷8am-11.30pm) and **Barista** (Map p160; 40 St Mark's Rd; ◷8am-11.30pm) have several outlets across town. For something different, try one of the following.

TOP CHOICE **Matteo**   CAFE
(Map p164; Church St; ◷9am-11pm) The hippest and newest cafe in Bengaluru serves first-rate brews (try the aromatic green tea), along with tasty side-orders such as shrimp and penne pasta or a filling chicken

baguette. The coolest rendezvous in the city centre.

Infinitea
CAFE

(Map p160; 2 Shah Sultan Complex, Cunningham Rd; ⏱9am-11pm) The service here can be patchy at times, but the steaming cuppa that follows more than makes up for it. Its menu features orthodox teas from the best estates, alongside a few fancy names such as chocolate tea milkshake.

☆ Entertainment

CINEMA

English-language films are popular, and tickets range from ₹150 to ₹300, depending on your theatre of choice and the show time.

INOX
CINEMA

(☑41128888; www.inoxmovies.com; 5th fl, Garuda Mall, Magrath Rd) Screens new releases from Bollywood and the West.

PVR Cinema
CINEMA

(☑22067511; www.pvrcinemas.com; Forum, 21 Hosur Rd) A megacinema with 11 screens showing Indian and international titles.

Nani Cinematheque
CINEMA

(☑22356262; 5th fl, Sona Tower, 71 Millers Rd) Classic Indian and European films are screened here Friday, Saturday and Sunday.

SPORT

Bengaluru's horse-racing seasons are from November to February and May to July. Contact the **Bangalore Turf Club** (Map p162; www.bangaloreraces.com; Racecourse Rd) for details.

For a taste of India's sporting passion up close, attend one of the regular cricket matches at **M Chinnaswamy Stadium** (Map p160; MG Rd). Details can be found at www.cricketkarnataka.com.

THEATRE

Ranga Shankara
THEATRE

(☑26592777; www.rangashankara.org; 36/2 8th Cross, JP Nagar) All kinds of interesting theatre (in a variety of languages and spanning various genres) and dance are held at this cultural centre.

🛍 Shopping

Bengaluru's shopping options are abundant, ranging from teeming bazaars to glitzy malls. Some good shopping areas include Commercial St (Map p160), Vittal Mallya Rd (Map p160) and the MG Rd area.

UB City
CLOTHING

(Map p160; Vittal Mallya Rd; ⏱11am-9pm) Global haute couture and Indian high fashion come to roost at this towering mall in the central district.

Cauvery Arts & Crafts Emporium
SOUVENIRS

(Map p164; 49 MG Rd; ⏱10am-7pm Mon-Sat) Showcases a great collection of sandalwood and rosewood products as well as textiles.

Ffolio
CLOTHING

(Map p160; 5 Vittal Mallya Rd; ⏱10.30am-8pm) A good place for high Indian fashion, with another branch at Leela Galleria (23 Airport Rd, Kodihalli).

Fabindia
CLOTHING

(54 17th Main Koramangala; ⏱10am-8pm) Commercial St (Map p160); Garuda mall (McGrath Rd) These branches contain Fabindia's full range of stylish clothes and homewares in traditional cotton prints and silks.

Magazines
BOOKSTORE

(Map p164; 55 Church St) An astounding collection of international magazines. Up to 70% discount on back issues.

Blossom
BOOKSTORE

(Map p164; 84/6 Church St) Great deals on new and second-hand books.

Bombay Store
SOUVENIRS

(Map p164; 99 MG Rd; ⏱10.30am-8.30pm) For gifts ranging from ecobeauty products to linens.

Mysore Saree Udyog
CLOTHING

(Map p160; 1st fl, 294 Kamaraj Rd; ⏱10.30am-8.30pm Mon-Sat) A great choice for top-quality silks and saris.

Some good malls in town include **Garuda Mall** (Map p160; McGrath Rd), **Forum** (Hosur Rd; Koramangala) and **Leela Galleria** (23 Airport Rd, Kodihalli).

ℹ Information

Internet Access

Being an IT city, internet cafes are plentiful in Bengaluru, as is wi-fi access in hotels.

Café Coffee Day (Map p160; Brigade Rd; ⏱8am-11.30pm) has a smoking deal comprising an hour's internet usage, cappuccino and cookies.

Left Luggage

The City train station (Map p162) and Central bus stand (Map p162) have 24-hour cloakrooms (per day ₹10).

KARNATAKA & BENGALURU SOUTHERN KARNATAKA

Maps

The tourist offices give out decent city maps. The excellent *Eicher City Map* (₹200) is sold at major bookshops.

Media

080 and *What's Up Bangalore* are great monthly magazines covering the latest in Bengaluru's social life. *Kingfisher Explocity Nights* (₹200) gives a low-down on the best night spots. All titles are available in major bookstores.

Medical Services

Most hotels here have doctors on call.

Hosmat (Map p160; ☑25593796; www.hosmat net.com; 45 Magrath Rd) For critical injuries and other general illnesses.

Mallya Hospital (Map p160; ☑22277979; www .mallyahospital.net; 2 Vittal Mallya Rd) With a 24-hour pharmacy and emergency services.

Money

ATMs are common.

Monarch (Map p164; ☑41123253; 54 Monarch Plaza, Brigade Rd; ☺10am-8pm Mon-Sat) Deals in foreign currency, travellers cheques and ticketing.

TT Forex (Map p160; ☑22254337; 33/1 Cunningham Rd; ☺9.30am-6.30pm Mon-Fri, 9.30am-1.30pm Sat) Changes travellers cheques and foreign currency.

Photography

Digital services are easy to come by.

GK Vale (89 MG Rd; ☺10am-7pm Mon-Sat) One-stop photography shop.

Post

Main post office (Map p160; Cubbon Rd; ☺10am-7pm Mon-Sat, 10am-1pm Sun)

Tourist Information

Government of India tourist office (Map p164; ☑25585417; 48 Church St; ☺9.30am-6pm Mon-Fri, 9am-1pm Sat)

Karnataka State Tourism Development Corporation (KSTDC; Badami House (Map p162; ☑43344334; Badami House, Kasturba Rd; ☺10am-7pm Mon-Sat); Karnataka Tourism House (Map p160; ☑41329211; 8 Papanna Lane, St Mark's Rd; ☺10am-7pm Mon-Sat). Bookings can be made for KSTDC city and state tours, as well as for luxury holidays such as the Golden Chariot.

Karnataka Tourism (Map p162; ☑22352828; 2nd fl, 49 Khanija Bhavan, Racecourse Rd; ☺10am-5.30pm Mon-Sat)

Travel Agencies

Skyway (Map p160; ☑22111401; www.sky waytour.com; 8 Papanna Lane, St Mark's Rd; ☺9am-6pm Mon-Sat) A thoroughly professional outfit with a satellite office in Mysore. Reliable for booking long-distance taxis and air tickets.

STIC Travels (Map p160; ☑22202408; www.stictravel.com; G5 Imperial Ct, 33/1 Cunningham Rd; ☺9.30am-6pm Mon-Sat) For ticketing, vehicles, hotels and holiday packages.

ℹ️ Getting There & Away

Air

Airline offices are generally open from 9am to 5.30pm Monday to Saturday. City offices and 24-hour helplines of domestic carriers serving Bengaluru include the following:

GoAir (☑9223222111; www.goair.in)

Indian Airlines (Map p162; ☑22277747; www.indian-airlines.nic.in; Unity Bldg, JC Rd)

DAILY FLIGHTS FROM BENGALURU

DESTINATION	STARTING FARE ₹	DURATION (HR)
Ahmedabad	3200	2
Chennai (Madras)	2300	1
Delhi	3700	2½
Goa	2600	1
Hyderabad	2400	1
Kochi	2300	1½
Kolkata (Calcutta)	3500	3
Mangalore	2300	1
Mumbai (Bombay)	3000	2
Pune	2600	1½
Trivandrum	3300	1½

MAJOR BUS SERVICES FROM BENGALURU

DESTINATION	FARE (₹)	DURATION (HR)	FREQUENCY
Chennai	274 (R)/472 (V)	7-8	15 daily
Ernakulam	484 (R)/598 (V)	10-12	7 daily
Hampi	316 (R)	8½	1 daily
Hospet	306 (R)/381 (V)	8	6 daily
Hyderabad	432 (R)/736 (V)	10-12	10 daily
Jog Falls	321 (R)	9	1 daily
Mumbai	1059 (V)	19	4 daily
Mysore	136 (R)/247 (V)	3	Every 30min
Ooty	262 (R)/357 (V)	8	8 daily
Panaji	473 (R)/779 (V)	12-14	4 daily
Puttaparthi	71 (R)/185 (V)	4	3 daily

R – Rajahamsa Semideluxe, V – Airavath AC Volvo

IndiGo (☑9910383838; www.goindigo.in)
Jet Airways (Map p162; ☑39893333, 39899999; www.jetairways.com; Unity Bldg, JC Rd)
Kingfisher Airlines (Map p160; ☑18002333131, 41148190; www.flykingfisher .com; 35/2 Cunningham Rd)
SpiceJet (☑18001803333; www.spicejet.com)

Bus

Bengaluru's huge, well-organised **Central bus stand** (Map p162; Gubbi Thotadappa Rd), also known as **Majestic**, is directly in front of the City train station. **Karnataka State Road Transport Corporation** (KSRTC; www.ksrtc .in) buses run throughout Karnataka and to neighbouring states. Other interstate bus operators:

Andhra Pradesh State Road Transport Corporation (APSRTC; www.apsrtc.gov.in)
Kadamba Transport Corporation (☑22351958, 22352922) Services for Goa.
Maharashtra State Road Transport Corporation (MSRTC; www.msrtc.gov.in)
Tamil Nadu State Transport Corporation (SETC; www.tnstc.in)

Computerised advance booking is available for most buses at the station. **KSRTC** (Map p160; Devatha Plaza, Residency Rd) also has convenient booking counters around town, including one at Devantha Plaza. It's wise to book long-distance journeys in advance.

Numerous private bus companies offer comfier and only slightly more expensive services. Private bus operators line the street facing the Central bus stand, or you can book through a travel agency.

For major KSRTC bus services from Bengaluru, see the boxed text above.

Train

Bengaluru's **City train station** (Map p162; Gubbi Thotadappa Rd) is the main train hub and the place to make reservations. **Cantonment train station** (Station Rd) is a sensible spot to disembark if you're arriving and headed for the MG Rd area, while **Yeshvantpur train station** (Rahman Khan Rd), 8km northwest of downtown, is the starting point for Goa trains.

If a train is booked out, foreign travellers can avail the foreign-tourist quota. Buy a wait-listed ticket, then fill out a form at the **Divisional Railway Office** (Map p162; Gubbi Thotadappa Rd) building immediately north of the City train station. You'll know about 10 hours before departure whether you've got a seat (a good chance); if not, the ticket is refunded. The computerised **train reservation office** (Map p162; ☑139; ⊙8am-8pm Mon-Sat, 8am-2pm Sun), on the left facing the station, has separate counters for credit-card purchase, women and foreigners. Luggage can be left at the 24-hour cloakroom on Platform 1 at the City train station (₹10 per bag per day).

See the boxed text p171 for information on major train services.

ⓘ Getting Around

To/From the Airport

The swish city **airport** (☑66782251; www.bengal uruairport.com) is in Hebbal, about 40km north from the MG Rd area. Prepaid taxis can take you from the airport to the city centre (₹700). You can also take the hourly shuttle Vayu Vajra AC bus service to Majestic or MG Rd (₹180).

Autorickshaw

The city's autorickshaw drivers are legally required to use their meters; few comply in reality. After 10pm, 50% is added onto the metered rate. Flag fall is ₹17 for the first 2km and then ₹9 for each extra kilometre.

Bus

Bengaluru has a thorough local bus network, operated by the **Bangalore Metropolitan Transport Corporation** (BMTC; www.bmtcinfo. com). Red AC Vajra buses criss-cross the city, while green Big10 deluxe buses connect the suburbs. Ordinary buses run from the City bus stand (Map p162), next to Majestic; a few operate from the City Market bus stand (Map p162) further south.

To get from the City train station to the MG Rd area, catch any bus from Platform 17 or 18 at the City bus stand. For the City market, take bus 31, 31E, 35 or 49 from Platform 8.

Taxi

Several places around Bengaluru offer taxi rental with driver. Standard rates for a long-haul Tata Indica cab are ₹7 per kilometre for a minimum of 250km, plus a daily allowance of ₹150 for the driver. For an eight-hour day rental, you're looking at around ₹1200. Luxury Renault cabs are also available for ₹60 for 4km kilometre and ₹15 for every subsequent kilometre. Try **Meru Cabs** (44224422) or **Skyway** (22111401).

Metro

Bengaluru's shiny new AC metro service was all set for inauguration at the time of research. With trains plying every four minutes and tickets costing marginally more than intra-city buses, the service comes as a welcome alternative to the city's congested public transport system. For the latest updates on the service, log on to www.bmrc.co.in.

Around Bengaluru

HESSARAGHATTA

Located 30km northwest of Bengaluru, Hessaraghatta is home to **Nrityagram** (080-28466313; www.nrityagram.org; 10am-2pm Tue-Sun), a leading dance academy established in 1990 to revive and popularise Indian classical dance.

The brainchild and living legacy of celebrated dancer Protima Gauri Bedi (1948–98), the complex was designed like a village by Goa-based architect Gerard da Cunha. Long-term courses in classical dance are offered to deserving students here, while local children are taught for free on Sundays. Self-guided tours cost ₹20 or you can book a tour, lecture and demonstration and vegetarian meal (₹1250, minimum 10 people).

Opposite the dance village, **Taj Kuteeram** (080-28466326; www.tajhotels.com; d ₹4000;

MAJOR TRAINS FROM BENGALURU

DESTINATION	TRAIN NO & NAME	FARE (₹)	DURATION (HR)	DEPARTURES
Chennai	12658 *Chennai Mail*	193/655	6	10.45pm
	12028 *Shatabdi*	510/1105	5	6am Wed-Mon
Delhi	12627 *Karnataka Exp*	546/2070	39	7.20pm
	12649 *Sampark Kranti Exp*	536/2020	35	10.10pm Mon, Wed, Fri, Sat & Sun
Hospet	16592 *Hampi Exp*	191/725	9½	9pm
Hubli	16589 *Rani Chennamma Exp*	203/745	8	9.15pm
Kolkata	12864 *YPR Howrah Exp*	508/1900	35	7.35pm
Mumbai	16530 *Udyan Exp*	363/1375	24	7.50pm
Mysore	12007 *Shatabdi*	305/590	2	11am Wed-Mon
	12614 *Tippu Exp*	62/225	2½	3pm
Trivandrum	16526 *Kanyakumari Exp*	325/1217	22	9.40pm

Shatabdi fares are chair/executive; Express (Exp/Mail) fares are 2nd/chair for day trains and sleeper/2AC for night trains.

✳@) is a hotel that combines comfort with rustic charm. It also offers ayurveda and yoga sessions.

🍃**Our Native Village** (☎080-41140909; www.ournativevillage.com; s/d incl full board ₹5000/6800; ✸), an ecofriendly organic farm and resort situated in the vicinity, is a great place to unwind in style while engaging in fun activities such as flying kites, riding bullock carts or milking cows.

From Bengaluru's City Market, buses 253, 253D and 253E run to Hessaraghatta (₹25, one hour), with bus 266 continuing on to Nrityagram.

NANDI HILLS

Rising to 1455m, the **Nandi Hills** (admission ₹5; ⏱6am-10pm), 60km north of Bengaluru, were once the summer retreat of Tipu Sultan. Today, it's the Bengaluru techie's favourite weekend getaway, and is predictably congested on Saturdays and Sundays. Nonetheless, it's a good place for hiking, with good views and two notable **Chola temples.** Buses head to Nandi Hills (₹50, two hours) from Bengaluru's Central bus stand.

JANAPADA LOKA FOLK ARTS MUSEUM

Situated 53km south of Bengaluru, this **museum** (adult/child ₹10/5; ⏱9am-5.30pm) dedicated to the preservation of rural cultures has a wonderful collection of folk art objects, including 500-year-old shadow puppets, festival costumes and musical instruments. Mysore-bound buses (one hour) can drop you here; get off 3km after Ramnagar.

Mysore

☎0821 / POP 799,200 / ELEV 707M

If you haven't been to Mysore, you just haven't seen South India. Conceited though it may sound, this is not an overstatement. An ancient city with more than 600 glorious years of legacy, Mysore is one of the most flamboyant places in India. Known for its glittering royal heritage, bustling markets, magnificent monuments, cosmopolitan culture and a friendly populace, it is also a thriving centre for the production of premium silk, sandalwood and incense. It also flaunts considerable expertise in yoga and ayurveda, two trades it markets worldwide.

The train station is northwest of the city centre, about 1km from the main shopping street, Sayyaji Rao Rd. The Central bus stand is on Bengaluru-Nilgiri (BN) Rd. The Maharaja's Palace sits in the heart of the buzzing quarters southeast of the city centre. The lofty Chamundi Hill is an ever-visible landmark to the south.

History

Mysore owes its name to the mythical Mahisuru, a place where the demon Mahisasura was slain by the goddess Chamundi. Its regal history began in 1399, when the Wodeyar dynasty of Mysore was founded, though they remained in service of the Vijayanagar empire until the mid-16th century. With the fall of Vijayanagar in 1565, the Wodeyars declared their sovereignty, which – save a brief period of Hyder Ali and Tipu Sultan's supremacy in the late 18th century – remained unscathed until 1947.

⊙ Sights

Maharaja's Palace   PALACE
(www.mysorepalace.tv; Indian/foreigner ₹20/200; ⏱10am-5.30pm) Among the grandest of India's royal buildings, this fantastic palace was the former seat of the Wodeyar maharajas. The old palace was gutted by fire in 1897; the one you see now was completed in 1912 by English architect Henry Irwin at a cost of ₹4.5 million.

The interior of this Indo-Saracenic marvel – a kaleidoscope of stained glass, mirrors and gaudy colours – is undoubtedly over the top. The decor is further embellished by carved wooden doors, mosaic floors and a series of paintings depicting life in Mysore during the Edwardian Raj. The way into the palace takes you past a fine collection of sculptures and artefacts. Don't forget to check out the armoury, with an intriguing collection of 700-plus weapons.

Every weekend, on national holidays, and through the Dasara celebrations, the palace is illuminated by nearly 100,000 light bulbs that accent its majestic profile against the night.

While you are allowed to snap the palace's exterior, photography within is strictly prohibited. Cameras must be deposited in lockers (₹5) at the palace entrance.

Also available within the compound is a multilingual guided audio tour of the palace, the price of which is included in the foreigners' ticket.

Devaraja Market   MARKET
(Sayyaji Rao Rd; ⏱6am-8.30pm) Dating from Tipu Sultan's reign, the spellbinding Devaraja Market is a lively bazaar that combines both the ancient and modern faces of India.

International brands compete for space here with local traders selling traditional items such as flower garlands, spices and conical piles of *kumkum* (coloured powder used for bindi dots), and their unique co-existence makes for some great photo-ops. Refresh your bargaining skills before shopping.

Chamundi Hill
SACRED SITE

At a height of 1062m, on the summit of Chamundi Hill, stands the **Sri Chamundeswari Temple** (⊙7am-2pm & 3.30-9pm), dominated by a towering 40m-high *gopuram* (entrance gateway). It's a fine half-day excursion, offering spectacular views of the city below; you can take bus 201 (₹15, 30 minutes) that rumbles up the narrow road to the summit. A return autorickshaw trip will cost about ₹300.

On your way down, you can also take the foot trail comprising 1000-plus steps that Hindu pilgrims use to visit the temple. One-third of the way down is a 5m-high statue of **Nandi** (Shiva's bull) that was carved out of solid rock in 1659.

Jayachamarajendra Art Gallery
ART GALLERY

(Jaganmohan Palace Rd; adult/child ₹20/10; ⊙8.30am-5pm) Built in 1861 as the royal auditorium, the **Jaganmohan Palace**, just west of the Maharaja's Palace, houses the Jayachamarajendra Art Gallery, with a collection of kitsch objects and regal memorabilia including rare musical instruments, Japanese art, and paintings by the noted artist Raja Ravi Varma.

FREE Indira Gandhi Rashtriya Manav Sangrahalaya
MUSEUM

(National Museum of Mankind; www.igrms.com; Wellington Lodge, Irwin Rd; ⊙10am-5.30pm Tue-Sun) This museum functions primarily as a cultural centre and exhibition space showcasing arts from rural India. Housing excellent rotating exhibitions and a souvenir shop, the centre organises two-week workshops in traditional art forms, which are open to the public. The interiors of the museum were under renovation at the time of research but should be completed by the time you read this. Don't miss the fantastic permanent terracotta exhibition – comprising artefacts from across the country – on the front lawn.

FREE Jayalakshmi Vilas Complex Museum
MUSEUM

(Mysore University Campus; ⊙10am-5.30pm Mon-Sat, closed alternate Sat) This museum, housed in a grand mansion, specialises in folklore. A wooden puppet of the 10-headed demon Ravana, leather shadow puppets, rural costumes and a 300-year-old temple cart are part of its fantastic collection.

Rail Museum
MUSEUM

(KRS Rd; adult/child ₹5/2, camera/video ₹10/25; ⊙9.30am-6.30pm Tue-Sun) This one's a real gem, and certainly not to be missed. Located behind the train station, the open-air museum bears testimony to the stylish way in which the royals once rode the railways. The chief exhibit is the Mysore maharani's saloon, a wood-panelled beauty dating from 1899. There are also five steam engines, each with its own story, and a large collection of instruments and memorabilia from the Indian Railways' chequered past. It's half a day of pure fun.

DUSSEHRA JAMBOREE

Mysore is at its carnivalesque best during the 10-day Dussehra (locally spelt 'Dasara') festival in October. Every evening, the Maharaja's Palace is dramatically lit up, while the town is transformed into a gigantic fairground, with concerts, dance performances, sporting demonstrations and cultural events running to packed houses. On the last day, the celebrations are capped off in grand style. A dazzling procession of richly costumed elephants, garlanded idols, liveried retainers and cavalry kicks off around 1pm, marching through the streets to the rhythms of clanging brass bands, all the way from the palace to the Bannimantap parade ground. A torchlight parade at Bannimantap and a spectacular session of fireworks then closes the festival for the year.

Mysore is choc-a-bloc with tourists during the festival, especially on the final day. To bypass suffocating crowds, consider buying a Dasara VIP Gold Card (₹6000 for two). Though expensive, it assures you good seats at the final day gala and helps you beat the entry queues at other events and performances, while providing discounts on accommodation, dining and shopping. It's also possible to buy tickets (₹250 to ₹1000) just for entering the palace and Bannimantap for the final day's parades. Contact the local Karnataka Tourism office or the **Dasara Information Centre** (✆2418888; www.mysore dasara.gov.in) for more details.

Mysore

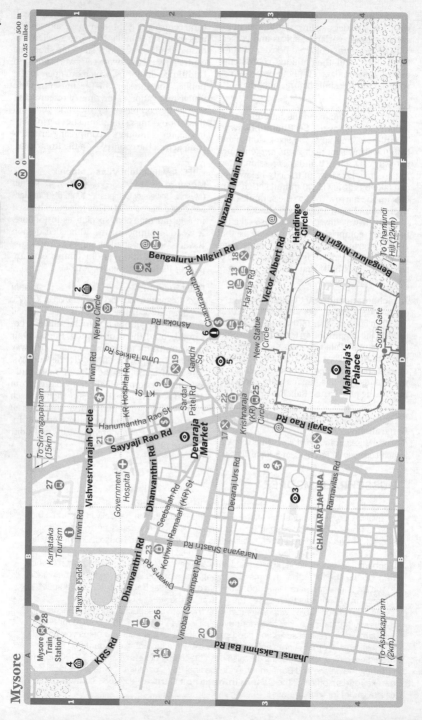

KARNATAKA & BENGALURU MYSORE

Other Sights · LANDMARKS

For architecture buffs, Mysore has quite a handful of charming buildings. Dating from 1805, **Government House** (Irwin Rd), formerly the British Residency, is a Tuscan Doric building set in 20 hectares of **gardens** (⊙5am-9pm). Facing the north gate of the Maharaja's Palace is the 1927 **Silver Jubilee Clock Tower** (Ashoka Rd); nearby stands the imposing **Rangacharlu Memorial Hall**, built in 1884. The beauty of towering **St Philomena's Cathedral** (St Philomena St; ⊙5am-6pm), built between 1933 and 1941 in neo-Gothic style, is emphasised by beautiful stained-glass windows.

Mysore's **zoo** (Indiranagar; adult/child ₹30/15, camera/video ₹10/150; ⊙8.30am-5.30pm Wed-Mon), set in pretty gardens on the eastern edge of the city, dates from 1892. A range of primates, tigers, elephants, bears, birds and rhinos live here.

🏃 Activities

Royal Mysore Walks · WALKING

(9632044188; www.royalmysorewalks.com; per person ₹495) A walking tour is an excellent way to familiarise yourself with Mysore's epic history and heritage. Run by techie-turned-historian Vinay, the outfit organises weekend walks with a specific focus on either the city's royal history, its markets, its old quarters or its handicrafts. Offbeat walks, such as a yoga and spirituality tour, can also be arranged at extra cost.

Emerge Spa · AYURVEDA

(☏2522500; www.emergespa.co.in; Windflower Spa & Resort, Maharanapratap Rd, Nazarbad) Mysore's spa operations are spearheaded by the slick, out-of-town Emerge Spa, where you can drop by for a pampering ayurvedic session (try the one-hour Abhayanga massage for ₹1600) or a range of Balinese massage, hydrotherapy and beauty treatments.

Swaasthya Ayurveda Retreat Village · AYURVEDA

(☏6557557, 9448056406; www.swaasthya.com; 69 Bommaru Agrahara; s/d incl full board ₹2000/3000; @) For an exceptionally peaceful and refreshing ayurvedic vacation, head 12km towards Srirangapatnam to this retreat, where you can spend some time in quiet meditation and feel your senses feast on the lush greenery, the aromatic herb gardens, the simple vegetarian food and the gurgling sounds of the Cauvery River. Daily rates include basic yoga sessions; for specific ayurvedic treatments, there are special packages on offer. Book well in advance.

Indus Valley Ayurvedic Centre AYURVEDA (✆2473263; www.ayurindus.com; Lalithadripura; s/d incl full board ₹8400/14,090) Set on 16 acres of gardens, this classy centre derives its therapies from ancient scriptures and prescriptions. A wide variety of treatments and basic training programs are on offer. The overnight package includes one session each of ayurveda, yoga and beauty therapy.

Karanji Lake Nature Park BIRDWATCHING (Indiranagar; admission ₹10, camera/video ₹10/25; ☉8.30am-5.30pm) Next to the zoo, ths nature park is the place to spy on various bird species, including great and little cormorants, purple and grey herons, egrets, black ibises, rose-ringed parakeets, green bee-eaters and painted storks, as well as several kinds of butterflies.

🎓 Courses

Yoga

The following places have put Mysore on the international yoga map. Unlike casual centres, they are all austerely committed to the art, and require at least a month's commitment on your part. You'll also need to register far in advance, as they are often booked out. Call or write to the centres for details.

Ashtanga Yoga Research Institute YOGA (AYRI; ✆9880185500; www.kpjayi.org; 3rd Stage, 235 8th Cross, Gokulam) Founded by the renowned Ashtanga teacher K Pattabhi Jois, who taught Madonna her yoga moves.

Atma Vikasa Centre YOGA (✆2341978; www.atmavikasayoga.com; Kuvempunagar Double Rd) 'Backbending expert' Yogacharya Venkatesh offers courses in yoga, Sanskrit and meditation. Call in advance to find out if they've already shifted to a new campus 2km away.

Sri Patanjala Yogashala YOGA (Yoga Research Institute; Sri Brahmatantra Swatantra Parakala Mutt, Jaganmohan Palace Circle; ☉6-8am & 5-7pm) The baby of well-respected Ashtanga practitioner BNS Iyengar (not to be confused with BKS Iyengar, famed exponent of Iyengar yoga).

Music

Jayashankar, the music teacher at **Shruthi Musical Works** (✆9845249518; 1189 3rd Cross,

ℹ NO 'TOURISTS', PLEASE

Yoga Institutes, as well as local laws, insist that all visitors arriving in Mysore to train in yoga must do so on a student visa, not a casual tourist visa. You are also required to register yourself at the local police station within 14 days of your arrival.

Irwin Rd; ☉10.30am-9pm Mon-Sat, 10.30am-2pm Sun) gets good reviews for his tabla instructions (₹200 per hour).

☞ Tours

KSTDC runs a daily Mysore city tour (₹175), taking in the entire city, Chamundi Hill, Srirangapatnam and Brindavan Gardens. It starts daily at 8.30am, ends at 8.30pm and is likely to leave you breathless!

Other KSTDC tours include one to Belur, Halebid and Sravanabelagola (₹450) on Tuesdays and Thursdays from 7.30am to 9pm. It requires a minimum of 10 people, so call in advance.

There's also a three-day tour of Ooty, Kodaikanal, Doddabetta and Coonoor every Monday, Thursday and Saturday (per person including accommodation is ₹2500) that starts off from Bengaluru; you can join at Mysore. These tours generally run during the high season.

All tours leave from the tours office at **Hotel Mayura Hoysala** (✆2423652; 2 Jhansi Lakshmi Bai Rd). Bookings can be made at the nearby **KSTDC Transport Office** (✆2423652; 2 Jhansi Lakshmi Bai Rd; ☉8.30am-8.30pm) or at travel agencies around town.

🛏 Sleeping

Mysore attracts tourists through the year and can fill up very quickly during Dussehra. Booking early is recommended. Check with the tourist office about government-approved homestays, offering rooms from around ₹400 per person.

The following have hot water (at least in the morning) and 24-hour checkout.

TOP CHOICE Parklane Hotel HOTEL $$ (✆4003500; www.parklanemysore.com; 2720 Harsha Rd; s/d from ₹900/1200; ✲🛜🐾) If there's one place in town that can spoil you for a grand a night, this is it. The travellers' central on Mysore's tourist circuit, the Parklane features snug and thoughtfully outfitted rooms (even mobile-phone chargers are provided), livened up by motley tilework on the walls and lovely city views framed in sheer-draped windows. The loos are the cleanest you'll find in town. And the restaurant on the first floor is one happy place to be in the evenings.

Mysore Youth Hostel   HOSTEL $
(☏2544704; www.yhmysore.com; Gangothri Layout; dm from ₹60) Shoestringers take note. This cutie is arguably the nicest hostel in all of India. Set against a patch of green lawns 3km west of town, it's clean, tidy, well-maintained and manned by an extremely professional staff. OK, there's an 11pm curfew, but then, there's also breakfast for ₹25 and dinner for ₹35. An age proof and identity document must be produced when checking in.

Hotel Mayura Hoysala   HOTEL $
(☏2426160; 2 Jhansi Lakshmi Bai Rd; s/d incl breakfast from ₹800/900; ❄) This government-owned hotel continues to offer its blend of mothballed heritage (lace-lined curtains, heavy wooden doors, assorted cane furniture and old photographs lining its corridors) at affordable prices, and the bar downstairs is popular with Mysore's tipplers.

Ginger   HOTEL $$
(☏6633333; www.gingerhotels.com; Nazarbad Mohalla; s/d ₹2499/2999; ❄🖥) An ultramodern, DIY business hotel, Ginger has slick and comfortable rooms painted in warm orange tones. Endless features such as a gymnasium, wi-fi, a 24-hour cafe, an ATM, snacks dispensers and juice vending machines complement the warm hospitality of its professional staff. The in-house spa offers ayurvedic sessions from ₹1200.

Royal Orchid Metropole   HERITAGE HOTEL $$$
(☏4255566; www.royalorchidhotels.com; 5 Jhansi Lakshmi Bai Rd; s/d incl breakfast from ₹4999/5999; ❄🖥🏊) Originally built by the Wodeyars to serve as the residence of the Maharaja's British guests, this is Mysore's leading heritage address. A fascinating colonial-era structure with bona fide old-world charm, it has 30 rooms oozing with character, and a stay here is spiced up with several add-ons such as occasional magic shows, music concerts, dance recitals, snake charming performances and astrological sessions.

Hotel Maurya Residency   HOTEL $$
(☏2523375; www.sangrouphotel.com; Harsha Rd; d from ₹995; ❄🖥) Along with Hotel Maurya

Palace, its twin establishment next door, the Maurya Residency remains a trusted name among the Harsha Rd midrange gang. It's a friendly place with well-appointed rooms and ecofriendly directives slapped all around. **Veg Kourt**, the restaurant downstairs, serves a sumptuous all-you-can-eat breakfast for ₹65.

Hotel Dasaprakash   HOTEL $
(☏2442444; www.mysoredasaprakashgroup.com; Gandhi Sq; s/d from ₹275/520, d with AC ₹1200; ❄) A stalwart in Mysore's hospitality industry, this hotel is particularly popular with local tourists and pilgrim groups. Rooms are well maintained; some get a touch of antiquity with old wooden furniture. However, maintenance may not always be up to expectations. An inexpensive veg restaurant, an ice-cream parlour and an astro-palmist are available within the complex.

Green Hotel   HERITAGE HOTEL $$
(☏4255000; www.greenhotelindia.com; 2270 Vinoba Rd; Jayalakshmipuram; s/d incl breakfast from ₹2250/2750) Given you're 3km west of town, you're largely paying for the ambience here, which is more prominent in the themed and moody rooms in the main palace building. Those overlooking the garden are bare, inadequately appointed for the price and sparsely evoke nostalgia.

Pai Vista   HOTEL $$
(☏2521111; www.paihotels.com; 35A BN Rd; s/d incl breakfast ₹3000/3500; ❄🖥🏊) A mint-fresh business hotel smack opposite the bus stand. Rooms and features are on par with any other hotel in its category. There's a pub called **Opium** that plays groovy music in the evenings.

Viceroy   HOTEL $$
(☏2425111; www.theviceroygroup.com; Harsha Rd; s/d from ₹1895/2295; ❄@) Very competitively priced, The Viceroy continues to stay abreast of the midrange race in town. However, the main reason for checking into one of its comfy rooms is the million-dollar view of the Maharaja's Palace from your window and the rooftop restaurant.

Eating & Drinking

Mysore is well served by Indian restaurants. For Western food you're best sticking with the major hotels. Unless otherwise mentioned, restaurants are open from noon to 3pm and 7pm to 11pm.

Malgudi Café   CAFE $
(Green Hotel, mains ₹60-80; ⏱9.30am-7pm) This ambient cafe set around an inner courtyard

within Green Hotel's main building brews some of the best South Indian coffees and Himalayan teas, coupling them with a number of tasty snacks. It actively promotes the causes of downtrodden communities while generating employment for them – all the attendants here come from underprivileged backgrounds. You can do your bit by ordering a second cuppa.

TOP CHOICE Pelican Pub
PUB $

(Hunsur Rd; mains ₹80-100; ⊙11am-11pm) A wonderful pub is the Pelican! Whether you love your Ogden Nash or not, you're bound to be one happy soul here. An alfresco-style watering hole located en route to Green Hotel, this laid-back joint serves beer for ₹50 a mug and some sinful pork chilli for ₹110 a platter. Happiness, of course, comes free.

Parklane Hotel
MULTICUISINE $$

(Parklane Hotel, 2720 Harsha Rd; mains ₹100-140) Choose from a wide selection of tasty Indian, Continental and Chinese dishes while lounging at one of the Parklane's picnic-style garden tables, lit up moodily by countless lanterns. The indoor seating area allows you to interact with house musicians who play popular Indian and Western tunes on request. A good place to exchange notes with fellow travellers.

Tiger Trail
INDIAN $$

(Royal Orchid Metropole, 5 Jhansi Lakshmi Bai Rd; mains ₹180-220) This sophisticated restaurant works up delectable Indian dishes in a courtyard that twinkles with torches and fairy lights at night. The best section on its menu comprises exotic jungle recipes collected from different tiger reserves across India.

Hotel RRR
SOUTH INDIAN $

(Gandhi Sq; mains ₹50-70) Classic Andhra-style food is ladled out at this ever-busy eatery, and you will likely have to queue for a table during meals. One item to try is the piping-hot veg thali (₹50) served on banana leaves. There's a second branch on Harsha Rd.

Vinayaka Mylari
SOUTH INDIAN $

(769 Nazarbad Main Rd; mains ₹30-50; ⊙7.30am-11.30am & 4-8pm) Local foodies say this is one of the best eateries in town to try local staples such as the *masala dosa* (papery lentil-flour pancakes stuffed with seasonal vegetables) and *idlis* (rice cakes) served with coconut chutney.

Café Aramane
SOUTH INDIAN $

(Sayyaji Rao Rd, mains ₹40-60; ⊙7.30am-10pm) Yet another of Mysore's august establishments, this busy cafe rolls out steaming breakfast platters for Mysore's office-goers, and welcomes them back in the evenings with aromatic filter coffee and a convoy of delicious snacks.

Café Coffee Day
CAFE $

(CCD; Devaraj Urs Rd; snacks ₹60-90; ⊙10am-11pm) Yes, these guys do have a gazillion outlets across India, but few other branches can match this lovely operation in terms of chill factor. The cool terrace sit-out is where you'll find Mysore's college brigade downing their joes with vigour.

🔒 Shopping

Mysore is a great place to shop for its famed sandalwood products, silk saris and wooden toys. It is also one of India's major incense-manufacturing centres.

Souvenir and handicraft shops are dotted around Jaganmohan Palace and Dhanvanthri Rd, while silk shops line Devaraj Urs Rd. Look for the butterfly-esque 'Silk Mark' on your purchase; it's an endorsement for quality silk.

Government Silk Factory
CLOTHING

(Mananthody Rd, Ashokapuram; ⊙10am-6.30pm Mon-Sat) Given that Mysore's prized silk is made under its very sheds, this is the best and cheapest place to shop for the exclusive textile. Behind the showroom is the factory, where you can drop by between 7.30am and 4pm to see how the fabric is made. There's an **outlet** (⊙10.30am-7.30pm Mon-Sat) on KR Circle as well.

Sandalwood Oil Factory
SOUVENIRS

(Ashokapuram; ⊙9.30-11am & 2-4pm Mon-Sat) This is a quality-assured place for sandalwood products such as incense, soap, cosmetic products and the prohibitively expensive pure sandalwood oil (₹1350 for 5ml!). Sandalwood is currently in short supply, so prices may escalate further in future. Guided tours are available to show you around the factory, and explain how the products are made.

Cauvery Arts & Crafts Emporium
CLOTHING

(Sayyaji Rao Rd; ⊙10am-7.30pm) Not the cheapest place, but the selection is extensive, the quality is unquestionable and there's no pressure to buy.

Fabindia
CLOTHING

(☑4259009; 451 Jhansi Lakshmi Bai Rd, Chamrajpuram; ⊙10am-8pm) A branch of the ever reliable clothing and homewares shop, en route to the silk and sandalwood factories.

Shruthi Musical Works MUSIC STORE
(1189 3rd Cross, Irwin Rd; ⊙10.30am-8pm Mon-Sat) Sells a variety of traditional musical instruments including tabla sets and assorted percussion instruments.

Sapna Book House BOOKSTORE
(1433 Narayan Shastry Rd; ⊙10.30am-8.30pm) A good collections of paperbacks and magazines, along with souvenirs.

ⓘ Information

Internet Access
Benaka Graphics (Sayyaji Rao Rd; per hr ₹20; ⊙10.30am-7.30pm) Internet, printing, image burning and photocopying facilities.
KSE Internet (Hotel Ramanashree Complex; BN Rd; per hr ₹30; ⊙10am-10pm) Fast internet connections.

Left Luggage
The City bus stand's cloakroom, open from 6am to 11pm, costs ₹10 per bag for 12 hours.

Medical Services
Government Hospital (☑4269806; Dhanvanthri Rd) Has a 24-hour pharmacy.

Money
HDFC Bank (Devaraj Urs Rd) ATM.
ICICI Bank (BN Rd) ATM location, below Hotel Pai Vista.
State Bank of Mysore (cnr Irwin & Ashoka Rds; ⊙10.30am-2.30pm & 3-4pm Mon-Fri, 10.30am-12.30pm Sat) Changes cash and travellers cheques.
Thomas Cook (☑2420090; Silver Tower, 9/2 Ashoka Rd; ⊙9.30am-6pm Mon-Sat) For foreign currency.

Photography
Danthi (44 Devaraj Urs Rd; ⊙10am-8pm)
Rekha Colour Lab (142 Dhanvanthri Rd; ⊙9am-9.30pm)

Post
DHL (Jhansi Lakshmi Bai Rd; ⊙9.30am-8.30pm Mon-Sat)
Main post office (cnr Irwin & Ashoka Rds; ⊙10am-6pm Mon-Sat)

Tourist Information
Karnataka Tourism (☑2422096; Old Exhibition Bldg, Irwin Rd; ⊙10am-5.30pm Mon-Sat) Extremely helpful.
KSTDC Transport Office (☑2423652; 2 Jhansi Lakshmi Bai Rd; ⊙8.30am-8.30pm) KSTDC has counters at the train station and Central bus stand, as well as this transport office next to KSTDC Hotel Mayura Hoysala.

ⓘ Getting There & Away

Air
Mysore's new airport had been freshly commissioned during research, with a solitary Kingfisher flight to Bengaluru (one hour) continuing to Chennai (three hours). **Indian Airlines** (☑2426317; Jhansi Lakshmi Bai Rd; ⊙10am-5pm Mon-Sat) has a booking office next to Hotel Mayura Hoysala for flights out of other cities. For booking on other carriers, try **Skyway** (☑2444444; 370/4 Jhansi Lakshmi Bai Rd; ⊙10am-6pm Mon-Sat).

Bus
The **Central bus stand** (BN Rd) handles all KSRTC long-distance buses. The **City bus stand** (Sayyaji Rao Rd) is for city, Srirangapatnam and Chamundi Hill buses. KSRTC bus services

BUSES FROM MYSORE

DESTINATION	FARE (₹)	DURATION (HR)	FREQUENCY
Bandipur	52 (O)	2	4 daily
Bengaluru	136 (R)/217 (V)	3	every 30min
Channarayapatna	56 (O)	2	hourly
Chennai	829 (V)	12	4 daily
Ernakulam	388 (R)/530 (V)	11	4 daily
Gokarna	323 (O)	12	1 daily
Hassan	76 (O)	3	hourly
Hospet	291 (O)	10	4 daily
Mangalore	252 (R)/350 (V)	7	hourly
Ooty	123 (R)/184 (V)	5	8 daily

O – Ordinary, R – Rajahamsa Semideluxe, V – Airavath AC Volvo

from Mysore include those listed in the boxed text p179.

For Belur, Halebid or Sravanabelagola, the usual gateway is Hassan. For Hampi, the best transfer point is Hospet.

The **Private bus stand** (Sayyaji Rao Rd) has services to Hubli, Bijapur, Mangalore, Ooty and Ernakulam. You'll find several ticketing agents around the stand.

Train

From Mysore's railway booking office, buy a ticket on the 6.45am *Chamundi Express* or the 11am *Tippu Express* to Bengaluru (2nd class/chair ₹66/195, three hours). The 2.15 *Shatabdi Express* also connects Bengaluru (chair/executive ₹275/550, two hours) and Chennai (chair/executive ₹695/1315, seven hours) daily except Tuesday. Several passenger trains to Bengaluru (₹35, 3½ hours), stop at Srirangapatnam (₹15, 20 minutes). The 10.15pm *Mysore Dharwad Express* goes to Hubli (sleeper/2AC ₹206/750, 9½ hours).

ⓘ Getting Around

Agencies at hotels and around town rent cabs for about ₹7 per kilometre, with a minimum of 250km per day, plus a daily allowance of ₹150 for the driver.

The flagfall on autorickshaws is ₹15, and ₹7 per kilometre is charged thereafter. Autorickshaws can also be hired along Harsha Rd for a day's sightseeing (₹900).

Around Mysore

SRIRANGAPATNAM
🖉08236

Steeped in bloody history, the fort town of Srirangapatnam, 16km for Mysore, is built on an island straddling the Cauvery River. The seat of Hyder Ali and Tipu Sultan's power, this town was the de facto capital of much of southern India during the 18th century. Srirangapatnam's glory days ended when the British waged an epic war again Tipu Sultan in 1799, when he was defeated and killed. However, the ramparts, battlements and some of the gates of the fort still stand, as do a clutch of monuments.

Close to the bus station is a handsome twin-tower mosque built by the sultan. Within the fort walls are the dungeon where Tipu held British officers captive, and the handsome **Sri Ranganathaswamy Temple** (☉7.30am-1pm & 4-8pm). Srirangapatnam's star attraction, however, is Tipu's summer palace, **Daria Daulat Bagh** (Indian/foreigner ₹5/100; ☉9am-5pm), which lies 1km east of the fort. Built largely out of wood, the palace is notable for the lavish decoration covering every inch of its interiors. The ceilings are embellished with floral designs, while the walls bear murals depicting courtly life and Tipu's campaigns against the British. There's a small museum within, which houses several artefacts including a portrait of Tipu Sultan, aged 30, painted by European artist John Zoffany in 1780.

About 2km further east, the remains of Hyder Ali, his wife and Tipu are housed in the impressive onion-domed **Gumbaz** (admission free; ☉8am-8pm), which stands amid serene gardens. Head 500m east of Gumbaz for the river banks to end your trip with a refreshing **coracle ride** (per boat ₹150, 15 min).

Just 3km upstream, the **Ranganathittu Bird Sanctuary** (Indian/foreigner ₹25/75, camera/video ₹25/100; ☉8.30am-6pm) is on one of three islands in the Cauvery River. Resident storks, ibises, egrets, spoonbills and cormorants are best seen at dawn or late afternoons on a **boat ride** (per person ₹100).

🛏 Sleeping & Eating

Mayura River View   HOTEL **$$**
(🖉252113; d from ₹1750; ✳) How we wish all government hotels were done up like the Mayura River View. Set on a quiet patch of riverbank, its cosy bungalows are custommade for unwinding in the lap of nature. And the **restaurant** (mains ₹90 to ₹120) has a wonderful sit-out from where you can gaze at the river while guzzling beer.

Royal Retreat New Amblee Holiday Resort   HOTEL **$$**
(🖉9845002665; www.ambleeresort.com; d from ₹1200; ✳✳) A menagerie of rabbits, ducks, turkeys and emus welcome you into the Amblee, which offers relatively good accommodation and a swimming pool to splash in. It has a pleasant riverside setting opposite the River View, and a reasonably priced restaurant that doesn't serve booze (although you can whisk it away to your room).

ⓘ Getting There & Away

Take buses 313 or 316 (₹14, one hour) that depart frequently from Mysore's City bus stand. Passenger trains travelling from Mysore to Bengaluru (₹12, 20 minutes) also stop here. The stand for private buses heading to Brindavan

Gardens (₹18, 30 minutes) is just across from Srirangapatnam's main bus stand.

ⓘ Getting Around

The sights are a little spread out, but walking isn't out of the question, especially in winter. For a quicker tour, an autorickshaw from Mysore is about ₹400 (three hours).

BRINDAVAN GARDENS

If you're familiar with Bollywood cinema, these ornamental **gardens** (adult/child ₹20/15, camera/video ₹50/100; ⊙8am-8.30pm) might give you a sense of déjà vu – they've indeed been the backdrop for many a gyrating musical number. The best time to visit is in the evening, when the fountains are illuminated and made to dance to popular film tunes.

There's no reason to halt a night in the gardens. For a special experience, however, you might consider checking into the swanky **Royal Orchid Brindavan Garden** (☑9945815566; www.royalorchidhotels.com; s/d incl breakfast from ₹4499/4999; ❉🛜🐾), an enormous luxury hotel perched atop a hillock overlooking the gardens. The rooms here are lavishly outfitted, and the strategically-located Elephant Bar is a vantage point from where to view the light-and-sound shows while sipping on your poison.

The gardens are 19km northwest of Mysore. One of the KSTDC tours stops here, and buses 301, 304, 305, 306 and 365 depart from Mysore's City bus stand hourly (₹15, 45 minutes).

MELKOTE

Life in the devout Hindu town of Melkote, about 50km north of Mysore, revolves around the atmospheric 12th-century **Cheluvanarayana Temple** (Raja St; ⊙8am-1pm & 5-8pm), with its rose-coloured *gopuram* (gateway tower) and ornately carved pillars. Get a workout on the hike up to the hilltop **Yoganarasimha Temple**, which offers fine views of the surrounding hills. The town comes alive for the **Vairamudi Festival** in March or April.

Three KSRTC buses shuttle daily between Mysore and Melkote (₹45, 1½ hours).

SOMNATHPUR

The astonishingly beautiful **Keshava Temple** (Indian/foreigner ₹5/100; ⊙8.30am-5.30pm) is one of the finest examples of Hoysala architecture, on par with the masterpieces of Belur and Halebid. Built in 1268, this star-shaped temple, 33km from Mysore, is adorned with superb stone sculptures depicting various scenes from the Ramayana, Mahabharata and Bhagavad Gita, and the life and times of the Hoysala kings.

On a tree in the temple grounds there's a red postbox, where prestamped mail posted by you will be collected by the local post office and marked with a special postmark bearing the temple's image – this is a great memento to send back home.

Somnathpur is 12km south of Bannur and 10km north of Tirumakudal Narsipur. Take one of the half-hourly buses from Mysore to either village (₹15, 30 minutes) and change there.

WORTH A TRIP

GO FISH

Game for some fishy gambolling? Then you're in luck. About 75km from Mysore, strung along the densely forested banks of the quiet-flowing Cauvery River, are the picturesque fishing camps of **Bheemeshwari**, **Galibore** and **Doddamakali**, teeming with their resident populations of carp, catfish and the venerable mahseer. Anglers are fast converging from around the world to hook these 45kg-plus beasts who (going by the trophy shots displayed in the dining hall) often seem to match their human captors in size. All fishing is on a catch-and-release policy. There's some equipment on hire, but get your own tackles, if possible.

Non-anglers, meanwhile, can engage in kayaking, coracle rides, biking or ayurveda sessions. Of the three camps, Bheemeshwari is the most developed in terms of facilities, and more easily accessible.

Accommodation is in a choice of ecofriendly cottages (per person incl full board Indian/foreigner from ₹2500/€70) operated by **Jungle Lodges & Resorts** (Map p164; ☑080-25597944; www.junglelodges.com; Shrungar Shopping Complex, MG Rd, Bengaluru; ⊙10am-5.30pm Mon-Sat). Book in Bengaluru or online.

The best way to reach the camps is by taxi. Drive past Malavalli, before turning right at Sathanur. It's 23km from here to Bheemeshwari. Resort jeeps connect the other camps from here.

About 60km east of Mysore is Sivasamu-dram, home to the twin waterfalls of Bara-chukki and Gaganachukki. The site of India's first hydroelectric project (1902), it's a place where you can spend a quiet time while indulging in natural bounties.

A few kilometres away is Hebbani village, where the affable Hatherell couple and their 10 dogs run the relaxing **Georgia Sunshine Village** (✆9448110660; www.georgiasunshine. com; d incl full board from ₹5000; ❈❋), a superb family getaway with accommodation in cosy bungalows, a sparkling swimming pool and delicious homemade food. Treks and fishing trips can be arranged on request.

Frequent buses run from Mysore (₹30, one hour) to Malavalli, 14km away. The Ha-therells can arrange an autorickshaw pick-up for ₹150. Call well in advance.

Hassan

✆08172 / POP 133,200

With a good range of hotels, a railhead and other conveniences, Hassan is a handy base for exploring Belur (38km), Halebid (33km) and Sravanabelagola (48km). Situated close to Mysore and Bengaluru, it's a bustling town with friendly people.

🛌 Sleeping

TOP CHOICE Hoysala Village Resort HOTEL **$$$**
(✆256764; www.hoysalavillageresorts.com; Belur Rd; cottage incl full board ₹6300; ❈❋) Located 6km from town on the road to Belur, this fantastic getaway is set amid a patch of manicured gardens, tucked around which are comfy cottages with large windows looking onto palms and hedges. There's a treehouse where you can laze away the evening, beer in hand, or flex your pectorals in the aqua-blue pool. And the food at the **restaurant** adjoining the reception area is scrummy to boot. The resort also has an ayurvedic massage centre; sessions kick off from around ₹700.

Hotel Suvarna Regency HOTEL **$$**
(✆266774; www.suvarnaregencyhotel.com; BM Rd; d from ₹750; ❈❋@) This place, just south of Gandhi Sq, is frequented by business people, and is one of Hassan's trusted oldies. It's often bulk-booked by organisers of conferences and conventions, so call early. The rooms are comfy, though dated in terms of decor.

Jewel Rock HOTEL **$**
(✆261048; BM Rd; d from ₹700; ❈) Close to the train station, this place is an absolute steal. The spacious rooms, with floral curtains, are comfortable and well-kept. Raucous private parties are often thrown by locals in the banquet hall downstairs; hopefully, you'll be checking in on a quieter day.

Hotel Hassan Ashhok HOTEL **$$**
(✆268731; www.hassanashok.com; BM Rd; s/d from ₹3000/3350; ❈❋) Clearly the classiest of Hassan's city options, this elegantly de-signed hotel offers you all the requisite luxe features, baskets full of herbal toiletries in the showers and plenty of fluffy white pil-lows to crash on. The **restaurant** works up a good range of Indian dishes, including a jumbo kebab platter (₹350).

Hotel Sri Krishna HOTEL **$**
(✆263240; BM Rd; s/d ₹350/725, d with AC ₹975; ❈) Hugely popular with local tourists, this place has biggish rooms done up in red-and-black checks, and large windows. There's a quality veg **restaurant** (mains ₹40 to ₹60) downstairs. Book well in advance.

🍴 Eating

Suvarna Gate MULTICUISINE **$$**
(Hotel Suvarna Regency, BM Rd; mains ₹90-130; ⊙noon-3.30pm & 6.30-11.30pm) Located to the rear of Hotel Suvarna Regency, this classy eatery tosses up some excellent Indian, Chi-nese and Continental mainstays – the chick-en tandoori masala is particularly delicious.

Mayur INDIAN **$$**
(Hotel Jewel Rock, BM Rd; mains ₹80-110; ⊙noon-3pm & 7-11pm) Hungry crowds flock to this eatery every evening for its lip-smacking South Indian as well as North Indian nonveg fare. The staff are patient and polite.

Hotel GRR SOUTH INDIAN **$**
(Bus Stand Rd; mains ₹30-60; ⊙11am-11pm) Top-of-the-line Andhra-style thalis (₹35) and a popular chicken biryani (₹60) personify this grubby joint next to the bus stand.

ℹ Information

The train station is 2km east of town on Bengaluru-Mangalore (BM) Rd. The Central bus stand is on the corner of AVK College and Bus Stand Rds. The helpful **tourist office** (✆268862; AVK College Rd; ⊙10am-5.30pm Mon-Sat) is 100m east of the bus stand. SBI and HDFC Bank have ATMs on BM Rd, but change foreign cur-rency in Bengaluru or Mysore. There's an internet cafe (per hr ₹20) below Hotel Suvarna Regency.

ⓘ Getting There & Away

Bus

Starting from 6am, buses leave the Central bus stand hourly for Halebid (₹18, one hour) and Belur (₹23, one hour). The last buses back from both places are around 8pm.

To get to Sravanabelagola, you must take one of the many buses to Channarayapatna (₹25, 45 minutes) and change there.

There are frequent services to Mysore (₹76, three hours), Bengaluru (semideluxe/deluxe ₹179/246, four hours) and Mangalore (₹166, five hours).

Taxi

Taxi drivers hang out on AVK College Rd, north of the bus stand. A day tour of Belur and Halebid or Sravanabelagola will cost you about ₹1000. Firmly set the price before departure.

Train

From the well-organised **train station**, three passenger trains head to Mysore daily (2nd class ₹120, three hours). For Bengaluru, take the 1.30am Yeshvantpur Express (sleeper ₹140, 5½ hours).

Belur & Halebid

📞08177 / ELEV 968M

Along with Somnathpur, the Hoysala temples at Halebid (also known as Halebeedu) and Belur (also called Beluru) are the apex of one of the most artistically exuberant periods of ancient Hindu cultural development. Architecturally, they are South India's answer to Khajuraho in Madhya Pradesh and Konark near Puri in Odisha (Orissa).

Only 16km lie between Belur and Halebid, and the towns are connected by frequent shuttle buses from 6.30am to 7pm (₹20, 40 minutes). See p183 for details of buses to/from Hassan. To get to Hampi, it's best to return to Bengaluru via Hassan and take an overnight bus to Hospet.

BELUR

The **Channakeshava Temple** (Temple Rd; ☉dawn-dusk) was commissioned in 1116 to commemorate the Hoysalas' victory over the neighbouring Cholas. It took more than a century to build, and is currently the only one among the three major Hoysala sites still in daily use – try to be there for the ritual *puja* ceremonies at 9am, 3pm and 7.30pm. Some parts of the temple, such as the exterior lower friezes, were not sculpted to completion and are thus less elaborate than those of the other Hoysala temples.

However, the work higher up is unsurpassed in detail and artistry, and is a glowing tribute to human skill. Particularly intriguing are the angled bracket figures depicting women in ritual dancing poses. While the front of the temple is reserved for images depicting erotic sections from the Kama Sutra, the back is strictly for gods. The roof of the inner sanctum is held up by rows of exquisitely sculpted pillars, no two of which are identical in design.

Scattered around the temple complex are other smaller temples, a marriage hall which is still used and the seven-storey *gopuram,* which has sensual sculptures explicitly portraying the activities of dancing girls.

Guides can be hired for ₹150; they help to bring some of the sculptural detail to life.

Hotel Mayura Velapuri (📞222209; Kempegowda Rd; d from ₹900; ❋), a state-run hotel gleaming with post-renovation glory, is located on the way to the temple, and is the best place to camp in Belur. The restaurant-bar serves a variety of Indian dishes and snacks (₹70 to ₹90) to go with beer.

Near Kempegowda's statue is **Shankar Hotel** (Temple Rd; mains ₹35; ☉7am-9.30pm), a busy place serving fine South Indian thalis, *masala dosas,* Indian sweets, snacks and drinks.

HALEBID

Construction of the **Hoysaleswara Temple** (☉dawn-dusk), Halebid's claim to fame, began around 1121 and went on for more than 80 years. It was never completed, but nonetheless stands today as a masterpiece of Hoysala architecture. The interior of its inner sanctum, chiselled out of black stone, is marvellous. On the outside, the temple's richly sculpted walls are covered with a flurry of Hindu deities, sages, stylised animals and friezes depicting the life of the Hoysala rulers. A huge statue of Nandi (Shiva's bull) sits to the left of the main temple, facing the inner sanctum. Guides are available to show you around for ₹150; the shoekeeper expects a wee tip for holding your shoes when you enter the temple.

The temple is set in large, well-tended gardens, adjacent to which is a small **museum** (admission ₹5; ☉10am-5pm Sat-Thu) housing a collection of sculptures.

If the pesky touts get on your nerves, take some time out to visit the nearby, smaller **Kedareswara Temple**, or a little-visited enclosure containing three **Jain** temples about 500m away, which also have fine carvings.

If you're stuck in Halebid for the night, the tidy rooms at **Hotel Mayura Shanthala** (☏273224; d ₹350), set around a leafy garden opposite the temple complex, is an OK fallback option.

Sravanabelagola

☏08176

Atop the bald rock of Vindhyagiri Hill, the 17.5m-high statue of the Jain deity Gomateshvara (Bahubali), said to be the world's tallest monolithic statue, is visible long before you reach the pilgrimage town of Sravanabelagola. Viewing the statue close up is the main reason for heading to this sedate town, whose name means 'Monk of the White Pond'.

◉ Sights

Gomateshvara Statue   MONUMENT
(Bahubali; ⊙6.30am-6.30pm) A steep climb up 614 steps takes you to the top of Vindhyagiri Hill, the summit of which is lorded over by the towering naked statue of Gomateshvara. Commissioned by a military commander in the service of the Ganga king Rachamalla and carved out of a single piece of granite by the sculptor Aristenemi in AD 981, its serenity and simplicity is in stark contrast to the Hoysala sites at Belur and Halebid.

Bahubali was the son of emperor Vrishabhadeva, who later became the first Jain *tirthankar* (revered teacher) Adinath. Embroiled in fierce competition with his brother Bharatha to succeed his father, Bahubali realised the futility of material gains and renounced his kingdom. As a recluse, he meditated in complete stillness in the forest until he attained enlightenment. His lengthy meditative spell is denoted by vines curling around his legs and an ant hill at his feet.

Leave shoes at the foot of the hill, but it's fine to wear socks. If you want it easy, you can hire a *dholi* (portable chair) with bearers for ₹400, from 6.30am to 11.30pm and 3.30pm to 6pm.

Every 12 years, millions flock here to attend the **Mastakabhisheka** ceremony, when the statue is dowsed in holy waters, pastes, powders, precious metals and stones. The next ceremony is slated for 2018.

Temples   JAIN TEMPLES
Apart from the Bahubali statue, there are several interesting Jain temples in town. The **Chandragupta Basti** (Chandragupta Community; ⊙6am-6pm), on Chandragiri Hill opposite Vindhyagiri, is believed to have been built by Emperor Ashoka. The **Bhandari Basti** (Bhandari Community; ⊙6am-6pm), in the southeast corner of town, is Sravanabelagola's largest temple. Nearby, **Chandranatha Basti** (Chandranatha Community; ⊙6am-6pm) has well-preserved paintings depicting Jain tales.

🛌 Sleeping & Eating

The local Jain organisation **SDJMI** (☏257258; d/tr ₹135/160) handles bookings for its 15 guesthouses. The office is behind the Vidyananda Nilaya Dharamsala, past the post office.

Hotel Raghu   HOTEL **$**
(☏257238; d from ₹500; ❄) This is the only privately owned hotel around, and offers basic but clean rooms. The real bonus is its vegetarian **restaurant** (⊙6am-9pm) downstairs, which works up an awesome veg thali (₹50), served with care by the staff and sometimes the owner himself.

ℹ Getting There & Away

There are no direct buses from Sravanabelagola to Hassan or Belur – you must go to Channarayapatna (₹15, 20 minutes) and catch an onward connection there. Four daily buses run direct to Bengaluru (₹92, 3½ hours) and Mysore (₹56, 2½ hours). Long-distance buses clear out before 3pm. If you miss these, catch a local bus to Channarayapatna and change there.

Nilgiri Biosphere Reserve

The pristine forests of the **Nilgiri Biosphere Reserve** are one of India's best-preserved wildernesses, and span about 5500 sq km across the states of Karnataka, Kerala and Tamil Nadu. Human access to the reserve is through a number of national parks, such as Wayanad (see p300) in Kerala and Mudumalai (see p367) in Tamil Nadu. In Karnataka, the best access points are Bandipur and Nagarhole, with the super-green forested region around the Kabini Lake boasting some of the top wildlife camps in the region.

Home to over 100 species of mammals and some 350 species of birds, the reserve is also a natural habitat for the prized but endangered Bengal tigers and Asiatic elephants; more than a fifth of the world's population of jumbos live here.

BANDIPUR NATIONAL PARK

About 80km south of Mysore on the Ooty road, the **Bandipur National Park** (Indian/foreigner ₹75/175, video ₹100) covers 880 sq km and was once the Mysore maharajas' private wildlife reserve. The park is noted for its herds of gaurs (Indian bison), chitals (spotted deer), sambars, panthers, sloth bears and langurs, as well as tigers and elephants. However, unrestricted traffic hurtling down the highway cutting through the forest has made animals wary of venturing close to safari areas.

Brief **elephant rides** (per person ₹100) are available for a minimum of four people. For a **safari** (per person Indian/foreigner ₹75/175; ⊙6.30am, 8.30am, 3.30pm & 5.30pm) there's the forest department's rumbling minibus, noisy enough to put off shy creatures. Resort vehicles are permitted to go into the forest; they are quieter and thus a better bet.

🍴 Sleeping & Eating

🏕 **Bandipur Safari Lodge** CAMPGROUND $$
(Mysore-Ooty Rd; person incl full board Indian/foreigner ₹3000/€70; ❄) Located on the fringes of the park is this largish government-owned ecotourism camp that offers luxurious but low-impact accommodation in well-maintained cottages. Rates include a safari, guided nature walks, entry fees and camera fees, and there are good Indian and Continental buffets for meals.

Tusker Trails CAMPGROUND $$
(☑080-23618024, 09845326467; per person incl full board Indian/foreigner ₹3000/4200; ☀) A lovely camp located on the eastern edge of the park, this place provides accommodation in simple huts backed by the forest. There's good food and an inviting pool. Rates include one daily safari, trekking with local guides, wildlife documentary screenings and a bonfire.

ℹ Getting There & Away

Buses between Mysore and Ooty will drop you at Bandipur (₹55, three hours). You can also book an overnight taxi from Mysore (about ₹2000).

NAGARHOLE NATIONAL PARK

West of the Kabini River is the 643-sq-km wildlife sanctuary of **Nagarhole National Park** (Rajiv Gandhi National Park; Indian/foreigner ₹50/150), pronounced *nag*-ar-hole-eh. The lush forests here are home to tigers, leopards, elephants, gaurs, muntjacs (barking deer), wild dogs, bonnet macaques and common langurs. The park can remain closed for long stretches between July and October, when the rains transform the forests into a giant slush-pit.

The park's main entrance is 93km southwest of Mysore. If you're not staying at a resort nearby, the only way to see the park is on the forest department's bus **tour** (per person ₹100; ⊙6-8am & 3-5.30pm). The best time to view wildlife is during summer (April to May), though winter (November to February) is kinder.

Decent sleeping options are limited in Nagarhole; you're better off in Kabini Lake. An OK place to camp is **Jungle Inn** (☑08222-246022; www.jungleinn.in; Hunsur-Nagarhole Rd; per head incl full board Indian/foreigner from ₹1800/US$60) about 35km from the park reception on the Hunsur road. With a welcoming atmosphere, evening campfires and simple, clean rooms, it also serves good organic food. Rates for safaris are extra.

KABINI LAKE

About 70km south of Mysore lies **Kabini Lake**, a giant forest-edged reservoir formed by the damming of the Kabini River. Endowed with rich and unspoilt vegetation, the area has rapidly grown to become one of Karnataka's best wildlife getaways. Positioned midway between the animal corridors of Bandipur and Nagarhole, the Kabini forests are also the habitat for a large variety of wildlife, and give you the chance to view the animals up close.

Tourism around Kabini is managed by a few resorts, most of which are founded on ecofriendly principles. Jungle safaris and other activities such as boat rides and birdwatching are conducted by the resorts, generally between 6.30am to 9.30am, and 4pm to 7pm.

🍴 Sleeping & Eating

⬛ TOP CHOICE **Kabini River Lodge** CAMPGROUND $$$
(☑08228-264402; per person (Indian) incl full board tents/r/cottages ₹3750/4500/5250, per foreigner (flat rate) €120; ❄) Rated consistently among the world's best wildlife getaways, this fascinating government-run luxury ecocamp is located on the serene, tree-lined grounds of the former Mysore maharaja's hunting lodge beside Kabini Lake. Promising an opulent yet idyllic experience, this showcase resort has hosted countless celebrities (Goldie Hawn is apparently an ardent fan) from around the world. Manned by an excellent staff, it offers accommodation in a choice of large canvas tents, regular rooms

and cottages. Rates include safaris, boat rides and forest entry fees. Book through **Jungle Lodges & Resorts Ltd** (Map p164; ☑080-25597944; www.junglelodges.com; Shrungar Shopping Complex, MG Rd, Bengaluru; ☺10am-5.30pm Mon-Sat).

Cicada Kabini CAMPGROUND $$$
(☑080-41152200, 9945602305; www.cicadaresorts .com; d incl full board ₹13,000; ✱@☲) Another highly recommended ecoresort, this well-conceived luxury option brings a dash of contemporary chic to the lakeside. The resort devotes itself to minimising environmental depletion while promoting rural empowerment. Rates are for accommodation and meals only; safaris (Indian/foreigner ₹750/1000) and kayaks and pedal boats (₹100) are extra.

ⓘ Getting There & Away

A few buses depart daily from Mysore and can drop you at Kabini village. However, it's better to have your own taxi. Enquire with the resorts while making a booking.

Kodagu (Coorg) Region

Nestled amid ageless hills that line the southernmost edge of Karnataka is the luscious Kodagu (Coorg) region, gifted with emerald landscapes and acres of plantations. A major centre for coffee and spice production, this rural expanse is also home to the unique Kodava race, believed to have descended from migrating Persians and Kurds or perhaps Greeks left behind from Alexander the Great's armies. The uneven terrain and cool climate make it a fantastic area for trekking, birdwatching or lazily ambling down little-trod paths winding around carpeted hills. All in all, Kodagu is rejuvenation guaranteed.

The best season for trekking is October to March. Guides are available for hire and can arrange food, transport and accommodation; see p186. Treks can last from a day to a week; the most popular routes are to the peaks of Tadiyendamol (1745m) and Pushpagiri (1712m), and to smaller Kotebetta. Adventure activities are conducted between November and May; the rest of the year is too wet for traipsing around.

Kodagu was a state in its own right until 1956, when it merged with Karnataka. The region's chief town and transport hub is Madikeri, but for an authentic Kodagu experience, you have to venture into the plantations. Avoid weekends, when places can quickly get filled up by weekenders from Bengaluru.

MADIKERI (MERCARA)
☑08272 / POP 32,400 / ELEV 1525M

Also known as Mercara, this congested market town is spread out along a series of ridges. The only reason for coming here is to organise treks or sort out the practicalities of travel. The Huthri festival, which falls sometime between November and December, is a nice time to visit.

In the chaotic centre around the KSRTC and private-bus stands, you'll find most hotels and restaurants.

◉ Sights

Madikeri's **fort**, now the municipal headquarters, was built in 1812 by Raja Lingarajendra II. There's an old church here, housing a quirky **museum** (admission free; ☺10am-5.30pm Tue-Sun) displaying dusty, poorly labelled artefacts. Panoramic views of the hills and valleys can be savoured from **Raja's Seat** (MG Rd; ☺5.30am-7.30pm). Behind are gardens, a toy-train line for kids and a tiny Kodava-style **temple**.

On the way to **Abbi Falls**, a pleasant 7km hike from the town centre, visit the quietly beautiful **Raja's Tombs**, better known as Gaddige. An autorickshaw costs about ₹200 return.

⚐ Activities

Trekking TREKKING

A trekking guide is essential for navigating the labyrinth of forest tracks. Most of the estates in Kodagu also offer trekking programs.

Veteran guides Raja Shekhar and Ganesh at **V-Track** (☑229102, 229974; Crown Towers, College Rd; ☺10am-2pm & 4.30-8pm Mon-Sat) can arrange one- to 10-day treks including guide, accommodation and food. Rates are around ₹750 per person per day, and can vary depending on the duration and number of people. For long treks, trips on obscure routes or big groups, it's best to give a week's notice.

Coorg Trails (☑9886665459; www.coorg trails.com; Main Rd; ☺9am-8.30pm) is another recommended outfit that can arrange day treks around Madikeri for ₹500 per person, and a 22km trek to Kotebetta, including an overnight stay in a village, for ₹1500 per person.

Coorg Planters' Camp OUTDOOR ADVENTURE
(☑080-41159270; www.coorgplanterscamp.com) Located in Kirudale, 25km from Madikeri, Coorg Planters' Camp is a fantastic ecoresort

featuring tented accommodation, which offers activities such as coffee plantation tours, trekking, birdwatching and nature walks through dense forests. However, large-scale renovation was on during research, and it appeared like the resort would only open sometime in early 2012. Hopefully, the wait will have been worth it.

Ayurjeevan
AYURVEDA

(Kohinoor Rd; ⊗9am-6pm) Ayurjeevan, a short walk from ICICI Bank, offers a whole range of rejuvenating ayurvedic packages, with 30-minute sessions kicking off at around ₹400.

🛌 Sleeping
Many hotels reduce their rates in the low season (June to September); all of those listed below have hot water, at least in the morning, and 24-hour checkout.

Hotel Mayura Valley View
HOTEL $$

(☑228387; near Raja's Seat; d incl breakfast from ₹1200; ❀) Despite being located out of town on a secluded hilltop past Raja's Seat, this is clearly Madikeri's best sleeping option. It has large bright rooms with fantastic views of the valley outside its floor-to-ceiling windows. Service – though patchy – could be bettered for a small tip. The all-new restaurant-bar (mains ₹70 to ₹100, open 7am to 10pm) with a terrace overlooking the valley is the coolest place for a drink.

Hotel Hill View
HOTEL $$

(☑223808; Hill Rd; d from ₹950) Situated at a far corner of the new town, this cosy hotel has small but well-kept rooms. The wall shades and the pruned hedges in the tiny sit-outs are perfectly colour coordinated with the green hills that overlook the rooms. Tours and bonfires can be arranged on request.

Hotel Chitra
HOTEL $

(☑225372; www.hotelchitra.net; School Rd; d from ₹600) A short walk off Madikeri's main traffic intersection is this austere hotel, providing low-cost, no-frills yet good-value rooms. The sheets are clean and service is efficient, which – coupled with its mid-town location – makes it a good budget option.

Hotel Cauvery
HOTEL $

(☑225492; School Rd; s/d ₹350/800) This geriatric hotel has just been given a facelift, and promises a rather unique mix of hospitality. The rooms are the same old holes, with a vivid sapphire blue livening up most walls. There's printed floral upholstery on the sturdy

beds, while the corridors outside have plastic creepers lining them. If kitsch is your thing, this might be your kind of place.

Hotel Coorg International
HOTEL $$$

(☑228071; www.coorginternational.com; Convent Rd; s/d incl half-board from ₹3500/4500; ❀❀) Madikeri's classiest option boasts a clean pool, a casual bar, a good multicuisine restaurant, a health club and – most importantly – comfortable rooms with bright upholstery and large windows. Rates include fixed-menu breakfast and dinner and snacks through the day.

🍴 Eating

Coorg Cuisinette
INDIAN $

(Main Rd; mains ₹70-90; ⊗noon-4pm & 6.30-10pm) Climb two flights up a commercial building by the main road to feast on endless Kodava specialities at this eatery. Some unique local dishes, such as *pandhi barthadh* (pork dry fry) and *kadambuttu* (rice dumplings) can make your day at the first bite.

Hotel Capitol
INDIAN $

(School Rd; mains ₹70-90; ⊗7am-9.30pm) Don't mind the shabby interiors – the locals certainly don't. All they care about is the great food that comes out of its kitchen, including the flavourful and spicy *pandhi* (pork) curry, best had with a pint of cold beer.

Athithi
SOUTH INDIAN $

(mains ₹30-50; ⊗7am-10pm) Lap it all up like a local at this busy pedestrian eatery, which serves a hot and tasty veg thali (₹45), followed by fruit salads, juices and shakes.

Popular Guru Prasad
SOUTH INDIAN $

(Main Rd; mains ₹30-40; ⊗7am-10pm) A hearty range of vegie options, including a value-for-money veg thali (₹40) and breakfast snacks are ever popular with diners here.

ℹ Information
A semi-functional **KSTDC Office** (☑228580; near Raja's Seat; ⊗10am-5.30pm Mon-Sat) offers basic tourist information about the region. If you need to change money, try **State Bank of India** (☑229959; College Rd; ⊗10.30am-5.30pm Mon-Fri). There's an internet cafe on Kohinoor Rd, opposite Ayurjeevan.

ℹ Getting There & Away
Seven deluxe buses a day depart from the **KSRTC bus stand** for Bengaluru (₹355, six hours), stopping in Mysore (₹165, three hours) en route. Deluxe buses go to Mangalore (₹170, three hours, three daily), while frequent ordinary

buses head to Hassan (₹80, three hours) and Shimoga (₹175, eight hours).

❶ Getting Around

Madikeri is a small town easy to negotiate on foot. For excursions around the region, several places rent out motorcycles for around ₹350 a day, with an initial refundable deposit of ₹500. Try **Spice's Mall** (opposite KSRTC bus stand) or **Coorg the Guide** (Chethana Complex). Carry your driver's licence, tank up on petrol and off you go!

THE PLANTATIONS

Spread around Madikeri are Kodagu's quaint and leafy spice and coffee plantations. Numerous estates here offer homestays, ranging from basic to quite luxurious, while high-end resorts have begun to spring up recently. The following are our pick of places within easy reach of Madikeri. Unless otherwise mentioned, rates include meals and trekking guides. Advance bookings should be made. Some options remain closed during the monsoons. Most arrange transport to/from Madikeri; enquire while booking.

TOP CHOICE Green Hills Estate HERITAGE HOTEL **$$**
(☎08274-254790; www.neemranahotels.com; Virajpet; r incl breakfast from ₹3000) Coorg's venerable old lady, carrying a burden of heritage on its back. A quaint planter's bungalow designed by a Swiss architect, this estate sits amid emerald plantations halfway between Madikeri and Kakkabe, with an air of nostalgia perpetually hanging heavy within its portals. Stacks of family memorabilia fill up its rosewood panelled interiors, and the rooms have quirky names such as Lord Jim and

❶ SPICE OF LIFE

If you have space in your bag, remember to pick up some local spices and natural produce from Madikeri's main market. There's a whole range of spices on offer at the shops lining the streets, including vanilla, nutmeg, lemongrass, pepper and cardamom, as well as the unbranded aromatic coffee that comes in from plantations. Look out for fruit juices and squashes, homemade wines, bottles of fresh wild honey sourced from the forests and packets of ready-made curry masala to flavour your dishes back home. Most items cost between ₹80 to ₹200.

Lady Madcap, supposedly named after racing thoroughbreds once owned by the planter's family. Lunch and dinner are ₹350 each.

Rainforest Retreat HOMESTAY **$$**
(☎08272-265636; www.rainforestours.com; Galibeedu; s/d incl full board from ₹1500/2000) A nature-soaked NGO and refuge located on an organic plantation, the Rainforest Retreat devotes itself to exploring organic and ecofriendly ways of life. Organic farming, sustainable agriculture and waste management are catchphrases here, and the hosts (who are a font of regional knowledge) can sufficiently enlighten you about their progressive projects through your stay. Accommodation is in tents and eco-chic cottages with solar power. Activities include plantation tours, birdwatching and treks, among others.

Golden Mist HOMESTAY **$$**
(☎08272-265629; www.golden-mist.net; Galibeedu; per person incl full board from ₹1500) A German-owned organic plantation, this is one of the nicest options near Madikeri town. Choose between its loft-style family cottage or individual rooms, and treat yourself to some fantastic rustic veg and nonveg food made from the farm's organic produce. Similar in atmosphere to Rainforest Retreat, it offers nature walks and plantation tours.

Alath-Cad Estate Bungalow HOMESTAY **$$**
(☎08274-252190; www.alathcadcoorg.com; Ammathi; d incl breakfast from ₹2300) A family estate set on a 26-hectare coffee plantation 28km from Madikeri, this is another good place to yield to unadulterated nature. Activities include plantation tours, trekking, fishing, birdwatching and even cooking classes. Accommodation is in simple but snugly done-up cottages, and there's a gracious family playing host.

Kadkani HOTEL **$$$**
(☎08274-254186; www.kadkani.com; Ammathi; d incl full board from ₹6500; ❋❀) An ultraluxurious retreat nestled in a dale amid silent forests by the Cauvery River, Kadkani effortlessly matches the best of modern comforts and rustic charm in its classy and plush ecocottages. An excellent place to unwind in style, with a 9-hole golf course and other activities such as river crossing, rafting and trekking thrown in. The evenings are reserved for listening to the cicadas.

KAKKABE

☑08272

About 40km from Madikeri, the village of Kakkabe is an ideal base to plan an assault on Kodagu's highest peak, Tadiyendamol. At the bottom of the summit, 3km from Kakkabe, is the picturesque **Nalakunad Palace** (admission free; ⊘9am-5pm), the restored hunting lodge of a Kodagu king dating from 1794. Within walking distance are several excellent places to camp.

Misty Woods (☑238561; www.coorgmisty.com; cottages from ₹3500), immediately uphill from Nalakunad Palace across a cascading waterfall, aptly complements the dreamy landscape that surrounds it. The tiled red-brick cottages adhering to *vastu shastra* (ancient science similar to Feng Shui) norms are both comfortable and stylish. Meals are extra.

Honey Valley Estate (☑238339; www.honeyvalleyindia.in; d from ₹800) is a wonderful place 1250m above sea level where you can wake to a chirpy dawn and cool, fresh air. The owners' friendliness, ecomindedness and scrumptious organic food make things even better. Advance bookings are essential.

Regular buses run to Kakkabe from Madikeri (₹25, 1½ hours) and from Virajpet (₹18, one hour).

DUBARE FOREST RESERVE

En route to Kushalnagar, Kodagu's second-largest town, is the Dubare Forest Reserve on the banks of the Cauvery River, where a team of elephants retired from forest department work live on pension. Cross the river (₹25) to participate in an **elephant interaction program** (Indian/foreigner ₹270/550; ⊘8.30-10.30am), when you can bathe, feed and then ride the jumbos.

Bookings can be made through **Jungle Lodges & Resorts Ltd** (Map p164; ☑080-25597944; www.junglelodges.com; Shrungar Shopping Complex, MG Rd, Bengaluru; ⊘10am-5.30pm Mon-Sat), which also runs the reserve's rustic but good **Dubare Elephant Camp** (☑9449599755; per person incl full board Indian/foreigner ₹2400/€70). Rates include the elephant-interaction program.

White-water rafting (per person ₹400) is also run from here, over an 8km stretch that features rapids up to grade IV.

BYLAKUPPE

☑08223

Tiny Bylakuppe, 5km southeast of Kushalnagar, was among the first refugee camps set up in South India to house thousands of Tibetans who fled from Tibet following the 1959 Chinese invasion. Comprising several clusters of settlements amid 1200 hectares of rolling sugarcane fields that rustle in the breeze, it has all the sights and sounds of a Tibetan colony, with resident maroon-and-yellow-robed monks and locals selling Tibetan food and handicrafts. The atmosphere is heart-warmingly welcoming. The settlement is also home to much festivity during the Tibetan New Year celebrations.

Foreigners are not allowed to stay overnight in Bylakuppe without a Protected Area Permit (PAP) from the Ministry of Home Affairs in Delhi. Contact the **Tibet Bureau Office** (☑26474798, 26439745; 10B Ring Rd, Lajpat Nagar IV, New Delhi) for details.

The area's highlight is the **Namdroling Monastery** (www.palyul.org), home to the jaw-droppingly spectacular **Golden Temple** (Padmasambhava Buddhist Vihara; ⊘7am-8pm), presided over by an 18m-high gold-plated Buddha. The temple is at its dramatic best when school is in session and it rings out with gongs, drums and chanting of hundreds of young novices. You're welcome to sit and meditate; look for the small blue guest cushions lying around. The **Zangdogpalri Temple** (⊘7am-8pm), a similarly ornate affair, is next door.

Opposite the Golden Temple is a shopping centre, where you'll find the simple **Paljor Dhargey Ling Guest House** (☑258686; pdguesthouse@yahoo.com; d from ₹280).

In the same shopping centre is **Shanti Family Restaurant** (mains ₹50-70; ⊘7am-9.30pm), offering a decent range of Indian meals and Tibetan dishes such as *momos* (dumplings) and *thukpa* (noodle soup).

Autorickshaws (shared/solo ₹10/50) ply to Bylakuppe from Kushalnagar. Buses frequently do the 34km run to Kushalnagar from Madikeri (₹30, 1½ hour) and Hassan (₹86, four hours). Most buses on the Mysore–Madikeri route stop at Kushalnagar.

KARNATAKA COAST

Mangalore

☑0824 / POP 539,300

Relaxed Mangalore sits at the estuaries of the picturesque Netravathi and Gurupur Rivers on the Arabian Sea coast. A major pit stop on international trade routes since the 6th century AD, it's the largest city on Karnataka's shoreline, and a nice place to break long-haul journeys along the western seaboard, or branch inland towards Bengaluru.

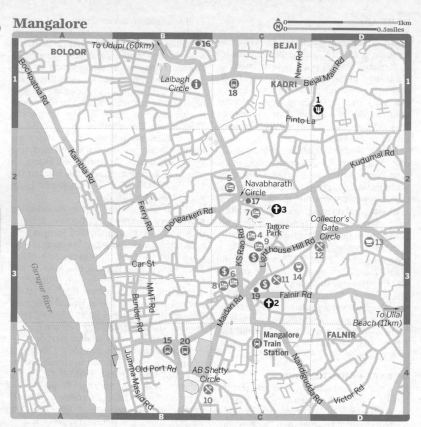

Once the main port of Hyder Ali's kingdom, Mangalore now ships out a bulk of the region's spice, coffee and cashew crops from the modern port, 10km north of the city. The city has a pleasant cosmopolitan air and, with a sprinkling of merry pubs and restaurants, makes for a relaxing stay.

Mangalore is hilly, with winding, disorienting and frenzied streets. Luckily, most hotels and restaurants, the bus stand and the train station are centrally located. The KSRTC bus stand is 3km to the north.

◉ Sights

Ullal Beach
BEACH

The ace up Mangalore's sleeve is serene Ullal Beach, a stretch of dazzling golden sands about an hour's drive south of town. It's best enjoyed from Summer Sands Beach Resort. An autorickshaw is ₹200 one way, or the frequent bus 44A (₹10) from the City bus stand will drop you right outside the gate.

St Aloysius College Chapel
CHURCH

(Lighthouse Hill; ⊙8.30am-6pm Mon-Sat, 10am-noon & 2-6pm Sun) Catholicism's roots in Mangalore date back to the arrival of the Portuguese in the early 1500s, and the city is liberally dotted with churches. One of the most impressive is the Sistine Chapel-like St Aloysius chapel, with its walls and ceilings painted with brilliant frescoes. Also worth checking out is the imposing Roman-style **Milagres Church** (Falnir Rd; ⊙8.30am-6pm) in the city centre.

Sultan's Battery
FORT

(Sultan Battery Rd; ⊙6am-6pm) The only remnant of Tipu Sultan's fort is 4km from the city centre on the headland of the old port; bus 16 will get you there.

Kadri Manjunatha Temple
HINDU TEMPLE

(Kadri; ⊙6am-1pm & 4-8pm) This Kerala-style temple houses a 1000-year-old bronze statue of Lokeshwara.

🛏 Sleeping

Nalapad Residency   HOTEL $$
(✆2424757; www.nalapad.com; Lighthouse Hill Rd; s/d incl breakfast from ₹900/1000; ❄) The best midrange option in Mangalore comes with spruce rooms featuring floor-to-ceiling windows and heavy red curtains. The rooftop restaurant, Kadal, spices up your stay. Ask for a fifth- or sixth-floor room with brilliant sea views.

Hotel Ocean Pearl   HOTEL $$
(✆2413800; www.theoceanpearl.in; Navabharath Circle; s/d from ₹3000/3600; ❄🛜) This brand-new designer hotel is clearly the talk of the town, with mint-fresh rooms featuring all the usual creature comforts paraded by business hotels. It's quite a steal for the price, but tariffs may go up once the inaugural offers draw to a close.

Summer Sands Beach Resort   HOTEL $$$
(✆2467690; www.summersands.in; d from ₹5000; ❄≋) Set amid palm groves on a remote patch along Ullal Beach, Summer Sands offers a series of ethno-chic bungalows done up in earth and floral shades, and is the ideal place for a quiet retreat. Memories of Joanna, its restaurant, has pastoral decor and an excellent menu. The resort can arrange sightseeing tours on request.

Hotel Poonja International   HOTEL $
(✆2440171; www.hotelpoonjainternational.com; KS Rao Rd; s/d incl breakfast from ₹900/1000; ❄) This well-managed place has faux creepers and sunflowers lining its lobby, and the rooms (a whopping 154 of them) are well-appointed though low on frills. There's a multi-cuisine restaurant with a decent selection of Continental dishes.

Hotel Srinivas   HOTEL $
(✆2440061; www.srinivashotel.com; GHS Rd; s/d from ₹550/700; ❄) It's centrally located and reasonably clean. There's an expo hall downstairs, which often organises sales (shoes, shirts and everything in between) at bumper discounts.

Hotel Shaan Plaza   HOTEL $
(✆2440313; KS Rao Rd, s/d from ₹500/600; ❄) Piped music and TVs are standard features in the well-maintained rooms at this budget address.

Hotel Manorama   HOTEL $
(✆2440306; KS Rao Rd; s/d from ₹400/600; ❄) A decent, centrally-located budget option, with clean and good-value rooms.

✕ Eating & Drinking

While in town, sample some Mangalorean delights such as *kane* (ladyfish) served in a spicy coconut curry, or the scrumptious deep-fried prawn *rawa* fry.

Kadal   SOUTH INDIAN $$
(Nalapad Residency, Lighthouse Hill Rd; mains ₹150-220) This high-rise restaurant has elegant and warmly lit interiors, with sweeping views all around. Try the spicy chicken *varval* (a coastal curry) or the yummy prawn ghee roast. Also enquire about the day's seafood specials.

Lalith Bar & Restaurant
SEAFOOD $$

(Balmatta Rd; mains ₹80-150) Unwind in the Lalith's cool, subterranean interior and pair a chilled beer with prawns, crab or kingfish from its extensive menu. The day's special seafood is usually the best bet.

Liquid Lounge
PUB $$

(☑4255175; Balmatta Rd; ☺7-11.30pm) A stiff Jack and Coke or the good old bottle of Corona, this trendy (and loud) pub has it all. With funky posters and neon-lit interiors upping its cool quotient, it's a great place to get happily drunk.

Janatha Deluxe
SOUTH INDIAN $

(Hotel Shaan Plaza, mains ₹50-70; ☺7am-11pm) This local favourite serves a great veg thali (₹50) and a range of North and South Indian veg dishes.

Pallkhi
SEAFOOD $$

(3rd fl, Tej Towers, Balmatta Rd; mains ₹140-170) A relatively smart and easygoing place, with stylish interiors and a formidable reputation for its coastal dishes.

Cochin Bakery
BAKERY $

(AB Shetty Circle; cakes ₹20-30; ☺9.30am-9pm Mon-Sat) An old-time place that works up delicious puffs and cakes.

Café Coffee Day
CAFE $

(Balmatta Rd; ☺9.30am-11pm) A range of good coffees and teas on offer, along with some tasty quick bites.

ℹ Information

State Bank of Mysore, Royal Bank of Scotland and ICICI Bank have ATMs on Balmatta Rd, Lighthouse Hill Rd and GHS Rd respectively.

Cyber Soft (Lighthouse Hill Rd; per hr ₹20; ☺10am-8pm) Fast internet access.

KSTDC tourist office (☑2453926; Lalbagh Circle; ☺10am-5pm Mon-Sat) Pretty useless.

Trade Wings (☑2427225; Lighthouse Hill Rd; ☺9.30am-5.30pm Mon-Sat) Travel agency. Changes travellers cheques.

ℹ Getting There & Away

Air

The **airport** is precariously perched atop a plateau in Bajpe, about 20km northeast of town. **Indian Airlines** (☑2496809; Hathill Rd) and **Jet Airways** (☑2441181; Ram Bhavan Complex, KS Rao Rd) both operate daily flights to Mumbai (1½ hours). Jet Airways also flies daily to Bengaluru (one hour).

Bus

The **KSRTC bus stand** is on Bejai Main Rd, 3km from the city centre; an autorickshaw there costs about ₹40. Several deluxe buses depart daily to Bengaluru (₹495, nine hours), via Madikeri (₹190, five hours) and Mysore (₹350, seven hours). Semideluxe buses go to Hassan (₹175, five hours). A 10.30pm deluxe bus heads to Panaji (₹399, seven hours). From opposite the City bus stand, private buses connect Udupi, Dharmasthala and Jog Falls. Tickets can be purchased at offices near Falnir Rd.

Roads around Mangalore are pothole hells, and journeys can be rough on the bum. Private bus drivers have a morbid fascination with speeding.

Train

The main **train station** is south of the city centre. The 12.20am *Netravati Express* stops at Margao in Goa (sleeper/2AC ₹194/702, 5½ hours), and continues to Mumbai (sleeper/2AC ₹361/1348, 15 hours). The 6.15pm *Malabar Express* heads to Thiruvananthapuram (Trivandrum; sleeper/2AC ₹257/941, 15 hours). The 9.30pm *West Coast Express* heads to Chennai (sleeper/2AC ₹317/1184, 18 hours).

Several Konkan Railway trains (to Mumbai, Margao, Ernakulam or Trivandrum) use **Kankanadi train station**, 5km east of Mangalore.

ℹ Getting Around

To get to the airport, take buses 47B or 47C from the City bus stand, or catch a taxi (₹400).

The City bus stand is opposite the State Bank of India. Flag fall for autorickshaws is ₹15, and ₹11 per kilometre thereafter. For late-night travel, add 50%. An autorickshaw to Kankanadi station costs around ₹60, or take bus 9 or 11B.

Dharmasthala

Inland from Mangalore are a string of Jain temple towns, such as Venur, Mudabidri and Karkal. The most interesting among them is Dharmasthala, 75km east of Mangalore by the Netravathi River. Some 10,000 pilgrims pass through this town every day. During holidays and major festivals such as **Lakshadeepotsava**, the footfall can go up tenfold.

The **Manjunatha Temple** (☺6.30am-2pm & 5-9pm) is Dharmasthala's main shrine, devoted to the Hindu lord Shiva. Men have to enter bare-chested, with legs covered. Simple free meals are available in the temple's **kitchen** (☺11.30am-2.15pm & 7.30-10pm), attached to a hall that can seat up to 3000.

Associated sights in town include the 12m-high **statue of Bahubali** at Ratnagiri Hill, and the **Manjusha Museum** (admission

₹2; ⊘10am-1pm & 4.30-7pm Mon-Sat), which houses a collection of sculptures, jewellery and local crafts. Don't forget to visit the fantastic **Car Museum** (admission ₹3; ⊘8.30am-1pm & 2-7pm), home to 48 vintage autos, including a 1903 Renault, a 1920s Studebaker President used by Mahatma Gandhi and a monster 1954 Cadillac.

Should you wish to stay, contact the helpful **temple office** (⌨08256-277121; www.shridharmasthala.org) for accommodation (per person ₹50) in pilgrim lodges.

There are frequent buses to Dharmasthala from Mangalore (₹40, two hours).

Udupi (Udipi)

⌨0820

Udupi is home to the atmospheric, 13th century **Krishna Temple** (Car St; ⊘3.30am-10pm), which draws thousands of Hindu pilgrims through the year. Surrounded by eight *maths* (monasteries), it's a hive of ritual activity, with musicians playing at the entrance, elephants on hand for *puja,* and pilgrims constantly passing through. Non-Hindus are welcome inside the temple; men must enter bare-chested. Elaborate rituals are also performed in the temple during the **Udupi Paryaya festival**.

Near the temple, above the Corp Bank ATM, the **tourist office** (⌨2529718; Krishna Bldg, Car St; ⊘10am-5.30pm Mon-Sat) is a useful source of advice on Udupi and around.

Udupi is famed for its vegetarian food, and recognised across India for its sumptuous thali. A good place to sample the local fare is the subterranean **Woodlands** (Dr UR Rao Complex; mains ₹60-90; ⊘8am-9.30pm), a short walk south of the temple.

Udupi is 58km north of Mangalore along the coast; regular buses ply the route (₹36, 1½ hours).

Malpe

⌨0820

A laid-back fishing harbour on the west coast 4km from Udupi, Malpe has fabulous beaches ideal for flopping about in the surf. A good place to stay is the **Paradise Isle Beach Resort** (⌨2538777; www.theparadiseisle.com; s/d from ₹3000/3500; ❉@☀), right on the sands, which has comfortable rooms and offers **water sports** such as bumpy rides, jet skiing, river rafting and kayaking (₹500 to ₹1500).

From Malpe pier, you can take a boat (₹70 per person) at 10.30am and 3.30pm out to tiny **St Mary's Island**, where Vasco da Gama supposedly landed in 1498. Over weekends the island is busy with locals inspecting the curious hexagonal basalt formations that jut out of the sand; during the week you might have it to yourself. An autorickshaw from Udupi to Malpe is around ₹70.

Devbagh

About 50km north of Gokarna, on one of the many islands that dot the Arabian Sea off the port town of Karwar, is the unspoilt and heavenly **Devbagh Beach Resort** (⌨08382-221603; per person incl full board Indian/foreigner from ₹2500/€70; ❉). It's the perfect place to play out your Robinson Crusoe fantasies, or stroll aimlessly along the sands. Accommodation comes in cute and comfy fishermen's huts, cottages, log huts and houseboats. **Water sports** such as kayaking (₹300), snorkelling (₹700) and parasailing (₹900) are extra.

FORMULA BUFFALO

Call it an indigenous take on the grand prix. Kambla, or traditional buffalo racing, is a hugely popular pastime among villagers along the southern Karnataka coast. Popularised in the early 20th century and born out of local farmers habitually racing their buffaloes home after a day in the fields, the races have now hit the big time. Thousands of spectators attend each edition, and racing buffaloes are pampered and prepared like thoroughbreds – a good animal can cost ₹300,000.

Kambla events are held between November and March, usually on weekends. Parallel tracks are laid out in a paddy field, along which buffaloes hurtle towards the finish line. In most cases, the man rides on a board fixed to a ploughshare, literally surfing his way down the track behind the beasts.

Keep your cameras ready, but don't even think of getting in the buffaloes' way to take that prize-winning photo. The faster creatures can cover the 120m-odd distance through water and mud in around 14 seconds!

You can reach Karwar by taking a slow bus from Gokarna (₹36, 1½ hours) or Panaji (₹50, three hours). Call the resort in advance to arrange a ferry from their satellite office in Karwar. Make bookings through **Jungle Lodges & Resorts Ltd** (Map p164; ☏080-25597944; www.junglelodges.com; Shrungar Shopping Complex, MG Rd, Bengaluru; ◷10am-5.30pm Mon-Sat).

Jog Falls

☏08186

Nominally the highest waterfalls in India, the Jog Falls only come to life during the monsoon. At other times, the Linganamakki Dam further up the Sharavati River limits the water flow and spoils the show. The tallest of the four falls is the Raja, which drops 293m.

To get a good view of the falls, bypass the scrappy area close to the bus stand and hike to the foot of the falls down a 1200-plus step path. Watch out for leeches during the wet season.

Hotel Mayura Gerusoppa (☏244732; d ₹650), near the car park, has a few enormous and musty doubles. Stalls near the bus stand serve omelettes, thalis, noodles and rice dishes, plus hot and cold drinks.

Jog Falls has buses roughly every hour to Shimoga (₹53, three hours), and three daily to Karwar via Kumta (₹51, three hours), where you can change for Gokarna (₹16, one hour). For Mangalore, change at Shimoga. A return taxi from Gokarna will cost around ₹1500.

Gokarna

☏08386

Quaint but vibrant Gokarna sits on a secluded seaside spot about 60km south of Karwar. A dazzling mix of Hindu rituals and a medieval way of life is on show at this village, whose dramatic ambience is heightened during **festivals** such as Shivaratri and Ganesh Chaturthi, when thousands of pilgrims throng its ancient temples. While the main village is rather conservative in its outlook, a few out-of-town beaches are custom-made for carefree sunbaking.

◉ Sights & Activities

Temples   HINDU TEMPLES

Foreigners and non-Hindus are not allowed inside Gokarna's temples. However, there are plenty of colourful rituals to be witnessed around town. At the western end of Car St is the **Mahabaleshwara Temple**, home to a revered lingam (phallic representation of Shiva). Nearby is the **Ganapati Temple**, while at the other end of the street is the **Venkataraman Temple**. About 100m further south is **Koorti Teertha**, the large temple tank (reservoir) where locals, pilgrims and immaculately dressed Brahmins perform their ablutions next to washermen on the ghats (steps or landings).

Beaches   BEACHES

Gokarna's 'town beach' is dirty, and not meant for casual bathing. The best sands are due south, and can be reached via a footpath that begins south of the Ganapati Temple and heads down the coast (if you reach the bathing tank, or find yourself clawing up rocks, you're on the wrong path).

A 20-minute hike on the path brings you to the top of a barren headland with expansive sea views. On the southern side is **Kudle** (pronounced kood-lay), the first of Gokarna's pristine beaches. Basic snacks, drinks and accommodation are available here, and it's a nice place to chill. South of Kudle Beach, a track climbs over the next headland, and a further 20-minute walk brings you to **Om Beach**, with a handful of chai shops, shacks and marauding groups of local tourists on weekends.

South of Om Beach lie the more isolated **Half-Moon Beach** and **Paradise Beach**, which come to life only between November and March. They are a 30-minute and one-hour walk, respectively.

Depending on demand, fishing boats can ferry you from Gokarna Beach to Kudle (₹100) and Om (₹200). An autorickshaw from town to Om costs around ₹200.

Don't walk around after dark, and not alone at any time – it's easy to slip on the paths or get lost, and muggings have occurred. For a small fee, most lodges in Gokarna will safely store valuables and baggage while you chill out on the beach.

Ayurveda   AYURVEDA

Well-trained masseurs at **Ayur Kuteeram** (☏9480575351; Gokarna Beach; ◷9am-8pm) can work magic on those knotty muscles. An *Abhayanga* treatment costs a mere ₹700.

Quality ayurvedic therapies and packages are also available at specialist ayurvedic centres at the SwaSwara resort and Om Beach Resort.

🛏 Sleeping

With a few exceptions, the choice here is between a rudimentary beach shack or a

WALK ON THE WILD SIDE

Located in the jungles of the Western Ghats about 100km from Goa, emerging **Dandeli** is a fantabulous wildlife getaway that promises close encounters with diverse exotic wildlife such as elephants, panthers, sloth bears, Indian bisons, wild dogs and flying squirrels. It's a chosen birding destination too, with resident hornbills, golden-backed woodpeckers, serpent eagles and white-breasted kingfishers. Also on offer are a slew of adventure activities ranging from kayaking to bowel-churning white-water rafting on the swirling waters of the Kali River.

Kali Adventure Camp (per person incl full board Indian/foreigner from ₹2300/€70; ☒) offers accommodation in tented cottages and rooms, done up lavishly while adhering to ecofriendly principles. Book through **Jungle Lodges & Resorts Ltd** (Map p164; ☎080-25597944; www.junglelodges.com; Shrungar Shopping Complex, MG Rd, Bengaluru; ☺10am-5.30pm Mon-Sat).

Frequent buses connect Dandeli to both Hubli (₹45, two hours) and Dharwad (₹35, 1½ hours), with onward connections to Goa, Gokarna, Hospet and Bengaluru.

basic but more comfortable room in town. Some guesthouses in town cater to pilgrims, and may come with certain rules and regulations. Prices can increase during festivals or the high season.

BEACHES
Both Kudle and Om beaches have shacks offering budget huts and rooms. Places open up on Half-Moon and Paradise beaches from November to March. Most places provide at least a bedroll; bring your own sheets or sleeping bag. Padlocks are provided and huts are secure. Communal washing and toilet facilities are simple.

TOP CHOICE SwaSwara HOTEL $$$
(☎257132, 0484-3011711; www.swaswara.com; Om Beach; d 7 nights Indian/foreigner ₹115,000/€2015; ☒@⚓) Clearly in a league of its own, this amazing health resort sits on the hill overlooking Om Beach. No short stays on offer here, but you can chill out at this elegant and superbly designed red-laterite-brick resort for a full week, and enjoy a holiday based around yoga and ayurvedic treatments. There's an interactive kitchen here, and the artists in residence can help you hone your creative skills. Rates include full board, transport, leisure activities and daily yoga sessions. Weeklong ayurvedic treatment packages kick off at around US$600.

Namaste Café GUESTHOUSE $
(☎257141; Om Beach; huts from ₹700; ☒@) In and out of season, Namaste is the place to hang. What's better, the place has upped its

luxuries since the last time we were here, and now offers AC and internet on its serene Om Beach premises. The restaurant-bar cooks up great bites and is the premier Om chill-out spot. In season, it also offers basic huts (₹150) at Paradise Beach and cottages at Namaste Farm (from ₹500) on the headland.

Hotel Gokarna International Kudle Resort HOTEL $$
(☎257843; Kudle Beach; d ₹1500; ☒) Run by the same management that owns Hotel Gokarna International in town, this midrange option has smart rooms and a lovely garden up front. The waves wash up to its gates during high tide, and seal the deal in its favour.

Nirvana Café GUESTHOUSE $
(☎329851; Om Beach; d ₹300; cottage ₹400) Located on the southern end of Om, this extremely pleasant guesthouse featuring huts within a shady garden should be done renovating by now.

GOKARNA
Om Beach Resort HOTEL $$
(☎257052; www.ombeachresort.com; Bangle Gudde; d incl breakfast Indian/foreigner ₹2800/US$105; ☒@) This little jewel sits on a headland 2km out of Gokarna, off the Om Beach road. Set amid lawns and shady trees, its red-brick cottages are excellently designed, and its restaurant serves good seafood to go with the booze. There's a professional ayurvedic centre on site, with seven-night treatment packages starting from US$490 per person.

Kamat Lodge
GUESTHOUSE $

(✆256035; Kamat Complex, Main St; s/d ₹200/300, d with AC ₹1200; ❇) A value-for-money place on Gokarna's main drag, this hotel offers clean rooms with fresh sheets and large windows. But don't expect room service and other such fluffs.

Nimmu House
GUESTHOUSE $

(✆256730; nimmuhouse@yahoo.com; s/d from ₹250/500; @) A pleasant option off Gokarna's main beach, run by a friendly family .

Vaibhav Lodge
GUESTHOUSE $

(✆256714; off Main St; d ₹250, s/d ₹150/200; @) A backpackers' dig, with mosquito nets, hot water in the morning and a rooftop restaurant.

Shastri Guest House
GUESTHOUSE $

(✆256220; Main St; s/d/tr ₹160/280/400) A hostel-like place with good, airy doubles in the new block out back. The singles are cramped, though.

✖ Eating

The chai shops on all of the beaches rustle up basic snacks and meals.

Namaste Café
CAFE $

(Om Beach; mains ₹80-100; ⊘7am-11pm) Om Beach's social centre serves some excellent Western staples such as pizzas, burgers and shakes. But the real draws are its tasty seafood dishes, especially the grilled calamari and the pomfret preparations. And remember, you're hogging it all up while sitting on a most beautiful seaside venue. Dinners are particularly enjoyable, after noisy local tourists have called it a day.

Prema Restaurant
MULTICUISINE $

(Gokarna Beach; mains ₹80-110; ⊘10am-8.30pm) A decent menu comprising Continental extempores and colourful ice-creams. Spice packs and herbal oils for sale at the counter.

Pai Restaurant
SOUTH INDIAN $

(Main St; mains ₹50-80; ⊘6.30am-9.30pm) Serves an awesome veg thali for ₹55.

Pai Hotel
INDIAN $

(Car St) A popular and freshly renovated eatery with an excellent vegetarian menu.

❶ Information

SBI (Main St) Has an ATM.

Shama Internet Centre (Car St; per hr ₹40; ⊘10am-11pm) Fast internet connections.

Sub post office (1st fl, cnr Car & Main Sts; 10am-4pm Mon-Sat)

❶ Getting There & Away

Bus

From the rudimentary **bus stand**, rickety buses roll to Karwar (₹33, 1½ hours), which has connections to Goa. Frequent direct buses run to Hubli (₹107, four hours), where you can change for Hospet and Hampi, while an evening bus goes to Bengaluru (₹402, 12 hours).

Train

Express trains stop at **Kumta station**, 25km away. The 3.30am *Matsyagandha Express* goes to Mangalore (sleeper ₹166, 3½ hours); the return train leaves Kumta at 6.20pm for Margao (sleeper ₹140, 2½ hours). Many of the hotels and small travel agencies in Gokarna can book tickets.

Autorickshaws charge ₹250 to go to Kumta station; a bus charges ₹15.

CENTRAL KARNATAKA

Hampi

✆08394

Unreal and bewitching, the forlorn ruins of Hampi dot an unearthly landscape that will leave you spellbound the moment you cast your eyes on it. Heaps of giant boulders perch precariously over miles of undulated terrain, their rusty hues offset by jade-green palm groves, banana plantations and paddy fields. The azure sky painted with fluffy white cirrus only adds to the magical atmosphere. A World Heritage Site, Hampi is a place where you can lose yourself among wistful ruins, or simply be mesmerised by the vagaries of nature, wondering how millions of years of volcanic activity and erosion could have resulted in a landscape so captivating.

Hampi is a major pit stop on the traveller circuit; November to March is the high season. While it's possible to see the main sites in a day or two, this goes against Hampi's relaxed grain. Plan on lingering for a while.

Hampi Bazaar and the southern village of Kamalapuram are the two main points of entry to the ruins. Kamalapuram has a government-run hotel and the archaeological museum. But the main travellers' ghetto is Hampi Bazaar, a village crammed with budget lodges, shops and restaurants, all

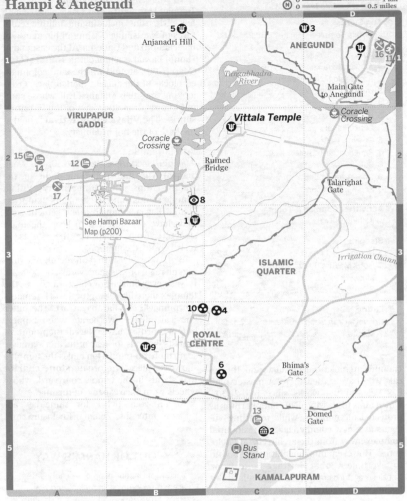

towered over by the majestic Virupaksha Temple. The ruins are divided into two main areas: the Sacred Centre, around Hampi Bazaar; and the Royal Centre, towards Kamalapuram. To the northeast across the Tungabhadra River is the historic village of Anegundi.

History

Hampi and its neighbouring areas find mention in the Hindu epic Ramayana as Kishkinda, the realm of the monkey gods. In 1336, Telugu prince Harihararaya chose Hampi as the site for his new capital Vijayanagar, which – over the next couple of centuries – grew into one of the largest Hindu empires in Indian history. By the 16th century, it was a thriving metropolis of about 500,000 people, its busy bazaars dabbling in international commerce, brimming with precious stones and merchants from faraway lands. All this, however, ended in a stroke in 1565, when a confederacy of Deccan sultanates razed Vijayanagar to the ground, striking it a death blow from which it never recovered.

A different battle rages in Hampi today, between conservationists bent on protecting

Hampi & Anegundi

Hampi's architectural heritage and the locals who have settled there. A master plan has been in the works since mid-2000s, which aims to classify all of Hampi's ruins as protected monuments, while resettling villagers at a new commercial and residential complex away from the architectural enclosures. However, implementation is bound to take time. **Global Heritage Fund** (www.globalheritagefund.org) has more details about Hampi's endangered heritage.

◉ Sights

Virupaksha Temple HINDU TEMPLE
(Map p200; admission ₹2; ⊘dawn-dusk) The focal point of Hampi Bazaar is the Virupaksha Temple, one of the city's oldest structures. The main *gopuram,* almost 50m high, was built in 1442, with a smaller one added in 1510. The main shrine is dedicated to Virupaksha, an incarnation of Shiva.

If Lakshmi (the **temple elephant**) and her attendant are around, she'll smooch (bless) you for a coin. The adorable Lakshmi gets her morning bath at 8.30am, just down the way by the river ghats.

To the south, overlooking Virupaksha Temple, **Hemakuta Hill** (Map p200) has a few early ruins, including monolithic sculptures of Narasimha (Vishnu in his man-lion incarnation) and Ganesha. At the east end of Hampi Bazaar is a monolithic **Nandi statue** (Map p200), around which stand colonnaded blocks of the ancient marketplace. Overlooking the site is Matanga Hill, whose summit affords dramatic views of the terrain at sunrise. The **Vijaya Utsav festival** is held at the base of the hill in January.

Vittala Temple HINDU TEMPLE
(Map p197; Indian/foreigner ₹10/250; ⊘8.30am-5.30pm) The undisputed highlight of the Hampi ruins, the 16th-century Vittala Temple stands amid the boulders 2km from Hampi Bazaar. Though a few cement scaffolds have been erected to keep the main structure from collapsing, the site is in relatively good condition.

Work possibly started on the temple during the reign of Krishnadevaraya (r 1509–29) It was never finished or consecrated, yet the temple's incredible sculptural work remains the pinnacle of Vijayanagar art. The outer 'musical' pillars reverberate when tapped, but authorities have placed them out of tourists' bounds for fear of further damage, so no more do-re-mi. Don't miss the temple's showcase piece, the ornate **stone chariot** that stands in the temple courtyard, whose wheels were once capable of turning.

Retain your ticket for same-day admission into the Zenana Enclosure and

ⓘ OUT OF HARM'S WAY

» Hampi Bazaar is an extremely safe area, but do not wander around the ruins after dark or alone. It's a dangerous terrain to get lost in; long-time guides have even sighted sloth bears prowling around Vittala Temple at night!

» Alcohol and narcotics are illegal in Hampi, and possession can get you in trouble. Cannabis peddlers lurk by the riverside after dark, but you'd do well to give them a wide berth.

» Local laws require all foreign travellers to report to the police station with their passports upon arrival, and notify the authorities about their proposed duration of stay.

Elephant Stables in the Royal Centre, and the archaeological museum in Kamalapuram.

Sule Bazaar & Achyutaraya Temple
HISTORIC SITE

Halfway along the path from Hampi Bazaar to the Vittala Temple, a track to the right leads over the rocks to deserted **Sule Bazaar** (Map p197), one of ancient Hampi's principal centres of commerce. At the southern end of this area is the deserted **Achyutaraya Temple** (Map p197).

Royal Centre
HISTORIC SITE

(Map p197) While it can be accessed by a 2km foot trail from the Achyutaraya Temple, the Royal Centre is best reached via the Hampi–Kamalapuram road. It's a flatter area compared to the rest of Hampi, where the boulders have been shaved off to create stone walls. A number of Hampi's major sites stand here, within the walled ladies' quarters called the **Zenana Enclosure** (Map p197; Indian/foreigner ₹10/250; ⊙8.30am-5.30pm). There's the **Lotus Mahal** (Map p197), a delicately designed pavilion which was supposedly the queen's recreational mansion. The Lotus Mahal overlooks the **Elephant Stables** (Map p197), a grand building with domed chambers. Your ticket is valid for same-day admission to the Vittala Temple and the archaeological museum in Kamalapuram.

Further south, you'll find various temples and elaborate waterworks, including the **Underground Shiva Temple** (Map p197; ⊙8.30am-5.30pm) and the **Queen's Bath** (Map p197; ⊙8.30am-5.30pm), deceptively plain on the outside but amazing within.

Archaeological Museum
MUSEUM

(Map p197; Kamalapuram; admission ₹5; ⊙10am-5pm Sat-Thu) The archaeological museum has collections of sculptures from local ruins, neolithic tools, 16th-century weaponry and a large floor model of the Vijayanagar ruins.

🛏 Sleeping

There's little to choose from between the many basic guesthouses in Hampi Bazaar and Virupapur Gaddi, some of which have lately undergone refitting to attract upmarket travellers. Between April and September you can shop around to get a good deal. The only government-run hotel (with a legal beer bar and a nonveg restaurant) is in Kamalapuram. Prices can shoot up depending on demand.

Also remember that most of the guesthouses in Hampi Bazaar are small operations, comprising only about half-a-dozen rooms of so. It might help to book early during high seasons.

HAMPI BAZAAR

TOP CHOICE Padma Guest House
GUESTHOUSE $$

(Map p200; ☎241331; padmaguesthouse@gmail.com; d from ₹600; ✳) In a quiet corner of Hampi Bazaar, the astute and amiable Padma has been quietly expanding her empire since we were last here. The basic but squeaky clean rooms are a pleasant deviation from Hampi's usual offerings, and those on the first floor have good views of the Virupaksha Temple. New rooms have been added to the west, with creature comforts (TV and AC) previously unheard of in Hampi. Well done, says 'Lovely Planet'.

Gopi Guest House
GUESTHOUSE $

(Map p200; ☎241695; kirangopi2002@yahoo.com; d ₹350-1000; ✳@) Centrally located amid the bustle of Hampi Bazaar, this pleasant dive continues to provide commendable service to travellers. The new block is quite upscale for Hampi's standards, with en suite rooms fronted by a sun-kissed terrace. The rooftop cafe – with a lovely view of the Virupaksha Temple – is a nice place to hang out.

Pushpa Guest House
GUESTHOUSE $

(Map p200; ☎241440; d from ₹500) This place was putting finishing touches to its terrace rooms during research, many of which already sported flowery pink walls and tiled floors. There is an extremely cordial family playing host, and a lovely sit-out on the first floor.

Shanthi Guest House
GUESTHOUSE $

(Map p200; ☎241568; s/d ₹300/350, without bathroom ₹150/250) An oldie but a goodie, Shanthi offers a peaceful courtyard with a swing chair, and has plastic creepers and colourful posters of a hundred gods decorating its basic rooms. There's a small souvenir shop at the entrance that operates on an honour system.

Ranjana Guest House
GUESTHOUSE $

(Map p200; ☎241696; d with/without AC ₹800/600; ✳) Almost on a par with Padma next door, this place also prides itself on well-appointed rooms; those on the terrace have killer views. There are a few cheapies adjoining the family quarters downstairs.

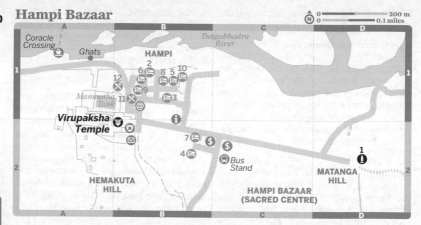

KARNATAKA & BENGALURU CENTRAL KARNATAKA

Rama Guest House GUESTHOUSE $
(☎241962; d ₹400-600) Sitting close to the river, this place seems a popular option with Bengaluru's young weekenders. Some rooms are a little low on light, though adequately appointed for a budget dig.

Vicky's GUESTHOUSE $
(Map p200; ☎241694; vikkyhampi@yahoo.co.in; d ₹350; @) A large operation done up in pop purple and green, with tiled floors, internet access and rooftop cafe. Fix the rate firmly while booking.

Rocky Guest House GUESTHOUSE $
(Map p200; ☎241951; rockyhampi@yahoo.co.in; d ₹400) A comfy option opposite Gopi, with clean rooms, friendly management and a travel desk.

Archana Guest House GUESTHOUSE $
(Map p200; ☎241547; addihampi@yahoo.com; d from ₹500) A quiet and cheerful establishment at the end of a lane, with decent rooms.

VIRUPAPUR GADDI

Many travellers prefer the tranquil atmosphere of Virupapur Gaddi, across the river from Hampi Bazaar. A small boat (₹10) shuttles frequently across the river from 7am to 6pm. During the monsoon, the river runs high and ferry services may be suspended.

Hema Guest House GUESTHOUSE $
(Map p197; ☎9449103008; d ₹250) Laid-back and happening, this is one of Virupapur Gaddi's most popular spots, with rows of cute and comfy cottages in a shady grove. The informal river-view cafe is perpetually full with lazing tourists.

Shanthi GUESTHOUSE $
(Map p197; ☎9449260162; shanthi.hampi@gmail.com; cottage ₹500-800; @) Shanthi's earth-themed, thatched cottages have rice-field, river and sunset views, with couch swings dangling in their front porches. The restaurant does good thalis and pizzas.

Mowgli GUESTHOUSE $$
(Map p197; ☎9448217588; hampimowgli@hotmail.com; d ₹500-1200; ❋@) A cluster of lilac cottages thrown around a sprawling garden complex with soothing views across the rice fields, Mowgli is a top-class chill-out spot this side of the river. It can fill up quickly over weekends, so book early.

KAMALAPURAM

Hotel Mayura Bhuvaneshwari HOTEL $$
(Map p197; ☎08394-241474; d from ₹1200; ❋) This tidy government operation, about 3km south of the Royal Centre, has well-appointed rooms (adorned with corny murals), a much-appreciated beer bar, a good multi-cuisine restaurant and ayurvedic sessions (from ₹1500) on request.

✕ Eating

Due to Hampi's religious significance, meat is strictly off the menu in all restaurants, and alcohol is banned. Places are open from 7am to 10pm.

TOP CHOICE Mango Tree MULTICUISINE $$
(Map p197; mains ₹70-100) Creativity blends with culinary excellence at this rural-themed chill-out joint, spread out under the eponymous mango tree by the river. Walk through

a banana plantation to get here, and try the special vegetable curry (₹100), the banana fritters (₹60) or the spaghetti with cashew nuts and cheese (₹100). The terraced seating is perfect for whiling away a lazy afternoon, book in hand.

New Shanthi MULTICUISINE **$$**
(Map p200; mains ₹80-120) A hippie vibe, complete with trance music and acid-blue lights, hangs over this popular option serving Mexican, Italian and Indian regulars, with cookies and crumbles on the side. A good range of teas (jasmine, lemongrass and herbal) are on offer.

Durga Huts CAFE **$**
(Map p200; mains ₹60-80) Clearly a hit with music lovers. Prem Joshua's fusion tracks get heavy airplay here, and there are a few guitars and drums on standby for an impromptu jam session. The food is of passable quality.

ⓘ Information

Aspiration Stores (◷10am-1pm & 4-8pm) Good for book guides. Try *Hampi* by John M Fritz and George Michell, a good architectural study.
Canara Bank (Map p200; ◷11am-2pm Mon-Tue & Thu-Fri, 11am-12.30pm Sat) Changes currency and has an ATM.
Hampi Heritage Gallery (◷10am-1pm & 3-6pm) Books and photo albums on Hampi's history and architecture, plus walking tours for ₹250.
Sree Rama Cyber Café (Map p200; per hr ₹40; ◷7am-11pm) Has printing and data burning facilities.
Tourist office (Map p200; ✆241339; ◷10am-5.30pm Sat-Thu) Arranges guides for ₹300/600 for a half/full day.

ⓘ Getting There & Away

A semideluxe bus connects Hampi Bazaar to Bengaluru (₹372, eight hours) leaving at 8.30pm. Overnight private sleeper buses ply to/from Goa (₹600) and Gokarna (₹500) from November through March. Numerous travel agents in Hampi Bazaar book onward tickets or arrange taxis.

Hospet is Hampi's nearest train station. The first bus from Hospet (₹12, 30 minutes, half-hourly) is at 6.30am; the last one back leaves Hampi Bazaar at 8.30pm. An autorickshaw costs around ₹150. See p203 for onward transport information.

ⓘ Getting Around

Once you've seen the main sights in Hampi, exploring the rest of the ruins by bicycle is the thing to do. The key monuments are haphazardly signposted all over the site. While they're not adequate, you shouldn't get lost. Bicycles cost about ₹30 per day in Hampi Bazaar. Mopeds can be hired for around ₹250, and petrol is ₹70 a litre. To cross the river, pile your vehicle onto a coracle for ₹10.

Walking the ruins is recommended too, but expect to cover at least 7km just to see the major sites. Autorickshaws and taxis are available for sightseeing, and will drop you as close to each of the major ruins as they can. A five-hour autorickshaw tour costs ₹500.

Organised tours depart from Hospet; see p203 for details.

Around Hampi

ANEGUNDI

Across the Tungabhadra, about 5km northeast of Hampi Bazaar, sits Anegundi, an ancient fortified village that's part of the Hampi World Heritage Site but predates Hampi by way of human habitation. Gifted with a landscape similar to Hampi, quainter Anegundi has been spared the blight of

DANCES WITH BEARS

About 15km south of Hampi, amid a scrubby undulated terrain, lies the **Daroji Sloth Bear Sanctuary** (admission ₹25; ⊘9.30am-6pm), which nurses a population of around 40 free-ranging sloth bears. It's possible to drive through the sanctuary and sight these furry creatures, along with leopards, wild boars, hyenas, jackals and others animals, as well as some exotic birds. Accommodation is in luxury cottages at the **Daroji Sloth Bear Resort** (per person incl full board Indian/foreigner from ₹3000/€70; ✺), located on the sanctuary's periphery. Book through **Jungle Lodges & Resorts Ltd** (Map p164; ⏧080-25597944; www.junglelodges.com; Shrungar Shopping Complex, MG Rd, Bengaluru; ⊘10am-5.30pm Mon-Sat). The resort can arrange pick-up and drop off from Hampi.

commercialisation, and thus continues to preserve the local atmosphere minus the touristy vibe.

◉ Sights & Activities

Temples   HINDU TEMPLES

Mythically referred to as Kishkinda, the kingdom of the monkey gods, Anegundi retains many of its historic monuments, such as sections of its defensive wall and gates, and the **Ranganatha Temple** (Map p197; ⊘dawn-dusk) devoted to Rama. The whitewashed **Hanuman Temple** (Map p197; ⊘dawn-dusk), accessible by a 570-step climb up the Anjanadri Hill, has fine views of the rugged terrain around. Many believe this is the birthplace of the Hindu monkey god Hanuman. On the pleasant hike up, you'll be courted by impish monkeys, and within the temple you'll find a horde of chillum-puffing resident sadhus. Also worth visiting is the **Durga Temple** (Map p197; ⊘dawn-dusk), an ancient shrine closer to the village.

◢ Kishkinda Trust   CULTURAL PROGRAMS, OUTDOOR ADVENTURE

(TKT; Map p197; ⏧08533-267777; www.thekishkindatrust.org) The Kishkinda Trust, an NGO that promotes sustainable tourism in Anegundi, organises soft adventure activities such as rock-climbing, camping, trekking and boating around the village. Equipment and trained instructors are provided. A slew of cultural programs, including performing arts sessions and classical and folk music concerts are also conducted from time to time. For more information on TKT, see the boxed text, p202.

🛏 Sleeping & Eating

Anegundi has several homestays managed by TKT. Contact the trust for bookings. Guesthouses listed can provide meals upon prior notice.

Naidile Guest House   GUESTHOUSE **$$**

(d ₹1500) A charmingly rustic air hangs over this renovated village home in the heart of Anegundi where you can savour all the sights and sounds of the ancient village. It can sleep up to five people.

Peshagar Guest House   GUESTHOUSE **$**

(d incl breakfast ₹600) Six simple rooms done up in rural motifs open around a pleasant common area in this new guesthouse. There's also a sumptuous breakfast platter available.

TEMA Guest House   GUESTHOUSE **$**

(d incl breakfast ₹700) The two rooms in this village quarters were undergoing renovation during research, and should be back in commission by now.

Champa Guest House   GUESTHOUSE **$**

(d incl breakfast ₹700) Champa offers basic but pleasant accommodation in two rooms, and is looked after by an affable village family.

Hoova Craft Shop & Café   CAFE **$**

(mains ₹40-60; ⊘9.30am-5pm Mon-Sat, 9.30am-2pm Sun) A lovely place for an unhurried meal. You can also shop for sundry souvenirs made by the village's women's self-help groups.

❶ Getting There & Away

Anegundi can be reached by crossing the river on a coracle (₹10) from the pier east of the Vittala Temple. The concrete bridge that was being erected across the river has mysteriously collapsed, taking away with it all hopes of cycling across.

You can also get to Anegundi by taking a bus (₹25, one hour) from Hospet.

Hospet

⏧08394 / POP 164,200

This busy regional centre is the main transport hub for Hampi. The Muslim festival of **Muharram** brings things to life in this otherwise dull transit town. With Hampi barely 30 minutes away, few choose to linger here.

Sleeping & Eating

Hotel Priyadarshini   HOTEL $
(☎227313; www.priyainhampi.com; Station Rd; d ₹800-950; ❄) This old-timer has a convenient location between the bus and train stations. The fresh rooms have balconies and TV, and its quality outdoor nonveg restaurant-bar **Manasa** (mains ₹60 to ₹120) stirs to life in the evenings.

Hotel Malligi   HOTEL $$
(☎228101; www.malligihotels.com; Jabunatha Rd; d Indian/foreigner ₹2800/3500; ❄@≋) Hospet's premier luxury option builds its reputation around clean and well-serviced rooms, an aquamarine swimming pool, a spa and a good multicuisine restaurant.

Udupi Sri Krishna Bhavan   SOUTH INDIAN $
(Bus stand; mains ₹30-50; ⊙6am-11pm) Opposite the bus stand, this clean spot dishes out Indian vegie fare, including thalis for ₹35.

ℹ Information

SBI, HDFC Bank and ICICI Bank have ATMs along the main drag and Shanbagh Circle. Internet joints are common, with connections costing ₹40 per hour.

KSTDC tourist office (☎221008; Shanbagh Circle; ⊙10am-5.30pm Mon-Sat) Offers an uninspiring Hampi tour (₹250) for groups of 10 or more.

ℹ Getting There & Away

Bus

The **bus stand** has services to Hampi from Bay 10 every half-hour (₹12, 30 minutes). Several express buses run to Bengaluru (ordinary/deluxe ₹212/306, nine hours). One bus goes to Badami (₹155, six hours) at 6.30am, or you can take a bus to Gadag (₹76, 2½ hours) and transfer. There are frequent buses to Bijapur (₹148, six hours) and overnight services to Hyderabad (₹335, 10 hours). For Gokarna, take a bus to Hubli (₹108, 4½ hours) and change. For Mangalore or Hassan, take a morning bus to Shimoga (₹203, five hours) and change there.

Train

Hospet's **train station** is a ₹20 autorickshaw journey from town. The 5.30am *Rayalaseema Express* heads to Hubli (2nd class ₹120, 3½ hours). For Bengaluru, take the 8.30pm *Hampi Express* (sleeper/2AC ₹187/720, nine hours). Every Monday, Wednesday, Thursday and Saturday, a 6.30am express train heads to Vasco da Gama (sleeper/2AC ₹176/630, 8½ hours).

For Badami, catch a Hubli train to Gadag and change there.

Hubli

☎0836 / POP 786,100
Prosperous Hubli is a hub for rail routes for Mumbai, Bengaluru, Goa and northern Karnataka. The train station is a 15-minute walk from the old bus stand. Most hotels sit along this stretch.

Sleeping & Eating

Ananth Residency   HOTEL $$
(☎2262251; ananthresidencyhubli@yahoo.co.uk; Jayachamaraj Nagar; d from ₹1100; ❄) A brand-new option that sports a sleek business-hotel look and feel. Has good-value rooms and efficient service.

Hotel Ajanta   HOTEL $
(☎2362216; Jayachamaraj Nagar; s/d from ₹250/330) This well-run place near the train station has basic, functional rooms. Its popular ground-floor restaurant serves delicious regional-style thalis for ₹35.

Sudarshan   INDIAN $$
(Jayachamaraj Nagar; mains ₹90-100) The non-veg bar-restaurant at Ananth Residency is a cheerful eatery with good food and chilled beer.

ℹ Information

SBI has an ATM opposite the bus stand. On the same stretch are several internet cafes, charging around ₹30 per hour.

ℹ Getting There & Away

Bus

Buses stop briefly at the **old bus stand** before moving to the **new bus stand** 2km away. There are numerous semideluxe services to Bengaluru (₹304, 10 hours), Bijapur (₹156, six hours) and Hospet (₹108, 4½ hours). There are regular connections to Mangalore (₹255, 10 hours, several daily), Borivali in Mumbai (semideluxe/sleeper ₹482/762, 14 hours, four daily), Mysore (₹299, 10 hours, three daily), Gokarna (₹110, five hours, two daily) and Panaji (₹204, six hours, six daily).

Private deluxe buses to Bengaluru (₹370) run from opposite the old bus stand.

Train

From the **train station**, expresses head to Hospet (2nd class ₹120, 3½ hours, three daily), Bengaluru (sleeper/2AC ₹203/910, 11 hours, four daily) and Mumbai (sleeper/2AC ₹285/1057,

THE KISHKINDA TRUST

Since 1995, the **Kishkinda Trust** (TKT; ☎08533-267777; www.thekishkindatrust.org) has been actively involved in promoting rural tourism, sustainable development and women's empowerment in Anegundi, as well as preserving the architectural, cultural and living heritage of the Hampi World Heritage Site. The first project in 1997 created a cottage industry of crafts using locally produced cloth, banana fibre and river grass. It now employs over 600 women, and the attractive crafts produced are marketed in ethnic product outlets across India.

For the benefit of tourists, TKT has a team featuring some of the best guides in the region, who are fluent in English and know the terrain like the back of their hands. Exploring the region while riding pillion on their motorcycles can be a truly enriching experience. Guides charge ₹300/600 for a half/full day. Contact the trust for details.

14 hours). The 11pm *Hubli-Vasco Link Express* goes to Goa (sleeper ₹153, six hours).

Air

From Hubli's basic **airport**, Kingfisher Red flies to Mumbai (from ₹5500, 1½ hours), Hyderabad (from ₹6800, 3½ hours) and Bengaluru (from ₹5500, 1½ hours).

NORTHERN KARNATAKA

Badami

☎08357 / POP 25,800

Now in a shambles, scruffy Badami is a far cry from its glory days, when it was the capital of the mighty Chalukya empire. Between the 6th and 8th century AD, the Chalukya kings shifted the capital here from Aihole, with a satellite capital in Pattadakal. The relocation of power saw Badami gifted with several temples and, most importantly, a group of magnificent rock-cut cave temples, which are the main reason for coming to the village today.

History

From about AD 540 to 757, Badami was the capital of an enormous kingdom stretching from Kanchipuram in Tamil Nadu to the Narmada River in Gujarat. It eventually fell to the Rashtrakutas, and changed hands several times thereafter, with each dynasty sculpturally embellishing Badami in their own way.

The sculptural legacy left by the Chalukya artisans in Badami includes some of the earliest and finest examples of Dravidian temples and rock-cut caves. During Badami's heydays, Aihole and Pattadakal served as trial grounds for new temple architecture; the latter is now a World Heritage Site.

◉ Sights

Cave Temples CAVES

(Indian/foreigner ₹5/100; ⊙dawn-dusk) Badami's highlight is its beautiful cave temples. Non-pushy and informed guides ask ₹200 for a tour of the caves, or ₹300 for the whole site. Watch out for pesky monkeys.

Cave one, just above the entrance to the complex, is dedicated to Shiva. It's the oldest of the four caves, probably carved in the latter half of the 6th century. On the wall to the right of the porch is a captivating image of Nataraja striking 81 dance poses. On the right of the porch area is a huge figure of Ardhanarishvara. The right half of the figure shows features of Shiva, while the left half has aspects of his wife Parvati. On the opposite wall is a large image of Harihara; half Shiva and half Vishnu.

Dedicated to Vishnu, **cave two** is simpler in design. As with caves one and three, the front edge of the platform is decorated with images of pot-bellied dwarfs in various poses. Four pillars support the verandah, their tops carved with a bracket in the shape of a *yali* (mythical lion creature). On the left wall of the porch is the bull-headed figure of Varaha, an incarnation of Vishnu and the emblem of the Chalukya empire. To his left is Naga, a snake with a human face. On the right wall is a large sculpture of Trivikrama, another incarnation of Vishnu.

Between the second and third caves are two sets of steps to the right. The first leads to a **natural cave**, where resident monkeys laze around. The eastern wall of this cave contains a small image of Padmapani (an incarnation of the Buddha). The second set of steps – sadly, barred by a gate – leads to the hilltop **South Fort**.

Cave three, carved in AD 578, has – on the left wall – a carving of Vishnu, to whom the cave is dedicated, sitting on a snake. Nearby is an image of Varaha with four hands. The pillars have carved brackets in the shape of *yalis*. The ceiling panels contain images, including Indra riding an elephant, Shiva on a bull and Brahma on a swan.

Dedicated to Jainism, **cave four** is the smallest of the set and dates between the 7th and 8th centuries. The pillars, with their roaring *yalis,* are similar to the other caves. The right wall has an image of Suparshvanatha (the seventh Jain *tirthankar*) surrounded by 24 Jain *tirthankars*. The inner sanctum contains an image of Adinath, the first Jain *tirthankar*.

Other Sights
HISTORIC SITES

Badami's caves overlook the 5th-century **Agastyatirtha Tank** and the waterside **Bhutanatha temples**. On the other side of the tank is an **archaeological museum** (admission ₹5; ☺10am-5pm Sat-Thu), which houses superb examples of local sculpture, including a remarkably explicit Lajja-Gauri image of a fertility cult that once flourished in the area. The stairway behind the museum climbs through a sandstone chasm and fortified gateways to reach the ruins of the **North Fort**.

It's also worth exploring Badami's laneways, where you'll find old houses with carved wooden doorways, the occasional Chalukyan ruin and flocks of curious kids.

🏃 Activities

The bluffs and the horseshoe-shaped red sandstone cliff of Badami offer some great low-altitude climbing. For more information, log on to www.dreamroutes.org.

🛏 Sleeping

Many of Badami's hotels offer discounts in the low season.

Mookambika Deluxe   HOTEL $

(☎220067; Station Rd; d ₹850-1100; ❄) Faux antique lampshades hang in the corridors of this friendly hotel, leading to comfy rooms done up in matte orange and green. It's Badami's de facto tourist office, and your best bet in town.

Hotel Mayura Chalukya   HOTEL $

(☎220046; Ramdurg Rd; d from ₹600) A government issue buried behind civic offices away from the bustle, this renovated hotel has large and clean (though featureless) rooms. There's a decent restaurant serving Indian staples.

Hotel Rajsangam   HOTEL $$

(☎221991; www.hotelrajsangam.com; Station Rd; d Indian/foreigner from ₹800/US$20; ❄@) This midrange place has slightly stuffy rooms that go unchallenged in their class. It sits right opposite the bus stand, in a commercial complex packing in sundry other utilities.

Hotel New Satkar   HOTEL $

(☎220417; Station Rd; d with/without AC ₹600/450; ❄) The best of the mediocre rooms in this budget dive are on the 1st floor. There was some refurbishing on during research, so things might have improved by now.

Hotel Badami Court   HOTEL $$

(☎220231; Station Rd; d incl breakfast from ₹3750; ❄☲) This luxury hotel sits amid a pastoral countryside 2km from town. Rooms are more functional than plush. Nonguests can use the pool for ₹150.

🍴 Eating

Banashree   INDIAN $

(Station Rd; mains ₹70-90; ☺7am-10.30pm) The awesome North Indian thalis (₹80) at this busy and popular eatery in front of Hotel Rajsangam are tasty to the last morsel.

Golden Caves Cuisine   MULTICUISINE $

(Station Rd; mains ₹70-100; ☺9am-11pm) A shabby place that produces palatable Indian, Chinese and Continental fare, and stocks ample chilled beer for its thirsty young clients.

Hotel Sanman   INDIAN $

(Station Rd; mains ₹70-90; ☺10am-11.30pm) You might call it ropey, but it feels kind of nice to disappear behind a curtain in the booths and sip your beer in peace. The food is borderline.

Geeta Darshini   FAST FOOD $

(Station Rd; snacks ₹15-20; ☺7am-9pm) Staple South Indian snacks are on endless demand here, washed down with milky tea.

ℹ Information

Station Rd, Badami's main street, has several hotels and restaurants; the old village is between this road and the caves. The **KSTDC tourist office** (☎220414; Ramdurg Rd; ☺10am-5.30pm Mon-Sat), adjoining Hotel Mayura Chalukya, is not very useful.

SBI has ATMs on Ramdurg Rd and Station Rd. Mookambika Deluxe hotel changes currency for guests, but at a lousy rate.

Internet is available at **Hotel Rajsangam** (Station Rd; per hr ₹20) in the town centre.

ℹ Getting There & Away

Buses regularly shuffle off from Badami's **bus stand** on Station Rd to Gadag (₹52, two hours), which has connections to Bijapur, Bengaluru and Hubli. Three buses go direct to Hospet (₹155, six hours). The tarmac's rough down this lane; mind your bum.

Broad-gauge railway has finally arrived in Badami. The 7.35am *Bijapur Express* now runs to Bijapur (2nd class ₹120, 3½ hours), while the 2.30am Hubli Express goes to Hubli (2nd class ₹120, 3½ hours). For Bengaluru, take the 8pm *Gol Gumbaz Express* (2nd class ₹244, 13 hours).

ℹ Getting Around

Frequent, on-time local buses make sightseeing in the area quite affordable. You can visit Aihole and Pattadakal in a day from Badami if you get moving early. Start with Aihole (₹20, one hour), then move to Pattadakal (₹15, 30 minutes), and finally return to Badami (₹18, one hour). The last bus from Pattadakal to Badami is at 5pm. Take food and water with you.

Taxis/autorickshaws cost around ₹1000/600 for a day trip to Pattadakal, Aihole and nearby Mahakuta. Badami's hotels can arrange taxis; alternatively, go to the **taxi stand** in front of the post office.

Around Badami

PATTADAKAL

A secondary capital of the Badami Chalukyas, Pattadakal is known for its group of **temples** (Indian/foreigner ₹10/250; ⊙6am-6pm), which are collectively a World Heritage Site. Barring a few temples that date back to the 3rd century AD, most others in the group were built during the 7th and 8th centuries AD. Historians believe Pattadakal served as an important trial ground for the development of South Indian temple architecture.

Two main types of temple towers were tried out here. Curvilinear towers top the Kadasiddeshwra, Jambulinga and Galaganatha temples, while square roofs and receding tiers are used in the Mallikarjuna, Sangameshwara and Virupaksha temples.

The main **Virupaksha Temple** is a massive structure, its columns covered with intricate carvings depicting episodes from the Ramayana and Mahabharata. A giant stone sculpture of Nandi sits to the temple's east. The **Mallikarjuna Temple**, next to the Virupaksha Temple, is almost identical in design. About 500m south of the main enclosure is the Jain **Papanatha Temple**, its entrance flanked by elephant sculptures. The tem-

ple complex also serves as the backdrop to the annual Classical Dance Festival, held between January and February.

Pattadakal is 20km from Badami. See p206 for transport details.

AIHOLE

Some 100 temples, built between the 4th and 6th centuries AD, speck the ancient Chalukyan regional capital of Aihole (*ay-ho-leh*). Most, however, are either in ruins or engulfed by the modern village. Aihole documents the embryonic stage of South Indian Hindu architecture, from the earliest simple shrines, such as the most ancient Ladkhan Temple, to the later and more complex buildings, such as the Meguti Temple.

The most impressive of them all is the 7th-century **Durga Temple** (Indian/foreigner ₹5/100; ⊙8am-6pm), notable for its semicircular apse (inspired by Buddhist architecture) and the remains of the curvilinear *sikhara* (temple spire). The interiors house intricate stone carvings. The small **museum** (admission ₹5; ⊙10am-5pm Sat-Thu) behind the temple contains further examples of Chalukyan sculpture.

To the south of the Durga Temple are several other temple clusters, including early examples such as the Gandar, Ladkhan, Kontigudi and Hucchapaya groups – all pavilion type with slightly sloping roofs. About 600m to the southeast, on a low hillock, is the Jain **Meguti Temple**. Watch out for snakes if you're venturing up.

Aihole is about 40km from Badami. See p206 for transport information.

Bijapur

☑ 08352 / POP 253,900 / ELEV 593M

A fascinating open-air museum dating back to the Deccan's Islamic era, dusty Bijapur tells a glorious tale dating back some 600 years. Blessed with a heap of mosques, mausoleums, palaces and fortifications, it was the capital of the Adil Shahi kings from 1489 to 1686, and one of the five splinter states formed after the Islamic Bahmani kingdom broke up in 1482. Despite its strong Islamic character, Bijapur is also a centre for the Lingayat brand of Shaivism, which emphasises a single personalised god. The **Lingayat Siddeshwara Festival** runs for eight days in January/February.

Bijapur's prime attractions, the Golgumbaz and the Ibrahim Rouza, are at opposite ends of town. Between them runs Station Rd

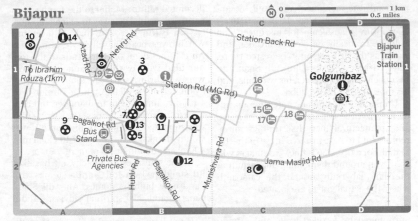

(also known as MG Rd), dotted with hotels and restaurants. The bus stand is a five-minute walk from Station Rd; the train station is 2km east of town.

⊙ Sights

Golgumbaz
MONUMENT

(Indian/foreigner ₹5/100, video ₹25; ⊙6am-5.40pm) Set in tranquil gardens, the magnificent Golgumbaz is big enough to pull an optical illusion on you; despite the perfect engineering, you might just think it's ill-proportioned! Golgumbaz is actually a mausoleum, dating back to 1659, and houses the tombs of emperor Mohammed Adil Shah (r 1627–56), his two wives, his mistress (Rambha), one of his daughters and a grandson.

Octagonal seven-storey towers stand at each corner of the monument, which is capped by an enormous dome. An astounding 38m in diameter, it's said to be the largest dome in the world after St Peter's Basilica in Rome. Climb the steep, narrow stairs up one of the towers to reach the 'whispering gallery' within the dome. An engineering marvel, its acoustics are such that if you whisper into the wall, a person on the opposite side of the gallery can hear you clearly. Unfortunately people like to test this out by hollering, so come early while most tourists are still snoozing.

Set in the lawns fronting the monument is a fantastic **archaeological museum** (admission ₹5; ⊙10am-5pm Sat-Thu). Skip the ground floor and head upstairs; there you'll find an excellent collection of artefacts, such as Persian carpets, china crockery, weapons, armours, scrolls and objects of daily use, dating back to Bijapur's heyday.

Bijapur

⊙ Top Sights

⊙ Sights

⊜ Sleeping

Eating

Ibrahim Rouza
MONUMENT

(Indian/foreigner ₹5/100, video ₹25; ⊙6am-6pm) The beautiful Ibrahim Rouza is among the most elegant and finely proportioned Islamic monuments in India. Its tale is rather poignant: the monument was built by emperor Ibrahim Adil Shah II (r 1580–1627) as a future mausoleum for his queen, Taj Sultana. Ironically, he died before her, and was thus the first person to be rested there. Interred here with Ibrahim Adil Shah and his queen are his daughter, his two sons, and his mother, Haji Badi Sahiba.

Unlike the Golgumbaz, noted for its immense size, the emphasis here is on grace and architectural finery. Its 24m-high minarets are said to have inspired those of the Taj Mahal. For a tip (₹150 is fine), caretakers will show you around the monument, including the dark labyrinth around the catacomb where the actual graves are located.

Citadel
FORT

Surrounded by fortified walls and a wide moat, the citadel once contained the palaces, pleasure gardens and durbar (royal court) of the Adil Shahi kings. Now mainly in ruins, the most impressive of the remaining fragments is the Gagan Mahal, built by Ali Adil Shah I around 1561 as a dual-purpose royal residency and durbar hall.

The ruins of Mohammed Adil Shah's seven-storey palace, the Sat Manzil, are nearby. Across the road stands the delicate Jala Manzil, once a water pavilion surrounded by secluded courts and gardens. On the other side of Station Rd are the graceful arches of Bara Kaman, the ruined mausoleum of Ali Roza.

Jama Masjid
MOSQUE

(Jama Masjid Rd; ⊙9am-5.30pm) Constructed by Ali Adil Shah I (r 1557–80), the finely proportioned Jama Masjid has graceful arches, a fine dome and a vast inner courtyard with room for more than 2200 worshippers. You can take a silent walk through its assembly hall, which still retains some of the elaborate murals. Women should make sure to cover their heads and not wear revealing clothing.

Other Sights
HISTORIC SITES

On the eastern side of the citadel is the tiny, walled Mecca Masjid, presumably built in the early 17th century. Some speculate that this mosque may have been for women. Further east, the Asar Mahal, built by Mohammed Adil Shah in about 1646 to serve as a Hall of Justice, once housed two strands of Prophet Mohammed's beard. The rooms on the upper storey are decorated with frescoes and a square tank graces the front. It's out of bounds for women. The stained but richly decorated Mihtar Mahal to the south serves as an ornamental gateway to a small mosque.

Upli Buruj is a 24m-high 16th-century watchtower near the city's western walls. An external flight of stairs leads to the top, mounted with two hefty cannons. A short walk west brings you to the Malik-e-Maidan (Monarch of the Plains), a huge cannon over 4m long, almost 1.5m in diameter and estimated to weigh 55 tonnes. Cast in 1549, it was supposedly brought to Bijapur as a war trophy thanks to the efforts of 10 elephants, 400 oxen and hundreds of men!

In the southwest of the city, off Bagalkot Rd, stand the twin Jod Gumbad tombs with handsome bulbous domes. An Adil Shahi general and his spiritual adviser, Abdul Razzaq Qadiri, are buried here.

Don't forget to spend a few hours in Bijapur's colourful central market, with its spice sellers, florists and tailors.

🛏 Sleeping

Hotel Pearl
HOTEL $

(☑256002; Station Rd; d from ₹550; ❄) As good as it gets for Bijapur, this excellent hotel features clean and bright rooms around a central atrium. It's very close to Golgumbaz. Ask for a room to the rear to avoid street noise.

Hotel Kanishka International
HOTEL $

(☑223788; Station Rd; s/d from ₹550/700; ❄) One of Bijapur's trusted options, this place has spacious and clean rooms, some with balconies. There's a small gym for guests' use, and the dealmaker is the excellent vegetarian restaurant downstairs. Book early.

Hotel Madhuvan International
HOTEL $

(☑255571; Station Rd; d ₹600-1000; ❄) Hidden down a lane off Station Rd, this pleasant hotel boasts lime-green walls, tinted windows and an amiable management. It's generally quiet and peaceful, but watch out for those boisterous wedding receptions often thrown at the garden restaurant.

Hotel Navaratna International
HOTEL $

(☑222771, Station Rd; d from ₹700; ❄) Bijapur's cheapest AC rooms are on offer at this well-managed hotel off Station Rd, with paintings à la Kandinsky and Chagall decorating the lobby. Rooms are sparkling clean, with shiny floor tiles.

Hotel Tourist
HOTEL $

(☑250655; Station Rd; d ₹190-350) Bang in the middle of the bazaar, with scrawny (but clean) rooms. Service is apathetic, so bring that DIY manual along.

Hotel Shashinag Residency
HOTEL $$
(☎260344; www.hotelshashinagresidency.com; Sholapur-Chitradurga Bypass Rd; s/d incl breakfast ₹2250/2750; ❄❈) Consider this place only if you can't do without a swimming pool or a snooker parlour. It's about 2km away from town.

✖ Eating & Drinking

Kamat Restaurant
SOUTH INDIAN $
(Station Rd; mains ₹60-80; ☺9am-11pm) Below Hotel Kanishka International, this popular joint serves diverse South Indian snacks and meals, including an awesome thali bursting with regional flavours.

Swapna Lodge Restaurant
PUB $
(Station Rd; mains ₹80-100; ☺noon-11pm) It's two floors up a dingy staircase next to Hotel Tourist, and has good grub, cold beer and a 1970s lounge feel. Its open-air terrace is a pleasant lounging spot, albeit a little noisy with maddening traffic below.

Hotel Madhuvan International
INDIAN $
(Station Rd; mains ₹60-80; ☺9am-11pm) Try the yummy *masala dosa* or the never-ending North Indian thalis dished out here by waiters in red turbans. The downside is that there's no alcohol on offer.

In the bustling market around Gandhi Circle on MG Rd, you'll find countless stalls flogging local snacks, roasted corn-on-the-cob, fresh fruits and sweetmeats such as *pedha* and *kalakandh*.

ⓘ Information

Cyber Park (Station Rd; per hr ₹20; ☺9am-10pm) Internet access.
Royal Internet Café (Station Rd, below Hotel Pearl; per hr ₹20; ☺9am-10pm) Internet access.
State Bank of India (Station Rd; ☺10.30am-4.30pm Mon-Fri, 10.30am-1.30pm Sat) Changes foreign currency and is super-efficient.
Tourist office (☎250359; Station Rd; ☺10am-5.30pm Mon-Sat) A poorly serviced office in the shabby Hotel Mayura Adil Shahi Annexe.

ⓘ Getting There & Away
Bus
From the **bus stand**, two early-morning buses run direct to Bidar (₹180, seven hours). Ordinary buses head frequently to Gulbarga (₹104, four hours) and Hubli (₹160, six hours). There are buses to Bengaluru (ordinary/sleeper ₹360/580, 12 hours, seven daily) via Hospet (₹148, five hours), Hyderabad (ordinary/semideluxe ₹239/348, 11

hours, five daily) and Mumbai (₹414, 12 hours, two daily) via Pune (₹293, 10 hours).

Train
From **Bijapur train station**, express trains go to Sholapur (2nd class ₹80, 2½ hours, three daily), Bengaluru (sleeper/2AC ₹288/1135, 17 hours, three daily), Mumbai (2nd class ₹149; 12 hours, four weekly) and Hyderabad (sleeper ₹121, 14 hours, one daily).

ⓘ Getting Around
Autorickshaws are expensive in Bijapur, so be prepared to haggle. ₹80 should get you from the train station to the town centre. Between the Golgumbaz and Ibrahim Rouza they cost about ₹50, unless you share with locals (₹10). Tonga drivers are eager for business but charge around the same. Autorickshaw drivers ask for about ₹350 for a sightseeing trip.

Bidar
☎08482 / POP 174,200 / ELEV 664M
Tucked away in Karnataka's far northeastern corner, Bidar is a little gem that most travellers choose to ignore, and no one quite knows why. At most an afterthought on some itineraries, this old walled town – first the capital of the Bahmani kingdom (1428–87) and later the capital of the Barid Shahi dynasty – is drenched in history. That apart, it is home to some amazing ruins and monuments, including the colossal Bidar Fort, the largest in South India. Wallowing in neglect, Bidar sure commands more than the cursory attention it gets today.

◉ Sights

Bidar Fort
FORT
(☺dawn-dusk) Keep aside a few hours for peacefully wandering around the remnants of this magnificent 15th-century fort. Sprawled across rolling hills 2km east of Udgir Rd, it was once the administrative capital of much of southern India. Surrounded by a triple moat hewn out of solid red rock and 5.5km of defensive walls (the second longest in India), the fort has a fairy-tale entrance that twists in an elaborate chicane through three gateways.

Inside the fort are many evocative ruins, including the **Rangin Mahal** (Painted Palace) which sports elaborate tilework, woodwork and panels with mother-of-pearl inlay, and the **Solah Khamba Mosque** (Sixteen-Pillared Mosque). There's also a small **museum** (admission free; ☺9am-5pm) in the former royal bath. Clerks at the **archaeological office** beside the museum often double as guides. For a small tip (₹150 is fine), they can show you many hidden places within the fort which otherwise remain locked.

Bahmani Tombs
HISTORIC SITE

(☉dawn-dusk) The huge domed tombs of the Bahmani kings in Ashtur, 3km east of Bidar, have a desolate, moody beauty that strikes a strange harmony with the rolling hills around them. These impressive mausoleums were built to house the remains of the sultans – their graves are still regularly draped with fresh satin and flowers – and are arranged in a long line along the edge of the road. The painted interior of Ahmad Shah Bahman's tomb is the most impressive, and is regularly prayed in.

About 500m prior to reaching the tombs, to the left of the road, is **Choukhandi** (admission free; ☉dawn-dusk), the serene mausoleum of Sufi saint Syed Kirmani Baba, who travelled here from Persia during the golden age of the Bahmani empire. An uncanny air of calm hangs within the monument, and its polygonal courtyard houses rows of medieval graves, amid which women in hijab sit quietly and murmur inaudible prayers. You are welcome to sit in or walk around, and soak up the ambience.

Both places are best visited early in the day, as it's difficult to find transport back to Bidar after dark.

Other Sights
HISTORIC SITES

Dominating the heart of the old town are the ruins of **Khwaja Mahmud Gawan Madrasa** (admission free; ☉dawn-dusk), a college for advanced learning built in 1472 by Mahmud Gawan, then chief minister of the empire. It was later used as an armoury by Mughal emperor Aurangzeb, when a gunpowder explosion ripped the building in half. To get an idea of its former grandeur, check out the remnants of coloured tiles on the front gate and one of the minarets which still stands intact.

Scattered around the town's bus stand are a handful of magnificent but forgotten **royal tombs**, including those of Ali Barid and his son Kasim Barid.

🛏 Sleeping & Eating

Hotel Mayura
HOTEL $

(☏228142; Udgir Rd; d from ₹400; ❄) Smart and friendly, with cheerful and well-appointed rooms, this is clearly the best hotel to camp in Bidar. It's bang opposite the bus stand, and there's an excellent **bar-restaurant** on the ground floor.

Hotel Mayura Barid Shahi
HOTEL $

(☏221740; Udgir Rd; d from ₹350; ❄) Otherwise featureless with simple, minimalist rooms (service is OK, though), this place scores due to its central location. The lovely garden **bar-restaurant** to the rear brims over with joy and merriment every evening.

Sapna International
HOTEL $

(☏220991; Udgir Rd; d from ₹400; ❄) This place is let down by slightly stiff service, but the rooms are just about fine for the price. In its favour are the two restaurants: the pure-veg Kamat and the nonveg Atithi, which offers meat dishes and booze (mains ₹80 to ₹100).

Nisarga Restaurant
INDIAN $

(Papanash Lake; mains ₹60-100; ☉noon-10pm) For a truly memorable meal, head out of town to the edge of placid Papanash Lake, where you can relish a train of local dishes and mash-ups (the pea and mushroom curry is yummy) in this laid-back restaurant under a shady tree. A return autorickshaw with waiting time would cost you about ₹100, but the extra expense is worth every penny.

Rasganga
SOUTH INDIAN $

(Udgir Rd, mains ₹30-50; ☉9am-10pm) A tasty South Indian thali (₹37) is on offer at this busy eatery located within the Hotel Mayura Barid Shahi complex.

ℹ Information

The modern town centre is along Udgir Rd, down which you will also find the bus station.

HDFC Bank (Udgir Rd) ATM opposite Sapna International.

Nisarga Internet (per hr ₹20; ☉9am-9pm) Internet access near Sapna International.

ℹ Getting There & Away

From the **bus stand**, frequent buses run to Gulbarga (₹75, three hours), which is connected to Mumbai and Bengaluru. Buses also go to Hyderabad (₹103, four hours), Bijapur (₹180, seven hours) and Bengaluru (semideluxe/AC ₹359/580, 12 hours).

The train station, around 1km southwest of the bus stand, has services to Hyderabad (sleeper ₹120, five hours, three daily) and Bengaluru (sleeper ₹280, 17 hours, one daily).

ℹ Getting Around

Rent a bicycle at **Sami Cycle Taxi** (Basveshwar Circle; per day ₹20; ☉10am-10pm) against your proof of identity. Or simply arrange a day tour in an autorickshaw for around ₹350.

Andhra Pradesh

Includes »

Best Places to Eat

» Waterfront (p221)

» Hotel Shadab (p221)

» Sandy Lane Restaurant
& Bar (p232)

» Fusion 9 (p223)

» Lotus Food City (p234)

Best Places to Stay

» Taj Mahal Hotel (p219)

» Taj Falaknuma Palace
(p219)

» Golden Glory Guesthouse
(p219)

» Sai Priya Resort (p232)

» Park (p232)

Why Go?

Andhra Pradesh won't hit you over the head with its attractions. It doesn't brag about its temples or its colourful history. It's forgotten most of its palaces and royal architecture – you'll have to purposely seek them out.

Andhra plays hard to get: its charms are subtle. But if you look closely, you'll find a long, fascinating history of arts, culture, spiritual scholarship and religious harmony. In Hyderabad's Old City, Islamic monuments, Persian-inspired architecture and the call of the muezzin speak of the city's unique heritage.

Dig a little deeper and you'll find another Andhran history: the region was an international centre of Buddhist thought for several hundred years from the 3rd century BC.

So come, but only if you're prepared to dig for the jewels to be found here. Keep your eyes open and your curiosity sharp and you're bound to find something that even Andhrans, in their modesty, hadn't thought to mention.

When to Go
Hyderabad

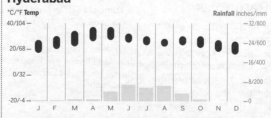

Dec–Jan Explore Hyderabad's sights in perfect 20-25°C weather.

Ramadan (around Jun–Aug) Join locals digging into *haleem*, a Ramzan favourite.

Jun–Sep Monsoons make travel tough, but surfing at beaches around Vizag is decent.

Hyderabad's new Rajiv Gandhi International Airport is the main arrival point. The main train stations are Nampally and Secunderabad in Hyderabad; Imlibun is the interstate bus station.

Visakhaptnam has monthly ferries leaving to Port Blair in the Andaman Islands.

Fast Facts

» Population: 84.7 million

» Area: 276,754 sq km

» Capital: Hyderabad

» Main languages: Telugu, Urdu, Hindi

» Sleeping prices: **$** below ₹800, **$$** ₹800 to ₹2500, **$$$** above ₹2500

Top Tip

Hotels charge a 5% 'luxury' tax on all rooms over ₹300; it's not included in the prices quoted in this chapter. All hotels listed have 24-hour checkout unless otherwise stated.

Resources

» APTDC tourism (www. aptdc.in)

» Deccan Chronicle (www. deccanchronicle.com)

» Fully Hyderabad (www. fullhyderabad.com)

Food

Hyderabad is a city known for its love of good food, and locals take great pride in their city's offerings. Andhra Pradesh's cuisine has two major influences. The Mughals brought tasty biryanis, *haleem* (pounded, spiced wheat with goat or mutton) and kebabs. The Andhra style is vegetarian and famous for its spiciness.

If you're travelling around Andhra Pradesh during Ramadan (known locally as Ramzan), look out for the clay ovens called *bhattis*. You'll probably hear them before you see them. Men gather around, taking turns to vigorously pound *haleem* inside purpose-built structures. Come nightfall, the serious business of eating begins. The taste is worth the wait. In September 2010, this love of the dish was taken a step further, being patented as 'Hyderabadi haleem'; prohibited to be served under that name unless it meets the strict quality guidelines.

DON'T MISS

The splendid architecture of **Hyderabad's** glory days is what brings most visitors to the region.

The 16th-century Qutb Shahi produced some masterful architecture including the stunning **Charminar**, **Golconda Fort** and their final resting place at the opulent tombs.

The lavish 18th-century nizam lifestyle is on display at sites such as **Chowmahalla Palace**, **Nizam's Museum** and the **Falaknuma Palace**, previously the residence of the sixth nizam and now a decadent hotel.

Top State Festivals

» Sankranti (Jan, statewide) This important Telugu festival marks the end of harvest season. Kite-flying abounds, women decorate their doorsteps with colourful *kolams* (or *rangolis* – rice-flour designs), and men decorate cattle with bells and fresh horn paint.

» Lumbini Festival (2nd Fri in Dec, Hyderabad, p214, Nagarjunakonda, p227) The three-day festival honours Andhra's Buddhist heritage.

» Visakha Utsav (Dec/Jan, Visakhapatnam, p231) A celebration of all things Visakhapatnam, with classical and folk dance and music performances; some events are staged on the beach.

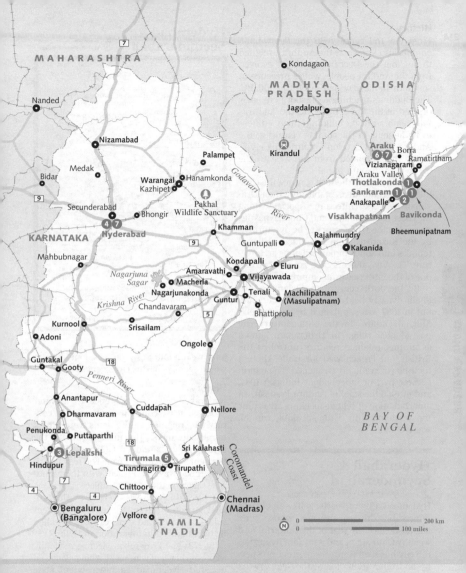

Andhra Pradesh Highlights

1 Absorb the meditative vibrations of monks past at **Sankaram** (p233), **Bavikonda** and **Thotlakonda** (p233)

2 Revel in the carnival beach atmosphere, at Visakhapatnam's **beaches** (p231)

3 Admire incredible carved images at **Veerbhadra Temple** in Lepakshi (p238).

4 Marvel at the genius design of **Golconda Fort** (p215)

5 Join millions of Hindu pilgrims taking *darshan* (deity viewing) at **Tirumala** (p235)

6 Sit back and enjoy the view on one of India's most scenic train trips to **Araku** (p233)

7 Learn about the state's rich ethnic diversity at the **tribal museums** in Hyderabad (p216) and Araku (p233)

History

From the 2nd century BC the Satavahana empire, also known as the Andhras, reigned throughout the Deccan plateau. It evolved from the Andhra people, whose presence in southern India may date back to 1000 BC. The Buddha's teaching took root here early on, and in the 3rd century BC the Andhras fully embraced it, building huge edifices in its honour. In the coming centuries, the Andhras would develop a flourishing civilisation that extended from the west to the east coasts of South India.

From the 7th to the 10th century, the Chalukyas ruled the area, establishing their Dravidian style of architecture, especially along the coast. The Chalukya and Chola dynasties merged in the 11th century to be overthrown by the Kakatiyas, who introduced pillared temples into South Indian religious architecture. The Vijayanagars then rose to become one of the most powerful empires in India.

By the 16th century the Islamic Qutb Shahi dynasty held the city of Hyderabad, but in 1687 was supplanted by Aurangzeb's Mughal empire. In the 18th century the post-Mughal rulers in Hyderabad, known as nizams, retained relative control as the British and French vied for trade, though their power gradually weakened. The region became part of independent India in 1947, and in 1956 the state of Andhra Pradesh, an amalgamation of Telugu-speaking areas plus the predominantly Urdu-speaking capital, was created.

Hyderabad & Secunderabad

🗷 040 / POP 5.5 MILLION / ELEV 600M

Hyderabad, City of Pearls, is like an elderly, impeccably dressed princess whose time has past. Once the seat of the powerful and wealthy Qutb Shahi and Asaf Jahi dynasties, the city has seen centuries of great prosperity and innovation. Today, the 'Old City' is full of centuries-old Islamic monuments and even older charms. In fact, the whole city is laced with architectural gems: ornate tombs, mosques, palaces and homes from the past are tucked away, faded and enchanting, in corners all over town. Keep your eyes open.

In the last decade, with the rise of Hyderabad's west side – our aged princess's sexy and popular granddaughter – a new decadence has emerged. 'Cyberabad', with Bengaluru (Bangalore) and Pune, is the seat of India's mighty software dynasty and generates

Hyderabad & Secunderabad

jobs, wealth and posh lounges. Opulence, it would seem, is in this city's genes.

History

Hyderabad owes its existence to a water shortage at Golconda in the late 16th century. The reigning Qutb Shahis were forced to relocate, and so Mohammed Quli and the royal family abandoned Golconda Fort for the banks of the Musi River. The new city of Hyderabad was established, with the brandnew Charminar as its centrepiece.

In 1687 the city was overrun by the Mughal emperor Aurangzeb, and subsequent rulers of Hyderabad were viceroys installed by the Mughal administration in Delhi.

In 1724 the Hyderabad viceroy, Asaf Jah, took advantage of waning Mughal power and declared Hyderabad an independent state with himself as leader. The dynasty of the nizams of Hyderabad began, and the traditions of Islam flourished. Hyderabad became a focus for the arts, culture and learning, and the centre of Islamic India. Its abundance of rare gems and minerals – the world-famous Kohinoor diamond is from here – furnished the nizams with enormous wealth. (William Dalrymple's *White Mughals* is a fascinating portrait of the city at this time.)

When Independence came in 1947, the then nizam of Hyderabad, Osman Ali Khan, considered amalgamation with Pakistan – and then opted for sovereignty. Tensions between Muslims and Hindus increased, however, and military intervention saw Hyderabad join the Indian union in 1948.

◉ Sights

Charminar
MONUMENT
(Four Towers; Map p220; Indian/foreigner ₹5/100; ⊙9am-5.30pm) Hyderabad's principal landmark was built by Mohammed Quli Qutb Shah in 1591 to commemorate the founding of Hyderabad and the end of epidemics caused by Golconda's water shortage. The dramatic four-column, 56m high and 30m wide structure has four arches facing the cardinal points. Minarets sit atop each column. The 2nd floor, home to Hyderabad's oldest mosque, and upper columns are not usually open to the public, but you can try your luck with the man with the key. The structure is illuminated from 7pm to 9pm.

Golconda Fort
FORT
(off Map p214; Indian/foreigner ₹5/100; ⊙9am-5pm) Although most of this 16th-century fortress dates from the time of the Qutb Shah kings, its origins as a mud fort have been traced to the earlier reigns of the Yadavas and Kakatiyas.

The citadel is built on a granite hill, 120m high and surrounded by crenellated ramparts constructed from large masonry blocks. The massive gates were studded with iron spikes to obstruct war elephants. Outside the citadel there stands another crenellated rampart, with a perimeter of 11km, and yet another wall beyond this. At Naya Quila (new fort), adjacent to the golf course, you can find a magnificent 400-year-old **baobab tree** (Hathiyan – elephant tree), with a circumference of 25m, said to be planted by seedlings carried by African regiments from Abyssiania. Exploring the crumbling rampart in the area you'll find cannons strewn about (some with beautiful inscriptions) and great views of the fort and tombs.

Survival within the fort was also attributable to water and sound. A series of concealed glazed earthen pipes ensured a reliable water supply, while the ingenious design of the diamond-shaped ceiling Grand Portico creates an acoustic system that carries even the smallest echo across the fort complex up to the highest point of the fort – used as a security system. Guides can also demonstrate the equally impressive acoustics in the royal palace where one's whisper into

the corner of the wall can be heard perfectly through the walls in the opposing corner, designed to catch out conspirators.

Knowledgeable **guides** (1½hr tour ₹600) are organised through the AP Tourism table in front of the entrance. Small guidebooks to the fort are also available.

Mornings are best for peace and quiet. An autorickshaw from Abids costs around ₹150. It's a one hour bus journey either with Bus 119 from Nampally station or Bus 66G from Charminar.

A trippy **sound-and-light show** (admission ₹50; ⊙in English 6.30pm Nov-Feb, 7pm Mar-Oct) is also held here.

Laad Bazaar
MARKET
(Map p220) West of the Charminar, the crowded Laad Bazaar is the perfect place to get lost. It has everything from fine perfumes, fabrics and jewels to musical instruments, secondhand saris and kitchen implements. Artisans are tucked away creating jewellery and scented oils, large pots and burkas. The lanes around the Charminar also form the centre of India's pearl trade. Some great deals can be had – if you know your stuff.

Salar Jung Museum
MUSEUM
(Map p220; www.salarjungmuseum.in; Salar Jung Marg; Indian/foreigner ₹10/150; ⊙10am-5pm Sat-Thu) The huge and varied collection, dating back to the 1st century, was put together by Mir Yusaf Ali Khan (Salar Jung III), the grand vizier of the seventh nizam, Osman Ali Khan (r 1910–49). The 35,000 exhibits from every corner of the world include sculptures, wood carvings, ivory (including a sadly ironic set of carved elephants), devotional objects, Persian miniature paintings, illuminated manuscripts, weaponry, toys and more than 50,000 books. The impressive nizams' jewellery collection is sometimes on display. Cameras are not allowed. Avoid Sunday, when it's bedlam. From any of the bus stands in the Abids area, take bus 7, which stops at **Afzal Gunj bus stop** (Map p220) on the north side of the nearby Musi River bridge.

Just west of the bridge is the spectacular **Osmania General Hospital** (Map p220), on the north side, and, on the south, the **High Court** (Map p220) and **Government City College** (Map p220), all built under the seventh nizam in the Indo-Saracenic style.

Chowmahalla Palace
MUSEUM
(Khilwat; Map p220; www.chowmahalla.com; Indian/foreigner ₹30/150, camera ₹50; ⊙10am-5pm Sat-Thu) The nizam family has sponsored a

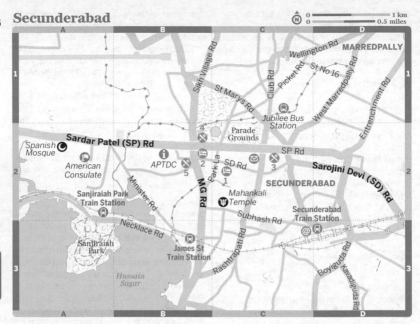

restoration of this dazzling palace – or, technically, four *(char)* palaces *(mahalla)*. Begun in 1750, it was expanded over the next 100 years, absorbing Persian, Indo-Saracenic, Rajasthani and European styles. The southern courtyard has one *mahal* with period rooms that have been reconstructed with the nizams' over-the-top furniture; another *mahal* with an exhibit on life in the zenana (women's quarters); antique cars; and curiosities like elephant seats, and a Remington Urdu typewriter.

In the northern courtyard is the **Khilwat Mubarak**, a magnificent durbar hall houses exhibitions of photos, arms and clothing.

HEH the Nizam's Museum   MUSEUM
(Purani Haveli; Map p220; adult/student ₹70/15, camera ₹150; ☺10am-5pm Sat-Thu) The 16th-century Purani Haveli was home of the sixth nizam, Fath Jang Mahbub Ali Khan (r 1869–1911), rumoured to have never worn the same garment twice. His 72m-long, two-storey Burmese teak wardrobe, the first room you'll enter, certainly seems to substantiate the claim. In the palace's former servants' quarters are personal effects of the seventh nizam, Osman Ali Khan (1886–1967) and gifts from his Silver Jubilee, lavish pieces that include an art deco silver letterbox collection. The museum's guides do an excellent job putting it all in context.

The rest of Purani Haveli is now a school, but you can wander around the grounds and peek in the administrative building, the nizam's former residence.

Qutb Shahi Tombs   TOMBS
(off Map p214; admission ₹10, camera/video ₹20/100; ☺9am-5pm) These graceful domed tombs sit serenely in landscaped gardens about 1.5km northwest of Golconda Fort's Balahisar Gate. Seven of the nine Qutb Shahi rulers were buried here, as well as members of the royal family and respected citizens from entertainers to doctors. You could easily spend half a day here taking photos and wandering in and out of the mausoleums. The upper level of Mohammed Quli's tomb, reached via a narrow staircase, has good views of the area. The Qutb Shahi Tombs **booklet** (₹20) may be available at the ticket counter.

The tombs are an easy walk from the fort, but an autorickshaw ride shouldn't be more than ₹25. Bus 80S also heads here from the fort.

Nehru Centenary Tribal Museum   MUSEUM
(Map p222; Masab Tank; Indian/foreigner ₹10/100; ☺10.30am-5pm Mon-Sat) Andhra Pradesh's 33 tribal groups, based mostly in the northeastern part of the state, comprise several

Secunderabad

🛏 Sleeping
1 Minerva Grand C2
2 YMCA...B2

🍴 Eating
3 Kamat Hotel..C2
4 Kamat Hotel..B2
5 Paradise Persis Restaurant...............B2

million people. The recently refurbished museum, run by the government's Tribal Welfare Department, exhibits photographs, dioramas of village life, musical instruments and some exquisite Naikpod masks. It's basic, but you'll get a glimpse into the cultures of these fringe peoples. There's an excellent library with 13,500 books covering tribal groups of India, and next door is the tiny **Girijan Sales Depot**, selling products made in tribal communities.

FREE **Paigah Tombs** TOMBS
(off Map p214; Phisalbanda, Santoshnagar; ☉10am-5pm Sat-Thu) The aristocratic Paigah family, purportedly descendents of the second Caliph of Islam, were fierce loyalists of the nizams, serving as statespeople, philanthropists and generals under and alongside them. The Paigahs' necropolis, tucked away in a quiet neighbourhood 4km southeast of Charminar, is a small compound of exquisite mausoleums made of marble from Agra and lime stucco. The main complex contains 27 tombs with intricate inlay work, surrounded by delicately carved walls and canopies, stunning filigree screens with geometric patterning and, overhead, tall, graceful turrets. The tombs are down a small lane across from Owasi Hospital. Look for the Preston Junior College sign. *The Paigah Tombs* (₹20) booklet is sold at the AP State Museum, but not here.

Buddha Statue & Hussain Sagar MONUMENT
Hyderabad has one of the world's largest free-standing stone **Buddha statues** (Map p218), completed in 1990 after five years of work. However, when the 17.5m-high, 350-tonne monolith was being ferried to its place in the Hussain Sagar, the barge sank. Fortunately, the statue was raised – undamaged – in 1992 and is now on a plinth in the middle of the lake. It's a magnificent sight when alit at night.

Frequent **boats** (adult/child ₹50/25) make the 30-minute return trip to the statue from both **Eat Street** (Map p222; ☉2-8.40pm)

and **Lumbini Park** (Map p218; admission ₹10; ☉9am-9pm), a pleasant place to enjoy sunsets and the popular musical fountain. The Tankbund Rd promenade, on the eastern shore of Hussain Sagar, has great views of the Buddha statue.

AP State Museum MUSEUM
(Map p218; Public Gardens Rd, Nampally; admission ₹10, camera/video ₹100/500; ☉10.30am-5pm Sat-Thu) The continually renovated State Museum hosts a rather dusty collection of important archaeological finds from the area, as well as a Buddhist sculpture gallery, with some relics of the Buddha and an exhibit on Andhra's Buddhist history. There are also Jain and bronze sculpture galleries, a decorative-arts gallery and a 4500-year-old Egyptian mummy. The museum, like the gorgeous **Legislative Assembly building** (Map p218) down the road (both commissioned by the seventh nizam), is floodlit at night.

Mecca Masjid MOSQUE
(Map p220; Shah Ali Banda Rd, Patthargatti; ☉9am-5pm) This mosque is one of the world's largest, with space for 10,000 worshippers. Women are not allowed inside.

Several bricks embedded above the gate are made with soil from Mecca – hence the name. To the left of the mosque, an enclosure contains the tombs of Nizam Ali Khan and his successors.

Since the 2007 bomb blasts here, security is tight; no bags are allowed inside.

**Birla Mandir &
Planetarium** HINDU TEMPLE, MUSEUM
(Map p218) The Birla **mandir** (☉7am-noon & 2-9pm), constructed of white Rajasthani marble in 1976, graces Kalabahad (Black Mountain), one of two rocky hills overlooking the Hussain Sagar. Dedicated to Venkateshwara, the temple is a popular Hindu pilgrimage centre and affords excellent views over the city, especially at sunset. The **library** (☉4-8pm) here is worth a visit

Next door are the **Birla Planetarium & Science Museum** (museum/planetarium ₹20/35; ☉museum 10.30am-8pm, to 3pm Fri, planetarium shows 11.30am, 4pm & 6pm) and the worthwhile **Birla Modern Art Gallery** (admission ₹10; ☉10.30am-6pm).

Hyderabad has a burgeoning contemporary art scene:

ICCR Art Gallery ART GALLERY
(Map p218; ☎23236398; Ravindra Bharati Theatre, Public Gardens Rd; ☉11am-7pm)

ANDHRA PRADESH HYDERABAD & SECUNDERABAD

ANDHRA PRADESH

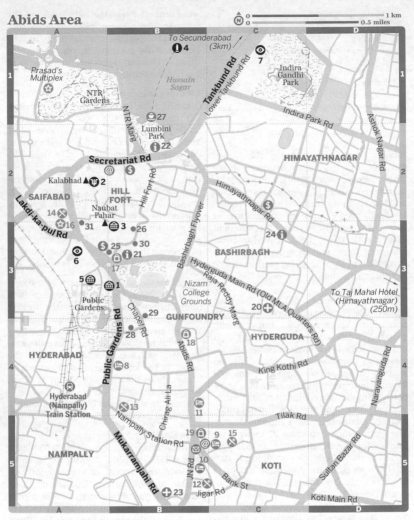

Kalakriti   ART GALLERY
(Map p222; www.kalakriti.in; Rd No 10, Banjara
Hills; ☉11am-7pm)

Shrishti   ART GALLERY
(www.shrishtiart.com; Rd No 15, Jubilee Hills;
☉11am-7pm)

☙ Courses

**Vipassana International
Meditation Centre**   BUDDHIST MEDITATION
(Dhamma Khetta; ☎24240290; www.khetta.
dhamma.org; Nagarjuna Sagar Rd, 12.6km) The
Vipassana International Meditation Centre
has intensive 10-day meditation courses in

its peaceful grounds 20km outside the city.
Apply online or at the Hyderabad **office**
(☎24732569). A shuttle runs to/from Hyderabad on the first and last day of courses.

☞ Tours

APTDC (p226) tours the city (₹270), Ramoji
Film City (₹600), Nagarjuna Sagar (weekends,
₹450) and Tirupathi/Tirumala (three days,
₹1950). The Sound & Light tour (₹200) takes
in Hitec City, the botanic gardens and Golconda Fort's sound-and-light show, but you may
spend much of it in traffic. Tours leave from
APTDC's Secunderabad branch (Map p216)

Passionate local **Abbas Tyabji** (☑9391010015) is an experienced guide/photojournalist who can take you to less-touristy sights – such as toddy tappers at work or nature walks in the city's outskirts.

Society To Save Rocks WALKING
(☑23552923; www.saverocks.org; 1236 Rd No 60, Jubilee Hills) This NGO organises monthly walks through the Andhran landscape and its surreal-looking boulders. Check website for details.

🛌 Sleeping

TOP CHOICE Taj Mahal Hotel (Himayathnagar) HOTEL $$
(off Map p218; ☑27637836-9; tajcafe@gmail.com; Himayathnagar; s/d from ₹900/1200; ❄☎) Despite its unfortunate location in front of an overpass on Himayathnagar Rd, the Taj is a peaceful, sunny, stylish place where the staff are warm and welcoming and the hallway floors look like Jaipuri marble. Rooms are surprisingly tasteful, with sleek lamps and chunky, contemporary wooden furniture. Comfy and classy for less than the going rate makes this a great choice.

Golden Glory Guesthouse HOTEL $
(Map p222; ☑23554765; www.goldengloryguesthouse.com; Rd No 3, Banjara Hills; s/d incl breakfast from ₹650/900, s incl breakfast without bathroom ₹290; ❄☎) Nestled among the mansions of ritzy Banjara Hills, this gem of a hotel scores big on location. Tucked down a quiet residential street, it's the perfect place to escape the madness of Hyderabad. First impressions are grand with sparkling lobby and spiral staircase, and while the cheaper rooms are boxy, they're very clean and good value (and include a simple breakfast). Pricier rooms are more spacious with balconies and bathtubs.

Taj Falaknuma Palace HOTEL $$$
(off Map p214; ☑24388888; www.tajhotels.com; Engine Bowli, Falaknuma; s/d from ₹16,500/17,625) Nowhere suits the term 'fit for royalty' better than at the Falaknuma Palace, the former residence of the sixth nizam. Taking over a decade to restore, the Taj Group's latest luxury hotel has most certainly been worth the wait. The 'cheapest' rooms have Italian marble floors, colonial furniture and great city views, while the Presidential Suite (an astounding ₹500,000 per night) was

ANDHRA PRADESH HYDERABAD & SECUNDERABAD

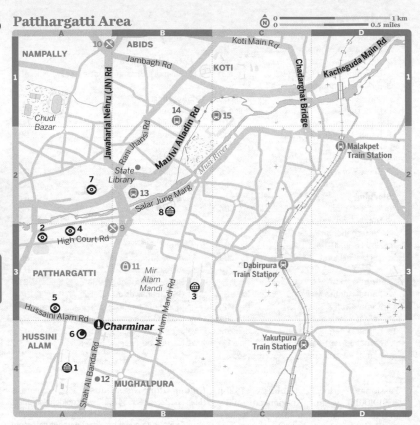

the nizam's living quarters and has its own swimming pool and personal butler! If you don't have a spare half million, you can still pop in for high tea in the Jade Room, which has hosted royalty from around the world.

Minerva Grand
HOTEL $$$

(Map p216; ☏66117373; www.minervagrand.com; SD Rd, Secunderabad; s/d incl breakfast from ₹4000 /4400; ❄@⊚) It's rare to find a hotel that has genuine style; this place has nailed it. Standard rooms (one wheelchair-accessible) have striking deep-fuchsia walls, white furniture, tasselled bedspreads and piles of pillows. More-expensive rooms are also bold in design, and all rooms have hardwood floors, gentle lighting and sleek, spacious bathrooms. A diamond in the rough of Sarojini Devi Rd.

Hotel Mandakini Jaya International
HOTEL $$

(Map p218; ☏9810068858; www.mandakinijayaintl -hyderabad.com; Hanuman Tekdi Rd; s/d incl breakfast from ₹1690/1790; ❄⊚) Under new management, the former budget Jaya International has reinvented itself as a smart and modern business hotel. Rooms are great value, comfortable and ultramodern. Its downside is the scungy hallways.

Nand International
HOTEL $

(☏24657511; www.nandhotels.com; Kacheguda Station Rd; s/d/tr from ₹535/635/735; ❄) The Nand is a pleasant surprise near Kacheguda Station. It has a roof garden with potted geraniums (and chai on order), sitting areas, water coolers, and well-looked-after peach-coloured rooms hung with weird mixed-media art.

YMCA
HOSTEL $

(Map p216; ☏27801190; secunderabadymca@ yahoo.co.in; cnr SP & SD Rd, Secunderabad; r from ₹500, without bathroom from ₹350; ❄) One of the better cheapies, this cheery hostel has clean, no frill rooms, some with private balcony. It's near the clock tower.

Hotel Suhail
HOTEL **$**

(Map p218; ☎24610299; www.hotel suhail.in; Troop Bazaar; s/d/tr from ₹475/620/900; ❄@) If all budget hotels were like the Suhail, we'd all be much better off. Staff are friendly and on top of it, the rooms are large and quiet, have balconies and constant hot water. It's tucked away on an alley behind the main post office and the Grand Hotel – away from the Hyderabad bustle, but it's also unlit at night; some readers find it sketchy.

Taj Mahal Hotel
HOTEL **$$**

(Map p218; ☎24758250; tajmahal_abid@rediffmail.com; cnr Abids & King Kothi Rds; s/d with AC from ₹1200/1650; ❄) This rambling 1924 heritage building has a magnificent exterior, plants peppered about and decent, though ultimately overpriced rooms. Each is different so ask to see a few: the better ones have boudoirs, crystal-knobbed armoires and wood-beam ceilings.

Hotel Harsha
HOTEL **$$**

(Map p218; ☎23201188; www.hotelharsha.net; Public Gardens Rd; s/d incl breakfast from ₹1600/1800; ❄🛜) Rooms don't have tonnes of character, and can be noisy (ask for a rear facing room) but they're bright, have fridges, the furniture is in good taste and the art is a step up from the usual schlock. The overall effect is polished but comfy. The lobby smells like success, with lots of glass and marble. One of the city's best deals.

Green Park
HOTEL **$$$**

(Map p222; ☎66515151; www.hotelgreenpark.com; Greenlands Rd, Begumpet; s/d incl breakfast from ₹5500/6500; ❄@🛜) Don't bother going beyond the standard rooms here, which are comfy and classy with sleek desks, bamboo flooring and flower petals in the bathroom. The lobby is a paragon of peace and gentle lighting, while smiley staff look on.

Secunderabad Retiring Rooms
RAILWAY RETIRING ROOMS

(Map p216; dm/s/d from ₹50/250/450; ❄) If you arrive late at Secunderabad train station, this is a good deal.

✕ Eating

Per local usage, we use the term 'meal' instead of 'thali' in this chapter.

CITY CENTRE

 Waterfront
ASIAN FUSION **$$$**

(Map p222; ☎65278899; Necklace Rd; mains ₹175-650; ⊙noon-2.30pm & 7-11pm) The outdoor deck here on the water (dinner service only) may have the best ambience in all of Hyderabad, with soft lighting overhead, the Buddha Statue and the entire Hussain Sagar and the Birla Mandir all twinkling in the distance. Eating indoors, alongside enormous picture windows, isn't bad either. But it's the Chinese, Indian and Thai food that's to die for – their take on *phad kea mou* (noodles with tasty bok choy) is a must-eat.

Hotel Shadab
INDIAN **$$**

(Map p220; High Court Rd, Patthargatti; mains ₹60-250; ⊙noon-midnight) One meal at Shadab and you'll be forever under its spell. The hopping restaurant is *the* place to get biryani (₹95 to ₹200) and, during Ramzan (Ramadan), *haleem*. It has even mastered veg biryani (!) and hundreds of other veg and non-veg delights (if you try the chocolate

chicken or pineapple mutton, let us know how it goes). Packed with Old City families and good vibes.

Kamat Hotel
INDIAN $
(Map p216; SD Rd, Secunderabad; mains ₹45-75; ☺7am-10pm) How much do we love Kamat Hotel? Words can't say. Each Kamat is slightly different, but they're all cheap and good. There are two branches on SD Rd; the others are in Saifabad and on Nampally Station Rd (Map p218). Meals (from ₹36) are reliably delish.

Kamat Andhra Meals
INDIAN $
(Map p218; Troop Bazaar; meals from ₹45; ☺noon-4pm & 7-11pm) Excellent authentic Andhra meals on banana leaves, topped up till you almost faint with pleasure, and finished off with a banana. Its sister restaurants in the same compound – **Kamat Jowar Bhakri** (Maharashtran), **Kamat Restaurant** with air-con (North and South Indian) and

Kamat Coffee Shop – are likewise friendly family joints full of happy diners. No relation to Kamat Hotel.

Also recommended:

Paradise Persis Restaurant
INDIAN $$
(Map p216; cnr SD & MG Rds, Secunderabad; mains ₹125-245; ☺11.30am-11pm) Ask any Hyderabadi about biryani, and they'll mention Paradise.

Mozamjahi Market
MARKET $
(Map p220; cnr Mukarramjahi & Jawaharlal Nehru Rds; ☺6am-6pm) A great place to buy fruit and vegies (or ice cream), while enjoying the alluring architecture of the stone building, commissioned by the seventh nizam and named after his son.

Sagar Papaji Ka Dhaba
INDIAN $
(Map p218; Hanuman Tekdi Rd; mains ₹45-110; ☺noon-4pm & 7-11pm) Always busy, Papaji's has profoundly delicious veg and non-veg biryanis, curries and tikkas. Watch the

ANDHRA PRADESH

guys making naan and throwing it in the tandoor while you wait for a table.

BANJARA HILLS & JUBILEE HILLS

Those looking for a finer dining experience should head to the hills, home to Hyderabad's more well-heeled residents.

Fusion 9 · CONTINENTAL $$$
(Map p222; ☑65577722; Rd No 1; mains ₹325-425; ☺12-3.30pm & 7-11pm) Soft lighting and cosy decor set off pan-fried Norwegian salmon (₹650), lamb cutlets with rosemary and crispy potatoes (₹395), or pork chops (₹425). One of the best international menus in town also features (less expensive) Mexican, Thai, pizzas and veg dishes, and lots of imported liquor.

Angeethi · PUNJABI $$
(Map p222; 7th fl, Reliance Classic Bldg, Rd No 1; mains ₹180-290; ☺noon-3.30pm & 7-11pm) Designed to resemble an old Punjabi *dhaba* (snack bar), jazzed up with vintage Bollywood posters on the walls, Angeethi does outstanding North Indian and Punjabi dishes, such as corn *methi malai* (sweet-corn stew with fenugreek leaves; ₹185).

Coco's · INDIAN/CONTINENTAL $$
(off Map p222; ☑23540600; Rd No 2; mains ₹120-325; ☺11.30am-11.30pm) This chilled-out rooftop restaurant/bar almost succeeds in resembling a bamboo beach shack, though it's position on a busy road above a Chinese restaurant was always going to make it tough. Looking out over KBR Park, relaxed Coco's

exudes ambience and serves decent Indian and Western dishes.

Big Dosa Company · INDIAN $
(Rd No 45, Jubilee Hills; dosas ₹75-135; ☺8am-11pm) There's a lot that's big about this dosa joint: the portions, the taste and the very idea itself of a gourmet dosa. The 'feta cheese and roasted pepper' dosa, served with sundried-tomato chutney or the 'shredded chicken' dosa make the journey out to Jubilee Hills worthwhile.

24-Lettered Mantra · GROCERY SHOP
(Map p222; www.24lettermantra.com; Rd No 12; ☺9.30am-10pm) Healthy people will appreciate this tiny grocery shop with organic produce, snacks and juices.

Ofen · BAKERY $$
(Map p222; www.theofen.com; Rd No 10; desserts ₹15-110; ☺11am-11pm Mon-Fri, 9am-11pm Sat & Sun) Two words: Linzer torte. Scrumptious desserts (some vegan and sugar-free), fresh-baked bread and comfort food like sandwiches and pasta (₹90 to ₹250). Does all-day continental breakfasts.

BBQ Nation · INDIAN, CONTINENTAL $$
(Map p222; www.barbeque-nation.com; Rd No 1; lunch Mon-Sat ₹344, Sun ₹544, dinner ₹600; ☺noon-3pm & 7-11pm) All you can eat BBQ meat, seafood and vegetarian skewers served at your table.

Little Italy · ITALIAN $$
(☑64566692; Apollo Rd, Jubilee Hills; mains ₹200-500 ☺noon-3pm & 7-11pm) Classy vegetarian Italian fare with good wine list.

KITSCHABAD

Mixed in with Hyderabad's world-class sights, you'll find some attractions that err on the more quirky side; which can provide some good relief from the 'proper' sightseeing.

Ramoji Film City
FILM STUDIO

(www.ramojifilmcity.com; adult/child ₹500/450; ⊙9.30am-5.30pm) The home of South India's burgeoning film industry, known as Tollywood, Ramoji Film City is undoubtedly the premier kitsch sight of Hyderabad. Set on more than 670 hectares, this is the world's largest movie-making complex, producing Telugu, Tamil, Hindi and the occasional foreign film. Though you won't actually get to see any being made, the four-hour bus tour will take you through flimsy film sets and gaudy fountains, stopping for dance routines and stunt shows. Located in the outskirts of town, around 20km from Abids, you can jump on bus 205 or 206 from Koti Women's College, northeast of Koti station, which take an hour to get here.

Health Museum
MUSEUM

(Map p218; Public Gardens Rd, Nampally; admission free; ⊙10.30am-5pm Sat-Thu) A throwback to a 1950s classroom, this museum houses a bizarre collection of medical and public-health paraphernalia. It features a rather terrifying giant model of a crab louse.

Snow World
AMUSEMENT PARK

(Map p218; Lower Tankbund; admission ₹300; ⊙11am-8pm) The perfect place to escape the heat, Snow World is, hands down, the coolest attraction in town (in a literal sense, of course...). It's a bizarre experience to suddenly find yourself in heavy-duty waterproof clothing amid people hurling snowballs, riding toboggans and playing snow volleyball. There's a snowfall on the hour, accompanied by cheers, a snow disco and lightshow.

Suddha Car Museum
MUSEUM

(www.sudhacars.net; Bahadurpura; Indian/foreigner ₹30/150; ⊙9.30am-6.30pm) Featuring the genius work of Sudhakar, here you'll find working cars in the shape of a toilet, computer, cricket bat, hamburger or condom, among other wacky designs. He holds the Guinness world record for the largest tricycle, standing a whopping 12.8m tall. You can poke your head into the workshop to see his latest project (at the time of research it was a 'stiletto shoe' car). It's located east of the Nehru Zoological Park.

NTR Park
PARK

(Map p218; child/adult ₹10/20; ⊙2.30-8.30pm) Making for a nice stroll about, with pleasant gardens, theme park rides and a games arcade, taking the cake in the kitsch stakes is the gaudy restaurant shaped like a giant fruit bowl.

Amurutha Castle
HOTEL

(www.bestwesternamruthacastle.com; Saifabad; d from ₹4800) Always dreamt of staying in a Bavarian castle while in Hyderabad? Probably not, but in case you did, this massive castle-hotel, based on the Schloss Neuschwanstein, is the place to do it. It ain't cheap though.

 ## Drinking & Entertainment

Hyderabad's scene is growing, but drinking establishments are limited by an 11.30pm curfew law. Unless stated otherwise, the following bars are open to 11.30pm (but don't get going till 9pm). All serve food and charge covers (₹500 to ₹1000) on certain nights – for couples, that is: guys usually need a gal to enter. Beer starts at ₹150, cocktails at ₹300.

TOP CHOICE Coco's
BAR

(off Map p222; ☑23540600; Rd No 2, Banjara Hills) Rooftop bar makes it the perfect place for a cold beer or cocktail on a balmy evening. Has live music.

Mocha
CAFE

(Map p222; Rd No 7, Banjara Hills; ⊙9am-11pm) Full of trendy twenty-somethings smoking hookahs (from ₹225), but the decor, the garden and the coffee are fabulous. Menu also has good breakfasts, paninis and shakes.

Liquids Et cera
BAR
(Map p222; ☎66259907; Bhaskar Plaza, Rd No 1, Banjara Hills) Regularly featured in the papers' Society pages, Liquids is the reigning queen of Hyderabad nightlife. There's no sign, and its name changes slightly each year.

Excess Club
BAR
(☎23542422; Novotel, Madhavpur; ☺7pm-2am Tue-Sun) Set over a huge space, Excess was the current most happening place; open the latest, the best DJs, but the furthest away – past Hitech City.

Touch
BAR
(Map p222; ☎23542422; Trendset Towers, Rd No 2, Banjara Hills); ☺7pm-midnight Wed, Sat & Sun) Touch is all about image. It's a stylish, comfy place to watch the beautiful people. Also has an 'ice bar' with temperatures set at -23°.

Café Coffee Day
CAFE
(Map p222; Eat Street, Necklace Rd; ☺7.30am-11pm) Decent coffee and snacks.

Barista
CAFE
(Map p222; Rd No 1, Banjara Hills; ☺8am-11pm) Another reliable coffee option.

Ravindra Bharati Theatre
THEATRE
(Map p218; ☎23233672; www.artistap.com; Public Gardens Rd) Regular music, dance and drama performances. Check local papers.

🛍 Shopping

The bazaars near the Charminar (p215) are the most exciting places to shop: you'll find exquisite pearls, silks, gold and fabrics alongside billions of bangles.

Hyderabad Perfumers
PERFUMERY
(Map p220; Patthargatti; ☺10am-8.30pm Mon-Sat) The family-run Hyderabad Perfumers, which has been in business for four generations, can whip something up for you on the spot.

Meena Bazar
CLOTHING
(Map p218; www.meenabazarhyd.co.in; Tilak Rd; ☺10.30am-8.30pm Mon-Sat) Gorgeous saris, *salwar* (trouser) suits and fabrics at fixed prices. Also has a branch in Banjara Hills (Map p222).

Kalanjali
HANDICRAFTS
(Map p218; Hill Fort Rd; ☺10am-9.30pm) With a huge range of arts, crafts, fabrics and clothing, Kalanjali (split between two buildings) has higher prices than the bazaar, but you can get a feel for what things cost in a relaxed environment.

Shilparamam Crafts Village
HANDICRAFTS
(off Map p222; www.shilparamam.org; Madhapur; adult/child ₹25/10; ☺10.30am-8.30pm) Near Hitech City, this government-initiative arts village has stalls selling handicrafts and clothes from all over India. A night bazaar is also planned. It has nice gardens with a pond to stroll about.

Fabindia
CLOTHING
(Map p222; www.fabindia.com; Rd No 9, Banjara Hills; ☺11am-8.30pm) Clothes and accessories in traditional artisanal fabrics.

Lepakshi
HANDICRAFTS
(Map p218; www.lepakshihandicrafts.gov.in; Gunfoundry; ☺10am-8pm Mon-Sat) Andhra crafts.

ℹ Information

Internet Access
Anand Internet (per hr ₹15; ☺10.30am-9.30pm) Opposite Secunderabad station.
Net World (Taramandal Complex, Saifabad; per hr ₹15; ☺9.30am-7pm Mon-Sat)
Reliance Internet (Himayathnagar; per hr ₹15; ☺8.30am-11pm)
Reliance Web World (MPM Mall, Abids Circle; per 4hr ₹100; ☺10.30am-9.30pm Mon-Sat, 12.30-9pm Sun)

Media
Good 'what's on' guides include *Channel 6* (www.channel6magazine.com), *GO Hyderabad* and *City Info*. The juiciest is *Wow! Hyderabad* (www.wowhyderabad.com; ₹25). The *Deccan Chronicle* is a good local paper; its *Hyderabad Chronicle* insert has info on happenings.

Medical Services
Apollo Pharmacy (Map p218; ☎23431734; Hyderguda Main Rd; ☺24hr) Delivers.
Care Hospital Banjara Hills (Map p222; ☎30418888; Rd No 1); Nampally (Map p218; ☎30417777; Mukarramjahi Rd) Reputable hospital with a 24-hour pharmacy.

Money
The banks offer the best currency-exchange rates here. ATMs are everywhere.
State Bank of India (☎23231986; HACA Bhavan, Saifabad; ☺10.30am-4pm Mon-Fri)

Post
Post office (☺8am-8.30pm Mon-Sat, 10am-2pm Sun) Secunderabad (Rashtrapati Rd); Abids (Abids Circle)

Tourist Information

Andhra Pradesh Tourism Development Corporation (APTDC; ☑24-hr info 23450444; www.aptdc.in; ☻7am-8.30pm) Bashirbagh (Map p218; ☑23298456; NSF Shakar Bhavan, opposite Police Control Room); Secunderabad (Map p216; ☑27893100; Yatri Nivas Hotel, Sardar Patel Rd); Tankbund Rd (Map p218; ☑65581555; ☻10.30am-5pm) Organises tours.

India Tourism (Government of India; Map p218; ☑23261360, 23260770; Netaji Bhavan, Himayathnagar Rd; ☻9.30am-6pm Mon-Fri, to noon Sat) Very helpful for information on Hyderabad, Andhra Pradesh and beyond.

❶ Getting There & Away

Air

Hyderabad's massive, modern **Rajiv Gandhi International Airport** (☑66546370; www. hyderabad.aero) is 22km southwest of the city in Shamshabad.

You'll get the best fares online or with a travel agent. Try **Neo Globe Tours & Travels** (Map p218; ☑66751786; Saifabad; ☻10am-7.30pm Mon-Sat, 11am-2pm Sun) beside the Nizam Club.

Airline offices are usually open from 9.30am to 5.30pm Monday to Friday, with a one-hour lunch break, and to 1.30pm Saturday.

Domestic airline offices:

GoAir (☑airport 9223222111, 1800222111; Rajiv Gandhi International Airport)

Indian Airlines (Map p218; ☑23430334, airport 24255161/2; HACA Bhavan, Saifabad)

IndiGo (Map p218; ☑23233590, airport 24255052; Interglobe Air Transport, Chapel Rd)

Jet Airways (Map p218; ☑39893333, airport 39893322; Hill Fort Rd; ☻9am-7pm Mon-Sat) Also handles bookings for JetLite.

JetLite (☑30302020; Rajiv Gandhi International Airport)

Kingfisher Airlines (Map p222; ☑40328400, airport 66605603; Balayogi Paryatak Bhavan,Begumpet)

SpiceJet (☑18001803333; Rajiv Gandhi International Airport)

International airlines:

Air India (Map p218; ☑1800227722, airport 66605163; HACA Bhavan, Saifabad)

AirAsia (Map p218; ☑66666464, airport 66605163; HACA Bhavan, Saifabad)

Emirates (Map p222; ☑66234444; Rd No 1, Banjara Hills)

GSA Transworld Travels (Map p218; ☑3298495; Chapel Rd) For Qantas.

Lufthansa (☑4888888; Rajiv Gandhi International Airport)

Sri Lankan Airlines (Map p222; ☑23372429/30; Raj Bhavan Rd, Somajiguda) Opposite the Yashoda Hospital.

Qatar Airways (Map p222; ☑01244566000, airport 66605121; Rd No 1, Banjara Hills)

Thai Airways (Map p222; ☑23333030; Rd No 1, Banjara Hills)

Bus

Hyderabad's long-distance bus stations are mind-bogglingly efficient. **Mahatma Gandhi bus station** (Map p220; ☑24614406), more commonly known as Imlibun, has **advance booking offices** (☑23434269; ☻8am-10pm). For trips to Karnataka, go with **KSRTC** (☑24656430). Visit www.apsrtc.co.in for timetables and fares.

Secunderabad's **Jubilee bus station** (Map p216; ☑27802203) operates Volvo AC buses to Bengaluru (₹801, 11 hours, six daily), Chennai (₹844, 12 hours, daily) and Visakhapatnam (₹701, 13 hours, daily).

Private bus companies with AC services are on Nampally High Rd, near the train station entrance.

Train

Secunderabad (Map p214), Hyderabad (Map p218) – also known as Nampally – and Kacheguda (off Map p218) are the three major train stations. Most through trains stop at Secunderabad

MAJOR DOMESTIC FLIGHTS FROM HYDERABAD

DESTINATION	LOWEST ONE-WAY FARE (₹)	DURATION (HR)	FLIGHTS PER DAY
Bengaluru	3000	1	20
Chennai	3000	1	15
Delhi	5000	2	12
Kolkata	5500	2	5
Mumbai	3000	1¼	25
Tirupathi	2800	1	3
Visakhapatnam	3500	1	5

DESTINATION	FARE (₹)	DURATION (HR)	FREQUENCY (DAILY)
Bengaluru	480-775	12-10	7 (evening)
Bidar	80	4	half-hourly
Chennai	550-880	12-14	3 (evening)
Hospet	280	9	2
Mumbai	550-985	14-12	6 (evening)
Mysore	599	15	1
Nagarjuna Sagar	85-116	4	8
Tirupathi	435-735	12	12
Vijayawada	197-390	6	hourly
Visakhapatnam	470-865	14	12
Warangal	77	3	half-hourly

and Kacheguda, which is convenient for Abids. See p228, for key routes. You can book at Hyderabad and Secunderabad stations from 8am to 8pm Monday to Saturday (to 2pm Sunday). Both stations have a tourist counter. For general enquiries, phone ☏139; for reservation status, ☏135.

❶ Getting Around

To/From the Airport

The new airport is fabulous, and is a 45 minute drive into town.

BUS Frequent public buses depart from the PTC for Jubilee and Imlibun stations. More comfy are AC **Aeroexpress** (☏18004192008; ☺24hr) buses (₹175), which run half-hourly to Charminar, Secunderabad, Begumpet, Mehdipatnam and Hitec City.

TAXI For prepaid taxis, pay at the counter inside the terminal, then get your cab at the PTC. **Meru** (☏44224422) and **Easy** (☏43434343) 'radio taxis' queue up outside arrivals and charge ₹15 per kilometre, ₹18.75 at night. The trip to Abids or Banjara Hills shouldn't exceed ₹450. Going to the airport, try **Yellow Taxi** (☏44004400).

Autorickshaw

Flag fall is ₹12 for the first kilometre, then ₹7 for each additional kilometre. Between 10pm and 5am a 50% surcharge applies. Unfortunately, the new electronic meters often don't work and lots of drivers won't use them: be prepared to negotiate.

Bus

Lots of local buses originate at **Koti bus station** (Map p220; ☏23443320; Rani Jhansi Rd), so if you come here you might get a seat. The 'travel as you like' ticket (ordinary/express ₹40/50),

available from bus conductors, permits unlimited travel anywhere within the city on the day of purchase. The tiny *City Bus Route Guide* (₹10) is available at bookshops around Koti.

Car

There are several car-hire places around Hyderabad station. **Links Travels** (☏9348770007) is reliable for local or long-distance day-hire.

Train

MMTS trains (www.mmts.co.in) are convenient, particularly for the three main train stations. There are two main lines: Hyderabad (Nampally) to Lingampalli (northwest of Banjara Hills) has 11 stops, including Lakdikapul, Khairatabad, Necklace Rd, Begumpet and Hitec City; the Falaknuma (south of Old City) to Secunderabad line passes by Yakutpura, Dabirpura, Malakpet and Kachiguda among others. Trains will be labelled with their start and end point: HL is Hyderabad–Lingampalli, FS is Falaknuma–Secunderabad and so on. Trains are efficient but only run every 30 to 40 minutes. Tickets are ₹3 to ₹10.

Nagarjunakonda

☏08680

The Hill of Nagarjuna, 150km southeast of Hyderabad, is a peaceful island in the middle of the Nagarjuna dam peppered with ancient Buddhist structures. From the 3rd century BC until the 4th century AD, the Krishna River valley was home to powerful empires that supported the sangha (Buddhist community of monks and nuns), including the Ikshvakus, whose capital was Nagarjunakonda. It's estimated that this area alone had 30 monasteries.

The remains here were actually discovered in 1926 by archaeologist AR Saraswathi in the adjacent valley. In 1953, when it became known that a massive hydroelectric project would soon create the **Nagarjuna Sagar** reservoir, flooding the area, a six-year excavation was launched to unearth the area's many Buddhist ruins: stupas, *viharas* (monasteries), *chaitya-grihas* (assembly halls with stupas) and *mandapas* (pillared pavilions), as well as some outstanding examples of white-marble depictions of the Buddha's life. The finds were reassembled on Nagarjunakonda.

◉ Sights & Activities

Nagarjunakonda Museum   MUSEUM
(Indian/foreigner ₹5/100; ◷8am-5pm) This thoughtfully laid-out museum, located on an island accessible by boat, has Buddha statues and beautifully carved limestone slabs that once adorned stupas. Most are from the 3rd century AD and depict scenes from the Buddha's life, interspersed with *mithuna* (paired male and female) figures languorously looking on. The reassembled **monuments** are spread around the hilltop outside.

Launches (₹90, one hour) depart from Vijayapuri, on the banks of Nagarjuna Sagar, at 9.30am, 11am and 1.30pm, and stay for one hour. To do the place justice, take the morning launch out and the afternoon one back. Extra morning launches usually run on weekends and holidays. Fisherman out in their dish-shaped coracle boats provide good photographic material.

Anupu   HISTORICAL SITE
Another Buddhist site 10km from the launch point is the peaceful **Anupu** with remains of a stupa, university and amphitheatre; likewise relocated piece by piece prior to the construction of the dam. A tree here was planted by the Dalai Lama during his visit in 2006.

MAJOR TRAINS FROM HYDERABAD & SECUNDERABAD

DESTINATION	TRAIN NO & NAME	FARE (₹)	DURATION (HR)	DEPARTURE TIME & STATION
Bengaluru	2430 *Rajdhani*	1025/1355 (A)	12	6.50pm Secunderabad (Tue, Wed, Sat & Sun)
	2785 *Secunderabad–Bangalore Exp*	274/715/970 (B)	11	7.05pm Kacheguda
Chennai	2604 *Hyderabad–Chennai Exp*	297/779/1058 (B)	13	4.55pm Hyderabad
	2760 *Charminar Exp*	312/837/1119 (B)	14	6.30pm Hyderabad
Delhi	2723 *Andhra Pradesh Exp*	465/1252/1715 (B)	26	6.25am Hyderabad
	2429 *Rajdhani*	1725/2245 (A)	26	7.50am Secunderabad (Mon, Tue, Thu & Fri)
Kolkata	2704 *Falaknuma Exp*	442/1187/1623 (B)	26	4pm Secunderabad
	8646 *East Coast Exp*	430/1178/1624 (B)	30	10am Hyderabad
Mumbai	2702 *Hussainsagar Exp*	312/823/1119 (B)	15	2.45pm Hyderabad
	7032 *Hyderabad–Mumbai Exp*	297/792/1089 (B)	16	8.40pm Hyderabad
Tirupathi	2734 *Narayanadri Exp*	284/794/1009 (B)	12	6.05pm Secunderabad
	2797 *Venkatadri Exp*	277/723/979 (B)	12	8.05pm Kacheguda
Visakhapatnam	2728 *Godavari Exp*	297/779/1058 (B)	13	5.15pm Hyderabad

Fares: A – 3AC/2AC; B – sleeper/3AC/2AC

BUS NO	ROUTE
65G/66G	Charminar–Golconda, via Abids
87	Charminar–Nampally
2/2V, 8A/8U	Charminar–Secunderabad station
20D	Jubilee station–Nampally
142K	Koti–Golconda
119OR, 142M	Nampally–Golconda
1P/25	Secunderabad station–Jubilee station
1K, 1B, 3SS, 40	Secunderabad station–Koti
20P, 20V, 49, 49P	Secunderabad station–Nampally

Ethipophala waterfall   WATERFALL
(admission ₹20; ☺8am-6pm) A further 18km
from the launch point is the 21m-high Ethipophala waterfall, which, after heavy rain can
be a spectacular sight.

☙ Courses

Dhamma Nagajjuna   MEDITATION
(Nagarjunasagar Vipassana Centre; ☎09440139329;
www.nagajjuna.dhamma.org; Hill Colony) Keeping the legacy of Buddhism alive in the
region, this centre offers intensive 10-day
meditation courses in the grounds overlooking Nagarjuna Sagar. Courses are run on a
donation basis.

🛏 Sleeping & Eating

Nagarjunakonda is popular, and accommodation can be tight during weekends and
holidays, though it's easily visited as a day
trip. Both hotels have restaurants.

Nagarjuna Resort   HOTEL $
(☎08642-242471; r from ₹750; 图) The most
convenient place to stay, across the road
from the boat launch. It has spacious,
slightly shabby rooms with geysers,
balconies and good views.

Vijay Vihar Complex   HOTEL $$
(☎277362; fax 276633; r with AC from ₹1800;
图图) Two kilometres up the hill from the
bus stand is the fancy government hotel
overlooking the lake. Room balconies have
excellent views.

❶ Information

AP Tourism (☎276634; ☺10am-5.30pm Mon-
Sat) Has an office at Project House, across
from the bus stand.

❶ Getting There & Away

The easiest way to visit Nagarjunakonda is with
APTDC (☎040-65581555) in Hyderabad. Tours
(₹450) depart on weekends at 7am returning at
9.30pm.

You can also make your own way there from
Hyderabad or Vijayawada. From Hyderabad, take
a bus to Nagarjuna Sagar (from ₹85, four hours).
From there, it's a ₹10 shared rickshaw to Pylon,
and another ₹10 to the boat launch. The nearest
train station is 22km away at Macherla, where
buses leave regularly for Nagarjuna Sagar.

Warangal

☎0870 / POP 528,570

Warangal was the capital of the Kakatiya
kingdom, which covered the greater part of
present-day Andhra Pradesh from the late
12th to early 14th centuries until it was con-
quered by the Tughlaqs of Delhi. The Hindu
Kakatiyas were great builders and patrons
of Telugu literature and arts, and during
their reign the Chalukyan style of temple
architecture reached its pinnacle.

Most buses and trains will stop en route
at **Bhongir**, 60km from Hyderabad. It's
worth jumping down for a couple of hours
to climb the fantastical-looking 12th-centu-
ry Chalukyan **hill fort** (admission ₹3; ☺9am-
6pm). Looking like a gargantuan stone egg,
the hill is mostly ringed by stairs.

Warangal, Hanamkonda and Kazhipet
are sister towns. The Warangal train station
and bus stand are opposite each other, and
the post office and police station are on Sta-
tion Rd. Main Rd connects Warangal and
Hanamkonda. It can be easily visited as a
day trip.

ANDHRA PRADESH WARANGAL

STATE OF GOOD KARMA

In its typically understated way, Andhra Pradesh doesn't make much of its vast archaeological – and karmic – wealth. But the state is packed with impressive ruins of its rich Buddhist history. Only a few of Andhra's 150 stupas, monasteries, caves and other sites have been excavated, turning up rare relics of the Buddha (usually pearl-like pieces of bone) with offerings such as golden flowers. Nagarjunakonda and Amaravathi were flourishing Buddhist complexes, and near Visakhapatnam were the incredibly peaceful sites of Thotlakonda, and Bavikonda and Sankaram, looking across seascapes and lush countryside.

They speak of a time when Andhra Pradesh – or Andhradesa – was a hotbed of Buddhist activity, when monks came from around the world to learn from some of the tradition's most renowned teachers. Andhradesa's Buddhist culture, in which sangha (community of monks and nuns), laity and statespeople all took part, lasted around 1500 years from the 6th century BC. There's no historical evidence for it, but some even say that the Buddha himself visited the area.

Andhradesa's first practitioners were likely disciples of Bavari, an ascetic who lived on the banks of the Godavari River and sent his followers north to bring back the Buddha's teachings. But the dharma really took off in the 3rd century BC under Ashoka, who dispatched monks across his empire to teach and construct stupas enshrined with relics of the Buddha. (Being near these was thought to help progress on the path to enlightenment.)

Succeeding Ashoka, the Satavahanas and then Ikshvakus were also supportive. At their capital at Amaravathi, the Satavahanas adorned Ashoka's modest stupa with elegant decoration. They built monasteries across the Krishna Valley and exported the dharma through their sophisticated maritime network.

It was also during the Satavahana reign that Nagarjuna lived. Considered by many to be the progenitor of Mahayana Buddhism, the monk was equal parts logician, philosopher and meditator, and he wrote several ground-breaking works that shaped contemporary Buddhist thought. Other important monk-philosophers would emerge from the area in the following centuries, making Andhradesa a sort of Buddhist motherland of the South.

👁 Sights

Fort   FORT
(Indian/foreigner ₹5/100; ⊙9am-6.30pm) Warangal's fort was a massive construction with three distinct circular strongholds surrounded by a moat. Four paths with decorative gateways, set according to the cardinal points, led to the Swayambhava, a huge Shiva temple. The gateways are still obvious, but most of the fort is in ruins. It's easily reached from Warangal by bus or autorickshaw (₹200 return). Admission includes entry to nearby **Kush Mahal**, a 16th century royal hall with artefacts on display.

1000-Pillared Temple   HINDU TEMPLE
(⊙6am-6pm) Built in 1163, the 1000-Pillared Temple on the slopes of Hanamkonda Hill, 400m from Hanamkonda crossroads, is a fine example of Chalukyan architecture in a peaceful, leafy setting. Dedicated to three deities – Shiva, Vishnu and Surya – it has been carefully restored with intricately carved pillars and a central, very impressive Nandi (bull; Shiva's mount) of black granite.

Down the hill and 3km to the right is the small **Siddheshwara Temple**. The **Bhadrakali Temple**, featuring a stone statue of Kali seated with a weapon in each of her eight hands, is high on a hill between Hanamkonda and Warangal.

🛏 Sleeping & Eating

Hotel Ashoka   HOTEL **$$**
(☎2578491; Main Rd, Hanamkonda; r from 600; ❄@) Good-value rooms near the Hanamkonda bus stand and the 1000-Pillared Temple. Also in the compound are a restaurant, a bar-restaurant, a pub and the veg **Kanishka** (mains ₹75 to ₹125).

Vijaya Lodge   HOTEL **$**
(☎2501222; fax 2446864; Station Rd; s/d from ₹150/240) About 100m from the train station, the Vijaya is well organised with helpful staff, but the rooms are becoming a little dreary.

❶ Information

Lots of ATMs and **SGS Internet** (per hr ₹10) are near Hotel Ratna on JPN Rd. The **Department** of Tourism (☑2459201; Hanamkonda-Kazhipet Rd, 3rd fl; ☺10.30am-5pm Mon-Sat), tucked off a sidestreet, opposite Indian Oil, is helpful.

❶ Getting There & Around

Frequent buses to Hyderabad (express/deluxe/luxury ₹77/87/100, four hours) depart from **Hanamkonda bus stand** (☑9959226056).

Warangal is a major rail junction. Trains go regularly to Hyderabad (2nd class/chair ₹67/229, three hours), Vijayawada (2nd class/chair ₹79/278, four hours) and Chennai (sleeper/3AC/2AC ₹277/723/979, 11 hours). Many trains go to Delhi daily.

Shared autorickshaws ply fixed routes around Warangal (including to the fort), Kazhipet and Hanamkonda. A shared autorickshaw ride costs ₹5 to ₹7.

Around Warangal

PALAMPET

About 65km northeast of Warangal, the stunning **Ramappa Temple** (☺6am-6.30pm), built in 1234, is an attractive example of Kakatiya architecture, although it was clearly influenced by Chalukya and Hoysala styles. Its pillars are ornately carved and its eaves shelter fine statues of female forms.

Just 1km south, the Kakatiyas constructed **Ramappa Cheruvu** to serve as temple tank. The lake, along with nearby Pakhal Lake 20km south, is popular with migrating birds.

The easiest way to get here is by private car (₹1000), but frequent buses also run from Hanamkonda to Mulugu (₹22), then a further 13km to Palampet (₹10). The temple is about 500m from here.

Visakhapatnam

☑0891 / POP 1.3 MILLION

Visit Visakhapatnam – also called Vizag (*vie*-zag) – during the holiday season and you'll see domestic tourism in rare form: balloons, fairy floss (cotton candy) and, of course, weddings! But the crowds only enhance the area's kitschy coasts. The rundown boardwalk along Ramakrishna Beach has lots of spunk, and the beach at nearby Rushikonda is Andhra's best.

The old beach-resort vibe exists despite the fact that Vizag is Andhra Pradesh's second-largest city, famous for shipbuilding, steel manufacturing and now, call centres, software and film production. It's a big, dusty city, but it's surrounded by little gems:

sweet beaches, a gorgeous temple and, further out, the Araku Valley and several ancient Buddhist sites.

For up-to-date social happenings, grab a copy of *Yo! Vizag* (₹25) from local bookstores.

◉ Sights & Activities

Beaches BEACH

The long beaches of **Waltair** overlook the Bay of Bengal, with its mammoth ships and brightly painted fishing boats. Its coastal **Beach Rd**, lined with parks and weird sculptures, is great for long walks.

The best beach for swimming is at **Rushikonda**, 10km north of town, one of the nicest stretches of coast you'll find this side of India. Weekends get busy and take on a carnival-like atmosphere. **Surfers** keen for a paddle can rent decent boards from local surf pioneer, Melville, at **SAAP** (Sports Authority of Andhra Pradesh, Rushikonda; ☑9848561052). To avoid unwanted attention, modest swim attire is recommended for females.

On the way to Rushikonda, **Kailasagiri Hill** has a cable car, gardens, playgrounds, toy train and a gargantuan Shiva and Parvati.

Bheemunipatnam, 25km north of Vizag, a former Dutch settlement and the oldest municipality in mainland India, is worth a visit. Here you'll find more bizarre sculptures, a lighthouse dating from 1861, an interesting Dutch cemetery and **Bheemli Beach**, where local grommets surf on crude homemade boards. To get here catch bus 999 (₹19), or otherwise a shared autorickshaw

Submarine Museum MUSEUM
(Beach Rd, adult/child ₹25/15; ☺2-8.30pm Tue-Sat, 10am-12.30pm & 2-8.30pm Sun) A fascinating opportunity to look inside the 91m-long Indian navy submarine. The soviet-built *Kursura* saw battle in 1971 during the Liberation War, (which saw India side with East Pakistan in their struggle for independence from Pakistan – resulting in the birth of Bangladesh) and, exploring within, you'll find a fantastic jumble of knobs, switches, wires, valves, gauges, nuts, bolts and dials.

☞ Tours

APTDC operates full-day tours of the city and surrounds (from ₹300) and Araku Valley.

⌷ Sleeping

Waltair along Beach Rd is the place to stay, but has few inexpensive hotels.

TOP CHOICE **Sai Priya Resort** HOTEL $

(☑2856330; www.saipriyabeachresorts.com; cottages/r from ₹700/1300; ❀@☎) Boasting a prime position right on Rushikonda beach, Sai Priya offers either modern rooms, some with sea views, or more rustic bamboo and cane cottages which have more of a beachy feel. The grounds are lush and *almost* really beautiful but, like the rest of the place, they fall short of their potential. Also, checkout's a rude 8am. Guests and nonguests can use the pool for two hours for ₹100.

Park HOTEL $$$

(☑2754488; www.theparkhotels.com; Beach Rd; s/d from ₹7000/9000; ❀@☎) Vizag's only five-star is very elegant, very high-design. Even if you don't stay here, visit Bamboo Bay, its beachfront restaurant, for a drink. Checkout is noon.

Haritha Hotel HOTEL $$

(☑2562333; Beach Rd, Appughar; r incl breakfast from ₹900; ❀) This APTDC hotel, formerly Punnami, is near Kailasagiri Hill and right across from the beach. The lowest-priced rooms (with no views) are only so-so; bump yourself up if you can. Checkout is 10am.

YMCA Tourist Hostel HOSTEL $

(☑2755826; ymca_visakha@yahoo.com; Beach Rd; dm/s/d from ₹150/550/650; ❀) Best value in town, with superb views, but always full. Call anyway; you might get lucky.

Gateway Hotel HOTEL $$$

(☑6623670; www.tajhotels.com/gateway; Beach Rd; s/d from ₹7000/8000; ❀@☎) The usual Taj classiness, with great sea views. Checkout is noon.

Dumpy budget hotels huddle around the train station:

Retiring rooms RAILWAY RETIRING ROOMS $

(dm/r from ₹100/350; ❀)

Sree Kanya Lodge HOTEL $

(☑5564881; Bowdara Rd; s/d from ₹250/500; ❀) Mostly characterless and a little dirty, but it's the best of the lot around the station.

✗ Eating & Drinking

At night, the snack stalls on Ramakrishna Beach and the beachfront restaurants at Rushikonda, next to Punnami, are hopping.

TOP CHOICE **Sandy Lane Restaurant & Bar** INDIAN $$

(Beach Rd; mains ₹80-160; ⊙11am-12.30pm) In a colonial building a few doors down from the Park hotel, out the back are tables in the sand on the edge of the beach where you can indulge in delicious spicy fried fish (₹120) and tiger prawns (₹160). It's also a great spot for a cold beer with ocean views and a big outdoor screen. It's an overwhelmingly male clientele, but isn't seedy like some Indian bars.

New Andhra Hotel INDIAN $

(Sree Kanya Lodge, Bowdara Rd; mains ₹25-75; ⊙11am-3.30pm & 7-10.30pm) An unassuming little place with *really* good, *really* hot Andhra dishes. Meals (₹50/130 for veg/non-veg) and biryani are top-notch.

Masala INDIAN $$

(Signature Towers, 1st fl, Asilmetta; mains ₹60-180; ⊙11.30am-3.30pm & 7-11pm) Near Sampath Vinayaka Temple, Masala does out-of-this-world Andhra, tandoori and Chinese. Try the *chepa pulusu* (Andhra-style fish; ₹130).

Kebabri INDIAN $$

(Siripuram Junction; kebabs ₹95-250; ⊙5.30-10.30pm) massive succulent BBQ kebabs, from tandoori chicken to seafood, to mouth-watering paneer skewers. Has another branch on Beach Rd.

Pastry, Coffee n' Conversation BAKERY $

(PCC; Siripuram Junction; ⊙11am-11pm) Hang-out spot for Vizag's hip young crowd, this is the place for pizza, burgers and delicious cakes.

ⓘ Information

ATMs are everywhere. RTC Complex has several internet cafes (per hour ₹15), some open 24 hours.

Apollo Pharmacy (☑2788652; Siripuram Junction; ⊙24hr)

APTDC RTC Complex (☑2788820; ⊙6.30am-9pm); Train station (☑2788821; ⊙6am-9pm) Information and tours.

Thomas Cook (☑2588112; Eswar Plaza, Dwarakanagar; ⊙9am-6.30pm Mon-Sat) Near ICICI Bank.

ⓘ Getting There & Around

You'll have to negotiate fares with autorickshaw drivers here. Most in-town rides will be around ₹20. **Guide Tours & Travels** (☑2754477), reliable for car hire, is opposite the RTC Complex 'out gate'.

Air

Take an autorickshaw (₹200), taxi (₹270) or bus 38 (₹6) to Vizag's airport, 13km west of town.

Domestic airlines and their daily services:

Indian Airlines (✆2746501, airport 2572521; LIC Bldg) Chennai, Delhi, Hyderabad and Mumbai.

Kingfisher (✆2503285, airport 2517614; Ardee Bldg, Siripuram Junction) Bengaluru, Chennai, Hyderabad, Kolkota, Pune and Tirupathi.

SpiceJet (✆airport 2010422) Delhi, Hyderabad, Kolkata and Mumbai .

Boat

Boats depart every month-ish for Port Blair in the Andaman Islands. Bookings for the 56-hour journey (from ₹1960) can be made at the **Shipping Office** (✆2565597, 9866073407; Av Bhanoji Row; ◷9am-5pm Mon-Sat) in the port complex. Bring your passport.

Bus

Vizag's well-organised **RTC Complex** (✆2746400) has frequent bus services to Vijayawada (deluxe/Volvo ₹250/530, eight/seven hours) and, in the afternoon, Hyderabad ('super-luxury'/Volvo ₹470/870, 14/12 hours).

Train

Vizag's train station is on the western edge of town, near the port. Visakhapatnam Junction station is on the Kolkata-Chennai line. The overnight *Coromandel Express* (sleeper/3AC/2AC ₹333/881/1199, 13½ hours) is the fastest of the five daily trains running to Kolkata. Heading south, it goes to Chennai (sleeper/3AC/2AC ₹310/817/1112, 14 hours). Frequent trains head to Vijayawada including 2717, the *Ratnachalam Express* (2nd-class/chair ₹108/477).

Around Visakhapatnam

ARAKU VALLEY

Andhra's best train ride is through the magnificent Eastern Ghats to the **Araku Valley**, 120km north of Vizag. The area is home to isolated tribal communities, and a small **Museum of Habitat** (admission ₹10; ◷10am-1pm & 2-5pm) with exhibits on indigenous life. APTDC runs **tours** (₹500) from Vizag, which take in a performance of Dhimsa, a tribal dance, and the million-year-old limestone **Borra Caves** (admission ₹40; camera ₹100; ◷10am-1pm & 2-5pm), 30km from Araku.

Araku itself is a small dusty town, but its surroundings are beautiful. A bicycle is the perfect way to explore the countryside. You can hire a bicycle (per hour/day ₹50/250) from Hill Resort Mayuri. It's best to check the security situation before heading out, with a reported Naxalite (members of an ultraleftist political movement) presence in the region.

Chandrika Guest House (✆9490430989; s/d ₹1000/1500), 2km from the station, is the most peaceful option with rooms looking out to fields, though it's overpriced. The **Hill Resort Mayuri** (✆958936-249204; cottages from ₹650; ✳), near the museum, has cottages with good views. There's also a few uninspiring options around the station, otherwise you could try the forest retreat of **Jungle Bells** (Tyda; cottages from ₹800; ✳), 45km from Araku, with cottages tucked away in woods. Book at APTDC. You can sample the local coffee at **Araku Valley Coffee House** (◷9am-9pm), next to the Museum of Habitat.

The Kirandol passenger train (₹20, five hours) leaves Vizag at 6.50am and Araku at 3pm. It's a slow, spectacular ride; sit on the right-hand side coming out of Vizag for best views. For Jungle Bells, get off at Tyda station, 500m from the resort. Frequent buses (₹58, 4½ hours) leave from Araku to Vizag every hour until 7pm.

BAVIKONDA & THOTLAKONDA

The Vizag area's natural harbours have long been conducive to dropping anchor, which helped monks from Sri Lanka, China and Tibet come here to learn and practice meditation. **Bavikonda** (◷9am-6pm) and **Thotlakonda** (◷10am-3pm) were popular hilltop monasteries on the coast that hosted up to 150 monks at a time – with the help of massive rainwater tanks and, at Thotlakonda, a natural spring.

The monasteries flourished during the Theravada period (Bavikonda, from the 3rd century BC to the 3rd century AD, and Thotlakonda, from the 2nd century BC to 2nd century AD) and had votive stupas, congregation halls, *chaitya-grihas*, *viharas* and refectories. Today only the ruins of these massive monastic compounds remain, but they're impressive nonetheless, with a placid, almost magical, air and sea views to meditate on. Bavikonda and Thotlakonda are 14km and 16km, respectively, from Vizag on Bheemli Beach Rd. Vizag's autorickshaw drivers charge around ₹400 return to see both.

SANKARAM

Forty kilometres southwest of Vizag is this stunning **Buddhist complex** (admission free; ◷9am-6pm), better known by the name of its two hills, Bojjannakonda and Lingalakonda. Used by monks from the 1st to 9th centuries AD (p230), the hills are covered with rock-cut caves, stupas, ruins of monastery structures, and reliefs of the Buddha that span the Theravada, Mahayana and Vajrayana periods. Bojjannakonda has a two-storey group of rock-cut caves flanked by *dwarapalakas* (doorkeepers) and containing a stupa and gorgeous carvings of the Buddha (some restored). Atop the hill sit the ruins of a huge stupa and a monastery; you can still make out the individual cells where monks meditated. Lingalakonda is piled high with stupas, some of them enormous.

A private car from Vizag costs around ₹800. Or, take a bus to Anakapalle (₹24, one hour, every 20 minutes), 3km away, and then an autorickshaw (₹150 return including waiting time).

Vijayawada

☏ 0866 / POP 1 MILLION

Vijayawada is a busy, rapidly growing city and an important port at the head of the delta of the mighty Krishna River. It's bustling, but it's also intersected by canals, lined with ghats and ringed by fields of rice and palm. The surrounding area is intensely lush and green.

Vijayawada is considered by many to be the heart of Andhra culture and language and has an important Durga temple. Nearby Amaravathi, meanwhile, was a centre of Buddhist learning and practice for many centuries.

Om Art Print (JD Hospital Rd, cnr Besant Rd; ⊙10am-8.30pm Mon-Sat) sells maps.

⊙ Sights

Undavalli Cave Temples   HINDU SITE
(Indian/foreigner ₹5/100; ⊙8am-5.30pm) Four kilometres southwest of Vijayawada, these stunning cave temples cut a fine silhouette against the palm trees and rice paddies. Shrines are dedicated to the Trimurti – Brahma, Vishnu and Shiva – and one cave on the third level houses a huge, beautiful statue of reclining Vishnu while seated deities and animals stand guard out front. The caves, in their Hindu form, date to the 7th century, but they're thought to have been constructed for Buddhist monks 500 years earlier. Bus 301 (₹9, 20 minutes) goes here.

Victoria Jubilee Museum   MUSEUM
(MGRd;admissionIndian/foreigner₹20/100,camera ₹3; ⊙10.30am-5pm Sat-Thu) The best part of this museum is the building itself, built in 1887 to honour Queen Victoria's coronation jubilee. In 1921 it hosted the Congress meeting where a new tricolour flag was introduced: Mahatma Gandhi added a wheel to the design and made it the Indian National Congress's official flag.

The interesting architecture outshines the museum's small collection of art and arms. But the **garden**, where temple sculptures from around the state (dating from the 3rd century AD) line shady paths, is lovely.

☕ Courses

Dhamma Vijaya   MEDITATION
(Vipassana Meditation Centre; ☏08812-225522; www.dhamma.org; Eluru-Chintalapudi Rd) Offers intensive 10-day *vipassana* meditation courses free of charge in lush palm- and cocoa-forested grounds. The centre is 15km from Eluru; call for details.

🛌 Sleeping

Hotel Sri Ram   HOTEL $
(☏2579377; Hanumanpet; s/d from ₹360/450; ✳) This cheapie has bright, clean, nondescript rooms near the train station. A conveniently located safe bet.

Swarna Palace   HOTEL $$
(☏2577222; swarnapalace@rediff.com; Eluru Rd, Governorpet; s/d with AC from ₹1400/1500; ✳) Swarna, along with Hotel Ilapuram, are Vijayawada's two best midrange places. Both fall short of the sleekness they aspire to. But they're professionally run – and a little bit sleek anyway.

Hotel Ilapuram   HOTEL $$
(☏2571282; ilapuram@hotmail.com; Prakasam Rd; s/d with AC from ₹1500/1700; ✳)

Gateway Hotel   HOTEL $$$
(☏6644444; www.thegatewayhotels.com; MG Rd; s/d from ₹3500/4250; ✳@) The most up-market option.

Retiring rooms   RAILWAY RETIRING ROOMS $
(dm/s/d from ₹75/180/375; ✳) The train station's clean and spacious rooms are a great option.

Bus station dorms   HOSTEL $
(☏3097809; from ₹100) The bus station, just north of the river, has dorms for gents.

🍴 Eating

Lotus Food City   INDIAN $$
(www.lotusthefoodcity.com; Seethanagaram; mains ₹80-150) Set up by APTDC, this food complex has a lovely spot on the Krishna River where you can dine in or outdoors looking out to the shimmering water.

TOP CHOICE **Minerva Coffee Shop** INDIAN $
(Museum Rd; mains ₹58-150; ⊙6.30am-11pm; ❀)
Just around the corner from Big Bazaar, this
outpost of the fabulous Minerva chain has
great North and South Indian, including top-
notch dosas (₹33 to ₹58). Its rava masala dosa
(made with semolina) is the best thing *ever*.

Modern Cafe INDIAN $
(Sree Lakshmi Vilas; Besant Rd, Governorpet;
meals ₹58; ⊙6.30am-10.30pm) With black-
and-white-check floors and mismatched
wooden chairs, this gritty, down-home veg
joint has a heavy 1940s vibe. The meals
are great, as are the fresh juices (₹15).

 Information

Apollo Pharmacy (Vijaya Talkies Junction,
Eluru Rd; ⊙24hr)
APTDC (✆2571393; MG Rd, opposite PWD
Grounds; ⊙9am-7pm) Don't bother, unless you
need brochures.
Department of Tourism (train station;
⊙10am-5pm)
KIMS Hospital (✆2570761; Siddhartha Nagar)
MagicNet (Swarnalok Complex, Eluru Rd; per
hr ₹20; ⊙9.30am-9pm) Internet access.
State Bank of Hyderabad (1st fl, Vijaya Com-
mercial Complex, Governorpet; ⊙10.30am-
3pm Mon-Fri) Changes currency and travellers
cheques.

Getting There & Around

The bus stand has a helpful **enquiry desk**
(✆2522200). Frequent services run to Hyderabad (deluxe/Volvo ₹193/375, six to seven
hours), Amaravathi (₹38, two hours), Warangal
(deluxe ₹180, 5½ hours) and Visakhapatnam
(deluxe/Volvo ₹270/540, nine hours).

Vijayawada is on the main Chennai–Kolkata
and Chennai–Delhi railway lines. The daily
Coromandel Express (2841) runs to Chennai
(sleeper/3AC/2AC ₹214/544/732, seven
hours) and, the other way, to Kolkata (2842;
sleeper/3AC/2AC ₹395/1054/1440, 20 hours).
Speedy *Rajdhani* (Thursday and Saturday)
and *Jan Shatabdi* (daily except Tuesday) trains
also ply the Vijayawada–Chennai route. Trains
galore run to Hyderabad (sleeper/3AC/2AC
₹190/478/639, 6½ hours) and Tirupathi
(sleeper/3AC/2AC ₹198/502/674, seven
hours). The **computerised advance-booking
office** (✆enquiry 2577775, reservations
2578955; ⊙8am-8pm Mon-Sat, till 2pm Sun) is
in the basement.

The train station has a prepaid autorickshaw
stand marked 'Traffic Police'.

Around Vijayawada

AMARAVATHI
Once the Andhran capital and a significant
Buddhist centre, Amaravathi is India's biggest **stupa** (Indian/foreigner ₹5/100; ⊙8am-
6pm), measuring 27m high and constructed
in the 3rd century BC, when Emperor Ashoka
sent monks south to spread the Buddha's
teaching. Located 60km west of Vijayawada,
all that remains are a mound and some
stones, but the nearby **museum** (admission
₹5; ⊙8am-5pm) has a small replica of the stupa, with its intricately carved pillars, marble-
surfaced dome and carvings of scenes from
the Buddha's life (no photography allowed
in the museum). In the courtyard is a recon-
struction of part of the surrounding gateway,
which gives you an idea of the stupa's massive scale. It's worth the trip, but many of
Amaravathi's best sculptures are in London's
British Museum and Chennai's Government
Museum in Tamil Nadu.

About 1km down the road is the **Dhyana
Buddha**, an imposing 20m-high seated Buddha built on the site where the Dalai Lama
spoke at the 2006 Kalachakra, which gives
the place added atmosphere.

Buses run from Vijayawada to Amaravathi every half-hour or so (₹24, two hours),
but it may be quicker to head to Guntur
(₹12, 45 minutes) and take another bus from
there. The drive here will take you through
some lovely lush scenery and memorable
glimpses of village life.

KONDAPALLI
Kondapalli fort (admission ₹5, camera ₹100;
⊙10.30am-5pm), strategically situated on the
old Machilipatnam–Golconda trade route,
was built in 1360 by the Reddy kings, and
was held by the Gajapathis, the Qutb Shahis,
the Mughals and the nizams before becoming a British military camp in 1767. Today
it's a quiet, lovely ruin. On weekdays, you'll
likely have the place to yourself and you
can easily spend a few hours hiking around.
Kondapalli village, 1km downhill, is famous
for its wooden dolls. The fort is 21km from
Vijayawada; an autorickshaw is ₹400 return.

Tirumala & Tirupathi
✆0877 / POP 302,000
The holy hill of **Tirumala** is, on any given
day, filled with tens of thousands of blissed-
out devotees, many of whom have endured

ANDHRA PRADESH

long journeys to see the powerful **Lord Venkateshwara** here, at his home. It's one of India's most visited pilgrimage centres: on average, 40,000 pilgrims come each day (the total often exceeds 100,000), and *darshan* (deity-viewing) runs 24/7. Temple staff alone number 12,000, and the efficient **Tirumala Tirupathi Devasthanams** (TTD; ☎2277777; www.tirumala.org) brilliantly administers the crowds. As a result, although the throngs can be overwhelming, a sense of order, serenity and ease mostly prevails, and a trip to the Holy Hill can be fulfilling, even if you're not a pilgrim.

'It is believed that Lord Sri Venkateshwara enjoys festivals', according to the TTD. And so do his devotees: *darshan* queues during October's **Brahmotsavam** can run up to several kilometres.

Tirupathi is the service town at the bottom of the hill, with hotels, restaurants, and transport; a fleet of buses constantly ferries pilgrims the 18km up and down. You'll find most of your worldly needs around the Tirupathi bus station (TP Area) and, about 500m away, the train station.

◉ Sights

Venkateshwara Temple   HINDU TEMPLE
Devotees flock to Tirumala to see Venkateshwara, an avatar of Vishnu. Among the many powers attributed to him is the granting of any wish made before the idol at Tirumala. Many pilgrims also donate their hair to the deity – in gratitude for a wish fulfilled, or to renounce ego – so hundreds of barbers attend to devotees. Tirumala and Tirupathi are filled with tonsured men, women and children, generating big money from exports to Western wig companies.

Legends about the hill itself and the surrounding area appear in the Puranas, and the temple's history may date back 2000 years. The main temple is an atmospheric place, though you'll be pressed between hundreds of devotees when you see it. The inner sanctum itself is dark and magical; it smells of incense, resonates with chanting and may make you religious. There, Venkateshwara sits gloriously on his throne, inspiring bliss and love among his visitors. You'll have a moment to make a wish and then you'll be shoved out again. Don't forget to collect your delicious *ladoo* (sweet made of flour, sugar, raisins and nuts) from the counter.

'Ordinary *darshan*' requires a wait of anywhere from two to six hours in the claustrophobic metal cages ringing the temple. 'Quick *darshan*' tickets (₹300) are recommended, and will get you through the queue faster, though you'll still have to brave the gauntlet of the cage, which is part of the fun, kind of... Upon entry you'll also have to sign a form declaring your support of Lord Vishnu.

☞ Tours

If you're pressed for time, APTDC runs three-day tours (₹1950) to Tirumala from Hyderabad. KSTDC and TTDC offer the same from Bengaluru and Chennai, respectively. APTDC also has a full-day tour (₹340) of temples in the Tirupathi area.

🛏 Sleeping & Eating

The TTD runs *choultries* (guesthouses) for pilgrims in Tirumala and Tirupathi, but most non-Hindu visitors stay in one of Tirupathi's many hotels.

Vast **dormitories** (beds free) and **guesthouses** (r ₹50-2500) surround the temple in Tirumala, but these are intended for pilgrims. To stay, check in at the Central Reception Office. Huge **dining halls** (meals free) serve thousands of pilgrims daily. Veg restaurants also serve meals for ₹15. The following places are all in Tirupathi.

Hotel Bliss   HOTEL $$
(☎2237773; www.blisstirupati.com; Reniguta Rd; s/d from ₹1710/1980; ❄@⊠) The most luxurious place in town with ultracomfortable rooms, professional staff and a glass lift with great views and droning pilgrim elevator music.

Hotel Annapurna   HOTEL $$
(☎2250666; Nethaji Rd; r from ₹850; ❄) A wee bit overpriced, but it's convenient and well organised. Rooms are clean, compact and pink, with constant hot water. Since it's on a corner (across from the train station), non-AC front rooms can be noisy. Its veg **restaurant** (mains ₹45-80) has fresh juices and Tirupathi's best food in sublime air-conditioning.

Hotel Mamata Lodge   HOTEL $
(☎2225873; 1st fl, 170 TP Area; s/d/tr & q ₹200/300/400) A friendly, spick-and-span cheapie. Some of the sheets are stained, but they're tucked in tight and lovingly patched with white squares. Avoid the downstairs lodge of the same name.

Retiring rooms   RAILWAY RETIRING ROOMS $
(dm/r from ₹45/150, with AC ₹400; ❄) The station retiring rooms are super value.

The following both serve hearty meals and juices:

Hotel Universal Deluxe INDIAN $
(49 G Car St; mains ₹35-65; ⊘5.30am-midnight) Near the train station.

Hotel Vikram INDIAN $
(☑2225433; TP Area; mains ₹43-85; ⊘5am-11pm) By the bus stand.

❶ Information

Anu Internet Centre (per hr ₹15; ⊘5.30am-10.30pm) Next to the bus stand.

Apollo Pharmacy (G Car St; ⊘24hr)

APTDC (☑2289120; Sridevi Complex, 2nd fl, Tilak Rd; ⊘8.30am-8pm) Tourist info and tour bookings.

Police station (☑2289006; Railway Station Rd)

❶ Getting There & Away

It's possible to visit Tirupathi on a (very) long day trip from Chennai. If travelling by bus or train, buy a 'link ticket', which includes transport from Tirupathi to Tirumala.

Air

Indian Airlines (☑2283992; Tirumala Bypass Rd; ⊘9.30am-5.30pm), 2km from town, has daily flights to Delhi via Hyderabad. **Kingfisher Red** (☑9849677008) plies the same route, including Bengaluru and Visakhapatnam. Book with **Mitta Travels** (☑2225981; Prakasam Rd; ⊘9am-7.30pm Mon-Sat, 9am-12.30pm Sun), next to Manasa Fast Foods, 2km from the train station.

Bus

Tirupathi's **bus station** (☑2289900) has buses to Chennai (deluxe/Volvo ₹70/155, four hours) and Hyderabad (deluxe/Volvo ₹408/717, 12/10 hours). Tonnes of APSRTC and KSTDC buses go to Bengaluru (deluxe/Volvo ₹153/365, six/five hours), and seven buses go to Puttaparthi daily (express/deluxe ₹165/227, eight hours).

Private buses depart from TP Area, opposite the bus stand.

Train

Tirupathi station is well served by express trains, running to Chennai (2nd-class chair/chair (₹62/206, three hours), Bengaluru (sleeper/3AC/2AC ₹168/470/628, seven hours), Hyderabad/Secunderabad (sleeper/3AC/2AC ₹284/764/1047, 12 hours) and Vijayawada (sleeper/3AC/2AC ₹198/502/674, seven hours). The **reservation office** (☑2225850; ⊘8am-8pm Mon-Sat, 8am-2pm Sun) is across the street.

❶ Getting Around

Bus

Tirumala Link buses have two bus stands in Tirupathi: next to the main bus stand and outside the train station. The scenic 18km trip to Tirumala takes one hour (₹54 return); if you don't mind heights, sit on the left side for views. A prepaid taxi is ₹350.

Walking

TTD has constructed probably the best footpath in India for pilgrims to walk up to Tirumala. It's about 15km from Tirupathi and takes four to six hours. Leave your luggage at the toll gate at Alipiri near the Hanuman statue. It will be transported free to the reception centre. At the time of research walking was prohibited from 4pm to 6am due to several leopard attacks on pilgrims. There are shady rest points along the way, and a few canteens.

Around Tirumala & Tirupathi

CHANDRAGIRI FORT

Only a couple of buildings remain from this 15th-century **fort** (Indian/foreigner ₹10/100; ⊘8am-5pm), 14km west of Tirupathi. Both the Rani Mahal and the Raja Mahal, which houses a small **museum** (⊘10am-5pm Sat-Thu), were constructed under Vijayanagar rule and resemble structures in Hampi's Royal Centre. There's a nightly **sound-and-light show** (admission ₹35; ⊘8pm Mar-Oct, 7.30pm Nov-Feb), narrated by Bollywood great Amitabh Bachchan. Buses for Chandragiri (₹10) leave Tirupathi bus station every half-hour. An autorickshaw is ₹200 return.

SRI KALAHASTI

Around 36km east of Tirupathi, Sri Kalahasti is known for its important **Sri Kalahasteeswara Temple** and for being, along with Machilipatnam near Vijayawada, a centre for the ancient art of *kalamkari*. These paintings are made with natural ingredients: the cotton is primed with *myrabalam* (resin) and cow's milk; figures are drawn with a pointed bamboo stick dipped in fermented jaggery and water; and the dyes are made from cow dung, ground seeds, plants and flowers. You can see the artists at work in the Agraharam neighbourhood, 2.5km from the bus stand. **Sri Vijayalakshmi Fine Kalamkari Arts** (☑9441138380; door No 15-890) is an old family business with 40 artists.

Buses leave Tirupathi for Sri Kalahasti every 10 minutes (₹23, 45 minutes); a prepaid taxi is ₹650 return.

Puttaparthi

📞08555

Prasanthi Nilayam (Abode of Highest Peace) is the main ashram of the late Sri Sathya Sai Baba (1926–2011), the deceased afro-haired guru revered by followers from around the world. Setting up the ashram in his hometown of Puttaparthi 60 years ago, he lived here for most of the year, though with his death from a respiratory-related illness on 24 April 2011, the town faces an uncertain future. While the millions of dollars pumped into the nearby hospital, schools and university will ensure the town continues to thrive upon his legacy, long-term it remains to be seen whether devotees will continue to arrive en masse without the presence of the man himself.

When he was 14, Sai Baba declared himself to be the reincarnation of another Sai Baba, a saintly figure who died in 1918 (p84). His millions of devotees regarded him as a true avatar and believed he performed miracles. Coming for the program of *darshan* (here that meant seeing Baba – though since poor health in 2005 his appearances were increasingly sporadic), they packed the ashram twice-daily for chanting and prayer. The sight of clean, well-paved streets lined with internet cafes might come as a surprise here, as will the prevalence of robed foreign devotees.

Everything about Sai Baba was big: the Afro hairdo, the big-name devotees, and the big controversies – allegations of sexual misconduct had led some devotees to lose faith. Others, however, regarded the controversy as simply another terrestrial test for their avatar. Sai Baba announced he would be reborn as Prema Sai in the district of Mandya in Karnataka, in what would be the third and final incarnation of Sai Baba, supposedly eight years after his own death.

Most people stay at the **ashram** (📞287390; www.srisathyasai.org.in), a small village with all amenities. Lodging is cheap but basic. Advance bookings aren't taken; visitors under 25 must be in a family or group.

Non-ashram options include the clean and simple **Sai Surya Guest House** (📞288134; Gopuram Rd, 1st Cross; r from ₹350), and the excellent-value **Sri Sai Sadan** (Meda's Guest House; 📞287507; srisaisadan@gmail.com; Gopuram Rd; r from ₹810; 🌐), near Venugopalaswamy Temple, with a roof garden and spacious rooms with fridges and balconies.

The rooftop **World Peace Café** (German Bakery; Main Rd; mains ₹95-145; 🕤7.30am-9.30pm) is an old favourite for saffron lassis,

good filter coffee and healthy food. The Tibetan **Bamboo Nest** (1st fl, Chitravathi Rd; mains ₹55-80; 🕤9.30am-2pm & 4.30-9pm) has a memorable veg wonton soup (₹60) and good *momos* (Tibetan dumplings; ₹70).

ℹ️ Getting There & Around

Puttaparthi is most easily reached from Bengaluru, 160km south; nine KSRTC buses (express/Volvo ₹110/220, four hours) and eight trains (sleeper/3AC/2AC ₹133/323/420, three hours) head here daily. The **KSRTC office** (📞288938) is next to the bus station.

From the **APSRTC bus station** (📞287313), uncomfortable buses run to/from Tirupathi (express/deluxe ₹160/200, eight hours, seven daily) and Chennai (₹342, 12 hours, two daily).

The bus station has a **train reservation booth** (🕤8am-noon & 5-7pm Mon-Sat, 8am-2pm Sun). For Hyderabad, an overnight train goes daily to Kacheguda (7604; sleeper/3AC/2AC ₹240/650/870, 10 hours). Overnight train 8564 runs to Visakhapatnam (sleeper/3AC/2AC ₹340/940/1300, 20 hours), stopping at Vijayawada. The daily *Udyan Express* (6530) heads to Mumbai (sleeper/3AC/2AC ₹350/950/1300, 21 hours).

A free shuttle for ashram visitors runs from the train station. An autorickshaw is ₹80.

Lepakshi

About 75km from Puttaparthi is Lepakshi, site of the **Veerbhadra Temple** (admission free). The town gets its name from the Ramayana: when demon Ravana kidnapped Rama's wife, Sita, the bird Jatayu fought him and fell, injured, at the temple site. Rama then called him to get up; 'Lepakshi' derives from the Sanskrit for 'Get up, bird'.

Look for the 9m-long monolithic **Nandi** – India's largest – at the town's entrance. From here, you can see the temple's **Naga-lingam** (a phallic representation of Shiva) crowned with a seven-headed cobra. The temple is known for its unfinished **Kalyana Mandapam** (Marriage Hall), depicting the wedding of Parvati and Shiva, and its **Natyamandapa** (Dance Hall), with carvings of dancing gods. The temple's most stunning features, though, are the Natyamandapa's ceiling **frescoes**.

To get here, take a Puttaparthi-Bengaluru bus and alight at Kodakonda Checkpost (₹40). From there, take a Hindupur-bound bus (₹14) or an autorickshaw (₹250 return) to Lepakshi. A private car from Puttaparthi is ₹1000. You can also go from Hindupur, a main stop on the Puttaparthi-Bengaluru train line, which has a few hotels. It's 11km from the temple.

ANDHRA PRADESH

Kerala

Beaches »
Backwaters »
Performing Arts »
Hill Stations »

Kettuvallam boat, Kerala backwaters

Beaches

Golden-sand beaches edge Kerala's coastline, fringed by palms and washed by the Arabian Sea. The southern beaches are the busiest, while less-discovered, wilder choices await in the north.

Most established of all the resorts along the coast is Kovalam, in the south, with two perfect crescents of beach. Once a quiet fishing village, it's now overlooked by a town that's almost entirely made up of hotels, fronted by a promenade and a strip of restaurants. If you're looking for something less built up: south of here are some lovely beaches, clustered in the area around Pulinkudi and Chowara.

Further north is Varkala, which straggles along its dramatic, streaked russet-and-gold cliffs. This has an entirely different flavour, with accommodation mostly in small guesthouses and homestays and a long line of laid-back cafes and restaurants.

There are also some fine beaches around the historic port of Fort Cochin. Best is Cherai Beach, a lovely stretch of white sand, with miles of lazy backwaters only a few hundred metres from the seafront.

And for the tropical desert island experience, there are the islands of Lakshadweep, a palm-covered archipelago 300km off the coast of Kerala.

Heading even further north, there are still deserted beaches along the coast, particularly around Bekal, and some stunning caramel-coloured beaches backed by palms close to the town of Kannur.

BEST BEACH TOWNS

» **Kovalam** (p256) Kerala's most commercial beach resort, but still fun and scenic despite the crowds and hawkers.

» **Varkala** (p260) This beautiful cliff-edged coastline is a Hindu holy place as well as a lively backpacker-focused resort.

» **Kochi** (p280) Combine a beach sojourn with a sense of history by heading to charismatic Kochi (Cochin) – the town beaches are nondescript, but you can visit those nearby.

Clockwise from top left
1. Papanasham Beach **2.** Beach trader **3.** Kovalam beach
4. Sunset at beach near Kovalam

MARK DAFFEY/LONELY PLANET IMAGES ©

Backwaters

Kerala's 900km of waterways spread watery tendrils through the region's lusciously green landscape. Palm-shaded, winding canals are lined by back-in-time villages, many of which are accessible only by boat.

It's one of India's most enchanting experiences to glide along the canals in a canoe, or sleep under a firmament of stars in a houseboat. The distinctive houseboats that cluster around the main hubs of Alappuzha (Alleppey) and Kollam (Quilon) are designed like traditional rice barges or *kettuvallam* ('boat with knots', so-called because the curvaceous structure is held together by knotted coir).

There are several ways to explore the backwaters. The most popular method is to rent a houseboat for a night or two, and these sleep anything from two up to 14 or more people. They vary wildly in luxury and amenities. The hire includes staff, so catering is included, and you'll eat traditional Keralan meals of fish and vegetables cooked in coconut milk. However, the popularity of these tours can mean that the main waterways get very busy, even gridlocked, in season. Another means of seeing the waterways is to take a public ferry. This is the cheapest way to travel, and you can take trips from town to town, though again you won't see much of the smaller canals where it is really tranquil. More expensive, but still very cheap, is the tourist cruise between Kollam and Alleppey, a scenic slow trip that takes all day.

The best way to explore deep into the network and escape the bigger boats is to take a canoe tour, as this will allow you to travel along the narrower canals and see village life in a way that's impossible on a house or ferry boat. Village tours with a knowledgeable guide are another tranquil way to explore the region and understand some of the local culture.

© V MUTHURAMAN/SUPERSTOCK/PHOTOLIBRARY

1

ECOFRIENDLY CRUISES

It's not all perfect in paradise. Pollution and land reclamation threaten the habitat of the waterways and the communities on their banks. It's estimated that the water levels have dropped by two-thirds since the mid-19th century, and many migratory birds no longer visit the area. The sheer numbers of houseboats mean that pollution is a major problem, and although outboard motors are not permitted, some operators use them on smaller boats. To ensure that your cruise is ecofriendly, ask to see operators' certification: those houseboat owners who have a 'Green Palm Certificate' are the ones to go for, which means they have installed solar panels and sanitary tanks. It's also better for the environment to avoid using AC as this requires a great deal more power. Best of all are the few remaining punting, rather than motorised, boats.

Clockwise from top left
1. Chinese fishing net (p281), Kochi **2.** Boat near Alleppey (p266) **3.** Smiles on the Kerala backwaters (p242)

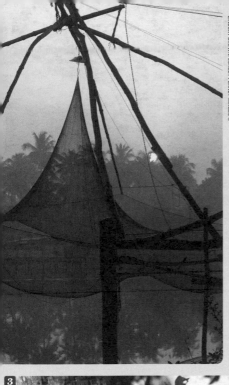

LINDSAY BROWN/LONELY PLANET IMAGES ©

Performing Arts

Kerala has an intensely rich culture of performing arts – living art forms that are passed on to new generations in specialised schools and arts centres.

Kathakali, with its elaborate ritualised gestures, heavy mask-like makeup, and dramatic stories of love, lust and power struggles based on the Ramayana, the Mahabharata and the Puranas, stems in part from 2nd-century temple rituals, though in its current form it developed around the 16th century. The actors tell the stories through precise mudras (hand gestures) and facial expressions. Traditionally performances start in temple grounds at around 8pm and go on all night, though versions for those with shorter attention spans are now performed in many tourist centres, to give a taste of the art.

Theyyam is an even earlier art, believed to be older than Hinduism, having developed from harvest folk dances. It's performed in *kavus* (sacred groves) in northern Kerala. The word refers to the ritual itself, and to the shape of the deity or hero portrayed, of which there are 450. The costumes are magnificent, with face paint, armour, garlands and huge headdresses. The performance consists of frenzied dancing to a wild drumbeat, creating a trance-like atmosphere.

Taking its moves from both these ancient arts is the martial art of *kalarippayat*, a ritualistic disclipline taught throughout Kerala. It's taught and displayed in an arena called a *kalari*, which combines gymnasium, school and temple.

PLACES TO SEE PERFORMING ARTS

» In the spring there are numerous festivals with the chance to see Kathakali, with Thirunakkara in Kottayam in March and the Pooram festival in Kollam in April.

» One of the best places to see Kathakali is **Kerala Kalamandalam** (p297) near Thrissur.

» You can also see performances at cultural centres across Kerala, such as **Kerala Kathakali** and **See India** (p290) in Kochi, **Mudra** (p276) in Kumily and **Margi Kathakali** (p251) school in Trivandrum. In Kovalam and Varkala there are short versions of the art in season.

» Both the **Kochi** and **Kumily** centres also have shows of *kalarippayat*, or you can visit the martial art training centres of **CVN Kalari Sangham** (p251) in Trivandrum and **Ens Kalari** (p284) in Nettoor, close to Ernakulam.

» The best areas to see *theyyam* performances are **Payyannur** and **Valiyaparamba**, in the northern backwater area, where there are more than 500 *kavus*. The season is from October to May. For advice on finding performances, contact the **Tourist Desk** (p284) in Kochi.

Clockwise from top left
1. Dancers at Elephant Festival, Ernakulam **2.** Kathakali dancer close up **2.** Kathakali dancers

EDDIE GERALD/LONELY PLANET IMAGES ©

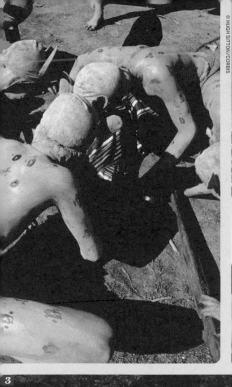

© HUGH SITTON / CORBIS

Hill Stations

Narrow roads wind up through jungle-thick vegetation providing dizzying views over deep peacock-green tea plantations. Spindly betel nut trees sway in the breeze and flame of the forest provides splashes of red.

Kerala's hill stations are set in sumptuous natural landscapes, where to visit and hang out for a few days in a plantation hideaway is an incredibly soothing way to escape the cares of the world.

The northern area around Wayanad Wildlife Sanctuary has shimmering green rice paddies and plantations of coffee, cardamom, ginger and pepper everywhere you look. The rolling hills are fragrant with wild herbs and punctuated by mammoth clumps of bamboo. It's one of the best places to spot wild elephants, but besides visiting the sanctuaries in the area, there are plenty of opportunities for trekking, such as up the area's highest mountain, Chembra Peak (2100m).

Around Munnar, further south, it's tea as far as the eye can see, with the clumpy green bushes carpeting the sculpted-seeming hills. This is the tea-growing heartland, but also a great place to trek and discover viewpoints across epic mountain scenery. There are some wonderful remote places to stay hidden in the hills, tucked deep into spice and flower gardens, or cardamom and coffee plantations.

Below
Picking tea leaves, Kerala

Kerala

Includes »

Why Go?

Kerala's thoughtful pace of life is as contagious as the Indian head-wobble – just setting foot on this swathe of soul-quenching green will slow your stride to a blissed-out amble. One of India's most beautiful and successful states, Kerala is a world away from the frenzy of elsewhere, as if India had passed through the Looking Glass and become an altogether more laid-back place.

Besides its famous backwaters, rice paddies, coconut groves, elegant houseboats and delicately spiced, taste-budtingling cuisine, Kerala also proffers azure seas, white crescents of beach, and evocative ex-colonial trading towns. Then there are the mountainous Ghats carpeted by spices and tea plantations, home to wild elephants, exotic birds and the odd tiger; and crazily vibrant traditions such as Kathakali – a blend of religious play and dance; *kalarippayat* – a gravity-defying martial art, and *theyyam* – a trance-induced ritual. The main problem a visitor might find here is choosing where to linger the longest.

Best Places to Eat

Best Places to Stay

When to Go
Thiruvananthapuram

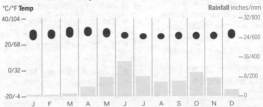

Jan–Feb
Perfect weather. Ernakulathappan Utsavam festival in Kochi.

Apr You can see Kathakali at Kottayam and Kollam festivals, and the elephant procession in Thrissur.

Aug–Sep
Tail-end of the monsoon period: prime time for ayurvedic treatments.

MAIN POINTS OF ENTRY

Thiruvanthapuram (Trivandrum), Kozhikode (Calicut) and Kochi (Cochin) are Kerala's air transport hubs; these and other towns are connected to everywhere else in India by bus and train.

Fast Facts

» Population: 33.4 million

» Area: 38,864 sq km

» Capital: Thiruvananthapuram (Trivandrum)

» Main language: Malayalam

» Sleeping prices: **$** below ₹800, **$$** ₹800 to ₹3000, **$$$** above ₹3000

Planning Your Trip

» High season in the backwaters and beach resorts is around November to March; between mid-December and mid-January, prices creep up further. There are great deals during the monsoon (June to September).

» Most Kerala national parks close for one week for a tiger census during the months of January or February. Check with Kerala Tourism for exact dates.

Resources

» Kerala Tourism (www.keralatourism.org) Kerala Tourist Board site.

» Manorama Online (www.manoramaonline.com) Local newspaper with an English edition on-line.

Food

Delicious breakfast dishes include *puttu* (rice powder and coconut, steamed in a metal or bamboo holder) eaten with steamed bananas and or with a spicy curry, *idlis* (spongy, round, fermented rice cakes) and *sambar* (fragrant vegetable dhal), dosas with coconut chutney, *idiyappam* (rice noodles) or *paalappam* (a kind of pancake) served with a meat or fish stew. *Appam* is a soft pancake made from toddy-fermented rice batter, with a soft spongy centre and crispy edges, also eaten with a coconut-mellowed stew.

The state's spice plantations, coconut-palm groves and long coastline shape the local cuisine, with deliciously delicate dishes such as fish *molee* (in coconut milk) or the spicy Malabar chicken curry. Dishes are mostly cooked in coconut oil.

For dessert, *payasam* is made of brown molasses, coconut milk and spices, garnished with cashew nuts and raisins.

DON'T MISS

Fort Cochin is an extraordinary town, resonant with 500 years of colonial history.

Floating along **Kerala's backwaters** on a houseboat, handmade in the style of traditional rice barges, or a canoe, is one of India's most magical experiences.

The plantation-cloaked hills of **Munnar** are a sight to soothe the soul, high in the lush mountains of Kerala's Western Ghats

---

Top State Festivals

» Ernakulathappan Utsavam (Jan/Feb, Shiva Temple, Ernakulam, Kochi, p284) Eight days of festivities culminating in a parade of 15 splendidly decorated elephants, music and fireworks.

» Thirunakkara Utsavam (Mar, Thirunakkara Shiva Temple, Kottayam, p271) All-night Kathakali dancing on the third and fourth nights of this 10-day festival; processions of elephants mark the finale.

» Pooram Festival (Apr, Asraman Shri Krishna Swami Temple, Kollam, p265) A 10-day festival with full-night Kathakali performances and a procession of 40 ornamented elephants.

» Thrissur Pooram (Apr/May, Vadakkumnathan Kshetram Temple, Thrissur, p295) The elephant procession to end all elephant processions.

» Nehru Trophy Snake Boat Race (2nd Sat in Aug, Alappuzha, p266) Most popular of Kerala's boat races.

» Onam (Aug/Sep, statewide) Kerala's biggest cultural celebration, when the entire state celebrates the golden age of mythical King Mahabali for 10 days.

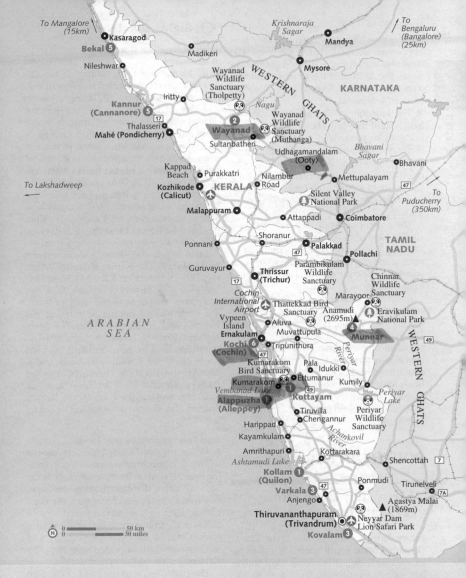

Kerala Highlights

1 Launch off in a houseboat or canoe from **Alleppey**, **Kottayam** or **Kollam**, slow down, and take a blissed-out glide on Kerala's fabled backwaters (p268)

2 Spot wild elephants at **Wayanad** (p300) amid spectacular mountain scenery and epic spice fields

3 Watch days slip slide away as you amble around the breathtaking beach resort of **Varkala** (p260) and have some laid-back fun in **Kovalam** (p256)

4 Hunker down in a beautifully remote resort and trek through the tea plantations around **Munnar** (p276)

5 Explore the golden-sand, unspoilt beaches around **Kannur** (p303) and **Bekal** (p305)

6 Feel the history in lovely, calm **Fort Cochin** (p285) in Kochi

History

Traders have been drawn to the scent of Kerala's spices for more than 3000 years. The coast was known to the Phoenicians, the Romans, the Arabs and the Chinese, and was a transit point for spices from the Moluccas (eastern Indonesia).

The kingdom of Cheras ruled much of Kerala until the early Middle Ages, competing with kingdoms and small fiefdoms for territory and trade. Vasco da Gama's arrival in 1498 opened the floodgates to European colonialism as Portuguese, Dutch and English interests fought Arab traders, and then each other, for control of the lucrative spice trade.

The present-day state of Kerala was created in 1956 from the former states of Travancore, Kochi and Malabar. A tradition of valuing the arts and education resulted in a post-Independence state that is one of the most progressive in India.

In 1957 Kerala had the first freely elected communist government in the world, which has gone on to hold power regularly since. The participatory political system has resulted in a more equitable distribution of land and income, and impressive health and education statistics (see boxed text, p260). Many Malayalis (speakers of Malayalam, the state's official language) work in the Middle East and their remittances play a significant part in the economy.

SOUTHERN KERALA

Thiruvananthapuram (Trivandrum)

☑ 0471 / POP 889,191

For obvious reasons, Kerala's capital Thiruvananthapuram is still often referred to by its colonial name: Trivandrum. Most travellers merely springboard from here to the nearby beachside resorts of Kovalam and Varkala, though laid-back, hill-enclosed Trivandrum, with its bevy of Victorian museums in glorious neo-Keralan buildings, is deserving of more time, if you can spare it. All you have to do is get off Trivandrum's racing-drag of a main street to find yourself immersed in old Kerala: surrounded by pagoda-shaped buildings, red-tiled roofs and narrow, winding lanes.

◉ Sights & Activities

TOP CHOICE Zoological Gardens
& Museums   ZOO, MUSEUMS

Yann Martel based the animals in his *Life of Pi* on those he observed in Trivandrum's **zoological gardens** (☑ 2115122; admission ₹10, camera ₹25; ◐ 9am-6pm Tue-Sun). Here are shaded paths meandering through woodland and lakes, where animals, such as tigers, macaques and birds frolic in massive open enclosures that mimic their natural habitats. There's a **reptile house** where cobras frequently flare their hoods – just don't ask what the cute guinea pigs are here for.

The park contains a gallery and two museums. Housed in an 1880 wooden building designed by Robert Chisholm, a British architect whose Fair Isle–style version of the Keralan vernacular shows his enthusiasm for local craft. The **Napier Museum** (admission ₹10; ◐ 9am-5pm Tue & Thu-Sun, 1-5pm Wed) has an eclectic display of bronzes, Buddhist sculptures, temple carts and ivory carvings. The carnivalesque interior is stunning and worth a look in its own right. The dusty **Natural History Museum** (admission ₹10; ◐ 9am-5pm Tue & Thu-Sun, 1-5pm Wed) has hundreds of stuffed animals and birds, and a fine skeleton collection. The **Shri Chitra Art Gallery** (admission ₹5; ◐ 9am-5pm Tue & Thu-Sun, 1-5pm Wed) has paintings by the Rajput, Mughal and Tanjore schools, and works by Ravi Varma.

Shri Padmanabhaswamy Temple   TEMPLE

(◐ Hindus only 4am-7.30pm) This 260-year-old temple is Trivandrum's spiritual heart, spilling over 2400 sq m. Its main entrance is the 30m-tall, seven-tier eastern *gopuram* (gateway tower). In the inner sanctum, the deity Padmanabha reclines on the sacred serpent and is made from over 10,000 *salagramam* (sacred stones) that were purportedly, and no doubt slowly, transported from Nepal by elephant.

The path around to the right of the gate offers good views of the *gopuram*.

Puthe Maliga Palace Museum   MUSEUM

(Indian/foreigner ₹10/30; ◐ 9am-1pm & 3-4.30pm) The 200-year-old palace of the Travancore maharajas has carved wooden ceilings, marble sculptures and even imported Belgian glass. Inside you'll find Kathakali images, an armoury, portraits of Maharajas, ornate thrones and other artefacts.

The annual **classical music festival** is held here in January.

Ayushmanbhava Ayurvedic Centre
AYURVEDA, YOGA

(☏4712556060; www.ayushmanbhava.com; Puthujanam) Offers treatments such as 60-minute massage (₹500), and daily therapeutic yoga classes (beginners 6.30am). Three kilometres west of the town centre, a one week package of treatments here costs ₹4700.

🎋 Courses

Margi Kathakali School
MARTIAL ARTS, DRAMA

(☏2478806; Fort) Conducts courses in Kathakali (p304) and *Kootiattam* (traditional Sanskrit drama) for beginner and advanced students. Fees average ₹300 per two-hour class. Visitors can peek at uncostumed practice sessions held 10am to noon Monday to Friday. It's in an unmarked building behind the Fort School, located 200m west of the fort.

CVN Kalari Sangham
MARTIAL ARTS

(☏2474182; www.cvnkalari.in; South Rd; 15-day/1-month course ₹1000/2000) Offers three-month courses in *kalarippayat* (p304) for serious students with some experience in martial arts. Contact Sathyan (☏2474182; sathyacvn@vsnl.net) for details. On Monday to Saturday at 6.30am to 8.30am, training sessions are open to visitors.

🖝 Tours

KTDC (Kerala Tourist Development Corporation) runs several tours, all leaving from the Tourist Reception Centre at the KTDC Hotel Chaithram on Central Station Rd. The **Kanyakumari Day Tour** (per person ₹550; ⊗8am-9pm Tue-Sun) visits Padmanabhapuram Palace (p260), Kanyakumari in Southern Tamil Nadu and the nearby Suchindram Temple. The **Narsa Darsan: Daily Half-day Tour** (per person ₹250; ⊗7.30am-1pm & 1.30-7pm Tue-Sun) visits Trivandrum's major sights.

🛏 Sleeping

🔺 Varikatt Heritage
HOMESTAY $$$

(☏2336057; www.varikattheritage.com; Punnen Rd; r ₹4000-5000) Trivandrum's most charismatic place to stay is the 250-year-old house of Colonel Roy Kuncheria. It's a wonderful bungalow flanked by verandas and a cinnamon tree, orchids in hanging pots. Every antique has a family story attached to it. Lunch and dinner available (₹300).

Graceful Homestay
HOMESTAY $$

(☏2444358; www.gracefulhomestay.com; Philip's Hill; downstairs s/d ₹1300/1500, upstairs s/d ₹2000/2500 incl breakfast; @🛜) In Trivan-

drum's leafy suburbs, this is owned by Sylvia and run by her brother Giles, and is an attractive house set in a couple of hectares of garden opposite AJ Hall. The pick of the rooms has an amazing covered terrace overlooking palm trees.

YMCA International Guesthouse
HOSTEL $

(☏2330059; YMCA Rd; s/d ₹485/620) Our value-ometer went off the scale when we saw this place – one of the less institutional among its brethren; rooms are spacious, spotless and come with tiled bathrooms and TV. Both men and women accepted.

Wild Palms Home Stay
HOMESTAY $$

(☏2471175; www.wildpalmsonsea.com; Mathrubhumi Rd; s ₹1495-1795, d ₹1795-2195; ❀) Trading on its touches of character and quiet setting, this is overpriced. Still, nowhere else has a Venus de Milo statue greeting you in the front garden. The ornate, comfortable family home here has well-furnished though faded rooms. The best has a terrace.

Sunday B&B
GUESTHOUSE $

(☏09746957056; opp Airport; s/d ₹400/500) This was fantastically well placed for a dawn flight, opposite the former international terminal. The terminal's move a few kilometres away has made it a little less convenient, but it's still handy, well priced and friendly with nicely kept, clean rooms with hot water.

Muthoot Plaza
HOTEL $$$

(☏2337733; www.themuthootplaza.com; Punnen Rd; s/d from ₹5800/6700, ste from ₹9500; ❀@🛜) Even though the arctic-level AC would make penguins shiver, this ultrachic business-focused hotel is still a great place to stay. The plush rooms are stuffed with pillows, couches and all mod cons.

Greenland Lodge
HOTEL $

(☏2328114; Thampanoor Junction; s/d ₹323/485, with AC ₹900/990; ❀) Close to the muted mayhem of the train station, Greenland lays out lots of serenity-inducing pastel colours to greet you. Inside, the rooms are spacious and come with hybrid squat/sit-down toilets. It's efficiently run, but expect to pay a hefty two-night deposit.

Princess Inn
HOTEL $

(☏2339150; Manjalikulam Rd; s/d ₹290/480, r with AC ₹650; ❀) In a modern (read: '80s) glass-fronted building, the Princess Inn promises a relatively quiet sleep in clean surrounds, plus satellite TV and immaculate green-tiled bathrooms.

Thiruvananthapuram (Trivandrum)

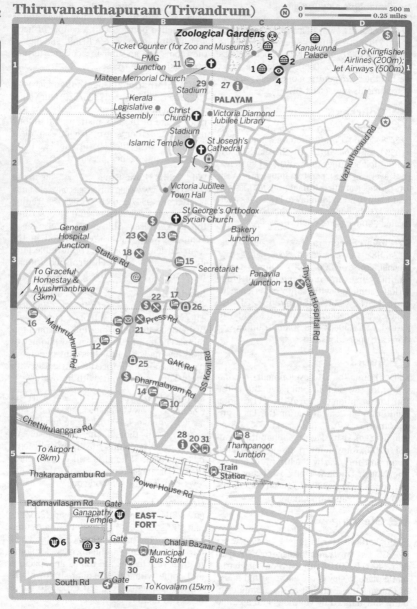

KTDC Mascot Hotel HOTEL $$$
(☎2318990; www.ktdc.com; Mascot Sq; s/d from ₹4000/4500; ❄@☎☀) Period touches, massive hallways and an imposing reception lend this place an aura of old-world charm. It has a monster pool and ayurvedic spa.

Hotel Regency HOTEL $
(☎2330377; www.hotelregency.com; Manjalikulam Cross Rd; s/d ₹540/788, with AC ₹900/1407; ❄) Offers small, cosy rooms with satellite TV, a leafy entryway, lots of hush and plenty of smiles at reception.

KERALA THIRUVANANTHAPURAM (TRIVANDRUM)

Kukie's Holiday Inn   GUESTHOUSE $
(☑2478530; Lukes Lane; s/d ₹220/275) At the end of a small lane in an appealingly quiet spot, this is centred around a little courtyard and offers bare-bones accommodation at rock-bottom prices. Rooms have hard beds and a cold water tap in the bathroom.

✗ Eating

For some unusual refreshments with your meal, look out for *karikku* (coconut water) and *sambharam* (buttermilk with ginger and chilli).

TOP CHOICE Indian Coffee House   INDIAN $
Station (Central Station Rd; dishes ₹12-50; ☺7am-11pm); Zoo (Museum Rd; ☺8.30am to 6pm) The Central Station Rd link of the chain serves its yummy coffee and snacks in a crazy red-brick tower that looks like a pigeon coop from outside, and has a spiralling interior lined inside by bench tables. You have to admire the hard-working waiters. It's a must-see. There's another, more run-of-the-mill branch near the museum.

Kalavara Family Restaurant   INDIAN $$
(Press Rd; dishes ₹60-140; ☺lunch & dinner) A bustling favourite of Trivandrum's middle class, this is decorated by curious half-awnings and serves up scrummy Keralan fish dishes. Our money's on the fish *molee* (fish in coconut sauce; ₹130).

Aroma   INDIAN $$
(☑4076000; Magic Days, Vanross Jn; dishes ₹50-100; ☺lunch & dinner) A smart hotel restaurant with a smashing buffet for lunch and dinner, as well as à la carte.

New Mubarak   MALABAR $
(off Statue Rd; dishes ₹20-60) A grand-sounding name for an ungrand restaurant, tucked away on a narrow lane off Statue Rd. However, it's a great place to sample Malabar Muslim cuisine such as crab masala or fresh fish cooked in coconut oil.

Ariya Nivaas   INDIAN $
(Manorama Rd; meals ₹45; ☺7am-9pm) Close to the train station and convenient for a quick feed between trains, this popular thali (traditional 'all-you-can-eat' meal) place gets positive reports.

Pizza Corner PIZZERIA $
(MG Rd; small pizzas ₹85-170; ⏰11am-11pm)
A bit of East meets West, with tasty pizzas sporting everything from traditional toppings (margherita) to Indian twists (eg Punjabi chicken tikka).

Ananda Bhavan INDIAN $
(☎2477646; MG Rd; dishes ₹22-31; ⏰lunch & dinner) A classic sit-down-and-dig-in-with-your-hands-type situation.

🔒 Shopping

Wander around **Connemara Market** (MG Rd) to see vendors selling vegetables, fish, live goats, fabric, clothes, spices and more bananas than you can poke a hungry monkey at.

SMSM Institute HANDICRAFTS
(YMCA Rd; ⏰9am-8pm Mon-Sat) No, it's not dedicated to the study of text messaging, but a Kerala Government-run handicraft emporium with an Aladdin's cave of well-priced goodies.

Sankers Coffee & Tea FOOD & DRINK
(☎2330469; MG Rd; ⏰9am-9pm Mon-Sat)
You'll smell the fresh coffee well before you reach this dainty shop. It sells Nilgiri Export OP Leaf Tea (₹260 per kilo) and a variety of coffees and nuts.

ℹ️ Information

ABC Internet (Capital Centre; MG Rd; per hr ₹20; ⏰8.30am-9pm) One of several good internet places in this small mall.

KIMS (Kerala Institute of Medical Sciences; ☎2447676; Kumarapuram) About 3km northwest of Trivandrum. For medical problems.

Main post office (☎2473071; MG Rd)
Thomas Cook (☎2338140-2; MG Rd; ⏰10.30am-6pm Mon-Sat) Changes cash and travellers cheques.

Tourist Facilitation Centre (☎2321132; Museum Rd; ⏰24hr) Supplies maps and brochures.
Tourist Reception Centre (KTDC Hotel Chaithram; ☎2330031; Central Station Rd; ⏰7am-9pm daily). Arranges KTDC-run tours.

ℹ️ Getting There & Away

Air

Between them, **Air India** (☎2317341; Mascot Sq), **Jet Airways** (☎2728864; Sasthamangalam Junction) and **Kingfisher Airlines** (☎18002333131; Star Gate Bldg; TC 9/888, Vellayambalam) fly to Mumbai (from ₹5200), Kochi (from ₹2300), Bengaluru (Bangalore; from ₹5400), Chennai (Madras; from ₹3800) and Delhi (from ₹7500).

There are regular flights from Trivandrum to Colombo and Male.

All airline bookings can be made at the efficient **Airtravel Enterprises** (☎3011412; www.ategroup.org; New Corporation Bldg, MG Rd).

Bus

For buses operating from the **KSRTC bus stand** (☎2323886), opposite the train station, see the table, p254.

For Tamil Nadu destinations, the State Express Transport Corporation (SETC) buses leave from the eastern end of the KSRTC bus stand.

Buses leave for Kovalam beach (₹15, 30 minutes, every 20 minutes) between 5.40am and 10pm from the southern end of the East Fort bus stand on MG Rd.

Buses leaving from Trivandrum (KSRTC Bus Stand):

MAJOR TRAINS FROM TRIVANDRUM

DESTINATION	TRAIN NO & NAME*	FARE (₹)	DURATION (HR)	DEPARTURES (DAILY)
Bengaluru	6525 *Bangalore Express*	307/833/1144	18	12.55pm
Chennai	2696 *Chennai Express*	166/799/1230	16½	5.10pm
Coimbatore	7229 *Sabari Express*	191/505/691	9¼	7.15am
Delhi	2625 *Kerala Express*	595/1616/2220	50	11.15am
Mangalore	6347 *Mangalore Express*	257/693/949	14½	8.45pm

*Sleeper/3AC/2AC

THE INDIAN COFFEE HOUSE STORY

The Indian Coffee House is a place stuck in time. Its India-wide branches feature old India prices and waiters dressed in starched white with peacock-style headdresses. It was started by the Coffee Board in the early 1940s, during British rule. In the 1950s the Board began to close down cafes across India, making employees redundant. At this point, the communist leader Ayillyath Kuttiari Gopalan Nambiar began to support the workers and founded with them the India Coffee Board Worker's Co-operative Society. The intention was to provide them with better opportunities and promote the sale of coffee. The Coffee House has remained ever since, always atmospheric, and always offering bargain snacks and drinks such as Indian filter coffee, rose milk and *idlis*. It's still run by its employees, all of whom share ownership.

DESTINATION	FARE (₹)	DURA-TION (HR)	FREQUENCY
Alleppey	97	3½	every 15min
Chennai	430	17	10 daily
Ernakulam (Kochi)	135	5	every 20min
Kanyakumari	56	2	6 daily
Kollam	42	1½	every 15min
Kumily (for Periyar)	126	8	2 daily
Madrai	195	7	9 daily
Munnar	193	7	2 daily
Neyyar Dam	20-26	1½	every 40min
Puducherry	375	16	1 daily
Thrissur	187	7½	every 30min
Udhagaman-dalam (Ooty)	365	14	1 daily
Varkala	36	1¼	hourly

Train

Trains are often heavily booked, so it's worth visiting the **reservation office** (☑139; ⊙8am-8pm Mon-Sat, to 2pm Sun) at the train station. See the table below for major long-distance services.

Within Kerala there are frequent trains to Varkala (2nd class/AC chair ₹36/279, one hour), Kollam (₹40/309, one hour) and Ernakulam (₹74/259, 4½ hours), with trains passing through either Alleppey (₹59/347, three hours) or Kottayam (₹62/396, 3½ hours). There are also numerous daily services to Kanyakumari (sleeper/3AC/2AC ₹140/272/396, 2½ hours).

ⓘ Getting Around

The **airport** (☑2501424) is 8km from the city and 15km from Kovalam; take local bus 14 from the East Fort and City Bus stand (₹6). Prepaid taxi vouchers from the airport cost ₹250 to the city and ₹400 to Kovalam.

Autorickshaws are the easiest way to get around, with short hops costing ₹10-20.

Around Trivandrum

NEYYAR DAM LION SAFARI PARK

This sanctuary, rebranded as the **Lion Safari Park** (☑2272182, 9744347582; Indian/foreigner ₹140/230; ⊙9.30am-5pm Tue-Sun), 35km north of Trivandrum, lies around an idyllic lake created by the 1964 Neyyar Dam. The fertile forest lining the shoreline is home to gaurs, sambar deer, sloth, elephants, lion-tailed macaques and the occasional tiger.

The park is usually visited via 1½-hour **lion safaris** (⊙9.30am-3.30pm) included in the admission fee, via boat and bus. This includes a 20-minute trek. Nearby there's a **Crocodile Protection Centre**, admission to which is also included. Get here from Trivandrum's KSRTC bus stand by frequent bus (₹20 to ₹26, 1½ hours). A taxi is ₹800 return (with two hours' waiting time) from Trivandrum, ₹1200 from Kovalam. The KTDC office in Trivandrum also run tours to Neyyar Dam (₹300).If you have your own transport, you can visit the park without a tour, which may enhance your chances of seeing wildlife.

SIVANANDA YOGA VEDANTA DHANWANTARI ASHRAM

Just before Neyyar Dam, this superbly located **ashram** (☑/fax 0471-2273093; www.sivananda.org/ndam), established in 1978, is renowned for its hatha yoga courses. Courses start on the 1st and 16th of each month, run for a minimum of two weeks and cost ₹700 per day for accommodation in a double room

(₹500 in dormitories). Low season (May to September) rates are ₹100 less. There's an exacting schedule (5.30am to 10pm) of yoga practice, meditation and chanting, though with plenty of breaks between sessions; and students rave about the food (included in the rates). Bookings are required. Month-long yoga-teacher training and ayurvedic massage courses are also available.

Kovalam

☎ 0471

Once a calm fishing village clustered around its crescents of beach, nowadays Kovalam is Kerala's most developed resort. It's a touristy place and the shore is built up with hotels, but it remains an appealing place to have some fun by the sea, though it has more than its fair share of resident touts and tourist tat.

Dangers & Annoyances

Bikini-clad women are likely to attract male attention, though this is definitely more of an annoyance than a danger. Cover up with a sarong when you're out of the water.

There are strong rips at both ends of Lighthouse Beach that carry away several swimmers every year. Swim only between the flags in the area patrolled by lifeguards – green flags show the area is safe, red flags warn of danger zones.

Kovalam has frequent blackouts and the footpaths behind Lighthouse Beach are un-lit, so carry a torch (flashlight) after dark.

◉ Sights & Activities

Lighthouse VIEWPOINT
(Indian/foreigner ₹10/25, camera/video ₹20/25; ⊙3-5pm) Check out the endless views along the coast by climbing Kovalam's lighthouse. Not recommended if you suffer from vertigo, or for small children.

Santhigiri MASSAGE
(☎2482800; www.santhigiriashram.org; nr Light-house Beach; ⊙8am-8pm) Try this place for ex-cellent massages and ayurvedic treatments. For ₹750/900 for 60/90 minutes you can have a four-handed massage while listening to the sound of the waves outside. Twenty-one-day panchakarma (internal purification) costs ₹64,250, including accommodation in big, airy rooms, and food.

🛏 Sleeping

Kovalam is chock-a-block with hotels, though budget places here cost more than usual and are becoming a dying breed. Beachfront properties are the most expen-sive and have great sea views. Look out for

Kovalam

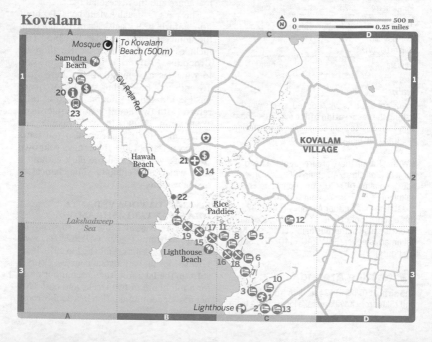

smaller places tucked away in the labyrinth of paths behind the beach among the palm groves and rice paddies; they're much better value. For more top-end accommodation choices, see the Around Kovalam section.

TOP CHOICE Beach Hotel II   HOTEL $$$
(☏2481937; www.thebeachhotel-kovalam.com; r ₹3000, with AC ₹4000; ❄) The Beach Hotel's upmarket new cousin, this is a stylish hotel with the best views on the seafront. Rooms have plate-glass windows opening onto terraces, and the decor is simple chic, with printed sheets and curtains and white walls. It's home to the new Oasia terrace restaurant.

Treetops   GUESTHOUSE $$
(☏2481363; treetopsofkovalam@yahoo.in; r ₹900; @) Indeed in the treetops, this friendly expat-owned place is a breath of fresh air, hidden away from the hustle. The three bright, sparkling-clean rooms have hanging chairs on the terraces, the view from the roof is awesome, and there's a yoga centre next door.

Paradesh Inn   GUESTHOUSE $$
(☏9995362952; inn.paradesh@yahoo.com; Paradesh House, Avaduthura; s/d ₹1250/1350; @) Next door to Treetops, tranquil Italian-run Paradesh Inn resembles a Greek island hideaway – a whitewashed building highlighted in blue. Each of the six fan-cooled rooms has a hanging chair outside, there are sweeping views from the rooftop and fab breakfasts.

Beach Hotel   GUESTHOUSE $$
(☏2481937; www.thebeachhotel kovalam.com; s/d ₹1500/2500;) Brought to you by the long-running German Bakery, this uberhip beachfront property has rooms designed with minimalist flair, ochre tones and finished with smart, arty touches. Plus Waves restaurant is just upstairs.

Leela   HOTEL $$$
(☏2480101; www.theleela.com; r from ₹14,000; ❄@❄☆) The only top-end option in town, the Leela is located in extensive grounds on the headland north of Hawah beach. There are three swimming pools, an ayurvedic centre, a gym, two private beaches, several restaurants and more. Rooms are sumptuous, with period touches, colourful textiles and Keralan artwork.

Sea Flower   HOTEL $
(☏2480554; www.seaflowerbeachresort.com; r downstairs ₹750, upstairs ₹900) Next door to Beach Hotel II, this dowdier place offers similar views at smaller prices. Rooms are simple and plain but freshly painted.

Dwaraka Lodge   GUESTHOUSE $
(☏2480411; d ₹450-500) With regular licks of paint helping to cover up the war wounds of this tired old-timer, friendly Dwaraka is the cheapest ocean-front property. There's nothing flash inside, just clean sheets and a basic bathroom.

Hotel Greenland   GUESTHOUSE $
(☏2486442; hotelgreenlandin@yahoo.com; r ₹500-1000) Family run and as friendly as they

Kovalam

come. The refurbished rooms in this multilevel complex have lots of natural light – some even have small kitchenettes for self-catering. Will cook up yummy food on request.

Green Valley Cottages GUESTHOUSE $
(☎2480636; indira_ravi@hotmail.com; r ₹500-1000) Also way back amongst the trees, this serene complex is the place to revel in serious shush time. The rooms are simple, but have good views from the terraces in front. They also have a house for rent, a short heft up the hill, for a ₹1000 per night.

Maharaju Palace GUESTHOUSE $$
(☎2485320; www.maharajupalace.in; d ₹1800) More of a quiet retreat than a palace, this place has more character than most, with wooden furnishings, including the odd four-poster, and different coloured mosquito nets. The breakfast terrace is hung with chintzy chandeliers.

Hotel Sky Palace GUESTHOUSE $
(☎9745841222; r downstairs/upstairs ₹500/900) This little two-storey place lies down a small lane; rooms are well kept, with a mix of colours and dark masculine tiling about the place; the ground-floor rooms are cheaper, but the same.

Varmas Beach Resort RESORT $$
(☎2480478; vijayavarmabeachresort@hotmail.com; Lighthouse Rd; s/d ₹1800/3000, with AC ₹2500/5500; ❄) Has a wood-panelled, Kerala-style facade and breezy rooms with exceptional views and comfy sitting areas on private balconies. However, this still doesn't justify these prices – try it off-season.

Jeevan Ayurvedic Beach Resort RESORT $$
(☎2480662; www.jeevanresort.net; d from ₹2400, with AC ₹3700; ❄☷) Expect inoffensively decorated, decent-sized rooms with bathtubs and an alluring, clean pool. Upstairs rooms have balconies with sea views.

Moon Valley Cottage GUESTHOUSE $
(☎9446100291; sknairkovalam@yahoo.com; d from ₹500, upstairs apt ₹1000) There's nothing but swaying palms around here, the rooms are a decent size and it's a peaceful spot.

Aparna GUESTHOUSE $$
(☎2480950; www.aparnahotelkovalam.com; s/d ₹1500/1750) Aparna has just a handful of cute, oddly shaped little rooms. All are cosy with private balconies, nice sea views and welcome sea breezes.

 Eating

Each evening, dozens of open-air restaurants line the beach promenade displaying the catch of the day – just pick a fish, settle on a price (per serve around ₹150, tiger prawns over ₹400) and decide how you want it prepared. Menus and prices are largely indistinguishable – it's more about which ambience takes your fancy. Unlicensed places will serve alcohol in mugs, or with the bottles hidden discreetly out of sight.

Malabar Cafe INDIAN $$
(mains ₹90-300) The busy tables tell their own story: this place, with its plastic chairs, candlelight at night, and view through pot plants to the crashing waves offers tasty food and good service.

Suprabhatham KERALAN $
(meals ₹45-80) This cosy little veggie place dishes up excellent, dirt-cheap and truly authentic Keralan cooking in a rustic setting. Out in the palm groves, it's secluded and intimate, and you can dine under the stars to a nightly orchestra of crickets.

Waves MULTICUISINE $$
(mains ₹100-480) With its broad, burnt-orange balcony, ambient soundtrack, and wide-roaming menu proffering everything from *weisskraut mit chinnken* (roast cabbage and bacon) to Thai curries, this is a foreign-tourist magnet.

Swiss Cafe CAFE $$
(mains ₹70-410) While the setting here is lovely, with an upstairs balcony and lots of wicker seating, the menu offers much the same choices as everywhere else, with a few token Swiss dishes (eg schnitzel) thrown in.

Fusion FUSION $$
(mains ₹120-440) This funky eatery has an inventive East-meets-West menu, with dishes such as oven-roasted tomatoes with spice crust on ginger cashew-nut noodles or lobster steamed in vodka. Also serves French press coffee and herbal teas.

Devi Garden Restaurant INDIAN $
(NUP Beach Rd; mains ₹50-150; ☉7.30am-11pm) Garden is overstating it, but this tiny, family-run eatery whips up great veg and nonveg Indian food for refreshingly reasonable prices.

☆ **Entertainment**

During high season, an abridged version of Kathakali is performed most nights –

enquire about locations and times at the Tourist Facilitation Centre.

ℹ Information

Almost every shop and hotel will change money. In Kovalam there's a National Bank of India and near the hospital a CBS **ATM** taking Visa cards. Otherwise, there are Federal Bank and ICICI ATMs at Kovalam Junction. There are lots of small **internet cafes** (per hr ₹30-50).

National Bank of India (☉10.30am-1.30pm Mon-Fri, ☉10.30am-noon Sat) Near the Leela resort. Changes cash.

Post office (Kovalam Beach Rd; ☉9am-1pm Mon-Sat)

Tourist Facilitation Centre (☑2480085; ☉9.30am-5pm) Helpful, inside the entrance to the Kovalam Beach Resort.

Upasana Hospital (☑2480632) Has English-speaking doctors who can take care of minor injuries.

ℹ Getting There & Away

BUS Buses connect Kovalam and Trivandrum every 20 minutes between 5.30am and 10.10pm (₹9, 30 minutes); catch them from the entrance to Leela resort. There are two buses daily to Ernakulam (₹140, 5½ hours), stopping at Kallambalam (for Varkala, ₹50, 1½ hours), Kollam (₹70, 2½ hours) and Alleppey (₹110, four hours). There's another 6.30am bus to Ernakulam via Kottayam that bypasses Varkala.

TAXI A taxi between Trivandrum and Kovalam beach is around ₹400.

MOTORBIKE HIRE Voyager Travels (☑9847065093) rents out scooters/Enfields for around ₹400/550 per day. It has no fixed office address.

Around Kovalam

SAMUDRA BEACH

Samudra beach, about 4km north of Kovalam by road, has seen a growing number of resorts edge out what was a small fishing village. Although more peaceful, the beach is steep and rough, and only accessible for swimming in December and January.

Set amid more than 5 hectares of lolling green grounds, **Taj Green Cove** (☑2487733; www.tajhotels.com; r ₹12,500-30,000; ✹@☎☎), the Kovalam branch of a swanky Indian hotel chain, has smashing individual chalets with sunken baths, an enticing infinity pool, several restaurants (one on the beach) and a spa.

PULINKUDI & CHOWARA

Around 8km south of Kovalam, amid endless-seeming swaying palms, colourful village life, and some empty golden-sand beaches, are some tantalising high-end alternatives to Kovalam's crowded centre.

For those serious about ayurvedic treatment, **Dr Franklin's Panchakarma Institute** (☑2480870; www.dr-franklin.com; Chowara; s from €38, d €55; @☎) is a reputable and less expensive alternative to the flashier resorts. Daily treatment with full board costs €56. Accommodation is tidy and comfortable but not resort style. There are therapy packages for whatever ails you, including spine problems, purification/detox treatments, as well as general rejuvenation and stress relief.

Surya Samudra Private Retreats (☑2480413; www.suryasamudra.com; Pulinkudi; r incl breakfast ₹14,100-42,900; ✹☎) proffers A-list-style seclusion, with 22 transplanted traditional Keralan homes, with four posters and open-air bathrooms, set in a palm grove above sparkling seas. There's an infinity pool carved out of a single block of granite, ayurvedic treatments, and spectacular outdoor yoga platforms.

In ayurvedic plant-filled gardens, **Somatheeram** (☑2266501; www.somatheeram.org; Pulinkudi; s/d from €72/80; ✹☎) is a good place to have an ayurvedic and yogic sojourn. The setting is paradisaical and rooms range from simple cottages to more luxurious houses. You can pay for treatments separately, or there are various packages (rejuvenation, slimming, etc).

☑Bethsaida Hermitage (☑2267554; www.bethsaidahermitage.com; Pulinkudi; AC s/d from €40/60, with sea view from €70/80; ✹) is a resort with a difference: this is a charitable organisation that helps support two nearby orphanages and an old people's home. It's also an inviting, somehow old-fashioned beachside escape, with sculpted gardens, a friendly welcome, and putting-green perfect lawns. It offers a variety of cottages, from large rooms with golden friezes to spacious, cool Kerala-style huts.

Thapovan Heritage Home (☑2480453; www.thapovan.com; s/d from ₹2650/3100) offers a midrange alternative next to a beautiful stretch of beach (no pool, AC or TV). There's a choice between pricier Keralan teak cottages, with wood-lined, slightly dated interiors, or some cheaper, plainer rooms, including a few overlooking the beach just a few paces away. Available ayurvedic treatments range from one-hour massages to 28-day treatment marathons.

Padmanabhapuram Palace

With a forest's worth of intricately carved ceilings and polished-teak beams, this **palace** (☎04651-250255; Indian/foreigner ₹25/200, camera/video ₹25/1500; ☺9am-1pm & 2-4.30pm Tue-Sun) is considered the best example of traditional Keralan architecture today. Parts of it date back to 1550; as the egos of successive rulers left their mark, it expanded into the magnificent conglomeration of 14 palaces it is today.

Asia's largest wooden palace complex, it was once the seat of the rulers of Travancore, a princely state taking in parts of Tamil Nadu and Kerala. Constructed of teak and granite, the exquisite interiors include carved rosewood ceilings, Chinese-style screens, and floors finished to a high black polish.

Padmanabhapuram is about 60km southeast of Kovalam. Catch a local bus from Kovalam (or Trivandrum) to Kanyakumari and get off at Thuckalay, from where it's a short autorickshaw ride or 15-minute walk. Alternatively, take one of the tours organised by the KTDC from Trivandrum, or hire a taxi (about ₹1500 return from Trivandrum or Kovalam).

Varkala

☎0470 / POP 42,273

Perched almost perilously along the edge of dizzying cliffs, Varkala has a naturally beautiful setting and is a low-key resort that's geared to a backpacker demographic. A strand of golden beach nuzzles Varkala's cliff edge, where restaurants play innocuous trance music and stalls sell the types of things every traveller might need: ethnic T-shirts, baggy trousers and silver jewellery. Even though this kind of tie-dye commercialism can grate on the nerves, Varkala is still a great place to watch the days slowly turn into weeks. The beach is a holy place, where Hindus come to make offerings for dead loved ones, assisted by priests who set up shop beneath the Hindustan Hotel. You can while away days watching the mix of fishermen, Hindu rituals, volleyball-playing visitors, locals gazing at the sea and strolling backpackers that make up the traffic on the beach.

Dangers & Annoyances

The beaches at Varkala have strong currents; even experienced swimmers have been swept away. This is one of the most dangerous beaches in Kerala, so be careful and swim between the flags or ask the lifeguards where's the safest place to swim.

If women wear bikinis or even swimsuits on the beach at Varkala, they are likely to feel uncomfortably exposed to stares – note that local people don't strip down on the beach. Wearing a sarong when out of the water will help avoid offending local sensibilities or attracting unwelcome attention, though it's worth noting that police patrol the beaches to keep male starers a-walkin' and the hawkers at bay. It pays to dress sensitively, especially if you're going into Varkala town.

It seems as if every man and his dog has an ayurvedic-related product or treatment to sell – many aren't qualified practitioners. Ask for recommendations before you go to get herbalised.

LEADER OF THE PACK

In 1957 Kerala democratically elected a communist government – the first place in the world to do so. Kerala's unique blend of democratic-socialist principles has a pretty impressive track record.

Kerala has been labelled 'the most socially advanced state in India' by Nobel prize-winning economist Amartya Sen. Land reform and a focus on infrastructure, health and education have played a large part in Kerala's success. The literacy rate (91%) is one of the highest of any developing nation, though a strong history of education stretches back centuries to the days of magnanimous rajas and active missionaries. The infant mortality rate in Kerala is one-fifth of the national average, while life expectancy stands at 73 years, 10 years higher than the rest of the country.

The picture is not all rosy, however. Lack of any industrial development or foreign investment means that the ambitions of many educated youth are curtailed. This might explain why Kerala also has the highest suicide rates and liquor consumption statistics in the country. A big hope for the economy's future is the recent boom in tourism, with Kerala emerging as one of India's most popular new tourist hot spots. So, thanks for coming, and congratulations on being a part of the solution.

⦿ Sights

Janardhana Temple   HINDU TEMPLE
Varkala is a temple town, and Janardhana Temple is the main event – its technicolour Hindu spectacle sits hovering above Beach Rd. It's closed to non-Hindus, but you may be invited into the temple grounds where there is a huge banyan tree and shrines to Ayyappan, Hanuman and other Hindu deities.

Sivagiri Mutt   SACRED SITE
(☏2602807; www.sivagiri.org) Sivagiri Mutt is the headquarters of the Shri Narayana Dharma Sanghom Trust, the ashram devoted to Shri Narayana Guru (1855–1928), Kerala's most prominent guru. This is a popular pilgrimage site and the resident swami is happy to talk to visitors.

🏃 Activities

Yoga is offered at several guesthouses for ₹200 to ₹300 per session. **Boogie boards** can be hired from places along the beach for ₹100; be wary of strong currents.

Laksmi's   MASSAGE
(☏9895948080; Clafouti Beach Resort; manicure/pedicure from ₹400/600, henna ₹300, massage ₹800; ⊙9am-7pm) This tiny place offers treatments such as threading and waxing as well as massages (women only).

Olympia House   MASSAGE
(☏9349439675; massages ₹600) Mr Omanakuttan is a qualified massage instructor, in both ayurveda and other schools.

Eden Garden   MASSAGE
(☏2603910; www.eden-garden.net; massage from ₹1000) Offers a more upmarket ayurvedic experience, and offers single treatments and packages.

🛏 Sleeping

Most places to stay are crammed in along the north cliff; some open only for the tourist onslaught in November. Less-developed Odayam beach, about 1km further north of Varkala's black beach, is a tranquil alternative.

The commission racket is alive and well – make sure that your rickshaw takes you to the place you've asked for.

⎡TOP⎤ Pink Aana   RESORT $
(☏9746981298; www.pinkaana.at; r ₹650-800) On the quiet Odayam Beach north of Varkala, there are just four wooden bungalows at the 'Pink Elephant'. Made of coconut wood

and bamboo, with private verandas, they're sparse but stylish, great value, and the best choice on this beach. There's a restaurant (meals around ₹200). Get here before the beach is ruined by any more buildings.

Villa Jacaranda   GUESTHOUSE $$$
(☏2610296; www.villa-jacaranda.biz; d incl breakfast ₹4600-5600) The ultimate in understated luxury, this romantic retreat has just a handful of huge, bright rooms in a large house, each with a balcony and decorated with a chic blend of minimalist modern and period touches. The delicious breakfast is served on your veranda.

Eden Garden   RESORT $$
(☏2603910; www.edengarden.in; r from ₹1200, luxury ste ₹5500) Overlooking peaceful paddy fields, this place has rooms with high wooden ceilings and attractive wooden furniture, set around a lush lily pond. Suites are organically shaped like white space-mushrooms, but inside they are romantic and fantastical, with intricate paintwork, round beds, and mosaic circular baths. A recommended ayurvedic resort is based here.

Taj Gateway Hotel   HOTEL $$$
(☏6673300; www.tajhotels.com/gateway; s/d ₹4400/5200; ✴@≋) Rebranded, revamped, refurbished, the Taj Varkala is looking hot – especially the new rooms, with beds covered in gleaming linen and mocha cushions, and with glass shower cubicles in the bathrooms, complete with electric blinds. There's a fantastic pool (nonguests ₹400).

Jicky's   GUESTHOUSE $$
(☏2606994; www.jickys.com; s ₹400, d ₹600-1750, cottage ₹900-1000) Way back in the palm groves, family-run Jicky's remains friendly as they come. The regular rooms are lovely and fresh, surrounded by lots of leafiness, and there are now also two double cottages, and some larger rooms for three to four in two smaller whitewashed, wooden-shuttered buildings.

Puthooram   RESORT $$
(☏3202007; www.puthooram.com; r ₹500-2000, with AC ₹2500-3000) If garden gnomes were on holiday, they'd probably come here, to stay in Puthooram's wood-lined bungalows set around a charming little garden. Rooms with sea view are pricier.

Villa Anamika   GUESTHOUSE $$
(☏2600096; www.villaanamika.com; r ₹500-2500, cottages ₹3500; ✴) This Keralan-German-run

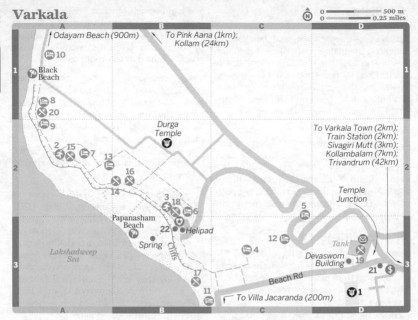

place has spacious rooms, all neatly furnished with homely decorations and art by owner Chicku. The pricier rooms have sea views, and the trim little garden out the back is a bonus.

Guest House Varkala GUESTHOUSE $
(☑2602227; d ₹220, with AC ₹440) A government-run guesthouse with several rooms in huge Keralan-styled bungalows that were once part of a palace complex. Though Spartan, each bargain-basement abode is finished with lots of polished wood and has incredibly high ceilings.

New Heaven GUESTHOUSE $$
(☑9846074818; newheavenbeachresort@yahoo.com; r ₹900-1000) New Heaven has easy access to Black Beach and great top-floor views. Bedrooms are roomy, basic and a tad drab, with big blue bathrooms and hanging wicker chairs out the front for lazing.

Sea Pearl Chalets RESORT $$
(☑2660105; www.seapearlchalets.com; d from ₹1500) Precariously perched on Varkala's southern cliff, these small, basic, podlike huts have unbeatable views and are surrounded by prim lawns. Definitely worth checking out before they tumble into the ocean.

Kerala Bamboo House RESORT $$
(☑9895270993; www.keralabamboohouse.com; huts d ₹1500-2000) For that bamboo-hut experience, this popular place squishes together dozens of pretty Balinese-style huts in a clifftop compound and a carefully maintained garden. Some of the huts are nicer than others (ie some have muralled outdoor showers and are wood-lined, some don't), so look at a few. Cheaper ones don't have hot water.

Santa Claus Village Resort RESORT $$
(☑9249121464; www.santaclausvillageresort.com; r from ₹500, with sea view ₹ 1000, with AC from ₹1500; ❋🌊) This simple but appealing cliff-front option has small rooms in traditional Keralan-themed buildings, with fetching bits of furniture and lots of teak-wood flair. The four rooms at the front are the money shot, with windows facing out to sea.

Sea Breeze GUESTHOUSE $$
(☑2603257; www.seabreezevarkala.com; r ₹1500, with AC ₹2200-3000; ❋) The large, orderly, if dull rooms in this pink building all offer sea views and share a large veranda – perfect for nightly sunset adulation.

🍴 Eating

Most restaurants in Varkala offer the same mishmash of Indian, Asian and Western

Varkala

fare to a soundtrack of easy-listening trance; they open from around 8am to 11pm. Join in the nightly Varkala saunter till you find a place that suits. Those who are unlicensed will usually serve alcohol discreetly.

Café del Mar   MULTICUISINE **$$**
(dishes ₹110-400) This is the kind of place you return to for its efficient service, good coffee, whirring fans, great position overlooking the cliffs, and the specials of the day chalked up on a board outside.

Trattorias   MULTICUISINE **$$**
(meals ₹80-200) Smarter than most Trattorias has an Italian coffee machine and the usual wide-ranging menu, but specialises in pasta and even has some Japanese dishes.

Nothin' Doing   INDIAN **$$**
(Hindustan Hotel; mains ₹120-280; ⊙7am-10.30am, noon-3pm & 7-10.15pm) The rooftop restaurant topping this carbuncle offers tasty enough nonveg and veg fare, but the real reason to come here is the view from the balcony (with just a couple of tables) over the action of the beach.

Oottupura Vegetarian Restaurant INDIAN **$**
(mains from ₹35) Bucking the trend and serving only veggie options, this budget eatery has a respectable range of yummy dishes, including breakfast *puttu* (flour with milk, bananas and honey).

Sreepadman   SOUTH INDIAN **$**
(thali ₹30) For dirt-cheap and authentic Keralan fare – think dosas (paper-thin lentil-flour pancakes) and thalis – where you can rub shoulders with rickshaw drivers rather than tourists, hit Sreepadman. This is a hole-in-the-wall with a view: there is neat seating out the back.

Hungry Eye Kitchen   MULTICUISINE **$$**
(meals ₹70-160) The multilevel design of Hungry Eye means everyone gets uninterrupted sea views. Thai food is a speciality – the kitchen can whip up red and green curries as well as the usual Varkala suspects.

Juice Shack   CAFE **$**
(juices ₹50, snacks ₹30-150; ⊙7am-7pm) A funky little health-juice bar that has a buffet on Wednesday and Saturday (₹250).

☆ Entertainment

Kathakali performances are organised during high season – look out for notices locally.

ⓘ Information

A 24-hour ATM at the temple junction takes Visa cards, and there are more ATMs in Varkala town. Many of the travel agents lining the cliff do cash advances on credit cards and change travellers cheques. **Internet cafes** (per hr around ₹40) dot the cliff top – save emails often, as power cuts are not uncommon.
Post office (⊙10am-2pm Mon-Sat) North of Temple Junction.

ⓘ Getting There & Away

There are frequent trains to Trivandrum (2nd class/AC chair ₹21/140, one hour) and Kollam (₹17/140, 30 minutes), as well as three daily services to Alleppey (₹35/153, two hours). It's feasible to get to Kollam in time for the morning backwater boat to Alleppey (p268). From Temple Junction, three daily buses pass by on their way to Trivandrum (₹30, 1½ to two hours), with one heading to Kollam (₹25, one hour).

ℹ️ Getting Around

It's about 2.5km from the train station to Varkala beach, with rickshaws going there for ₹40 to ₹50. Local buses also travel regularly between the train station and the temple junction (₹4).

Many places along the cliff hire out scooters/ Enfields for ₹250/350 per day.

Kollam (Quilon)

📞 0474 / POP 380,100

Small but busy, untouristy Kollam (Quilon) is the southern approach to Kerala's backwaters. One of the oldest ports in the Arabian Sea, it was once a major commercial hub that saw Roman, Arab, Chinese and later Portuguese, Dutch and British traders jostle into port – eager to get their hands on spices and the region's cashew crops. The centre of town is reasonably hectic, but surrounding it are the calm waterways of Ashtamudi Lake, fringed with coconut palms, cashew plantations and traditional villages.

⊙ Sights

The best thing to do from Kollam is explore the backwaters around **Munroe Island** (see Tours, p264). There's a rowdy **fish market** at Kollam Beach where customers and fisherfolk alike pontificate on the value of the

day's catch; there's also an evening fish market from 5pm to 9pm. The **beach** (long, but nothing special) is 2km south of town, a ₹30 rickshaw ride away.

🏃 Activities

Janakanthi Panchakarma Centre AYURVEDA (📞 2763014; www.santhigiri.co.in; Vaidyasala Nagar, Asraman North) An ayurvedic centre with more of an institutional than a spa vibe, 5km from Kollam, popular for its seven- to 21-day treatment packages – accommodation is available for ₹500 a night. You can also just visit for a rejuvenation massage (₹750). An autorickshaw from Kollam should cost around ₹140.

👉 Tours

TOP
CHOICE **Canoe-boat tours** BOATING (per person ₹400; ⏱ 9am-1.30pm & 2pm-6.30pm) Excellent tours through the canals of Munroe Island and across Ashtamudi Lake are organised by the DTPC (District Tourism Promotion Council). You're first driven 25km to the starting point, then take a three-hour trip via punted canoe. On these excursions (with knowledgeable guides) you can observe daily village life, see *kettuvallam* (rice barge) construction, toddy (palm beer) tapping, coir-making (coconut fibre),

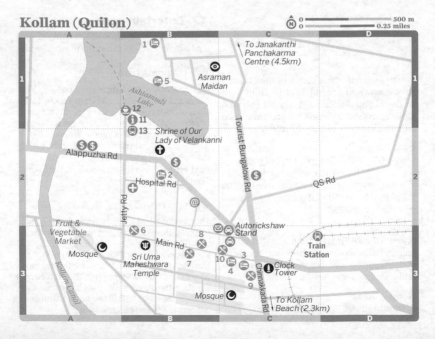

Kollam (Quilon)

prawn and fish farming, and do some bird-watching on spice-garden visits.

Houseboat cruises
BOATING
(2/4 people 24hr cruise ₹4000/4500, Kollam to Alappuzha cruise ₹10,000/12,000) The DTPC organises these houseboat cruise packages.

Festivals & Events
The **Pooram festival** is held in Kollam every April; the **Ashtamudi Craft & Art festival** (December/January) is every two years.

Sleeping
The DTPC office keeps a list of **homestays** in and around Kollam.

Valiyavila Homestay
GUESTHOUSE $$
(☎2701546, 9847132449; www.kollamlakeview resort.com; Panamukkom; r ₹1000-2000, with AC ₹2500; ❋@) This has an amazing location, crowning a breezy peninsula surrounded by leisurely backwaters on three sides. The four enormous rooms come with lots of windows to enjoy the views and the breeze. It's a good choice for families. Call ahead for a boat pick-up, catch a public ferry from Kollam (₹3), or grab an autorickshaw (₹100) to get here. The tourist boat from Alleppey also stops here before it docks at Kollam.

Get here before 2013, when it's set to close. The host, Joseph Prabath, has set up

Kollam (Quilon)

🛌 Sleeping

✕ Eating

Information

Transport

Ashtamudi Villas (www.ashtamudivillas.com; d ₹1000), simple brick huts set on the water's edge, among nodding palms, which are much closer to town.

Nani Hotel
HOTEL $$
(☎2751141; Chinnakada Rd; r ₹1050, with AC ₹1600-3000; ❋@) This boutique business hotel is a surprise in Kollam's busy centre, and exceptionally good value. Built by a cashew magnate, it's gorgeously designed and mixes traditional Keralan elements and modern lines for a sleek look. Even the cheaper rooms have flat-screen TVs, feathery pillows and sumptuous bathrooms.

Tamarind
HOTEL $$
(☎2745538; r with AC ₹1400; ❋) Overlooking the backwaters, across the lake from the ferry terminal, this has big, airy, bright orange, slightly tired rooms, with great views.

Government Guest House
GUESTHOUSE $
(☎2743620; s/d ₹220/440) In a colonial-era relic that's all whitewashed walls, tall varnished shutters and dusty grandeur, this guesthouse offers crumbling rooms with high ceilings and wooden floors. They're a bargain, but isolated 3km north of the centre on Ashtamudi Lake. Book ahead.

Hotel Sudarsan
HOTEL $$
(☎2744322; Alappuzha Rd; www.hotelsudarsan. com; s/d with AC from ₹900/1000, deluxe ₹1200/1400; ❋) Sudarsan is welcoming enough, set around a car-park-courtyard, but rooms are plain and dull, if comfortable. Those at the front are noisy. There's a good restaurant.

Kodiylil Residency
GUESTHOUSE $
(☎3018030; Main Rd; s/d ₹440/550, with AC ₹800/900; ❋) Bright red hallways are moodily lit, if at all, and the rooms here come in shades of lime that could do with a lick of paint. Shame about the lack of windows.

Karuna Residency
GUESTHOUSE $
(☎3263240; Main Rd; s/d ₹350/450, r with AC ₹700; ❋) This little budgeteer is starting to show its age, but is still maintained in decent condition. The central location close to the train station is probably its biggest asset.

✕ Eating

Prasadam
MULTICUISINE $$
(☎2751141; Chinnakada Rd; mains ₹60-150) The restaurant at the swish Nani Hotel has a comely setting amid intricate copper-relief

artwork depicting Kollam history. The meals are well prepared and include tasty thalis.

Kedar Restaurant
INDIAN $$
(Hotel Sudarsan; meals ₹90-150; ⊙7am-11pm) This small glass-walled eatery is recommended for its tasty veg and nonveg cuisine, including special chicken masala.

Fayalwan Hotel
INDIAN $
(Main Rd; meals ₹10-40) This is a real Indian working-man's diner, packed to the rafters come lunchtime. There are concrete booths and long benches for sitting and tucking in – try the mutton biryani (₹45).

Hotel Guru Prasad
INDIAN $
(Main Rd; meals ₹24) In a neat colonial building still clinging to remnants of a once-cheery paint job, this busy lunchtime place draws the punters with dirt-cheap set meals.

Indian Coffee House
INDIAN $
(Main Rd) Reliable for a decent breakfast and strong coffee.

Vijayalaxmi Cashew Co
FOODSTUFFS $
(Main Rd; ⊙10am-7pm) A major exporter of Kollam's famous cashews; quality nuts are around ₹260 per 500g.

ⓘ Information

DTPC information centre (☑2745625; info@ dtpckollam.com; ⊙8am-7pm) Helpful; near the KSRTC bus stand and boat jetty.

Post office (☑2746607; Alappuzha Rd)

Silver Net (per hr ₹25; ⊙10.30am-6.30pm Mon-Sat) The most convenient of numerous internet cafes at the Bishop Jerome Nagar Complex.

UAE Exchange (☑2751240-1; Alappuzha Rd; ⊙9.30am-6pm Mon-Fri, to 4pm Sat, to 1.30pm Sun) For changing cash and travellers cheques.

ⓘ Getting There & Away

Boat

See p268 for information on cruises to Alleppey. From the main boat jetty there are frequent public ferry services across Ashtamudi Lake to Guhanandapuram (one hour). Fares are around ₹10 return, or ₹3 for a short hop.

Bus

Kollam is on the Trivandrum–Kollam–Alleppey–Ernakulam bus route, with superfast/fast buses departing every 10 or 20 minutes to Trivandrum (₹44/42, 1¾/two hours), Alleppey (₹55/52, two/2½ hours) and Ernakulam (Kochi, ₹90/85, 3¼/3½ hours). Buses depart from the **KSRTC bus stand** (☑2752008) near the boat jetty.

Train

There are frequent trains to Ernakulam (2nd class/AC chair ₹61/210, 3½ hours, six daily) and Trivandrum (₹40/165, one hour) via Varkala (₹36/165, 30 minutes). A couple of trains daily go to Alappuzha (Alleppey; ₹59/202, 1½ hours).

Around Kollam

KRISHNAPURAM PALACE MUSEUM

Two kilometres south of Kayamkulam (between Kollam and Alleppey), this restored **palace** (☑0479-2441133; admission ₹10, camera/ video ₹25/250; ⊙9am-1pm & 2-5pm Mon-Sat) is a fine example of grand Keralan architecture. Now a museum, inside are paintings, antique furniture, sculptures, and a renowned 3m-high mural depicting the Gajendra Moksha (the liberation of Gajendra, chief of the elephants) as told in the Mahabharata. The **Bharni Utsavam festival** is held at the nearby Chettikulangara Bhaghavathy Temple in February/March.

Buses (₹25) leave Kollam every few minutes for Kayamkulam. Get off at the bus stand near the temple gate, 2km before the palace.

Alappuzha (Alleppey)

☑0477 / POP 282,700

Hmm, those Venice comparisons might work if Venice shrank, acquired a few breeze-block buildings, and imported some tooting rickshaws.

But step out of the hectic centre, and Alappuzha is graceful and greenery-fringed, set around its grid of canals. Explore the vast watery highways of the region and you'll experience one of Kerala's most mesmerisingly beautiful and relaxing experiences.

It's the gateway to the fabled backwaters, a sprawling network of canals – float along and gaze over rice fields of succulent green, curvaceous rice barges, and village life along the banks. Most people in town would like to organise you some houseboat or canoe action. It's also home to the famous **Nehru Trophy Snake Boat Race**.

🏃 Activities

Ayurveda: Shri Krishna Ayurveda Panchkarma Centre
AYURVEDA
(☑3290728, 9847119060; www.krishnayurveda. com) For ayurvedic treatments; one-hour rejuvenation massages are ₹600. It's near the Nehru race finishing point.

Alappuzha (Alleppey)

Sleeping
1	Dream Nest	A2
2	Palmy Residency	B1

Eating
3	Indian Coffee House	B2
4	Indian Coffee House	A4
5	Kream Korner	B3
6	Kream Korner	A2
7	Royale Park Hotel	A2
8	Thaff	A4
9	Thaff	B1

Information
10	DTPC Tourist Reception Centre	B1

Transport
11	Boat Jetty	B1
12	KSRTC Bus Stand	B2

Tours

Any of the dozens of travel agencies in town, guesthouses, hotels, or the KTDC can arrange canoe-boat tours of the backwaters; also see p268.

Sleeping

For lovely canalside lazing, try the relaxed sleeping options on the backwaters a few kilometres north of Alleppey; all can arrange town pick-ups and drop offs.

The rickshaw-commission racketeers are at work here; ask to be dropped off at a landmark close to your destination if you're having problems getting where you want to go.

TOP CHOICE Raheem Residency HOTEL **$$$**
(☎2239767; www.raheemresidency.com; Beach Rd; s/d from €140/170; ❉☞⊛) This thoughtfully renovated 1860s heritage home is a delight to visit, let alone stay in. The 10 rooms here have been restored to their former glory and have bathtubs, antique furniture and period fixtures. The common areas are airy and comfortable, there are pretty indoor courtyards, a well-stocked library, a great little pool and an excellent restaurant.

Palmy Residency GUESTHOUSE **$**
(☎2235938; www.palmyresort.com; Opposite Matha Jetty, Finishing Point Rd; r ₹350) Run by the friendly folk of Palmy Resort, this has to be the best deal in town. It's in a brand-new building in a fab location – just over the new Matha footbridge from the bus station, but set back from the road amid lush greenery. Rooms are spacious and floored in Italian marble.

Cherukara Nest HOMESTAY **$**
(☎2251509; www.cherukaranest.com; d incl breakfast ₹750, with AC ₹1200; ❉@) Set in well-tended gardens, with a pigeon coop at the back, this lovely heritage home has the sort of welcoming family atmosphere that makes you miss your grandma. There are four large characterful rooms, each sporting lots of polished wood touches and antediluvian doors with ornate locks. Great value.

Palmy Lake Resort HOMESTAY **$**
(☎2235938; www.palmyresorts.com; Punnamada Rd East; cottages d ₹750) With six handsome cottages, some in bamboo and some in concrete, there's loads of charm and peace at this stunning value homestay, 3.5km north of Alleppey. It's set among palm groves near the backwaters, with gracious owner Bigi and his wife Macy providing delicious meals on request.

THE BACKWATERS

The undisputed main attraction of a trip to Kerala is travelling through the 900km network of waterways that fringe the coast and trickle inland. Long before the advent of roads, these waters were the slippery highways of Kerala, and many villagers still use paddle-power as their main form of transport. Trips through the backwaters traverse palm-fringed lakes studded with cantilevered Chinese fishing nets, and wind their way along narrow, shady canals where coir (coconut fibre), copra (dried coconut kernels) and cashews are loaded onto boats. Along the way are isolated villages where farming life continues as it has for eons. For information on the northern backwaters, see p306.

Tourist Cruises

The popular tourist cruise between Kollam and Alleppey (₹400) departs at 10.30am, arriving at 6.30pm, daily from August to March and every second day at other times. Generally, there's a 1pm lunch stop (with a basic lunch provided) and a brief afternoon chai stop. The crew has an ice box full of fruit, soft drinks and beer to sell. Bring sunscreen and a hat.

It's a scenic and leisurely way to get between the two towns, but the boat travels along only the major canals – you won't have many close-up views of the village life that makes the backwaters so magical. Some travellers say they found the eight-hour trip boring.

Another option is to take the trip halfway (₹200) and get off at the **Matha Amrith-anandamayi Mission** (☏0476-2897578; www.amritapuri.org; Amrithapuri), the incongruously pink ashram of Matha Amrithanandamayi. One of India's few **female gurus**, Amrithanandamayi is also known as Amma (Mother), or 'The Hugging Mother', because of the darshan (audience) she offers, often hugging thousands of people in marathon all-night sessions. The ashram runs official tours at 5pm each day. It's a huge complex, with about 2000 people living here permanently – monks, nuns, students and families, both Indian and foreign. It offers food, ayurvedic treatments, yoga and meditation, as well as souvenirs; everything from books to postcards of Amma's toes. Amma travels around for much of the year, so you might be out of luck if in need of a cuddle.

Visitors should dress conservatively and there is a strict code of behaviour. With prior arrangement, you can stay at the ashram for ₹150 per day (including simple vegetarian meals) and pick up an onward or return cruise a day or two later. Alternatively, you can take the free ferry to the other side of the canal and grab a rickshaw to Karunagappally, 10km away (around ₹170), from where you can catch buses to Alleppey (₹35, 1½ hours).

Houseboats

Renting a houseboat designed like a kettuvallam (rice barge) could be one of your most expensive experiences in India, but it's usually worth every rupee. Drifting through quiet canals lined with coconut palms, eating delicious Keralan food, meeting local villagers and sleeping on the water – it's a world away from the clamour elsewhere.

Houseboats cater for couples (one or two double bedrooms) and groups (up to seven bedrooms!). Food (and an onboard chef to cook it) is generally included in the quoted cost. Houseboats can be chartered through a multitude of private operators in Kollam (book ahead here as there are fewer boats) and Alleppey. This is the biggest business in Kerala:

Tharavad HOMESTAY **$$**
(☏242044; www.tharavadheritageresort.com; West of North Police Station; d ₹1000, with AC ₹2000; ﹡) Between the town centre and beach, in a quiet canalside location, this ancestral home (the owner's grandfather was an ayurvedic doctor) has lots of glossy teak and antiques, five characterful rooms, and well-maintained gardens.

Gowri Residence GUESTHOUSE **$**
(☏2236371; www.gowriresidence.com; r ₹600-900, with AC ₹1200; ﹡) This rambling complex

has traditional wood-panelled rooms in the main house, several types of bungalows made from either stone, wood, bamboo or thatch, and a towering treehouse. Good food is served, and there's an aviary that even includes an emu.

Sona GUESTHOUSE **$$**
(☏2235211; www.sonahome.com; Lakeside, Finishing Point; r ₹800, with AC ₹1100) Run by the affable Joseph, this old heritage home has slightly shabby but high-ceilinged rooms with

some operators are unscrupulous. The quality of boats varies widely, from rust buckets to floating palaces – try to check out the boat before agreeing on a price. Travel-agency reps will be pushing you to book a boat as soon as you set foot in Kerala, but it's better to wait till you reach a backwater hub: choice is greater in Alleppey (500 boats and counting), and you're much more likely to be able to bargain down a price if you turn up and see what's on offer.

In the high season you're likely to get caught in backwater-gridlock – some travellers are disappointed by the number of boats on the water. It's not possible to travel by houseboat between Alleppey and Kollam, or between Alleppey and Kochi. Expect a boat for two people for 24 hours to cost about ₹4500–6000; for four people, ₹5500-8000; more for larger boats or for AC. Shop around to negotiate a bargain – though this will be harder in the busier seasons. Prices triple from around 20 December to 5 January.

Village Tours & Canoe Boats

More and more travellers are opting for village tours or canal-boat trips. Village tours usually involve small groups of five to six people, a knowledgeable guide and an open canoe or covered *kettuvallam*. The tours (from Kochi, Kollam or Alleppey) last from 2½ to six hours and cost between ₹300 and ₹650 per person. They include visits to villages to watch coir-making, boat building, toddy (palm beer) tapping and fish farming. On longer trips a traditional Keralan lunch is often provided. The Munroe Island trip from Kollam (p264) is an excellent tour of this type; the tourist desk in Ernakulam also organises recommended tours.

In Alleppey, rented canoe boats offer a nonguided laze through the canals on a small, covered canoe for up to four people (two people for two/four hours ₹150/₹600) – a great way to spend a relaxing afternoon.

Public Ferries

If you want the local backwater transport experience, there are State Water Transport boats between Alleppey and Kottayam (₹10 to ₹11, 2½ hours) depart Alleppey at 7.30am, 9.35am, 11.30am, 2.30pm and 5.15pm; they leave Kottayam at 6.40am, 11.30am, 1pm, 3.30pm and 5.15pm. The trip crosses Vembanad Lake and has a more varied landscape than the Alleppey cruise.

Environmental Issues

Pollution from houseboat motors is becoming a major problem as boat numbers swell every season. The Keralan authorities have introduced an ecofriendly accreditation system for houseboat operators. Among the criteria an operator must meet before being issued with the 'Green Palm Certificate' are the installation of solar panels and sanitary tanks for the disposal of waste – ask operators whether they have the requisite certification. There's been talk of running boats on cleaner natural gas, though we've yet to see this being implemented. Consider choosing one of the few remaining punting, rather than motorised, boats if possible.

---

faded flowered curtains, and four-poster beds overlooking a well-kept garden.

Malayalam RESORT **$$**
(☑2234591; malayalamresorts@yahoo.com; Punnamada; r ₹1200) With one of best locations in Alleppey, this little family-run pad has four cute cottages that practically play footsies with the backwaters. It's a bit hard to find: walk past the Keraleeyam resort reception and along the canal bank.

Palm Grove Lake Resort RESORT **$$**
(☑2235004; www.palmgrovelakeresort.com; Punnamada; cottages d ₹1750, with AC ₹3500) Close to the starting point of the Nehru Trophy Snake Boat Race on Punnamada Lake, this isolated option has stylish, airy double cottages set amid palms, on the lake. Each plainly furnished but appealing hut has a secluded veranda, eye-catching, if jaded, outdoor showers and lake views.

Johnson's GUESTHOUSE $
(2245825; www.johnsonskerala.com; r ₹400-650) On a quiet street just west of town, this is a backpackers' favourite in a quirky modern mansion. Captained by the zealous Johnson Gilbert (who is keen to sell his pricey houseboat tours), this rambling residence is filled with funky furniture and loads of plants. A cheaper bamboo hut (₹250) is in the garden.

Dream Nest GUESTHOUSE $
(9895543080; www.thedreamnest.com; Cullen Rd; d & tr ₹500-600; ❋@) With a cheery welcome, this offers fairly clean, spacious, if drab rooms in a central villa, and a slightly blokish atmosphere. There's a nothing-special terrace out the back where you can hang out and shoot the breeze.

✗ Eating

Royale Park Hotel INDIAN $$
(YMCA Rd; meals ₹90-200; ⊗7am-10pm; ⊛) There is an extensive menu at this swish hotel restaurant, and the food is excellent, including scrumptious veg thalis for ₹100. You can order from the same menu in the upstairs bar and wash down your meal with a cold Kingfisher.

Chakara Restaurant MULTICUISINE $$$
(2230767; Beach Rd; mini Kerala meal ₹350, mains ₹420; ⊗1-3pm & 7-9.30pm) The restaurant at Raheem Residency is Alleppey's finest, with seating on a bijou open rooftop with views over to the beach. The menu creatively combines traditional Keralan and European cuisine. Local Indian wine is available.

Harbour Restaurant MULTICUISINE $$
(2230767; Beach Rd; meals ₹90-120; ⊗10am-10pm) This beachside, casual little brick hut is run by the swish Raheem Residency. It's more casual and budget-conscious than the hotel's restaurant, but promises equally well prepared cuisine, and is good to drop by for a cold beer (large Kingfisher ₹110).

Kream Korner MULTICUISINE $
(Mullackal Rd; dishes ₹20-80; ⊗8.30am-10pm) This relaxed airy place is popular with Indian and foreign families and offers a tasty menu. There's another, pint-sized branch on Cullan Rd.

Thaff INDIAN $
(YMCA Rd; meals ₹35-110) An absurdly popular joint that has scrumptious Indian bites,

with some Arabic flavours mixed in, to boot. It does succulent roast spit-chicken, scrumptious *shawarma* and brain-freezing ice-cream shakes. There's another location on Punnamada Rd.

Vembanad Restaurant INDIAN $
(Alleppey Prince Hotel; AS Rd; mains ₹50-170) Reliable dining pool-side; occasional live music, located 3km northwest of town.

Indian Coffee House CAFE $
(snacks around ₹10) Branches on Mullackal Rd, YMCA Rd, and Beach Rd – the latter is a pavilion in a great, breezy beachside location.

ℹ Information

DTPC Tourist Reception Centre (2253308; www.alappuzhatourism.com; ⊗8.30am-6pm) Remarkably rudimentary tourist info.

Mailbox (2339994; Boat Jetty Rd; per hr ₹40; ⊗8am-9.30pm) Internet access.

National Cyber Park (2238688; YMCA Compound; per hr ₹30; ⊗10am-9pm) Internet access.

Tourist Police (2251161; ⊗24hr) Next door to the DTPC.

UAE Exchange (2264407; cnr Cullan & Mullackal Rds; ⊗9.30am-6pm to 4pm Sat, to 1pm Sun) For changing cash and travellers cheques.

ℹ Getting There & Away

Boat
Ferries run to Kottayam from the boat jetty on VCSB (Boat Jetty) Rd; see the boxed text, p268.

Bus
From the KSRTC bus stand, frequent buses head to Trivandrum (₹97, 3½ hours, every 20 minutes), Kollam (₹54) and Ernakulam (Kochi, ₹39, 1½ hours). Buses to Kottayam (₹30, 1¼ hours, every 30 minutes) are much faster than the ferry. One bus daily leaves for Kumily at 6.40am (₹110, 5½ hours). The Varkala bus (₹97, 3½ hours) leaves at 10.40am daily.

Train
There are several trains to Ernakulam (2nd class/AC chair ₹59/202, 1½ hours) and Trivandrum (₹59/202, three hours) via Kollam (₹45/165, 1½ hours). Four trains a day stop at Varkala (2nd class/AC chair ₹50/178, two hours). The train station is 4km west of town.

ℹ Getting Around
An autorickshaw from the train station to the boat jetty and KSRTC bus stand is around ₹50. Several guesthouses around town hire out scooters for ₹200 per day.

Around Alleppey

Kerala's backwaters snake in all directions from Alleppey and, while touring on a houseboat is a great experience, taking time to slow down and stay in a village can be just as rewarding.

Just 10km from Alleppey, **Green Palms Homes** (☎0477-2724497; www.greenpalmshomes. com; Chennamkary; r without bathroom incl full board ₹2250, r ₹3250-4000) is a series of homestays that seem a universe away, set in a picturesque backwater village, where you will sleep in basic rooms in villagers' homes among rice paddies. It's splendidly quiet, there are no roads in sight and you can take a guided walk (₹200), hire bicycles (₹50 per hour) and canoes (₹100 per hour) or take cooking classes with your hosts (₹150). Book ahead.

To get here, call ahead and catch one of the hourly ferries from Alleppey to Chennamkary (₹5, 1¼ hours). Please remember this is a traditional village; dress appropriately.

Kottayam

☎0481 / POP 172,867

Sandwiched between the Western Ghats and the backwaters, Kottayam is renowned for being the centre of Kerala's spice and rubber trade rather than for its aesthetic appeal. For most travellers it's a hub town, well connected to both the mountains and the backwaters.

Kottayam has a bookish history: the first Malayalam-language printing press was established here in 1820, and this was the first district in India to achieve 100% literacy. A place of churches and seminaries, it was a refuge for the Orthodox church when the Portuguese began forcing Keralan Christians to switch to Catholicism in the 16th century.

The **Thirunakkara Utsavam festival** is held in March at the Thirunakkara Shiva Temple.

🛏 Sleeping

Accommodation options are pretty dire in Kottayam – you're better off heading to Kumarakon for some great top-end hotels. Also try checking for homestays at the **DTPC office** (☎2560479), which range from basic (₹1000 per person full board) to deluxe (up to US$100).

Homestead Hotel　　　　　　HOTEL $
(☎2560467; KK Rd; s/d from ₹350/548, d with AC ₹1500; ❄) Easily the pick of the budget lit-

ter, this place has painstakingly maintained rooms in a blissfully quiet building off the street. The foyer sports '60s-style decor that's accidentally stumbled into vogue again, and Thali and Meenachil restaurants are right out the front. Book ahead.

Windsor Castle　　　　　　HOTEL $$$
(☎2363637; www.thewindsorcastle.net; MC Rd; s/d from US$80/100, cottages US$155; ❄❄) This grandiose carbuncle has some of the better rooms in Kottayam – spacious and with bathtubs, and some with attractive river views, but overpriced. You may as well go for the deluxe dark wood-furnished cottages, strewn around the private backwaters. There's a pleasant restaurant overlooking landscaped waterways.

Pearl Regency　　　　　　HOTEL $$
(☎2561123; www.pearlregencyktm.com; TB Junction, MC Rd; s/d from ₹1900/2200; ❄@) This business-focused contender has roomy-but-dull, comfily inoffensive abodes. It's efficient, decent value, and a passable stay if you're stuck in Kottayam.

Ambassador Hotel　　　　　　HOTEL $
(☎2563293; KK Rd; www.fhrai.com; s/d from ₹376/550) A respectable budget sleeping option, the rooms here are spartan but fairly clean, spacious and quiet. It has a bakery, bar, an adequate restaurant, and a boat-shaped fish tank in the lobby.

✖ Eating

Thali　　　　　　SOUTH INDIAN $
(1st fl, KK Rd; meals ₹53-63; ☺8am-8.30pm) A lovely, spotlessly kept 1st-floor room, with slatted blinds, this place is a swankier version of the typical Keralan set-meal place. The food here is great, including Malabar fish curry (₹45) and thalis (₹70-85).

Meenachil　　　　　　MULTICUISINE $
(2nd fl, KK Rd; dishes ₹60-110; ☺noon-3pm & 6-10pm) This is our favourite place in Kottayam to fill up on scrumptious Indian and Chinese fare. The family atmosphere is friendly, the dining room modern and tidy and the menu expansive.

Nalekattu　　　　　　SOUTH INDIAN $$
(Windsor Hotel; MC Rd; dishes ₹140-190; ☺lunch & dinner) The traditional Keralan restaurant at the Windsor Castle overlooks some neat backwaters and serves tasty Keralan specialities like *chemeen* (mango curry) and *tharavu mappas* (duck in coconut gravy). There's also a recommended buffet at ₹249.

Hotel Suryaas INDIAN $

(Baker Junction, SB Rd; dishes ₹38-50; ⊙8am-10pm) It's no surprise this dark and cosy, vintage wood-lined dining room is packed to the rafters with hungry families come mealtime – the North and South Indian food here is excellent.

Indian Coffee House CAFE $

(TB Rd) We just can't get enough of this South Indian institution serving the whole gamut of tasty Indian snacks.

ℹ Information

The KSRTC bus stand is 1km south of the centre; the boat jetty is a further 2km (at Kodimatha). The train station is 1km north of Kottayam. There's a handful of ATMs around.

DTPC office (☎2560479; dtpcktm@sanchar-net.in; ⊙10am-5pm Mon-Sat) At the boat jetty.

UAE Exchange (☎2303865; 1st fl, MC Rd; ⊙9.30am-6pm Mon-Sat, 9.30am-1pm Sun) Changes cash and travellers cheques.

ℹ Getting There & Away

Boat

Ferries run to Alleppey; see the boxed text, p268.

Bus

The **KSRTC bus stand** has buses to Trivandrum (₹93, four hours, every 20 minutes), Alleppey (₹31, 1¼ hours, every 30 minutes) and Ernakulam (Kochi, ₹42, two hours, every 20 minutes). There are also frequent buses to nearby Kumarakom (₹8, 30 minutes, every 15 minutes), to Thrissur (ordinary ₹79, four hours), Calicut (₹162, seven hours, 13 daily), Kumily for Periyar Wildlife Sanctuary (₹69, four hours, every 30 minutes) and Munnar (₹100, five hours, five daily). There are also buses to Kollam (₹60, four daily) and Varkala (₹78, three hours).

Train

Kottayam is well served by frequent trains running between Trivandrum (2nd class/AC chair ₹62/214, 3½ hours) and Ernakulam (₹40/165, 1½ hours).

ℹ Getting Around

An autorickshaw from the jetty to the KSRTC bus stand is around ₹30, and from the bus stand to the train station about ₹20. Most trips around town cost ₹20.

Around Kottayam

KUMARAKOM
☎0481

Kumarakom, 16km west of Kottayam and on the shore of Vembanad Lake, is an unhurried backwater town with a smattering of dazzling top-end sleeping options. You can arrange houseboats through Kumarakom's less-crowded canals, but expect to pay considerably more than in Alleppey.

Arundhati Roy, author of the 1997 Booker Prize-winning *The God of Small Things,* was raised in the nearby Aymanam village.

◉ Sights & Activities

Kumarakom Bird Sanctuary NATURE RESERVE
(Indian/foreigner ₹5/45; ⊙6am-6pm) This reserve on the 5-hectare site of a former rubber plantation is the haunt of a variety of domestic and migratory birds. October to February is the time for travelling birds like the garganey teal, osprey, marsh harrier and steppey eagle; May to July is the breeding season for local species such as the Indian shag, pond herons, egrets and darters. Early morning is the best viewing time.

Buses between Kottayam's KSRTC stand and Kumarakom (₹8, 30 minutes, every 15 minutes) stop at the entrance to the sanctuary.

⊨ Sleeping

Cruise 'N Lake RESORT $$
(☎2525804; www.homestaykumarakom.com; Puthenpura Tourist Enclave; r ₹1000-1500, with AC ₹1500-2000; ❀) As any estate agent will tell you, it's all about location, location, location. Crowning the tip of a small peninsula surrounded by backwaters on one side and a lawn of rice paddies on the other, this is the ideal affordable getaway. The rooms are plain, but it's lovely and secluded out here, surrounded by bucolic villages where houseboats are made by hand. To get to it, go several kilometres past the sanctuary and take a left, it's then 2km down a dirt road. Management can arrange pick-ups from Kottayam, and houseboats are available from here.

Coconut Lagoon RESORT $$$
(☎0484-3011711; www.cghearth.com; r incl breakfast & tax from ₹13,000; ❀@☒) Spread languidly over 9 hectares of grounds, this luxurious resort offers the ultimate in seclusion: it's accessible only by private boat. Surrounded by backwaters and with perfect sunsets guaranteed, the different *tharawad* (ancestral home) cottages on offer here are variously filled with polished wood, classy antique-style furnishings and neat open-air bathrooms. This place might be familiar to those who have read Arundhati Roy's *The God of Small Things.*

Tharavadu Heritage Home GUESTHOUSE $$$
(☏2525230; www.tharavaduheritage.com; r from ₹1200, with AC ₹2000; ❄) Tharavadu means 'large family house', an apt description. Rooms are either in the superbly restored 1870s teak family mansion or in equally comfortable individual creekside cottages. All abodes are excellently crafted and come with arty touches – some have glistening teak beams while others have big bay windows and relaxing patios. It's 4km before the bird sanctuary.

ETTUMANUR

The **Shiva Temple** at Ettumanur, 12km north of Kottayam, has inscriptions dating from 1542, but parts of the building may be even older. The temple is noted for its exceptional woodcarvings and murals similar to those at Kochi's Mattancherry Palace. The annual **festival**, involving exposition of the idol (Shiva in his fierce form) and elephant processions, is held in February/March.

SREE VALLABHA TEMPLE

Devotees make offerings at this temple, 2km from Tiruvilla, in the form of traditional, regular all-night **Kathakali** performances that are open to all. Tiruvilla, 35km south of Kottayam, is on the rail route between Ernakulam and Trivandrum. Around 10km east of here, the **Aranmula Boat Race** is held in August/September.

THE WESTERN GHATS

Periyar Wildlife Sanctuary

☏04869
South India's most popular wildlife sanctuary, **Periyar** (☏224571; www.periyartigerreserve.org; Indian/foreigner ₹25/300; ⊙6am-6pm) encompasses 777 sq km and a 26-sq-km artificial lake created by the British in 1895. The vast region is home to bison, sambar, wild boar, langur, 900 to 1000 elephants and 35 to 40 tigers. Firmly established on both the Indian and foreigner tourist trails, the place can sometimes feel a bit like Disneyland-in-the-Ghats, but its mountain scenery and jungle walks make for an enjoyable visit. Bring warm and waterproof clothing.

Kumily, 4km from the sanctuary, is a growing strip of hotels, spice shops and Kashmiri emporiums. Thekkady is the sanctuary centre with the KTDC hotels and boat jetty. Confusingly, when people refer to the sanctuary they tend to use Kumily, Thekkady and Periyar interchangeably.

◉ Sights & Activities

Various tours and trips enable you to visit the Periyar Wildlife Sanctuary. Most hotels and agencies around town can arrange all-day 4WD **Jungle Safaris** (per person ₹1600-2000; ⊙5am-6.30pm), which cover over 40km of trails in jungle bordering the park. Tours include meals as well as a paddleboat trip.

You can arrange **elephant rides** (per 30min ₹350) at most hotels and agents in town. If you want the extended elephant experience, you can pay ₹2500 for a 2½-hour ride that includes elephant feeding and cleaning. **Cooking classes** (around ₹250) are offered by many local homestays.

Forest Department boats BOATING
(per adult/child ₹40/20; ⊙departures 7.30am, 10am, 11.30am, 1.30pm & 3.30pm) These smaller, more decrepit boats offer a chance to get a bit closer to the animals than on KTDC trips, and are driven by sanctuary workers who may offer commentary. Entry to the park doesn't guarantee a place on the boat; get to the **ticket office** (⊙6.30am-4pm) 1½ hours before each trip to buy tickets. The first and last departures offer the best prospects for wildlife spotting, and October to March are generally the best times to see animals.

KTDC boat trips BOATING
(lower/upper deck ₹75/150) ⊙departures 2hr tours 7.30am & 3.30pm, 1hr tours 10am, 7am, 11.30am & 1.30pm) One- or two-hour trips around the lake are the usual way of touring the sanctuary. They can be enjoyable, though often packed, rowdy and not ideal for wildlife-spotting.

Ecotourism Centre OUTDOOR ADVENTURES
(☏224571; www.periyartigerresereve.org; Thekkady Rd; ⊙9am-5pm) A number of more adventurous explorations of the park can be arranged by the Ecotourism Centre, run by the Forest Department. These include border hikes (₹750; 8am to 5pm), three-hour elevated cloud walks (₹200), 4 to 5km nature walks (₹100), full-day bamboo rafting (₹1000) and 'jungle patrols' (₹500), which cover 4 to 5km and are the best way to experience the park close up, accompanied by a trained tribal guide. Trips usually require a minimum of four or five people. There are also two-day 'tiger trail' treks (per person ₹3000, solo ₹5000), which are run by former poachers and cover 20 to 30km. On any of the tours, you can request special birdwatching guides.

Spice Gardens & Plantations GARDENS

Interesting spice tours cost around ₹450/750 by autorickshaw/taxi (two to three hours) and can be arranged by most hotels. If you want to see a tea factory in operation, do it from here – tea-factory visits are not permitted in Munnar.

If you'd rather do a spice tour independently, you can visit a few excellent gardens outside Kumily. The one-hectare **Abraham's Spice Garden** (222919; tours ₹100; 7am-6.30pm) has been going for 56 years. **Highrange Spices** (222117; tours ₹100; 7am-6pm), 3km from Kumily, has 4 hectares where you can see ayurvedic herbs and vegetables growing. A rickshaw to either spice garden and back will be around ₹250. About 13km away from Kumily is a working **tea plantation** (8am-5pm) where you can wander around the grounds and see displays of the tea-making process for free.

Santhigiri Ayurveda AYURVEDA

(223979; Vandanmedu Junction) An excellent and authentic place for the ayurvedic experience, offering top-notch massage (₹650 to ₹1500), sirovasthi (₹1200) and long-term treatments lasting seven to 14 days.

🛏 Sleeping

INSIDE THE SANCTUARY

The Ecotourism Centre can arrange park accommodation in a basic **tent/bamboo cottage** (d incl breakfast ₹1000/1500), and the KTDC runs three steeply priced hotels in the park. It's a good idea to make reservations (at any KTDC office), particularly for weekends. Note that there's effectively a curfew at these places – guests are not permitted to roam the sanctuary after 6pm.

Lake Palace HOTEL $$$

(223888; www.ktdc.com; r incl all meals ₹16,000-25,000) Located on an island in the middle of the Periyar Lake, this is the best value of the government hotels inside the park. It is a stunningly restored old palace that has six charismatic rooms, all decorated with flair using antique furnishings and a selection of modern conveniences (like flat-screen TVs). Staying in the midst of the sanctuary gives you the best chance of seeing wildlife, from your private terrace. Transport is by boat across the lake.

KUMILY

Green View Homestay HOMESTAY $$

(224617; www.sureshgreenview.com; Bypass Rd; r incl breakfast ₹600-1750) Grown from its

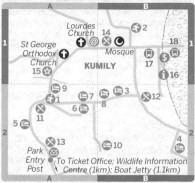

Kumily & Periyar Wildlife Sanctuary

humble homestay origins to be practically hotel-size today, Greenview is a smashing place that manages to retain its personal and friendly family welcome, and continues to get rave reviews. The buildings house several classes of immaculately maintained rooms with private balconies, bamboo or wood furniture and loads of greenery. Vegetarian **meals** (₹65) and **cooking lessons** (₹250) are available.

Claus Garden HOMESTAY $$

(222320; www.homestay.in; r ₹800-1000) Set well away from the hustle and bustle, this lovely big building has gently curving balconies, warm, bright colours in spades, and is surrounded by a lush green garden. The excellent rooms are spacious and have neat touches like colourful blankets, rugs, and artwork. Two doubles sharing one bathroom would be an ideal family choice (₹2000). Top value.

Spice Village HOTEL $$$

(0484-3011711; crs@cghearth.com; Thekkady Rd; villas ₹12,000-22,000;) This place has captivating, spacious cottages that are smart yet cosily rustic, in pristinely kept grounds. Its restaurant does lavish lunch and dinner buffets (₹1000 each) and you can find the **Wildlife Interpretation Centre** (7.30am-9.30pm) here, which has a resident naturalist showing slides and answering questions about the park.

Mickey Homestay GUESTHOUSE $

(223196; www.mickeyhomestay.com; Bypass Rd; r ₹350-850) Mickey has just a handful of intimate rooms in a family house, all with homely touches that make them some of the most comfortable in town. Balconies have rattan furniture and hanging bamboo seats and the whole place is surrounded by greenery.

Chrissie's Hotel   GUESTHOUSE **$$**
(☎224155; www.chrissies.in; Bypass Rd; r ₹1600-2000) This four-storey building behind the popular expat-run restaurant of the same name somehow manages to blend in with the forest-green surrounds. The chic rooms are spacious and bright, with cheery furnishings, lamps and colourful pillows – the more expensive ones, with balconies, are much better than the cheaper ground-floor options.

Coffee Inn   GUESTHOUSE **$**
(☎222763; coffeeinn@sancharnet.in; Thekkady Rd; huts ₹250-700, r from ₹1000) With rustic bamboo huts, tree houses and cottages in a garden overlooking the sanctuary, Coffee Inn has swankier digs in its main building, where the wood-lined rooms have a cosy, characterful feel, several offering balconies with sweeping views. However, some readers say the rooms can be musty.

Tranquilou   HOMESTAY **$$**
(☎223269; Bypass Rd; r ₹1000-1200;@) Friendly family homestay huddled among some hush; the two doubles that adjoin a shared sitting room are a good family option.

El-Paradiso   HOMESTAY **$$**
(☎222350; www.goelparadiso.com; Bypass Rd; r ₹1250;@) This family homestay has fresh rooms, with balconies with hanging

chairs, or opening onto a terrace overlooking greenery at the back.

Eating

There are plenty of good cheap veg restaurants in the bazaar area.

Periyar Cafe   INDIAN **$**
(meals ₹40-140) Painted in kindergarten-bright colours and papered with zinging advertisements, this cheery diner serves up loads of North and South Indian dishes at sensible prices. Near the park entrance, it's perfect for an early breakfast or quick lunch between animal-spotting trips.

Chrissie's Cafe   MULTICUISINE **$$**
(Bypass Rd; snacks ₹50-80, meals ₹110-180) A perennially popular haunt, this airy 1st-floor cafe satisfies travellers with cakes and snacks, excellent coffee, and well-prepared Western faves like pizza and pasta.

Ebony's Cafe   MULTICUISINE **$**
(Bypass Rd; meals ₹70-100) This small, friendly 1st-floor joint serves up a tasty assortment of Indian and Western food with a smile and a background of traveller-friendly music.

Shri Krishna   INDIAN **$**
(Bypass Rd; meals ₹35-85) A great local favourite, serving up spicy pure veg meals including several takes on thali.

Coffee Inn   MULTICUISINE **$$**
(meals ₹75-200) This laid-back restaurant serves just a few Indian and Western meals. The food is reasonable and the spice-garden setting is nice, but be warned, it can take a while to arrive: bring a book.

Ambadi Restaurant INDIAN $$
(dishes ₹80-100) At the hotel of the same name, this popular place serves OK North and South Indian dishes (more importantly, Kingfisher beer, ₹100) in a smart, breezy indoor dining room.

☆ Entertainment

Kerala Cultural Centre CULTURAL PROGRAM
(☑9446072901; admission ₹150) For **Kathakali** performances, visit this centre, which comprises the Mudra Kathakali Centre, for shows at 4.30pm and 7pm (make-up starts 30 minutes before each show; visitors can attend and it's very photogenic), and the Kerala Kalari Centre, for hour-long **Kalaripayattu demonstrations** (admission ₹200) at 6pm daily.

❶ Information

DTPC office (☑222620; ⊙10am-5pm Mon-Sat) Behind the bus stand, not as useful as the Ecotourism Centre.
Ecotourism Centre (☑224571; ⊙9am-5pm) For park tours and walks.
Kumily Internet (☑222170; Thekkady Junction; per hr ₹40; ⊙9am-9.30pm)
State Bank of Travancore (⊙10am-3.30pm Mon-Fri, to 12.30pm Sat) Changes travellers cheques and currency; has an ATM accepting foreign cards.
Wildlife Information Centre (☑222028; ⊙6am-6pm) Above the boat jetty in Thekkady.

❶ Getting There & Away

Buses originating or terminating at Periyar start and finish at Aranya Nivas, but they also stop at the Kumily bus stand, at the eastern edge of town.

Eight buses daily operate between Ernakulam (Kochi) and Kumily (₹110, five hours). Buses leave every 30 minutes for Kottayam (₹69, four hours), with two direct buses to Trivandrum at 8.45am and 11am (₹145, eight hours) and one daily bus to Alleppey at 1.10pm (₹85, 5½ hours).

Tamil Nadu buses leave every 30 minutes to Madurai (₹42-56, four hours) from the Tamil Nadu bus stand just over the border.

❶ Getting Around

Kumily is about 4km from Periyar Lake; you can catch the bus (almost as rare as the tigers), take an autorickshaw (₹40) or set off on foot; it's a pleasant, shady walk into the park. **Bicycle hire** is available from many guesthouses.

Munnar

☑04865 / ELEV 1524M / POP 68,000
Wander just a few kilometres outside the scruffy little hill station of Munnar and you'll be engulfed in a sea of a thousand shades of green. The lolling hills all around are covered by a sculptural carpet of tea-trees, and the mountain scenery is magnificent – you're often up above the clouds, watching veils of mist cling below the mountaintops. Once known as the High Range of Travancore, today Munnar is the commercial centre of some of the world's highest tea-growing estates.

◉ Sights & Activities

The main reason to be in Munnar is to explore the lush, tea-filled hillocks that surround it. Hotels, homestays, travel agencies, autorickshaw drivers and practically every passer-by will want to organise a day of sightseeing for you: shop around.

Tata Tea Museum MUSEUM
(☑230561; adult/child ₹75/35; ⊙10am-4pm Tue-Sun) Located around 1.5km north of town, this museum is, unfortunately, about as close as you'll get to a working tea factory around Munnar. It's a slightly sanitised version of the real thing, but it still shows the basic process. A collection of old bits and pieces from the colonial era, including photographs and a 1905 tea-roller, are also kept here. The short walk to here from town is lovely, passing some of the most accessible tea plantations from Munnar town.

☞ Tours

The DTPC runs a couple of fairly rushed full-day tours to points around Munnar. The **Sandal Valley Tour** (per person ₹350; ⊙9am-6pm) visits Chinnar Wildlife Sanctuary, several viewpoints, waterfalls, plantations, a sandalwood forest and villages. The **Tea Valley tour** (per person ₹300; ⊙10am-6pm) visits Echo Point, Top Station and Rajamalai (for Eravikulam National Park), among other places. You can hire a day's taxi to visit the main local sights for around ₹1100 – there's a taxi office in Munnar.

⊨ Sleeping

The best options are mostly outside Munnar town centre.

AROUND TOWN

TOP CHOICE **Zina Cottages** HOMESTAY $
(☑230349; r incl tax ₹800-1000) On the outskirts of town but immersed in lush tea plantations, the 10 rooms in this hospitable homestay are an outstanding deal. Frilly touches in the rooms and stunning vistas

Munnar

come as standard, as do the local information and hospitable cups of tea provided by the legendary Mr Iype, from the Tourist Information Service, who has been name-checked in travel books by Devla Murphy and Bill Aitken. However, wild boars mean going out for a wander after 7pm is a no-no.

JJ Cottage   HOMESTAY **$**

(☎230104;jjcottagemunnar@sancharnet.in;d₹350-800) The mothering family at this superb place will go out of its way to make sure your stay is comfortable. The varied and uncomplicated rooms are ruthlessly clean, bright and have TV and geysers. The one deluxe room has frilly pink curtains and sweeping views.

Green View   GUESTHOUSE **$**

(☎230940; greenview_munnar@sify.com; d ₹400-600) With a friendly welcome, this tidy house next door to JJ Cottage has fresh budget rooms. And the young owner is setting up a new place – **Green Woods Anachal** (d ₹750) outside Munnar that's a budget option out in the tea plantations; there are four rooms.

Westwood Riverside Resort   RESORT **$$$**

(☎230884-6; www.westwoodmunnar.com; Alwaye-Munnar (AM) Rd; r incl breakfast & dinner ₹3000-5000) It doesn't appear promising from outside, but inside is surprisingly nice, with lots of polished wood floors, heartfelt murals on the walls, and rooms that are plain, spotless and inviting – the pick have river views.

Kaippallil Homestay   GUESTHOUSE **$**

(☎230203; www.kaippallil.com; r ₹200-600) Up the hill and away from (most of) the clatter of the bazaar, Kaippallil is the best budget

bet in town, though by no means a 'homestay'. A new part to the building is unfinished, giving it a half-built look, but the rooms are reasonably clean and have balconies and sweeping views. Two basic but characterful small rooms in a neighbouring cottage are the cheapest option.

MUNNAR HILLS

TOP CHOICE **Rose Gardens**   HOMESTAY **$$$**

(☎04864-278243; www.rosegardens.com; NH49 Rd, Karadipara; r ₹3500) Around 10km south of Munnar. Despite its handy location on the main road, with good bus connections, this is a peaceful spot overlooking Tomy's idyllic plant nursery, with over 240 types of plants. Rooms are large and comfortable, and the family are charming. Rajee's home cooking is delicious, the coffee home-grown, the honey from their hives. Cooking lessons are free, including fresh coconut pancakes for breakfast and delicately spiced Keralan dishes for dinner.

Dew Drops   GUESTHOUSE **$$**

(☎0484-2216455; wilsonhomes2003@yahoo.co.in, www.dewdropsmunnar.com; Kallar; r incl breakfast ₹1200) Set in the thick forest around 20km south of Munnar, this fantastic, remote place lies on 97 hectares of spice plantation and farmland. The resplendent building is expertly constructed, with seven bright, simple rooms. Each room has a veranda on which you can sit and enjoy the hush, and the small restaurant has expansive views. The peace here is zen. It's 20km from Munnar; call for a pick-up (₹50 per person).

British County
GUESTHOUSE $$

(☎2371761; touristdesk@satyam.net.in; ET City Rd, Anachal person full board ₹2000) Around 11km southeast of Munnar, with its veranda facing a stunning panorama, this appealing little guesthouse has two nice fresh rooms with views. There's a simple little treehouse for rent too, and steps lead down into the valley. A taxi from Munnar will cost ₹400. This is the overnight base for the Tourist Desk's Munnar Hillstation Tour from Kochi.

Bracknell Forest
GUESTHOUSE $$$

(☎231555; www.bracknellforestmunnar.com; Ottamaram; r ₹5000; ☏) A remote-feeling 9.5km south of Munnar, this place houses neat, handsome rooms with balconies and great views overlooking a lush valley. It's surrounded by deep forest on all sides. Breakfast and a few hours trekking are included; meals cost ₹350 – the small restaurant has wraparound views. A transfer from Munnar costs ₹400.

Windermere Estate
RESORT $$$

(☎reservations 0484-2425237; www.windermere munnar.com; Pothamedu; AC r ₹6900-14,800; ✺) Windermere is a boutique-meets-country-retreat 4km south of Windermere. There are farmhouse rooms and newer, swankier cottages with spectacular views, surrounded by shush and 26 hectares of cardamom and coffee plantations. Book ahead.

✕ Eating

Early-morning food stalls in the bazaar serve breakfast snacks and cheap meals.

SN Annexe
INDIAN $$

(AM Rd; meals ₹55-130; ⊘7am-10pm) SN restaurant's little sis has a nice deep-orange look with slatted blinds at the windows. It's madly popular with families for its great range of thalis: take your pick from special, Rajasthani, Gujarati, Punjabi and more, plus a dazzling array of veg dishes.

Eastend
INDIAN $$

(Temple Rd; dishes ₹120-170; ⊘noon-3.30pm & 6.30-10.30pm) In the same-named hotel, this frilly-curtained, smartish place is the best place in town to head for nonveg Indian dishes, with Chinese, North and South Indian and Kerala specialities on the menu.

Royal Retreat
INDIAN $

(Kannan Devan Hills; www.royalretreat.co.in; dishes ₹50-75; ⊘7am-9.30pm) This longstanding favourite has reliably tasty and fresh Indian

cooking served in nicely twee rooms with checked tablecloths, in a hotel set amid gardens. Try specialities such as Alleppey fish curry and *bhindi masala* (okra curry).

Rapsy Restaurant
INDIAN $

(Bazaar; dishes ₹30-80; ⊘6am-10pm) This hole-in-the-wall is packed at lunchtime, with locals lining up for Rapsy's famous *paratha* or biryani (from ₹40). It also makes a decent stab at fancy international dishes like Spanish omelette and Israeli *shakshuka* (scrambled eggs with tomatoes and spices).

SN Restaurant
INDIAN $

(AM Rd; meals ₹35-90; ⊘6am-10pm) Just south of the tourist office, SN is a cheery place with an attractive red interior, which seems to be perpetually full of people digging into masala dosas (₹35) and other Indian veg and nonveg dishes.

❶ Information

There are ATMs near the bridge, south of the bazaar.

DTPC Tourist Information Office (☎231516; Alway-Munnar Rd; ⊘8.30am-7pm) Marginally helpful.

Forest Information Centre (☎231587; enpmunnar@sify.com; ⊘8am-5pm)

Olivia Communications (per hr ₹35; ⊘9am-10.30pm) Surprisingly fast internet.

State Bank of Travancore (☎230274; ⊘10am-3.30pm Mon-Sat, to noon Sun) Has an ATM.

Tourist Information Service (☎230349, 9447190954) Joseph Iype is a walking Swiss-army knife of Munnar information – he no longer has an office in town, but will supply information on trekking, taxis and so on, if you call.

❶ Getting There & Away

Roads around Munnar are in poor condition and can be affected by monsoon rains, so bus times may vary. The main **KSRTC bus station** (AM Rd) is south of town, but it's best to catch buses from stands in Munnar town (where more frequent private buses also depart).

There are around 10 buses a day to Ernakulam (Kochi, ₹80, 5½ hours) and a few services to Kottayam (₹85/101 ordinary/super fast, five hours), and Trivandrum (₹191, nine hours).

❶ Getting Around

DTPC rents out bicycles for ₹15/150 per hour/day. **Gokulam Bike Hire** (☎9447237165; per day ₹250; ⊘7.30am-7pm) has several motorbikes for hire, as does SN Restaurant (per day ₹250).

Autorickshaws ply the hills around Munnar with bone-shuddering efficiency; they charge up to ₹650 for a full day's sightseeing.

Around Munnar

ERAVIKULAM NATIONAL PARK

Sixteen kilometres from Munnar, **Eravikulam National Park** (Indian/foreigner ₹15/200; ⊗8am-5pm Mar-Dec) is home to the endangered, but almost tame, Nilgiri tahr (a type of mountain goat). From Munnar, an autorickshaw/taxi costs ₹250/500 return; a government bus takes you the final 4km from the checkpoint (₹20).

CHINNAR WILDLIFE SANCTUARY

About 10km past Marayoor and 60km northeast of Munnar, this **wildlife sanctuary** (www.chinnar.org; Indian/foreigner ₹10/100, camera/video ₹25/150; ⊗7am-6pm) hosts deer, leopards, elephants and the endangered grizzled giant squirrel. **Trekking** (3hr trek ₹150) and **tree house** (s/d ₹1000/1250) or **hut** (s/d ₹1500/1800) accommodation within the sanctuary are available, as well as eco-tour programs like river-trekking, cultural visits, and waterfall treks (around ₹150). For details contact the Forest Information Centre in Munnar. Buses from Munnar can drop you off at Chinnar (₹35, 1½ hours), or taxi hire for the day will cost around ₹1100.

TOP STATION

Come here, on Kerala's border with Tamil Nadu, for spectacular views over the Western Ghats. From Munnar, four daily buses (₹35, from 7.30am, 1½ hours) make the steep 32km climb in around an hour, or you could book a return taxi (₹750).

THATTEKKAD BIRD SANCTUARY

A serene 25-sq-km park in the foothills of the West Ghats, cut through by two rivers and two streams, **Thattekkad Bird Sanctuary** (☎0485-2588302; Indian/foreigner ₹10/100, camera/video ₹25/150; ⊗6.30am-6pm) is home to over 320 fluttering species – unusual in that they are forest, rather than water birds – including Malabar grey hornbills, Ripley owl, jungle nightjar, grey drongo, darters and rarer species like the Sri Lankan frogmouth. There are kingfishers, flycatchers, warblers, sunbirds and flower peckers (who weigh only 4g). There's lots of other wildlife, including the occasional elephant, leopard, bear, snakes (including cobras), sambar monkey and flying squirrels, and 120 species of butterflies. You can arrange two- or three-hour **treks** (up to 5/10 people per person ₹500/250). To stay in the **Treetop Machan** (Indian/Foreigner dm ₹80/150, d incl meals ₹1500-2500) in the sanctuary, contact the **assistant wildlife warden** (☎0485-2588302) at Kothamangalam. Another option is the **homestay** (☎9947506188; per person incl meals ₹750) of the enthusiastic Ms Sudah.

For more luxury, visit the lovely **Birds Lagoon Resort** (☎0485-2572444; www.birds lagoon.com; Palamatton, Thattekkad; s/d incl breakfast €60/70, with AC from €65/75; ✴❄). Set deep in the villages near Thattekkad, this low-key resort lies on a seasonal lake among spacious and manicured grounds. The basic rooms here are roomy and comfy, with lots of wood trim and lamp lighting. The whole place feels refreshingly remote and is particularly popular with visiting ornithologists. It's 16km from Kothamangalam. There's also the tented **Hornbill Camp** (☎0484 2092280; www.thehornbillcamp.com; d full board ₹5000) with accommodation in large permanent tents, in a sublimely peaceful location, cooled by fans and facing the Periyar River. Kayaking, cycling and a spice-garden tour are included in the price. It's around 8km from Thattekkad by road.

Thattekkad is on the Ernakulam-Munnar road. Take a direct bus from either Ernakulam (₹29, two hours) or Munnar (₹50, three hours) to Kothamangalam, from where a Thattekkad bus travels the final 12km (₹6, 25 minutes).

Parambikulam Wildlife Sanctuary

Possibly the most protected environment in South India – it's nestled behind three dams in a valley surrounded by Keralan and Tamil Nadu sanctuaries – **Parambikulam Wildlife Sanctuary** (www.parambikulam.org; Indian/foreigner ₹10/100, video/camera ₹100/25; ⊗7am-6pm) constitutes 285 sq km of Kipling-storybook scenery and wildlife-spotting goodness. It's home to elephants, bison, gaur, sloths, sambar, crocodiles, tigers, panthers and some of the largest teak trees in Asia. The sanctuary is best avoided during monsoon (June to August) and it sometimes closes in March and April.

Contact the **Ecocare Centre** (☎04253-245025) in Palakkad to arrange tours of the park, **hikes** (1-/2-day trek ₹3000/6000) and stays on the reservoir's freshwater island (r ₹5000). There are 150 beds in **tree-top huts** (from ₹2500) throughout the park; book through the ecocare centre. Boating or rafting costs ₹600 for one hour.

You have to enter the park from Pollachi (40km from Coimbatore and 49km from Palakkad in Tamil Nadu. There are at least two buses in either direction between Pollachi and Parambikulam via Annamalai daily (₹15, 1½ hours). The nearest train station is Coimbatore, Tamil Nadu, from where you can board buses to Pollachi.

CENTRAL KERALA

Kochi (Cochin)

☏ 0484 / POP 1.36 MILLION

Serene Kochi has been drawing traders and explorers to its shores for over 600 years. Nowhere in India could you find such a mix: giant fishing nets from China, a 400-year-old synagogue, ancient mosques, Portuguese houses, and crumbling remains of the British Raj. The result is an unlikely blend of medieval Portugal, Holland and an English village grafted onto the tropical Malabar Coast. It's a delightful place to spend some time and nap in some of India's finest heritage accommodation.

Mainland Ernakulam is the hectic transport and cosmopolitan hub of Kochi, while the historical towns of Fort Cochin and Mattancherry remain wonderfully serene – thick with the smell of the past.

While you're here, the perfect read is Salman Rushdie's the *Moor's Last Sigh,* which bases much action around Mattancherry and the Synagogue.

◉ Sights

FORT COCHIN

TOP CHOICE **Mattancherry Palace** PALACE

(Map p284; Dutch Palace; ☏ 2226085; Bazaar Rd; admission ₹5; ◷8am-5pm) Admission is a bargain to this interesting building. Presented by the Portuguese in 1555, Mattancherry Palace was a generous gift presented to the Raja of Kochi, Veera Kerala Varma (1537–61), as a gesture of goodwill. More probably, it was a used as a sweetener to securing trading privileges. The Dutch renovated the palace in 1663, hence its alternative name, the Dutch Palace.

The star attractions here are the astonishingly preserved Hindu **murals**, depicting scenes from the Ramayana, Mahabharata and Puranic legends in intricate detail. The central hall on the 1st floor is now a portrait gallery of maharajas from 1864. There's an impressive collection of palanquins (hand-carried carriages), bejewelled outfits and splendidly carved ceilings in every room. The ladies' bedchamber downstairs features a cheerful, impressively multitasking Krishna, using his eight hands and two feet to engage in foreplay with eight happy milkmaids, whilst also managing to play the flute. Photography is prohibited.

TOP CHOICE **Kerala Folklore Museum** MUSEUM

(☏ 0484-2665452; Folklore Junction, Thevara; admission ₹200; ◷9.30am-7pm) This incredible place is well worth the journey – on the southeast outskirts of Ernakulam. It's a private museum created from ancient temples and beautiful old houses collected by its owner, an antique dealer, over three years. It includes over 5000 artefacts and covers three architectural styles: Malabar on the ground floor, Kochi on the 1st, Travanbur on the 2nd. There are 3000-year-old burial urns *'nannangadi'*, in which people were buried in the foetal position, and *Where the Wild Things Are*–style masks carved from jack-fruit trees. Upstairs is a beautiful wood-lined theatre, with a 17th-century wooden ceiling, where **performances** (Indian/foreigner ₹100/350; ◷6.30-8pm Sep-Mar) take place nightly. A rickshaw here should cost ₹70, or you can take any bus to Thivara from where it's a ₹20 rickshaw ride. An autorickshaw from Fort Cochin will cost ₹150.

Look out for the owner's new cultural museum, which is due to open in Mattancherry in a vast old godown (warehouse) close to the synagogue.

TOP CHOICE **Pardesi Synagogue & Jew Town** SYNAGOGUE

(Map p284; admission ₹5; ◷10am-1pm & 3-5pm Sun-Thu, closed Jewish hols) Originally built in 1568, this synagogue was partially destroyed by the Portuguese in 1662, and rebuilt two years later when the Dutch took Kochi. It features an ornate gold pulpit and elaborate hand-painted, willow-pattern floor tiles from Canton, China, which were added in 1762. It's magnificently illuminated by chandeliers (from Belgium) and coloured-glass lamps. The graceful clock tower was built in 1760. There is an upstairs balcony for women who worshipped separately according to

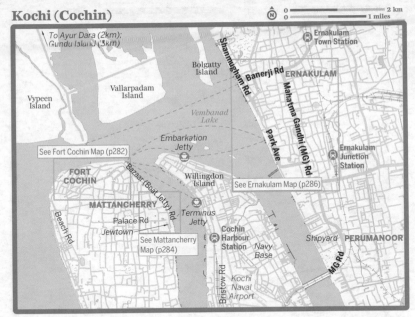

Orthodox rites. Note that shorts or sleeveless tops are not allowed inside.

Jew Town AREA

The synagogue is smack in the middle of Jew Town (Map p284), a bustling port area and centre of the Kochi spice trade. Scores of small firms huddle together in old, dilapidated buildings and the air is filled with the biting aromas of ginger, cardamom, cumin, turmeric and cloves, though the lanes around the Dutch Palace and synagogue are packed with antique and tourist-curio shops rather than spices. Look out for the Jewish names on some of the buildings.

At the tip of Fort Cochin sit the unofficial emblems of Kerala's backwaters: cantilevered **Chinese fishing nets** (Map p282). A legacy of traders from the AD 1400 court of Kubla Khan, these enormous, spiderlike contraptions require at least four people to operate their counterweights at high tide. Unfortunately, modern fishing techniques are making these labour-intensive methods less and less profitable.

Indo-Portuguese Museum MUSEUM

(Map p282; ☎2215400; Indian/foreigner ₹10/25; ☺9am-1pm & 2-6pm Tue-Sun) This museum in the garden of the Bishop's House preserves the heritage of one of India's earliest Catholic communities, including vestments, silver processional crosses and altarpieces from the Cochin diocese. The basement contains remnants of the Portuguese Fort Immanuel.

St Francis Church CHURCH

(Map p282; Bastion St) Believed to be India's oldest European-built church, it was originally constructed in 1503 by Portuguese Franciscan friars. The edifice that stands here today was built in the mid-16th century to replace the original wooden structure. Adventurer Vasco da Gama, who died in Cochin in 1524, was buried in this spot for 14 years before his remains were taken to Lisbon – you can still visit his tombstone in the church.

Dutch Cemetery HISTORIC SITE

(Map p282; Beach Rd) Consecrated in 1724, this cemetery contains the worn and dilapidated graves of Dutch traders and soldiers. Its gates are normally locked but a caretaker might let you in, or ask at St Francis Church.

Santa Cruz Basilica CHURCH

(Map p282; cnr Bastion St & KB Jacob Rd) The imposing Catholic basilica was originally built on this site in 1506, though the current building dates to 1902. Inside you'll find artefacts from the different eras in Kochi and a striking pastel-coloured interior.

Fort Cochin

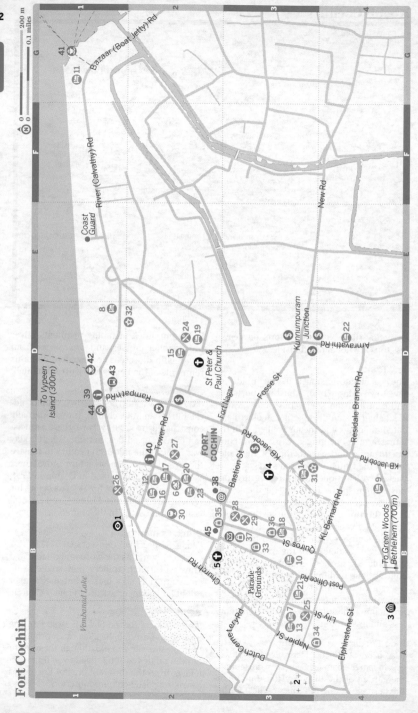

Kashi Art Cafe GALLERY
(Map p282; Burgher St; ⊙8.30am-7.30pm) The pioneer of Fort Cochin's art revival, Kashi displays changing exhibitions of local artists. There's another gallery on Bazaar Rd, which opens if there's an exhibition on.

Activities

Grande Residencia Hotel SWIMMING
(Map p282; Princess St, Fort Cochin) Nonguests can swim at the hotel's small pool for ₹350 per person.

Cherai Beach (Vypeen Island) SWIMMING
For a dip in the ocean, you can make a day trip out to the lovely white-sand Cherai

Beach (p294), a short journey by ferry to Vypeen Island.

Ayur Dara AYURVEDA
(☑2502362; www.ayurdara.com; Murikkumpadam, Vypeen Island; ⊙9am-5.30pm) Run by third-generation ayurvedic practitioner Dr Subhash, this delightful waterside treatment centre specialises in long-term treatments. By appointment only. Massage and *sirodara* (steady stream of oil poured onto the forehead) costs ₹1000. It's 4km from the Vypeen Island ferry (autorickshaw ₹35).

Ayush AYURVEDA
(Map p282; ☑6456566; KB Jacob Rd, Fort Cochin; massage from ₹900; ⊙8am-8pm) Part of an

India-wide chain of ayurvedic centres, this place also does long-term treatments.

Kerala Ayurveda AYURVEDA
(Kerala Ayurveda Pharmacy Ltd; Map p286; ☑2378198; www.kaplayurveda.com; AM Thomas Rd, Ernakulam; massage from ₹600; ⊙7am-8pm) This government-approved centre comes recommended for all types of ayurvedic treatments.

SVM Ayurveda Centre AYURVEDA
(Kerala Ayurveda Pharmacy Ltd; ☑9847371667; www.svmayurveda.com; Quiero St; massage from ₹600; ⊙9.30am-7pm) A small Fort Cochin centre, this offers relaxing massages and Hatha yoga (₹400, 1½ hours) daily at 8am. Longer rejuvenation packages are also available.

✎ Courses

The Kerala Kathakali Centre (p291) has lessons in classical Kathakali dance, music and make-up (from ₹350 per hour).

For a crash course in the martial art of *kalarippayat*, head out to Ens Kalari (p291), a famed training centre, which offers short intensive courses from one week to one month.

Cook & Eat COOKING
(☑2215377; simonroy@hotmail.com; Quiros St; classes ₹550; ⊙11am & 6pm) Mrs Leelu Roy runs a popular two-hour cooking class called 'Cook & Eat' in her great big family kitchen, teaching five dishes to classes of five to 10 people. Several of the homestays in towns are also happy to organise cooking classes for their guests.

☞ Tours

Most hotels and tourist offices can arrange a day trip out to the **Elephant training camp** (⊙7am-6pm) at Kudanadu, 50km from Kochi. Here you can go for a ride (₹200) and even help out with washing the gentle beasts if you arrive at 8am. Entry is free, though the elephant trainers will expect a small tip. A return trip out here in a taxi should cost around ₹700 to ₹1200.

Tourist Desk Information Counter
BOATING, WILDLIFE WATCHING
This private tour agency (p292) runs the popular full-day **Water Valley Tour** (day tour ₹650) through local canals and lagoons. A canoe trip through smaller canals and villages is included, as is lunch and hotel pickups. It also offers a **Wayanad Wildlife tour** (2 nights ₹5500), and **Munnar Hillstation tour** (1 night ₹2500). Prices include accommodation, transport and meals.

KTDC BOATING
The KTDC (p292) has **backwater tours** (½-day tour ₹450) at 8.30am and 2pm, and tourist **motor-boat tours** (2½hr tour ₹150) around Fort Cochin at 9am and 2pm. Its full-day **houseboat backwater trips** (day tour ₹800; ⊙8am-6.30pm) stops for you to see local weaving factories, spice gardens and, most importantly, toddy tapping!

✦ Festivals & Events

The eight-day **Ernakulathappan Utsavam festival**, in January/February, culminates in a procession of 15 decorated elephants, ecstatic music and fireworks.

🛏 Sleeping

Fort Cochin is an ideal place to escape the noise and chaos of the mainland – it's tranquil and romantic, with some excellent accommodation choices. This could be India's homestay capital, with hundreds of family houses offering near-identical, large and clean budget rooms.

Ernakulam is much cheaper and more convenient for onward travel, but the ambiance and accommodation choices there are less inspiring. Regardless of where you stay, book ahead during December and January.

FORT COCHIN

Malabar House `TOP CHOICE` HOTEL $$$
(Map p282; ☑2216666; www.malabarhouse.com; Parade Ground Rd; r €220, ste incl breakfast €300-360; ❈@❅) What may just be one of the fanciest boutique hotels in Kerala, Malabar flaunts its uberhip blend of modern colours and period fittings like it's not even trying. It has a restaurant and wine bar. While the suites are huge and lavishly appointed, the standard rooms are more snug. Also check out their lush retreat **Privacy at Sanctuary Bay** (cottage/ste €220/360) or gorgeous ecofriendly house boat, **Discovery** (d full board €450).

Brunton Boatyard `TOP CHOICE` HOTEL $$$
(Map p282; ☑2215461; brunton boatyard@cg hearth.com; River Rd; r ₹18,700-25,000; ❈@❅) This imposing hotel faithfully reproduces 16th- and 17th-century Dutch and Portuguese architecture in its grand complex. All of the rooms look out over the harbour, and have bathtub and balconies with a refreshing sea breeze that beats AC any day.

Noah's Ark HOMESTAY $$
(Map p282; ☑2215481; www.noahsarkcochin.com; 1/508 Fort Kochi Hospital Rd; r ₹2750-2900; ❈@) An upmarket, huge modern house, with a sweeping spiral staircase from the reception room and a variety of gleamingly clean, appealing rooms (one with a balcony), plus a friendly welcome.

Walton's Homestay GUESTHOUSE $$
(Map p282; ☑2215309; www.waltonshomestay. com; Princess St; r incl breakfast ₹1200-2400, with AC ₹1600-2600; ❈) The fastidious Mr Walton offers big wood-furnished rooms in his lovely old house that's painted a nautical white with blue trim. There's a lush garden

out the back and a large secondhand bookshop downstairs. The bird-filled garden has one AC garden **cottage** (d ₹1200) available for rent.

Tea Bungalow HOTEL $$$
(Map p282; ☑3019200; www.teabungalow.in; 1/1901 Kunumpuram; r ₹7500; ❈@❅) This mustard-coloured colonial building was built in 1912 as headquarters of a UK spice trading company before being taken over by Brooke Bond tea. Graceful rooms are decorated with flashes of strong colour and carved wooden furniture, and have Bassetta-tiled bathrooms.

Raintree Lodge GUESTHOUSE $$
(Map p282; ☑3251489; www.fortcochin.com; Peter Celli St; r ₹2300; ❈) The intimate and comfortable rooms at the Raintree flirt with boutique-hotel status. Each room has a great blend of contemporary style and carved wood furniture. Try to get an upstairs room with a (tiny) balcony.

Bernard Bungalow GUESTHOUSE $$
(Map p282; ☑2216162; www.bernardbungalow. com; Parade Ground Rd; r ₹2500-3500; ❈) This gracious place has the look of a 1940s summer cottage, housed in a fine 350-year-old house that boasts a large collection of interesting rooms. The house has polished floorboards, wooden window shutters, balconies and verandas, and is filled with lovely period furniture.

Sui House HOMESTAY $$$
(☑2227078; http://suihousecochin.com; Maulana Azad Rd; r incl breakfast & tax ₹4000; ❈) This is the home of the antique-dealer owner of gorgeous Caza Maria in Jew Town Rd. There are four mammoth turquoise rooms in this grand family villa. The sumptuous communal drawing room is filled with more antiques, and a hearty breakfast is served in the outdoor courtyard.

Old Harbour Hotel HOTEL $$$
(Map p282; ☑2218006; www.oldharbourhotel.com; Tower Rd; r incl tax ₹8250-14200; ❈@❅) Set around an idyllic garden, with lily ponds and a small pool, the dignified Old Harbour is housed in a 300-year-old Dutch/Portuguese heritage building. The elegant mix of period and modern styles and bright colour accents are luxurious without being over the top, lending the place a much more intimate feel than some of the more grandiose competition. There are 13 rooms here, some

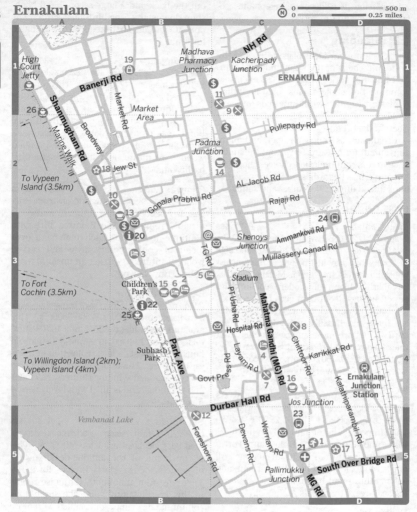

facing directly onto the garden, and some with plant-filled, open-air bathrooms.

Mother Tree   HOMESTAY **$**
(Map p282; ☏9447464906; www.hotelmothertree. com; KL Bernard Master Rd; r ₹700, with AC ₹1000; ✳) There are just a few miniscule rooms in this compact homestay, but the immaculate cleanliness and neat rooftop chill-out space make this place worth seeking out.

Dream Catcher   HOMESTAY **$**
(☏2217550; www.dreamcatcherhomestays.com; KB Jacob Rd; r from ₹600, d/tr AC from ₹2500/3500; ✳) Tucked away on a narrow laneway, this rambling old colonial house has budget rooms, an almost gothic sitting room and balconies lined with pot plants: it offers a backpacker-friendly welcome from the Portuguese-descended family.

Green Woods Bethlehem   HOMESTAY **$$**
(off Map p282; ☏3247791; greenwoodsbethle hem1@vsnl.net; opposite ESI Hospital; d incl breakfast ₹900) Owner Sheeba looks ready to sign your adoption papers the minute you walk through her front door. What might just be the cutest guesthouse in Kochi lies in a quiet

residential area cocooned in its own thick jungle of plants and palms. The rooms are humble but cosy; breakfast is served in the fantastic, leafy rooftop cafe, where cooking classes/demonstrations are often held.

Princess Inn GUESTHOUSE $
(Map p282; ☎2217073; princessinnfortkochi@ gmail.com; Princess St; r ₹400-800) Sticking to its budget guns, the friendly Princess Inn spruces up its dull, tiny rooms with cheery bright colours. The comfy communal spaces are a treat, and the three large, front-facing rooms are good value.

Sonnetta Residency GUESTHOUSE $$
(Map p282; ☎2215744; www.sonnettaresidency. com; Princess St; r ₹1000, with AC ₹1500; ﹡) Right in the thick of the Fort Cochin action, the plain rooms at this Portuguese-era building are small, but come with nice, chintzy touches like curtains and indoor plants to make you feel at home.

Delight Home Stay GUESTHOUSE $$
(Map p282; ☎2217658; www.delightfulhomestay. com; Post Office Rd; r ₹1400-1800, with AC ₹2500; ﹡) And delightful it is. This grand house's exterior is adorned with frilly white wood-work, and the rooms are spacious and polished. It overlooks the parade ground and has a charming little garden, and an imposing sitting room covered in wall-to-wall teak.

Koder House HOTEL $$$
(Map p282; ☎2217988; www.koderhouse.com; Tower Rd; r from ₹11,300 with AC; ﹡) A historic mansion overlooking the Chinese fishing nets, this fine heritage property has characterful rooms and an atmospheric, high-ceiling restaurant with whirring fans that serves nice food. Rooms are overpriced in season, but worthwhile at other times.

Spencer Home GUESTHOUSE $$
(Map p282; ☎2215049; spencerhomstayfc@rediff mail.com; 1/298 Parade Ground Rd; d ₹1500-2500) This handsomely restored heritage home has top-value, snug rooms set around a charming little garden courtyard. It has great period highlights, like high wood-beam ceilings and amazingly intricate antique locks. Breakfast is served garden-side, in front of your room.

Fort House Hotel HOTEL $$$
(☎2217103; www.hotelforthouse.com; 2/6A Calvathy Rd; r from ₹3800; ﹡@) With lush gardens, on the waterfront, this offers smart, chic rooms in soft earth and ochre colours and with solid wooden furnishings, opening onto a long veranda. There's a recommended waterside restaurant.

Costa Gama Home Stay HOMESTAY $
(☎2216122; www.stayincochin.com; Thamaraparambu Rd; s/d from ₹400/650) Cosy little place that gets rave reviews. South off KB Jacob Rd.

Homested HOMESTAY $
(☎9388600512; http://homestedcochin.com; 1386 A Thamarakulam Rd; s/d ₹600/700, d with AC ₹900; ❄) With three spic-and-span rooms in a well-kept family house tucked into one of Fort Cochin's backstreets, away from the melee.

Daffodil HOMESTAY $$
(Map p282; ☎2218686; www.cochinhomestays. org; Njaliparambu Junction; s/d ₹1500/2000, with AC ₹2500/3000; ❄) Run by a local couple, this has big and brightly painted modern rooms, with an upstairs carved-wood Keralan balcony.

Royal Grace Tourist Home GUESTHOUSE $
(Map p282; ☎2216584; Amaravathi Rd; r ₹400-600) This old-timer is one of the rare budget stalwarts still left in Fort Cochin. There are loads of rooms on offer in a large multistorey building, each with little more than a bed, four walls and a pint-sized bathroom.

MATTANCHERRY & JEW TOWN

Caza Maria HOMESTAY $$$
(Map p284; ☎3258837; cazamaria@rediffmail.com; Jew Town Rd; r incl breakfast ₹4500; ❄) Right in the heart of Jew Town, this unique place has just two enormous, gorgeous heritage rooms overlooking the bazaar. Fit for a maharaja, the rooms feature an idiosyncratic style – with each high-ceilinged room painted in bright colours, filled to the brim with antiques, and with tall windows looking onto the bustling market street below.

ERNAKULAM

TOP CHOICE Olavipe HOMESTAY $$
(☎0478-2522255; www.olavipe.com; Olavipe; s/d incl meals ₹5100/8500) This gorgeous 1890s traditional Syrian-Christian home is on a 16-hectare farm surrounded by backwaters, 28km south of Kochi. A restored mansion of rosewood and glistening teak, it has several large and breezy rooms beautifully decorated in the original period decor (only the ceiling fans are new). There are lots of shady awnings and sitting areas, a fascinating archive with six generations of family history, and the gracious owners will make you feel like a welcome friend rather than a guest. A taxi to/from Fort Cochin is less than ₹1000.

Grand Hotel HOTEL $$
(Map p286; ☎2382061; www.grandhotelkerala. com; MG Rd; s/d from ₹1900/2200; ❄) This 1960s hotel on Mahatma Gandhi (MG) Rd,

with its polished original art deco fittings, oozes the sort of retro cool that modern hotels would kill to re-create. The spacious rooms have gleaming parquet floors and large modern bathrooms, and the foyer has beautiful vintage furniture. Definitely fine enough to tempt a stay in Ernakulam.

John's Residency HOTEL $
(Map p286; ☎2355395; TG Rd; s/d from ₹310/380, with AC ₹1050; ❄) With a cool, yellow foyer featuring interesting clutter such as vintage fans, this is a refreshing place to enter from the busy street. Rooms are small but decorated with flashes of colour: red curtains and bathrooms, that give them a funky feel that's a welcome surprise in this price bracket.

Government Guest House GUESTHOUSE $$
(Map p286; ☎2360502; Shanmughan Rd; s/d ₹980/1380; ❄) We secretly love Kerala's government guesthouses – they usually manage to be the best deal in town. Right in the city's heart and near the sea, this eight-storey monolith of a building has huge, neat rooms. It probably won't win any style awards, but some of the upper-floor rooms have balconies with sweeping sea vistas.

Bijus Tourist Home HOTEL $
(Map p286; ☎2361661; www.bijustouristhome.com; Market Rd; s/d from ₹475/725, d with AC ₹1350; ❄) This friendly, popular choice is handy for the main jetty and has reasonable, drab but clean rooms and a friendly welcome. **Day tours** to the elephant training camp from here are only ₹700.

Saas Tower HOTEL $
(Map p286; ☎2365319; www.saastower.com; Cannon Shed Rd; s/d ₹500/800, with AC from ₹750/1400; ❄) It has 'facilities to match your fantasies' but this will only be the case if you fantasise about a low-end business hotel, with clean smart rooms filled with wooden furniture, handily located near the boat jetty.

Eating & Drinking

Covert beer consumption is *de rigueur* at most of the Fort Cochin restaurants, and more expensive in the licensed ones (₹100 to ₹165).

FORT COCHIN

Behind the Chinese fishing nets are several **fishmongers** (Map p282; seafood per kg ₹200-400), from whom you can buy fish (or prawns, scampi, lobster), then take your selection to the nearby row of shacks where the folks there will cook it and serve it to you (cooking is an extra ₹100 per kg).

TOP CHOICE Dal Roti   INDIAN $$

(Map p282; Lily St; meals ₹70-170; ⊙lunch & dinner) Friendly and knowledgeable owner Ramesh will hold your hand through his expansive North Indian menu, which even sports its own glossary, and help you dive in to his delicious range of vegetarian, eggetarian and nonvegetarian options. The setting is chic minimalist, with whitewashed walls and bench seating, helping you focus on the yummy dishes here.

Teapot   CAFE $

(Map p282; Peter Celli St; snacks ₹40-60, meals ₹140-180) This atmospheric place is the perfect venue for 'high tea', with teas, sandwiches and full meals served in chic, airy rooms. Witty tea-themed accents include loads of antique teapots, tea chests for tables and a gnarled, tea-tree based glass table. The cheesecake is divine.

Shala   KERALAN $$

(Map p282; Peter Celli St; meals ₹180-220; ⊙noon-3.30pm & 6.30-11pm) With high ceilings, whirring fans, and white walls adorned with striking paintings, Shala is owned by the same management as Kailah Art Cafe, and serves well-presented meals that include a vegetable side dish and rice, such as coconut fish curry or vegetable of the day, all made by local women.

Solar Cafe   CAFE $$

(Bazaar Rd; meals ₹80-130; ⊙8am-8pm) This arty and funky cafe serves up organic breakfasts and lunches, with dishes such as fruit with wild honey and drinks such as cinnamon coffee, in a lime-bright, book-lined and friendly setting.

Arca Nova   SOUTH INDIAN $$

(2/6A Calvathy Rd; mains ₹225-290; ⊙12.30-2.30pm & 7.30-10.30pm) The waterside restaurant at the Fort House Hotel is a prime choice for a leisurely lunch (mosquitoes may join you for dinner), particularly specialising in fish, with dishes such as fish wrapped in banana leaf or spicy peppered fish, set in a serenely spacious covered area in the garden.

Casa Linda   MULTICUISINE $$

(Map p282; Dispensary Rd; mains ₹85-300) This modern dining room above the hotel of the same name might not be much to look at,

but it's all about the food here. Chef Dipu once trained with a Frenchman and whips up delicious local Keralan dishes alongside French imports like Poisson de la Provencale (fish fried in oil and herbs, Provence-style). The Keralan dry-fried coconut prawns, made to a loving mother's recipe, are scrumptious.

Kashi Art Cafe   CAFE $$

(Map p282; Burgher St; breakfast & snacks ₹60-95; ⊙8.30am-7.30pm) An institution in Fort Cochin, this place has a hip-but-casual vibe and solid wood tables that spread out into a semi-courtyard space. The coffee is as strong as it should be and the daily Western breakfast and lunch specials are excellent. A small gallery shows off local artists.

Menorah Restaurant   KERALAN $$

(Map p282; Korder House; dishes ₹175-275; ⊙lunch & dinner) In the gracious hall of Korder House, now a heritage hotel, with tall wooden ceilings and chessboard black-and-white-tiled flooring, with whirring fans. It serves wine and beer, and tasty Keralan dishes, if tweaked for tourist tastes.

Malabar Junction   INTERNATIONAL $$$

(Map p282; ☎2216666; Parade Ground Rd; mains ₹380-600) Set in an open-sided pavilion, the restaurant at Malabar House is movie-star cool, with white-tableclothed tables in a courtyard close to the small pool. There's a seafood-based, European-style menu and Grover's Estate wine (quaffable Indian) is served. The signature dish is the impressive seafood platter with grilled vegetables (₹1500). Upstairs, the bar serves upmarket snacks such as tapioca-and-cumin fritters in funkily clashing surroundings.

Old Harbour Hotel   MULTICUISINE $$$

(Map p282; ☎2218006; www.oldharbourhotel.com; Tower Rd; mains ₹400-500; ⊙10.30am-10pm) Certainly one of Cochin's most enchanting settings for an evening meal, in the poolside candlelit garden of the Old Harbour Hotel, serenaded by traditional musicians. The food is bland but acceptable, but it gets a thumbs up for ambience and you can order wine (from ₹1350 a bottle) and beer (₹175).

XL   BAR

(Map p282; ⊙10am-10.30pm) This slightly dingy bar-restaurant, with whirring fans and big windows, is a hugely popular place to settle down for a cold Kingfisher, with reasonable prices, palatable snacks and meals such as beef deep fry.

KERALA CENTRAL KERALA

Ramathula Hotel　　　　INDIAN $
(Map p284; Kayees Junction, Mattancherry; biryani ₹40-45; ⊙lunch & dinner) This place is legendary among locals for its chicken and mutton biryanis – get here early or you'll miss out. It's better known by the chef's name, Kayikka's.

Caza Maria　　　　MULTICUISINE $$
(Map p284; Bazaar Rd; mains around ₹120-200) With cooks trained by a travelling Frenchman, this is an enchanting, bright blue, antique-filled space with funky music and a changing daily menu of North Indian, South Indian and French dishes.

Ginger House　　　　INDIAN $$$
(Map p284; Bazaar Rd; meals ₹400-600) Walk through the massive antique-filled godown and you'll find the attached restaurant, with a fantastic setting right on the waterfront, where you can relax on mismatched chairs (straight from the shop) and feast on Indian dishes and snacks.

Shri Krishna　　　　INDIAN $
(Map p284; thali ₹24, dishes ₹4-23; ⊙7am-9.30pm) A simple, basic, but tasty thali.

Café Jew Town　　　　CAFE $$
(Map p284; Bazaar Rd; snacks around ₹100-200) A Swiss-owned cafe, this chi-chi little place running alongside an upmarket antique shop has a few tables and proffers good cakes, snacks and coffee.

ERNAKULAM

TOP CHOICE **Grand Pavilion**　　　　INDIAN $$
(Map p286; MG Rd; meals ₹90-350; ✳) This is the restaurant at the Grand Hotel and is as retro-stylish as the hotel itself. It serves a tome of a menu that covers dishes from the West, North India, South India and most of the rest of the Asian continent. The *meen pollichathu* (fish cooked in banana leaves) gets the thumbs up.

Frys Village Restaurant　　　　KERALAN $
(Map p286; Veekshanam Rd; dishes ₹50-100; ⊙noon-3.30pm & 7-10.30pm; ✳) This brightly decorated place with an arched ceiling is a great family restaurant with authentic Keralan food, especially seafood like *pollichathu* or crab roast (₹50–200 depending on size). Fish/veg thalis (and much more) are available for lunch.

Subhiksha　　　　INDIAN $
(Map p286; Gandhi Sq, D.H. Road; dishes ₹30-100; ⊙7.30am-3.30pm & 7-11pm; ✳) A popular pure-veg hotel restaurant, this is a smart place to dig into tasty thalis (₹90). It's rammed for breakfast and lunch. The hotel also has a busy, breezy coffee shop serving dosas and the like.

Aruvi Nature Restaurant　　　　KERALAN $
(Map p286; Chittoor Rd; dishes ₹10-25; ⊙noon-2.30pm & 6-9pm) An interesting twist on the traditional Keralan set meal – the menu is created according to ayurvedic principles and contains no dairy, spicy peppers or salt. And with dishes such as pumpkin dosas, it's definitely worth a try!

Andhra Meals　　　　INDIAN $$
(Map p286; meals ₹70-125; ⊙11.30am-3.30pm & 7-11.30pm) A dark, buzzing 1st-floor place, serving spicy Andhra cuisine on banana leaves. Try a thali, for all-you-can-eat joy.

South Star　　　　MULTICUISINE $$
(Map p286; Shanmughan Rd; meals ₹70-140; ✳) This upmarket version of the Bimbis chain of restaurants is in a moodily lit space that's plushed out in nice chairs and dark-wood tables. The bulky menu has North and South Indian victuals, as well as a massive choice of Chinese dishes.

Spencer's Daily　　　　SUPERMARKET $
(Map p286; Veekshanam Rd; ⊙7.30am-10.30pm) Well-stocked supermarket.

Indian Coffee House　　　　CAFE
(Map p286; Cannon Shed Rd) Also has branches on Jos Junction and MG Rd near Padma Junction.

Coffee Beanz　　　　CAFE
(Map p286; Shanmugham Rd; snacks ₹40-140; ⊙9am-10.30pm; ✳) For a hip coffee hit.

☆ Entertainment

There are several places in Kochi where you can view Kathakali (see p304). The performances are certainly made for tourists, but they're also a good introduction to this intriguing art form. The standard program starts with the intricate make-up application, followed by a demonstration and commentary on the dance and then the performance. The fast-paced traditional martial art of *kalarippayat* can now be easily seen in Fort Cochin.

See India Foundation　　　　CULTURAL PROGRAM
(Map p286; ☑2376471; devankathakali@yahoo.com; Kalathiparambil Lane, Ernakulam; admission ₹150; ⊙make-up 6pm, show 6.45-8pm) One of the oldest Kathakali theatres in Kerala, it

has small-scale shows with an emphasis on the religious and philosophical roots of Kathakali.

Kerala Kathakali Centre
CULTURAL PROGRAM

(Map p282; ☎2217552; www.kathakalicentre.com; KB Jacob Rd, Fort Cochin; admission ₹250; ☺make-up from 5pm, show 6-7.30pm) In an intimate, wood-lined theatre, this place provides a useful introduction to Kathakali, complete with amazing demonstrations of eye movements, plus handy translations of the night's story. The centre also hosts performances of the martial art of *kalarippayat* at 4 to 5pm daily, traditional music at 8 to 9pm Sunday to Friday and classical dance at 8 to 9pm on Saturday.

Ens Kalari
CULTURAL PROGRAM

(☎2700810; www.enskalari.org.in; Nettoor, Ernakulam) If you want to see real professionals have a go at *kalarippayat,* it's best to travel out to this renowned *kalarippayat* learning centre, 8km southeast of Ernakulam. There are one-hour demonstrations Monday to Saturday at 5.30pm (one day's notice required, admission by donation).

Sridar Cinema
CINEMA

(Map p286; Shanmugham Rd, Ernakulam) Screens films in Malayalam, Hindi, Tamil and English.

🛍 Shopping

Broadway in Ernakulam (p286) is good for local shopping, spice shops and clothing, and around Convent and Market Rds is a huddle of tailors. On Jew Town Rd in Mattancherry there's a plethora of Gujarati-run shops selling genuine antiques mingled with knock-offs and copies. A couple of shops close to the synagogue sell exquisite lace work. Most of the shops in Fort Cochin are identikit Kashmiri-run shops selling a mixed bag of north Indian crafts. Many shops around Fort Cochin and Mattancherry operate lucrative commission rackets, with autorickshaw drivers getting huge kickbacks (added to your price) for dropping tourists at their door.

Niraamaya
CLOTHING

Fort Cochin (Map p282; ☎3263465; Quiros St, Fort Cochin; ☺10am-5.30pm Mon-Sat); Mattancherry (Map p284; VI/217 A.B. Salam Rd, Jew Town) Popular throughout Kerala, Niraamaya sells 'ayurvedic' clothing and fabrics – all made of organic cotton, coloured with natural herb dyes, or infused with ayurvedic oils.

DC Books
BOOKSTORE

(Map p286; ☎2391295; Banerji Rd, Ernakulam; ☺9.30am-7.30pm Mon-Sat) This has a typically great English-language selection of fiction and nonfiction.

Idiom Bookshop
BOOKSTORE

Fort Cochin (Map p282; ☎2217075; Bastion St; ☺10.30am-9pm Mon-Sat); Mattancherry (☎2225604; opposite boat jetty; ☺10am-6pm) Huge range of quality new and used books.

Fabindia
CLOTHING, HOMEWARES

(Map p282; ☎2217077; www.fabindia.com; Napier St, Fort Cochin; ☺10.30am-8.30pm) Fab Fabindia has heaps of fine Indian textiles, fabrics, clothes and household linen.

Cinnamon
CLOTHING

(Map p282; ☎2217124; Post Office Rd, Fort Cochin; ☺10am-7pm Mon-Sat) Cinnamon sells gorgeous Indian-designed clothing, jewellery and homewares in an ultrachic white retail space.

🍃 Tribes India
HANDICRAFTS

(Map p282; ☎2215077; c/o Head Post Office, Fort Cochin; ☺10am-6.30pm Mon-Sat) Tucked behind the post office, this TRIFED (Ministry of Tribal Affairs) enterprise sells tribal artefacts, paintings, shawls, figurines, etc, at reasonable fixed prices and the profits go towards supporting the artisans.

ℹ Information

Internet access

Net Park (Map p286; Convent Rd, Ernakulam; per hr ₹15; ☺9am-8pm)

Sify iWay (Map p282; per hr ₹40; ☺9am-10pm) Fast computers in a spacious upstairs cafe setting above the Shop-n-Save.

Medical Services

Lakeshore Hospital (☎2701032; NH Bypass, Marudu) It's 8km southeast of central Ernakulam.

Medical Trust (Map p286; ☎2358001; www.medicaltrusthospital.com; MG Rd)

Money

UAE Exchange (☺9.30am-6pm Mon-Fri, to 4pm Sat) Ernakulam (☎2383317; Perumpillil Bldg, MG Rd); Ernakulam (☎3067008; Chettupuzha Towers, PT Usha Rd Junction); Fort Cochin (☎2216231; Amravathi Rd) Foreign exchange and travellers cheques.

Post

College post office (☎2369302; Convent Rd, Ernakulam; ☺9am-5pm Mon-Sat)

Ernakulam post office branches (☎2355467; Hospital Rd; ☺9am-8pm Mon-Sat, 10am-5pm Sun) Also branches on MG Rd and Broadway.

Main post office (Post Office Rd, Fort Cochin; ⊘9am-5pm Mon-Fri, to 3pm Sat)

Tourist information

There's a tourist information counter at the airport. Many places distribute a free brochure that includes a neat map and walking tour entitled *Historical Places in Fort Cochin.*

KTDC Tourist Reception Centre (Map p286; ☑2353234; Shanmugham Rd, Ernakulam; ⊘8am-7pm) Also organises tours.

Tourist Desk Information Counter Ernakulam (Map p286; ☑2371761; touristdesk@satyam. net.in; ⊘8am-6pm); Fort Cochin (Map p282; ☑2216129) A private tour agency that's extremely knowledgeable and helpful about Kochi and beyond. Runs several popular and recommended tours, and its Ernakulam office displays a board showing recommended cultural events on in town that day, has a secondhand book exchange, and produces the 'Village Astrologer', a monthly free newsletter about cultural events in Kerala.

Tourist Police Ernakulam (☑2353234; Shanmugham Rd, Ernakulam; ⊘8am-6pm); Fort Cochin (Map p282; ☑2215055; ⊘24hr)

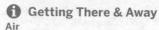

Getting There & Away

Air

The following airlines have offices in Kochi:

Air India (☑2351295; MG Rd)

Jet Airways (☑2358582; MG Rd)

Kingfisher Airlines (☑1800 2093030; Spencer Travels, 2nd fl, Sreekandath Rd)

Bus

The **KSRTC bus stand** (Map p286; ☑2372033; ⊘reservations 6am-10pm) is in Ernakulam next to the railway halfway between the two train stations. Many buses passing through Ernakulam originate in other cities – you may have to join the scrum when the bus pulls in. You can make reservations up to 20 days (30 for Tamil Nadu) in advance for buses originating here. There's a separate window for reservations to Tamil Nadu. See p293 for more information on buses from Ernakulam.

DOMESTIC FLIGHTS FROM ERNAKULAM

DESTINATION	AIRLINE	FARE (₹)	DURATION (HR)	FREQUENCY
Agatti	IT	₹10,000	1½	5 weekly
Bengaluru	9W	₹2200	1¼	1 daily
	IT	3500	1¼	4 daily
Chennai	IC	2300	1	1 daily
	9W	2900	1½	3 daily
	IT	2800	1½	1 daily
Delhi	IC	5900	3	2 daily
	9W	6300	3	3 daily
Goa	IT	6200	5	1 daily
	SG	9350	5	1 daily
Kozhikode	IC	2000	3/4	2 daily
Mumbai	IC	5500	2	1 daily
	9W	5300	2	1 daily
	IT	4700	2	1 daily
	SG	4900	2	2 daily
Trivandrum	IC	2300	¾	1 daily
	6E	2200	¾	1 daily

Note: Fares are one way. Airline codes: IC – Air India; 9W – Jet Airways; IT – Kingfisher; 6E – IndiGo; SG – SpiceJet.

The following bus services operate from the KSRTC bus stand (Map p286).

DESTINATION	FARE (₹)	DURATION (HR)	FREQUENCY
Alleppey	34	1½	every 20min
Bengaluru	302 (AC 576)	14	4 daily
Calicut	120 (AC 190)	5	1-2 hourly
Chennai	465	16	1 daily, 2pm
Coimbatore	130	4½	9 daily
Kannur	170	8	2 daily
Kanyakumari	170	8	2 daily
Kollam	90	3½	every 20min
Kothamangalam	30	2	every 10min
Kottayam	40	2	every 30min
Kumily (for Periyar)	90	5	8 daily
Madurai	160	9	1 daily, 7.45pm
Munnar	86	4½	every 30min
Mangalore	286	12	1 daily
Thrissur	46	2	every 10min
Trivandrum	140	5	every 30min

Several private bus companies have super-deluxe, AC, video buses to Bengaluru, Chennai, Mangalore and Coimbatore; prices are around 75% higher than government buses. There are stands selling tickets all over Ernakulam. **Kaloor bus stand** is the main private bus station; it's 1km north of the city.

Train

Ernakulam has two train stations, **Ernakulam Town** and **Ernakulam Junction**. Reservations for both are made at the Ernakulam Junction **reservations office** (132; ⊘8am-8pm Mon-Sat, 8am-2pm Sun).

There are trains to Trivandrum (2nd class/AC chair ₹70/255, 4½ hours), via either Alleppey (₹39/165, 1½ hours) and Kollam (₹60/210, 3½ hours), or via Kottayam (₹40/165, 1½ hours). Trains also run to Thrissur (₹43/165, 1½ hours), Calicut (₹67/237, 4½ hours) and Kannur (₹85/300, 6½ hours). For long-distance trains, see p294.

ℹ️ Getting Around

To/From the Airport

Kochi International Airport (☏610125; http://cochinairport.com) is at Nedumbassery, 30km northeast of Ernakulam. Taxis to/from Ernakulam cost around ₹500, and to/from Fort Cochin around ₹650; a bumpy rickshaw dash from Ernakulam would cost ₹350. Ernakulam's mad traffic means that the trip can take over 1½

hours in the daytime, though usually less than one hour at night.

Boat

Ferries are the fastest form of transport between Fort Cochin and the mainland. The jetty on the eastern side of Willingdon Island is called **Embarkation** (Map p281); the west one, opposite Mattancherry, is **Terminus** (Map p281); and the main stop at Fort Cochin is **Customs**, with another stop at the **Mattancherry Jetty** near the synagogue (Map p284). One-way fares are ₹2.50 (₹3.50 between Ernakulam and Mattancherry).

ERNAKULAM There are services to both Fort Cochin jetties (Customs and Mattancherry) every 25 to 50 minutes (5.55am to 9.30pm) from Ernakulam's **main jetty** (Map p286).

Ferries also run every 20 minutes or so to Willingdon and Vypeen Islands (6am to 10pm).

FORT COCHIN Ferries run from Customs Jetty to Ernakulam between 6.20am and 9.50pm. Ferries also hop between Customs Jetty and Willingdon Island 18 times a day from 6.40am to 9.30pm (Monday to Saturday).

Car and passenger ferries cross to Vypeen Island from Fort Cochin virtually nonstop from 6am until 10pm.

Local Transport

There are no real bus services between Fort Cochin and Mattancherry Palace, but it's an

MAJOR TRAINS FROM ERNAKULAM

The following are major long-distance trains departing from Ernakulam Town.

DESTINATION	TRAIN NO & NAME*	FARE (₹)	DURATION (HR)	DEPARTURES (DAILY)
Bengaluru	6525 *Bangalore Express*	264/688/949	13	5.55pm
Chennai	2624 *Chennai Mail*	289/758/1028	12	10.52
Delhi	2625 *Kerala Express***	579/1572/2159	46	3.45pm
Goa	6312 *Bikaner Express*	305/827/1137	15	8.00pm (Sat only)
Kanyakumari	6526 *Kanyakumari Express*	155/404/551	8	10.10am
Mangalore	6347 *Malabar Express*	187/496/679	10½	1.30am
Mumbai	6382 *Mumbai Express*	465/1277/1762	40	1.20pm

*Sleeper/3AC/2AC

**Departs from Ernakulam Junction

enjoyable 30-minute walk through the busy warehouse area along Bazaar Rd. Autorickshaws should cost around ₹20-30. Most autorickshaw trips around Ernakulam shouldn't cost more than ₹25.

To get to Fort Cochin after ferries stop running, catch a bus in Ernakulam on MG Rd (₹8, 45 minutes), south of Durbar Hall Rd. From Fort Cochin, buses head out to Ernakulam from opposite the Vypeen Island ferry jetty. Taxis charge round-trip fares between the islands, even if you only go one way – Ernakulam Town train station to Fort Cochin should cost around ₹200.

Scooters/Enfields can be hired for ₹250/350-600 per day from **Vasco Tourist Information Centre** (Map p282; ☑2216267; vascoinformations@yahoo.co.uk; Bastion St, Fort Cochin).

Around Kochi

TRIPUNITHURA

Hill Palace Museum (☑0484-2781113; admission ₹20; ◷10am-12.30pm & 2-4.30pm Tue-Sun) At Tripunithura, 16km southeast of Ernakulam en route to Kottayam, this museum was formerly the residence of the Kochi royal family and is an impressive 49-building palace complex. It now houses the collections of the royal families, as well as 19th-century oil paintings, old coins, sculptures and paintings, and temple models. From Ernakulam catch the bus to Tripunithura from MG Rd or Shanmugham Rd, behind the Tourist Reception Centre (₹5 to ₹10, 45 minutes); an autorickshaw should cost around ₹300 return with one-hour waiting time.

CHERAI BEACH

On Vypeen Island, 25km from Fort Cochin, Cherai Beach might just be Kochi's best-kept secret. It's a lovely stretch of as-yet undeveloped white sand, with miles of lazy backwaters just a few hundred metres from the seafront. Best of all, it's close enough to visit on a day trip from Kochi.

If you plan to stay for more than a day, there are a few low-key resorts here.

Brighton Beach House (☑9946565555; www.brightonbeachhouse.org; r ₹1500, with AC ₹2000) has a few basic rooms in a small building right near the shore. The beach is rocky here, but the place is wonderfully secluded, filled with hammocks to loll in, and has a neat, elevated stilt-restaurant that serves perfect sunset views with dinner.

An excellent collection of distinctive cottages lying around a meandering lagoon, **Cherai Beach Resort** (☑0484-2416949; www.cheraibeachresorts.com; Vypeen Island; r from ₹2500; ※@) has the beach on one side and backwaters on the other. Bungalows are individually designed using natural materials, with curving walls, or split-levels, or lookouts onto the backwaters. There's even a tree growing inside one room. Check out a few to find one to your liking.

To get here from Fort Cochin, catch a car-ferry to Vypeen Island (per person ₹2) and either hire an autorickshaw from the jetty (around ₹300) or catch one of the frequent buses (₹14, one hour).

PARUR & CHENNAMANGALAM

Nowhere is the tightly woven religious cloth that is India more apparent than in **Parur**, 35km north of Kochi. Here, one of the oldest synagogues (admission ₹5; ⊙9am-5pm Tue-Sun) in Kerala, at **Chennamangalam**, 8km from Parur, has been fastidiously renovated. Inside you can see door and ceiling wood reliefs in dazzling colours, while just outside lies one of the oldest tombstones in India – inscribed with the Hebrew date corresponding to 1269. The Jesuits first arrived in Chennamangalam in 1577 and there's a **Jesuit church** and the ruins of a Jesuit college nearby. Nearby is a **Hindu temple** on a hill overlooking the Periyar River, a 16th-century **mosque**, and Muslim and Jewish **burial grounds**.

In Parur town, you'll find the **agraharam** (place of Brahmins) – a small street of closely packed and brightly coloured houses originally settled by Tamil Brahmins.

Parur is compact, but Chennamangalam is best visited with a guide. **Indoworld** (Map p282; ☑9447037527; www.indoworldtours.com; Princess St) can organise tours; a day trip is around ₹2200 including guide and car.

Buses for Parur leave from the KSRTC bus stand in Kochi (₹16, one hour, every 10 minutes). From Parur catch a bus (₹3) or autorickshaw (₹60) to Chennamangalam.

Thrissur (Trichur)

☑0487 / POP 330,100

While the rest of Kerala has its fair share of celebrations, untouristy, bustling Thrissur is the cultural cherry on the festival cake. With a list of energetic festivals as long as a temple-elephant's trunk, the region supports several institutions that nurse the dying classical Keralan performing arts back to health. This busy, bustling place is home to a Nestorian Christian community whose denomination dates to the 3rd century AD. The popular performing-arts school Kerala Kalamandalam (p297) and Shri Krishna Temple (p297) are nearby. Plan to arrive during the rambunctious festival season (November to mid-May).

◉ Sights & Activities

Thrissur is famed for its central temple, as well as for its numerous impressive churches.

Vadakkunathan Kshetram Temple   TEMPLE
One of the oldest in the state, Vadakkunathan Kshetram Temple crowns the hill at the epicentre of Thrissur. Finished in classic Keralan architecture, only Hindus are allowed inside, though the mound surrounding the temple has sweeping metropolis views and is a popular spot to linger.

Archaeology Museum   MUSEUM
(admission ₹6; ⊙9am-1pm & 2pm-4.30pm Tue-Sun) The Archaeology Museum is housed in the wonderful 200-year-old Sakthan Thampuran Palace. Its mix of artefacts include fragile palm-leaf manuscripts, 12th-century Keralan bronze sculptures, earthenware pots big enough to cook children in, and an extraordinary 1500kg wooden treasury box covered in locks and iron spikes.

Our Lady of Lourdes Cathedral   CHURCH
This massive cathedral has an underground shrine.

Puttanpalli (New) Church   CHURCH
Recognisable from its towering, pure-white spires.

Chaldean (Nestorian) Church   CHURCH
This church is unique in its complete lack of pictorial representations of Jesus.

✯ Festivals & Events

In a state where festivals are a way of life, Thrissur still manages to stand out for temple revelry. Highlights include **Thrissur Pooram** (April/May) – the most colourful and biggest of Kerala's temple festivals with wonderful processions of elephants; **Uthralikavu Pooram** (March/April), whose climactic day sees 20 elephants circling the shrine; and **Thypooya Maholsavam** (January/February), with a *kavadiyattam* (a form of ritualistic dance) procession in which dancers carry tall, ornate structures called *kavadis*.

🛏 Sleeping

Hotel Luciya Palace   HOTEL $$
(☑2424731; www.hotelluciyapalace.com; s/d with AC ₹1250/1400; ✳) In a cream, colonial-themed building, this is one of the few places in town that has some character. Sitting in a quiet cul-de-sac, this grandiose-looking hotel has comfortable and spacious rooms.

Joys Palace   HOTEL $$
(☑2429999; www.joyshotels.com; TB Rd; s/d from ₹2400/2900; ✳@) This ornate 10-storey meringue caters to Thrissur's jet set. Thankfully, the rooms are not too over the top, are quite comfy and have big windows to enjoy the upper floor's sweeping views. There's a 2nd-floor **restaurant** with an outdoor balcony, and a cool glass-fronted elevator that feels like a fun-park ride.

KERALA CENTRAL KERALA

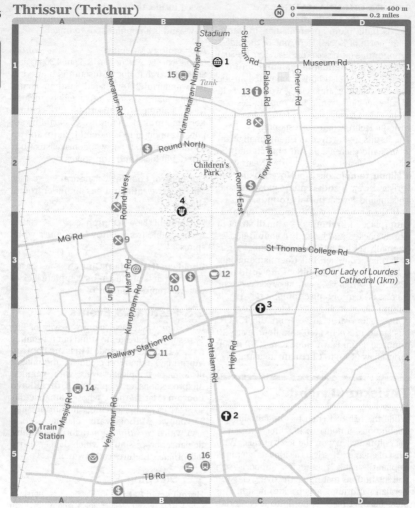

Pathans Hotel   HOTEL **$**

(☎2425620; www.pathansresidentialhotel.com; Round South; s/d from ₹400/539, with AC ₹700/1000; ❄) With no-frills rooms at no-frills prices, this is probably the best budget value in town. The basic and clean rooms are on the 5th and 6th floors and have TV and occasional hot water.

🍴 Eating & Drinking

India Gate   INDIAN **$**

(Town Hall Rd; dishes ₹30-60) In the same building as the HDFC Bank, this is a bright, pure-veg place, with a vintage feel, serving an unbeatable range of dosas, including jam, cheese and cashew versions, and *uttapams* (thick savoury rice pancakes – a Tamil Nadu version of a pizza).

Navaratna Restaurant   NORTH INDIAN **$**

(Round West; dishes ₹57-96; ⊙lunch & dinner) Cool dark and intimate, this is the classiest dining joint in town, with seating on raised platforms and piped music. Expect lots of veg and nonveg dishes from North India, plus a few Keralan specialities, served in AC surrounds.

Pathans Hotel   INDIAN **$**

(1st fl, Round South; dishes ₹30-40; 7am-9.30pm) A little cafeteria-like, this atmospheric

Thrissur (Trichur)

Sights
1 Archaeology Museum C1
2 Chaldean (Nestorian) Church C5
3 Puttanpalli (New) Church C3
4 Vadakkunathan Kshetram
    Temple..B2

Sleeping
5 Hotel Luciya Palace A3
6 Joys Palace B5
    Pathans Hotel ....(see 10)

Eating
7 Ambady Restaurant B2
8 India Gate...C2

9 Navaratna Restaurant B3
10 Pathans Hotel B3

Drinking
11 Indian Coffee House............................B4
12 Indian Coffee House............................C3

Information
13 DTPC Office C1

Transport
14 KSRTC Bus Stand A4
15 Priyadarshini (North) Bus
    Stand...B1
16 Sakthan Thampuran Bus Stand B5

place is popular with families for lunch (thali ₹40) and has a sweets counter downstairs.

Ambady Restaurant INDIAN $
(Round West; dishes ₹30-40) A little way off the street, this dark-brown place is a huge hit with families tucking into several different varieties of set meals.

Indian Coffee House CAFE
Has branches at Round South and Railway Station Rd.

ℹ Information

There are several ATMs around town.
DTPC office (District Tourism Promotion Council; ☑2320800; Palace Rd; ☉10am-5pm Mon-Sat)
Lava Rock Internet Cafe (Kuruppam Rd; per hr ₹30; ☉8.30am-9pm)
UAE Money Exchange (☑2445668; TB Rd; ☉9am-6.30pm Mon-Fri, to 1pm Sat, to 4pm Sun)

ℹ Getting There & Away

Bus
KSRTC buses leave around every 30 minutes from the **KSRTC bus stand** bound for Trivandrum (₹193, 7½ hours), Ernakulam (Kochi, ₹51, two hours), Calicut (₹80, 3½ hours), Palakkad (₹43, 1½ hours) and Kottayam (₹83, four hours). Hourly buses go to Coimbatore (₹77, three hours). From here there are buses to Ponnani (₹35, 1½ hours, four daily) and Prumpavoor (₹37, two hours), where you can connect with buses bound for Munnar.

Regular services also chug along to Guruvayur (₹22, one hour), Irinjalakuda (₹13, one hour) and Cheruthuruthy (₹20, 1½ hours). Two private bus stands (**Sakthan Thampuran** and **Priyadarshini**) have more frequent buses to these destinations, though the chaos involved in navigating each station hardly makes using them worthwhile.

Train
Services run regularly to Ernakulam (2nd class/AC chair ₹43/165, 1½ hours) and Calicut (₹53/180, three hours). There are also regular trains running to Palakkad (sleeper/3AC/2AC ₹120/265/306, 1½ hours) via Shoranur.

Around Thrissur

The Hindu-only **Shri Krishna Temple** at Guruvayur, 33km northwest of Thrissur, is the most famous in Kerala. Said to have been created by Guru, preceptor of the gods, and Vayu, god of wind, the temple is believed to date from the 16th century and is renowned for its healing powers. An annual and spectacular **Elephant Race** is held here in February or March.

Kerala Kalamandalam (☑04884-262305; info@kalamandalam.org; ☉June-Mar), 32km northeast of Thrissur at Cheruthuruthy, is a champion of Kerala's traditional-art renaissance. Using an ancient Gurukula system of learning, students undergo intensive study in Kathakali, *mohiniyattam* (dance of the enchantress), *Kootiattam,* percussion, voice and violin. Structured **visits** (per person ₹1000; ☉9.30am-12.30pm) are available, including a tour around the theatre and classes. Individually tailored **introductory courses** (per month around ₹2500) are offered one subject at a time and last from six to 12 months. The school can help you find local homestay accommodation. For visits, email to book in advance.

Natana Kairali Research & Performing Centre for Traditional Arts (✆0480-2825559; natanakairali@gmail.com), 20km south of Thrissur near Irinjalakuda, offers training in traditional arts, including rare forms of puppetry and dance. Short **appreciation courses** (per class about ₹400) lasting up to a month are sometimes available to keen foreigners. In December each year, the centre holds five days of *mohiniyattam* **performances**, a form of classical Keralan women's dance.

River Retreat (✆04884-262244; www.river retreat.in; Palace Rd; Cheruthuruthy; d ₹2520-4725) is only 1km from Kerala Kalamandalam. It's a hotel in the former summer palace of the Maharajas of Cochin. The more expensive rooms in the main building have river views. They're much nicer and discounts may be available, so ask.

Regular bus services connect each of these destinations with Thrissur (p297).

NORTHERN KERALA

Kozhikode (Calicut)

✆0495 / POP 880,168

Always a prosperous trading town, Calicut was once the capital of the formidable Zamorin dynasty. Vasco da Gama first landed near here in 1498, on his way to snatch a share of the subcontinent for king and country (Portugal that is). These days, trade depends mostly on exporting Indian labour to the Middle East. There's not a lot for tourists to see, though it's a nice break in the journey and the jumping-off point for Wayanad Wildlife Sanctuary.

◉ Sights

Mananchira Square was the former courtyard of the Zamorins and preserves the original spring-fed tank. The 650-year-old **Kuttichira Mosque** is in an attractive wooden four-storey building that is supported by impressive wooden pillars and painted brilliant aqua, blue and white. Burnt down by the Portuguese in 1510, it was protected then rebuilt to tell the tale. The central **Church of South India** was established by Swiss missionaries in 1842 and has unique Euro-Keralan architecture. At Beypore, 10km south, it's possible to see the traditional craft of **dhow** (boat) building.

🛏 Sleeping

Harivihar TOP CHOICE HOMESTAY **$$$**
(✆2765865; www.harivihar.com; Bilathikulam; s/d from ₹4800/6600) In northern Calicut, the ancestral home of the Kadathanadu royal family is as serene as it gets, a traditional Keralan family compound with pristine lawns. Rooms are large and furnished with darkwood antiques. There's an ayurvedic centre, with packages available. The food is delicious.

Beach Hotel HOTEL **$$**
(✆2762055; www.beachheritage.com; Beach Rd; r ₹2500; ☀) Built in 1890 to house the Malabar British Club, this place is now a delightful 10-room hotel. Some rooms have bathtubs and secluded verandas; others have original polished wooden floors and private balconies. All are tastefully furnished and drip with character. Dinner is often served in the little garden.

Hyson Heritage HOTEL **$$**
(✆4081000; www.hysonheritage.com; Bank Rd; s/d from ₹1800/2300; ☀☎) At this business-

Kozhikode (Calicut)

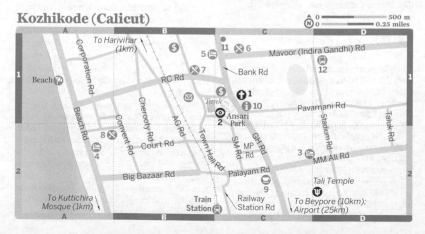

focused, friendly place you get a fair bit of swank for your rupee. All rooms are spic and span, large, comfortable and with inoffensive decor, while the massive deluxe rooms have views over town too.

Alakapuri
HOTEL **$**

(☑2723451; www.alakapurihotels.com; MM Ali Rd; s/d from ₹250/700, with AC ₹625/800; ✳) Built motel-style around a green lawn (complete with fountain!) this place is off the road and quieter than most. Rooms come in different sizes and prices and, while a little scuffed, are tidy and reasonable value.

✗ Eating & Drinking

Paragon Restaurant
INDIAN **$$**

(Kannur Rd; dishes ₹50-220) This always packed restaurant was founded in 1939. The menu is embarrassingly vast, and it's famous for fish dishes such as fish in tamarind sauce, and its legendary chicken biryani.

Zains
INDIAN **$**

(Convent Cross Rd; dishes ₹60-100; ⊙noon-11pm) This historic, authentic Mappila restaurant cooks up delicious authentic dishes such as deep fried beef *pathiri* (pastry) and unnakaya (*plantain snack*).

Hotel Sagar
INDIAN **$**

(Mavoor Rd; dishes ₹20-80) With a dark wood interior and latticework on the front, this eatery is a tad more stylish than the competition. Veg and nonveg thali meals are

served, with yummy biryanis (including fish) and other dishes offered at lunchtime.

Indian Coffee House
CAFE **$**

(GH Rd) For tasty snacks and great coffee.

ℹ Information

There are HDFC and State Bank of India ATMs in town, and several internet cafes.

KTDC Tourist Information (☑2373862; GH Rd; ⊙10.15am-5.15pm Mon-Sat) Cursory tourist information.

UAE Exchange (☑2762772; Bank Rd; ⊙9.30am-6pm Mon-Fri, to 4pm Sat, to 1pm Sun) Close to the Hyson Heritage Hotel.

Thomas Cook (☑2762681; Bank Rd; ⊙9.30am-6.30pm Mon-Sat)

ℹ Getting There & Away

Air

Air India (☑2771974; Eroth Centre, Bank Rd) flies daily to Mumbai (from ₹4700), Chennai (₹5600) and Kochin (₹6000). **Jet Airways** (☑2740518; 29 Mavoor Rd) has one daily flight to Mumbai (₹2300), while **Kingfisher** (☑1800 2093030) flies to Chennai (₹5700), Mangalore (₹6300) and Kochi (from ₹6200).

Bus

The **bus stand** (Mavoor Rd) has government buses to Bengaluru (Bangalore; via Mysore, ₹226, AC ₹391, eight hours, 10 daily), Mangalore (₹260, seven hours, three daily) and to Ooty (₹100, 5½ hours, four daily). There are frequent buses to Thrissur (₹81, 3½ hours), Trivandrum (via Alleppey and Ernakulam; ordinary/Express/ deluxe ₹260/300/335, 10 hours, eight daily) and Kottayam (₹160, seven hours, 13 daily). For Wayanad district, buses leave every 15 minutes heading to Sultanbatheri (₹63, three hours) via Kalpetta (₹51, two hours). Private buses for various long-distance locations also use this stand.

Train

The train station is 1km south of Mananchira Sq. There are trains to Mangalore (sleeper/3AC/2AC ₹130/330/448, five hours), Kannur (2nd class/3AC/2AC ₹46/210/279, two hours), Ernakulam (2nd class/AC chair ₹67/237, 4½ hours) via Thrissur (₹67/237, three hours), and all the way to Trivandrum (sleeper/3AC/2AC ₹181/500/680, 11 hours).

Heading southeast, trains go to Coimbatore (sleeper/3AC/2AC ₹120/292/394, 4½ hours), via Palakkad (₹120/243/356, 3½ hours). These trains then head north to the centres of Bengaluru, Chennai and Delhi.

ℹ Getting Around

Calicut has a glut of autorickshaws and most are happy to use the meter. It's about ₹20 from the station to the KSRTC bus stand or most hotels.

AYURVEDA

With its roots in Sanskrit, the word ayurveda is from *ayu* (life) and *veda* (knowledge); it is the knowledge or science of life. Principles of ayurvedic medicine were first documented in the Vedas some 2000 years ago, but may have been practised centuries earlier.

Ayurveda sees the world as having an intrinsic order and balance. It argues that we possess three *doshas* (humours): *vata* (wind or air); *pitta* (fire); and *kapha* (water/earth), known together as the *tridoshas*. Deficiency or excess in any of them can result in disease: an excess of *vata* may result in dizziness and debility; an increase in *pitta* may lead to fever, inflammation and infection. *Kapha* is essential for hydration.

Ayurvedic treatment aims to restore the balance, and hence good health, principally through two methods: panchakarma (internal purification), and herbal massage. Panchakarma is used to treat serious ailments, and is an intense detox regime, a combination of five types of different therapies (*panchakarma* means 'five actions') to rid the body of built-up endotoxins. These include: *vaman* – therapeutic vomiting; *virechan* – purgation; *vasti* – enemas; *nasya* – elimination of toxins through the nose; and *raktamoksha* – detoxification of the blood. Before panchakarma begins, the body is first prepared over several days with a special diet, oil massages (*snehana*) and herbal steambaths (*swedana*). Although it may sound pretty grim, panchakarma purification might only use a few of these treatments at a time, with therapies like bloodletting and leeches only used in rare cases. Still, this is no spa holiday. The herbs used in ayurveda grow in abundance in Kerala's humid climate – the monsoon is thought to be the best time of year for treatment, when there is less dust in the air and the pores are open and the body is most receptive to treatment – and every village has its own ayurvedic pharmacy.

Wayanad Wildlife Sanctuary

☑04936 / POP 780.200

Ask any Keralan what the prettiest part of their state is and most will whisper: Wayanad. Encompassing part of a remote forest reserve that spills into Tamil Nadu, Wayanad's landscape is combines rice paddies of ludicrous green, skinny betel nut trees, bamboo, red earth, spiky ginger fields, and rubber, cardamom and coffee plantations. Tourist infrastructure is beginning, though it's still fantastically unspoilt, with epic views. Surprisingly few tourists make it here, a shame since it's one of the few places you're almost guaranteed to spot wild elephants.

The 345 sq km sanctuary has two separate pockets – **Muthanga** in the east bordering Tamil Nadu, and **Tholpetty** in the north bordering Karnataka. Three major towns in Wayanad district make good bases for exploring the sanctuary – **Kalpetta** in the south, **Sultanbatheri** (Sultan Battery) in the east and **Mananthavadi** in the northwest.

◉ Sights & Activities

TOP CHOICE **Visiting the Sanctuary** NATURE RESERVE
Entry to both parts of the **sanctuary** (admission to each part ₹110, camera/video ₹25/150;

◷7-10.30am & 3-6.30pm) is only permitted as part of a guided trek or jeep safari, both of which can be arranged at the sanctuary entrances. Tholpetty closes during the monsoon period, while Muthanga remains open.

At **Tholpetty** (☑04935-250853; jeep ₹300, guide ₹200; ◷Sept-Mar), the 1½-hour **jeep tours** (7am to 9am and 3pm to 5pm) are a great way to spot wildlife. Rangers organise **guided treks** (up to 5 people ₹1500, extra people ₹400) from here.

At **Muthanga** (☑271010; jeep ₹300 guide ₹100), two-hour **jeep tours** are available in the mornings and afternoons. During the monsoon period, with a minimum of four people, **rafting trips** (2½hr trip ₹800-900) may also be arranged .

The DTPC, as well as most hotels, arrange guided **jeep tours** (up to 5 people with/without guide ₹2200/1700) of the Muthanga sanctuary and surrounding Wayanad sights.

Kannur Ayurvedic Centre AYURVEDA
(☑0436-203001; www.ayurvedawayanad.com; Kalpetta; massage from ₹500) For ayurvedic treatments, visit this excellent small, government-certified and family-run clinic, tucked away in the leafy backstreets of Kalpetta. Ayurvedic massage starts at ₹500, longer treatments like full 21-day panchakarma cleansing costs around ₹20,000, including food.

There are nice **rooms** (r ₹500) – some with balconies and views. There are also daily yoga classes (per week ₹400; ◎6-7am).

Trekking & Rafting
OUTDOOR ACTIVITIES

There are some top opportunities for independent **trekking** around the district, including a climb to the top of Chembra Peak, at 2100m the area's tallest summit; Vellarimala, with great views and lots of wildlife-spotting opportunities; and **Pakshipathalam**, a formation of large boulders deep in the forest. Permits are necessary and can be arranged at forest offices in South or North Wayanad. The **DTPC office** in Kalpetta organises trekking guides (₹600 per day), camping equipment (around ₹250 per person) and transport – pretty much anything you might need to get you hiking. It also runs four-hour bamboo **rafting trips** (₹1000) from June to September.

Thirunelly Temple
TEMPLE

(◎dawn-dusk) Thought to be one of the oldest on the subcontinent, Thirunelly Temple is 10km from Tholpetty. Non-Hindus cannot enter, but it's worth visiting to experience the otherworldly cocktail of ancient and intricate pillars and stone carvings, set against a backdrop of mist-covered peaks.

Jain temple
TEMPLE

(◎8am-noon & 2-6pm) The 13th-century Jain temple near Sultanbatheri, has splendid stone carvings and is an important monument to the region's strong historical Jain presence.

Edakal Caves
CAVES

(admission ₹10; ◎9am-5pm) Close to the Jain temple, near Ambalavayal, these caves have petroglyphs thought to date back over 3000 years and jaw-dropping views of Wayanad district.

Wayanad Heritage Museum
MUSEUM

(Ambalavayal; admission ₹10; ◎9am-5pm) In the same area as the caves, this museum exhibits its headgear, weapons, pottery, carved stone and other artefacts dating back to the 15th century that shed light on Wayanad's significant Adivasi population.

Uravu
HANDICRAFTS

(☏04936-231400/275 443; Thrikkaippetta; www.uravu.net; ◎8.30am-5pm Mon-Sat) Around 6km southeast of Kalpetta is where a collective of bamboo workers create all sorts of artefacts from bamboo. You can visit the artists' workshops, where they work on looms, painting and carving, and support their work by buying vases, lampshades, bangles, baskets, and much more at bargain prices from the small fixed-price shop. A return jeep from Kalpetta will cost around ₹250.

Pookot Lake
PARK, BOATING

(admission ₹10; ◎9am-6pm) is 3km before Vythiri, a beautiful mirror framed by forest. Geared up for visitors, it has well-maintained gardens, a cafeteria, playground and **boats** (paddle/row boats per 20min ₹30/50) for hire. It gets packed on the weekends, though feels quite peaceful during the week.

🛏 Sleeping & Eating

<u>TOP CHOICE</u> **Tranquil**
HOMESTAY $$$

(☏04936-220244; www.tranquilresort.com; Kuppamudi Estate, Kolagapara; full board & tax s/d from ₹10,101/13,750, tree villa ₹14,850/19,500, tree house ₹13,000/17,900;✺) This wonderful homestay is in the middle of an incredible lush 160 hectares of pepper, coffee, vanilla and cardamom plantations. The elegant house has sweeping verandas filled with plants and handsome furniture, and there are two treehouses that have to be the finest in the state – most romantic is the tree house, which is at a dizzying height and has a branch growing through the bathroom. Victor, the plantation owner, will welcome you in like an old friend of the family. There are 12 walks marked around the plantation.

Pachyderm Palace
GUESTHOUSE $$

(☏reservations0484-2371761;touristdesk@satyam.net.in; Tholpetty; r per person incl meals ₹1250-1500) This fine old Keralan house lies just outside the gate of Tholpetty Wildlife Sanctuary – handy for early-morning treks, tours and wildlife viewing. The varied rooms are simple and tidy, with polished wood ceilings, tiled floors and mosquito nets. There's one stilt-bungalow surrounded by forest. Venu is a stupendous cook, and his son Dilip is a great guide to the surrounds. Besides trekking, they can arrange night **animal-spotting safaris** (30-60min ₹200) – not inside the park – where your chances of spotting wild elephants are pretty phenomenal.

Ente Veedu
HOMESTAY $$

(☏0435-220008; www.ente veedu.co.in; Panamaram; r incl breakfast ₹2500-3000; @) It's isolated

KERALA NORTHERN KERALA

and set in a stunning location overlooking sprawling banana plantations and rice paddies, so this homestay halfway between Kalpetta and Manthavady is definitely worth seeking out. Surrounded by bucolic villages, it has several large rooms that come thoughtfully and colourfully furnished. Two rooms are bamboo-lined and offer private balconies. There are hammocks and wicker lounges here to enjoy the sensational views. Call to arrange a pick-up.

Stream Valley Cottages RESORT $$
(☑04936-255860; www.streamvalleycottages.com; Vythiri; d ₹2500-3000, cottages sleeping 8 ₹6000) These plain modern cottages lie on the banks of a small stream, several hundred metres off the main road (2.5km before Vythiri). Each cottage has a separate sitting area, private veranda, dark-wood interior and comes with a hushed soundtrack of singing birds and bubbling brooks. Traditional Keralan meals (₹390) are available.

Tamarind HOTEL $$
(☑0493-5210475; info@tamarindthirunelly.com; Thirunelly; d with AC ₹1400) With a fantastic setting 750m from the Thirunelly Temple, this remote-feeling KTDC property is set on its own in the countryside, has large rooms

with verdant views, and is a good deal. There's a restaurant.

Haritagiri HOTEL $$
(☑04936-203145; www.hotelharitagiri.com; Kalpetta; s/d ₹900/1200, executive ₹1200/1600; ✳) Somewhat set away from Kalpetta's busy main streets, this is a reasonable, comfortable hotel, and some of the rooms, with lively orange, green and blue colour schemes, have good views across the town's greenery from their balconies.

PPS Tourist Home HOTEL $
(☑04936-203431; Kalpetta; s/d ₹440/550, deluxe d ₹670; ✳) This agreeable and friendly place in the middle of Kalpetta has budget rooms in a motel-like compound that are fairly clean and comfy. The helpful management can arrange trips around Wayanad (₹2000 per carload) and hikes up Chembra Peak (₹1000 plus permit fees, six hours).

Hotel Regency HOTEL $$
(☑04936-220512; www.issacsregency.com; Sultanbatheri; s/d/tr from ₹800/1200/1400, with AC from ₹1200/1600/1800; ✳) The pick of Sultanbatheri's bunch of hotels, this quiet and no-nonsense place has routine, large and relatively tidy rooms in a U-shaped building.

The deluxe rooms differ from the standard ones in price only.

ℹ Information

The somewhat disorganised **DTPC office** (☎04936-202134; www.dtpcwayanad.com; Kalpetta; ⏰10am-5pm Mon-Sat) at Kalpetta can help organise tours, permits and trekking. There are UAE Exchange offices in Kalpetta and Sultanbatheri, and Federal Bank and Canara Bank ATMs can be found in each of the three main towns, as can a smattering of internet cafes.

ℹ Getting There & Around

Autorickshaw & Jeep

There are plenty of autorickshaws and jeeps for short trips within the towns.

Bus

Buses brave the winding roads between Calicut and Sultanbatheri (₹62/70 ordinary/Express, three hours), via Kalpetta (₹51), every 15 minutes. Private buses also run between Kannur and Mananthavadi every 45 minutes (₹62, 2½ hours). From Sultanbatheri, an 8am bus heads out for Ooty (₹56, four hours), with a second one passing through town at around 1pm. Buses for Mysore (₹78, three hours) leave every 30 minutes or so.

Plenty of private buses connect Mananthavadi, Kalpetta and Sultanbatheri every 10 to 20 minutes during daylight hours (₹14 to ₹22, 45 minutes to one hour). From Mananthavadi, regular buses also head to Tholpetty (₹14, one hour), Mysore (₹70, three hours, five buses) and Ooty (₹82, 5 to 6 hours, two daily). You can hire jeeps to get from one town to the next for around ₹400 to ₹600 each way.

Car hire

DTPC can help arrange car hire (from around ₹1700 per day).

Kannur (Cannanore)

☎0497 / POP 498,200

Under the Kolathiri rajas, Kannur was a major port bristling with international trade – explorer Marco Polo christened it a 'great emporium of spice trade'. Since then, the usual colonial suspects, including the Portuguese, Dutch and British, have had a go at exerting their influence on the region. Today it is an unexciting, though agreeable, town known mostly for its weaving industry and cashew trade, with some stunning, off-the-beaten track beaches nearby; bear in mind you can't swim during the monsoon season because of rough seas. This is a dominantly

Muslim area, so local sensibilities should be kept in mind: wear a sarong over your bikini on the beach. It's also a great base for seeing incredible *theyyam* possession performances.

◉ Sights & Activities

Theyyam Rituals   CULTURAL PROGRAM

Kannur is the best place to see the spirit-possession ritual called *theyyam* (p304); on most nights of the year there should be a *theyyam* ritual on somewhere in the vicinity. The easiest way to find out is to contact Kurien at Costa Malabari guesthouse. Alternatively, you can visit the **Kerala Folklore Academy** (☎2778090), near Chirakkal Pond, Valapattanam, 20km north of Kannur, where you can see vibrantly coloured costumes up close and sometimes catch a performance.

FREE **St Angelo Fort**   FORT

(⏰9am-6pm) The Portuguese built the St Angelo Fort in 1505 from brilliantly red laterite stone on a promontory a few kilometres south of town. It has a serene garden and excellent views of nearby palm-fringed beaches.

Loknath Weavers'
Co-operative   HANDICRAFTS

(☎2726330; ⏰8.30am-5.30pm Mon-Sat) Established in 1955, this is one of the oldest co-operatives in Kannur and occupies a large building busily clicking with the sound of looms. You can stop by for a quick tour and visit the small shop here that displays the fruits of their labours. It's 4km south of Kannur.

Kerala Dinesh Beedi
Co-Operative   HANDICRAFTS

(☎2835280; ⏰8am-5pm Tue-Sat) This region is also known for the manufacture of *beedis,* those tiny Indian cigarettes deftly rolled inside green leaves. This is one of the largest and purportedly best manufacturers, with a factory at Thottada, 7km south of Kannur. Either of these cooperatives is a ₹80 to ₹100 (return) autorickshaw ride from Kannur town.

Kairail   BOATING

(☎0460-2243460; barge hire per hr ₹1600) Kairail, 20km north of Kannur, offers rice-barge trips on the unspoilt northern Kerala backwaters; you can rent a barge by the hour but it's worth enquiring about day trips.

🛏 Sleeping & Eating

TOP CHOICE Ezhara Beach House   HOMESTAY **$$**
(☎0497-2835022; www.ezharabeachhouse.com;
7/347 Ezhara Kadappuram; r per person incl meals
₹1500; 🛜) Beside the unspoilt Kizhunna
Ezhara beach, midway between Kannur
and Telicherry railway stations (11km from
each), hidden amongst palms alongside sim-
ilar traditional Keralan houses, is the blue
Ezhara Beach House, run by the magnifi-
cent, straight-talking Hyancinth. Rooms are
simple and small, but the house has charac-
ter and there's a brilliant terrace where you
can sit and gaze out to sea through swaying
palms and spot sea eagles swooping, plus
wi-fi if you should want to keep in touch
with the world.

Ayisha Manzil   HOMESTAY **$$**
(☎0490-2341590; Court Rd, Tellicherry; d incl
meals & tax ₹9750) Around 25km south of
Kannur is Ayisha Manzil, a lovely 1862 colonial-era building perched on a cliff top,
with stunning sea views and faded, antique-
decorated rooms, run by the perfect hosts,
CP Moosa and his wife Faiza Moosa, who is
a renowned cook and cookery teacher, spe-

TRADITIONAL KERALAN ARTS

Kathakali

The art form of Kathakali crystallised at around the same time as Shakespeare was scribbling his plays. The Kathakali performance is the dramatised presentation of a play, usually based on the Hindu epics the Ramayana, the Mahabharata and the Puranas. All the great themes are covered – righteousness and evil, frailty and courage, poverty and prosperity, war and peace.

Drummers and singers accompany the actors, who tell the story through their pre-cise movements, particularly mudras (hand gestures) and facial expressions.

Preparation for the performance is lengthy and disciplined. Paint, fantastic costumes, ornamental headpieces and meditation transform the actors both physically and men-tally into the gods, heroes and demons they are about to play.

You can see cut-down performances in tourist hot spots all over the state, and there are Kathakali schools in Trivandrum and near Thrissur that encourage visitors.

Kalarippayat

Kalarippayat is an ancient tradition of martial training and discipline, still taught throughout Kerala. Some believe it is the forerunner of all martial arts, with roots tracing back to the 12th-century skirmishes among Kerala's feudal principalities.

Masters of *kalarippayat*, called Gurukkal, teach their craft inside a special arena called a *kalari*.

Kalarippayat movements can be traced in Kerala's performing arts, such as Kathakali and *kootiattam*, and in ritual arts such as *theyyam*.

Theyyam

Kerala's most popular ritualistic art form, *theyyam*, is believed to pre-date Hinduism, originating from folk dances performed during harvest celebrations. An intensely local ritual, it's often performed in *kavus* (sacred groves) throughout northern Kerala.

Theyyam refers both to the shape of the deity/hero portrayed, and to the actual ritual. There are around 450 different *theyyams*, each with a distinct costume; face paint, bracelets, breastplates, skirts, garlands and especially headdresses are exuber-ant, intricately crafted and sometimes huge (up to 6m or 7m tall).

During performances, each protagonist loses his physical identity and speaks, moves and blesses the devotees as if he were that deity. Frenzied dancing and wild drumming create an atmosphere in which a deity indeed might, if it so desired, manifest itself in human form.

During October to May there are an annual rituals at each of the hundreds of *kavus*. *Theyyam*s are often held to bring good fortune to important events such as marriages and housewarmings. See p303 for details on how to find one.

cialising in Mopla cuisine (Keralan Islamic cooking). Pick up may be arranged,

Costa Malabari
GUESTHOUSE $$

(☑reservations 0484-2371761; touristdesk@saty am.net.in; Thottada Beach; r per person incl meals from ₹1250) In a small village and five minutes' walk from an idyllic beach, Costa Malabari pioneered tourism in this area with its spacious rooms in an old hand-loom factory, surrounded by lush greenery. There's a huge communal space and comfy lounging areas outside. Extra rooms are offered in two other buildings, the pick of which is perched dramatically just above the beach, where you fall asleep to the crashing of waves, and there are steps directly down to the beach. The home-cooked Keralan food is plentiful, varied, and delicious. Kurien, your gracious host, is an expert on the astonishing *theyyam* ritual and can help arrange a visit. It's 8km from Kannur town; a rickshaw/taxi from the train station is around ₹120/200.

Kannur Beach House
HOMESTAY $$

(☑0497-2708360, 9847184535; www.kannurbeach house.com; Thottada Beach; r ₹2200-2500) Near Costa Malabari and in an idyllic spot right behind the beach, the rooms in this traditional Keralan building are presentably furnished and boast handsome wooden shutters. Four rooms overlook the sea, with either a balcony or porch to enjoy the sensational ocean sunset views through swaying palms, and you can spot cuckoos and bramini kites in the nearby mangroves. It's 8km from Kannur.

Government Guest House
GUESTHOUSE $

(☑2706426; d ₹440; ✱) This place has the air of torpor that is the speciality of government-run hotels, but rooms in the 'new block' are enormous, simply furnished and sport balconies that look right onto the sea – they're phenomenal value.

Hotel Meridian Palace
HOTEL $

(☑2761676; www.hotelmeridianpalace.com; Bellard Rd; s from ₹200/250, d with AC ₹600-900) In the market area opposite the main train station, this is not quite a palace, but is friendly enough and offers a cornucopia of budget rooms. If you manage to decide on one, chances are it will be fairly clean, basic and convenient for an early train departure.

Mascot Beach Resort
HOTEL $$

(☑2708115; www.mascotresort.com; d with AC from ₹2200; ✱✱) A few hundred metres south of the Government Guest House, this place is a small, reasonable hotel and also has grand views of the ocean from its 30 neat and comfy AC rooms. It's worth angling for a discount.

❶ Information

The **DTPC Office** (☑2706336; ◷10am-5pm Mon-Sat), opposite the KSRTC bus stand, supplies basic maps of Kannur. There are Federal Bank and State Bank of India ATMs adjacent to the bus stand. A **UAE Exchange** (☑2709022; City Centre, Fort Rd; ◷9.30am-6pm Mon-Sat, 11am-1pm Sun) office changes travellers cheques and cash; it's located in City Centre mall, five minutes from the train station.

❶ Getting There & Away

There are daily buses to Mysore (₹164/188 ordinary/deluxe, eight hours, five daily), Mangalore (₹109, four hours, two daily), Ernakulam (₹187, eight hours, four daily), and Kalpetta (₹70, four hours, two daily) for Wayanad. There's one daily bus to Ooty (via Wayanad, ₹135, nine hours) at 10pm.

There are several daily trains to Mangalore (sleeper/3AC/2AC ₹100/218/301, three hours), Calicut (2nd class/AC chair ₹31/140, two hours) and Ernakulam (₹69/272, 6½ hours).

Bekal & Around

☑0467

Bekal and nearby Palakunnu and Udma, in Kerala's far north, have some long white-sand beaches begging for DIY exploration. The area is beginning to be colonised by glitzy, unreal five-star resorts catering to fresh-from-the-Gulf millionaires, but it's still worth the trip for off-the-beaten-track adventurers intent on discovering the beaches before they get swallowed up by developers with dollar-signs in their eyes. Because it's a predominantly Muslim area, it's important to keep local sensibilities in mind, especially at the beach.

The laterite-brick **Bekal Fort** (Indian/foreigner ₹5/100; ◷8am-5pm), built between 1645 and 1660, sits on Bekal's rocky headland and houses a small Hindu temple and plenty of goats. Next door, **Bekal Beach** (admission ₹5) encompasses a grassy park and a long, beautiful stretch of sand that

WORTH A TRIP

VALIYAPARAMBA BACKWATERS

For those seeking to escape the burgeoning commercialism around Alleppey, what are often referred to as the northern backwaters offer an intriguing alternative. This large body of water is fed by five rivers and fringed by ludicrously green lands punctuated by rows of nodding palms. One of the nearest towns is **Payyanur**, 50km north of Kannur. It's possible to catch the ferry from Kotti, from where KSWTD operates local ferries to the surrounding islands. It's five minutes' walk from Payyanur railway station. The 2½-hour trip (₹9) from Kotti takes you to the **Ayitti Jetty** (☏0467-2213577), 8km from Payyanur; then catch the return ferry.

You can stay at the tiny **Valiyaparamba Retreat** (☏2371761; touristdesk@satyam.net. in; d full board ₹3000), a secluded place 15km north of Payyanur and 3km from Ayitti Jetty. It has two simple rooms and two stilted bungalows, fronted by an empty golden-sand beach and backed by backwaters. Kochi's Tourist Desk (contactable via the Retreat, or in Kochi, p292) also runs **day trips** (per person incl lunch ₹600) for groups of four to 15 people, on a traditional houseboat around the Valiyaparamba Backwaters.

Otherwise, 22km south of Bekal, **Bekal Boat Stay** (☏0467-2282633; www.bekal boatstay.com; Kottappuram, Nileshwar) is one of the few enterprises in the region to offer overnight **houseboat trips** (2-4 people per 24hr ₹7000-9500) around the Valiyaparamba backwaters. Cheaper sunset or day cruises are also available. You can also try Kairail (p303) near Kannur.

turns into a circus on weekends and holidays when local families descend here for rambunctious leisure time. Isolated **Kappil Beach**, 6km north of Bekal, is a beautiful, lonely stretch of fine sand and calm water, but beware of shifting sandbars.

There are lots of cheap, poor quality hotels scattered between Kanhangad (12km south) and Kasaragod (10km north), with a few notable exceptions that could work well as Bekal bases.

TOP CHOICE **Neeleshwar Hermitage** (☏0467-2288876; www.neeleshwarhermitage.com; Neeleshwar; r from ₹8000) consists of 16 fishermen's cottages that have been converted into a stand-out eco resort. Built according to the principles of Kerala Vastu, it has an infinity pool that gazes out to sea, nearly 5 hectares of lush gardens fragrant with frangipani, smashing organic food and little comforts like iPod docks.

Gitanjali Heritage (☏0467-2234159; www. gitanjaliheritage.com; s/d full-board ₹2500/3500) This lovely place lies surrounded by rice paddies, deep among Kasaragod's inland villages. It is just 5km from Bekal and is an intimate heritage home with comfortable, higgledy-piggledy rooms filled with ancestral furniture and polished wood. Call ahead for pick-ups.

ⓘ Getting There & Around

A couple of local trains stop at Fort Bekal station, right on Bekal beach. Kanhangad, 12km south, is a major train stop, while Kasaragod, 10km to the north, is the largest town in the area. Both Kanhangad and Kasaragod have frequent buses running to and from Bekal (around ₹10, 20 minutes). An autorickshaw from Bekal Junction to Kappil beach is around ₹40.

LAKSHADWEEP

POP 60,700

Comprising a string of 36 palm-covered, white sand-skirted coral islands 300km off the coast of Kerala, Lakshadweep is as stunning as it is isolated. Only 10 of these islands are inhabited, mostly with Sunni Muslim fishermen, and foreigners are only allowed to stay on a few of these. With fishing and coir production the main sources of income, local life on the islands remains highly traditional, and a caste system divides the islanders between Koya (land owners), Malmi (sailors) and Melachery (farmers).

The real attraction of the islands lies under the water: the 4200 sq km of pristine archipelago lagoons, unspoiled coral reefs and warm waters are a magnet for flipper-toting travellers and divers alike. Diving, snorkelling, kayaking, boat trips, sailing and jaunts to nearby islands can be arranged by most resorts. At the time of research, the resort on the 20-hectare, white-sand-fringed Bangaram island was closed – enquire locally to find out if it's reopened.

Lakshadweep can only be visited on a prearranged package trip – all listed accommodation prices are for the peak October to May season and include permits and meals.

ℹ Information

SPORTS (Society for the Promotion of Recreational Tourism & Sports; ☎0484-2668387; www.lakshadweeptourism.com; IG Rd, Willingdon Island; ☺10am-5pm Mon-Sat) is the main organisation for tourist information.

PERMITS Foreigners are limited to staying in the resorts, none of which are budget places; a special permit (one month's notice) is required and organised by tour operators, hotels or SPORTS in Kochi. Most of the islands have only recently been opened up to foreigners, who are now allowed to stay on Bangaram, Agatti, Kadmat, Minicoy and Kavaratti Islands.

ℹ Getting There & Away

Kingfisher Airlines (www.flykingfisher.com) flies regularly between Kochi and Agatti Island (₹9700 return). At the time of research, there were no ferry services between Agatti and Bangaram. Boat transport between Agatti and Kadmat is included in the package tours available, and the same goes for transport from Kochi to Kadmat and the Mincoy Islands. See the package section of www.lakshwdeeptourism.com for more details.

Agatti Island

The village located on this 2.7-sq-km island has several **mosques**, which you can visit if dressed modestly. There's no alcohol on the island.

Agatti Island Beach Resort (☎0484-2362232; www.agattiislandresorts.com; d full board €155, with AC €210; ❄) sits on two beaches at the southern tip of the island and offers a range of packages. The resort has simple, low-rise beach cottages, designed to be comfortably cool without AC, and a restaurant for 20 people.

Kadmat Island

Kadmat Beach Resort (☎0484-4011134; www.kadmat.com; d from €185 per person; ❄) has 28 modern cottages, administered by Mint Valley (www.mintvalley.com) and can be reached by overnight boat from Kochi (p280).

Lakshadweep

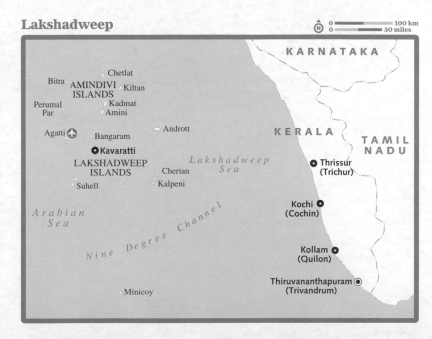

DIVING

Lakshadweep is a diver's dream, with excellent visibility and an embarrassment of marine life living on undisturbed coral reefs. The best time to dive is between mid-October and mid-May when the seas are calm and visibility is 20m to 40m.

Lacadives (☑022-66627381; www.lacadives.com) runs dive centres on Bangaram and Kadmat Islands. Costs can vary: a four-day PADI open-water course costs ₹28,000, while experienced divers pay ₹3000 per dive (including equipment hire), with discounts available for multiple dives. Information is available through the hotels or directly through Lacadives at 14C Bungalow, Boran Rd, Opposite Elco Market, Off Hill Rd, Bandra (W), Mumbai.

From Kadmat Island, dives range from 9m to 40m in depth. Some of the better sites include North Cave, the Wall, Jack Point, Shark Alley, the Potato Patch, Cross Currents and Sting Ray City. Around Bangaram good spots include the 32m-deep wreck of the *Princess Royale*, Manta Point, Life, Grand Canyon and the impressive sunken reef at Perumal Par.

Minicoy Island

You can stay on the remote island of Minicoy, the second largest island and the closest to the Maldives, in modern cottages or a 20-room guesthouse at **Minicoy Island Resort** (☑0484-2668387; www.lakshadweeptourism.com; s/d ₹3000/4000, with AC ₹5000/6000; ❄) via SPORTS Swaying Palms and Coral Reef Packages.

Tamil Nadu & Chennai

Best Places to Eat

» Any branch of Hotel
Saravana Bhavan (p322)

» Bangala (p362)

» Satsanga (p346)

Best Places to Stay

» Calve (p343)

» Visalam (p362)

» 180 McIver (p379)

» Carlton Hotel (p373)

Why Go?

Tamil Nadu is the homeland of one of humanity's living classical civilisations, a people whose culture has grown, but in many ways not fundamentally altered, since the Greeks sacrificed goats to Zeus.

But this state is as dynamic as it is drenched in history. In Tamil Nadu's famous temples, fire-worshipping devotees smear tikka on their brows before heading to IT offices to develop new software applications. Tamil Nadu has one foot in the 21st century and the other in the poetry of one of the oldest literary languages on Earth.

Here you can reach the ends of India, where three oceans mingle. See the tiger-prowled hills of the Nilgiris, the Mother Temple of the triple-breasted, fish-eyed goddess and the Mountain of Fire, where god manifests as a pillar of flame. It's all packed into a state that manages to remain fiercely distinct from the rest of India, while exemplifying her oldest and most adventurous edges.

When to Go
Chennai

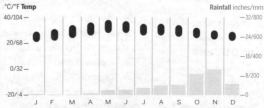

Jan Pongal (harvest festival) celebrations spill into the streets.

May Head to the hill stations for the summer 'season'.

Nov The full-moon festival of lights.

Fast Facts

» Population: 72.1 million

» Area: 130,058 sq km

» Capital: Chennai (Madras)

» Main language: Tamil

» Sleeping prices: **$** below ₹1000, **$$** ₹1000 to ₹3000, **$$$** above ₹3000

Top Tip

If you need train tickets in a hurry, the Foreign Tourist Assistance Cell at Chennai Central (p327) is the most helpful and efficient we've ever come across; tickets for booked-up trains anywhere in India seem to become magically available here.

Resources

» TamilNadu.Com (www. tamilnadu.com) News and directory.

» Tamil Nadu Forest Department (www.forests.tn.nic. in) National parks, ecotourism and permit information.

» Tamil Nadu Tourism (www.tamilnadutourism.org)

Food

Tamil Nadu's favourite foods are overwhelmingly vegetarian, with lots of coconut and chilli. No matter where you go you'll find dosas, *idlis* (spongy, round fermented rice cakes) and *vada* (deep-fried lentil-flour doughnuts), all of which are always served with coconut chutney and *sambar* (lentil broth). These will sometimes be your only options, and luckily they're very, very tasty (though you want to eat your *idlis* fresh and warm) – and they're generally vegan friendly, too. Thalis – all-you-can-eat meals based around rice, lentil dishes, *rasam* (hot and sour tamarind soup) and chutneys, often served on a banana leaf – are also good, ubiquitous, cheap and filling.

The exception to the all-veg diet is Chettinad food, derived from food traditionally prepared in the southern region around Pudukkottai and Karaikkudi but available at restaurants in most of the bigger towns. Chettinad menus often feature mutton, chicken and fish; it's less fiery and more about the use of fresh spices like cinammon, cumin and star anise. Pepper Chicken is a classic Chettinad dish.

For a state that grows a lot of tea, Tamil Nadu really loves its coffee; filtered coffee (mixed with milk and sugar, of course) is more readily available than tea in many cheap thali joints.

DON'T MISS

Escape from the heat of the plains by taking the **toy train** from Mettapulayam up into the Nilgiri hills; the tracks cut through tropical palms and paddy fields, then through green, monkey-infested jungles, crosses bridges over gushing streams and finally chugs through European-looking forest into the cool of Ooty.

You can't come to Tamil Nadu without admiring its ancient **temples**; see p351 for a selection with the most stunning architecture, rituals and festivals.

Top State Festivals

» International Yoga Festival (4-7 Jan, Puducherry, p343)

» Chennai Sangamam (mid-Jan, Chennai, p320)

» Pongal (mid-Jan, statewide, p312) Harvest festival.

» International Music festival (Jan, Thiruvaiyaru, p355)

» Teppam (Float) Festival (Jan/Feb, Madurai, p365)

» Natyanjali Dance Festival (Feb/Mar, Chidambaram, p350)

» Chithrai Festival (Apr/May, Madurai, p365)

» Summer festivals (May-Jun, statewide, p312)

» Bastille Day (14 Jul, Puducherry, p343)

» Karthikai Deepam Festival (Nov/Dec, statewide, p312)

» Chennai Festival of Music & Dance (mid-Dec–mid-Jan, Chennai, p320)

» Mamallapuram Dance Festival (Dec-Jan, Mamallapuram, p334)

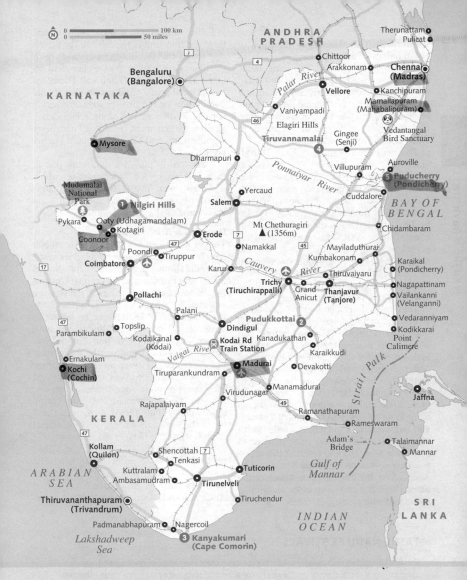

Tamil Nadu Highlights

① Climb into the cool of the **Western Ghats** (p372)

② Spend the night in a Chettiar mansion in **Pudukkottai district** (p361)

③ Watch the sun set over three oceans at once in **Kanyakumari** (p369)

④ See god manifest as a lingam of fire in **Tiruvannamalai** (p340)

⑤ Explore the Gallic roots of **Puducherry** (Pondicherry; p342)

History

It's ironic that the bearers of the torch of South Indian identity may have their origins in Punjab and Pakistan. The early Indus civilisations display elements of Dravidian thought, language, culture and art, including a meditating god seated in the lotus position. This may be the world's first depiction of the yogi archetype, who has come to symbolise, for many, Asian spirituality.

The nomadic Aryans drove the Dravidians south around 1500 BC. Here, a classical language and classical civilisations developed, cushioned by geography against North Indian invasion. By 300 BC the region was controlled by three major dynasties – Cholas in the east, Pandyas in the central area and Cheras in the west. This was the classical period of Tamil literature and myth – the Sangam Age – when kingdoms were ruled by feuding poet-kings and romantic epics; a visitor at the time described the Tamils as favouring rose petals over gold.

The Tamils developed their own aesthetic style, constructing huge cities that rivalled population centres in China and Europe, and magnificent steeped temples that wouldn't look out of place in Mayan Central America. Although each kingdom left notable achievements, the Cholas deserve some special mention. This remarkable nation maintained one of the great maritime empires of history, extending its influence to Cambodia, Vietnam and Indonesia, and spreading Tamil ideas of reincarnation, karma and yogic practice to Southeast Asia. The end result of this cross-pollination was architectural wonders like Angkor Wat, the intellectual gestation of Balinese Hinduism and much of the philosophy associated with classical Buddhism.

Before the Mughals could fully extend their reach to India's tip, in 1640 the British negotiated the use of Madraspatnam (now Chennai) as a trading post. Subsequent interest by the French, Dutch and Danes led to continual conflict and, finally, almost total domination by the British, when the region became known as the Madras Presidency. Small pocketed areas, including Puducherry (Pondicherry) and Karaikal, remained under French control.

Many Tamils played a significant part in India's struggle for independence, which was finally won in 1947. In 1956 the Madras Presidency was disbanded and Tamil Nadu was established as an autonomous state.

Dangers & Annoyances

The big draw in Tamil Nadu is the 5000-odd temples, but this is a very religious state, and non-Hindus are generally not allowed inside inner sanctums. This can be frustrating, as large areas of the best temples are essentially inaccessible to many travellers. Even nonresident Indians can be subject to scrutiny, and non-Indian Hindus may have to provide proof of conversion. Temple touts are fairly common and can be a nuisance, but don't dismiss every one as a scammer. There are many excellent guides here and they deserve both your time and rupees; use your best judgement, ask other travellers which guides they'd recommend and be on the lookout for badge-wearing official guides, who tend to be excellent resources.

Don't expect the Hindi slang you picked up in Rishikesh to go over well here. The Tamils are fiercely proud of their language and some consider Hindi to be North Indian cultural imperialism. North Indian tourists

---

TAMIL NADU FESTIVALS

Pongal is held in mid-January. As the rice boils over the new clay pots, this festival symbolises the prosperity and abundance a fruitful harvest brings. For many, the celebrations begin with temple rituals, followed by family gatherings. Later it's the animals, especially cows, that are honoured for their contribution to the harvest.

Summer festivals are held from May through June throughout the hills, but especially in Ooty and Kodaikanal, where there are boat races on the lake, horse racing (in Ooty), flower shows and music.

Held during full moon in November/December, the **Karthikai Deepam Festival** (Nov/Dec; statewide) is Tamil Nadu's 'festival of lights'. It is celebrated throughout the state with earthenware lamps and firecrackers, but the best place to see it is Tiruvannamalai (see boxed text, p340), where the legend began.

Many other temple-centred festivals are held in towns around the state; see p310 for a rundown and individual town sections for details.

are often as confused as you are down here; more Tamils speak English than Hindi.

ℹ Information

The state tourism body is **Tamil Nadu Tourism** (www.tamilnadutourism.org), which runs tourist offices of varying degrees of uselessness in most cities and large towns, plus a reliably average chain of hotels. You can also check www.tamilnadu-tourism.com for package-tour options. Accommodation costing more than ₹200 in Tamil Nadu (but not Puducherry) is subject to a government 'luxury' tax – 5% on rooms between ₹200 and ₹500, 10% on rooms between ₹501 and ₹1000, and 12.5% on rooms over ₹1000. There's often an additional 'service tax' at upmarket hotels. Prices throughout this chapter do not include tax, unless stated otherwise.

CHENNAI (MADRAS)

🖉044 / POP 6.6 MILLION

Chennai doesn't always make a good first impression. The streets are clogged with traffic, the weather is oppressively hot, the air is heavy with smog and sights of any great interest are thin on the ground.

The city's charm lies in its inhabitants; the enthusiasm of Chennaites for their hometown starts to infect you after a while, and they're friendlier and more down to earth than most big-city dwellers. Chennai is so chilled out you wouldn't even know it's an economic powerhouse, much less a queen of showbiz: India's fourth-largest city is its most humble.

The major transport hub of the region, this 70-sq-km city is a conglomerate of urban villages connected by a maze of roads ruled by hard-line rickshaw drivers. Its central location and excellent plane, train and bus connections actually make it an interesting alternative entry point into India. If you do happen to be caught here between connections, it's certainly worth your while poking around the markets of George Town or taking a sunset stroll along pretty Marina Beach.

Bordered on the east by the Bay of Bengal, Chennai is a sprawling combination of several small districts. George Town, a jumble of narrow streets, bazaars and the court buildings, is in the north, near the harbour. To the southwest is the major thoroughfare of Anna Salai (Mount Rd) and the two main train stations: Egmore, for destinations in Tamil Nadu, and Central, for interstate trains.

History

Chennai and surrounds have been attracting seafaring traders for centuries. As long as 2000 years ago, its residents traded and haggled with Chinese, Greek, Phoenician, Roman and Babylonian merchants. The Portuguese and the Dutch muscled in on this lucrative trade in the 16th century. The British, initially content to purchase spices and other goods from the Dutch, soon had enough of that and in 1639 established a settlement in the fishing village of Madraspatnam. The British East India Company erected Fort St George in 1653.

By the 18th century, the British East India Company had to contend with the French. Robert Clive (Clive of India), a key player in the British campaign, recruited an army of 2000 sepoys (Indian soldiers in British service) and launched a series of military expeditions that developed into the Carnatic Wars. Facing defeat, the French withdrew to Pondicherry (now Puducherry) in 1756.

In the 19th century, the city became the seat of the Madras Presidency, one of the four divisions of British Imperial India. After Independence, growth continued until the city became the significant southern gateway it is today.

Dangers & Annoyances

Convincing a Chennai autorickshaw driver to use the meter is a Vatican-certified miracle; fares border on the astronomical; and post-arrival disputes over pre-agreed fares are not uncommon. Avoid paying up front, and never get into an autorickshaw before reaching an agreement.

Tempting offers of ₹50 'tours' of the city sound too good to be true. They are. Expect to spend the day being dragged from one shop or emporium to another. Some travellers report negotiating cheap fares by agreeing to visit 'just one shop'.

If you have a serious problem with a driver, mentioning a call to the **traffic police** (🖉103) can defuse the conflict. See p328 for details on other modes of transport.

◉ Sights

EGMORE & CENTRAL CHENNAI

Government Museum MUSEUM

(Map p318; www.chennaimuseum.org; 486 Pantheon Rd, Egmore; Indian/foreigner ₹15/250, camera/video ₹200/500; ☺9.30am-5pm Sat-Thu) Housed across several British-built buildings known as the Pantheon Complex, this excellent museum is Chennai's best.

Chennai (Madras)

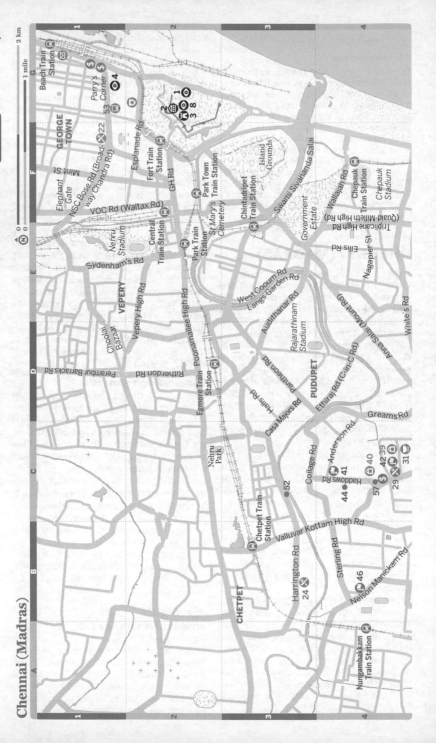

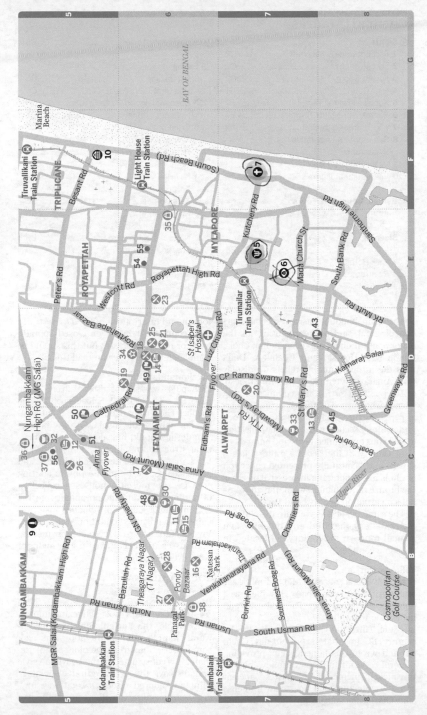

BAY OF BENGAL

Marina Beach

Tiruvallikani Train Station

TRIPLICANE

Besant Rd

Light House Train Station

(South Beach Rd)

MYLAPORE

Kutchery Rd

Santhome High Rd

Peter's Rd

ROYAPETTAH

Westcott Rd

Royapettah High Rd

Mada Church St

South Bank Rd

RK Mutt Rd

Royathape Bazaar

St Isabel's Hospital

Luz Church Rd

Tirumaillar Train Station

Kamaraj Salai

Greenway's Rd

Nungambakkam High Rd (MG Salai)

Cathedral Rd

CP Rama Swamy Rd

Flyover

(Mowbray's Rd)

St Mary's Rd

TTK Rd

ALWARPET

Boat Club Rd

Adyar River

TEYNAMPET

Eldham's Rd

Chamiers Rd

Anna Flyover

Anna Salai (Mount Rd)

Anna Salai (Mount Rd)

NUNGAMBAKKAM

MGR Salai (Kodambakkam High Rd)

GN Chetty Rd (MG Salai)

Bazullah Rd

Theagaraya Nagar (T Nagar)

Thanikachalam Rd

Boag Rd

Pondy Bazaar

Natesan Park

Venkatanarayana Rd

Burkit Rd

Southwest Boag Rd

Cosmopolitan Golf Course

North Usman Rd

Panagal Park

Usman Rd

South Usman Rd

Kodambakkam Train Station

Mambalam Train Station

The main building has a respectable **archaeological section** representing all the major South Indian periods, including Chola, Vijayanagar, Hoysala and Chalukya. Don't miss the intricate marble reliefs on display from Amaravathi temple in Andhra Pradesh, or the poignant *sati* stones commemorating women who burned on their husbands' funeral pyres. Further along is a **natural history and zoology** section with a motley collection of skeletons and stuffed birds and animals.

In Gallery 3, the **bronze gallery** has a superb and beautifully presented collection of Chola art. Among the impressive pieces is the bronze of Ardhanariswara, the androgynous incarnation of Shiva and Parvati.

The same ticket gets you into the **National Art Gallery**, the **children's museum** and a small **modern art gallery**, all located in the same complex.

Valluvar Kottam   MONUMENT
(Map p314; Valluvar Kottam High Rd, Kodambakkam; adult/child ₹3/2; ☉8am-6pm) This memorial honours the Tamil poet Thiruvalluvar and his classic work, the *Thirukural*. A weaver by trade, Thiruvalluvar lived around the 1st century BC in what is present-day Chennai and wrote this famed poem, providing a moral code for millions of followers. The three-level memorial replicates ancient Tamil architecture and boasts an immense 35m chariot, as well as an enormous audi-torium and inscriptions of the *Thirukural's* 1330 couplets. It has been closed sporadically for renovation work but this should be completed by the time you read this.

Vivekanandar Illam   MUSEUM
(Map p314; www.sriramakrishnamath.org; South Beach Rd; adult/child ₹2/1; ☉10am-noon & 3-7pm Thu-Tue) The Vivekananda House is interesting not only for the displays on the famous 'wandering monk', but also for the semicircular structure in which it's housed. Swami Vivekananda stayed here briefly in 1897 and preached his ascetic philosophy to adoring crowds. The museum houses a collection of photographs and memorabilia from the swami's life, a gallery of religious historical paintings and the 'meditation room' where Vivekananda stayed. Free one-hour meditation classes are held on Wednesday nights at 7pm (over-15s only).

SOUTH CHENNAI

Kapaleeshwarar Temple   HINDU TEMPLE
(Map p314; Kutchery Rd, Mylapore; ☉5am-12.30pm & 4-10pm) Chennai's most active and impressive temple, the ancient Shiva Kapaleeshwarar Temple was rebuilt 300 years ago; some inscriptions from the older temple remain. It is constructed in the Dravidian style and displays the architectural elements – rainbow-coloured *gopuram* (gateway tower), *mandapams* (pavilions in front of a

temple) and a huge tank – found in the famous temple cities of Tamil Nadu.

Ramakrishna Mutt Temple HINDU TEMPLE
(Map p314; RK Mutt Rd; ☺4.30-11.45am & 3-9pm, puja 8am) The tranquil, leafy grounds of the Ramakrishna Mutt Temple are a world away from the chaos and crazy rickshaw drivers outside. Monks glide around and there's a reverential feel here. The temple itself is a handsome shrine incorporating aspects of Hindu, Christian and Islamic styles; like the Belur Math in Kolkata, it's surprisingly architecturally coherent. It's open to followers of any faith for meditation.

San Thome Cathedral CHURCH
(Map p314; Kamarajar Salai) Originally built by the Portuguese in 1504, then rebuilt in neo-Gothic style in 1893, San Thome Cathedral is a soaring Roman Catholic church between Kapaleeshwarar Temple and Marina Beach. In the basement is a modern chapel housing the tomb of St Thomas the Apostle (Doubting Thomas), who it is said brought Christianity to the subcontinent in the 1st century; above is a museum containing Thomas-related artefacts of varying degrees of historical dubiousness.

Marina Beach BEACH
Take an early-morning or evening stroll (you really don't want to fry here at any other time) along the 13km sandy stretch of Marina Beach (Map p314) and you'll pass cricket matches, flying kites, fortune-tellers, fish markets and families enjoying the sea breeze. This beach was especially hard hit by the 2004 tsunami, with around 200 recorded casualties, most of them children. Don't swim here – strong rips make it dangerous.

Theosophical Society GARDEN, HISTORIC SITE
(Map p314; Lattice Bridge Rd; ☺8.30-10am & 2-4pm Mon-Sat) Between the Adyar River and the coast, the 100 hectares of the Theosophical Society provide a green and peaceful retreat from the city. It's a lovely spot to just wander; the sprawling grounds contain a church, mosque, Buddhist shrine and Hindu temple. There's a huge variety of native and introduced trees, including a famed 400-year-old **banyan tree** whose branches offer reprieving shade for over 40,000 sq ft. The **Adyar Library** (☺9am-4.30pm) here has an immense collection of books on religion and philosophy, some of which are on display, from thousand-year-old Buddhist scrolls to intricate, handmade 19th-century bibles.

GEORGE TOWN
Fort St George HISTORICAL BUILDING, MUSEUM
(Map p314; ☺8am-5pm) Finished around 1653 by the British East India Company, the fort has undergone many facelifts over the years. Inside the vast perimeter walls is now a precinct housing the **Secretariat &**

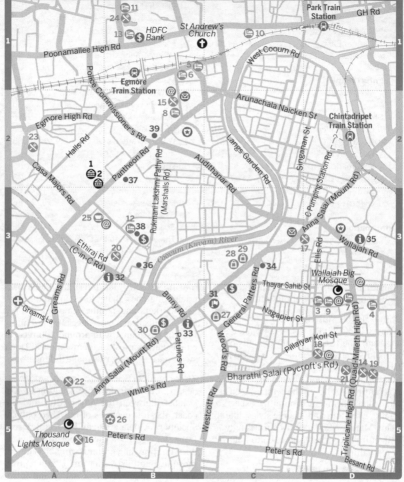

N 0 ___ 500 m
0 ___ 0.25 miles

Legislative Assembly. The 46m-high **flag-staff** at the main entrance is a mast salvaged from a 17th-century shipwreck.

The **Fort Museum** (Indian/foreigner ₹5/100, video ₹25; ⊙8am-5pm) has some interesting military memorabilia from the British and French East India Companies, as well as the Raj and Muslim administrations. Fascinating 18th-century etchings show European-looking families being rowed to shore from their ships by *lung-hi*-clad fishermen who look just like their modern-day counterparts on the beach across the street.

High Court   HISTORICAL BUILDING
Built in 1892, this red Indo-Saracenic structure (Map p314)at Parry's Corner is said to be the largest judicial building in the world after the Courts of London. You can wander around the court buildings and sit in on sessions.

OTHER SIGHTS
Little Mount & St Thomas Mount   SHRINE
It is believed that from around AD 58, St Thomas lived in hiding at **Little Mount** (Chinnamalai). The cave still bears what some believe to be Thomas' handprint, left when he escaped through an opening that

TAMIL NADU & CHENNAI CHENNAI (MADRAS)

miraculously appeared. You may be offered water drawn up from the St Thomas miracle spring. Three kilometres on, **St Thomas Mount** (Parangi Malai) is thought to be the site of Thomas' martyrdom in AD 72. The shrine supposedly contains a fragment of Thomas' bone and a cross he carved, among other relics; the views across the city from here are wonderful. Both mounts are about 1km from the Saidapet and St Thomas Mount train stations, respectively.

 Activities

Go for a 45-minute *abhyangam* (oil treatment; ₹750) or an extended ayurvedic treatment at **Amrit** (Map p314; ☑65195195; amrit.chennai@gmail.com; 6 Khader Nawaz Khan Rd, Nungambakkam; ☺7am-7pm). It also offers one-hour yoga classes (₹200) or month-long courses (₹1200).

 Courses

**International Institute of
Tamil Studies** LANGUAGE
(☑22542781; www.ulakaththamizh.org; Central Polytechnic Campus, Adyar) Runs intensive one-month and three-month courses in Tamil. It also sells an instructional CD of Tamil lessons, available through the website.

Vivekanandar Illam MEDITATION
(Map p314; ☑28446188; Kamarajar Salai, Triplicane) Free one-hour meditation classes (over-15s only) on Wednesday nights at 7pm.

 Tours

TTDC (Map p318; ☑25367850; www.tamilnadu tourism.org; 2 Wallajah Rd, Triplicane; ☺10am-5.30pm Mon-Fri) conducts half-day city tours (non-AC/AC ₹140/200) and day trips to

DEFINING DRAVIDIANS

The Tamils consider themselves the standard bearers of Dravidian – pre-Aryan Indian – civilisation. Their culture, language and history are distinctive from North India (although more related than some Tamil nationalists claim), and their ability to trace Tamil identity to classical antiquity is a source of considerable pride.

During the Indus Valley period (2600-1900 BC), the nomadic Aryans drove the city-dwelling Dravidians south while incorporating elements of the latter's beliefs into their holy texts, the Vedas. Later, south–north and class tensions were encouraged by the British, who used these strains to facilitate divide-and-conquer policies.

Ever since Indian independence in 1947, Tamil politicians have railed against caste (which they see as favouring light-skinned Brahmins) and Hindi (as unrelated to Tamil as Russian). The post-independence 'Self Respect' movement, influenced by Marxism, mixed South Indian communal values with class warfare rhetoric and spawned Dravidian political parties that remain major regional powers today.

Many Tamil politicians loudly defend the Tamil Tigers, the same organisation that assassinated Rajiv Gandhi in 1991 (imagine a viable, sitting opposition party in your country openly supporting a group that killed your president or prime minister to get an idea of how separate some Tamil parties still consider themselves from India), and there is an unfortunate prejudice among the generally tolerant Tamils towards anything Sinhalese. Throughout the state, male politicians don a white shirt and white *mundu* (sarong), the official uniform of Tamil pride.

Mamallapuram (₹385/550), Puducherry (₹500/750) and Tirupathi (AC ₹915/1135). Every full moon there's an overnight pilgrimage trip to Tiruvannamalai (₹385/630).

Storytrails (☑9600080215, 42124214; www.storytrails.in) runs highly recommended neighbourhood walking tours based around themes such as dance, jewellery and bazaars, as well as tours specially aimed at children.

The classic Enfield Bullet motorcycle has been manufactured in India since 1955 and remains in production today at the **Enfield Factory** (☑42230208; www.royalenfield.com; Tiruvottiyur), 17km out of Chennai. Tours (₹600) run on Saturday from 10am to noon.

✹ Festivals & Events

**Chennai Festival of
Music & Dance** MUSIC, DANCE
(mid-Dec–mid-Jan) One of the largest of its type in the world, this festival is a celebration of Tamil music and dance.

Chennai Sangamam ARTS
(mid-Jan; www.chennaisangamam.com) Arts and culture festival held in venues around the city, coinciding with the statewide Pongal festival.

🛏 Sleeping

Hotels in Chennai are pricier than in the rest of Tamil Nadu and don't as a rule offer much bang for your buck.

The Triplicane High Rd area is best for budget accommodation. There are some cheapies in Kennet Lane in Egmore, and Egmore is also where you'll find the majority of midrange sleeping options, while the top-end hotels lie further out in leafy, southwest Chennai.

Top-end hotels have central AC and multicuisine restaurants and bars, and they accept credit cards. Note that many hotels in Chennai fill up by noon.

EGMORE

Hotel Chandra Park HOTEL $
TOP CHOICE
(Map p318; ☑28191177; info@hotelchandrapark.com; 9 Gandhi Irwin Rd; s/d with AC incl breakfast from ₹899/999; ❄) How do they do it? Prices keep rising around Chennai but Chandra Park's prices remain mysteriously low. Standard rooms are small but have clean towels and tight, white sheets. Throw in a decent bar, a hearty buffet breakfast and classy front lobby, and this place offers superb value by Chennai standards.

**YWCA International
Guest House** GUESTHOUSE $
(Map p318; ☑25324234; ywcaigh@indiainfo.com; Poonamallee High Rd; s/d incl breakfast from ₹700/900; ❄@) Set around sprawling, green and shady grounds right near the Egmore train station, the YWCA manages to offer up healthy doses of hush. There's a slight atmo-

sphere of colonial missionary guesthouse (in a good way), and the rooms adhere to the most demanding levels of cleanliness. It's worth booking in for home-style buffet lunch and/or dinner in the pleasant dining room (₹150/225 for veg/nonveg).

Fortel
HOTEL $$$

(Map p318; ☑30242424; info@cischennai.in; 3 Gandhi Irwin Rd; s/d incl breakfast from ₹3500/4000; ✸) Right opposite Egmore train station and remarkably quiet for it, the Fortel is cool and stylish in a dark wood-and-white-walls way, with comfy cushion-laden beds and two good restaurants.

Vestin Park
HOTEL $$$

(Map p318; ☑28527171; vestinpark@vsnl.com; 39 Montieth Rd; s/d incl breakfast from ₹2800/3300; ✸@) More charming on the outside than in, this corporate-feeling hotel has the kind of bland, reliably clean and comfortable rooms you'd expect at this price. The real draws are the excellent ₹348 lunch and dinner buffet at the **Splendour** restaurant, and the fast and free internet.

Masa
HOTEL $

(Map p318; ☑28193344; 15/1 Kennet Lane; r from ₹460; ✸) The once-grotty Masa has built new budget rooms that were still reasonably fresh at the time of research; the old Masa rooms next door are now called **Hotel Regal**, where you can usually find a fairly grim room (singles/doubles ₹340/420) if all other places are full (as they often are).

Salvation Army Red Shield Guest House
HOSTEL $

(Map p318; ☑25321821; 15 Ritherdon Rd; dm ₹100-150, d ₹300-350) This cheapie lies in a quiet spot north of Egmore train station. It's dingy and grim, believe us, but it's probably the safest sleep in town if you're genuinely down to your last ₹100, and the sheets ain't too bad. Checkout is 9am, and booking ahead *doesn't* guarantee there'll be a bed for you when you arrive.

Royal Regency
HOTEL $$

(Map p318; ☑25611777; www.regencygroupch.com; 26-27 Poonamallee High Rd; s/d from ₹2300/2600; ✸☎) Smack-bang between Central and Egmore train stations. By no means the best-value hotel in Chennai, but if you want AC and wi-fi near the train station, it's clean and friendly if a tad battered.

TRIPLICANE

Cristal Guest House
HOTEL $

(Map p318; ☑28513011; 34 CNK Rd; r from ₹250) In a modern building adhering to the white-tile-on-every-surface school of interior design, the clean abodes here win our 'cheapest rooms in Chennai' award (second edition in a row!).

Broad Lands Lodge
HOTEL $

(Map p318; ☑28545573; broadlandshotel@yahoo.com; 18 Vallabha Agraharam St; r ₹350-600) At this old-school favourite of the dreadlocked brigade, rooms (some much fresher than others) are scattered through a creaky, peeling, colonial-era building that has a certain faint charm. Visitors don't seem to mind the bare-bone, idiosyncratic rooms, the plain concrete floors or the dank shared bathrooms – perhaps the leafy, subdued courtyards and happy communal vibe trumps these shortcomings.

Paradise Guest House
HOTEL $

(Map p318; ☑28594252; paradisegh@hotmail.com; 17 Vallabha Agraharam St; d from ₹400; ✸) Travellers agree that the Paradise boasts some of the best-value digs on this street. Expect simple rooms with clean tiles, a breezy rooftop, friendly staff and hot water by the steaming bucket.

Hotel Comfort
HOTEL $$

(Map p318; ☑28587661; reservations@hotelcomfortonline.com; 22 Vallabha Agraharam St; s/d from ₹1000/1200; ✸) Clean, fresh, smallish rooms with flat-screen TVs and bright-orange bathrooms. Perfectly comfy.

TRADITIONAL TRADERS

George Town, the area that grew around the fort, retains much of its original flavour. This is the wholesale centre of Chennai (Madras). Many backstreets, bordered by NSC Bose Rd, Krishna Koil St, Mint St and Rajaji Salai, are entirely given over to selling one particular type of merchandise as they have for hundreds of years – paper goods in Anderson St, fireworks in Badrian St and so on. Even if you're not in the market for anything, wander the maze-like streets to see another aspect of Indian life flowing seamlessly from the past into the present.

SOUTH CHENNAI

TOP CHOICE **The Lotus** HOTEL **$$**
(Map p314; ☏28157272; www.thelotus.inn; 15 Venkatraman St, T Nagar; s/d incl breakfast from ₹2000/2700; ❄️🛜) An absolute gem, the Lotus offers a quiet setting away from the main roads, a great veg restaurant, and fresh, stylish, sparkling rooms with wood floors and cheerful decor. There are good deals if you stay for a while, and if you want a kitchen nook with gadgets ahoy, the ₹3800 suite is excellent value.

Residency Towers HOTEL **$$**
(Map p314; ☏28156363; www.theresidency.com; Sir Theagaraya Nagar Rd, T Nagar; s/d incl breakfast from ₹5200/5700; ❄️@🛜🏊) At this price, it's like Residency Towers doesn't know what a good thing it has going: five-star elegance with personality. Every floor is decorated differently, but rooms all have sliding doors in front of windows to block out light and noise, dark-wood furniture and thoughtful touches. Wi-fi is free.

Park Hotel BOUTIQUE HOTEL **$$$**
(Map p314; ☏42676000; www.theparkhotels.com; 601 Anna Salai; s/d from ₹10,500/11,500; ❄️@🛜) We love this uberchic boutique hotel, which flaunts stylish elements like framed old Bollywood posters, towering indoor bamboo gardens and oversized doors. The rooms are petite but have lovely lush bedding, and all the mod cons, including funky bathrooms separated from the boudoir by an opaque glass wall. It's all pretty swish, and as a bonus the pricier rooms include airport pickup and drop-off.

Raintree HOTEL **$$$**
(Map p314; ☏24304050; www.raintreehotels.com; 120 St Mary's Rd, Mylapore; r from ₹8500; ❄️@🏊) At this 'ecofriendly' lodge, floors are made of bamboo, wastewater is treated and used for gardening, and electricity conservation holds pride of place. The sleek, minimalist rooms are stylish and comfortable around, and the rooftop infinity pool (which doubles as insulation) has a gorgeous wooden terrace with views of the sea. There's a newer, second branch on Anna Salai.

Raj Park HOTEL **$$$**
(☏42257777; www.rajpark.com; 180 TTK Rd, Alwarpet; s/d incl breakfast from ₹4200/4800; ❄️🛜🏊) Not the best value in town, but this 'business hotel' is comfy and plush in a corporate kind of way, with friendly staff and lots of little extras. The cheaper rooms are on the small

side. It has one of the more relaxed and affordable hotel bars around.

 Eating

Chennai is packed with classic 'meals' joints, which serve thalis for lunch and dinner, and tiffin (snacks) such as *idlis* and dosas the rest of the day. It's tempting – and feasible – to eat every meal at one of Chennai's dozen or so Saravana Bhavan restaurants, where you can count on quality vegetarian food. In the Muslim area around Triplicane High Rd you'll find great biryani joints every few steps – try any of them.

Spencer Plaza has an impressive 3rd-floor food mall with a couple of Western chains, a branch of Hotel Saravana Bhavan (hey, it's Chennai), various fast foods and Chinese options.

EGMORE

TOP CHOICE **Hotel Saravana Bhavan** SOUTH INDIAN **$**
Egmore (Map p318; 21 Kennet Lane; ⏰6am-10.30pm); George Town (Map p314; 209 NSC Bose Rd); Mylapore (Map p314; 101 Dr Radhakrishnan Salai; ⏰7am-11pm); Thousand Lights (Map p318; 293 Peter's Rd; ⏰lunch & dinner); Triplicane (Map p318; Shanthi Theatre Complex, 48 Anna Salai; ⏰7am-11pm) Dependably delish, 'meals' at the Saravana Bhavans run around ₹50, though the Mylapore locale has some 'special meals' for ₹100 and up. The Thousand Lights branch is more upscale, with silver cutlery.

Ponnusamy Hotel INDIAN **$**
(Map p318; Wellington Estate, 24 Ethiraj Rd; mains ₹80-110; ⏰lunch & dinner) This well-known nonveg place serves curry, biryani and Chettinad specialities. Look out for interesting options like brain fry and rabbit masala. You may be ordered to wash your hands before you can sit down.

Sparky's Diner AMERICAN **$$**
(Map p318; Ramanathan Salai, Spur Tank Rd; meals ₹180-280; ⏰lunch & dinner) An expat-run American diner plastered with US licence plates and movie posters, with Sinatra crooning on the stereo. Come for reliably good Western food, especially the pasta, and a bottomless cup of iced tea (₹45). If you're craving a US-style burger you might have to adjust your expectations a little (they're not bad though).

Basil MULTICUISINE **$$**
(Map p318; Fortel, 3 Gandhi Irwin Rd; mains ₹150-300) The bigger of the two restaurants at the Fortel hotel has an impressive Western

breakfast range, if you're really after hash browns, as well as tasty North Indian and Continental dishes in a pleasant setting.

TRIPLICANE

A2B
SOUTH INDIAN **$**

(Map p318; Bharathi Salai; mains ₹20-50) Enjoy South Indian classics, veg biryani, a wide range of sweets and savoury snacks in clean, AC surrounds. If you've got any room for food left, head a few doors down the road, closer to the beach, where you'll find excellent ice cream at **Natural Fresh** (Map p318; 35 Bharathi Salai).

Ratna Cafe
SOUTH INDIAN **$**

(Map p318; 255 Triplicane High Rd; dishes ₹30-60) Though often crowded and cramped, Ratna is renowned in Triplicane and beyond for its scrumptious *idlis* and the hearty doses of *sambar* that go with it.

NUNGAMBAKKAM & AROUND

Tuscana Pizzeria
ITALIAN **$$$**

(Map p314; www.tuscanarestaurants.com; 19, 3rd St, Wallace Garden, Nungambakkam; large pizzas ₹295-525; ☺lunch & dinner) This, my pizza-loving friends, is the real deal, and Chennai is embracing it fast. Tuscana serves authentic thin-crust pizzas with toppings like prosciutto, as well as interesting takes like hoi sin chicken pizza. Pasta and desserts are also top-notch. The expat owner, who is serious about food, also runs a Greek restaurant, **Kryptos**, just round the corner in Kader Nawaz Khan Rd.

Kumarakom
INDIAN **$$**

(Map p314; Kodambakkam High Rd, Nunganbakkam; mains ₹60-160; ☺lunch & dinner) You may have to queue for a table at this classy, popular Keralan restaurant with dark-wood furniture, cool AC and busy waiters. The seafood is the standout – try the prawns masala – but everything's fresh and tasty.

Sea Shell
MIDDLE EASTERN, INDIAN **$**

(Map p318; ☑28295788; 55 Greams Rd, Thousand Lights; mains ₹50-150; ☺lunch & dinner) A bustling, super-popular spot with Middle Eastern favourites like hummus and shawarma in addition to a big menu of North Indian and Chinese. Choose from a long list of bizarrely named mocktails: 'Carbuncle', 'Rolex' or 'Flosberry Flop' anyone?

Kailash Parbat
NORTH INDIAN **$**

(Map p314; 1st fl, 9 Harrington Rd, Chetpet; mains ₹60-130; ☺lunch & dinner) A huge range of tasty street-stall food – *pani puri, chaat pav, bhaji* and more – at decent prices in AC comfort. Specialises in veg-only Sindhi and Punjabi dishes, including paneer cooked a bunch of different ways. There's a wee branch in the food court at Ampa Skywalk mall.

SOUTH CHENNAI

Copper Chimney
NORTH INDIAN **$$$**

(Map p314; 74 Cathedral Rd, Teynampet; mains ₹250-350; ☺noon-3pm & 6-11.30pm) The vegetarian dishes aren't the priority here, but meat eaters will drool over the yummy North Indian tandoori dishes served among plush furnishings. The fish tikka – lumps of skewered tandoori-baked fish – is supurb.

Murugan Idly Shop
SOUTH INDIAN **$**

(Map p314; 77 GN Chetty Rd, T Nagar; dishes ₹25-60) Those in the know generally agree this particular branch of the small chain serves some of the best *idli* and South Indian meals in town. We heartily concur. For afters there's a branch of the very good **Natural Fresh** ice-cream chain just across the road.

Crust
CAFE **$$**

(Map p314; 18 Bheemanna Garden Rd, Abhiramapuram; sandwiches ₹70-140, pasta ₹150-180; ☺lunch) In a leafy courtyard, enjoy sandwiches on bread like you've never tasted in India, as well as quiche, fresh salads and delicious brownies, cakes and tiramisu (made with marscapone flown all the way from Delhi!). Plans are in the works for an expanded restaurant and menu.

Chit Chat
CAFE **$$**

(Map p314; 532 Anna Salai, Teynampet; mains ₹100-250; ☺lunch & dinner) This spot presents as a casual, clean Western-style cafe, and has a wide menu of sandwiches, pizza, kebabs and posh North Indian lunch combos (₹140 to ₹190). It's famous for its milkshakes, and has a cake shop out the front.

Coconut Lagoon
SEAFOOD **$$**

(Map p314; cnr Cathedral & TTK Rds, Alwarpet; mains ₹100-200; ☺noon-3pm & 7-11.45pm) Excellent Keralan and Goan fare with a focus on seafood delicacies, such as *kari meen polli chathu* (fish masala steamed in banana leaf). If you've got room there's good ice cream across the road at **Kulfi Corner**.

Self-Catering

Big Bazaar
SUPERMARKET

(Map p314; Sir Theagaraya Nagar Rd, T Nagar) Americans, they've got Oreos. Aussies, they've got Tim Tams. You're welcome.

Heritage Fresh SUPERMARKET
(Map p314; TTK Rd, Alwarpet; ⊗9am-8.30pm)

Jam Bazaar MARKET
(Map p318; cnr Ellis Rd & Bharathi Salai, Triplicane)
Animated market bursting with fruit,
vegetables and spices.

Spencer's Daily SUPERMARKET
(Map p318; Ritherdon Rd; ⊗9.30am-9pm)

Drinking

Cafes
Popular coffee chains are dotted around
Chennai, including **Barista** (Map p314; Rosy
Towers, Nungambakkam High & D Khader Nawaz
Khan Rds, Nungambakkam; ⊗7.30am-11.30pm)
and **Café Coffee Day** (⊗10am-11pm) Aminjikarai (Ampa Skywalk mall, Poonamallee High Rd;
⊗9am-9pm); Egmore (Map p318; Alsa Mall, Montieth Rd); Nungambakkam (Map p314; 123/124 Nungambakkam High Rd).

Bars & Nightclubs
Chennai's nightlife throbs that little bit more
every year, though it doesn't help that bars
and clubs are supposed to close by midnight
and are restricted to hotels. The very pricey
(by any standards) bars at the five-star hotels are about the only place to get a drink
without thumpingly loud music in the background.

Nightclubs attached to five-star hotels
draw big crowds; at the time of research
the hottest clubs were **Pasha** (Park Hotel, 601
Anna Salai; ⊗8.30-11.30pm Wed-Sun) and **Dub-
lin** (Sheraton Park, 132 TTK Rd; ⊗8-11.30pm Wed-
Sun). Admission is around the ₹1000 mark
for couples and solo guys, and usually free
for women.

Geoffrey's Pub BAR
(Radha Regent, 171 Jawaharlal Nehru Salai, Arum-
bakkam; ⊗4-11pm) This basement 'English'
pub is one of the few places in Chennai
that hosts live music nightly (save Sundays, when there's a DJ). Not always great
music, but music nonetheless. The atmosphere is casual, with Kollywood types
occasionally gracing the place with their
presence.

Leather Bar BAR
(Map p314; Park Hotel, 601 Anna Salai; ⊗8.30-
11.30pm) 'Leather' refers to floor and wall
coverings rather than anything kinky. This
tiny, modish pad has mixologists dishing
up fancy drinks and DJs spinning dance
tunes. How half of Chennai fits into this
teensy space on Friday and Saturday
nights is a mystery.

10D PUB
(10 Downing St; Map p314; www.10ds.net; North
Boag Rd, T Nagar; ⊗11am-11pm) An English-
themed pub (pictures of Big Ben on the
wall, devilled eggs and fish fingers on the
menu), often packed with a mixed bag of
punters. Wednesday is Ladies Night. (Pro
tip: skip the devilled eggs and go for the
tasy tandoori snacks.)

☆ Entertainment

Classical Music & Dance
Kalakshetra Arts Village DANCE, MUSIC
(☑24521169; kshetra@vsnl.com; Dr Muthulakshmi
Rd, Tiruvanmiyu) Founded in 1936, Kalakshetra is committed to reviving classical dance
and music. Check out one of its regular performances. Four-month courses in music
and dance are available.

Music Academy DANCE, MUSIC
(Map p314; ☑28112231; www.musicacademymya
dras.com; cnr Roytthahape & Cathedral Rds) This
is Chennai's most popular public venue
for Carnatic classical music and Bharata
Natyam dance. Many performances are free.
Check the website for upcoming events.

Cinema
Chennai has more than 100 cinemas, a re-
flection of the vibrant film industry here.
Most screen Tamil films, but **PV Cinema**
(www.pvrcinemas.com; Ampa Skywalk mall, Poonamallee High Rd, Aminjikarai) regularly shows
English-language films, as does **Sathyam
Cinema** (Map p318; www.sathyamcinemas.com;
8 Thiruvika Rd, Royapettah). Tickets are around
₹120, and you can book online.

🔒 Shopping
Theagaraya Nagar (aka T Nagar; Map p314)
has greata shopping, especially at Pondy Bazaar and around Panagal Park. Nungambakkam's shady D Khader Nawaz Khan Rd
(Map p314) is a pleasant lane of shops, cafes
and galleries. There's a good branch of the
fixed-price government handicrafts chain
Poompuhar (Map p318; ⊗10am-8pm Mon-Sat)
in Anna Salai.

The best commercial shopping malls include **Spencer Plaza** (Map p318; Anna Salai),
Ampa Skywalk (Poonamallee High Rd, Aminjikarai) and **Chennai Citicentre** (Map p314; Dr
Radhakrishnan Salai, Mylapore). Ampa Skywalk
is the poshest and hosts mostly international chains, while Spencer Plaza is better for
slightly cheaper shops, including Kashmiri
souvenir stores and lots of clothes.

Fabindia
HOMEWARES & FOOD

Spencer Plaza (Map p318; Anna Salai; ⊘11am-8pm), Woods Rd (Map p318; ⊘10am-8pm) The Woods Rd shop has home and food sections, along with fabulous clothes.

Naturally Auroville
HOMEWARES

(Map p314; D Khader Nawaz Khan Rd, Nungambakkam; ⊘10.30am-8pm Mon-Sat, 11.30am-7pm Sun) *Objets* (pottery, bedspreads, scented candles) and fine foods (organic coffees, breads and cheeses) from Auroville, near Pondicherry.

Good Earth
HOMEWARES

(Map p314; www.goodearth.in; 3 Rutland Gate, 4th St, Thousand Lights; ⊘11am-8pm Mon) Gorgeous homewares, furniture, original artwork and more. All Indian inspired and themed, it often has a sense of humour – look for the series of autorickshaw-themed products.

Silk

Many of the finest Kanchipuram silks turn up in Chennai, so consider doing your silk shopping here. The streets around Panagal Park are filled with silk shops; if you're lucky enough to be attending an Indian wedding this is where you buy your sari. Try one of these:

Nalli Silks
FABRIC

(Map p314; 9 Nageswaran Rd, T Nagar; ⊘9.30am-9.30pm) The granddaddy of silk shops. There's a big readymades shop next door with gorgeous *salwar kameez*.

Kumaran Textiles
FABRIC

(Map p314; 12 Nageswaran Rd, T Nagar; ⊘9am-9.30pm) Saris, saris and plenty of Kanchipuram silk.

Bookshops

Higginbothams
BOOKSTORE

(Map p318; higginbothams@vsnl.com; 116 Anna Salai; ⊘9am-8pm Mon-Sat, 10.30am-7.30pm Sun) Decent English-language book selection. Has a branch at the airport.

Landmark
BOOKSTORE

Aminjikarai (Ampa Skywalk mall, Poonamallee High Rd; ⊘10am-9pm); Anna Salai (Map p318; Spencer Plaza, Phase II; ⊘9am-9pm Mon-Sat, 10.30am-9pm Sun); Nungambakkam (Map p314; Apex Plaza, Nungambakkam High Rd; ⊘9am-9pm Mon-Sat, 10.30am-9pm Sun)

Oxford Book Stores
BOOKSTORE

(Map p314; 39/12 Haddows Rd, Nungambakkam; ⊘9.30am-9.30pm) A big selection, tables and colouring-in equipment for kiddies, and a cafe.

ℹ Information

Internet Access

There are 'browsing centres' all over town; most charge between ₹20 and ₹30 an hour.

Cyber Palace (Map p318; Bharathi Salai; per hr ₹20; ⊘9am-10pm)

Dreamzzz Zone (Map p318; Alsa Mall, Egmore; per hr ₹20; ⊘8.30am-10.30pm) Clean, fast, AC.

Internet Zone (Map p318; 1 Kennet Lane, Egmore; per hr ₹30; ⊘8am-10pm)

Log In Net Cafe (Map p318; 35 Triplicane High Rd, Triplicane; per hr ₹15; ⊘9am-11pm)

SGee (Map p318; ☑42310391; 20 Vallabha Agraharam St, Triplicane; per hr ₹20; ⊘24hr)

Left Luggage

Egmore and Central train stations have left-luggage counters, as do the international and domestic airports.

Medical Services

Apollo Hospital (Map p318; ☑28293333, emergency 28290792; www.apollohospitals.com; 21 Greams Lane) Cutting-edge hospital popular with international 'medical tourists'.

St Isabel's Hospital (Map p314; ☑24991081; 18 Oliver Rd, Mylapore)

Money

ATMs are everywhere; there's a cluster at the front of Central train station.

HDFC Bank (Map p318; Poonamallee High Rd, Egmore; ⊘10am-4pm Mon-Fri, 10am-1pm Sat) Foreign exchange and ATM; handy to the YWCA and Salvation Army guesthouses.

State Bank of India Anna Salai (Map p318; Anna Salai; ⊘10am-4pm Mon-Fri, 10am-1pm Sat); George Town (Map p314; 22 Rajaji Salai, George Town; ⊘10am-4pm Mon-Fri, 10am-1pm Sat)

Thomas Cook Anna Salai (Map p318; Spencer Plaza, Phase I; ⊘9.30am-6.30pm); Egmore (Map p318; 45 Montieth Rd; ⊘9.30am-6pm Mon-Sat, 10am-4pm Sun); George Town (Map p314; 20 Rajaji Salai; ⊘9.30am-6pm Mon-Sat); Nungambakkam (Map p314; Eldorado Bldg, 112 Nungambakkam High Rd; ⊘9.30am-6.30pm Mon-Fri, 9.30am-noon Sat) Changes currency and travellers cheques with no commission.

Post

DHL (Map p318; ☑4214886/7; 85 Pantheon Rd, Egmore; ⊘8am-11pm) For secure international parcel delivery. There's a few branches around, including one on Esplanade Rd in George Town.

Post office Anna Salai (Map p318; ⊘8am-8.30pm Mon-Sat, 10am-4pm Sun, poste restante 10am-6pm Mon-Sat); Egmore (Map p318; Kennet Lane; ⊘10am-6pm Mon-Sat); George Town (Map p314; Rajaji Salai; ⊘8am-8.30pm Mon-Sat, 10am-4pm Sun)

Tourist Information

Check out **Chennai Best** (www.chennaibest.com) and **Chennai Online** (www.chennaionline.com).

India Tourism Development Corporation (ITDC; Map p318; ☎28281250; www.attindia tourism.com; 29 Cherian Cres, Egmore; ☉10am-5.30pm Mon-Sat) Hotel and tour bookings only; they're not very helpful.

Indiatourism (Map p318; ☎28460285; ind-tour@dataone.in; 154 Anna Salai; ☉9am-6pm Mon-Fri, 9am-1pm Sat) Maps and information on all of India.

Tamil Nadu Tourism Complex (TTDC; Map p318; ☎25367850; www.tamilnadutourism. org; 2 Wallajah Rd, Triplicane; ☉10am-5.30pm Mon-Fri) Brochure-filled state tourist offices from all over India. The tour-booking desk at the Tamil Nadu office (☎25383333) is suppos-edly open 24 hours.

Travel Agencies

South Tourism (☎42179092; www.south tourism.in; 1 Z-Block, 19th St, Anna Nagar West) Recommended agency for tours and bookings.

SP Travels & Tours (Map p318; ☎28604001; sptravels1@eth.net; 90 Anna Salai, Triplicane; ☉9.30am-6.30pm Mon-Sat)

Visa Extensions

Foreigners' Regional Registration Office (Map p314; ☎28251721; Shastri Bhavan, Haddows Rd, Nungambakkam; ☉9.30am-12.30pm Mon-Fri) Everything will take complicated wrangling and copious doses of patience (we had to sit in a queue for half an hour just to be told the open-ing hours), but you can usually get extensions for all visas except tourist here (tourist visas are only extended in cases of medical emergency). Theoretically, they take 10 days to process.

✈ Getting There & Away

Air

AIRPORTS The international **Anna terminal** (☎22560551) of Chennai Airport in Tirusulam, 16km southwest of the centre, is efficient and not too busy, making Chennai a good entry or exit point. The domestic **Kamaraj terminal** (☎22560551) is next door.

DOMESTIC AIRLINES

Indian Airlines (Map p318; ☎28578153/4, airport 22561906; 19 Rukmani Lakshmi Pathy Rd (Marshalls Rd), Egmore)

IndiGo (☎22560286; airport)

Jet Airways (Map p318; ☎domestic 39893333, international 1800 225522; 41/43 Montieth Rd, Egmore; ☉9am-5.30pm Mon-Sat)

Kingfisher Airlines (Map p318; ☎43988400; 19 Rukmani Lakshmi Pathy Rd (Marshalls Rd), Egmore)

SpiceJet (☎1800 1803333; airport)

INTERNATIONAL AIRLINES

Air France (Map p318; ☎1800 1800033; Kuber's Bldg, 42 Pantheon Rd, Egmore)

Air India (Map p318; ☎1800 1801407; 19 Rukmani Lakshmi Pathy Rd (Marshalls Rd), Egmore) Air India Express has a desk here.

Air Mauritius (Map p318; ☎43508811; Prince Plaza, Pantheon Rd, Egmore; ☉9.30am-5.30pm Mon-Fri, to 1pm Sat)

Cathay Pacific Airways (Map p314; ☎18002091616; 47 Major Ramanathan Salai (Spur Tank Rd), Chetpet)

KLM (Map p318; ☎1800 1800044; Kuber's Bldg, 42 Pantheon Rd, Egmore)

Lufthansa (☎22569393; airport)

Malaysia Airlines (Map p314; ☎42199999; 90 Dr Radhakrishnan Salai, Mylapore)

Singapore Airlines (Map p314; ☎45921921; Westminster, 108 Dr Radhakrishnan Salai, Mylapore)

Sri Lankan Airlines (Map p314; ☎43921100; 4 Kodambakkam High Rd, Nungambakkam)

Thai Airways International (Map p314; ☎22561928; 31 Haddows Rd, Nungambakkam)

Boat

Passenger ships sail from the George Town har-bour to Port Blair in the Andaman Islands (see p398) every five to 10 days or so. The **Director of Shipping Services** (Map p314; ☎25226873; fax 25220841; Shipping Corporation Bldg, Rajaji Salai, George Town; ☉10am-4pm Mon-Sat) sells tickets (₹1962 to ₹7642) for the 60-hour trip. You will need two photographs and three photocopies each of your passport identity page and visa. Bring a book, take a number and try to position yourself near a fan – it can be a long process.

Bus

Most Tamil Nadu (SETC) and other government buses operate from the chaotic **Chennai Mofus-sil Bus Terminus** (CMBT; off Map p314; Jawaha-rlal Nehru Salai, Koyambedu), better known as Koyambedu CMBT, 7km west of town.

Bus 15 or 15B from Parry's Corner or Central train station, and 27B from Anna Salai or Egmore train station, all head there (₹5, 45 minutes). An autorickshaw charges around ₹150 for the same ride.

SETC, Karnataka (KSRTC) and Andhra Pradesh (APRSTC) bus services cover the desti-nations listed in the table (p328), usually in the morning and late afternoon.

Several companies operate Volvo AC buses to the same destinations from the less overwhelm-ing private-bus station next door to CMBT. There's another, smaller private bus stand (Map p318) opposite Egmore train station. These

DOMESTIC FLIGHTS FROM CHENNAI (MADRAS)

DESTINATION	AIRLINE	FARE FROM (₹)	DURATION (HR)	FREQUENCY
Bengaluru	IC	2115	¾	3 daily
	9W	3333	1	4 daily
	6E	2033	1	daily
Delhi	IC	4071	2½	4 daily
	9W	5475	2½	6 daily
	SG	3432	2½	4 daily
	6E	3432	2½	4 daily
Goa	IC	2666	1¼	4 weekly
	SG	2312	1¼	daily
Hyderabad	IC	2115	1	2 daily
	9W	3333	1	2 daily
	6E	2033	1	2 daily
	SG	2033	1	daily
Kochi	IC	2115	1	2 daily
	9W	3333	1	2 daily
Kolkata	IC	5971	2	2 daily
	9W	5844	2	2 daily
	SG	3033	2	daily
	6E	3033	2	3 daily
Mumbai	IC	3325	2	4 daily
	9W	5589	2	6 daily
	SG	3033	2	daily
	6E	3033	2½	2 daily
Port Blair	IC	6376	2	daily
	9W	5787	2	daily
Trivandrum	IC	2115	1½	2 daily
	9W	3700	1½	daily

Note: fares are one-way only

Airline codes: 6E – IndiGo, 9W – Jet Airways, IC – Indian Airlines, SG – SpiceJet

super-deluxe buses usually leave at night and cost two to three times more than ordinary buses.

Train

Interstate trains and those heading west generally depart from Central train station (Map p314), while trains heading south depart from Egmore (Map p318). The **Train Reservation Complex** (☎general 139; ☺8am-8pm Mon-Sat, 8am-2pm Sun) is in a separate 10-storey building just west of Central train station; the Foreign Tourist Assistance Cell (one of the best ever) is on the 1st floor. Egmore's **booking office** (☎28194579) keeps the same hours.

BUS SERVICES FROM CHENNAI (MADRAS)

DESTINATION	FARE (₹)	DURATION (HR)	FREQUENCY
Bengaluru	180-260	9	every 30min
Chidambaram	80-90	7	6 daily
Coimbatore	220-300	11½	9 daily
Ernakulam (Kochi)	420-600	16½	2 daily
Kodaikanal	200-230	13	daily
Madurai	160-190	10	every 30min
Mamallapuram	35	2	every 15-30min
Mysore	200-240	11	10 daily
Ooty	250-320	14	daily
Puducherry	45-90	3½	every 30min
Thanjavur	130-150	8½	hourly
Tirupathi	60-70	3½	every 30min
Trichy	120-190	7	every 15-30min
Trivandrum	330-450	17	7 daily

❶ Getting Around

To/From the Airport

The cheapest way to reach the airport is by MRTS train to Tirusulam station, 300m across the road from the terminals. An autorickshaw will cost you at least ₹250/350 for a day/night trip. Both terminals have prepaid taxi kiosks, where tickets are ₹500 to Egmore or Anna Salai/Triplicane, or out to CMBT (main bus terminus). If you want to bypass Chennai, the kiosks can organise taxis straight from here to destinations including Mahabalipuram (₹2000) or Puducherry (₹4000).

Autorickshaw

Rickshaw drivers in Chennai routinely quote astronomical fares for both locals and tourists alike. Since you have no chance of getting a driver to use the meter, expect to pay at least ₹40 for a short trip down the road. From Egmore to George Town, Triplicane or Anna Salai will cost around ₹70, to Nungambakkam ₹90. Prices are at least 25% higher after 10pm. There's a prepaid booth outside Central station.

Bus

Chennai's bus system is worth getting to know. The main city bus stand (Map p314) is at Parry's Corner, and fares are between ₹5 and ₹12. Some useful routes are listed in the table, p330.

Car & Taxi

For an extended hire, organise a driver through a travel agent or large hotel. You might pay a little more, but the driver should be reliable and you'll have a point of contact should something go wrong. Non-AC rates are around ₹600 per half-day (five hours) within the city.

Train

Efficient MRTS trains run every 15 minutes from Beach station to Fort, Park (at Central station), Egmore, Chetpet, Nungambakkam, Kodambakkam, Mambalam, Saidapet, Guindy, St Thomas Mount, Tirusulam (for the airport), and on down to Tambaram. The second line branches off at Park and hits Light House and Tirumailar (at Kapaleeshwarar Temple).

NORTHERN TAMIL NADU

Chennai to Mamallapuram

Chennai's sprawl peters out after an hour or two heading south on the coastal road, at which point Tamil Nadu becomes open road, red dirt, khaki sand and blue skies (or, if you take the inland road being developed as an 'information technology corridor', huge new buildings). Currently this stretch of sand is the only area of Tamil Nadu's 1076km coastline that's being developed for traditional beachside tourism.

There's a tropical bohemian groove floating around Injambalkkam village, site of the **Cholamandal Artists' Village** (☑044-4926092; www.cholamandalartistsvillage.org; admission free; ☉9.30am-9pm). This 4-hectare

MAJOR TRAINS FROM CHENNAI (MADRAS)

DESTINATION	TRAIN NO & NAME	FARE (₹)	DURATION (HR)	DEPARTURE
Bengaluru	2007 *Shatabdi Express**	510/995	4½	6am CC
	2609 *Bangalore Express*	108/380	6	1.35pm CC
Delhi	2615 *Grand Trunk Express*	528/1429/1960	35	7.15pm CC
	2621 *Tamil Nadu Express*	528/1429/1960	33	10pm CC
Coimbatore	6627 *West Coast Express*	212/564/772	8½	11.30am CC
	2671 *Nilgiri Express*	232/594/802	8	9pm CC
Goa	7311 *Vasco Express***	347/947/1302	22	1.40pm CC
Hyderabad	2759 *Charminar Express*	312/823/1119	14	6.10pm CC
	2603 *Hyderabad Express*	297/779/1095	13	4.45pm CC
Kochi	6041 *Alleppey Express*	269/728/998	11¾	9.15pm CC
Kolkata	2842 *Coromandel Express*	461/1242/1700	27	8.45am CC
	2840 *Howrah Mail*	461/1242/1700	28½	11.40pm CC
Madurai	6127 *Guruvayur Express*	212/564/772	8¾	7.50am CE
	2635 *Vaigai Express*	132/471	8	12.40pm CE
Mumbai	1042 *Mumbai Express*	383/1046/1440	26	11.55am CC
	2164 *Dadar Express*	403/1076/1470	23	6.50am CE
Mysore	2007 *Shatabdi Express**	655/1265	7	6am CC
	6222 *Kaveri Express*	212/564/772	10½	9.30pm CC
Tirupathi	6053 *Tirupathi Express*	60/206	3	1.50pm CC
Trichy	2605 *Pallavan Express*	104/367	5½	3.45pm CE
Trivandrum	2695 *Trivandrum Express*	341/903/1230	16	3.25pm CC

Departure codes: CC – Chennai Central, CE – Chennai Egmore

*Daily except Wednesday; ** Friday only

Shatabdi fares are chair/executive; Express and Mail fares are 2nd/chair car for day trains, sleeper/3AC/2AC for overnight trains

artists' cooperative (18km south of Chennai) is a serene muse away from the world and a quiet chance to both see and purchase contemporary Indian art direct from the source. There are two simple studio-cum-guesthouses but they are available for visiting artists only (₹500; book well in advance).

As Cholamandal is to contemporary Indian expression, **DakshinaChitra** (☎044-27472603; www.dakshinachitra.net; Indian adult/student ₹75/30, foreign adult/student ₹200/75; ☺10am-6pm Wed-Mon) is to traditional arts and crafts. Located about 12km south of Cholamandal, this is a jumble of open-air museum, preserved village and artisan workshops – another well-worth-it stop (especially for the kids) for learning about the Dravidian crafts of Tamil Nadu, Kerala, Karnataka and Andhra Pradesh. DakshinaChitra means 'A Picture of the South', which is essentially what you're provided via local pottery, silk-weaving, puppet-building and basket-making workshops, traditional theatre performances and art studios.

Along this stretch of road the TTDC runs the **Muttukadu Boat House** (☺9am-6pm), where you can take a 45-minute boat trip (per person from ₹45) out on the backwaters.

One of the best institutions of its kind in India, **Crocodile Bank** (☎044-27472447; www.madrascrocodilebank.org; adult/child ₹35/10,

CHENNAI BUS ROUTES

BUS NO	ROUTE
29K	Koyambedu CMBT–Guindy–Adyar–Mylapore
9, 10	Parry's–Central–Egmore–T Nagar
11/11A	Parry's–Anna Salai–T Nagar
15B	Parry's–Central–Koyambedu CMBT
18	Parry's–Saidapet
19G	Parry's–Central–Adyar
27B	Egmore–Chetpet–Koyambedu CMBT
31	Parry's–Central–Vivekananda Illam
32	Central–Triplicane–Vivekananda Illam
51M	T Nagar–St Thomas Mount

camera/video ₹20/100; ⊘8.30am-5.30pm Tue-Sun), 40km south of Chennai, is a fascinating peek into a world of reptiles, and an incredible conservation trust to boot. The Bank does crucial work towards protecting the critically endangered gharial, an enormous but harmless (to humans) species of crocodilian that feeds on fish and has a long, thin nose. There are thousands of other reptiles here, including the Indian mugger and saltwater crocs of the Andaman and Nicobar Islands. If you have a spare evening on the weekend, come for the **night safari** (adult/child ₹60/20; ⊘7-8pm Sat & Sun), when you can shine a flashlight over the water and catch the staring eyes of thousands of the Bank's local residents. Volunteer opportunities are available here; see the website for details.

About 5km north of Mamallapuram in the village of Salavankuppam, beside the East Coast Rd, the **Tiger Cave** is a rock-cut shrine, possibly dating from the 7th century. It's dedicated to Durga and has a small *mandapam* featuring a crown of carved *yali* (mythical lion creature) heads.

To reach these places, take any bus heading south from Chennai to Mamallapuram and ask to be let off at the appropriate destination. Another option is the TTDC's hop-on, hop-off **bus tour** (✆044-25383333; www.tamilnadutourism.org/hopontour.html; ₹250) that runs between Chennai and Mamallapuram on the half-hour between 9am and 11am, and in the other direction between 4.15pm and 6pm. A taxi for a full-day tour costs from about ₹1600. You can swim along the coast, but beware of strong currents and tides as there are no lifeguards around.

Mamallapuram (Mahabalipuram)

✆044 / POP 12,345

This World Heritage Site was once a major seaport and second capital of the Pallava kings, and a saunter through the town's great carvings and temples at sunset, when the sandstone turns bonfire orange and blood red and modern carvers *tink-tink* with their chisels on the street, enflames the imagination.

And then, in addition to ancient archaeological wonders, there's the traveller ghetto of Othavadai Cross St. You'll hear the mellow trills of Jack Johnson. Bob Marley flags hang from the balconies. Stores sell things from Tibet, 'Indian' clothes that few Indians would probably ever wear, toilet paper, hand sanitiser and used books, and you know you have landed, once again, in the Kingdom of Backpackistan.

'Mal', as many travellers call it, is less than two hours by bus from Chennai, and many travellers make a beeline here straight from Chennai. The village is tiny and laid-back, and the surrounding sites of interest can be explored on foot or by bicycle.

◉ Sights

You can easily spend a full day exploring the temples, *mandapams* and rock carvings around Mamallapuram. Apart from the Shore Temple and Five Rathas, admission is free. Official guides from the Archaeological Survey of India can be found at archaeological sites and hired for around ₹50 (give more if the tour is good); they're well worth the money.

Shore Temple
HINDU TEMPLE

(combined ticket with Five Rathas Indian/foreigner ₹10/250, video ₹25; ⊙6.30am-6pm) Standing like a magnificent fist of rock-cut elegance overlooking the sea, the Shore Temple symbolises the heights of Pallava architecture and the maritime ambitions of the Pallava kings. Its small size belies its excellent proportion and the supreme quality of the carvings, many of which have been eroded into vaguely Impressionist embellishments. Originally constructed in the 7th century, it was later rebuilt by Narasimhavarman II and houses two central shrines to Shiva. The layout is meant to resemble the perfect cosmic body, with the head and heart located over the spire that dominates the structure. Facing east and west, the original linga (phallic images of Shiva) captured the sunrise and sunset. The temple is believed to be the last in a series of buildings that extended along a since submerged coastline; this theory gained credence during the 2004 tsunami, when receding waters revealed the outlines of what may have been sister temples.

Five Rathas
HINDU TEMPLES

(Five Rathas Rd; combined ticket with Shore Temple Indian/foreigner ₹10/250, video ₹25; ⊙6.30am-6pm) Carved from single pieces of rock, the Five Rathas are low-laying monoliths that huddle in more ancient subtlety than grandeur. Each temple is dedicated to a Hindu god and named for one of the Pandavas, the five hero-brothers of the epic Mahabharata, plus their common wife, Draupadi.

The shrines are meant to resemble chariots (ratha is Sanskrit for chariot), and were hidden in the sand until excavated by the British 200 years ago. Outside each ratha is a carving of an animal mount of the gods. Taken together, the layout theme of God, Pandava and animal mount is remarkable for its architectural consistency, considering everything here was cut from single chunks of rock.

The first ratha, Draupadi Ratha, on the left after you enter the gate, is dedicated to Draupadi and the goddess Durga, who represents the sacred femininity and fertility of the Indian soil. The goddess looks out at her worshippers from a carved lotus throne, while outside, a huge sculpted lion stands guard.

Behind the goddess shrine, a huge Nandi (bull, vehicle of Shiva) heralds the chariot of the most important Pandava. Arjuna Ratha is appropriately dedicated to Shiva, the most important deity of the Pallavas. Other gods, including the Vedic Indra, are depicted on the outer walls

Look around the lintels of the middle temple, Bhima Ratha, and you'll notice faded faces that some archaeologists believe possess Caucasian features, evidence of Mamallapuram's extensive trade ties with ancient Rome. Inside is a shrine to Vishnu.

Guides may tell you the carving of Pallava king Narasimhavarman on Dharmaraja Ratha, the tallest of the chariots, resembles an Egyptian pharaoh, suggesting even earlier trade ties across the Indian Ocean. The theory is tantalising, but not terribly well substantiated. The final ratha, Nakula-Sahadeva Ratha, is dedicated to Indra and has a fine sculptured elephant standing nearby. As you enter the gate, approaching from the north, you see its back first, hence its name gajaprishthakara (elephant's backside). The life-sized image is regarded as one of the most perfectly sculptured elephants in India.

Arjuna's Penance
HISTORIC SITE

(West Raja St) As if we couldn't wax more poetic on Mamallapuram's stonework, along comes this relief carving, one of the greatest of its age and certainly one of the most convincing and unpretentious works of ancient art in India. Inscribed into a huge boulder, the penance bursts with scenes of Hindu myth (notice the nagas, or snake-beings, that descend a cleft once filled with water, meant to represent the Ganges) and everyday vignettes of South Indian life. A herd of elephants marches under armies of celestial beings, while Arjuna performs self-mortification so he can be granted Shiva's most powerful weapon, the god-slaying Pasupata. In Hinduism, 'penance' does not mean suffering that erases sins, but distress undertaken for the sake of boons from the gods. Another interpretation: the carving depicts the penance of the sage Bhagaritha, who asked the Ganges to fall to the earth and cleanse the ashes (and ergo, sins) of his dead relatives. There's humour amid the holy: notice the cat performing his own penance to a crowd of appreciative mice.

Ganesh Ratha & Around
HINDU TEMPLE

This ratha is northwest of Arjuna's Penance. Once a Shiva temple, it became a shrine to Ganesh (Shiva's elephant-headed son) after the original lingam was removed. Just north of the ratha is a huge boulder known as Krishna's Butter Ball. Immovable, but apparently balancing precariously, it's a

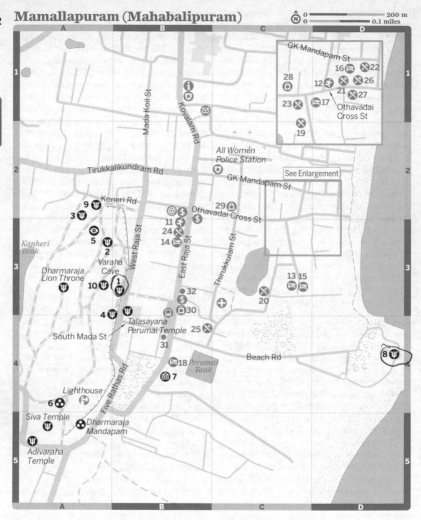

TAMIL NADU & CHENNAI NORTHERN TAMIL NADU

favourite photo opportunity. The nearby **Kotikal Mandapam** is dedicated to Durga. Southwest of here is **Varaha Mandapam II**, dominated by an incredibly active panel of Vishnu manifested as a boar avatar. Early Hindu art is rife with depictions of Vishnu in animal form, as opposed to today, when he is primarily worshipped as Rama or Krishna, which suggests this nascent phase of Hindu theology was more closely tied to tribal religions. Nearby, the **Trimurti Cave Temple** honours the Hindu trinity – Brahma, Vishnu and Shiva – with a separate section dedicated to each deity.

Mandapams
HISTORIC SITES

Mamallapuram's main hill, which dominates the town (and is in turn dominated by a red-and-brownstone lighthouse), makes for an excellent hour or two of low-key hiking (it's a good spot for the sunset as well). Many *mandapams* are scattered over this low rise of rock, including **Krishna Mandapam**, one of the earliest rock-cut temples around the region. The famous carving depicts both a rural pastiche and Krishna lifting up Govardhana mountain to protect his kinsfolk from the wrath of Indra. Other shrines include **Mahishamardini Mandapam**, just a few metres southwest of the lighthouse. Scenes from the Puranas (Sanskrit stories dating from the 5th century AD) are depicted on the *mandapam,* with the sculpture of the goddess Durga considered one of the finest.

Above the *mandapam* are the remains of the 8th-century **Olakkannesvara Temple,** and spectacular views of Mamallapuram.

Sculpture Museum   MUSEUM
(East Raja St; adult/child ₹5/2, camera ₹10; ⊙9.30am-5pm) This museum contains more than 3000 sculptures and paintings that run the gamut from interesting stonework to still-life depictions of fruit bowls. Parts of the building are as interesting as the exhibits.

🏃 Activities

Beach
Mamallapuram's beach, or at least the bit that fronts the village, isn't exactly pristine and gets downright dingy in some spots, but if you walk a bit north or south of the Shore Temple it clears into very fine sand. You'll also be further away from the leers of men who spend their days out here gawking at tourists. It's not a great place for swimming – there are dangerous rips – but it's possible to

go fishing in one of local outriggers; negotiate a price with the owner.

Therapies
There are numerous places offering massage, reiki, yoga and ayurvedic practices. Sessions cost around ₹400 for 30 to 45 minutes. The more upmarket hotels tend to have reliable inhouse massage options; the GRT Temple Bay hotel has a branch of the popular Chennai massage centre Ayush.

Sri Chakra (Othavadai St; massage per hr ₹450; ⊙9am-9pm) offers ayurvedic massage as well as yoga sessions (₹200) at 7am and 4pm, and there are many other operators in town with similar rates and timings. As always, and especially for such an intimate service, ask fellow travellers, question the massage therapist carefully and if you have any misgivings, don't proceed.

👉 Tours
Hi! Tours (☎27443360; www.hi-tours.com; 123 East Raja St; ⊙9.30am-6pm) runs bicycle tours to sights like the Tiger Cave. Tours run from 8am to 2pm and include guide and lunch; prices are around ₹350 per person. Hi! Tours also organises day trips to Kanchipuram

and Vedantangal Bird Sanctuary and fishing trips at certain times of the year.

✦ Festivals & Events

The **Mamallapuram Dance Festival** (Dec-Jan) is a four-week dance festival showcasing dances from all over India, with many performances on an open-air stage against the imposing backdrop of Arjuna's Penance. Dances include the Bharata Natyam (Tamil Nadu), Kuchipudi (Andhra Pradesh) tribal dance and Kathakali (Kerala drama); there are also puppet shows and classical music performances. Performances are held only from Friday to Sunday.

🛏 Sleeping

In addition to the following there's a cluster of cheap family-run places and budget lodges near the Five Rathas.

Hotel Mamalla Heritage　HOTEL $$
(☏27442060; www.hotelmamallaheritage.com; 104 East Raja St; s/d from ₹1600/1800; ❄❂☎) In town, this corporate-y place has large, comfortable rooms, all with fridge, spotlessly sparkling bathrooms and charmingly friendly service. The pool's a decent size, and there's a quality veg and rooftop restaurant.

**Tina Blue View Lodge
& Restaurant**　HOTEL $
(☏27442319; 34 Othavadai St; r ₹250-500) Tina is one of Mamallapuram's originals and kind of looks it, with some frayed and faded edges, but remains deservedly popular for its whitewashed walls, blue accents and tropically pleasant garden, as well as tireless original owner Xavier ('I am same age as Tony Wheeler!').

Ideal Beach Resort　RESORT $$$
(☏27442240; www.idealresort.com; s/d from ₹4500/5000; ❄@❂☎) With a landscaped garden setting, its own stretch of (pretty nice) beachfront and comfortable rooms or cottages, this low-key, laid-back beachfront resort is popular with families and Chennai expats. The design is small and secluded enough to have an intimate atmosphere and there's a lovely open-air poolside restaurant where live classical music is sometimes performed. It's about 3.5km north of town.

La Vie en Rose　HOTEL $
(☏9444877544; East Raja St; d from ₹450; ❂) Simple, decent-sized and very clean rooms, friendly staff and a restaurant with some not-bad French dishes.

GRT Temple Bay　RESORT $$$
(☏27443636; www.radisson.com/mamallapuramin; s/d incl breakfast from ₹8000/9000; ❄@❂☎) This is the best of the luxury resorts that lie to the north of town. It's got everything you need to feel like waterfront royalty, including 24-hour service, a spa, sauna, health club and prices that are probably a little much, all things considered. Prices jump in December/January.

Bharath Guest House　HOTEL $
(☏274434304; barathguesthouse@gmail.com; 6 Othavadai Cross St; d from ₹400; ❂) One of a string of similarly priced places in a row along Othavadai Cross St (Siva Guest House and Greenlands are just as good), Bharath is painted a cheerful sunflower yellow and has big, colourful, simple rooms at a decent price.

Galaxy Guest House　HOTEL $
(☏9940171595; Othavadai St; r ₹300-500) Central to the action, this is a family-run place with basic, clean rooms around a courtyard and flashier (ie more tackily decorated), bigger rooms upstairs.

Hotel Daphne　HOTEL $
(☏27442811; hoteldaphne1@yahoo.com; 17 Othavadai Cross St; s/d from ₹250/350; ❂) Part of the Moonrakers mini-empire, this place isn't the standout it used to be, but it still offers decent value for money; walls and sheets are fresh, even if the furniture isn't, and the leafy setting and rooftop garden restaurant are big drawcards.

Hotel Sea Breeze　HOTEL $$
(☏27443035; www.nivalink.com/seabreeze; Othavadai Cross St; r incl breakfast from ₹900; ❄❂☎) The Sea Breeze is a bland, slightly overpriced hotel of the reliably midrange beachfront-escape school of design, but the real draw is the pool, which nonguests can use for ₹150. Breakfast is free, which is too expensive for cold *idlis*.

Try Residency　HOTEL $
(☏27442728; tryresidency@gmail.com; 7 Old College Rd; r from ₹800; ❂) Rooms aren't too stylish but they're big and clean; if you need some Western-style amenities, it's not a bad option. There's a wee garden ruled by some ducks, and the world's tiniest pool.

Guru Lodge　HOTEL $
(☏27443093; East Raja St; r from ₹300) Just outside the Othavadai ghetto, the simple, clean, peach-coloured rooms here offer good value.

New Manoj Cottage HOMESTAY **$**
(⌨9840387095; newmanojcottage@yahoo.com;
136 Fisherman Colony; r ₹400-600) A friendly,
family-run homestay with three well-kept
rooms.

✖ Eating & Drinking

Restaurateurs near Othavadai Cross St provide open-air ambience, decent Western mains and bland Indian curries. If you want real Indian food, there are good cheap veg places and biryani joints near the bus stand. Most places – licensed or not – serve beer, but be sensitive to the 11pm local curfew; if you persuade a restaurant to allow you to linger over drinks, it's the owner, not you, who faces a hefty fine. All places listed are open for breakfast, lunch and dinner.

In addition the places reviewed here, beachside and nearly beachside Dreamlands, Seashore Restaurant, Santana Beach Restaurant and Luna Magica, are all recommended for fresh seafood; you'll get a good plate of fish for around ₹150 to ₹200.

Self-caterers should head to **Nilgiris Supermarket** (East Raja St; ⊙9.30am-9pm), between Othavadai St and the bus stand.

TOP CHOICE Gecko Café MULTICUISINE **$$**
(www.gecko-web.com; off Othavadai Cross St; mains ₹100-200) Two friendly brothers run this cute little spot on a thatch-covered rooftop above the family home. The menu choices and prices aren't that different to other tourist-oriented spots, but there's more love put into the cooking here, and the decor is fun: we liked the wall of goddesses, with Laxmi hanging next to the Virgin and Child. There's internet and a book exchange downstairs.

Le Yogi MULTICUISINE **$$**
(Othavadai St; mains ₹90-160) This is some of the best Western food in town; the steaks, pastas and pizzas are genuine and tasty (if small), service is good, and the airy dining area, with wooden accents and flickering candlelight, is romantic as all get out.

Rose Garden INDIAN **$**
(Beach Rd; mains around ₹50) This is one of the better biryani shops in a town that's surprisingly full of joints serving this tasty Hyderabadi rice dish.

Freshly 'N Hot CAFE **$$**
(Othavadai Cross St; mains ₹50-180) Yes, the name makes no sense. A comparatively small menu of perfectly OK pizza, pasta and sandwiches, and a long, long list of coffees, hot and cold. The ice coffees are excellent.

Moonrakers MULTICUISINE **$$**
(34 Othavadai St; mains ₹60-150) Like it or not, you're likely to end up here at some stage; it's the sort of place that magnetises travellers and dominates the backpacker-ghetto streetscape. Food is OK, ambience is better and beer is enjoyable from the top-floor veranda. It's a mystery why the opposite-facing Blue Elephant, with almost identical food and nicer decor, isn't as popular as Moonrakers, though they both get pretty packed out with visitors from Chennai on weekend evenings.

🛍 Shopping

Mamallapuram wakes to the sound of sculptors' chisels on granite, and you'll inevitably be approached by someone trying to sell you everything from a ₹100 stone pendant to a ₹400,000 Ganesh that needs to be lifted with a crane. There are lots of good art galleries, tailors and antique shops here. For clothes, we recommend **Ponn Readymade Tailoring** (Othavadai St). Nice prints, cards and original art can be found at **Shriji Art Gallery** (11/1 Othavadai St) and expensive but beautiful curios culled from local homes at **Southern Arts and Crafts** (⌨27443675; www.southernarts.in; 72 East Raja St).

A number of shops have books for sale or exchange. **JK Bookshop** (⌨9880552200; 143 Othavadai St; ⊙9am-12.30pm & 2-8.30pm) is a small bookshop where you can buy or swap books in several languages, including English, French and German. Proceeds support education for local 'untouchable' children.

ℹ Information

Internet access is everywhere.
Indian Overseas Bank ATM (East Raja St)
KK Netscape (East Raja St; per hr ₹30; ⊙9am-10pm)
Ruby Forex (East Raja St; ⊙9.30am-7pm Mon-Sat)
South India Browsing Centre (Mango Leaf restaurant, Othavadai St; per hr ₹30; ⊙8am-8pm) Also has a decent book exchange.
State Bank of India ATM (East Raja St)
Suradeep Hospital (⌨27442390; 15 Thirukulam St; ⊙24hr) Recommended by travellers.
Tourist office (⌨27442232; Kovalam Rd; ⊙10am-5.45pm Mon-Fri) Staff treat visitors as a major inconvenience; someone will probably sigh and point you to a table of maps and brochures.

❶ Getting There & Away

There are at least 30 buses a day running to/from Chennai (₹30, two hours, 30 daily). To Chennai Airport take bus 108B (₹25, two hours, 9am and 8pm daily). There are also at least nine daily buses to Puducherry (₹35, two hours), and Kanchipuram (₹24, two hours) via Tirukkalikundram; there's a faster direct private bus to Kanchipuram daily at 6am. Two daily buses run to Tiruvannamalai (₹36, three hours, 9.30am and 8pm)

Taxis are available from the bus station. Long-distance trips require plenty of bargaining. It's about ₹1400 to Chennai or the airport.

You can make train reservations at the **Southern Railway Reservation Centre** (East Raja St).

❶ Getting Around

The easiest way to get around is on foot, though on a hot day it's quite a hike to see all the monuments. Bicycles can be rented through most guesthouses and at numerous stalls along East Raja St.

Vedantangal Bird Sanctuary

Located about 52km southwest of Mamallapuram, this wildlife **sanctuary** (admission ₹20; ⊘6am-6pm) is an important breeding ground for waterbirds – cormorants, egrets, herons, ibises, spoonbills, storks, grebes and pelicans – that migrate here from October to March. At the height of breeding season (December and January) there can be up to 30,000 birds nesting in the mangroves. The best viewing times are early morning and late afternoon; head for the watchtower and look down on the noisy nests across the water.

Basic rooms are available at the **Forest Department Resthouse** (d ₹525, with AC ₹725), 500m before the sanctuary. You're supposed to book in advance with the **Wildlife Warden's Office** (WWO; Map p314; ☎22351471; 4th fl, DMS office, 259 Anna Salai, Teynampet) in Chennai – it's not easy, and do phone first as there was talk of the office moving at the time of research. It can be easier through a tour operator (such as Hi! Tours in Mamallapuram), or if you turn up the caretaker may just find a room if one's available. You may or may not be offered food if you arrive unexpectedly; if you have transport, it's 10km or so to the nearest evening food stall.

To get here by public transport, first get to Chengalpattu, an hour's bus ride from Mamallapuram. From here you can take a bus to Vedantangal via Padalam, where you may have to change buses at the road junction. Most Vedantangal buses go directly to the sanctuary entrance, others to the village bus station, from where the sanctuary is a 1km walk south. Visitors also often make a day trip by AC taxi from Mamallapuram; this should cost around ₹1400.

Kanchipuram

☎044 / POP 188,763

The old capital of the Pallava dynasty is a typical Tamil Nadu temple town: modern India at her frenetic best dappled with houses of worship that form a veritable dialogue with history in stone. Kanchi (as it's often called) is also a centre of silk production and famed for its high-quality saris. It's usually (and best) visited as a day trip from Mamallapuram or Chennai, as there's not a lot to see outside of the justifiably famous temples. Don't make a special trip just to shop, as silk is generally no cheaper here than in Chennai.

The city is on the main road between Chennai and Bengaluru (Bangalore), 76km southwest of Chennai. There's no tourist office, but for information online check out www.hellokanchipuram.com.

◉ Sights

All temples are open from 6am to 12.30pm and 4pm to 8.30pm. All have free admission, though you may have to pay for shoe-keeping and/or to bring in a camera.

Kailasanatha Temple   HINDU TEMPLE

The oldest temple in Kanchi is the most impressive, not for its size but weight of historical presence. Dedicated to Shiva, the Kailasanatha Temple was built by the Pallava king Rajasimha in the 7th century. The low-slung sandstone compound has fascinating carvings, including many half-animal deities that were in vogue during the period of early Dravidian architecture.

Non-Hindus are allowed into the inner sanctum here, where there is a prismatic lingam – the largest in town and third-largest in Asia.

Sri Ekambaranathar Temple   HINDU TEMPLE

This Shiva temple is one of the largest in the city, covering 12 hectares and dominated by a 59m-high *gopuram*. The carvings feel alive and beautiful, but still weighted with five centuries of history; they were chiselled by artisans in 1509 during the Vijayanagar

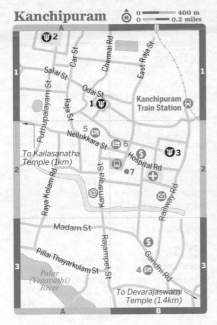

0 — 400 m
0 — 0.2 miles

⊙ Sights

1 Kamakshi Amman Temple A1
2 Sri Ekambaranathar Temple A1
3 Vaikunta Perumal Temple B2

🛏 Sleeping

4 GRT Regency B3
5 MM Hotel A2
6 Sri Sakthi Residency B2

Eating

Dakshin .... (see 4)
Saravana Bhavan .... (see 4)

Transport

7 Bicycle Rental B2

TAMIL NADU & CHENNAI VEDANTANGAL BIRD SANCTUARY

empire. The temple's name is said to derive from Eka Amra Nathar – Lord of the Mango Tree – and there is an old mango tree, with four branches representing the four Vedas (sacred Hindu texts) on-site. Of the five elemental temples of Shiva, this is the shrine of Earth.

According to legend, the goddess Kamakshi worshipped Shiva here in the form of a linga made of sand, which still lies at the heart of the temple. Non-Hindus cannot see the mirror chamber, where worshippers enter with candles. The central image of Shiva is reflected in the candlelight across the mirrored walls, creating countless images of the god that allude to his infinite presence.

Kamakshi Amman Temple　HINDU TEMPLE
This imposing temple is dedicated to the goddess Parvati in her guise as Kamakshi (She Whose Eyes Awaken Desire). To the right of the temple's entrance is the marriage hall, with wonderful ornate pillars, and directly ahead is the main shrine topped with a golden *vimana* (legendary flying chariot). Again, non-Hindus cannot enter the sanctum, where Kamakshi/Parvati is depicted, uncharacteristically, in the lotus position. Each February/March carriages housing statues of the temple deities are hauled

through the streets; this procession should not be missed if you're in the vicinity.

Devarajaswami Temple　HINDU TEMPLE
(camera/video ₹5/100) Dedicated to Vishnu, this enormous monument was built by the Vijayanagars and is among the most impressive of Kanchipuram's temples. It has a beautifully sculptured '1000-pillared' hall (admission ₹1; only 96 of the original 1000 remain) as well as a marriage hall commemorating the wedding of Vishnu and Lakshmi. One of the temple's most notable features is a huge chain carved from a single piece of stone, which can be seen at each corner of the *mandapam*. The temple is supposedly the place to go to receive cures from lizard-related illnesses, thanks to twin silver- and gold-plated reptiles that crawl over the temple ceiling.

Every 40 years the waters of the temple tank are drained, revealing a huge wooden statue of Vishnu that is worshipped for 48 days. You may like to hang around for the next viewing – in 2019. Otherwise, float festivals (when deities are literally floated across the reservoir) are held on the tank three times a year.

Vaikunta Perumal Temple　HINDU TEMPLE
Roughly 1200 years old and dedicated to Vishnu, this temple was built shortly after the Kailasanatha. The cloisters inside the outer wall consist of lion pillars and are representative of the first phase in the architectural evolution of the grand 1000-pillared halls. The main shrine, which is uniquely spread over three levels, contains images of Vishnu standing, sitting, reclining and riding his preferred mount, the garuda (half-eagle,

half-man). There's another monitor lizard icon here.

Sleeping & Eating

Kanchi's cheap pilgrims' lodges are shabby, but there are a few decent midrange options.

GRT Regency
HOTEL $$

(☎27225250; www.grthotels.com; 487 Gandhi Rd; s/d incl breakfast ₹2250/2750; ❋☎) Set back from the noisy main road, this place probably has the cleanest and most comfortable rooms you'll find in Kanchi. The attached **Dakshin** restaurant (mains ₹180 to ₹375) is a tad overpriced but is a plush AC spot that offers a big multicuisine menu including Western-style breakfast, good seafood (especially the Indian dishes) and tasty tandoori.

Sri Sakthi Residency
HOTEL $

(☎27233799; www.sreesakthiresidency.com; 71 Nellukkara St; s/d from ₹800/900; ❋) Not bad value; simple blonde-wood furniture and coloured walls make the rooms fairly modern, with only a touch of fraying round the edges. There's a fine veg restaurant under the hotel.

MM Hotel
HOTEL $

(☎27227250; www.mmhotels.com; 65 Nellukkara St; d from ₹800; ❋) A busy and clean hotel, with shiny floors and flatscreen TVs, frequented by Indian businesspeople. A Saravana Bhavan veg restaurant is next door, with a welcome AC dining room.

Information

Axis Bank ATM (Gandhi Rd)
Googly (144 Kamaraja St; per hr ₹20; ◷7.30am-10.30pm) Internet access.
State Bank of India ATM (Hospital Rd)

Getting There & Away

Regular suburban trains direct to Kanchipuram leave from Beach, Fort or Egmore stations in Chennai.The busy bus stand is in the centre of town. Destinations from the bus stand include:
Bengaluru ₹110 to ₹160, six hours, two daily
Chennai ₹26, two hours, every 15 minutes
Mamallapuram ₹27, two hours, nine daily
Puducherry ₹36, three hours, 12 daily
Tiruvannamalai ₹38, three hours, hourly
Trichy ₹110, seven hours, four daily
Vellore ₹26, two hours, every 15 minutes

Getting Around

Bicycles can be hired from stalls around the bus stand. An autorickshaw for a half-day tour of the

five main temples (around ₹400) will inevitably involve a stop at a silk shop.

Vellore

☎0416 / POP 386,746

For a dusty bazaar town, Vellore feels kinda cosmopolitan, thanks to a couple of tertiary institutions and the Christian Medical College (CMC) Hospital, one of the finest hospitals in India. The hospital attracts international medical students as well as patients from all over India, and the town is worth a day for soaking up both its historical ambience – the massive Vijayanagar fort rewards a wander – and small-town-but-international vibe. The new Sripuram Golden Temple, just out of town, draws pilgrims from all over India.

Sights

Sripuram Golden Temple
HINDU TEMPLE

(Mahalakshmi Temple; admission free) This controversial temple (it was built just a few years ago with 1½ tons of gold on the roof, and some have questioned whether the money could have been better spent) is in a lovely garden setting 7km south of town, and is popular with pilgrims; there's a certain thrill in seeing all that carved gold up close. There's a huge security presence, with no electronic items allowed inside the gates (your bag will be searched and screened), as well as an enforced dress code (no shorts, no legs or shoulders on display), and you have to keep strictly to the roped-off walkway that's lined with quotes from the temple's guru and strident calls for donations. You can pay ₹250 to walk straight in, otherwise there are long queues in hot caged corridors. Buses (₹8) run regularly from the New Bus Stand; an autorickshaw costs ₹80.

Vellore Fort
FORT COMPLEX

The solid walls and dry moat of the splendid Vellore Fort dominate the west side of town. It was built in the 16th century and passed briefly into the hands of the Marathas in 1676 and the Mughals in 1708. The British occupied the fort in 1760 following the fall of Srirangapatnam and the death of Tipu Sultan. These days it houses various government offices, parade grounds, a university, a church, an ancient mosque and a police recruiting school.

At the west side of the fort complex, the small **Archaeological Survey Museum** (admission free; ◷9am-5pm Sat-Thu) contains

TAMIL NADU & CHENNAI NORTHERN TAMIL NADU

sculptures dating back to Pallava and Chola times. Next door, pretty **St John's Church** (1846) is only open for Sunday services. On the east side, the **Government Museum** (Indian/foreigner ₹5/100; ☺9.30am-5pm Sat-Thu) displays hero stones in the forecourt dating from the 8th century and depicting the stories of war heroes in battle. The dusty exhibits have seen much better days, but the small collection of tribal clothes and artefacts is interesting.

Near the fort entrance, **Jalakanteshwara Temple** (☺6am-1pm & 3-8.30pm), a gem of late Vijayanagar architecture, was built about 1566. Check out the small, detailed sculptures on the walls of the marriage hall. For many years the temple was occupied by garrisons and temple rituals ceased. Now it's once again a place of worship after it was reconsecrated in the mid-1980s.

🛏 Sleeping & Eating

Vellore's cheap hotels are concentrated along the roads south of and parallel to the hospital, mostly catering to people in town for treatment. The cheapest are pretty grim, and there's not much at the top end, but Vellore's your city when it comes to bland rooms in the space between budget and midrange.

Darling Residency   HOTEL $$
(✐2213001; darling_residency@yahoo.com; 11/8 Officer's Line; s/d from ₹1400/1700; ✱✦☊) It's no five-star, but rooms are clean and comfortable (if forgettable), staff are friendly and there's even a small fitness room with exercise bike. The rooftop **Aranya Roof Garden Restaurant** (open lunch and dinner) is cool and breezy.

Hotel Palm Tree   HOTEL $
(✐2222960; hotelpalmtree@yahoo.in; 10 Thennamaram Rd; s/d from ₹850/950; ✱@) Down a lane just off Officer's Line, not far south of the fort. Rooms are clean and spruce, with IKEA-style furniture and coloured feature walls, and staff are helpful.

Ismail Residency   HOTEL $
(✐2223216; Ida Scudder Rd (Arcot Rd); s/d from ₹600/700; ✱) A five-room lodge with clean rooms that are a tad bigger than others along this stretch.

Hotel River View   HOTEL $$
(✐2225251; Katpadi Rd; d from ₹1000; ✱) North of the town centre and close to the New Bus Stand, this hotel benefits from a relatively quiet location and pleasant gardens, but the 'river view' is hardly that. Rooms are spacious, and the restaurants are both good, but service is odd-to-rude and bathroom cleaning isn't quite up to scratch for these prices.

Meher Hotel   HOTEL $
(✐2220992; Ida Scudder Rd; s/d ₹600/700) Right across from the hospital entrance, this is one of a string of similarly priced places with smallish, clean, undecorated rooms that get a bit of street noise.

Hotel Arthy   INDIAN $
(Ida Scudder Rd; mains ₹10-50) A bunch of cheap veg restaurants line Ida Scudder Rd, but this place is one of the cleanest, with tasty South Indian favourites plus cheap-and-yummy biryani; the rather good 'special thali' is ₹50.

❶ Information

There are several internet cafes around town, including a few opposite the hospital on Ida Scudder Rd (Arcot Rd).
Axis Bank ATM (Officer's Line) A couple of blocks south of the fort.
Geo Wings Internet (Ida Scudder Rd; per hr ₹30; ☺9am-9pm)
State Bank of India ATM (Bangalore Rd) There's another ATM a couple of blocks north of the hospital on Katpadi Rd.
Tourist office (Vellore Fort; ☺10am-1pm & 2-2.30pm Mon-Fri)
UAE Exchange (Ida Scudder Rd; ☺9.30am-6pm Mon-Fri, to 4pm Sat) Foreign exchange, in the same building as the Meher Hotel.

❶ Getting There & Away

Bus
The New Bus Stand is about 500m from the Hotel River View, 1.5km to the north of town. AC Volvo buses run 12 times a day to Chennai (₹145). Government bus services from the New Bus Stand include:
Chennai ₹54, three daily, every 15 minutes
Bengaluru ₹87, five daily, every 30 minutes
Kanchipuram ₹26, two hours, every 15 minutes
Tiruvannamalai ₹38, two hours, every 30 minutes
Trichy ₹120, seven hours, three daily

Train
Vellore's main train station is 5km north at Katpadi. Bus 192 shuttles between the station and town. There are at least six daily express trains to/from Chennai Central (2nd class/sleeper ₹76/133).

Tiruvannamalai

📞 04175 / POP 130,567

There are temple towns, there are mountain towns, and there are temple-mountain towns where God appears as a phallus of fire. Welcome to Tiruvannamalai. About 85km south of Vellore and flanked by boulder-strewn Mt Arunachala, this is one of the five 'elemental' cities of Shiva; here the god is worshipped in his fire incarnation as Arunachaleswar (see boxed text, p340). At each full moon Mt Arunachala swells with thousands of pilgrims who circumnavigate the base of the mountain, but at any time you'll see Shaivite priests, sadhus (spiritual men) and devotees gathered around the temple. Tiruvannamalai is also home to the Sri Ramana (also known as Sri Ramanasramam) Ashram.

Budget and spiritual-minded travellers who see the Mamallapuram scene as played out are increasingly making their way here; in the streets near the ashram you'll find a few congenial cafes and hotels, and the ubiquitous Kashmiri souvenir shops.

⊙ Sights & Activities

Arunachaleswar Temple   HINDU TEMPLE
(🕙5am-12.30pm & 3.30-9pm) The Arunachaleswar is awash in golden flames and the roasting scent of burning ghee, as befits the fire incarnation of the Destroyer of the Universe. Covering some 10 hectares, this vast temple is one of the largest in India. Four large unpainted *gopurams,* one for each cardinal point, front the approaches, with the eastern tower rising 13 storeys and an astonishing 66m.

You enter Arunachaleswar through concentric rings of profanity evolving into sacredness, from the outer wall of beggars and merchants, past dark corridors recessed with bejewelled gods and, finally, into the heart of the temple, where a roaring oven that looks like a walnut shell spewing fire is tended by temple Brahmins in front of a lingam. *Puja* is performed about seven times daily; a notice displays the times. This is a remarkably hassle-free temple to wander through.

Mt Arunachala   MOUNTAIN
Known as Sonachalam (Red Mountain) in Sanskrit, this 800m-high extinct volcano dominates Tiruvannamalai and local conceptions of the element of fire, which supposedly finds its sacred abode in Arunachala's heart. On full-moon and festival days, thousands of pilgrims circumnavigate the 14km base of the mountain. If you're not quite that devoted, an autorickshaw will take you around for about ₹200 if things are quiet, or up to double that on festival days. An alternative is to pick up a circle map from the ashram office, hire a bicycle from the road near the entrance and ride your way around.

You can make a sort of phallus pilgrimage here by visiting eight famous linga dotted around the mountain's cardinal and subcardinal spokes. Also, watch out for the field of a thousand lingam, 'planted' by domestic and overseas donators from Malaysia to the USA.

For a superb view of the Arunachaleswar Temple, climb part or all the way up the hill (about four hours return). There's a signed path that leads up through village homes near the northwest corner of the temple, passing two caves, **Virupaksha** and **Skandasramam**. Sri Ramana Maharshi lived and meditated in these caves for more than 20 years from 1899 to 1922, after which he and his growing band of spiritual followers established the ashram.

THE LINGAM OF FIRE

Legend has it that Shiva appeared as a column of fire on Mt Arunachala, creating the original symbol of the lingam. Each November/December full moon, the **Karthikai Deepam Festival** celebrates this legend throughout India but becomes particularly significant at Tiruvannamalai. Here, a huge fire, lit from a 30m wick immersed in 2000L of ghee, blazes from the top of Mt Arunachala for days. In homes, lamps honour Shiva and his fiery lingam. The fire symbolises Shiva's light, which eradicates darkness and evil.

At festival time up to half a million people come to Tiruvannamalai. In honour of Shiva, they scale the mountain or circumnavigate its base. On the upward path, steps quickly give way to jagged and unstable rocks. There's no shade, the sun is relentless and the journey must be undertaken in bare feet – a mark of respect to the deity. None of this deters the thousands of pilgrims who quietly and joyfully make their way to the top and the abode of their deity.

Sri Ramana Ashram
ASHRAM

(✐237200; www.sriramanamaharshi.org; ☉office 7.30am-12.30pm & 2-6.30pm) This tranquil ashram, 2km southwest of Tiruvannamalai, draws devotees of Sri Ramana Maharshi, a guru who died in 1950 after nearly 50 years in contemplation. It's a very relaxed place, set in green surrounds, where visitors are able to meditate or worship the shrine where the guru achieved samadhi (conscious exit from the body). Day visits are permitted but *devotees only* may stay at the ashram by applying in writing (email is acceptable), preferably at least three months in advance.

☞ Tours

Bougainvillea Tours (✐9500325159; www.bougainvilleatours.com) offers a range of guided walks around the mountain and to the temples, as well as a bullock-cart circumnavigation of the mountain. Full-moon pilgrimage tours are also run from Chennai by the TTDC (p326).

🛏 Sleeping & Eating

Tiruvannamalai can be visited as a day trip from Puducherry or Chennai, but more and more travellers are staying on. There are budget lodges around the temple, but quality is generally lacking. During festival time (November/December) prices can rise by a staggering 1000%.

Arunachala Ramana Home
HOTEL $

(✐236120; www.arunachalaramanahome.com; 70 Ramana Nagar, Chengam Rd; s/d from ₹300/400, d with AC ₹ 700; ❄) Basic, clean and friendly, this popular place is not far from the ashram. Next door is the excellent Manna Cafe, which answers any need for non-Indian food, including salads, pasta and bread. Plenty of chai stalls and veg cafes are nearby.

Hotel Ganesh
HOTEL $

(✐2226701; 111A Big St; d ₹275-₹605; ❄) On the busy bazaar road running along the north side of the temple, Ganesh is a little haven of peace and value. Some rooms are poky, but they're clean enough and the inner courtyard balcony is pleasant. There's a decent veg restaurant downstairs.

Hotel Arunachala Residency
HOTEL $

(✐228300; www.hotelarunachala.com; 5 Vada Sannathi St; s/d/tr from ₹400/600/750; ❄) The best of the temple-adjacent hotels, this place right next to the main temple entrance is clean and fine with pretentions to luxury apparent in the marblesque floors and ugly furniture. The veg restaurant downstairs has simple, very good, South Indian dishes. It's a much better option than the inexplicably popular Hotel Ramakrishna, nearby on the highway, which has run-down rooms at similar prices.

Shanti Internet Café
CAFE $

(www.shanticafe.com; 115 Chengam Rd; ☎) Near the ashram. A popular, relaxed spot with cushion seating on the floor and a small menu of sandwiches, salads, shakes and cakes. There's internet access downstairs (per hour ₹25) and wi-fi in the cafe.

ℹ Getting There & Away

There are buses every half-hour to Chennai (₹66, 3½ hours) and Vellore (₹38, two hours). There are at least three daily buses to Puducherry (₹40, three hours). A taxi to Puducherry (via Gingee) costs around ₹1500 return, or ₹900 one way.

Only local passenger trains use Tiruvannamalai train station – two trains a day pass through between Vellore and Villupuram (where you can change for Puducherry).

Gingee (Senji)
✐04145

Somewhere 37km east of Tiruvannamalai, nature sprinkled a smattering of marbles – rounded boulders and lumpy rocks – in shades of grey, brown and red over the flat green paddies of Tamil Nadu. Then man turned two of these stony protrusions into the **Rajagiri & Krishnagiri** (King & Queen Fort; Indian/foreigner ₹5/150; ☉9am-5pm). Constructed mainly in the 16th century by the Vijayanagars (though some structures date from the 13th century), these edifices, which poke out of the Tamil plain like castles misplaced by the *Lord of the Rings*, have been occupied by the Marathas, the Mughals, the French and, finally, the British.

It's a good hike to the top of either fort, but along the way you'll pass through several monuments, from *gopurams* to granaries. A walk around will take half a day, especially if you cross the road and make the steep ascent to Krishnagiri. Buildings within Rajagiri (on the south side of the road) include a Shiva temple, a mosque and – most prominent – the restored audience hall. Almost all have been marred by graffiti.

It's easy to day trip to Gingee from Puducherry (67km) or Tiruvannamalai (37km). Buses leave every 30 minutes from

Tiruvannamalai (₹13, 1½ hours). Ask to be let off at 'the fort', 2km before Gingee town. An autorickshaw from Gingee to the fort costs about ₹90 one way.

Puducherry (Pondicherry)

☑0413 / POP 220,749

Let's get something clear: if you came to Puducherry (which used to be called Pondicherry and is almost always referred to as 'Pondy') expecting a Provençal village in South India, you're in for some sore disappointment, *mon ami.* Most of Pondy is Tamil Nadu: honk-scream-screech-honk-chaos Tamil Nadu. Running through this is a thin trickle of colonial Pondy: some cobblestones, mustard-yellow townhouses, and here and there a shady boulevard that could put you in mind of gendarmes marching past sari-clad belles – HONK!

On top of everything are hotels, restaurants and 'lifestyle' shops that sell a vision of *vieux Asie* created by savvy entrepreneurs and embellished by Gallic creative types who arrived here on the French hippie trail. Their presence has in turn attracted Indian artists and designers, and thus, Pondy's vibe: less faded colonial *ville*, more contemporary bohemian, vaguely New Age – but also faintly Old World – node on the international travel trail.

Enjoy the shopping, the French food (hello steak!), the beer (goodbye Tamil Nadu alcohol taxes – Pondy is a Union Territory) and, if you like, yoga and meditation at the Sri Aurobindo Ashram.

Puducherry is split from east to west by a partially covered sewer...we mean, canal. The more 'French' part of town is on the east side (towards the sea), the more typically Indian portion to the west. Nehru St and Lal Bahadur Sastri, better known as Rue Bussy, are the main east–west streets; Mahatma Gandhi (MG) Rd and Mission St (Cathedral St) are the north–south thoroughfares. Pondy's grid design makes it relatively easy to follow, although many streets have one name at one end and another at the other, while others use the French 'Rue' instead of 'Street'.

◉ Sights & Activities

French Quarter   OLD NEIGHBOURHOOD

Pocketed away in the eastern alleys are a series of cobbled roads, white and mustard buildings in various states of romantic *déshabillé,* and a slight sense of Gallic glory gone by, otherwise known as the French Quarter. The best way to explore these streets is via Puducherry's **heritage walk.** Start at the north end of Goubert Ave, the seafront promenade, and wander south past the **French consulate** and the **Gandhi Statue.** Turn right at the **Hôtel de Ville** (Town Hall) on Rue Mahe Labourdonnais, past the shady **Bharathi Park.** From there it's a matter of pottering south through Dumas, Romain Rolland and Suffren Sts. You may also want to take a look down Vysial St, between MG Rd and Mission St; locals say this tree-lined block is one of the last faithfully maintained slices of old Pondy.

Sri Aurobindo Ashram   ASHRAM

(cnr Marine & Manakula Vinayagar Koil Sts) Founded in 1926 by Sri Aurobindo and a French woman known as 'the Mother' (whose visage is *everywhere* here), this ashram seeks to synthesise yoga and modern science. After Aurobindo's death, spiritual authority (and minor religious celebrity) passed to the Mother, who died in 1973 aged 97. A constant flow of visitors files through the **main ashram building** (⊙8am-noon & 2-5pm), which has the flower-festooned samadhi of Aurobindo and the Mother in the central courtyard. Opening hours are longer for guests of any of the ashram's accommodation around the town.

Puducherry Museum   MUSUEM

(15 St Louis St; adult/child ₹2/1; ⊙9.40am-1pm & 2-5.20pm Tue-Sun) Goodness knows how this cute little museum keeps its artefacts from rotting, considering there's a whole floor of French-era furniture sitting in the South Indian humidity. As you amble through the colonial-era building, keep an eye peeled for Pallava and Chola sculptures, French Union-era bric-a-brac, and coins and shards of pottery excavated from Arikamedu, a once-major seaport a few kilometres south of Puducherry that traded with the Roman Empire during the 1st century BC.

Churches   CHURCHES

Puducherry has one of the best collections of over-the-top cathedrals in India. *Merci,* French missionaries. The **Church of Our Lady of the Immaculate Conception** (Mission St), completed in 1791, is a robin's-egg-blue-and-cloud-white typically Jesuit edifice, while the brown-and-white grandiosity of the **Sacred Heart Church** (Subbayah Salai) is set off by stained glass and a Gothic sense of proportion. The mellow pink-and-cream **Notre Dame de Anges** (Dumas St), built in

1858, looks sublime in the late-afternoon light. The smooth limestone interior was made using eggshells in the plaster.

Sri Manakula Vinayagar Temple   HINDU TEMPLE
(Manakula Vinayagar Koil St; ⊘5.45am-12.30pm & 4-9.30pm) Pondy may have more churches than most towns, but this is still India, and the Hindu faith still reigns supreme. Don't miss the chance to watch tourists, pilgrims and the curious get a head pat from the temple elephant who stands outside Sri Manakula Vinayagar Temple, dedicated to Ganesh and tucked down a backstreet just south of the Sri Aurobindo Ashram. The temple also contains over 40 skillfully painted friezes.

Botanical Gardens   GARDEN
(admission free; ⊘10am-5pm) Established by the French in 1826, the botanical gardens form a green, if somewhat litter-strewn, oasis on the southwest side of town.

Beaches   BEACHES
Pondy is a seaside town, but that doesn't make it a beach destination; the city's sand is a thin strip of dirty brown blah that slurps into a seawall of jagged rocks. With that said, Goubert Ave (Beach Rd) is a killer stroll, especially at dawn and dusk when everyone in town takes a constitutional or romantic stroll. There are a few decent beaches to the north and south of town. Quiet, Reppo and Serenity Beaches are all north of the centre, within 8km of Puducherry. Chunnambar, 8km south, has Paradise Beach, water sports and backwater boat cruises. Both areas are becoming inundated with high-end resorts. The tourist office has details.

Yoga
Puducherry has an annual International Yoga Festival. **Ayurvedic Holistic Healing Centre** (☏6537651; 6 Sengeniammal Koil St) performs detox services, back procedures, varna point massage, skin treatment, and offers ayurvedic massages and yoga courses. You can practise (and study) yoga at Sri Aurobindo Ashram. **International Centre for Yoga Education & Research** (ICYER; ☏2241561; www.icyer.com; 16A Mettu St, Chinnamudaliarchavady, Kottukuppam), also known as the Ananda Ashram, conducts annual six-month yoga teacher-training courses and 10-day introductory summer courses (€500, including food and lodging).

☞ Tours
The local tourist office runs half-day sightseeing tours (₹100 to ₹150, 1.30pm to 5pm) to the Sacred Heart Church, Auroville and Sri Aurobindo Ashram. Full-day tours (₹200 to ₹250, 9.45am to 5pm) cover the same area plus the botanical gardens, Puducherry Museum, Sri Manakula Vinayagar Temple and the Chunnambar water sports complex.

Shanti Tours (Romain Rolland St; ⊘8am-9pm Mon-Sat, 9am-6pm Sun) offers recommended two-hour **walking tours** (per person ₹200) of Puducherry with informed, multilingual guides.

🎊 Festivals & Events

International Yoga Festival   YOGA
(4-7 Jan) Puducherry's ashrams and yoga culture are put on show with workshops, classes, and music and dance events. Held throughout the city, the event attracts yoga masters from all over India.

Bastille Day   PARADE
(14 Jul) Street parades and a bit of French pomp and ceremony are all part of the fun at this celebration.

🛏 Sleeping
If you've been saving for a special occasion, splurge here, because Puducherry's lodgings are as good as South India gets. Local heritage houses manage to combine colonial romanticism with modern spoilage and, dare we say, French playfulness, like vintage movie posters and colour schemes that run from monochrome to neon-bright; these same rooms are likely to run to hundreds of dollars in the West.

Sri Aurobindo Ashram runs a lot of local budget accommodation. The lodgings are clean and you'll be around like-minded souls (ie the budget – and karma – conscious). But they come with rules: 10.30pm curfew and no smoking or alcohol. For information and reservations, contact the **Sri Aurobindo information centre** (☏2233604; bureaucentral@sriaurobindoashram.org; Cottage Complex, cnr Rangapillai St & Ambour Salai; ⊘6am-8pm).

It's smart to book ahead if you plan on arriving at a weekend; hotels tend to fill up with Indian tourists.

[TOP CHOICE] Calve   BOUTIQUE HOTEL $$$
(☏2224261; www.calve.in; 36 Vysial St; r incl breakfast ₹3555-5355; ❋) This excellent heritage option, located on a quiet, tree-shaded boulevard, combines a soaring sense of high-ceilinged space with egg-white walls, wooden shutters, flat-screen TVs, huge niche-embedded mattresses and a warm backdrop

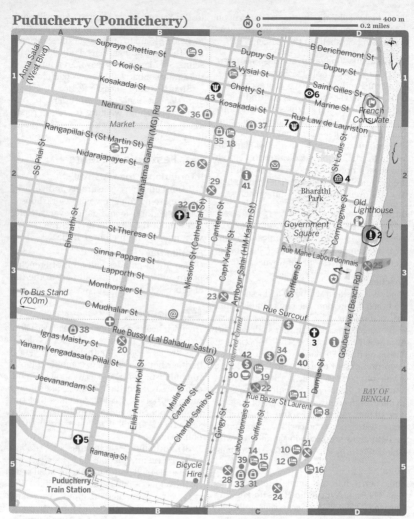

of Burmese teak floors and banisters. Add gorgeous tiled floors, beautiful furniture and big baths, and you've got a winner.

Dumas Guest House BOUTIQUE HOTEL **$$**
(☏2225726; www.dumasguesthouse.com; 36 Dumas St; d from ₹2000; ❄) All whitewash and dark wood, this antique-filled heritage option has real personality. Enjoy the carved doors, quiet gardens, slight quirkiness in the decor and very friendly multilingual staff.

Les Hibiscus BOUTIQUE HOTEL **$$**
(☏2227480; www.leshibiscus.com; 49 Suffren St; d incl breakfast ₹2500; ❄@) Not dissimilar to the

Dumas in its white-and-wood heritage style, Hibiscus has just four high-ceilinged rooms with gorgeous antique beds and flatscreen TVs. Travellers have raved about the friendly, helpful owner, and the tasty complimentary breakfast that will set you up for the day.

Kailash Guest House HOTEL **$**
(☏2224485; www.kailashguesthouse.in; cnr Vysial & Mission Sts; s/d from ₹500/750; ❄) The best value for money in this price range; Kailash has simple, super-clean rooms and friendly management. It's geared to traveller needs, with communal areas, shared fridge and clothes-drying facilities, and bike rental.

TAMIL NADU & CHENNAI PUDUCHERRY (PONDICHERRY)

Villa Helena BOUTIQUE HOTEL **$$**
(☎2226789; villahelena@satyam.net.in; 13 Lal Bahadur Shastri St; r ₹2200-2800; ❉) What sits Helena apart from her heritage siblings is the dash of vintage fun she overlays on respectable colonial facades. With 1930s-era Chinese movie posters, wrought-iron beds and high-ceilinged rooms, you feel caught between a black-and-white colonial noir flick and a modern designer's dream.

Hotel De L'Orient BOUTIQUE HOTEL **$$$**
(☎2343067; www.neemranahotels.com; 17 Romain Rolland St; r ₹3000-6500; ❉) This is as grand as it gets in Puducherry: a restored colonial mansion with rooms that appeal to your inner pith-helmeted aristocrat. Should you need a sense of columned regal importance, the hush of breezy verandas and the scurrying service of men in clean white uniforms,

this is the place to book. An attached shop has beautiful, wildly overpriced souvenirs.

Park Guest House ASHRAM HOTEL **$**
(☎2224644; 1 Goubert Ave; s/d from ₹450/600) This is the most soughtafter ashram address in town thanks to its wonderful seafront position. All front rooms face the sea and have their own porch or balcony, and there's a large garden area for morning yoga or meditation. These are the best-value AC rooms in town. Prebooking is technically possible but can be difficult, and reception staff can be unfriendly until they're sure you're going to obey the house rules.

New Guest House ASHRAM HOTEL **$**
(☎2221553; 64 Romain Rolland St; d ₹200, r up to 8 people ₹480) Sparse, huge and packed with the ashram faithful; this is a great spot for those who love the monastery cubicle school of lodging.

Santhi Inn HOTEL $
(☏2220946; 57 Nehru St; s/d ₹900/1000; ❋)
The multistorey Santhi certainly isn't a
heritage house, but it's a clean, bland
spot with comfy beds, a rooftop bar and a
conveniently central location.

Ajantha Beach Guest House HOTEL $$
(☏2338898; 1 Rue Bazar St Laurent; d with sea
view ₹1500; ❋) The location is the only real
selling point – right on the beachfront
promenade. The four sea-view rooms are
plain but comfortable and have balconies;
others are drab and windowless. Next-
door **Lotus Bay View Hotel** has shinier,
much more luxurious but equally charac-
ter-free rooms at nearly twice the price.

Hotel de Pondichery BOUTIQUE HOTEL $$
(☏2227409; 38 Dumas St; s/d ₹ 1800/2500; ❋)
Yet another heritage home, this place has
colonial-style rooms and outdoor terraces.
It's more Old World than luxurious, but
rooms are private and quiet, and staff are
lovely.

Raj Lodge HOTEL $
(☏2337346; www.rajlodge.in; 57 Rangapillai St;
s/d ₹300/450, d with AC ₹750; ❋) A friendly,
central lodge with basic, dark but clean
rooms.

✖ Eating

Puducherry is a culinary highlight of Tamil
Nadu; you get the best of South Indian cooking plus several restaurants specialising in
well-prepped French and Italian cuisine. If
you've been missing cheese or have a hankering for pâté, you're in luck, and *everyone* in the French quarter offers crepes and
good brewed coffee. There's a string of cheap
street stalls open past 11pm on Anna Salai
and Lal Bahadur Shastri St, and more good
cheap Indian eateries around the market.

For self-caterers, **Nilgiris Supermarket**
(cnr Mission & Rangapillai Sts; ☻9am-9pm) has a
big range of supplies (in addition to toilet-
ries, children's books and toys.)

TOP CHOICE Satsanga MULTICUISINE $$
(☏2225867; 30-32 Labourdonnais St; mains ₹170-
350; ☻lunch & dinner) This deservedly popular
garden spot serves excellent Continental
cuisine and, like most places in this genre, a
full Indian menu as well. The large variety of
sausages, pâté and lovely home-made bread
and butter goes down a particular treat,
as do the steaks. **Satsanga Epicerie**, next
door, sells French and Italian food supplies;
pasta, cheese, even vacuum-packed *jamon*.

Salle a Manger INDO-FRENCH $$
(www.calve.in; Calve hotel, 36 Vysial St; mains
₹150-300; ❋) The speciality here is 'Creole'
food, using recipes sourced from Pondy's
French-Indian families and using lots of seafood and spices: try the Fish Vindali, full of
fresh flavours. Like the decor – all teak and
teal-coloured walls – the food has an Indo-
Chinese vibe.

kasha ki aasha CAFE $$
(www.kasha-ki-aasha.com; 23 Rue Surcouf; mains
₹125-225; ☻8am-7pm Mon-Sat) You'll get a
great pancake breakfast, good lunches (try
the 'European-style thali') and delicious
cakes served on the pretty rooftop of this
colonial-house-cum-craftshop-cum-cafe.
Indo-European fusion food includes chips
with chutney, and pizza dosa. The heat in
some dishes has been dialled back a bit for
Western tastes, but it's all delicious.

Le Club MULTICUISINE $$
(38 Dumas St; mains ₹120-330; ☻lunch & dinner)
This place wraps three restaurants into one,
with heavy French fare at Le Bistro, a simple
garden terrace at Le Club, and Vietnamese
and Southeast Asian fare in the attached
Indochine. Le Club also offers Contintental
breakfasts.

Surguru SOUTH INDIAN $
(99 Mission St; mains ₹40-100; ☻lunch & dinner)
Simple South Indian served in a posh setting. Surguru is the fix for thali addicts who
like their veg accompanied by the strongest
AC this side of Chennai. There's a couple of
branches round town.

Le Café CAFE $$
(Goubert Ave; mains ₹50-170; ☻24hr) Situated
near the Gandhi statue, this is a good spot
for sandwiches, cake, coffee (hot or ice), wel-
come fresh breezes and clean views over the
Bay of Bengal. Be warned, service can be se-
riously slow; but it's one of the nicest spots
in town to wait.

La Terrasse CONTINENTAL $$
(5 Subbayah Salai; pizzas ₹120-200; ☻breakfast,
lunch & dinner Thu-Tue) This simple semi-open-
air place near the southern end of the promenade has a wide menu but is best known
for good pizzas and safe salads, as opposed
to its rather ordinary Indian food. No alcohol is served.

Café des Artes CAFE $
(Labourdonnais St; ☻breakfast, lunch & dinner;
☎) Good brekky and coffee, wi-fi and a

nice outdoor/veranda setting outside a small gallery.

Café de Flore
CAFE $$

(Maison de Colombani, Dumas St; ☺8.30am-8pm) In the Alliance Française's performance space, on an airy veranda overlooking a garden, you'll find mocktails, great coffee, sandwiches and chips, along with copies of *Le Monde* to browse.

Baker St
BAKERY $

(Rue Bussy; pastries ₹35-120) A very popular upmarket, French-style bakery with cakes, brownies, meringues, quiches, baguettes and croissants. Eat in or takeaway.

Saravana Bhavan
SOUTH INDIAN $

(Nehru St; mains ₹30-50) A clean setting with good cheap South Indian – all the thalis, dosa and *vada* you could want.

🍷 Drinking & Entertainment

Although this is one of the better spots in Tamil Nadu to sink a beer, closing time is a decidedly un-Gallic 11pm. If you're here on a Friday or Saturday, get ready for some late-night fun, when Pondy stays open until (drum roll)...11.30pm! With low taxes on alcohol, Puducherry has a reputation for cheap booze. The reality is you'll really only find cheap beer in 'liquor shops' or the darkened bars attached to them. Many of the garden and rooftop restaurants in the French Quarter have pleasant bar areas, especially Satsanga and Le Club.

L'e-Space Coffee & Arts
CAFE

(2 Labourdonnais St; ☺8am-11pm) A battered, quirky little semi-open-air cafe for breakfasts, juice, coffee, a bite and some fine cocktails (₹160 to ₹180). Staff are friendly, locals and tourists congregate here, and all in all it's the most social traveller spot in Pondy.

🛍 Shopping

With all the yoga yuppies congregating here, Pondy specialises in the boutique-chic-meets-Indian-bazaar school of fashion, accessories and souvenirs. Every Sunday evening the central shopping area on and around Nehru St is packed with clothes stalls strung up in front of closed shopfronts. Among other things, you'll find the kind of cotton pants and shirts that would cost *waaaay* more in Pondy's boutiques.

Fabindia
CLOTHING

(www.fabindia.com; 59 Suffren St; ☺10am-8pm) Opposite Alliance Française, this shop has a good variety of quality woven goods and furnishings, traditionally made but with a contemporary feel. This chain has been in operation since 1960, and one of its selling points is its 'fair, equitable and helpful relationship' with village producers. Next door **Pondy Cre'Art** is also worth checking out, with handbags, handmade paper journals and clothes.

Geethanjali
ANTIQUES

(20 Lal Bahadur Shastri St; ☺10am-7pm) The sort of place where Indiana Jones gets the sweats, this antique and curio shop sells statues, sculptures, paintings and furniture culled from Puducherry's colonial and even pre-colonial history.

Kalki
ACCESSORIES

(134 Mission St; ☺9.30am-8.30pm) Beautiful, jewel-coloured silk clothes, scarves and shoes, as well as jewellery, candles, knick-knacks and more.

kasha ki aasha
CLOTHING, HANDICRAFTS

(www.kasha-ki-aasha.com; 23 Rue Surcouf; ☺8am-7pm Mon-Sat) Fabulous fabrics, gorgeous garments and comfy handmade leather sandals, as well as crafts, are sourced directly from their makers and sold by an all-women staff in this lovely old colonial house. There's a breezy rooftop eatery on-site.

La Boutique d'Auroville
HANDICRAFTS

(38 Nehru St; ☺9.30am-1pm & 3.30-8pm Mon-Sat) It's fun browsing through the crafts here, including jewellery, batiks, *kalamkari* (similar to batik) drawings, carpets and woodcarvings. For more Auroville products head west to the **Sri Aurobindo Handmade Paper Factory** (50 SV Patel Salai; ☺8.30am-noon & 1.30-5pm Mon-Sat) for fine handmade paper; ask at the counter about tours of the factory.

Hidesign
BAGS

(cnr Nehru & Mission Sts) Established in Pondy in the 1970s, this boutique sells beautifully made designer leather handbags and 'man bags' in a range of colours, at prices that are very reasonable for what you get. We bought a bag here in 1985 that's still going strong. The 3rd-floor cafe has pasta, burgers and tapas, great coffee and free wi-fi.

Bookshops

French Bookshop
BOOKSTORE

(Suffren St; ☺9am-12.30pm & 3.30-7.30pm Mon-Sat) This small shop next to Alliance Française carries many French titles.

Libraire Kailash　BOOKSTORE
(169 Lal Bahadur Shastri St; ⊙9am-8pm Mon-Sat) Another excellent collection of titles, particularly coffee-table books, in French.

Focus Books　BOOKSTORE
(204 Mission St; ⊙9.30am-1.30pm & 3.30-9pm Mon-Sat) A big range of English-language books, friendly staff, Lonely Planet guides.

ⓘ Information

Puducherry keeps European hours and takes a long lunch break; you can expect most businesses to be closed from about 1pm to 3.30pm.

Cultural Centres

Alliance Française (☎2338146; afpondy@satyam.net.in; 58 Suffren St; ⊙9am-noon & 3-6pm Mon-Sat) The French cultural centre has a library, computer centre and art gallery, and conducts French-language classes. Films are shown regularly. The monthly newsletter, *Le Petit Journal,* details forthcoming events. Maison Colombani, its associated exhibition and performance space, is on Dumas St.

Internet Access

Coffee.Com (236 Mission St; per 30min ₹30; ⊙10am-10pm) There might be some pressure to buy a drink; don't feel obliged.

Wi Corner (1 Caziavar St, cnr Lal Bahadur Shastri St; per hr ₹30; ⊙10am-10pm Mon-Sat)

Medical Services

Lal Bahadur Shastri St between Bharathi St and MG Rd is packed with clinics, pharmacies and two 24-hour hospitals.

New Medical Centre (☎2225289; 470 MG Rd; ⊙24hr)

Money

Nilgiris Supermarket has a **forex counter** (⊙9am-5.30pm Mon-Sat) upstairs.

Citibank ATM (cnr Lal Bahadur Shastri & Suffren Sts)

ICICI Bank ATM (47 Mission St)

State Bank of India (15 Suffren St)

Thomas Cook (Labourdonnais St; ⊙9.30am-6.30pm Mon-Sat) Foreign exchange next to L'e-Space Coffee & Arts.

UTI Bank ATM (164 Rue Bussy)

Tourist Information

Puducherry tourist office (☎2339497; 40 Goubert Ave; ⊙9am-5pm)

Travel Agencies

Shanti Travels (Romain Rolland St; ⊙8am-9pm Mon-Sat, 9am-6pm Sun) Helpful French-run agency offering bus, train and air ticketing, as well as walking tours, day trips, longer tours and airport pick-ups from Chennai.

ⓘ Getting There & Away

Bus

The bus stand is 500m west of town. See the boxed text for details of services. There's a **booking office** (⊙7am-2pm & 4-9pm) at the station.

Taxi

Air-conditioned taxis between Puducherry and Chennai cost around ₹3500; it should be cheaper to/from Chennai Airport.

Train

There are two direct services a day to Chennai Egmore (₹52, five hours, 5.35am and 2.35pm), and one to Tirupathy (₹79, nine hours, 1.40pm). There's a computerised booking service for southern trains at the station.

ⓘ Getting Around

One of the best ways to get around Pondy is by walking. Large three-wheelers shuttle between the bus stand and Gingy St for ₹5, but they're

BUSES FROM PUDUCHERRY (PONDICHERRY)

DESTINATION	FARE (₹)	DURATION (HR)	FREQUENCY (DAILY)
Bengaluru	150	8	4
Chennai	56	3½	50
Chidambaram	36	2	50
Coimbatore	170	9	7
Kanchipuram	40	3	6
Kumbakonam	42	4	6
Mamallapuram	35	2	5
Tiruvannamalai	40	3	10
Trichy	80	5	4

hopelessly overcrowded. Autorickshaws are plentiful – a trip across town costs about ₹50.

Since the streets are broad and flat, the most popular transport is pedal power. Bicycle-hire shops line many of the streets, especially MG Rd and Mission St. You'll also find hire shops in Subbayah Salai and Goubert Ave. The usual rental is ₹10/50 per hour/day.

Mopeds or motorbikes are useful for getting out to the beaches or to Auroville and can be rented from a number of shops and street stalls. The going rate is about ₹150 a day for a gearless scooter and ₹200 for a motorbike.

Auroville

📞 0413 / POP 1800

Auroville is one of those ideas anyone with a whiff of New Age will love: an international community built on soil donated by 124 countries, where dedicated souls, ignoring creed, colour and nationality, work to build a universal township and realise interconnectedness, love and good old human oneness.

In reality, Auroville is both its high ideals and some not-as-glamorous reality. Imagine over 80 rural settlements encompassing scrubby Tamil countryside, where harmony is strived for if not always realised between 1800 residents representing almost 40 nationalities. Two-thirds of Aurovillians are foreign, and outside opinions of them range from positive vibes to critics who say the town is an enclave for expats seeking a self-indulgent rustic escape.

Ultimately, Auroville encompasses all of the above, and anyone interested in the experiment may want to visit on a day trip from Puducherry. Be prepared for lots of posters celebrating 'The Mother', the French traveller-turned-guru, and founder of the Sri Aurobindo Ashram (p342). Be warned: Auroville is not that tourist friendly. Each settlement has its own area of expertise and most Aurovillians are busy simply getting on with their work. Still, you may get a sense of the appeal of the place after a visit to the visitor centre and the **Matrimandir**, Auroville's spiritual heart. One of those unfortunate buildings that tries to look futuristic and ends up coming off dated, this giant golden golf ball/faux Epcot Center contains an inner chamber lined with white marble that houses a solid crystal (the largest in the world), 70cm in diameter, which you won't actually see, since the Matrimandir is not open to casual visitors. But there is a pleasant plot of **gardens** (⊘10am-1pm & 2-4.30pm daily except Sun afternoon), from where you can spy the struc-

ture; you need to pick up a pass (free) from the information service in the visitor centre.

🛏 Sleeping & Eating

You can only stay in Auroville if you're serious about contributing to it. A stay of at least a week is preferred and while work isn't obligatory, it is appreciated. Accommodation isn't offered in exchange for work; rooms range from ₹300 to more than ₹1000, and guests are also required to contribute towards the 'maintenance and development' of Auroville.

There are more than 40 guesthouses in Auroville, each tied to communities with specific work missions (women's education, farming etc). The best way to match your interests with the community you'll stay in is to check out the website and, preferably, get suggestions from and make arrangements with the **Auroville Guest Service** (📞2622704; avguests@auroville.org.in) before arriving.

Although there are stores and small roadside eateries in Auroville, and communities have communal dining areas, many Aurovillians gather at the Solar Kitchen – powered by solar energy – which dishes out more than 400 meals daily from its buffet. The cafe at the visitor centre is open to day visitors.

ℹ Information

There's a photographic exhibition and video room at the **Auroville Information Service** (www.auroville.org; admission free; ⊘9.15am-1pm & 1.30-5.30pm), which also issues garden passes for external views of the Matrimandir (from 9.45am to 12.30pm and 2pm to 4pm; morning only on Sunday). In the same complex, the **visitor centre** (📞2622239; www.auroville.org; ⊘9am-6pm) contains a bookshop, a nice cafe and Boutique d'Auroville, which sells Aurovillian handicrafts.

ℹ Getting There & Away

The best way to enter Auroville is from the coast road, at the village of Periyar Mudaliarchavadi. Ask around as it's not well signposted. A return autorickshaw ride from Puducherry is about ₹300, but a better option is to hire a moped or bicycle. It's about 12km from Puducherry to the visitor centre.

CENTRAL TAMIL NADU

Chidambaram

📞 04144 / POP 67,795

There's basically one reason to visit Chidambaram: the great temple complex of Nataraja, Shiva as the Dancer of the Universe.

The greatest Nataraja temple in India also happens to be a Dravidian architectural highlight and one of the holiest Shiva sites in South India. Chidambaram can be visited as a day trip from Puducherry, or as a stopover between Puducherry and Kumbakonam or Trichy.

Of the many festivals, the two largest are the **10-day chariot festivals**, which are celebrated in April/May and December/January. In February/March the five-day **Natyanjali Dance Festival** attracts performers from all over the country to celebrate Nataraja (Shiva) – Lord of the Dance.

The small town is developed around the Nataraja Temple with streets named after the cardinal points. Accommodation is close to the temple and the bus stand a five-minute walk to the southeast. The train station is about 1km further south.

◉ Sights

Nataraja Temple HINDU TEMPLE
(☉courtyard & shrines 6am-noon & 4-10pm) The legend goes: one day, in a nearby forest, Shiva and Kali got into a dance-off that was judged by the assembled gods. Shiva finished his routine with a high kick to the head that Kali could not duplicate and won the title Nataraja (Lord of the Dance). It is in this form he is worshipped at the great Shiva temple, which draws a regular stream of pilgrims and visitors. The region was a Chola capital from 907 to 1310 and the temple was erected during the later time of the administration, although local guides claim some of the complex was built by the Pallavas in the 6th century. The high-walled 22-hectare complex has four towering *gopurams* decked out in schizophrenic Dravidian stonework.

The main entrance, through the east *gopuram*, off East Car St, depicts the 108 sacred positions of classical Tamil dance. In the northeast of the complex, to the right as you enter, is the 1000-pillared **Raja Sabha** (King's Hall), open only on festival days, and to the left is the **Sivaganga** (Temple Tank), which is thick with mudfish and worshippers performing ritual ablutions. To the west of the entrance to the inner sanctum is a depiction of Shiva as Nataraja that is underlined by a distinctly European pair of cherubic angels. In the southwest corner of the second enclosure is the Dance Hall, decorated with 56 pillars, that marks the spot where Shiva outdanced Kali.

Cameras are not allowed inside the temple, and non-Hindus cannot enter the inner sanctum, although you can glimpse its golden roof and its 21,600 tiles (one for every breath a human takes a day). Nataraja images abound, wherein Shiva holds the drum that beats the rhythm of creation and the fire of destruction in his outstretched hands, ending one cycle of creation, beginning another and uniting all opposites – light and dark, good and evil.

Try to catch the fire ceremony, which occurs six times a day and pulls in hundreds of worshippers who watch a ritual essentially unchanged for thousands of years. The entire complex erupts in drum beats and bells, while fires of clarified oil and butter are passed under the image of the deity, thus ensuring the cycle of creation continues.

Brahmin priests will usually guide you for a fee (anywhere from ₹30 up to ₹300, depending on the language skills and knowledge of the guide) around the temple complex. Since the Brahmins work as a cooperative to fund the temple, you may wish to support this magnificent building by way of donation or hiring a guide (but don't feel bound to do so).

🛏 Sleeping & Eating

Chidambaram has many cheap pilgrims' lodges clustered around the temple, but some of these spots come off as pretty dire. If there's anywhere really nice to stay in Chidambaram, we haven't found it yet.

Hotel Saradharam HOTEL $
(☑221336; www.hotelsaradharam.co.in; 19 VGP St; d incl breakfast ₹770, with AC ₹1400; ❋☞) The busy and friendly Saradharam is as good as it gets, and is conveniently located across from the bus stand. It's a bit worn (readers have met bedbugs here, though we remained unbitten), but it's comfortable enough and a welcome respite from the frenzy of the town centre. The good breakfast buffet is a bonus.

Hotel Akshaya HOTEL $
(☑220192; www.hotel-akshaya.com; 17-18 East Car St; d from ₹600; ❋) Close to the temple and also a bit grotty round the edges, this hotel has a wide range of rooms that run the gamut from boxy singles to quite good-value AC 'suites'.

The best places to eat are in hotels. **Anu-upallavi** (mains ₹50-120; ☉lunch & dinner) is an excellent AC multicuisine restaurant in

TOP FIVE TEMPLES

Tamil Nadu is nirvana for anyone wanting to explore South Indian temple culture and architecture. Many of the temples are important places of pilgrimage for Hindus, where daily *puja* (offering or prayer) rituals and colourful festivals will leave a deep impression on even the most temple-weary traveller. Other temples stand out for their stunning architecture, soaring *gopurams* (gateway towers) and intricately carved, pillared *mandapams* (pavilions in front of the temple). Almost all have free admission. There are so many that it pays to be selective, but the choice is subjective. Here's our top five:

» Sri Meenakshi Temple (p364) This elaborately carved temple complex in Madurai is considered the crowning achievement of South Indian temple architecture.

» Arunachaleswar Temple (p340) Fire rituals – and the smell of roasting ghee – dominate this huge temple in Tiruvannamalai.

» Brihadishwara Temple (p353) Thanjavur recently celebrated the thousand-year anniversary of this beautiful sandstone temple and fort.

» Sri Ranganathaswamy Temple (p357), Trichy (Tiruchirappalli) One of the biggest temples in India, this city-like complex in Trichy has fine carvings and a lively cart festival.

» Nataraja Temple (p350) Fire ceremonies commemorate Shiva's role as Lord of the Dance in Chidambaram.

the Saradharam, and the **Golden Roof** (RK Residency, 30 VGP St; mains ₹30-50) does a decent job of Indian and 'Chinese' basics. Just across the bus stand is vegetarian **Ishwarya** (thalis ₹30; ⊘breakfast, lunch & dinner), which does fine thalis. There are lots of cheap veg eats in the area immediately surrounding the temple complex.

❶ Information

Bank of India ATM (VGP St)

Cybase (Pillaiyar Koil St; per hr ₹30; ⊘9am-9pm) Fast internet access.

ICICI Bank ATM (Hotel Saradharam, VGP St)

Tourist office (☑238739; Railway Feeder Rd; ⊘9am-5pm Mon-Fri) Frequently deserted.

UAE Exchange (Pillaiyar Koil St; ⊘closed Sun afternoon) Best place in town to exchange money.

❶ Getting There & Away

The bus stand is very central – within walking distance to the temple and accommodation. There are hourly buses to Chennai (₹98, seven hours), and buses to Puducherry (₹36, two hours) and Kumbakonam (₹37, 2½ hours) run regularly. There are also five direct buses daily to Madurai (₹155, eight hours).

Chidambaram is on the Chennai–Trichy gauge line, with services to Kumbakonam, Thanjavur and once a day to Rameswaram (10 hours). The station is a 20-minute walk southeast of the temple (₹50 by autorickshaw).

Kumbakonam

☑0435 / POP 160,767

At first glance Kumbakonam is another Indian junction town, but then you notice the temples that sprout out of this busy city like mushrooms, a reminder that this was once a seat of medieval South Indian power. It's an easy day trip from Thanjavur, and makes a good base for exploring the coastal towns of the Cauvery Delta.

◉ Sights

Dozens of colourfully painted *gopurams* point skyward from Kumbakonam's 18 temples, most of which are dedicated to Shiva or Vishnu, but probably only the most dedicated temple goer would tackle visiting more than a few. All temples are open from 6am to noon and 4pm to 10pm, and admission is free.

The largest Vishnu temple in Kumbakonam, with a 50m-high east gate, is **Sarangapani Temple**, just off Ayikulam Rd. The temple shrine, in the form of a chariot, was the work of the Cholas during the 12th century.

Kumbeshwara Temple, about 200m west and entered via a nine-storey *gopuram,* is the largest Shiva temple. It contains a lingam said to have been made by Shiva himself when he mixed the nectar of immortality with sand.

The 12th-century **Nageshwara Temple**, from the Chola dynasty, is also dedicated to

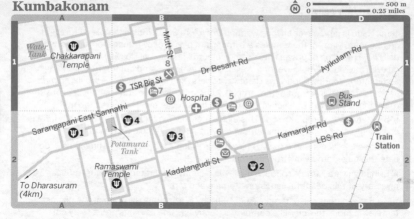

Shiva in the guise of Nagaraja, the serpent king. On three days of the year (in April or May) the sun's rays fall on the lingam. The main shrine here is in the form of a chariot.

The huge **Mahamakham Tank**, 600m southeast of the Nageshwara Temple, is the most sacred in Kumbakonam. It's believed that every 12 years the waters of the Ganges flow into the tank, and at this time a festival is held; the next is due in 2016.

🛏 Sleeping & Eating

Hotel Rayas   HOTEL $
(☑2422545, 2423170; 18 Post Office Rd; d from ₹800; ﹡) Friendly service and reliably spacious (and clean) rooms make this your best lodging option in town.

Paradise Resort   RESORT $$
(☑2416469; www.paradiseresortindia.com; Tanjore Rd, Darasuram; s/d from ₹3200/3800; ﹡) Out of town, this is an atmospheric resort constructed around heritage buildings and thatch and teak cottages. The rooms here have cool tiles and verandas overlooking quiet and spacious gardens, and a plethora of ayurvedic spa treatment options.

Hotel Kanishka   HOTEL $
(☑2425231; www.hotelkanishka.in; Ayikulam Rd; d from ₹700; ﹡) A sparkling new (at our visit) place with smallish and simple but cheerful rooms with yellow feature walls. It's owned and run by a young couple who aim to keep the hotel family friendly.

Pandian Hotel   HOTEL $
(☑2430397; 52 Sarangapani East St; s/d ₹190/300) It feels a bit institutional, but in

general you're getting good value at this clean-enough budget standby.

Hotel Sri Venkkatramana   INDIAN $
(TSR Big St; thalis ₹30; ⊘breakfast, lunch & dinner) Serves good fresh veg food and is very popular with locals.

🛈 Information

There's no tourist office in Kumbakonam, and road names and signs here are more erratic than usual.

Ashok Net Café (24 Ayikulam Rd; per hr ₹20; ⊘9am-10.30pm)
Axis Bank ATM (Ayikulam Rd)
Speed Browsing Centre (Sarangapani East St; per hr ₹20; ⊘9am-9pm)
State Bank of India ATM (TSR Big St)
UAE Exchange (☑2423212; 134 Kamarajar Rd) The best place to exchange money.

🛈 Getting There & Away

The bus stand and train station are east of the town centre.

Trains to/from Chennai Egmore include the overnight *Rock Fort Express* (sleeper/3AC ₹191/505), going via Thanjavur and Trichy, and the faster *Chennai Egmore Express/Rameswaram Express* (₹158/413). Passenger trains run to Chidambaram (two hours) and Thanjavur.

For the Cauvery Delta area there are buses running every half-hour to Karaikal (₹20, two hours), via Tranquebar and then on to Nagapattinam. Government buses from the bus stand include:

Chennai ₹110, seven hours, every 30 min
Chidambaram ₹37, 2½ hours, every 20 minutes

Kumbakonam

Coimbatore ₹140, 10 hours, daily
Madurai ₹72, five hours, eight daily
Puducherry ₹42, four hours, every 30 minutes
Thanjavur ₹15, one hour, every 30 minutes

Around Kumbakonam

Only 4km west of Kumbakonam in the village of Dharasuram, the **Airatesvara Temple** (☉6am-noon & 4-8pm), constructed by Rajaraja II (1146–63), is a superb example of 12th-century Chola architecture. Fronted by columns overflowing with miniature sculptures, the temple art depicts, among other things, Shiva in the rare incarnation as Kankalamurti, the mendicant.

At Gangakondacholapuram, 35km north of Kumbakonam, you'll find a Shiva **temple** (☉6am-noon & 4-8pm) built by Rajendra I that represents a latter, somewhat more developed phase of Chola art. Note the 49m-tall *vimana* (tower) that tops the temple; its elegant up-sloping curves stand in stark contrast to the Brihadishwara's angular lines, and as a result the Gangakondacholapuram is often described as the feminine counterpart to the Thanjavur edifice.

Buses go from Kumbakonam bus stand to Gangakondacholapuram every half-hour (₹18, 1½ hours). A rickshaw to Dharasuram costs about ₹90 round trip. Frequent buses head to Dharasuram as well; ask at the bus stand, as these tend to be village buses that will have to drop you off on their way out of town.

Cauvery Delta

The Cauvery River is the beating heart of South Indian agriculture and, back in its day, connected the entire region via river-

ine routes. Today the Cauvery's delta, which spills into Tamil Nadu's east coast, is one of the prettiest and poorest parts of the state. This green and pleasant region can be visited on a lovely day drive (expect to pay about ₹3000 for a return taxi from Kumbakonam).

About 80km south of Chidambaram, **Tranquebar** was a Danish post established in 1620 by the Danish East India Company. The seafront **Danesborg Fort** houses a small museum on the region's Danish history. To get here, take a bus from Chidambaram (₹32, 2½ hours).

Just south of the district capital, Nagapattinam, the main draw of the little town of **Vailankanni**, is the basilica of **Our Lady of Good Health**, built on the spot where a young buttermilk boy glimpsed the Virgin Mary in the 15th century. Distinctly Hindu styles of worship are popular here, and an annual nine-day festival culminates on 8 September, the celebration of Mary's birth. There are daily bus services between Vailankanni and Chidambaram, as well as Chennai, Coimbatore, Bengaluru and Thiruvananthapuram (Trivandrum).

Thanjavur (Tanjore)

⊿ 04362 / POP 215,314

Here are the ochre foundation blocks of one of the most remarkable nations of Dravidian history, one of the few kingdoms to expand Hinduism beyond India, a bedrock for aesthetic styles that spread from Madurai to the Mekong. A dizzying historical legacy was once administered from Thanjavur, ancient capital of the great Chola Empire, which today...is a chaotic, messy, modern Indian town. Oh, how the good times have gone. But their presence is still remarkably evident; past the honking buses and happy public urination are the World Heritage–listed Brihadishwara Temple and the sprawling Maratha palace complex.

⊙ Sights

Brihadishwara Temple & Fort   HINDU TEMPLE
(☉6am-noon & 4-8.30pm) Come here twice: in the morning, when the tawny sandstone begins to assert its dominance over the white dawn sunshine, and in the evening, when the rocks capture a hot palette of reds, oranges, yellows and pinks on the Brihadishwara Temple, the crowning glory of Chola temple architecture. The temple was commissioned in 1010 by Rajaraja (whose name literally

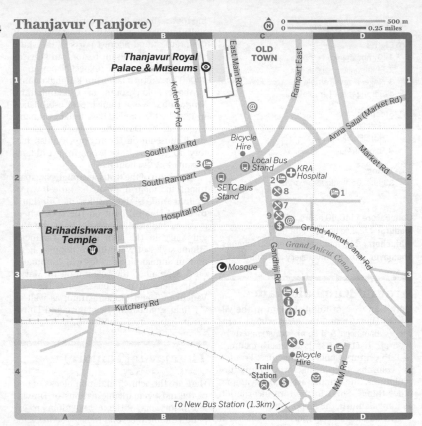

means 'king of kings'), a well-regarded monarch so organised he had the names and addresses of all his dancers, musicians, barbers and poets inscribed into the temple wall. Thousand-year anniversary celebrations and renovations were held in 2010.

Note the covered statue of Nandi (Shiva's sacred bull) – 6m long by 3m high – that faces the inner sanctum. Created from a single piece of rock, it weighs 25 tonnes and is one of India's largest Nandi statues. There's also a well-executed interpretive centre set along the side alcoves, which includes sculptures and paintings culled from the temple walls (including a particularly energetic Shiva slaying an army of demons while Buddha hovers above. Not for enlightenment either; the demons were Shiva worshippers, and the Buddha took them on as devotees so the Destroyer could justify killing them).

Unlike most South Indian temples where the *gopurams* are the highest towers, here

the 13-storey, 66m *vimana* (centre tower) dominates. There's not a lot of touting here, and the grounds are nice spot to sit awhile.

Thanjavur Royal Palace & Museums
HISTORICAL BUILDING

The pink walls hold court for crows; the queen's courtyard is overrun with weeds; the inner corridors stink of bat guano. And yet... amid the decay are expertly carved bodies of gods and goddesses, sky-bright tile work, massive columns of preserved, chocolate-coloured teak and the incredible murals of one of the great dynasties of South Indian royalty. The labyrinthine complex was constructed partly by the Nayaks of Madurai and partly by the Marathas.

Walk by a local school to enter the main hall of the **palace** (Indian adult/child ₹10/5, foreign adult/child ₹50/25 incl entry to the Durbar Hall & bell tower, camera/video ₹30/250; ⊙9am-1pm & 3-6pm) and follow the signs to the elegantly faded **Durbar Hall** (Royal Court). An incred-

Thanjavur (Tanjore)

ible profusion of murals erupts here, unrestored and elegantly faded, bursting with geometric designs, scenes of Hindu legend and a flock of vaguely European-yet-almost-Indian cherubs. With a torch you can peek into a 6km secret passage that runs under the palace and reeks of bat poo.

In the former Sadar Mahal Palace is the **Raja Serfoji Memorial Hall** (admission ₹2), with a small collection of thrones, weapons and photographs; there's a similar collection in the **Royal Palace Museum** (admission ₹1, camera/video ₹30/250). Many of the artefacts date from the early 19th century when the enlightened and far-sighted scholar-king Serfoji II ruled (six generations later, his descendants still lives here).

An extensive **gallery** (Indian adult/child ₹17/2, foreigner ₹30) of Chola bronzes sits between the Royal Palace Museum and the bell tower. Nearby, the **bell tower** is worth a climb for views right across Thanjavur and the palace itself. The spiral stone staircase is dark, narrow and slippery; watch your head and your step.

Perhaps Serfoji II's greatest contribution to posterity is the **Saraswati Mahal Library** (admission free; ⊙10am-1pm & 1.30-5.30pm Tue-Thu) between the gallery and the palace museum. It's a monument to both universal knowledge and an eclectic mind that collected prints of Chinese torture methods, Audubon-style sketches of Indian flora and fauna, sketches of

the London skyline, and a collection of some 60,000 palm-leaf and paper manuscripts in Indian and European languages.

✦ Festivals & Events

Two important festivals are held about 13km north of Thanjavur in Thiruvaiyaru. The January **International Music Festival** honours saint and composer Thyagaraja, and the Thyagararajaswami Temple has a 10-day **car festival** in April/May when the largest temple chariot in Tamil Nadu is hauled through the streets.

⌷ Sleeping

There's a bunch of nondescript cheap lodges opposite the SETC bus stand.

Hotel Gnanam HOTEL $$
(☎278501; www.hotelgnanam.com; Anna Salai; s/d from ₹1350/1550; ❄@⌘) The best place in town, the Gnanam has stylish, comfy rooms (the more expensive rooms have bathtubs – the cleanest we've seen in the whole state) and is perfect for anyone needing wi-fi and other modern amenities while they're plopped in Thanjavur's geographic centre. Guests are greeted with chilled face cloths – perfect in such a humid town.

Hotel Valli HOTEL $
(☎231580; arasu_tnj@rediffmail.com; 2948 MKM Rd; s/d from ₹340/360; ❄) Near the train station, the green-painted (inside and out) Valli is a good choice for budget travellers; the non-AC rooms are better value than the more expensive ones. Staff are personable and the rooms themselves are spic-and-span. It's in a reasonably peaceful location beyond a bunch of greasy backyard workshops.

Hotel Tamil Nadu HOTEL $$
(☎231325; www.ttdconline.com; Gandhiji Rd; d from ₹600; ❄) The Tamil Nadu is appealing from the outside; the architecture is sultan chic (makes sense, given this is a former royal guesthouse), an atmosphere accentuated by a quiet, leafy courtyard and wide balconies. But inside the rooms are dank, if spacious, and overpriced.

Hotel Ramnath HOTEL $
(☎272567; hotel_ramnath@yahoo.com; 1335 South Rampart; s/d from ₹550/600; ❄) Just across from the SETC bus stand (the attendant noise is not as bad as you might expect), a nice 'upmarket budget' option with fresh rooms.

TAMIL NADU & CHENNAI CENTRAL TAMIL NADU

Ashoka Lodge HOTEL $
(☏230022; 93 Abraham Pandithar Rd; dm/s/d
₹150/195/325, r with AC ₹700; ❄) The Ashoka's been in business for 44 years, and
is frankly looking its age. That said, the
rooms are, if a little gloomy, surprisingly
spacious for the cost and kept clean.

Eating

There's a cluster of simple veg restaurants,
open for breakfast, lunch and dinner, near
the local bus stand and along Gandhiji Rd.

Sahana INDIAN $
(Hotel Gnanam, Anna Salai; mains ₹70-90; ☺break-
fast, lunch & dinner) This classy hotel restaurant does a nice line in fresh, tasty, mainly
Indian veg dishes. This might be the only
place in town to get a Continental breakfast
if you're not up to *idlis* first thing. The hotel's pricier nonveg restaurant, **Diana**, is also
very good, with a wide range of tandoori and
other northern dishes.

Sri Venkata Lodge SOUTH INDIAN $
(Gandhiji Rd; thalis ₹30) A few minutes from
the local bus stand, this veg-only place
does a nice thali.

Bombay Sweets INDIAN $
(Gandhiji Rd; snacks ₹15-30) Near the train
station, a clean, popular spot with good
sweets (halwa, *burfi*) and snacks like
samosas and *bhelpuri*.

Thevar's Biryani INDIAN $
(Gandhiji Rd; mains ₹50-150; ☺closed Fri) Thevar's specialises in exactly what the name
suggests, and it specialises in the Mughal
rice dish (done up with southern influences here, like sour tamarind sauce) well.
Chicken and fish dishes are also good.

Sathars INDIAN $
(167 Gandhiji Rd; mains ₹45-100) Good service
and quality food make this place popular.
Downstairs is a veg restaurant with lunchtime thalis, upstairs is an AC section with
good-value nonveg food.

🛍 Shopping

Thanjavur is a good place to shop for handicrafts and arts, especially around the palace,
though beware of rickshaw drivers wanting to take you to a particular shop (their
commission will be reflected in the price
you pay). Numerous shops along East Main
and Gandhiji Rds sell everything from quality crafts and ready-made clothes to inexpensive kitsch. For fixed prices and hassle-
free shopping, try **Poompuhar** (Gandhiji Rd;
☺10am-8pm Mon-Sat).

ℹ Information

24Hrs Internet (Golden Plaza, Ganhiji Rd; per
hr ₹20) We can't swear by the claimed opening
hours.
ICICI Bank ATM (New Bus Station)
Indian Bank ATM (train station)
Sify iWay (East Main Rd; per hr ₹20; ☺10am-
9pm)
State Bank of India ATM (Hospital Rd)
Tourist office (☏230984; Gandhiji Rd;
☺10am-5pm Mon-Fri) On the corner of the
Hotel Tamil Nadu complex.
VKC Forex (Golden Plaza, Gandhiji Rd;
☺9.30am-9pm) Changes cash and travellers
cheques.

ℹ Getting There & Away

Bus
The two city bus stands are for local and
SETC buses. SETC has a **reservation office**
(☺7.30am-9.30pm). Destinations from here
include Chennai (₹120, eight hours, 20 daily)
and Ooty (₹135, 10 hours, daily).

The New Bus Station, 2.5km south of the cen-
tre, services local areas and destinations south.
Bus 74 shuttles between the three bus stations
(₹4). Buses from the New Bus Station include:
Chidambaram ₹54, four hours, every 30
minutes
Kumbakonam ₹15, one hour, every 30 minutes
Madurai ₹56, four hours, every 15 minutes
Trichy ₹24, 1½ hours, every 15 minutes

Train
The station is conveniently central at the south
end of Gandhiji Rd. Thanjavur is off the main
Chennai–Madurai line, so there's only one
express train direct to Chennai – the overnight
Rock Fort Express (sleeper/3AC ₹178/472, 9½
hours) departing at 8.30pm. For more frequent
trains north or south, including to Madurai,
take a passenger train to Trichy (₹22, 1½ hours,
eight daily) and change there. There's a couple
of express and three passenger trains daily to
Kumbakonam (₹20, one hour).

The *Thanjavur-Mysore Express* leaves daily at
7.15pm for Bengaluru (sleeper/3AC ₹206/547,
10 hours) and Mysore (sleeper/3AC ₹237/627,
14 hours).

ℹ Getting Around

The main attractions of Thanjavur are close
enough to walk between, but this can make for
a tiring day depending on your fitness. Bicycles
can be hired from stalls opposite the train station and local bus stand (per hour ₹5). An au-

torickshaw into town from the New Bus Station costs around ₹100.

Trichy (Tiruchirappalli)

☏ 0431 / POP 866,354

Welcome to (more or less) the geographic centre of Tamil Nadu. Fortunately, this hub isn't just a travel junction, although it does make a good base for exploring large swatches of central Tamil Nadu. But Tiruchirappalli, universally known as Trichy, also mixes up a throbbing bazaar with several major must-see temples.

Trichy's long history dates back to before the Christian era when it was a Chola citadel. Since then it's passed into the hands of the Pallavas, Pandyas, Vijayanagars and Deccan sultans. The modern town and the Rock Fort Temple were built by the Nayaks of Madurai.

Trichy's places of interest are scattered over a large area from north to south, but for travellers the city is conveniently split into three distinct areas. The Trichy Junction, or Cantonment, area in the south has most of the hotels and restaurants, the bus and train stations and tourist office. This is where you're likely to arrive and stay. The Rock Fort Temple and main bazaar area is 2.5km north of here; the other important temples are in an area called Srirangam, a further 3km to 5km north again,

across the Cauvery River. Fortunately, the whole lot is connected by a good bus service.

◉ Sights

Rock Fort Temple   HINDU TEMPLE

(Map p357; admission ₹3, camera/video ₹20/100; ⊗6am-8pm) The Rock Fort Temple, perched 83m high on a massive outcrop, lords over Trichy with stony arrogance. The ancient rock was first hewn by religious-minded Pallavas, who cut small cave temples into the southern face, but it was the war-savvy Nayaks who later made strategic use of the naturally fortified position. There are two main temples: **Sri Thayumanaswamy Temple**, halfway to the top (there may be some bats snoozing in the ceiling), and **Vinayaka Temple**, at the summit, dedicated to Ganesh. There are 437 stone-cut steps to climb, and the hike is worth the effort – the view is wonderful, with eagles wheeling beneath and Trichy sprawling all around into the greater Cauvery. Non-Hindus are not allowed inside either temple.

Sri Ranganathaswamy Temple   HINDU TEMPLE

(Map p357; camera/video ₹50/100; ⊗6am-1pm & 3-9pm) Alright temple-philes, here's the one you've been waiting for: quite possibly the biggest temple in India. Located about 3km north of the Rock Fort, it feels more like a self-enclosed city than a house of worship,

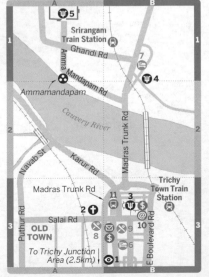

Trichy (Tiruchirappalli)

and in truth, that's the idea: entering this temple's inner sanctum requires passing through seven *gopuram* (the largest is 73m high). Inside the fourth wall is a kiosk where you can buy a ticket (₹10) and climb the wall for a semi-panoramic view of the complex that delineates levels of existence and consciousness. You'll proceed past rings of beggars, merchants and Brahmins, then plazas of *devas* (celestial beings) and minor deities before reaching the inner chamber, dedicated to Vishnu. Here, the god is worshipped as Sheshashayana, Vishnu who sleeps on a bed made of the king of *nagas*.

Take note of the numerous carvings and statues of *vanaras* (literally 'forest people'), monkey warriors and princesses from the Ramayana, as well as avatars (incarnations) of Vishnu in one of his animal forms, such as the half-lion Nairarishma. These may have been tribal pre-Hindu deities that were folded into the religion, and remain popular objects of worship.

If you turn right just before you go through the fifth gate there's a small, dusty **Art Museum** (admission ₹5; ⊙9am-1pm & 2-6pm) with some fascinating exhibits, including bronze statues, the tusks of former temple elephants, and copper edict plates. The highlight is a collection of beautifully detailed 17th-century (Nayak period) ivory carvings of gods, kings and queens (some of them erotically engaged), demons and even a Portuguese soldier; they look Balinese in style, although of course the influence flowed in the other direction.

A **Temple Chariot Festival** where statues of the deities are paraded aboard a fine chariot is held here each January, but the most important festival is the 21-day **Vaikunta Ekadasi** (Paradise Festival) in mid-December, when the celebrated Vaishnavaite text, Tiruvaimozhi, is recited before an image of Vishnu.

Bus 1 from Trichy Junction or Rock Fort stops right outside this temple.

Sri Jambukeshwara Temple   HINDU TEMPLE
(Tiruvanakoil; Map p357; camera/video ₹20/150; ⊙6am-1pm & 3-9pm) If you're visiting the five elemental temples of Shiva, you need to visit Sri Jambukeshwara Temple, dedicated to Shiva, Parvati and the medium of water. The liquid theme of the place is realised in the central shrine, which houses a partially submerged Shiva lingam. The outer chambers are full of carvings, including several of an elephant being freed from a spiderweb by Shiva, which provoked the pachyderm to perform *puja* for the Destroyer.

If you're taking bus 1, ask for 'Tiruvanakoil'; the temple is about 100m east of the main road.

Lourdes Church   CHURCH
(Map p357; Madras Trunk Rd) This church is heavily decked out in Gallo-Catholic design, from neo-Gothic spires to the anguished scenes of crucifixion and martyrdom painted inside. The hush of the nave makes an interesting contrast to the frenetic activity that characterises Trichy's Hindu temples. The **Feast of Our Lady of Lourdes** is held on 11 February. The entrance to Lourdes is on Madras Trunk Rd, and when you're finished you can escape into the green and cool campus of Jesuit St Joseph's College (where classes run from Intro to Javascript to Comparative Theology). An eccentric and dusty **museum** (admission free; ⊙10am-noon & 2-4pm Mon-Sat) contains the natural history collections of the Jesuit priests' summer excursions to the Western Ghats in the 1870s. Bang on the door and the caretaker will let you in – or not, depending on if he's there.

Hazrat Nathervali Dargah   TOMB
(Map p357) This is the tomb of popular Muslim saint Natther. From a distance the mausoleum is a minaret-ensconced compound

Trichy (Tiruchirappalli) Junction Area

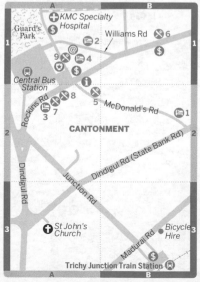

with distinctly Arab sea-green embellishments, but the *puja*-like worship of Natther has strong Hindu overtones. If you're asking for directions most people will know it as 'the Muslim shrine'.

🛏 Sleeping

The majority of Trichy's hotels are in the Junction/Cantonment area around the bus station and a short walk north of the train station. Most budget hotels have either doubled their prices or halved their cleaning budgets in the last couple of years; the upper budget and midrange spots here are much better value, charging only a little more for good non-AC rooms than you'd pay for a grim cheapie.

Femina Hotel   HOTEL **$**
(Map p358; ☎2414501; try_femina@sancharnet. in; 104C Williams Rd; d incl breakfast from ₹770; ❀⊛🛜) Femina is one of those Indian business hotels that manages to be affordable even if you're on a budget – and the staff don't look at travellers as if they've just crawled out of a swamp. Nonguests can use the pool and small gym (per hour ₹75). Good buffet breakfast including toast and eggs as well as the full traditional South Indian.

Ramyas Hotel   HOTEL **$**
(Map p358; ☎2412626; www.ramyas.com; Williams Rd; s/d from ₹650/750; ❀🛜) Another good corporate spot, although it *has* been known to be unfriendly to backpackers. Rooms in the new block are clean and stylish, some with pleasant balconies overlooking the trees, and the non-AC rooms are good value, though some are a bit smoky smelling. There's a couple of decent restaurants on-site; the **Meridien** has excellent local Chettinad-style dishes.

Hotel Royal Sathyam   HOTEL **$$**
(Map p357; ☎4011414; www.hotelsathyam.co.in; 42A Singarathope; s/d from ₹1200/1400; ❀) Towering over a posh jewellery shop, this is the classiest place to stay if you want to be close to the temple and market action. Rooms are small but stylish, with extra-comfy mattresses and a fresh wood-and-whitewash theme that's almost but not quite 'boutique'.

Breeze Residency   HOTEL **$$**
(Map p358; ☎2414414; www.breezehotel.com; 3/14 McDonald's Rd; s/d from ₹2300/2700; ❀@🛜) Undergoing a name change and a noisy refurbishment when we visited, the Breeze is enormous, semiluxurious and in a relatively quiet location. The best rooms are on the top floors but all are well appointed. Hotel facilities include a health club; a very good restaurant, the **Madras** (mains ₹90-250); and a bizarre Wild West theme bar.

Hotel Temple In   HOTEL **$**
(Map p357; ☎4250304; 139 Madras Trunk Rd; s/d from ₹450/750; ❀) Opened literally the day before we visited, this friendly, very clean (for now) spot near the two major temples in the Srirangam area was a much better choice than the budget options in the Cantonment at the time of research.

Hotel Meega   HOTEL **$**
(Map p358; ☎2414092; 3 Rockins Rd; d from ₹425; ❀) It's friendly and still reasonably cheap (though not as cheap as it should be), but rooms are worn and grubby and the creaky lift gave us some scary moments. There's a popular veg restaurant downstairs. Next-door **Hotel Mathura** is another cheapie with peeling walls that's hiked its prices for no good reason, but if you're really on a budget it's clean and spacious enough.

🍴 Eating

Femina Food Court   MULTICUISINE **$**
(Map p358; Williams Rd; mains ₹60-35, snacks ₹10-30; ☉lunch & dinner) Next to the Femina 'shopping mall' (two large shops) is a shaded outdoor-seating area with a Chinese restaurant, an Indian snack bar, and a juice and cake

Trichy (Tiruchirappalli) Junction Area

shop; the Chinese is especially tasty and it's a good spot to take a break.

Banana Leaf   INDIAN $
(Map p357; ☑271101; Madras Trunk Rd; mains ₹30-90; ☺lunch & dinner) A big menu of regional favourites. The speciality is the fiery, vaguely vinegary cuisine of Andhra Pradesh. Another branch is next to the Hotel Tamil Nadu in Trichy Junction.

Shree Krishnas   INDIAN $
(Map p358; 1 Rockins Rd; mains ₹20-40; ☺breakfast, lunch & dinner) On the lower floor of Hotel Mathura, with a nice view of the buses playing plough-the-pedestrian across the road, this is a reliable spot for veg goodness and milky-sweet desserts.

Vasanta Bhavan   INDIAN $
(Map p357; West Blvd; mains ₹30-60; ☺breakfast, lunch & dinner) Pop in here for North Indian veg – that of the paneer and naan genre – if you're tired of dosas and *idlis* (of course you can get them too, along with excellent lassi). There's another branch in the Cantonment, next to Shree Krishnas.

Marrybrown   FAST FOOD $$
(Map p358; Williams Rd; burger ₹70-150; ☺11am-11pm) Join the cool kids for burgers, fries and chicken at this popular chain.

Shopping

The main bazaar, which runs by the entrance to the Rock Fort, is as chaotic and crowded as you like; it constantly feels like all of Trichy is strolling the strip. The usual array of plastic toys and silk saris is on sale. Try **Poompuhar** (Map p357; West Blvd Rd; ☺9am-8pm) for fixed-price crafts.

ⓘ Information

Axis Bank ATM (Map p357; Chinnar Bazaar)
Canara Bank (Map p358; Royal Rd)
ICICI Bank ATM Junction Rd (Map p358); West Blvd Rd (Map p357)
Indian Bank ATM (Map p358; Rockins Rd)
Indian Panorama (☑4226122; www.indian panorama.in) Trichy based and covering all of India, this professional and reliable travel agency/tour operator is run by an Indian-Australian couple.
KMC Speciality Hospital (Map p358; ☑4077777; Royal Rd) A large hospital in the Cantonment.
Sify iWay (internet per hr ₹30; ☺9am -9pm) Chinnar Bazaar (Map p357); Williams Rd (Map p358)
State Bank of India ATM (Map p358; Williams Rd)
Tourist office (Map p358; ☑2460136; 1 Williams Rd; ☺10am-5.45pm Mon-Fri) One of the more helpful tourism info offices in the state.

ⓘ Getting There & Away

Trichy is virtually in the geographical centre of Tamil Nadu and it's well connected by air, bus and train.

Air

As well as domestic flights, Trichy's airport has opened up to international flights in the last couple of years. **Sri Lankan Airlines** (Map p358; ☑2460844; ☺9am-5.30pm Mon-Sat, 9am-1pm Sun), with an office at Femina Hotel, has 10 flights a week to Colombo (₹8700). **Air Asia** (☑4540393) flies daily to Kuala Lumpur, and **Air India Express** (☑2341744; trzapt@airindiaexpress.in) flies to Kulala Lumpur, Singapore and Abu Dhabi.

Bus

Most buses head to the **Central bus station** (Map p358; Rockins Rd) on Rockins Rd. If you're

BUSES FROM TRICHY (TIRUCHIRAPPALLI)

DESTINATION	FARE (₹)	DURATION (HR)	FREQUENCY
Bengaluru	160	8	3 daily
Chennai	120-190	7	every 15min
Chidambaram	55	3½	hourly
Coimbatore	80	7	every 30min
Kodaikanal	65	5½	3 daily
Madurai	42	3	every 15min
Ooty	100	8	daily
Puducherry	80	5	3 daily
Thanjavur	24	1½	every 15min

travelling to Kodaikanal, a good option is to take one of the frequent buses to Dindigul (₹25, two hours) and change there. For details of services, see the boxed text, opposite.

Train

Trichy is on the main Chennai–Madurai line so there are lots of rail options in either direction. Of the nine daily express services to Chennai, the quickest are the *Vaigai Express* (2nd/chair class ₹104/367, 5½ hours) departing Trichy at 8.50am, and the *Pallavan Express*, which leaves at 6.30am. The best overnight train is the *Rock Fort Express* (sleeper/3AC ₹164/432, 7½ hours) at 10pm.

For Madurai the best train is the *Guruvaya Express* (2nd class/sleeper ₹62/120, three hours), which leaves at 1.15pm. The *Mysore Express* goes daily to Bengaluru at 8.35pm (sleeper/3AC ₹187/496, 8½ hours) and Mysore (₹236/636, 12½ hours).

ℹ️ Getting Around

To/From the Airport

The 6km ride into town is about ₹300 by taxi and ₹100 by autorickshaw; there's a prepaid taxi stand at the airport. Otherwise, take bus 7, 59, 58 or 63 to/from the airport (30 minutes).

Bicycle

Trichy lends itself to cycling as it's flat; it's a reasonably easy ride from Trichy Junction to the Rock Fort Temple, but a long haul to Srirangam and back. There are a couple of places on Madurai Rd near the train station where you can hire bicycles (per hr ₹5).

Bus

Trichy's local bus service is easy to use. Bus 1 (any letter) from the **Central bus station** (Map p358; Rockins Rd) goes every few minutes via the Rock Fort Temple, Sri Jambukeshwara Temple and the main entrance to Sri Ranganathaswamy Temple (₹5). To see them all, get off in that order (ask the conductor or driver where the stops are), as it runs in a one-way circuit.

SOUTHERN TAMIL NADU

Trichy to Rameswaram

In Pudukkottai district, between Trichy and Rameswaram, is Tamil Nadu's best example of temples, cave art, the homeland of the region's greatest traders and bankers, and has a few other stops that make a good road trip (or day tour from Trichy, Madurai or Rameswaram).

PUDUKKOTTAI & AROUND

Some 34km south of Trichy is the nondescript town of Pudukkottai, which has historical importance in inverse proportion to its current obscurity; from 1680 to 1947 this was one of the great princely states of South India.

Pudukkottai Museum MUSEUM
(Indian/foreigner ₹5/100; ⊘9.30am-5pm) The relics of bygone days are on display in this wonderful museum, located in a renovated palace building in Pudukkottai town. Its eclectic collection includes musical instruments, megalithic burial artefacts, and some remarkable paintings and miniatures.

Vijayalaya Cholisvaram HINDU TEMPLE
(Natharmalai; admission free) About 16km north of Pudukkottai, above the village of Natharmalai, is this small but stunning 10th-century rock-cut temple, remniscent of the famous carvings at Mamallapuram but almost always deserted. Villagers will point you to the site, which takes a quick walk up a rocky hill with views of the green and serene countryside around. If the caretaker's around he'll give you an enthusiastic tour and open up the temple to show scraps of ancient frescoes, and may direct you to other temples being restored in the area. Further up the road is **Sittannavasal** (admission ₹100), where you'll find a small Jain cave temple that conceals more frescoes and statues of Jain saints sitting in cross-legged repose.

Tirumayam Fort FORT
(Indian/foreigner ₹5/100; ⊘9am-5pm) Simple and imposing, the renovated Tirumayam Fort, located about 17km south of Pudukkottai, is worth a climb for the 360-degree views from the battlements onto the surrounding countryside. Or you can take a shady rest with local goats under a banyan tree.

KARAIKKUDI & AROUND

In the backstreets of small **Kanadukathan** are the wedding-cake houses of the Chettiars, an interrelated clan of bankers, merchants and traders. The mansions of the community are decked out in the cosmopolitan goods bought home by Chettiars during their extensive trading forays: Belgian chandeliers, Italian granite, Burmese teak and artwork from around the world.

To get a feel for the royal life, book a night in one of the following heritage houses; they're pricey but they provide a fantastic experience. All have kitchens producing authentic Chettinad cuisine, which is not as chilli-laden as traditional South Indian food (and less likely to be vegetarian); Visalam has an 'interactive kitchen' and Bangala offers cooking courses for groups.

TOP CHOICE Visalam BOUTIQUE HOTEL $$$
(☑4564-273301; www.cghearth.com; Local Fund Rd, Kanadukathan; r from ₹10,700; ❋@☀) Stunningly restored and professionally run by a Malayali hotel chain, it's no longer in the hands of the original family but it's still decorated with their old photos, furniture and paintings, and staff can tell you the sad story of the young woman the house was built for. The garden is lovely and the pool setting is magical, with a low-key cafe alongside it.

Bangala BOUTIQUE HOTEL $$$
(☑4565-220221; www.thebangala.com; Devakottai Rd, Karaikkudi; d ₹4500-5400; ❋@☀) This lovingly restored whitewashed home ('bungalow') is quirkily decorated with locally sourced antique furniture, fascinating old photos of the owner's family, film posters and traditional crafts. Famous for its Chettinad food (₹500 for the set meal, and worth every paisa), it has a beautiful outdoor/indoor dining area. Rooms are spacious, comfy and individually styled; the 'honeymoon room' has a private veranda and an enclosed, carved wooden bed with a mirror in the roof!

Chettinadu Mansion BOUTIQUE HOTEL $$$
(☑4564-273080; www.chettinadumansion.com; Kanadukathan; s/d ₹4700/6400; ❋@☀) Slightly shabbier than some of the Chettiar joints, and much more colourfully decorated, this house is still owned by the original family. Service is top-notch, and all rooms have private balconies looking over other mansions in the village.

❶ Getting There & Away

This region is an easy day tour from Trichy (taxi ₹1600) or Madurai (a little more). Otherwise catch one of the many daily buses from Trichy to Karaikkudi (₹56, three hours) and get on and off at the sights along the way. Coming from Madurai, get a bus to Karaikkudi and take a local bus or hire a taxi. Kanadukathan is about a 500m walk off the main road. Regular buses run between Karaikkudi, via Ramanathapuram, to Rameswaram.

Rameswaram

☑04573 / POP 37,968
Rameswaram was once the southernmost point of sacred India; to leave her boundaries was to abandon caste and fall below the status of the lowliest skinner of sacred cows. Then Rama, incarnation of Vishnu and hero of the Ramayana, led an army of monkeys and bears to the ocean and crossed into the kingdom of (Sri) Lanka, where he defeated the demon Ravana and rescued his wife, Sita. Afterwards, prince and princess came to this spot to offer thanks to Shiva.

If all this seems like so much folklore, it's absolute truth for millions of Hindus, who flock to the Ramanathaswamy Temple to worship where a god worshipped a god.

Apart from these pilgrims, Rameswaram is a sleepy fishing village. It's also an island, connected to the mainland by the Indira Gandhi bridge, and used to serve as a ferry link to Sri Lanka.

Most hotels and restaurants are clustered around the Ramanathaswamy Temple. The bus stand, 2km to the west, is connected by shuttle bus to the town centre.

◎ Sights

Ramanathaswamy Temple HINDU TEMPLE
(camera ₹25; ⊙4am-1pm & 3-8.30pm) When Rama decided to worship Shiva, he figured he'd need a lingam to do the thing properly. Being a god, he sent a flying monkey to find the biggest lingam around – in this case, a Himalayan mountain. But the monkey took too long, so Rama's wife Sita made a simple lingam of sand, which Shiva approved of, and which is enshrined today in the centre of this temple. Besides housing the world's holiest sand mound, the structure is notable for its horizon-stretching thousand-pillar halls and 22 *theerthams* (tanks), which pilgrims are expected to bathe in and drink from. Only Hindus may enter the inner sanctum.

Even when the temple is closed, it is possible to take a peaceful amble through the extensive corridors. In the evening, before the temple is closed, you may see temple Brahmins take some of the residing deities on a parade through the halls of Ramanathaswamy.

Gandamadana Parvatham HINDU TEMPLE
This temple, located 3km northwest of Rameswaram, is a shrine reputedly containing Rama's footprints. The two-storey *mandapam* is on a small hill – the highest point on the island – and has good views out over the coastal landscape. Pilgrims visit at dawn and dusk.

Dhanushkodi & Adam's Bridge
Kanyakumari may technically be India's land's end, but **Dhanushkodi** plays the part better. About 18km southwest of town, this is a long, low sweep of sand, dust devils, fish-

ing hamlets, donkeys and green waves. It's tempting to swim here, but be careful of strong rips. You can ride a passenger truck for a few rupees, or walk 2½ hours (one way!) to the edge: **Adam's Bridge**, the chain of reefs, sandbanks and islets that almost connects India with Sri Lanka, 33km away, was supposedly built by Rama and his monkey army. Buses (₹5, hourly) from the local bus stand on East Car St stop about 4km before the beach so you have to walk the rest of the way, and an autorickshaw costs ₹300 return.

About 10km before Dhanushkodi, the **Kothandaraswamy Temple** was the only structure to survive a cyclone that destroyed the village in 1964. Legend has it Rama, overcome with guilt at having killed Ravana, performed a *puja* on this spot and thereafter the temple was built.

★☆ Festivals & Events

During the **car festival** (February/March), a huge decorated chariot with idols of the deities installed is hauled through the streets in a pulsating parade. **Thiru Kalyana** (July/August) is a festival celebrating the celestial marriage of Shiva and Parvati.

🛏 Sleeping & Eating

Budget travellers should drop in at the **rooms booking office** (East Car St; ⊘24hr), opposite the main temple entrance, which can score doubles for as low as ₹300 a night. Many hotels here are geared towards pilgrims, which means staff can be conservative, often refusing to take in single travellers; this is the case for most of the cheapies (and at the rooms booking office). The cheapest rooms tend to be dire, but there's a string of reasonable midrange hotels. Book ahead before festivals.

Hotel Royal Park   HOTEL $$
(⊘221680; Ramnad Hwy; s/d ₹ 1250/1650; ❄) It sounds like a contrdiction in terms, but this place on the main road near the bus stand is actually the most peaceful hotel in town. A couple of kilometres from the main temple action, it bills itself as a 'budget luxury hotel'; rooms are standard midrange with some nice artwork, and the attached AC veg restaurant is good value (mainly South Indian, but the cheese and tomato toastie is perfect too).

Hotel Sunrise View   HOTEL $$
(⊘223434; East Car St; d ₹1300; ❄) The best of the newish midrange places near the temple, this has sparkling tiles and wooden furniture that's a tad better quality than at

other spots. Some rooms have good sea views; just try to look out at the ocean rather than down at the rubbish on the ground.

Hotel Sri Saravana   HOTEL $
(⊘223367; htl_saravana@yahoo.com; South Car St; r from ₹770; ❄) This is a friendly, clean hotel with good service and spacious rooms, and it's not averse to single travellers. Rooms towards the top have sea views (and increased rates).

Hotel Shanmuga Paradise   HOTEL $
(⊘222984; www.shanmugaparadise.com; Middle St; d from ₹500, with AC from ₹800; ❄) This is another reasonable midrange place, just removed from the eastern temple entrance. Rooms are a fraction more tired than at some of the newer spots.

Lodge Santhya   HOTEL $
(⊘221329) This grotty spot offers singles for as low as ₹190. You get what you pay for, but, if you must, pinch that penny. Next-door **Santhana Lodge** is similar; neither place will take singles.

Guru Lodge   HOTEL $
(⊘221531; East Car St; d ₹475) Right by the main temple entrance, this place isn't great value for money (it's not a lot cleaner than the real cheapies) but it's the cheapest place we found that would accept single travellers.

A number of inexpensive vegetarian restaurants such as **Ashok Bhavan** (West Car St) and **Vasantha Bhavan** (East Car St) serve thalis for around ₹40. As you might guess there's a focus on South Indian food here, but **Ram Nivas** (West Car St; mains ₹20-50) does a nice line in North Indian veg, such as paneer and dhal fry. You can find fish in a few restaurants, but we didn't find anything else carnivore friendly.

ℹ Information

You can't change money here but the **State Bank of India** (East Car St) has an ATM accepting international cards.

Siva Net (Middle St; per hr ₹40; ⊘8am-9pm) Internet.

Tourist Office (⊘221371; bus stand; ⊘10am-6pm Mon-Fri) Friendly but not terribly helpful.

ℹ Getting There & Away

Bus
Buses run to Madurai every 10 minutes (₹50, four hours). There are SETC buses to Chennai (₹248, 12 hours, daily), Kanyakumari (₹125,

10 hours, two daily) and Trichy every half-hour (₹90, seven hours). There are also private buses and minibuses from the town centre to Chennai and Madurai.

Train

The overnight *Sethu Express* leaves for Chennai daily at 8pm (sleeper/3AC ₹246/665, 12 hours).

❶ Getting Around

Town buses 1 and 2 (₹2) travel between the temple and the bus stand from early morning until late at night. Cycling is a good way to get around, with many stalls renting old rattlers for ₹5 per hour.

Madurai

📞 0452 / POP 1.2 MILLION

Chennai may be the heart of Tamil Nadu, but Madurai claims her soul. Madurai is Tamil borne and Tamil rooted, one of the oldest cities in India, a metropolis that traded with ancient Rome and outlasted her destruction.

Tourists, Indian and foreign, usually come here to see the temple of Sri Meenakshi Amman, a labyrinthine structure that ranks among the greatest temples of India. Otherwise, Madurai, perhaps appropriately given her age, captures many of India's most glaring dichotomies: a city centre dominated by a medieval temple, an economy increasingly driven by IT, all overlaid with the energy and excitement of a typically Indian city slotted into a much more manageable package than Chennai's sprawl.

History

Tamil and Greek documents record the existence of Madurai from the 4th century BC. It was popular for trade, especially in spices, and was also the home of the *sangam,* the academy of Tamil poets. Over the centuries Madurai has come under the jurisdiction of the Cholas, the Pandyas, Muslim rulers, the Hindu Vijayanagar kings, and the Nayaks, who ruled until 1781. During the reign of Tirumalai Nayak (1623–55), the bulk of the Sri Meenakshi Temple was built, and Madurai became the cultural centre of the Tamil people, playing an important role in the development of the Tamil language.

Madurai then passed into the hands of the British East India Company. In 1840 the company razed the fort, which had previously surrounded the city, and filled in the moat. Four broad streets – the Veli streets – were constructed on top of this fill and to this day define the limits of the old city.

✦ Sights

Sri Meenakshi Temple   HINDU TEMPLE

(camera ₹30; ⊙4am-12.30pm & 4-9.30pm) The Sri Meenakshi Temple, abode of the triple-breasted, fish-eyed goddess Meenakshi Amman ('fish-eyed' is an adjective for perfect eyes in classical Tamil poetry), is considered by many to be the height of South Indian temple architecture, as vital to the aesthetic heritage of this region as the Taj Mahal is to North India. It's not so much a temple as a 6-hectare complex enclosed by 12 *gopurams,* the highest of which towers 52m over Madurai, and all of which are carved with a staggering array of gods, goddesses, demons and heroes.

According to legend, the beautiful Meenakshi was born with three breasts and this prophecy: her superfluous breast would melt away when she met her husband. The event came to pass when she met Shiva and took her place as his consort. The temple of the cosmic couple was designed in 1560 by Vishwanatha Nayak and built during the reign of Tirumalai Nayak, but its history goes back 2000 years to the time when Madurai was a Pandyan capital.

Much of the temple is off-limits to non-Hindus, but lay people can enter at the eastern *gopuram.* From here you can see the outer rings of the concentric corridors that enclose the sanctums of Meenakshi and Shiva, worshipped here as Sundareswarar, the beautiful lord. Be on the lookout for statues of deities encrusted in small balls of butter, thrown at the gods as offerings from their devout worshippers.

Also within the temple complex, housed in the 1000-Pillared Hall, is the **Temple Art Museum** (adult/child/foreigner ₹ 5/2/50, camera/video ₹50/250; ⊙7am-7.30pm). It contains painted friezes and stone and brass images and good exhibits on Hindu deities.

Allow plenty of time to see this temple and be warned: dress codes have been tightened, and no legs should be exposed for either gender, or shoulders (for women). If you're deemed to be immodestly dressed an enterprising young man from the shop across the road will sell you a dhoti. Early mornings or late evenings are the best times to avoid crowds, and there's often classical dance somewhere in the complex at the weekends. 'Temple guides' charge negotiable fees, rarely below ₹200, so prepare to negotiate and be aware that they are often fronts for emporiums and tailor shops.

Gandhi Memorial Museum
MUSEUM

(admission free, camera ₹50; ⊙10am-1pm & 2-5.30pm) Housed in an old *tamukkam* (old exhibition pavilion), this excellent museum is set in spacious and relaxing grounds. The maze of rooms contains an impressively moving and detailed account of India's struggle for independence from 1757 to 1947, and the English-language signs pull no punches about British rule. Included in the exhibition is the blood-stained dhoti (long loincloth) that Gandhi was wearing at the time he was assassinated in Delhi in 1948; it's here because he first took up wearing the dhoti as a sign of native pride in Madurai in 1921. The **Gandhian Literary Society Bookstore** (⊙Mon-Sat) is behind the museum. The **Madurai Government Museum** (Indian/foreigner ₹ 5/100, camera ₹20; ⊙9.30am-5pm Sun-Thu) is next door in the same grounds. Inside is a small collection of archaeological finds, sculpture, bronzes, costumes and paintings.

Tirumalai Nayak Palace
HISTORICAL BUILDING

(Indian/foreigner ₹10/50, camera/video ₹30/100; ⊙9am-1pm & 2-5pm) What the Meenakshi Temple is to Nayak religious architecture, the Tirumalai palace is to the secular, although it's just a shell that's in a state of rot today. The main event is the entrance gate, main hall and Natakasala (Dance Hall), with their faded yellow plasterwork, lion and *makara* (crocodile-elephant creature) sculptures and a series of murals that hints at the opulence the Nayak rulers once enjoyed. The rectangular courtyard is known as Swargavilasa (Celestial Pavilion).

Mariamman Teppakkulam Tank
HISTORICAL BUILDING

This vast tank, 5km east of the old city, covers an area almost equal to that of Sri Meenakshi Temple and is the site of the incredible Teppam (Float) Festival. The tank is empty for most of the year and primarily serves as a cricket ground for local kids. It was built by Tirumalai Nayak in 1646 and is connected to the Vaigai River by underground channels.

★ Festivals & Events

Teppam (Float) Festival
TEMPLE FESTIVAL

(Jan/Feb) A popular event held on the full moon of the Tamil month of Thai, when Meenakshi temple deities are taken on a tour of the town and floated on the huge Mariamman Teppakkulam Tank. The evening culminates in Shiva's seduction of his wife, whereupon the icons are brought back to the temple to make love and, in so doing, regenerate the universe (Meenakshi's diamond nose stud is even removed so it doesn't irritate her lover).

Chithrai Festival
TEMPLE FESTIVAL

(Apr/May) The main event on Madurai's busy festival calendar is this 14-day event that celebrates the marriage of Meenakshi to Sundareswarar (Shiva). The deities are wheeled around the Sri Meenakshi Temple in massive chariots that form part of long, colourful processions.

🛏 Sleeping

Most of Madurai's accommodation is concentrated in the area between the train station and Sri Meenakshi Temple.

Town Hall Rd, running eastwards from the train station, has a knot of budget hotels, but Madurai's best-value accommodation is the string of almost identical midrange hotels along West Perumal Maistry St, near the train station. Rooms without AC are generally good value and it's worth taking the step up from budget joints. Most have rooftop restaurants with temple and sunset views.

Madurai Residency
HOTEL $$

(☎2343140; www.madurairesidency.com; 15 West Marret St; s/d incl breakfast from ₹800/1000; ❄@) The service is stellar and the rooms are comfy and fresh at this winner, which has the highest rooftop restaurant in town. There's 24-hour internet in the lobby.

Hotel Keerthi
HOTEL $$

(☎4377788; www.hellomadurai.in/hotelkeerthi; 40 West Perumal Maistry St; r from ₹990; ❄) Don't be fooled by the nondescript lobby. This spotless, shiny hotel has rooms that are small but surprisingly stylish and modern, with groovy bedspreads, funky wall mirrors, picture walls and flatscreen TV.

Royal Court Madurai
HOTEL $$$

(☎4356666; www.royalcourtindia.com; 4 West Veli St; s/d from ₹2800/3100; ❄@☎) The Royal Court manages to blend a bit of white-sheeted, hardwood-floored colonial elegance with modern amenities, such as wi-fi in all rooms, that makes it an excellent, centrally located top-end choice for someone who needs a bit of spoiling.

Hotel Park Plaza
HOTEL $$

(☎3011111; www.hotelparkplaza.net; 114 West Perumal Maistry St; s/d incl breakfast ₹1900/2300; ❄)

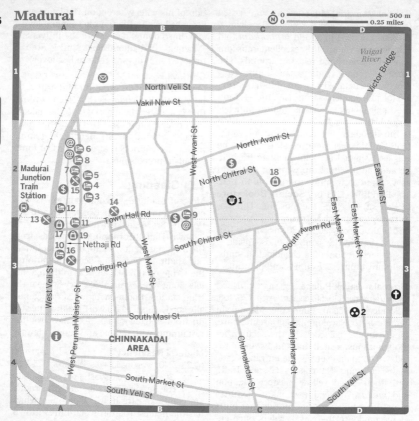

The Plaza's rooms are standard midrange: comfortable and simply furnished, with modern TVs. The front rooms have temple views from the 3rd floor up. There's a good multicuisine rooftop restaurant and the (inappropriately named) **Sky High Bar** – on the 1st floor. Perks include free breakfast and free pick-up from the airport or train station.

Hotel Supreme HOTEL **$$**
(☑2343151; www.hotelsupreme.in; 110 West Perumal Maistry St; d ₹720, s/d with AC from ₹1320/1500; ❄) This is another large, well-presented hotel that is very popular with domestic tourists. Don't miss the chance to walk into **Apollo**, a bar built to look like a spaceship, and wonder if someone laced your lassi last night. There's good food at the on-site **Surya Restaurant**.

Hotel Rathna Residency HOTEL **$$**
(☑4374444; www.hotelrathnaresidency.com; 109 West Perumal Maistry St; s/d incl breakfast from

₹1150/1200; ❄) There's not a lot to distinguish this bland, clean, vaguely corporate midrange spot from its neighbours, other than it has nicer pictures on its walls (Mughal-style miniatures) and doesn't offer any non-AC rooms.

Hotel West Tower HOTEL **$**
(☑2346908; West Tower St; s/d from ₹450/650; ❄) Somewhere between budget and midrange, this place is all about the location (right near the temple) but it's also acceptably clean and friendly.

Hotel Grand Central HOTEL **$**
(☑2343940; 82 West Perumal Maistry St; d from ₹350; ❄) Grand it ain't, but the cheap rooms aren't bad for the price, with clean sheets, cleanish bathrooms, tile floors and TVs.

New College House HOTEL **$**
(☑4372900; collegehouse_mdu@yahoo.co.in; 2 Town Hall Rd; r from ₹275; ❄) FYI: it's spelled 'Neww College House', in huge letters, in

Madurai

case you get confused. There's some 250 rooms scattered over this concrete complex. Some are fine, some not so much, and street noise often permeates, so try and get something away from the bustle.

Hotel International   HOTEL **$**
(☏4377463; 46 West Perumal Maistry St; s/d from ₹280/380) Shabby walls and dank bathrooms; but clean sheets, TVs and wee balconies.

 Eating

Along West Perumal Maistry St the rooftop restaurants of a string of hotels offer breezy night-time dining and temple views (don't forget the mosquito repellent); most also have AC restaurants open for breakfast and lunch. Street stalls selling sweets, dosas, *idli* and the like are ubiquitous, especially near the train station. **Shoppers Shop** (Town Hall Rd; ⊙8am-11pm) is a well-stocked grocery store that has a good selection of Western foods.

British Bakery   CAFE **$**
(West Velli St; mains ₹30-75; ⊙lunch & dinner) A clean, popular snack joint with shakes, ice cream, iced tea and other refreshing drinks, along with fries, sandwiches, fried rice and Indian snacks.

Surya Restaurant   MULTICUISINE **$**
(110 West Perumal Maistry St; mains ₹45-115; ⊙dinner) The rooftop restaurant of Hotel Supreme offers a superb view over the city, stand-out service and a nice pure veg menu, but the winner here has got to be the cold coffee, which might as well have been brewed by God when you sip it on a dusty, hot (ie every) day.

Jayaram Fast Foods   MULTICUISINE **$**
(5-8 Nethaji Rd; mains ₹45-90; ⊙lunch & dinner) There's a busy (and yummy) bakery downstairs, and a crisp and clean restaurant up top that does a nice line in Indian fare, plus burgers and pizzas. While the latter dishes aren't winning any awards, this is as good a piece of pie as you'll find in Madurai. It's a small spot that gets very busy.

Dhivyar Mahal Restaurant   MULTICUISINE **$**
(☏2342700; 21 Town Hall Rd; mains ₹30-110; ⊙lunch & dinner) One of the better multicuisine restaurants not attached to a hotel, Dhivyar Mahal is clean, bright and friendly. The curries go down a treat, and where else are you going to find roast leg of lamb in Madurai?

Emperor Restaurant   MULTICUISINE **$**
(☏2350490; Hotel Chentoor, 106 West Perumal Maistry St; mains ₹35-90; ⊙breakfast, lunch & dinner) It's all veg all the time at Hotel Chentoor's rooftop restaurant, but that karmic goodness is a bit undone by the fact this spot basically becomes a very popular bar come nightfall.

🛍 **Shopping**

Madurai teems with cloth stalls and tailors' shops, which you may notice upon being approached for the umpteenth time by a tailor tout. A great place for getting cottons and printed fabrics is **Puthu Mandapam**, the pillared former entrance hall at the eastern side of Sri Meenakshi Temple. Here you'll find rows of tailors, all busily treadling away and capable of whipping up a good replica of whatever you're wearing in an hour or two. Quality, designs and prices vary greatly depending on the material and complexity of the design, but you can have a shirt made up for as little as ₹200. Every driver, temple guide and tailor's brother will lead you to the Kashmiri craft shops in North Chitrai St, offering to show you the temple view from the rooftop – the views are good, and so is the inevitable sales pitch. For fixed-price crafts try **Poompuhar** (West Velli St; ☺10am-1pm & 3-8pm Mon-Sat).

There's a couple of good English-language bookshops in town: try **Malligai Book Centre** (11 West Veli St; ☺9am-2pm & 4.30-9pm Mon-Sat) and **Turning Point Books** (75 Venkatesh Towers, Town Hall Rd; ☺10am-9pm); the latter is a 1st-floor shop opposite New College with a good selection of titles on Indian religion.

Information

Internet access
You can't walk without tripping over an internet cafe. There are several 24-hour Sify iWays, including a couple adjoining hotels in West Perumal Maistry St.
Web Tower Internet (West Tower Rd; per hr ₹20; ☺10.30am-10pm) Downstairs from Hotel West Tower.

Money
ATMs are plentiful.
ICICI Bank ATM (North Chitrai St)
State Bank of India (West Veli St) Has foreign-exchange desks and an ATM; almost next door to Royal Court.
VKC Forex (Zulaiha Towers, Town Hall Rd; ☺9am-6pm) An efficient place to change travellers cheques and cash.

Tourist Information
Madurai tourist office (☎2334757; 180 West Veli St; ☺10am-5.45pm Mon-Fri) Not a lot of help, but staff will give you a brochure and map if you ask.

Getting There & Away

Air
Indian Airlines (☎2341234, airport 2690771; West Veli St; ☺10am-5pm Mon-Sat) flies daily to Mumbai and Chennai, as does SpiceJet, which also flies to Delhi. Jet Airways flies daily to Chennai, and Kingfisher Airlines flies daily to Chennai and Bengaluru. None of these last three airlines has an office in town, but airport counters open at flight times.

Bus
Most long-distance buses arrive and depart from the **Central bus station** (☎2580680; Melur Rd; ☺24hr), 6km northeast of the old city. It appears chaotic but is actually a well-organised 24-hour operation. Local buses shuttle into the city every few minutes for ₹3. An autorickshaw to the train station (where most of the hotels are located) is about ₹100. The boxed text on p368 lists prices for government buses; some express services run to Bengaluru, Chennai, Mysore and Puducherry.

The Arapalayam bus stand, northwest of the train station on the river bank, has regular services to Coimbatore (₹76, six hours), two daily to Kodaikanal (₹48, four to five hours) and to Palani every half-hour (₹38, five hours).

Train
Madurai Junction train station is on the main Chennai–Kanyakumari line. There are at least nine daily trains to Chennai, and three daily services to Kanyakumari.

Some other services include Madurai to Coimbatore (2nd class/sleeper ₹74/155, seven hours) and Bengaluru (sleeper/3AC ₹209/555, 11 hours), as well as Trivandrum and Mumbai.

BUSES FROM MADURAI

DESTINATION	FARE (₹)	DURATION (HR)	FREQUENCY
Bengaluru	190	12	7 daily
Chennai	160-190	10	every 30min
Chidambaram	95	8	daily
Coimbatore	90	7	daily
Kochi	145	8	daily
Kanyakumari	94	6	hourly
Mysore	280	16	daily (via Ooty)
Puducherry	110	8	2 daily
Rameswaram	58	4	every 30min
Trichy	42	3	every 15min

Getting Around

The airport is 12km south of town and taxis cost ₹250 to the town centre. Autorickshaws ask around ₹130. Alternatively, bus 10A from the Central bus station goes to the airport, but don't rely on it being on schedule.

Central Madurai is small enough to get around on foot.

Kanyakumari (Cape Comorin)

☏04652 / POP 19,739

The end of India has more appeal than just being the end of the road. There's a whiff of accomplishment (along with dried fish) upon making it to the tip of the country, the terminus of a narrowing funnel of rounded granite mountains – some of India's oldest – green fields plaided with silver-glinting rice paddies and slow-looping turbines on wind farms. Like all edges, there's a sense of the surreal here. You can see three seas mingle, the sunset over the moonrise and the Temple of the Virgin Sea Goddess within minutes of each other. But beyond that, Kanyakumari is a genuinely friendly village that is a nice respite from the dust of the Indian road.

The main temple is right on the point of Kanyakumari and leading north from it is a small bazaar lined with restaurants, stalls and souvenir shops.

◉ Sights & Activities

Kumari Amman Temple   HINDU TEMPLE
(☺4.30am-12.30pm & 4-8pm) The legends say the *kanya* (virgin) goddess Kumari, a manifestation of the Great Goddess Devi, single-handedly conquered demons and secured freedom for the world. At this temple pilgrims give her thanks in an intimately spaced, beautifully decorated temple, where the nearby crash of waves from three oceans can be heard through the twilight glow of oil fires clutched in vulva-shaped votive candles (a reference to the sacred femininity of the goddess). Men must remove their shirts to enter and cameras are forbidden.

Gandhi Memorial   MONUMENT
(admission by donation; ☺7am-7pm) Poignantly and appropriately placed at the end of the nation Gandhi fathered is this memorial, which purposely resembles an Orissan temple embellished by Hindu, Christian and Muslim architects. The central plinth was used to store some of the Mahatma's ashes, and each year, on Gandhi's birthday (2 October), the sun's rays fall on the stone. Guides may ask for an excessive donation, but ₹10 is enough; try and keep an air of silence (even if locals don't).

Kamaraj Memorial   MONUMENT
(☺7am-7pm) Just next to the Gandhi memorial is this shrine to K Kamaraj, known as 'the Gandhi of the South'; Chennai's domestic airport is named after him. One of the most powerful politicians of post-independence India, Kamaraj held the chief ministership of both Madras State and latter-day Tamil Nadu. The shrine is just a collection of dusty blown-up photographs with almost no space given to context or explanation.

Vivekananda Exhibition   MUSEUM
(Main Rd; admission ₹2; ☺8am-noon & 4-8pm) This exhibition, which was closed for refurbishment at the time of research, details the life and extensive journey across India made by the philosopher Swami Vivekananda (the 'Wandering Monk', 1863–1902), who developed a synthesis between the tenets of Hinduism and concepts of social justice. Another exhibition can be found at **Vivekanandapuram** (☏247012; admission free; ☺9am-1pm & 5-9pm), an ashram 3km north of town that provides a snapshot of Indian philosophy, religion, leaders and thinkers.

Vivekananda Memorial   MONUMENT
(admission ₹10; ☺8am-5pm) Four hundred metres offshore is the rock where Swami Vivekananda meditated and chose to take his moral message beyond India's shores. A memorial was built in Vivekananda's memory in 1970, and reflects architectural styles drawn from all over India. It can be a loud place when packed with tourists, but the islet is big enough to provide moments of seclusion.

The huge **statue** on the smaller island, which looks like an Indian Colossus of Rhodes, is not of Vivekananda but Tamil poet Thiruvalluvar. India's 'Statue of Liberty' was the work of more than 5000 sculptors. It was erected in 2000 and honours the poet's 133-chapter work *Thirukural* – hence its height of exactly 133ft (40.5m).

Ferries shuttle between the port and the islands between 8am and 4pm; tickets are ₹20 return.

Seafront   BEACH
There's a crowded beach here and **ghats** that lead down to a lingam half submerged in a

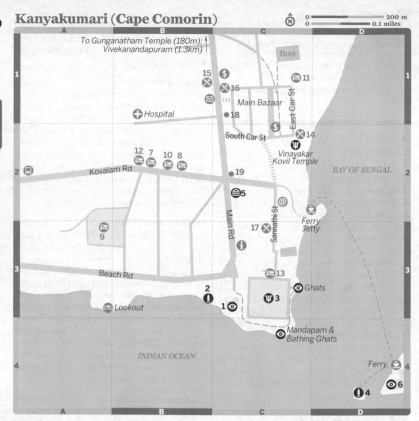

wave-driven tidal pool. Past the ice-cream and *chaat* (snack) sellers above the beach is a **memorial** to victims of the 2004 tsunami.

🛏 Sleeping

As befits a holiday destination, Kanyakumari's hoteliers have generally gone for bright colours and, dare we say, tackily cheerful decorations; after the bland sameness of midrange hotels around the state, it's quite exciting to find a large neon-coloured tiger painted on your bedhead. Some hotels, especially midrange places around the bazaar, have seasonal rates, so some prices double during April and May, and late October to January.

Manickhan Tourist Home HOTEL $
(☏246387; East Car St; d from ₹770; ❄) This very friendly hotel is professionally run and a real pleasure to doss in; the large rooms are all outfitted with clean bathrooms, TV and, if you're willing to shell out a bit, superb

sea views. Next-door **Hotel Maadhini** has almost identical rates and service, with the addition of a garden restaurant that's very pleasant in the evening.

Santhi Residency HOTEL $
(☏247091; Kovalam Rd; d from ₹700; ❄) A smaller, older restored house with a more restrained sense of style than the hotels (the only decoration in each simple room is a picture of Jesus), this place is quiet and very clean with a nice patch of leafy garden.

Hotel Tri Sea HOTEL $$
(☏246586; triseahotel@yahoo.com; Kovalam Rd; r from ₹1600; ❄❄) As you walk west of the town you can't miss the high-rise Tri Sea, which offers huge, spotless, airy rooms, most with balconies facing the ocean. The colour schemes are hectic, to say the least, but there are big flatscreen TVs, a great rooftop pool and viewing platforms that make a perfect spot for sunrise and sunset.

Kanyakumari (Cape Comorin)

TAMIL NADU & CHENNAI KANYAKUMARI (CAPE COMORIN)

Hotel Narmadha HOTEL $
(✆246365; Kovalam Rd; r ₹250-400) This big concrete block conceals some friendly staff and a range of cheap rooms, some of which are better than others; the good-value ₹400 doubles with sea views had crisp white sheets when we visited, while the cheaper rooms didn't look so hot. It's popular with pilgrims and is set to the west of the main bazaar, next to Hotel Tri Sea.

Hotel Tamil Nadu HOTEL $
(✆246257; www.ttdconline.com; Beach Rd; r from ₹800; ✶) Despite the usual quirks of a government-run hotel (and – surprise – it's overpriced), this is a great location if you want to get away from the (slight) bustle of town; balcony rooms have ocean, though not temple, views.

Saravana Lodge HOTEL $
(✆246007; Sannathi St; r ₹200-600) It's basic, but you can get a reasonable deal at this place just outside the temple entrance. All rooms have private bathrooms with squat toilets. A whole new block of rooms with a rooftop viewing platform should be complete by the time you read this.

Hotel Sun World HOTEL $$
(✆247755; hotelsunworld@sancharnet.in; Kovalam Rd; d from ₹1500; ✶) Everything's very bright and glossy at this higher-end spot, where most rooms have a private balcony with fab three-ocean views.

✖ Eating

There are plenty of fruit stalls and basic veg restaurants in the bazaar area, open for breakfast, lunch and dinner. Hotel Saravana has two clean, busy veg restaurants with thalis (₹30).

Sangam Restaurant MULTICUISINE $$
(Main Rd; mains ₹55-190) It's as if the Sangam started in Kashmir, trekked across the entirety of India, and stopped here to open a restaurant that features top culinary picks culled from every province encountered along the way. The food is good and the joint is bustling. The biggest downer is a height-and-weight machine by the front door that calculates your BMI and lets you know if eating here has made you obese.

Sri Krishna CAFE $
(Sannathi St; mains ₹30-90) If you need fresh juice, good ice cream or Indian takes on pizza, chips and burgers, try this clean and busy corner cafe.

Hotel Seaview MULTICUISINE $$
(East Car St; mains ₹60-200) This hotel has an excellent AC multicuisine restaurant specialising in fresh local seafood and posh takes on North and South Indian faves. The vibe is upmarket and waiters are very attentive.

Hotel Triveni SOUTH INDIAN $
(Main Rd; mains ₹20-50) The fans might blow you clear into the ocean, but this place also has clean tables, efficient service and good-value, mainly South Indian veg dishes. A good spot for breakfast.

ℹ Information

Janaki Forex (🕘9.30am-6.30pm Mon-Sat) Off South Car St. Change cash and travellers cheques here.

Tamil Mercantile Bank ATM (Main Rd)

Tony's Internet (Sannathi St; per hr ₹50; 🕘10am-8pm) Friendly – possibly over-friendly (but not unsafe) if you're a lone woman.

Tourist office (✆246276; Main Rd; 🕘8am-6pm Mon-Fri)

ℹ Getting There & Away

Bus

The surprisingly sedate bus stand is a 10-minute walk west of the centre along Kovalam Rd and there's a handy **SETC booking office** (◷7am-9pm) on Main Rd. Almost all buses go via Madurai; the exception is the Rameswaram service. Buses from here include:

Bengaluru ₹430, 15 hours, daily
Chennai ₹390, 16 hours, seven daily
Kodaikanal ₹225, 10 hours, daily
Madurai ₹94, six hours, eight daily
Ooty ₹330, 14 hours, two daily
Rameswaram ₹145, nine hours, two daily

Train

The train station is about 1km north of the bazaar and temple. There are three daily trains to Chennai, the fastest of which is the *Kanyakumari Express*, departing at 5.20pm (sleeper/3AC ₹305/801, 13 hours) and stopping at Madurai and Trichy.

There are two daily express trains to Trivandrum (2nd class/3AC ₹30/238, two hours).

For the real long-haulers or train buffs, the weekly *Himsagar Express* runs all the way to Jammu Tawi, a distance of 3715km, in 70 hours – the longest single train ride in India. It departs 2pm Friday (sleeper/3AC ₹629/1741).

THE WESTERN GHATS

Welcome to the lush mountains of the Western Ghats, some of the most welcome heat relief in India. Rising like an impassable bulwark of evergreen and deciduous tangle from the north of Mumbai to the tip of Tamil Nadu, the Ghats (with an average elevation of 915m) contain 27% of all India's flowering plants, 60% of its medicinal plants and an incredible array of endemic wildlife. It's not just the air and (relative) lack of pollution that's refreshing, either – there's a general acceptance of quirkiness and eccentricity in the hills that is hard to find in the lowlands. Think hippie cafes, handlebar-moustachioed trekking guides and tiger-stripe earmuffs for sale in the bazaar. On the downside is the state of local tribal groups whose identity is in danger of both over-exploitation and assimilation.

Kodaikanal (Kodai)

☑04542 / POP 32,969 / ELEV 2100M

Kodai is small, intimate, misty and mountainous; there are few more refreshing Tamil Nadu moments than boarding a bus in the heat-soaked plains and disembarking in the sharp pinch of a Kodaikanal night. It's not all cold though; during the day the weather is positively pleasant, more reminiscent of deep spring than early winter.

Located in the Palani knolls some 120km northwest of Madurai, Kodai clings to a mountainside draped in *sholas* (forests) of pine, gum trees and *kurinji* shrub, unique to the Western Ghats. The light, purple-blue-coloured blossoms flower every 12 years; next due date 2018. If you don't feel like waiting, the many treks by nearby dark rock faces and white waterfalls are still rewarding.

The renowned Kodaikanal International School provides a bit of cosmopolitan influence, with students from around the globe. Compared to Ooty, the town is relaxed (tourist brochures call it the 'Princess of Hills', while Ooty is the Queen), but it's still popular with Indian tourists (especially honeymooners). For a hill station, it's remarkably compact and the central town area can easily be explored on foot.

◉ Sights & Activities

**Sacred Heart Natural
History Museum**   MUSEUM
(Sacred Heart College, Law's Ghat Rd; admission ₹5; ◷9am-5pm) In the extensive old college grounds (now being marketed as an 'eco sanctuary') a couple of kilometres out of town, this museum has a hodge-podge collection of flora and fauna put together over more than 100 years by Jesuit priests; the amateur (and therefore rather charming) nature of the collection is displayed through dodgy taxidermy, hand drawings, odd commentary, and old black-and-white photos of solemn-looking priests with huge snakes draped over them. There are some pleasant walks around the grounds.

Walking & Trekking

Assuming it's not cloaked in opaque mist, the valley views along paved **Coaker's Walk** (admission ₹3, camera ₹5; ◷7am-7pm) are superb. There's a small **observatory** (admission ₹3) with a telescope at the southern end. You can start near Greenlands Youth Hostel or Villa Retreat – where **stained glass** in the nearby Church of South India (CSI) is stunning in the morning light – and the stroll takes all of five minutes. The 5km **lake circuit** is pleasant in the early morning when you can count the kingfishers before the tourist traffic starts.

The views from **Pillar Rocks**, a 7km hike (one way, beginning near Bryant Park), are excellent (again, assuming fine weather), and there are some wonderful hiking trails through pockets of forest, including **Bombay Shola** and **Pambar Shola**, that meander around Lower Shola Rd and St Mary's Rd. You'll need a guide; talk to the staff at Greenlands Youth Hostel; other hotels might also be able to help. Guides of varying quality will approach you in the street.

Parks & Waterfalls

Near the start of Coaker's Walk is **Bryant Park** (adult/child ₹20/10, camera/video ₹30/75; ⊙9am-6.30pm), landscaped and stocked by the British officer after whom it's named. **Chettiar Park** (admission free; ⊙8.30am-5pm), about 1.5km uphill from town on the way to the Kurinji Andavar Temple, is small, pretty and landscaped. Both get crowded with school groups and canoodling couples. Nearby waterfalls include **Silver Cascade**, on the road outside Kodai and often full of interstate tourists bathing on the rocks, and compact **Bear Shola Falls**, in a pocket of forest about a 20-minute walk from the town centre.

Boating & Horse Riding

If you're sappy in love like a bad Bollywood song, the thing to do in Kodai is rent a pedal boat (₹50 per half-hour), rowboat (₹120) or Kashmiri *shikara* (covered gondola, aka 'honeymoon boat'; ₹260 including boatman) from either the Kodaikanal Boat and Rowing Club or Tamil Nadu Tourist Development Corporation; screechy crooning to your significant other is strictly optional.

There's a few horse-riding stands on the lake. The rate is ₹300 per hour unaccompanied or ₹400 with a guide.

🛏 Sleeping

Hotel prices can jump by as much as 300% during the high season (from 1 April to 30 June). Prices listed here are low-season rates. There are some lovely heritage places, and a couple of good-value midrange options if you live without colonial ambience.

Most hotels in Kodai have a 9am or 10am checkout time in high season, but for the rest of the year it's usually 24 hours.

TOP CHOICE Carlton Hotel HOTEL **$$$**
(☏240056; www.krahejahospitality.com; Lake Rd; s/d/cottages from ₹6245/7130/10,695) The cream of Kodai's hotels is a magnificent five-star colonial mansion that overlooks the lake and the international school. Rooms are bright, spacious and some have private balconies with lake views. The lobby and grounds very much succeed at re-creating hill station ambience, with stone walls, dark-wood flooring and roaring fireplaces that make you want to demand a scotch now, dammit, from the eager staff. There's a pricey and rather wonderful buffet lunch and dinner available.

Villa Retreat HOTEL **$$**
(☏240940; www.villaretreat.com; Club Rd; r ₹1350-2813, ste ₹3375) The terrace garden of this lovely old stone-built family hotel at the northern end of Coaker's Walk offers awesome valley views. Most rooms have fireplaces and TV; new rooms should be ready by the time you read this. Prices include taxes.

Hotel Cokkers Tower HOTEL **$**
(☏240374; cokkers.tower@yahoo.com; Woodville Rd; dm/d ₹125/750) Just near the Church of South India, this is a clean, straightforward hotel with simple, light-coloured rooms (no colonial wood here). The dorm beds are narrow and reminiscent of train bunks, but the shared bathroom is sparkling and you can't top the price.

Hilltop Towers HOTEL **$$**
(☏240413; www.hilltopgroup.in; Club Rd; d from ₹1200) Although it comes off as boxy and corporate, rustic accents like polished teak floors and wooden embellishments, plus friendly staff and excellent upper-floor views, make the Hilltop a good midrange choice.

Hotel Astoria HOTEL **$**
(☏240524; www.astoriaveg.com; Anna Salai; r from ₹700) You wouldn't expect it from the outside, which is mainly all about the popular restaurant (and we'll admit the curry smell occasionally wafts through the lower corridors), but this central hotel has clean, wood-floored, very pleasant rooms with colonial-style furniture. Prices are reasonable.

Greenlands Youth Hostel HOSTEL **$**
(☏240899; www.greenlandskodaikanal.com; Coaker's Walk; dm ₹200, d ₹500-1800) We're a bit ambivalent about this popular, long-running spot; the grounds and views are excellent, guides can be organised here and it's a great spot to socialise with other budget travellers in the cosy, crowded dorms. But the rooms are overpriced (negotiating might lower

Kodaikanal (Kodai)

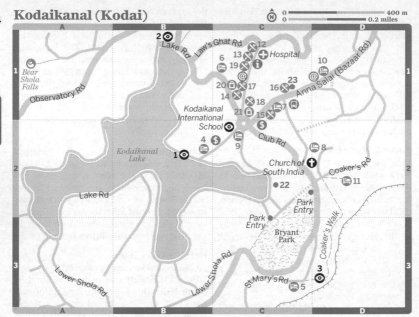

TAMIL NADU & CHENNAI THE WESTERN GHATS

them), management can be unhelpful and hot water appears less often than is claimed.

RR Residency HOTEL **$$**
(📞244301; rrresidency@rediffmail.com; Boat House Rd; r ₹1490; 📶) Tasteful artwork, comfy beds and slightly dank bathrooms for the price.

Snooze Inn HOTEL **$$**
(📞240873; snoozeinnslaes@jayarajgroup.com; Anna Salai; r from ₹600) The outside has a bit more character than the rooms, but this is another decent-value budget choice with clean bathrooms and plenty of blankets.

✗ Eating

PT Rd is the best place for cheap restaurants and it's here that most travellers and students from the international school congregate.

Hotel New Punjab NORTH INDIAN **$**
(PT Rd; mains ₹30-100; ☺lunch & dinner) For North Indian cuisine, including tandoori (and any nonveg curries in general), this is Kodai's favourite. It serves the best tandoori chicken in South India, according to locals.

Cloud Street MULTICUISINE **$$**
(PT Rd; mains ₹50-200; ☺lunch & dinner Tue-Sun, breakfast Sat & Sun) Why yes, that is a real Italian-style woodfire pizza oven. And yes, that's hummus, felafel and nachos on the menu,

alongside pasta and pizza – it's all great food in a simple, relaxed setting. (Also, ask the owners about their lovely homestay getaway 20km out of Kodai.)

Tava INDIAN **$**
(PT Rd; mains ₹40; ☺lunch & dinner Thu-Tue) A clean, fast and cheap veg option, this place has a wide menu; try the cauliflower-stuffed *gobi paratha* (spicy cauliflower bread) and *sev puri* (crisp, puffy fried bread with potato and chutney).

Royal Tibet TIBETAN **$**
(PT Rd; mains ₹40-80; ☺lunch & dinner) If you're missing Tibetan food, come here for the chewy but tasty *momos* (dumplings) and *thukpa* (noodle soup). A nearby competitor, **Tibetan Brothers**, offers almost the exact same menu; they're both good.

Red Apple MULTICUISINE **$**
(Anna Salai; mains ₹50-80; ☺lunch & dinner) A pure-veg multicuisine spot (well there's a few Chinese dishes, as well as North and South Indian) that's cheap, clean and cheerful. There's a posh thali for ₹60. It's just opposite the bus stand.

Pot Luck CAFE **$**
(PT Rd; snacks ₹20-50; ☺10.30am-7pm Wed-Mon) Sandwiches, pancakes, coffee and

Kodaikanal (Kodai)

quesadillas (!) served up on a pretty, tiny terrace attached to a pottery shop. There are delicious chutneys, lemon curd and biscuits to takeaway, too.

Hotel Astoria   INDIAN $

(Anna Salai; mains ₹30-50, thalis ₹35-60; ⊙breakfast, lunch & dinner) This veg restaurant is always packed with locals and tourists, especially come lunchtime when it serves excellent all-you-can-eat thalis.

Self-Catering

Excellent homemade chocolates and dried fruit are sold all over town.

Eco Nut   HEALTH FOOD $

(☑243296; PT Rd; ⊙10am-5pm Mon-Sat) This interesting shop sells a wide range of locally produced organic health food –

wholewheat bread, muffins, cheese, salad greens – and essential oils, herbs and herb remedies.

Pastry Corner   BAKERY $

(Anna Salai; ⊙9am-9pm) Pick up great picnic sandwiches and yummy brownies here, or squeeze onto the benches with a cuppa to watch the world go by.

Hilltop Bake   BAKERY $

(Club Rd; pastries ₹18-40; ⊙11am-9pm) A wide range of fresh savoury pastries, including good approximations of pizza, as well as cakes and brownies.

Shopping

The many handicraft stores stock good craftwork, and several also reflect a local low-key but long-term commitment to social justice. On PT Rd you'll find small Kashmiri shops and South Indian handicrafts stalls.

Cottage Crafts   HANDICRAFTS

(PT Rd; ⊙10am-730pm) Run by the voluntary organisation Coordinating Council for Social Concerns in Kodai (Corsock), here you'll find goods crafted by disadvantaged groups, with about 80% of the purchase price returned to the craftspeople.

Re Shop   HANDICRAFTS

(Seven Roads Junction; ⊙10am-7pm Mon-Sat) Stylish jewellery, bags, cards and more, at reasonable prices, made by and benefiting vllage women around Tamil Nadu. It's run by the **Blue Mango Trust** (www.bluemangoindia.com).

Information

Alpha Net (PT Rd; internet per hr ₹50; ⊙9am-10pm)

Apollo Communications (Anna Salai; internet per hr ₹40; ⊙9.30am-8pm)

Indian Bank (Anna Salai; ⊙10am-2pm & 2.30-3.30pm Mon-Fri, 10am-12.30pm Sat) Has a foreign-exchange desk.

Kurinji Tours & Travel (☑240008; kodai-kurinji@sancharnet.in; Club Rd; ⊙9am-9pm) Reliable help with onward travel arrangements; also does foreign exchange.

State Bank of India ATM (Anna Salai)

Tourist office (☑241675; PT Rd; ⊙10am-5.45pm Mon-Fri) No brochures, maps or tours; 'just information, madam'.

ⓘ Getting There & Away

The nearest train station is Kodai Road, about two hours away at the foot of the mountain, where taxis (around ₹1000) and buses (₹17) wait. There's a **train booking office** (off Anna Salai; ☺9am-5pm Mon-Sat, 1.30-5pm Sun) in town.

Don't expect a bus to depart from Kodaikanal immediately. Tickets for private buses can be booked at travel agents near the bus stand. Buses from Kodai include:

Bengaluru ₹283, 11 hours, daily
Chennai ₹230, 11 hours, daily
Coimbatore ₹74, five hours, two daily
Madurai ₹48, four hours, hourly
Ooty ₹260, eight hours, daily
Palani ₹34, two hours, 10 daily
Trichy ₹65, 5½ hours, four daily

ⓘ Getting Around

The central part of Kodaikanal is compact and very easy to get around on foot. There are no autorickshaws (believe it or not) but plenty of taxis willing to take you to various sightseeing points. Charges are fixed; sightseeing tours cost from ₹600 to ₹1200 for a day trip. There's a stand opposite the bus station.

If you fancy a ride around the lake or you're fit enough to tackle the hills, mountain bikes can be hired from several **bicycle stalls** (per hr ₹20; ☺8am-6pm) around the lake.

Around Kodaikanal

One of the better high-end escapes in the hills, about three hours' drive below Kodaikanal off the Palani–Dindigul road, is the fabulous **Cardamom House** (☎0451-2556765, 09360-691793; www.cardamomhouse.com; r from ₹3300). Created with love and care by a retired Brit, this comfortable guesthouse – at the end of a scenic road beside bird-rich Lake Kamarajar – runs on solar power, uses water wisely, farms organically, trains and employs only locals (who produce terrific meals), and supports several village development initiatives. You'll need to book well in advance, hire a driver to take you there, and prepare for some serious relaxation.

Coimbatore

☎0422 / POP 1.46 MILLION

Coimbatore may be one of the largest cities in Tamil Nadu, but most travellers use it as either a step towards getting into Ooty, or a step down from the hills and into Kerala. Which isn't a bad idea; this is a large business and junction city that's friendly enough (and its proximity to the hills means temperatures are just a little cooler than average), but it's short on sights. Sometimes known as the Manchester of India for its textile industry, it's in the process of becoming a major IT centre. It has plenty of accommodation and eating options if you need to spend the night.

🛏 Sleeping

Legend's Inn   HOTEL **$$**
(☎4350000; legends_inn@yahoo.com; Geetha Hall Rd; s/d from ₹900/990; ❄) Some of the best-value midrange rooms in town, with comfortable furnishings, bamboo blinds and shiny bathrooms.

Residency   HOTEL **$$$**
(☎2241414; www.theresidency.com; 1076 Avanashi Rd; s/d incl breakfast from ₹4750/5100; ❄@🛜♨) Coimbatore's finest hotel has all the five-star trimmings, along with friendly staff and immaculate rooms. There's a well-equipped health club and pool, two excellent restaurants, a coffee shop and a bookshop in the lobby.

Sabari's Nest   HOTEL **$$**
(☎4505500; nest.coimbatore@sabarihotels.com; 739A Avanashi Rd; s/d incl breakfast from ₹2000/2300; ❄🛜) A change of name and ownership doesn't seem to have damaged this long-standing favourite; rooms are very comfortable, with wooden floors and tasteful Audubon-esque prints of local birdlife.

Hotel ESS Grande   HOTEL **$$**
(☎2230271; hessgrande@gmail.com; Nehru St; s/d incl breakfast from ₹1300/1600; ❄@) The best of the bus-stand-adjacent hotels, the ESS has small but very clean, fresh rooms, and possibly the sparkliest bathrooms in Coimbatore.

Hotel Rathna Regent   HOTEL **$$$**
(☎4294444; www.rathnaregent.com; Avanashi Rd; s/d incl breakfast from ₹2800/3300; ❄🛜) Not quite the top spot in town (hint: it's just opposite it), but a very comfortable place to lay your head all the same. The more expensive rooms are more like apartments, and all the facilities are here, including a couple of great restaurants, a bar and a cafe.

Hotel Shri Shakti   HOTEL **$**
(☎2234225; Sastri Rd; s/d from ₹260/380; ❄) There's not much character here, but there are a lot of rooms, and probably the cheapest AC in town; if you need a cheap, basic place to crash that's near the bus stands, look no further.

Hotel AP
HOTEL **$**

(☏2301773; hotelap@yahoo.com; s/d from ₹420/510, d with AC ₹990, ✉) Basic, clean-enough rooms near the train station. The AP's tucked down a back street, but you'll recognise it by its oddly cubist exterior. Singles are real singles, not the usual single-occupancy doubles, and are a bit cell-like.

✗ Eating

There's a fast-food hall and supermarket underneath Sabari's Nest hotel.

Malabar
INDIAN **$**

(7 Sastri Rd; mains ₹60-120; ☉lunch & dinner) In the KK Residency Hotel, this restaurant specialises in Keralan and North Indian food. The Keralan chicken roast (₹150 for half a chicken) is a spicy treat and there are seafood choices like crab masala.

Annalakshmi
INDIAN **$$**

(☏2212142; 106 Racecourse Rd; set meals ₹200; ☉lunch & dinner Tue-Sun) The top veg restaurant in town, this is run by devotees of Swami Shatanand Saraswati; the price of your meal helps support underprivileged children.

Annalakshmi Hotel
SOUTH INDIAN **$**

(Geetha Hall Rd; mains ₹20-80) A lot more down-market than the posh restaurant it probably borrowed its name from, but this cheap-and-cheerful place is probably the best of the cluster of mainly South Indian restaurants on Geetha Hall Rd. Mushroom dishes are particulary good, and the biryani ain't bad.

KR Food Mall
INDIAN **$**

(cnr State Bank & Geetha Hall Rds) Indian snacks and sweets all day, a good veg restaurant with a decent range of North and South Indian upstairs (breakfast, lunch and dinner), and an evening-only, super-popular halal takeaway stall that's heavy on spicy chicken dishes.

Naalukattu
SOUTH INDIAN **$**

(Nehru St; mains ₹50-140; ☉lunch & dinner) Like a dark-wood-accented Keralan veranda, with Malayalam-inspired food that's all good – especially the seafood.

Hot Chocolate
WESTERN **$$$**

(Avanashi Rd; mains ₹80-200; ☉lunch & dinner) Not bad at all if you're hankering after cakes, pasta or burgers.

ℹ Information

There's a string of internet joints along Geetha Hall Rd, opposite the train station, all charging about ₹20 per hour.

HSBC ATM (Racecourse Rd) Next to Annalakshmi restaurant.

Oscar Browsing Centre (cnr Kalingaray & Sastri Sts; per hr ₹20; ☉9.30am-10pm) Internet access near the bus stands.

Coimbatore

N 0 ——— 500 m
0 ——— 0.25 miles

Coimbatore

State Bank of India ATM (Avanashi Rd) Opposite Sabari's Nest.

VKC Forex (Raheja Centre, Avanashi Rd; ⊙9.30am-6.30pm Mon-Sat) Currency exchange and travellers cheques cashed, next door to the Residency hotel.

ⓘ Getting There & Away

Air

The airport is 10km east of town, with domestic flights to many destinations, including Chennai, Delhi, Bengaluru, Mumbai and Kochi. SilkAir also runs three flights a week direct to/from Singapore. Airlines include **Air India** (☑2399833), **Jet Airways** (☑2243465), Kingfisher Airlines, **SilkAir** (☑4370271) and SpiceJet.

Bus

There are three bus stands in the city centre.

From the Central bus station services depart to northern destinations such as Salem and Erode. From Thiruvalluvar bus station you can catch regular state and interstate buses to Bengaluru (₹180 to ₹230, nine hours), Mysore (₹80 to ₹100, five hours) and Chennai (₹300, 11½ hours). The Town bus stand is for local city buses.

Ukkadam bus station, south of the city, is for buses to nearby southern destinations, including Palani (₹35, three hours), Pollachi (₹16, one hour) and Madurai (₹74, five hours). The Ooty bus stand, aka 'new bus stand', is a couple of kilometres west of the centre on the Mettupalayam road; regular services run to Mettupalayam (45 minutes), Ooty (3½ hours; via Coonoor) and Kotagiri.

Taxi

A taxi up the hill to Ooty (2½ hours) costs about ₹1500; Ooty buses are often so crowded that it's an option worth considering.

Train

Coimbatore Junction is on the main line between Chennai and Ernakulam (Kerala). For Ooty, catch the daily 12671 *Nilgiri Express* at 5.15am; it connects with the miniature railway departure from Mettupalayam to Ooty at 7.10am. The whole trip to Ooty takes about seven hours. For other train services, see the boxed text, p378.

ⓘ Getting Around

For the airport take bus 20 from the Town bus stand or bus 90 from the train station. Many buses run between the train station and the Town bus stand, and between the Central bus station and Ooty and Ukkadam stands. Autorickshaw drivers charge around ₹50 between the bus and train stations. An autorickshaw from the centre out to the Ooty bus stand will cost up to ₹100 depending on your bargaining skills.

Around Coimbatore

The **Isha Yoga Center** (☑0422-2515345; www.ishafoundation.org), an ashram in Poondi, 30km west of Coimbatore, is also a yoga retreat and place of pilgrimage. The centrepiece is a multi-religious temple housing the Dhyanalingam, said to be unique in that it embodies all seven chakras of spiritual energy. Visitors are welcome to the temple to meditate, or to take part in yoga courses, for which you should register in advance.

The commercial town of **Mettupalayam** is the starting point for the miniature train to Ooty. There's little of interest for travellers, but if you want to sleep in a little longer before you catch the train, there is plenty of accommodation. There are various cheap lodges right by the bus and train stations, and **Hotel EMS Mayura** (☑04254-227936; 212 Coimbatore Rd; r ₹700, with AC ₹1200; ❄), a fine, clean, bland midrange hotel with a decent restaurant, is just 1km from the train station.

MAJOR TRAINS FROM COIMBATORE

DESTINATION	TRAIN NO & NAME	FARE (₹)	DURATION (HR)	DEPARTURE
Bengaluru	6525 *Island Express*	191/505	7½	10.50pm
Chennai*	2672 *Kovai Express*	132/471	7½	2.20pm
	2674 *Cheran Express*	232/594	8½	10.20pm
Kochi	7230 *Sabari Express*	122/311	5	8.35am
Madurai	6610 *Nagercoil Express*	155/404	6	8.30pm

*2nd class/AC chair
All other fares sleeper/3AC

Coonoor

📞0423 / POP 101,000 / ELEV 1850M

Coonoor is one of the three Nilgiri hill stations – Ooty, Kotagiri and Coonoor– that lie above the southern plains. Like Kotagiri, Coonoor is a place for quiet and isolation, and it's emerging as a centre for foodies and upmarket homestays. From Upper Coonoor's accommodation, 1km to 2km above the town centre, you can look down over the sea of red-tile rooftops to the slopes behind and soak up the peace, cool climate and beautiful scenery. Just note you get none of the above in central Coonoor, which is a bustling, honking mess.

◉ Sights & Activities

There are several popular viewpoints around Coonoor. **Dolphin's Nose**, about 10km from town, exposes a vast panorama encompassing **Catherine Falls** across the valley. **Lamb's Rock**, named after the British captain who created a short path to this favourite picnic spot in a pretty patch of forest, has amazing views past the hills into the hazy plains. The easiest way to see these sights – all on the same road – is on a rickshaw tour for around ₹500. If you're feeling energetic, walk the 6km or so back into town from Lamb's Rock (it's mostly, but not entirely, downhill).

Sim's Park   PARK
(adult/child ₹10/5, camera/video ₹25/250; ⏱8.30am-6pm) In Upper Coonoor, the 12-hectare Sim's Park is a peaceful oasis of manicured lawns and more than 1000 plant species, including magnolia, tree ferns and camellia. Buses heading to Kotagiri can drop you here.

🛏 Sleeping & Eating

You'll need a rickshaw (or good legs) to reach all these places. If you're self-catering, try the **Green Shop** (Jograj Bldg, Bedford Circle) for honey and other local goodies, and the well-stocked supermarket in **Tulsi Mall** for a range of packaged Western goods.

TOP CHOICE **180 McIver**   BOUTIQUE HOTEL $$$
(📞2233323; 180mciver@gmail.com; McIver Villa, Orange Grove Rd; d incl breakfast ₹3000-4500) A French couple has turned the four bedrooms in this classic Nilgiri bungalow into something really special; bright-coloured walls, antique furniture and floorboards, working fireplaces and big fresh bathrooms

blend French and local sensibilities in the best possible way. The multicuisine restaurant, **La Belle Vie**, uses organic produce and has guests driving a long way to sample the Indian-French menu (mains ₹140 to ₹350).

Acres Wild   FARMSTAY $$
(📞2232621; www.acres-wild.com; Upper Meanjee Estate, Kannimariamman Kovil St; cottages incl breakfast ₹2000-4000) This gorgeously situated farm outside Coonoor makes cheese like you've never tasted in India, and invites guests to help in the production. Cottages are simple and stylish, with fireplaces for chilly nights and views over the valley; your hosts are friendly and the food is great. No walk-ins – book in advance.

Tryst   GUESTHOUSE $$$
(📞2207057; www.trystindia.com; s/d incl breakfast & dinner ₹5500/6600) If you're looking for a gregarious accommodation experience that's quirky and classy, check out the website of this extraordinary guesthouse and book ahead. It's beautifully located in a former tea plantation manager's bungalow.

YWCA Wyoming Guesthouse   GUESTHOUSE $
(📞2234426; ywcacoonoor@gmail.com; s/d ₹500/700) This ramshackle guesthouse, a hill-station gem of a structure nestled into an upslope of Upper Coonoor, is a budget favourite. Although ageing and draughty, the 150-year-old colonial house oozes character with wooden terraces and serene views over Coonoor.

Hotel Vivek Coonoor   HOTEL $
(📞2230658; www.hotelvivek.com; Figure of Eight Rd; r from ₹600) A good 'upper budget' option. Many of the wide range of rooms here have balconies (screened to avoid the 'monkey menace') from which you can watch the tea fields.

❶ Getting There & Away

Coonoor is on the miniature train line between Mettupalayam (28km) and Ooty (18km) – see p387. Buses to Ooty (₹8, one hour) and Kotagiri (₹10, one hour) leave roughly every 15 minutes.

Kotagiri

📞04266 / POP 29,184

The oldest of the three Nilgiri hill stations, Kotagiri is about 28km from Ooty. It's a quiet, unassuming place with a forgettable town centre, but we're assuming you're not here for the nightlife. Rather, the appeal is the escape from the overdevelopment in Ooty: red dirt tracks in the pines, blue skies and the high green walls of the Nilgiris.

From Kotagiri you can visit **Catherine Falls**, 8km away near the Mettupalayam road (the last 3km is by foot only, and the falls only flow after rain), **Elk Falls** (6km) and **Kodanad Viewpoint** (22km), where there's a view over the Coimbatore Plains and Mysore Plateau. A half-day taxi tour to all three will cost around ₹800. The scenery on the road to Mettupalayam is gorgeous, so you may want to detour this way if you're heading down from Ooty.

If you've any interest at all in the history of the Nilgiris, it's worth visiting the **Sullivan Memorial** (Nilgiri Documentation Centre; ☑9486639092; Kannerimukku; ◷10am-5pm Mon-Sat). The bungalow that belonged to John Sullivan, the founder of Ooty, has been refurbished and filled with fascinating photos and artefacts about local tribal groups, European settlement and icons like the toy train. Call if nobody's there, or to arrange visits out of hours.

Also located here are the offices of the **Keystone Foundation** (☑272277; www.keystone-foundation.org; Groves Hill Rd), an NGO that works to improve environmental conditions in the Nilgiris while working with, and creating better living standards for, indigenous communities. The foundation's **Green Shop** (Johnstone Circle) has goodies for picnics – local organic cheese, honey and more.

A couple of very basic lodges are in the small town centre, and you won't go short of *idlis* or dosas. A combination of splendid 1915 colonial building and flashy new block, **Nahar Retreat** (☑273300; www.naharretreat.com; r from₹2000) has very comfortable rooms, great views and a very simple veg restaurant, but charges a lot for extras. Closer to the centre, **Hope Park** (☑271229; www.hopeparkhotel.com; r from ₹1200) has big, clean rooms, a decent restaurant and friendly staff.

Buses stop at the edge of town, about 1km from the centre. Buses to Ooty depart hourly (₹12, 1½ hours), crossing one of Tamil Nadu's highest passes. Buses to Mettupalayam leave every 30 minutes and to Coonoor every 15 minutes.

Ooty (Udhagamandalam)

☑0423 / POP 93,921 / ELEV 2240M

Ooty may be a bit bustling for some tastes, but most travellers quickly fall in love with this pine-clad retreat, where trekkers congregate in front of roaring fires before setting out into the surrounding green dream. Even the typical chaos of India becomes somehow subdued in the shadow of the hills. Therein lays Ooty's charm, especially when you throw in her quirks: a jumble of Hindu temples and ecotourism, overlaid by a veneer of manicured British aesthetic.

This is South India's most famous (and certainly best-named) hill station, established by the British in the early 19th century as the summer headquarters of the then-Madras government and memorably nicknamed 'Snooty Ooty'. Development ploughed through a few decades ago, and continues, but somehow old Ooty survives – you just have to walk a bit further out from the town centre to find it.

The journey up to Ooty on the miniature train is romantic and the scenery stunning – try to get a seat on the left-hand side where you get the best views across the mountains. With that said, even the bus ride is pretty impressive (if not nearly as relaxing). From April to June (the *very* busy season) Ooty is a welcome relief from the hot plains, and in the colder months (October to March) you'll need warm clothing – which you can buy cheap here – as overnight temperatures occasionally drop to 0°C.

The train station and bus station are next to the racecourse, which is surrounded by cheap hotels. Further downhill is the lake, while the valley slopes up on either side, studded with colonial houses and guest lodges with good views. From the bus station it's a 10-minute walk to the bazaar area and a 20-minute walk to Ooty's commercial centre, Charing Cross. Like Kodai, Ooty has an international school whose students can often be seen around town.

◉ Sights

St Stephen's Church   CHURCH
(Church Hill Rd; ◷10am-1pm & 3-5pm Mon-Sat, services 8am & 11am Sun) Perched above the town centre, the immaculate St Stephen's Church, built in 1829, is the oldest church in the Nilgiris. Throughout its history, St Stephen's has racially shifted from hosting an exclusively British congregation to an Anglo-Indian orphanage to falling under the auspices of the Church of South India. Look out for lovely stained glass, huge wooden beams hauled by elephant from the palace of Tipu Sultan some 120km away, and the sometimes kitschy, sometimes touching, slabs and plaques donated by colonial-era

churchgoers. In the quiet, overgrown cemetery you'll find headstones commemorating many an Ooty Brit, including the wife and daughter of John Sullivan, the town's founder. If you're partial to colonial cemeteries, the quiet yard overlooking the lake at **St Thomas Church** (Racecourse Rd) is also worth a wander.

Botanical Gardens   GARDEN

(adult/child ₹20/10, camera/video ₹30/75; ⊙7am-6.30pm) Established in 1848, these lovely gardens are a living gallery of the natural fauna of the Nilgiris. Look out for a fossilised tree trunk believed to be around 20 million years old, and on busy days, roughly 20 million Indian tourists.

Doddabetta Lookout   VIEWPOINT

(admission ₹5; ⊙7am-6pm) This is it: the highest point (2633m) of the Nilgiris and one of the best viewpoints around, assuming, as usual, the day is clear. It's about 10km out of town; go early for better chances of a mist-free view. Any Kotagiri buses will drop you at the Dodabetta junction, from where it's a fairly energetic 3km walk or a quick jeep ride. A taxi will do the round trip from Charing Cross for ₹350.

Centenary Rose Park   GARDEN

(Selbourne Rd; adult/child ₹20/10, camera/video ₹30/50; ⊙9am-6.30pm) With its terraced lawns and colourful flowerbeds – best between May and July – this terraced rose garden is a pleasant place for a stroll. There are good views over Ooty from the hilltop location.

Thread Garden   GARDEN

(☎2445145; North Lake Rd; admission ₹10, camera/video ₹15/30; ⊙8.30am-8pm) If your expectations aren't too high, you may enjoy the 'miracle' (official description and just *slight* hyperbole) that is 150 species of 'plants' from around the world meticulously re-created using 'hand-wound' thread. The technique was perfected by Keralan artist Anthony Joseph and the work took 50 craftspeople 12 years to complete.

Tribal Research Centre Museum   MUSEUM

(Muthorai Palada; admission free; ⊙10am-5pm Mon-Fri) It's hard to say why you should love this museum more than most: for its decently executed exhibits on Nilgiri and Andaman tribal groups, or the decomposing corpses of badly stuffed local wildlife, including a rotting mongoose that just arrived from hell's deepest pit. Seriously, the artefacts are fantastic – you may never get the chance to hold a Stone Age bow in your life again – and descriptions of the tribes are good, if written by anthropologists with no filter from academia to normal English. The museum is just beyond the village of Muthorai Palada

Nilgiri Hills

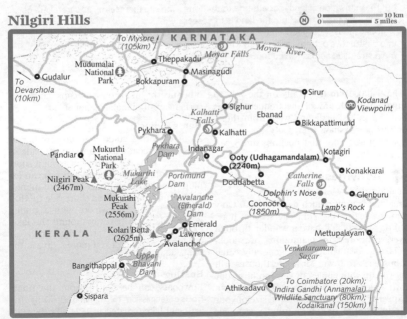

For centuries, the Nilgiris have been home to hill tribes. While retaining integrity in customs, dress and language, the tribes were economically, socially and culturally interdependent. The British concept of exclusive property rights disenfranchised many tribespeople, as did exploitative commercial practices that undermined their barter-based economy. Today, many eke out a living in poverty gathering honey or herbs for the ayurveda industry.

The Toda tribe's social, economic and spiritual system centred on the buffalo, whose milk and ghee was integral to their diet and used as currency – in exchange for grain, tools and medical services. Most importantly, the dairy produce provided offerings to the gods as well as fuel for the funeral pyre. It was only at the ritual for human death that the strictly vegetarian Toda killed a buffalo, not for food but to provide company for the deceased.

The Badagas are believed to have migrated to the Nilgiris from the north around 1600 AD, in the wake of Muslim invasions in the north, and are thus not officially a tribal people. With knowledge of the world outside the hills, they became effective representatives for the hill tribes. Their agricultural produce, particularly grain, added a further dimension to the hill diet.

The Kotas lived in the Kotagiri area and were considered by other tribes to be lower in status. They still undertake ceremonies in which the gods are beseeched for rains and bountiful harvests.

The Kurumbas inhabited the thick forests of the south. They gathered bamboo, honey and materials for housing, some of which were supplied to other tribes. They also engaged in a little agriculture, and at sowing and harvest times they employed the Badaga to perform rituals entreating the gods for abundant yields.

The Irulus, also from the southern slopes, produced tools and gathered honey and other forest products that they converted into brooms and incense. They are devotees of Vishnu and often perform rituals for other tribes.

British colonialism and lowland migration have undermined tribal cultural systems to the point of collapse. Displaced tribes have been 'granted' land by the Indian government, but the cultivation of land is anathema to the Toda, who see themselves as caretakers of the soil – for them, to dig into the land is to desecrate it.

Today many tribal people have assimilated to the point of invisibility. Some have fallen into destructive patterns associated with displacement and alienation, while others remain straddled across two cultures.

(M Palada), 11km from Ooty on the way to Emerald. Catch any of the frequent buses heading to M Palada and walk from there, or hire a rickshaw from Ooty for around ₹300 return. Note that opening times can be a bit iffy.

🏃 Activities

Trekking

Trekking is pretty much de rigueur in Ooty and the reason most travellers come here. On day trips you'll have a wander through evergreen forest, tea plantations, over lookouts, into local villages and, generally, catch a bus back to town. Most guesthouses will set you up with guides, or you can hire your own – plenty will offer their services to you. Expect to pay depending on the size of your group, ₹300 to ₹900 for a full-day trek. For

other nearby hiking options, consider the resorts near Mudumalai National Park.

Horse Riding

Alone or with a guide, you can hire horses outside the boathouse on the north side of the lake; the rides mostly consist of a short amble along bitumen, although you can explore the woods and hills for more money. Prices run from ₹50 for a short ride to ₹100 to ₹200 for an hour (more with a guide), which takes you partway around the lake. Some horses look in pretty bad shape. A white horse will cost you more – do ask the guide why that is.

Boating

Rowboats can be rented from the **boathouse** (admission ₹5; ⊘9am-5.30pm) by the artificial lake (created in 1824). Prices start from ₹80 for a two-seater pedal boat (30 minutes) and go up to ₹280 for a 15-seater motorboat (20 minutes).

Horse Racing

Ooty's racecourse dominates the lower part of the hill station between Charing Cross and the lake. The horse-racing season runs from mid-April to June and on race days the town is a hive of activity; it's an event you can't miss if you're in town. Outside the season, the 2.4km racecourse just becomes a cricket field/trash dump/public toilet.

☞ Tours

The tourist office can put you in touch with agencies that run day trips to Mudumalai National Park via the Pykhara Dam. Trips to Coonoor and surrounds are also possible. A better alternative is to hire a taxi for the day and go as you please. Rates run for about ₹800 for a four-hour trip around Ooty, or ₹1600 to ₹1800 for a full day depending on where you're heading.

🛌 Sleeping

Ooty has some good rustic lodges in the budget-midrange scale, gorgeous colonial-era residences at the high end, and even some decent backpacker dosses. Be warned: it's a sellers' market in the high season (1 April to 15 June), when many hotel prices double and checkout time is often 9am. Prices listed here are for the low season when most places are good value.

Hotel Sweekar HOTEL $
(☑2442348; Race View Rd; d ₹350-400) Definitely the best value for money in town, the Sweekar hosts guests in simple but very clean rooms in a traditional Ooty cottage that sits at the end of a lavender-lined path. It's run by an incredibly friendly Bahai manager.

Willow Hill HOTEL $$
(☑2223123; www.willowhill.in; 58/1 Havelock Rd; d ₹900-2000) Sitting high above town, Willow Hill's large windows provide great views of Ooty. The rooms, all with wooden floors, have a distinct alpine chalet chic, with the most expensive rooms offering a private garden.

Fernhills Palace HOTEL $$$
(☑2443911; www.fernhillspalace.co.in; Fernhill Post; 2-night packages ₹13,250-33,950) The Maharaja of Mysore's summer palace has been lovingly restored in colourfully gorgeous,

ridiculously over-the-top princely colonial style; if you can afford to stay here, you really should. Play billiards, walk in the garden and check out old photos of the Ooty Hunt while sipping Scotch in the atmospheric Fox **Hunt Bar**.

YWCA Anandagiri HOTEL $
(☑2442218; www.ywcaagooty.com; Ettines Rd; dm from ₹99, r from ₹345) This former brewery and sprawling complex of hill cottages is dotted with flower gardens; throw in elegant lounges and fireplaces and you've got some excellent budget accommodation going on. High ceilings can mean cold nights; ask for extra blankets if you think you might need them.

Hotel Welbeck Residency HOTEL $$
(☑2223300; www.welbeck.in; Club Rd; r from ₹1800) An attractive older building that's been thoroughly tarted up with very comfortable rooms, a touch of colonial class (miniature cannons at the front door!) and a good restaurant. Staff are very helpful.

King's Cliff HOTEL $$
(☑2224545; www.littlearth.in; Havelock Rd; d from ₹1475) High above Ooty on Strawberry Hill is this gorgeous residence, a colonial house with wood panelling, antique furnishings and cosy lounge. If you plan on living large, Raj style, go for the more expensive rooms; the cheaper doubles don't quite reflect the old-world charm of the rest of the place. To really get out into the hills, ask the staff about **Destiny**, their delightful farmstay property an hour's drive from Ooty.

Lymond House HOTEL $$
(☑2223377; www.serendipityo.com; 77 Sylks Rd; d from ₹2250) If Mucha and F Scott Fitzgerald partnered up to open a hotel in Ooty, it'd probably come out looking something like this restored English villa. Rooms are all ensconced in Old World/Jazz Age opulence, the dining room (with limited, but very good, menu) and gardens are gorgeous, and the period atmosphere is thick enough to swim in.

Savoy Hotel HOTEL $$$
(☑2444142; www.tajhotels.com; 77 Sylks Rd; s/d from ₹5800/6800; 🖥) The Savoy is one of Ooty's oldest hotels, with parts dating back to 1829. Big cottages are arranged around a beautiful garden of flowerbeds, lawns and clipped hedges. The quaint rooms have large bathrooms, polished floors, log fires and bay windows. Modern facilities include a

Ooty (Udhagamandalam)

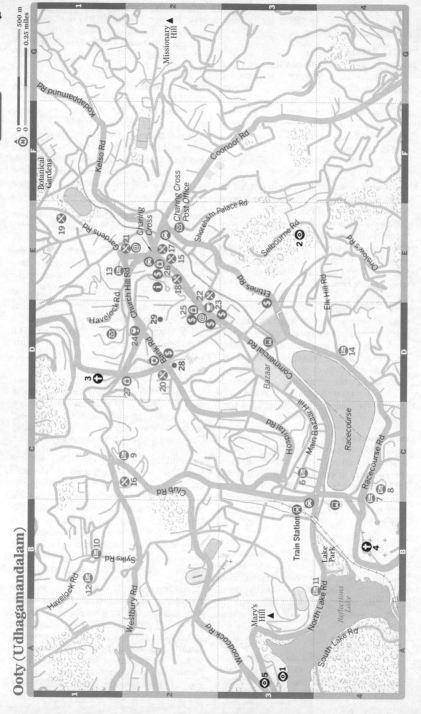

500 m
0.25 miles

24-hour bar, wi-fi, an excellent multicuisine dining room and an ayurvedic centre.

Hotel Mountview HOTEL **$**
(☎2443307; Racecourse Rd; r ₹660-1700) Perched on a quiet driveway directly above the bus station, this elegant old bungalow has eight simple, enormous (no, really) rooms, all wood lined and high ceilinged and slightly draughty, with unused fireplaces. There's enough untapped renovation potential here to make a decorator weep.

Reflections Guest House HOTEL **$**
(☎2443834; North Lake Rd; d ₹500-700) Judging by reader feedback, there must be two Reflections. One has helpful and welcoming staff, good food, and a great common area that's excellent for meeting other hill-bound travellers and trekkers. The other has curt staff who demand extra cash for everything from loo rolls to blankets. Either way, rooms are clean and decent value, and the setting very pleasant.

Hotel Maneck HOTEL **$**
(☎2443494; Main Bazaar; r ₹600-800) A small, friendly Jain-run hotel in the market; the slightly more expensive rooms are clean and comfortable.

TTDC Youth Hostel HOTEL **$**
(☎2443665; yhttdc@yahoo.in; Gardens Rd; dm/d from ₹100/350) This state-run hostel is reliably mediocre, clean and busy; you may want to call ahead to book a dorm bed if you're in the area.

✖ Eating & Drinking

Ooty has two branches each of **Café Coffee Day** and **Barista**, both with the usual range of reliably fine coffee, tea, cakes and sandwiches; the Club Rd branch of Barista has nice views and does a good toast-and-eggs breakfast. The more upmarket hotels all have atmospheric, multicuisine restaurants.

For self-caterers, **Modern Stores** (Garden Rd) is a mini-supermarket with all kinds of Western packaged food, as well as Nilgiri-produced bread and cheese, and the **Green Shop** (Club Rd) has honey, cheese and other local foods. **Virtue Bake** (Charing Cross) has excellent cakes, pastries and brownies to take away.

Kabab Corner NORTH INDIAN **$$**
(Commercial Rd; mains ₹60-200; ☺lunch & dinner) This is the place for meat eaters who are tiring of the nonstop veg of South India. It might not look like much from the outside, but here you can tear apart perfectly grilled and spiced chunks of lamb, chicken and, if you like, paneer, sopping up the juices with pillowy triangles of naan. The ₹450 tandoori platter is exceptionally good if you're in a group; if there's fewer than four of you, it may defeat you.

Garden Restaurant
SOUTH INDIAN $

(Nahar Hotel, Commercial Rd; mains ₹50-90; ⊗lunch & dinner) Slightly upmarket South Indian food in a clean hotel-restaurant setting, along with juices, ice creams, snacks and even pizza; the pizza's made in the hotel's **Sidewalk Café**, which has good vegetarian Western food at fairly high prices.

Shinkow's Chinese Restaurant
CHINESE $$

(☑2442811; 38/83 Commissioner's Rd; mains ₹50-150; ⊗lunch & dinner) Shinkow's is an Ooty institution and the simple menu of chicken, pork, beef, fish, noodles and rice dishes is reliably good and quick to arrive at your table.

Hotel Blue Hills
INDIAN $

(Commercial Rd; mains ₹20-80; ⊗lunch & dinner) Downstairs, dimly lit and feeling slightly disreputable, Blue Hills has been serving up good meals, huge crispy dosas and a range of other Indian standards for decades.

Willy's Coffee Pub
CAFE $

(mains ₹30-80; ⊗lunch & dinner) Climb the stairs and join international students and local cool kids for board games, magazines and very reasonably priced pizzas, fries, toasted sandwiches, cakes and cookies.

🔒 Shopping

The main places to shop are along Commercial Rd, where you'll find Kashmiri shops as well as government outlets for Kairali and Khadi Gramodyog Bhavan. The **Big Shop** (Commercial Rd) sells lovely new and antique jewellery and knick-knacks at fairly inflated prices. For cheaper but equally attractive silver and Toda (tribal) jewellery, there's a string of shops stretching along Main Bazaar in the direction of the train station; **Mahaveerchand** (291 Main Bazaar), next to Hotel Maneck, sells particularly nice work. Near the entrance to the botanical gardens you'll find Tibetan refugees selling sweaters and shawls, which you may appreciate on a chilly Ooty evening.

Higginbothams Commercial Rd (☑2443736; ⊗9am-1pm & 3.30-7.30pm Mon-Sat); Commissioner's Rd (☑2442546; ⊗9am-1pm & 2-6pm Mon-Sat) Has a good selection of contemporary English-language Indian and other fiction, and Lonely Planet guides.

ℹ Information

Internet Access

Global Net (Commercial Rd; per hr ₹30; ⊗9.30am-9pm)

Cyber Planet (Garden Rd; per hr ₹30; ⊗10am-7.30pm)

Library

Nilgiri Library (Bank Rd; temporary membership ₹200; ⊗9.30am-1pm & 2.30-6pm, reading room 9.30am-6pm Sat-Thu) Quaint little haven in a crumbling 1867 building with a collection of more than 40,000 books, including rare titles on the Nilgiris and hill tribes. Unless you're a student it costs an extra ₹500 for temporary membership if you want to actually take a book away with you.

Money

Axis Bank ATM (Commercial Rd)

Canara Bank (Commercial Rd) The only bank in town that does cash advances on credit cards.

State Bank of India (Bank Rd; ⊗10am-4pm Mon-Fri, 10am-1pm Sat) Changes travellers cheques and has an ATM.

State Bank of India ATM (Commercial Rd)

UK Forex (137 Commercial Rd) Changes travellers cheques and cash.

UTI Bank ATM (Ettines Rd)

National Park Information

Office of the Field Director (☑2444098; fdmtr@tn.nic.in; ⊗10am-5.45pm Mon-Fri) Manages Mudumalai National Park, including advance bookings for park accommodation.

Tourist Information

Tourist office (⊗2443977; ⊗10am-5.45pm Mon-Fri) Maps, brochures and tour information.

ℹ Getting There & Away

Without doubt the most romantic way to arrive in Ooty is aboard the miniature train, and you'll need to book ahead in the high season. Buses also run regularly up and down the mountain, both from other parts of Tamil Nadu and from Mysore in Karnataka.

Bus

The state bus companies all have **reservation offices** (⊗9am-5.30pm) at the busy bus station. There are two routes to Karnataka – the main bus route via Gudalur and the shorter, more arduous route via Masinagudi. The latter is tackled only by minibuses and winds through 36 hairpin bends! Frequent buses leave for Mettupalayam and Coimbatore, and there's daily service to Chennai, Bengaluru and Mysore.

Connect with trains to Chennai or Kochi (Cochin, Kerala) at Coimbatore.

To get to Mudumalai National Park (₹30, 2½ hours, 11 daily), take one of the Mysore buses that will drop you at park headquarters at Theppakadu, or one of the small buses that go via the narrow and twisting Sighur Ghat road. Some of these rolling wrecks travel only as far as Masinagudi (₹16, 1½ hours), from where there are buses every two hours to Theppakadu.

Local buses leave every 30 minutes for Kotagiri (₹10, 1½ hours) and every 10 minutes to Coonoor (₹12, one hour).

Train

The miniature train – one of the Mountain Railways of India given World Heritage status by Unesco in 2005 – is the best way to get here. There are fine views of forest, waterfalls and tea plantations along the way, especially from the front 1st-class carriage; the steam engine pushes, rather than pulls, the train up the hill, so the front carriage leads the way. Note that this route has been suspended on and off in the last few years after heavy rains led to landslides over the tracks; it was back on schedule at the time of research.

Departures and arrivals at Mettupalayam connect with those of the *Nilgiri Express,* which runs between Mettupalayam and Chennai. The miniature train departs Mettupalayam for Ooty at 7.10am daily (1st/2nd class ₹142/21, five hours). If you want a seat in either direction, be at least 45 minutes early or make a reservation at least 24 hours in advance.

From Ooty the train leaves at 3pm and takes about 3½ hours. There are also three daily passenger trains between Ooty and Coonoor (₹15, 1½ hours).

ⓘ Getting Around

Plenty of autorickshaws hang around the bus station – a ride from the train or bus stations to Charing Cross costs about ₹40, and lists of autorickshaw fixed prices can be found at the steps on Commercial Rd leading to the tourist information office, at the lake and outside the Botanical Gardens.

Taxis cluster at several stands in town. There are fixed fares to most destinations, including Coonoor (₹600), Kotagiri (₹800), Gudalur (₹1200), Mudumalai National Park (₹900) and Coimbatore (₹1800).

There's a jeep hire near the main bazaar, although it's best to rent these out in groups; expect to pay about 1.5 times more than local taxi fares.

Mudumalai National Park

☏ 0423

In the foothills of the Nilgiris, this 321-sq-km park is like a classical Indian landscape painting given life: thin, spindly trees and light-slotted leaves concealing spotted chital deer and slow herds of gaur (Indian bison).

Somewhere in the hills are tigers, although you're very lucky if you spot one.

Part of the Nilgiri Biosphere Reserve (3000 sq km), the park is the best place for spotting wildlife in Tamil Nadu, although there's still a good chance you won't see more than some deer and kingfishers. Vegetation ranges from grasslands to semi-evergreen forests to foothill scrub; besides the above species, panthers, wild boars, jackals and sloth bears prowl the reserve. Otters and crocodiles both inhabit the Moyar River, and the park's wild elephant population numbers about 600.

A good time to visit is between December and June, although the park may be closed during the dry season (February to March). Heavy rain is common in October and November.

The main service area in Mudumalai is Theppakadu, on the main road between Ooty and Mysore. Here you'll find the park's **reception centre** (☏ 2526235; ⊙ 6.30-9am & 3-5.30pm) and some park-run accommodation. The closest village is Masinagudi, 7km from Theppakadu.

◉ Sights & Activities

It's not possible to hike in the park and tours are limited to sanctuary minibuses; private vehicles are not allowed in the park except on the main Ooty–Mysore road that runs through it. Most people see the park via the fun 45-minute **minibus tours** (per person ₹35, camera/video ₹ 25/150) that run between 7am and 9am and 3pm and 6pm. The tour makes a 15km loop through part of the park in buses painted in camoflague stripes.

You can also hire a guide for a foot **trek** outside the park boundaries, but the only way to do this safely and legally is through one of the better resorts, where guides are experts who know where it's OK to walk. Tourists have been killed after getting too close to wild elephants on dodgy treks, and park rules have since tightened up considerably.

Early-morning **elephant rides** in the jungle are available but must be booked in advance at the Office of the Field Director in Ooty (p386); it costs ₹460 per group of four.

Near the reception centre, and sharing the same hours, the **elephant camp** (per person ₹15) is a spot on the river where you can watch elephants being fed and bathed in the morning or evening.

🛏 Sleeping & Eating

There are budget and midrange lodges inside the park at Theppakadu; budget rooms and midrange cottages in Masinagudi; and midrange and upmarket jungle resorts in Bokkapuram (4km south of Masinagudi). For meals at the resorts, expect to pay from ₹400 per person per day.

IN THE PARK

For most accommodation in the park, book in advance, in person, with the Office of the Field Director (p386) in Ooty. The first three places listed here are park-run accommodation on the banks of the river and are all walking distance from park reception.

Minivet Dormitory HOTEL $
(q ₹310) A simple place, with two four-bed rooms, each with private bathroom with cold water only. Expect vociferous demands for extra rupees for the most basic services here.

Theppakadu Log House HOTEL $$
(d/q ₹1030/1500) Comfortable rooms, well maintained.

Sylvan Lodge HOTEL $$
(d/q ₹530/1080) Not a very big drop in quality from Log House, and with the addition of a kitchen that prepares meals for booked guests.

Hotel Tamil Nadu HOTEL $
(📞2526580; dm/d/q ₹125/550/950) A nearby government-run hotel providing basic accommodation and meals.

BOKKAPURAM

This area south of Masinagudi is home to a gaggle of fine forest resorts, mostly family-run businesses with a warm, homely atmosphere, high standards and breathtaking views. Don't wander outside your resort at night; leopards, among other wild animals, are very much present.

Jungle Retreat RESORT $$
(📞2526469; www.jungleretreat.com; dm ₹525, bamboo huts/standard r ₹1969/2532, tree house ₹4500; 🏊) One of the most stylish resorts in the area, with lovingly built stone cottages decked out in classic furniture and sturdy bamboo huts, all spread out to give a feeling of seclusion. It's possible to camp, and there's a dormitory for groups. The bar, restaurant and common area is a great place to meet fellow travellers and the owners are knowledgeable and friendly, with a large area of private forest at their disposal. The

pool and its setting are stunning. All prices include taxes.

Jungle Hut RESORT $$
(📞2526463; www.junglehut.in; s/d incl taxes & 3 meals ₹2970/4000) Similar in style to Jungle Retreat, with cottages spread across the property, this resort has the best food in Bokkapuram (if you're visiting the restaurant from another resort after dark, don't walk home on your own!). If you're up for fishing you can relax by the ponds fed from waterfalls you can see in the distant hills.

Safari Land Resort RESORT $$
(📞2526937; www.safarilandresorts.com; r from ₹1800, tree house from ₹3500; 🛜) This jungle complex has comfortable rooms and cottages as well as well-decked-out tree houses above a gurgling stream. The views into the surrounding jungle hills are stunning, but the pace, for all the dramatic scenery, is supremely relaxed. Your host is a Hyderabadi prince and former rifle-shooting champ.

Forest Hills Guest House RESORT $$
(📞2526216; www.foresthillsindia.com; r incl taxes from ₹1743) Forest Hills is a family-run, family-sized guesthouse (10 rooms on 5 hectares) with a few cute bamboo huts, some clean spacious rooms, and a fabulous watchtower for wildlife-watching and birdwatching. There's a slight colonial air here with a gazebo-style bar, games rooms and a barbecue pit. It's popular with Indian families.

Bear Mountain Jungle Retreat RESORT $$
(📞2526505; www.bearmountainjungleresort.com; cottages from ₹2000) Good for groups, this resort has stunning jungle and mountain views and simple, clean rooms.

❶ Getting There & Around

Bus services run every two hours between Theppakadu and Masinagudi (7km); shared jeeps ply this route for ₹7 if there's enough passengers, or you can have one to yourself for ₹100. Costs are similar for jeeps between Masinagudi and Bokkapuram.

Buses from Ooty to Mysore and Bengaluru stop at Theppakadu (2½ hours, 11 daily). There's another, more direct route between Ooty and Masinagudi, an interesting 'short cut' (₹13, 1½ hours, 36km) which involves taking one of the small government buses that make the trip up (or down) the tortuous (but very pretty) Sighur Ghat road. The bends are so tight and the gradient so steep that large buses simply can't use it, and accidents are not uncommon. A taxi from Ooty to Masinagudi using this route takes an hour and costs ₹750.

Andaman Islands

Best Places to Stay

» Eco Villa (p401)

» Aashiaanaa Rest Home (p396)

» Pristine Beach Resort (p405)

» Blue View (p405)

» Blue Planet (p404)

Best Beaches

» Radha Nagar (p400)

» Merk Bay (p404)

» Ross & Smith Islands (p404)

» Beach 5 (p400)

» Butler Bay (p405)

Why Go?

On old maps, the Andamans and Nicobars were the kind of islands whose inhabitants were depicted with dog's heads or faces in their chests, surrounded by sea serpents in a tempest-lashed sea known to Indians as Kalapani: the Black Waters. These were the islands that someone labelled, with a shaky hand, 'Here be Monsters' – probably an early traveller who didn't want to share this delightful place with the rest of us.

Lovely opaque emerald waters are surrounded by primeval jungle and mangrove forest; snow-white beaches melt under flame-and-purple sunsets; and the population is a friendly masala of South and Southeast Asian settlers, as well as Negrito ethnic groups whose arrival here still has anthropologists baffled. And geographically, the Andamans are more Southeast Asia – 150km from Indonesia and 190km from Myanmar – making them all the more intriguing.

The Nicobars are off-limits to tourists, but that still leaves hundreds of islands to explore.

When to Go
Port Blair

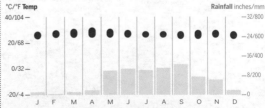

Dec–Apr High tourist season: perfect sunny days, optimal diving conditions.

Oct–Dec & Apr–mid-May Weather's a mixed bag, but fewer tourists and lower costs

Dec–Mar Best time to see turtles nesting

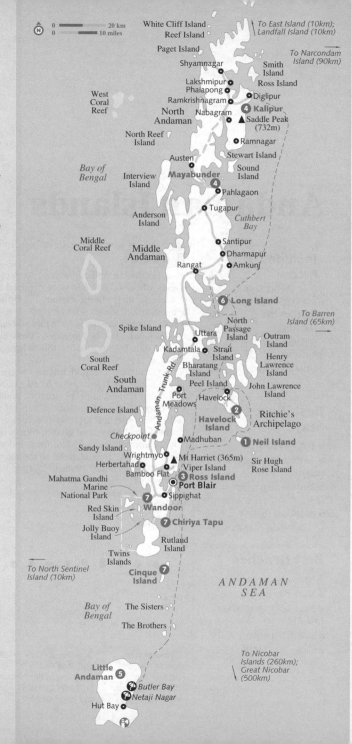

Andaman Islands Highlights

1 Regress to infantile laziness and happiness on **Neil Island** (p402)

2 Dive, snorkel and socialise on **Havelock Island** (p400)

3 Glimpse Port Blair's colonial history at **Ross Island** (p399)

4 Travel through the jungle heart of the Andamans around **Mayabunder** (p404) and **Kalipur** (p404)

5 Find Butler Bay and paradise on **Little Andaman** (p405)

0 ———— 20 km
0 ———— 10 miles

To East Island (10km);
Landfall Island (10km)

White Cliff Island
Reef Island
Paget Island
Shyamnagar
Smith Island
To Narcondam Island (90km)
Lakshmipur
Phaiapong
Ramkrishnagram
West Coral Reef
North Andaman
Nabagram
Ross Island
Diglipur
4 **Kalipur**
▲ Saddle Peak (732m)
North Reef Island
Ramnagar
Stewart Island
Bay of Bengal
Austen
Interview Island
Mayabunder
Sound Island
4
Pahlagaon
Cuthbert Bay
Anderson Island
Tugapur
Middle Coral Reef
Middle Andaman
Santipur
Dharmapur
Rangat
Amkunj
6 **Long Island**
To Barren Island (65km)
Spike Island
Uttara
North Passage Island
Outram Island
Kadamtala
Strait Island
Henry Lawrence Island
South Coral Reef
South Andaman
Bharatang Island
Peel Island
John Lawrence Island
Defence Island
Port Meadows
Havelock
Checkpoint
Madhuban
Havelock Island
2
Ritchie's Archipelago
Sandy Island
Wrightmyo
Herbertahad
▲ Mt Harriet (365m)
Viper Island
1 **Neil Island**
Mahatma Gandhi Marine National Park
Bamboo Flat
3 **Ross Island**
● **Port Blair**
Sir Hugh Rose Island
Red Skin Island
7 Sippighat
Wandoor
Jolly Buoy Island
7 **Chiriya Tapu**
Rutland Island
Twins Islands
To North Sentinel Island (10km)
Cinque Island **7**
ANDAMAN SEA
Bay of Bengal
The Sisters
The Brothers
To Nicobar Islands (260km); Great Nicobar (500km)
Little Andaman **5**
7 Butler Bay
7 Netaji Nagar
Hut Bay

FAST FACTS

» Population: 380,000

» Area: 8248 sq km

» Telephone code: ☎03192

» Main languages: Hindi, Bengali, Tamil

» Sleeping prices: $ below ₹800, $$ ₹800 to ₹2500, $$$ above ₹25,000

History

The date of initial human settlement in the Andamans and Nicobars is lost to history. Anthropologists say stone-tool crafters have lived here for 2000 years, and scholars of human migration believe local indigenous tribes have roots in Negrito and Malay ethnic groups in Southeast Asia. Otherwise, these specks in the sea have been a constant source of legend to outside visitors.

The name 'Andaman' is thought to derive from 'Hanuman'; the Hindu monkey god supposedly used the islands as a stepping stone between India and Sri Lanka. Anthropologists say stone-tool crafters were here 2000 years ago but the date of initial human settlement is not known.

The 10th-century Persian adventurer Buzurg Ibn Shahriyar described an island chain inhabited by cannibals, Marco Polo added that the natives had dogs' heads, and tablets in Thanjavur (Tanjore) in Tamil Nadu named the archipelago Timaittivu: the Impure Islands.

None of the above was exactly tourism-brochure stuff, but visitors kept coming: the Marathas in the late 17th century and 200 years later, the British, who used the Andamans as a penal colony for political dissidents. In WWII some islanders greeted the invading Japanese as liberators, but despite installing Indian politicians as (puppet) administrators, the Japanese military proved to be harsh occupiers.

Following Independence in 1947, the Andaman and Nicobar Islands were incorporated into the Indian Union. With migration from the mainland (including Bengali refugees fleeing the chaos of partition), the population has grown from a few thousand to more than 350,000. During this influx, tribal land rights and environmental protection were often disregarded; some conditions are improving but indigenous tribes remain largely in decline.

The islands were devastated by the 2004 Indian Ocean earthquake, offshore aftershocks and the resulting tsunami. The Nicobars were especially hard hit; some estimate a fifth of the population was killed; others were relocated to Port Blair and many have yet to return. But by and large normalcy has returned, along with tourists, although places like Little Andaman remain practically deserted by visitors (so visit).

Climate

Sea breezes keep temperatures within the 23°C to 31°C range and the humidity at around 80% all year. It's very wet during the southwest (wet) monsoon between roughly mid-May and early October, while the northeast (dry) monsoons between November and December also have their fair share of rainy days.

Geography & Environment

The islands form the peaks of the Arakan Yoma, a mountain range that begins in Western Myanmar (Burma) and extends into the ocean running all the way to Sumatra in Indonesia.

The isolation of the Andaman and Nicobar Islands has led to the evolution of many endemic plant and animal species. Of 62 identified mammals, 32 are unique to the islands, including the Andaman wild pig, crab-eating macaque, masked palm civet, and species of tree shrews and bats. Almost 50% of the islands' 250 bird species are endemic, including ground-dwelling megapodes, *hawabills* (swiftlets) and the emerald Nicobar pigeon. The isolated beaches are breeding grounds for turtles; rivers are prowled by saltwater crocodiles; and dolphins are frequently sighted, but the once abundant dugongs have all but vanished.

Mangroves provide a protective barrier between land and sea. Inland forests contain important tree species, including the renowned padauk – a hardwood with light and dark timber occurring in the same tree.

🏃 Activities

The Andamans are one of the world's great **diving** locations, as much for their relative isolation as their crystal-clear waters, superb coral and kaleidoscopic marine life.

The main dive season is roughly November to April, but trips still occur during the summer wet season (June to August) – just closer to the shore. Diving conditions are generally fine in September and October; there's just rain to contend with.

Centres offer fully equipped boat dives, discover scuba diving courses (from ₹4000), PADI open water (₹18,000) and advanced courses (₹13,500), as well as Divemaster training. Prices vary depending on the location, number of participants and duration of the course, but diving in the Andamans costs around ₹2000/3500 for a one/two boat dive. In national parks an additional ₹500 per person per day is payable directly to the park.

Havelock Island is far and away the main diving centre in the islands, although outfits have expanded to Neil and South Andaman. See relevant sections for details.

Much easier and cheaper to arrange than diving, **snorkelling** can be highly rewarding. Havelock Island is one of the best, and certainly easiest, places for snorkelling as many accommodation places organise boat trips out to otherwise inaccessible coral reefs and islands. There's also excellent snorkelling offshore on Neil Island and Kalipur.

Some reefs have been damaged by coral bleaching in recent times, but diving still remains world-class, and new sites are still being discovered.

ⓘ Information

Even though they're 1000km east of the mainland, the Andamans still run on Indian time. This means that it can be dark by 5pm and light by 4am; people here tend to be very early risers. All telephone numbers must include the ☎03192 area code, even when dialling locally.

Andaman & Nicobar Tourism (IP&T; ☎232747; www.tourism.andaman.nic.in; Kamaraj Rd, Port Blair; ⊗8.30am-1pm & 2-5pm Mon-Fri, 8.30am-noon Sat) Pick up a copy of the useful tourist booklet the *Emerald Islands* (₹100) either here or from the small branch at the airport.

ACCOMMODATION Prices given in this chapter are for midseason (1 October to 30 April, excluding peak times). They shoot up in peak season (15 December to 15 January). May to September is low season. Camping is currently not permitted on public land or national parks in the islands.

PERMITS Most civil servants come to Port Blair on two-year postings from the mainland. With such a turnover of staff, be aware rules and regulations regarding permits are subject to sudden changes.

All foreigners need a permit to visit the Andaman Islands; it's issued free on arrival. The 30-day permit allows foreigners to stay in Port Blair, South and Middle Andaman (excluding tribal areas), North Andaman (Diglipur), Long Island, North Passage, Little Andaman (excluding tribal areas), and Havelock and Neil Islands. It's possible to get a 15-day extension from either Port Blair at the **Immigration Office** (☎03192-239247; ⊗8.30am-1pm & 2-5.30pm Mon-Fri, until 1pm Sat) or the police station in Havelock.

The permit also allows day trips to Jolly Buoy, South Cinque, Red Skin, Ross, Narcondam, Interview and Rutland Islands, as well as the Brothers and the Sisters.

To obtain the permit, air travellers simply present their passport and fill out a form on arrival at Port Blair airport. Permits are usually issued up to the 30-day maximum (be sure to check).

Boat passengers will probably be met by an immigration official on arrival; if not, seek out the immigration office at Haddo Jetty immediately. Keep your permit on you at all times – you won't be able to travel without it. Police frequently ask to see it, especially when you're disembarking on other islands, and hotels will need permit details. Check current regulations regarding boat travel with any of the following:

Andaman & Nicobar Tourism (☎03192-238473)

Foreigners' Registration Office Chennai (☎044-23454970, 044-28278210); Kolkata (☎033-22470549, 033-22473300)

Shipping Corporation of India (SCI; www.shipindia.com) Chennai (☎044-5231401; Jawahar Bldg, 6 Rajaji Salai); Kolkata (☎033-2482354; 1st fl, 13 Strand Rd)

NATIONAL PARKS & SANCTUARIES Additional permits are required to visit some national parks and sanctuaries. At the tourism office in Port Blair, there's a **Forestry Department Desk** (⊗9am-3pm Mon-Fri, until 1pm Sat) where you can find out whether a permit is needed, how to go about getting it, how much it costs and whether it is in fact possible to get one.

If you plan to do something complicated, you'll be sent to the **Chief Wildlife Warden** (CWW; ☎233321; Haddo Rd, Pt Blair; ⊗8.30am-noon & 1-4pm Mon-Fri) where your application should

---

CAREFUL WITH THE CORAL!

In general, you should only snorkel during high tide in the Andamans. At low tide it's easy to step on coral, irreparably damaging the delicate organisms. Even the sweep of a strong flipper kick can do harm. You also risk a painful sea-urchin spine if you set foot on the seabed. Divers should be extra cautious about descents near reefs; colliding with coral at a hard pace with full gear is environmentally disastrous.

consist of a letter stating your case, the name of the boat and the dates involved; all things being equal, the permit should be issued within the hour.

For most day permits it's not the hassle but the cost. For areas such as Mahatma Gandhi Marine National Park, and Ross and Smith Islands near Diglipur, the permits cost ₹50/500 for Indians/foreigners. For Saddle Peak National Park, also near Diglipur, the cost is ₹25/250.

Students with valid ID pay minimal entry fees, so don't forget to bring your card.

The Nicobar Islands are off-limits to all except Indian nationals engaged in research, government business or trade.

ⓘ Getting There & Away

AIR There are daily flights to Port Blair from Delhi, Kolkata and Chennai, although flights from Delhi and Kolkata are often routed through Chennai. Round-trip fares are between US$250 and US$500 depending on how early you book; some airlines offer one-way flights for as low as US$80, but these need to be booked months in advance. At the time of research, **Kingfisher Airlines** (☑1800 2093030; www.flyingfisher. com) had the cheapest last-minute flights to the islands. Other options include **Air India** (Chennai ☑044-28554747; Kolkata ☑033-22117879; Port Blair ☑03192-233108; www.airindia.com) and **JetLite** (Chennai ☑080-39893333; Kolkata ☑033-25110901; Port Blair ☑03192- 242707; www.jetlite.com).

There are no direct flights from Port Blair to Southeast Asia, though at the time of research a chartered flight was scheduled to fly direct from Kuala Lumpur. But don't get your hopes up.

BOAT Depending on who you ask, the infamous boat to Port Blair is either 'the only *real* way to get to the Andamans' or a hassle and a half. The truth lies somewhere in between. There are usually four to six sailings a month between Port Blair and the Indian mainland – fortnightly to/from Kolkata (56 hours), weekly (in high season) to/from Chennai (60 hours) and monthly to/from Vizag (56 hours). In Chennai you can book tickets through the **Assistant Director of Shipping Services** (☑044-25226873; Rajaji Salai, Chennai Port). **Shipping Corporation of India** (SCI; www.shipindia.com; ☑033-22482354 in Kolkata, 0891-2565597 in Vizag) operates boats from Kolkata and Vizag. The schedule is erratic, so call SCI in advance. All ferries from the mainland arrive at Haddo Jetty.

Take sailing times with a large grain of salt – travellers have reported sitting on the boat at Kolkata harbour for up to 12 hours, or waiting to dock near Port Blair for several hours. With holdups and variable weather and sea conditions, the trip can take three to four days. You can organise your return ticket at the **ferry ticket office** at

Phoenix Bay. Bring two passport photos and a photocopy of your permit. Updated schedules and fares can be found at www.and.nic.in/spsch/sailing.htm.

Classes vary slightly between boats, but the cheapest is bunk (₹1700 to ₹1960), followed by 2nd class B (₹3890), 2nd class A (₹5030), 1st class (₹6320) and deluxe cabins (₹7640). The MV *Akbar* also has AC dorm berths (₹3290). Higher-end tickets cost as much as, if not more than, a plane ticket. If you go bunk, prepare for waking up to a chorus of men 'hwwaaaaching' and spitting, little privacy and toilets that tend to get...unpleasant after three days at sea. That said, it's a good way to meet locals.

Food (tiffin for breakfast, thalis for lunch and dinner) costs around ₹150 per day and are pretty much glop on rice. Bring something (fruit in particular) to supplement your diet. Some bedding is supplied, but if you're travelling bunk class bring a sleeping sheet. Many travellers take a hammock to string up on deck.

There is no official ferry between Port Blair and Thailand, but if there are yachts around you could try to crew. You can't legally get from the Andamans to Myanmar (Burma) by sea, although we hear it's been done with their own boats. Be aware you risk imprisonment or worse from the Indian and Burmese navies if you give this a go.

Bad weather can seriously muck up your itinerary: ferry services are cancelled if the sea is too rough. Build in a few days' buffer to avoid being marooned and missing your flight (which perhaps isn't always a bad thing...).

ⓘ Getting Around

AIR A subsidised interisland helicopter service runs from Port Blair to Little Andaman (₹1488, 35 minutes, Tuesday, Friday and Saturday), Havelock Island (₹850, 20 minutes) and Diglipur via Mayabunder (₹2125 or ₹1915 from Mayabunder, one hour). Priority is given to government workers and the 5kg baggage limit precludes most tourists from using this service. You can chance your luck by applying at the **Secretariat** (☑230093) in Port Blair, returning at 4pm to see if you were successful.

BOAT Most islands can only be reached by water. While this sounds romantic, ferry ticket offices can be hell: expect hot waits, slow service, queue-jumping and a rugby scrum to the ticket window. To hold your spot and advance you need to be a little aggressive (but don't be a jerk) – or be a woman; ladies' queues are a godsend, but they really only apply in Port Blair. You can buy tickets the day you travel by arriving at the appropriate jetty an hour beforehand, but this is risky during high season and not a guarantee on Havelock any time of year. In towns like Rangat, ferry ticket office opening hours are erratic and

ISLAND INDIGENES

The Andaman and Nicobar Islands' indigenous peoples constitute just 12% of the population and, in most cases, their numbers are decreasing. The Onge, Sentinelese, Andamanese and Jawara are all of Negrito ethnicity, who share a strong resemblance to people from Africa. Tragically, numerous groups have become extinct over the past century. In February 2010 the last survivor of the Bo tribe passed away, bringing an end to both the language and 65,000 years of ancestry.

Onge

Two-thirds of Little Andaman's Onge Island was taken over by the Forest Department and 'settled' in 1977. The 100 or so remaining members of the Onge tribe live in a 25-sq-km reserve covering Dugong Creek and South Bay. Anthropologists say the Onge population has declined due to demoralisation through loss of territory.

Sentinelese

The Sentinelese, unlike the other tribes in these islands, have consistently repelled outside contact. For years, contact parties arrived on the beaches of North Sentinel Island, the last redoubt of the Sentinelese, with gifts of coconuts, bananas, pigs and red plastic buckets, only to be showered with arrows, although some encounters have been a little less hostile. About 150 Sentinelese remain.

Andamanese

As they now number only about 50, it seems impossible the Andamanese can escape extinction. There were around 7000 Andamanese in the mid-19th century, but friendliness to colonisers was their undoing, and by 1971 all but 19 of the population had been swept away by measles, syphilis and influenza epidemics. They've been resettled on tiny Strait Island.

Jarawa

The 350 remaining Jarawa occupy the 639-sq-km reserve on South and Middle Andaman Islands. In 1953 the chief commissioner requested that an armed sea plane bomb Jarawa settlements and their territory has been consistently disrupted by the Andaman Trunk Rd, forest clearance and settler and tourist encroachment. Most Jarawa remain hostile to contact.

Shompen

Only about 250 Shompen remain in the forests on Great Nicobar. Seminomadic hunter-gatherers who live along the riverbanks, they have resisted integration and avoid areas occupied by Indian immigrants.

Nicobarese

The 30,000 Nicobarese are the only indigenous people whose numbers are not decreasing. The majority have converted to Christianity and been partly assimilated into contemporary Indian society. Living in village units led by a head man, they farm pigs and cultivate coconuts, yams and bananas. The Nicobarese, who probably descended from people of Malaysia and Myanmar, inhabit a number of islands in the Nicobar group, centred on Car Nicobar, the region worst affected by the 2004 tsunami.

unreliable. At the time of research it was a requirement to bring a photocopy of your permit: organise this before you arrive.

There are regular boat services to Havelock and Neil Islands, as well as Rangat, Mayabunder, Diglipur and Little Andaman. If all else fails, fishermen may be willing to give you a ride for around ₹2000 between, say, Port Blair and Havelock. A schedule of inter-island sailing times can be found at the website www.and.nic.in/spsch/iisailing.htm.

BUS All roads – and ferries – lead to Port Blair, and you'll inevitably spend a night or two here booking onward travel. The main island group –

South, Middle and North Andaman – is connected by road, with ferry crossings and bridges. Cheap state and more expensive private buses run south from Port Blair to Wandoor, and north to Bharatang, Rangat, Mayabunder and finally to Diglipur, 325km north of the capital. The Jarawa reserve closes to most traffic at around 3pm; thus, buses that pass through the reserve leave from around 4am up till 11am.

PRIVATE JEEPS & MINIVANS Hop-on, hop-off affairs connect many villages; you can hire a whole vehicle for an inflated price.

TRAIN Mainland train bookings can be made at the **Railway Bookings office** (☑233042; ⊘8am-12.30pm & 1-2pm), located in the Secretariat's office south of Aberdeen Bazaar, Port Blair; your hotel owners should also be able to help with any onward rail enquires.

Port Blair

POP 100,186

Green, laid-back and occasionally attractive, Port Blair is the main town in the Andamans; a vibrant mix of Indian Ocean inhabitants – Bengalis, Tamils, Nicobarese, Burmese and Telugus. Most travellers don't hang around any longer than necessary (usually one or two days while waiting to book onward travel in the islands, or returning for departure), instead hell-bent on heading straight to the islands. And while 'PB' can't compete with the beaches of Havelock, its fascinating history makes for some outstanding sightseeing.

◉ Sights

Cellular Jail National Memorial   HISTORICAL BUILDING

(GB Pant Rd; admission ₹10, camera/video ₹25/100; ⊘8.45am-12.30pm & 1.30-5pm Tue-Sun) A former British prison that is now a shrine to the political dissidents it once jailed, Cellular Jail National Memorial is worth visiting to understand the important space the Andamans occupy in India's national memory. Construction of the jail began in 1896 and it was completed in 1906 – the original seven wings (several of which were destroyed by the Japanese during WWII) contained 698 cells radiating from a central tower. Like many political prisons, Cellular Jail became something of a university for freedom fighters, who exchanged books, ideas and debates despite walls and wardens.

There's a **sound-and-light show** (adult/child ₹20/10) in English at 6.45pm on Monday, Tuesday and Wednesday.

Anthropological Museum   MUSEUM

(☑03192-232291; MG Rd; admission ₹10; ⊘9am-1pm & 1.30-4.30pm Fri-Wed) The best museum in Port Blair provides a thorough and sympathetic portrait of the islands' indigenous tribal communities. The glass display cases may be old school, but they don't feel anywhere near as ancient as the simple geometric patterns etched into a Jarawa chest guard, a skull left in a Sentinelese lean-to or the totemic spirits represented by Nicobarese shamanic sculptures. Pick up a pamphlet (₹20) on indigenous culture, written by local anthropologists, in the gift shop.

Samudrika Marine Museum   MUSEUM

(Haddo Rd; adult/child ₹20/10, camera/video ₹20/50; ⊘9am-1pm & 2-5pm Tue-Sun) Run by the Indian Navy, this museum has a diverse range of exhibits with informative coverage of the islands' ecosystem, tribal communities, plants, animals and marine life (including a small aquarium). Outside is a skeleton of a blue whale washed ashore on Kamorta Island in the Nicobars.

Chatham Saw Mill   HISTORICAL SITE

(admission ₹10; ⊘8.30am-2.30pm Mon-Sat) Located on Chatham Island (reached by a road bridge), the saw mill was set up by the British in 1836 and was one of the largest wood processors in Asia. The mill is still operational and, while it may not be to everyone's taste – especially conservationists – it's an interesting insight to the island's history and economy. There's also a large crater from a bomb dropped by the Japanese in WWII, and a rather dismal forest museum.

Corbyn's Cove   BEACH

No one comes to Port Blair for the beach but, if you need a sand fix, Corbyn's Cove, 7km south of town, is your best bet. It's a small curve of coast backed by palms that's popular with locals and Indian tourists, and it's a good spot for swimming and sunset. An autorickshaw ride from town costs about ₹200. Otherwise hiring a motorcycle is a good way to travel this coastal road, and you'll encounter numerous Japanese WWII bunkers along the way.

Burmese Buddhist Mission   SACRED SITE

This tiny bell-shaped stupa (shrine) is not particularly impressive, but it's an incongruous example of Burmese Buddhist architecture in India and a reminder that you're way closer to Southeast Asia than the subcontinent.

Port Blair

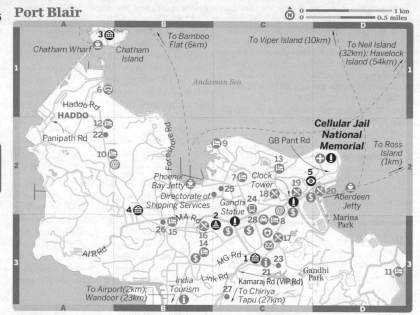

Activities

The following dive companies specialise in sites south of Port Blair. All are fairly new on the scene, but offer a great alternative to diving outside Ritchie's Archipelago. Suited for divers of all levels.

Planet Scuba India DIVING
(242287; www.planetscubaindia.com; Foreshore Rd, Haddo) The only dive company in Port Blair, Planet Scuba runs dives to Mahatma Gandhi NP and Cinque. Stocks diving equipment.

Lacadives DIVING
(9679532104; www.lacadives.com) Based just outside Wandoor, specialising in more remote areas of Mahatma Gandhi National Park, avoiding the crowds of Red Skin and Jolly Buoy.

Infinity Scuba DIVING
(281183; www.infinityscubandamans.com) Located in Chiriya Tapu, Infinity's main destination is Cinque Island; also visiting Rutland Island and a wrecked ship.

Tours

Andaman & Nicobar Tourism TOURS
(IP&T; 232694; www.tourism.andaman.nic. in; Kamaraj Rd; 8.30am-1pm & 2-5pm Mon-Fri, 8.30am-noon Sat) Runs Port Blair city tours

(₹52), as well tours to Ross Island (₹75), Mt Harriet (₹157), Wandoor via spice and rubber plantations (₹105), Corbyn's Cove (₹52), Chiriya Tapu (₹105) snorkelling trips to Jolly Buoy and Redskin Islands (₹450), and a tour of Ross and Viper Islands and North Bay (₹360). Trip times vary throughout the week.

Sleeping

Most of the hotels are around the Aberdeen Bazaar area. The airport is about 4km south of town. Midrange accommodation is often booked out solidly from September to December by Indian package tours.

TOP CHOICE Aashiaanaa Rest Home GUESTHOUSE $
(09474217008; shads_maria@hotmail; Marine Hill; r ₹300-900; ✵) Run by the incredibly friendly Shadab and his lovely family, the Aashiaanaa has a lot of 'As' in the name and love in its heart. Rooms are spotless and spacious, and the more expensive ones have nice views over town. It's conveniently just up the hill from Phoenix Bay Jetty.

Hotel Sinclairs Bayview HOTEL $$$
(03192-227824; www.sinclairshotels.com; South Point; r from ₹5300; ✵≋) Located 2km outside town, on the road to Corbyn's Cove, Sinclairs' big comfy rooms have the best views in town, opening right out to the water. It has nice

seaside gardens with hammocks to lounge in, and several Japanese WWII bunkers on-site.

Fortune Resort – Bay Island   HOTEL $$$
(☎03192-234101; www.fortunehotels.in, reserva tions.frbi@fortunehotels.in; Marine Hill; s/d from ₹5500/6200; ❉@☲) Perched above the ocean with fine sea views from its terraced garden and balcony restaurant, Fortune boasts a fine location. The rooms, while comfortable with polished floors, balconies and island bric-a-brac, are small; make sure to ask for a sea-facing room.

Hotel Tejas   HOTEL $$
(☎03192-221698; www.hoteltejas.mobi; Haddo Rd; r from ₹750; ❉) Sparkling rooms of the linoleum-floor-and-comfy-enough-bed sort perch over a hill, a tangled clump of jungle and a sweeping view of Haddo Jetty.

Azad Lodge   GUESTHOUSE $
(☎03192-242646; MA Rd, Aberdeen Bazaar; s/d from ₹250/450, without bathroom ₹150/250) One of the best budget options in town, Azad's rooms are clean and cheap, though singles without bathroom are like prison cells.

Hotel Driftwood   HOTEL $$
(☎03192-244044; hoteldriftwood@rediffmail.com; JN Rd, Haddo; r from ₹1600; ❉☏) The mid-range Driftwood makes a fine choice for those wanting comfort at reasonable prices. Rooms are sunny and a decent size; the pricier ones have lovely views of lush jungle. It has smiley staff, a good restaurant with an attached outdoor bar (karaoke night Saturdays), and wi-fi access in the lobby.

TSG Emerald   HOTEL $$
(☎03192-246488; www.andamantsghotels.com; MA Rd, Haddo; r from ₹2000; ❉☏) While a business-chic hotel may not necessarily suit the Andamans, this place is pretty plush with sleek, sparkling, modern rooms. Also has a nautical themed bar upstairs.

Other good cheapies:

Amina Lodge   GUESTHOUSE $
(☎9933258703; aminalodge@ymail.com; Aberdeen Bazaar; s/d ₹300/400) Run by a friendly couple, Amina has good-value rooms in the thick of the action. It can get noisy, so ask for a room away from the main road. Bicycle hire is possible.

Lalaji Bay View   GUESTHOUSE $
(☎9933222010; lalajibayviewbookings@gmail. com; RP Rd, Dugnabad; r from ₹250) Set among ramshackle colonial buildings, Lalaji Bay is a good budget option with clean rooms and attractive bedspreads.

Sai Residency GUESTHOUSE $
(☎9434262965; r from ₹400; ✸) This small, family-run affair has some spic-and-span rooms in a central location tucked down a small street.

✗ Eating

TOP CHOICE Bayview MULTICUISINE $$$
(Southpoint; mains from ₹110-500; ⊙11am-11pm) Right on the water with a lovely cool sea breeze, the Bayview is a great spot for lunch. While the grilled fish is delicious and the beer cold, this place is still more about the location than the food. Ask the friendly staff to show you the Japanese WWII bunkers on the premises. An autorickshaw will cost ₹40.

Lighthouse Residency INDIAN $$
(MA Rd, Aberdeen Bazaar; mains ₹60-280; ⊙11am-11pm) The Lighthouse is lit like a fluorescent nightmare, but the air-conditioning is cranked, the beer's cold and seafood fresh. Choose from the display of red snapper, crab or tiger prawns. The BBQ fish is sensational. Its sister restaurant, **New Lighthouse Residency**, further up the road, is open air, but there's no alcohol.

Annapurna INDIAN $
(MG Rd; mains from ₹40) Annapurna is an extremely popular veg option that looks like a high-school cafeteria and serves consistently good karma-friendly fare, ranging from crisp southern dosas to rich North Indian-style curries.

Mandalay Restaurant INDIAN, WESTERN $$$
(Marine Hill; buffet breakfast/lunch or dinner ₹200/350) If you need to splurge, you can do a lot worse than the Mandalay's excellent buffet meals, heavy with Indian and Western faves served on either an attractive deck or in a not-quite-as-appealing Burmese-themed interior.

Gagan Restaurant INDIAN $
(Clock tower, Aberdeen Bazaar; mains from ₹40; ⊙7am-9pm) Popular with locals, this hole-in-the-wall place serves up great food at good prices, including seafood curries, coconut chicken, and dosas for breakfast.

Adi Bengali Hotel BENGALI $
(MA Rd; mains from ₹30; ⊙7am-3pm & 6-10pm) This energetic canteen does a brisk stock-in-trade in spicy fish curries and other West Bengal staples. Everything's prepared pretty well, if the usual clientele of silent, satisfied Bengali labourers is any proof.

ℹ Information

Port Blair is the only place in the Andamans where you can change cash or travellers cheques. There are ATMs all over town, and a Western Union office by the post office. There are a few internet places in Aberdeen Bazaar.

Aberdeen Police Station (☎03192-232400; MG Rd)

Andaman & Nicobar Tourism (IP&T; ☎232694; www.tourism.andaman.nic.in; Kamaraj Rd; ⊙8.30am-1pm & 2-5pm Mon-Fri, 8.30am-noon Sat) The main island tourist office, and place to book government accommodation and get wildlife permits. Staff are helpful, if laid-back.

e-Cafe (internet per hr ₹30; ⊙8am-midnight) In Aberdeen Bazaar, just before the Clock Tower.

GB Pant Hospital (☎03192-233473, 232102; GB Pant Rd)

Main post office (MG Rd; ⊙9am-7pm Mon-Sat)

State Bank of India (MA Rd; ⊙9am-noon & 1-3pm Mon-Fri, 10am-noon Sat) Travellers cheques and foreign currency can be changed here.

ℹ Getting There & Away

See p398 for details on transport to and from the Andaman Islands. The airport is about 4km south of town.

Boat

All interisland ferries depart from Phoenix Bay Jetty. Tickets can be purchased from the **ferry booking office** (⊙9am-1pm & 2-4pm Mon-Sat). On some boats tickets can be purchased on board, but in high season you risk missing out. Most people head straight to Havelock (₹195, 2½ hours), with two or more ferries departing daily; those not wanting to hang around Port Blair should make the jetty their first port of call to book tickets. Don't forget to bring a photocopy of your permit. Another option is the privately owned **Makruzz ferry** (www.makruzz.com) operating on Tuesday, Thursday and Saturday in high season (from ₹650, two hours). Tickets are available from the airport or travel agents in Aberdeen Bazaar.

From Chatham Wharf there are hourly passenger ferries to Bamboo Flat (₹3, 15 minutes).

Bus

There are buses all day from the bus stand at Aberdeen Bazaar to Wandoor (₹12, 1½ hours) and Chiriya Tapu (₹10, 1½ hours). Two buses run at 4am and 4.30am to Diglipur (₹170, 12 hours) and at 5am and 9.30am to Mayabunder (₹130, nine hours) via Rangat (₹95, seven hours) and Baratang (₹55, three hours). More comfortable private buses are also available; their 'offices' (a guy with a ticket book) are located across from the main bus stand.

ℹ Getting Around

TO/FROM THE AIRPORT A taxi or autorickshaw from the airport to Aberdeen Bazaar costs around ₹50. There are also hourly buses (₹5) to/from airport, located 100m outside the complex, to the main bus stand.

BUS The central area is easy enough to walk around, but to get out to Corbyn's Cove, Haddo or Chatham Island you'll need some form of transport.

MOTORBIKE Unfortunately you can no longer hire bicycles in Port Blair, but you can hire a motorbike or scooter from **Govindamma & Co** (☑9732486858; MA Rd; per 24hr ₹400), which is a perfect way to explore south of Port Blair.

AUTORICKSHAW From Aberdeen Bazaar to Phoenix Bay Jetty is about ₹20 and to Haddo Jetty it's around ₹40.

Around Port Blair & South Andaman

ROSS ISLAND

Visiting Ross Island (not to be confused with its namesake island in North Andaman) feels like discovering a jungle-clad Lost City, à la Angkor Wat, where the ruins happen to be Victorian English rather than ancient Khmer. The former administrative headquarters for the British in the Andamans, **Ross Island** (admission ₹20) is an essential half-day trip from Port Blair. In its day, little Ross was fondly called the 'Paris of the East' (along with Pondicherry, Saigon etc...). But the cute title, vibrant social scene and tropical gardens were all wiped out by the double whammy of a 1941 earthquake and the invasion of the Japanese (who left behind some machine-gun nests that are great fun to poke around in).

Today the old English architecture is still standing, even as it is swallowed by a green wave of fast-growing jungle. Landscaped paths cross the island and most of the buildings are labelled. There's a small museum with historical displays and photos of Ross Island in its heyday, and a small park where resident deer nibble on bushes.

Ferries to Ross Island (₹75, 20 minutes) depart from the jetty behind the aquarium in Port Blair at 8.30am, 10.30am, 12.30pm and 2pm every day other than Wednesday; check when you buy your ticket, as times can be affected by tides.

You can also catch a 9.30am ferry to **Viper Island** (₹75), where you'll find the ruins of gallows built by the British in 1867, but it's a fairly forgettable excursion.

WANDOOR & MAHATMA GANDHI MARINE NATIONAL PARK

Wandoor, a tiny speck of a village 29km southwest of Port Blair, has a nice beach (though at the time of research, swimming was prohibited due to crocodiles being sighted in the area), but is better known as a jumping-off point for **Mahatma Gandhi Marine National Park** (Indian/foreigner ₹50/500). Covering 280 sq km it comprises 15 islands of mangrove creeks, tropical rainforest and reefs supporting 50 types of coral. The marine park's snorkelling sites alternate between **Jolly Buoy** (☉1 Nov-15 May) and **Red Skin** (☉16 May-30 Oct), a popular day trip from Wandoor Jetty (₹450; Tuesday to Sunday). That said, if Havelock or Neil Islands are on your Andamans itinerary, it's probably easier and cheaper to wait until you reach them for your underwater experience; unless you're willing to pay through the nose, boats simply don't linger long enough for you to get a good snorkelling experience. **Lacadives** (☑9679532104; www.lacadives.com) is worth getting in touch with if you want to explore the area properly. There are several places to stay in Wandoor. Permits can be arranged at Wandoor jetty or the tourist office in Port Blair.

Buses run from Port Blair to Wandoor (₹12, 1½ hours).

CHIRIYA TAPU

Chiriya Tapu, 30km south of Port Blair, is a tiny village of beaches, mangroves and, about 2km south, some of the best **snorkelling** outside Havelock and Neil Islands. It's a great spot place to watch the sunset. There are seven buses a day to the village from Port Blair (₹10, 1½ hours) and it's possible to arrange boats from here to Cinque Island. The new **biological park** (Indian/foreigner ₹20/50; ☉9am-4pm Tue-Sun) is still a work in progress (scheduled for completion in 2015), but has a pleasant forested setting with spacious, natural enclosures for crocodiles, deer and wart hog.

CINQUE ISLAND

The uninhabited islands of North and South Cinque, connected by a sandbar, are part of the wildlife sanctuary south of Wandoor. The islands are surrounded by coral reefs, and are among the most beautiful in the Andamans.

Only day visits are allowed but, unless you're on one of the day trips occasionally organised by travel agencies, you need to get permission in advance from the Chief Wildlife Warden (p398). The islands are two hours by boat from Chiriya Tapu or 3½ hours from Wandoor, and are covered by the **Mahatma Gandhi Marine National Park permit** (Indian/foreigner ₹50/500). See p396 for info on diving opportunities in Cinque Island.

Havelock Island

With snow-white beaches, teal shallows, dark jungle hills, a coast crammed with beach huts and backpackers from around the world, Havelock's one of those budget-travel tropical gems that, in a few years, will have the same cachet as Thailand's Ko Pha-Ngan if not the nightlife. There are quietly buzzing social scenes concentrated around the common area of the beach hut resorts, but nothing approaching full-moon party madness. Besides for doing nothing, Havelock is a popular spot for snorkelling and diving, and many are content to stay here for the entire duration of their visit to the Andamans.

◉ Sights & Activities

Havelock is the premier spot for **scuba diving** on the Andamans, and the main reason why most tourists jump straight on the ferry here. There's no shortage of dive operator options, with places set up along the main tourist strip; it's just a matter of checking out a few and going with the one you feel most comfortable with.

The **snorkelling** here is equally impressive. The best way to get out is to organise a *dunghi* (motorised wooden boat) through your hotel. Trips cost from ₹1000 to ₹2000, depending on the number of people going, distance involved etc – if you go with a good-sized group you may pay as low as ₹250 per head. Snorkelling gear is widely available on Havelock from resorts and small restaurants, but is generally very low quality.

Fishing is another popular activity, likewise best organised through your hotel. There are also several sports-fishing operators in town.

Some resorts can organise guided **jungle treks** for keen walkers or birdwatchers, but be warned the forest floor turns to glug after rain. The inside rainforest is a spectacular, emerald cavern, and the **birdwatching** – especially on the forest fringes – is rewarding; look out for the blue-black racket-tailed drongo trailing his fabulous tail feathers and, by way of contrast, the brilliant golden oriole.

About 5km beyond No 5 Village, you'll find Kalapathar, where there's an **elephant training camp**; at the time of research there were plans to give demonstrations of working elephants in action. Beyond Kalapathar the road passes another pristine beach and then peters out into forest.

Radha Nagar Beach   BEACH

The prettiest and most popular stretch of stretch of sand is the critically acclaimed Radha Nagar Beach, also known as **beach No 7**. It's a beautiful curve of sugar fronted by perfectly spiralled waves, all backed by native forest that might have grown out of a postcard. And the sunsets? Pretty damn nice. The drive out to the beach, located on

---

CROCODILES

The tragic death of an American tourist attacked by a saltwater crocodile while snorkelling in Havelock on April 2010 sent shockwaves through the community. While crocodiles are a way of life in many parts of the Andamans, they've never been sighted where the incident took place at Neil's Cove, near Radha Nagar. Furthermore, an attack occurring in the open ocean on a coral reef was considered extremely unusual. There are numerous theories about how the crocodile got there; most likely it was ousted from its mangrove habitat on the western side of the island, in a territorial dispute. The crocodile was eventually captured (now residing in Port Blair's zoo) and there have been no sightings since – a high level of vigilance remains in place. General consensus is that it was an isolated incident, and it should not deter people from swimming, though it's important you keep informed, heed any warnings by authorities and, on the western side of the island, don't swim alone and avoid being in the water at dawn or dusk.

Other tourist spots for which warnings have been issued include Corbyn's Cove, Wandoor Beach, Baratang and all over Little Andaman.

the northwestern side of the island about 12km from the jetty, runs through the green dream that is inland Havelock (autorick-shaws will take you for about ₹150), or otherwise the bus runs here from No 1 Village when it pleases. Ten minutes' walk along the beach to the northwest is the gorgeous '**lagoon**' at Neils Cove, another gem of sheltered sand and crystalline water. There was a crocodile attack here in 2010, so it might be worth checking if it's safe for swimming (see boxed text, p400). In high season you can take an **elephant ride** (adult/child ₹25/15; ⊙11am-2pm Mon-Sat) along the beach, posing for that quintessential cheesy snap.

Elephant Beach BEACH

Elephant Beach, where there's good **snorkelling**, is further north and reached by a 40-minute walk through a muddy elephant logging trail; it's well marked (off the cross-island road), but hard going after rain. The beach itself virtually disappeared after the 2004 tsunami and at high tide it's impossible to reach – ask locally. Lots of snorkelling charters come out this way, and there are lifeguards who will reprimand anyone who litters – God bless them.

Beach 5 BEACH

On the other side of the island from Radha Nagar, Beach No 5 is paradise. Its palm-ringed beaches give it that added relaxed feel, and it has shady patches and less sandflies than Radar Nagar. However, swimming is very difficult in low tide when water becomes shallow for miles. Most of the island's accommodation is out this way.

Dive India DIVING
(☏091-9932082204; www.diveindia.com; btwn No 3 & 5 Village)

Andaman Bubbles DIVING
(☏282140; www.andamanbubbles.com; No 5 Village)

Barefoot Scuba DIVING
(☏282181; www.barefootindia.com; No 3 Village)

🛏 Sleeping & Eating

Most hotels in Havelock are of the cluster-of-beach-hut genre. They all claim to be 'eco' huts ('eco' apparently meaning 'cheap building material'), but they are great value for money, especially in low season.

All listed accommodation has passable menus of backpacker-oriented Western and Indian food. If you desire something more authentically Indian, head to the cheap food stalls in town (No 1 Village) or the main bazaar (No 3 Village). There's a 'wine shop' in No 1 Village.

Most of the accommodation is strung along the east coast between villages No 2 and No 5.

TOP CHOICE **Eco Villa** BUNGALOWS $$
(☏282212; www.havelock.co.in/ecovilla; Beach 2; huts ₹300-3000) The original, and still the best, Eco Villa is the only place with huts right on the beachfront. It caters to all budgets, from the two-storey bamboo duplex huts, tastefully decorated with pot plants, to simple bamboo bungalows, all of which open up to the water. The restaurant gets pretty damn romantic at night, when the moon rises over deep-blue ocean evenings. Accepts credit cards.

Orient Legend Resort GUESTHOUSE $
(☏282389; Beach 5; huts ₹300-1000, without bathroom ₹100-250) A very popular choice, this sprawling place covers most budgets, and is one of the few guesthouses where you can actually see the water from your room.

Wild Orchid HOTEL $$$
(☏282472; www.wildorchidandaman.com; d cottages from ₹3000; ✳@) Set back from a secluded beach, this is a mellow, friendly place with tastefully furnished cottages designed in traditional Andamanese style. The restaurant, **Red Snapper** (mains ₹100-350), is the best in town, with a great islander ambience. The fresh tuna pasta is magnifico, and tiger prawns out of this world.

Emerald Gecko BUNGALOWS $$
(☏282170; www.emerald-gecko.com; huts ₹750-2250) This is a step up in quality from other hut resorts. There are four comfortable double-storey huts with open-roofed bathrooms, lovingly constructed from bamboo rafts that drifted ashore from Myanmar. There are some budget huts too, and the **Blackbeard** restaurant has a quality menu designed by the same folk as Wild Orchid.

Barefoot at Havelock HOTEL $$$
(☏reservation 044-24341001; www.barefootindia.com; cottages ₹7100-9700; ✳) For the location alone – ensconced in bird-filled forest grounds just back from Radha Nagar Beach – this is Havelock's most luxurious resort, boasting beautifully designed timber and bamboo-thatched cottages. The **restaurant** (mains ₹180-450) with Italian chef serves up

everything from Indian to Thai, making for a nice romantic splurge.

Dreamland Resort   GUESTHOUSE $
(☎9474224164; Beach 5; huts ₹300) In a prime location, only 50m from Radha Nagar 7, Dreamland has simple thatched bungalows and very friendly owners.

Green Land Resort   GUESTHOUSE $
(☎9933220620; huts ₹200-250, without bathroom ₹150-200) This is the spot for those wanting peace and quiet, with simple huts arranged in a jungle of fruit trees. It's only a 15-minute walk to Radha Nagar.

Coconut Lodge   GUESTHOUSE $
(☎282056; huts ₹200-500) Popular with Israeli travellers, Coconut Lodge is the place to head to if you want to party. Huts are arranged in a weird circular outlay that directs everyone to a raised, concrete platform where the entire lodge usually ends up carousing.

Anju-coco Resto   INDIAN, CONTINENTAL $
(mains ₹120-250) Charming little restaurant run by a friendly owner, features a varied menu with tasty BBQ fish in the high season. The big breakfast (₹60) is indeed big, and a good choice.

B3 – Barefoot Bar & Restaurant   PIZZA $$
(Village No 1; mains ₹150-500; ⊙11am-4pm & 6-9.30pm) Modern decor with classic movie posters on the walls; there's a Western-heavy menu, with the best pizzas in Havelock. Outdoor seating is pleasant, but overlooks the unattractive jetty.

These places also have great Western food and a relaxed ambience:

Full Moon Cafe   WESTERN $
(mains ₹90-180) At Dive India.

Café Del Mar   WESTERN $
(mains ₹70-200) At Barefoot Scuba.

❶ Information

There are two ATMs side by side in No 3 Village, where you can also find painfully slow **internet** (per hour ₹80).

❶ Getting There & Away

Ferry times are changeable, but there are always direct sailings to and from Havelock from Port Blair at least once daily, and often twice or more (tourist ferry ₹195, 2½ hours). You'd best book tickets at least a day in advance. The ticket office is open between 9am and 11am. Otherwise you could try the more comfortable Makruzz (from ₹650, two hours).

Several government ferries a week link Havelock with Neil Island (₹195). It's also the most convenient launching point to get to Long Island (₹195), en route to Rangat where buses continue to North Andaman.

❶ Getting Around

A local bus (₹7) connects the jetty and villages on a roughly hourly circuit, but having your own transport is useful here. You can hire mopeds or motorbikes (per day from ₹250) and bicycles (per day ₹40 to ₹50) from your hotel or otherwise in No 3 Village.

An autorickshaw from the jetty to No 3 Village is ₹30, to No 5 ₹50 and to No 7 ₹150 to ₹200.

Neil Island

Happy to laze in the shadows of its more famous island neighbour, Neil is still the place for that added bit of relaxation. Its beaches may not be quite as luxurious as Havelock's, but they have ample character and are a perfect distance apart to explore by bicycle. There's a lovely unhurried pace of life here; cycling through picturesque villages you'll get many friendly hellos from kids and adults alike. In Neil Island you're about 40km from Port Blair, a short ferry ride from Havelock and several universes away from life at home

At the time of research there were no internet or moneychanging facilities. There's a post office in the bazaar.

◉ Sights & Activities

Neil Island's five **beaches** (numbered one to five) all have their unique charms. **No 1** is the prettiest and most accessible, a 40-minute walk west of the jetty and village. The island's best **snorkelling** is around the coral reef at the far (western) end of this beach at high tide. There's a good sunset viewpoint out this way accessed via Pearl Park Resort, which becomes a communal spot in the sand for tourists and locals come early evening.

No 2, on the north side of the island, has the **Natural Bridge** rock formation, accessible only at low tide by walking around the rocky cove. To get here by bicycle take the side road that runs through the bazaar, then take a left where the road forks. The best swimming is at **No 4**, though its proximity to the jetty is a slight turn off. **No 3** is a secluded powdery sand cove, which is best accessed via Blue Sea Restaurant. Further ahead the more wild and rugged **No 5**

(5km from the village), reached via the village road to the eastern side of the island, is a nice place to walk along the beach, with small limestone caves accessible at low tide.

You can dive with **India Scuba Explorers** (☑9474238646; www.indiascubaexplorers.com), while snorkelling gear can hired (per day ₹150) at your hotel or around town. If you're extremely lucky you may spot a **dugong** at No 1 Beach feeding in the shallows at high tide. Hiring a fishing boat to go to offshore snorkelling or fishing will cost between ₹1000 and ₹2000 depending on how far out you want to travel, how long you choose to snorkel etc; several people can usually fit on board.

The main bazaar has a mellow vibe, and is a popular gathering spot in the early evening. **Cooking classes** (from ₹200) can be arranged at Gyan Garden Restaurant. Behind the restaurant is a track up the small hill that leads to a **viewpoint** across the island and out to sea.

🛏 Sleeping & Eating

In the low season there are great deals on simple beach huts. The most popular places to stay are **Tango Beach Resort** (☑03192-282583; huts ₹50-350, cottages ₹600-1000) and **Pearl Park Resort** (☑03192-282510; huts ₹100-250, cottages & r ₹400-1600) both at No 1 Beach. Their proximity and same-sameness makes them feel like identical sides of a double-headed coin; both offer nice thatch huts and less interesting, if more comfortable, concrete rooms. The main difference is that Tango has ocean views and a sea breeze, while Pearl Park has the sunset point and lush garden surrounds. **A-N-D Beach Resort** (☑214722; huts ₹300-700) is another good option on No 4 Beach.

Eating is surprisingly good on Neil Island. You'll find cheap and delicious Bengali food in the market.

Moonshine (mains ₹40-150) on the road to No 1 Beach is a backpacker favourite, cooking up excellent home-made pasta dishes (the prawn pasta is amazing), with cold beer. In the market, **Chand Restaurant** (mains ₹50-200) is also popular, with strong filter coffee and delicious BBQ fish. **Gyan Garden Restaurant** (mains ₹50-200) has a good seafood selection.

❶ Getting There & Around

A ferry makes a round trip each morning from Phoenix Bay Jetty in Port Blair (₹195, two hours). There's also a daily ferry to Havelock in either the morning or early afternoon.

Hiring a bicycle (per day from ₹50) is the best way to get about; roads are flat and distances short. An autorickshaw will take you to No 1 Beach from the jetty for ₹50.

Middle & North Andaman

The Andamans aren't just sun and sand. They're also jungle that feels as primeval as the Jurassic and as thick as the Amazon, a green tangle of ancient forest that could have been birthed in Mother Nature's subconscious. This shaggy, wild side of the islands can be seen on a long, loping bus ride up the Andaman Trunk Rd (ATR). Going to Diglipur by road thrusts you onto bumpy roads framed by antediluvian trees and roll-on, roll-off ferries that cross red-tannin rivers prowled by saltwater crocodiles.

But there's a negative side to riding the ATR: the road cuts through the homeland of the Jarawa and has brought the tribe into incessant contact with the outside world. Modern Indian and tribal life do not seem able to coexist – every time Jarawa and settlers interact, misunderstandings have led to friction, confusion and, at worst, violent attacks and death. Indian anthropologists and indigenous rights groups like Survival International have called for the ATR to be closed; its status is under review at time of writing (see p394). At present, vehicles are permitted to travel only in convoys at set times from 6am to 3pm. Photography is strictly prohibited, as is stopping or any other interaction with the Jarawa people – who are becoming increasingly reliant on handouts from passing traffic.

The first place of interest north of Port Blair is the impressive **limestone caves** (☺closed Mon) at Baratang. It's a 45-minute boat trip (₹200) from the jetty, a scenic trip through mangrove forest. A **permit** is required, organised at the jetty.

Rangat is the next main town, a transport hub with not much else going for it. If you do get stuck here, try **Hotel PLS Bhawan** (s/d from ₹150/250; ✸), the best of a bad bunch. There's an ATM nearby. Ferries depart to/from Port Blair and Havelock Island (₹50/195, nine hours), as well as Long Island (₹7) from Yeratta Jetty, 8km from Rangat. A daily bus goes to Port Blair (₹95, seven hours).

Between December and March, Hawksbill turtles nest on the beaches at **Cuthbert Bay**, a 45-minute drive from Rangat. Any northbound bus will drop you here. **Hawksbill Nest** (☎03192-279022; 4-bed dm ₹600, d ₹400, with AC ₹800; ❋) is the only place to stay; bookings must be made at A&N Tourism in Port Blair. A permit (₹250) can be organised at the ranger office in Betapur

LONG ISLAND

With its friendly island community and lovely slow pace of life, Long Island is perfect for those wanting to take the pace down even a few more notches. There are no motorised vehicles on the island, and at times you're likely to be the only tourist here.

A 1½-hour trek in the jungle (not advisable after heavy rain) will lead you to the secluded **Lalaji Bay**, a beautiful white-sand beach with good swimming. Hiring a *dunghi* (₹1500 return) makes it much easier – especially if you don't like leeches. You can also get a *dunghi* to North Passage island for snorkelling at the stunning **Merk Bay** with its blinding white sand and translucent waters. Trips to South Button are also possible from here.

🏝 **Blue Planet** (☎9474212180; www.blue planetandamans.com; r with/without bathroom from ₹300/700; @) is not only a great place to stay, it also sets an excellent example by incorporating bottles washed ashore into its architecture. Its simple rooms are set around a lovely Padauk tree, with hammocks strung about. Food is available, as well as very slow internet. Follow the blue arrows from the jetty to get here. It also has private cottages (₹2000 to ₹3000) at a nearby location. No alcohol is sold on Long Island, so you'll have to stock up beforehand.

There are three ferries a week to Havelock and Port Blair (₹195), and daily service to Rangat (₹8).

MAYABUNDER & AROUND

In 'upper' Middle Andaman, there are several villages inhabited by Karen, members of a Burmese hill tribe who were relocated here during the British colonial period. In Mayabunder, stop at **Sea'n'Sand** (☎03192-273454; thanzin_the_great@yahoo.co.in; r from ₹200; ❋), a simple lodge, restaurant and bar overlooking the water 1km south of the town centre. Run by Titus and Elizabeth and their extended Karen family, it's low-key and will appeal to travellers looking for an experience away from the crowds. You can go on a range of **boat-based day tours** (per tour from ₹500-2500) that, depending on the season, may include visits to **Forty One Caves** where

hawabills make their highly prized edible nests; snorkelling off **Avis Island**; or jungle trekking at creepy **Interview Island**, where there's a small population of wild elephants, released after a logging company closed for business in the 1950s. You'll feel very off the beaten trek here. A permit (₹500) is required, best organised through Sea'n'Sand.

Mayabunder, 71km north of Rangat, is linked by daily buses from Port Blair (₹130, 10 hours) and by thrice-weekly ferries (Tuesday, Thursday and Friday). There's an unreliable ATM here.

DIGLIPUR & AROUND

Those who make it this far north are well rewarded with some impressive attractions in the area. Though don't expect anything of **Diglipur**, the northernmost major town in the Andamans, which is a sprawling, gritty bazaar town with an ATM and slow **internet connection** (per hr ₹40). You should instead head straight for **Kalipur**, where you'll find lodging and vistas of the ocean and outlying islands.

Ferries arrive at Aerial Bay Jetty from where it's 11km southwest to Diglipur, the bus stand and Administration Block, where boat tickets can be booked. Kalipur is on the coast 8km southeast of the jetty.

◉ Sights & Activities

Leatherback, hawksbill, olive ridley and green **turtles** all nest along the Diglipur coastline between December and April. Tourists can assist with collecting eggs for hatching; contact Pristine Beach Resort for more information. The area also has a number of caves.

Islands   BEACH, SNORKELLING

Like lovely tropical counterweights, the twin islands of **Smith** and **Ross** are connected by a narrow sandbar. Since this is designated as a marine sanctuary, to visit you must get a permit from the **Forest Office** (Indian/foreigner ₹50/500; ⊙6am-2pm Mon-Sat) opposite Aerial Bay Jetty. These islands are up there with the best in the Andamans, and the snorkelling is amazing. You can charter a boat to take you for the day from the village for ₹1000.

Craggy Island, a small island off Kalipur, also has good snorkelling. Strong swimmers can reach here, otherwise a *dunghi* is available (₹200 return).

Saddle Peak   TREKKING

At 732m, Saddle Peak is the highest point in the Andamans. You can trek through subtropical forest to the top and back from Kalipur in about six hours; the views from the peaks onto the archipelago are incredible. Again, a permit (Indian ₹25, foreigner ₹250) is required from the Forest Office and a local guide will make sure you don't get lost – ask at Pristine Beach Resort. Otherwise follow the red arrows marked on the trees.

🍴 Sleeping & Eating

TOP CHOICE **Pristine Beach Resort** GUESTHOUSE (☏9474286787; www.andamanpristineresorts.com; tents ₹150, huts ₹250-1000, r ₹2500; ❉@) This pretty spot huddled among the palms between paddy fields and the beach has several simple bamboo huts on stilts, as well as more romantic bamboo 'tree houses' and upmarket rooms, and a restaurant-bar. Alex, the super-friendly owner, is a great source of information. The resort also rents bicycles/motorcycles (per day ₹60/250).

ℹ Getting There & Around

Diglipur, located about 80km north of Mayabunder, is served by daily buses to/from Port Blair (₹170, 12 hours), as well as buses to Mayabunder (₹50, 2½ hours) and Rangat (₹70, 4½ hours). There are also daily ferries from Port Blair to Diglipur, returning overnight from Diglipur (seat/bunk ₹100/295, 10 hours).

Buses run from Diglupur to Kalipur (₹10) every 30 minutes; an autorickshaw costs about ₹100.

Little Andaman

Named Gaubolambe by the indigenous Onge, Little Andaman is as far south as you can go in the islands. There's an end-of-the-world (in tropical paradise) feeling here: barely any tourists visit, the locals are so friendly they feel like family, and the island itself is a gorgeous fist of mangroves, jungle and teal plucked from a twinkle in nature's eye.

Badly hit by the 2004 Boxing Day tsunami, Little Andaman has slowly rebuilt itself, and while there's still zero tourist infrastructure, new guesthouses are starting to open up. Located about 120km south of Port Blair, the main settlement here is **Hut Bay**, a pleasant small town that primarily produces smiling Bengalis and Tamils. North of here you'll find isolated beaches as fresh as bread out of the oven.

◎ Sights & Activities

Netaji Nagar Beach, 11km north of Hut Bay, and **Butler Bay**, a further 3km north, are gorgeous, deserted (apart from the odd cow) and great for surfing.

Inland, the **White Surf** and **Whisper Wave waterfalls** offer a forest experience (the latter involves a 4km jungle trek and a guide is highly recommended); they're pleasant falls and you may be tempted to swim in the rock pools, but beware local crocodiles.

Little Andaman lighthouse, 14km from Hut Bay, is another worthwhile excursion. Standing 41m high, exactly 200 steps lead you up to magnificent views over the coastline and forest. The easiest way to get here is by motorcycle, or otherwise a sweaty bicycle journey. You could also take an autorickshaw until the road becomes unpassable, and walk for an hour along the blissful stretch of deserted beach.

Harbinder Bay and **Dugong Creek** are designated tribal areas for the Nicobarese and Onge, respectively, and are off-limits.

Intrepid surfing travellers have been whispering about Little Andaman since it first opened up to foreigners several years ago. The reef breaks are legendary, but best suited for more experienced surfers; and then there's the sharks and crocodiles to contend with. Get in touch with surfing nut, **Muthu** (☏9775276182), based in Havelock, who can provide info on waves for Little Andaman and around. Several surfing liveaboard yachts make the trip out here, taking you to more remote, inaccessible sites. Try **Surf Andamans** (www.surfandamans.com).

🍴 Sleeping & Eating

There's no great reason to stay in Hut Bay, an inconvenient 10km away from the nicer beaches, but if you do, **Nandhini Tourist Home** (☏9933259090; s/d ₹150/250) has rooms looking onto the tsunami-scarred beach. There are plenty of cheap thali and tiffin places (we recommend the unnamed Bengali eatery across from the police station).

TOP CHOICE **Blue View** (☏9531802037; Km11.5; s/d ₹150/250) has prime real estate across the road from Netaji Nagar Beach. Rooms are simple, adjoined shacks, and it has a friendly owner, Azad. You can rent bicycles/motorbikes (per day ₹50/250). The food here is very good. Otherwise you could try the less appealing concrete **Ananta Lodge** (☏744207; Km16; s/d ₹200/300) in the bazaar just beyond Butler's Bay.

🛈 Getting There & Around

Ferries land at Hut Bay Jetty on the east coast; from there the beaches lay to the north. Buses (₹10) leave when they want for Butler Bay, or you can hire a local jeep (₹100).

Boats sail to Little Andaman from Port Blair daily, alternating between the overnight eight-hour slow boat, and the afternoon six-hour 'speedboat' (seat/bunk ₹25/70).

If you're planning on getting a helicopter, this is the place to chance your luck. Not only will it save you from a 7½-hour boat trip, but the aerial views are incredible – though the 5kg baggage limit makes it tricky.

Understand
South India

population per sq km

INDIA   CHINA   USA

👤 ≈ 30 people

South India Today

The Kashmir Epic

In 2010 the violence between pro-independence protesters and Indian security forces in the Kashmir Valley had turned deadly. The protesters called for India to remove its troops from Kashmir. They stoned police and paramilitary and burned police vehicles, all while demanding *azadi* – freedom. Security forces responded with gunfire, and more than 100 protesters died.

The predominantly Muslim Kashmir Valley is claimed by both India and Pakistan – and now, Kashmiris – and the impasse has plagued relations between the two countries since Partition in 1947 (see p424). After three India-Pakistan wars and countless skirmishes, there's still no solution in sight – this is a hot topic of debate right around India, including the south.

By 1989, Kashmir had an armed insurgency. A militant fringe of Kashmiris revolted against the Indian government, joined by armed supporters from Afghanistan and Pakistan. India accused Pakistan of assisting insurgents; Pakistan countered that India was denying Kashmiris the right to self-determination. Thousands of civilians have been killed in the course of the conflict. India-Pakistan relations sunk even lower in 1998 when the Bharatiya Janata Party (BJP; Indian People's Party) government detonated five nuclear devices in the Rajasthan desert and Pakistan responded in kind. A border conflict was averted, but nukes were now in the picture.

By the time the Congress Party government of Prime Minister Manmohan Singh came to power in 2004, relations were strained but cordial; the reopening of cross-border transport links, among other measures, helped calm the situation. But talks were derailed when in Mumbai (Bombay) in 2008, a team of terrorists killed at least 163 people, some of whom were tortured, at 10 sites around the city during three days of coordinated bombings and shootings. The one sniper caught alive, a Pakistani, had ties to

» Population:
1.21 billion

» GDP: US$1.4
trillion (2009)

» Unemployment rate:
10.8%

» Employed
in agriculture:
52%

» Literacy rate
(female/male):
65/82%

» Sex ratio
(female/male):
940/1000

Dos & Don'ts

» Dress conservatively. Avoid tight clothes and keep shoulders and knees covered. Outside Goa, this applies to swimming too.

» Public kissing, cuddling or holding hands is not condoned.

» Remove shoes before entering people's homes and holy sites.

» Your right hand is for eating and shaking hands; don't use the left (aka 'toilet') hand.

» Ask before photographing people or holy places.

» That head wobble? It can mean yes, maybe or I have no idea. Just go with the flow.

Greetings

» Saying 'namaste' with hands together in a prayer gesture is a traditional, respectful Hindu greeting and a universally accepted way to say hello or goodbye.

» Hugs between strangers don't really happen.

belief systems
(% of population)

80.5	13.4	2.3
Hindu	Muslim	Christian

1.9	0.8	1.1
Sikh	Buddhist	Other

if India were 100 people

41 would speak Hindi
55 would speak one of 21 other official languages
4 would speak one of around 400 other languages
Note: 10 of these 100 will speak English as a second language

---

Lashkar-e-Taiba, a militant group that formed to assist the Pakistani army in Kashmir in the 1990s. Pakistan denied any involvement.

Communal Tension

Kashmir is India's most persistent conflict – frequently making national news headlines – but religion-based confrontation further south may be its most insidious. One of the most violent episodes occurred in 1992, when Hindu zealots destroyed a mosque, the Babri Masjid, in Ayodhya, Uttar Pradesh (revered by Hindus as the birthplace of Rama). The Hindu-revivalist BJP, the main opposition party, reportedly did little to discourage the acts, and rioting across the north killed thousands.

The BJP grew in popularity and won the elections in 1998 and again in 1999. Prime Minister Atal Bihari Vajpayee appeared moderate, but there were purportedly belligerent elements within and beyond the party ranks.

The year 2008 was one of India's darkest: bomb blasts in Jaipur, Ahmedabad and Delhi each killed dozens of people. Investigations pointed at hardline Islamist groups, but no sooner had Delhi vowed to rein in terrorism than terror struck again with the bombings and shootings in Mumbai on 26 November, now known as 26/11.

At the time of writing tensions seemed to have diminished post-26/11, with extremist groups softening their rhetoric. And in late 2010, when an Uttar Pradesh court announced that the Ayodhya site would be split between Hindus and Muslims, the response was peaceful. The verdict is being appealed, but for now, the whole of India breathed a collective sigh of relief.

> India's national anthem, 'Jana Gana Mana' (Thou Art the Ruler of the Minds of All People), was written and composed by Bengali poet and Nobel Laureate Rabindranath Tagore. Another of his poems became Bangladesh's national anthem.

Congress Today

When the Congress Party regained power in 2004, it was under the leadership of Sonia Gandhi – the Italian-born wife of the late Rajiv Gandhi,

---

Top Fiction

The White Tiger Aravind Adiga's Booker Prize–winning novel.
A Fine Balance Rohinton Mistry's masterfully crafted (Mumbai-based) tragic tale.
The God of Small Things Arundhati Roy's 1997 Man Booker Prize winner.

The Guide and **The Painter of Signs** Classic RK Narayan novels set in the fictional South Indian town of Malgudi.
Midnight's Children Salman Rushdie's allegory about Independence and Partition.

Political Nonfiction

India After Gandhi: The History of the World's Largest Democracy By Ramachandra Guha.

The Elephant, the Tiger and the Cellphone By Shashi Tharoor. Reflections on 21st-century India.

who had served as prime minister from 1984 to 1989 (after his mother, Prime Minister Indira Gandhi, was assassinated). The BJP's planned national agitation campaign against Sonia Gandhi's foreign origins was subverted when she stepped aside to allow Manmohan Singh to be sworn in as prime minister. However, many believe that Gandhi wields substantial influence behind the scenes.

Under Singh's leadership, India has carried out a program of economic liberalisation along with a number of education, health and other social-reform initiatives. The prime minister made international headlines in 2006 by concluding a civilian nuclear agreement with the US, which grants India access to nuclear fuel and technology in exchange for following International Atomic Energy Agency safeguards. However, recent times have seen Singh come under increasing criticism for weak leadership regarding a series of corruption allegations levelled towards his government.

Belonging to the Sikh faith, India's prime minister Manmohan Singh (of the Congress Party) was the first member of any religious minority community to hold India's highest elected office.

It's the Economy

India's socialist-leaning economy was shaken up in 1991 when Manmohan Singh, then finance minister, took the momentous step of partially floating the rupee against a basket of 'hard' currencies. State subsidies were phased out and the economy was opened up to foreign investment, with multinationals drawn by educated professionals and relatively low wages.

With one of the world's fastest growing economies, India has made giant strides since then. But despite its healthy annual growth rate of around 9% in recent years, huge sections of the country's billion-plus population have benefited little from this boom. Indeed, the government's ongoing challenge is to spread the bounty of India's fiscal prosperity – not an easy task given that the gap between the haves and the have-nots, and the sheer number of have-nots, is vast.

Top Films

Fire (1996), **Earth** (1998) and **Water** (2005) The Deepa Mehta trilogy was popular abroad, controversial in India.
Lagaan (2001) Written and directed by Ashutosh Gowariker; set in the British Raj with an epic cricket match climax.

Pyaasa (Thirst; 1957) and **Kaagaz Ke Phool** (Paper Flowers; 1959) Two bittersweet films directed by and starring film legend Guru Dutt.

Gandhi (1982) Academy-awarded film starring Ben Kingsley.

History

South India has always laid claim to its own unique history, largely resulting from its insulation by distance from the political developments up north. The cradle of Dravidian culture, it has a long and colourful historical tapestry of wrangling dynasties and empires, interwoven with the influx of traders and conquerors arriving by sea. Evidence of human habitation in South India dates back to the Stone Age; discoveries include hand axes in Tamil Nadu and a worn limestone statue of a goddess, believed to be between 15,000 and 25,000 years old, from an excavation in the Vindhya Range.

India's first major civilisation flourished around 2500 BC in the Indus River valley, much of which lies within present-day Pakistan. This civilisation, which continued for a thousand years and is known as the Harappan culture, appears to have been the culmination of thousands of years of settlement. The Harappan civilisation fell into decline from the beginning of the 2nd millennium BC. Some historians attribute the end of the empire to floods or decreased rainfall, which threatened the Harappans' agricultural base. The more enduring, if contentious, theory is that an Aryan invasion put paid to the Harappans, despite little archaeological proof or written reports in the ancient Indian texts to that effect. As a result, some nationalist historians argue that the Aryans (from a Sanskrit word meaning 'noble') were in fact the original inhabitants of India and that the invasion theory was invented by self-serving foreign conquerors. Others say that the arrival of the Aryans was more of a gentle migration that gradually subsumed Harappan culture, rather than an invasion. Those who defend the invasion theory believe that from around 1500 BC Aryan tribes from Afghanistan and Central Asia began to filter into northwest India. Despite their military superiority, their progress was gradual, with successive tribes battling over territory and new arrivals pushing further east into the Ganges plain. Eventually these tribes controlled northern India as far as the

To learn more about the ancient Indus Valley civilisation, ramble around Harappa (www. harappa.com), which presents an illustrated yet scholarly overview.

TIMELINE	2600–1700 BC	1500 BC	1500–1200 BC
	The heyday of the Indus Valley civilisation, which spans parts of Rajasthan, Gujarat and the Sindh province in present-day Pakistan, and includes cities such as Harappa and Moenjodaro.	The Indo-Aryan civilisation takes root in the fertile plains of the Indo-Gangetic basin. Settlers speak an early form of Sanskrit, from which several Indian vernaculars, including Hindi, later evolve.	The *Rig-Veda*, the first and longest of Hinduism's canonical texts, the Vedas, is written; three more books follow. Earliest forms of priestly Brahmanic Hinduism emerge.

Vindhya Range. As a consequence, many of the original inhabitants, the Dravidians, were forced south.

Influences from the North

While the Indus Valley civilisation may not have affected South India, the same cannot be said for the Aryan invasion. The Aryanisation of the south was a slow process, but it had a profound effect on the social order of the region and the ethos of its inhabitants. The northerners brought their literature (the four Vedas – a collection of sacred Hindu hymns), their gods (Agni, Varuna, Shiva and Vishnu), their language (Sanskrit) and a social structure that organised people into castes, with Brahmins at the top.

Over the centuries other influences flowed from the north, including Buddhism and Jainism. Sravanabelagola in Karnataka, an auspicious place of pilgrimage to this day, is where over 2000 years ago the northern ruler Chandragupta Maurya, who had embraced Jainism and renounced his kingdom, arrived with his guru. Jainism was then adopted by the trading community (its tenet of ahimsa, or nonviolence, precluded occupations tainted by the taking of life), who spread it through South India.

Emperor Ashoka, a successor of Chandragupta who ruled for 40 years from about 272 BC, was a major force behind Buddhism's inroads into the south. Once a campaigning king, his epiphany came in 260 BC when, overcome by the horrific carnage and suffering caused by his campaign against the Kalingas (a powerful kingdom), he renounced violence and embraced Buddhism. He sent Buddhist missionaries far and wide, and his edicts (carved into rock and incised into specially erected pillars) have been found in Andhra Pradesh and Karnataka. Stupas were also built in South India under Ashoka's patronage, mostly along the coast of Andhra Pradesh (see the boxed text, p230), although at least one was constructed as far south as Kanchipuram in Tamil Nadu.

The appeal of Jainism and Buddhism was that they rejected the Vedas and condemned the caste system. Buddhism, however, gradually lost favour with its devotees, and was replaced with a new brand of Hinduism, which emphasised devotion to a personal god. This bhakti (surrendering to the gods) order developed in South India around AD 500. Bhakti adherents opposed Jainism and Buddhism, and the movement hastened the decline of both in South India.

The concepts of zero and infinity are widely believed to have been devised by eminent Indian mathematicians during the reign of the Guptas.

Mauryan Empire & Southern Kingdoms

Chandragupta Maurya was the first in a line of Mauryan kings to rule what was effectively the first Indian empire. The empire's capital was in present-day Patna in Bihar. Chandragupta's son, Bindusara, who came to the throne around 300 BC, extended the empire as far as Karnataka.

1000 BC	599–528 BC	563–483 BC	326 BC
Indraprastha, Delhi's first incarnation, comes into being. Archaeological excavations at the site, where the Purana Qila now stands, continue even today, as more facts about this ancient capital keep emerging.	The life of Mahavir, the 24th and last *tirthankar* (enlightened teacher) who established Jainism. Like Buddha, he preaches compassion and a path to enlightenment for all castes.	The life of Siddhartha Gautama. The prince is born in modern-day Nepal and attains enlightenment beneath the Bodhi Tree in Bodhgaya (Bihar), thereby transforming into Buddha (Awakened One).	Alexander the Great invades India. He defeats King Porus in Punjab to enter the subcontinent, but a rebellion within his army keeps him from advancing beyond Himachal Pradesh's Beas River.

Apart from the Mughals and then the British many centuries later, no other power controlled more Indian territory than the Mauryan empire. It's therefore fitting that it provided India with one of its most significant historical figures.

Emperor Ashoka's rule was characterised by flourishing art and sculpture, while his reputation as a philosopher-king was enhanced by the rock-hewn edicts he used both to instruct his people and to delineate the enormous span of his territory.

Ashoka's reign also represented an undoubted historical high point for Buddhism: he embraced the religion in 269 BC, declaring it the state religion and cutting a radical swathe through the spiritual and social body of Hinduism. The emperor also built thousands of stupas and monasteries across the region. Ashoka sent missions abroad, and he is revered in Sri Lanka because he sent his son and daughter to carry Buddha's teaching to the island.

The long shadow this emperor of the 3rd century BC still casts over India is evident from the fact that the central design of the Indian national flag is the Ashoka Chakra, a wheel with 24 spokes. Ashoka's standard, which topped many pillars, is also the seal of modern-day India (four lions sitting back-to-back atop an abacus decorated with a frieze and the inscription 'truth alone triumphs') and its national emblem, chosen to reaffirm the ancient commitment to peace and goodwill.

However, he seems to have stopped there, possibly because the Mauryan empire was on cordial terms with the southern chieftains of the day.

The identity and customs of these chiefdoms have been gleaned from various sources, including archaeological remains and ancient Tamil literature. These literary records describe a land known as the 'abode of the Tamils', within which resided three major ruling families: the Pandyas (Madurai), the Cheras (Malabar Coast) and the Cholas (Thanjavur and the Cauvery Valley). The region described in classical Sangam literature (written between 300 BC and AD 200) was still relatively insulated from Sanskrit culture, but from 200 BC this was starting to change.

A degree of rivalry characterised relations between the main chiefdoms and the numerous minor chiefdoms, and there were occasional clashes with Sri Lankan rulers. Sangam literature indicates that Sanskrit traditions from the old Aryan kingdoms of the north were taking root in South India around 200 BC. Ultimately, the southern powers all suffered at the hands of the Kalabhras, about whom little is known except that they appeared to have originated from somewhere north of the Tamil region.

By around 180 BC the Mauryan empire, which had started to disintegrate soon after the death of Emperor Ashoka in 232 BC, had been

321–185 BC	c 235 BC	3rd century BC	1st century AD
Rule of the Maurya kings. Founded by Chandragupta Maurya, this pan-Indian empire is ruled from Pataliputra (present-day Patna) and briefly adopts Buddhism during the reign of Emperor Ashoka.	Start of Chola reign. The Tamil dynasty, known for the power and territory it accreted in the 9th to 13th centuries, ruled in India's south for more than 1500 years.	The Satavahana empire, of Andhran origin, rules over a huge central Indian area. Their interest in art and maritime trade combines to influence artistic development regionally and in Southeast Asia.	International trade booms: the region's elaborate overland trade networks connect with ports linked to maritime routes. Trade to Africa, the Gulf, Socotra, Southeast Asia, China and even Rome thrives.

overtaken by a series of rival kingdoms that were subjected to repeated invasions from northerners such as the Bactrian Greeks. Despite this apparent instability, the post-Ashokan era produced at least one line of royalty whose patronage of the arts and ability to maintain a relatively high degree of social cohesion have left an enduring legacy. This was the Satavahanas, who eventually controlled all of Maharashtra, Madhya Pradesh, Chhattisgarh, Karnataka and Andhra Pradesh. Under their rule, between 200 BC and AD 200, the arts blossomed, especially literature, sculpture and philosophy. Buddhism reached a peak in Maharashtra under the Satavahanas, although the greatest of the Buddhist cave temples at Ajanta and Ellora were built later by the Chalukya and Rashtrakuta dynasties.

Most of all, the subcontinent enjoyed a period of considerable prosperity. South India may have lacked vast and fertile agricultural plains on the scale of North India, but it compensated by building strategic trade links via the Indian Ocean.

The Fall & Rise of the Chola Empire

After the Kalabhras suppressed the Tamil chiefdoms, South India split into numerous warring kingdoms. The Cholas virtually disappeared and the Cheras on the west coast appear to have prospered through trading, although little is known about them. It wasn't until the late 6th century AD, when the Kalabhras were overthrown, that the political uncertainty in the region ceased. For the next 300 years the history of South India was dominated by the fortunes of the Chalukyas of Badami, the Pallavas of Kanchi (Kanchipuram) and the Pandyas of Madurai.

The Chalukyas were a far-flung family. In addition to their base in Badami, they established themselves in Bijapur, Andhra Pradesh and near the Godavari Delta. The Godavari branch of the family is commonly referred to as the Eastern Chalukyas of Vengi. It's unclear from where the Pallavas originated, but it's thought they may have emigrated to Kanchi from Andhra Pradesh. After their successful rout of the Kalabhras, the Pallavas extended their territory as far south as the Cauvery River, and by the 7th century were at the height of their power, building monuments such as the Shore Temple and Arjuna's Penance at Mamallapuram (Mahabalipuram). They engaged in long-running clashes with the Pandyas, who, in the 8th century, allied themselves with the Gangas of Mysore. This, combined with pressure from the Rashtrakutas (who were challenging the Eastern Chalukyas), had by the 9th century snuffed out any significant Pallava power in the south.

At the same time as the Pallava dynasty came to an end, a new Chola dynasty was establishing itself and laying the foundations for what was to become one of the most significant empires on the subcontinent. From their base at Thanjavur, the Cholas spread north absorbing what was left

AD 52	**319–510**	**4th–9th centuries**
Possible arrival of St Thomas the Apostle on the coast of Kerala. Christianity thought to have been introduced to India with his preaching in Kerala and Tamil Nadu.	The golden era of the Gupta dynasty, the second of India's great empires after the Mauryas. This era is marked by a creative surge in literature and the arts.	The Pallavas enter the shifting landscape of southern power centres, eventually establishing dominance in Andhra Pradesh and northern Tamil Nadu from their base in Kanchipuram.

» Carvings, Kanchipuram

© V MUTHURAMAN/ PHOTOLIBRARY

of the Pallavas' territory, and made inroads into the south. But it wasn't until Rajaraja Chola I (r 985–1014) ascended the throne that the Chola kingdom really started to emerge as a great empire. Rajaraja Chola I successfully waged war against the Pandyas in the south, the Gangas of Mysore and the Eastern Chalukyas. He also launched a series of naval campaigns that resulted in the capture of the Maldives, the Malabar Coast and northern Sri Lanka, which became a province of the Chola empire. These conquests gave the Cholas control over critical ports and trading links between India, Southeast Asia, Arabia and East Africa. They were therefore in a position to grab a share of the huge profits involved in selling spices to Europe.

Rajaraja Chola's son, Rajendra Chola I (r 1014–44), continued to expand the Chola's territory, conquering the remainder of Sri Lanka and campaigning up the east coast as far as Bengal and the Ganges River. Rajendra also launched a campaign in Southeast Asia against the Srivijaya kingdom (Sumatra), reinstating trade links that had been interrupted and sending trade missions as far as China. In addition to both its political and economic superiority, the Chola empire produced a brilliant legacy in the arts. Sculpture, most notably bronze sculpture, reached astonishing new heights of aesthetic and technical refinement.

Music, dance and literature flourished and developed a distinctly Tamil flavour, enduring in South India long after the Cholas had faded from the picture. Trade wasn't the only thing the Cholas brought to the shores of Southeast Asia; they also introduced their culture. That legacy lives on in Myanmar (Burma), Thailand, Bali (Indonesia) and Cambodia in dance, religion and mythology.

But the Cholas, eventually weakened by constant campaigning, succumbed to expansionist pressure from the Hoysalas of Halebid and the Pandyas of Madurai, and by the 13th century were finally supplanted by the Pandyas. The Hoysalas were themselves eclipsed by the Vijayanagar empire, which arose in the 14th century. The Pandyas prospered and their achievements were much admired by Marco Polo when he visited in 1288 and 1293. But their glory was short-lived, as they were unable to fend off the Muslim invasion from the north.

Muslim Invasion & the Vijayanagar Empire

The Muslim rulers in Delhi campaigned in South India from 1296, rebuking a series of local rulers, including the Hoysalas and Pandyas, and by 1323 had reached Madurai.

Mohammed Tughlaq, the sultan of Delhi, dreamed of conquering the whole of India, something not even Emperor Ashoka had managed. He rebuilt the fort of Daulatabad in Maharashtra to keep control of South India, but eventually his ambition led him to overreach his forces. In

India: A History by John Keay is an astute and readable account of subcontinental history spanning from the Harappan civilisation to Indian Independence.

History and Society in South India by Noboru Karashima is an academic compilation focusing on the development of South Indian society during the Chola dynasty and the rule of the Vijayanagars.

HISTORY MUSLIM INVASION & THE VIJAYANAGAR EMPIRE

610	850	12th–19th centuries	13th century
Prophet Mohammed establishes Islam. He soon invites the people of Mecca to adopt the new religion under the command of God, and his call is met with eager response.	The Chola empire emerges anew in South India, establishing itself as a formidable economic and military presence in Asia under Rajaraja Chola I and his son Rajendra Chola I.	Africans are brought to the Konkan coast as part of trade with the Persian Gulf; the slaves become servants, dock workers and soldiers, and are known as Siddis or Habshis.	The Pandyas, a Tamil dynasty dating to the 6th century BC, assumes control of Chola territory, expanding into Andhra Pradesh, Kalinga (Odisha) and Sri Lanka from their capital in Madurai.

1334 he had to recall his army in order to quash rebellions elsewhere and, as a result, local Muslim rulers in Madurai and Daulatabad declared their independence.

At the same time, the foundations of what was to become one of South India's greatest empires, Vijayanagar, were being laid by Hindu chiefs at Hampi.

The Vijayanagar empire is generally said to have been founded by two chieftain brothers who, having been captured and taken to Delhi, converted to Islam and were sent back south to serve as governors for the sultanate. The brothers, however, had other ideas; they reconverted to Hinduism and around 1336 set about establishing a kingdom that was eventually to encompass southern Karnataka, Tamil Nadu and part of Kerala. Seven centuries later, the centre of this kingdom – the ruins and temples of Hampi – is now one of South India's biggest tourist drawcards.

The Bahmanis, who were initially from Daulatabad, established their capital at Gulbarga in Karnataka, relocating to Bidar in the 15th century. Their kingdom eventually included Maharashtra and parts of northern Karnataka and Andhra Pradesh – and they took pains to protect it.

Not unnaturally, ongoing rivalry characterised the relationship between the Vijayanagar and Bahmani empires until the 16th century when both went into decline. The Bahmani empire was torn apart by factional fighting and Vijayanagar's vibrant capital of Hampi was laid to waste in a six-month sacking by the combined forces of the Islamic sultanates of Bidar, Bijapur, Berar, Ahmednagar and Golconda. Much of the conflict centred on control of fertile agricultural land and trading ports; at one stage the Bahmanis wrested control of the important port of Goa from their rivals (although in 1378 the Vijayanagars seized it back).

The Vijayanagar empire is notable for its prosperity, which was the result of a deliberate policy of giving every encouragement to traders from afar, combined with the development of an efficient administrative system and access to important trading links, including west-coast ports. Hampi became quite cosmopolitan, with people from various parts of India as well as from abroad mingling in the bazaars.

Portuguese chronicler Domingo Paez arrived in Vijayanagar during the reign of one of its greatest kings, Krishnadevaraya (r 1509–29). During his rule Vijayanagar enjoyed a period of unparalleled prosperity and power.

Paez recorded the achievements of the Vijayanagars and described how they had constructed large water tanks and irrigated their fields. He also described how human and animal sacrifices were carried out to propitiate the gods after one of the water tanks had burst repeatedly.

A History of South India from Prehistoric Times to the Fall of Vijayanagar by KA Nilakanta Sastri is arguably the most thorough history of this region; especially recommended if you're heading for Hampi.

1336	**1345**	**1469**	**1484**
Foundation of the mighty Vijayanagar empire, named after its capital city, the ruins of which can be seen today in the vicinity of Hampi (in modern-day Karnataka).	Bahmani sultanate is established in the Deccan following a revolt against the Tughlaqs of Delhi. The capital is set up at Gulbarga, in today's northern Karnataka, later shifting to Bidar.	Guru Nanak, founder of the Sikh faith, which has millions of followers within and beyond India to the present day, is born in a village near Lahore (in modern-day Pakistan).	Bahmani sultanate begins to break up following independence movements; Berar is the first to revolt. By 1518 there are five Deccan sultanates: Berar, Ahmadnagar, Bidar, Bijapur and Golconda.

ENTER THE PORTUGUESE

By the time Krishnadevaraya ascended to the throne, the Portuguese were well on the way to establishing a firm foothold in Goa. It was only a few years since they had become the first Europeans to sail across the Indian Ocean from the east coast of Africa to India's shores.

On 20 May 1498 Vasco da Gama dropped anchor off the South Indian coast near the town of Calicut (now Kozhikode). It had taken him 23 days to sail from the east coast of Africa, guided by a pilot named Ibn Masjid, sent by the ruler of Malindi in Gujarat.

The Portuguese sought a sea route between Europe and the East so they could trade directly in spices. They also hoped they might find Christians cut off from Europe by the Muslim dominance of the Middle East, while at the same time searching for the legendary kingdom of Prester John, a powerful Christian ruler with whom they could unite against the Muslim rulers of the Middle East. However, in India they found spices and the Syrian Orthodox community, but not Prester John.

Vasco da Gama sought an audience with the ruler of Calicut, to explain himself, and seems to have been well received. The Portuguese engaged in a limited amount of trading, but became increasingly suspicious that Muslim traders were turning the ruler of Calicut against them. They resolved to leave Calicut, which they did in August 1498.

He included detail about the fine houses that belonged to wealthy merchants and the bazaars full of precious stones (rubies, diamonds, emeralds, pearls), textiles (including silk) and 'every other sort of thing there is on earth and that you may wish to buy'.

Like the Bahmanis, the Vijayanagar kings invested heavily in protecting their territory and trading links. Krishnadevaraya employed Portuguese and Muslim mercenaries to guard the forts and protect his domains. He also fostered good relations with the Portuguese, upon whom he depended for access to trade goods, especially the Arab horses he needed for his cavalry.

Thousands were burned at the stake during the Goa Inquisition, which lasted more than 200 years. The judgment ceremony took place outside the Se Cathedral in Old Goa.

Arrival of the Europeans & Christianity

And so began a new era of European contact with the East. After Vasco da Gama's arrival in 1498 came Francisco de Ameida and Alfonso de Albuquerque, who established an eastern Portuguese empire that included Goa (first taken in 1510). Albuquerque waged a constant battle against the local Muslims in Goa, finally defeating them. But perhaps his greatest achievement was in playing off two deadly threats against each other – the Vijayanagars (for whom access to Goa's ports was extremely important) and the Bijapuris (who had split from the Bahmanis in the early 16th century and who controlled part of Goa).

1498	1510	1526	1542–45
Vasco da Gama, a Portuguese voyager, discovers the sea route from Europe to India. He arrives in (present-day) Kerala and engages in trade with the local nobility.	Portuguese forces capture Goa under the command of Alfonso de Albuquerque, whose initial attempt was thwarted by then-ruler Sultan Adil Shah of Bijapur. He succeeds following Shah's death.	Babur becomes the first Mughal emperor after conquering Delhi. He stuns Rajasthan by routing its confederate force, gaining an edge with the introduction of matchlock muskets in his army.	St Francis Xavier's first mission to India. He preaches Catholicism in Goa, Tamil Nadu and Sri Lanka, returning in 1548–49 and 1552 in between travels in the Far East.

VASCO DA GAMA

The Bijapuris and Vijayanagars were sworn enemies, and Albuquerque skilfully exploited this antipathy by supplying Arab horses, which had to be constantly imported because they died in alarming numbers once on Indian soil. Both kingdoms bought horses from the Portuguese to top up their warring cavalry, thus keeping Portugal's Goan ports busy and profitable.

The Portuguese also introduced Catholicism, and the arrival of the Inquisition in 1560 marked the beginning of 200 years of religious suppression in the Portuguese-controlled areas on the west coast of India. Not long after the beginning of the Inquisition, events that occurred in Europe had major repercussions for European relations with India. In 1580 Spain annexed Portugal, and until it regained its independence in 1640, Portugal's interests were subservient to Spain's. After the defeat of the Spanish Armada in 1588, the sea route to the East lay open to the English and the Dutch.

Today the Portuguese influence is most obvious in Goa, with its chalk-white Catholic churches dotting the countryside, Christian festivals and unique cuisine, although the Portuguese also had some influence in Kerala in towns such as Kochi (Cochin). By the mid-16th century, Old Goa had grown into a thriving city said to rival Lisbon in magnificence, and although only a ruined shadow of that time, its churches and buildings are still a stunning reminder of Portuguese rule. It wasn't until 1961 – 14 years after national Independence – that the Portuguese were finally forced out by the Indian military.

The Dutch got to India first but, unlike the Portuguese, were more interested in trade than in religion and empire. Indonesia was used as the main source of spices, and trade with South India was primarily for pepper and cardamom. So the Dutch East India Company set up a string of trading posts (called factories), which allowed them to maintain a complicated trading structure all the way from the Persian Gulf to Japan. They set up trading posts at Surat (Gujarat) and on the Coromandel Coast in South India, and entered into a treaty with the ruler of Calicut. In 1660 they captured the Portuguese forts at Cochin (now Kochi) and Kodungallor.

The English also set up a trading venture, the British East India Company, which in 1600 was granted a monopoly. Like the Dutch, the English were at that stage interested in trade, mainly in spices, and Indonesia was their main goal. But the Dutch proved too strong there and the English turned instead to India, setting up a trading post at Madras (now Chennai). The Danes traded off and on at Tranquebar (on the Coromandel Coast) from 1616, and the French acquired Pondicherry (now Puducherry) in 1673.

The Career and Legend of Vasco da Gama by Sanjay Subrahmanyam is one of the better recent investigations of the person credited with 'discovering' the sea route to India.

1560–1812

Portuguese Inquisition in Goa. Trials focus on converted Hindus and Muslims thought to have 'relapsed'. Thousands were tried and several dozen were executed before it was abolished in 1812.

1600

Britain's Queen Elizabeth I grants the first trading charter to the East India Company, with the maiden voyage taking place in 1601 under the command of Sir James Lancaster.

CHRISTINE OSBORNE/LONELY PLANET IMAGES ©

» Portuguese church, Fort Aguada, Goa

The name Chhatrapati Shivaji is revered in Maharashtra, with statues of the great warrior astride his horse gracing many towns, and street names and monuments being named (or renamed in the case of Mumbai's Victoria Terminus, among others) after him.

Shivaji was responsible for leading the powerful Maratha dynasty, a sovereign Hindu state that controlled the Deccan region for almost two centuries, at a time when much of India was under Islamic control. A courageous warrior and charismatic leader, Shivaji was born in 1627 to a prominent Maratha family at Shivneri. As a child he was sent to Pune with his mother, where he was given land and forts and groomed as a future leader. With a very small army, Shivaji seized his first fort at the age of 20 and over the next three decades he continued to expand Maratha power around his base in Pune, holding out against the Muslim invaders from the north (the Mughal empire) and the south (the forces of Bijapur) and eventually controlling the Deccan. He was shrewd enough to play his enemies (among them Mughal emperor Aurangzeb) off against each other, and in a famous incident in 1659 he killed Bijapuri general Afzal Khan in a face-to-face encounter at Pratapgad Fort (see p112).

In 1674 Shivaji was crowned Chhatrapati (Lord of the Universe) of the Marathas at Raigad Fort. He died six years later and was succeeded by his son Sambhaji, but almost immediately the power Shivaji had built up began to wane.

Mughals Versus Marathas

Around the late 17th century the Delhi-based Mughals were making in-roads into South India, gaining the sultanates of Ahmednagar, Bijapur and Golconda (including Hyderabad) before moving into Tamil Nadu. But it was here that Emperor Aurangzeb (r 1658–1707) came up against the Marathas who, in a series of guerrilla-like raids, captured Thanjavur and set up a capital at Gingee near Madras.

Although the Mughal empire gradually disintegrated following Aurangzeb's death, the Marathas went from strength to strength, and they set their sights on territory to the north. But their aspirations brought them into conflict with the rulers of Hyderabad, the Asaf Jahis, who had entrenched themselves here when Hyderabad broke away from the declining Mughal rulers of Delhi in 1724. The Marathas discovered that the French were providing military support to the Hyderabadi rulers in return for trading concessions on the Coromandel Coast. However, by the 1750s Hyderabad had lost a lot of its power and became landlocked when much of its coast was controlled by the British.

Down in the south, Travancore (Kerala) and Mysore were making a bid to consolidate their power by gaining control of strategic maritime

Amar Chitra Katha, a popular publisher of comic books about Indian folklore, mythology and history, has several books about Shivaji, including *Shivaji: The Great Maratha*, *Tales of Shivaji* and *Tanaji, the Maratha Lion*, about Shivaji's close friend and fellow warrior.

1673	1674	1707	1757
The Compagnie française des Indes orientales (French East India Company) establishes an outpost at Pondicherry (now Puducherry), which the French, Dutch and British fight over.	Shivaji establishes the Maratha kingdom, spanning western India and parts of the Deccan and North India. He assumes the imperial title of Chhatrapati, which means 'Great Protector'.	Death of Aurangzeb, the last of the Mughal greats. His demise triggers the gradual collapse of the Mughal empire, as anarchy and rebellion erupts across the country.	The East India Company registers its first military victory on Indian soil. Siraj-ud-Daulah, nawab of Bengal, is defeated by Robert Clive in the Battle of Plassey.

regions and access to trade links. Martanda Varma (r 1729–58) of Travancore created his own army and tried to keep the local Syrian Orthodox trading community onside by limiting the activities of European traders. Trade in many goods, with the exception of pepper, became a royal monopoly, especially under Martanda's son Rama Varma (r 1758–98).

Mysore started off as a landlocked kingdom, but in 1761 a cavalry officer, Hyder Ali, assumed power and set about acquiring coastal territory. Hyder Ali and his son Tipu Sultan eventually ruled over a kingdom that included southern Karnataka and northern Kerala. Tipu conducted trade directly with the Middle East through the west-coast ports he controlled. But Tipu was prevented from gaining access to ports on the eastern seaboard and the fertile hinterland by the British East India Company.

The British Take Hold

The British East India Company at this stage was supposedly interested only in trade, not conquest. But Mysore's rulers proved something of a vexation. In 1780 the Nizam of Hyderabad, Hyder Ali, and the Marathas joined forces to defeat the company's armies and take control of Karnataka. The Treaty of Mangalore, signed by Tipu Sultan in 1784, restored the parties to an uneasy truce. But meanwhile, within the company there was a growing body of opinion that only total control of India would really satisfy British trading interests. This was reinforced by fears of a renewed French bid for land in India following Napoleon's Egyptian expedition of 1798–99. It was the governor general of Bengal, Lord Richard Wellesley, who launched a strike against Mysore, with the Nizam of Hyderabad as an ally (who was required to disband his French-trained troops and in return gained British protection). Tipu, who may have counted on support from the French, was killed when the British stormed the river-island fortress of Seringapatam (present-day Srirangapatnam, near Mysore) in 1799.

Wellesley restored the old ruling family, the Wodeyars, to half of Tipu's kingdom – the rest went to the Nizam of Hyderabad and the British East India Company – and laid the foundations for the formation of the Madras Presidency. Thanjavur and Karnataka were also absorbed by the British, who, when the rulers of the day died, pensioned off their successors. By 1818 the Marathas, racked by internal strife, had collapsed.

By now most of India was under British influence. In the south the British controlled the Madras Presidency, which stretched from present-day Andhra Pradesh to the southern tip of the subcontinent, and from the east coast across to the western Malabar Coast. Meanwhile, a fair chunk of the interior was ruled by a bundle of small princely states. Much of Maharashtra was part of the Bombay Presidency, but there were a dozen or so small princely states scattered around, including Kolhapur,

In 1839 the British government offered to buy Goa from the Portuguese for half a million pounds.

1857	1858	1869	1869
The First War of Independence against the British. In the absence of a national leader, freedom fighters coerce the Mughal king, Bahadur Shah Zafar, to proclaim himself emperor of India.	British government assumes control over India – with power officially transferred from the East India Company to the Crown – beginning the period known as the British Raj.	The birth of Mohandas Karamchand Gandhi in Porbandar (Gujarat) – the man who would later become popularly known as Mahatma Gandhi and affectionately dubbed 'Father of the Nation'.	Opening of the Suez Canal accelerates trade from Europe and makes Bombay India's first port of call; journey from England goes from three months to three weeks. Bombay's economic importance skyrockets.

Sawantwadi, Aundh and Janjira. The major princely states were Travancore, Hyderabad and Mysore, though all were closely watched by the Resident (the British de facto governor, who officially looked after areas under British control).

The First War of Independence: The Indian Uprising

In 1857, half a century after having established firm control of India, the British suffered a serious setback. To this day, the causes of the Uprising (known at the time as the Indian Mutiny and subsequently labelled by nationalist historians as a War of Independence) are the subject of debate. The key factors included the influx of cheap goods, such as textiles, from Britain that destroyed many livelihoods; the dispossession of territories from many rulers; and taxes imposed on landowners.

The incident that's popularly held to have sparked the Uprising, however, took place at an army barracks in Meerut in Uttar Pradesh on 10 May 1857. A rumour leaked out that a new type of bullet was greased with what Hindus claimed was cow fat, while Muslims maintained that it came from pigs; pigs are considered unclean to Muslims, and cows are sacred to Hindus. Since loading a rifle involved biting the end off the waxed cartridge, these rumours provoked considerable unrest.

In Meerut, the situation was handled with a singular lack of judgment. The commanding officer lined up his soldiers and ordered them to bite off the ends of their issued bullets. Those who refused were immediately marched off to prison. The following morning, the soldiers of the garrison rebelled, shot their officers and marched to Delhi. Of the 74 Indian battalions of the Bengal army, seven (one of them Gurkhas) remained loyal, 20 were disarmed and the other 47 mutinied. The soldiers and peasants rallied around the ageing Mughal emperor in Delhi. They held Delhi for some months and besieged the British Residency in Lucknow for five months before they were finally suppressed. The incident left festering sores on both sides.

Almost immediately the East India Company was wound up, and direct control of the country was assumed by the British government, which announced its support for the existing rulers of the princely states, claiming they would not interfere in local matters as long as the states remained loyal to the British.

The Road to Independence

The desire among many Indians to be free from foreign rule remained. Opposition to the British began to increase at the turn of the 20th century, spearheaded by the Indian National Congress (Congress Party), the

1885	1891	1919	1940
The Indian National Congress, India's first home-grown political organisation, is set up. It brings educated Indians together and plays a key role in India's enduring freedom struggle.	BR Ambedkar, activist, economist, lawyer and writer, is born to a poor outcaste family. He earns several advanced degrees, becomes a Buddhist and advocates forcefully for Dalit rights.	The massacre, on 13 April, of unarmed Indian protesters at Jallianwala Bagh in Amritsar (Punjab). Gandhi responds with his program of civil (nonviolent) disobedience against the British government.	The Muslim League adopts its Lahore Resolution, which champions greater Muslim autonomy in India. Subsequent campaigns for the creation of a separate Islamic nation follow.

nation's oldest political party. The fight for independence gained momentum when, in April 1919, following riots in Amritsar (Punjab), a British army contingent was sent to quell the unrest. Under direct orders of the officer in charge the army ruthlessly fired into a crowd of unarmed protesters attending a meeting, killing an estimated 1500 people. News of the massacre spread rapidly throughout India, turning huge numbers of otherwise apolitical Indians into Congress supporters. At this time, the Congress movement found a new leader in Mohandas Gandhi.

After some three decades of intense campaigning for an independent India, Mahatma Gandhi's dream finally materialised. However, despite Gandhi's plea for a united India – the Muslim League's leader, Mohammed Ali Jinnah, was demanding a separate Islamic state for India's sizeable Muslim population – the decision was made to split the country.

The partition of India in 1947 contained all the ingredients for an epic disaster, but the resulting bloodshed was far worse than anticipated. Massive population exchanges took place. Trains full of Muslims, fleeing westward, were held up and slaughtered by Hindu and Sikh mobs. Hindus and Sikhs fleeing to the east suffered the same fate. By the time the chaos had run its course, more than 10 million people had changed sides and at least 500,000 had been killed.

India and Pakistan became sovereign nations under the British Commonwealth in August 1947 as planned, but the violence, migrations and the integration of a few states, especially Kashmir, continued. The Constitution of India was at last adopted in November 1949 and went into effect on 26 January 1950 and, after untold struggle, independent India officially became a republic.

A golden oldie, *Gandhi*, directed by Richard Attenborough, is one of the few films to engagingly capture the grand canvas that is India in tracing the country's rocky road to Independence.

Mahatma Gandhi

One of the great figures of the 20th century, Mohandas Karamchand Gandhi was born on 2 October 1869 in Porbandar, Gujarat. After studying in London (1888–91), he worked as a barrister in South Africa. Here, the young Gandhi became politicised, railing against the discrimination he encountered. He soon became the spokesman for the Indian community and championed equality for all.

Gandhi returned to India in 1915 with the doctrine of ahimsa (nonviolence) central to his political plans, and committed to a simple and disciplined lifestyle. He set up the Sabarmati Ashram in Ahmedabad, which was innovative for its admission of Untouchables (the lowest caste Dalits).

Within a year, Gandhi had won his first victory, defending farmers in Bihar from exploitation. It's said that this was when he first received the title 'Mahatma' (Great Soul) from an admirer. The passage of the discriminatory Rowlatt Acts (which allowed certain political cases to be

GANDHI

1942
Mahatma Gandhi launches the Quit India campaign, demanding that the British leave India without delay and allow the country to get on with the business of self-governance.

1947
India gains independence on 15 August. Pakistan is formed a day earlier. Partition is followed by mass cross-border exodus, as Hindus and Muslims migrate to their respective nations.

1947–48
First war between India and Pakistan takes place after the (procrastinating) Maharaja of Kashmir signs the Instrument of Accession that cedes his state to India. Pakistan challenges the document's legality.

DALLAS STRIBLEY LONELY PLANET IMAGES ©

» Statue of Gandhi

tried without juries) in 1919 spurred him to further action and he organised a national protest. In the days that followed this hartal (strike), feelings ran high throughout the country. After the massacre of unarmed protesters in Amritsar (Punjab), a deeply shocked Gandhi immediately called off the movement.

By 1920 Gandhi was a key figure in the Indian National Congress, and he coordinated a national campaign of noncooperation or satyagraha (passive resistance) to British rule, with the effect of raising nationalist feeling while earning the lasting enmity of the British. In early 1930, Gandhi captured the imagination of the country, and the world, when he led a march of several thousand followers from Ahmedabad to Dandi on the coast of Gujarat. On arrival, Gandhi ceremoniously made salt by evaporating sea water, thus publicly defying the much-hated salt tax; not for the first time, he was imprisoned. Released in 1931 to represent the Indian National Congress at the second Round Table Conference in London, he won the hearts of many British people but failed to gain any real concessions from the government.

Disillusioned with politics, he resigned his parliamentary seat in 1934. He returned spectacularly to the fray in 1942 with the Quit India campaign, in which he urged the British to leave India immediately. His actions were deemed subversive and he and most of the Congress leadership were imprisoned.

In the frantic Independence bargaining that followed the end of WWII, Gandhi was largely excluded and watched helplessly as plans were made to partition the country – a dire tragedy in his eyes. Gandhi stood almost alone in urging tolerance and the preservation of a single India, and his work on behalf of members of all communities drew resentment from some Hindu hardliners. On his way to a prayer meeting in Delhi on 30 January 1948, he was assassinated by a Hindu zealot.

In 21st-century India, Mahatma Gandhi continues to be an iconic figure and is still widely revered as the 'Father of the Nation'.

Carving up the South

While the chaos of Partition was mostly felt in the north – mainly in Punjab and Bengal – the south faced problems of its own. Following Independence, the princely states and British provinces were dismantled and South India was reorganised into states along linguistic lines. Though most of the princely states acceded to India peacefully, an exception was that of the Nizam of Hyderabad. He wanted Hyderabad to join Islamic Pakistan, although only he and 10% of his subjects were Muslims. Following a time of violence between Hindu and Islamic hardliners, the Indian army moved in and forcibly took control of Hyderabad state in 1949.

The Nehrus and the Gandhis is Tariq Ali's astute portrait-history of these families and the India over which they cast their long shadow.

1948	17 September 1948	November 1949	26 January 1950
Mahatma Gandhi is assassinated in New Delhi by Nathuram Godse on 30 January. Godse and his co-conspirator Narayan Apte are later tried, convicted and executed (by hanging).	Asaf Jah VII, the last Nizam of Hyderabad, surrenders to the Indian government. The Muslim dynasty was receiving support from Pakistan but had refused to join either new nation.	The Constitution of India, drafted over two years by a 308-member Constituent Assembly, is adopted. The Assembly included dozens of members from Scheduled Castes.	India becomes a republic. Date commemorates the Purna Swaraj Declaration, or Declaration of Independence, put forth by the Indian National Congress in 1930.

THE KASHMIR CONFLICT

Kashmir is the most enduring symbol of the turbulent partition of India. In the lead-up to Independence, the delicate task of drawing the India–Pakistan border was complicated by the fact that India's 'princely states' were nominally independent. As part of the settlement process, local rulers were asked which country they wished to belong to. Kashmir was a predominantly Muslim state with a Hindu maharaja, Hari Singh, who tried to delay his decision. A ragtag Pashtun (Pakistani) army crossed the border, intent on racing to Srinagar and annexing Kashmir for Pakistan. In the face of this advance, the maharaja panicked and requested armed assistance from India. The Indian army arrived only just in time to prevent the fall of Srinagar, and the maharaja signed the Instrument of Accession, tying Kashmir to India, in October 1947. The legality of the document was immediately disputed by Pakistan, and the two nations went to war, just two months after Independence.

In 1948 the fledgling UN Security Council called for a referendum (which remains a central plank of Pakistani policy) to decide the status of Kashmir. A UN-brokered ceasefire in 1949 kept the countries on either side of a demarcation line, called the Cease-Fire Line (later to become the Line of Control, or LOC), with little else resolved. Two-thirds of Kashmir fell on the Indian side of the LOC, which remains the frontier, but neither side accepts this as the official border. The Indian state of Jammu & Kashmir, as it has stood since that time, incorporates Ladakh (divided between Muslims and Buddhists), Jammu (with a Hindu majority) and the 130km-long, 55km-wide Kashmir Valley (with a Muslim majority and most of the state's inhabitants). On the Pakistani side, over three million Kashmiris live in Azad (Free) Kashmir. Since the frontier was drawn, incursions across the LOC have occurred with dangerous regularity.

The Wodeyars in Mysore, who also ruled right up to Independence, were pensioned off. But they were so popular with their subjects that the maharaja became the first governor of the post-Independence state of Mysore. The boundaries of Mysore state were redrawn on linguistic grounds in 1956, and the extended Kannada-speaking state of Greater Mysore was established, becoming Karnataka in 1972.

Kerala, as it is today, was created in 1956 from Travancore, Cochin (now Kochi) and Malabar (formerly part of the Madras Presidency). The maharajas in both Travancore and Cochin were especially attentive to the provision of basic services and education, and their legacy today is India's most literate state. Kerala also blazed a trail in post-Independence India by becoming the first state in the world to freely elect a communist government in 1957.

Andhra Pradesh was declared a state in 1956, having been created by combining Andhra state (formerly part of the Madras Presidency)

1961	**1965**	**1966**	**1971**
In a military action code-named 'Operation Vijay' the Indian government sends armed troops into Goa and – with surprisingly little resistance – ends over four centuries of Portuguese colonial rule in the region.	Skirmishes in Kashmir and the disputed Rann of Kutch in Gujarat flare into the Second India-Pakistan War, said to have involved the biggest tank battles since WWII. The war ends with a UN-mandated ceasefire.	Indira Gandhi, daughter of independent India's first prime minister, Jawaharlal Nehru, becomes prime minister of India. She has so far been India's only female prime minister.	East Pakistan seeks independence from West Pakistan. India gets involved, sparking the Third India-Pakistan War. West Pakistan surrenders, losing sovereignty of East Pakistan, which becomes Bangladesh.

with parts of the Telugu-speaking areas of the old Nizam of Hyderabad's territory.

Tamil Nadu emerged from the old Madras Presidency, although until 1969 Tamil Nadu was known as Madras State. In 1956, in a nationwide reorganisation of states, it lost Malabar district and South Canara to the fledgling state of Kerala on the west coast. However, it also gained new areas in Trivandrum (now Thiruvananthapuram), district including Kanyakumari. In 1960, 1049 sq km of land in Andhra Pradesh was exchanged for a similar amount of land in Salem and Chengalpattu districts.

The creation of Maharashtra was one of the most contested issues of the language-based demarcation of states in the 1950s. After Independence, western Maharashtra and Gujarat were joined to form Bombay state, but in 1960, after agitation by pro-Marathi supporters, the modern state of Maharashtra was created, separating from Gujarat while gaining parts of Hyderabad and Madhya Pradesh.

The French relinquished Pondicherry in 1954 – 140 years after claiming it from the British. It's a Union Territory (controlled by the government in Delhi), though a largely self-governing one. Lakshadweep was granted Union Territory status in 1956, as were the Andaman and Nicobar Islands.

Throughout most of this carve-up, the tiny enclave of Goa was still under the rule of the Portuguese. Although a rumbling Independence movement had existed in Goa since the early 20th century, the Indian government was reluctant to intervene and take Goa by force, hoping the Portuguese would leave of their own volition. The Portuguese refused, so in December 1961 Indian troops crossed the border and liberated the state with surprisingly little resistance. It became a Union Territory of India, but after splitting from Daman and Diu (Gujarat) in 1987, it was officially recognised as the 25th state of the Indian Union.

In 1997 KR Narayanan became India's president, the first member of the lowest Hindu caste (the Dalits; formerly known as Untouchables) to hold the position.

HISTORY CARVING UP THE SOUTH

1984	May 2004	December 2004	2008
Prime Minister Indira Gandhi is assassinated by two of her Sikh bodyguards after her highly controversial decision to have Indian troops storm Amritsar's Golden Temple, the Sikhs' holiest shrine.	Belonging to the Sikh faith, Manmohan Singh of the Congress Party becomes the first member of any religious minority community to hold India's highest elected office.	On 26 December a catastrophic tsunami batters coastal parts of eastern and South India as well as the Andaman and Nicobar Islands, killing over 10,000 people and leaving hundreds of thousands homeless.	On 26 November a series of coordinated bombing and shooting attacks on landmark Mumbai sites (primarily in the city's south) begins; the attacks last three days and kills at least 163 people.

The South Indian Way of Life

For travellers, one of the most enduring impressions of South India is the way everyday life is intimately intertwined with the sacred: from the housewife who devoutly performs *puja* (prayers) each morning to the shopkeeper who – regardless of how many tourists may be in the store – rarely commences business until blessings have been sought from the gods.

Along with religion, family lies at the heart of Indian society. For most, the idea of being unmarried and without children by one's mid-30s is unthinkable. Despite the rising number of nuclear families the extended family remains a cornerstone in both urban and rural South India, with males generally considered the head of the household.

With religion and family deemed so sacrosanct, don't be surprised or miffed if you are grilled about these subjects yourself, especially beyond the larger cities, and receive curious (possibly disapproving) gawps if you don't 'fit the mould'. The first question travellers are usually asked is their country of origin. This may be followed by a string of queries on topics that might be considered somewhat inappropriate elsewhere, especially coming from a complete stranger. Apart from religion and marital status, frequently asked questions include age, qualifications, profession (possibly even income) and your impressions of India. This is generally innocuous probing, not intended to offend.

National pride has long existed on the subcontinent but has swelled in recent years as India attracts ever-increasing international kudos in various fields including information technology (IT), science, medicine, literature, film and, of course, cricket. Speaking of the sporting arena, although there are rising stars on the tennis front, it is cricket that by far reigns supreme, with top players afforded superhero status.

The country's robust economy – one of the world's fastest growing – is another source of prolific national pride. Also widely embraced as potent symbols of Indian honour and sovereignty are the advancements in nuclear and space technology – in 2008 India joined the elite global lunar club with its maiden unmanned mission to the moon.

India has one of the world's largest diasporas – over 26 million people – with Indian banks holding an estimated US$55 billion in Non-Resident Indian (NRI) accounts.

Marriage, Birth & Death

Marriage is an auspicious event for Indians and although 'love marriages' have spiralled upwards in recent times (mainly in urban hubs), most Hindu marriages are arranged. Discreet enquiries are made within the community. If a suitable match is not found, the help of professional matchmakers may be sought or advertisements may be placed in newspapers and/or on the internet. The horoscopes are checked and, if propitious, there's a meeting between the two families. The legal marriage age in India is 18.

Dowry, although illegal, is still a key issue in many arranged marriages (primarily in the more conservative communities), with some families plunging into debt to raise the required cash and merchandise, which ranges from washing machines and televisions to cars and computers. Health workers claim that India's high rate of abortion of female foetuses (despite sex-determination ultrasounds being banned in India, they still clandestinely occur in some clinics) is predominantly due to the financial burden of providing a daughter's dowry.

The Hindu wedding ceremony is officiated over by a priest and the marriage is formalised when the couple walk around a sacred fire seven times. Despite the existence of nuclear families, it's still the norm for a wife to live with her husband's family once married and assume the household duties outlined by her mother-in-law. Not surprisingly, the mother–daughter-in-law relationship can be a prickly one, as portrayed in the various Indian TV soap operas that largely revolve around this theme.

Divorce and remarriage is becoming more common (primarily in India's bigger cities), but divorce is still not granted by courts as a matter of routine and is generally not looked upon favourably by society. Among the higher castes, widows are traditionally expected not to remarry and are admonished to wear white and live pious, celibate lives.

The birth of a child is another momentous occasion, with its own set of special ceremonies, which take place at various auspicious times during the early years of childhood. These include the casting of the child's first horoscope, name-giving, feeding the first solid food, and the first hair cutting.

Hindus cremate their dead and funeral ceremonies are designed to purify and console both the living and the deceased. An important aspect of the proceedings is the *sharadda,* paying respect to one's ancestors by offering water and rice cakes. It's an observance that's repeated at each anniversary of the death. After the cremation the ashes are collected and, 13 days after the death (when blood relatives are deemed ritually pure), a member of the family usually scatters them in a holy river, such as the Ganges, or in the ocean.

The Caste System

Although the Indian constitution does not recognise the caste system, caste still wields considerable influence, especially in rural India, where the caste you are born into largely determines your social standing in the community. It can also influence one's vocational and marriage prospects. Castes are further divided into thousands of *jati,* groups of 'families' or social communities, which are sometimes but not always

Read more about India's tribal communities at www. tribal.nic.in, a site maintained by the Indian government's Ministry of Tribal Affairs.

Matchmaking has embraced the cyber age, with popular sites including www. shaadi.com, www. bharatmatrimony. com and, more recently, www. secondshaadi. com – for those seeking a partner again.

THE SOUTH INDIAN WAY OF LIFE

INDIAN ATTIRE

Widely worn by Indian women, the elegant sari comes in a single piece (between 5m and 9m long and 1m wide) and is ingeniously tucked and pleated into place without the need for pins or buttons. Worn with the sari is the choli (tight-fitting blouse) and a drawstring petticoat. The *palloo* is the part of the sari draped over the shoulder. Also commonly worn is the *salwar kameez,* a traditional dresslike tunic and trouser combination accompanied by a dupatta (long scarf). Saris and *salwar kameez* come in an appealing range of fabrics, designs and prices.

Traditional attire for men includes the dhoti, and in the south the lungi and the *mundu* are also commonly worn. The dhoti is a loose, long loincloth pulled up between the legs. The lungi is more like a sarong, with its end usually sewn up like a tube. The *mundu* is like a lungi but is always white.

There are regional and religious variations in costume – for example, you may see Muslim women wearing the all-enveloping burka.

linked to occupation. Conservative Hindus will only marry someone of the same *jati*.

According to tradition, caste is the basic social structure of Hindu society. Living a righteous life and fulfilling your dharma (moral duty) raises your chances of being reborn into a higher caste and thus into better circumstances. Hindus are born into one of four varnas (castes): Brahmin (priests and scholars), Kshatriya (soldiers and administrators), Vaishya (merchants) and Shudra (labourers). The Brahmins were said to have emerged from the mouth of Lord Brahma at the moment of creation, Kshatriyas were said to have come from his arms, Vaishyas from his thighs and Shudras from his feet.

Beneath the four main castes are the Dalits (formerly known as Untouchables), who hold menial jobs such as sweepers and latrine cleaners. The word *pariah* is derived from the name of a Tamil Dalit group, the Paraiyars. Some Dalit leaders, such as the renowned Dr BR Ambedkar (1891–1956), sought to change their status by adopting another faith; in his case it was Buddhism. At the bottom of the social heap are the Denotified Tribes. They were known as the Criminal Tribes until 1952, when a reforming law officially recognised 198 tribes and castes. Many are nomadic or seminomadic tribes, forced by the wider community to eke out a living on society's fringes.

To improve the Dalits' position, the government reserves considerable numbers of public-sector jobs, parliamentary seats and university places for them. Today these quotas account for almost 25% of government jobs and university (student) positions. The situation varies regionally, as different political leaders chase caste vote-banks by promising to include them in reservations. The reservation system, while generally regarded in a favourable light, has also been criticised for unfairly blocking tertiary and employment opportunities for those who would have otherwise got positions on merit.

Pilgrimage

Devout Hindus are expected to go on a *yatra* (pilgrimage) at least once a year. Pilgrimages are undertaken to implore the gods or goddesses to grant a wish, to take the ashes of a cremated relative to a holy river, or to gain spiritual merit. India has thousands of holy sites to which pilgrims travel; the elderly often make Varanasi their final one, as it is believed that dying in this sacred city releases a person from the cycle of rebirth.

Most festivals in India are rooted in religion and are thus a magnet for pilgrims. This is something that travellers should keep in mind, even at those festivals that may have a carnivalesque sheen.

Women in South India

South Indian women have traditionally had a greater degree of freedom than their northern sisters. This is especially so in Kerala. Unique in many ways, Kerala is the most literate state in India and is also famous for its tradition of matrilineal kinship. Exactly why the matrilineal

If you're keen to learn more about India's caste system, these two books are a good start: *Interrogating Caste* by Dipankar Gupta and *Translating Caste* edited by Tapan Basu.

The Wonder That was India by AL Basham proffers descriptions of Indian civilisations, major religions and social customs – a good thematic approach to weave the disparate strands together.

RANGOLIS

Rangolis, the striking and breathtakingly elaborate chalk, rice-paste or coloured-powder design (also called *kolams*) that adorn thresholds, especially in South India, are both auspicious and symbolic. *Rangolis* are traditionally drawn at sunrise and are sometimes made of rice-flour paste, which may be eaten by little creatures – symbolising a reverence for even the smallest living things. Deities are deemed to be attracted to a beautiful *rangoli*, which may also signal to sadhus (ascetics) that they will be offered food at a particular house. Some people believe that *rangolis* protect against the evil eye.

ADIVASIS

India's Adivasis (tribal communities; Adivasi translates to 'original inhabitant' in Sanskrit) have origins that precede the Vedic Aryans and the Dravidians of the south. According to the 2001 census, India's Adivasis constitute 8.2% of the population (over 84 million people), with more than 400 different tribal groups. The literacy rate for Adivasis, as per the 2001 census, is just 29.6%; the national average is 65.4%.

Historically, contact between Adivasis and Hindu villagers on the plains rarely led to friction as there was little or no competition for resources and land. However, in recent decades an increasing number of Adivasis have been dispossessed of their ancestral land and turned into impoverished labourers. Although they still have political representation thanks to a parliamentary quota system, the dispossession and exploitation of Adivasis has reportedly sometimes been with the connivance of officialdom – an accusation the government denies. Whatever the arguments, unless more is done, the Adivasis' future is an uncertain one.

Read more about Adivasis in *Archaeology and History: Early Settlements in the Andaman Islands* by Zarine Cooper, *The Tribals of India* by Sunil Janah and *Tribes of India: The Struggle for Survival* by Christoph von Fürer-Haimendorf.

family became established in this region is subject to conjecture, although one explanation is that it was in response to ongoing warfare in the 10th and 11th centuries. With the military men absent, women invariably took charge of the household. It has also been argued that the men would very likely form alliances wherever they found themselves and that the children of these unions would become the responsibility of the mother's family. Whatever the reason, by the 14th century a matrilineal society was firmly established in many communities across Kerala, and it lasted pretty much unchallenged until the 20th century. Kerala was also India's first state to break societal norms by recruiting female police officers in 1938. On top of that, it was the first state to establish an all-female police station (1973).

In other parts of South India, such as Tamil Nadu, women also had more freedom than was the norm elsewhere in India. Matriarchy was a long-standing tradition within Tamil communities and the practice of marriage between cousins meant that young women did not have to move away and live among strangers. Dowry deaths and female infanticide were virtually unknown in India until relatively recent times, but the imposition of consumerism on old customs and conventions, making dowries more expensive, has resulted in increased instances.

Women throughout India are entitled to vote and own property. While the percentage of women in politics has risen over the past decade, they're still notably underrepresented in the national parliament, accounting for around 10% of parliamentary members.

Although the professions are still very much male dominated, women are steadily making inroads, most noticeably in the bigger cities. For village women it is much more difficult to get ahead, and an early marriage to a suitable provider (often arranged years beforehand) is usually regarded as essential.

In low-income families in particular, girls can be regarded as a serious financial liability because at marriage a dowry must often be supplied.

For the urban middle-class woman, life is materially much more comfortable, but pressures still exist. Broadly speaking, she is far more likely to receive a tertiary education, but once married is still usually expected to fit in with her in-laws and be a homemaker above all else. Like her village counterpart, if she fails to live up to expectations – even if it's just not being able to produce a grandson – the consequences can

Sati: A Study of Widow Burning in India by Sakuntala Narasimhan explores the history of *sati* (a widow's suicide on her husband's funeral pyre; now banned) on the subcontinent.

HIJRAS

India's most visible nonheterosexual group is the *hijras*, a caste of transvestites and eunuchs who dress in women's clothing. Some are gay, some are hermaphrodites and some were unfortunate enough to be kidnapped and castrated. Since it has long been traditionally frowned upon to live openly as a gay man in India, *hijras* get around this by becoming, in effect, a third sex of sorts. They work mainly as uninvited entertainers at weddings and celebrations of the birth of male children, and possibly as prostitutes.

Read more about *hijras* in *The Invisibles* by Zia Jaffrey and *Ardhanarishvara the Androgyne* by Dr Alka Pande.

Based on Rabindranath Tagore's novel, *Chokher Bali* (directed by Rituparno Ghosh) is a poignant film about a young widow living in early 20th-century Bengal who challenges the 'rules of widowhood' – something unthinkable in that era.

sometimes be dire, as demonstrated by the extreme practice of 'bride burning', where the husband or a member of his family inflicts pain, disfigurement or death on his wife. It may take the form of dousing her with fuel and setting her alight or scalding her with boiling water, and is usually intentionally designed to look like an accident or suicide. Reliable statistics are unavailable; however, some women's groups claim that for every reported case, roughly 250 go unreported, and that less than 10% of the reported cases are pursued through the legal system.

In October 2006, following women's civil-rights campaigns, the Indian parliament passed a landmark bill (on top of existing legislation) that gives women who are suffering domestic violence increased protection and rights. The new law purports that any form of physical, sexual (including marital rape), emotional and economic abuse entails not only domestic violence but also human-rights violations. Perpetrators face imprisonment and fines.

Although the constitution allows for divorcees (and widows) to remarry, relatively few reportedly do so, simply because divorcees are traditionally considered outcasts from society, especially beyond big cities. Divorce rates in India are among the world's lowest, and have risen only from 0.7% in 1991 to 0.11% in 2009.

Cricket

FOOTBALL

In India, it's all about cricket, cricket and cricket! Travellers who show even a slight interest in the game can expect to strike passionate conversations with people of all stripes, from taxi drivers to IT yuppies. Cutting across all echelons of society, cricket is more than just a national sporting obsession – it's a matter of enormous patriotism (some say jingoism), especially evident whenever India plays against Pakistan. Matches between these South Asian neighbours – which have had rocky relations since Independence – attract especially high-spirited interest, and the players of both sides are under colossal pressure to do their respective countries proud.

India's first recorded cricket match was in 1721. It won its first test series in 1952 in Chennai against England.

Today cricket – especially the recently rolled-out Twenty20 format (see www.cricket20.com) – is big business in India, attracting lucrative sponsorship deals and celebrity status for its players. The sport has not been without its murky side, though, with Indian cricketers among those embroiled in match-fixing scandals over past years.

International games are played at various centres – see Indian newspapers or surf the web for details about matches that coincide with your visit.

Keep your finger on the cricketing pulse at www.espncricinfo.com (rated most highly by many cricket aficionados) and www.cricbuzz.com.

In South India, football (soccer) has a reasonably strong following, especially in Goa and Kerala. In early 2011 India occupied the 145th spot in the FIFA world rankings.

Delicious South India

Through its legendary cuisine, you'll swiftly discover that South India is a culinary carnival expressed in a symphony of colours, aromas, flavours and textures. Like so many aspects of South India, its food, too, is an elusive thing to define because it's made up of many different dishes, all with their own special preparation techniques and ingredients. Indeed, this wonderful diversity is what makes munching your way through the steamy south so deliciously rewarding.

Dakshin Bhog by Santhi Balaraman offers a yummy jumble of southern stars, from iconic dosas and *idlis* to *kootan choru* (vegetable rice).

Although South Indian meals may at times appear quite simple – mounds of rice, spiced vegetables, curd and a splodge of fresh pickles, sometimes served on a banana-leaf plate – within this deceptive simplicity hides a sensual and complex repertoire of taste sensations. Add to this the distinct regional variations, from the colonial-influenced fare of Goa to the traditional seafood specialities of Kerala – along with a bounty of exotic fruits and vegetables – and there's more than enough to get the tastebuds tingling.

A Culinary Carnival

South India's culinary story is an ancient one. The cuisine that exists today reflects an extraordinary amalgam of regional and global influences. From the traditional Indian fare faithfully prepared in simple village kitchens to the piled-high Italian-style pizzas served in cosmopolitan city restaurants, the carnival of flavours available in this part of the world is nothing short of spectacular.

Spices

Christopher Columbus was searching for the famed black pepper of Kerala's Malabar Coast when he stumbled upon America. Turmeric is the essence of most Indian curries, but coriander seeds are the most widely used spice and lend flavour and body to just about every savoury dish. Most Indian 'wet' dishes – commonly known as curries in the West – begin with the crackle of cumin seeds in hot oil. Tamarind is sometimes known as the 'Indian date' and is a particularly popular souring agent in the south. The green cardamom of Kerala's Western Ghats is regarded as the world's best and you'll find it in savoury dishes, desserts and warming chai (tea). Saffron, the dried stigmas of crocus flowers grown in Kashmir, is so light it takes more than 1500 hand-plucked flowers to yield just 1g. Cinnamon, curry leaves, nutmeg and garlic are also widely used in cooking.

Fish is a staple of non-vegetarian Marathi food; Maharashtra's signature fish dish is *bombil* (Bombay duck; a misnomer for this slimy, pikelike fish), which is eaten fresh or sun-dried.

A masala is a blend of dry-roasted ground spices (the word loosely means 'mixed'), the most popular being garam masala (hot mix), a combination of up to 15 spices used to season dishes.

Red chillies are another common ingredient. Often dried or pickled (in rural areas you may see chillies laid out to dry on the roadside), they are used as much for flavour as for heat.

Rice Paradise

Rice is the most popular staple of South India. It's served with virtually every meal, and is used to make anything and everything from spongy *idlis* (fermented rice cakes) and dosas (large savoury crepes) to exquisite *mithai* (Indian sweets).

After China, India is the world's second-largest producer and consumer of rice, and the majority of it is grown in the south. Long-grain white rice is the most common and is served boiled with any 'wet' dish. It can be cooked up in a spicy biryani or a pilau (or pilaf; rice cooked in stock and flavoured with spices), or simply flavoured with a dash of turmeric or saffron.

Containing handy tips, including how to best store spices, Monisha Bharadwaj's *Indian Spice Kitchen* is a slick cookbook with more than 200 traditional recipes.

Flippin' Fantastic Bread

Although traditional-style subcontinental breads are more commonly associated with North India, you'll certainly encounter them at plenty of places in the south. Roti, the generic term for Indian-style bread, is a name used interchangeably with chapati to describe the most common variety: the irresistible unleavened round bread made with whole-wheat flour and cooked on a *tawa* (flat hotplate). *Puri* is deep-fried dough puffed up like a crispy balloon. Kachori is somewhat similar, but the dough has been pepped up with corn or dhal, which makes it considerably thicker. Flaky, unleavened *paratha* can be eaten as is or jazzed up with fillings such as paneer (soft, unfermented cheese). The thick, usually teardrop-shaped naan is cooked in a tandoor (clay oven) and is especially scrummy when flavoured with garlic.

Dhal-icious!

Dhal, along with rice, is a mainstay of the South Indian diet. The most common forms of dhal in South India are *sambar* and *tuvar* (yellow lentils). You may encounter up to 60 different pulses including *channa*, a slightly sweeter version of the yellow split pea; tiny yellow or green ovals called *moong* (mung beans); salmon-coloured *masoor* (red lentils); *rajma* (kidney beans); *urad* (black gram or lentils); and *lobhia* (black-eyed peas).

The Fruits (and Vegetables) of Mother Nature

A visit to any South Indian market will reveal a vast and vibrant assortment of fresh fruit and vegetables, overflowing from large baskets or stacked in neat pyramids. The south is especially well known for its abundance of tropical fruits such as pineapples and papaya. Mangos abound during the summer months (especially April and May), with India boasting more than 500 varieties, the pick of the luscious bunch being the sweet Alphonso.

DEEP-SEA DELIGHTS

With around 7500km of coastline, it's no surprise that seafood is an important staple on the subcontinent, especially on the west coast, from Mumbai (Bombay) down to Kerala. Goa is particularly known among tourists for its succulent prawn dishes and fiery fish curries, but the fishing communities dotted along South India's entire Konkan Coast deserve praise for their unique seafood creations.

THE GREAT SOUTH INDIAN THALI

In South India, the thali is a favourite lunchtime meal. Inexpensive, satiating, wholesome and incredibly tasty, this is Indian food at its simple best. Whereas in North India the thali is usually served on a steel plate with indentations for the various side dishes (thali gets its name from the plate), in the south a thali is traditionally served on a flat steel plate that may be covered with a fresh banana leaf, or on a banana leaf itself.

In a restaurant, when the steel plate is placed in front of you, you may like to follow local custom and pour some water on the leaf then spread it around with your right hand. Soon enough a waiter with a large pot of rice will come along and heap mounds of it onto your plate, followed by servings of dhal, *sambar* (soupy lentils), *rasam* (dhal-based broth flavoured with tamarind), vegetable dishes, chutneys, pickles and *dahi* (curd/yoghurt). Using the fingers of your right hand, start by mixing the various side dishes with the rice, kneading and scraping it into mouth-sized balls, then scoop it into your mouth using your thumb to push the food in. It is considered poor form to stick your hand right into your mouth or to lick your fingers. Observing fellow diners will help get your thali technique just right. If it's all getting a bit messy, there should be a finger bowl of water on the table. Waiters will continue to fill your plate until you wave your hand over one or all of the offerings to indicate you have had enough.

DELICIOUS SOUTH INDIA A CULINARY CARNIVAL

Naturally in a region with so many vegetarians, *sabzi* (vegetables) make up a predominant part of the diet. Vegetables can be fried, roasted, curried, baked, mashed and stuffed into dosas or wrapped in batter to make deep-fried *pakoras* (fritters). Potatoes are ubiquitous and popularly cooked with various masalas, mixed with other vegetables, or mashed and fried for the street snack *aloo tikka* (mashed-potato patties). Onions are fried with other vegetables, ground into a paste for cooking with meats, and served raw as relishes. Heads of cauliflower are usually cooked dry on their own, with potatoes to make *aloo gobi* (potato-and-cauliflower curry), or with other vegetables such as carrots and beans. Also popular is *saag* (a generic term for leafy greens), which can include mustard, spinach and fenugreek. Something a little more unusual is the bumpy-skinned *karela* (bitter gourd) which, like the delicious *bhindi* (okra), is commonly prepared dry with spices.

Dakshin: Vegetarian Cuisine from South India by Chandra Padmanabhan is an easy-to-read and beautifully illustrated book of southern recipes.

Vegetarians & Vegans

South India is absolutely phenomenal when it comes to vegetarian food. There's little understanding of veganism (the term 'pure vegetarian' means without eggs) and animal products such as milk, butter, ghee and curd are included in most dishes. If you are vegan your first problem is likely to be getting a chef to completely understand your requirements.

For further information, surf the web – good places to begin include: Indian Vegan (www.indianvegan.com) and Vegan World Network (www.vegansworldnetwork.org).

Pickles, Chutneys & Relishes

No Indian meal is really complete without one, and often all, of the above. A relish can be anything from a tiny pickled onion to a delicately crafted fusion of fruit, nuts and spices. One of the most popular meal accompaniments is raita (mildly spiced yoghurt, often containing shredded cucumber or diced pineapple; served chilled), which makes a tongue-cooling counter to spicy food. *Chatnis* can come in any number of varieties (sweet or savoury) and can be made from many different vegetables, fruits, herbs and spices. But you should proceed with caution before polishing off that pickled speck sitting on your thali; it may quite possibly be the hottest thing that you have ever tasted.

In coastal areas, especially Goa and Kerala, it's hard to beat the beach shacks for a fresh, inexpensive seafood meal – from fried mussels, prawns and calamari to steamed fish, crab and lobster.

Dairy

Milk and milk products make a staggering contribution to Indian cuisine: *dahi* (curd/yoghurt) is commonly served with meals and is great for subduing heat; paneer is a godsend for the vegetarian majority; lassi is one in a host of nourishing sweet and savoury beverages; ghee is the traditional and pure cooking medium; and some of the finest *mithai* (Indian sweets) are made with milk.

Sweet at Heart

India has a fabulously colourful kaleidoscope of often sticky and squishy *mithai* (Indian sweets), most of them sinfully sugary. The main categories are *barfi* (a fudgelike milk-based sweet), soft *halwa* (made with vegetables, cereals, lentils, nuts or fruit), *ladoos* (sweet balls made of gram flour and semolina) and sweet balls made from *chhana* (unpressed paneer) such as *rasgullas* (cream-cheese balls flavoured with rose water). There are also simpler – but equally scrumptious – offerings such as crunchy *jalebis* (orange-coloured coils of deep-fried batter dunked in sugar syrup; served hot) that you'll see all over the country.

Payasam (called *kheer* in the north) is one of the most popular after-meal desserts. It's a creamy rice pudding with a light, delicate flavour, enhanced with cardamom, saffron, pistachios, flaked almonds, chopped cashews or slivered dried fruit. Other favourites include *gulab jamuns,* deep-fried balls of dough soaked in rose-flavoured syrup, and *kulfi,* a firm-textured ice cream made with reduced milk and flavoured with any number of nuts (often pistachio), fruits and berries. In the hill areas of Maharashtra you'll find *chikki,* a rock-hard, toffee-like confectionery.

Each year, an estimated 14 tonnes of pure silver is converted into the edible foil that decorates many Indian sweets, especially during the Diwali festival.

Street Food

Whatever the time of day, food vendors are frying, boiling, roasting, peeling, simmering, mixing, juicing or baking some type of food and drink to lure peckish passers-by. Small operations usually have one special that they serve all day, while other vendors have different dishes for breakfast, lunch and dinner. The fare varies as you venture between neighbourhoods, towns and regions; it can be as simple as puffed rice or peanuts roasted in hot sand, as unexpected as a spiced fried-egg sandwich, or as complex as the riot of different flavours known as *chaat* (savoury snack).

Devilishly delicious deep-fried fare is the staple of South Indian streets, and you'll find satiating samosas (deep-fried pastry triangles filled with spiced vegetables and less often meat) and *bhajia* (vegetable fritters) in

The fiery cuisine of the Karnatakan coastal city of Mangalore is famed for its flavour-packed seafood dishes. Mangalorean cuisine is diverse, distinct and characterised by its liberal use of chilli and fresh coconut.

Thin and crispy, pappadams (commonly referred to as pappad) are circle-shaped lentil- or chickpea-flour wafers served either before or with a meal.

PAAN

Meals are often rounded off with *paan,* a fragrant mixture of betel nut (also called areca nut), lime paste, spices and condiments wrapped in an edible, silky *paan* leaf. Peddled by *paan*-wallahs, who are usually strategically positioned outside busy restaurants, *paan* is eaten as a digestive and mouth-freshener. The betel nut is mildly narcotic and some aficionados eat *paan* the same way heavy smokers consume cigarettes – over the years these people's teeth can become rotted red and black.

There are two basic types of *paan:* mitha (sweet) and *saadha* (with tobacco). A parcel of *mitha paan* is a splendid way to finish a satisfying meal. Pop the whole parcel in your mouth and chew slowly, allowing the juices to ooooooooze.

RAILWAY SNACK ATTACK

One of the thrills of travelling by rail in India is the culinary circus that greets you at almost every station. Roving vendors accost arriving trains, yelling and scampering up and down the carriages; fruit, *namkin* (savoury nibbles), omelettes, nuts and sweets are offered through the grilles on the windows; and platform cooks try to lure you from the train with the sizzle of spicy goodies such as fresh samosas. Frequent rail travellers know which station is famous for which food item: Lonavla station in Maharashtra is largely known for *chikki* (a rock-hard, toffeelike confectionery).

varying degrees of spiciness. Much loved in Maharasthra is *vada pao*, a veg-burger of sorts, with a deep-fried potato patty in a bread bun served with hot chillies and tangy chutneys. Sublime kebabs doused in smooth curd and wrapped in warm Indian-style bread are most commonly found in neighbourhoods with a large Muslim community.

Daily Dining Habits

Three main meals a day is the norm. South Indians generally have an early breakfast, then a thali for lunch and/or several tiffin (an all-purpose Raj-era term for between-meal snacks) during the day. Dinner, usually large serves of rice, vegetables, curd and spicy side dishes, can be a late affair (post 9pm) depending on personal preference and possibly the season (eg late dinners during the warmer months). Restaurants usually spring to life after 9pm. Dishes are usually served all at once rather than as courses. Desserts are optional and most prevalent during festivals or other special occasions. Fruit often wraps up a meal.

Spiritual Sustenance

For many in India, food is considered just as critical for fine-tuning the spirit as it is for sustaining the body. Broadly speaking, Hindus traditionally avoid foods that are thought to inhibit physical and spiritual development, although there are few hard-and-fast rules. The taboo on eating beef (the cow is holy to Hindus) is the most rigid restriction. Jains avoid foods such as garlic and onions, which, apart from harming insects in their extraction from the ground, are thought to heat the blood and arouse sexual desire. You may come across vegetarian restaurants that make it a point to advertise the absence of onion and garlic in their dishes for this reason. Devout Hindus may also avoid garlic and onions. These items are also banned from most ashrams.

Some foods, such as dairy products, are considered innately pure and are eaten to cleanse the body, mind and spirit. Ayurveda, the ancient science of life, health and longevity, also influences food customs (see the boxed text, p300).

Pork is taboo for Muslims and stimulants such as alcohol are avoided by the most devout. *Halal* is the term for all permitted foods and *haram* for those prohibited. Fasting is considered an opportunity to earn the approval of Allah, to wipe the sin-slate clean and to understand the suffering of the poor.

Buddhists and Jains subscribe to the philosophy of ahimsa (nonviolence) and are mostly vegetarian. Jainism's central tenet is ultra-vegetarianism, and rigid restrictions are in place to avoid even potential injury to any living creature.

India's Sikh, Christian and Parsi communities have few or no restrictions on what they can eat.

CURRY

Technically speaking, there's no such thing as an Indian 'curry' – the word, an Anglicised derivative of the Tamil word *kari* (sauce), was used by the British as a term for any dish that includes spices.

For recipes online, try:

www.recipes indian.com

www.thokalath. com/cuisine

www.indianfood forever.com

STREET FOOD: TIPS

Tucking into street food is one of the joys of travelling in South India – here are some tips to help avoid tummy troubles.

» Give yourself a few days to adjust to the local cuisine, especially if you're not used to spicy food.

» You know the rule about following a crowd – if the locals are avoiding a particular vendor, you should too. Also take notice of the profile of the customers – any place popular with families will probably be your safest bet.

» Check how and where the vendor is cleaning the utensils, and how and where the food is covered. If the vendor is cooking in oil, have a peek to check it's clean. If the pots or surfaces are dirty, there are food scraps about or too many buzzing flies, don't be shy about making a hasty retreat.

» Don't be put off when you order some deep-fried snack and the cook throws it back into the wok. It's common practice to partly cook the snacks first and then finish them off once they've been ordered. In fact, frying them hot again will kill any germs.

» Unless a place is reputable (and busy), it's best to avoid eating meat from the street.

» The hygiene standard at juice stalls is wildly variable, so exercise caution. Have the vendor press the juice in front of you and steer clear of anything stored in a jug or served in a glass (unless you're absolutely convinced of the washing standards).

» Don't be tempted by glistening pre-sliced melon and other fruit, which keeps its luscious veneer with the regular dousing of (often dubious) water.

The Celebration Table

Although most Hindu festivals have a religious core, many are also great occasions for spirited feasting. Sweets rate among the most luxurious of foods and almost every special occasion is celebrated with a spectacular range. *Karanjis,* crescent-shaped flour parcels stuffed with sweet *khoya* (milk solids) and nuts, are synonymous with Holi, the most rambunctious Hindu festival, and it wouldn't be the same without sticky *malpuas* (wheat pancakes dipped in syrup), *barfis* and *pedas* (multicoloured pieces of *khoya* and sugar). Pongal is the major harvest festival of the south and is most closely associated with the dish of the same name, made with the season's first rice, along with jaggery, nuts, raisins and spices. Diwali, the festival of lights, is the most widely celebrated national festival, and some regions have specific Diwali sweets; if you're in Mumbai dive into delicious *anarsa* (rice-flour cookies).

Ramadan (Ramazan) is the Islamic month of fasting, when Muslims abstain from eating, drinking or smoking between sunrise and sunset. Each day's fast is often broken with dates – considered auspicious – followed by fruit and/or fruit juices. On the final day of Ramadan, Eid al-Fitr, a lavish feast celebrates the end of the fast with hearty nonvegetarian biryanis and a huge proliferation of special sweets.

Those curious about ayurvedic treatments that include food might be interested in *Healthy Living with Ayurveda* by Anuradha Singh.

Drinks, Anyone?

Nonalcoholic Drinks

Gujarat is India's only dry state but there are drinking laws in place all over the country, and each state may have regular dry days when the sale of alcohol from liquor shops is banned. To avoid paying high taxes, head for Goa, where booze isn't subject to the exorbitant levies of other states. Very few vegetarian restaurants serve alcohol,

South India grows both tea and coffee but unlike North India, where it has only fairly recently become all the rage to guzzle cappuccinos and lattes, coffee has long been popular down south. In the larger cities, you'll find ever-multiplying branches of hip coffee chains, such as Barista and Café Coffee Day, widely found in what were once chai strongholds. Meanwhile, on today's tea front, you can expect to find a wide assortment, from peppermint to rosehip and good old-fashioned Indian chai – the ultrasweet milky concoction that still reigns supreme.

In cities and towns particularly, you'll come across sugar-cane juice and fruit-juice vendors – be wary of hygiene standards. Some restaurants think nothing of adding salt or sugar to juice to intensify the flavours; ask the waiter to omit these if you don't want them. Coconut water is also popular in the south and you'll see vendors just about everywhere standing by mounds of green coconuts, machete at the ready. Finally, there's lassi, a refreshing and delicious iced curd (yoghurt) drink that comes in sweet and savoury varieties, or mixed with fruit.

For information about safely drinking water in India, see the boxed text, p506.

The Booze Files

An estimated three-quarters of India's drinking population quaffs 'country liquor' such as the notorious arak (liquor distilled from coconut-palm sap, potatoes or rice) of the south. This is widely known as the poor man's drink and millions are addicted to the stuff. Each year, many people are blinded or even killed by the methyl alcohol in illegal arak.

In Kerala, Goa and parts of Tamil Nadu, toddy (palm 'beer') is a milky white local brew made from the sap of the coconut palm. It's collected in pots attached to the tree by toddy-tappers and drunk either straight from the pot or distilled. In Goa toddy is called feni and is made either from coconut or – the more popular and potent version – from the fruit of the cashew tree. The fermented liquid is double-distilled to produce a knockout concoction that can be as much as 35% proof. Although usually drunk straight by locals, feni virgins should consider mixing it with a soft

Legend says that Buddha, after falling asleep during meditation, decided to cut his eyelids off in an act of penance. The lids grew into the tea plant, which, when brewed, banished sleep.

Complete Indian Cooking by Mridula Baljekar, Rafi Fernandez, Shehzad Husain and Manisha Kanani contains a host of southern favourites including chicken with green mango, masala mashed potatoes and Goan prawn curry.

SOUTHERN BELLES

Dosas (also spelt dosais), a family of large papery rice-flour crepes, usually served with a bowl of hot *sambar* (a soupy lentil dish with cubed vegetables) and another bowl of cooling coconut *chatni* (chutney), are a South Indian speciality that can be eaten at any time of day. The most popular is the masala dosa (stuffed with spiced potatoes), but there are also other fantastic dosa varieties – the *rava* dosa (batter made with semolina), the Mysore dosa (like masala dosa but with more vegetables and chilli in the filling), and the *pessarettu* dosa (batter made with mung-bean dhal) from Andhra Pradesh.

The humble *idli,* a traditional South Indian snack, is low-cal and nutritious, providing a welcome alternative to oil, spice and chilli. *Idlis* are spongy, round, white fermented rice cakes that you dip in *sambar* and coconut *chatni. Dahi idli* is an idli dunked in very lightly spiced yoghurt – brilliant for tender tummies. Other super southern snacks include *vadas* (doughnut-shaped deep-fried lentil savouries) and *appams* or *uttappams* (thick, savoury South Indian rice pancake with finely chopped onions, green chillies, coriander and coconut).

The subcontinent's wine industry is an ever-evolving one – take a cyber-sip of Indian wine at www.indianwine. com. Cheers!

drink. Decorative feni bottles can be found in Goan shops; they make a great gift or souvenir.

About a quarter of India's drinks market comprises Indian Made Foreign Liquors (IMFLs), produced with a base of rectified spirit. Recent years have seen a rise in the consumption of imported spirits, with a spiralling number of city watering holes and restaurants flaunting a dazzling array of domestic and foreign labels.

Beer is a hit everywhere, with the more upmarket bars and restaurants stocking local and foreign brands (Budweiser, Heineken, Corona and the like). Most of the domestic brands are straightforward Pilsners around the 5% alcohol mark; travellers largely champion Kingfisher.

Wine is steadily on the rise, despite the domestic wine-producing industry still being relatively new. The favourable climate and soil conditions in certain areas – such as parts of Maharasthra and Karnataka – have spawned some commendable Indian wineries including Indage, Grover Vineyards (www.groverwines.com) and Sula Vineyards (www.sulawines.com). Domestic offerings include chardonnay, chenin blanc, sauvignon blanc, cabernet sauvignon, shiraz and zinfandel. Also see the 'Grapes of Nasik' box on p82.

Naturally Beautiful

With its tremendous mix of landscapes, from lush rice paddies and breezy coconut groves to postcard-perfect beaches and mountain ranges, the great South Indian outdoors is nature at its spectacular best.

The most prominent geographical feature of the region is its dramatic mountain ranges. The Vindhya Range, which stretches nearly the entire width of peninsular India (roughly contiguous with the Tropic of Cancer), is the symbolic division between the north and the south. South of the Vindhya Range lies the Deccan plateau (Deccan is derived from the Sanskrit word *dakshina,* meaning south), a triangular-shaped mass of ancient rock that slopes gently towards the Bay of Bengal. On its western and eastern borders, the Deccan plateau is flanked by the Western and Eastern Ghats. Pockets of the ghats are now protected in forest reserves and national parks.

The Western Ghats (known in Goa and Maharashtra as the Sahyadris) start to rise just north of Mumbai (Bombay) and run parallel to the coast, gaining height as they go south until they reach the tip of the peninsula. The headwaters of southern rivers, such as the Godavari and Cauvery, rise in the peaks of the Western Ghats and drain into the Bay of Bengal.

The Eastern Ghats, a less dramatic chain of low, interrupted ranges, sweep northeast in the direction of Chennai (Madras) before turning northward, roughly parallel to the coast bordering the Bay of Bengal, until they merge with the highlands of central Odisha (Orissa).

At 2695m, Anamudi in Kerala is South India's highest peak. The Western Ghats have an average elevation of 915m, and are covered with tropical and temperate evergreen forest and mixed deciduous forest. The western coastal strip between Mumbai and Goa, known as the Konkan Coast, is studded with river estuaries and sandy beaches. Further south, the Malabar Coast forms a sedimentary plain into which are etched the sublime waterways and lagoons that characterise Kerala. The eastern coastline (known as the Coromandel Coast where it tracks through Tamil Nadu) is wider, drier and flatter.

Offshore from India are a series of island groups, politically part of India but geographically linked to the landmasses of Southeast Asia and islands of the Indian Ocean. The Andaman and Nicobar Islands sit far out in the Bay of Bengal (they comprise 572 islands and form the peaks of a vast submerged mountain range extending almost 1000km between Myanmar and Sumatra), while the coral atolls of Lakshadweep (300km west of Kerala) are a northerly extension of the Maldives islands, with a land area of just 32 sq km.

To stay abreast of current wildlife and wilderness issues, explore Indian Jungles (www.indian jungles.com).

Wonderful Wildlife

The subcontinent has some of the richest biodiversity in the world, with 2546 fish, 1250 bird, 460 reptile, 397 mammal and 240 amphibian species – among the highest counts for any country in the world. Understandably, wildlife-watching has become one of the country's prime tourist activities and there are dozens of national parks offering opportunities to spot rare and unusual wildlife. To find out where and when to get close to nature, see the boxed text at the end of this chapter.

India is one of around a dozen 'megadiversity' countries, which together make up an estimated 70% of the world's biodiversity. South India has three recognised biogeographic zones: the forested, wet and elevated Western Ghats, which run parallel to the west coast from Mumbai to Kerala; the flat, dry Deccan plateau; and the islands, including the Andaman and Nicobar Islands and Lakshadweep.

To keep your finger on the Indian government's green pulse, click on the Ministry of Environment & Forests site at www.envfor.nic.in.

Animals, Animal, Animals

Most people know that India is the natural home of the tiger and Indian elephant, but the forests, jungles, coastlines, waters and plains actually provide a habitat for a staggering multitude of species.

In South India, the tropical forests of the Western Ghats contain one of the rarest bats on earth – the small Salim Ali's fruit bat – as well as flying lizards (technically gliders), sloth bears, leopards, jungle cats, hornbills, parrots and hundreds of other bird species.

Offshore, the Lakshadweep in the Indian Ocean and the Andaman and Nicobar Islands in the Bay of Bengal preserve classic coral atoll ecosystems. Bottlenose dolphins, coral reefs, sea turtles and tropical fish flourish beneath the water, while seabirds, reptiles, amphibians and butterflies thrive on land. Members of the Andamans' small population of elephants have been known to swim up to 3km between islands.

Endangered Species

Despite having amazing biodiversity, India faces a growing challenge from its exploding human population. At last count, India had 569

THE INDIAN ELEPHANT

Revered in Hindu mythology and admired for its strength and stamina, the elephant traditionally appears in various guises in South India's history and culture.

Today, however, Indian elephants are exploited as well as honoured: tamed elephants are used in religious ceremonies or in logging (though they have largely been replaced by heavy machinery), while farmers fear the destructive capabilities of their wild brethren. Indian elephants weigh up to 5 tonnes and live in family groups, usually led by the oldest females. At puberty, males leave to pursue solitary lives. Elephants live in forest or grassland habitats and have voracious appetites, eating for up to 18 hours per day and wolfing down some 200kg of food, mostly grass, leaves and shrubs. While in search of food, elephants have been known to leave the forest and demolish farmers' entire crops, bringing themselves into unwanted human contact. Indeed, humans are the elephant's sole enemy. Along with loss of habitat from urban development and logging, elephants face an ongoing threat from poachers. The tusk of the male elephant is valued for its ivory, and illegal poaching has had serious effects on the gender balance.

The cultural significance of the elephant can be seen at temples and during festivals, where they may be colourfully decorated and lead processions. In Hindu creation myths, the elephant is the upholder of the universe and the foundation of life, while the elephant-headed deity Ganesh is the god of good fortune and remover of obstacles. Some temples have their own elephant, which takes part in rituals or waits patiently at the entrance with its mahout (keeper), accepting offers or coins with its trunk.

Safaris through forest reserves give you the opportunity to spot elephants in the wild, and some national parks offer elephant treks through the jungle.

threatened species, comprising 247 species of plants, 89 species of mammals, 82 species of birds, 26 species of reptiles, 68 species of amphibians, 35 species of fish and 22 species of invertebrates.

Prior to 1972 India had only five national parks, so the Wildlife Protection Act was introduced that year to set aside parks and stem the abuse of wildlife. The act was followed by a string of similar pieces of legislation with bold ambitions but few teeth with which to enforce them. A rare success story has been Project Tiger, launched in 1973 to protect India's big mammals. The main threats to wildlife continue to be habitat loss due to human encroachment and poaching by criminals, corrupt officials and businessmen at all levels of society. It is estimated that 846 tigers and 3140 leopards were poached between 1994 and 2008, while 320 elephants were poached from 2000 to 2008.

All of India's wild cats, from snow leopards to panthers and jungle cats, are facing extinction from habitat loss and poaching for the lucrative trade in skins and body parts for Chinese medicine. There are thought to be fewer than 1500 tigers, 200 to 600 snow leopards and 300 Asiatic lions still alive in the wild. Spurious health benefits are linked to every part of the tiger, from the teeth to the penis, and a whole tiger carcass can fetch upwards of US$53,000. Government estimates suggest that India is losing 1% of its tigers every year to poachers.

Even highly protected rhinos are poached for the medicine trade – rhino horn is highly valued as an aphrodisiac and as a material for making handles for daggers in the Persian Gulf. Elephants are also poached for ivory – we implore you not to support this trade by buying ivory souvenirs. Various species of deer are threatened by hunting for food and trophies, and the chiru, or Tibetan antelope, is nearly extinct because its hair is woven into wool for expensive shahtoosh shawls.

Other threatened species include lion-tailed macaques, glossy black Nilgiri langurs and the slender loris, an adept insect-catcher with huge eyes for nocturnal hunting. Sadly, there is still illegal trade in South India for live loris – their eyes are believed by some to be a powerful medicine for human-eye diseases, as well as a vital ingredient for love potions. South India's hilly regions are the last remaining stronghold of the endangered Nilgiri tahr (cloud goat).

In the Andaman Islands, the once-common dugong (*Dugong dugon;* a large herbivorous aquatic mammal with flipper-like forelimbs) has almost disappeared. It was hunted by mainland settlers for its meat and oil, and has also suffered from a loss of natural habitat (seagrass beds).

Birds

Birdlife is where South India really comes into its own, and there are several wetlands and sanctuaries supporting a large percentage of the country's water birds. Many species, including herons, cranes, storks and even flamingos, can be spotted at various sanctuaries.

In village ponds, you can often see a surprising array of birds, from the common sandpiper to the Indian pond heron, or paddy bird, surveying its domain. Waterways are particularly rich in birdlife; graceful white egrets and colourful kingfishers (including the striking storkbilled kingfisher, with its massive red bill) are common, as are smaller species, such as plovers, water hens and coots. Red-wattled and yellow-wattled lapwings can be readily recognised by the coloured, fleshy growths on their faces.

Birds of prey, such as harriers and buzzards, soar over open spaces searching for unwary birds and small mammals. Around rubbish dumps and carcasses, the black or pariah kite is a frequent visitor. Birds inhabiting forested areas include woodpeckers, barbets and

Visitors seeking an in-depth overview of India's habitats should take a look at *Ecosystems of India*, edited by JRB Alfred.

India's national animal is the tiger, its national bird is the peacock and its national flower is the lotus. The national emblem of India is a column topped by three Asiatic lions.

ELEPHANTS

malkohas (a colourful group of large, forest-dwelling cuckoos). Fruit-eaters include a number of pigeons (including the Nilgiri wood-pigeon and pompadour green-pigeon), doves, colourful parrots (including Malabar and plum-headed parakeets), minivets and various cuckoo-shrikes and mynas.

Hornbills are forest-dwelling birds similar to toucans, with massive curved bills. The largest is the great hornbill, sporting a large bill and a horny growth on its head (called a casque); the Malabar grey hornbill is endemic to the Malabar region.

Fish

The still-pristine coral around the archipelagos of Lakshadweep, Andaman and Nicobar supports a diverse marine ecosystem that hosts a myriad of tropical fish, including butterfly fish, parrotfish, the ugly porcupine fish and the light-blue surgeonfish. Along the Goan and Malabar Coasts, mackerel and sardines are prevalent, although overfishing from mechanised trawlers is an increasing problem. Other marine life off the coast of South India includes moray eels, crabs and sea cucumbers. Migratory visitors include the sperm whale.

Invertebrates

South India has some truly stunning butterflies and moths, including the Malabar banded swallowtail (*Papilio liomedon*) and the peacock hair-streak (*Thelca pavi*).

In the Andaman and Nicobar Islands, you may come across the coconut or robber crab (*Birgus latro*), a 5kg tree-climbing creature that combs the beaches for coconuts.

Leeches are common in the forests, especially during and immediately after the monsoon.

Mammals

The nocturnal sloth bear (*Melursus ursinus*) has short legs and shaggy black or brown hair, with a splash of white on its chest. It roams in the forested areas of the national parks and in the Nilgiri Hills.

The gaur (*Bos gaurus*), a wild ox (sometimes referred to as the Indian bison), can be seen in major national parks in Karnataka, Goa and Kerala. Up to 2m tall, it's born with light-coloured hair that darkens as it ages. With its immense bulk and white legs, the gaur is easily recognised. It prefers the wet *sholas* (virgin forests) and bamboo thickets of the Western Ghats.

The common dolphin (*Delphinus delphis*) is found off both coastlines of the Indian peninsula, and dugongs, although elusive, can sometimes be spotted off the Malabar Coast and the Andaman Islands.

ANTELOPES, GAZELLES & DEER

You'll see plenty of these grazers in South India's national parks, but keep your eyes peeled for the chowsingha (*Tetracerus quadricornis*), the only animal in the world with four horns. Also unusual is the nilgai (*Boselaphus tragocamelus*), the largest Asiatic antelope.

The blackbuck (*Antilope cervicapra*) has distinctive spiral horns and an attractive dark coat, making it a prime target for poachers. The dominant males develop dark, almost black, coats (usually dark brown in South India), while the 20 or so females and subordinate males in each herd are fawn in colour.

The slender chinkara (*Gazella gazella*; Indian gazelle), with its light-brown coat and white underbelly, favours the drier foothills and plains. It can be seen in small herds in national parks and sanctuaries in Karnataka and Andhra Pradesh.

Cheetal Walk: Living in the Wilderness by ERC Davidar describes the author's life among the elephants of the Nilgiri Hills and examines how they can be saved from extinction.

Read about wildlife, conservation and the environment in *Sanctuary Asia* (www.sanctuaryasia.com), a laudable publication raising awareness about India's precious natural heritage.

The Wildlife Protection Society of India (www.wpsi-india.org) is a premier wildlife conservation organisation campaigning for animal welfare via education, lobbying and legal action against poachers.

In many parts of South India, plastic bags and bottles clog drains, litter city streets and beaches, and even stunt grass growth in parks. Animals choke on the waste and the plastic also clogs water courses, heightening the risk of malaria and water-borne diseases. Campaigners estimate that about 75% of plastics used are discarded within a week and only 15% are recycled.

Fed up with ineffectual government policies to address the plastic problem, an increasing number of local initiatives are being pursued. For instance, in Kodaikanal (Kodai) shopping bags are now made from paper instead of plastic, while Goa has imposed various 'plast-free' zones, including on a number of its beaches.

Tourists can assist by not buying anything in plastic bags or bottles and encouraging hotels and shops to use environmentally friendly alternatives. Shopkeepers almost invariably put your purchases in plastic bags and, without turning it into a battle, it does help to request they use paper bags or nothing at all. Other ways to help include buying tea in terracotta cups at train stations and purifying your own drinking water (see the boxed text, p506).

The little mouse deer *(Tragulus meminna)* grows only 30cm tall. Delicate and shy, its speckled olive-brown/grey coat provides excellent camouflage in the forest. The common sambar *(Cervus unicolor)*, the largest of the Indian deer, sheds its impressive horns at the end of April; new ones start growing a month later. Meanwhile, the attractive chital *(Axis axis;* spotted deer) can be seen in most of South India's national parks, particularly those with wet evergreen forests. The barking deer *(Muntiacus muntjak)* is a small deer that bears tushes (elongated canine teeth) as well as small antlers, and its bark is said to sound much like that of a dog. It's a difficult animal to spot in its habitat, the thick forests of Tamil Nadu, Karnataka and Andhra Pradesh.

A Pictorial Guide to the Birds of the Indian Subcontinent, by Salim Ali and S Dillon Ripley, is a comprehensive field reference to birds found in South India.

TIGERS & LEOPARDS

The tiger *(Panthera tigris)* is the prize of wildlife-watchers in India, but being a shy, solitary animal, it's a rare sight. India has the world's largest tiger population, but most of the famous tiger reserves are in North India. Tigers prefer to live under the cover of tall grass or forest and can command vast areas of territory.

The leopard *(Panthera pardus)* does not stick exclusively to heavy forest cover, but it is possibly even harder to find than the tiger. Leopards are golden brown with black rosettes, although in the Western Ghats they may be almost entirely black.

DOG FAMILY

The wild dog, or dhole *(Cuon alpinus)*, is a tawny predator that hunts during the day in packs that have been known to bring down animals as large as a buffalo.

The Indian wolf *(Canis lupus linnaeus)* has suffered from habitat destruction and hunting, and is now rare in South India. Its coat is fawn with black stipples, and it's generally a much leaner-looking animal than its European or North American cousins. For a chance to see the Indian wolf, head to its preferred habitat of dry, open forest and scrubland of the Deccan plateau.

The Indian fox *(Vulpes bengalensis)* has a black-tipped tail and a greyish-coloured coat, and because of its appetite for rodents, it can coexist much more comfortably with farming communities than other carnivores.

The WWF (www.wwfindia. org) promotes environmental protection and wildlife conservation throughout India.

PRIMATES

You can't miss these cheeky creatures, whether it's passing through sign-posted 'monkey zones' as you traverse the Western Ghats or fending off overfriendly macaques at temples.

The little pale-faced bonnet macaque *(Macaca radiata)* is so named for the 'bonnet' of dark hair that covers its head. These macaques live in highly structured troops where claims on hierarchy are commonly and noisily contested. They are opportunistic feeders – barely a grub, berry or leaf escapes their alert eyes and nimble fingers – and they love to congregate at tourist spots where excited families throw fruit their way. The crab-eating macaque *(Macaca fascicularis),* found in the Nicobar Islands, looks rather like a rhesus or a bonnet macaque, but has a longer, thicker tail. In contrast, the lion-tailed macaque *(Macaca silenus)* has a thick mane of greyish hair that grows from its temples and cheeks.

Less shy is the common langur *(Presbytis entellus)* or Hanuman monkey, recognisable by its long limbs and black face. India's most hunted primate is the Nilgiri langur *(Trachypithecus johni),* which inhabits the dense forests of the Western Ghats, including the *sholas* of the Nilgiri and Annamalai ranges. This vegetarian monkey is pursued by poachers for the supposed medicinal qualities of its flesh and viscera.

The peculiar-looking slender loris *(Loris tardigradus)* has a soft, woolly, brown or grey coat and huge, bushbaby eyes. Nocturnal, this endangered species comes down from the trees only to feed on insects, leaves, berries and lizards.

Reptiles & Amphibians

Of the 32 species of turtles and tortoises in India, you may see the hawks-bill, leatherback, loggerhead or endangered olive ridley species in the waters of South India. Turtles are protected, but it's possible to see them nesting in some areas, notably at Morjim in Goa. If you're lucky, you may see the Indian star tortoise *(Geochelone elegans)* waddling along the forest floor in Andhra Pradesh.

Three species of crocodiles are found in India, two of them in South India – the mugger, or marsh, crocodile *(Crocodylus palustris)* and the saltwater crocodile *(Crocodylus porosus).* The latter lives in the Andaman and Nicobar Islands, while the mugger is extensively distributed in rivers and freshwater lakes in South India thanks to government breeding programs. If you don't see them in the wild, you certainly will at the Crocodile Bank, a breeding farm 40km south of Chennai.

The Plant Kingdom

Once almost entirely covered in forest, India's total forest cover is now estimated to be around 20%, although the Forest Survey of India has set an optimistic target of 33%. Despite widespread clearing of native habitats, the country boasts 49,219 plant species, of which around 5200 are endemic. Species on the southern peninsula show Malaysian ancestry, while desert plants in Rajasthan are more clearly allied with the Middle East and conifer forests of the Himalaya derive from European and Siberian origins.

Forest types in South India include tropical, wet and semi-evergreen forests of the Andaman and Nicobar Islands and Western Ghats; tropical, moist deciduous forests in the Andamans, southern Karnataka and Kerala; tropical thorn forests, found in much of the drier Deccan plateau; and montane and wet temperate forests in the higher parts of Tamil Nadu and Kerala.

Characteristic of the Nilgiri and Annamalai Hills in the Western Ghats are the patches of moist evergreen forest restricted to the valleys and steep, protected slopes. Known as *sholas,* these islands of dark green are

---

Get the inside track on Indian environmental issues at Down to Earth (www.downtoearth.org.in), an online magazine that dives into subjects often overlooked by the mainstream media.

Fish Curry & Rice published by the Goa Foundation is an incisive study of the Goan environment and the threats facing it.

surrounded by expansive grasslands covering the more exposed slopes. They provide essential shelter and food for animals, but their limited size and patchy distribution make *sholas* vulnerable to natural and human disturbances.

Indian rosewood *(Dalbergia latifolia)*, Malabar kino *(Pterocarpus marsupium)* and teak have been virtually cleared from some parts of the Western Ghats, and sandalwood *(Santalum album)* is diminishing across India due to illegal logging for the incense and wood-carving industries. A bigger threat to forestry is firewood harvesting, often carried out by landless peasants who squat on gazetted government land.

Widely found in the south are banyan figs with their dangling aerial roots, bamboo (in the Western Ghats), coconut palms (on the islands and along the coastal peninsula), Indian coral trees (along the coasts) and tiny pockets of mangroves. India is home to around 2000 species of orchid, about 10% of those found worldwide. The Nilgiri Hills is one of the finest places to spot orchids, such as the Christmas Orchid *(Calanthe triplicata)*.

Around 2000 plant species are described in ayurveda (traditional Indian herbal medicine), while close to 100 plant species are used in *amchi* (Tibetan traditional medicine).

National Parks & Wildlife Sanctuaries

India has 97 national parks and 486 wildlife sanctuaries, which constitute about 5% of India's territory. An additional 70 parks have been authorised on paper but not yet implemented on the ground. There are also 14 biosphere reserves, overlapping many of the national parks and sanctuaries, providing safe migration channels for wildlife and allowing scientists to monitor biodiversity. In South India, most of the parks were established to protect wildlife from loss of habitat, so entry is often restricted to tours.

We heartily recommend visiting at least one national park/sanctuary on your travels – the experience of coming face to face with a wild animal will stay with you for a lifetime, while your visit adds momentum to efforts to protect India's natural resources. Wildlife reserves tend to be off the beaten track and infrastructure can be limited – book transport and accommodation in advance, and check opening times, permit requirements and entry fees before you visit. Many parks close to conduct a census of wildlife in the off-season, while monsoon rains can make wildlife-viewing tracks inaccessible.

Almost all parks offer jeep or van tours, but you can also search for wildlife on guided treks, boat trips and elephant safaris.

Environmental Challenges

With more than a billion people, ever-expanding industrial and urban centres, and an expansive growth in chemical-intensive farming, India's environment is under tremendous threat. An estimated 65% of India's land is degraded in some way and nearly all of that land is seriously degraded, with the government consistently falling short on most of its environmental protection goals due to lack of enforcement or willpower.

Despite numerous new environmental laws since the 1984 Bhopal disaster (for further information see www.bhopal.org), corruption continues to exacerbate environmental degradation – companies involved in hydroelectricity, mining, and uranium and oil exploration provide the worst examples of the flagrant flouting of environmental rules. Usually, the people most affected are low-caste rural farmers and Adivasis (tribal people) who have limited political representation and few resources to fight big businesses.

Between 11% and 27% of India's agricultural output is lost because of soil degradation from over-farming, rising soil salinity, loss of tree cover and poor irrigation. The human cost is heart-rending and lurking behind all these problems is a basic Malthusian truth: there are too many people for India to support at its current level of development.

NATURALLY BEAUTIFUL ENVIRONMENTAL CHALLENGES

PARK/SANCTUARY	PAGE	LOCATION	FEATURES	BEST TIME TO VISIT
Calimere (Kodikkarai) Wildlife & Bird Sanctuary	n/a	near Thanjavur, Tamil Nadu	coastal wetland; dolphins, sea turtles, crocodiles, flamingos, waterfowl, wading birds, mynas & barbets	Nov-Jan
Dubare Forest Reserve	p189	near Madikeri, Karnataka	interactive camp for retired working elephants	Sep-May
Indira Gandhi Wildlife Sanctuary (Annamalai)	n/a	near Pollachi, Tamil Nadu	forested mountains; elephants, gaurs, tigers, jungle cats, bears, flying squirrels, civet cats	year-round, except in periods of drought
Mahatma Gandhi Marine National Park	p399	Andaman & Nicobar Islands	mangrove forests & coral reefs	Nov-Apr
Nilgiri Biosphere Reserve, including Wayanad Wildlife Sanctuary, Bandipur National Park, Nagarhole National Park, Mudumalai National Park	Wayanad p300, Bandipur p185, Nagarhole p185, Mudumalai p387	Tamil Nadu, Karnataka & Kerala	forest; elephants, tigers, deer, gaurs, sambars, muntjacs, mouse deers, chitals & bonnet macaques	Mar-May (some areas year-round)
Periyar Wildlife Sanctuary	p273	Kumily, Kerala	wooded hills; lion-tailed macaques, elephants, gaurs, otters, dholes, pythons, kingfishers & fishing owls	Oct-Jun
Ranganathittu Bird Sanctuary	p180	near Mysore, Karnataka	river & islands; storks, ibises, egrets, spoonbills & cormorants	Jun-Nov
Sanjay Gandhi National Park	p51	near Mumbai, Maharashtra	scenic city park; water birds, flying foxes & leopards	Aug-Apr
Tadoba-Andhari Tiger Reserve	p96	south of Nagpur, Maharashtra	deciduous forest, grasslands & wetlands; tigers, dholes, nilgais & gaurs	Feb-May
Vedantangal Bird Sanctuary	p336	near Chengalpattu, Tamil Nadu	forest & lake; cormorants, egrets, herons, storks, ibises, spoonbills, grebes & pelicans	Nov-Jan

While the Indian government could undoubtedly do more, some blame must also fall on Western farm subsidies that artificially reduce the cost of imported produce, undermining prices for Indian farmers.

As anywhere, tourists tread a fine line between providing an incentive for change and making the problem worse.

Deforestation

Since Independence, some 53,000 sq km of India's forests have been cleared for logging and farming, or damaged by urban expansion, mining, industrialisation and river dams. The number of mangrove forests has halved since the early 1990s, reducing the nursery grounds for the fish that stock the Indian Ocean and Bay of Bengal. Demand for fuel and building materials, natural fires and traditional slash-and-burn farming, destruction of forests for mining or farmland, and illegal smuggling of teak, rosewood and sandalwood have all contributed to this drastic deforestation.

One of the most dramatic examples of deforestation is in the Andaman and Nicobar Islands, where forest cover has been slashed from 90% to a mere 20%. Although protected forest reserves have been established on most islands here, illegal and sanctioned logging continues.

India's first Five Year Plan in 1951 recognised the importance of forests for soil conservation and various policies have been introduced to increase forest cover. However, over the years there have been allegations of haphazard implementation by officials as well as cases of ordinary people clearing forests for firewood and grazing in forest areas. Try to minimise the use of wood-burning stoves while you travel (this is less of an issue in areas with fast-growing pine species in the hills).

Marine Matters

The marine life along the 3000km-long coastline of South India and around the outlying archipelagos is under constant threat from pollution, sewage and harmful fishing methods. Ports, dams and tourism all contribute to the degradation of South India's marine environment.

India's seas have been overfished to such an extent that stocks are noticeably dwindling. Trawlers and factory fishing ships have largely replaced traditional log boats, and in some areas – eg the coast of Kerala – fishing communities are struggling to find other sources of income. Over the past decade, the international demand for prawns saw a plethora of prawn farms set up in South India, resulting in environmental damage to the coastline and birdlife as well as to farmland. There are now laws in place to curtail the effects of prawn farming, although these are not always adhered to.

Mangroves

About 2.5 million hectares of mangroves have been destroyed in India since 1900. Mangroves are home to migratory birds and marine life, and are the first defence against soil erosion. They also help protect the coast from natural disasters, such as tidal waves and cyclones. Destruction of South India's mangroves has been caused by cattle grazing, logging, water pollution, prawn farming and tidal changes caused by the erosion of surrounding land. On the coast of Tamil Nadu and in the Andaman and Nicobar Islands, there have been efforts to reintroduce mangroves around fishing villages as a protective barrier following the damage caused by the devastating 2004 tsunami.

Coral Reefs

Three major coral reefs are located around the islands of Lakshadweep, Andaman and Nicobar, as well as the Gulf of Mannar (near Sri Lanka). Coral is a crucial part of the fragile marine ecology, but is under constant threat from overfishing and bottom-of-the-sea trawling. Other factors contributing to the onslaught against the reefs are shipping, pollution, sewage, poaching, and excessive silt caused by deforestation and urban development on the land.

The Kurinji shrub, which produces bright purple-blue coloured blossoms only every 12 years, is unique to the hills of South India's Western Ghats. Unfortunately, the next blossom isn't due until 2016!

The Foundation for Revitalisation of Local Health Traditions has a search engine for medicinal plants at www.medicinalplants.in. Travellers with a strong interest should get CP Khare's *Encyclopedia of Indian Medicinal Plants*.

The Goa Foundation (http://goafoundation.org) is the primary environmental monitoring group in Goa.

NATURALLY BEAUTIFUL ENVIRONMENTAL CHALLENGES

Spiritual India

From a mother performing *puja* (prayers) for her child's forthcoming exams to a mechanic who has renounced his material life and set off on the path to self-realisation, religion suffuses almost every aspect of life in India.

India's major religion, Hinduism, is practised by 80.5% of the population. Along with Buddhism, Jainism and Zoroastrianism, Hinduism is one of the world's oldest extant religions, with roots extending beyond 1000 BC.

Islam is India's largest minority religion; 13.4% of the population is Muslim. Islam is believed to have been introduced to northern India by invading armies (in the 16th and 17th centuries the Mughal empire controlled much of North India) and to the south by Arab traders.

Christians comprise about 2.3% of the population, with approximately 75% living in South India, while the Sikhs – estimated at around 1.9% of the population – are mostly found in the northern state of Punjab. Around 0.8% of the population is Buddhist, with Bodhgaya (Bihar) being a major pilgrimage destination. Jainism is followed by about 0.4% of the population, with the majority of Jains living in Gujarat and Mumbai. Parsis, adherents of Zoroastrianism, today number somewhere between 60,000 and 69,000 – a mere drop in the ocean of India's billion-plus population. Historically, Parsis settled in Gujarat and became farmers; however, during British rule they moved into commerce, forming a prosperous community in Mumbai. Newspaper reports indicate that there are less than 5000 Jews left in India, most living in Mumbai and parts of South India.

Tribal religions have so merged with Hinduism and other mainstream religions that very few are now clearly identifiable. It's believed that some basic tenets of Hinduism may have originated in tribal culture.

For details about India's major religious festivals, see the Month by Month chapter.

Communal Conflict

Religion-based conflict has been a bloody part of India's history. The post-Independence partition of the country into Hindu India and Muslim Pakistan resulted in horrendous carnage and epic displacement (see p421).

Later bouts of major sectarian violence in India include the Hindu/Sikh riots of 1984, which led to the assassination of then prime minister Indira Gandhi, and the politically fanned 1992 Ayodhya calamity, which sparked ferocious Hindu/Muslim clashes.

The ongoing dispute between India and Pakistan over Kashmir is also perilously entwined in religious conflict. Since Partition, India and Pakistan have fought two wars over Kashmir and have had subsequent artillery exchanges, coming dangerously close to war in 1999. The festering dispute over this landlocked territory continues to fuel Hindu/Muslim animosity on both sides of the border.

Hinduism

Hinduism has no founder or central authority and is not a proselytising religion. Essentially, Hindus believe in Brahman, who is eternal, uncreated and infinite; everything that exists emanates from Brahman and will ultimately return to it. The multitude of gods and goddesses are merely manifestations – knowable aspects of this formless phenomenon.

Hindus believe that earthly life is cyclical; you are born again and again (a process known as samsara), the quality of these rebirths being dependent upon your karma (conduct or action) in previous lives. Living a righteous life and fulfilling your dharma (moral code of behaviour; social duty) will enhance your chances of being born into a higher caste and better circumstances. Alternatively, if enough bad karma has accumulated, rebirth may take animal form. But it's only as a human that you can gain sufficient self-knowledge to escape the cycle of reincarnation and achieve moksha (liberation).

Gods & Goddesses

All Hindu deities are regarded as a manifestation of Brahman, who is often described as having three main representations (the Trimurti): Brahma, Vishnu and Shiva.

Brahman

The One; the ultimate reality. Brahman is formless, eternal and the source of all existence. Brahman is *nirguna* (without attributes), as opposed to all the other gods and goddesses, which are manifestations of Brahman and therefore *saguna* (with attributes).

Brahma

Only during the creation of the universe does Brahma play an active role. At other times he is in meditation. His consort is Saraswati, the goddess of learning, and his vehicle is a swan. He is sometimes shown sitting on a lotus that rises from Vishnu's navel, symbolising the interdependence of the gods. Brahma is generally depicted with four (crowned and bearded) heads, each turned towards a point of the compass.

Vishnu

The preserver, Vishnu is associated with 'right action'. He protects and sustains the good in the world. He is usually depicted with four arms, holding a lotus, a conch shell (as it can be blown like a trumpet it symbolises the cosmic vibration from which all existence emanates), a discus and a mace. His consort is Lakshmi, the goddess of wealth, and his vehicle is Garuda, the man-bird creature. The Ganges is said to flow from his feet.

Shiva

Shiva is the destroyer, but without whom creation couldn't occur. Shiva's creative role is phallically symbolised by his representation as the frequently worshipped lingam. With 1008 names, Shiva takes many forms, including Nataraja, lord of the *tandava* (cosmic victory dance), who paces out the cosmos' creation and destruction.

Sometimes Shiva has snakes draped around his neck and is shown holding a trident (representative of the Trimurti) as a weapon while riding Nandi, his bull. Nandi symbolises power and potency, justice and moral order. Shiva's consort, Parvati, is capable of taking many forms.

Murugan

One of Shiva's sons, Murugan is a popular deity in South India, especially in Tamil Nadu. He is sometimes identified with another of Shiva's sons,

Unravelling the basic tenets of Hinduism are *Hinduism: An Introduction* by Shakunthala Jagannathan and *Hinduism: An Introduction* by Dharam Vir Singh.

The Hindu pantheon is said to have around 330 million deities; those worshipped are a matter of personal choice or tradition.

SPIRITUAL INDIA HINDUISM

HINDU PANTHEON

Skanda, who enjoys a strong following in North India. Murugan's main role is that of protector and he is depicted as young and victorious.

Ayyappan

Ayyappan is another of Shiva's sons who is identified with the role of protector. It's said that he was born from the union of Shiva and Vishnu, both male. Vishnu is said to have assumed female form (as Mohini) to give birth. Ayyappan is often depicted riding on a tiger and accompanied by leopards, symbols of his victory over dark forces. Today, the Ayyappan following has become something of a men's movement, with devotees required to avoid alcohol, drugs, cigarettes and general misbehaviour before making the pilgrimage.

Other Prominent Deities

Elephant-headed Ganesh is the god of good fortune, remover of obstacles, and patron of scribes (the broken tusk he holds was used to write sections of the Mahabharata). His animal vehicle is Mooshak (a ratlike creature). How exactly Ganesh came to have an elephant's head is a story with several variations. One legend says that Ganesh was born to Parvati in the absence of his father (Shiva), so initially grew up not knowing him. One day, as Ganesh stood guard while his mother bathed, Shiva returned and asked to be let into Parvati's presence. Ganesh, who didn't recognise Shiva, refused. Enraged, Shiva lopped off Ganesh's head, only to later discover, much to his horror, that he had slaughtered his own son. He vowed to replace Ganesh's head with that of the first creature he came across, which happened to be an elephant.

Another prominent deity, Krishna is an incarnation of Vishnu sent to earth to fight for good and combat evil. His alliances with the *gopis* (milkmaids) and his love for Radha have inspired countless paintings and songs. Depicted with blue-hued skin, Krishna is often seen playing the flute.

Hanuman is the hero of the Ramayana and loyal ally of Rama; he embodies the concept of bhakti (devotion). Hanuman is the king of the monkeys, but is capable of taking on other forms.

Among the Shaivite (followers of the Shiva movement), Shakti – the goddess as mother and creator – is worshipped as a force in her own right. The concept of *shakti* is embodied in the ancient goddess Devi (divine mother), who is also manifested as Durga and, in a fiercer evil-destroying incarnation, Kali. Other widely worshipped goddesses include Lakshmi, the goddess of wealth, and Saraswati, the goddess of learning.

Sacred Texts

Hindu sacred texts fall into two categories: those believed to be the word of god (*shruti,* meaning 'heard') and those produced by people (*smriti,* meaning 'remembered'). The Vedas are regarded as *shruti* knowledge and are considered the authoritative basis for Hinduism. The oldest of the Vedic texts, the Rig-Veda, was compiled over 3000 years ago. Within its 1028 verses are prayers for prosperity and longevity as well as an explanation of the universe's origins. The Upanishads, the last parts of the Vedas, reflect on the mystery of death and emphasise the oneness of the universe. The oldest of the Vedic texts were written in Vedic Sanskrit (related to Old Persian). Later texts were composed in classical Sanskrit, but many have been translated into the vernacular.

The *smriti* texts comprise a collection of literature spanning centuries and include expositions on the performance of domestic ceremonies as well as the proper pursuit of government, economics and religious law. Among its well-known works are the Ramayana and Mahabharata, as well as the Puranas, which expand on the epics and promote the notion

Shiva is sometimes characterised as the lord of yoga, a Himalaya-dwelling ascetic with matted hair, an ash-smeared body and a third eye symbolising wisdom.

Did you know that blood-drinking Kali is another form of milk-giving Gauri? *Myth = Mithya: A Handbook of Hindu Mythology* by Devdutt Pattanaik sheds light on this and other fascinating Hindu folklores

THE SACRED SEVEN

The number seven has special significance in Hinduism. There are seven sacred Indian cities, each of which are major pilgrimage centres: Varanasi, associated with Shiva; Haridwar, where the Ganges enters the plains from the Himalaya; Ayodhya, birthplace of Rama; Dwarka, with the legendary capital of Krishna thought to be off the Gujarat coast; Mathura, birthplace of Krishna; Kanchipuram, site of historic Shiva temples; and Ujjain, venue every 12 years of the Kumbh Mela.

There are also seven sacred rivers: the Ganges (Ganga), Saraswati (thought to be underground), Yamuna, Indus, Narmada, Godavari and Cauvery.

of the Trimurti. Unlike the Vedas, reading the Puranas is not restricted to initiated higher-caste males.

The Mahabharata

Thought to have been composed at some time around the 1st millennium BC, the Mahabharata focuses on the exploits of Krishna. By about 500 BC the Mahabharata had evolved into a far more complex creation with substantial additions, including the Bhagavad Gita (where Krishna proffers advice to Arjuna before a battle).

The story centres on conflict between the heroic gods (Pandavas) and the demons (Kauravas). Overseeing events is Krishna, who has taken on human form. Krishna acts as charioteer for the Pandava hero Arjuna, who eventually triumphs in a great battle with the Kauravas.

The Ramayana

Composed around the 3rd or 2nd century BC, the Ramayana is believed to be largely the work of one person, the poet Valmiki. Like the Mahabharata, it centres on conflict between the gods and demons.

The story goes that Dasharatha, the childless king of Ayodhya, called upon the gods to provide him with a son. His wife duly gave birth to a boy. But this child, named Rama, was in fact an incarnation of Vishnu, who had assumed human form to overthrow the demon king of Lanka, Ravana. The adult Rama, who won the hand of the princess Sita in a competition, was chosen by his father to inherit his kingdom. At the last minute Rama's stepmother intervened and demanded that her son, Barathan, take Rama's place. Barathan, upon hearing the unjust news, was very upset and implored Rama to take his rightful place on the throne. However, Rama refused to disobey the wishes of his parents, so Barathan ruled on his behalf.

Rama, Sita and Rama's brother, Lakshmana, were exiled and went off to the forests, where Rama and Lakshmana battled demons and dark forces. Rama's father died of grief when he heard the news of his son's exile.

Ravana's sister attempted to seduce Rama. She was rejected and, in revenge, Ravana captured Sita and spirited her away to his palace in Lanka. Rama, assisted by an army of monkeys led by the loyal monkey god Hanuman, eventually found the palace, killed Ravana and rescued Sita. All returned victorious to Ayodhya, where Rama was welcomed by Barathan and crowned king.

Two recommended publications containing English translations of holy Hindu texts are *The Bhagavad Gita* by S Radhakrishnan and *The Valmiki Ramayana* by Romesh Dutt.

Sacred Flora & Fauna

Animals, particularly snakes and cows, have long been worshipped in the subcontinent. For Hindus, the cow represents fertility and nurturing, while snakes (especially cobras) are associated with fertility and welfare. Naga stones (snake stones) serve the dual purpose of protecting humans from snakes and propitiating snake gods.

OM

One of Hinduism's most venerated symbols is 'Om'. Pronounced 'aum', it's a highly propitious mantra (sacred word or syllable). The 'three' shape symbolises the creation, maintenance and destruction of the universe (and thus the holy Trimurti). The inverted *chandra* (crescent or half moon) represents the discursive mind and the *bindu* (dot) within it, Brahman.

Buddhists believe that, if repeated often enough with complete concentration, it will lead to a state of blissful emptiness.

Plants can also have sacred associations, such as the banyan tree, which symbolises the Trimurti, while mango trees are symbolic of love – Shiva is believed to have married Parvati under one. Meanwhile, the lotus flower is said to have emerged from the primeval waters and is connected to the mythical centre of the earth through its stem. Often found in the most polluted of waters, the lotus has the remarkable ability to blossom above murky depths. The centre of the lotus corresponds to the centre of the universe, the navel of the earth; all is held together by the stem and the eternal waters. This is how Hindus are reminded their own lives should be – like the fragile yet resolute lotus, an embodiment of beauty and strength. So revered is the lotus that today it's India's national flower.

Worship

Worship and ritual play a paramount role in Hinduism. In Hindu homes you'll often find a dedicated worship area, where members of the family pray to the deities of their choice. Beyond the home, Hindus worship at temples. *Puja* is a focal point of worship and ranges from silent prayer to elaborate ceremonies. Devotees leave the temple with a handful of *prasad* (temple-blessed food), which is humbly shared among friends and family. Other forms of worship include *aarti* (the auspicious lighting of lamps or candles) and the playing of soul-soothing bhajans (devotional songs).

Islam

Islam was founded in Arabia by the Prophet Mohammed in the 7th century AD. The Arabic term *islam* means to surrender, and believers (Muslims) undertake to surrender to the will of Allah (God), which is revealed in the scriptures, the Quran. In this monotheistic religion, God's word is conveyed through prophets (messengers), of whom Mohammed is the most recent.

Following Mohammed's death, a succession dispute split the movement, and the legacy today is the Sunnis and the Shiites. Most Muslims in India are Sunnis. The Sunnis emphasise the 'well-trodden' path or the orthodox way. Shiites believe that only imams (exemplary leaders) can reveal the true meaning of the Quran.

All Muslims, however, share a belief in the Five Pillars of Islam: the shahada (declaration of faith: 'There is no God but Allah; Mohammed is his prophet'); prayer (ideally five times a day); the zakat (tax), in the form of a charitable donation; fasting (during Ramadan) for all except the sick, young children, pregnant women, the elderly and those undertaking arduous journeys; and the haj (pilgrimage) to Mecca, which every Muslim aspires to do at least once.

Sikhism

Sikhism, founded in Punjab by Guru Nanak in the 15th century, began as a reaction against the caste system and Brahmin domination of ritual. Sikhs believe in one god and, although they reject the worship of idols, some keep pictures of the 10 gurus as a point of focus. The Sikhs' holy book, the Guru Granth Sahib, contains the teachings of the 10 Sikh gurus, among others.

SADHU

A sadhu is someone who has surrendered all material possessions in pursuit of spirituality through meditation, the study of sacred texts, self-mortification and pilgrimage. Read more in *Sadhus: India's Mystic Holy Men* by Dolf Hartsuiker.

Like Hindus and Buddhists, Sikhs believe in rebirth and karma. In Sikhism, there's no ascetic or monastic tradition ending the cycles of rebirth.

Fundamental to Sikhs is the concept of Khalsa, or belief in a Sikh brotherhood of saint-soldiers who abide by strict codes of moral conduct (abstaining from alcohol, tobacco and drugs) and engage in a crusade for *dharmayudha* (righteousness). There are five *kakkars* (emblems) denoting the Khalsa brotherhood: *kesh* (the unshaven beard and uncut hair symbolising saintliness); *kangha* (comb to maintain the ritually uncut hair); *kaccha* (loose underwear symbolising modesty); *kirpan* (sabre or sword symbolising power and dignity); and *karra* (steel bangle symbolising fearlessness). Singh, literally 'Lion', is the name adopted by many Sikhs.

A belief in the equality of all beings lies at the heart of Sikhism. It's expressed in various practices, including *langar*, whereby people from all walks of life – regardless of caste and creed – sit side by side to share a complimentary meal prepared by volunteers in the communal kitchen of the *gurdwara* (Sikh temple).

To grasp the intricacies of Sikhism dive into *A History of the Sikhs* by Khushwant Singh, which comes in Volume 1 (1469–1839) and Volume 2 (1839–2004).

SPIRITUAL INDIA BUDDHISM

Buddhism

Buddhism developed in India when it was embraced by Emperor Ashoka during his reign (272–232 BC). It appears that Buddhist communities were quite influential in Andhra Pradesh between the 2nd and 5th centuries AD; missionaries from Andhra helped establish monasteries and temples in countries such as Thailand. However, Buddhism's influence waned as Hinduism's waxed in South India, about 1000 years after it was first introduced. It underwent a sudden revival in the 1950s when the Dalit leader, Dr Ambedkar, converted to Buddhism and brought many Dalit followers with him. Today these Neo-Buddhists, as they are often called, number about six million and are concentrated in Dr Ambedkar's home state of Maharashtra.

There are several communities of Tibetan refugees in South India, who have established a number of new monasteries and convents since the 1960s. The Bylakuppe area of Karnataka is one of the more easily accessible Tibetan settlements – see p189 for more information.

Both the current Dalai Lama and the 17th Karmapa reside in the north Indian state of Himachal Pradesh.

Jainism

Jainism arose in the 6th century BC as a reaction against the caste restraints and rituals of Hinduism. It was founded by Mahavira, a contemporary of the Buddha.

Jains believe that liberation can be attained by achieving complete purity of the soul. Purity means shedding all *karman*, matter generated by one's actions that binds itself to the soul. By following various austerities

---

GURU NANAK: SIKHISM'S FIRST GURU

Born in present-day Pakistan, Guru Nanak (1469-1539), the founder of Sikhism, was unimpressed with both Muslim and Hindu religious practices. Unlike many Indian holy men, he believed in family life and the value of hard work – he married, had two sons and worked as a farmer when not travelling around, preaching and singing self-composed *kirtan* (Sikh devotional songs) with his Muslim musician, Mardana. He performed miracles and emphasised meditation on God's name as the best way to enlightenment.

Nanak believed in equality centuries before it became fashionable and campaigned against the caste system. He was a practical guru – 'a person who makes an honest living and shares earnings with others recognises the way to God'. He appointed his most talented disciple to be his successor, not one of his sons.

His *kirtan* are still sung in *gurdwaras* (Sikh temples) and his picture hangs in millions of homes.

Buddhism arose in the 6th century BC as a reaction against the strictures of Brahminical Hinduism. Buddha (Awakened One) is believed to have lived from about 563 BC to 483 BC. Formerly a prince (Siddhartha Gautama), Buddha, at the age of 29, embarked on a quest for emancipation from the world of suffering. He achieved nirvana (the state of full awareness) at Bodhgaya (Bihar), aged 35.

Buddha taught that existence is based on Four Noble Truths – that life is rooted in suffering, that suffering is caused by craving, that one can find release from suffering by eliminating craving, and that the way to eliminate craving is by following the Noble Eightfold Path. This path consists of right understanding, right intention, right speech, right action, right livelihood, right effort, right awareness and right concentration. By successfully complying with these one can attain nirvana.

(eg fasting and meditation) one can shed *karman* and purify the soul. Right conduct is essential, and fundamental to this is ahimsa (nonviolence) in thought and deed towards any living thing.

The religious disciplines of the laity are less severe than for monks, with some Jain monks going naked. The slightly less ascetic maintain a bare minimum of possessions including a broom, with which to sweep the path before them to avoid stepping on any living creature, and a piece of cloth that is tied over their mouth to prevent the accidental inhalation of insects.

One notable Jain holy site in South India is Sravanabelagola in Karnataka.

Christianity

There are various theories circulating about Christ's link to the subcontinent. Some, for instance, believe that Jesus spent his 'lost years' in India, while others say that Christianity came to South India with St Thomas the Apostle in AD 52. However, many scholars say it's more likely Christianity is traced to around the 4th century with a Syrian merchant, Thomas Cana, who set out for Kerala with around 400 families to establish what later became a branch of the Nestorian church. Today, the Christian community is fractured into a multitude of established churches and new evangelical sects.

Set in Kerala against the backdrop of caste conflict and India's struggle for independence, *The House of Blue Mangoes* by David Davidar spans three generations of a Christian family.

The Nestorian church sect survives today; services are in Armenian, and the Patriarch of Baghdad is the sect's head. Thrissur (Trichur) is the church's centre. Other Eastern Orthodox sects include the Jacobites and the Syrian Orthodox churches.

Catholicism established a strong presence in South India in the wake of Vasco da Gama's visit in 1498. Catholic orders that have been active in the region include the Dominicans, Franciscans and Jesuits. The faith is most noticeable in Goa, not only in the basilicas and convents of Old Goa but also in the dozens of active whitewashed churches scattered through towns and villages. Protestant missionaries are believed to have arrived in South India from around the 18th century and today most of this minority group belong to the Church of South India, which comprises various denominations including Anglican, Methodist and Presbyterian.

Evangelical Christian groups have made inroads both into the other Christian communities and into lower caste and tribal groups across South India. According to news reports, some congregations have been seen as being aggressive in seeking converts, and in retaliation a number of Christian communities have been targeted by Hindu nationalist groups.

Zoroastrianism

Zoroastrianism, founded by Zoroaster (Zarathustra) in Persia in the 6th century BC, is based on the concept of dualism, whereby good and evil are locked in a continuous battle. Zoroastrianism isn't quite monotheistic: good and evil entities coexist, although believers are urged to honour only the good. Both body and soul are united in this struggle of good versus evil. Although humanity is mortal it has components that are timeless, such as the soul. On judgement day the soul isn't called to account – but a pleasant afterlife does depend on one's deeds, words and thoughts during earthly existence. Zoroastrianism was eclipsed in Persia by the rise of Islam in the 7th century and its followers, many of whom openly resisted Islam, suffered persecution. Over the following centuries, some emigrated to India, where they became known as Parsis.

The Zoroastrian funerary ritual involves the 'Towers of Silence' where the corpse is laid out and exposed to vultures, which pick the bones clean.

Judaism

There are fewer than 5000 Jews left in India, most living in Mumbai and scattered pockets of South India. South India's Jews first settled in the region from the Middle East as far back as the 1st century. They became established at Kochi (Cochin), and their legacy continues in the still-standing synagogues and trading houses – see p280.

Tribal Religions

Tribal religions have merged with Hinduism and other mainstream religions so that very few are now clearly identifiable. It's believed that some basic tenets of Hinduism may have originated in ancient tribal culture.

Village and tribal people in South India have their own belief systems, which are much less accessible or obvious than the temples, rituals and other outward manifestations of the mainstream religions. The village deity may be represented by a stone pillar in a field, a platform under a tree or an iron spear stuck in the ground. Village deities are generally seen as less remote and more concerned with the immediate happiness and prosperity of the community; in most cases they are female. There are also many beliefs about ancestral spirits, including those who died violently.

To learn more about some of South India's tribal groups, see the Nehru Centenary Tribal Museum (p216), Island Indigenes boxed text (p394) and Hill Tribes of the Nilgiri boxed text (p382).

The Last Jews of Kerala by Edna Fernandes proffers an interesting window on the last remaining members of Kerala's dwindling Jewish community.

RELIGIOUS ETIQUETTE

Whenever visiting a sacred site, always dress and behave respectfully – don't wear shorts or sleeveless tops (this applies to men and women) and refrain from smoking. Loud and intrusive behaviour isn't appreciated, and neither are public displays of affection or kidding around.

Before entering a holy place, remove your shoes (tip the shoe-minder a few rupees when retrieving them) and check if photography is allowed. You're permitted to wear socks in most places of worship – often necessary during warmer months, when floors can be uncomfortably hot.

Religious etiquette advises against touching locals on the head, or directing the soles of your feet at a person, religious shrine or image of a deity. Protocol also advises against touching someone with your feet or touching a carving of a deity.

Head cover (for women and sometimes men) is required at some places of worship – especially *gurdwaras* (Sikh temples) and mosques – so carry a scarf just to be on the safe side. There are some sites that don't admit women and some that deny entry to nonadherents of their faith – enquire in advance. Women may be required to sit apart from men. Jain temples request the removal of leather items you may be wearing or carrying and may also request menstruating women not to enter.

Taking photos inside a shrine, at a funeral, at a religious ceremony or of people taking a holy dip can be offensive – ask first. Flash photography may be prohibited in certain areas of a shrine, or may not be permitted at all.

CRAFTS

The Great Indian Bazaar

South India is filled with bustling old bazaars and modern shopping malls that sell a staggering range of goodies: glossy gemstones, exquisite sculptures, sumptuous silks, chunky tribal jewellery, traditional shawls, beautiful woodwork and rustic village handicrafts. Many crafts fulfil a practical need as much as an aesthetic one.

Every region has its own special arts and crafts, usually showcased in state emporiums and cottage industries' (fair-trade) cooperatives. These shops normally charge fair fixed prices; almost everywhere else, you'll have to don your haggling hat (read the 'Art of Haggling' boxed text in this chapter). Opening hours for shops vary – consult the Shopping sections of regional chapters for details.

Be cautious when buying items that include delivery to your country of residence and be wary of being led to shops by smooth-talking touts (see 'Touts & Commission Agents' on p477). Exporting antiques is prohibited (read the 'Prohibited Exports' box on p483).

So much to buy, so little luggage space...Happy shopping!

Crafts aren't necessarily confined to their region of origin – artists migrate and have sometimes been influenced by the ideas of other regions – which means you can come across, for example, a Kashmiri handicraft emporium anywhere in India.

Bronze Figures, Pottery, Stone Carving & Terracotta

In southern India and parts of the Himalaya, small images of deities are created by the age-old lost-wax process. A wax figure is made, a mould is formed around it, and the wax is melted and poured out and replaced with molten metal; the mould is then broken open to reveal the figure inside. Figures of Shiva as dancing Nataraja are the most popular items, but you can also find images of Buddha and numerous deities from the Hindu pantheon.

The West Bengalese also employ the lost-wax process to make Dokra tribal bell sculptures, while in the Bastar region of Chhattisgarh, the Ghadwa Tribe has an interesting twist on the lost-wax process by using a fine wax thread to cover the metal mould, leaving a lattice-like design on the final product.

In Buddhist areas, you can find very striking bronze statues of Buddha and the Tantric gods, finished off with finely polished and painted faces.

In Mamallapuram in Tamil Nadu, craftsmen using local granite and soapstone have revived the ancient artistry of the Pallava sculptors; souvenirs range from tiny stone elephants to enormous deity statues weighing half a tonne. Tamil Nadu is also known for the bronzeware from Thanjavur and Trichy (Tiruchirappalli).

A number of places produce attractive terracotta work, ranging from vases and decorative flowerpots to terracotta images of deities, and children's toys.

At temples across India you can buy small clay or plaster effigies of Hindu deities.

Carpets, Carpets, Carpets!

Carpet-making is a living craft in India, with workshops across the country producing fine wool and silkwork in traditional and contemporary designs. The finest carpets are produced in Kashmir and the Buddhist heartlands of Ladakh, Himachal Pradesh, Sikkim and West Bengal. These can be bought around the country. Carpet-making is also a major revenue earner for Tibetan refugees; most refugee settlements have cooperative carpet workshops. You can also find reproductions of tribal Turkmen and Afghan designs in some states. Antique carpets usually aren't antique – unless you buy from an internationally reputable dealer; stick to 'new' carpets.

The price of a carpet will be determined by the number and the size of the hand-tied knots, the range of dyes and colours, the intricacy of the design and the material. Silk carpets cost more and look more luxurious, but wool carpets usually last longer. Expect to pay upwards of US$200 for a good quality 90cm by 1.5m (or 90cm by 1.8m, depending on the region) wool carpet, and around US$2000 for a similar sized carpet in silk. Tibetan carpets are cheaper, reflecting the relative simplicity of the designs; many refugee cooperatives sell 90cm by 1.5m carpets for around US$100 or less.

A number of people buy carpets under the mistaken belief that they can be sold for a profit back home. Unless you really know your carpets and the carpet market in your home country, it's best to buy a carpet simply because you love it. Many places can ship carpets home for a fee – although it may be safest to send things independently to avoid scams (depending on the shop; use your instinct) – or you can carry them in the plane's hold (allow 5kg to 10kg of your baggage allowance for a 90cm by 1.5m carpet).

CARPETS & CHILD LABOUR

Children have been employed as carpet weavers in the subcontinent for centuries, and many child-care charities from within and beyond India are campaigning against the use of child labour by the carpet industry. Although it's impossible to get accurate figures, various published reports suggest there are upwards of 100,000 child carpet weavers in India.

Unfortunately, the issue is more complicated than it first appears. In many areas, education is often not an option, for both economic and cultural reasons, and the alternative to child labour may not be school but hunger for the whole family. We encourage travellers to buy from carpet-weaving cooperatives that employ adult weavers *and* provide education for their children, breaking the cycle of child labour.

India's Carpet Export Promotion Council (www.india-carpets.com) is campaigning to eliminate child labour from the carpet industry by penalising factories that use children, and by founding schools to provide an alternative to carpet-making. Ultimately, the only thing that can stop child labour is compulsory education for children. However, the economic and social obstacles are significant, often making new initiatives difficult to implement.

Unfortunately for the buyer, there's no easy way of knowing whether a carpet has been made by children. Shops are unlikely to admit to using child labour and most of the international labelling schemes for carpets have been discredited. The carpets produced by Tibetan refugee cooperatives are almost always made by adults, while Uttar Pradesh is the capital of child labour in India. Government emporiums and charitable cooperatives are usually the best places to buy.

PRETTY PEARLS

Pearls are produced at many Indian seaside states, but are a particular speciality of Hyderabad. You'll find them sold at most state emporiums across the country. Prices vary depending on the colour and shape – you pay more for pure white pearls or rare colours like black. Perfectly round pearls are generally more expensive than misshapen or elongated pearls; however, the quirky shapes of Indian pearls can actually be more alluring than the perfect round balls. A single strand of seeded pearls can cost as little as ₹400, but a strand of better-quality pearls starts at around ₹1000.

In some areas you may come across coarsely woven woollen *numdas* (or *namdas*), which are much cheaper than knotted carpets. Various regions also manufacture flat-weave *dhurries* (kilimlike cotton rugs) and striking *gabbas,* made from chain-stitched wool or silk.

Cuttack (Odisha) is famed for making lacelike silver filigree work known as *tarakasi*. A silver framework is made and then filled in with delicate curls and ribbons of thin silver.

The Jewellery Box

Virtually every town in South India has at least one bangle shop selling an extraordinary variety ranging from colourful plastic and glass to shiny brass and silver. Gold, precious and semi-precious gem jewellery is similarly widespread.

Heavy folk-art jewellery is also popular and in tourist centres is pitched at foreign tastes. Chunky Tibetan jewellery made from silver (or white metal) and semiprecious stones is another red-hot favourite. In tourist hot spots many pieces feature Buddhist motifs and text in Tibetan script, including the famous mantra *Om Mani Padme Hum.* Some of the pieces sold are genuine antiques, but be aware that there's a huge industry in India, Nepal and China that makes artificially aged souvenirs.

If you feel like being creative, loose beads of agate, turquoise, carnelian and silver are in abundance, while Buddhist meditation beaded strings made of gems or wood make good souvenirs.

Leatherwork

As cows are sacred in India, leatherwork is made from buffaloes, camels, goats or some other substitute. Kanpur in Uttar Pradesh is the country's major leatherwork centre.

Most large cities offer a smart range of modern leather footwear at very reasonable prices, some stitched with zillions of sparkly sequins – marvellous partywear!

The northern states of Punjab and Rajasthan (especially Jaipur) are famed for jootis (traditional, often pointy-toed slip-in shoes) – these can be found in a number of South Indian shops.

In most big cities you'll find well-made, competitively priced leather handbags, wallets, belts and other accessories.

Metal & Marble Masterpieces

You'll find copper and brassware throughout India. Candleholders, trays, bowls, tankards and ashtrays are particularly popular buys.

Many Tibetan religious objects (sold nationwide) are created by inlaying silver in copper; prayer wheels, ceremonial horns and traditional document cases are all inexpensive buys. Resist the urge to buy *kangling* (Tibetan horns) and *kapala* (ceremonial bowls) made from inlaid human leg bones and skulls – they are illegal!

In all Indian towns, you can find *kadhai* (Indian woks, also known as *balti*) and other items of cookware for incredibly low prices. Beaten-brass pots are particularly attractive, while steel storage vessels, copper-bottomed cooking pans and steel thali trays are also popular souvenirs.

Throughout India you can find finely crafted gold and silver rings, anklets, earrings, toe rings, necklaces and bangles, and pieces can often be crafted to order.

The people of Bastar in Chhattisgarh discovered a method of smelting iron some 35,000 years ago. Similar techniques are used today to create abstract depictions of spindly, pointillist animal and human figures, which are often also made into functional items such as lamp stands and coat racks.

A sizeable cottage industry has sprung up in Agra reproducing the ancient Mughal art form of *pietra dura* (inlaying marble with semiprecious stones) and these can be found in some South Indian handicraft stores. The inspiration for most pieces is derived from the Taj Mahal.

Musical Instruments Galore

Quality Indian musical instruments are mostly available in the larger cities. Prices vary according to the quality – and sound – of the instrument.

Decent tabla sets with a wooden tabla (tuned treble drum) and metal *doogri* (bass tone drum) cost upwards of ₹3000. Cheaper sets are generally heavier and often sound inferior.

Sitars range anywhere from ₹4000 to ₹20,000 (possibly even more). The sound of each sitar will vary with the wood used and the shape of the gourd, so try a few. Note that some cheaper sitars can warp in colder or hotter climates. On any sitar, make sure the strings ring clearly and check the gourd carefully for damage. Spare string sets, sitar plectrums and a screw-in 'amplifier' gourd are sensible additions.

Other popular instruments include the *shehnai* (Indian flute), the *sarod* (like an Indian lute), the harmonium and the *esraj* (similar to an upright violin). Conventional violins are great value – prices start at ₹3000, while quality acoustic guitars are from just ₹2500).

Exquisite Paintings

India is known for its rich painting history. Reproductions of Indian miniature paintings are widely available but the quality varies, with the cheaper ones having less detail and mostly using inferior materials.

In places such as Kerala and Tamil Nadu, you'll come across miniature paintings on leaf skeletons portraying domestic life, rural scenes and deities.

The artists' community of Raghurajpur, near Puri (Odisha), preserves the age-old art of *pattachitra* painting. Cotton or *tassar* (silk cloth) is covered with a mixture of gum and chalk, which is then polished; images of deities and scenes from Hindu legends are painted on with exceedingly fine brushes. Odisha also produces *chitra pothi,* where images are etched onto dried palm-leaf sections with a fine stylus.

Bihar's unique folk art is Mithila (or Madhubani) painting, an ancient art form preserved by the women of Madhubani. These captivating paintings are most easily found in Patna but are also sold in big city emporiums.

In some areas (primarily with sizeable Tibetan Buddhist communities) you can find exquisite *thangkas* (rectangular Tibetan paintings on cloth) of Tantric Buddhist deities and ceremonial mandalas. Some perfectly reproduce the glory of the murals in India's medieval gompas (Buddhist monasteries); others are much simpler. Prices vary, but bank on at least ₹3000 for a decent quality *thangka* of A3 size and a lot more for large intricate *thangkas*. The selling of antique *thangkas* is illegal, and you would be unlikely to find the real thing anyway.

Throughout South India, especially in Mumbai, Chennai and Bengaluru, keep your eyes peeled for shops and galleries selling brilliant contemporary paintings by local artists.

Chappals, those wonderful (often curly-toed) leather sandals, are sold throughout India but are particularly good in the Maharashtrian cities of Kolhapur, Pune and Matheran.

Bidri – a form of damascening where silver is inlaid in gunmetal (an alloy of zinc, copper, lead and tin) – is used to make boxes and ornaments in Bidar (Karnataka).

Government emporiums, fair-trade cooperatives, department stores and modern shopping centres almost always charge fixed prices. Anywhere else you need to bargain. Shopkeepers in tourist hubs are accustomed to travellers who have lots of money and little time to spend it, so you can often expect to be charged double or triple the 'real' price. Souvenir shops are generally the most notorious.

The first 'rule' to haggling is never to show too much interest in the item you've set your heart upon. Secondly, resist purchasing the first thing that takes your fancy. Wander around and price items, but don't make it too obvious – if you return to the first shop the vendor will know it's because they are the cheapest (resulting in less haggling leeway).

Decide how much you would be happy paying and then express a casual interest in buying. If you have absolutely no idea of what something should really cost, start by slashing the price by half. The vendor will, most likely, look utterly aghast, but you can now work up and down respectively in small increments until you reach a mutually agreeable price. You'll find that many shopkeepers lower their so-called 'final price' if you head out of the store saying you'll 'think about it'.

Haggling is a way of life in India and is usually taken in good spirit. It should never turn ugly. Always keep in mind exactly how much a rupee is worth in your home currency to put things in perspective. If a vendor seems to be charging an unreasonably high price, simply look elsewhere.

Sumptuous Shawls, Silk & Saris

Indian shawls are famously warm and lightweight – they're often better than the best down jackets. It's worth buying one to use as an emergency blanket on cold night journeys. Shawls are made from all sorts of wool, from lambswool to fibres woven from yak, goat and angora-rabbit hair. Many are embroidered with intricate designs.

The undisputed capital of the Indian shawl is the Kullu Valley in Himachal Pradesh, with dozens of women's cooperatives producing very fine woollen pieces – these are exported right around the country as well as overseas.

Shawls made in other northern states are also widely found in South India: Ladakh and Kashmir are major centres for *pashmina* (wool shawl) production – you'll pay at least ₹6000 for the authentic article – however, be aware that many so-called *pashmina* shawls are actually made from a mixture of yarns. Shawls from the Northeast States are famously warm, with bold geometric designs. Gujarat's Kutch region produces some particularly distinctive woollen shawls, patterned with subtle embroidery and mirrorwork.

Be aware that it's illegal to buy *shahtoosh* shawls, as rare Tibetan antelopes are slaughtered to provide the wool. If you come across anyone selling these shawls, inform local authorities.

Saris are a very popular souvenir, especially given that they can be easily adapted to other purposes (from cushion covers to skirts). Real silk saris are the most expensive, and the silk usually needs to be washed before it becomes soft. The 'silk capital' of India is Kanchipuram in Tamil Nadu, but you can also find fine silk saris (and cheaper scarves) in other southern centres such as Mysore. Meanwhile, Assam is renowned for its *muga, endi* and *pat* silks (produced by different species of silkworm). You'll pay upwards of ₹3000 for a quality embroidered silk sari, no matter which state it comes from.

Patan, in Gujarat, is the centre for the ancient and laborious craft of *patola*-making – every thread in these fine silk saris is individually hand-dyed before weaving, and patterned borders are woven with real gold. Slightly less involved versions are produced in Rajkot (also in Gujarat) – only the warp threads are dyed. Gold thread is also used in the famous *kota doria* saris of Kota in Rajasthan.

Aurangabad, in Maharashtra, is the traditional centre for the production of *himroo* shawls, sheets and saris, which are made from a blend of cotton, silk and silver thread. Silk and gold-thread saris produced at Paithan (near Aurangabad) are some of India's finest – prices range from around ₹6000 to a mind-blowing ₹300,000. Other states that are famous for sari production include Madhya Pradesh for *maheshwari* (cotton saris from Maheshwar), *chanderi* saris (silk saris from Chanderi) and Bishnupur (West Bengal) for *baluchari* saris, which employ a traditional form of weaving with untwisted silk thread.

Terrific Textiles

Textile production is India's major industry and around 40% takes place at the village level, where it's known as *khadi* (homespun cloth) – hence the government-backed *khadi* emporiums around the country. These inexpensive superstores sell all sorts of items made from homespun cloth, including the popular Nehru jackets and kurta pyjamas (long shirt and loose-fitting trousers) with sales benefiting rural communities.

You'll find a truly amazing variety of weaving and embroidery techniques around India. In tourist centres, especially, textiles are stitched into popular items such as shoulder bags, wall hangings, cushion covers, bedspreads, clothes and much more.

Appliqué is an ancient art in India, with most states producing their own version, often featuring abstract or anthropomorphic patterns. The traditional lampshades and *pandals* (tents) used in weddings and festivals are usually produced using the same technique.

In some Adivasi (tribal) areas, small pieces of mirrored glass are embroidered onto fabric, creating eye-catching bags, cushion covers and wall hangings. Jamnagar, in Gujarat, is famous for its vibrant *bandhani* (tie-dye work) used for saris, scarves and anything else that stays still for long enough.

Block-printed and woven textiles are sold by fabric shops all over India, often in incredibly vivid colour combinations. Each region generally has its own speciality. The India-wide chain store Fabindia (www.fabindia.com) is one retail outlet striving to preserve traditional patterns and fabrics, transforming them into highly accessible items for home decoration and Indian and Western-style fashions.

The techniques used to create *kalamkari* cloth paintings in Andhra Pradesh (a centre for this ancient art is Sri Kalahasti) and Gujarat are also used to make lovely wall hangings and lamp shades.

Lucknow, in Uttar Pradesh, is noted for hand-woven embroidered *chikan* cloth, which features incredibly intricate floral motifs. Punjab is famous for the attractively folksy *phulkari* embroidery (flowerwork with stitches in diagonal, vertical and horizontal directions), while women in West Bengal use chain stitches to make complex figurative designs called

In Andhra Pradesh you can buy exquisite cloth paintings called *kalamkari*, which depict deities and historic events; see www.kalamkariart.org for more on this interesting art form.

Traditional Indian Textiles by John Gillow and Nicholas Barnard explores India's beautiful regional textiles and includes sections on tie-dye, weaving, beadwork, brocades and even camel girths.

ON THE PAPIER-MÂCHÉ TRAIL

Artisans in Srinagar have been producing lacquered papier-mâché for centuries, and papier-mâché-ware is now sold across India. The basic shape is made in a mould from layers of paper (often recycled newsprint), then painted with fine brushes and lacquered for protection. Prices depend upon the complexity and quality of the design and the amount of gold leaf used. Many pieces feature patterns of animals and flowers, or hunting scenes from Mughal miniature paintings. You can find papier-mâché bowls, boxes, letter holders, coasters, trays, lamps, puppets and Christmas decorations (stars, crescent moons, balls and bells). Weight for weight, these are probably the most cost-effective souvenirs in India, but you need to transport them carefully.

kantha. A similar technique is used to make *gabba,* women's kurtas and men's wedding jackets in Kashmir. All of these can be found in major southern centres.

Batik, available throughout India, is often used for saris and *salwar kameez* (traditional dresslike tunic and trouser combination for women). Big Indian cities such as Mumbai and Bengaluru are top spots to pick up haute couture by talented Indian designers, as well as moderately priced Western fashions.

Beautiful Woodcarving

Wood inlay is one of India's oldest crafts – you'll find lovely wooden wall hangings, tabletops, trays and boxes inlaid with metals and bone.

WOOD INLAY

Woodcarving is an ancient art form throughout India. Sandalwood carvings of Hindu deities is one of Karnataka's specialities, but you'll pay a king's ransom for the real thing – a 10cm-high Ganesh costs around ₹3000 in sandalwood, compared to roughly ₹300 in kadamb wood. However, the sandalwood will release fragrance for years.

The carved wooden massage wheels and rollers available at many Hindu pilgrimage sites make good gifts for friends and family back home, while Buddhist woodcarvings are a speciality of all Tibetan refugee areas. You'll find wall plaques of the eight lucky signs, dragons and *chaam* masks, used for ritual dances. Most of the masks are artless reproductions, but you can sometimes find genuine *chaam* masks made from lightweight whitewood or papier-mâché from ₹3000 upwards.

Other Treasures

Virtually all towns have bazaars selling locally made spices at terrific prices. Karnataka, Kerala, Uttar Pradesh, Rajasthan and Tamil Nadu produce most of the spices that go into garam masala (the 'hot mix' used to flavour Indian curries), while the Northeast States and Sikkim are known for black cardamom and cinnamon bark.

Attar (essential oil mostly made from flowers) shops can be found right around the country. Mysore is especially famous for its sandalwood oil, while Mumbai is a major centre for the trade of traditional fragrances, including valuable *oud,* made from a rare mould that grows on the bark of the agarwood tree. Ooty and Kodaikanal (both in Tamil Nadu) produce aromatic and medicinal oils from herbs, flowers and eucalyptus.

Indian incense is exported worldwide, with Bengaluru and Mysore being major producers, and incense from Auroville is also well regarded.

GANDHI'S CLOTH

More than 80 years ago Mahatma Gandhi sat by his spinning wheel and urged Indians to support the freedom movement by ditching their foreign-made clothing and turning to *khadi* – homespun cloth. Like the spinning wheel itself, *khadi* became a symbol of the struggle for freedom and of Indian independence, and the fabric is still closely associated with politics. The government-run, nonprofit group, Khadi and Village Industries Commission (www.kvic.org.in), serves to promote khadi; many politicians still wear it and the Indian flag is supposed to be made from only *khadi* cloth. In recent years the fashion world too has taken a growing interest in this simple fabric, which is usually cotton, but can also be silk or wool.

Khadi outlets are listed in the Shopping sections of various chapters in this book, but you'll find them all over India. Prices are reasonable and are often discounted in the period around Gandhi's birthday (2 October). A number of outlets also have a tailoring service.

They are simple, no-nonsense places from which to pick up genuine Indian clothing such as kurta (long, collarless shirt), pyjamas, headscarves, saris and, at some branches, assorted handicrafts.

Overall, a comparatively small proportion of the money brought to India by tourism reaches people in rural areas. Travellers can make a greater contribution by shopping at community cooperatives, set up to protect and promote traditional cottage industries and to provide education, training and a sustainable livelihood at the grassroots level. Many of these projects focus on refugees, low-caste women, tribal people and others living on society's fringes.

The quality of products sold at cooperatives is high and the prices are usually fixed, which means you won't have to haggle. A share of the sales money is channelled directly into social projects such as schools, healthcare, training and other advocacy programs for socially disadvantaged groups. Shopping at the national network of Khadi & Village Industries emporiums will also contribute to rural communities (also see the box on Gandhi's Cloth in this chapter).

Wherever you travel, keep your eyes open for fair-trade cooperatives and also see this book's regional chapters for recommendations, where they exist.

Meanwhile, a speciality of Goa is feni (liquor distilled from coconut milk or cashews) – a head-spinning spirit that often comes in decorative bottles.

Quality Indian tea is sold in Darjeeling and Kalimpong (both in West Bengal), Assam and Sikkim, as well as parts of South India. All varieties can usually be found nationwide at major tea retailers.

Fine-quality handmade paper – often fashioned into cards, boxes and notebooks – is worth seeking out, with good places to start including Puducherry and Mumbai.

India has a phenomenal range of books at very competitive prices, including gorgeous leather-bound titles. Music CDs by local musicians are also super value.

The Arts

Immerse yourself in India's incredibly vibrant performing-arts scene – especially classical dance and music – at Art India (www.artindia.net).

Over the centuries India's many ethnic groups have spawned a vivid artistic heritage that is both inventive and spiritually significant. Today, artistic beauty lies around almost every corner, whether it's the garishly painted trucks rattling down dusty country roads or the exquisite, spidery body art of *mehndi* (henna). Indeed, a glowing highlight of subcontinental travel is its wealth of art treasures, from ancient temple dances to a dynamic performing-arts scene. Contemporary Indian artists have fused historical elements with edgy modern influences, creating art, dance and music that have won acclaim on both the domestic and international arenas.

Dance

Dance is an ancient and revered Indian art form that is traditionally linked to mythology and classical literature. Historically, accomplished artists were a matter of prolific pride among royal houses; the quality of their respective dance troupes was at one stage the cause of intense competition between the maharajas of Mysore and Travancore. Between the 2nd and 8th centuries, trade between South India and Southeast Asia brought a cultural legacy that endures in the dance forms of Bali (Indonesia), Thailand, Cambodia and Myanmar (Burma). Today, dance – classical, popular and folk – thrives on city stages, on the cinema screen and in towns and villages throughout South India.

South India has many kinds of folk dance: these include the Puraviattams of Karnataka and Tamil Nadu, where dancers are dressed in horse costumes; the Koklikatai dance of Tamil Nadu, in which dancers move about on stilts that have bells attached; and the Kolyacha fishers' dance from the Konkan Coast. Goa's stylised Mando song and dance is a waltz-like blend of Indian rhythms and Portuguese melody accompanied by Konkani words.

MEHNDI

Mehndi is the traditional art of painting a woman's hands (and sometimes feet) with intricate henna designs for auspicious ceremonies, such as marriage. If quality henna is used, the design, which is orange-brown, can last up to one month.

In touristy areas, *mehndi*-wallahs are adept at applying henna tattoo 'bands' on the arms, legs and lower back. If you're thinking about getting *mehndi* applied, allow at least a couple of hours for the design process and required drying time (during drying you can't use your hennaed hands). Once applied, henna usually fades faster the more you wash it and apply lotion.

It's always wise to request the artist to do a 'test' spot on your arm before proceeding, as nowadays some dyes contain chemicals that can cause allergies. If good-quality henna is used, you should not feel any pain during or after the procedure.

Various forms of trance-dancing and dances of exorcism occur throughout the south, and almost all tribal peoples, including the Todas of Tamil Nadu and the Banjaras of Andhra Pradesh, retain unique dance traditions.

The major classical dance forms of South India are as follows:

» Bharata Natyam (also spelt *bharatanatyam*) is Tamil Nadu's unique performing art and is believed to be India's oldest continuing classical dance. It was originally known as Dasi Attam, a temple art performed by young women called *devadasis*. After the 16th century, however, it fell into disrepute, largely because it became synonymous with prostitution. It was revived in the mid-19th century by four brothers from Thanjavur (Tanjore), who are credited with restoring the art's purity by returning to its ancient roots.

» Kathakali, one of South India's most renowned forms of classical dance-drama, is a Keralan form of play, usually based on Hindu epics; also see the boxed text, p304.

» Kuchipudi is a 17th-century dance-drama that originated in the Andhra Pradesh village from which it takes its name. Like Kathakali, its present-day form harks back to the 17th century, when it became the prerogative of Brahmin boys from this village. It often centres on the story of Satyambhama, wife of Lord Krishna.

» Mohiniyattam, from Kerala, is a semiclassical dance form that is based on the story of Mohini, the mythical seductress. Known for its gentle and poetic movements, it contains elements of Bharata Natyam and Kathakali.

» *Theyyam,* seen in Kannur (Kerala; see the boxed text, p304), is an ancient dance form practised by tribal people and villagers in the north Malabar region. The headdresses, costumes, body painting and trancelike performances are truly extraordinary. The Parasinikadavu Temple (near Kannur) stages *theyyam* performances.

» Yakshagana is unique to the Tulu-speaking region of Karnataka's south coast. The focus in Yakshagana is less on the dance or movement aspect of performance, since (unlike Kathakali) the actors have vocal roles to play, both singing and speaking. As in Kathakali, the costumes and make-up are not only visually striking but also symbolic of a particular character's personality.

Music

Indian classical music traces its roots back to Vedic times, when religious poems chanted by priests were first collated in an anthology called the Rig-Veda. Over the millennia classical music has been shaped by many influences, and the legacy today is Carnatic (characteristic of South India) and Hindustani (the classical style of North India) music. With common origins, both share a number of features. Both use the raga (the melodic shape of the music) and tala (the rhythmic meter characterised by the number of beats); *tintal,* for example, has a tala of 16 beats. The audience follows the tala by clapping at the appropriate beat, which in *tintal* is at beats one, five and 13. There's no clap at the beat of nine; that's the *khali* (empty section), which is indicated by a wave of the hand. Both the raga and the tala are used as a basis for composition and improvisation.

Both Carnatic and Hindustani music are performed by small ensembles, generally comprising three to six musicians, and both have many instruments in common. There's no fixed pitch, but there are differences between the two styles. Hindustani has been more heavily influenced by Persian musical conventions (a result of Mughal rule); Carnatic music, as it developed in South India, cleaves more closely to theory. The most striking difference, at least for those unfamiliar with India's classical forms, is Carnatic's greater use of voice.

One of the best-known Indian instruments is the sitar (large stringed instrument) with which the soloist plays the raga. Other stringed instruments include the sarod (which is plucked) and the sarangi (which is played with a bow). Also popular is the tabla (twin drums), which

Indian Classical Dance by Leela Venkataraman and Avinash Pasricha is a lavishly illustrated book covering various Indian dance forms, including Bharata Natyam and Kathakali.

To tune into the melodious world of Hindustani classical music, including a glossary of musical terms, get a copy of Nād: Understanding Raga Music by Sandeep Bagchee.

provides the tala. The drone, which runs on two basic notes, is provided by the oboelike *shehnai* or the stringed *tampura* (also spelt taboura). The hand-pumped keyboard harmonium is used as a secondary melody instrument for vocal music.

Indian regional folk music is widespread and varied. Wandering musicians, magicians, snake charmers and storytellers often use song to entertain their audiences; the storyteller usually sings the tales from the great epics.

Although more prominent in North India, you may come across *qawwali* (Islamic devotional singing), performed at mosques or at musical concerts. *Qawwali* concerts usually take the form of a *mehfil* (gathering) with a lead singer, a second singer, harmonium and tabla players, and a thunderous chorus of junior singers and clappers, all sitting cross-legged on the floor. The singer whips up the audience with lines of poetry, dramatic hand gestures and religious phrases as the two voices weave in and out, bouncing off each other to create an improvised, surging sound. On command the chorus dives in with a hypnotic and rhythmic refrain. Members of the audience often sway and shout in ecstatic appreciation.

To delve into the beguiling world of Carnatic music, check out www.carnaticcorner.com, www.carnatic.com and www.carnaticindia.com.

A completely different genre altogether, filmi music entails musical scores from Bollywood movies – modern (slower-paced) love serenades feature among the predominantly hyperactive dance songs. To ascertain the latest filmi favourites, as well as in-vogue Indian pop singers, enquire at music stores.

Radio and TV have played a vital role in broadcasting different music styles – from soothing bhajans to booming Bollywood hits – to even the remotest corners of South India.

Cinema

The nation's film industry was born in the late 19th century – the first major Indian-made motion picture, *Panorama of Calcutta,* was screened in 1899. India's first real feature film, *Raja Harishchandra,* was made during the silent era in 1913 and it's ultimately from this that Indian cinema traces its vibrant lineage.

Today, India's film industry is the biggest in the world – larger than Hollywood – and Mumbai, the Hindi-language film capital, is affectionately dubbed 'Bollywood'. India's other major film-producing centres include Chennai, Hyderabad and Bengaluru, with a number of other southern centres also producing films in their own regional vernacular.

As well as the obvious Bollywood blockbusters, most states in South India have their own regional film industry. Tamil-language films from Tamil Nadu and Telugu films from Andhra Pradesh are the most numerous, but there are strong Malayalam films from Kerala and Kannada films from Karnataka.

Encyclopedia of Indian Cinema by Ashish Rajadhyaksha and Paul Willemen chronicles India's dynamic cinematic history, spanning from 1897 to the 21st century.

Big-budget films are often partly or entirely shot abroad, with some countries vigorously wooing Indian production companies because of the potential spin-off tourism revenue these films generate.

An average of 1000 feature films are produced annually in India. Apart from hundreds of millions of local Bollywood buffs, there are also millions of Non-Resident Indian (NRI) fans, who have played a significant role in catapulting Indian cinema into the international arena.

Broadly speaking, there are two categories of Indian films. Most prominent is the mainstream movie – three hours and still running, these blockbusters are often tear-jerkers and are packed with dramatic twists interspersed with numerous song-and-dance performances. There are no explicit sex, or even kissing, scenes in Indian films made for the local market (although smooching is creeping into some Bollywood movies);

however, lack of nudity is often compensated for by heroines dressed in skimpy or body-hugging attire.

The second Indian film genre is art house, which adopts Indian 'reality' as its base. Generally speaking they are, or at least supposed to be, socially and politically relevant. Usually made on infinitely smaller budgets than their commercial cousins, these films are the ones that win kudos at global film festivals and award ceremonies.

For information about Bollywood and working as a film extra, read the boxed text, p54.

Literature

South India's main languages – Tamil, Kannada, Telugu, Malayalam and Marathi – each have a long literary history. Tamil is considered a case apart (some early works date from the 2nd century) because it evolved independently from the others, which all have their roots in Sanskrit.

In the 19th century, South Indian literature began to reflect the influence of European genres. Where literature had once been expressed primarily in verse, now it was widely seen in prose. By the end of the 19th century, South Indian writers were pioneering new forms; among them Subramanya Bharathi and VVS Aiyar, who are credited with transforming Tamil into a modern language.

India boasts an ever-growing list of internationally acclaimed authors. Some particularly prominent writers include Vikram Seth, best known for his award-winning epic novel *A Suitable Boy,* and Amitav Ghosh, who has won a number of accolades; his *Sea of Poppies* was shortlisted for the 2008 Man Booker Prize. Indeed, recent years have seen a number of India-born authors win the prestigious Man Booker Prize, the most recent being Chennai-born Aravind Adiga, who won in 2008 for his debut novel, *The White Tiger.* The prize went to Kiran Desai in 2006 for *The Inheritance of Loss;* Kiran Desai is the daughter of the award-winning Indian novelist Anita Desai, who has thrice been a Booker Prize nominee. In 1997, Arundhati Roy won the Booker Prize for her novel, *The God of Small Things,* while Mumbai-born Salman Rushdie took this coveted award in 1981 for *Midnight's Children.*

Trinidad-born Indian writer VS Naipaul has written widely about India and won many notable awards including the Booker Prize (1971) and the Nobel Prize in Literature (2001). UK-born Bengali writer Jhumpa Lahiri was awarded the 2000 Pulitzer Prize for Fiction for *Interpreter of Maladies,* a collection of short stories.

For the latest film fare, check out Bollywood World (www.bollywood world.com) and Tamil Cinema World (www.tamil cinemaworld. com).

RABINDRANATH TAGORE: A LITERARY LEGEND

The brilliant and prolific poet, writer, artist and patriot Rabindranath Tagore has had an unparalleled impact on Bengali – and wider Indian – culture. Born to a prominent family in Kolkata (Calcutta) in 1861, he began writing as a young boy and never stopped, said to have been dictating his last poem only hours before his death in 1941.

Tagore is also largely credited with introducing India's historical and cultural richness to the Western world. He won the Nobel Prize in Literature in 1913 with his mystical collection of poems *Gitanjali* (Song Offerings), and in later years his lecture tours saw him carrying his message of human unity around Asia, America and Europe.

But for all his internationalism, Tagore's heart was firmly rooted in his homeland; a truth reflected in his many popular songs, sung by the masses, and in the lyrics of the national anthems of both India and Bangladesh. In 1915 Tagore was awarded a knighthood by the British, but he later surrendered it in protest of the 1919 Jallianwala Bagh Massacre in Amritsar (Punjab).

For a taste of Tagore's work, dip into his *Selected Short Stories.*

Painting

Around 1500 years ago artists covered the walls and ceilings of the Ajanta caves (p92) in western India with scenes from the Buddha's life. The figures are endowed with an unusual freedom and grace, and contrast with the next major style that emerged from this part of India in the 11th century.

India's Jain community created some particularly lavish temple art. However, after the Muslim conquest of Gujarat in 1299, the Jains turned their attention to illustrated manuscripts, which could be hidden away. These manuscripts are the only known form of Indian painting that survived the Islamic conquest of North India.

The Indo-Persian style – characterised by geometric design coupled with flowing form – developed from Islamic royal courts, although the depiction of the elongated eye is one convention that seems to have been retained from indigenous sources. The Persian influence blossomed when artisans fled to India following the 1507 Uzbek attack on Herat (in present-day Afghanistan), and with trade and gift-swapping between the Persian city of Shiraz, an established centre for miniature production, and Indian provincial sultans.

The 1526 victory by Babur at the Battle of Panipat ushered in the era of the Mughals in India. Although Babur and his son Humayun were both patrons of the arts, it's Humayun's son Akbar who is generally credited with developing the characteristic Mughal style. This painting style, often in colourful miniature form, largely depicts court life, architecture, battle and hunting scenes, as well as detailed portraits. Akbar recruited artists from far and wide, and artistic endeavour first centred on the production of illustrated manuscripts (topics varied from history to mythology), but later broadened into portraiture and the glorification of everyday events. European painting styles influenced some artists, and this influence occasionally reveals itself in experiments with motifs and perspective.

Akbar's son Jehangir also patronised painting, but he preferred portraiture, and his fascination with natural science resulted in a vibrant legacy of paintings of flowers and animals. Under Jehangir's son Shah Jahan, the Mughal style became less fluid, and although the bright colouring was eye-catching, the paintings lacked the vigour of before.

Various schools of miniature painting (small paintings crammed with detail) emerged in Rajasthan from around the 17th century. The subject matter ranged from royal processions to shikar (hunting expeditions), with many artists influenced by Mughal styles. The intense colours, still evident today in miniatures and frescoes in some Indian palaces, were often derived from crushed semiprecious stones, while the gold and silver colouring is in fact finely pounded pure gold and silver leaf.

By the 19th century, painting in North India was notably influenced by Western styles (especially English watercolours), giving rise to what has been dubbed the Company School, which had its centre in Delhi.

Pottery

The potter's art is steeped in mythology. Although there are numerous stories that explain how potters came to be, they usually share the notion that a talent for working with clay is a gift from the god Brahma. This gives potters a very special status; on occasion they are said to act directly as intermediaries between the spiritual and the temporal worlds.

The name for the potter caste, Kumbhar, is taken from *kumbha* (water pot), which is itself an essential component in a version of the story that explains how potters found their calling. The water pot is still an indispensable item in South India. The narrow-necked, round-based design

Legends of Goa, by Mario Cabral E Sa, is an illustrated compilation of Goan folktales that offers an insight into the state's colourful traditions and history.

Get arty with *Indian Art* by Roy Craven, *Contemporary Indian Art: Other Realities* edited by Yashodhara Dalmia, and *Indian Miniature Painting* by Dr Daljeet and Professor PC Jain.

In the 21st century, paintings by contemporary Indian artists have been selling at record numbers (and prices) around the world. One especially innovative and successful online art auction house, the Mumbai-based **Saffronart** (www.saffronart.com), has reportedly surpassed heavyweights like Sotheby's and Christie's in terms of its online Indian art sales.

Online auctions promote feisty global bidding wars, largely accounting for the high success rate of Saffronart, which also previews its paintings in Mumbai and New York prior to its major cyber auctions. Many bidders are wealthy NRIs (Non-Resident Indians) who not only appreciate Indian art but have also recognised its investment potential. However, there is also mounting demand from non-Indian collectors, with recent years witnessing spiralling sales in Europe, the USA, UK, Southeast Asia and the Middle East.

International auction houses have been descending upon India, either to set up offices or to secure gallery alliances, in order to grab a piece of what they have identified as a major growth market. Although the bulk of demand, on both the domestic and international fronts, is generally for senior Indian artists' works, such as those of Francis Newton Souza, Tyeb Mehta, Syed Haider Raza, Akbar Padamsee, Ram Kumar and Maqbool Fida Husain, there's a steadily growing interest in emerging Indian artists.

means that women can carry the water-filled pots on their heads with less risk of spillage. The shape is also symbolic of the womb and hence fertility.

Apart from water pots, potters create a variety of household items, including all manner of storage and cooking pots, dishes and *jhanvan* (thick, flat pieces of fired clay with one rough side used for cleaning the feet). The ephemeral nature of clay-made items means the potter never wants for work. Potters all over Tamil Nadu are kept especially busy at their wheels thanks to such traditions as the Pongal harvest festival in mid-January. On the day before the festival starts, clay household vessels are smashed and replaced with new ones.

Potters are also called upon to create votive offerings. These include the guardian horse figures (which can be huge creations) that stand sentry outside villages in Tamil Nadu, images of deities such as Ganesh, and other animal effigies. Clay replicas of parts of the human body are sometimes commissioned by those seeking miraculous cures and are then placed before a shrine. Clay toys and beads are also among a potter's repertoire.

Glazing pottery is rare in South Indian states; one exception is Tamil Nadu, where a blue or green glaze is sometimes applied.

Architectural Splendour

The History of Architecture in India: From the Dawn of Civilisation to the End of the Raj by Christopher Tadgell is an illustrated overview of the subject that includes significant sites in South India.

From looming temple gateways adorned with a rainbow of delicately carved deities to whitewashed cube-like village houses, South India has a rich architectural heritage. Traditional buildings, such as temples, often have a superb sense of placement within the local environment, whether perched on a boulder-strewn hill or standing by a large artificial reservoir.

The influence of British architecture is most obvious in cities such as Chennai, Bengaluru and Mumbai, which have scores of grand neoclassical structures. British bungalows with corrugated iron roofs and wide verandahs are a feature of many hill stations, including Ooty (Udhagamandalam). More memorable are the attempts to meld European and Indian architecture, such as in the great 19th-century public buildings of Mumbai and the breathtaking Maharaja's Palace in Mysore.

Sacred Creations

Complex rules govern the location, design and building of each temple, based on numerology, astrology, astronomy and religious principles. Essentially, a temple represents a map of the universe. At the centre is an unadorned space, the *garbhagriha* (inner sanctum), which is symbolic of the 'womb-cave' from which the universe is believed to have emerged. This provides a residence for the deity to which the temple is dedicated.

Above the shrine rises a superstructure known as a *vimana* in South India and a *sikhara* in North India. The *sikhara* is curvilinear and topped with a grooved disk, on which sits a pot-shaped finial, while the *vimana* is stepped, with the grooved disk replaced with a solid dome. Some temples have a *mandapa* (temple forechamber) connected to the sanctum by vestibules. These *mandapas* may also contain *vimanas* or *sikharas*.

A *gopuram* is a soaring pyramidal gateway tower of a Dravidian temple. The towering *gopurams* of various South Indian temple complexes (eg Madurai's Sri Meenakshi Temple) took ornamentation and monumentalism to new levels.

From the outside, Jain temples can resemble Hindu ones, but inside they're often a riot of sculptural ornamentation, the very opposite of ascetic austerity. Meanwhile, gurdwaras (Sikh temples) can usually be identified by a *nishan sahib* (flagpole flying a triangular flag with the Sikh insignia).

Stupas, which characterise Buddhist places of worship, essentially evolved from burial mounds. They served as repositories for relics of

Buddha and, later, other venerated souls. A relatively recent innovation is the addition of a *chaitya* (hall) leading up to the stupa itself.

The subcontinent's Muslim rulers contributed their own architectural conventions – arched cloisters and domes among them. One of the most striking differences between Hinduism and Islam is religious imagery – while Islamic art eschews any hint of idolatry or portrayal of God, it has developed a rich heritage of calligraphic and decorative designs.

In terms of mosque architecture, the basic design elements are similar worldwide. A large hall is dedicated to communal prayer and within the hall is a mihrab (niche) indicating the direction of Mecca. The faithful are called to prayer from minarets, placed at cardinal points. Many large towns have at least one mosque; some fine examples of Islamic architecture in South India include Mecca Masjid and Golconda Fort in Hyderabad and Golgumbaz in Bijapur.

Churches in India reflect the fashions and trends of typically European ecclesiastical architecture with many also incorporating Hindu decorative flourishes. The Portuguese, among others, made impressive attempts to replicate the great churches and cathedrals of their day. Today, Goa has some particularly impressive churches and cathedrals, especially Old Goa.

Forts & Palaces

A typical South Indian fort is situated on a hill or rocky outcrop, ringed by moated battlements. It usually has a town nestled at its base, which would have developed after the fortifications were built. Gingee (Senji) in Tamil Nadu is a particularly good example. Vellore Fort, also in Tamil Nadu, is one of India's best-known moated forts, while Bidar and Bijapur in Karnataka are home to great metropolitan forts.

Daulatabad in Maharashtra is another magnificent structure, with 5km of walls surrounding a hilltop fortress. The fortress is reached by passageways filled with ingenious defences, including spike-studded doors and false tunnels, which in times of war led either to a pit of boiling oil or to a crocodile-filled moat!

Few old palaces remain in South India, as conquerors often targeted these for destruction. The remains of the royal complex at Vijayanagar, near Hampi, indicate that local engineers weren't averse to using the sound structural techniques and fashions (such as domes and arches) of their Muslim adversaries, the Bahmanis. Travancore's palace of the maharajas at Padmanabhapuram, which dates from the 16th century, has private apartments for the king, a zenana (women's quarters), rooms dedicated to public audiences, an armoury, a dance hall and temples. Meanwhile, the Indo-Saracenic Maharaja's Palace in Mysore is the best known and most opulent in the south, its interior a kaleidoscope of stained glass, mirrors and mosaic floors.

Discover more about India's diverse temple architecture (in addition to other temple-related information) at Temple Net (www. templenet.com).

Temples of South India by Sunil Vaidyanathan is rich in images and covers major South Indian temples.

ARCHITECTURAL SPLENDOUR FORTS & PALACES

TEMPLE TANKS

Commonly used for ritual bathing and religious ceremonies, as well as adding aesthetic appeal to places of worship, temple tanks have long been a focal point of temple activity. These often vast, angular, engineered reservoirs of water, sometimes fed by rain, sometimes fed – via a complicated drainage system – by rivers, serve both sacred and secular purposes. The waters of some temple tanks are believed to have healing properties, while others are said to have the power to wash away sins. Devotees (as well as travellers) may be required to wash their feet in a temple tank before entering a place of worship.

Sculpture

Sculpture and religious architecture are closely related in South India, and it's difficult to consider them separately. Sculpture is invariably religious in nature and isn't generally an art form through which individuals express their own creativity.

The 7th-century relief Arjuna's Penance, at Mamallapuram (Mahabalipuram), is one of the most sublime examples of early sculpture. Its fresh, lively touch is also reflected in later 9th-century Chola shrine sculptures. The legacy and tradition of sculptors from the Pallava dynasty live on in Mamallapuram, where hundreds of modern-day sculptors work with stone to produce freestanding sculptures of all shapes and sizes (see the Sculpture Museum in Mamallapuram). Some even mix the old with the brand new – such as a sculpture of Ganesh chatting on a mobile phone!

Unlike in the north of India, a tradition of South Indian sculpture was able to develop without serious interruption from Muslim invasions. But curiously, despite a high level of technical skill, the 17th-century work often appears to lack the life and quality of earlier examples. However, South India remains famous for its bronze sculptures, particularly those of the 9th and 10th centuries, created during the highly artistic Chola dynasty. Artisans employed the lost-wax technique to make their pieces, which were usually of Hindu deities such as Vishnu and – in the south especially – Shiva in his adored form as Lord of the Dance, Nataraja. This technique, still in use in South India, involves carving a model out of wax, then painting on a claylike mixture to form a mould. The wax is melted out, leaving a hollow mould into which molten bronze (or silver, copper, lead etc) is poured. Some of the most exuberant sculptural detail comes from the Hoysala period, and can be seen at the temples of Belur and Halebid in Karnataka.

Architecture and Art of Southern India by George Michell provides details on the Vijayanagar empire and its successors, encompassing a period of some 400 years.

Window on Goa by Maurice Hall is an authoritative labour of love featuring descriptions of Goa's churches, forts, villages and more.

Survival Guide

Women & Solo Travellers

Women and solo travellers may encounter a few extra hurdles when travelling in South India – from cost (for those travelling by themselves) to clothing (women). As with anywhere else, it pays to be prepared.

Women Travellers

Although Bollywood might suggest otherwise, India remains a largely conservative society. As such, female travellers should be aware that their behaviour and dress code are under scrutiny, particularly away from cities and towns popular with tourists.

Attention

» Be prepared to be stared at; it's something you'll have to live with so don't allow it to get the better of you.

» Refrain from returning male stares, as this may be considered a come-on.

» Dark glasses, MP3 players and books are useful for averting unwanted conversations.

Clothing

Avoiding culturally inappropriate clothing will help to make your travels stress-free.

» Steer clear of sleeveless tops, shorts, miniskirts (ankle-length skirts are recommended) and anything else that's skimpy, see-through or tight fitting.

» Wearing Indian-style clothes makes a positive impression and can considerably deflect harassment.

» Draping a dupatta (long scarf) over T-shirts is another good way of staving off unwanted stares – it's also handy if you visit a shrine that requires your head to be covered.

» Wearing a salwar kameez will show your respect for local dress etiquette; it's also surprisingly cool in the hot weather.

» A smart alternative is a kurta (long shirt) worn over jeans or trousers.

» Going out in public wearing a *choli* (sari blouse) or a sari petticoat (which some foreign women mistake for a skirt) is rather like strutting around half dressed – avoid it.

» Most Indian women wear long shorts and a T-shirt whenever swimming in public view; when returning from the beach use a sarong to avoid stares on the way back to your hotel.

Health & Hygiene

» Sanitary pads are widely available but tampons are usually restricted to pharmacies in big cities and some tourist towns (even then, the choice may be limited).

» Carry additional stocks for travel off the beaten track.

» For gynaecological health issues, most women prefer to seek out a female doctor – see p508 for more information.

Sexual Harassment

Many female travellers have reported some form of sexual harassment while in India.

» Most cases are reported in urban centres and prominent tourist towns elsewhere, and have involved lewd comments, invasion of privacy and sometimes groping.

» Other cases have included provocative gestures, jeering, getting 'accidentally' bumped into on the street and being followed.

» Incidents are particularly common at exuberant (and crowded) special events such as the Holi festival

» Women travelling with a male partner are less likely to be hassled.

» Mixed couples of Indian and non-Indian descent may get disapproving stares, even if neither individual actually lives in India.

Taxis & Public Transport

Being a woman has some advantages; women are able to queue-jump for buses and trains without consequence and on trains there are special ladies-only carriages.

» Solo women should prearrange an airport pick-up from their hotel if their flight is scheduled to arrive after dark.

» Mumbai (and some other cities) have prepaid radio cab services – it's more expensive than the regular prepaid taxis, but promotes itself as a safe service, with drivers who have been vetted as part of their recruitment.

» If you do catch a regular prepaid taxi, make a point of writing down the car registration and driver's name – in front of the driver – and giving it to one of the airport police.

» Avoid taking taxis alone late at night and never agree to have more than one man (the driver) in the car – ignore claims that this is 'just my brother' or 'for more protection'.

» Solo women have reported less hassle by opting for the more expensive classes on trains, especially for overnight trips.

» If you're travelling overnight in a three-tier carriage, try to get the uppermost berth, which will give you more privacy (and distance from potential gropers).

» On public transport, don't hesitate to return any errant limbs, put some item of luggage in between you, be vocal (so as to attract public attention, thus shaming the fellow), or simply find a new spot.

Staying Safe

The following tips may help you on your travels:

» Keep conversations with unknown men short – getting involved in an inane conversation with someone you barely know can be misinterpreted as a sign of sexual interest.

» Questions and comments such as 'Do you have a boyfriend?' or 'You're very beautiful' are indicators that the conversation may be taking a steamy tangent.

» Some women wear a pseudo wedding ring, or announce early on in the conversation that they're married or engaged (regardless of the reality).

» If you get the feeling that a guy is encroaching on your space, he probably is. A firm request to keep away usually does the trick, especially if your tone is loud and curt enough to draw the attention of passers-by.

» The silent treatment can also be very effective.

» Follow local women's cues and instead of shaking hands say *namaste* – the traditional, respectful Hindu greeting.

» Avoid wearing expensive-looking jewellery.

» Check the reputation of any teacher or therapist before going to a solo session (get recommendations from other travellers – some women have reported being molested by masseurs and other therapists). If you feel uneasy at any time, leave.

» Female filmgoers will probably feel more comfortable (and lessen the chances of potential harassment) by going to the cinema with a companion.

» At hotels keep your door locked, as staff (particularly at budget places) can knock and automatically walk in without waiting for your permission.

» Try to arrive in towns before dark. Don't walk alone at night and avoid wandering alone in isolated areas even during daylight.

Solo Travellers

Travellers often move in roughly the same direction throughout South India, so it's not unusual to see the same faces over and over again on your trip. Tourist hubs such as Goa and Kerala are good places to meet fellow travellers, swap stories, get up-to-the-minute travel tips and find others to travel with. You may also be able to find travel companions on

HANDY WEBSITES

You can read personal experiences proffered by fellow women travellers at www.journey woman.com and www. wanderlustandlipstick. com.

Lonely Planet's **Thorn Tree Travel Forum** (www.lonely planet.com/thorntree).

Cost

The most significant issue facing solo travellers is cost.

» Single-room rates at guest houses and hotels are sometimes not much lower than double rates; some midrange and top-end places don't even offer a single tariff.

» Always try negotiating a lower rate for single occupancy.

Transport

» You'll save money if you find others to share taxis and autorickshaws, as well as when hiring a car for longer trips.

» Solo bus travellers may be able to get the 'co-pilot' (near the driver) seat on buses, which not only has a good view out front but is also handy if you've got a big bag.

Safety

Most solo travellers experience no major problems in South India, but some less honourable souls (locals and travellers alike) view lone tourists as an easy target for theft.

» There have been muggings of single men wandering around isolated areas, even during the day.

» Don't be paranoid, but like anywhere else in the world, it's wise to stay on your toes in unfamiliar surroundings.

Scams

India has its fair share of scams and some places are dodgier than others, but most problems can be avoided with common sense and an appropriate amount of caution. The main places to be wary in South India are big cities and tourist centres. Scams change as tricksters try to stay ahead of the game so chat with travellers and tourism officials to keep abreast of the latest cons. Look at the India branch of Lonely Planet's **Thorn Tree Travel Forum** (www.lonelyplanet.com/thorntree), where travellers often post timely warnings about problems they've encountered on the road.

Contaminated Food & Drink

» Some private medical clinics have given patients more treatment than necessary to procure larger payments from travel insurance companies – get a second opinion if possible.

» Most bottled water is legit, but always ensure the lid seal is intact and check that the bottom of the bottle hasn't been tampered with.

• Crush plastic bottles after use to prevent them being misused later.

• Better still, use your own water bottle and water-purification tablets or a filtration system to avoid adding to India's plastic waste mountain.

Credit Card Con

» Be careful when paying for souvenirs with a credit card. While government shops are usually legitimate, private souvenir shops have been known to surreptitiously run off extra copies of the credit-card imprint slip, used for phoney transactions later. Insist that the trader carries out any credit-card transaction in front of you. Alternatively, take out cash from an ATM to avoid this risk altogether.

Gem Scams

» This long-running scam involves charming con artists who promise foolproof 'get rich quick' schemes.

» Travellers are asked to carry or mail gems home and then sell them to the trader's (non-existent) overseas representatives at a profit.

» Without exception, the goods – if they arrive at all – are worth a fraction of what you paid, and the 'representatives' never materialise.

» Don't believe hard-luck stories about an inability to obtain an export licence, and don't believe the testimonials they show you from other travellers – they are usually all fake.

» Carpets are another favourite for this particular con.

KEEPING SAFE

» A good travel-insurance policy is essential (p484).

» Email copies of your passport identity page, visa page, and a copy of your airline ticket to yourself, and keep copies on you.

» Keep your money and passport in a concealed money belt or a secure place under your shirt and never keep your wallet in your back pocket.

» Store at least US$100 separately from your main stash but keep the rest of your cash and other valuables on your person.

» Separate big currency notes from small bills so you don't publicly display large wads of cash when paying for services or checking into hotels.

» Consider using your own padlock at cheaper hotels where doors are locked with a padlock.

» If you cannot lock your hotel room securely from the inside at night, stay somewhere else.

Overpricing & Photography

» Agree on prices beforehand, particularly if eating in places without menus, flagging down an autorickshaw or arranging an airport pick-up from your hostel or hotel. This will save you money and could deflect potentially ugly misunderstandings later.

» When photographing people use your instincts; some people may demand money afterwards. Also see the Photography section in the Directory A-Z (p486).

TOP SCAMS

These long-running scams have been separating travellers from their money for years; keep an eye out.

» Gunk (dirt, paint, poo) suddenly appears on your shoes, only for a shoe cleaner to magically appear and offer to clean it off – for a price.

» Shops and restaurants 'borrow' the name of their more successful and popular competitor.

» Taxi drivers insist that they don't know the way to your hotel, or that the place you're looking for has moved or is closed – but they'll happily take you to their 'friend's' place (where they'll receive a nice commission).

» Touts claim to be 'government-approved' guides or 'tour operators' and sting you for large sums of cash. Inquire at the tourist office about recommended guides and ask to see evidence from the guides themselves.

Theft & Druggings

Druggings

» Very occasionally, tourists (especially those travelling solo) are drugged and robbed during train or bus journeys. A spiked drink is the most commonly used method for sending travellers off to sleep. Fortunately, reports of this are relatively rare in South India.

» Use your instincts. If you're unsure then politely decline drinks or food offered by strangers; stomach upsets are a convenient excuse.

Theft

» Theft is a risk in India, as it is anywhere else.

» Keep luggage securely locked on buses and trains.

» Be extra alert just before the train departs; thieves often take advantage of the confusion and crowds.

» Take extra care in dormitories and never, ever leave your valuables in the room when you go out unless there is a safe.

» For lost credit cards/travellers cheques, immediately contact the relevant office to lodge a report.

Touts & Commission Agents

» Many hotels and shops drum up extra business by paying commission to local fixers who bring tourists through the doors. Prices in these places will invariably be raised (by as much as 50%) to pay the fixer's commission.

» Train and bus stations are often swarming with touts – if anyone asks if this is your first trip to India, say you've been here several times, even if you haven't.

» Telling touts that you have already prepaid your transfer/tour/onward journey can help dissuade them.

» Where possible, prearrange hotel pick-ups, particularly in big cities.

» You'll often hear stories about hotels that refuse to pay commissions as being 'full' or 'closed' – check things out yourself.

» Be very sceptical of phrases like 'my brother's shop' and 'special deal at my friend's place'.

» Touts can be beneficial if you arrive in a town without a hotel reservation when some big festival is on, or during the peak season – they'll know which places have beds.

Transport Scams

» Make sure you're completely clear what is included in the price of any tour to avoid charges for hidden 'extras' later; get this in writing.

» Be extremely wary of anyone offering tours to Kashmir – see Lonely Planet India for comprehensive coverage of northern scams.

» Some travel agents exploit travellers' safety concerns to make extra money from tours that you can do just as easily (and safely) on public transport.

» When buying a bus, train or plane ticket anywhere other than the registered office of the transport company, make certain you're getting the ticket class you paid for.

• It's not uncommon for travellers to book a deluxe bus or AC train berth and arrive to find an ordinary bus or a less comfortable sleeper seat.

» Some tricksters pose as India Rail officials and insist that you pay to have your e-ticket validated; ignore them.

» Ignore taxi drivers outside airports who say they are prepaid taxi drivers; your prepaid taxi receipt will have the designated drivers' licence plate number printed on it.

Directory A-Z

Accommodation

Accommodation in South India ranges from grungy backpacker hostels with concrete floors and cold 'bucket' showers to opulent heritage hotels. In this guide, we've listed reviews by author preference; standout options are indicated by ![TOP CHOICE].

Categories

As a general rule, budget (₹) covers everything from basic hostels and railway retiring rooms to simple guest houses in traditional village homes. Midrange hotels (₹₹) tend to be modern-style concrete blocks that usually offer extras such as cable/satellite TV and air-conditioning (although some just have noisy 'air-coolers' that cool air by blowing it over cold water). Top End places (₹₹₹) stretch from luxury five-star chains to gorgeous heritage lodgings.

Costs

Given that the cost of budget, midrange and top-end hotels varies so much across South India, it would be misleading of us to provide a 'southern' price strategy for each category. The best way to gauge accommodation costs is to go directly to the Fast Facts and the Sleeping sections of this book's regional chapters. Keep in mind that most establishments raise tariffs annually, so the prices may have risen by the time you read this.

Price Icons

The price indicators in this book refer to the cost of a double room, including private bathroom, unless otherwise noted. The following table is based on price indicators for Kerala, Tamil Nadu and Goa and gives an example of the difference in accommodation costs across South India.

Reservations

» The majority of top-end and some midrange hotels require a deposit at the time of booking, which can usually be done with a credit card.

» Some midrange places may ask for a cheque or cash deposit into a bank account to secure a reservation. This is usually more hassle than it's worth.

» Some budget options won't take reservations as they don't know when people are going to check-out; call ahead to check.

» Other places will ask for a deposit at check in – ask for a receipt and be wary of any request to sign a blank impression of your credit card. If the hotel insists, consider going to the nearest ATM and paying cash.

» Verify the check-out time when you check-in – some hotels have a fixed check-out time (usually 10am or noon), while others give you 24-hour check-out.

» Reservations by phone without a deposit are usually fine, but call to confirm the booking the day before you arrive.

Seasons

» Rates in this guide are full price in high season. The definition of the high and low seasons varies depending on location. For places like Goa and Kerala high season is basically one month before and two months after Christmas; in the hill stations it's usually from around April to July.

» Tourist hubs such as Goa can triple their rates in season – advance bookings are highly recommended.

» At other times you may find significant discounts; if the hotel seems quiet ask for a discount. Some hotels in places like Goa shut during the monsoon.

» Many temple towns have additional peak seasons around major festivals and

---

BOOK YOUR STAY ONLINE

For more reviews by Lonely Planet authors, check out hotels.lonelyplanet.com/India. You'll find independent reviews, as well as recommendations on the best places to stay. Best of all, you can book online.

SAMPLE ACCOMMODATION COSTS

CATEGORY	COST KERALA	COST TAMIL NADU	COST GOA
₹ budget	<₹800	<₹1000	<₹1000
₹₹ midrange	₹800-3000	₹1000-3000	₹1000-2500
₹₹₹ top end	>₹3000	>₹3000	>₹2500

pilgrimages; for festival details see the Month by Month (p17) chapter and Festivals & Events section of the regional chapters.

Taxes & Service Charges

» State governments slap a variety of taxes on hotel accommodation (except at the cheaper hotels), and these are added to the cost of your room.

» Taxes vary from state to state and are detailed in the regional chapters.

» Many upmarket hotels also levy an additional 'service charge' (usually around 10%).

» Rates quoted in this book's regional chapters exclude taxes unless otherwise noted.

Budget & Midrange Hotels

Apart from some traditional guesthouses, most budget and midrange hotels are modern-style concrete blocks. Some are charming, clean and good value, others less so.

» Room quality can vary considerably within hotels so try to inspect a few rooms first, and avoid carpeted rooms at cheaper hotels unless you like the smell of mouldy socks.

» Shared bathrooms (often with squat toilets) are usually only found at the cheapest lodgings.

» Most rooms have ceiling fans and better rooms have electric mosquito-killers and/or window nets, although cheaper rooms may lack windows altogether.

» You may like to bring your own sheet or sleeping-bag liner – sheets and bed covers at cheap hotels can be stained, well worn and in need of a wash.

» Sound pollution can be irksome (especially in urban hubs); pack good-quality earplugs and request a room that doesn't face a busy road.

» It's wise to keep your door locked, as some staff (particularly in budget accommodation) may knock and automatically walk in without first seeking your permission.

» Blackouts are common (especially during summer and the monsoon) so double-check that the hotel has a back-up generator if you're paying for electric 'extras' such as air-conditioners and TVs.

» Note that some hotels lock their doors at night. Members of staff may sleep in the lobby but waking them up can be a challenge. Let the hotel know in advance if you'll be arriving or coming back to your room late in the evening.

GET TO KNOW YOUR BATHROOM

Most of South India's midrange hotels and all top-end ones have sit-down toilets with toilet paper and soap supplied. In ultra-cheap hotels, and in places off the tourist trail, squat toilets are the norm and toilet paper is rarely provided. Squat toilets are variously described as 'Indian-style', 'Indian' or 'floor' toilets, while the sit-down variety may be called 'Western' or 'commode' toilets. In a few places, you'll find the curious 'hybrid toilet', a sit-down version with footpads on the edge of the bowl.

Terminology for hotel bathrooms varies. 'Attached bath', 'private bath' or 'with bath' means that the room has its own en suite bathroom. 'Common bath', 'no bathroom' or 'shared bath' means communal bathroom facilities.

Not all rooms have hot water. 'Running', '24-hour' or 'constant' water means that hot water is available round-the-clock (not always the case in reality). 'Bucket' hot water is only available in buckets (sometimes for a small charge).

Many places use wall-mounted electric geysers (water heaters) that need to be switched on up to an hour before use. Note that the geyser's main switch can sometimes be located outside the bathroom.

Hotels that advertise 'room with shower' may be misleading – sometimes the shower is just a pipe sticking out of the wall. Meanwhile, some hotels surreptitiously disconnect showers to cut costs, while showers at other places render a mere trickle of water.

In this book, hotel rooms have their own private bathroom unless otherwise indicated.

CARBON-MONOXIDE POISONING

Some mountain areas rely on charcoal burners for warmth, but these should be avoided due to the risk of fatal carbon-monoxide poisoning. The thick, mattress-like blankets used in many mountain areas are amazingly warm once you get beneath the covers. If you're still cold, improvise a hot-water bottle by filling your drinking-water bottle with boiled water and covering it with a sock.

» Away from tourist areas, cheaper hotels may not take foreigners because they don't have the necessary foreigner-registration forms.

Camping

» There are few official camping sites in South India, but campers can usually find hotels with gardens where they can camp for a nominal fee and use the bathroom facilities. Wild camping is often the only accommodation option on trekking routes.

Dormitory Accommodation

» A number of hotels have cheap dormitories, although these may be mixed and, in less touristy places, full of drunken drivers – not ideal conditions for women. More traveller-friendly dorms are found at the handful of hostels run by the YMCA, YWCA and Salvation Army as well as at HI-associated hostels.

Government Accommodation & Tourist Bungalows

» The Indian government maintains a network of guest houses for travelling officials and public workers, known variously as rest houses, dak bungalows, circuit houses, PWD (Public Works Department) bungalows and forest rest houses.

» These places may accept travellers if no government employees need the rooms, but permission is sometimes required from local officials and you'll probably have to find the chowkidar (caretaker) to open the doors.

» 'Tourist bungalows' are run by state governments – rooms are usually midpriced (some with cheap dorms) and have varying standards of cleanliness and service.

» Some state governments also run chains of more expensive hotels, including some lovely heritage properties. Details are normally available through the state tourism office.

Homestays/B&Bs for Paying Guests

» These family-run guest houses will appeal to those seeking a small-scale, uncommercial setting with home-cooked meals.

» Standards range from mud-and-stone huts with hole-in-the-floor toilets to comfortable middle-class homes.

» Be aware that some hotels market themselves as 'home-stays' but are run like hotels with little (or no) interaction with the family.

» Contact the local tourist office for a full list of participating families, or see entries in the regional chapters.

Railway Retiring Rooms

» Most large train stations have basic rooms for travellers holding an ongoing train ticket or Indrail Pass. Some are grim, others are surprisingly pleasant, but all are noisy from the sound of passengers and trains. Nevertheless, they're useful for early-morning train departures and there's usually a choice of dormitories or private rooms (24-hour checkout).

Temples & Pilgrims' Rest houses

» Accommodation is available at some ashrams (spiritual retreats), gurdwaras (Sikh temples) and dharamsalas (pilgrims' guest houses) for a donation, but these places have been established for genuine pilgrims so please exercise judgment about the appropriateness of staying (some regional chapters have further details). Always abide by any protocols.

Top-End & Heritage Hotels

» South India has plenty of top-end properties, from modern five-star chain hotels to unique heritage abodes.

» Most top-end hotels have rupee rates for Indian guests and US dollar rates for foreigners (including Non-Resident Indians, or NRIs).

» Officially, you're supposed to pay the dollar rates in foreign currency or by credit card, but many places will accept rupees adding up to the dollar rate (verify this when checking-in).

» The Government of India tourism website, **Incredible India** (www.incredibleindia. org), has a useful list of palaces, forts and other erstwhile royal retreats that accept paying guests – click on the 'Royal Retreats' heading.

Activities

South India offers a range of fantastic activities

from jungle safaris and scuba-diving to yoga and meditation. For details on regional activities, courses, equipment hire, clubs and companies, see this book's Plan Your Trip and If You Like... chapters.

Business Hours

» Official business hours are from 9.30am to 5.30pm Monday to Friday but many offices open later and close earlier.

» Most offices have an official lunch hour from around 1pm.

» Bank opening hours vary from town to town so check locally; foreign-exchange offices may open longer and operate daily.

» Some larger post offices have a full day on Saturday and a half-day on Sunday.

» All timings vary regionally; exceptions are noted in the regional chapters.

Courses

You can pursue all sorts of courses in South India, from yoga and meditation to cooking and classical dancing. See the Courses section of the regional chapters for details.

Language Courses

The places that are listed below offer language courses, some requiring a minimum time commitment.

Mumbai Beginners' courses in Hindi, Marathi and Sanskrit at Bharatiya Vidya Bhavan (p51).

Tamil Nadu Tamil courses in Chennai (p319).

Customs Regulations

Technically you're supposed to declare any amount of cash/travellers cheques over US$5000/10,000 on arrival. Indian rupees shouldn't be taken out of India; however, this is rarely policed. Officials very occasionally ask tourists to enter expensive items such as video cameras and laptop computers on a 'Tourist Baggage Re-export' form to ensure they're taken out of India at the time of departure.

Electricity

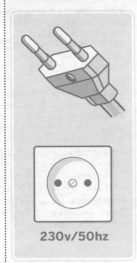

230v/50hz

230v/50hz

STANDARD HOURS

We've listed business hours only where they differ from the following standards.

BUSINESS	OPENING HOURS
Airline Office	9.30am-5.30pm Mon-Sat
Bank	9.30 or 10am-2 or 4pm Mon-Fri, to noon or 1pm Sat
Government Office	9.30am-1pm & 2-5.30pm Mon-Fri, closed alternate Sat (usually 2nd and 4th)
Post Office	9am-6pm Mon-Fri, to noon Sat
Museum	10am-5pm Tue-Sun
Restaurant	lunch noon-2.30 or 3pm, dinner 7-10 or 11pm
Shop	10am-7pm, some closed Sun
Sights	10am-5pm

Embassies & Consulates

Most foreign diplomatic missions are based in Delhi, but several nations operate consulates in other Indian cities (see websites, where

PRACTICALITIES

» **Newspapers & Magazines** Major English-language dailies include the *Hindustan Times, Times of India, Indian Express, Hindu, Daily News & Analysis (DNA)* and *Economic Times*. Regional English-language and local vernacular publications are found nationwide. Incisive current-affairs magazines include *Frontline, India Today*, the *Week, Tehelka* and *Outlook*.

» **Radio** Government-controlled All India Radio (AIR) is India's national broadcaster with over 220 stations broadcasting local and international news. There are also private FM channels broadcasting music, current affairs, talkback and more.

» **TV & Video** The national (government) TV broadcaster is Doordarshan. More people watch satellite and cable TV; English-language channels include BBC, CNN, Star World, HBO and Discovery.

» **Weights & Measures** Officially India is metric. Terms you're likely to hear are: lakhs (one lakh = 100,000) and crores (one crore = 10 million).

provided, in the following Delhi addresses). Many missions have certain timings for visa applications, usually mornings; phone for details. The following are just some of the many foreign missions found in India.

Australia Chennai (Map p318; ☑044-43913200; 512 Alpha Wing, Raheja Towers, 177 Anna Salai); Delhi ☑011-41399900; www.india.highcommission.gov.au; 1/50G Shantipath, Chanakyapuri); Mumbai (Map p44; ☑022-61167100; 36 Maker Chambers VI, 220 Nariman Point).

Bangladesh Delhi ☑011-24121394; www.bhcdelhi.org; EP39 Dr Radakrishnan Marg, Chanakyapuri); Kolkata ☑033-40127500; 9 Bangabandhu Sheikh Mujib Sarani).

Bhutan ☑011-26889230; www.bhutan.gov.bt; Chandragupta Marg, Chanakyapuri, Delhi).

Canada Chennai (Map p314; ☑044-28330888; 18, 3rd fl YAFA Tower, Khader Nawaz Khan Rd); Delhi ☑011-41782000; www.canadainternational.gc.ca/india-inde; 7/8 Shantipath, Chanakyapuri); Mumbai (Map p50; ☑022-67494444; 6th fl, Fort House, 221 Dr DN Rd).

France Delhi ☑011-24196100; http://ambafrance-in.org/; 2/50E Shantipath, Chanakyapuri); Mumbai (Map p44; ☑022-56694000; Wockhardt Towers, East Wing, 5th fl, Bandra Kurla Complex, Bandra East).

Germany Chennai (Map p314; ☑044-24301600; 9 Boat Club Rd, RA Puram); Delhi ☑011-44199199; www.new-delhi.diplo.de; 6/50G Shantipath, Chanakyapuri); Kolkata ☑033-24791141; 1 Hastings Park Rd, Alipore); Mumbai (Map p44; ☑022-22832422; 10th fl, Hoechst House, Nariman Point).

Ireland Delhi ☑011-24626733; www.irelandindia.com; 203 Jor Bagh).

Israel Delhi ☑011-30414500; http://delhi.mfa.gov.il; 3 Aurangzeb Rd); Mumbai (Map p44; ☑022-22822822; Earnest House, 16th fl, NCPA Marg, 194 Nariman Point).

Malaysia Chennai (Map p314; ☑044-28226888; 44 Tank Bund Rd, Nungambakkam); Delhi ☑011-26111291/97; www.kln.gov.my/web/ind_new-delhi/home; 50M Satya Marg, Chanakyapuri); Mumbai (Map p62; ☑022-

26455751/2; 4B, 4th fl, Notan Plaza, Turner Rd, Bandra West).

Maldives Delhi ☑011-41435701; www.maldiveshighcom.in/; B2 Anand Niketan).

Myanmar Delhi ☑011-24678822; 3/50F Nyaya Marg); Kolkata ☑033-24851658; 57K Ballygunge Circular Rd).

Nepal Delhi ☑011-23327361; Mandi House, Barakhamba Rd); Kolkata ☑033-24561224; 1 National Library Ave, Alipore).

Netherlands Chennai (Map p314; ☑044-43535381; 76 Venkata Krishan Rd, Mandaveli); Delhi ☑011-24197600; http://india.nlembassy.org/; 6/50F Shantipath, Chanakyapuri); Mumbai (Map p44; ☑022-22194200; Forbes Bldg, Charanjit Rai Marg, Fort).

New Zealand Chennai (Map p314; ☑044-28112472; Rane Engine Valves Ltd, 132 Cathedral Rd); Delhi ☑011-46883170; www.nzembassy.com/india; Sir Edmund Hillary Marg, Chanakyapuri); Mumbai (Map p44; ☑022-66151155; 1007, 10th fl, Dalamal House, Nariman Point).

Pakistan ☑011-24676004; 2/50G Shantipath, Chanakyapuri, Delhi).

Singapore Chennai (Map p314; ☑044-28158207; 17-A North Boag Rd, T. Nagar); Delhi ☑011-46000915; www.mfa.gov.sg/newdelhi; E6 Chandragupta Marg, Chanakyapuri); Mumbai (Map p44; ☑022-22043205; 152, Maker Chambers IV, 14th fl, 222 Jamnalal Bajaj Rd, Nariman Point).

Sri Lanka Chennai (Map p314; ☑044-24987896; 196 TTK Rd, Alwarpet); Delhi ☑011-23010201; www.newdelhi.mission.gov.lk; 27 Kautilya Marg, Chanakyapuri); Mumbai (Map p50; ☑022-22045861; Mulla House, 34 Homi Modi St, Fort).

Switzerland Delhi ☑011-26878372; www.eda.admin.ch; Nyaya Marg, Chanakyapuri); Mumbai (Map p44; ☑022-22884563-65; 102 Maker Chambers IV, 10th fl, 222 Jamnalal Bajaj Marg, Nariman Point).

Thailand Chennai (off Map p314; ☎044-42300730; 21/22 Arunaoholam Rd, Kotturpuram); Delhi ☎011-26118103-4; www.thaiemb.org.in; 56N Nyaya Marg, Chanakyapuri); Kolkata ☎033-24407836; 18B Mandeville Gardens, Ballygunge); Mumbai (Map p44; ☎022-22823535; Dalamal House, 1st fl, Jamnalal Bajai Marg, Nariman Point).

UK Chennai (Map p314; ☎044-42192151; 20 Anderson Rd); Delhi ☎011-24192100; http://ukinindia.fco.gov.uk; Shantipath, Chanakyapuri); Kolkata ☎033-22885172-6; 1A Ho Chi Minh Sarani); Mumbai (Map p44; ☎022-66502222; Naman Chambers, C/32 G Block Bandra Kurla Complex, Bandra East).

USA Chennai (Map p314; ☎044-28574000; Gemini Circle, 220 Anna Salai); Delhi ☎011-24198000; http://newdelhi.usembassy.gov/; Shantipath, Chanakyapuri); Kolkata ☎033-39842400; 5/1 Ho Chi Minh Sarani); Mumbai (Map p44; ☎022-23633611; Lincoln House, 78 Bhulabhai Desai Rd, Breach Candy).

Gay & Lesbian Travellers

In July 2009, Delhi's High Court overturned India's 148-year-old anti-homosexuality law. Prior to this landmark ruling, homosexual relations for men were illegal with penalties for transgression theoretically up to life imprisonment (there was no law against lesbian sexual relations).

However, the country remains largely conservative and public displays of affection are generally frowned upon for heterosexual couples as well as gay and lesbian couples.

There are low-key gay scenes in a number of southern cities including Mumbai and Bengaluru.

Publications

Time Out Mumbai (www.timeoutmumbai.net) Gay events in Mumbai.

Websites

Gay Bombay (www.gaybombay.org) Lists gay events as well as offering support and advice.

Indian Dost (www.indiandost.com/gay.php) News and information including contact groups in India.

India Pink (www.indiapink.co.in) India's first 'gay travel boutique' founded by a well-known Indian fashion designer.

A number of South Indian cities have support groups including the following:

Bengaluru

Good As You (www.goodasyou.in) Support group for gay, lesbian, bisexual and transgender people. It's part of the NGO **Swabhava**, which works for the LGBT community and operates the **Sahaya Helpline** (☎080-22230959).

Sangama (www.sangama.org) Deals with crisis intervention and provides a community outreach service for gay and bisexual men and women, transgenders and *hijra*s (transvestites and eunuchs).

Chennai

Shakti Center (☎044-45587071; www.shakticenter.org) Is a collective of LGBT activists and artists, which holds workshops, exhibitions and other activities.

Mumbai

Humsafar Trust (☎022-26673800; www.humsafar.org) Runs gay and transgender support groups and advocacy programs. Their drop-in centre in Santa Cruz East

---

PROHIBITED EXPORTS

To protect India's cultural heritage, the export of certain **antiques** is prohibited. Many 'old' objects are fine, but the difficulties begin if something is verifiably more than 100 years old. Reputable antique dealers know the laws and can make arrangements for an export-clearance certificate for any old items that you're permitted to export. If in doubt, contact Delhi's **Archaeological Survey of India** (☎011-23010822; www.asi.nic.in; Janpath; ⊙9.30am-1pm & 2-6pm Mon-Fri) next to the National Museum. The rules may seem stringent but the loss of artworks and traditional buildings due to the international trade in antiques and carved windows and doorframes has been alarming. Look for quality reproductions instead.

The Indian Wildlife Protection Act bans any form of **wildlife trade**. Don't buy any products that endanger threatened species and habitats – doing so can result in heavy fines and even imprisonment. This includes ivory, *shahtoosh* shawls (made from the down of rare Tibetan antelopes), and anything made from the fur, skin, horns or shell of any endangered species. Products made from certain rare plants are also banned.

Note that your home country may have additional laws forbidding the import of restricted items and wildlife parts. The penalties can be severe so know the law before you buy.

hosts workshops and has a library – pick up a copy of the pioneering gay-and-lesbian magazine *Bombay Dost*. It's also one of the venues for 'Sunday High', a monthly screening of queer-interest films.

Insurance

» Comprehensive travel insurance to cover theft, loss and medical problems (as well as air evacuation) is strongly recommended; also see p502.

» Some policies specifically exclude potentially dangerous activities such as scuba diving, motorcycling and even trekking: read the fine print.

» Some trekking agents may accept customers only who have cover for emergency helicopter evacuation.

» If you plan to hire a motorcycle in India, make sure the rental policy includes at least third-party insurance; see p497.

» Check in advance if your insurance policy will pay doctors and hospitals directly or reimburse you later for overseas health expenditures (keep all documentation for your claim).

LEGAL AGE

» **Age of Majority** 18

» **Buying Alcohol** 18-25 depending on state

» **Driving** 18

» **Sexual Consent** 16 heterosexual sex, 18 homosexual sex

» **Voting** 18

Travellers should note that they can be prosecuted under the law of their home country regarding age of consent, even when abroad.

» It's crucial to get a police report in India if you've had anything stolen; insurance companies may refuse to reimburse you without one.

» Worldwide travel insurance is available at www.lonely-planet.com/travel_services. You can buy, extend and claim online any time – even if you're already on the road.

Internet Access

Internet cafes are widespread and connections are usually reasonably fast, except in more remote areas. Wireless (wi-fi) access is available in an increasing number of hotels and some coffee shops in larger cities. In this book, hotels offering internet access are marked by @.

Practicalities

» Internet charges vary regionally (see regional chapters); charges fall anywhere between ₹15 and ₹90 per hour and often with a 15- to 30-minute minimum.

» Power cuts are not uncommon; avoid losing your email by writing and saving messages in a text application before pasting them into your browser.

» Bandwidth load tends to be lowest in the early morning and early afternoon.

» Some internet cafes may ask to see your passport; carrying photocopies of the relevant pages (information and visa) saves you having to dig your passport out each time.

» See p13 for useful India-specific web resources.

Security

» Be wary of sending sensitive financial information from internet cafes; some places are able to use keystroke-capturing technology to access passwords and emails.

» Avoid sending credit-card details or other personal data

---

over a wireless connection; using online banking on any nonsecure system is generally unwise.

Laptops

» Many internet cafes can supply laptop users with internet access over a LAN Ethernet cable; alternatively join an international roaming service with an Indian dial-up number, or take out an account with a local Internet Service Provider (ISP).

» Make sure your modem is compatible with the telephone and dial-up system in India (an external global modem may be necessary).

» Companies including Reliance, Airtel and Vodafone offer 3G Data Cards, which can be plugged into the USB port of your laptop and will allow you to access the internet.

• Tariffs start from ₹800 per month for 3 GB up to ₹1500 per month for 15 GB.

• Make sure you check to see if the area you're travelling to is covered by your service provider.

» Consider purchasing a fuse-protected universal AC adaptor to protect your circuit board from power surges.

» Plug adaptors are widely available throughout India, but bring spare plug fuses from home.

Legal Matters

If you're in a sticky legal situation, contact your embassy as quickly as possible. However, be aware that all your embassy may be able to do is monitor your treatment in custody and arrange a lawyer.

Antisocial Behaviour

» Smoking in public places is illegal throughout India but this is very rarely enforced; if caught you'll be fined ₹200.

» People can smoke inside their homes and in most open spaces such as streets (heed any signs stating otherwise).

» A number of Indian cities have banned spitting and littering, but this is also variably enforced.

Drugs

» Indian law does not distinguish between 'hard' and 'soft' drugs; possession of any illegal drug is regarded as a criminal offence.

» If convicted, the *minimum* sentence is 10 years, with very little chance of remission or parole.

» Cases can take months, even several years, to appear before a court while the accused may have to wait in prison. There's also usually a hefty monetary fine on top of any custodial sentence.

» Be aware that travellers have been targeted in sting operations in backpacker enclaves.

» Marijuana grows wild in various parts of India, but consuming it is still an offence, except in towns where bhang is legally sold for religious rituals.

» Police are getting particularly tough on foreigners who use drugs, so you should take this risk very seriously.

Police

» You should always carry your passport; police are entitled to ask you for identification at any time.

» If you're arrested for an alleged offence and asked for a bribe, the prevailing wisdom is to pay it as the alternative may be a trumped up charge; although there are no 'rules' guiding how much you should pay.

» Corruption is rife so the less you have to do with local police the better; try and avoid potentially risky situations in the first place.

Maps

Maps available inside India are of variable quality. Some

of the better map series include:

Eicher (http://maps.eicher world.com/)
Nelles (www.nelles-verlag.de)
Nest & Wings (www.nestwings.com)
Survey of India (www.survey ofindia.gov.in) Decent city, state and country maps but some titles are restricted for security reasons.

All of these maps are available at good bookshops, or you can buy them online from Delhi's **India Map Store** (www.indiamapstore.com). Throughout India, most state-government tourist offices stock basic local maps.

Money

The Indian rupee (₹) is divided into 100 paise (p), but paise coins are becoming increasingly rare. Coins come in denominations of ₹1, ₹2 and ₹5; notes come in ₹5, ₹10, ₹20, ₹50, ₹100, ₹500 and ₹1000 (this last one is handy for large bills but can pose problems in regard to getting change for small services). The Indian rupee is linked to a basket of currencies and has been subject to fluctuations in recent years; see p13 for exchange rates.

ATMs

» ATMs are found in most urban centres and Visa, MasterCard, Cirrus, Maestro and Plus are the most commonly accepted cards.

» Some banks in India that accept foreign cards include Citibank, HDFC, ICICI, HSBC and the State Bank of India.

» Before your trip, check whether your card can reliably access banking networks in India and ask for details of charges.

» Notify your bank that you'll be using your card in India (provide dates) to avoid having your card blocked;

WARNING: BHANG LASSI

Although it's rarely printed in menus, some restaurants in popular tourist centres will clandestinely whip up bhang lassi, a yoghurt and iced-water beverage laced with cannabis (occasionally other narcotics). Commonly dubbed 'special lassi', this often potent concoction can cause varying degrees of ecstasy, drawn-out delirium, hallucination, nausea and paranoia. Note that some travellers have been ill for several days, robbed or hurt in accidents after drinking this fickle brew. A few towns have legal (controlled) bhang outlets.

take along your bank's phone number just in case.

» The ATMs listed in this book's regional chapters accept foreign cards (but not necessarily all types of card).

» Always keep the emergency lost-and-stolen numbers for your credit cards in a safe place, separate from your cards, and report any loss or theft immediately.

» Away from major towns, always carry cash or travellers cheques as back-up.

Black Market

» Black-market moneychangers exist but legal moneychangers are so common that there's no reason to use them. Exceptions may be to change small amounts of cash at land border crossings. As a rule, if someone approaches you on the street and offers to change money, you're probably being set up for a scam.

Cash

» Major currencies such as US dollars, British pounds and Euros are easy to change throughout India, although some bank branches insist on travellers cheques only.

» Some banks also accept other currencies such as Australian and Canadian dollars, and Swiss francs.

» Private moneychangers deal with a wider range of currencies, but Pakistani, Nepali and Bangladeshi currency can be harder to change away from the border.

» When travelling off the beaten track, always carry an adequate stock of rupees.

» Whenever changing money, check every note. Don't accept any filthy, ripped or disintegrating notes, as these may be difficult to use.

» It can be tough getting change in India so keep a stock of smaller currency; ₹10, ₹20 and ₹50 notes are helpful.

» Officially, you cannot take rupees out of India, but this is laxly enforced. You can change any leftover rupees back into foreign currency, most easily at the airport (some banks have a ₹1000 minimum). You may have to present encashment certificates or credit-card/ATM receipts, and show your passport and airline ticket.

Credit Cards

» Credit cards are accepted at a growing number of shops, upmarket restaurants, and midrange and top-end hotels, and they can usually be used to pay for flights and train tickets.

» Cash advances on major credit cards are also possible at some banks.

» MasterCard and Visa are the most widely accepted cards.

Encashment Certificates

» Indian law states that all foreign currency must be changed at official money-changers or banks.

» For every (official) foreign-exchange transaction, you'll receive an encashment certificate (receipt), which will allow you to re-exchange rupees into foreign currency when departing India.

» Encashment certificates should total the amount of rupees you intend changing back to foreign currency.

» Printed receipts from ATMs are also accepted as evidence of an international transaction at most banks.

International Transfers

» If you run out of money, someone back home can wire you cash via money-changers affiliated with **Moneygram** (www.moneygram.com) or **Western Union** (www.westernunion.com). A fee is added to the transaction. To collect cash, bring your passport and the name and reference number of the person who sent the funds.

Moneychangers

» Private moneychangers are usually open for longer hours than banks, and are found almost everywhere (many also double as internet cafes and travel agents). Upmarket hotels may also change money, but their rates are usually not as competitive.

Tipping, Baksheesh & Bargaining

» In tourist restaurants or hotels, a service fee is usually already added to your bill and tipping is optional. Elsewhere, a tip is appreciated.

» Hotel bellboys and train/airport porters appreciate anything around ₹50, and hotel staff should be given similar gratuities for services above and beyond the call of duty.

» It's not mandatory to tip taxi or rickshaw drivers, but it's good to tip drivers who are honest about the fare.

» If you hire a car with driver for more than a couple of days, a tip is recommended for good service – details on p495.

» Baksheesh can loosely be defined as a 'tip'; it covers everything from alms for beggars to bribes.

» Many Indians implore tourists not to hand out sweets, pens or money to children, as it encourages them to beg. To make a lasting difference, donate to a reputable school or charitable organisation (see p26).

» Unless shopping in fixed-price shops (such as government emporiums and fair-trade cooperatives), bargaining is the norm.

Travellers Cheques

» All major brands are accepted, but some banks may accept cheques only from American Express (Amex) and Thomas Cook.

» Pounds sterling and US dollars are the safest currencies, especially in smaller towns.

» Keep a record of the cheques' serial numbers separate from your cheques, along with the proof-of-purchase slips, encashment vouchers and photocopied passport details. If you lose your cheques, contact the American Express or Thomas Cook office in Delhi.

» To replace lost travellers cheques, you need the proof-of-purchase slip and the numbers of the missing cheques (some places require a photocopy of the police report and a passport photo). If you don't have the numbers of your missing cheques, Amex (or whichever company has issued them) will contact the place where you bought them.

Photography

For useful tips and techniques on travel photography, read Lonely Planet's guide to *Travel Photography*.

Digital

» Memory cards for digital cameras are available from photographic shops in most large cities and towns. However, the quality of memory cards is variable – some don't carry the advertised amount of data.

» Expect to pay upwards of ₹500 for a 1GB card.

» To be safe, regularly back up your memory card to CD; internet cafes may offer this service for ₹60 to ₹120 per disk.

» Some photographic shops make prints from digital photographs for roughly the standard print-and-processing charge.

Print & Slide

» Colour-print film-processing facilities are readily available in most urban centres.

» Film is relatively cheap and the quality is usually good, but you'll find colour-slide film only in the major cities towns.

» On average, developing costs around ₹5 per 4x6 print, plus ₹20 for processing.

» Passport photos are available from many photo shops for around ₹100 to ₹135 (four visa-size shots).

» Always check the use-by date on local film and slide stock, and make sure you get a sealed packet.

» It's best to buy film only from reputable stores – and preferably film that's been refrigerated (rather than sitting in a glass cabinet in the sunshine).

Restrictions

» India is touchy about anyone taking photographs of military installations – this can include train stations, bridges, airports, military sites and sensitive border regions.

» Photography from the air is officially prohibited, although airlines rarely enforce this.

» Many places of worship – such as monasteries, temples and mosques – also prohibit photography. Taking photos inside a shrine, at a funeral, at a religious ceremony or of people publicly bathing (including rivers) can also be offensive – ask first.

» Flash photography may be prohibited in certain areas of a shrine, or may not be permitted at all.

» Exercise sensitivity when taking photos of people, especially women, who may find it offensive – obtain permission in advance.

Post

India has the biggest postal network on earth, with over 155,500 post offices. Mail and poste-restante services are generally good, although the speed of delivery will depend on the efficiency of any given office. Airmail is faster and more reliable than sea mail, although it's best to use courier services (such as DHL) to send and receive items of value – expect to pay around ₹3000 per kilogram to Europe, Australia or the USA. Private couriers are often cheaper, but goods may be repacked into large packages to cut costs and things sometimes go missing.

Receiving Mail

» Ask senders to address letters to you with your surname in capital letters and underlined, followed by poste restante, GPO (main post office), and the city or town in question. To claim mail you'll need to show your passport.

» Many 'lost' letters are simply misfiled under given/first names, so check under both your names and ask senders to provide a return address.

» Letters sent via poste restante are generally held for around one to two months before being returned.

» It's best to have any parcels sent to you by registered post.

Sending Mail

LETTERS

» Posting letters/aerogrammes to anywhere overseas costs ₹20/15.

» International postcards cost around ₹7.

» For postcards, stick on the stamps *before* writing on them, as post offices can give you as many as four stamps per card.

» Sending a letter overseas by registered post adds ₹15 to the stamp cost.

PARCELS

» Posting parcels can either be relatively straightforward or involve multiple counters and lots of queuing; get to the post office in the morning.

» Prices vary depending on weight (including packing material).

» A small package (unregistered) costs ₹40 (up to 100g) to any country and ₹30 per additional 100g (up to a maximum of 4000g; different charges apply for higher weights than this).

» Parcel post has a maximum of 20kg to 30kg depending on the destination.

» There is the choice of airmail (delivery in one to three weeks), sea mail (two to four months), or Surface Air-Lifted (SAL) – a curious hybrid where parcels travel by both air and sea (around one month).

» There is also EMS (express mail service; delivery within three days) for around 30% more than the normal airmail price.

» Parcels must be packed up in white linen and the seams sealed with wax – local tailors offer this service if the post office doesn't.

» The post office can provide the necessary customs declaration forms and these must be stitched or pasted to the parcel. If the contents are a gift under the value of ₹1000, you won't have to pay duty at the delivery end.

» Carry a permanent marker to write on the parcel any information requested by the desk.

» Books or printed matter can go by international book post for ₹350 (maximum 5kg), but the package must be wrapped with a hole that reveals the contents for inspection by customs – tailors can do this in such a way that nothing falls out.

» India Post (www.indiapost. gov.in) has an online calculator for domestic and international postal tariffs.

Public Holidays

There are officially three national public holidays. Every state celebrates its own official holidays, which cover bank holidays for government workers as well as major religious festivals. Most businesses (offices, shops etc) and tourist sites close on public holidays, but transport is usually unaffected. It's wise to make transport and hotel reservations well in advance if you intend visiting during major festivals.

Public Holidays

Republic Day 26 January
Independence Day 15 August
Gandhi Jayanti 2 October

Major Religious Festivals

Mahavir Jayanti (Jain) February
Holi (Hindu) March
Easter (Christian) March/April
Buddha Jayanti (Buddhist) April/May
Eid al-Fitr (Muslim) August/September
Dussehra (Hindu) October
Diwali (Hindu) October/November
Nanak Jayanti (Sikh) November
Christmas (Christian) 25 December

Safe Travel

Travellers to India's major cities may fall prey to petty and opportunistic crime but most problems can be avoided with a bit of common sense and an appropriate amount of caution – see p476 for more information. Women and solo travellers should read p474. Also have a look at the India branch of Lonely Planet's **Thorn Tree Travel Forum** (www.lonelyplanet.com/thorn tree), where travellers often post timely warnings about problems they've encountered on the road. Always check your government's travel advisory warnings.

Rebel Violence

India has a number of (sometimes armed) dissident groups championing various causes. These groups have employed the same tried and tested techniques of rebel groups everywhere – assassinations and bomb attacks on government infrastructure, public transport, religious centres, tourist sites and markets.

» International terrorism is as much of a risk in Europe or America, so this is no reason not to go to India, but it makes sense to check the local security situation carefully before travelling.

Telephone

» There are few payphones in India (apart from in airports), but private PCO/STD/ISD call booths do the same job, offering local, interstate and international calls at lower prices than calls made from hotel rooms.

» These booths are found around the country. A digital meter displays how much the call is costing and usually provides a printed receipt when the call is finished.

» Costs vary depending on the operator and destination but can range from ₹1 per minute for local calls and between ₹5 and ₹10 for international calls.

» Some booths also offer a 'call-back' service – you ring home, provide the phone number of the booth and wait for people at home to call you back, for a fee of around ₹10 on top of the cost of the preliminary call.

» Getting a line can be difficult in remote country and mountain areas – an engaged signal may just mean that the exchange is overloaded, so keep trying.

GOVERNMENT TRAVEL ADVICE

The following government websites offer travel advice and information on current hot spots.

» **Australian Department of Foreign Affairs** (www.smartraveller.gov.au)
» **British Foreign Office** (www.fco.gov.uk/en)
» **Canadian Department of Foreign Affairs** (www.voyage.gc.ca)
» **German Foreign Office** (www.auswaeriges-amt.de)
» **Japan Ministry of Foreign Affairs** (www.mofa.go.jp)
» **Ministry of Foreign Affairs Netherlands** (www.government.nl/Subjects/Advice_to_travellers)
» **Switzerland** (www.eda.admin.ch)
» **US State Department** (http://travel.state.gov)

» Useful online resources include the **Yellow Pages** (www.indiayellowpages.com) and **Justdial** (www.justdial.com).

Mobile Phones

» Indian mobile phone numbers usually have 10 digits typically beginning with ♪9.

» There's roaming coverage for international GSM phones in most cities and large towns.

» To avoid expensive roaming costs (often highest for incoming calls), get hooked up to the local mobile-phone network.

» Note that mobiles bought in some countries may be locked to a particular network; you'll have to get the phone unlocked, or buy a local phone (available from ₹2000) to use an Indian SIM card.

GETTING CONNECTED

» Getting connected is inexpensive but increasingly complicated owing to security concerns and involves a lot of paperwork.

» Foreigners must supply between one and five passport photos, their passport, and photocopies of their passport identity and visa pages.

» You must also supply a residential address, which can be the address of the hotel where you're staying (ask the hotel to write a letter on your behalf by way of confirmation).

» Some phone companies send representatives to the listed address, or at the very least call to verify that you are actually staying there.

» Some travellers have reported their SIM card being suspended once the phone company realised that they had moved on from the hotel where they registered their phone. Others have been luckier and used the same SIM card throughout their travels.

» Another option is to get a friendly local to register the phone using their local ID.

» Prepaid mobile-phone kits (SIM card and phone number, plus an allocation of calls) are available in most Indian towns from around ₹200 from a phone shop or local PCO/STD/ISD booth, internet cafe or grocery store.

» You must then purchase new credits on that network, sold as scratch cards in shops and call centres.

» Credit must usually be used within a set time limit and costs vary with the amount of credit on the card. The amount you pay for a credit top-up is not the amount you get on your phone – state taxes and service charges come off first.

» For some networks, recharge cards are being replaced by direct credit, where you pay the vendor and the credit is deposited straight to your phone – ask which system is in use before you buy.

CHARGES

» Calls made within the state or city in which you bought the SIM card are cheap – ₹1 per minute – and you can call internationally for less than ₹10 per minute.

» SMS messaging is even cheaper – usually, the more credit you have on your phone, the cheaper the call rate.

» The most popular (and reliable) companies include Airtel, Vodaphone and BSNL.

» Most SIM cards are state specific; they can be used in other states, but you pay for calls at roaming rates and you'll be charged for incoming calls as well as outgoing calls.

» If you buy a SIM card in Mumbai, calls ex-Mumbai will be around ₹1.50 per minute, while the charge to receive a call from anywhere in India (ex-Mumbai) is around ₹1 per minute.

» Be aware that unreliable signals and problems with international texting (with messages or replies being delayed or failing to get through) are not uncommon.

» As the mobile-phone industry continues to evolve, mobile rates, suppliers and coverage are all likely to develop over the life of this book.

Phone Codes

» Calling India from abroad: dial your country's international access code, then ♪91 (India's country code), then the area code (without the initial zero), then the local number.

» Calling internationally from India: dial ♪00 (the international access code), then the country code of the country you're calling, then the area code (without the initial zero if there is one) and the local number.

» Phone numbers have an area code followed by up to eight digits.

» Toll-free numbers begin with 1800.

» The government is slowly trying to bring all numbers in India onto the same system, so area codes may change and new digits may be added to numbers with limited warning.

Time

India uses the 12-hour clock and the local standard time is known as IST (Indian Standard Time). IST is 5½ hours ahead of GMT/UTC. The floating half-hour was added to maximise daylight hours over such a vast country.

Toilets

» Public toilets are most easily found in major cities and tourist sites and the cleanest toilets (usually with sit-down and squat choices) are most

CITY	NOON IN DELHI
Beijing	2.30pm
Dhaka	12.30pm
Islamabad	11.30am
London	6.30am
Kathmandu	12.15pm
New York	1.30am
San Francisco	10.30pm
Sydney	5.30pm
Tokyo	3.30pm

reliably found at modern restaurants, shopping complexes and cinemas.

» Beyond urban centres toilets are of the squat variety and locals may use the 'hand-and-water' technique, which involves cleaning one's bottom with a small jug of water and the left hand. It's always a good idea to carry your own toilet paper, just in case.

Tourist Information

In addition to the Government of India tourist offices (also known as 'India Tourism') each state maintains its own network of tourist offices. These vary in their efficiency and usefulness – some are run by enthusiastic souls who go out of their way to help, others are little more than a means of drumming up business for State Tourism Development Corporation tours. Most of the tourist offices have free brochures and often a free (or inexpensive) local map (for further map information see p485).

The first stop for information should be the tourism website of the Government of India, **Incredible India** (www.incredibleindia.org). For details of its regional offices around India, click on the 'Help Desk' tab at the top of the homepage.

See regional chapters for contact details of relevant tourist offices.

Travel Permits

Even with a visa, you're not permitted to travel everywhere in South India. Some national parks and forest reserves call for a permit.

A permit is required to visit the Andaman Islands (see p398) and Lakshadweep (see 306).

Travellers with Disabilities

India's crowded public transport, crush of humanity and variable infrastructure can test even the hardiest able-bodied traveller. If you have a physical disability or you are vision impaired, these can pose even more of a challenge. If your mobility is considerably restricted you may like to ease the stress by travelling with an able-bodied companion.

Accommodation Wheelchair-friendly hotels are almost exclusively top end. Make pre-trip inquiries and book ground-floor rooms at hotels that lack adequate facilities.

Accessibility Some restaurants and offices have ramps, most tend to have at least one step. Staircases are often steep; lifts frequently stop at mezzanines between floors.

Footpaths Where pavements exist, they can be riddled with holes, littered with debris and packed with pedestrians. If using crutches, bring along spare rubber caps.

Transport Hiring a car with driver will make moving around a lot easier (see p495); if you use a wheelchair, make sure the car-hire company can provide an appropriate vehicle to carry it.

For further advice pertaining to your specific requirements, consult your doctor before heading to India.

The following organisations may be able to proffer further information or at least point you in the right direction.

Access-Able Travel Source (www.access-able.com).

Accessible Journeys (www.disabilitytravel.com).

Global Access News (www.globalaccessnews.com).

Mobility International USA (MIUSA; www.miusa.org).

Royal Association for Disability & Rehabilitation (RADAR; www.radar.org.uk).

Visas

A pilot scheme is currently in place to provide visas on arrival to nationals of Japan, New Zealand, Singapore, Luxembourg and Finland at Mumbai, Chennai, Kolkata and New Delhi airports. This scheme has been introduced on a one-year 'experimental' basis so double-check before you fly. All other nationals – except Nepal and Bhutan – must get a visa *before* arriving in India. These are available at Indian missions worldwide. Note that your passport needs to be valid for at least six months beyond your intended stay in India with at least two blank pages.

Entry Requirements

» In 2009 a large number of foreigners were found to be working in India on tourist visas so regulations surrounding who can get a visa and for how long have been tightened. These rules are likely to change, however, so double-check with the Indian embassy in your country prior to travel.

» Most people travel on the standard six-month tourist visa. Student and business visas have strict conditions (consult the Indian embassy for details).

» Tourist visas are valid from the date of issue, not the date you arrive in the country. You can spend a total of 180 days in India.

» Five- and 10-year tourist visas are available to US citizens *only* under a bilateral arrangement; however, you can only still stay in the country for up to 180 days continuously. Currently, you are required to submit two passport photographs with your visa application; these must be in colour and 2 inches x 2 inches.

» An onward travel ticket is a requirement for most visas, but this isn't always enforced (check in advance).

» There are additional restrictions on travellers from Bangladesh and Pakistan, as well as certain Eastern European, African and Central Asian countries. Check any special conditions for your nationality with the Indian embassy in your country.

» Visas are priced in the local currency and may have an added service fee (contact your country's Indian embassy for current prices).

» Extended visas are possible for people of Indian origin (excluding those in Pakistan and Bangladesh) who hold a non-Indian passport and live abroad.

» For visas lasting more than six months, you're supposed to register at the Foreigners' Regional Registration Office (FRRO) within 14 days of arriving in India; inquire about these special conditions when you apply for your visa.

Re-entry Requirements

» Current regulations dictate that when you leave the country, you will receive a stamp in your passport indicating you may not re-enter India for two months, regardless of how much longer your visa may be valid for.

» If you wish to return to India before the two-month period has passed, you will have to visit the Indian High Commission or Consulate in the country where you've travelled to, or are resident, and apply for a Permit to Re-enter. This permit is granted only if urgent or in extreme cases.

» If you're travelling to multiple countries then a permit is not needed as long as your trip follows an itinerary, which you can show at immigration (if you're transiting back through India from Nepal on your way home for example).

» If granted a permit, you must register with the FRRO/ FRO within 14 days.

Visa Extensions

» At the time of writing, the **Ministry of Home Affairs** (☏011-23385748; Jaisalmer House, 26 Man Singh Rd, Delhi; ◷inquiries 9-11am Mon-Fri) were not granting visa extensions. The only circumstances where this might conceivably happen are in *extreme* medical emergencies or if you were robbed of your passport just before you planned to leave the country (at the end of your visa).

» In such cases, you should contact the **Foreigners' Regional Registration Office** (FRRO; ☏011-26195530; frrodelhi@hotmail.com; Level 2, East Block 8, Sector 1, Rama Krishna (RK) Puram, Delhi; ◷9.30am-5.30pm Mon-Fri), just around the corner from the Hyatt Regency hotel. This is also the place to come for a replacement visa if you need your lost/stolen passport replaced (required before you can leave the country). Note that regional FRROs are even less likely to grant an extension.

» Assuming you meet the stringent criteria, the FRRO is permitted to issue an extension of 14 days (free for nationals of most countries; inquire on application). You must bring your confirmed air ticket, one passport photo (take two, just in case) and a photocopy of your passport identity and visa pages. Note that this system is designed to get you out of the country promptly with the correct official stamps, not to give you two extra weeks of travel.

Transport

GETTING THERE & AWAY

South India is most easily accessed via its major international airports of Mumbai and Chennai. Some countries also offer charter flights to Goa. The South can also be reached overland from elsewhere in and near India.

Entering India

Entering India by air or land is relatively straightforward, with standard immigration and customs procedures (p481).

Passport

To enter India you need a valid passport, visa (p491) and an onward/return ticket.

Your passport should be valid for at least six months beyond your intended stay in India. If your passport is lost or stolen, immediately contact your country's representative (p481). Keep photocopies of your airline ticket and the identity and visa pages of your passport in case of emergency. Better yet, scan and email copies to yourself. Check with the Indian embassy in your home country for any special conditions that may exist for your nationality.

Air

Airports & Airlines

India is a big country so it makes sense to fly into the airport that's nearest to the area you'll be visiting. South India has two main gateways for international flights (listed here); however, there are a number of other cities servicing international carriers – for details see regional chapters. Direct charter flights from the UK, Russia and certain parts of Europe land at Goa's Dabolim Airport and, while you can get some cheap deals, you must also return via a charter flight.

India's national carrier is **Air India** (www.airindia. com), of which the former state-owned domestic carrier, Indian Airlines, is now a part, following a merger deal. Air India has had a relatively decent air safety record in recent years.

Chennai (Madras; MAA; Anna International Airport; ☎044-22560551; www.chennaiairport guide.com)

Mumbai (Bombay; BOM; Chhatrapati Shivaji International Airport; ☎022-2626 4000; www.csia.in)

Tickets

An onward or return air ticket is usually a condition of the Indian tourist visa, so few visitors buy international tickets inside India. Only designated travel agencies can book international flights, but fares may be the same if you book directly with the airlines. Departure tax and other charges are included in airline tickets. You are required to show a copy of your ticket or itinerary in order to enter the airport, whether flying internationally or within India.

Land

It's possible, of course, to get to South India overland via the long haul through North India. The classic hippie route from Europe to Goa involves travelling via Turkey, Iran and Pakistan. Other popular overland options are via Bangladesh

---

THINGS CHANGE...

The information in this chapter is particularly vulnerable to change. Check directly with the airline or a travel agent to make sure you understand how a fare (and the ticket you may buy) works and be aware of the security requirements for international travel. Shop carefully. The details given in this chapter should simply be regarded as pointers and not as a substitute for your own careful up-to-date research.

CLIMATE CHANGE & TRAVEL

Every form of transport that relies on carbon-based fuel generates CO_2, the main cause of human-induced climate change. Modern travel is dependent on aeroplanes, which might use less fuel per person than most cars but travel much greater distances. The altitude at which aircraft emit gases (including CO_2) and particles also contributes to their climate change impact. Many websites offer 'carbon calculators' that allow people to estimate the carbon emissions generated by their journey and, for those who wish to do so, to offset the impact of the greenhouse gases emitted with contributions to portfolios of climate-friendly initiatives throughout the world. Lonely Planet offsets the carbon footprint of all staff and author travel.

or Nepal. If you enter India by bus or train you'll be required to disembark at the border for standard immigration and customs checks.

You *must* have a valid Indian visa in advance, as no visas are available at the border – see p491 for more information.

Drivers of cars and motorbikes will need the vehicle's registration papers, liability insurance and an international drivers' permit in addition to their domestic licence. You'll also need a *Carnet de passage en douane,* which acts as a temporary waiver of import duty.

To find out the latest requirements for the paperwork and other important driving information, contact your local automobile association.

See the relevant sections in this chapter for more on car and motorcycle travel.

For detailed information about crossing into India from neighbouring countries, consult Lonely Planet's *India.*

Sea

There are several sea routes between India and surrounding islands but none leave Indian sovereign territory. There has long been talk of a passenger ferry service between southern India and Colombo in Sri Lanka but this has yet to materialise. Inquire locally to see if there has been any progress.

GETTING AROUND

Air
Airlines in South India

India has a very competitive domestic airline industry. Some well-established players are Air India (which now includes Indian Airlines), Kingfisher and Jet Airways. There are also a host of budget airlines offering discounted fares on a variety of domestic sectors. Airline seats can be booked directly by telephone, through travel agencies or cheaply over the internet. Domestic airlines set rupee fares for Indian citizens, while foreigners may be charged US dollar fares (usually payable in rupees).

At the time of writing, the following airlines were operating across various destinations in India – see regional chapters for specifics about routes, fares and booking offices. Keep in mind, however, that the competitive nature of the aviation industry means that fares fluctuate dramatically. Holidays, festivals and seasons also have a serious affect on ticket prices, so check for the latest fares online.

Air India (☑1800 1801407; www.airindia.com) India's national carrier operates many domestic and international flights.

GoAir (☑1800 222111; www.goair.in) Reliable low-cost carrier servicing Goa and Cochin among other destinations.

IndiGo (☑1800 1803838; www.goindigo.in) Good, reliable budget airline flying to numerous cities including Mumbai and Chennai.

Jagson Airlines (☑011-23721593; http://jagsonairlines.biz) Regular planes and tiny Dornier carriers to access the country's smaller runways.

Jet Airways (☑011-39893333; www.jetairways.com) Rated by many as India's best airline, with growing domestic and international services.

JetLite (☑1800 223020; www.jetlite.com) Jet Airways' budget carrier flies to numerous destinations including Chennai.

Kingfisher Airlines (☑1800 2093030; www.flykingfisher.com) Domestic and international flights.

Kingfisher Red (☑1800 2093030; www.flykingfisher.com) Kingfisher Airlines' low-cost option.

Spicejet (☑1800 1803333; www.spicejet.com) Budget carrier servicing domestic destinations in addition to international ports such as Colombo (Sri Lanka) and Kathmandu (Nepal).

Security at airports is generally stringent. All hold baggage must be X-rayed prior to check-in and every item of cabin baggage needs a label, which must be stamped as part of the security check (don't forget to collect tags at the check-in counter).

PREPAID TAXIS

Most Indian airports and many train stations have a prepaid-taxi booth, normally just outside the terminal building. Here, you can book a taxi for a fixed price (which will include baggage) and thus avoid commission scams. However, officials advise holding on to the payment coupon until you reach your chosen destination, in case the driver has any other ideas! Smaller airports and stations may have prepaid autorickshaw booths instead.

The recommended check-in time for domestic flights is one hour before departure. The usual luggage allowance is 20kg (10kg for smaller aircraft) in economy class and 30kg in business.

Bicycle

South India offers loads of variety for the cyclist, from pretty coastal routes to winding roads passing fragrant spice plantations and breezy coconut groves.

There are no restrictions on bringing a bicycle into the country. However, bicycles sent by sea can take a few weeks to clear customs in India, so it's better to fly bikes in. It may actually be cheaper – and less hassle – to hire or buy a bicycle in India itself. Read up on bicycle touring before you travel – Rob Van Der Plas' *Bicycle Touring Manual* and Stephen Lord's *Adventure Cycle-Touring Handbook* are good places to start. Consult local cycling magazines and cycling clubs for useful information and advice.

The **Cycling Federation of India** (☎011-23753529; www. cyclingfederationofindia.org; 12 Pandit Pant Marg; ◷10am-5pm Mon-Fri) can provide local information.

Hire

» Tourist centres and traveller hang-outs are the easiest spots to find bicycles for hire – simply inquire locally.

» Prices vary; places charge anywhere between ₹40 and ₹100 per day for a road-worthy, Indian-made bicycle. Mountain bikes, where available, are usually upwards of ₹350 per day).

» Hire places may require a cash security deposit (avoid leaving your airline ticket or passport).

Practicalities

» Mountain bikes with off-road tyres give the best protection against India's puncture-prone roads.

» Roadside cycle mechanics abound but you should still bring spare tyres and brake cables, lubricating oil and a chain repair kit, and plenty of puncture repair patches.

» Bikes can often be carried for free, or for a small luggage fee, on the roof of public buses – handy for uphill stretches.

» Contact your airline for information about transporting your bike and customs formalities in your home country.

Purchase

Mountain bikes with reputable brands, including Hero (www.herocycles.com) and Atlas (www.atlascycle sonepat.com), generally start at around ₹3500.

» Reselling is usually fairly easy – ask at local cycle or hire shops or put up an advert on travel noticeboards.

» If you purchased a new bike and it's still in reasonably good condition, you should be able to get back around 50% of what you originally paid.

Road Rules

» Vehicles drive on the left in India but otherwise road rules are virtually nonexistent. Cities and national highways can be hazardous places to cycle so, where possible, stick to back roads.

» Be conservative about the distances you expect to cover – an experienced cyclist can manage around 60km to 100km a day on the plains, 40km to 60km on sealed mountain roads and 40km or less on dirt roads.

Boat

» Scheduled ferries connect mainland India to Port Blair in the Andaman Islands.

» There are sporadic ferries from Visakhapatnam (Andhra Pradesh) to the Andaman Islands.

» Between October and May, there are boat services from Kochi (Kerala) to the Lakshadweep Islands.

» There are also numerous shorter ferry services across rivers, from chain pontoons to coracles, and various boat cruises – see the regional chapters for more information.

Bus

» Buses go almost everywhere in South India and tend to be the cheapest way to travel. Services are fast and frequent, and buses are the only way to get around many mountainous areas.

» Roads in curvaceous terrain can be especially perilous; buses are often driven with wilful abandon and accidents are always a risk.

» Avoid night buses unless there's no alternative. Driving conditions are more hazardous and drivers may also be suffering from lack of sleep.

» All buses make snack and toilet stops (some more frequently than others), providing a break but possibly adding hours to journey times.

» Shared jeeps complement the bus service in many mountain areas.

Classes

» There are state-owned and private bus companies and both offer 'ordinary' buses and more expensive 'deluxe' buses. Many state tourist offices run their own reliable deluxe bus services.

» 'Ordinary' buses tend to be ageing rattletraps while 'deluxe' buses range from less decrepit versions of ordinary buses to flashy Volvo buses with AC and reclining two-by-two seating.

» Buses run by the state government are usually the more reliable option (if there's a breakdown, another bus will be sent to pick up passengers), and seats can usually be booked up to a month in advance.

» Private buses are either more expensive (but more comfortable), or cheaper but with kamikaze drivers and conductors who try and cram in as many passengers as possible to maximise profits.

» Travel agencies in many tourist towns offer relatively expensive private two-by-two buses, which tend to leave and terminate at conveniently central stops.

» Be warned that some agencies have been known to book people onto ordinary buses at super-deluxe prices – if possible, book directly with the bus company.

» Timetables and destinations may be displayed on signs or billboards at travel agencies and tourist offices.

» Earplugs are a boon on all long-distance buses to muffle the often deafening music. On any bus, try to sit between the axles to minimise the bumpy effect of potholes.

Costs

» The cheapest buses are 'ordinary' government buses, but prices vary from state to state (consult regional chapters).

» Add around 50% to the ordinary fare for deluxe services, double the fare for AC, and triple or quadruple the fare for a two-by-two service.

Luggage

» Luggage is either stored in compartments underneath the bus (sometimes for a small fee) or it can be carried on the roof.

» Arrive at least an hour ahead of the departure time – some buses cover the roof-stored bags with a large sheet of canvas, making last-minute additions inconvenient or impossible.

» If your bags go on the roof, make sure they're securely locked and tied to the metal baggage rack – some unlucky travellers have seen their belongings go bouncing off the roof on bumpy roads!

» Theft is a minor risk so keep an eye on your bags at snack and toilet stops and *never* leave your day-pack or valuables unattended inside the bus.

Reservations

» Most deluxe buses can be booked in advance – usually up to a month in advance for government buses – at the bus station or local travel agencies.

» Reservations are rarely possible on 'ordinary' buses and travellers often get left behind in the mad rush for a seat.

» To maximise your chances of securing a seat, either send a travelling companion ahead to grab some space, or pass a book or article of clothing through an open window and place it on an empty seat. This 'reservation' method rarely fails.

» If you board a bus midway through its journey, you'll often have to stand until a seat becomes free.

» Many buses only depart when full – you may find your bus suddenly empties to join another bus that's ready to leave before yours.

» At many bus stations there's a separate women's queue, although this isn't always obvious because signs are often not in English and men frequently join the melee. Women have an unspoken right to elbow their way to the front of any bus queue in India, so don't be shy, ladies!

Car

Self-drive car hire is possible in South India's larger cities, but given the hair-raising driving conditions most travellers opt for a car with driver. Hiring a car with driver is wonderfully affordable, particularly if several people share the cost. Seatbelts are either nonexistent or of variable quality. International rental companies with representatives in India include **Budget** (www.budget.com) and **Hertz** (www.hertz.com).

Hiring a Car & Driver

» Most towns have taxi stands or car-hire companies where you can arrange short or long tours (see regional chapters).

» Not all hire cars are licensed to travel beyond their home state. Even those vehicles that are licensed to enter different states have to pay extra (often hefty) state taxes, which will add to the rental charge.

» Ask for a driver who speaks some English and knows the region you intend to visit, and try to see the car and meet the driver before paying any money.

» Ambassador cars look great but can be rather slow and uncomfortable if travelling long distances – keep them for touring cities.

» For multiday trips, the charge should cover the driver's meals and accommodation. Drivers should make their own sleeping and eating arrangements.

» It is *essential* to set the ground rules from day one; politely but firmly let the driver know that you're boss in order to avoid anguish later.

Costs

» The price depends on the distance and the terrain (driving on mountain roads uses more petrol, hence the higher cost).

» One-way trips usually cost the same as return ones (to cover the petrol and driver charges for getting back).

» Hire charges vary from state to state. Some taxi unions set a time limit or a maximum kilometre distance for day trips – if you go over, you'll have to pay extra.

» To avoid potential misunderstandings, ensure you get *in writing* what you've been promised (quotes should include petrol, sightseeing stops, all your chosen destinations, and meals and accommodation for the driver). If a driver asks you for money to pay for petrol en route because he is short of cash, get receipts so you can be reimbursed later.

» For sightseeing day trips around a single city, expect to pay anywhere upwards of ₹800/1000 for a non-AC/AC car with an eight-hour, 80km limit per day (extra charges apply beyond this).

» A tip is customary at the end of your journey; ₹125-150 per day is fair (more if you're really pleased with the driver's service).

Hitching

Hitching is not much of an option in South India, as the concept of a 'free ride' – considering the inexpensive public transport options available – is relatively unknown. Be aware that truck drivers have a reputation for driving under the influence of alcohol.

Travellers who decide to hitch should understand that they're taking a small but potentially serious risk. As anywhere, women are strongly advised against hitching alone or even as a pair. Always use your instincts.

Local Transport

» Buses, cycle-rickshaws, autorickshaws, taxis, boats and urban trains provide transport around South India's cities. Costs for public transport vary from town to town (consult regional chapters).

» On any form of transport without a fixed fare, agree on the price *before* you start your journey and make sure that it covers your luggage and every passenger.

» Even where local transport is metered, drivers may refuse to use the meter, demanding an elevated 'fixed' fare. If this happens, insist on the meter – if that fails, find another vehicle.

» Fares usually increase at night (by up to 100%) and some drivers charge a few rupees extra for luggage.

» Carry plenty of small bills for taxi and rickshaw fares as drivers rarely have change.

» Some taxi/autorickshaw drivers are involved in the commission racket – for more information see p476.

Autorickshaw, Tempo & Vikram

» The Indian autorickshaw is basically a three-wheeled motorised contraption with a tin or canvas roof and sides, providing room for two passengers (although you'll often see many more bodies squeezed in) and limited luggage. They are also referred to as autos, scooters, riks or tuk-tuks.

» They are mostly cheaper than taxis and are usually metered, although getting the driver to turn on the meter can be a challenge.

» Travelling by auto is great fun but, thanks to the open windows, can be smelly, noisy and hot!

» Tempos and *vikrams* (large tempos) are outsized autorickshaws with room for more passengers, running on fixed routes for a fixed fare.

» In country areas, you may also see the fearsome-looking 'three-wheeler' – a crude, tractor-like tempo with a front wheel on an articulated arm.

Boat

Various kinds of local boats offer transport across and down rivers in South India, from big car ferries to wooden canoes and wicker coracles – see regional chapters for details. Most of the larger boats carry bicycles and motorcycles for a fee. Kerala is especially renowned for its breathtaking backwater boat cruises (see the boxed text, p269).

Bus

Urban buses, particularly in the big cities, are fume-belching, human-stuffed mechanical monsters that travel at breakneck speed (except during morning and evening rush hours, when they can be endlessly stuck in traffic). It's usually far more convenient and comfortable to opt for an autorickshaw or taxi.

Cycle-Rickshaw

» A cycle-rickshaw is a pedal cycle with two rear wheels, supporting a bench seat for passengers. Most have a canopy that can be raised in wet weather, or lowered to provide extra space for luggage.

» Many of the big cities have phased out (or reduced) the number of cycle-rickshaws, but they are still a major means of local transport in many smaller towns.

Fares must be agreed upon in advance – speak to locals to get an idea of what is a fair price for the distance you intend travelling. Tips are always appreciated, given the slog involved.

Taxi

» Most towns have taxis with meters; however, getting drivers to use them can be a major hassle. Drivers often claim that the meter is broken and proceed to request a hugely elevated 'fixed' fare instead. Threatening to get another taxi will often miraculously fix the meter. In tourist areas especially, some taxis flatly refuse to use the meter – if this happens, just find another cab.

» To avoid fare-setting shenanigans, use prepaid taxis where possible (regional chapters contain details).

» Be aware that many taxi drivers supplement their earnings with commissions – see p477.

Other Local Transport

In some towns, *tongas* (horse-drawn two-wheelers) and *victorias* (horse-drawn carriages) still operate. Mumbai and Chennai, among other centres, have suburban trains that leave from ordinary train stations. See regional chapters for comprehensive details.

Motorcycle

In terms of motorcycles as public transport, Goa is the only place in South India where they are a licensed form of conveyance. They take one person on the back and are a quick, inexpensive way to cover short distances.

Despite the traffic challenges, South India is an amazing region for long-distance motorcycle touring. Motorcycles generally handle the pitted roads better than four-wheeled vehicles, and you'll have the added bonus of being able to stop when and where you want. However, motorcycle touring can be quite an undertaking – there are some popular motorcycle tours for those who don't want the rigmarole of going it alone.

Weather is an important factor to consider – for the best times to visit different areas see the Climate Chart at the start of regional chapters. To cross from neighbouring countries, check the latest regulations and paperwork requirements from the relevant diplomatic mission.

Driving Licence

To hire a motorcycle in India, technically you're required to have a valid international drivers' permit in addition to your domestic licence. In tourist areas, some places may rent out a motorcycle without asking for a driving permit/licence, but you won't be covered by insurance in the event of an accident and may also face a fine.

Hire

» The classic way to motorcycle around India is on an Enfield Bullet, still built to the original 1940s specifications. As well as making a satisfying chugging sound, these bikes are fully manual, making them easy to repair (parts can be found almost everywhere in India). However, Enfields are often less reliable than many of the newer, Japanese-designed bikes.

» Plenty of places rent out motorcycles for local trips and longer tours. Japanese- and Indian-made bikes in the 100cc to 150cc range are cheaper than the big 350cc to 500cc Enfields.

» As a deposit, you'll need to leave a large cash lump sum (ensure you get a receipt that also stipulates the refundable amount), your passport or your air ticket. It's strongly advisable to avoid leaving your air ticket and passport, the latter of which you'll need to check in at hotels and which the police can demand to see at any time.

» For three weeks' hire, a 500cc Enfield costs from ₹22,000; a European style is ₹23,000; and a 350cc costs ₹15,000. The price includes excellent advice and an invaluable crash course in Enfield mechanics and repairs.

» See the regional chapters for other recommended rental companies and their charges.

Purchase

» If you're planning a longer tour, consider purchasing a motorcycle. Secondhand bikes are widely available and the paperwork is a lot easier than buying a new machine. Finding a secondhand motorcycle is a matter of asking around. Check travellers' noticeboards and approach local motorcycle mechanics and other bikers.

» A well-looked-after secondhand 350cc Enfield will cost anywhere from ₹25,000 to ₹50,000. A more modern version, with European-style

MANNING THE METRE

Getting a metered ride is only half the battle. Meters are almost always outdated, so fares are calculated using a combination of the meter reading and a complicated 'fare adjustment card'. Predictably, this system is open to abuse. If you spend a few days in any town, you'll soon get a feel for the difference between a reasonable fare and a blatant rip-off. When in doubt, seek advice from locals.

configuration, costs ₹45,000 to ₹65,000. The 500cc model costs anywhere from ₹60,000 to ₹85,000. You will also have to pay for insurance.

» It's advisable to get any secondhand bike serviced before you set off.

» When reselling your bike, expect to get between half and two-thirds of the price you paid if the bike is still in reasonable condition.

» Shipping an Indian bike overseas is complicated and expensive – ask the shop you bought the bike from to explain the process.

» Helmets are available for ₹500 to ₹2,000 and extras like panniers, luggage racks, protection bars, rear-view mirrors, lockable fuel caps, petrol filters and extra tools are easy to come by. One useful extra is a customised fuel tank, which will increase the range you can cover between fuel stops. An Enfield 500cc gives about 25km/L: the 350cc model gives slightly more.

» A useful website for Enfield models is www.royalenfield.com.

Ask around for dealer recommendations. One place that gets good reports in Mumbai is:

Allibhai Premji Tyrewalla (☎022-23099313; www.premjis.com; 205 Dr D Bhadkamkar (Lamington) Rd) Sells new and secondhand motorcycles with a buy-back option.

OWNERSHIP PAPERS

» There's plenty of paperwork associated with owning a motorcycle; the registration papers are signed by the local registration authority when the bike is first sold and you'll need these papers when you buy a secondhand bike.

» Foreign nationals cannot change the name on the registration. Instead, you must fill out the forms for a change of ownership and transfer of insurance. If you buy a new bike, the company selling it must register the machine for you, adding to the cost.

» For any bike, the registration must be renewed every 15 years (for around ₹5000) and you must make absolutely sure that it states the 'fitness' of the vehicle, and that there are no outstanding debts or criminal proceedings associated with the bike.

» The whole process is complicated and it makes sense to seek advice from the company selling the bike. Allow around two weeks to tackle the paperwork and get on the road.

Fuel, Spare Parts & Extras

» Petrol and engine oil are widely available in the plains, but petrol stations are widely spaced in the mountains. If you intend to travel to remote regions, ensure you carry enough extra fuel (seek local advice about fuel availability before setting off). At the time of research, petrol cost around ₹55 per litre.

» If you're going to remote regions it's also important to carry basic spares (valves, fuel lines, piston rings etc). Spare parts for Indian and Japanese machines are widely available in cities and larger towns.

» For all machines (particularly older ones), make sure you regularly check and tighten all nuts and bolts, as Indian roads and engine vibration tend to work things loose quite quickly.

» Check the engine and gearbox oil level regularly (at least every 500km) and clean the oil filter every few thousand kilometres.

» Given the road conditions, the chances are you'll make at least a couple of visits to a puncture-wallah – start your trip with new tyres and carry spanners to remove your own wheels.

» It's a good idea to bring your own protective equipment (jackets etc).

Insurance

» Only hire a bike with third-party insurance – if you hit someone without insurance, the consequences can be very costly. Reputable companies will include third-party cover in their policies; those that don't probably aren't trustworthy.

» You must also arrange insurance if you buy a motorcycle (usually you can organise this through the person selling the bike).

» The minimum level of cover is third-party insurance – available for ₹300 to

---

RIDING THE RAILS WITH YOUR BIKE

For long hauls, transporting your bike by train can be a convenient option. Buy a standard train ticket for the journey, then take your bike to the station parcel office with your passport, registration papers, driver's licence and insurance documents. Packing-wallahs will wrap your bike in protective sacking for around ₹50 to ₹250 and you must fill out various forms and pay the shipping fee – around ₹2000 to ₹3500 (charges are less on an ordinary train) – plus an insurance fee of 1% of the declared value of the bike. Bring the same paperwork to collect your bike from the goods office at the other end. If the bike is left waiting at the destination for more than 24 hours, you'll pay a storage fee of around ₹50 to ₹100 per day.

₹600 per year. This will cover repair and medical costs for any other vehicles, people or property you might hit, but no cover for your own machine. Comprehensive insurance (recommended) costs upwards of ₹800 per year.

Road Conditions

Given the varied road conditions, India can be challenging for novice riders. Hazards range from cows and chickens crossing the carriageway to broken-down trucks, pedestrians on the road, and perpetual potholes and unmarked speed humps. Rural roads sometimes have grain crops strewn across them to be threshed by passing vehicles – a serious sliding hazard for bikers.

Try not to cover too much territory in one day and avoid travelling after dark – many vehicles drive without lights, and dynamo-powered motorcycle headlamps are useless at low revs while negotiating potholes.

On busy national highways expect to average 40 to 50km/h without stops; on winding back roads and dirt tracks this can drop to 10km/h.

Organised Motorcycle Tours

Dozens of companies offer organised motorcycle tours around India with a support vehicle, mechanic and guide. Below are some reputable outfits (see websites for contact details, itineraries and prices):

Blazing Trails (www.blazing trailstours.com)

Classic Bike Adventure (www.classic-bike-india.com)

Ferris Wheels (www.ferris wheels.com.au)

H-C Travel (www.hctravel. com)

Indian Motorcycle Adventures (www.indianmotorcycle adventures.com)

Lalli Singh Tours (www. lallisingh.com)

Moto Discovery (www. motodiscovery.com)

Royal Expeditions (www. royalexpeditions.com)

Saffron Road Motorcycle Tours (www.saffronroad.com)

Wheel of India (www. wheelofindia.com)

Shared Jeeps

» In mountain areas, such as those around Aurangabad in Maharashtra, shared jeeps supplement the bus service, charging similar fixed fares – see regional chapters for routes and costs.

» Although nominally designed for five to six passengers, most shared jeeps squeeze in many more people. The seats beside and immediately behind the driver are more expensive than the cramped bench seats at the rear.

» Four-wheel-drives leave only when full, and it is not uncommon for everyone to bail out of a half-full jeep and pile into a fuller vehicle that is ready to depart. Drivers will leave immediately if you pay for all the empty seats in the vehicle.

» Four-wheel-drives run from jeep stands and 'passenger stations' at the junctions of major roads; ask locals to point you in the right direction.

» In some states, jeeps are known as 'sumos' after the Tata Sumo, a popular jeep.

» Be warned that some people can suffer from travel sickness, particularly on winding mountain roads; be prepared to give up your window seat to queasy fellow passengers.

Tours

Tours are available all over South India, run by tourist offices, local transport companies and travel agencies. Organised tours can be an inexpensive way to see several places on one trip,

although you rarely get much time at each place. If you arrange a tailor-made tour, you'll have more freedom about where you go and how long you stay.

Drivers may double as guides or you can hire a qualified local guide for a fee. In tourist towns, be wary of touts claiming to be professional guides – see p477. See the Tours section in the regional chapters for details about local tours.

International Tour Agencies

Many international companies offer tours to India, from straightforward sightseeing trips to adventure tours and activity-based holidays. To find current tours that match your interests, quiz travel agents and surf the web. Some good places to start your tour hunt:

Dragoman (www.dragoman. com) One of several reputable overland tour companies offering trips on customised vehicles.

Exodus (www.exodustravels. co.uk) A wide array of specialist trips, including tours with a holistic, wildlife and adventure focus.

India Wildlife Tours (www. india-wildlife-tours.com) All sorts of wildlife tours, plus jeep/horse/camel safaris and bird-watching.

Indian Encounter (www. indianencounters.com) Special-interest tours that include wildlife spotting, river-rafting and Ayurvedic treatments.

Intrepid Travel (www. intrepidtravel.com) Endless possibilities from wildlife tours to sacred rambles.

Peregrine Adventures (www.peregrine.net.au) Popular cultural and trekking tours.

Sacred India Tours (www. sacredindia.com) Includes tours with a holistic focus such as yoga and Ayurveda, as well as architectural and cultural tours.

Shanti Travel (http://shantitravel.com) A range of tours including family and adventure run by a Franco-Indian team.

World Expeditions (www.worldexpeditions.com.au) An array of options that includes trekking and cycling tours.

Train

Travelling by train is a quintessential Indian experience. Trains offer a smoother ride than buses and are especially recommended for long journeys that include overnight travel. India's rail network is one of the largest and busiest in the world and Indian Railways is the largest utility employer on earth, with roughly 1.5 million workers. There are around 6900 train stations scattered across the country.

We've listed useful trains throughout this book but there are hundreds more services. The best way of sourcing updated railway information is to use relevant internet sites such as **Indian Railways** (www.indianrail.gov.in) and the

TOP SCENIC TRAIN JOURNEYS

A handful of delightful toy trains still ply the metre-gauge lines from the plains to the hills, offering sterling views and a hint of colonial-era charm. Here are our top South Indian scenic rail journeys.

» Mettupalayam-Ooty Miniature Train (p387)

» Matheran Toy Train (p101)

» Visakhapatnam through Eastern Ghats (p233)

useful www.seat61.com/India.htm. There's also *Trains at a Glance* (₹35), available at many train station bookstands and better bookshops and newsstands, but it's published annually so it's not as up to date as websites. Nevertheless, it offers comprehensive timetables covering all the main lines.

Booking Tickets in India

You can either book tickets through a travel agency or hotel (for a commission) or in person at the train station. Big stations often have English-speaking staff who can help with choosing the best train. At smaller stations, midlevel officials such as the deputy station master usually speak English. It's also worth approaching tourist office staff if you need advice about booking tickets, deciding train classes etc. The nationwide railways inquiries number is ☑139.

For information on the ins and outs of booking tickets from outside of India and recommended websites for booking tickets online see p24.

AT THE STATION

» Get a reservation slip from the information window, fill in the name of the departure station, destination station, the class you want to travel and the name and number of the train. Join the long queue to the ticket window where your ticket will be printed. Women should avail themselves of the separate women's queue – if there isn't one, go to the front of the regular queue.

TOURIST RESERVATION BUREAU

» Larger cities and major tourist centres have an International Tourist Bureau, which allows you to book tickets in relative peace – check www.indianrail.gov.in for a list of these stations.

FARE FINDER

To find out which trains travel between any two destinations, go to www.trainenquiry.com and click on 'Find Your Train' – type in the name of the two destinations (you may then be prompted to choose from a list of stations) and you'll get a list of every train (with the name, number and arrival/departure times). Then, armed with these details, you can find the fare for your chosen train by going to www.indianrail.gov.in and clicking on 'Fare Enquiry'.

Reservations

» Bookings open 90 days before departure and you must make a reservation for all chair-car, sleeper, and 1AC, 2AC and 3AC carriages. No reservations are required for general (2nd-class) compartments. Trains are always busy in India so it's wise to book as far in advance as possible; advance booking for overnight trains is strongly recommended. Train services to certain destinations are often increased during major festivals but it's still worth booking well in advance. For details on classes of travel see p24.

» Reserved tickets show your seat/berth number and the carriage number. When the train pulls in, keep an eye out for your carriage number written on the side of the train (station staff and porters can also point you in the right direction). A list of names and berths is also posted on the side of each reserved carriage.

EXPRESS TRAIN FARES IN RUPEES

DISTANCE (KM)	1AC	2AC	3AC	EXECUTIVE CHAIR	CHAIR CAR (CC)	SECOND (II)
100	541	322	267	424	212	65
200	814	480	363	594	297	90
300	1,077	633	473	764	382	115
400	1,313	770	572	918	459	135
500	1,499	879	650	1,040	520	150
1000	2,451	1,432	1,048	NA	760	230
1500	3,069	1,791	1,306	NA	825	224
2000	3,316	1,935	1,410	NA	893	243

» Refunds are available on any ticket, even after departure, with a penalty – the rules are complicated so check when you book.

» Be aware that train trips can be delayed at any time of the journey so, to avoid stress, factor some leeway into your travel plans.

» Also be mindful of potential passenger drugging and theft – see p477.

If the train you want to travel on is sold out, make sure to inquire about the following possibilities:

TOURIST QUOTA

» A special (albeit small) tourist quota is set aside for foreign tourists travelling between popular stations. These seats can be booked only at dedicated reservation offices in major cities (see regional chapters for details), and you need to show your passport and visa as ID. Tickets can be paid for in rupees (some offices may ask to see foreign exchange certificates – ATM receipts will suffice), British pounds, US dollars or Euros (all in cash), or Thomas Cook and American Express travellers cheques.

TAKTAL TICKETS

» Indian Railways holds back a (very) small number of tickets on key trains and releases them at 8am two days before the train is due to depart. A charge of between ₹10 and ₹300 is added to each ticket price. First AC and Executive Chair tickets are excluded from the scheme.

WAITLIST (WL)

» Trains are frequently overbooked, but many passengers cancel and there are regular no-shows. So if you buy a ticket on the waiting list you're quite likely to get a seat, even if there are a number of people ahead of you on the list. Check your booking status at www.indianrail.gov.in/pnr_stat.html by entering your tickets' PNR number. A refund is available if you fail to get a seat – ask the ticket office about your chances.

RESERVATION AGAINST CANCELLATION (RAC)

» Even when a train is fully booked, Indian Railways sells a handful of seats in each class as 'Reservation Against Cancellation' (RAC). This means that if you have an RAC ticket and someone cancels before the departure date, you will get his or her seat (or berth). You'll have to check the reservation list at the station on the day of travel to see where you've been allocated to sit. Even if no one cancels, as an RAC ticket holder you can still board the train, and even if you don't get a seat, you can still travel.

Costs

Fares are calculated by distance and class of travel; Rajdhani and Shatabdi trains are slightly more expensive, but the price includes meals. Most air-conditioned carriages have a catering service (meals are brought to your seat). In unreserved classes it's a good idea to carry portable snacks. Seniors (those over 60) get 30% off all fares in all classes on all types of train. Children below the age of five travel free; those aged between five and 12 are charged half price.

Health

There is huge geographical variation in India, so environmental issues like heat, cold and altitude can cause health problems. Hygiene is poor in most regions so food and water-borne illnesses are common. Many insect-borne diseases are present, particularly in tropical areas. Medical care is basic in many areas (especially beyond the larger cities) so it's essential to be well prepared.

Pre-existing medical conditions and accidental injury (especially traffic accidents) account for most life-threatening problems. Becoming ill in some way, however, is very common. Fortunately, most travellers' illnesses can be prevented with some common-sense behaviour or treated with a well-stocked travellers' medical kit – however, never hesitate to consult a doctor while on the road, as self-diagnosis can be hazardous.

The following advice is a general guide only and certainly does not replace the advice of a doctor trained in travel medicine.

BEFORE YOU GO

You can buy many medications over the counter in India without a doctor's prescription, but it can be difficult to find some of the newer drugs, particularly the latest antidepressant drugs, blood-pressure medications and contraceptive pills. Bring the following:

» medications in their original, labelled containers

» a signed, dated letter from your physician describing your medical conditions and medications, including generic names

» a physician's letter documenting the medical necessity of any syringes you bring

» if you have a heart condition, a copy of your ECG taken just prior to travelling

» any regular medication (double your ordinary needs)

Insurance

Don't travel without health insurance. Emergency evacuation is expensive – bills of over US$100,000 are not uncommon. Consider the following when buying insurance:

» You may require extra cover for adventure activities such as rock climbing and scuba diving.

» In India, doctors usually require immediate payment in cash. Your insurance plan may make payments directly to providers or it will reimburse you later for overseas health expenditures. If you do have to claim later, make sure you keep all relevant documentation.

» Some policies ask that you telephone back (reverse charges) to a centre in your home country where an immediate assessment of your problem will be made.

Vaccinations

Specialised travel-medicine clinics are your best source of up-to-date information; they stock all available vaccines and can give specific recommendations for your trip. Most vaccines don't give immunity until *at least* two weeks after they're given, so visit a doctor four to eight weeks before departure. Ask your doctor for an International Certificate of Vaccination (otherwise known as the 'yellow booklet'), which will list all the vaccinations you've received.

Medical checklist

Recommended items for a personal medical kit:

» Antifungal cream, eg Clotrimazole

» Antibacterial cream, eg Mupirocin

» Antibiotic for skin infections, eg Amoxicillin/Clavulanate or Cephalexin

» Antihistamine – there are many options, eg Cetrizine for daytime and Promethazine for night

» Antiseptic, eg Betadine

» Antispasmodic for stomach cramps, eg Buscopam

» Contraceptive

» Decongestant, eg Pseudoephedrine

» DEET-based insect repellent

» Diarrhoea medication – consider an oral

REQUIRED & RECOMMENDED VACCINATIONS

The only vaccine required by international regulations is **yellow fever**. Proof of vaccination will only be required if you have visited a country in the yellow-fever zone within the six days prior to entering India. If you are travelling to India from Africa or South America, you should check to see if you require proof of vaccination.

The World Health Organization (WHO) recommends the following vaccinations for travellers going to India (as well as being up to date with measles, mumps and rubella vaccinations):

» **Adult diphtheria & tetanus** Single booster recommended if none in the previous 10 years. Side effects include sore arm and fever.

» **Hepatitis A** Provides almost 100% protection for up to a year; a booster after 12 months provides at least another 20 years' protection. Mild side effects such as headache and sore arm occur in 5% to 10% of people.

» **Hepatitis B** Now considered routine for most travellers. Given as three shots over six months. A rapid schedule is also available, as is a combined vaccination with Hepatitis A. Side effects are mild and uncommon, usually headache and sore arm. In 95% of people lifetime protection results.

» **Polio** Only one booster is required as an adult for lifetime protection. Inactivated polio vaccine is safe during pregnancy.

» **Typhoid** Recommended for all travellers to India, even those only visiting urban areas. The vaccine offers around 70% protection, lasts for two to three years and comes as a single shot. Tablets are also available, but the injection is usually recommended as it has fewer side effects. Sore arm and fever may occur.

» **Varicella** If you haven't had chickenpox, discuss this vaccination with your doctor.

These immunisations are recommended for long-term travellers (more than one month) or those at special risk (seek further advice from your doctor):

» **Japanese B Encephalitis** Three injections in all. Booster recommended after two years. Sore arm and headache are the most common side effects. In rare cases, an allergic reaction comprising hives and swelling can occur up to 10 days after any of the three doses.

» **Meningitis** Single injection. There are two types of vaccination: the quadravalent vaccine gives two to three years' protection; meningitis group C vaccine gives around 10 years' protection. Recommended for long-term backpackers aged under 25.

» **Rabies** Three injections in all. A booster after one year will then provide 10 years' protection. Side effects are rare – occasionally headache and sore arm.

» **Tuberculosis (TB)** A complex issue. Adult long-term travellers are usually recommended to have a TB skin test before and after travel, rather than vaccination. Only one vaccine given in a lifetime.

rehydration solution (og Gastrolyte), diarrhoea 'stopper' (eg Loperamide) and antinausea medication (eg Prochlorperazine). Antibiotics for diarrhoea include Ciprofloxacin; for bacterial diarrhoea Azithromycin; for giardia or amoebic dysentery Tinidazole.

» First-aid items such as scissors, elastoplasts, bandages, gauze, thermometer (but not mercury), sterile needles and syringes, safety pins and tweezers

» Ibuprofen or another anti-inflammatory

» Iodine tablets (unless you are pregnant or have a thyroid problem) to purify water

» Migraine medication if you suffer from migraines

» Paracetamol

» Pyrethrin to impregnate clothing and mosquito nets

» Steroid cream for allergic or itchy rashes, eg 1% to 2% hydrocortisone

» High-factor sunscreen

» Throat lozenges

» Thrush (vaginal yeast infection) treatment, eg Clotrimazole pessaries or Diflucan tablet

» Ural or equivalent if prone to urine infections

Websites

There is a wealth of travel-health advice on the internet. www.lonelyplanet.com is a good place to start. Some other suggestions:

Centers for Disease Control and Prevention (CDC; www.cdc.gov) Good general information.

MD Travel Health (www.mdtravelhealth.com) Provides complete travel-health recommendations for every country, updated daily.

World Health Organization (WHO; www.who.int/ith) Its helpful book *International Travel & Health* is revised annually and is available online.

Further Reading

Lonely Planet's *Healthy Travel – Asia & India* is a handy pocket size and packed with useful information, including pre-trip planning, emergency first aid, immunisation and disease information, and what to do if you get sick on the road. Other recommended references include *Travellers' Health* by Dr Richard Dawood and *Travelling Well* by Dr Deborah Mills – check out the website of **Travelling Well** (www.travellingwell.com.au).

IN INDIA

Availability of Health Care

Medical care is hugely variable in India. Some cities now have clinics catering specifically to travellers and expatriates; these clinics are usually more expensive than local medical facilities, and offer a higher standard of care. Additionally, they know the local system, including reputable local hospitals and specialists. They may also liaise with insurance companies should you require evacuation. It is usually difficult to find reliable medical care in rural areas.

Self-treatment may be appropriate if your problem is minor (eg traveller's diarrhoea), you are carrying the relevant medication and you cannot attend a recommended clinic. If you suspect

a serious disease, especially malaria, travel to the nearest quality facility.

Before buying medication over the counter, check the use-by date, and ensure the packet is sealed and properly stored (eg not exposed to the sunshine).

Infectious Diseases

Malaria

This is a serious and potentially deadly disease. Before you travel, seek expert advice according to your itinerary (rural areas are especially risky) and on medication and side effects.

Malaria is caused by a parasite transmitted by the bite of an infected mosquito. The most important symptom of malaria is fever, but general symptoms, such as headache, diarrhoea, cough or chills, may also occur. Diagnosis can only be properly made by taking a blood sample.

Two strategies should be combined to prevent malaria: mosquito avoidance and antimalarial medications. Most people who catch malaria are taking inadequate or no antimalarial medication.

Travellers are advised to prevent mosquito bites by taking these steps:

» Use a DEET-containing insect repellent on exposed skin. Wash this off at night, as long as you are sleeping under a mosquito net. Natural repellents such as citronella can be effective, but must be

applied more frequently than products containing DEET.

» Sleep under a mosquito net impregnated with pyrethrin.

» Choose accommodation with proper screens and fans (if not air-conditioned).

» Impregnate clothing with pyrethrin in high-risk areas.

» Wear long sleeves and trousers in light colours.

» Use mosquito coils.

» Spray your room with insect repellent before going out for your evening meal. There are a variety of medications available:

Chloroquine & Paludrine combination Limited effectiveness in many parts of South Asia. Common side effects include nausea (40% of people) and mouth ulcers.

Doxycycline (daily tablet) A broad-spectrum antibiotic that helps prevent a variety of tropical diseases, including leptospirosis, tick-borne disease and typhus. Potential side effects include photosensitivity (a tendency to sunburn), thrush (in women), indigestion, heartburn, nausea and interference with the contraceptive pill. More serious side effects include ulceration of the oesophagus – take your tablet with a meal and a large glass of water, and never lie down within half an hour of taking it. It must be taken for four weeks after leaving the risk area.

Lariam (mefloquine) This weekly tablet suits many people. Serious side effects are rare but include depression, anxiety, psychosis and seizures. Anyone with a history of depression, anxiety, other psychological disorders or epilepsy should not take Lariam. It is considered safe in the second and third trimesters of pregnancy. Tablets must be taken for four weeks after leaving the risk area.

Malarone A combination of atovaquone and proguanil.

HEALTH ADVISORIES

It's a good idea to consult your government's travel-health website before departure, if one is available:
Australia (www.dfat.gov.au/travel)
Canada (www.travelhealth.gc.ca)
New Zealand (www.mfat.govt.nz/travel)
UK (www.fco.gov.uk/en/travelling-and-living-overseas)
US (www.cdc.gov/travel)

Side effects are uncommon and mild, most commonly nausea and headache. It is the best tablet for scuba divers and for those on short trips to high-risk areas. It must be taken for one week after leaving the risk area.

Other diseases

Avian Flu 'Bird flu' or Influenza A (H5N1) is a subtype of the type A influenza virus. Contact with dead or sick birds is the principal source of infection and bird-to-human transmission does not easily occur. Symptoms include high fever and flu-like symptoms with rapid deterioration, leading to respiratory failure and death in many cases. Immediate medical care should be sought if bird flu is suspected. Check www.who.int/en/or www.avianinfluenza.com.au.

Coughs, Colds & Chest Infections Around 25% of travellers to India will develop a respiratory infection. If a secondary bacterial infection occurs – marked by fever, chest pain and coughing up discoloured or blood-tinged sputum – seek medical advice or consider commencing a general antibiotic.

Dengue Fever This mosquito-borne disease is becoming increasingly problematic, especially in the cities. As there is no vaccine available it can only be prevented by avoiding mosquito bites at all times. Symptoms include high fever, severe headache and body ache and sometimes a rash and diarrhoea. Treatment is rest and paracetamol – do not take aspirin or ibuprofen as it increases the likelihood of haemorrhaging. Make sure you see a doctor to be diagnosed and monitored.

Hepatitis A This food- and water-borne virus infects the liver, causing jaundice (yellow skin and eyes), nausea and lethargy. There is no specific treatment for hepatitis A, you just need to allow time for the liver to heal. All travellers to India should be vaccinated against hepatitis A.

Hepatitis B This sexually transmitted disease is spread by body fluids and can be prevented by vaccination. The long-term consequences can include liver cancer and cirrhosis.

Hepatitis E Transmitted through contaminated food and water, hepatitis E has similar symptoms to hepatitis A, but is far less common. It is a severe problem in pregnant women and can result in the death of both mother and baby. There is no commercially available vaccine, and prevention is by following safe eating and drinking guidelines.

HIV Spread via contaminated body fluids. Avoid unsafe sex, unsterile needles (including in medical facilities) and procedures such as tattoos. The growth rate of HIV in India is one of the highest in the world.

Influenza Present year-round in the tropics, influenza (flu) symptoms include fever, muscle aches, a runny nose, cough and sore throat. It can be severe in people over the age of 65 or in those with medical conditions such as heart disease or diabetes – vaccination is recommended for these individuals. There is no specific treatment, just rest and paracetamol.

Japanese B Encephalitis This viral disease is transmitted by mosquitoes and is rare in travellers. Most cases occur in rural areas and vaccination is recommended for travellers spending more than one month outside of cities. There is no treatment, and it may result in permanent brain damage or death. Ask your doctor for further details.

Rabies This fatal disease is spread by the bite or possibly even the lick of an infected animal – most commonly a dog or monkey. You should seek medical advice immediately after any animal bite and commence postexposure treatment. Having pre-travel vaccination means the postbite treatment is greatly simplified. If an animal bites you, gently wash the wound with soap and water, and apply iodine-based antiseptic. If you are not pre-vaccinated you will need to receive rabies immunoglobulin as soon as possible, and this is very difficult to obtain in much of India.

STDs Sexually transmitted diseases most common in India include herpes, warts, syphilis, gonorrhoea and chlamydia. Condoms will prevent gonorrhoea and chlamydia but not warts or herpes. If after a sexual encounter you develop any rash, lumps, discharge or pain when passing urine, seek immediate medical attention. If you have been sexually active during your travels, have an STD check on your return home.

Tuberculosis While TB is rare in travellers, those who have significant contact with the local population (such as medical and aid workers and long-term travellers) should take precautions. Vaccination is usually only given to children under the age of five, but adults at risk are recommended to have pre- and post-travel TB testing. The main symptoms are fever, cough, weight loss, night sweats and fatigue.

Typhoid This serious bacterial infection is also spread via food and water. It gives a high and slowly progressive fever and headache, and may be accompanied by a dry cough and stomach pain. It is diagnosed by blood tests and treated with antibiotics. Vaccination is recommended for all travellers who are spending more than a week in India. Be aware that vaccination is not 100% effective, so you must still be careful with what you eat and drink.

Travellers' Diarrhoea

This is by far the most common problem affecting travellers in India – between 30% and 70% of people will suffer from it within two weeks of starting their trip. It's usually caused by a bacteria, and thus responds promptly to treatment with antibiotics.

Travellers' diarrhoea is defined as the passage of more than three watery bowel actions within 24 hours, plus at least one other symptom, such as fever, cramps, nausea, vomiting or feeling generally unwell.

Treatment consists of staying well hydrated; rehydration solutions like Gastrolyte are the best for this. Antibiotics such as ciprofloxacin or azithromycin should kill the bacteria quickly. Seek medical attention quickly if you do not respond to an appropriate antibiotic.

Loperamide is just a 'stopper' and doesn't get to the cause of the problem. It can be helpful, though (eg if you have to go on a long bus ride). Don't take loperamide if you have a fever or blood in your stools.

Amoebic Dysentery Amoebic dysentery is very rare in travellers but is often misdiagnosed by poor-quality labs. Symptoms are similar to bacterial diarrhoea: fever, bloody diarrhoea and generally feeling unwell. You should always seek reliable medical care if you have blood in your diarrhoea. Treatment involves two drugs: Tinidazole or Metronidazole to kill the parasite in your gut and then a second drug to kill the cysts. If left untreated complications such as liver or gut abscesses can occur.

Giardiasis Giardia is a parasite that is relatively common in travellers. Symptoms include nausea, bloating, excess gas, fatigue and intermittent diarrhoea. The parasite will eventually go away if left untreated but this can take months; the best advice is to seek medical treatment. The treatment of choice is Tinidazole, with Metronidazole being a second-line option.

Environmental Hazards

Air Pollution

Air pollution, particularly vehicle pollution, is an increasing problem in most of India's urban hubs. If you have severe respiratory problems, speak with your doctor before travelling to India.

Diving & Surfing

Divers and surfers should seek specialised advice before they travel to ensure their medical kit contains treatment for coral cuts and tropical ear infections. Divers should ensure their insurance covers them for decompression illness – get specialised dive insurance through an organisation such as **Divers Alert Network**

(DAN; www.danasiapacific.org). Certain medical conditions are incompatible with diving; check with your doctor.

Food

Eating in restaurants is a big risk for contracting diarrhoea. Ways to avoid it include:

» eating only freshly cooked food
» avoiding shellfish and buffets
» peeling fruit
» cooking vegetables
» soaking salads in iodine water for at least 20 minutes
» eating in busy restaurants with a high turnover of customers.

Heat

Many parts of India, especially down south, are hot and humid throughout the year. For most people it takes at least two weeks to adapt to the hot climate. Swelling of the feet and ankles is common, as are muscle cramps caused by excessive sweating. Prevent these by avoiding dehydration and excessive activity in the heat. Don't eat salt tablets (they aggravate the gut); drinking rehydration solution or eating salty food helps. Treat cramps by resting, rehydrating with double-

---

DRINKING WATER

» Never drink tap water.

» Bottled water is generally safe – check the seal is intact at purchase.

» Avoid ice unless you know it has been safely made.

» Be careful of fresh juices served at street stalls in particular – they may have been watered down or may be served in unhygienic jugs/glasses.

» Boiling water is usually the most efficient method of purifying it.

» The best chemical purifier is iodine. It should not be used by pregnant women or those with thyroid problems.

» Water filters should also filter out viruses. Ensure your filter has a chemical barrier such as iodine and a small pore size (less than four microns).

strength rehydration solution and gently stretching.

Dehydration is the main contributor to heat exhaustion. Recovery is usually rapid and it is common to feel weak for some days afterwards. Symptoms include:

» feeling weak
» headache
» irritability
» nausea or vomiting
» sweaty skin
» a fast, weak pulse
» normal or slightly elevated body temperature.
Treatment:
» get out of the heat
» fan the sufferer
» apply cool, wet cloths to the skin
» lay the sufferer flat with their legs raised
» rehydrate with water containing one-quarter teaspoon of salt per litre.

Heat stroke is a serious medical emergency. Symptoms include:

» weakness
» nausea
» a hot dry body
» temperature of over 41°C
» dizziness
» confusion
» loss of coordination
» seizures
» eventual collapse.
Treatment:
» get out of the heat
» fan the sufferer
» apply cool, wet cloths to the skin or ice to the body, especially to the groin and armpits.

Prickly heat is a common skin rash in the tropics, caused by sweat trapped under the skin. Treat it by moving out of the heat for a few hours and by having cool showers. Creams and ointments clog the skin so they should be avoided. Locally bought prickly-heat powder can be helpful.

Altitude Sickness

If you are going to altitudes above 3000m, Acute Mountain Sickness (AMS) is an issue. The biggest risk factor is going too high too quickly – follow a conservative acclimatisation schedule found in good trekking guides, and *never* go to a higher altitude when you have any symptoms that could be altitude related. There is no way to predict who will get altitude sickness and it is often the younger, fitter members of a group who succumb.

Symptoms usually develop during the first 24 hours at altitude but may be delayed up to three weeks. Mild symptoms include:

» headache
» lethargy
» dizziness
» difficulty sleeping
» loss of appetite.
AMS may become more severe without warning and can be fatal. Severe symptoms include:

» breathlessness
» a dry, irritative cough (which may progress to the production of pink, frothy sputum)
» severe headache
» lack of coordination and balance
» confusion
» irrational behaviour
» vomiting
» drowsiness
» unconsciousness.
Treat mild symptoms by resting at the same altitude until recovery, which usually takes a day or two. Paracetamol or aspirin can be taken for headaches. If symptoms persist or become worse, immediate descent is necessary; even 500m can help. Drug treatments should never be used to avoid descent or to enable further ascent.

The drugs acetazolamide and dexamethasone are recommended by some doctors for the prevention of AMS; however, their use is controversial. They can reduce the symptoms, but they may also mask warning signs; severe

and fatal AMS has occurred in people taking these drugs.

To prevent acute mountain sickness:

» ascend slowly – have frequent rest days, spending two to three nights at each rise of 1000m
» sleep at a lower altitude than the greatest height reached during the day, if possible. Above 3000m, don't increase sleeping altitude by more than 300m daily
» drink extra fluids
» eat light, high-carbohydrate meals
» avoid alcohol and sedatives.

Insect Bites & Stings

Bedbugs Don't carry disease but their bites can be very itchy. They live in furniture and walls and then migrate to the bed at night. You can treat the itch with an antihistamine.

Lice Most commonly appear on the head and pubic areas. You may need numerous applications of an antilice shampoo such as pyrethrin. Pubic lice are usually contracted from sexual contact.

Ticks Contracted walking in rural areas. Ticks are commonly found behind the ears, on the belly and in armpits. If you have had a tick bite and have a rash at the site of the bite or elsewhere, fever or muscle aches, you should see a doctor. Doxycycline prevents tick-borne diseases.

Leeches Found in humid rainforest areas. They do not transmit any disease but their bites are often intensely itchy for weeks and can easily become infected. Apply an iodine-based antiseptic to any leech bite to help prevent infection.

Bee and wasp stings Anyone with a serious bee or wasp allergy should carry an injection of adrenalin (eg an Epipen). For others pain is the main problem – apply ice to the sting and take painkillers.

Skin Problems

Fungal rashes There are two common fungal rashes that affect travellers. The first occurs in moist areas, such as the groin, armpits and between the toes. It starts as a red patch that slowly spreads and is usually itchy. Treatment involves keeping the skin dry, avoiding chafing and using an antifungal cream such as clotrimazole or Lamisil. The second, *Tinea versicolor*, causes light-coloured patches, most commonly on the back, chest and shoulders. Consult a doctor.

Cuts and scratches These become easily infected in humid climates. Immediately wash all wounds in clean water and apply antiseptic. If you develop signs of infection (increasing pain and redness), see a doctor.

Sunburn

Even on a cloudy day sunburn can occur rapidly. Always adhere to the following:

» Use a strong sunscreen (factor 30) and reapply after a swim

» Wear a wide-brimmed hat and sunglasses

» Avoid lying in the sun during the hottest part of the day (10am to 2pm)

» Be vigilant above 3000m – you can get burnt very easily at altitude.

If you become sunburnt, stay out of the sun until you have recovered, apply cool compresses and, if necessary, take painkillers for the discomfort. One per cent hydrocortisone cream applied twice daily is also helpful.

Women's Health

For gynaecological health issues, seek out a female doctor.

Birth control Bring adequate supplies of your own form of contraception.

Sanitary products Pads, rarely tampons, are readily available.

Thrush Heat, humidity and antibiotics can all contribute to thrush. Treatment is with antifungal creams and pessaries such as clotrimazole. A practical alternative is a single tablet of Fluconazole (Diflucan).

Urinary-tract infections These can be precipitated by dehydration or long bus journeys without toilet stops; bring suitable antibiotics.

Language

WANT MORE?

For in-depth language information and handy phrases, check out Lonely Planet's *India Phrasebook*. You'll find it at **shop .lonelyplanet.com**, or you can buy Lonely Planet's iPhone phrasebooks at the Apple App Store.

The number of languages spoken in India helps explain why English is still widely spoken there, and why it's still in official use. Another 22 languages are recognised in the constitution, and more than 1600 other languages are spoken throughout the country.

The native languages of the southern regions covered in this book – and in this chapter – are Tamil, Kannada, Konkani, Malayalam, Marathi, Oriya and Telugu. Most of them belong to the Dravidian language family, although they have been influenced to varying degrees during their development by Hindi and Sanskrit. As the predominant languages in specific geographic areas, they have in effect been used to determine the regional boundaries for the southern states.

Major efforts have been made to promote Hindi as the national language of India and to gradually phase out English. However, while Hindi is the predominant language in the north, it bears little relation to the Dravidian languages of the south. Consequently, very few people in the south speak Hindi.

Many educated Indians speak English as virtually their first language. For the large number of Indians who speak more than one language, it's often their second tongue. Although you'll find it very easy to get around South India with English, it's always good to know a little of the local language.

Pronunciation

The pronunciation systems of all languages covered in this chapter include a number of 'retroflex' consonants (pronounced with the tongue bent backwards), and all languages except for Tamil also have 'aspirated' consonants (pronounced with a puff of air). Our simplified pronunciation guides don't distinguish the retroflex consonants from their nonretroflex counterparts. The aspirated sounds are indicated with an apostrophe (') after the consonant. If you read our coloured pronunciation guides as if they were English, you'll be understood. The stressed syllables are indicated with italics for languages that have noticeable word stress; for others, all syllables should be equally stressed.

TAMIL

Tamil is the official language in the South Indian state of Tamil Nadu (as well as a national language in Sri Lanka, Malaysia and Singapore). It is one of the major Dravidian languages of South India, with records of its existence going back more than 2000 years. Tamil has about 62 million speakers in India.

Note that aw is pronounced as in 'law' and ow as in 'how'.

Basics

Hello.	வணக்கம்.	va·*nak*·kam
Goodbye.	போய் வருகிறேன்.	po·i va·*ru*·ki·reyn
Yes./No.	ஆமாம்./இல்லை.	aa·maam/il·lai
Excuse me.	தயவு செய்து.	ta·ya·vu sei·du
Sorry.	மன்னிக்கவும்.	man·nik·ka·vum
Please.	தயவு செய்து.	ta·ya·vu chey·tu
Thank you.	நன்றி.	nan·dri

Question Words – Tamil

What's that?	அது என்ன?	a·tu en·na
When?	எப்பொழுது?	ep·po·zu·tu
Where?	எங்கே?	eng·key
Who?	யார்?	yaar
Why?	ஏன்?	eyn

How are you?
நீங்கள் நலமா? · neeng·kal na·la·maa

Fine, thanks. And you?
நலம், நன்றி. நீங்கள்? · na·lam nan·dri neeng·kal

What's your name?
உங்கள் பெயர் என்ன? · ung·kal pe·yar en·na

My name is ...
என் பெயர் ... · en pe·yar ...

Do you speak English?
நீங்கள் ஆங்கிலம் பேசுவீர்களா? · neeng·kal aang·ki·lam pey·chu·veer·ka·la

I don't understand.
எனக்கு விளங்கவில்லை. · e·nak·ku vi·lang·ka·vil·lai

Accommodation

Where's a ... nearby?	அருகே ஒரு ... எங்கே உள்ளது?	a·ru·ke o·ru ... eng·ke ul·la·tu
guesthouse	விருந்தினர் இல்லம	vi·run·ti·nar il·lam
hotel	ஹோட்டல	hot·tal

Do you have a ... room?	உங்களிடம் ஓர் ... அறை உள்ளதா?	ung·ka·li·tam awr ... a·rai ul·la·taa
single	தன	ta·ni
double	இரட்டை	i·rat·tai

How much is it per ...?	ஓர் ... என்னவிலை?	awr ... en·na·vi·lai
night	இரவுக்கு	i·ra·vuk·ku
person	ஒருவருக்கு	o·ru·va·ruk·ku

air-conditioned	குளிர்சாதன வசதியுடையது	ku·lir·chaa·ta·na va·cha·ti·yu·tai·ya·tu
bathroom	குளியலறை	ku·li·ya·la·rai
bed	படுக்கை	pa·tuk·kai
window	சன்னல	chan·nal

Directions

Where's the ...?
... எங்கே இருக்கிறது? · ... eng·key i·ruk·ki·ra·tu

What's the address?
வீலாசம் என்ன? · vi·laa·cham en·na

Can you show me (on the map)?
எனக்கு (வரைபடத்தில்) காட்ட முடியுமா? · e·nak·ku (va·rai·pa·tat·til) kaat·ta mu·ti·yu·maa

How far is it?
எவ்வளவு தூரத்தில் இருக்கிறது? · ev·va·la·vu too·rat·til i·ruk·ki·ra·tu

Turn ...	... புறத்தில் திரும்புக.	pu·rat·til ti·rum·pu·ka
left	இடது	i·ta·tu
right	வலது	va·la·tu

It's ...	அது இருப்பது ...	a·tu i·rup·pa·tu ...
behind ...	... க்குப் பின்னால	... kup pin·naal
in front of ...	... க்கு முன்னால	... ku mun·naal
near (to ...)	(... க்கு) அருகே	(... ku) a·ru·key
on the corner	ஓரத்தில	aw·rat·til
straight ahead	நேரடியாக முன்புறம்	ney·ra·di·yaa·ha mun·pu·ram

Eating & Drinking

Can you recommend a ...?	நீங்கள் ஒரு ... பரிந்துரைக்க முடியுமா?	neeng·kal o·ru ... pa·rin·tu·raik·ka mu·ti·yu·maa
bar	பார்	paar
dish	உணவு வகை	u·na·vu va·kai
place to eat	உணவகம்	u·na·va·ham

I'd like (a/the) ..., please.	எனக்கு தயவு செய்து ... கொடுங்கள்.	e·nak·ku ta·ya·vu chey·tu ... ko·tung·kal
bill	வீலைச்சீட்டு	vi·laich·cheet·tu
menu	உணவுப்– பட்டியல்	u·na·vup· pat·ti·yal
that dish	அந்த உணவு வகை	an·ta u·na·vu va·hai

(cup of) coffee/tea ...	(கப்) காப்பி/ தேனீர் ...	(kap) kaap·pi/ tey·neer ...
with milk	பாலுடன்	paa·lu·tan
without sugar	சர்க்கரை– இல்லாமல	chark·ka·rai· il·laa·mal

a bottle/ glass of ... wine	ஒரு பாட்டில்/ கிளாஸ ... வைன்	o·ru paat·til/ ki·laas ... vain
red	சிவப்பு	chi·vap·pu
white	வெள்ளை	vel·lai

Do you have vegetarian food?

உங்களுடைய காசை உணவு உள்ளதா? — ung·ka·li·tam chai va u·na·vu ul·la·taa

I'm allergic to (nuts).

எனக்கு (பருப்பு வகை) உணவு சேராது. — e·nak·ku (pa·rup·pu va·kai) u·na·vu chey·raa·tu

beer	பீர்	peer
breakfast	காலை உணவு	kaa·lai u·na·vu
dinner	இரவு உணவு	i·ra·vu u·na·vu
drink	பானம்	paa·nam
fish	மீன்	meen
food	உணவு	u·na·vu
fruit	பழம்	pa·zam
(orange) juice	(ஆரஞ்சு) சாறு	(aa·ra·nyu) chaa·ru
lunch	மதிய உணவு	ma·ti·ya u·na·vu
meat	இறைச்சி	i·raich·chi
milk	பால்	paal
soft drink	குளிர் பானம்	ku·lir paa·nam
vegetable	காய்கறி	kai·ka·ri
water	தண்ணீர்	tan·neyr

Emergencies

Help!	உதவ!	u·ta·vi
Stop!	நிறுத்து!	ni·rut·tu
Go away!	போய் வீடு!	pow·i vi·tu

Call a doctor!

ஐ அழைக்கவும் ஒரு மருத்துவர்! — i a·zai·ka·vum o·ru ma·rut·tu·var

Call the police!

ஐ அழைக்கவும் போலிஸ்! — i a·zai·ka·vum pow·lees

I'm lost.

நான் வழி தவறி போய்விட்டேன். — naan va·zi ta·va·ri pow·i·vit·teyn

It hurts here.

இங்கே வலிக்கிறது. — ing·key va·lik·ki·ra·tu

I have to use the phone.

நான் தொலைபேசியை பயன்படுத்த வேண்டும. — naan to·lai·pey·chi·yai pa·yan·pa·tut·ta veyn·tum

Where are the toilets?

கழிவறைகள் எங்கே? — ka·zi·va·rai·kal eng·key

Shopping & Services

Where's the market?

எங்கே சந்தை இருக்கிறது? — eng·key chan·tai i·ruk·ki·ra·tu

Can I look at it?

நான் இதைப் பார்க்கலாமா? — naan i·taip paark·ka·laa·maa

How much is it?

இது என்ன வீலை? — i·tu en·na vi·lai

That's too expensive.

அது அதிக விலையாக இருக்கிறது. — a·tu a·ti·ka vi·lai·yaa·ka i·ruk·ki·ra·tu

There's a mistake in the bill.

இந்த வீலைச்சீட்டில் ஒரு தவறு இருக்கிறது. — in·ta vi·laich·cheet·til o·ru ta·va·ru i·ruk·ki·ra·tu

bank	வங்கி	vang·ki
credit card	கிரேடிட் அட்டை	ki·rey·tit at·tai
internet	இணையம்	i·nai·yam
post office	தபால் நிலையம்	ta·paal ni·lai·yam
tourist office	சுற்றுப்பயண அலுவலகம்	chut·rup·pa·ya·na a·lu·va·la·kam

Numbers

1	ஒன்று	on·dru
2	இரண்டு	i·ran·tu
3	மூன்று	moon·dru
4	நான்கு	naan·ku
5	ஐந்து	ain·tu
6	ஆறு	aa·ru
7	ஏழு	ey·zu
8	எட்டு	et·tu
9	ஒன்பது	on·pa·tu
10	பத்து	pat·tu
20	இருபது	i·ru·pa·tu
30	முப்பது	mup·pa·tu
40	நாற்பது	naar·pa·tu
50	ஐம்பது	aim·pa·tu
60	அறுபது	a·ru·pa·tu
70	எழுபது	e·zu·pa·tu
80	எண்பது	en·pa·tu
90	தொன்னூறு	ton·noo·ru
100	நூறு	noo·ru
1000	ஓராயிரம்	aw·raa·yi·ram

Time & Dates

What time is it?

மணி என்ன? — ma·ni en·na

It's (two) o'clock.

மணி (இரண்டு). — ma·ni (i·ran·tu)

Half past (two).

(இரண்டு) முப்பது. — (i·ran·tu) mup·pa·tu

yesterday	நேற்று	neyt·tru
today	இன்று	in·dru
tomorrow	நாளை	naa·lai

day	நாள்	naal
morning	காலை	kaa-*lai*
evening	மாலை	maa-*lai*
night	இரவு	i-ra-vu

Monday	திங்கள்	*ting*-kal
Tuesday	செவ்வாய்	chev-*vai*
Wednesday	புதன்	pu-*tan*
Thursday	வியாழன்	vi-*yaa*-zan
Friday	வெள்ளி	vel-*li*
Saturday	சனி	cha-*ni*
Sunday	ஞாயிறு	nyaa-yi-ru

Transport

Is this the ... to (New Delhi)?	இது தாணா (புது– டில்லிக்குப்) புறப்படும் ...?	i-*tu* taa-*naa* (pu-*tu* til-lik-*kup*) pu-*rap*-pa-tum ...
bus	பஸ்	pas
plane	வீமானம்	vi-*maa*-nam
train	இரயில்	i-ra-*yil*

One ... ticket (to Madurai), please.	(மதுரைக்கு) தயவு செய்து ... டிக்கட் கொடுங்கள்.	(ma-tu-raik-*ku*) ta-ya-vu chey-*tu* ... tik-*kat* ko-tung-kal
one-way	ஒரு வழிப்பயண	o-ru va-*zip*-pa-ya-na
return	இரு வழிப்பயண	i-*ru* va-*zip*-pa-ya-na

What time's the first/last bus?
எத்தனை மணிக்கு முதல்/இறுதி பஸ் வரும்? — et-ta-nai ma-*nik*-ku mu-*tal*/i-ru-ti pas va-*rum*

How long does the trip take?
பயணம் எவ்வளவு நேரம் எடுக்கும்? — pa-ya-*nam* ev-va-la-vu ney-*ram* e-*tuk*-kum

How long will it be delayed?
எவ்வளவு நேரம் அது தாமதப்படும்? — ev-va-la-vu ney-ram a-*tu* taa-ma-*tap*-pa-tum

Please tell me when we get to (Ooty).
(ஊட்டிக்குப்) போனவுடன் தயவு செய்து எனக்குக கூறுங்கள். — (oot-tik-*kup*) paw-na-vu-*tan* ta-ya-*vu* chey-*tu* e-*nak*-kuk koo-rung-kal

Please take me to (this address).
தயவு செய்து என்னை இந்த (விலாசத்துக்குக்) கொண்டு செல்லுங்கள். — ta-ya-vu chey-*tu* en-*nai* in-ta (vi-*laa*-chat-tuk-kuk) kon-tu *chel*-lung-kal

Please stop/wait here.
தயவு செய்து இங்கே நிறுத்துங்கள்/ காத்திருங்கள். — ta-ya-vu chey-*tu* ing-key ni-*rut*-tung-kal/ *kaat*-ti-rung-kal

I'd like to hire a car (with a driver).
நான் ஒரு மோட்டார் வண்டி. (ஓர் ஓட்டுநருடன்) வாடகைக்கு எடுக்க விரும்புகிறேன். — naan o-ru mowt-taar van-ti (awr aw-*tu*-na-ru-tan) vaa-ta-*haik*-ku e-*tuk*-ka vi-*rum*-pu-ki-reyn

Is this the road to (Mamallapuram)?
இது தான் (மாமல்லபுரத்துக்கு) செல்லும் சாலையா? — i-*tu* taan (maa-mal-*la*-pu-rat-*tuk*-ku) *chel*-lum chaa-lai-*yaa*

airport	வீமான நிலையம்	vi-maa-na ni-*lai*-yam
bicycle	சைக்கிள்	chaik-kil
boat	படகு	pa-ta-ku
bus stop	பஸ் நிறுத்தும்	pas ni-*rut*-tum
economy class	சீக்கன வகுப்பு	chik-ka-na va-*kup*-pu
first class	முதல் வகுப்பு	mu-*tal* va-*kup*-pu
motorcycle	மோட்டார் சைக்கிள்	mowt-taar chaik-kil
train station	நிலையம்	ni-*lai*-yam

KANNADA

Kannada is the official language of the state of Karnataka. It is a Dravidian language and has about 38 million speakers.

The symbol oh is pronounced as the 'o' in 'note' and ow as in 'how'.

Basics

Hello.	ನಮಸ್ಕಾರ.	na-mas-*kaa*-ra
Goodbye.	ಸಿಗೋಣ.	si-*goh*-na
How are you?	ಹೇಗಿದ್ದೀರಿ?	hey-gi-dee-ri
Fine, thanks.	ಚೆನ್ನಾಗಿದೇನಿ, ವಂದನೆಗಳು.	chen-naa-gi-dee-ni, van-da-ne-ga-lu
Yes./No.	ಹೌದು./ಇಲ್ಲ.	how-du/il-la
Please.	ದಯವಿಟ್ಟು.	da-ya-vit-tu
Thank you.	ಥ್ಯಾಂಕ್ಯೂ.	t'ank-yoo
Excuse me.	ಸ್ವಲ್ಪ ದಾರಿ ಬಿಡಿ.	sval-pa daa-ri bi-di
Sorry.	ಕ್ಷಮಿಸಿ.	ksha-mi-si

What's your name?
ನಿಮ್ಮ ಹೆಸರೇನು? — nim-ma he-sa-rey-nu

My name is ...
ನನ್ನ ಹೆಸರು ... — nan-na he-sa-ru ...

Do you speak English?
ನೀವು ಇಂಗ್ಲೀಷ್ ಮಾತಾಡುತ್ತೀರಾ? — nee-vu ing-lee-shu maa-taa-dut-tee-ra

I don't understand.
ನನಗೆ ಅರ್ಥವಾಗುವುದಿಲ್ಲ. — na-na-ge ar-t'a-aa-gu-vu-dil-la

How much is it?
ಎಷ್ಟು ಇದು? — esh·tu i·du

Where are the toilets?
ಟಾಯ್ಲೆಟ್‌ಟುಗಳು ಎಲ್ಲಿ? — taay·let·tu·ga·lu el·li

Emergencies

Help! — ಸಹಾಯ ಮಾಡಿ! — sa·haa·ya maa·di
Go away! — ದೂರ ಹೋಗಿ! — doo·ra hoh·gi

Call ...! — ... ಕಾಲ್ ಮಾಡಿ! — ... kaal maa·di
 a doctor — ಡಾಕ್ಟರಿಗೆ — daak·ta·ri·ge
 the police — ಪೋಲೀಸಿಗೆ — poh·lee·si·ge

I have to use the phone.
ನಾನು ಫೋನ್ ಬಳಸಬೇಕು. — naa·nu foh·nu ba·la·sa·bey·ku

I'm lost.
ನಾನು ಕಳೆದುಹೋಗಿರುವೆ. — naa·nu ka·le·du·hoh·gi·ru·ve

Numbers

1	ಒಂದು	on·du
2	ಎರಡು	e·ra·du
3	ಮೂರು	moo·ru
4	ನಾಲ್ಕು	naa·ku
5	ಐದು	ai·du
6	ಆರು	aa·ru
7	ಏಳು	ey·lu
8	ಎಂಟು	en·tu
9	ಒಂಬತ್ತು	om·bat·tu
10	ಹತ್ತು	hat·tu
20	ಇಪ್ಪತ್ತು	ip·pat·tu
30	ಮೂವತ್ತು	moo·vat·tu
40	ನಲವತ್ತು	na·la·vat·tu
50	ಐವತ್ತು	ai·vat·tu
60	ಆರವತ್ತು	a·ra·vat·tu
70	ಎಪ್ಪತ್ತು	ep·pat·tu
80	ಎಂಬತ್ತು	em·bat·tu
90	ತೊಂಬತ್ತು	tom·bat·tu
100	ನೂರು	noo·ru
1000	ಸಾವಿರ	saa·vi·ra

KONKANI

Konkani is the official language of the state of Goa. It's an Indo-Aryan language and has 2.5 million speakers. The Devanagari script (also used to write Hindi and Marathi) is the official writing system for Konkani in Goa. However, many Konkani speakers in Karnataka use the Kannada script, as given in this section.

A few pronunciation tips: eu is pronounced as the 'u' in 'nurse', oh as the 'o' in 'note' and ts as in 'hats'.

Basics

Hello. — ಹಲ್ಸೋ. — hal·lo
Goodbye. — ಮೆಳ್ಯಾಂ. — mel·yaang
How are you? — ಕಸೊ/ಕಶಿ ಆಸಾಯ್? — keu·so/keu·shi aa·saay (m/f)
Fine, thanks. — ಹಾಂವ್ ಬರೊಂ ಆಸಾ. — haang·ung beu·rong aa·saang
Yes. — ವ್ಯ್. — weu·i
No. — ನಾ. — naang
Please. — ಉಪ್ಕಾರ್ ಕರ್ನ್. — up·kaar keurn
Thank you. — ದೇವ್ ಬರೆಂ ಕರುಂ. — day·u bo·reng ko·roong
Excuse me. — ಉಪ್ಕಾರ್ ಕರ್ನ್. — up·kaar keurn
Sorry. — ಚೂಕ್ ಜಾಲಿ, ಮಾಫ್ ಕರ್. — ts'ook zaa·li maaf keur

What's your name?
ತುಜೆಂ ನಾಂವ್ ಕಿತೆಂ? — tu·jeng naang·ung ki·teng

My name is ...
ಮ್ಹಜೆಂ ನಾಂವ್ ... — m'eu·jeng naang·ung ...

Do you speak English?
ಇಂಗ್ಲಿಶ್ ಉಲೈತಾಯ್ಗೀ? — ing·leesh u·leuy·taay·gee

Do you understand?
ಸಮ್ಜಾಲೆಂಗೀ? — som·zaa·leng·gee

I understand.
ಸಮ್ಜಾಲೆಂ. — som·zaa·leng

I don't understand.
ನಾ, ಸಮ್ಜೊಂಕ್–ನಾ. — naang som·zonk·naang

How much is it?
ತಾಕಾ ಕಿಲ್ಲೆ ಪೈಶೆ? — taa·kaa kit·le peuy·she

Where are the toilets?
ಟೊಯ್ಲೆಟ್ ಕೈಂಚರ್ ಆಸಾತ್? — toy·let k'eu·ing·ts'eur aa·saat

Emergencies

Help! — ಮ್ಹಾಕಾ ಕುಮಕ್ ಕರ್! — m'aa·kaa ku·meuk keur
Go away! — ವಚ್! — weuts'

Call ...! — ... ಆಪೈ! — ... aa·pai
 a doctor — ಡಾಕ್ಟರಾಕ್ — daak·te·raak
 the police — ಪೊಲಿಸಾಂಕ್ — po·li·saank

I have to use the phone.
ಮ್ಹಾಕಾ ಫೊನಾಚಿ ಘರ್ಜ್ ಆಸಾ. — m'aa·kaa fo·na·chi g'eurz aa·saa

I'm lost.
ಮ್ಹಜೀ ವಾಟ್ ಚುಕ್ಲ್ಯಾ. — m'eu·ji waat ts'uk·lyaa

Could you help me, please?
ಮ್ಹಾಕಾ ಇಲ್ಲೊಚೊ ಉಪ್ಕಾರ್ ಕರ್ಶಿಗೀ? — m'aa·kaa il·lo·ts'o up·kaar keur·shi·gee

Numbers

1	ഒക്	ayk
2	ഡോന്	dohn
3	തീന്	teen
4	ചാര്	chaar
5	പാംഛ്	paants'
6	ീഛ	so
7	സാത്	saat
8	ആട്	aat'
9	നോഹ്	nohw
10	ഡാ	d'aa
20	വീസ്	wees
30	തീസ്	tees
40	ചാളീസ്	ts'aa·lees
50	പന്യാസ്	pon·naas
60	സാട്	saat'
70	സത്തര്	seut·teur
80	ാംഠം	euyng·shing
90	നോവ്ോദ്	no·wod
100	ഷ്ംഭര്	shem·bor
1000	ഹജ്ഝാര്	ha·zaar

MALAYALAM

Malayalam is the official language of the state of Kerala. It belongs to the Dravidian language family and has around 33 million speakers.

Note that zh is pronounced as the 's' in 'measure'.

Basics

Hello.	ഹലോ.	ha·lo
Goodbye.	ഗുഡ് ബൈ.	good bai
Yes./No.	അതെ./അല്ല.	a·t'e/al·la
Please.	ദയവായി.	da·ya·va·yi
Thank you.	നന്ദി.	nan·n'i
Excuse me.	ക്ഷമിക്കണം.	ksha·mi·ka·nam
Sorry.	ക്ഷമിക്കുക.	ksha·mi·ku·ka
How are you?	താങ്കള്ക്ക് സുഖമാണോ?	t'ang·al·ku su·k'a·maa·no
Fine, thanks.	അതെ, നന്ദി.	a·t'e nan·d'i

Do you speak English?
നിങ്ങള് ഇംഗ്ലീഷ് സംസാരിക്കുമോ? — ning·al in·glish sam·saa·ri·ku·mo

I don't understand.
എനിക്ക് മനസ്സിലാകില്ല. — e·ni·ku ma·na·si·la·ki·la

What's your name?
താങ്കളുടെ പേര് എന്താണ്? — t'ang·a·lu·te pey·ru en·t'aa·nu

My name is ...
എന്റെ പേര് ... — en·te pey·ru ...

How much is it?
എത്രയാണ് ഇതിന്? — et·ra·yaa·nu i·t'i·nu

Where are the toilets?
എവിടെയാണ് കക്കൂസ്? — e·vi·de·yaa·nu ka·koo·su

Emergencies

Help!	സഹായിക്കൂ!	sa·ha·yi·koo
Go away!	ഇവിടുന്ന് പോകൂ!	i·vi·du·nu po·koo
Call ...!	... വിളിക്കൂ!	... vi·li·koo
a doctor	ഒരു ഡോക്ടറെ	o·ru dok·ta·re
the police	പൊലീസിനെ	po·li·si·ne

I have to use the phone.
എനിക്ക് ഈ ഫോൺ ഒന്നു വേണമായിരുന്നു. — e·ni·ku ee fon o·nu vey·na·maa·yi·ru·nu

I'm lost.
എനിക്ക് വഴി അറിഞ്ഞുകൂട. — e·ni·ku va·zhi a·ri·nyu·koo·da

Numbers

1	ഒന്ന്	on·na
2	രണ്ട്	ran·d'a
3	മൂന്ന്	moo·na
4	നാല്	naa·la
5	അഞ്ച്	an·ja
6	ആറ്	aa·ra
7	ഏഴ്	e·zha
8	എട്ട്	e·t'a
9	ഒമ്പത്	on·pa·t'a
10	പത്ത്	pa·t'a
20	ഇരുപത്	i·ru·pa·t'a
30	മുപ്പത്	mu·p'a·t'a
40	നാല്പത്	naal·pa·t'a
50	അമ്പത്	an·ba·t'a
60	അറുപത്	a·ru·pa·t'a
70	എഴുപത്	e·zhu·pa·t'a
80	എൺപത്	en·pa·t'a
90	തൊണ്ണൂറ്	t'on·noo·ra
100	നൂറ്	n'oo·ra
1000	ആയിരം	aa·ye·ram

MARATHI

Marathi is the official language of the state of Maharashtra. It belongs to the Indo-Aryan language family and is spoken by an estimated 71 million people. Marathi is written in the Devanagari script (also used for Hindi).

Keep in mind that oh is pronounced as the 'o' in 'note'.

Basics

Hello.	नमस्कार.	na·mas·kaar
Goodbye.	बाय.	bai
Yes.	होय.	hoy
No.	नाही.	naa·hee
Please.	कृपया.	kri·pa·yaa
Thank you.	धन्यवाद.	d'an·ya·vaad
Excuse me.	क्षमस्व.	ksha·mas·va
Sorry.	खेद आहे.	k'ed aa·he

How are you?
आपण कसे आहात ? — aa·pan ka·se aa·haat

Fine, thanks.
छान आहे, आभार. — ch'aan aa·he aa·b'aar

What's your name?
आपले नाव ? — aa·pa·le naa·nav

My name is ...
माझे नाव ... — maa·j'e naa·nav ...

Do you speak English?
आपण इंग्रजी बोलता का ? — aa·pan ing·re·jee bol·taa kaa

I don't understand.
मला समजत नाही. — ma·laa sam·jat naa·hee

How much is it?
याची काय किंमत आहे ? — yaa·chee kaay ki·mat aa·he

Where are the toilets?
शौचालय कुठे आहे ? — shoh·chaa·lai ku·t'e aa·he

Emergencies

Help!	मदत !	ma·dat
Go away!	दूर जा !	door jaa

Call ...!	कॉल करा ... !	kaal ka·raa ...
a doctor	डॉक्टरांना	dok·ta·raan·naa
the police	पोलिसांना	po·li·saa·naa

I have to use the phone.
मला फोन वापरायचा आहे. — ma·laa fon vaa·pa·raa·ya·chaa aa·he

I'm lost.
मी हरवले आहे. — mee ha·ra·va·le aa·he

Numbers

1	एक	ek
2	दोन	don
3	तीन	teen
4	चार	chaar
5	पाच	paach
6	सहा	sa·haa
7	सात	saat
8	आठ	aat'
9	नऊ	na·oo
10	दहा	da·haa
20	वीस	vees
30	तीस	tees
40	चाळीस	chaa·lees
50	पन्नास	pan·naas
60	साठ	saat'
70	सत्तर	sat·tar
80	ऐंशी	ain·shee
90	नव्वद	nav·vad
100	शंभर	sham·b'ar
1000	एक हजार	ek ha·jaar

ORIYA

Oriya is the official language of the state of Orissa, spoken by around 31 million people. It belongs to the Indo-Aryan language family.

Basics

Hello.	ଆଜ୍ଞେ.	aa·he
Goodbye.	ବିଦାୟ.	bi·daa·ya
Yes.	ହଁ.	han
No.	ନା.	naa
Please.	ଦୟାକରି.	da·yaa·ka·ri
Thank you.	ଧନ୍ୟବାଦ.	d'an·ya·baa·da
Excuse me.	କ୍ଷମା କରନ୍ତୁ.	k'ya·maa ka·ran·tu
Sorry.	ଦୁଃଖିତ.	du·k'i·ta

How are you?
ଆପଣ କେମିତି ଅଛନ୍ତି ? — aa·pa·na ke·mi·ti a·chan·ti

Fine, thanks.
ଉତ୍ତମ, ଧନ୍ୟବାଦ. — u·t'a·ma d'an·ya·bad

What's your name?
ଆପଣଙ୍କ ନାମ କ' ଣ ? — aa·pa·na·ka naa·ma ka·na

My name is ...
ମୋ ନାମ ହେଲା ... — mo naa·ma he·laa ...

Do you speak English?
ଆପଣ ଇଂଲିଶ୍ କୁହନ୍ତି କି? — aa·pa·na eng·li·sha ku·han·ti ki

I understand.
ମୁଁ ବୁଝେ. — mu bu·j'e

I don't understand.
ମୁଁ ବୁଝେ ନାହିଁ. — mu bu·j'e naa·hi

How much is it?
ଏହା କେତେ ? — e·ha ke·te

Where are the toilets?
ସୌଚାଗାର ବେଢ଼ିଆରେ ଅଛି? — so·u·cha·gaa·ra ke·un·t'aa·re aa·chi

Emergencies

Help!	ରକ୍ଷା କର!	rak·hya ka·ra
Go away!	ଏଠାରୁ ଚାଲିଯାଅ!	e·t'aa·ru cha·li·jaa·a
Call ...!	ଡାକ ... କୁ!	daa·ka ... ku
a doctor	ଡାକ୍ତର	daak·ta·ra
the police	ପୋଲିସ୍	po·li·sa

I have to use the phone.
ମୋର ଦୂରଭାଷ mo·ra du·ra·b'aa·sha
ବ୍ୟବହାର bya·ba·haa·ra
କରିବାର ଅଛି. ka·ri·baa·ra aa·chi

I'm lost.
ମୁଁ ହଜିଯାଇଛି. mu ha·ji·jaa·e·chi

Numbers

1	ଏକ	e·ka
2	ଦୁଇ	do·e
3	ତିନ	ti·ni
4	ଚାରି	cha·ri
5	ପାନ୍ଚ	pan·cha
6	ଛଅ	cha·a
7	ସାତ	saa·t'a
8	ଆଠ	aa·t'a
9	ନଅ	na·aa
10	ଦଶ	da·sa
20	କୋଡିଏ	ko·dee·e·a
30	ତିରିଶ	ti·ri·si
40	ଚାଳିଶ	cha·li·si
50	ପଚାଶ	pa·cha·sa
60	ଷାଠିଏ	sha·t'i·e
70	ସତୁରି	sa·tu·ri
80	ଅଶୀଏ	a·see·e
90	ନବେ	na·be
100	ଶହେ	sa·he
1000	ଏକ ହଜାର	e·ka ha·ja·ra

TELUGU

Telugu is the official language of the state of Andhra Pradesh. It's a Dravidian language and has around 70 million speakers.

Remember to pronounce oh as the 'o' in 'note'.

Basics

Hello.	నమస్కారం.	na·mas·kaa·ram
Goodbye.	వెళ్ళొస్తాను.	vel·loh·staa·nu
Yes./No.	అవును./కాదు.	a·vu·nu/kaa·du
Please.	దయచేసి.	da·ya·chay·si

Thank you.	ధన్యవాదాలు.	d'an·ya·vaa·daa·lu
Excuse me.	ఏమండి.	ay·an·di
Sorry.	క్షమించండి.	ksha·min·chan·di
How are you?	ఎట్లా ఉన్నారు?	et·laa un·naa·ru
Fine, thanks.	బాగున్నాను.	baa·gun·naa·nu

What's your name?
మీ పేరేంటి? mee pay·rayn·ti

My name is ...
నా పేరు ... naa pay·ru ...

Do you speak English?
మీరు ఇంగ్లిషు mee·ru ing·lee·shu
మాట్లాడుతారా? maat·laa·du·taa·raa

I don't understand.
అర్థం కాదు. ar·t'am kaa·du

How much is it?
అది ఎంత? a·di en·ta

Where are the toilets?
బాత్రూములు ఎక్కడ baat·room·lu ek·ka·da
ఉన్నాయి? un·naa·yi

Emergencies

Help!	సహాయం కావాలి!	sa·haa·yam kaa·vaa·li
Go away!	వెళ్ళిపో!	vel·li·poh
Call ...!	... పిలవండి!	... pi·la·van·di
a doctor	డాక్టర్ని	daak·tar·ni
the police	పోలీసుల్ని	poh·lee·sul·ni

I have to use the phone.
నేను ఫోను nay·nu p'oh·nu
వాడుకోవాలి. vaa·du·koh·vaa·li

I'm lost.
నేను దారి తప్పి nay·nu daa·ri tap·pi
పోయాను. poh·yaa·nu

Numbers

1	ఒకటి	oh·ka·ti
2	రెండు	ren·du
3	మూడు	moo·du
4	నాలుగు	naa·lu·gu
5	ఐదు	ai·du
6	ఆరు	aa·ru
7	ఏడు	ay·du
8	ఎనిమిది	e·ni·mi·di
9	తొమ్మిది	tohm·mi·di
10	పది	pa·di
20	ఇరవై	i·ra·vai
30	ముప్పై	mup·p'ai

40	నలబై	na·la·b'ai	80	ఎనబై	e·na·b'ai
50	యాబై	yaa·b'ai	90	తొంబై	tohm·b'ai
60	అరవై	a·ra·vai	100	వంద	van·da
70	డెబ్బై	deb·b'ai	1000	వెయ్యి	vey·yi

GLOSSARY

This glossary has some words and terms you may encounter during your South Indian wanderings. For food and drink definitions, see p431 and for an overview of the various vernaculars spoken in South India, see p509.

abbi – waterfall

Adivasi – tribal person

agarbathi – incense

Agni – major deity in the *Vedas*; mediator between men and the gods; also fire

ahimsa – discipline of non-violence

AIR – All India Radio, the national broadcaster

air-cooler – noisy water-filled cooling fan

amrita – immortality

Ananta – serpent on whose coils *Vishnu* reclined

Annapurna – form of *Durga*; worshipped for her power to provide food

apsara – heavenly nymph

Aranyani – Hindu goddess of forests

Ardhanariswara – *Shiva*'s half-male, half-female (*Parvati*) form

Arjuna – *Mahabharata* hero and military commander who married Subhadra (*Krishna*'s incestuous sister), took up arms and overcame many demons; he had the *Bhagavad Gita* related to him by Krishna, led Krishna's funeral ceremony and finally retired to the Himalaya

Aryan – Sanskrit for 'noble'; those who migrated from Persia and settled in northern India

Ashoka – ruler in the 3rd century BC; responsible for spreading Buddhism throughout South India

ashram – spiritual community or retreat

ASI – Archaeological Survey of India; an organisation involved in monument preservation

attar – essential oil; used as a base for perfumes

autorickshaw – noisy, three-wheeled, motorised contraption for transporting passengers, livestock etc for short distances; found throughout the country, they are cheaper than taxis

Avalokiteshvara – in *Mahayana* Buddhism, the *bodhisattva* of compassion

avatar – incarnation, usually of a deity

ayurveda – the ancient and complex science of Indian herbal medicine and healing

azad – free (Urdu), as in Azad Jammu & Kashmir

baba – religious master or father; term of respect

babu – clerk

bagh – garden

baksheesh – tip, donation (alms) or bribe

banyan – Indian fig tree; spiritual to many Indians

Bhagavad Gita – Hindu Song of the Divine One; *Krishna*'s lessons to *Arjuna*, the main thrust of which was to emphasise the philosophy of bhakti; it's part of the *Mahabharata*

bhajan – devotional song

bhakti – surrendering to the gods; faith

bhang – dried leaves and flowering shoots of the marijuana plant

bhangra – rhythmic Punjabi music/dance

Bharata – half-brother of *Rama*; ruled while Rama was in exile

bhavan – house, building; also spelt *bhawan*

Bhima – *Mahabharata* hero; he is the brother of *Hanuman* and renowned for his great strength

bidi – small, hand-rolled cigarette

bindi – forehead mark (often dot shaped) worn by women

BJP – Bharatiya Janata Party; political party

bodhisattva – literally 'one whose essence is perfected wisdom'; in Early Buddhism, bodhisattva refers only to the Buddha during the period between his conceiving the intention to strive for Buddhahood and the moment he attained it; in *Mahayana* Buddhism, it is one who renounces nirvana in order to help others attain it

Bollywood – India's answer to Hollywood; the film industry of Mumbai (Bombay)

Brahma – Hindu god; worshipped as the creator in the *Trimurti*

Brahmin – member of the priest/scholar caste, the highest Hindu caste

Buddha – Awakened One; the originator of Buddhism; also regarded by Hindus as the ninth incarnation of *Vishnu*

bund – embankment or dyke

cantonment – administrative and military area of a Raj-era town

Carnatic music – classical music of South India

caste – a Hindu's hereditary station (social standing) in life; there are four castes: the *Brahmins,* the *Kshatriyas,* the *Vaishyas* and the *Shudras;* the Brahmins occupy the top spot

chaitya – Sanskrit form of 'cetiya', meaning shrine or object of worship; has come to mean temple, and more specifically, a hall divided into a central nave and two side aisles by a line of columns, with a votive *stupa* at the end

chandra – moon; the moon as a god

chappals – sandals or leather thonglike footwear; flip-flops

charas – resin of the marijuana plant; also referred to as 'hashish'

chillum – pipe of a *hookah;* commonly used to describe the pipes used for smoking *ganja* (dried flowering tips of the marijuana plant)

chinkara – gazelle

chital – spotted deer

choli – sari blouse

chowk – town square, intersection or marketplace

chowkidar – night watchman; caretaker

crore – 10 million

dagoba – see *stupa*

Dalit – preferred term for India's *Untouchable* caste

dargah – shrine or place of burial of a Muslim saint

darshan – offering or audience with someone; auspicious viewing of a deity

Deccan – meaning 'South', this refers to the central South Indian plateau

devadasi – temple dancer

Devi – *Shiva*'s wife; goddess

dhaba – basic restaurant or snack bar; especially popular with truck drivers

dharamsala – pilgrims' rest house

dharma – for Hindus, the moral code of behaviour or social duty; for Buddhists, following the law of nature, or path, as taught by the Buddha

dhobi – person who washes clothes; commonly referred to as *dhobi-wallah*

dhobi ghat – place where clothes are washed by the *dhobi*

dhol – traditional double-sided drum

dholi – people-powered portable 'chairs'; people are carried in them to hilltop temples etc

dhoti – like a *lungi,* but the ankle-length cloth is then pulled up between the legs; worn by men

dhurrie – rug

dowry – money and/or goods given by a bride's parents to their son-in-law's family; it's illegal but still exists in many arranged marriages

Draupadi – wife of the five Pandava princes in the *Mahabharata*

Dravidian – general term for the cultures and languages of the deep south of India, including Tamil, Malayalam, Telugu and Kannada

dupatta – long scarf for women often worn with the *salwar kameez*

durbar – royal court; also a government

Durga – the Inaccessible; a form of *Shiva*'s wife, *Devi,* a beautiful, fierce goddess riding a tiger/lion

dwarpal – doorkeeper; sculpture beside the doorways to Hindu or Buddhist shrines

Emergency – period in the 1970s during which Indira Gandhi suspended many political rights

Eve-teasing – sexual harassment

filmi – slang term describing anything to do with Indian movies

gaddi – throne of a Hindu prince

Ganesh – Hindu god of good fortune and remover of obstacles; popular elephant-headed son of *Shiva* and *Parvati,* he is also known as Ganpati; his vehicle is a ratlike creature

Ganga – Hindu goddess representing the sacred Ganges River; said to flow from *Vishnu*'s toe

garbhagriha – the inner, or 'womb' chamber of a Hindu temple

Garuda – man-bird vehicle of *Vishnu*

gaur – Indian bison

geyser – hot-water unit found in many bathrooms

ghat – steps or landing on a river, range of hills, or road up hills

giri – hill

gopuram – soaring pyramidal gateway tower of *Dravidian* temples

gumbad – dome on an Islamic tomb or mosque

gurdwara – Sikh temple

guru – holy teacher; in Sanskrit literally *goe* (darkness) and *roe* (to dispel)

Guru Granth Sahib – Sikh holy book

haj – Muslim pilgrimage to Mecca

haji – Muslim who has made the *haj*

Hanuman – Hindu monkey god, prominent in the *Ramayana,* and a follower of *Rama*

hartal – strike

haveli – traditional, often ornately decorated, residences

hijra – eunuch, transvestite

hindola – swing

hookah – water pipe used for smoking *ganja* (dried flowering tips of the marijuana plant) or strong tobacco

imam – Muslim religious leader

IMFL – Indian-made foreign liquor

Indo-Saracenic – style of colonial architecture that integrated Western designs with Islamic, Hindu and Jain influences

Indra – significant and prestigious Vedic god; god of rain, thunder, lightning and war

Jagannath – Lord of the Universe; a form of *Krishna*
jali – carved lattice (often marble) screen, also refers to the holes or spaces produced through carving timber or stone
jhula – bridge
ji – honorific that can be added to the end of almost anything as a form of respect; thus 'Babaji', 'Gandhiji'
jootis – traditional, often pointy-toed, slip-in shoes
jyoti linga – most important shrines to *Shiva*, of which there are 12

Kailasa – sacred Himalayan mountain; home of *Shiva*
kalamkari – designs painted on cloth using vegetable dyes
Kali – the ominous-looking evil-destroying form of *Devi*; commonly depicted with dark skin, dripping with blood, and wearing a necklace of skulls
kameez – woman's shirtlike tunic
Kannada – state language of Karnataka
karma – Hindu, Buddhist and Sikh principle of retributive justice for past deeds
khadi – homespun cloth; Mahatma Gandhi encouraged people to spin this rather than buy English cloth
Khalistan – former Sikh secessionists' proposed name for an independent Punjab
Khalsa – Sikh brotherhood
Khan – Muslim honorific title
kolam – elaborate chalk, rice-paste or coloured powder design; also known as *rangoli*
Konkani – state language of Goa
Krishna – *Vishnu's* eighth incarnation, often coloured blue; he revealed the *Bhagavad Gita* to *Arjuna*

Kshatriya – Hindu caste of soldiers or administrators; second in the caste hierarchy
kurta – long shirt with either short collar or no collar

lakh – 100,000
Lakshmana – half-brother and aide of *Rama* in the *Ramayana*
Lakshmi – *Vishnu's* consort, Hindu goddess of wealth; she sprang forth from the ocean holding a lotus
lama – Tibetan Buddhist priest or monk
lingam – phallic symbol; auspicious symbol of *Shiva*; plural 'linga'
lungi – worn by men, this loose, coloured garment (similar to a sarong) is pleated at the waist to fit the wearer

maha – prefix meaning 'great'
Mahabharata – Great Hindu Vedic epic poem of the Bharata dynasty; containing approximately 10,000 verses describing the battle between the Pandavas and the Kauravas
mahal – house or palace
maharaja – literally 'great king'; princely ruler
maharani – wife of a princely ruler or a ruler in her own right
mahatma – literally 'great soul'
Mahavir – last *tirthankar*
Mahayana – the 'greater-vehicle' of Buddhism; a later adaptation of the teaching which lays emphasis on the *bodhisattva* ideal, teaching the renunciation of nirvana (ultimate peace and cessation of rebirth) in order to help other beings along the way to enlightenment
mahout – elephant rider or master
maidan – open (often grassed) area; parade ground
Makara – mythical sea creature and *Varuna's* vehicle; crocodile

mala – garland or necklace
Malayalam – state language of Kerala
mandapa – pillared pavilion; a temple forechamber
mandir – temple
Mara – Buddhist personification of that which obstructs the cultivation of virtue, often depicted with hundreds of arms; also the god of death
Maratha – central Indian people who controlled much of India at various times and fought the *Mughals* and *Rajputs*
marg – road
masjid – mosque
mehndi – henna; ornate henna designs on women's hands (and often feet), traditionally for certain festivals or ceremonies (eg marriage)
mela – fair or festival
mithuna – pairs of men and women; often seen in temple sculpture
Mohini – *Vishnu* in his female incarnation
moksha – liberation from *samsara*
mudra – ritual hand movements used in Hindu religious dancing; gesture of Buddha figure
Mughal – Muslim dynasty of subcontinental emperors from Babur to Aurangzeb

Naga – mythical serpentlike beings capable of changing into human form
namaskar – see *namaste*
namaste – traditional Hindu greeting (hello or goodbye), often accompanied by a respectful small bow with the hands together at the chest or head level
Nanda – in Hinduism, cowherd who raised *Krishna*; in Buddhism, *Buddha's* half-brother
Nandi – bull, vehicle of *Shiva*
Narasimha – man-lion incarnation of *Vishnu*
Narayan – incarnation of *Vishnu* the creator

Nataraja – *Shiva* as the cosmic dancer

nilgai – antelope

nizam – hereditary title of the rulers of Hyderabad

NRI – Non-Resident Indian

Om – sacred invocation representing the essence of the divine principle; for Buddhists, if repeated often enough with complete concentration, it leads to a state of emptiness

paise – the Indian rupee is divided into 100 paise

palanquin – boxlike enclosure carried on poles on four men's shoulders; the occupant sits inside on a seat

Pali – the language; related to Sanskrit, in which the Buddhist scriptures were recorded; scholars still refer to the original Pali texts

Parasurama – *Rama* with the axe; sixth incarnation of *Vishnu*

Parsi – adherent of the Zoroastrian faith

Partition – formal division of British India in 1947 into two separate countries, India and Pakistan

Parvati – a form of *Devi*

PCO – Public Call Office from where to make local, interstate and international phone calls

pietra dura – marble inlay work characteristic of the Taj Mahal

Pongal – Tamil harvest festival

pradesh – state

pranayama – study of breath control; meditative practice

prasad – temple-blessed food offering

puja – literally 'respect'; offering or prayers

Puranas – set of 18 encyclopaedic Sanskrit stories, written in verse, relating to the three gods, dating from the 5th century AD

purdah – custom among some conservative Muslims (also adopted by some Hin-

dus, especially the *Rajputs*) of keeping women in seclusion; veiled

Purnima – full moon; considered to be an auspicious time

qawwali – Islamic devotional singing

Radha – favourite mistress of *Krishna* when he lived as a cowherd

raga – any of several conventional patterns of melody and rhythm that form the basis for freely interpreted compositions

railhead – station or town at the end of a railway line; termination point

raj – rule or sovereignty; British Raj (sometimes just Raj) refers to British rule

raja – king; sometimes *rana*

Rajput – Hindu warrior caste, former rulers of northwestern India

rakhi – amulet

Rama – seventh incarnation of *Vishnu*

Ramadan – the Islamic holy month of sunrise-to-sunset fasting (no eating, drinking or smoking); also referred to as Ramazan

Ramayana – the story of *Rama* and *Sita* and their conflict with *Ravana* is one of India's best-known epics

rana – king; sometimes *raja*

rangoli – see *kolam*

rani – female ruler or wife of a king

rathas – rock-cut *Dravidian* temples

Ravana – demon king of Lanka who abducted *Sita*; the titanic battle between him and *Rama* is told in the *Ramayana*

rickshaw – small, two- or three-wheeled passenger vehicle

sadhu – ascetic, holy person; one who is trying to achieve enlightenment; often addressed as *swamiji* or *babaji*

sagar – lake, reservoir

sahib – respectful title applied to a gentleman

salwar – trousers usually worn with a *kameez*

salwar kameez – traditional dresslike tunic and trouser combination for women

samadhi – in Hinduism, ecstatic state, sometimes defined as 'ecstasy, trance, communion with God'; in Buddhism, concentration; also a place where a holy man has been cremated/buried, usually venerated as a shrine

sambar – deer

samsara – Buddhists, Hindus and Sikhs believe earthly life is cyclical; you are born again and again, the quality of these rebirths being dependent upon your karma in previous lives

Sangam – ancient academy of Tamil literature; means literally 'the meeting of two hearts'

sangha – community of monks and nuns

Saraswati – wife of *Brahma*; goddess of learning; sits on a white swan, holding a *veena*

Sati – wife of *Shiva*; became a *sati* ('honourable woman') by immolating herself; although banned more than a century ago, the act of *sati* is still (very) occasionally performed

satyagraha – nonviolent protest involving a hunger strike, popularised by Mahatma Gandhi; from Sanskrit, literally meaning 'insistence on truth'

Scheduled Castes – official term used for the *Untouchables* or *Dalits*

sepoy – formerly an Indian solider in British service

shahadah – Muslim declaration of faith ('There is no God but Allah; Mohammed is his prophet')

Shaivism – worship of *Shiva*

Shaivite – follower of *Shiva*

Shakti – creative energies perceived as female deities; devotees follow Shaktism

shikara – covered gondola-like boat used on lakes

Shiv Sena – Hindu nationalist political party

Shiva – the Destroyer; also the Creator, in which form he is worshipped as a lingam

Shivaji – great Maratha leader of the 17th century

shola – virgin forest

Shudra – caste of labourers

sikhara – Hindu temple-spire or temple

Sita – the Hindu goddess of agriculture; more commonly associated with the *Ramayana*

sitar – Indian stringed instrument

Sivaganga – water tank in temple dedicated to *Shiva*

Skanda – Hindu god of war, *Shiva's* son

stupa – Buddhist religious monument composed of a solid hemisphere topped by a spire, containing relics of the Buddha; also known as a *dagoba* or pagoda

Sufi – Muslim mystic

Sufism – Islamic mysticism

Surya – the sun; a major deity in the *Vedas*

swami – title of respect meaning 'lord of the self'; given to initiated Hindu monks

tabla – twin drums

Tamil – language of Tamil Nadu; people of *Dravidian* origin

tandava – *Shiva's* cosmic victory dance

tank – reservoir; pool or large receptacle of holy water found at some temples

tempo – noisy three-wheeler public-transport vehicle; bigger than an autorickshaw

theertham – temple tank

Theravada – orthodox form of Buddhism practiced in Sri Lanka and Southeast Asia that is characterised by its adherence to the *Pali* canon; literally, 'dwelling'

tikka – a mark Hindus put on their foreheads

tilak – auspicious forehead mark of devout Hindu men

tirthankars – the 24 great Jain teachers

tonga – two-wheeled horse or pony carriage

toy train – narrow-gauge train; mini-train

Trimurti – triple form; the Hindu triad of *Brahma*, *Shiva* and *Vishnu*

Untouchable – lowest caste or 'casteless', for whom the most menial tasks are reserved; the name derives from the belief that higher castes risk defilement if they touch one; now known as *Dalit*

Vaishya – member of the Hindu caste of merchants

Varuna – supreme Vedic god

Vedas – Hindu sacred books; collection of hymns composed in preclassical Sanskrit during the second millennium BC and divided into four books: Rig-Veda, Yajur-Veda, Sama-Veda and Atharva-Veda

veena – stringed instrument

vihara – Buddhist monastery, generally with central court or hall off which open residential cells, usually with a Buddha shrine at one end

Vijayanagar empire – one of South India's greatest empires; lasted from the 14th to 17th century

vikram – *tempo* or a larger version of the standard tempo

vimana – principal part of Hindu temple; a tower over the sanctum

vipassana – the insight meditation technique of *Theravada* Buddhism in which mind and body are closely examined as changing phenomena

Vishnu – part of the *Trimurti*; Vishnu is the Preserver and Restorer who so far has nine avatars: the fish Matsya, the tortoise Kurma, the wild boar Naraha, *Narasimha*, Vamana, *Parasurama*, *Rama*, *Krishna* and *Buddha*

wallah – man; added onto almost anything, eg *dhobi*-wallah, chai-wallah, taxi-wallah

yali – mythical lion creature

yatra – pilgrimage

zakat – tax in the form of a charitable donation; one of the five 'Pillars of Islam'

zenana – area of a home where women are secluded; women's quarters

behind the scenes

SEND US YOUR FEEDBACK

We love to hear from travellers – your comments keep us on our toes and help make our books better. Our well-travelled team reads every word on what you loved or loathed about this book. Although we cannot reply individually to postal submissions, we always guarantee that your feedback goes straight to the appropriate authors, in time for the next edition. Each person who sends us information is thanked in the next edition – and the most useful submissions are rewarded with a free book.

Visit **lonelyplanet.com/contact** to submit your updates and suggestions or to ask for help. Our award-winning website also features inspirational travel stories, news and discussions.

Note: We may edit, reproduce and incorporate your comments in Lonely Planet products such as guidebooks, websites and digital products, so let us know if you don't want your comments reproduced or your name acknowledged. For a copy of our privacy policy visit lonelyplanet.com/privacy.

OUR READERS

Many thanks to the travellers who used the last edition and wrote to us with helpful hints, useful advice and interesting anecdotes:

Keith Abraham, Fern Albert, Liz Allam, Rossen Arnaoudov, Else Bavinck, Annika Bratt, Marie Brown, Jim Burt, Aaron Chew, Stephanie Coontz, Stephanie Costello, Camilla Cramsie, Olivia Dalzell, Frankowski Dariusz, Walter Denzel, Wilson Dominic, Lou Elliott, Debbie Epstein, Alexander Erskine, Alex Fraser, Jerry Haigh, Don Hansen, Nick Hearn, Carol Hobart, Kat Hull, Vanessa Hyde, Julia Kozitsyna, P Krishnasamy, Doris Kudla, Damian Lidgard, Robert Linden, Jasmin Löffler, Kate Lyons-Priker, Christie Maccallum, Antonio Marreiros, Sanson Melissa, Aglaia Molinari, Emily Moss, Urs Naef, Brian O'Neill, Petra O'Neill, Peter Openshaw, Dyrla Podedworna, Katherine Robins, Anne Roskott, Brittany Scheid, Saurabh Sharma, Emma Sherwood, Elise Snyder, Rosemary Srinivasan, Willi Suter, Steve Tanner, Lauren Thomas, Yossi Tor, Nadia Trebbi, Aleksei Trofimov, Harold Verbakel, Mikolaj Wabia, Franc Walsh, Jay A Waronker, Katrin Wiebus, Leslie Young

AUTHOR THANKS

Sarina Singh

Thank you to those at Lonely Planet who played a part on this beautiful behemoth, especially Suzannah and Brigitte. Gratitude also goes to those in India and beyond who kindly proffered feedback, with extra special thanks to Shiv – for being a pillar of strength at a particularly challenging time. Bless. Massive thanks to the authors – you were a veritable dream team! Your enthusiasm, tenacity, humour and warmth is tremendously appreciated. I'd like to dedicate this – my 31st Lonely Planet book – to my wonderful parents, who are a constant source of strength, love and wisdom.

Trent Holden

Biggest thanks to all the good folk I met on the road who helped me out with some great tips. Thanks to Suzannah Shwer, who gave me the opportunity to work on my dream book, Sarina Singh for her calming presence throughout, as well as Amy Karafin and Paul Harding for the info. Thanks to Nigel Chin, Alex Leung and Wibowo Rusli for their great work inhouse. Finally, lots of love to my family, grandmother (Bushia) and my girlfriend Kate.

Abigail Hole

Many thanks to all at Lonely Planet, especially to Suzannah Shwer. Special thanks to the amazing Sarina Singh and my coauthors – thanks for the tips Amy, Daniel, Mark, and Michael. Thanks very much to PJ Varghese for help in Kerala. Thanks also to Umesh and Sudir in Kerala, and to Sunny Singh for his recommendation, as well as to all the readers who wrote in with useful advice and updates. Last but not least, many, many thanks to the baby-sitting team: Luca, Mum, Ant and Karen, and to Gabriel and Jack for being so good.

Kate James

At Lonely Planet, thanks to Sarina Singh and Suzannah Shwer for support, particularly during my credit-card crisis (thanks Sarina for the tip about purloining breakfast-buffet *idlis* when you're cash-poor). For exceptional assistance, thanks goes to Suzan and Michael Clements in Ooty, Pandian in Trichy, John Sinclair Willis in Bokkapuram, Bob Naik in Coimbatore and Luke Caleo in Chennai, as well as Jyothi Doreswamy for the cross-border holiday in Mysore. Thanks go out to Prema and all the friendly staff at the Textech office in Chennai for helpful tips and party invitations. As always, thanks to Chris for encouragement and animal-wrangling.

Amy Karafin

I'm very thankful to the people of Goa for putting up with my questions, especially the bus- and train-station guys (shout-out to Mr Sandesh Varai!), and to readers who wrote in with excellent tips. I'm also deeply grateful to Akash Bhartiya, who provided invaluable assistance, Manik and Surekha Bhartiya, Malini Harihaman, Sarina Singh, Suzannah Shwer, Brigitte Ellemor, the Fernandeses in Panaji, Serafin Fernandes, Pamela Maria Mascarenhas e Menezes Pereira, Saaz and Veda Aggarwal, David Gélinas, Eva Bollman, Francesco Vitelli, Kevin Raub, Michael Benanav,

and SN Goenka and everyone at Dhamma Pattana. *Bhavatu sabba mangalam.*

Anirban Mahapatra

Thanks, first of all, to Suzannah, Sarina, Brigitte, Adrian, the entire team at Lonely Planet and all my coauthors for making this a dream project to work on. Thanks to Bengaluru buddies Priya, Rajesh, Swagata and Himu for their help and hospitality. Thanks to Shama Pawar, Vinay Parameswarappa, Chris and Laila Baker, Roop Deb and Suvam Pal for patiently helping with my research. Sridhar and Vivek, thanks for your sincere duties behind the steering wheel, you made it happen. And finally, thanks to Bhutu, Baghira, Kelu, Buro, Goopi, Caesar, Elsa, Dotty and Magic for being around, in person or in spirit.

Kevin Raub

Special thanks to my wife, Adriana Schmidt Raub, who puts up with the insane travel. (Seriously.) On and from the road in India: Sarita Hegde Roy, Daniel D'Mello, Dhanya Pilo, Sarina Singh, Amy Karafin, Ellie Girdwood, Emma Weeks, Nikhila Palat, Tanvi Madkaiker, Chris Way, Sudeip Nair, DJ Pramz, Sanghamitra Jena, Neeranjan 'Tutu' Rout, Bubu Yugabrata, Biswajit Mohanty, Claire Prest, Pulak Mohanty, Chiya Sethi, Mohammed Salim, Nick Hansen, Samiur Rahman, Daniel McCrohan and the three rickshaw drivers that didn't try to fleece me.

ACKNOWLEDGMENTS

Climate map data adapted from Peel MC, Finlayson BL & McMahon TA (2007) 'Updated World Map of the Köppen-Geiger Climate Classification', *Hydrology and Earth System Sciences*, 11, 163344.
Cover photograph: Boat cruising along Kerala's backwaters/Felix Hug, LPI
Many of the images in this guide are available for licensing from Lonely Planet Images: www.lonelyplanetimages.com.

This Book

This 6th edition of Lonely Planet's *South India* guidebook was researched and written by Sarina Singh, Trent Holden, Abigail Hole, Kate James, Amy Karafin, Anirban Mahapatra and Kevin Raub. Katja Gaskell contributed to the Plan Your Trip chapters and Survival Guide. Amelia Thomas wrote the Travel with Children chapter. Dr Trish Batchelor wrote the Health chapter. Sarina also coordinated the previous two editions. This guidebook was commissioned in Lonely Planet's Melbourne office, and produced by the following:

Commissioning Editors Kate Morgan, Suzannah Shwer

Coordinating Editor Jeanette Wall

Coordinating Cartographer Andrew Smith

Coordinating Layout Designer Lauren Egan

Managing Editor Brigitte Ellemor

Managing Cartographers Alison Lyall, Adrian Persoglia

Managing Layout Designer Chris Girdler

Assisting Editors Cathryn Game, Karyn Noble, Christopher Pitts, Gabrielle Stefanos

Cover Research Naomi Parker

Internal Image Research Rebecca Skinner

Language Content Annelies Mertens, Branislava Vladisavljevic

Thanks to Ryan Evans, Lisa Knights, Averil Robertson, Gerard Walker

index

000 Map pages
000 Photo pages

how to use this book

These symbols will help you find the listings you want:

◉	Sights	⚜	Festivals & Events	☆	Entertainment
🏃	Activities	🛏	Sleeping	🏠	Shopping
🍃	Courses	✕	Eating	ℹ	Information/Transport
👉	Tours	🍷	Drinking		

These symbols give you the vital information for each listing:

☎	Telephone Numbers	🛜	Wi-Fi Access	🚌	Bus
⊙	Opening Hours	🏊	Swimming Pool	🚢	Ferry
P	Parking	🥗	Vegetarian Selection	M	Metro
⊖	Nonsmoking	📋	English-Language Menu	S	Subway
❄	Air-Conditioning	👪	Family-Friendly	⊖	London Tube
@	Internet Access	🐾	Pet-Friendly	🚊	Tram
				🚆	Train

Look out for these icons:

TOP CHOICE	Our author's recommendation
FREE	No payment required
🍃	A green or sustainable option

Our authors have nominated these places as demonstrating a strong commitment to sustainability – for example by supporting local communities and producers, operating in an environmentally friendly way, or supporting conservation projects.

Reviews are organised by author preference.

Map Legend

Sights
- ◉ Beach
- ◉ Buddhist
- ◉ Castle
- ◉ Christian
- ◉ Hindu
- ◉ Islamic
- ◉ Jewish
- ◉ Monument
- ◉ Museum/Gallery
- ◉ Ruin
- ◉ Winery/Vineyard
- ◉ Zoo
- ◉ Other Sight

Activities, Courses & Tours
- ◉ Diving/Snorkelling
- ◉ Canoeing/Kayaking
- ◉ Skiing
- ◉ Surfing
- ◉ Swimming/Pool
- ◉ Walking
- ◉ Windsurfing
- ◉ Other Activity/Course/Tour

Sleeping
- ◉ Sleeping
- ◉ Camping

Eating
- ◉ Eating

Drinking
- ◉ Drinking
- ◉ Cafe

Entertainment
- ◉ Entertainment

Shopping
- ◉ Shopping

Information
- ◉ Bank
- ◉ Embassy/Consulate
- ◉ Hospital/Medical
- ◉ Internet
- ◉ Police
- ◉ Post Office
- ◉ Telephone
- ◉ Toilet
- ◉ Tourist Information
- • Other Information

Transport
- ◉ Airport
- ◉ Border Crossing
- ◉ Bus
- ◉ Cable Car/Funicular
- ◉ Cycling
- ◉ Ferry
- ◉ Metro
- ◉ Monorail
- ◉ Parking
- ◉ Petrol Station
- ◉ Taxi
- ◉ Train/Railway
- ◉ Tram
- • Other Transport

Routes
- Tollway
- Freeway
- Primary
- Secondary
- Tertiary
- Lane
- Unsealed Road
- Plaza/Mall
- Steps
- Tunnel
- Pedestrian Overpass
- Walking Tour
- Walking Tour Detour
- Path

Geographic
- ◉ Hut/Shelter
- ◉ Lighthouse
- ◉ Lookout
- ▲ Mountain/Volcano
- ◉ Oasis
- ◉ Park
-)(Pass
- ◉ Picnic Area
- ◉ Waterfall

Population
- ◉ Capital (National)
- ◉ Capital (State/Province)
- ◉ City/Large Town
- ◉ Town/Village

Boundaries
- — — — International
- — — — — State/Province
- — - — Disputed
- — - - Regional/Suburb
- Marine Park
- Cliff
- Wall

Hydrography
- River, Creek
- Intermittent River
- Swamp/Mangrove
- Reef
- Canal
- Water
- Dry/Salt/Intermittent Lake
- Glacier

Areas
- Beach/Desert
- + + + Cemetery (Christian)
- × × × Cemetery (Other)
- Park/Forest
- Sportsground
- Sight (Building)
- Top Sight (Building)